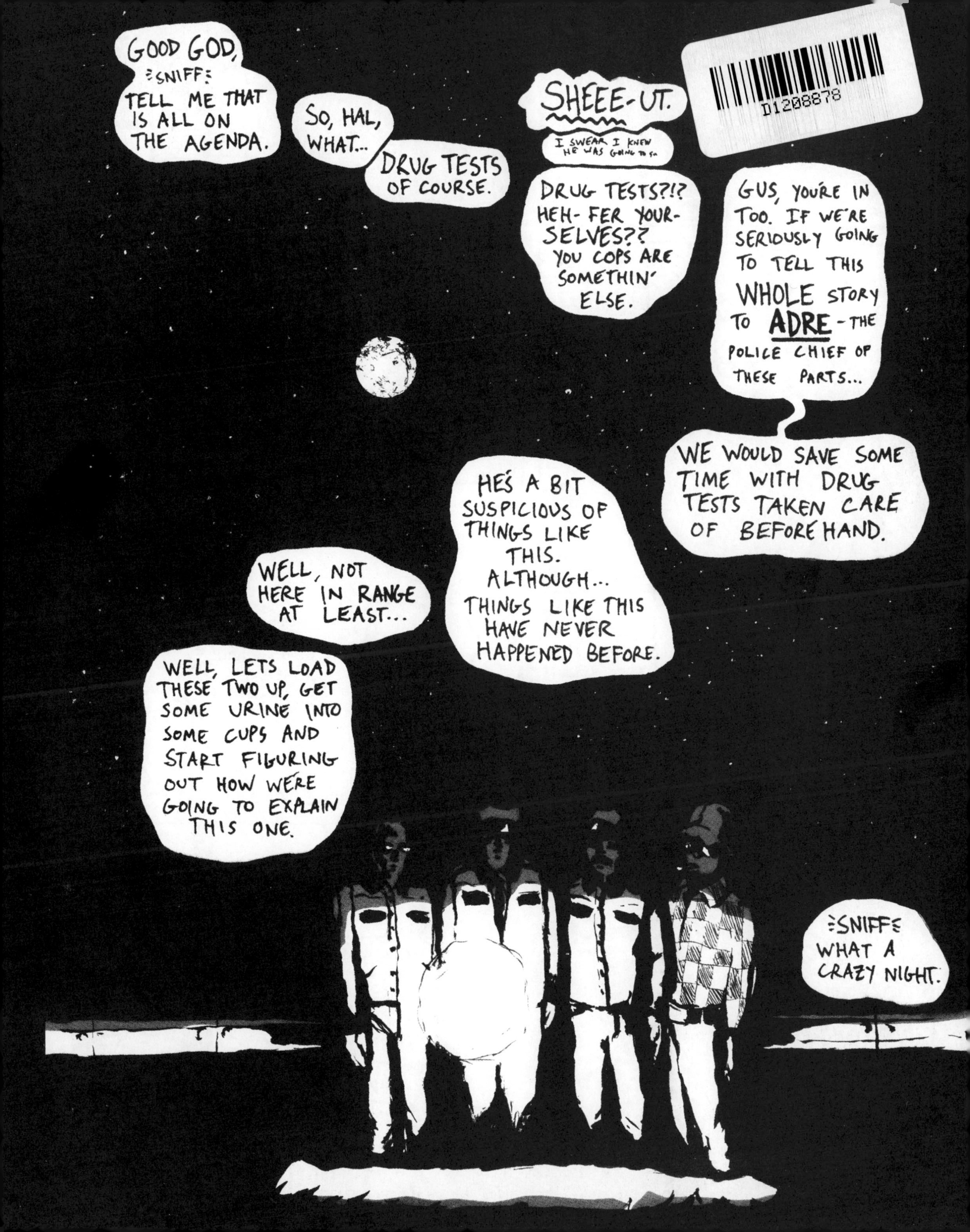
GOOD GOD, ≡SNIFF≡ TELL ME THAT IS ALL ON THE AGENDA.
SO, HAL, WHAT...
DRUG TESTS OF COURSE.
SHEEE-UT.
I SWEAR I KNEW HE WAS GOING TO
DRUG TESTS?!? HEH- FER YOUR-SELVES?? YOU COPS ARE SOMETHIN' ELSE.
GUS, YOU'RE IN TOO. IF WE'RE SERIOUSLY GOING TO TELL THIS WHOLE STORY TO ADRE - THE POLICE CHIEF OF THESE PARTS...
WE WOULD SAVE SOME TIME WITH DRUG TESTS TAKEN CARE OF BEFORE HAND.
HE'S A BIT SUSPICIOUS OF THINGS LIKE THIS. ALTHOUGH... THINGS LIKE THIS HAVE NEVER HAPPENED BEFORE.
WELL, NOT HERE IN RANGE AT LEAST...
WELL, LETS LOAD THESE TWO UP, GET SOME URINE INTO SOME CUPS AND START FIGURING OUT HOW WERE GOING TO EXPLAIN THIS ONE.
≡SNIFF≡ WHAT A CRAZY NIGHT.

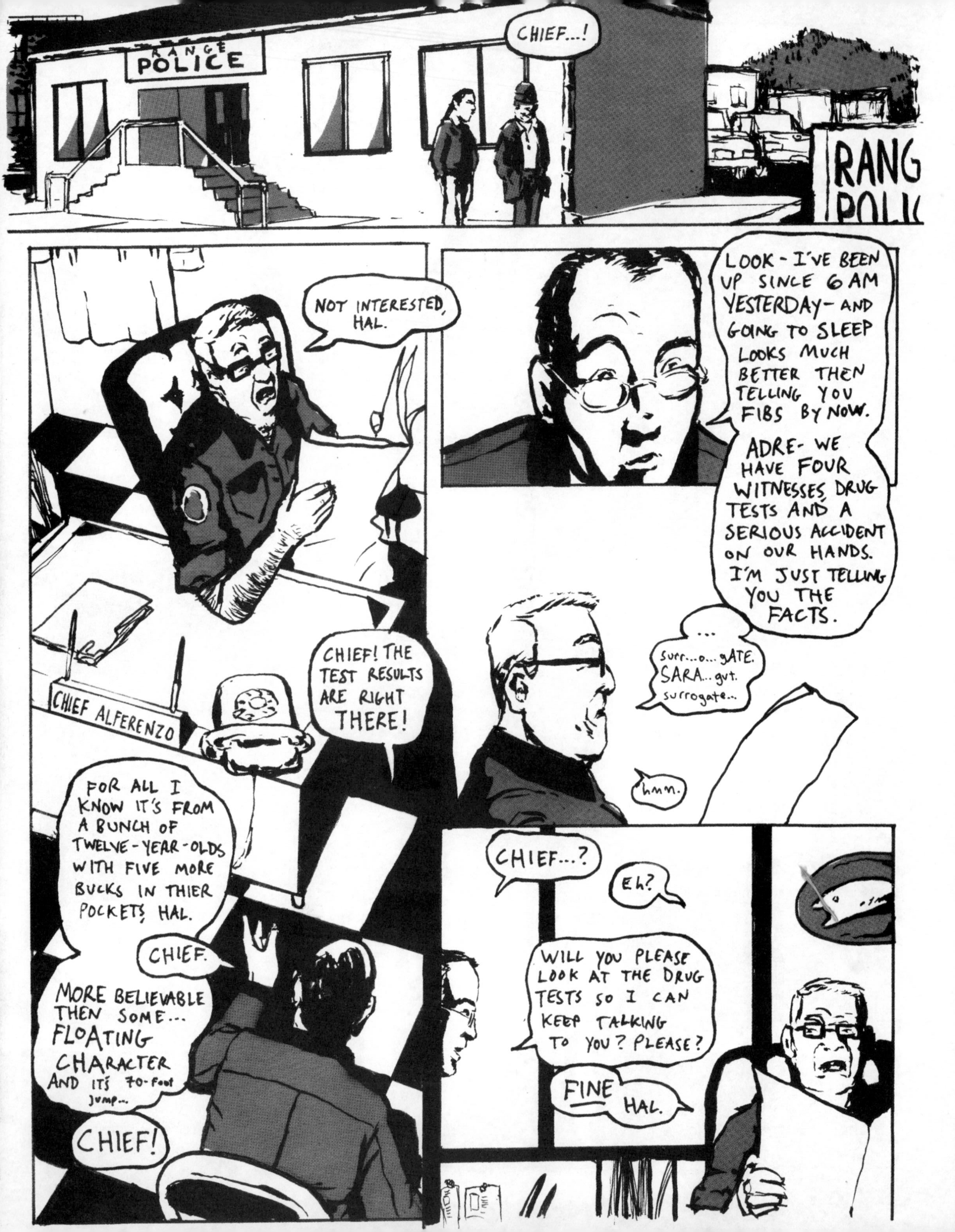
RANGE POLICE
CHIEF...!
RANG POLI
NOT INTERESTED, HAL.
LOOK - I'VE BEEN UP SINCE 6 AM YESTERDAY - AND GOING TO SLEEP LOOKS MUCH BETTER THEN TELLING YOU FIBS BY NOW.
ADRE- WE HAVE FOUR WITNESSES, DRUG TESTS AND A SERIOUS ACCIDENT ON OUR HANDS. I'M JUST TELLING YOU THE FACTS.
CHIEF! THE TEST RESULTS ARE RIGHT THERE!
CHIEF ALFERENZO
...
surr...o...gATE. SARA...gut. surrogate...
FOR ALL I KNOW IT'S FROM A BUNCH OF TWELVE-YEAR-OLDS WITH FIVE MORE BUCKS IN THIER POCKETS, HAL.
hmm.
CHIEF.
MORE BELIEVABLE THEN SOME... FLOATING CHARACTER AND ITS 70-FOOT jump...
CHIEF!
CHIEF...?
Eh?
WILL YOU PLEASE LOOK AT THE DRUG TESTS SO I CAN KEEP TALKING TO YOU? PLEASE?
FINE HAL.

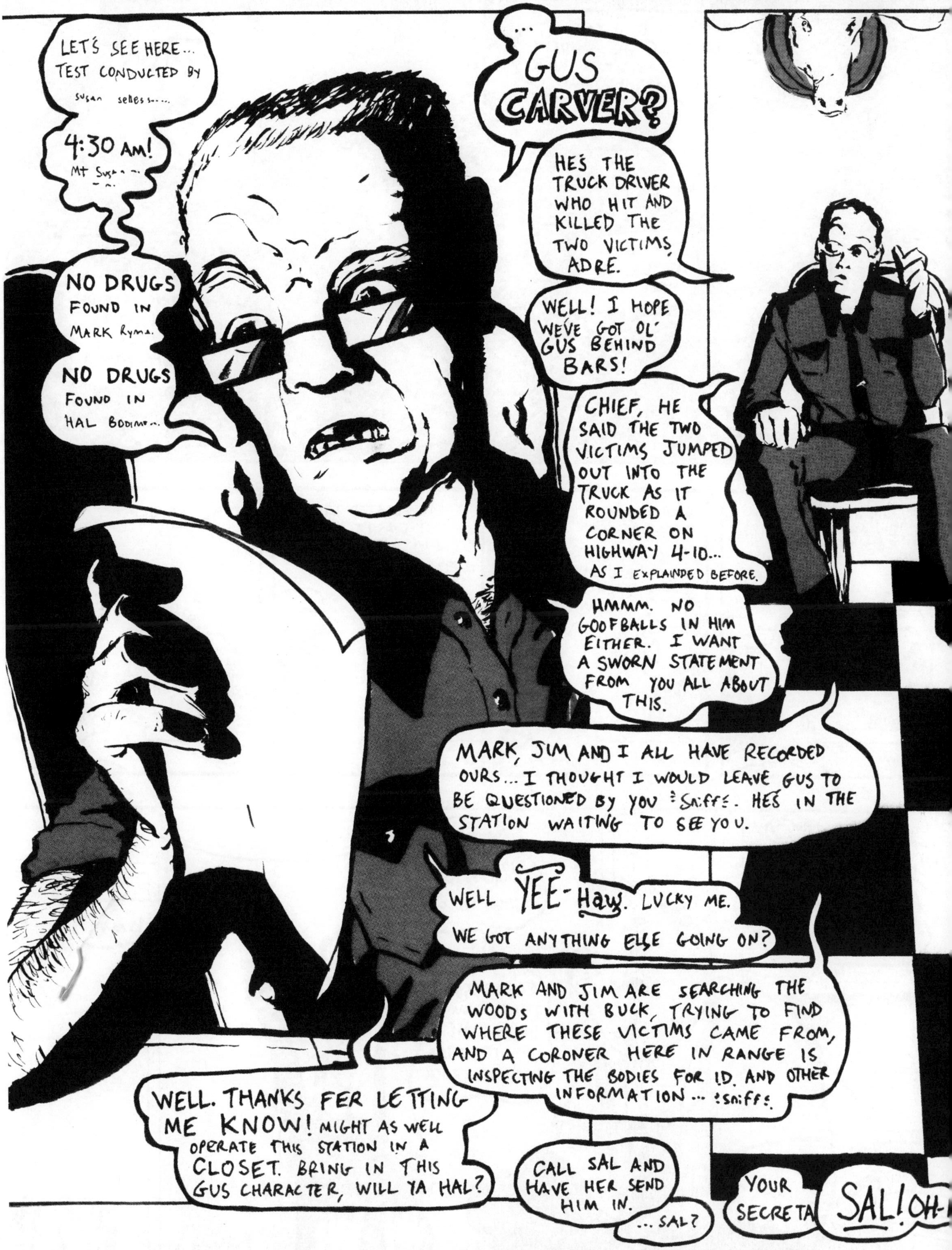
LET'S SEE HERE... TEST CONDUCTED BY
4:30 AM!
NO DRUGS FOUND IN MARK
NO DRUGS FOUND IN HAL
... GUS CARVER?
HE'S THE TRUCK DRIVER WHO HIT AND KILLED THE TWO VICTIMS, ADRE.
WELL! I HOPE WE'VE GOT OL' GUS BEHIND BARS!
CHIEF, HE SAID THE TWO VICTIMS JUMPED OUT INTO THE TRUCK AS IT ROUNDED A CORNER ON HIGHWAY 4-10... AS I EXPLAINDED BEFORE.
HMMM. NO GOOFBALLS IN HIM EITHER. I WANT A SWORN STATEMENT FROM YOU ALL ABOUT THIS.
MARK, JIM AND I ALL HAVE RECORDED OURS... I THOUGHT I WOULD LEAVE GUS TO BE QUESTIONED BY YOU :SNIFF:. HE'S IN THE STATION WAITING TO SEE YOU.
WELL YEE-HAW. LUCKY ME. WE GOT ANYTHING ELSE GOING ON?
MARK AND JIM ARE SEARCHING THE WOODS WITH BUCK, TRYING TO FIND WHERE THESE VICTIMS CAME FROM, AND A CORONER HERE IN RANGE IS INSPECTING THE BODIES FOR I.D. AND OTHER INFORMATION... :SNIFF:
WELL. THANKS FER LETTING ME KNOW! MIGHT AS WELL OPERATE THIS STATION IN A CLOSET. BRING IN THIS GUS CHARACTER, WILL YA HAL?
CALL SAL AND HAVE HER SEND HIM IN.
... SAL?
YOUR SECRETA
SAL! OH-

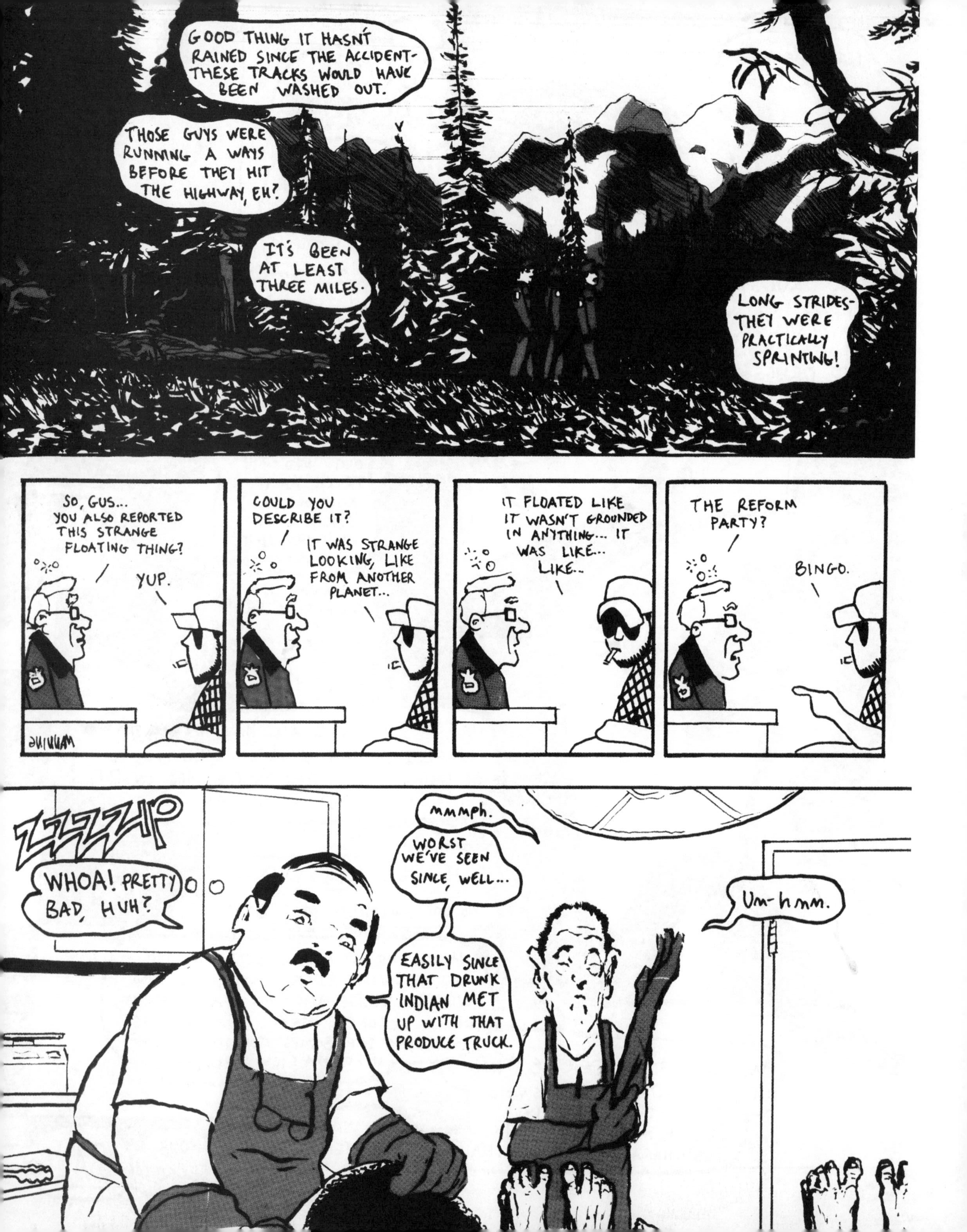
GOOD THING IT HASN'T RAINED SINCE THE ACCIDENT- THESE TRACKS WOULD HAVE BEEN WASHED OUT.
THOSE GUYS WERE RUNNING A WAYS BEFORE THEY HIT THE HIGHWAY, EH?
IT'S BEEN AT LEAST THREE MILES.
LONG STRIDES- THEY WERE PRACTICALLY SPRINTING!
SO, GUS... YOU ALSO REPORTED THIS STRANGE FLOATING THING?
YUP.
COULD YOU DESCRIBE IT?
IT WAS STRANGE LOOKING, LIKE FROM ANOTHER PLANET...
IT FLOATED LIKE IT WASN'T GROUNDED IN ANYTHING... IT WAS LIKE... LIKE..
THE REFORM PARTY?
BINGO.
ZZZZZIP
WHOA! PRETTY BAD, HUH?
mmmph.
WORST WE'VE SEEN SINCE, WELL...
EASILY SINCE THAT DRUNK INDIAN MET UP WITH THAT PRODUCE TRUCK.
Um-hmm.

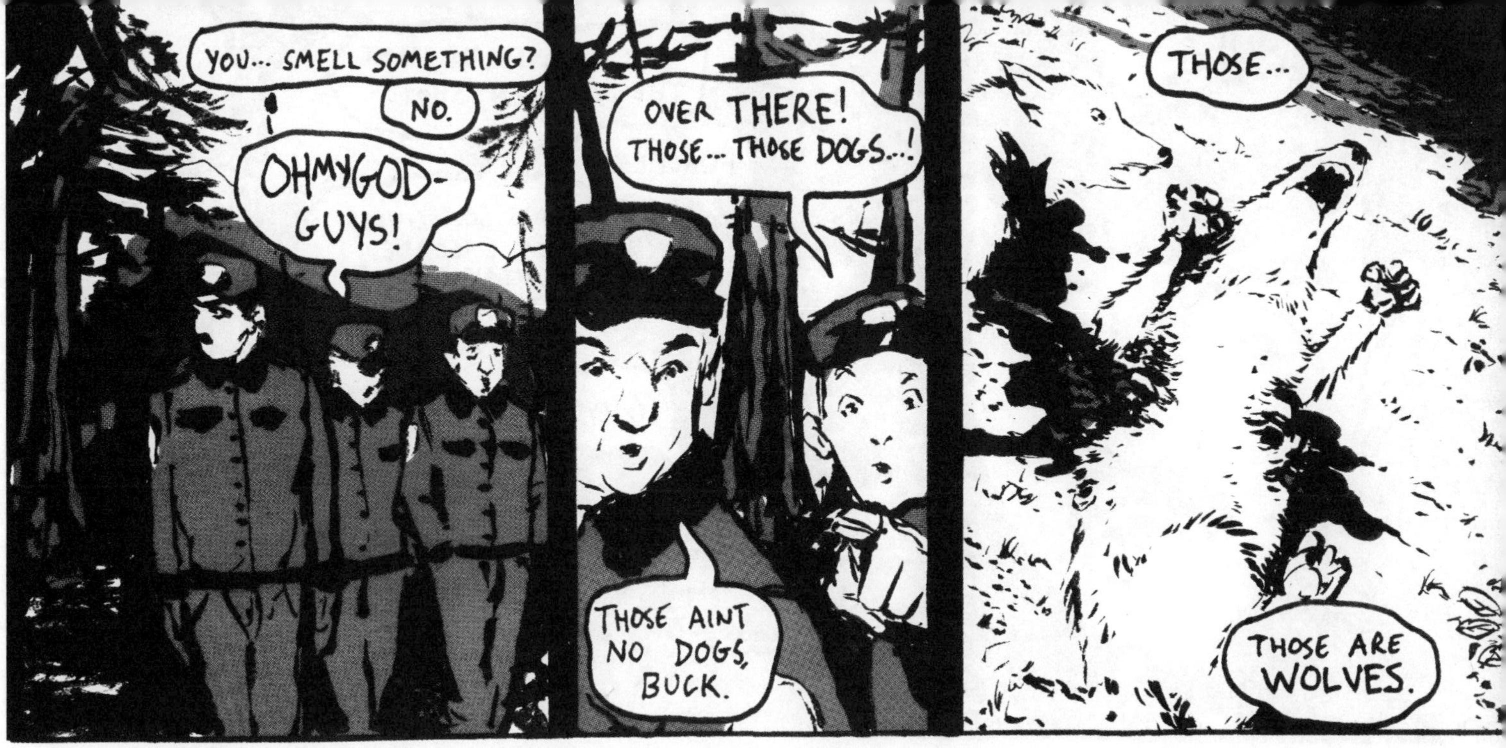
YOU... SMELL SOMETHING?
NO.
OHMYGOD-GUYS!
OVER THERE! THOSE... THOSE DOGS...!
THOSE AINT NO DOGS, BUCK.
THOSE...
THOSE ARE WOLVES.

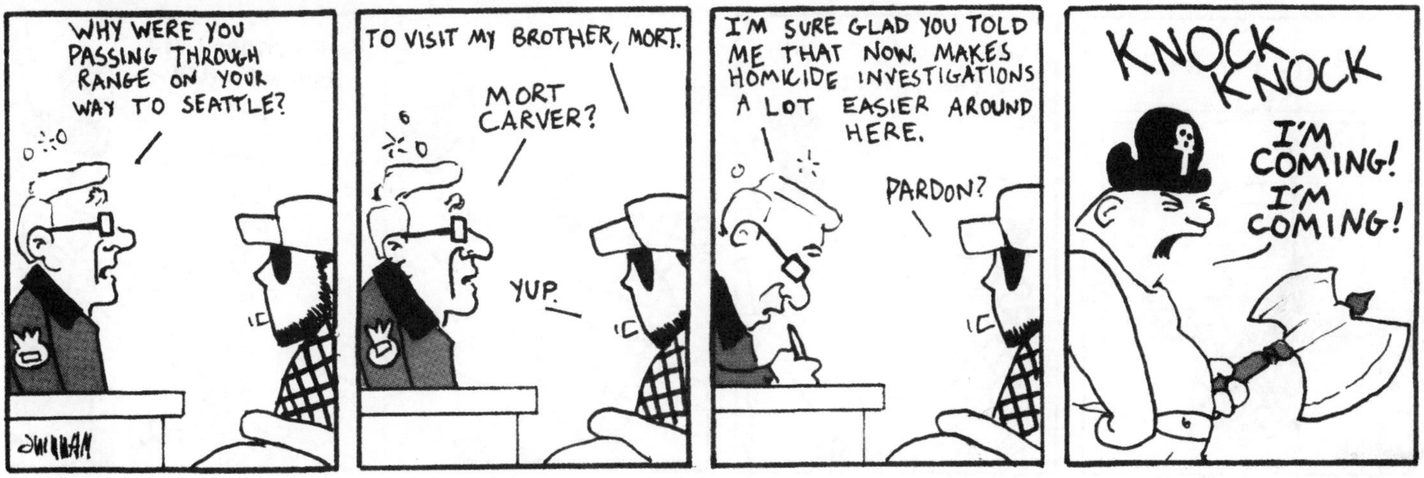
WHY WERE YOU PASSING THROUGH RANGE ON YOUR WAY TO SEATTLE?
TO VISIT MY BROTHER, MORT.
MORT CARVER?
YUP.
I'M SURE GLAD YOU TOLD ME THAT NOW. MAKES HOMICIDE INVESTIGATIONS A LOT EASIER AROUND HERE.
PARDON?
KNOCK KNOCK
I'M COMING! I'M COMING!

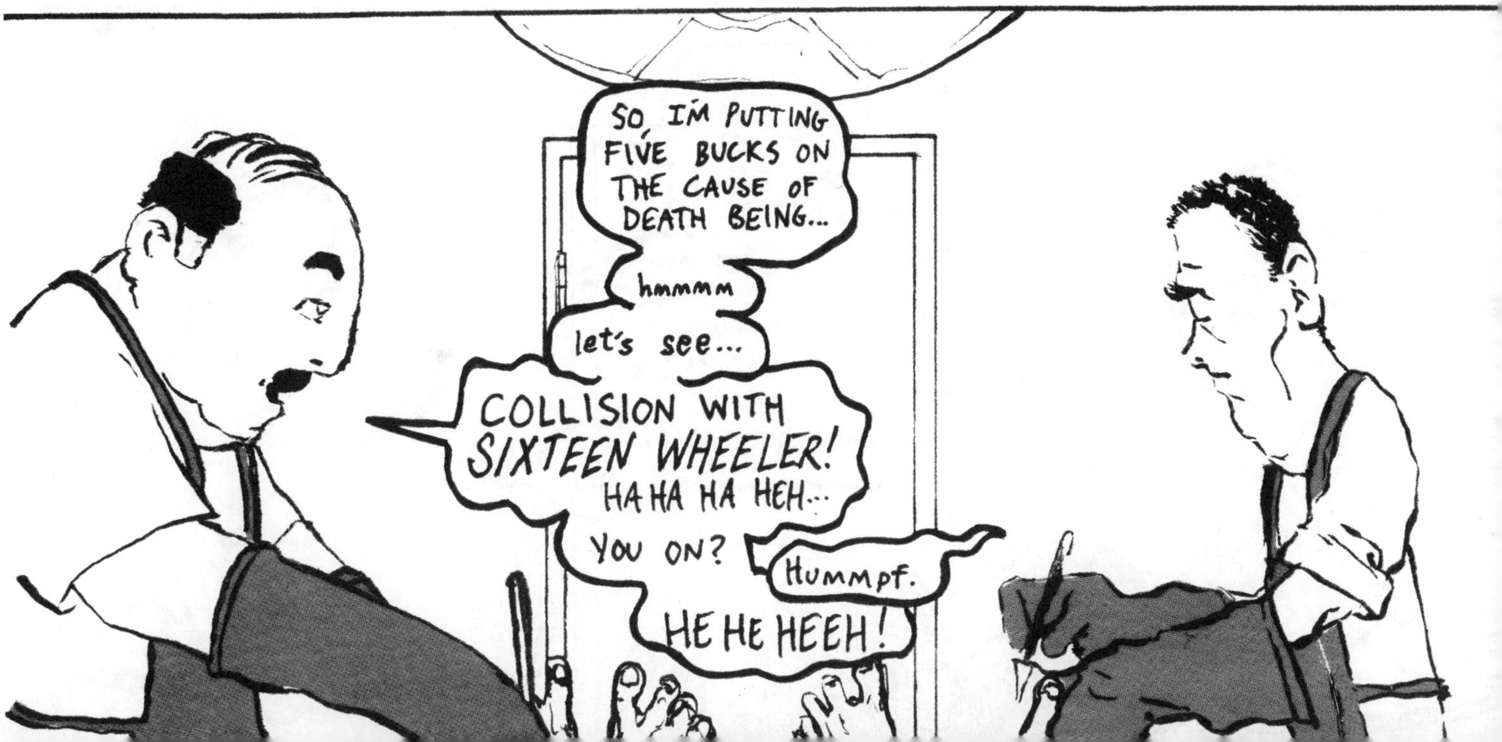
SO, I'M PUTTING FIVE BUCKS ON THE CAUSE OF DEATH BEING...
hmmmm
let's see...
COLLISION WITH SIXTEEN WHEELER! HA HA HA HEH...
YOU ON?
HUMMPF.
HE HE HEEH!

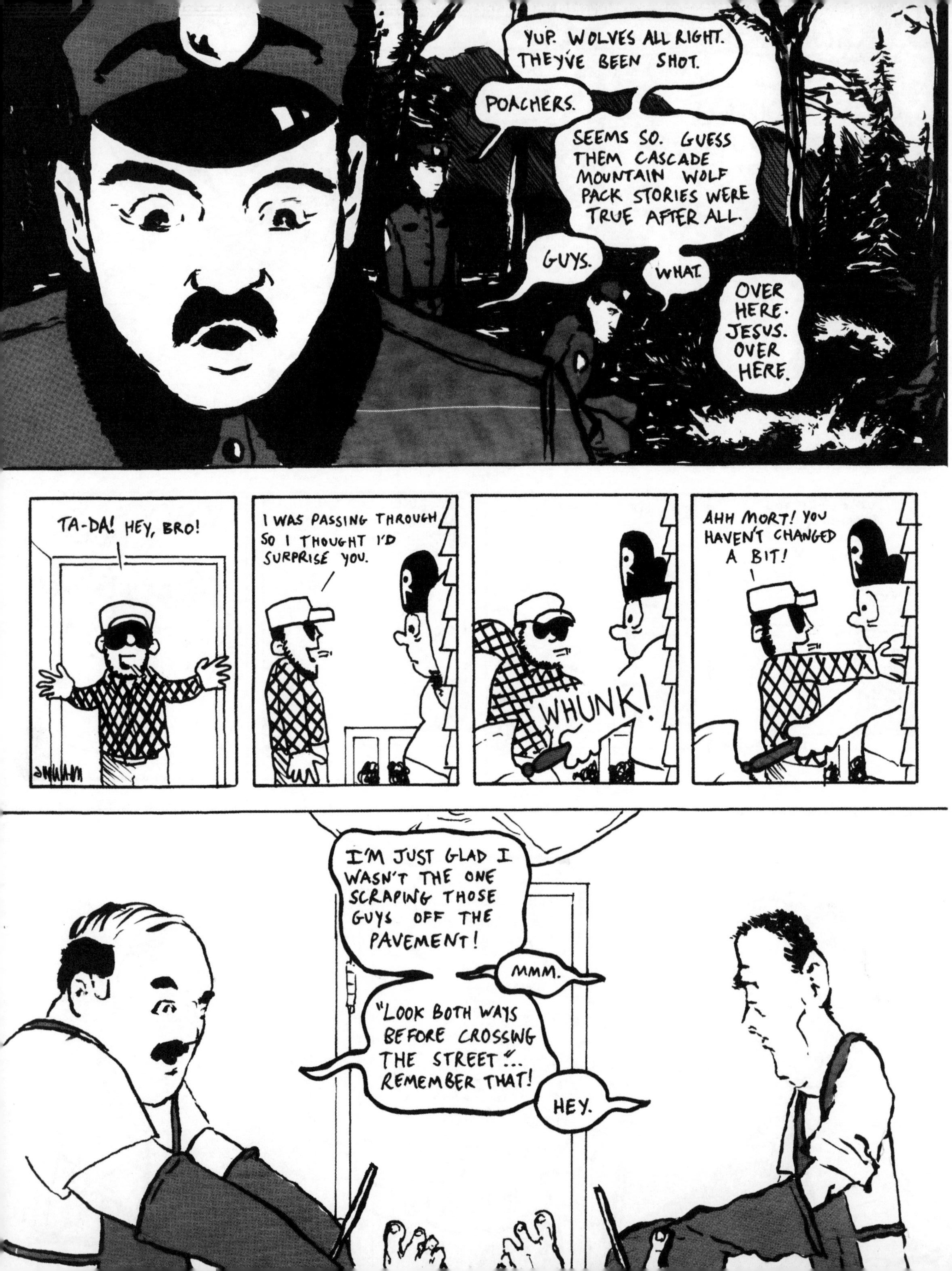
YUP. WOLVES ALL RIGHT. THEY'VE BEEN SHOT.
POACHERS.
SEEMS SO. GUESS THEM CASCADE MOUNTAIN WOLF PACK STORIES WERE TRUE AFTER ALL.
GUYS.
WHAT.
OVER HERE. JESUS. OVER HERE.
TA-DA! HEY, BRO!
I WAS PASSING THROUGH SO I THOUGHT I'D SURPRISE YOU.
WHUNK!
AHH MORT! YOU HAVEN'T CHANGED A BIT!
I'M JUST GLAD I WASN'T THE ONE SCRAPING THOSE GUYS OFF THE PAVEMENT!
MMM.
"LOOK BOTH WAYS BEFORE CROSSING THE STREET"... REMEMBER THAT!
HEY.

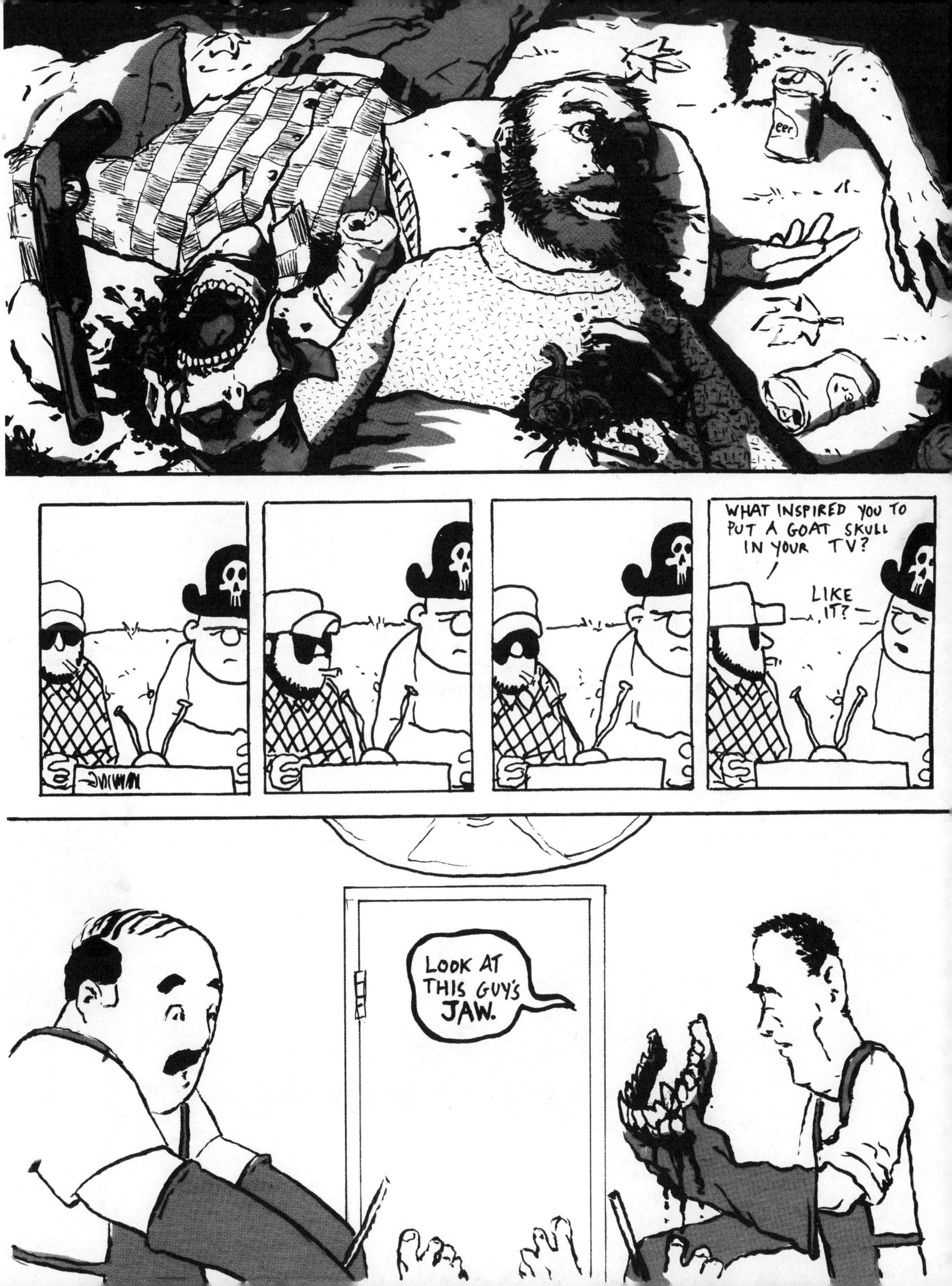
WHAT INSPIRED YOU TO PUT A GOAT SKULL IN YOUR TV?
LIKE IT?
LOOK AT THIS GUY'S JAW.

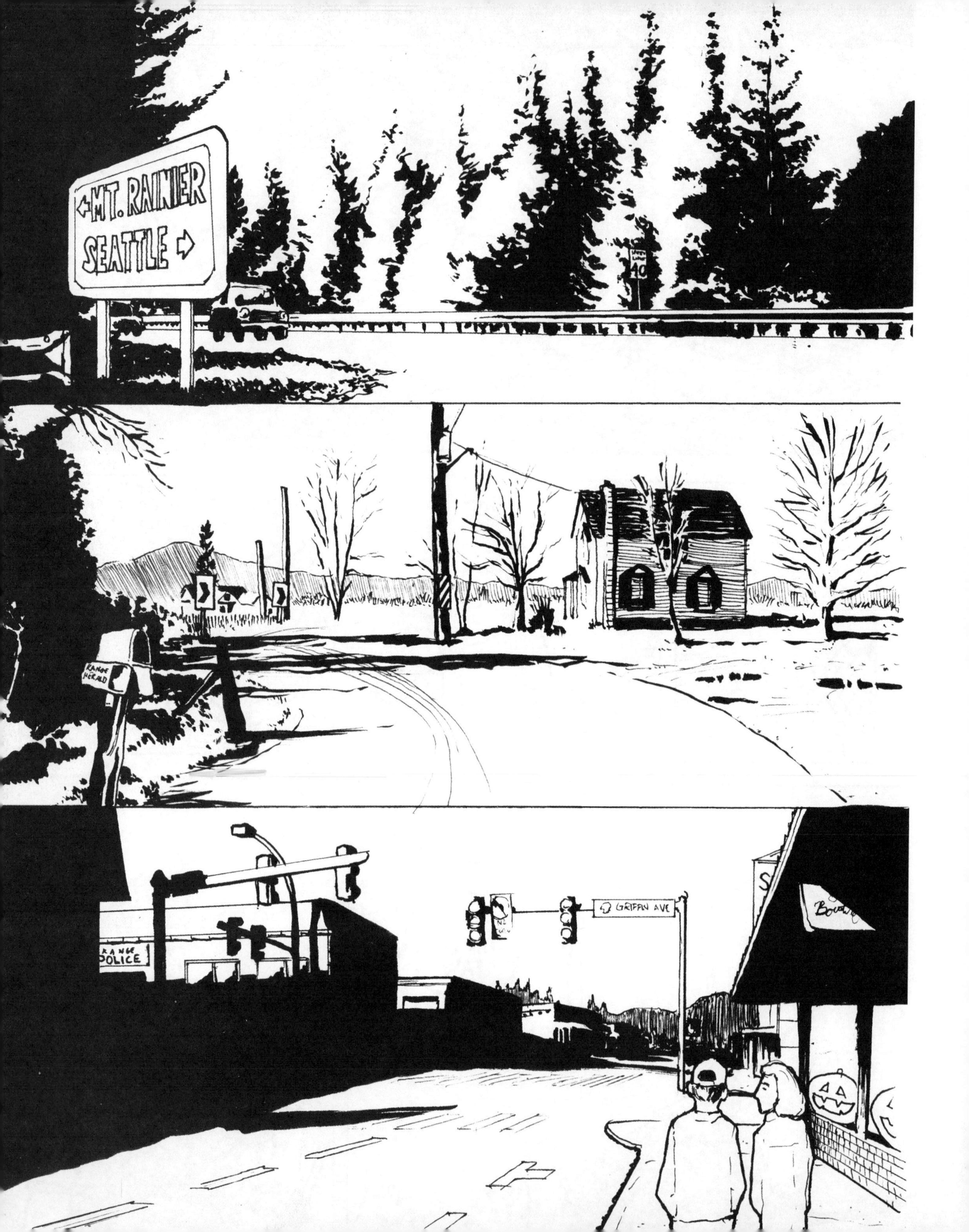
MT. RAINIER
SEATTLE
GRIFFIN AVE
POLICE

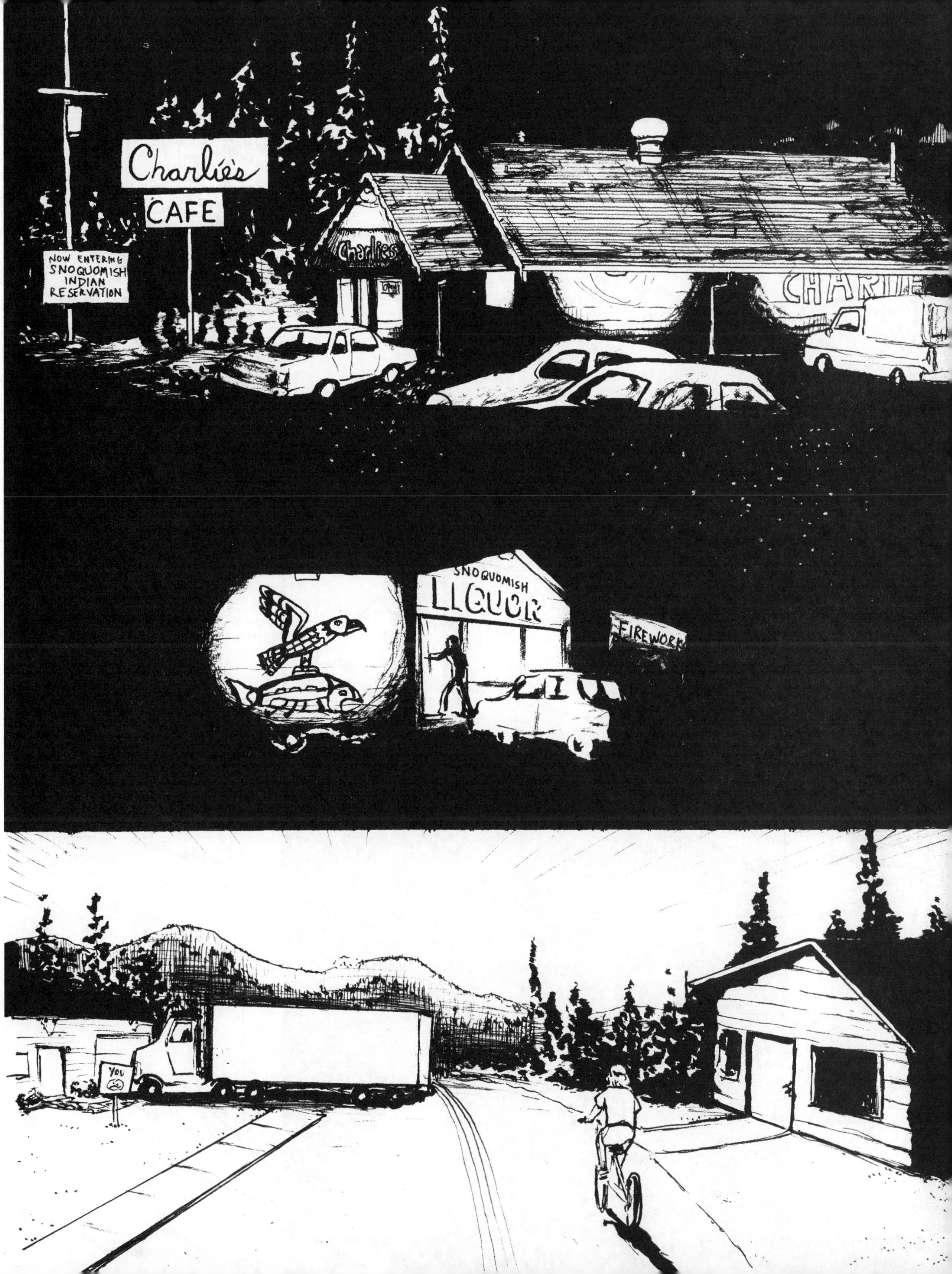
Charlie's
CAFE
NOW ENTERING SNOQUOMISH INDIAN RESERVATION
Charlie's
SNOQUOMISH
LIQUOR
FIREWORK
YOU

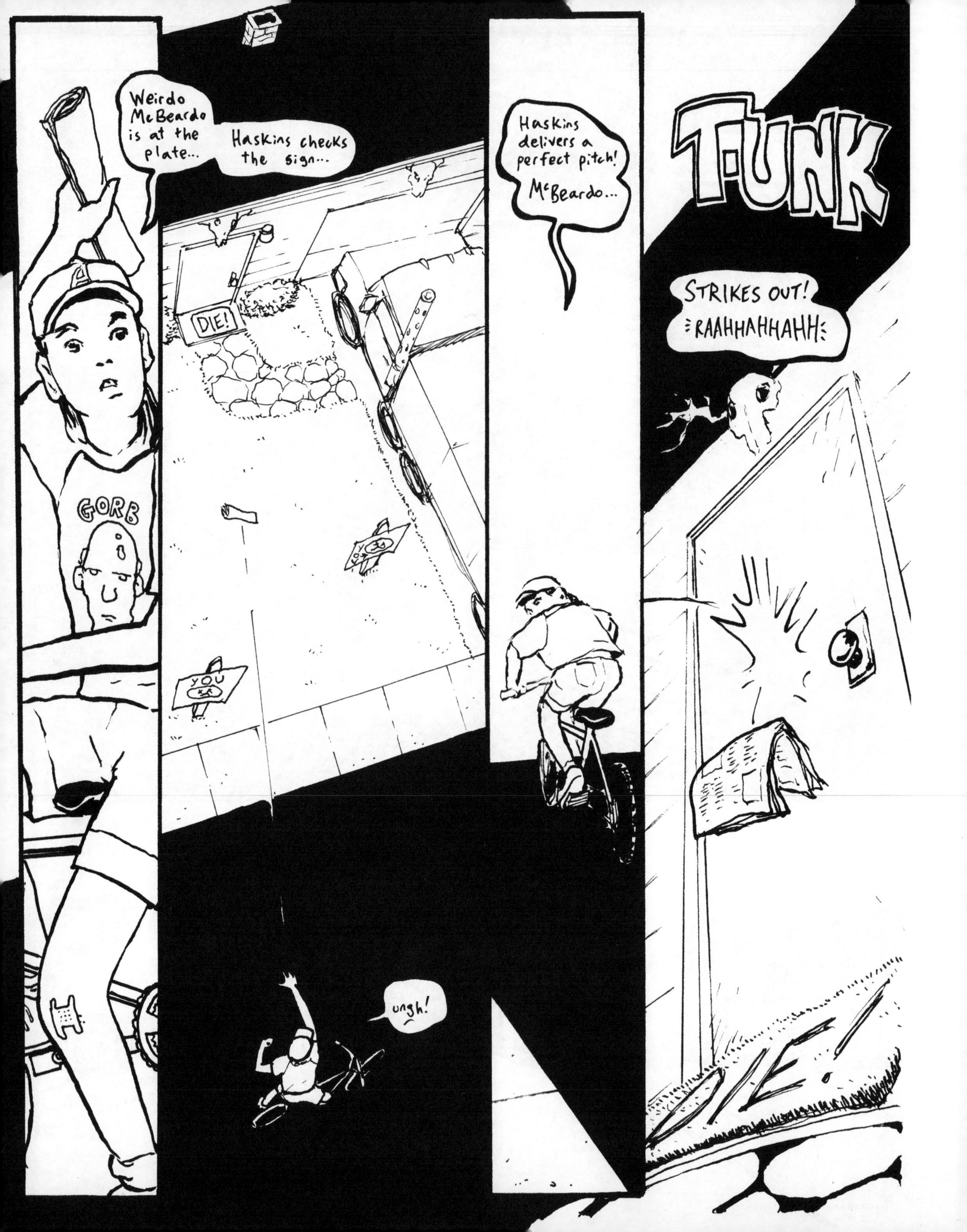
Weirdo McBeardo is at the plate...
Haskins checks the sign...
DIE!
YOU
GORB
ungh!
Haskins delivers a perfect pitch! McBeardo...
T-UNK
STRIKES OUT! RAAHHAHHAHH

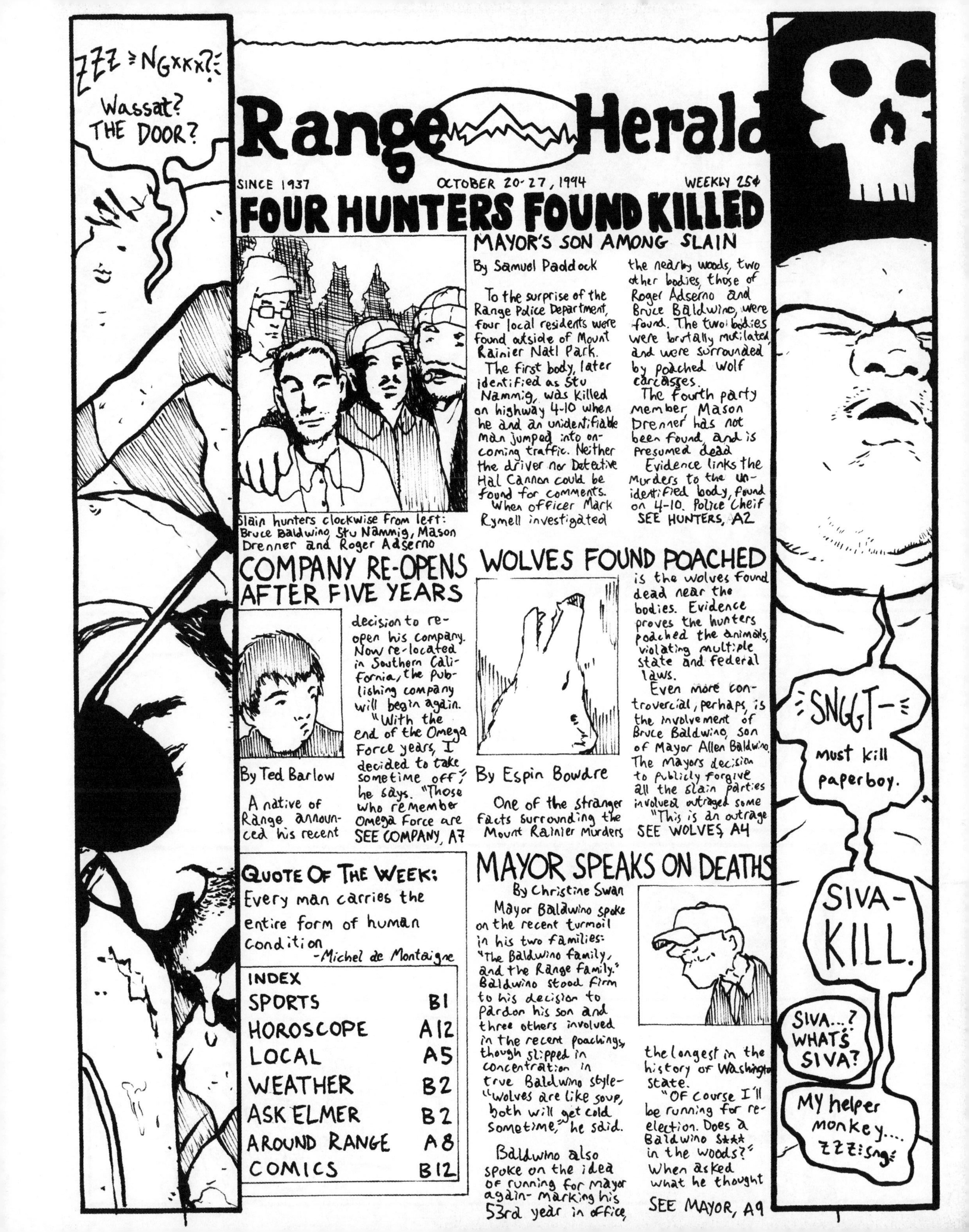
ZZZ ≡ NGxxx?≡
Wassat? THE DOOR?
Range Herald
SINCE 1937
OCTOBER 20-27, 1994
WEEKLY 25¢
FOUR HUNTERS FOUND KILLED
MAYOR'S SON AMONG SLAIN
Slain hunters clockwise from left: Bruce Baldwino, Stu Nammig, Mason Drenner and Roger Adserno
By Samuel Paddock
To the surprise of the Range Police Department, four local residents were found outside of Mount Rainier Natl Park.
The first body, later identified as Stu Nammig, was killed on highway 4-10 when he and an unidentifiable man jumped into on-coming traffic. Neither the driver nor Detective Hal Cannon could be found for comments.
When officer Mark Rymell investigated the nearby woods, two other bodies, those of Roger Adserno and Bruce Baldwino, were found. The two bodies were brutally mutilated and were surrounded by poached wolf carcasses.
The fourth party member Mason Drenner has not been found, and is presumed dead.
Evidence links the murders to the unidentified body, found on 4-10. Police Cheif
SEE HUNTERS, A2
COMPANY RE-OPENS AFTER FIVE YEARS
By Ted Barlow
A native of Range announced his recent decision to re-open his company. Now re-located in Southern California, the publishing company will begin again.
"With the end of the Omega Force years, I decided to take sometime off," he says. "Those who remember Omega Force are
SEE COMPANY, A7
WOLVES FOUND POACHED
By Espin Bowdre
One of the stranger facts surrounding the Mount Rainier Murders is the wolves found dead near the bodies. Evidence proves the hunters poached the animals, violating multiple state and federal laws.
Even more controvercial, perhaps, is the involvement of Bruce Baldwino, son of Mayor Allen Baldwino. The Mayors decision to publicly forgive all the slain parties involved outraged some.
"This is an outrage
SEE WOLVES, A4
QUOTE OF THE WEEK:
Every man carries the entire form of human condition
-Michel de Montaigne
INDEX
SPORTS B1
HOROSCOPE A12
LOCAL A5
WEATHER B2
ASK ELMER B2
AROUND RANGE A8
COMICS B12
MAYOR SPEAKS ON DEATHS
By Christine Swan
Mayor Baldwino spoke on the recent turmoil in his two families: "The Baldwino family, and the Range family." Baldwino stood firm to his decision to pardon his son and three others involved in the recent poachings, though slipped in concentration in true Baldwino style- "Wolves are like soup, both will get cold sometime," he said.
Baldwino also spoke on the idea of running for mayor again- marking his 53rd year in office, the longest in the history of Washington state.
"Of course I'll be running for re-election. Does a Baldwino S*** in the woods?" When asked what he thought
SEE MAYOR, A9
≡SNGGT-≡
Must kill paperboy.
SIVA-KILL.
SIVA...? WHAT'S SIVA?
My helper monkey.... ZZZ≡Sng≡

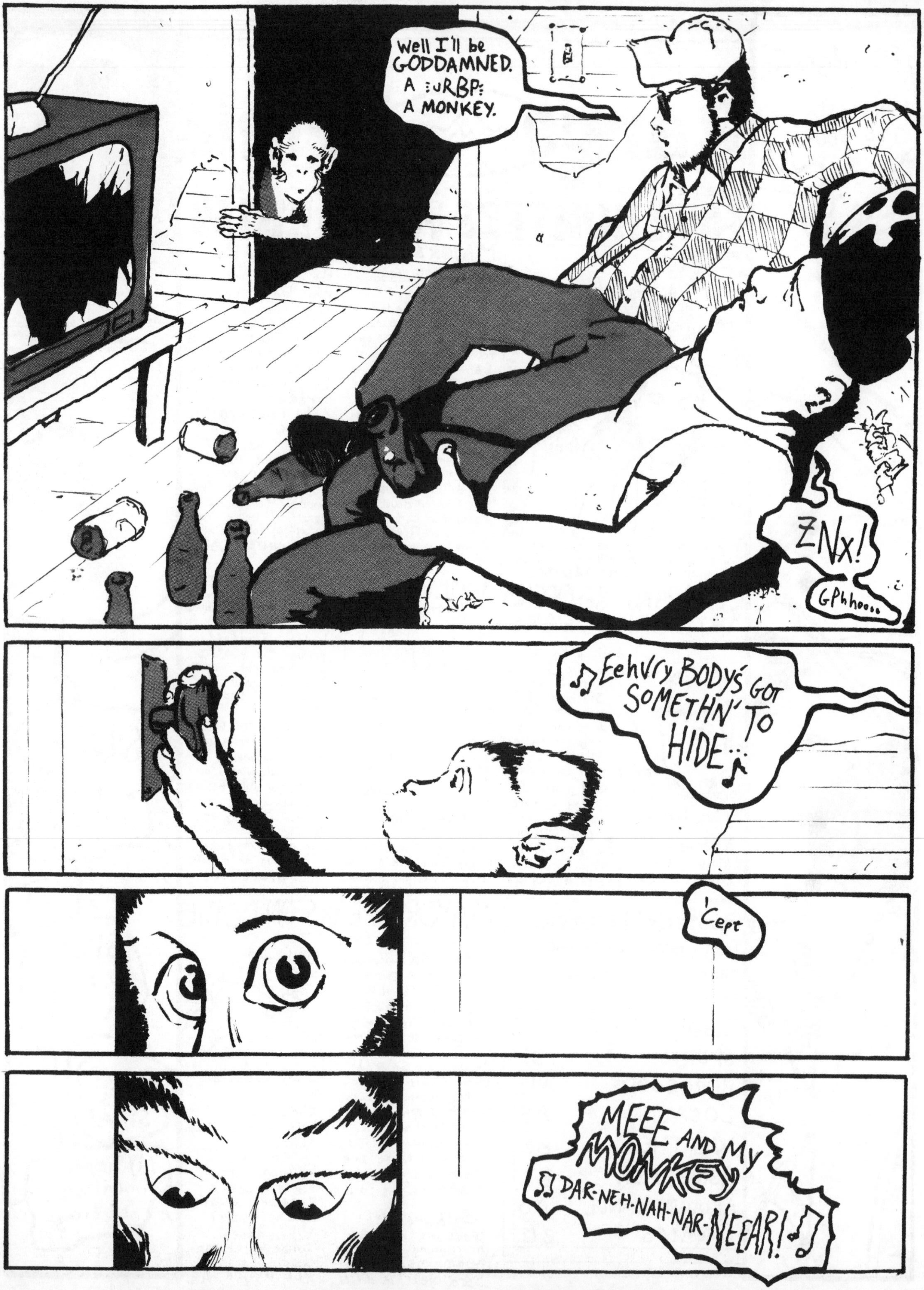
Well I'll be GODDAMNED. A :uRBP: A MONKEY.
ZNx!
GPhhooo..
Eehvry BODY's GOT SOMETHN' TO HIDE..
'Cept
MEEE AND MY MONKEY DAR-NEH-NAH-NAR-NEEAR!

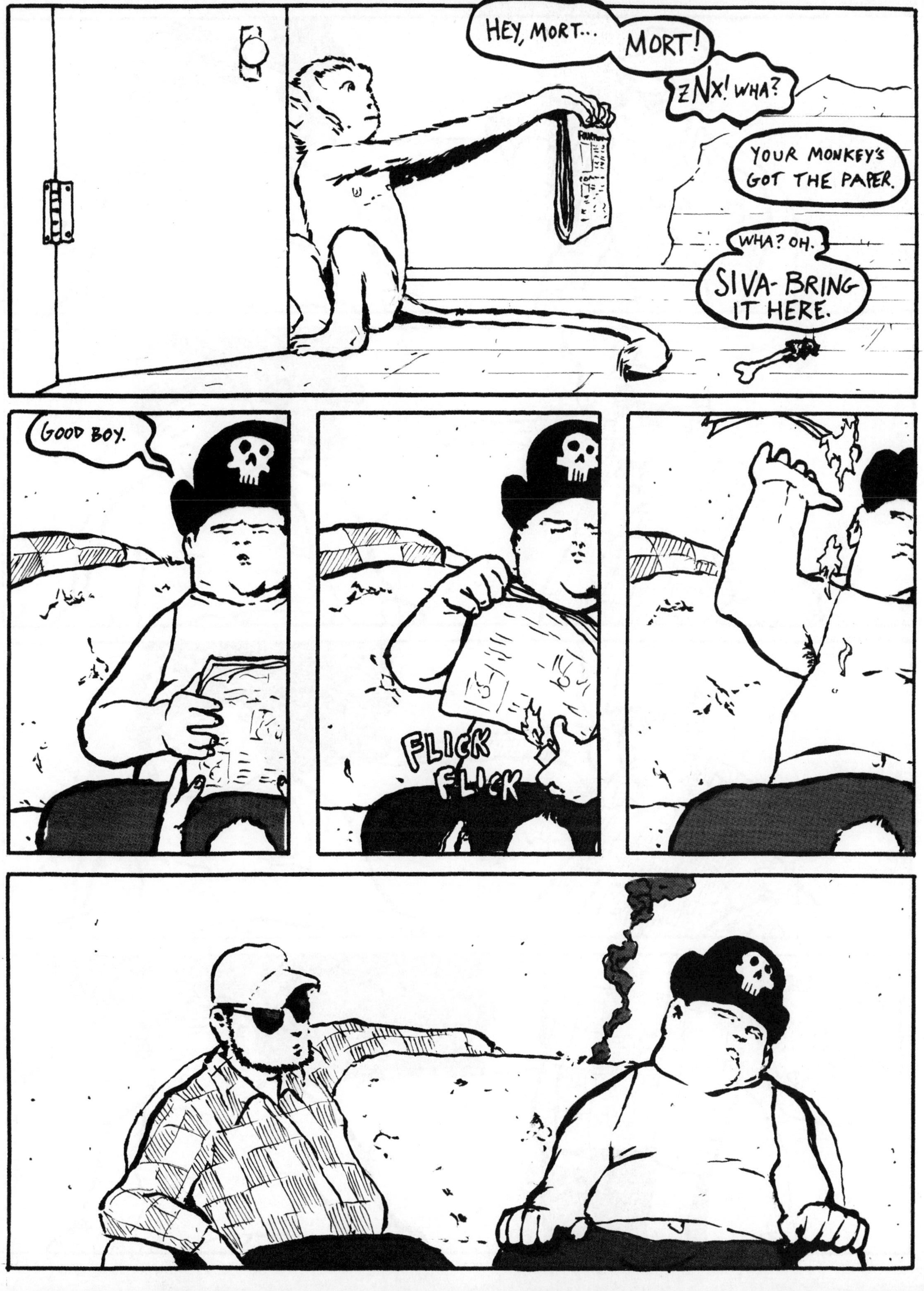
HEY, MORT...
MORT!
ZNX! WHA?
YOUR MONKEY'S GOT THE PAPER.
WHA? OH.
SIVA- BRING IT HERE.
GOOD BOY.
FLICK
FLICK

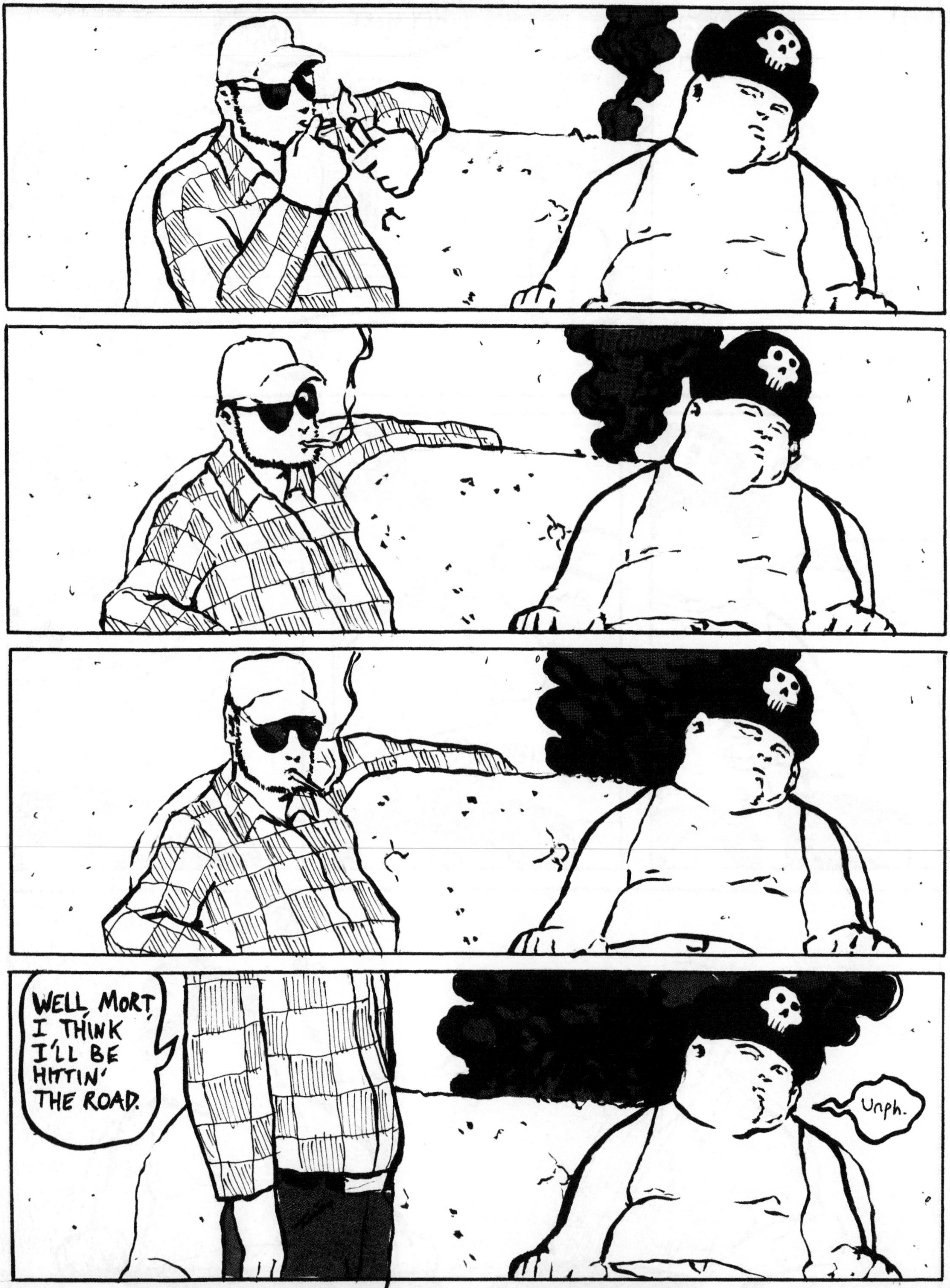
WELL, MORT, I THINK I'LL BE HITTIN' THE ROAD.
Unph.

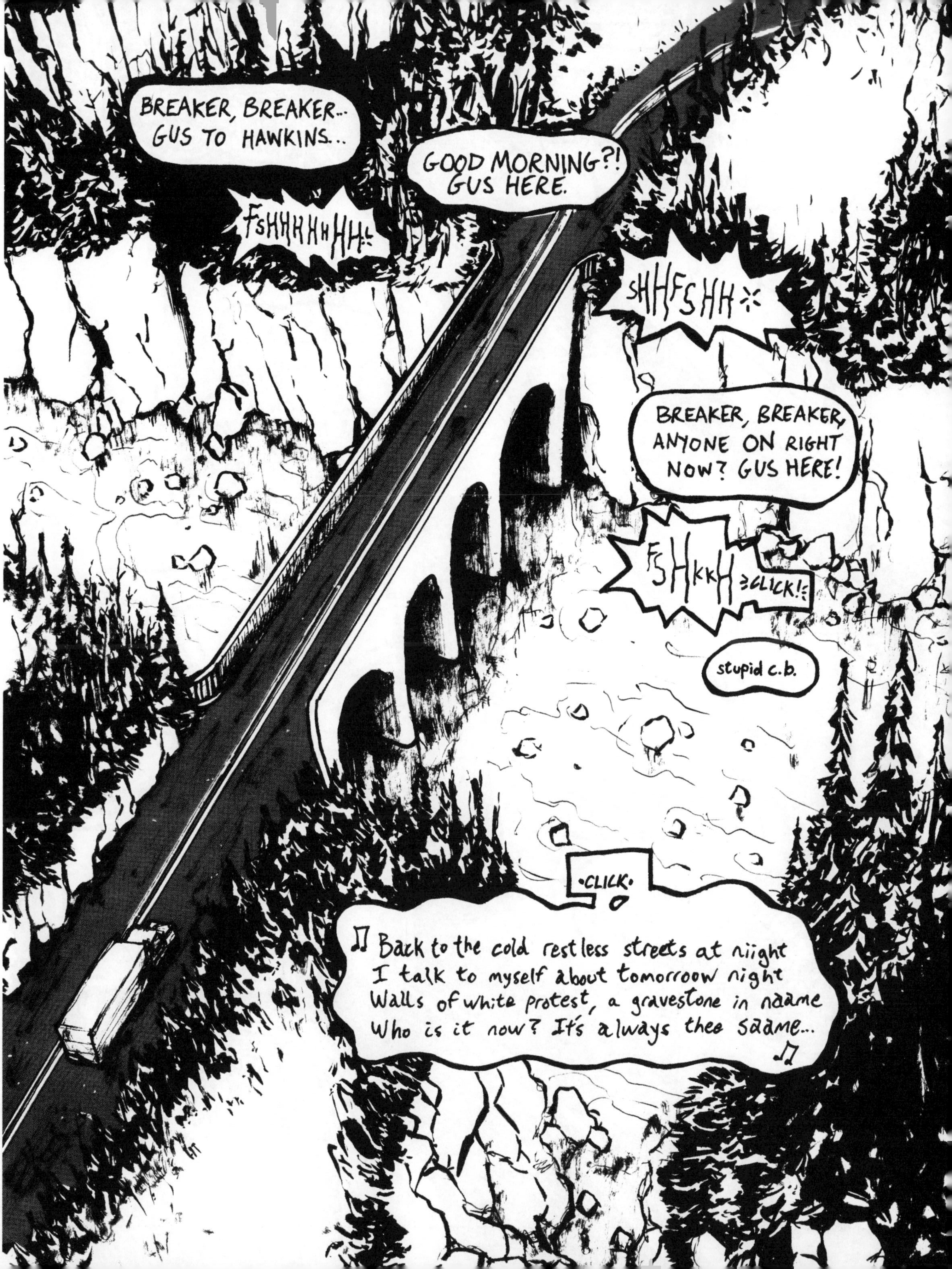
BREAKER, BREAKER... GUS TO HAWKINS...
FSHHHHHHHH
GOOD MORNING?! GUS HERE.
SHHFSHH
BREAKER, BREAKER, ANYONE ON RIGHT NOW? GUS HERE!
FSHKKH
CLICK!
stupid c.b.
•CLICK•
Back to the cold restless streets at niight
I talk to myself about tomorroow night
Walls of white protest, a gravestone in naame
Who is it now? It's always thee saame...

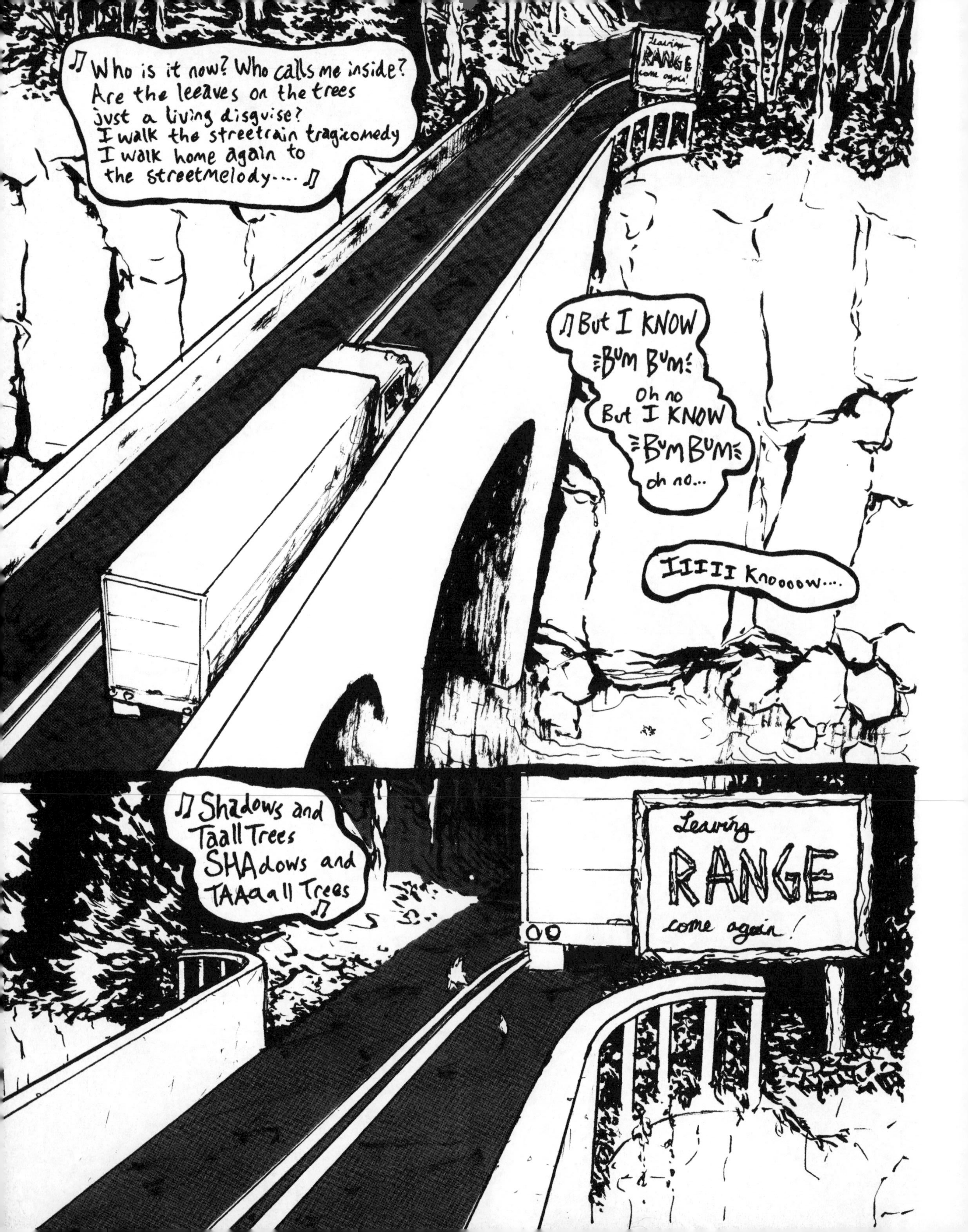
♫ Who is it now? Who calls me inside? Are the leeaves on the trees just a living disguise? I walk the streetrain tragicomedy I walk home again to the streetmelody.... ♫
Leaving RANGE come again!
♫ But I KNOW BUM BUM oh no But I KNOW BUM BUM oh no...
IIIII Knooooow....
♫ Shadows and Taall Trees SHAdows and TAAaall Trees ♫
Leaving RANGE come again!

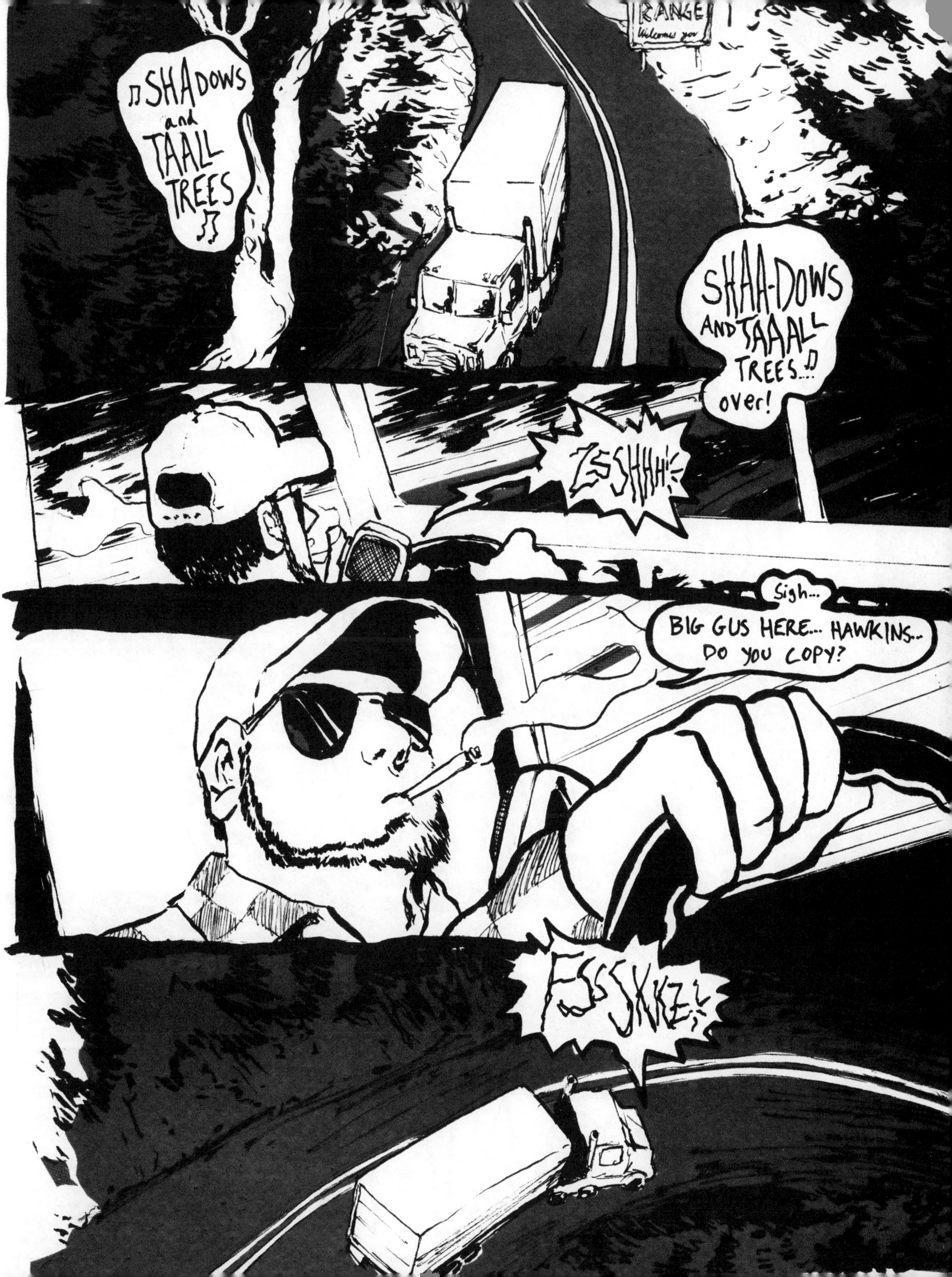

♫SHADOWS and TAALL TREES♫
SHAA-DOWS AND TAAALL TREES...♫ over!
ZSSHHH!
Sigh...
BIG GUS HERE... HAWKINS... DO YOU COPY?
FSSSKKZ!

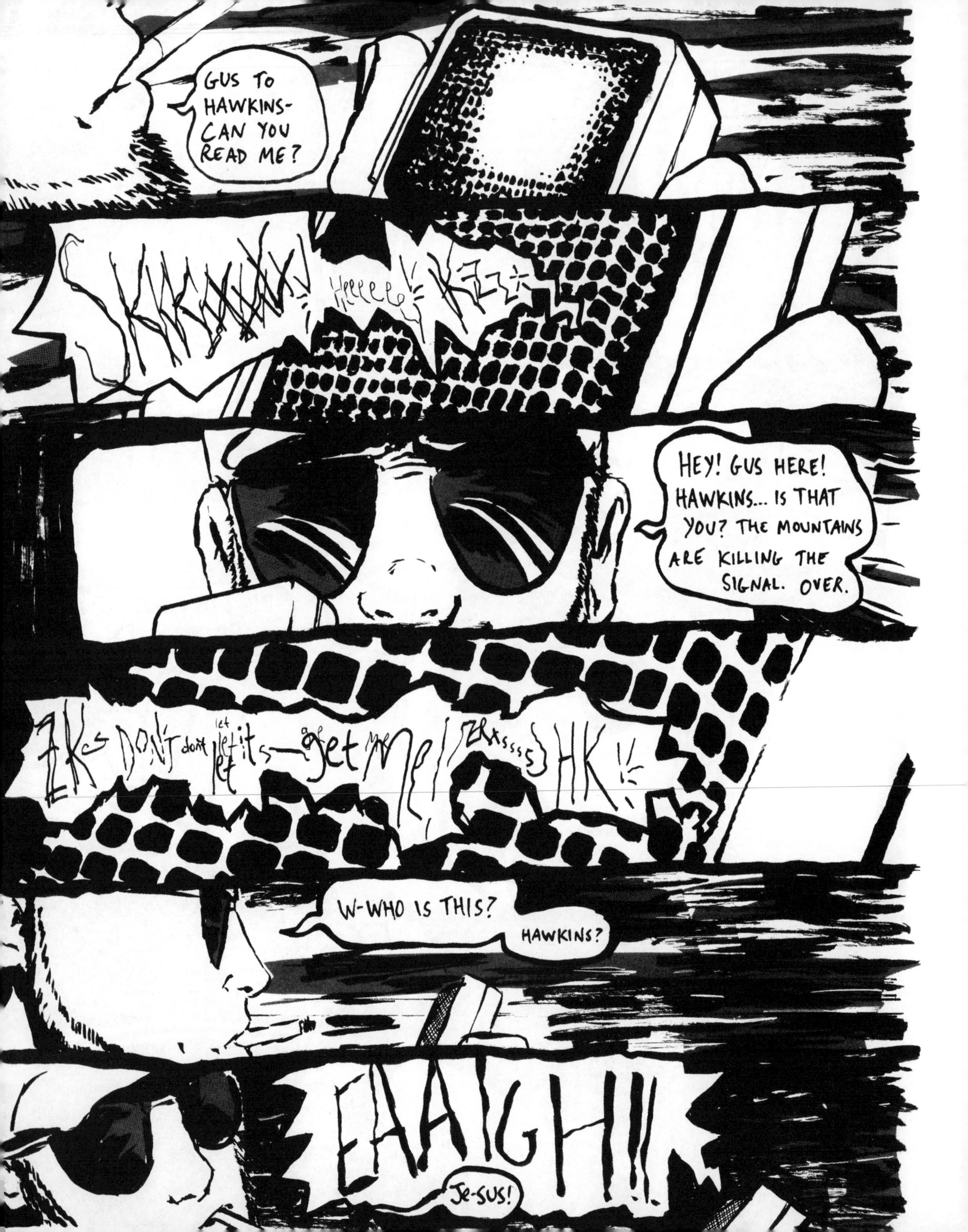
GUS TO HAWKINS- CAN YOU READ ME?
SKKKAAAAK!
Heeeee!
KZZZ
HEY! GUS HERE! HAWKINS... IS THAT YOU? THE MOUNTAINS ARE KILLING THE SIGNAL. OVER.
ZKs DON'T dont let let its—get me! ZRAssss SHK!
W-WHO IS THIS?
HAWKINS?
EAAIGH!!
Je-SUS!

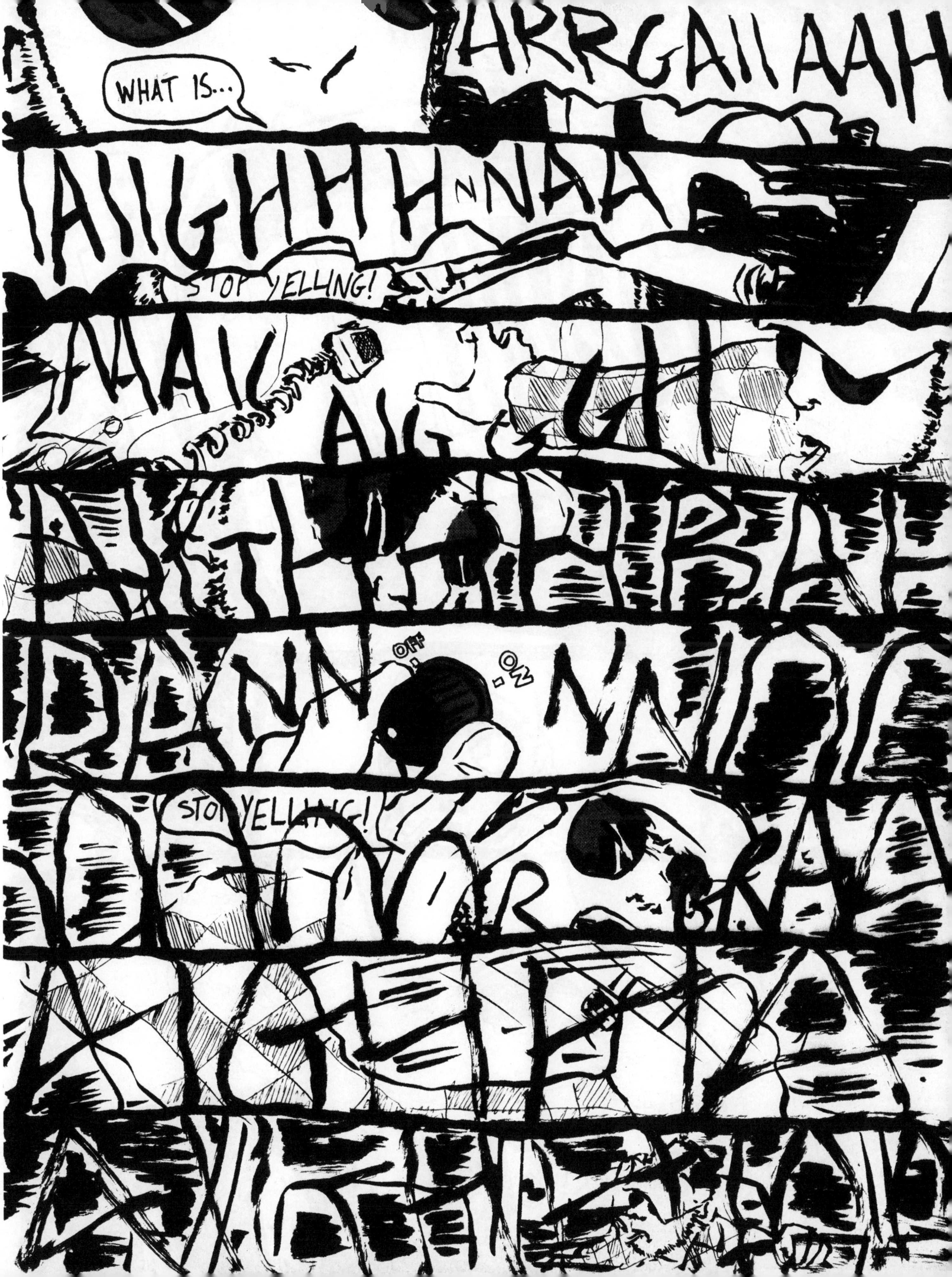
WHAT IS...
HRRGAIIAAH
AIIGHHHNNAA
STOP YELLING!
OFF
ON
STOP YELLING!

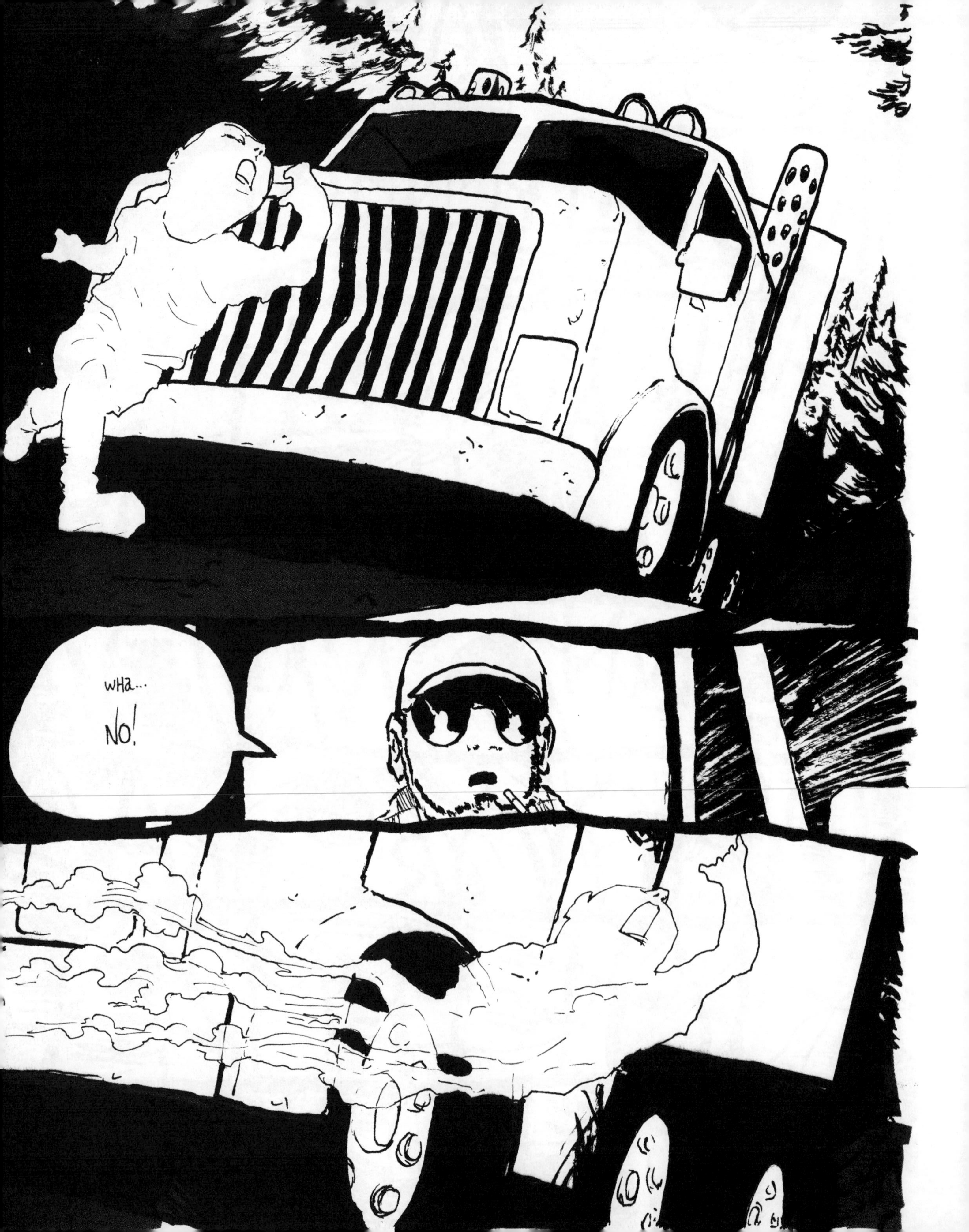
wha...
No!

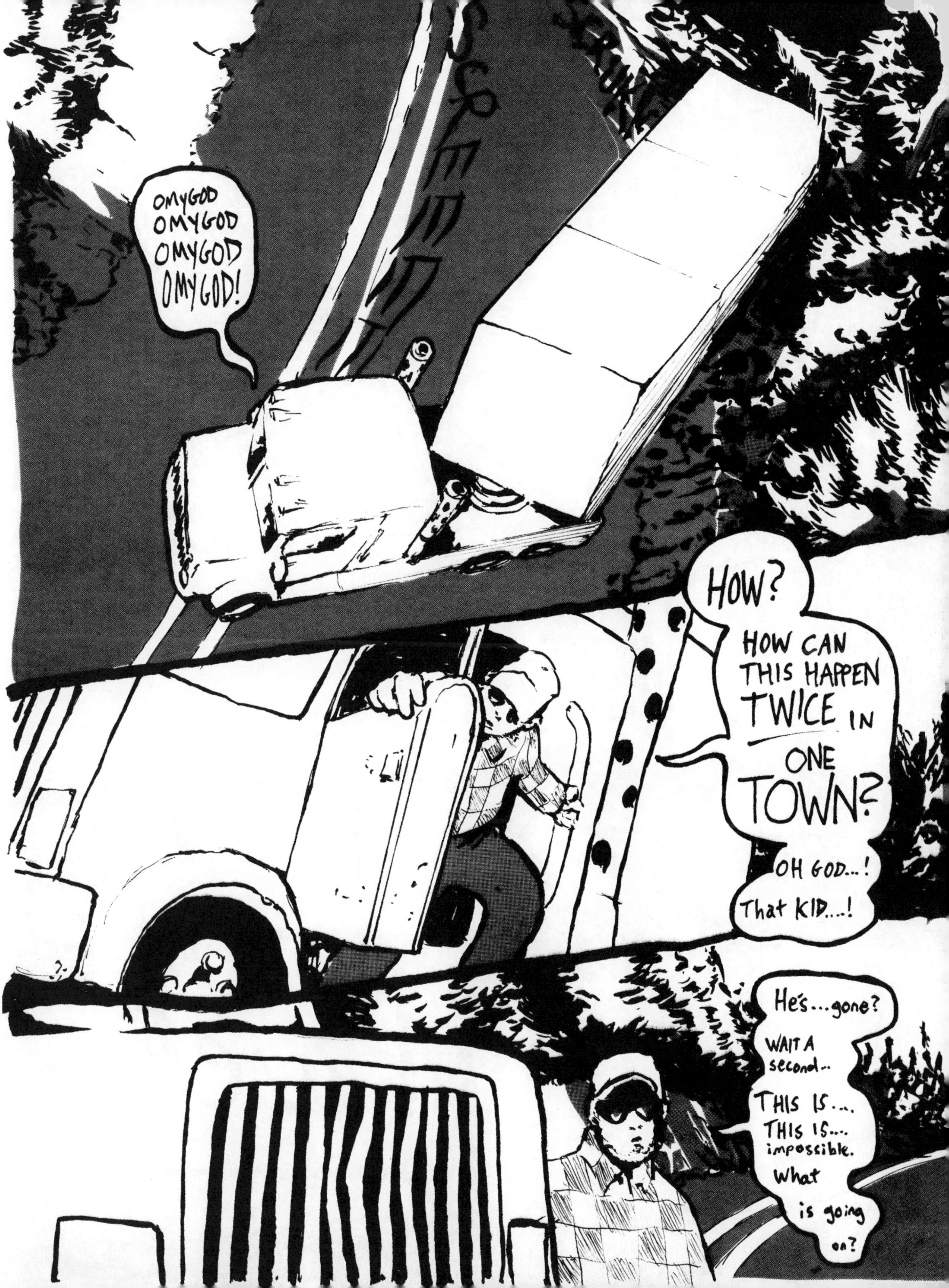
SCREEEE
SCRUK
OMYGOD OMYGOD OMYGOD OMYGOD!
HOW?
HOW CAN THIS HAPPEN TWICE IN ONE TOWN?
OH GOD...! That KID....!
He's...gone?
WAIT A second..
THIS IS.... THIS IS.... impossible.
What is going on?

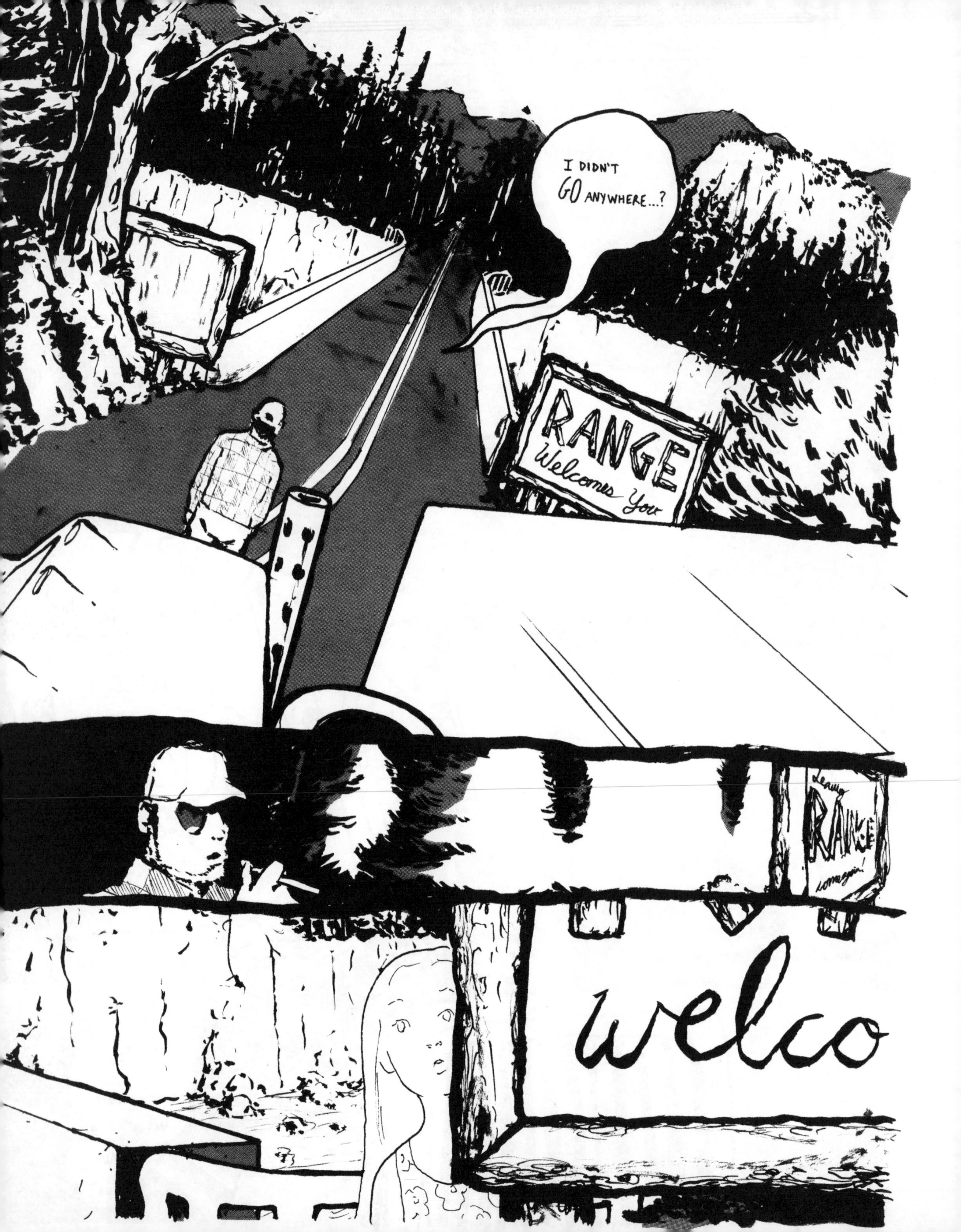
I DIDN'T GO ANYWHERE...?
RANGE
Welcomes You
welco

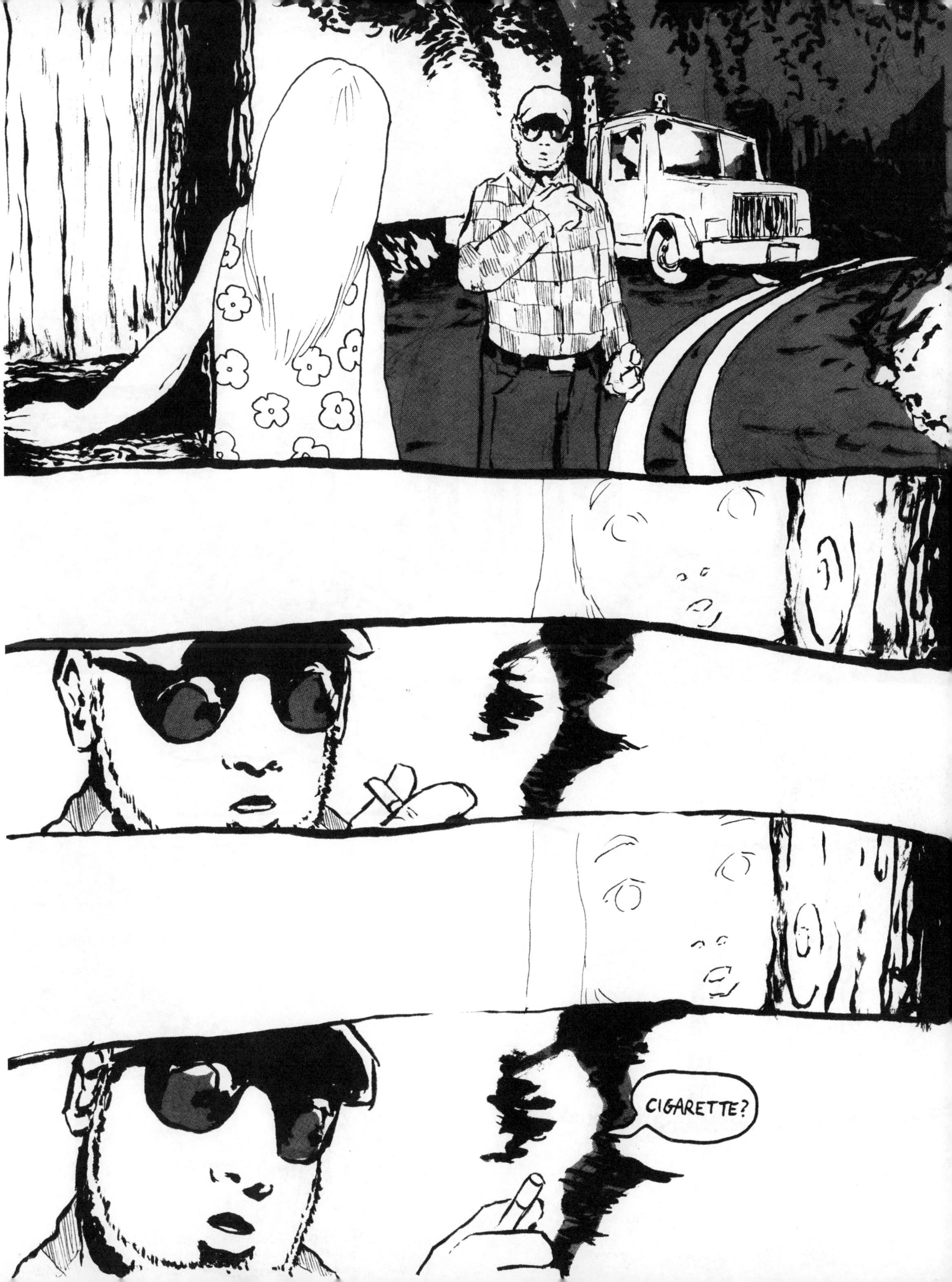
CIGARETTE?

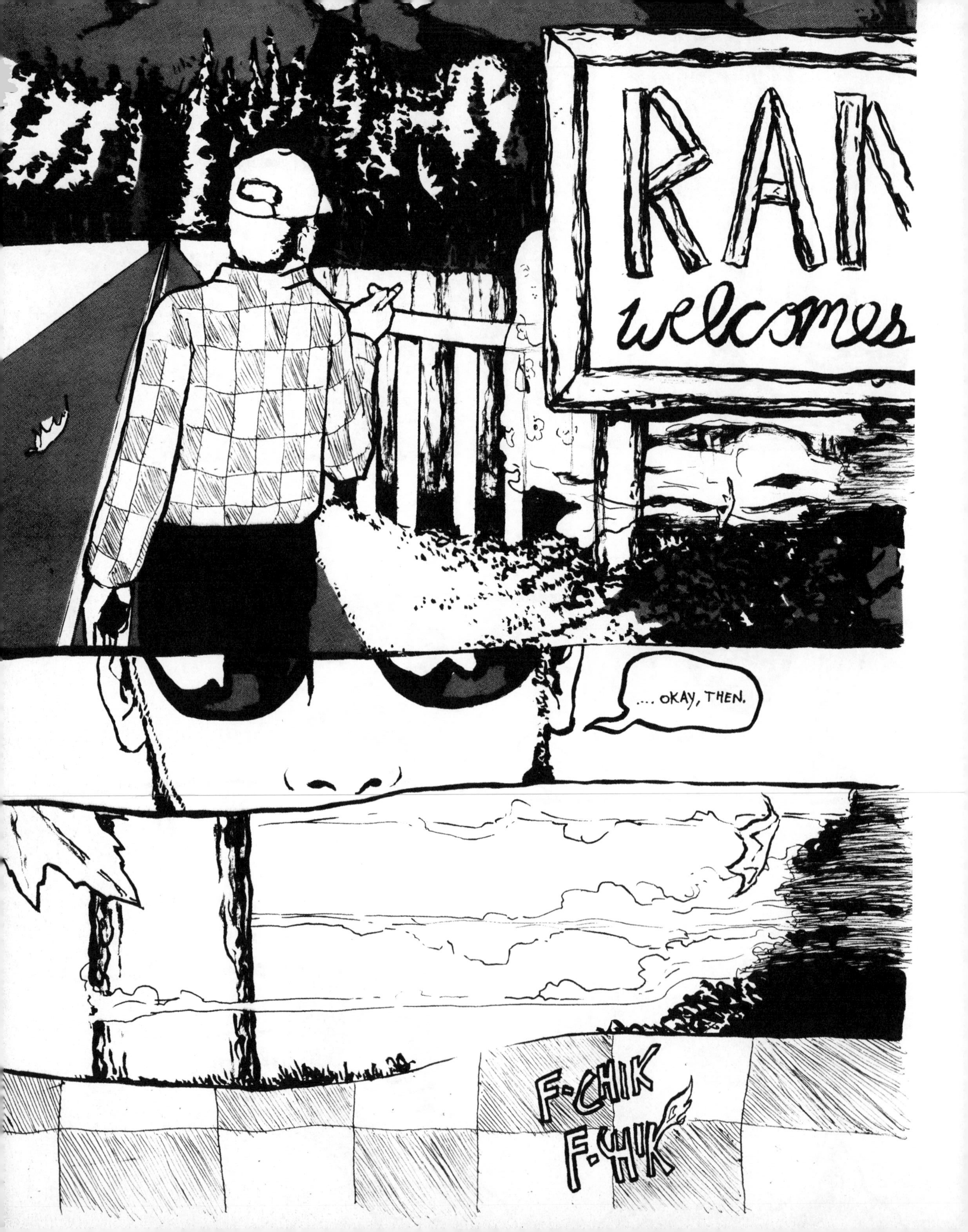
RAN
welcomes
.... OKAY, THEN.
F-CHIK
F-CHIK

2.
OUR FENCES

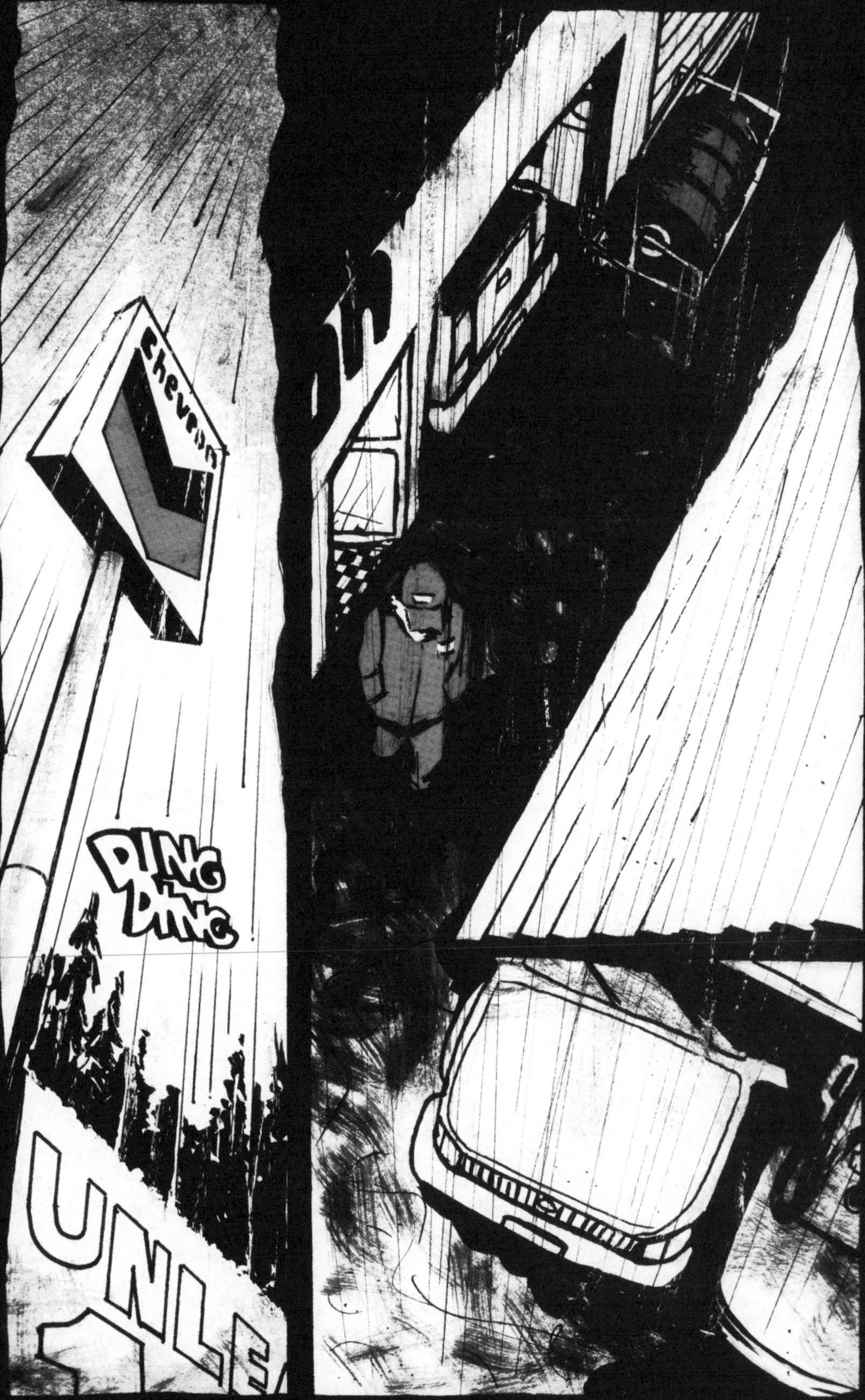
Chevron
DING DING
UNLE

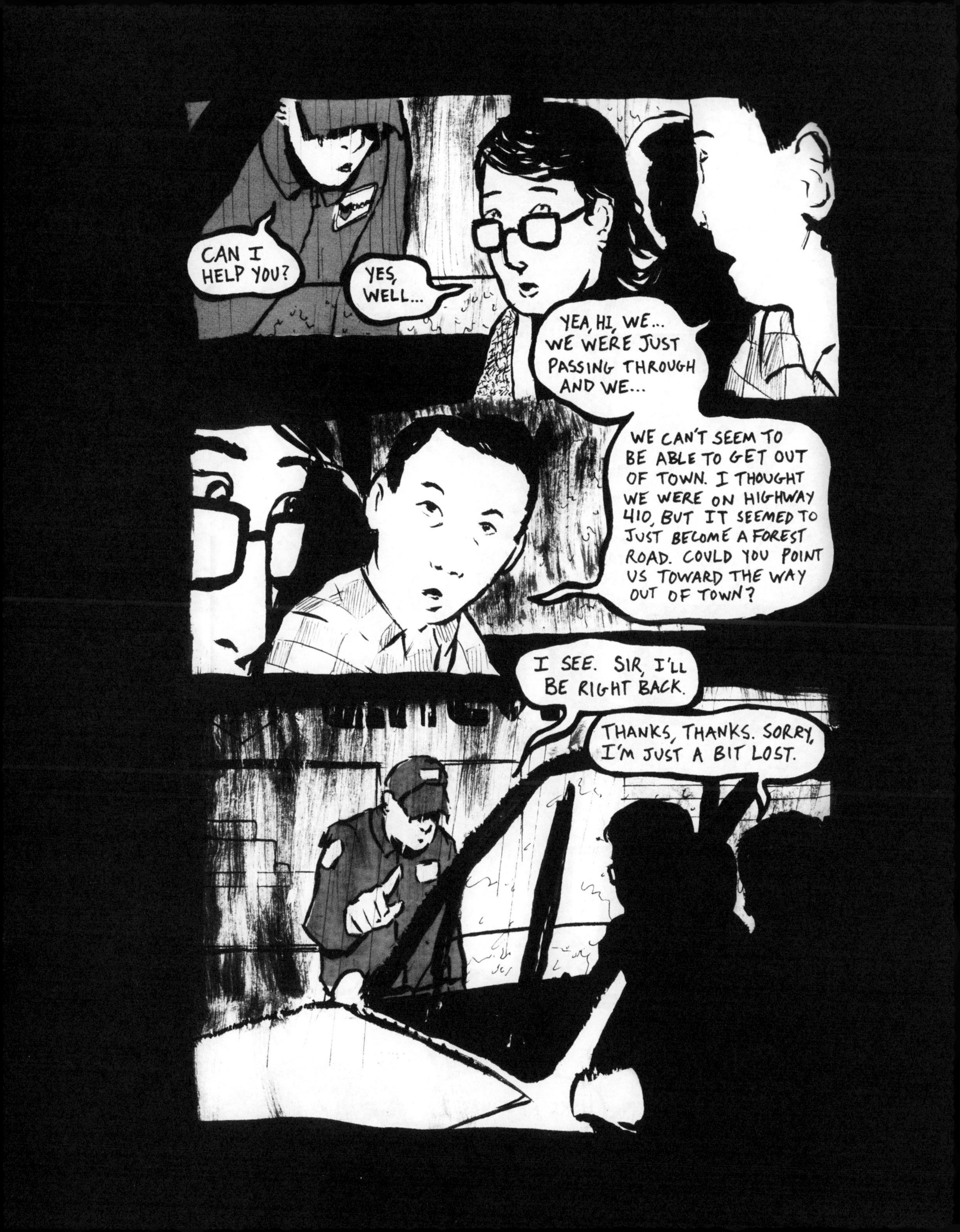
CAN I HELP YOU?
YES, WELL...
YEA, HI, WE... WE WERE JUST PASSING THROUGH AND WE...
WE CAN'T SEEM TO BE ABLE TO GET OUT OF TOWN. I THOUGHT WE WERE ON HIGHWAY 410, BUT IT SEEMED TO JUST BECOME A FOREST ROAD. COULD YOU POINT US TOWARD THE WAY OUT OF TOWN?
I SEE. SIR, I'LL BE RIGHT BACK.
THANKS, THANKS. SORRY, I'M JUST A BIT LOST.

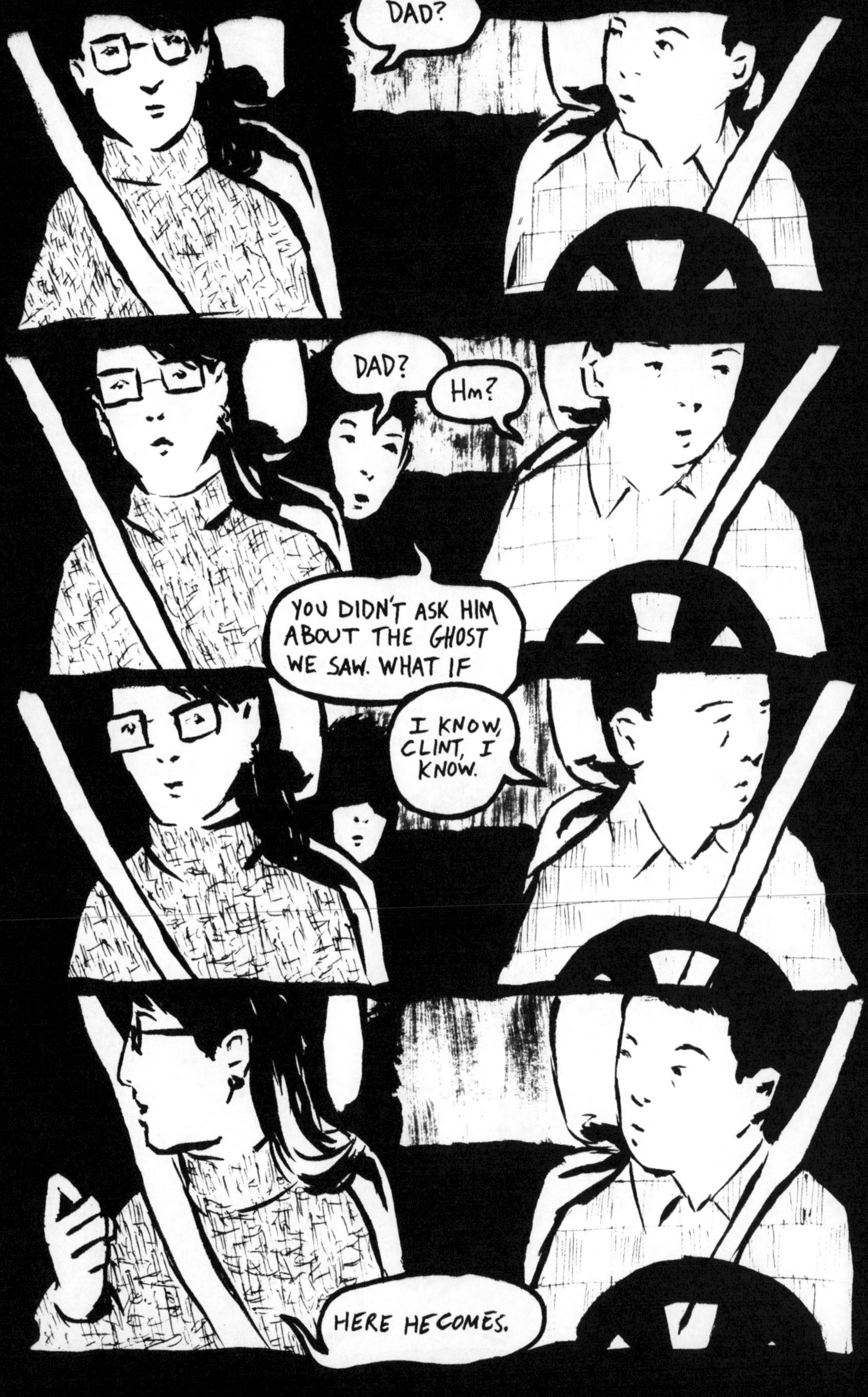
DAD?
DAD?
Hm?
YOU DIDN'T ASK HIM ABOUT THE GHOST WE SAW. WHAT IF
I KNOW, CLINT, I KNOW.
HERE HE COMES.

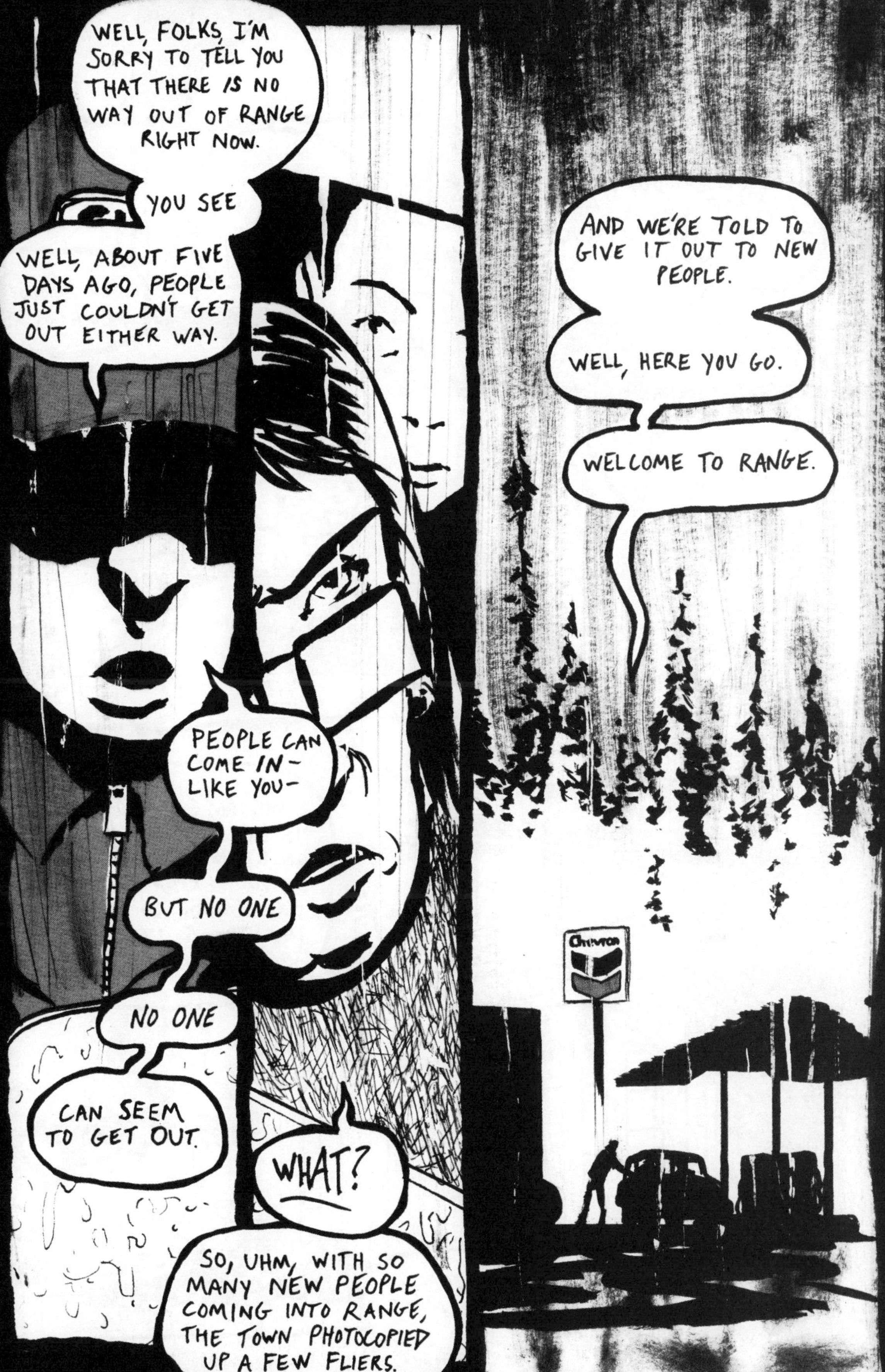
WELL, FOLKS, I'M SORRY TO TELL YOU THAT THERE IS NO WAY OUT OF RANGE RIGHT NOW.
YOU SEE
WELL, ABOUT FIVE DAYS AGO, PEOPLE JUST COULDN'T GET OUT EITHER WAY.
PEOPLE CAN COME IN- LIKE YOU-
BUT NO ONE
NO ONE
CAN SEEM TO GET OUT.
WHAT?
SO, UHM, WITH SO MANY NEW PEOPLE COMING INTO RANGE, THE TOWN PHOTOCOPIED UP A FEW FLIERS.
AND WE'RE TOLD TO GIVE IT OUT TO NEW PEOPLE.
WELL, HERE YOU GO.
WELCOME TO RANGE.
Chevron

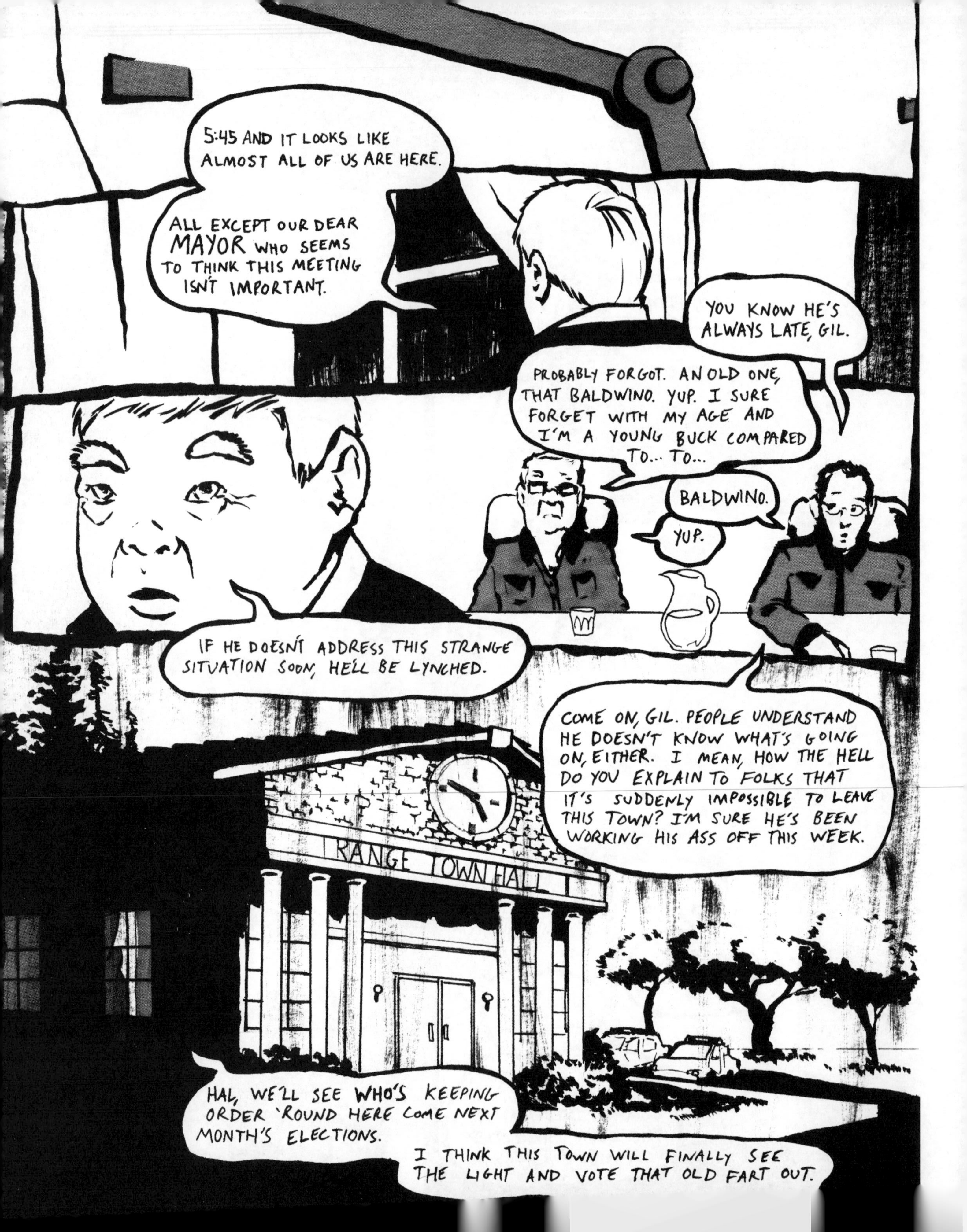
5:45 AND IT LOOKS LIKE ALMOST ALL OF US ARE HERE.
ALL EXCEPT OUR DEAR MAYOR WHO SEEMS TO THINK THIS MEETING ISN'T IMPORTANT.
YOU KNOW HE'S ALWAYS LATE, GIL.
PROBABLY FORGOT. AN OLD ONE, THAT BALDWINO. YUP. I SURE FORGET WITH MY AGE AND I'M A YOUNG BUCK COMPARED TO... TO...
BALDWINO.
YUP.
IF HE DOESN'T ADDRESS THIS STRANGE SITUATION SOON, HE'LL BE LYNCHED.
COME ON, GIL. PEOPLE UNDERSTAND HE DOESN'T KNOW WHAT'S GOING ON, EITHER. I MEAN, HOW THE HELL DO YOU EXPLAIN TO FOLKS THAT IT'S SUDDENLY IMPOSSIBLE TO LEAVE THIS TOWN? I'M SURE HE'S BEEN WORKING HIS ASS OFF THIS WEEK.
RANGE TOWN HALL
HAL, WE'LL SEE WHO'S KEEPING ORDER 'ROUND HERE COME NEXT MONTH'S ELECTIONS.
I THINK THIS TOWN WILL FINALLY SEE THE LIGHT AND VOTE THAT OLD FART OUT.

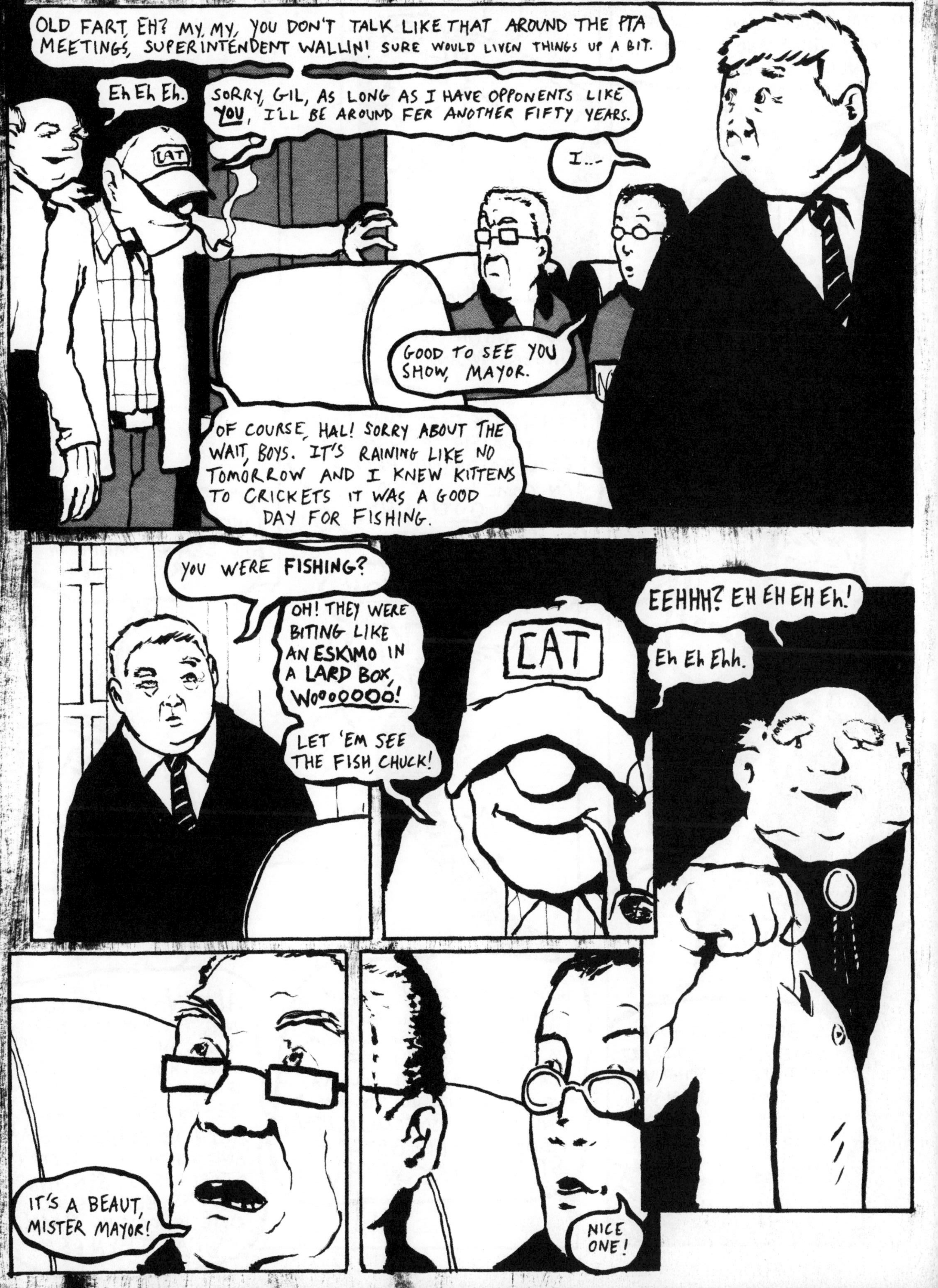
OLD FART, EH? MY, MY, YOU DON'T TALK LIKE THAT AROUND THE PTA MEETINGS, SUPERINTENDENT WALLIN! SURE WOULD LIVEN THINGS UP A BIT.
Eh Eh Eh.
SORRY, GIL, AS LONG AS I HAVE OPPONENTS LIKE YOU, I'LL BE AROUND FER ANOTHER FIFTY YEARS.
I...
GOOD TO SEE YOU SHOW, MAYOR.
OF COURSE, HAL! SORRY ABOUT THE WAIT, BOYS. IT'S RAINING LIKE NO TOMORROW AND I KNEW KITTENS TO CRICKETS IT WAS A GOOD DAY FOR FISHING.
YOU WERE FISHING?
OH! THEY WERE BITING LIKE AN ESKIMO IN A LARD BOX, WOOOOOOO!
LET 'EM SEE THE FISH, CHUCK!
EEHHH? EH EH EH Eh!
Eh Eh Ehh.
IT'S A BEAUT, MISTER MAYOR!
NICE ONE!

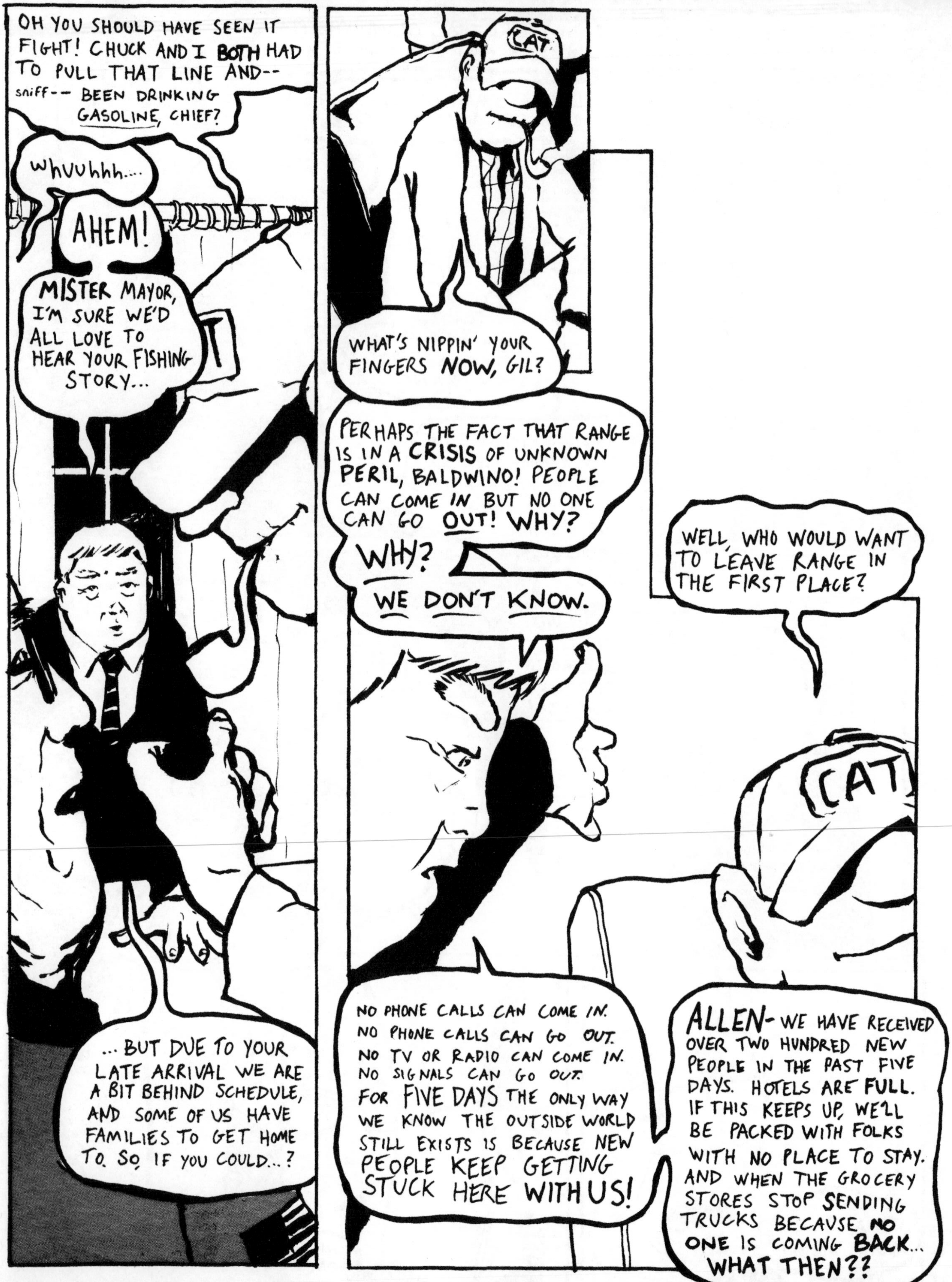
OH YOU SHOULD HAVE SEEN IT FIGHT! CHUCK AND I BOTH HAD TO PULL THAT LINE AND--
sniff-- BEEN DRINKING GASOLINE, CHIEF?
whuuhhh....
AHEM!
MISTER MAYOR, I'M SURE WE'D ALL LOVE TO HEAR YOUR FISHING STORY...
...BUT DUE TO YOUR LATE ARRIVAL WE ARE A BIT BEHIND SCHEDULE, AND SOME OF US HAVE FAMILIES TO GET HOME TO. SO, IF YOU COULD...?
CAT
WHAT'S NIPPIN' YOUR FINGERS NOW, GIL?
PERHAPS THE FACT THAT RANGE IS IN A CRISIS OF UNKNOWN PERIL, BALDWINO! PEOPLE CAN COME IN BUT NO ONE CAN GO OUT! WHY?
WHY?
WE DON'T KNOW.
WELL, WHO WOULD WANT TO LEAVE RANGE IN THE FIRST PLACE?
CAT
NO PHONE CALLS CAN COME IN. NO PHONE CALLS CAN GO OUT. NO TV OR RADIO CAN COME IN. NO SIGNALS CAN GO OUT. FOR FIVE DAYS THE ONLY WAY WE KNOW THE OUTSIDE WORLD STILL EXISTS IS BECAUSE NEW PEOPLE KEEP GETTING STUCK HERE WITH US!
ALLEN- WE HAVE RECEIVED OVER TWO HUNDRED NEW PEOPLE IN THE PAST FIVE DAYS. HOTELS ARE FULL. IF THIS KEEPS UP, WE'LL BE PACKED WITH FOLKS WITH NO PLACE TO STAY. AND WHEN THE GROCERY STORES STOP SENDING TRUCKS BECAUSE NO ONE IS COMING BACK... WHAT THEN??

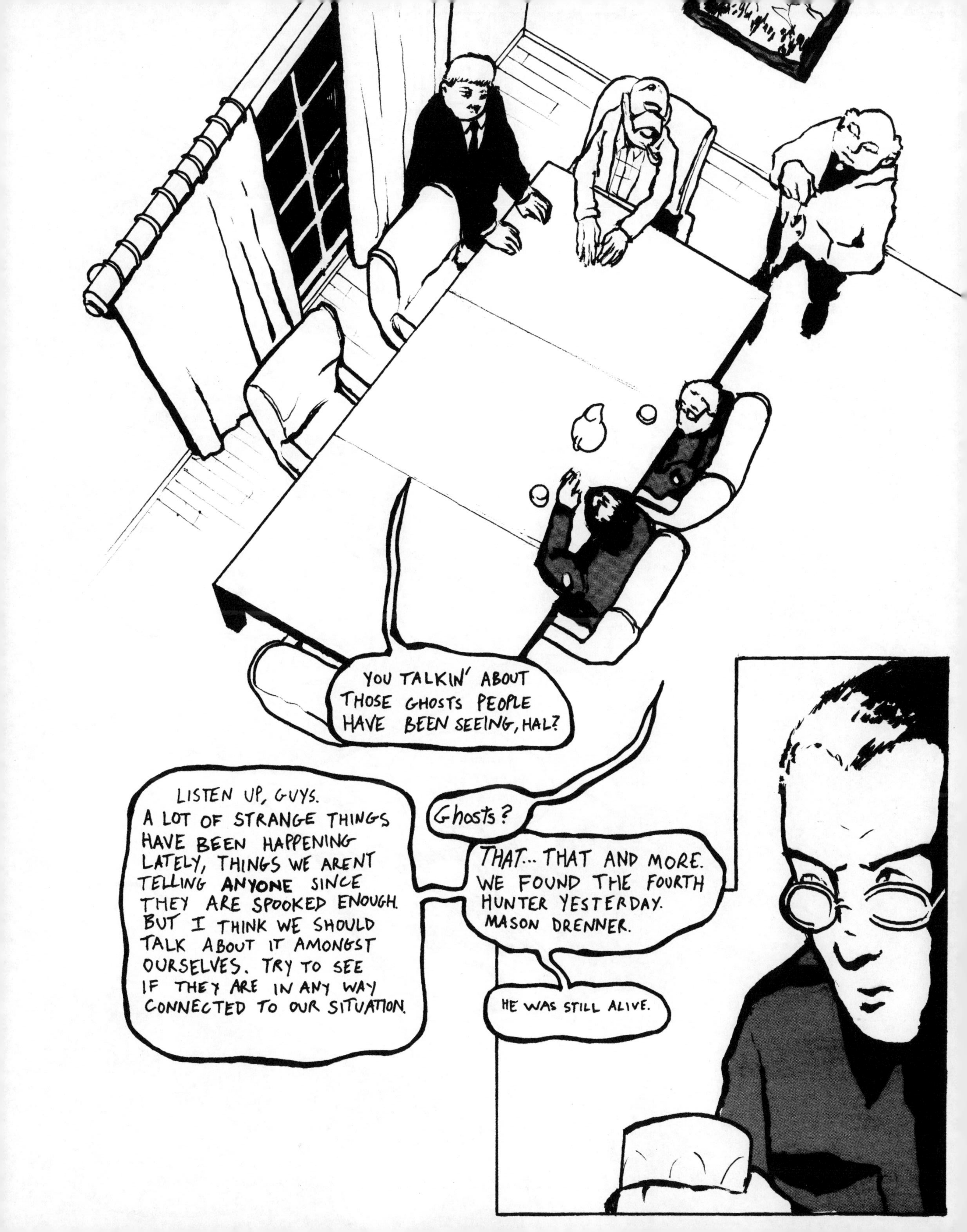
LISTEN UP, GUYS. A LOT OF STRANGE THINGS HAVE BEEN HAPPENING LATELY, THINGS WE ARENT TELLING ANYONE SINCE THEY ARE SPOOKED ENOUGH. BUT I THINK WE SHOULD TALK ABOUT IT AMONGST OURSELVES. TRY TO SEE IF THEY ARE IN ANY WAY CONNECTED TO OUR SITUATION.
YOU TALKIN' ABOUT THOSE GHOSTS PEOPLE HAVE BEEN SEEING, HAL?
Ghosts?
THAT... THAT AND MORE. WE FOUND THE FOURTH HUNTER YESTERDAY. MASON DRENNER.
HE WAS STILL ALIVE.

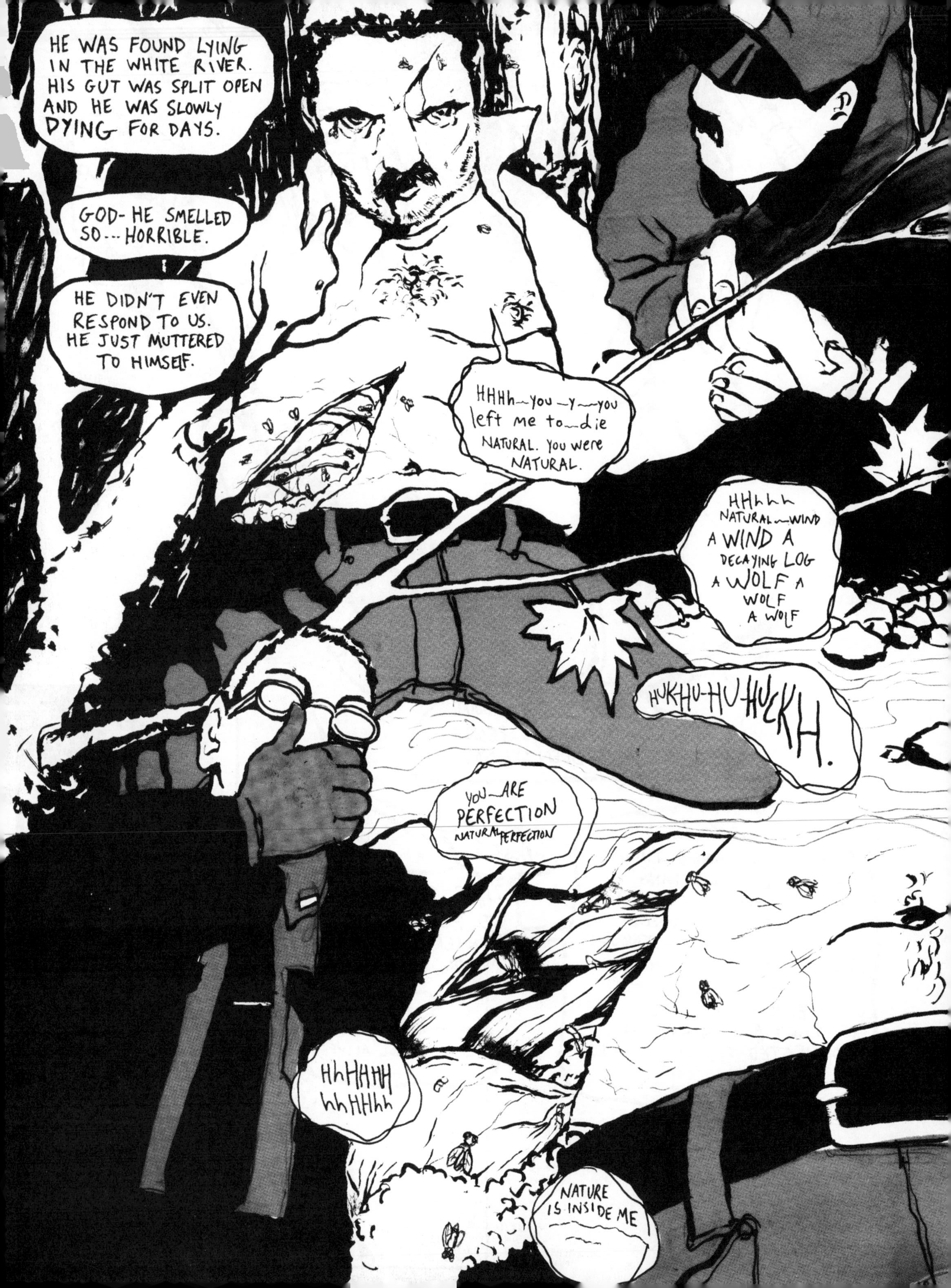
HE WAS FOUND LYING IN THE WHITE RIVER. HIS GUT WAS SPLIT OPEN AND HE WAS SLOWLY DYING FOR DAYS.
GOD- HE SMELLED SO... HORRIBLE.
HE DIDN'T EVEN RESPOND TO US. HE JUST MUTTERED TO HIMSELF.
HHHh—you—y—you left me to—die NATURAL. You were NATURAL.
HHhhh NATURAL—WIND A WIND A DECAYING LOG A WOLF A WOLF A WOLF
HUK-HU-HU-HUCKH.
YOU—ARE PERFECTION NATURAL PERFECTION
HhHHHH hhHHhh
NATURE IS INSIDE ME

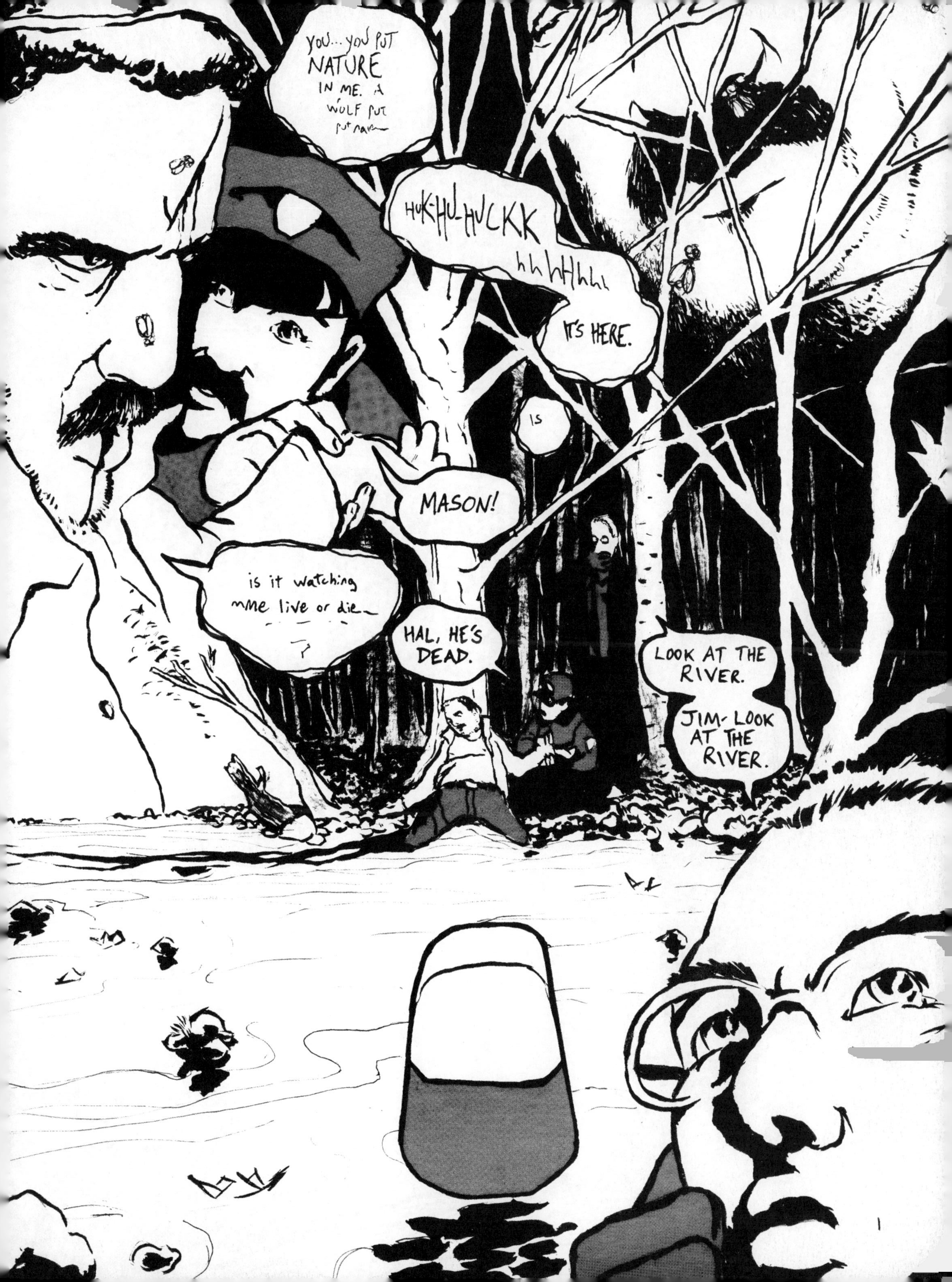
YOU... YOU PUT NATURE IN ME. A WOLF PUT
HUK-HU-HUCKK hhhHHhhh
IT'S HERE.
IS
MASON!
is it watching mme live or die—
HAL, HE'S DEAD.
LOOK AT THE RIVER.
JIM- LOOK AT THE RIVER.

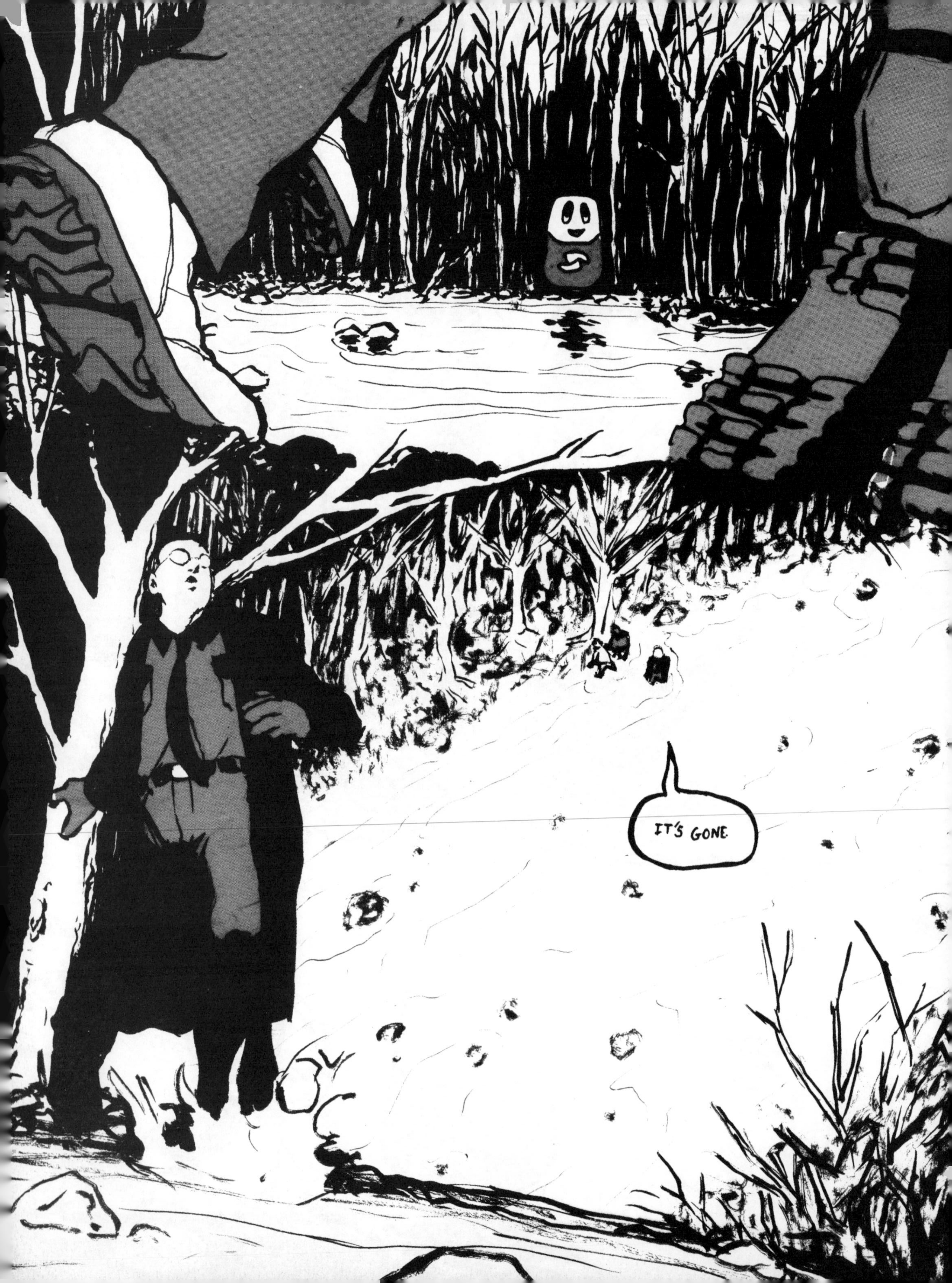
IT'S GONE

Welcome to Beautiful Range, Washington

Range was founded in 1920 as a logging town. Loggers used the White River to transport timber and the land that is now Range was used by loggers as a processing plant. Range now is best known for the McKee Timber Plant and crisp Far-Far's Pickles!

TO AUBURN, SEATTLE
410
Explore the ancient ways of the Snoquomish
SNOQUOMISH INDIAN RESERVATION
RANGE
Try our dandy pickles!
GRIFFIN AVE.
See our history at the McKee Timber Plant!
WHITE RIVER
TO MT. RAINIER
N
Range is known as "The Inland Island" because the White River actually breaks into two-- surrounding the town!

A GREETING FROM

MAYOR ALLEN BALDWINO

While I sure can't remember the first time I saw Range, (because I was born here and you don't remember much of that time due either to bad eyesight, bad mind or bad smell) I sure haven't tried to find a better place.

Enjoy your stay,

Allen Baldwino

Need a place to stay?

- ALPINE INN 825-4333
- THE TIMBER LODGE 825-5711
- THE ROADSIDE MOTEL 825-3925

OR STAY WITH OUR "OPEN HOUSE VOLUNTEERS." CALL 825-4999 TO LOCATE A VOLUNTEER.

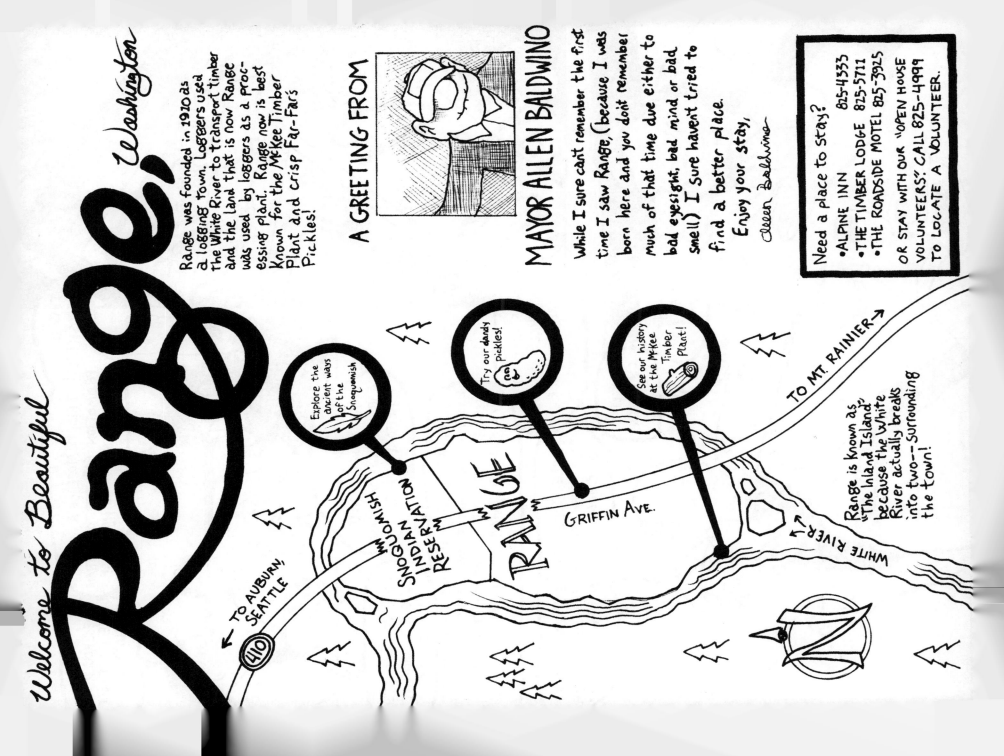

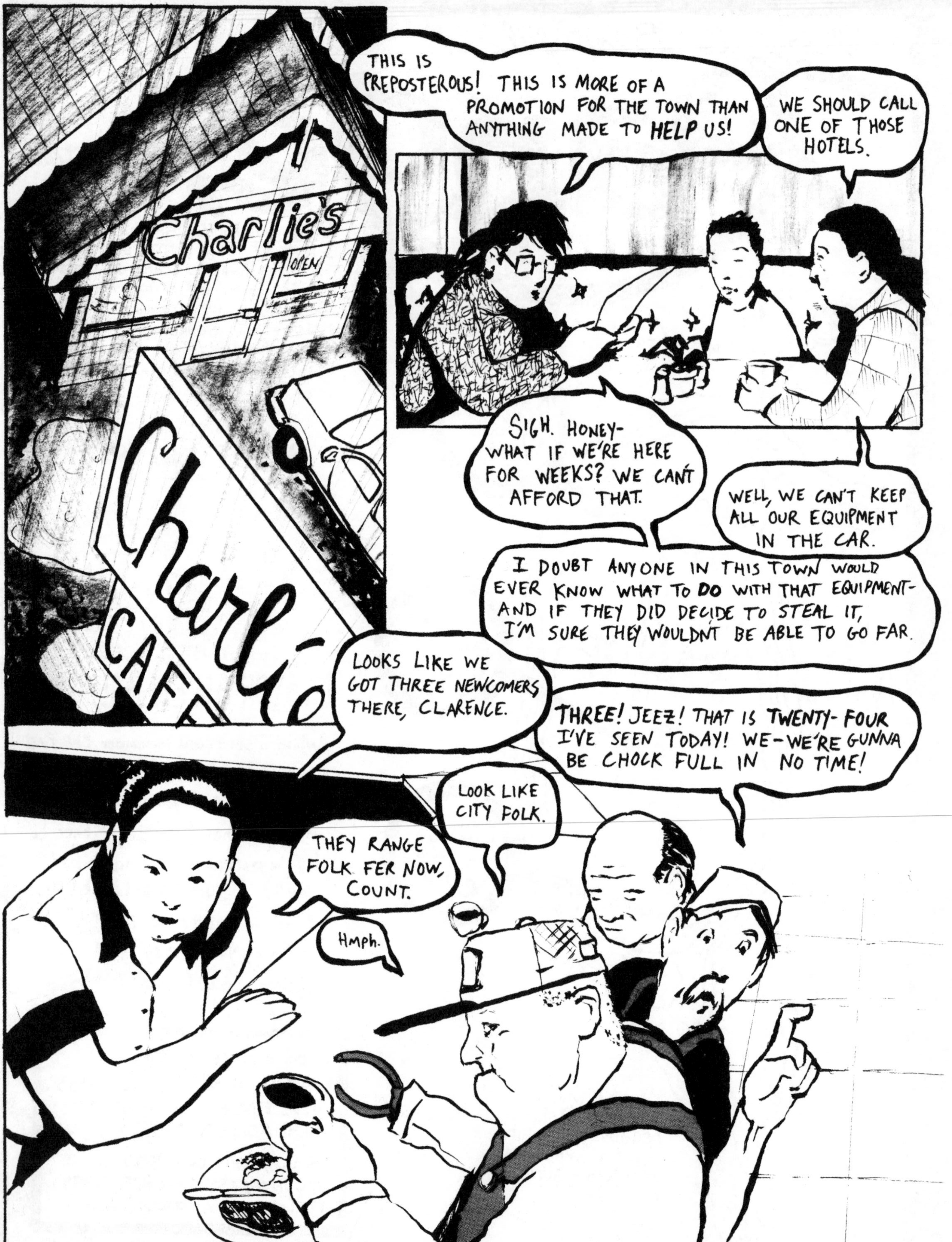
Charlie's
OPEN
Charlie's CAFE
THIS IS PREPOSTEROUS! THIS IS MORE OF A PROMOTION FOR THE TOWN THAN ANYTHING MADE TO HELP US!
WE SHOULD CALL ONE OF THOSE HOTELS.
SIGH. HONEY- WHAT IF WE'RE HERE FOR WEEKS? WE CAN'T AFFORD THAT.
WELL, WE CAN'T KEEP ALL OUR EQUIPMENT IN THE CAR.
I DOUBT ANYONE IN THIS TOWN WOULD EVER KNOW WHAT TO DO WITH THAT EQUIPMENT- AND IF THEY DID DECIDE TO STEAL IT, I'M SURE THEY WOULDN'T BE ABLE TO GO FAR.
LOOKS LIKE WE GOT THREE NEWCOMERS THERE, CLARENCE.
THREE! JEEZ! THAT IS TWENTY-FOUR I'VE SEEN TODAY! WE-WE'RE GUNNA BE CHOCK FULL IN NO TIME!
LOOK LIKE CITY FOLK.
THEY RANGE FOLK FER NOW, COUNT.
Hmph.

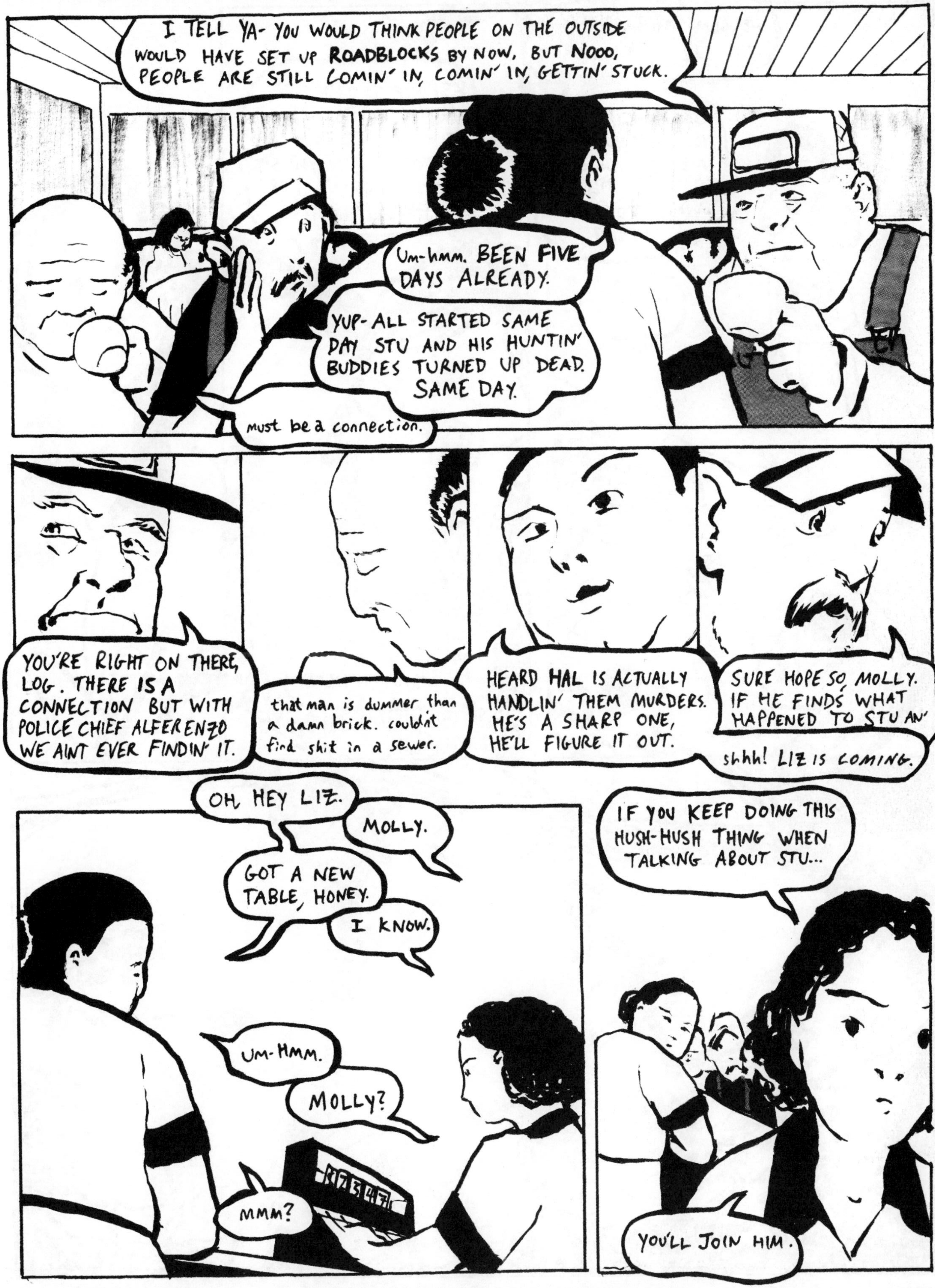
I TELL YA- YOU WOULD THINK PEOPLE ON THE OUTSIDE WOULD HAVE SET UP ROADBLOCKS BY NOW, BUT NOOO, PEOPLE ARE STILL COMIN' IN, COMIN' IN, GETTIN' STUCK.
Um-hmm. BEEN FIVE DAYS ALREADY.
YUP- ALL STARTED SAME DAY STU AND HIS HUNTIN' BUDDIES TURNED UP DEAD. SAME DAY.
must be a connection.
YOU'RE RIGHT ON THERE, LOG. THERE IS A CONNECTION BUT WITH POLICE CHIEF ALFERENZO WE AINT EVER FINDIN' IT.
that man is dummer than a damn brick. couldn't find shit in a sewer.
HEARD HAL IS ACTUALLY HANDLIN' THEM MURDERS. HE'S A SHARP ONE, HE'LL FIGURE IT OUT.
SURE HOPE SO, MOLLY. IF HE FINDS WHAT HAPPENED TO STU AN'
shhh! LIZ IS COMING.
OH, HEY LIZ.
MOLLY.
GOT A NEW TABLE, HONEY.
I KNOW.
UM-HMM.
MOLLY?
MMM?
IF YOU KEEP DOING THIS HUSH-HUSH THING WHEN TALKING ABOUT STU...
YOU'LL JOIN HIM.

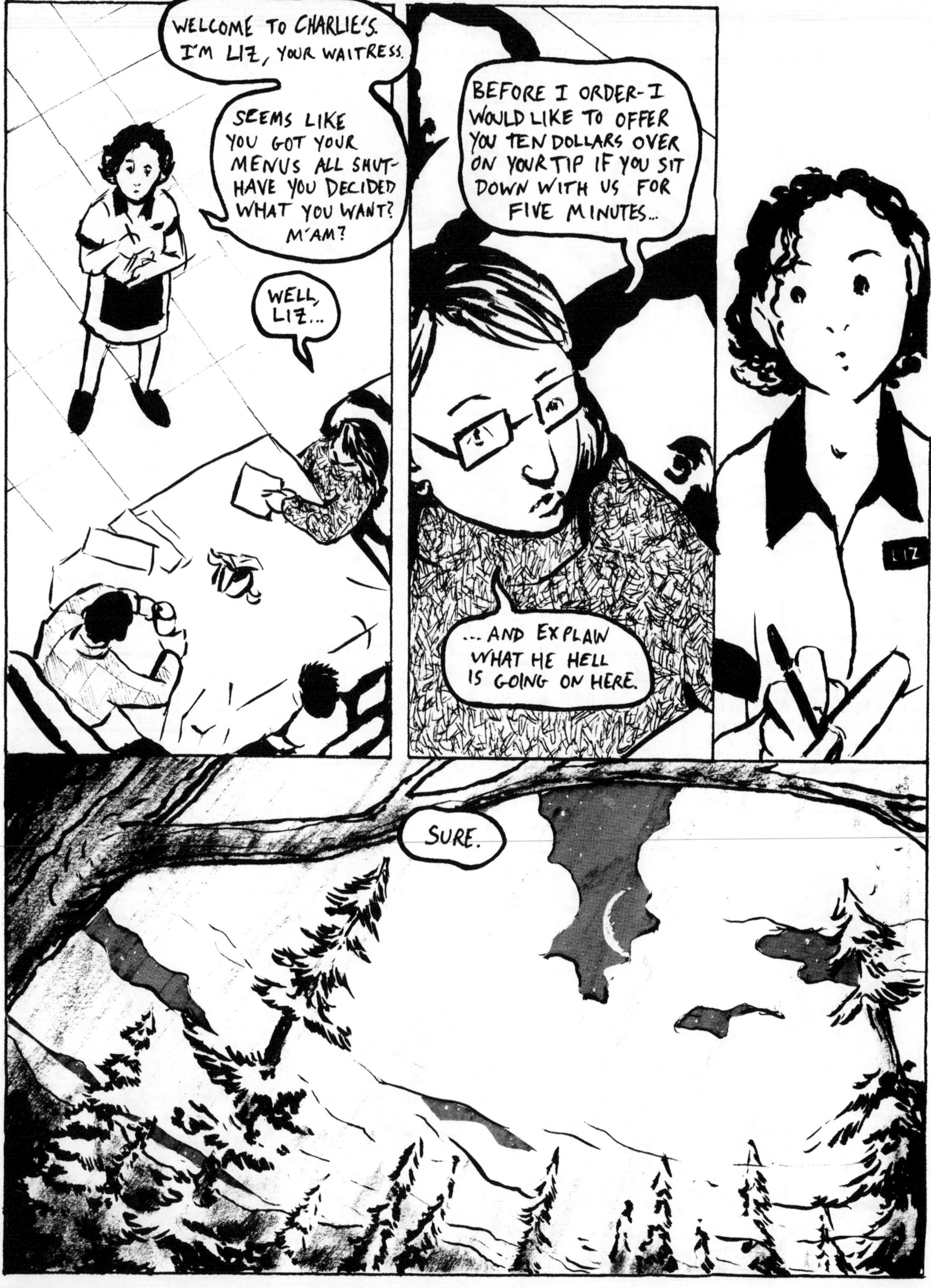
WELCOME TO CHARLIE'S. I'M LIZ, YOUR WAITRESS.
SEEMS LIKE YOU GOT YOUR MENUS ALL SHUT- HAVE YOU DECIDED WHAT YOU WANT? M'AM?
WELL, LIZ...
BEFORE I ORDER- I WOULD LIKE TO OFFER YOU TEN DOLLARS OVER ON YOUR TIP IF YOU SIT DOWN WITH US FOR FIVE MINUTES...
... AND EXPLAIN WHAT HE HELL IS GOING ON HERE.
LIZ
SURE.

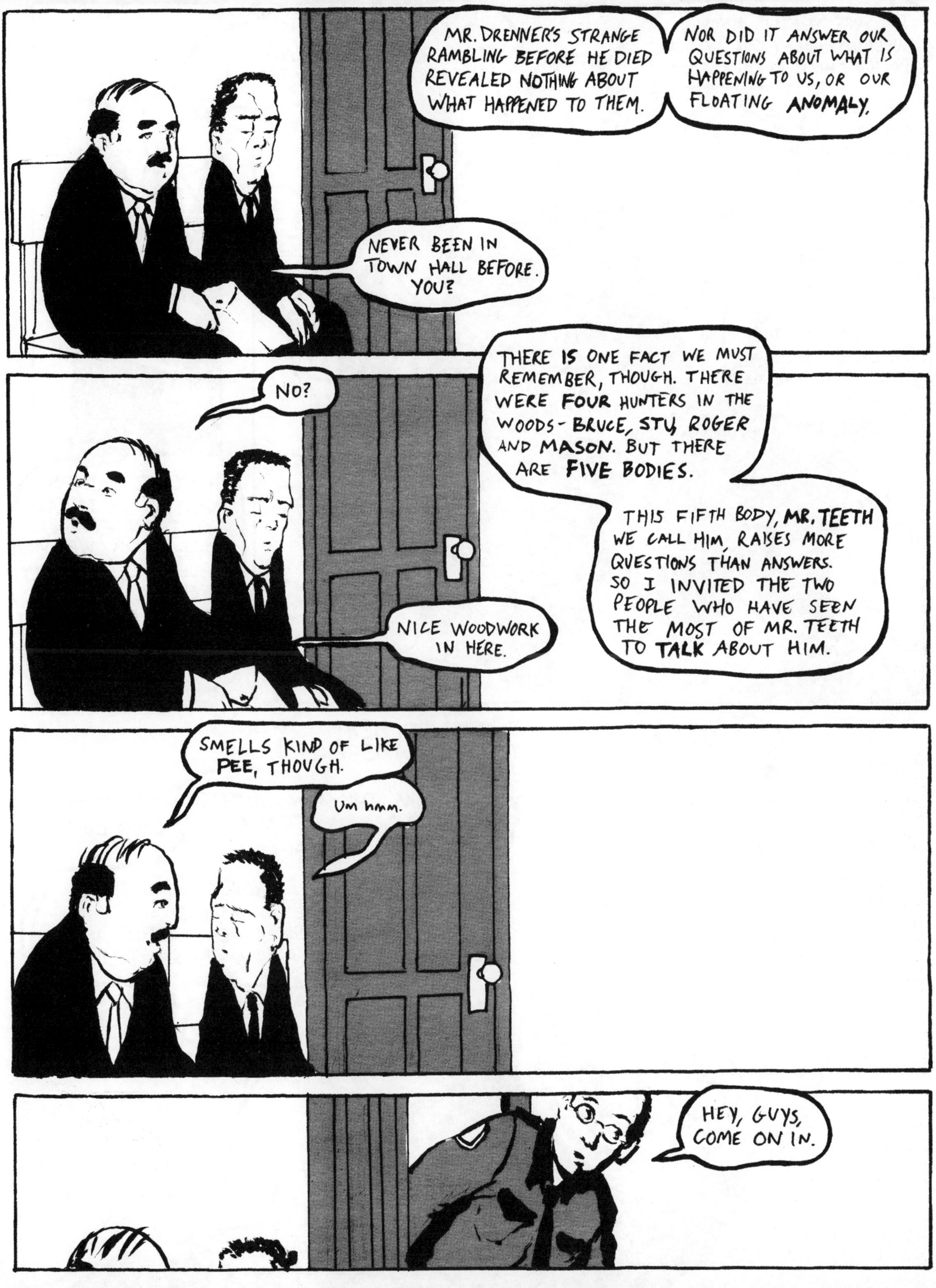
MR. DRENNER'S STRANGE RAMBLING BEFORE HE DIED REVEALED NOTHING ABOUT WHAT HAPPENED TO THEM.
NOR DID IT ANSWER OUR QUESTIONS ABOUT WHAT IS HAPPENING TO US, OR OUR FLOATING **ANOMALY**.
NEVER BEEN IN TOWN HALL BEFORE. YOU?
THERE **IS** ONE FACT WE MUST REMEMBER, THOUGH. THERE WERE **FOUR** HUNTERS IN THE WOODS - **BRUCE**, **STU**, **ROGER** AND **MASON**. BUT THERE ARE **FIVE BODIES**.
NO?
THIS FIFTH BODY, **MR. TEETH** WE CALL HIM, RAISES MORE QUESTIONS THAN ANSWERS. SO I INVITED THE TWO PEOPLE WHO HAVE SEEN THE MOST OF MR. TEETH TO **TALK** ABOUT HIM.
NICE WOODWORK IN HERE.
SMELLS KIND OF LIKE **PEE**, THOUGH.
Um hmm.
HEY, GUYS, COME ON IN.

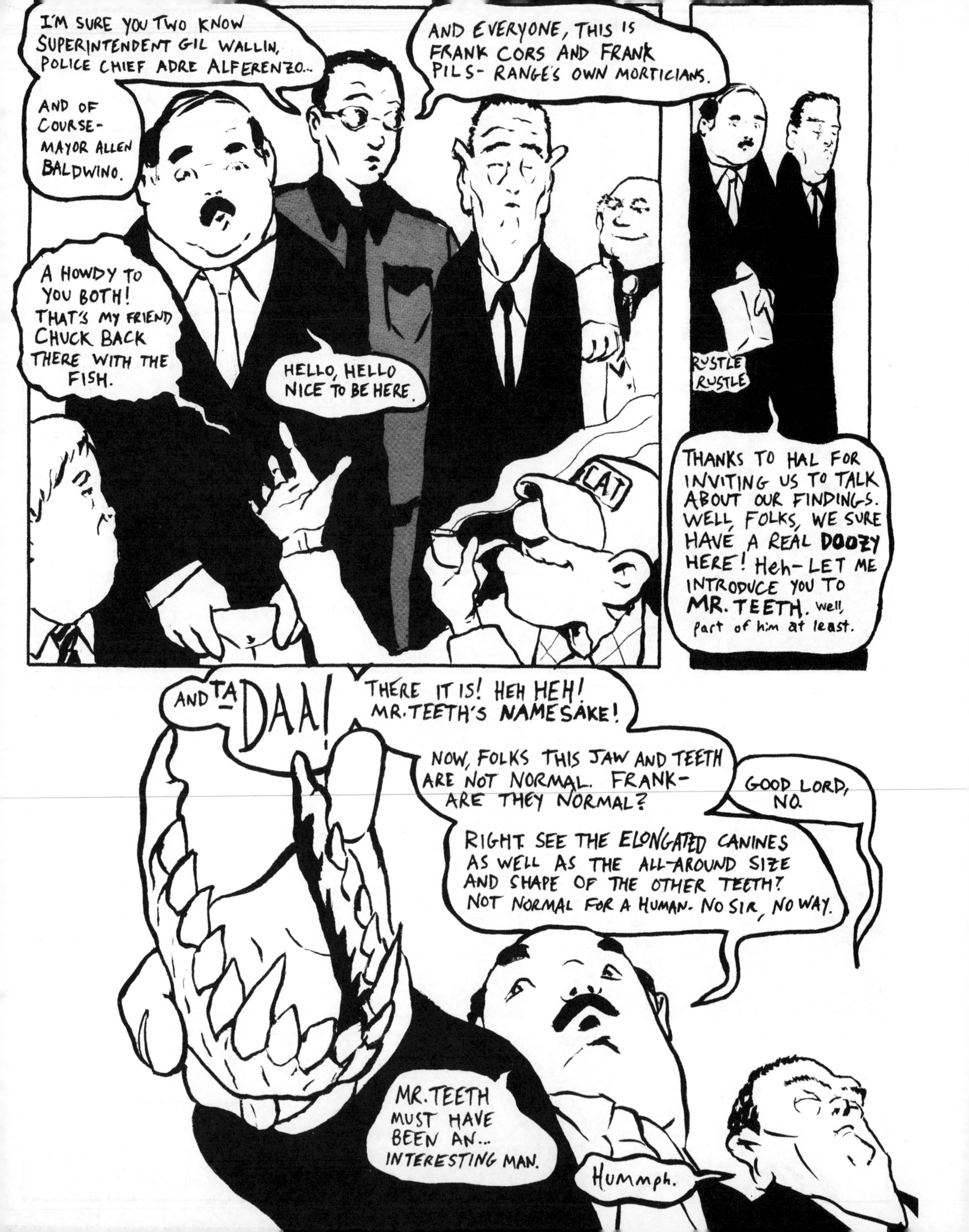
I'M SURE YOU TWO KNOW SUPERINTENDENT GIL WALLIN, POLICE CHIEF ADRE ALFERENZO...
AND OF COURSE- MAYOR ALLEN BALDWINO.
AND EVERYONE, THIS IS FRANK CORS AND FRANK PILS- RANGE'S OWN MORTICIANS.
A HOWDY TO YOU BOTH! THAT'S MY FRIEND CHUCK BACK THERE WITH THE FISH.
HELLO, HELLO NICE TO BE HERE.
CAT
RUSTLE RUSTLE
THANKS TO HAL FOR INVITING US TO TALK ABOUT OUR FINDINGS. WELL, FOLKS, WE SURE HAVE A REAL DOOZY HERE! Heh- LET ME INTRODUCE YOU TO MR. TEETH. Well, part of him at least.
AND TA DAA!
THERE IT IS! HEH HEH! MR. TEETH'S NAMESAKE!
NOW, FOLKS THIS JAW AND TEETH ARE NOT NORMAL. FRANK- ARE THEY NORMAL?
GOOD LORD, NO.
RIGHT. SEE THE ELONGATED CANINES AS WELL AS THE ALL-AROUND SIZE AND SHAPE OF THE OTHER TEETH? NOT NORMAL FOR A HUMAN. NO SIR, NO WAY.
MR. TEETH MUST HAVE BEEN AN... INTERESTING MAN.
Hummph.

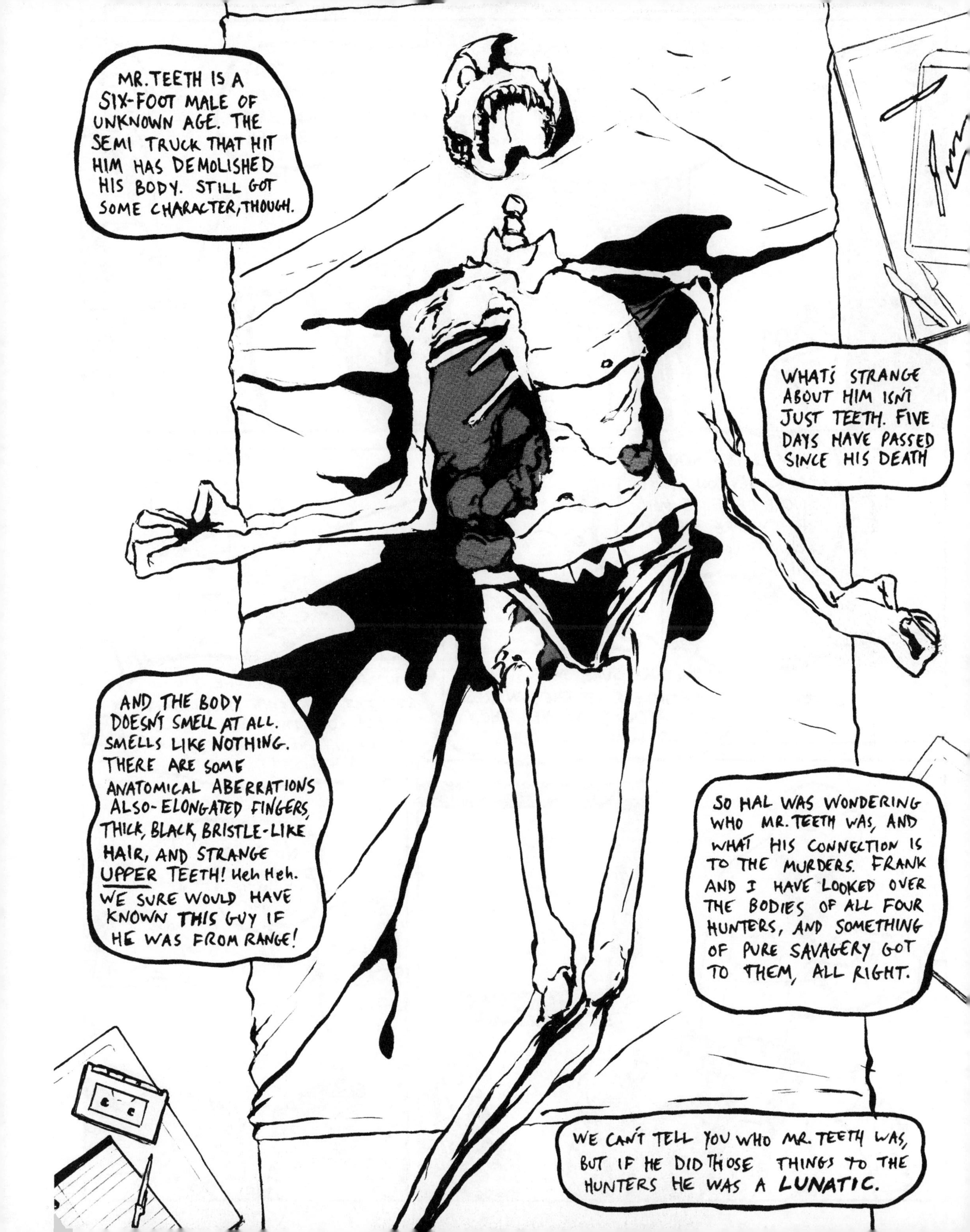
MR. TEETH IS A SIX-FOOT MALE OF UNKNOWN AGE. THE SEMI TRUCK THAT HIT HIM HAS DEMOLISHED HIS BODY. STILL GOT SOME CHARACTER, THOUGH.
WHAT'S STRANGE ABOUT HIM ISN'T JUST TEETH. FIVE DAYS HAVE PASSED SINCE HIS DEATH
AND THE BODY DOESN'T SMELL AT ALL. SMELLS LIKE NOTHING. THERE ARE SOME ANATOMICAL ABERRATIONS ALSO- ELONGATED FINGERS, THICK, BLACK, BRISTLE-LIKE HAIR, AND STRANGE UPPER TEETH! Heh Heh. WE SURE WOULD HAVE KNOWN THIS GUY IF HE WAS FROM RANGE!
SO HAL WAS WONDERING WHO MR. TEETH WAS, AND WHAT HIS CONNECTION IS TO THE MURDERS. FRANK AND I HAVE LOOKED OVER THE BODIES OF ALL FOUR HUNTERS, AND SOMETHING OF PURE SAVAGERY GOT TO THEM, ALL RIGHT.
WE CAN'T TELL YOU WHO MR. TEETH WAS, BUT IF HE DID THOSE THINGS TO THE HUNTERS HE WAS A LUNATIC.

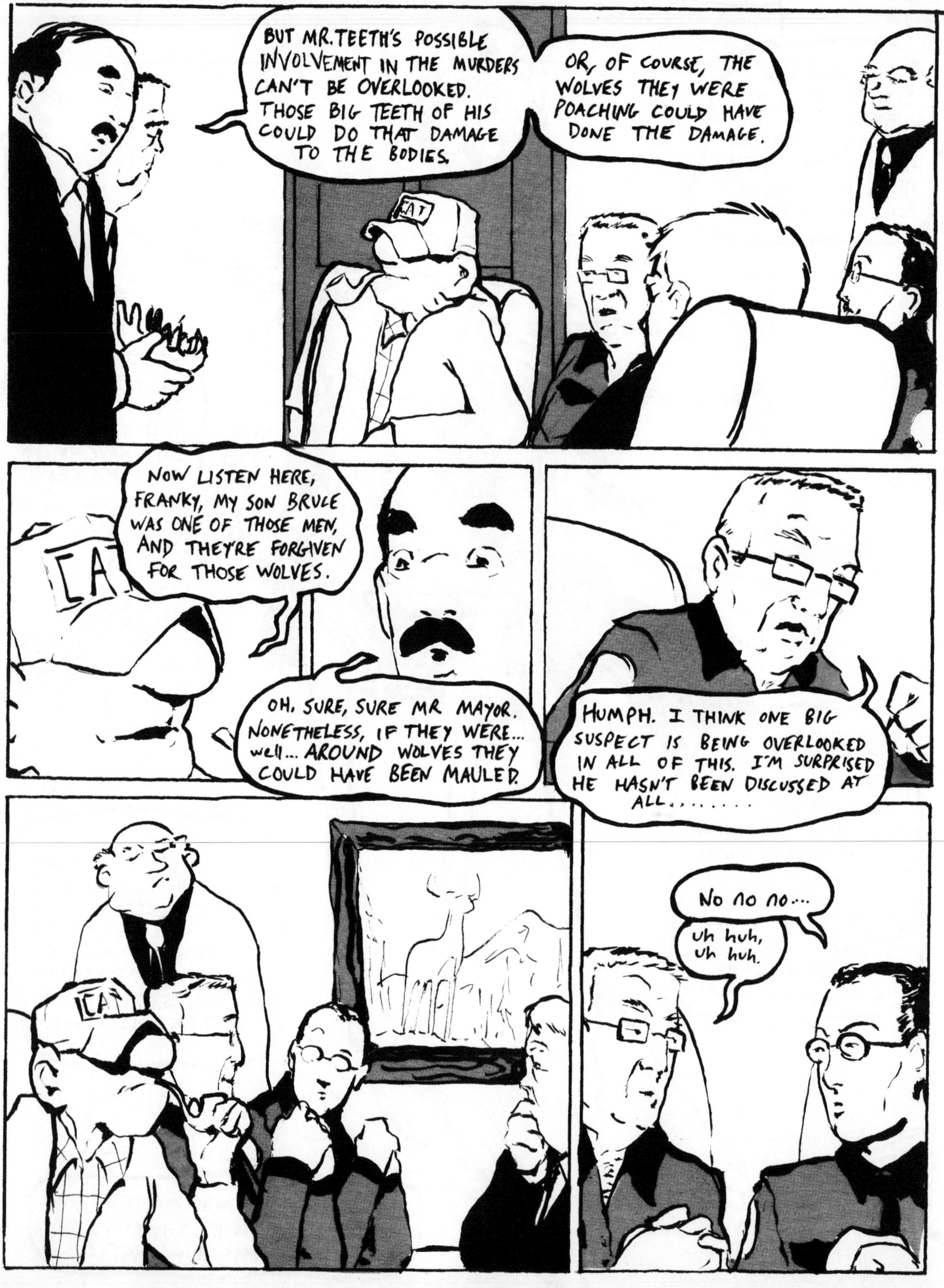
BUT MR. TEETH'S POSSIBLE INVOLVEMENT IN THE MURDERS CAN'T BE OVERLOOKED. THOSE BIG TEETH OF HIS COULD DO THAT DAMAGE TO THE BODIES.
OR, OF COURSE, THE WOLVES THEY WERE POACHING COULD HAVE DONE THE DAMAGE.
CAT
NOW LISTEN HERE, FRANKY, MY SON BRUCE WAS ONE OF THOSE MEN, AND THEY'RE FORGIVEN FOR THOSE WOLVES.
OH. SURE, SURE MR MAYOR. NONETHELESS, IF THEY WERE... well... AROUND WOLVES THEY COULD HAVE BEEN MAULED.
HUMPH. I THINK ONE BIG SUSPECT IS BEING OVERLOOKED IN ALL OF THIS. I'M SURPRISED HE HASN'T BEEN DISCUSSED AT ALL........
No no no....
uh huh, uh huh.

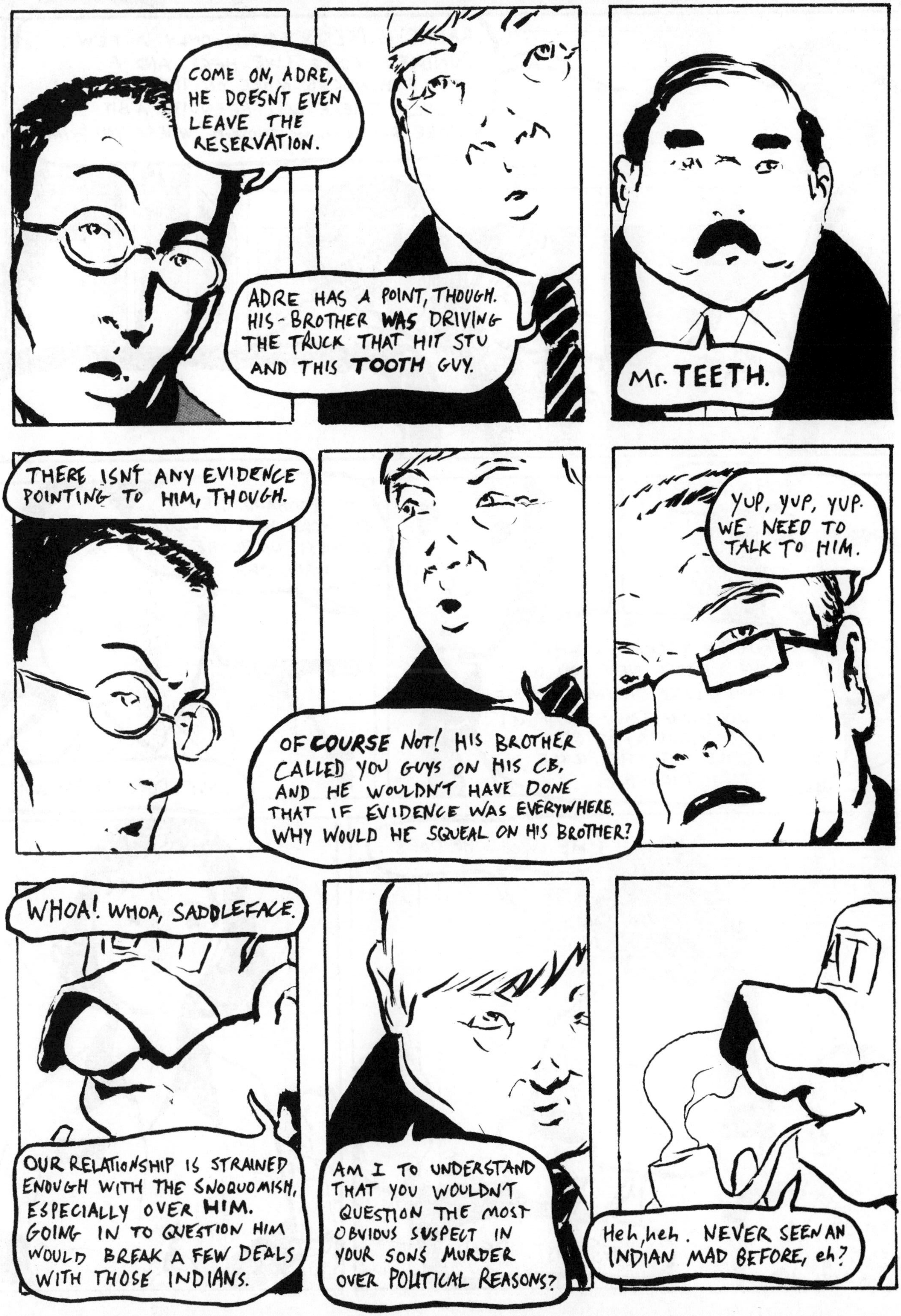
COME ON, ADRE, HE DOESN'T EVEN LEAVE THE RESERVATION.
ADRE HAS A POINT, THOUGH. HIS-BROTHER WAS DRIVING THE TRUCK THAT HIT STU AND THIS TOOTH GUY.
Mr. TEETH.
THERE ISN'T ANY EVIDENCE POINTING TO HIM, THOUGH.
OF COURSE NOT! HIS BROTHER CALLED YOU GUYS ON HIS CB, AND HE WOULDN'T HAVE DONE THAT IF EVIDENCE WAS EVERYWHERE. WHY WOULD HE SQUEAL ON HIS BROTHER?
YUP, YUP, YUP. WE NEED TO TALK TO HIM.
WHOA! WHOA, SADDLEFACE.
OUR RELATIONSHIP IS STRAINED ENOUGH WITH THE SNOQUOMISH, ESPECIALLY OVER HIM. GOING IN TO QUESTION HIM WOULD BREAK A FEW DEALS WITH THOSE INDIANS.
AM I TO UNDERSTAND THAT YOU WOULDN'T QUESTION THE MOST OBVIOUS SUSPECT IN YOUR SONS MURDER OVER POLITICAL REASONS?
Heh, heh. NEVER SEEN AN INDIAN MAD BEFORE, eh?

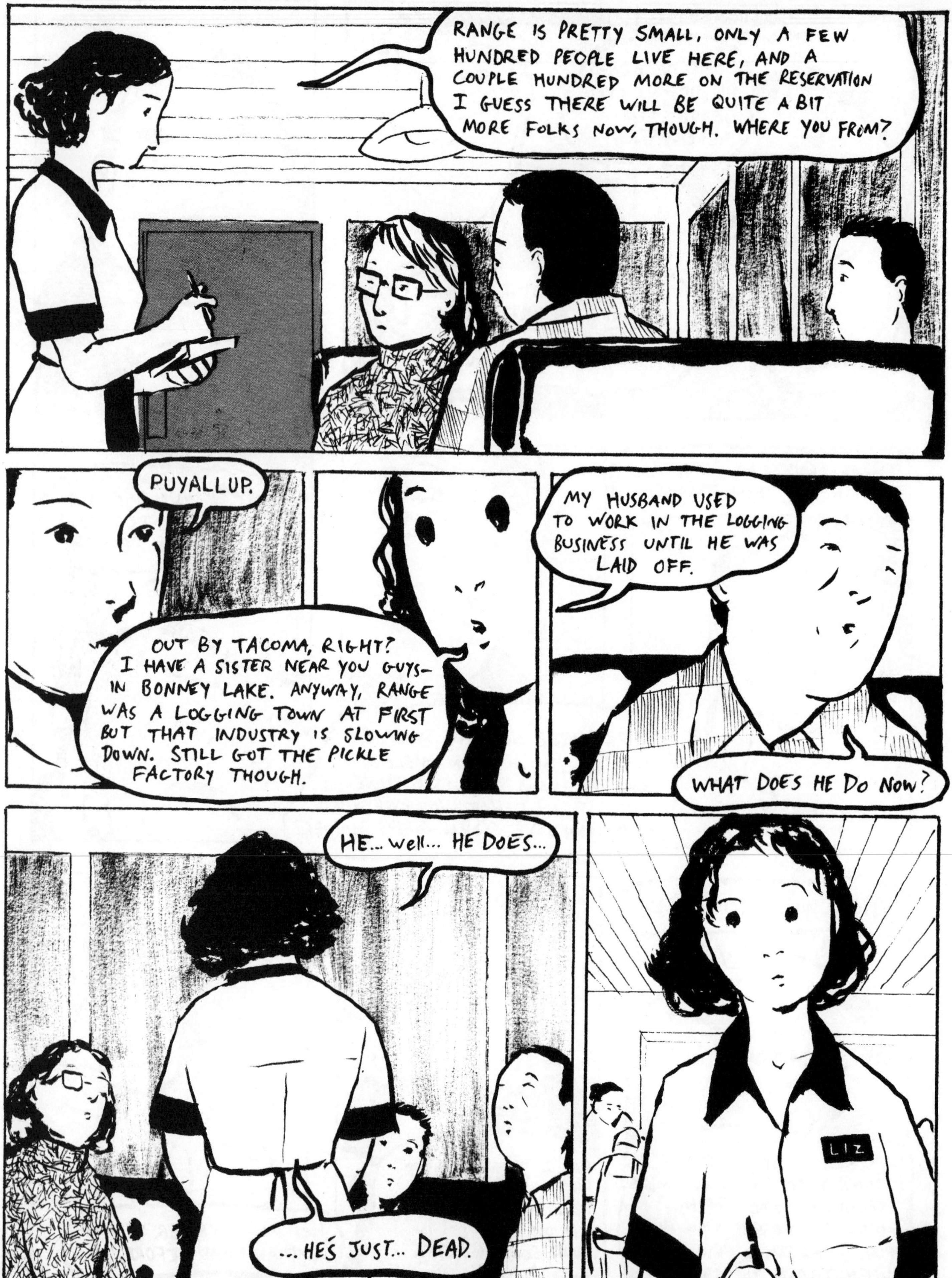
RANGE IS PRETTY SMALL, ONLY A FEW HUNDRED PEOPLE LIVE HERE, AND A COUPLE HUNDRED MORE ON THE RESERVATION I GUESS THERE WILL BE QUITE A BIT MORE FOLKS NOW, THOUGH. WHERE YOU FROM?
PUYALLUP.
OUT BY TACOMA, RIGHT? I HAVE A SISTER NEAR YOU GUYS—IN BONNEY LAKE. ANYWAY, RANGE WAS A LOGGING TOWN AT FIRST BUT THAT INDUSTRY IS SLOWING DOWN. STILL GOT THE PICKLE FACTORY THOUGH.
MY HUSBAND USED TO WORK IN THE LOGGING BUSINESS UNTIL HE WAS LAID OFF.
WHAT DOES HE DO NOW?
HE... well... HE DOES...
...HE'S JUST... DEAD.
LIZ

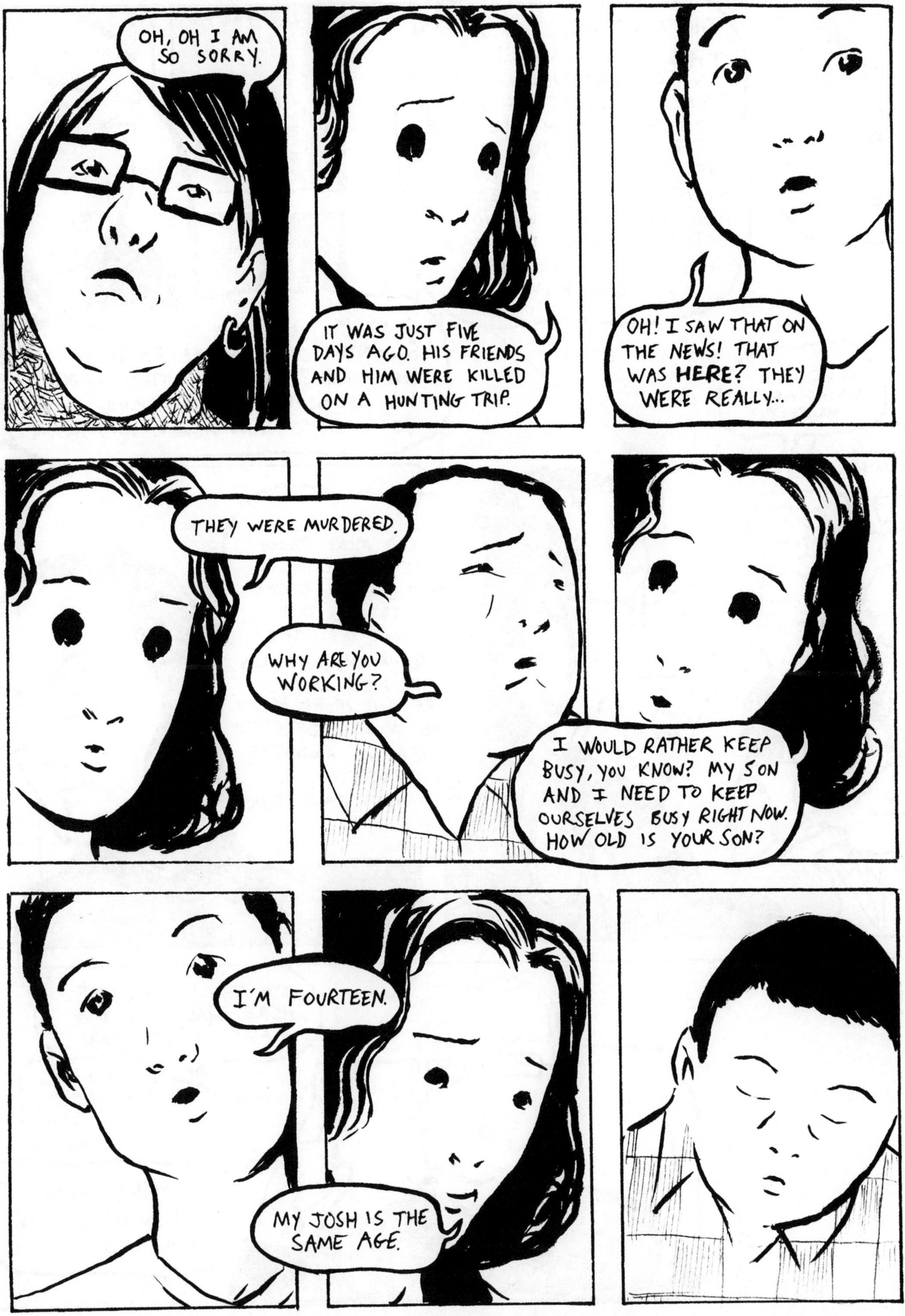
OH, OH I AM SO SORRY.
IT WAS JUST FIVE DAYS AGO. HIS FRIENDS AND HIM WERE KILLED ON A HUNTING TRIP.
OH! I SAW THAT ON THE NEWS! THAT WAS **HERE**? THEY WERE REALLY...
THEY WERE MURDERED.
WHY ARE YOU WORKING?
I WOULD RATHER KEEP BUSY, YOU KNOW? MY SON AND I NEED TO KEEP OURSELVES BUSY RIGHT NOW. HOW OLD IS YOUR SON?
I'M FOURTEEN.
MY JOSH IS THE SAME AGE.

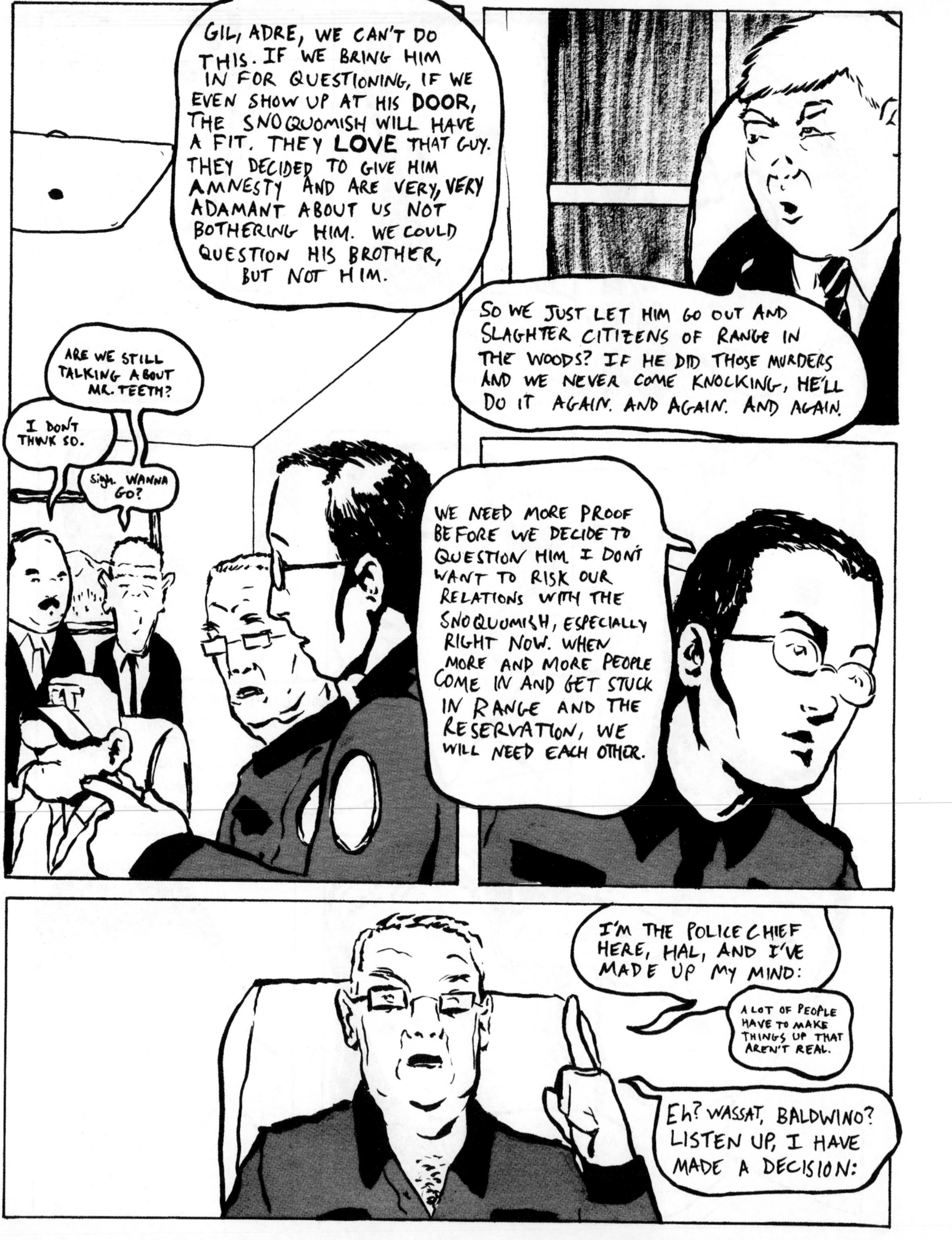
GIL, ADRE, WE CAN'T DO THIS. IF WE BRING HIM IN FOR QUESTIONING, IF WE EVEN SHOW UP AT HIS DOOR, THE SNOQUOMISH WILL HAVE A FIT. THEY LOVE THAT GUY. THEY DECIDED TO GIVE HIM AMNESTY AND ARE VERY, VERY ADAMANT ABOUT US NOT BOTHERING HIM. WE COULD QUESTION HIS BROTHER, BUT NOT HIM.
SO WE JUST LET HIM GO OUT AND SLAGHTER CITIZENS OF RANGE IN THE WOODS? IF HE DID THOSE MURDERS AND WE NEVER COME KNOCKING, HE'LL DO IT AGAIN. AND AGAIN. AND AGAIN.
ARE WE STILL TALKING ABOUT MR. TEETH?
I DON'T THINK SO.
Sigh. WANNA GO?
WE NEED MORE PROOF BEFORE WE DECIDE TO QUESTION HIM. I DON'T WANT TO RISK OUR RELATIONS WITH THE SNOQUOMISH, ESPECIALLY RIGHT NOW. WHEN MORE AND MORE PEOPLE COME IN AND GET STUCK IN RANGE AND THE RESERVATION, WE WILL NEED EACH OTHER.
I'M THE POLICE CHIEF HERE, HAL, AND I'VE MADE UP MY MIND:
A LOT OF PEOPLE HAVE TO MAKE THINGS UP THAT AREN'T REAL.
Eh? WASSAT, BALDWINO? LISTEN UP, I HAVE MADE A DECISION:

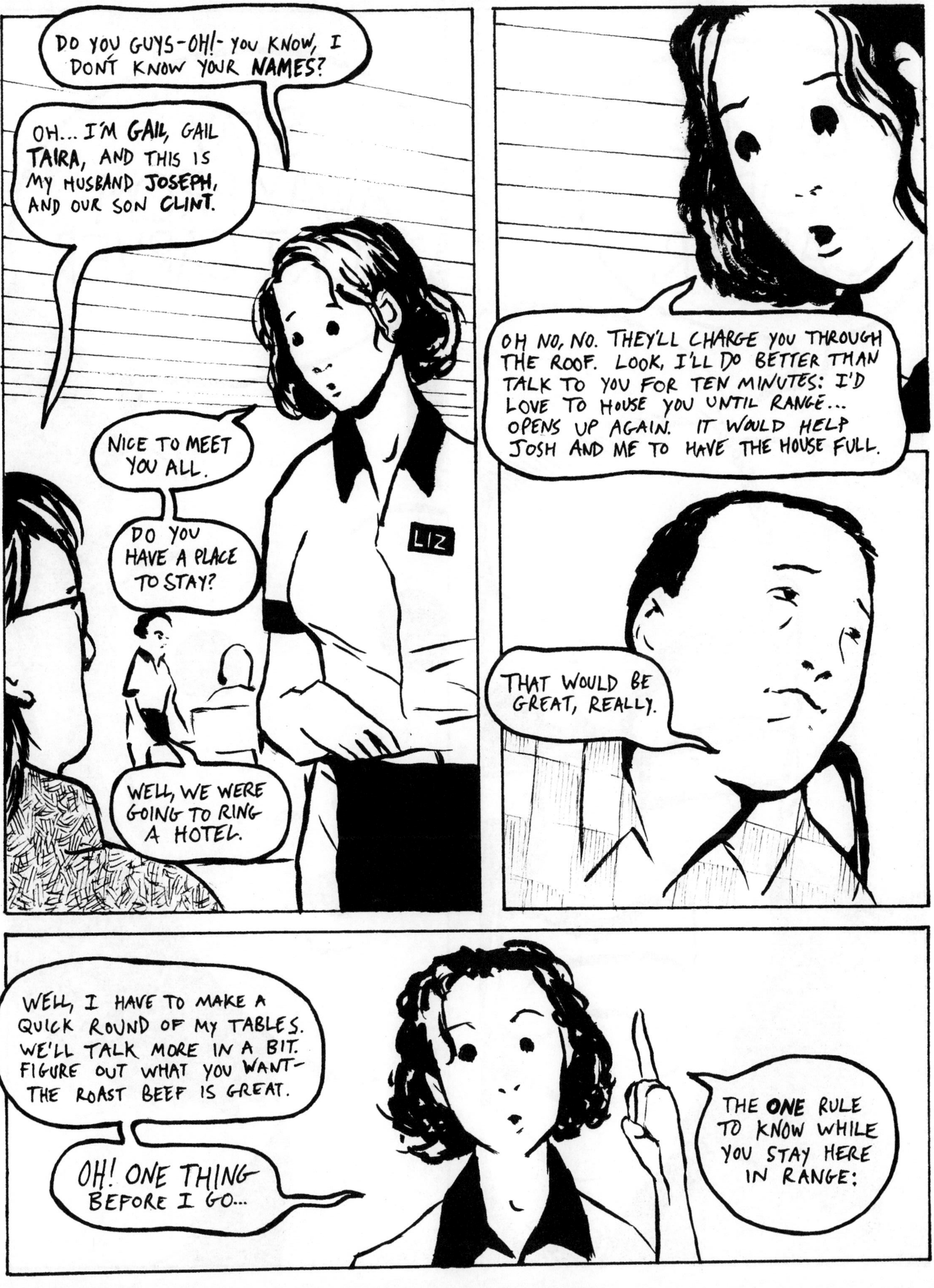
DO YOU GUYS-OH!- YOU KNOW, I DON'T KNOW YOUR **NAMES**?
OH... I'M **GAIL**, GAIL **TAIRA**, AND THIS IS MY HUSBAND **JOSEPH**, AND OUR SON **CLINT**.
NICE TO MEET YOU ALL.
DO YOU HAVE A PLACE TO STAY?
LIZ
WELL, WE WERE GOING TO RING A HOTEL.
OH NO, NO. THEY'LL CHARGE YOU THROUGH THE ROOF. LOOK, I'LL DO BETTER THAN TALK TO YOU FOR TEN MINUTES: I'D LOVE TO HOUSE YOU UNTIL RANGE... OPENS UP AGAIN. IT WOULD HELP JOSH AND ME TO HAVE THE HOUSE FULL.
THAT WOULD BE GREAT, REALLY.
WELL, I HAVE TO MAKE A QUICK ROUND OF MY TABLES. WE'LL TALK MORE IN A BIT. FIGURE OUT WHAT YOU WANT- THE ROAST BEEF IS GREAT.
OH! ONE THING BEFORE I GO...
THE **ONE** RULE TO KNOW WHILE YOU STAY HERE IN RANGE:

GET ME MORT CARVER.
STAY AWAY FROM MORT CARVER.

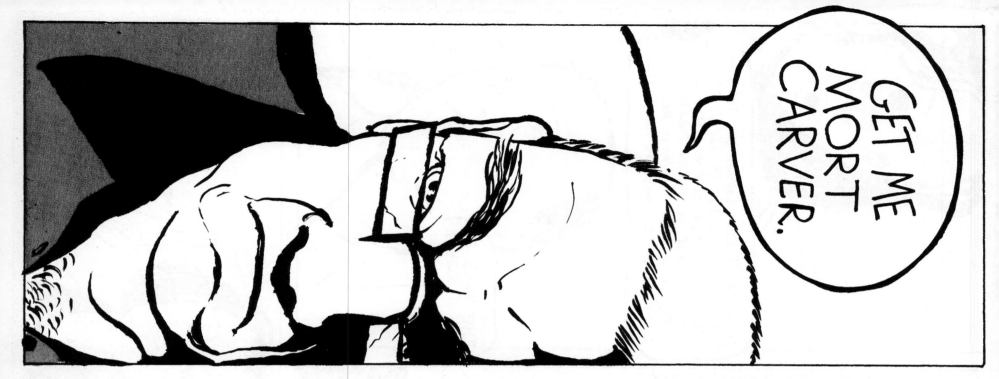

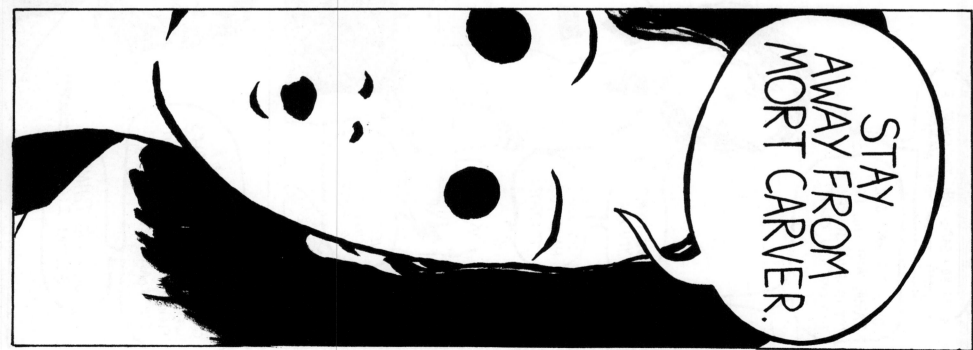

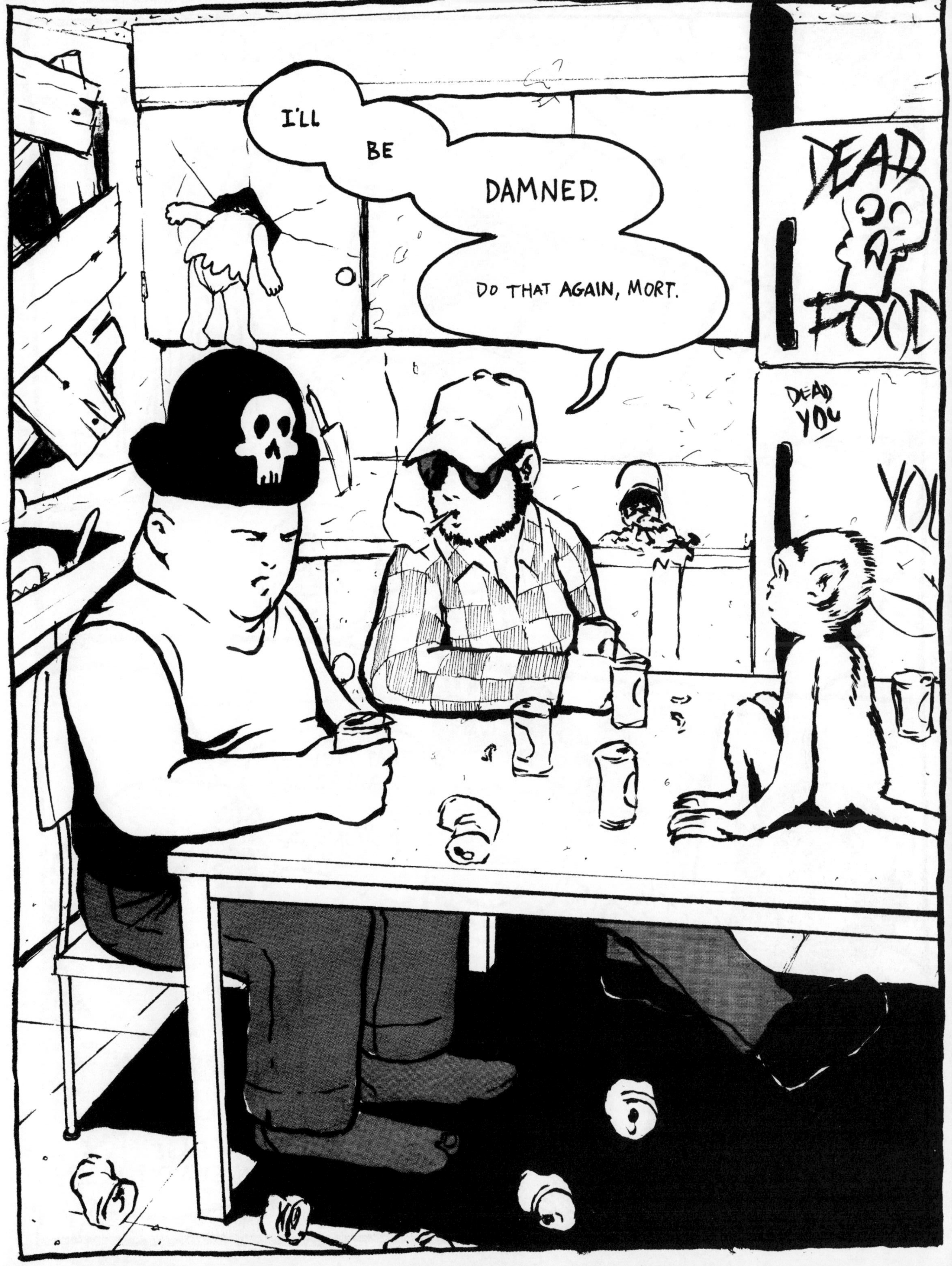
I'LL BE DAMNED.
DO THAT AGAIN, MORT.
DEAD FOOD
DEAD YOU

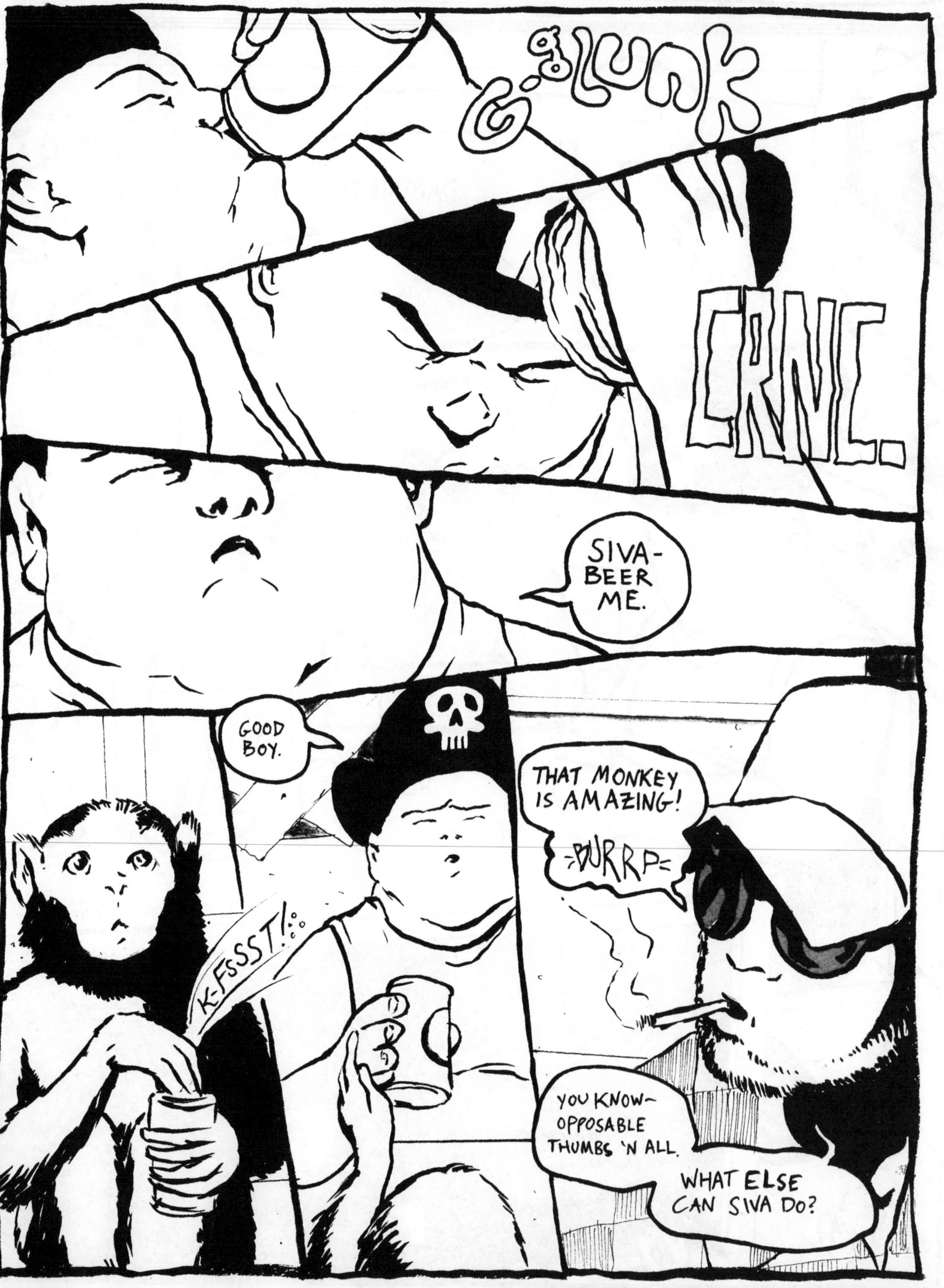
G-GLUNK
CRNC.
SIVA-BEER ME.
GOOD BOY.
K-FSSST!
THAT MONKEY IS AMAZING!
-BURRP-
YOU KNOW-OPPOSABLE THUMBS 'N ALL.
WHAT ELSE CAN SIVA DO?

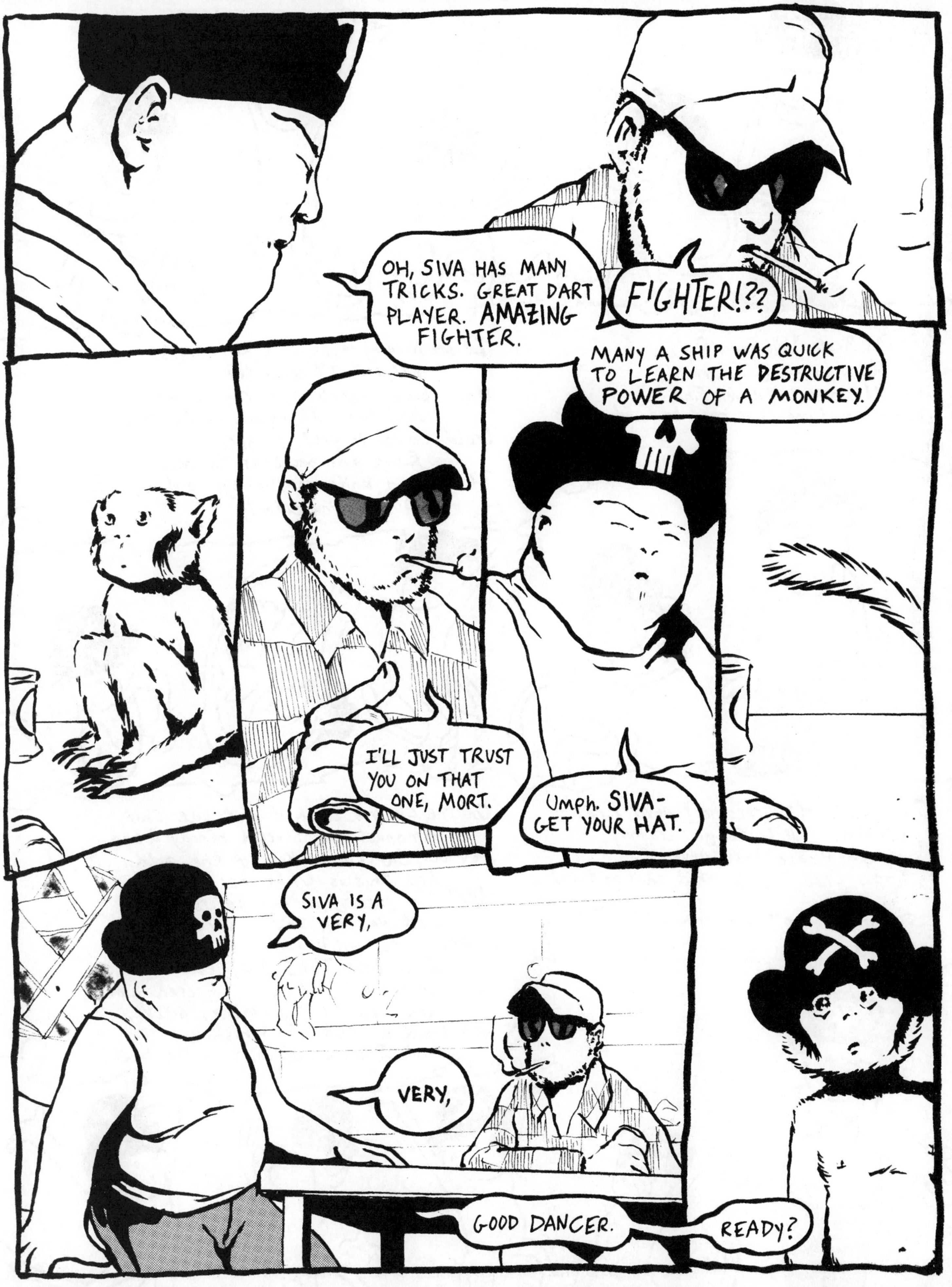
OH, SIVA HAS MANY TRICKS. GREAT DART PLAYER. AMAZING FIGHTER.
FIGHTER!??
MANY A SHIP WAS QUICK TO LEARN THE DESTRUCTIVE POWER OF A MONKEY.
I'LL JUST TRUST YOU ON THAT ONE, MORT.
Umph. SIVA- GET YOUR HAT.
SIVA IS A VERY,
VERY,
GOOD DANCER.
READY?

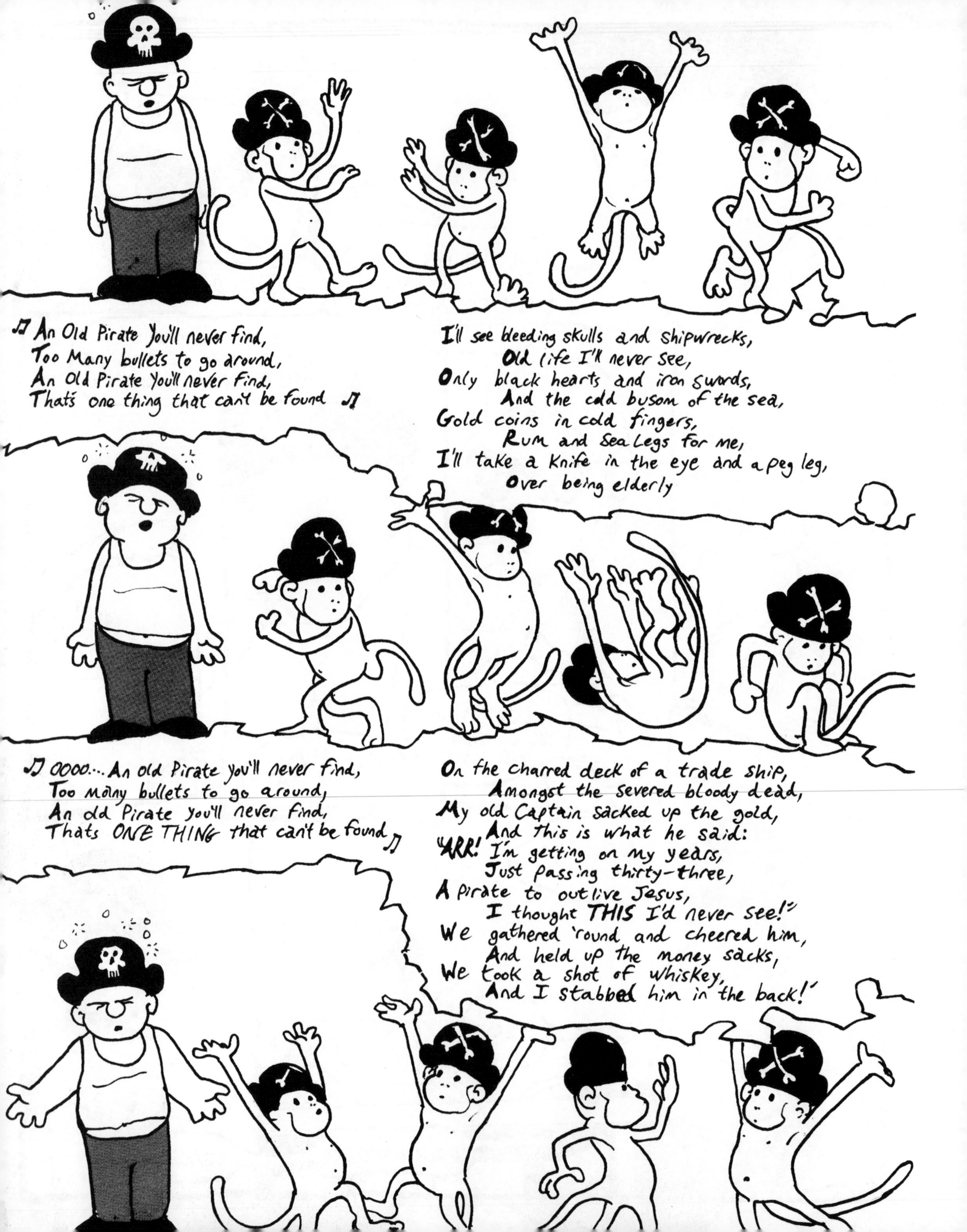
♫ An Old Pirate You'll never find,
Too Many bullets to go around,
An Old Pirate You'll never find,
That's one thing that can't be found ♫
I'll see bleeding skulls and shipwrecks,
Old life I'll never see,
Only black hearts and iron swords,
And the cold busom of the sea,
Gold coins in cold fingers,
Rum and Sea Legs for me,
I'll take a knife in the eye and a peg leg,
Over being elderly
♫ oooo... An old Pirate you'll never find,
Too many bullets to go around,
An old Pirate you'll never find,
Thats ONE THING that can't be found ♫
On the charred deck of a trade ship,
Amongst the severed bloody dead,
My old Captain sacked up the gold,
And this is what he said:
"ARR! I'm getting on my years,
Just passing thirty-three,
A pirate to outlive Jesus,
I thought THIS I'd never see!"
We gathered 'round and cheered him,
And held up the money sacks,
We took a shot of whiskey,
And I stabbed him in the back!'

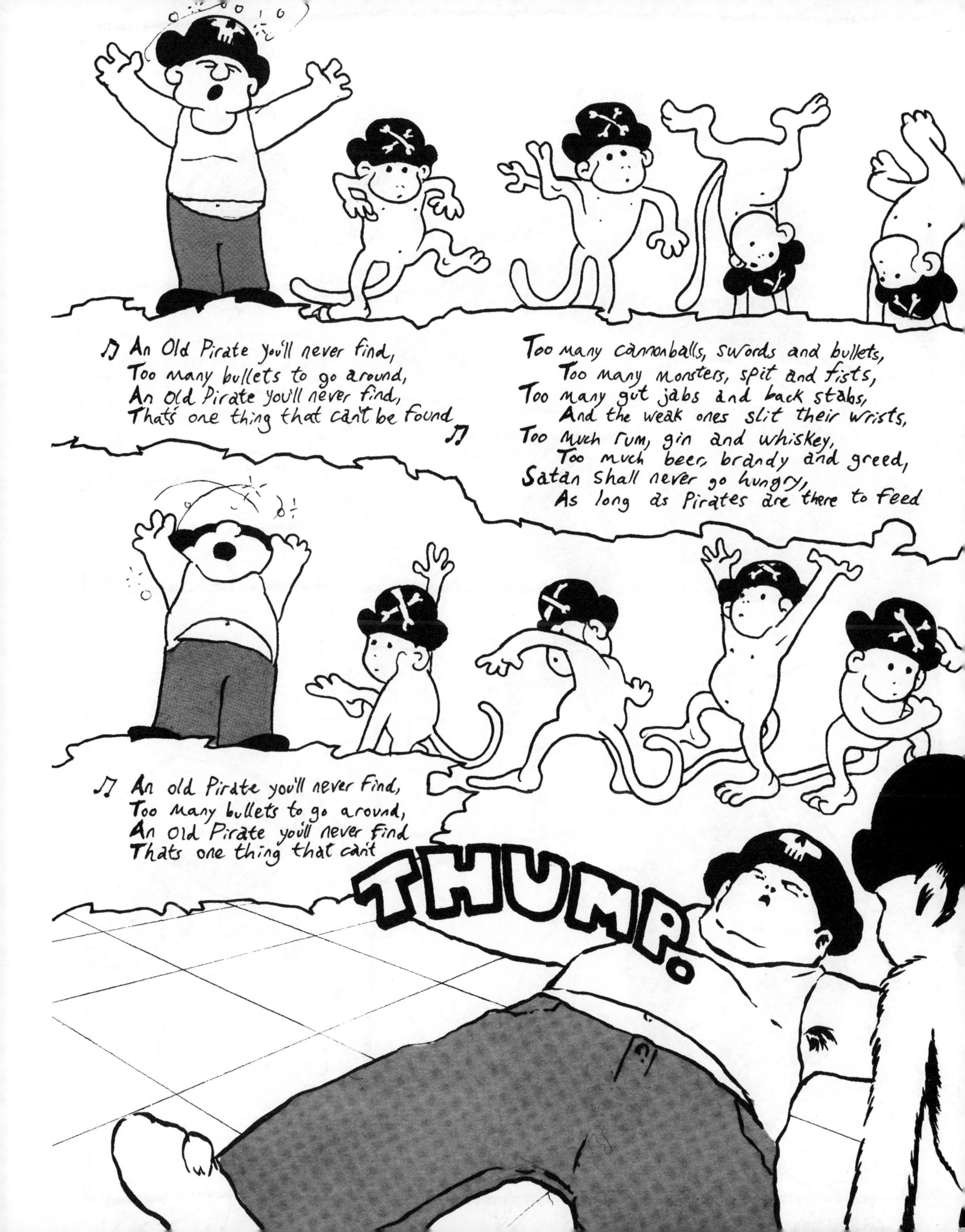
♫ An Old Pirate you'll never find,
Too many bullets to go around,
An Old Pirate you'll never find,
That's one thing that can't be found ♫
Too many cannonballs, swords and bullets,
Too many monsters, spit and fists,
Too many gut jabs and back stabs,
And the weak ones slit their wrists,
Too much rum, gin and whiskey,
Too much beer, brandy and greed,
Satan shall never go hungry,
As long as Pirates are there to feed
♫ An old Pirate you'll never find,
Too many bullets to go around,
An Old Pirate you'll never find
Thats one thing that can't
THUMP.

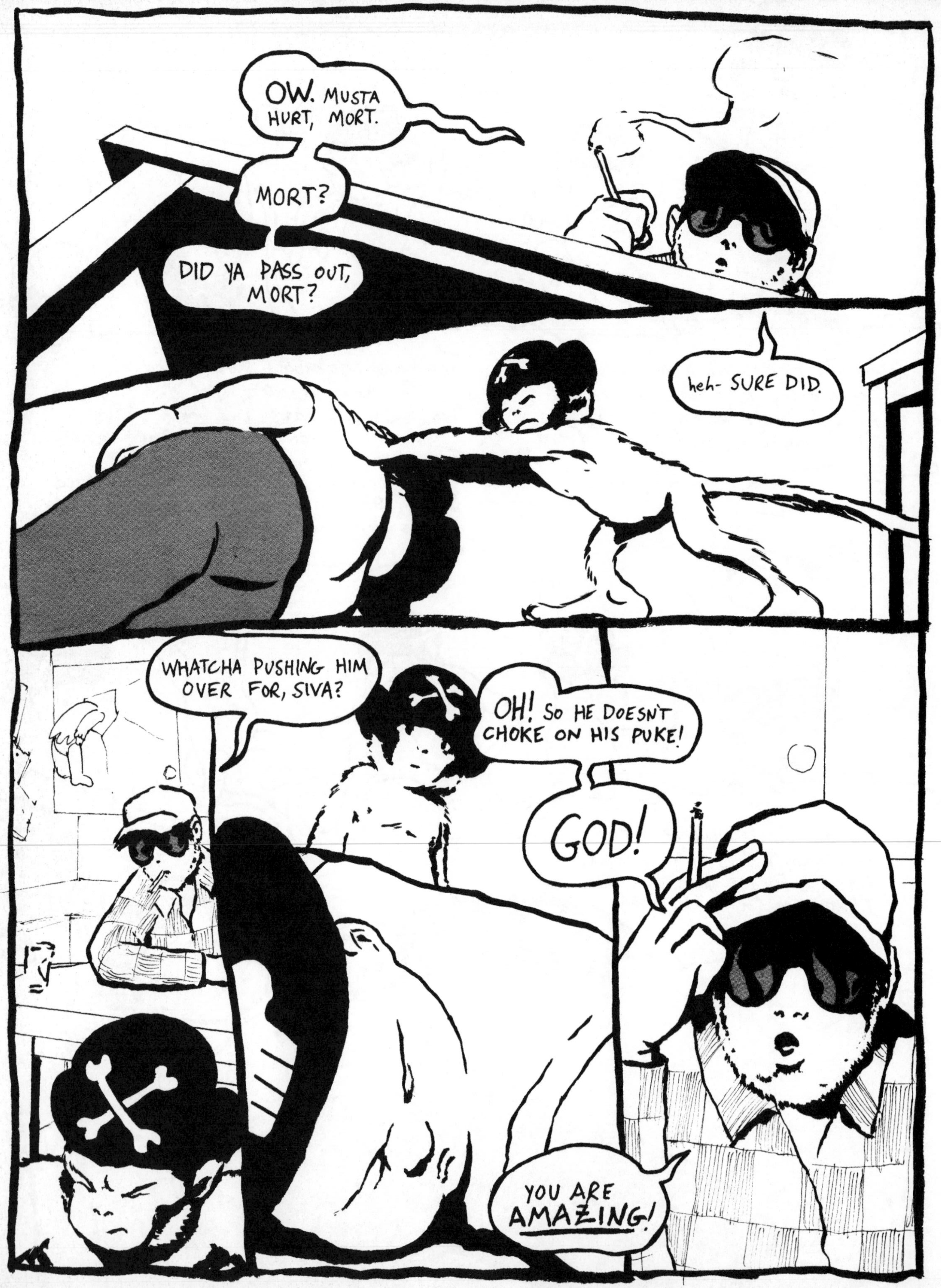
OW. MUSTA HURT, MORT.
MORT?
DID YA PASS OUT, MORT?
heh- SURE DID.
WHATCHA PUSHING HIM OVER FOR, SIVA?
OH! SO HE DOESN'T CHOKE ON HIS PUKE!
GOD!
YOU ARE AMAZING!

3.
CANNONADE

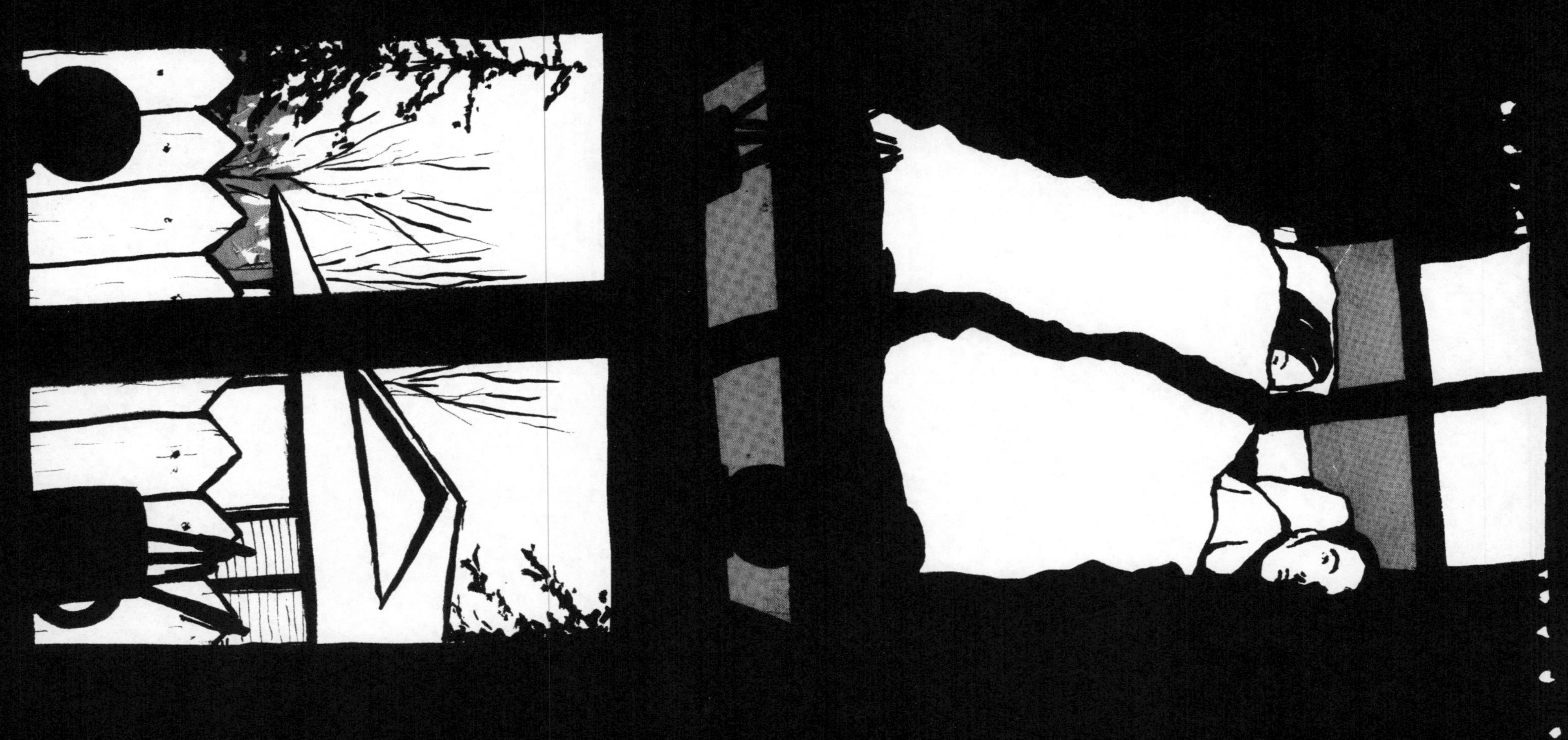

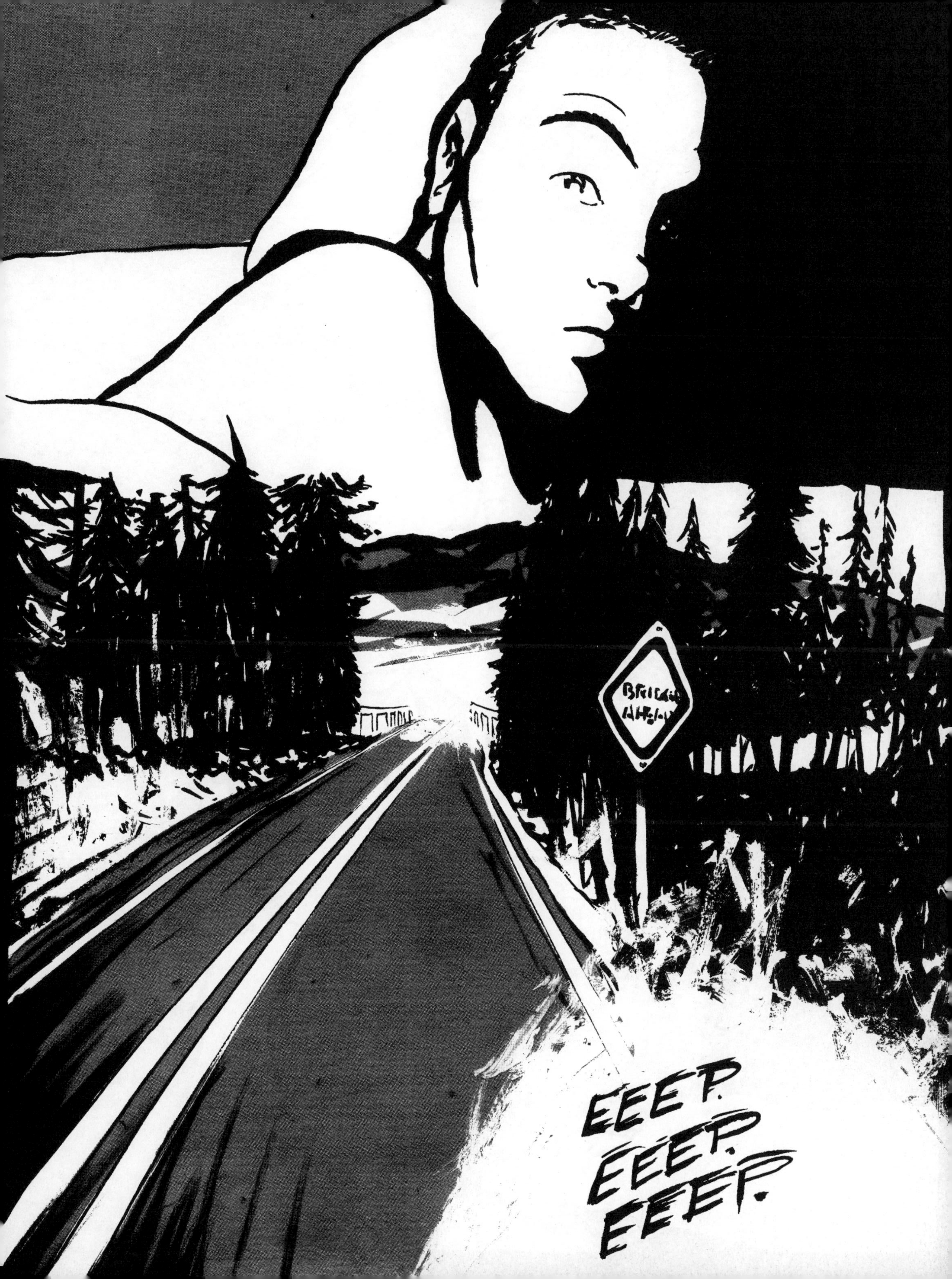
EEEP.
EEEP.
EEEEP.

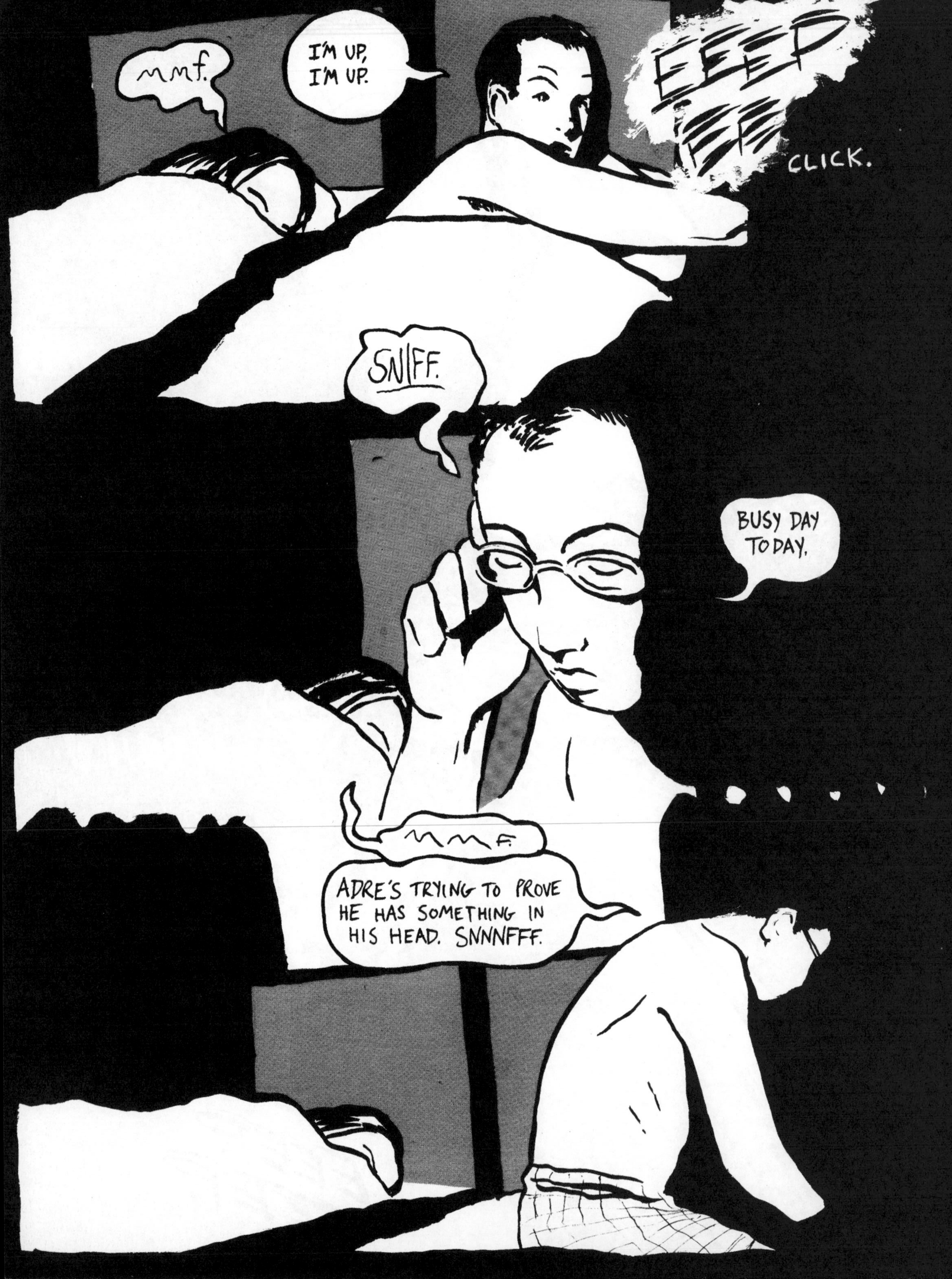
EEEP
CLICK.
I'M UP, I'M UP.
mmf.
SNIFF.
BUSY DAY TODAY.
MMF.
ADRE'S TRYING TO PROVE HE HAS SOMETHING IN HIS HEAD. SNNNFFF.

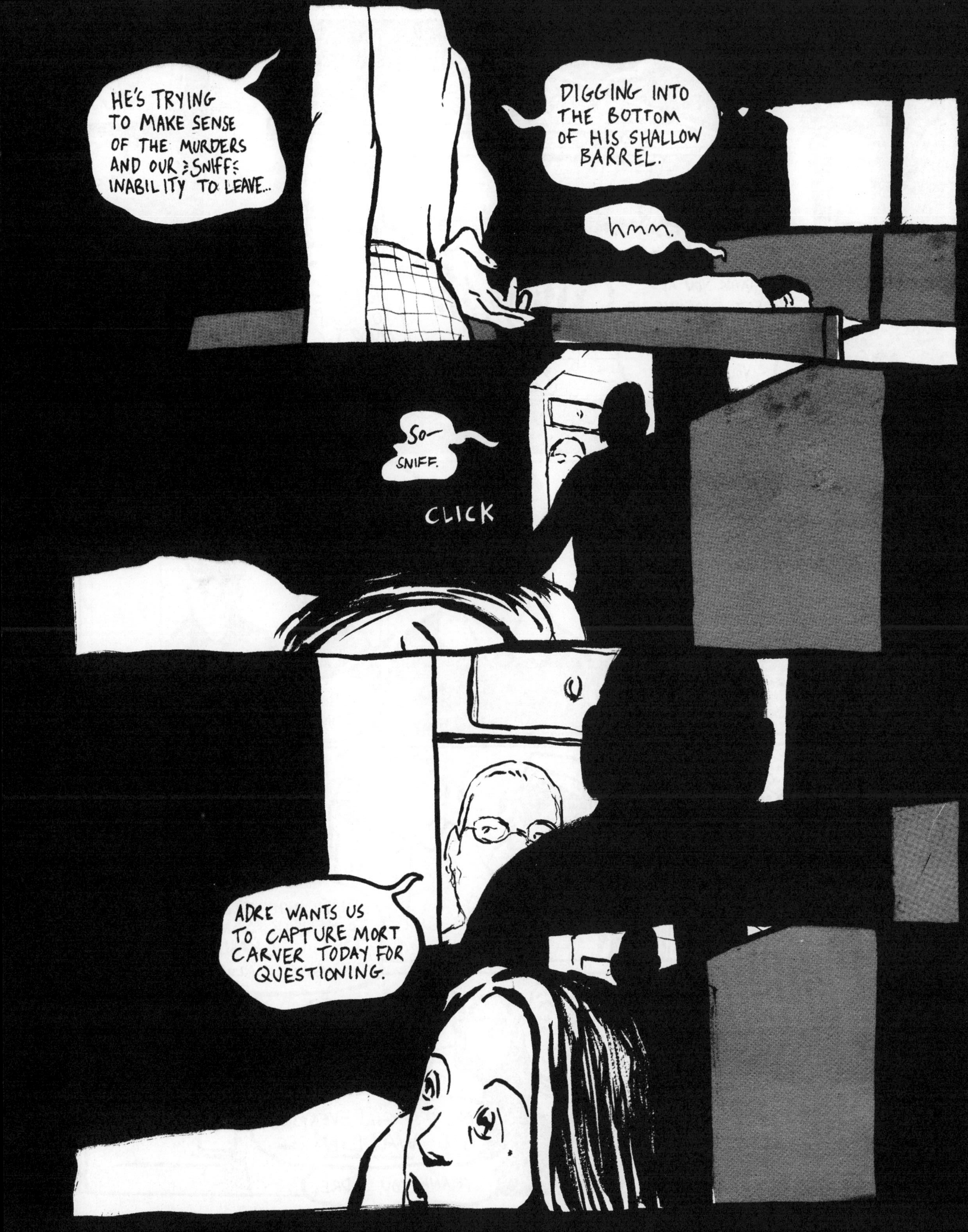
HE'S TRYING TO MAKE SENSE OF THE MURDERS AND OUR ≥SNIFF≤ INABILITY TO LEAVE...
DIGGING INTO THE BOTTOM OF HIS SHALLOW BARREL.
hmm.
So— SNIFF.
CLICK
ADRE WANTS US TO CAPTURE MORT CARVER TODAY FOR QUESTIONING.

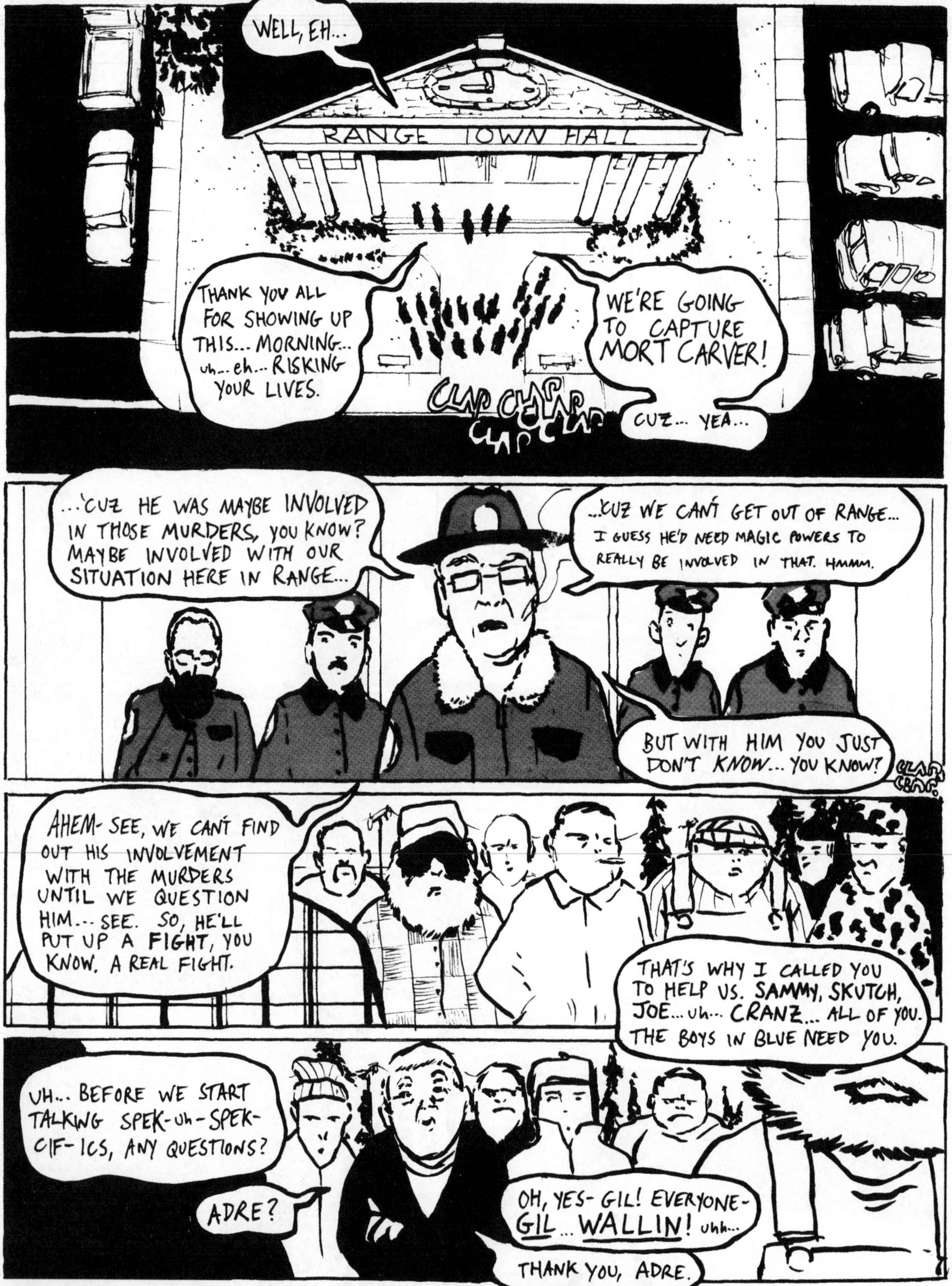
WELL, EH...
RANGE TOWN HALL
THANK YOU ALL FOR SHOWING UP THIS... MORNING... uh... eh... RISKING YOUR LIVES.
WE'RE GOING TO CAPTURE MORT CARVER!
CLAP CLAP CLAP CLAP CLAP
CUZ... YEA...
...'CUZ HE WAS MAYBE INVOLVED IN THOSE MURDERS, YOU KNOW? MAYBE INVOLVED WITH OUR SITUATION HERE IN RANGE...
...'CUZ WE CAN'T GET OUT OF RANGE... I GUESS HE'D NEED MAGIC POWERS TO REALLY BE INVOLVED IN THAT. HMMM.
BUT WITH HIM YOU JUST DON'T KNOW... YOU KNOW?
CLAP CLAP
AHEM- SEE, WE CAN'T FIND OUT HIS INVOLVEMENT WITH THE MURDERS UNTIL WE QUESTION HIM... SEE. SO, HE'LL PUT UP A FIGHT, YOU KNOW. A REAL FIGHT.
THAT'S WHY I CALLED YOU TO HELP US. SAMMY, SKUTCH, JOE... uh... CRANZ... ALL OF YOU. THE BOYS IN BLUE NEED YOU.
UH... BEFORE WE START TALKING SPEK-uh-SPEK-CIF-ICS, ANY QUESTIONS?
ADRE?
OH, YES- GIL! EVERYONE- GIL... WALLIN! uhh...
THANK YOU, ADRE.

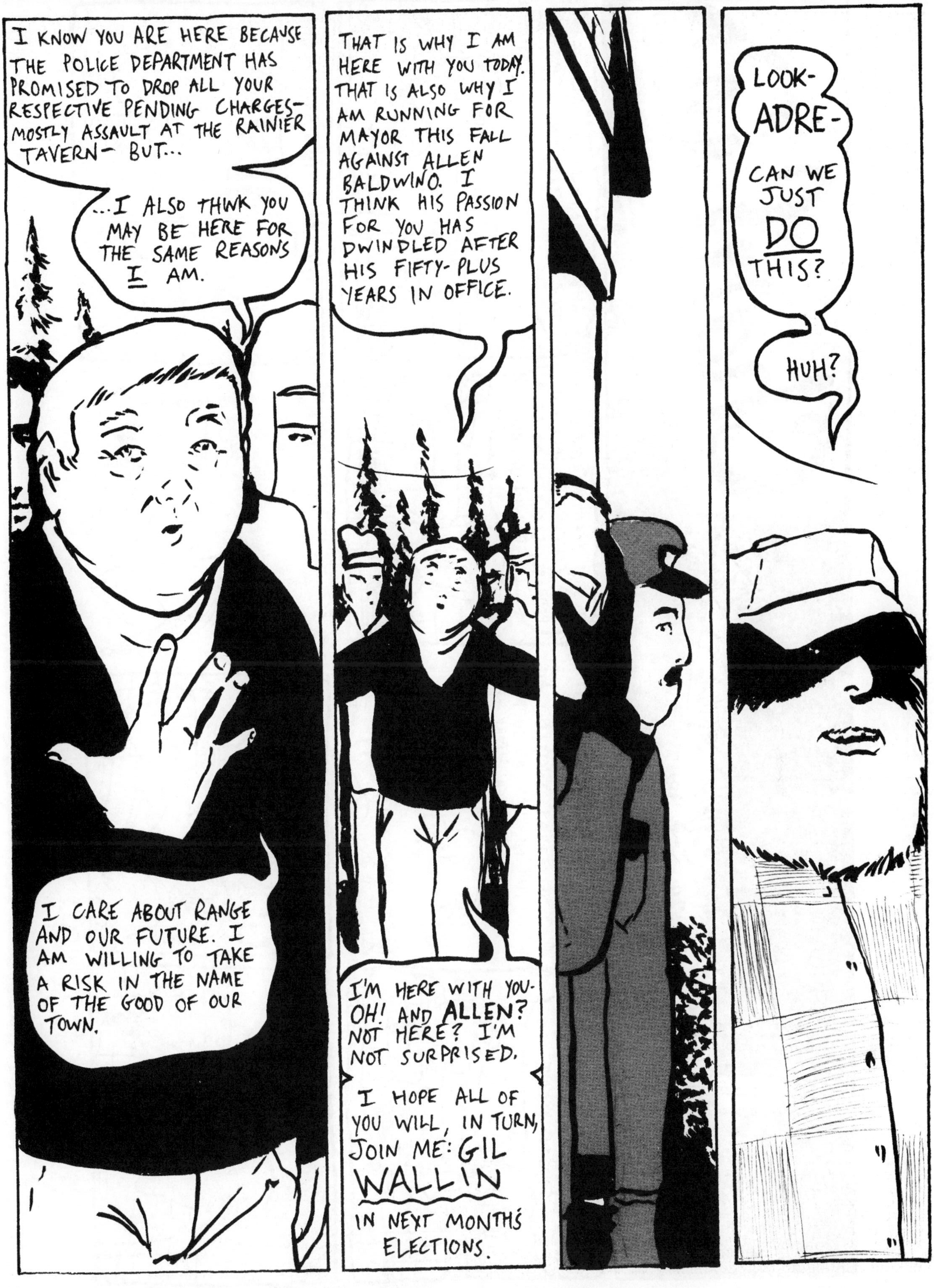
I KNOW YOU ARE HERE BECAUSE THE POLICE DEPARTMENT HAS PROMISED TO DROP ALL YOUR RESPECTIVE PENDING CHARGES- MOSTLY ASSAULT AT THE RAINIER TAVERN- BUT...
...I ALSO THINK YOU MAY BE HERE FOR THE SAME REASONS I AM.
I CARE ABOUT RANGE AND OUR FUTURE. I AM WILLING TO TAKE A RISK IN THE NAME OF THE GOOD OF OUR TOWN.
THAT IS WHY I AM HERE WITH YOU TODAY. THAT IS ALSO WHY I AM RUNNING FOR MAYOR THIS FALL AGAINST ALLEN BALDWINO. I THINK HIS PASSION FOR YOU HAS DWINDLED AFTER HIS FIFTY-PLUS YEARS IN OFFICE.
I'M HERE WITH YOU- OH! AND ALLEN? NOT HERE? I'M NOT SURPRISED.
I HOPE ALL OF YOU WILL, IN TURN, JOIN ME: GIL WALLIN IN NEXT MONTH'S ELECTIONS.
LOOK- ADRE-
CAN WE JUST DO THIS?
HUH?

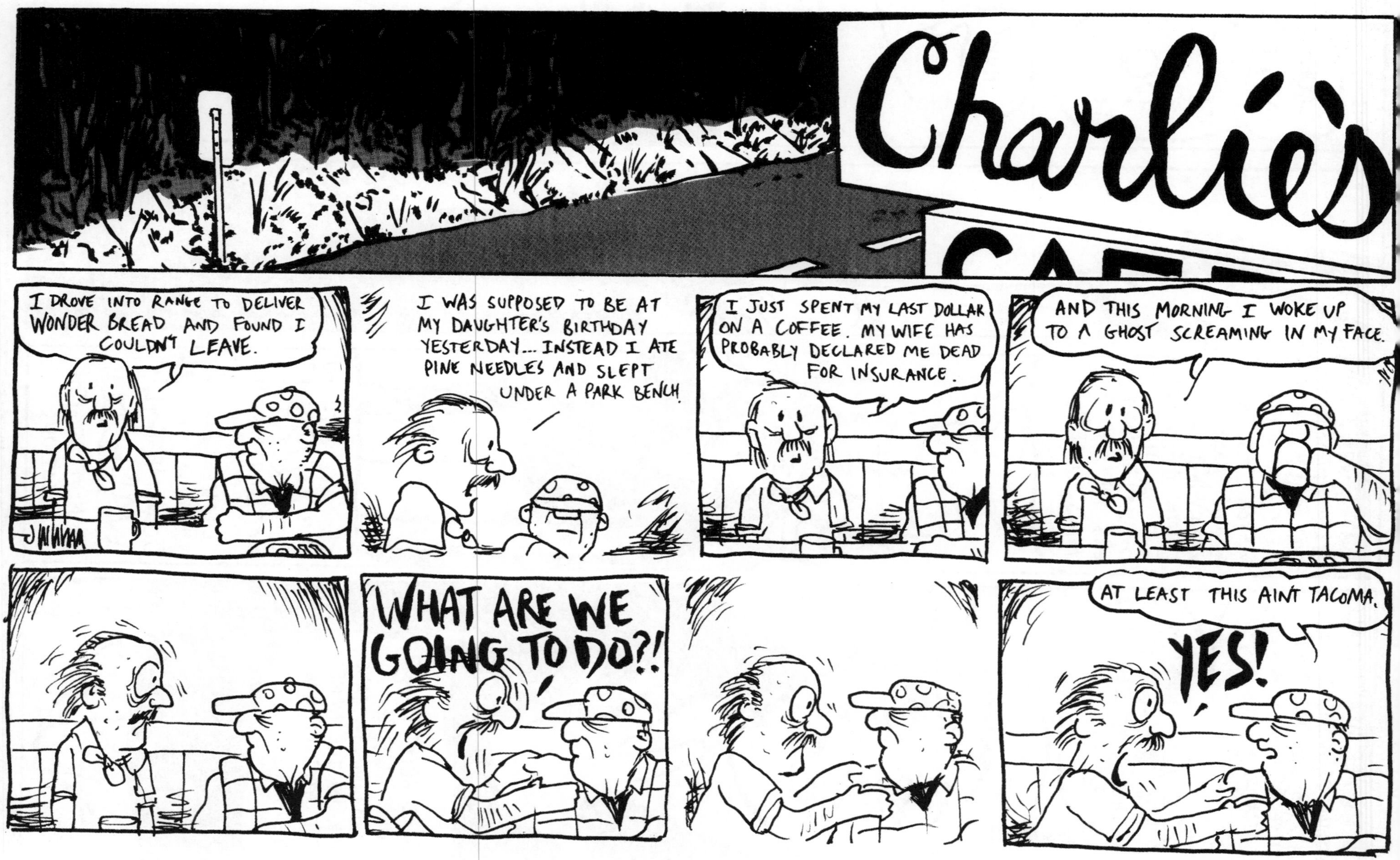
Charlie's
CAF
I DROVE INTO RANGE TO DELIVER WONDER BREAD AND FOUND I COULDN'T LEAVE.
I WAS SUPPOSED TO BE AT MY DAUGHTER'S BIRTHDAY YESTERDAY... INSTEAD I ATE PINE NEEDLES AND SLEPT UNDER A PARK BENCH.
I JUST SPENT MY LAST DOLLAR ON A COFFEE. MY WIFE HAS PROBABLY DECLARED ME DEAD FOR INSURANCE.
AND THIS MORNING I WOKE UP TO A GHOST SCREAMING IN MY FACE.
WHAT ARE WE GOING TO DO?!
AT LEAST THIS AINT TACOMA.
YES!

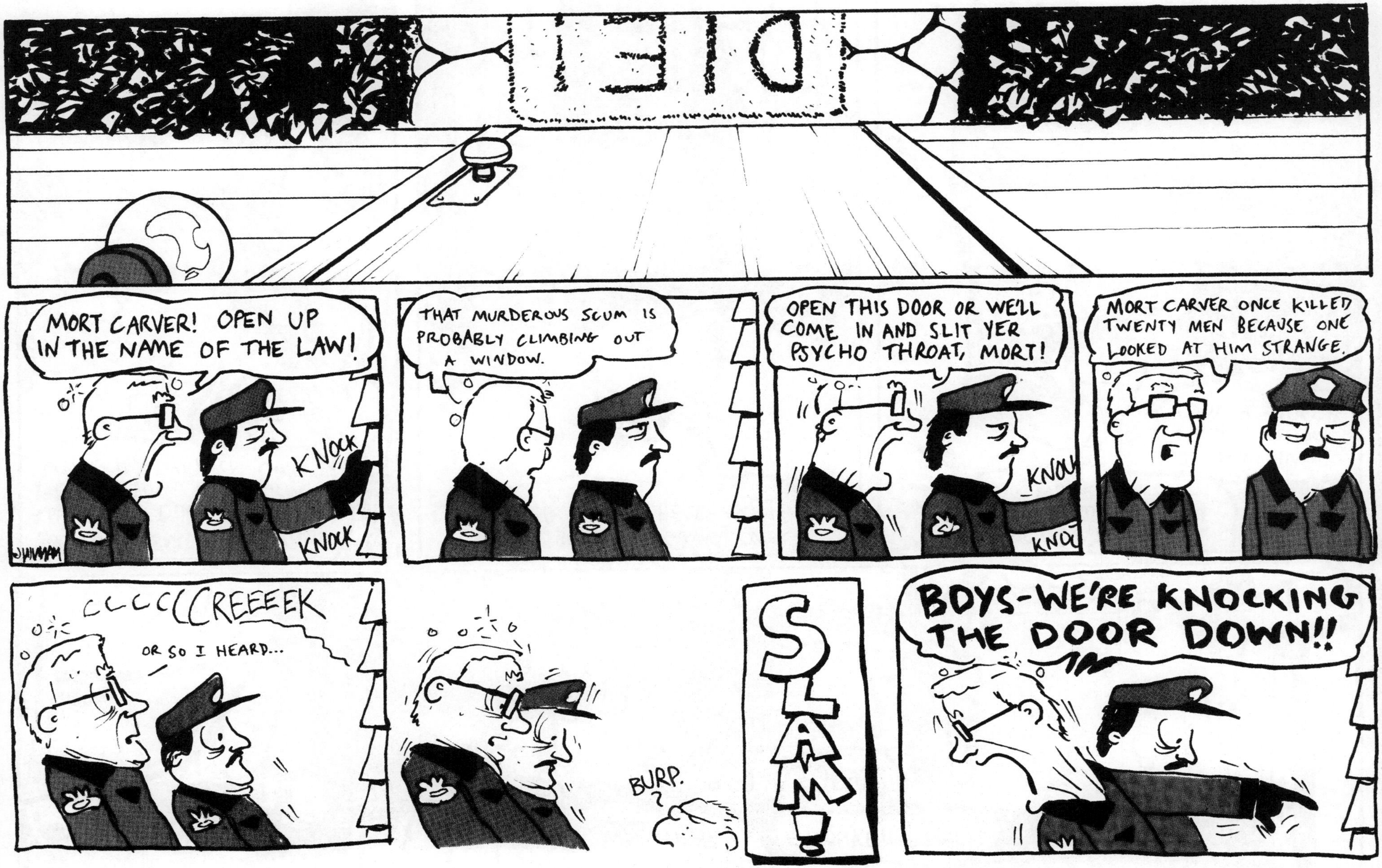

DIE!
MORT CARVER! OPEN UP IN THE NAME OF THE LAW!
KNOCK
KNOCK
THAT MURDEROUS SCUM IS PROBABLY CLIMBING OUT A WINDOW.
OPEN THIS DOOR OR WE'LL COME IN AND SLIT YER PSYCHO THROAT, MORT!
MORT CARVER ONCE KILLED TWENTY MEN BECAUSE ONE LOOKED AT HIM STRANGE.
CCCCCCREEEEEK
OR SO I HEARD...
BURP.
SLAM!
BOYS-WE'RE KNOCKING THE DOOR DOWN!!

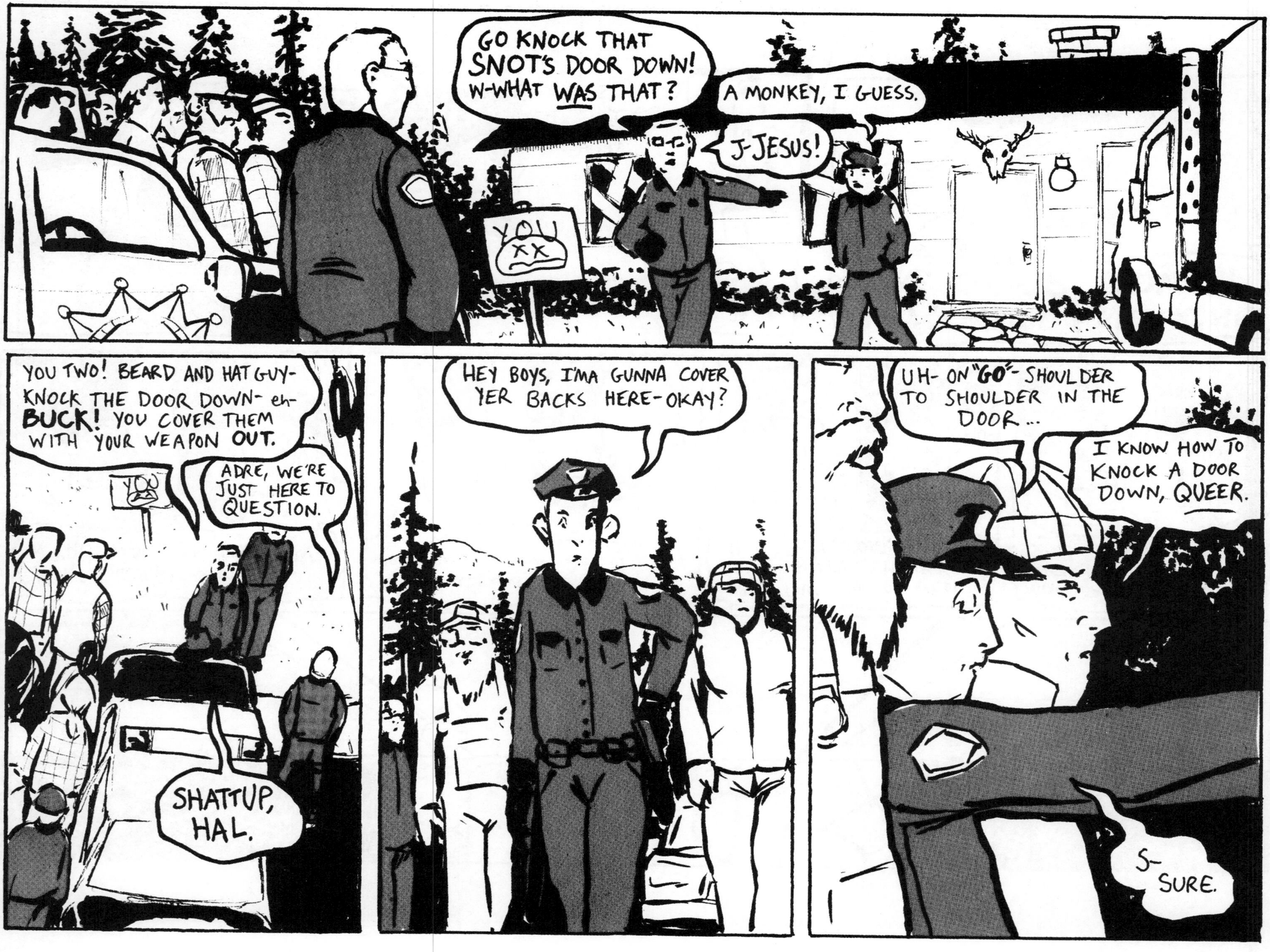
GO KNOCK THAT SNOT'S DOOR DOWN! W-WHAT WAS THAT?
A MONKEY, I GUESS.
J-JESUS!
YOU
YOU TWO! BEARD AND HAT GUY- KNOCK THE DOOR DOWN- eh- BUCK! YOU COVER THEM WITH YOUR WEAPON OUT.
ADRE, WE'RE JUST HERE TO QUESTION.
SHATTUP, HAL.
HEY BOYS, I'MA GUNNA COVER YER BACKS HERE-OKAY?
UH- ON "GO"- SHOULDER TO SHOULDER IN THE DOOR...
I KNOW HOW TO KNOCK A DOOR DOWN, QUEER.
S- SURE.

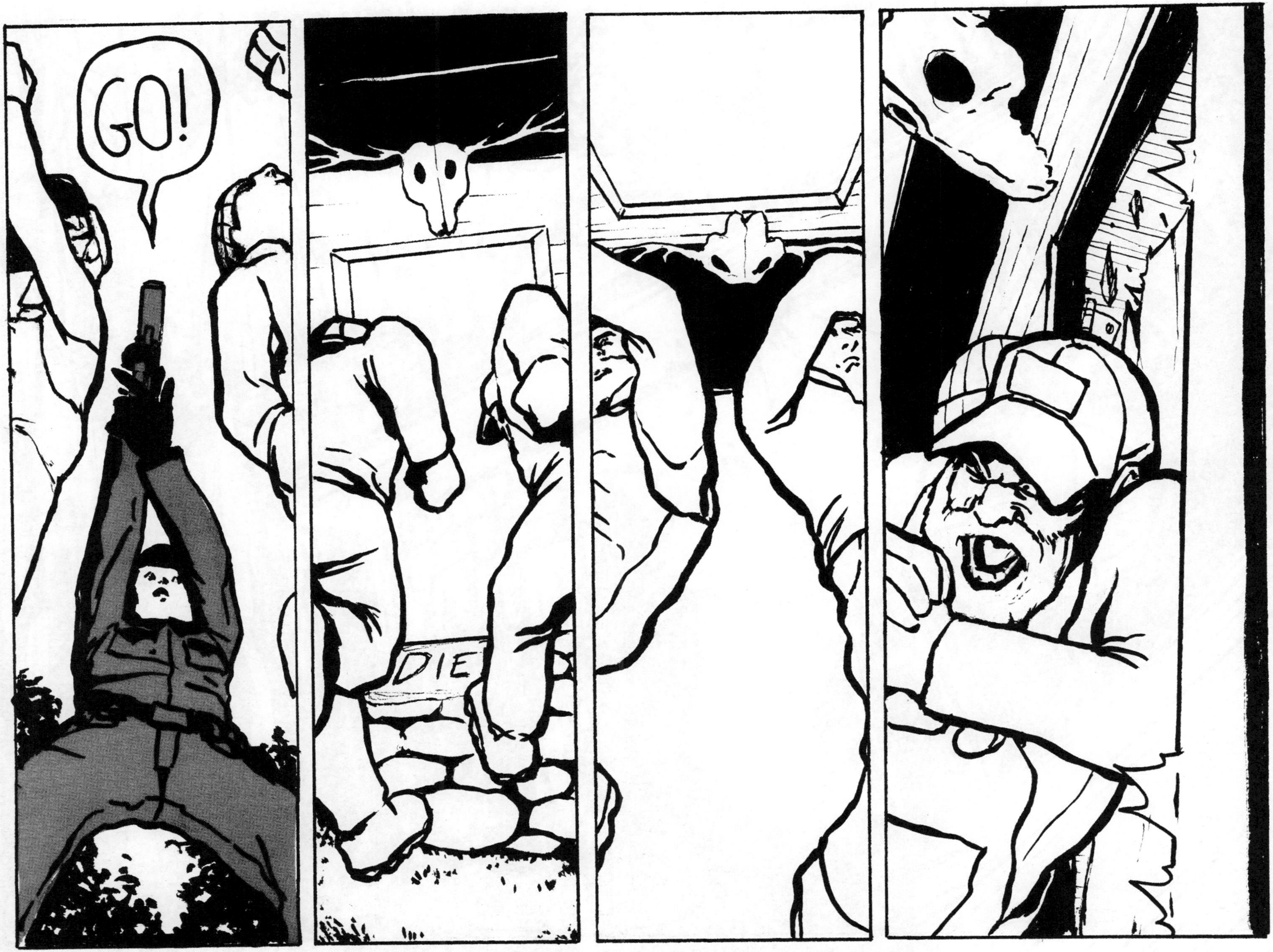
GO!
DIE

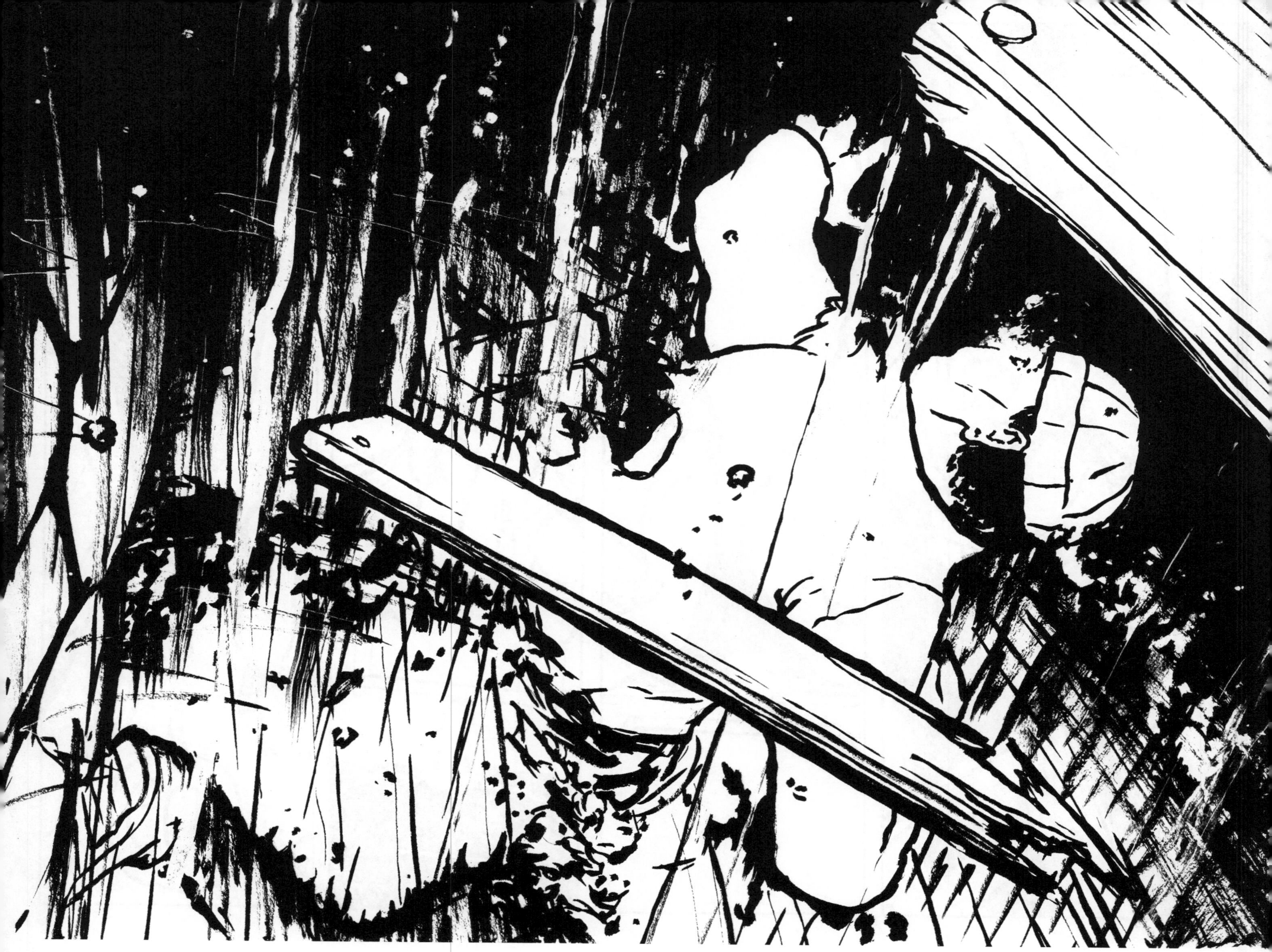

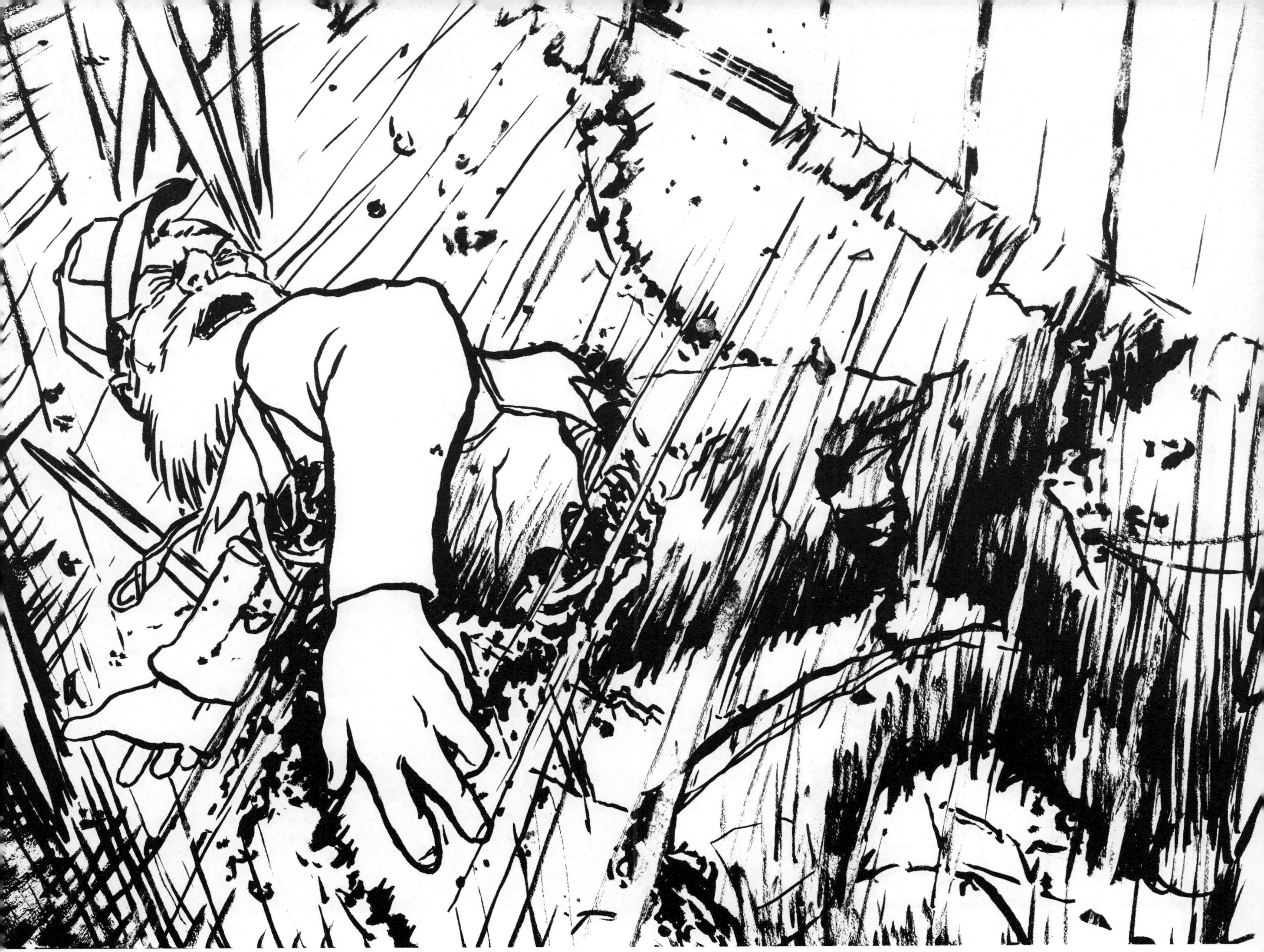

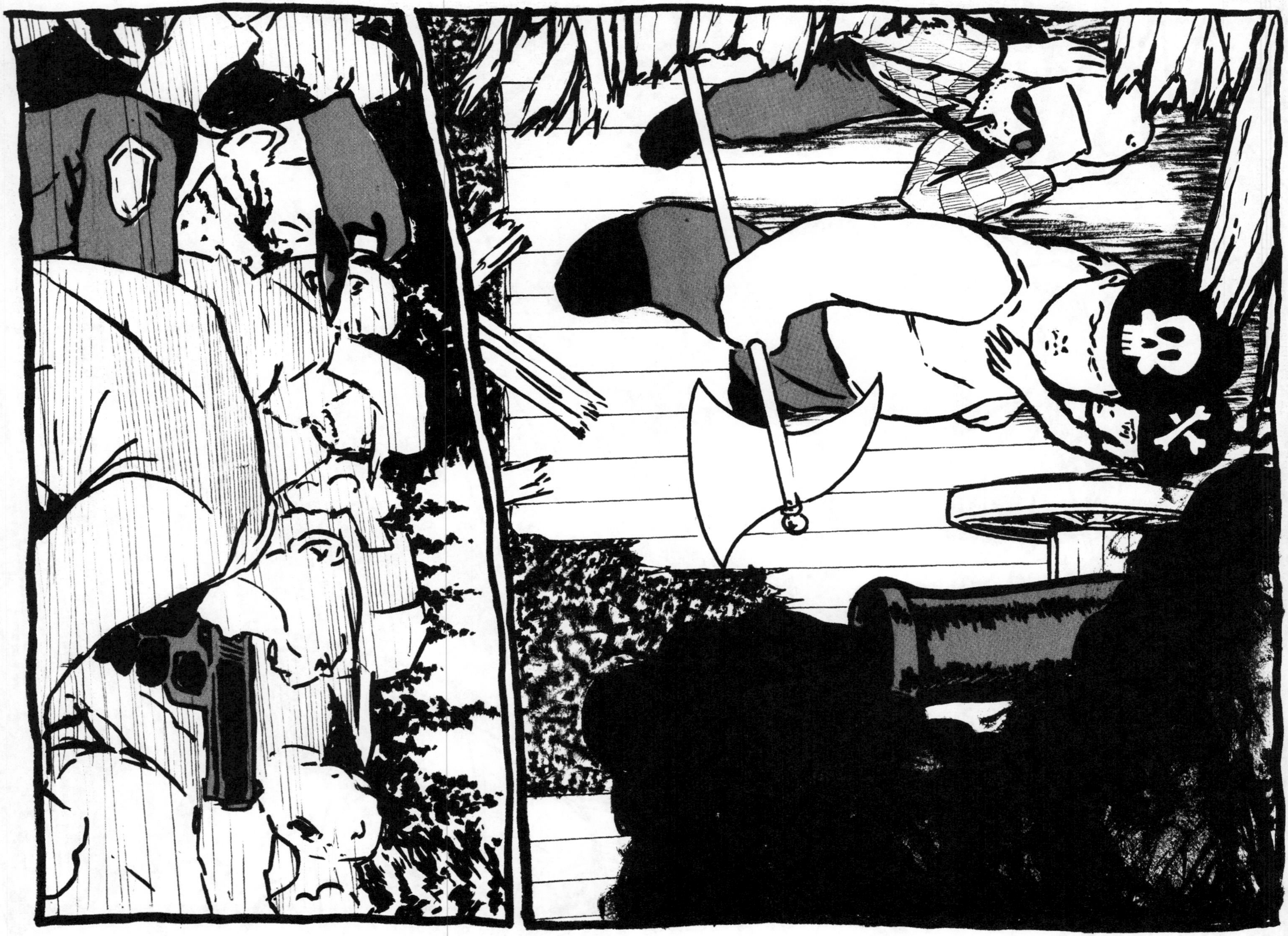

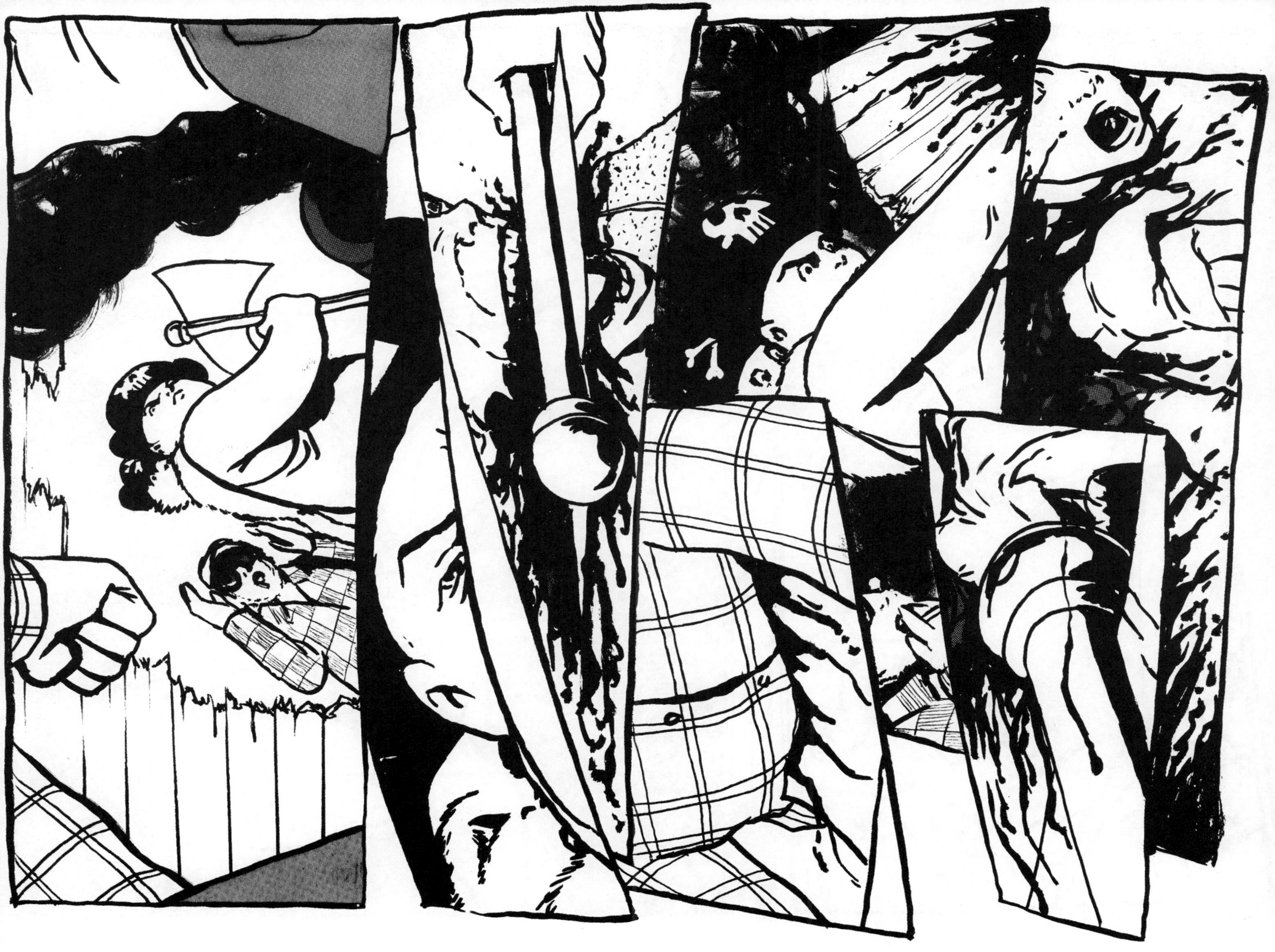

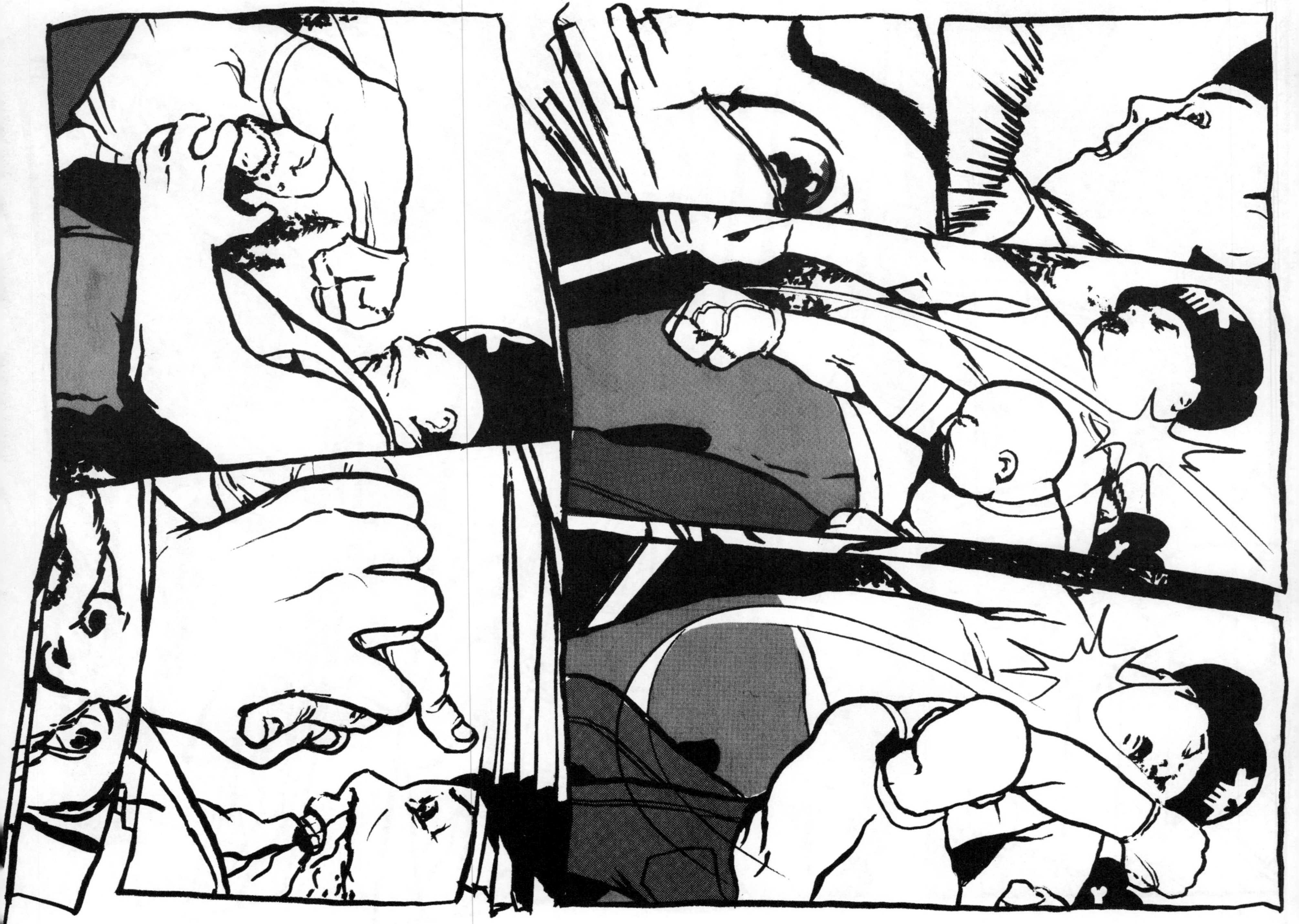

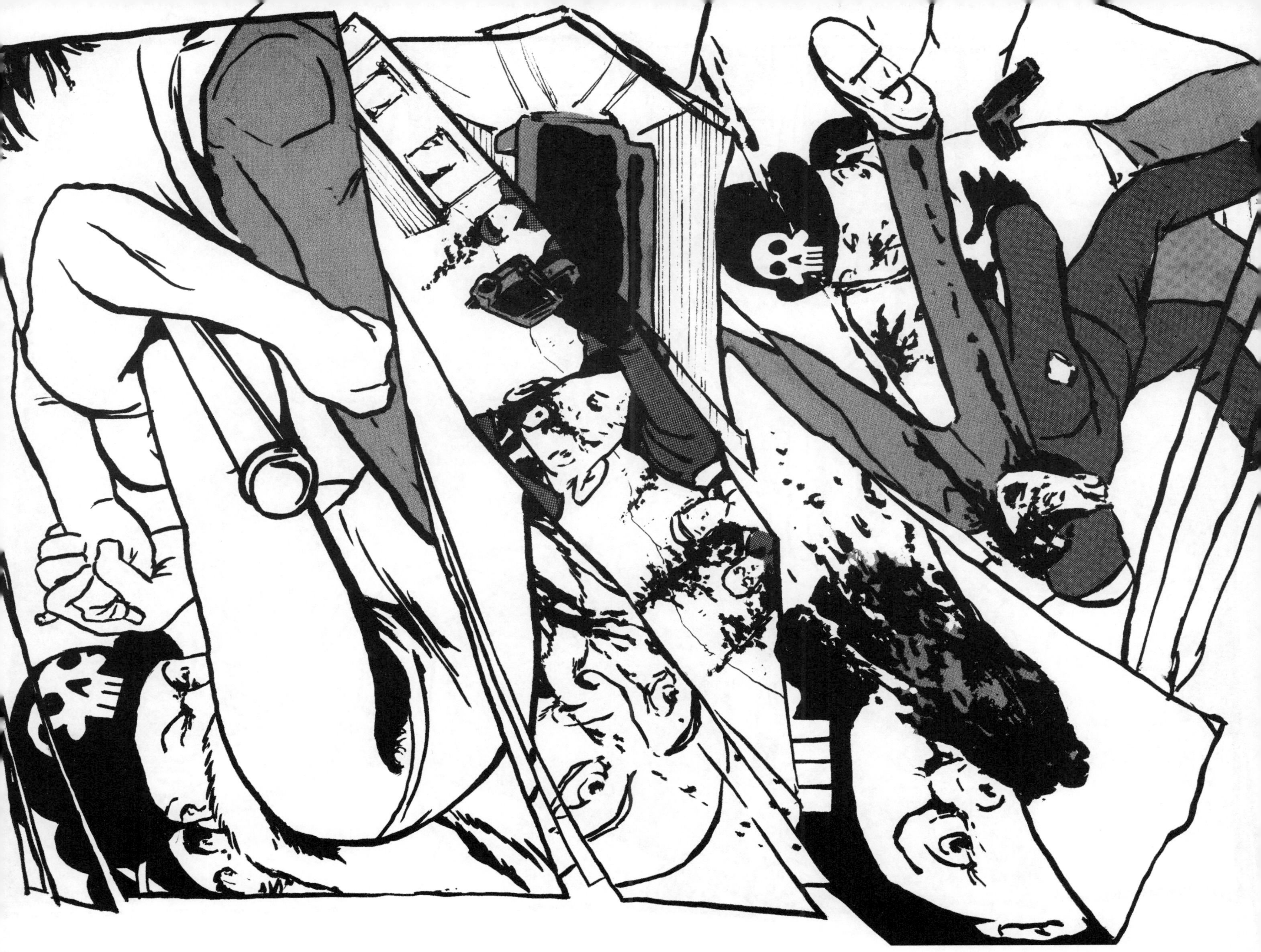

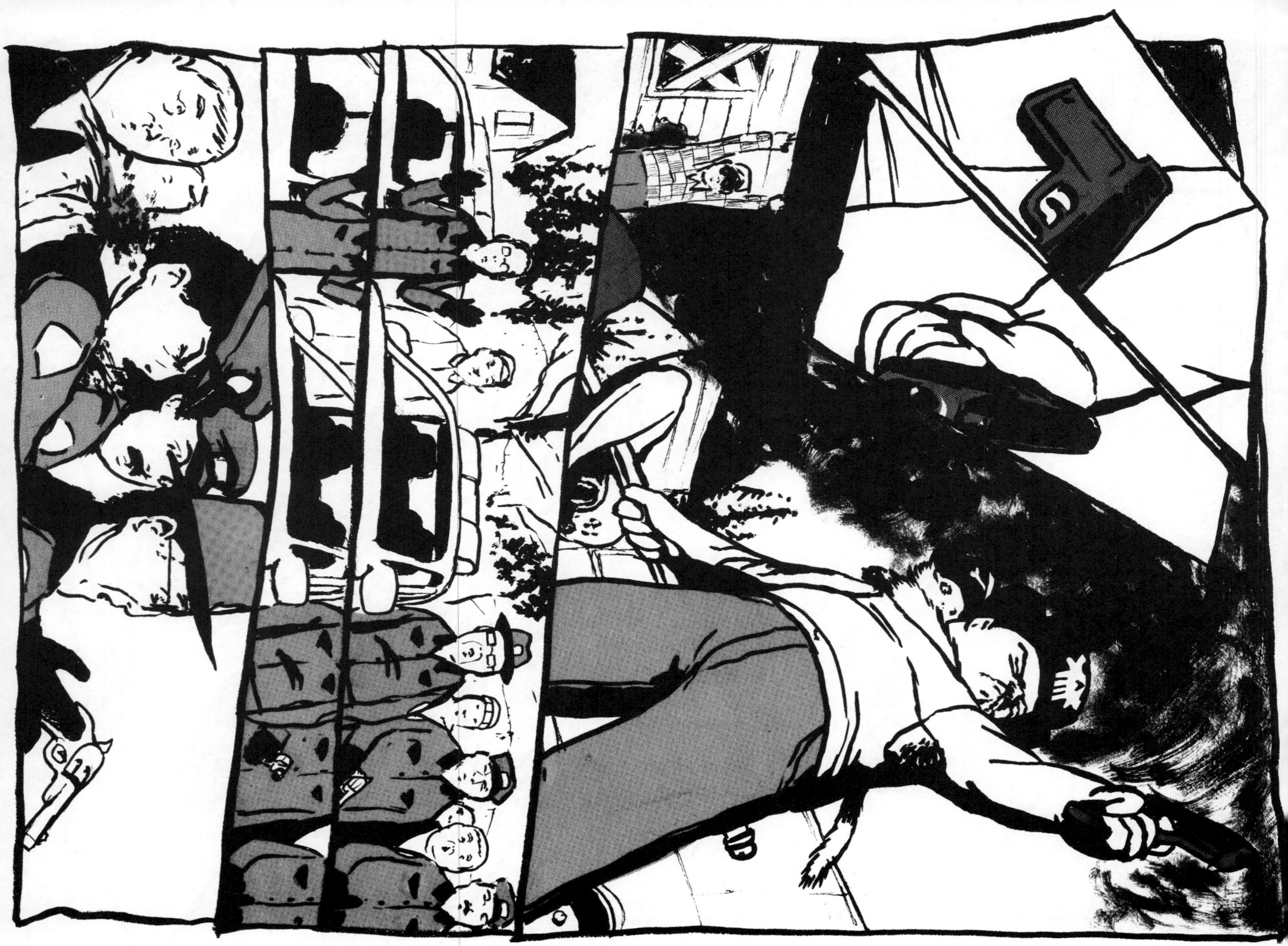

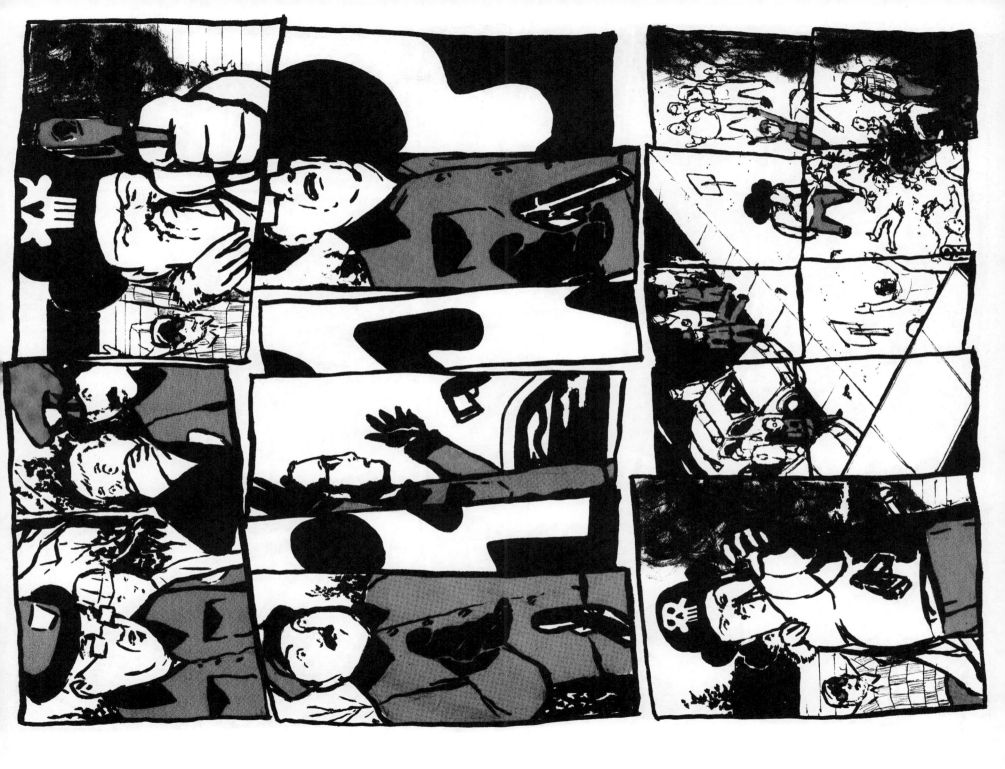

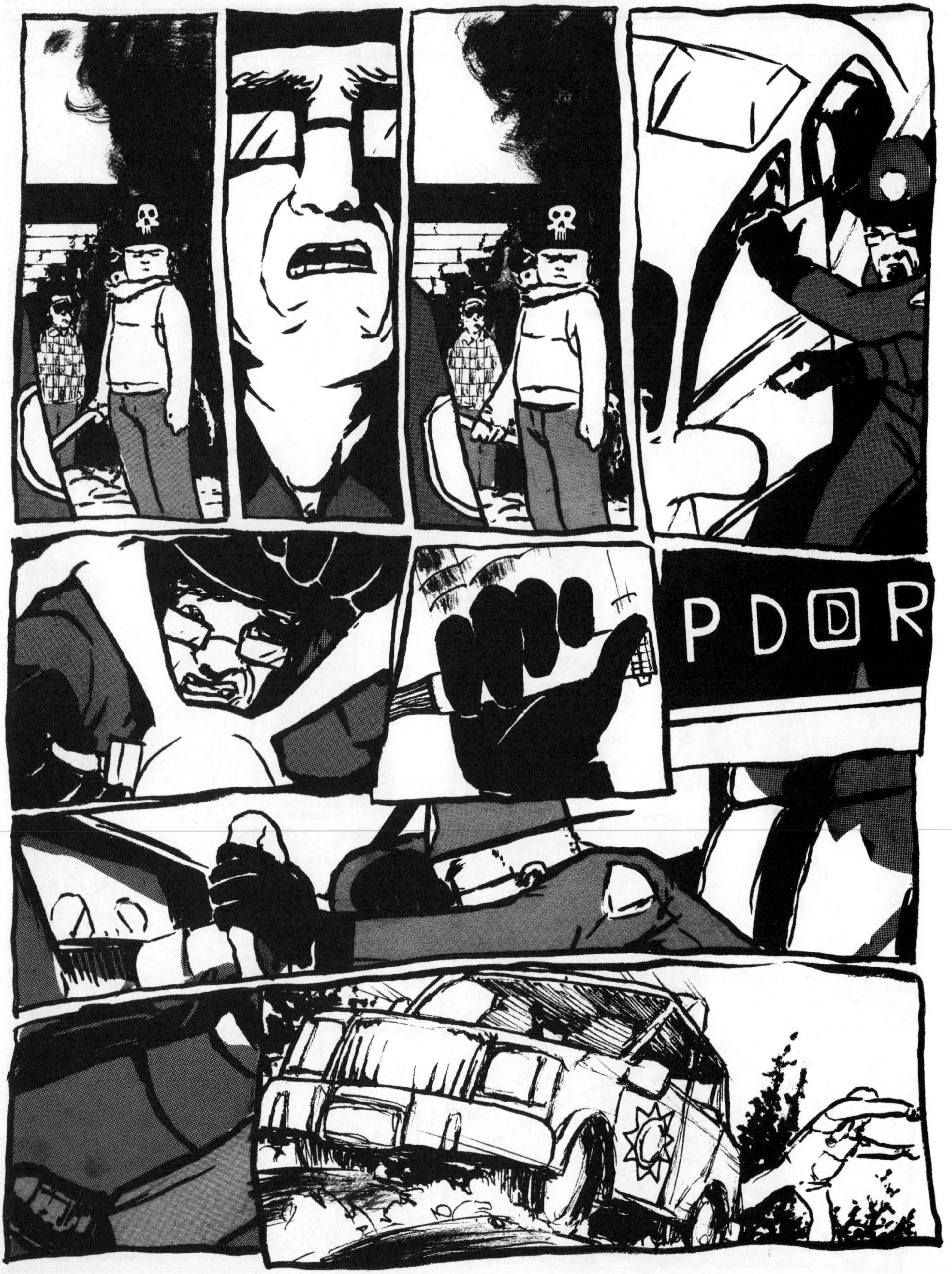
PDDR

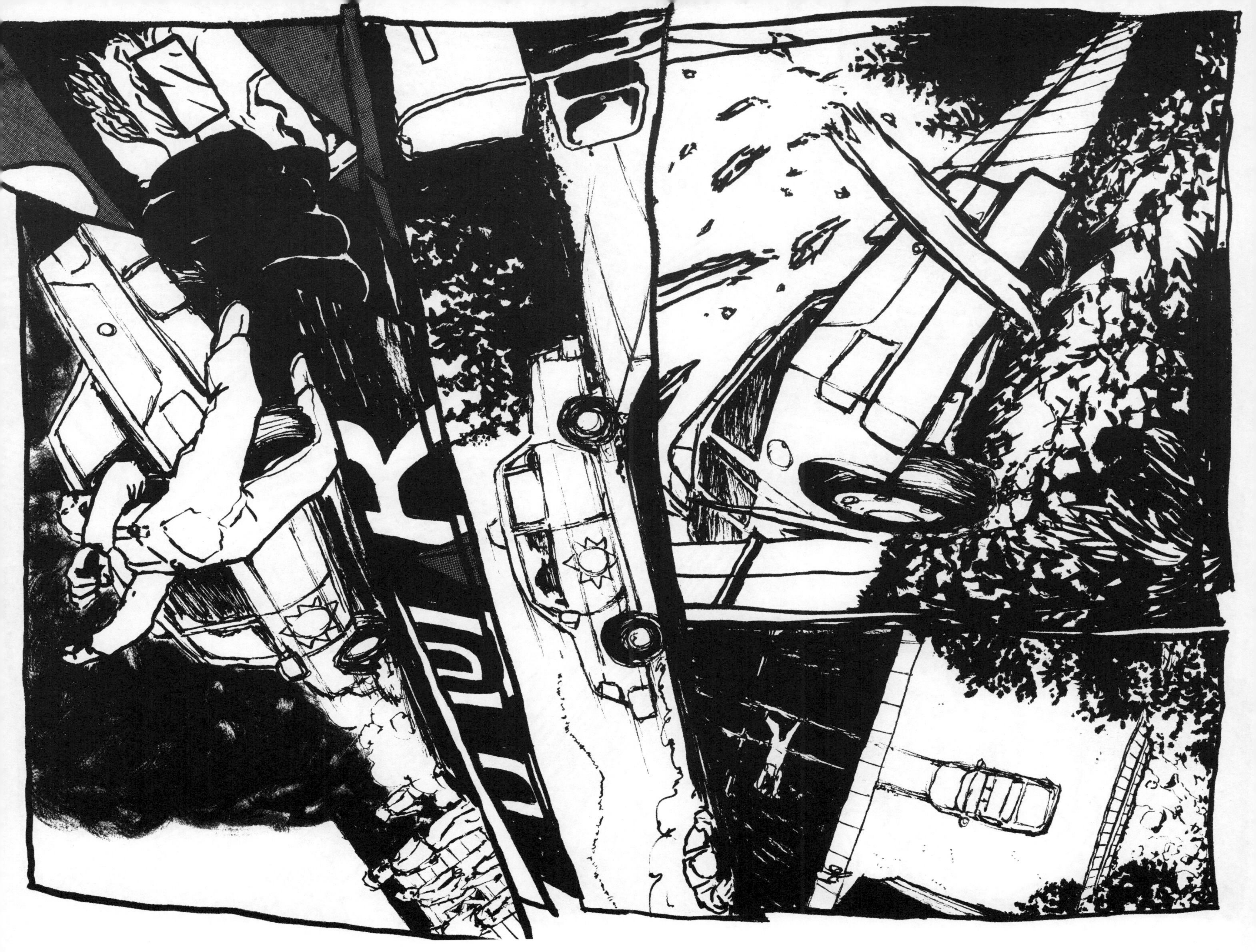

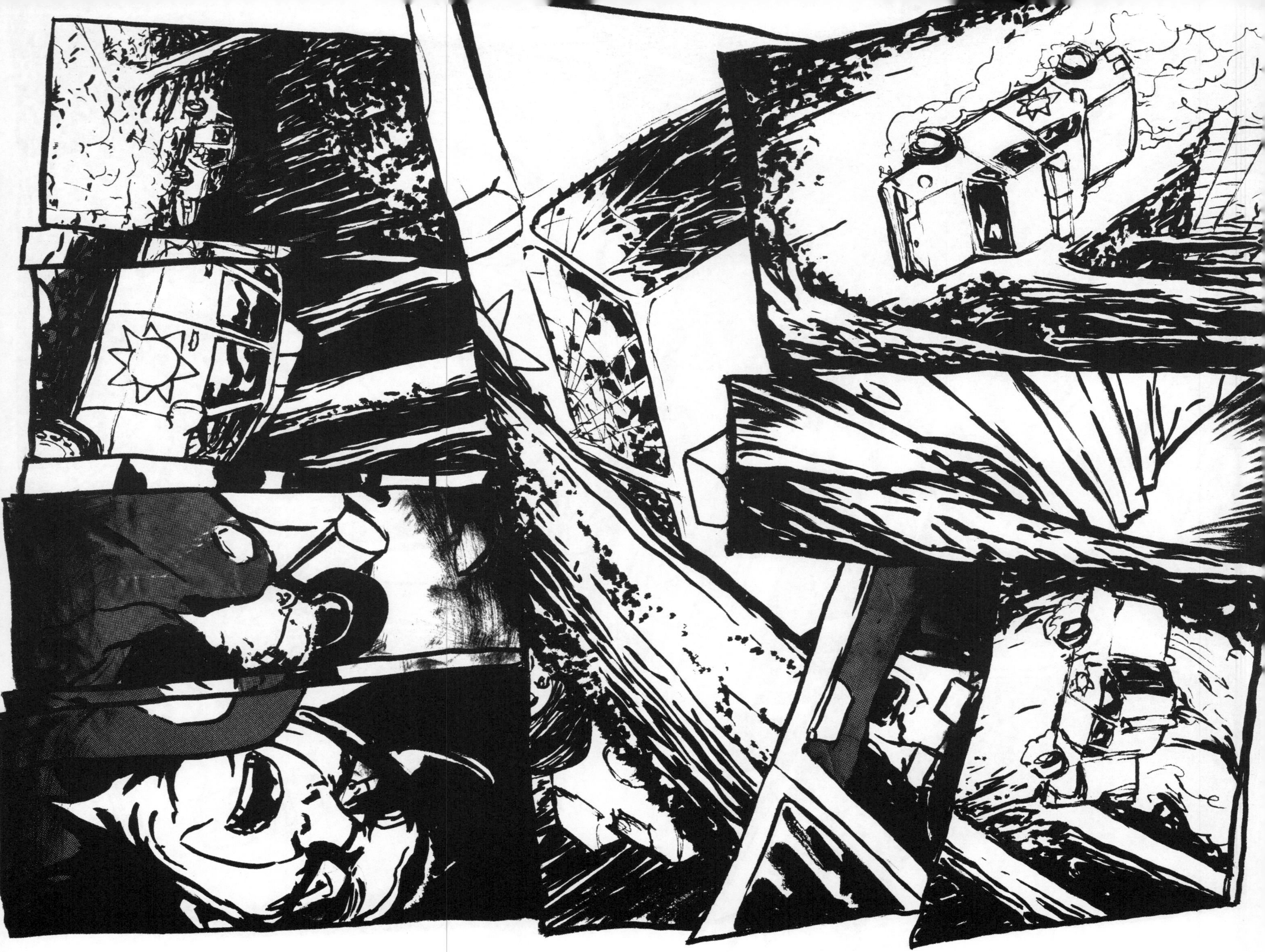

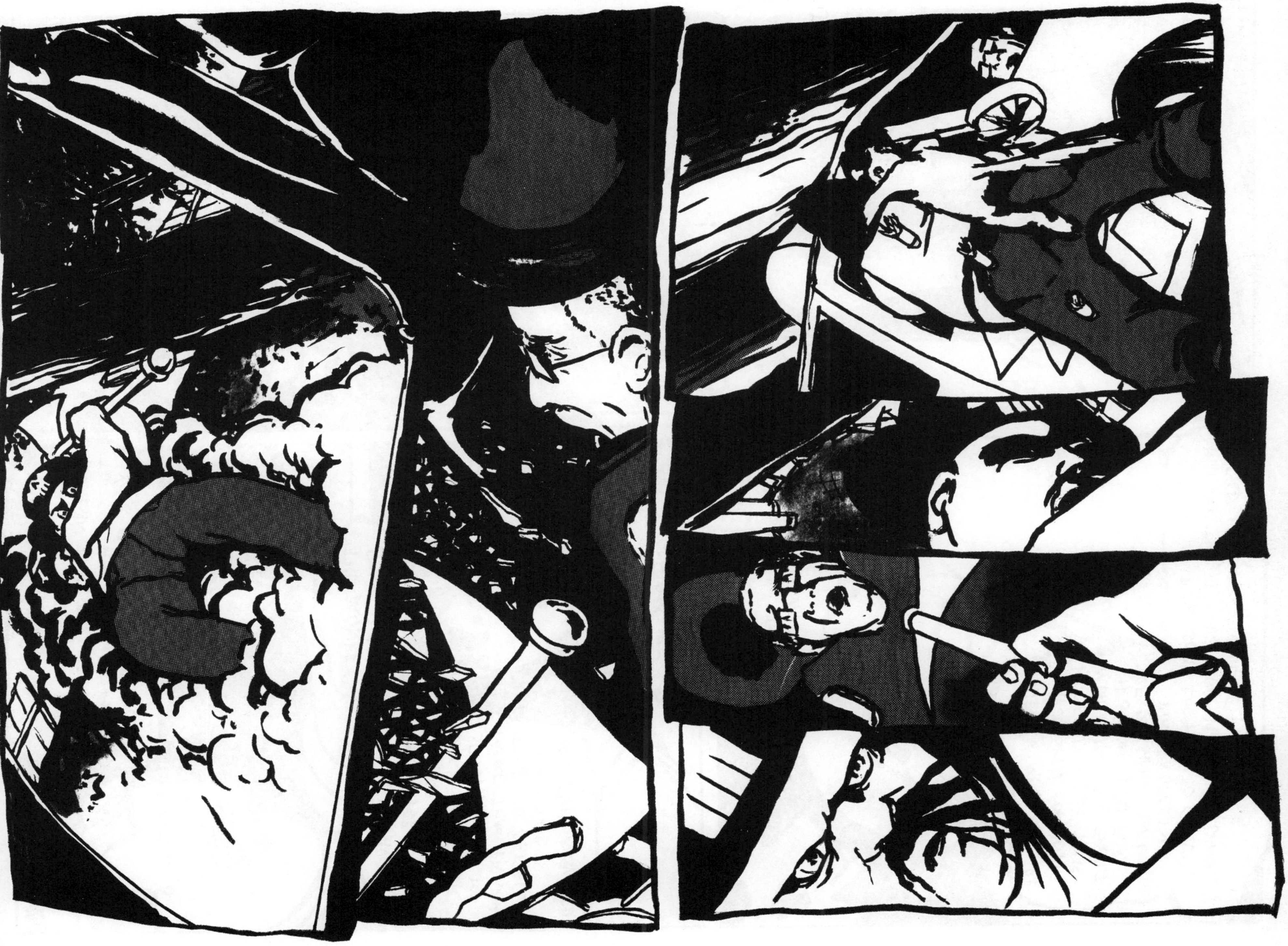

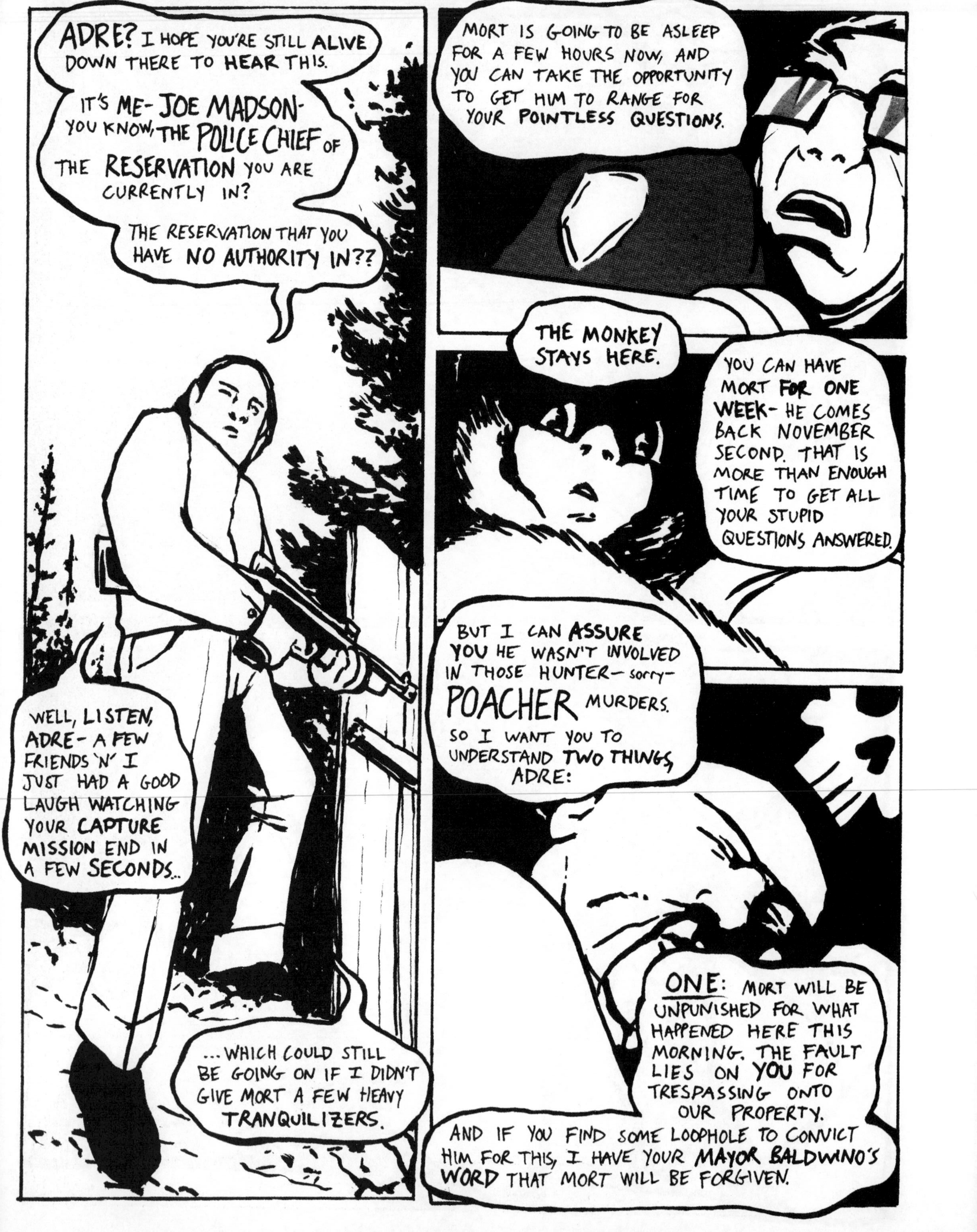
ADRE? I HOPE YOU'RE STILL ALIVE DOWN THERE TO HEAR THIS.
IT'S ME- JOE MADSON- YOU KNOW, THE POLICE CHIEF OF THE RESERVATION YOU ARE CURRENTLY IN?
THE RESERVATION THAT YOU HAVE NO AUTHORITY IN??
WELL, LISTEN, ADRE- A FEW FRIENDS 'N' I JUST HAD A GOOD LAUGH WATCHING YOUR CAPTURE MISSION END IN A FEW SECONDS...
...WHICH COULD STILL BE GOING ON IF I DIDN'T GIVE MORT A FEW HEAVY TRANQUILIZERS.
MORT IS GOING TO BE ASLEEP FOR A FEW HOURS NOW, AND YOU CAN TAKE THE OPPORTUNITY TO GET HIM TO RANGE FOR YOUR POINTLESS QUESTIONS.
THE MONKEY STAYS HERE.
YOU CAN HAVE MORT FOR ONE WEEK- HE COMES BACK NOVEMBER SECOND. THAT IS MORE THAN ENOUGH TIME TO GET ALL YOUR STUPID QUESTIONS ANSWERED.
BUT I CAN ASSURE YOU HE WASN'T INVOLVED IN THOSE HUNTER— sorry— POACHER MURDERS.
SO I WANT YOU TO UNDERSTAND TWO THINGS, ADRE:
ONE: MORT WILL BE UNPUNISHED FOR WHAT HAPPENED HERE THIS MORNING. THE FAULT LIES ON YOU FOR TRESPASSING ONTO OUR PROPERTY.
AND IF YOU FIND SOME LOOPHOLE TO CONVICT HIM FOR THIS, I HAVE YOUR MAYOR BALDWINO'S WORD THAT MORT WILL BE FORGIVEN.

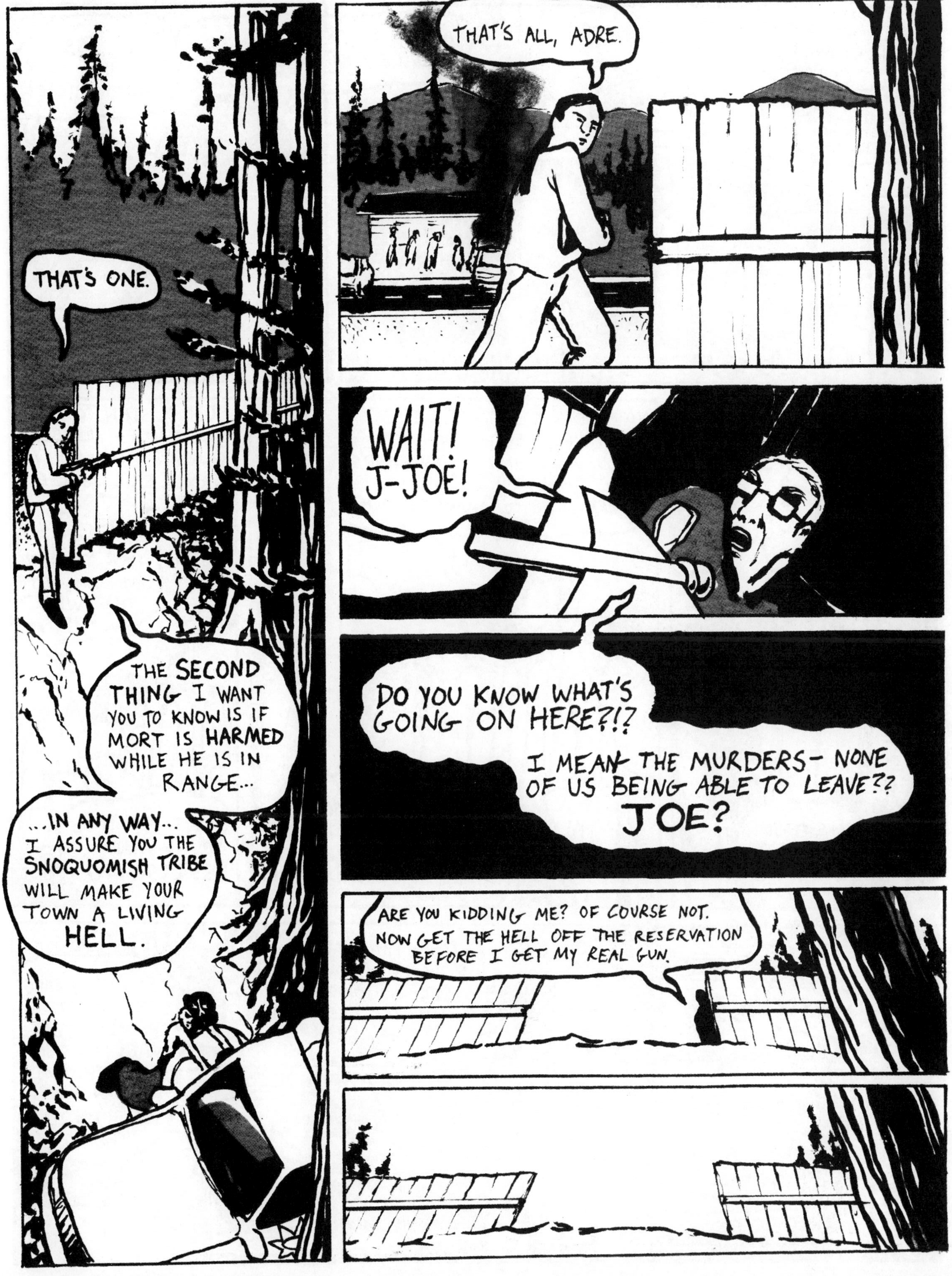
THAT'S ONE.
THE SECOND THING I WANT YOU TO KNOW IS IF MORT IS HARMED WHILE HE IS IN RANGE...
...IN ANY WAY... I ASSURE YOU THE SNOQUOMISH TRIBE WILL MAKE YOUR TOWN A LIVING HELL.
THAT'S ALL, ADRE.
WAIT! J-JOE!
DO YOU KNOW WHAT'S GOING ON HERE?!?
I MEAN THE MURDERS- NONE OF US BEING ABLE TO LEAVE?? JOE?
ARE YOU KIDDING ME? OF COURSE NOT. NOW GET THE HELL OFF THE RESERVATION BEFORE I GET MY REAL GUN.

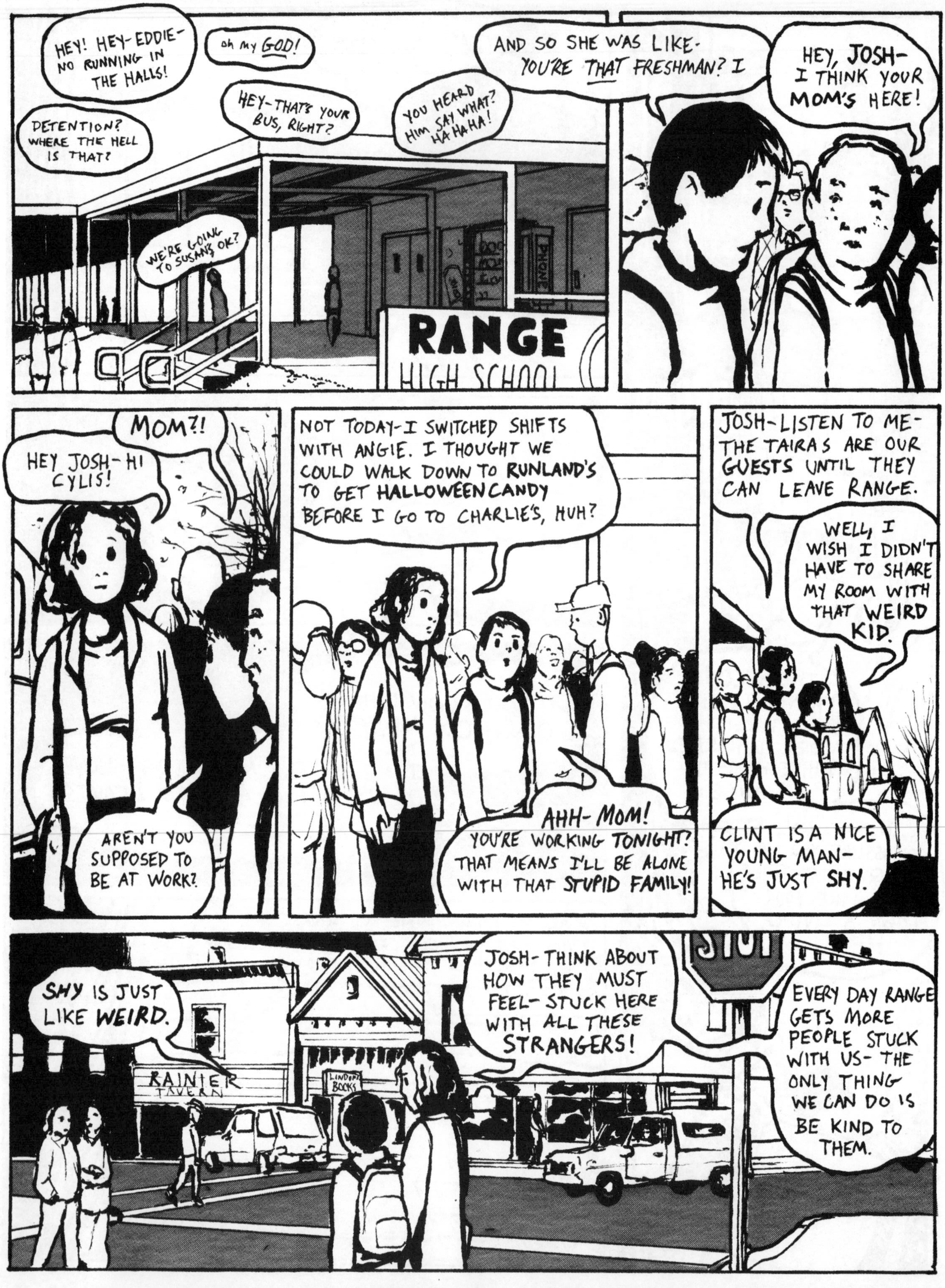
HEY! HEY-EDDIE- NO RUNNING IN THE HALLS!
DETENTION? WHERE THE HELL IS THAT?
oh my GOD!
HEY-THAT'S YOUR BUS, RIGHT?
WE'RE GOING TO SUSAN'S OK?
YOU HEARD HIM SAY WHAT? HA HA HA!
RANGE
HIGH SCHOOL
AND SO SHE WAS LIKE- YOU'RE THAT FRESHMAN? I
HEY, JOSH- I THINK YOUR MOM'S HERE!
HEY JOSH- HI CYLIS!
MOM?!
AREN'T YOU SUPPOSED TO BE AT WORK?
NOT TODAY-I SWITCHED SHIFTS WITH ANGIE. I THOUGHT WE COULD WALK DOWN TO RUNLAND'S TO GET HALLOWEEN CANDY BEFORE I GO TO CHARLIE'S, HUH?
AHH- MOM! YOU'RE WORKING TONIGHT? THAT MEANS I'LL BE ALONE WITH THAT STUPID FAMILY!
JOSH-LISTEN TO ME- THE TAIRAS ARE OUR GUESTS UNTIL THEY CAN LEAVE RANGE.
WELL, I WISH I DIDN'T HAVE TO SHARE MY ROOM WITH THAT WEIRD KID.
CLINT IS A NICE YOUNG MAN- HE'S JUST SHY.
SHY IS JUST LIKE WEIRD.
RAINIER TAVERN
BOOKS
JOSH-THINK ABOUT HOW THEY MUST FEEL-STUCK HERE WITH ALL THESE STRANGERS!
EVERY DAY RANGE GETS MORE PEOPLE STUCK WITH US- THE ONLY THING WE CAN DO IS BE KIND TO THEM.

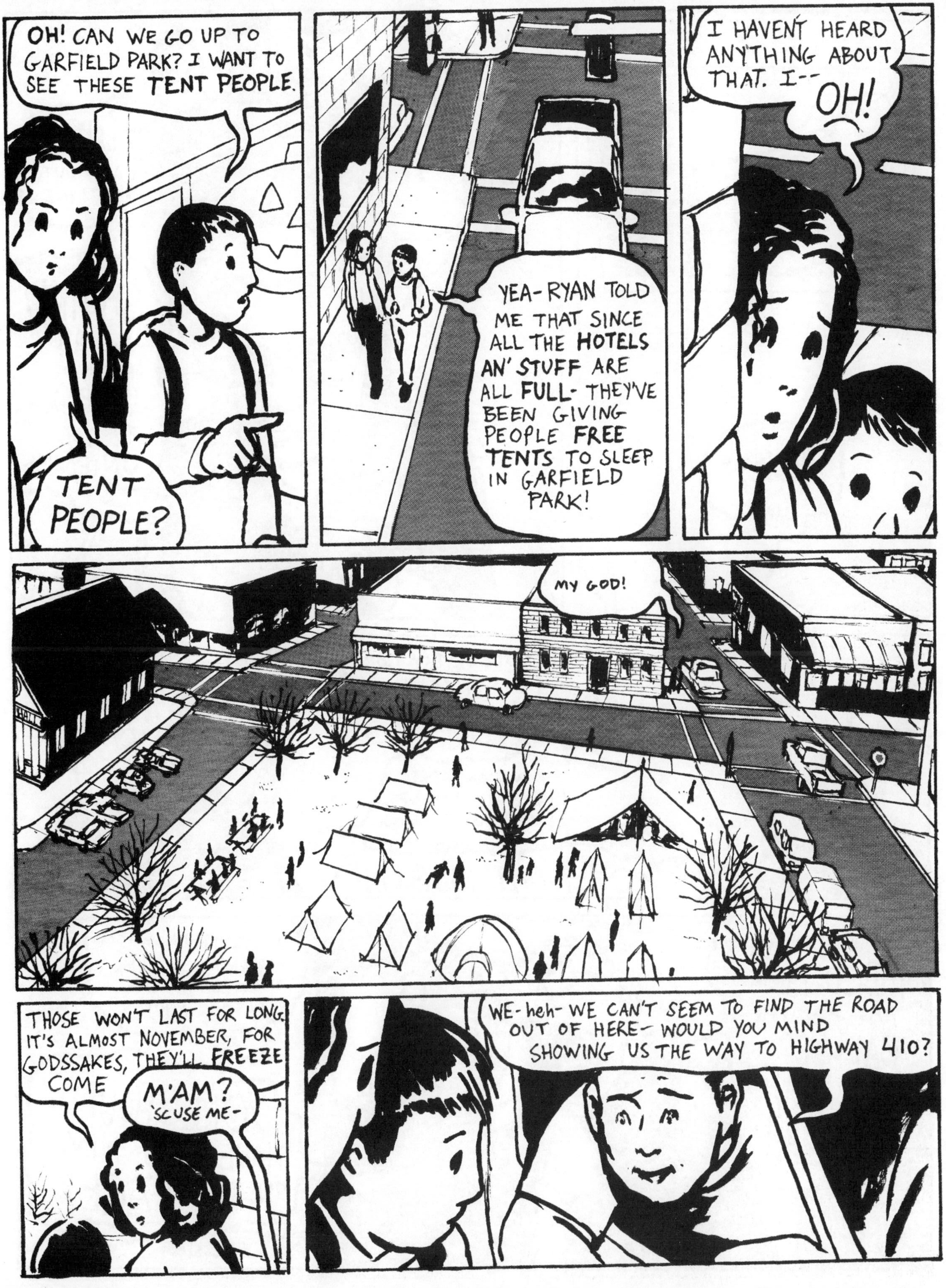
OH! CAN WE GO UP TO GARFIELD PARK? I WANT TO SEE THESE TENT PEOPLE.
TENT PEOPLE?
YEA-RYAN TOLD ME THAT SINCE ALL THE HOTELS AN' STUFF ARE ALL FULL- THEY'VE BEEN GIVING PEOPLE FREE TENTS TO SLEEP IN GARFIELD PARK!
I HAVEN'T HEARD ANYTHING ABOUT THAT. I--
OH!
MY GOD!
THOSE WON'T LAST FOR LONG. IT'S ALMOST NOVEMBER, FOR GODSSAKES, THEY'LL FREEZE COME
M'AM? 'SCUSE ME-
WE-heh-WE CAN'T SEEM TO FIND THE ROAD OUT OF HERE- WOULD YOU MIND SHOWING US THE WAY TO HIGHWAY 410?

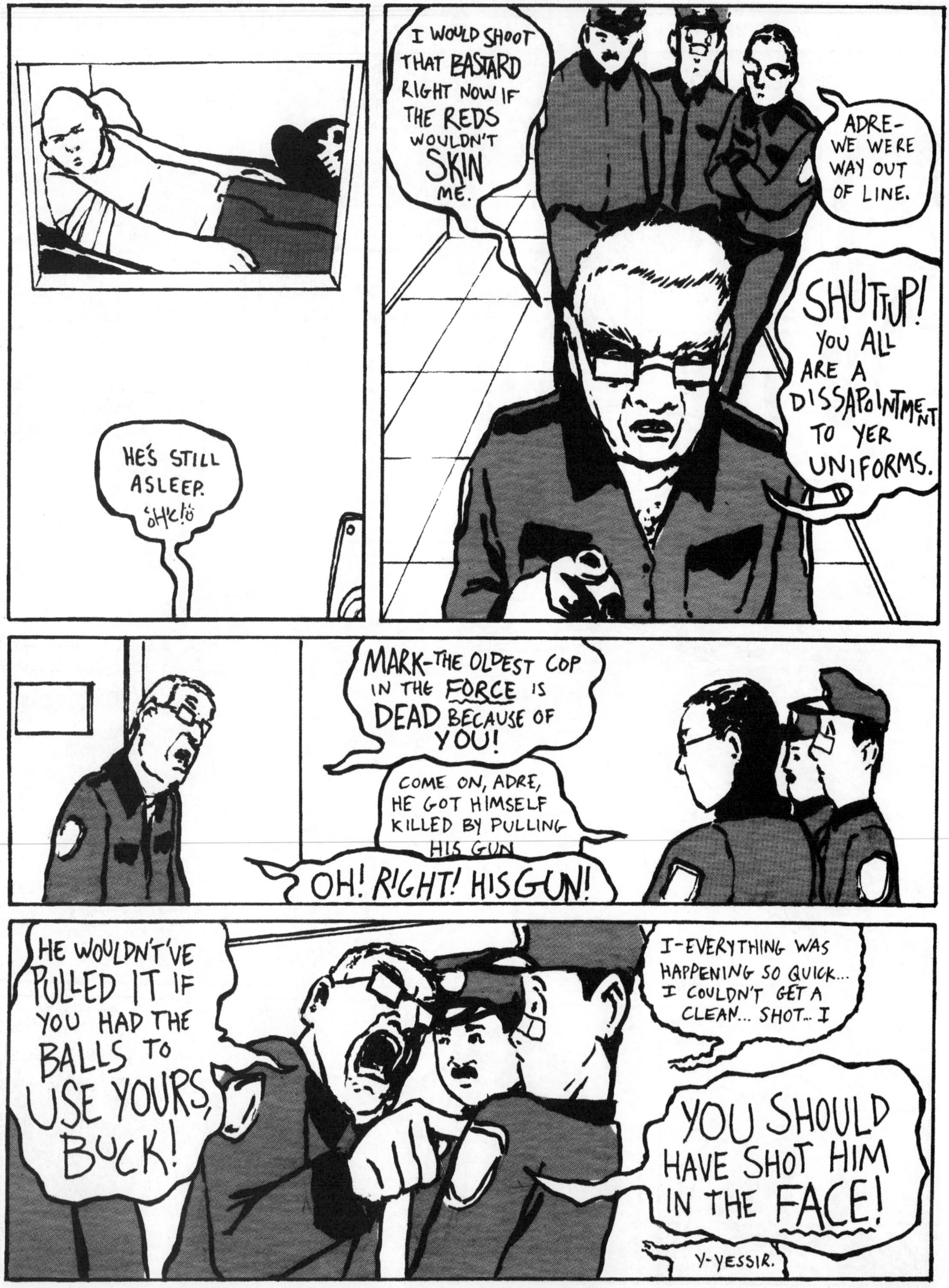
HE'S STILL ASLEEP.
I WOULD SHOOT THAT BASTARD RIGHT NOW IF THE REDS WOULDN'T SKIN ME.
ADRE- WE WERE WAY OUT OF LINE.
SHUTTUP! YOU ALL ARE A DISSAPOINTMENT TO YER UNIFORMS.
MARK-THE OLDEST COP IN THE FORCE IS DEAD BECAUSE OF YOU!
COME ON, ADRE, HE GOT HIMSELF KILLED BY PULLING HIS GUN
OH! RIGHT! HIS GUN!
HE WOULDN'T'VE PULLED IT IF YOU HAD THE BALLS TO USE YOURS, BUCK!
I-EVERYTHING WAS HAPPENING SO QUICK... I COULDN'T GET A CLEAN... SHOT... I
YOU SHOULD HAVE SHOT HIM IN THE FACE!
Y-YESSIR.

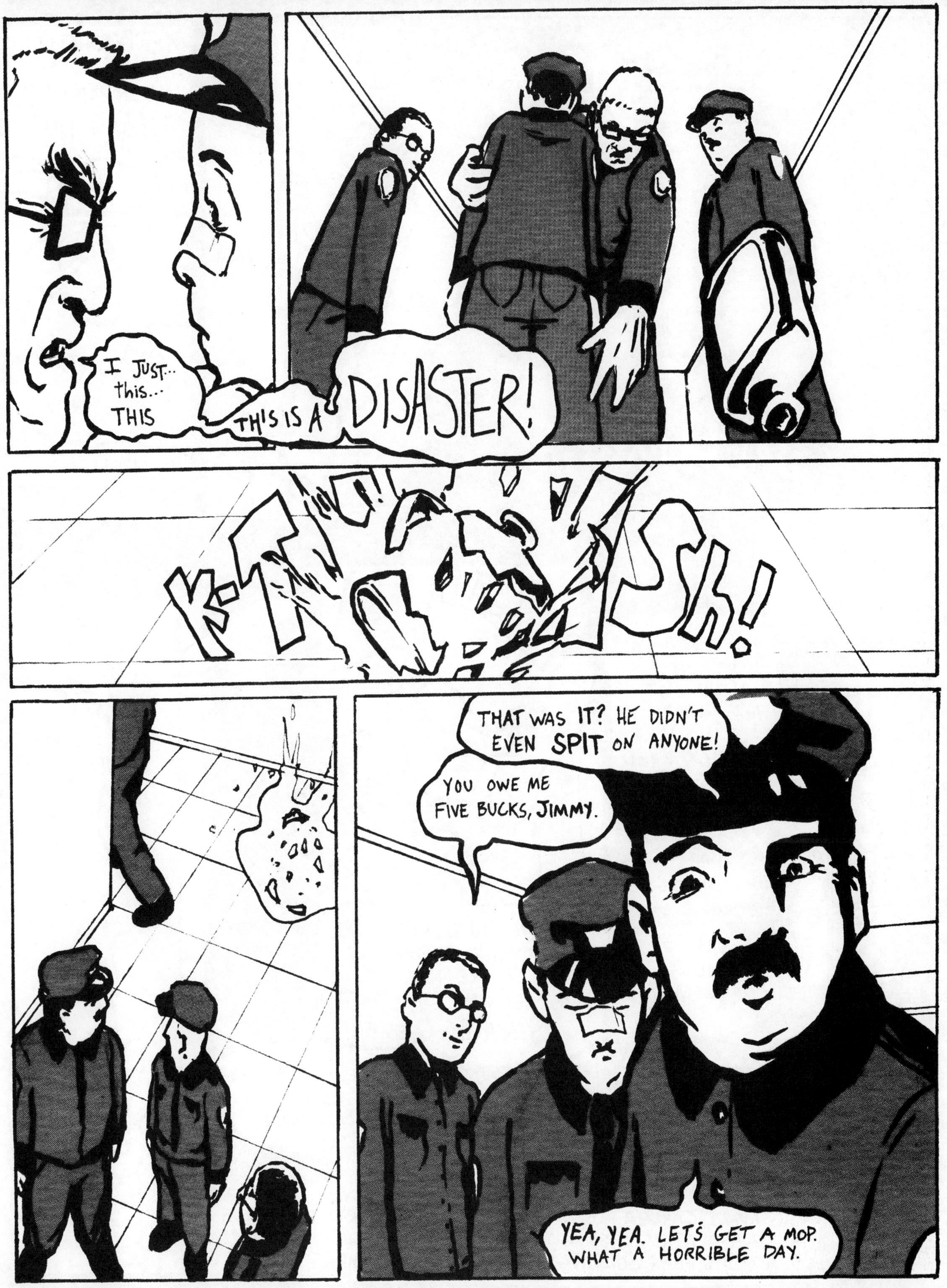
I JUST... this... THIS
THIS IS A DISASTER!
THAT WAS IT? HE DIDN'T EVEN SPIT ON ANYONE!
YOU OWE ME FIVE BUCKS, JIMMY.
YEA, YEA. LET'S GET A MOP. WHAT A HORRIBLE DAY.

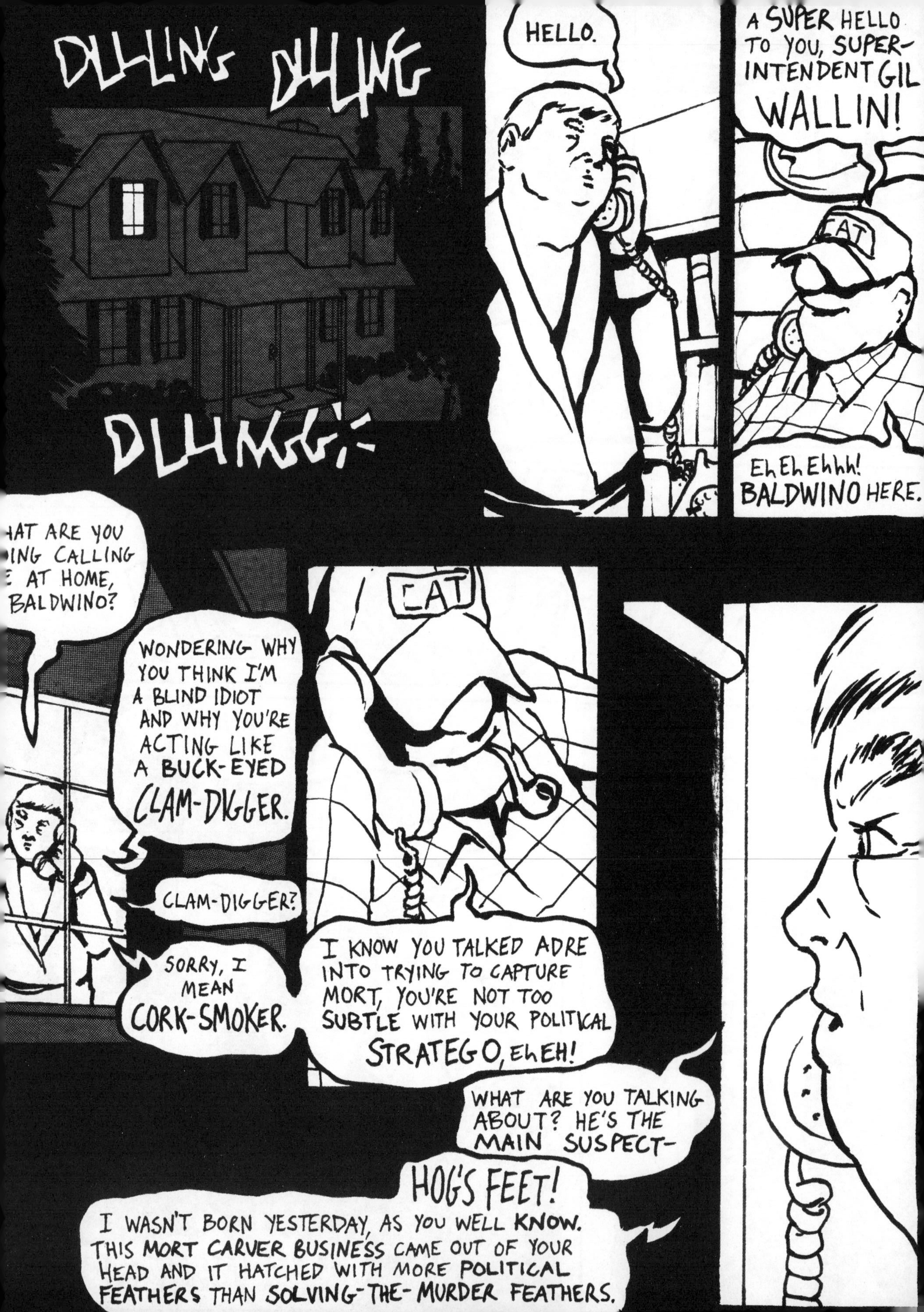
DLLLING DLLLING
DLLLNGG!
HELLO.
A SUPER HELLO TO YOU, SUPER-INTENDENT GIL WALLIN!
EH EH EHHH! BALDWINO HERE.
HAT ARE YOU
ING CALLING
AT HOME,
BALDWINO?
WONDERING WHY YOU THINK I'M A BLIND IDIOT AND WHY YOU'RE ACTING LIKE A BUCK-EYED CLAM-DIGGER.
CLAM-DIGGER?
SORRY, I MEAN CORK-SMOKER.
I KNOW YOU TALKED ADRE INTO TRYING TO CAPTURE MORT, YOU'RE NOT TOO SUBTLE WITH YOUR POLITICAL STRATEGO, EH EH!
WHAT ARE YOU TALKING ABOUT? HE'S THE MAIN SUSPECT-
HOG'S FEET!
I WASN'T BORN YESTERDAY, AS YOU WELL KNOW. THIS MORT CARVER BUSINESS CAME OUT OF YOUR HEAD AND IT HATCHED WITH MORE POLITICAL FEATHERS THAN SOLVING-THE-MURDER FEATHERS.

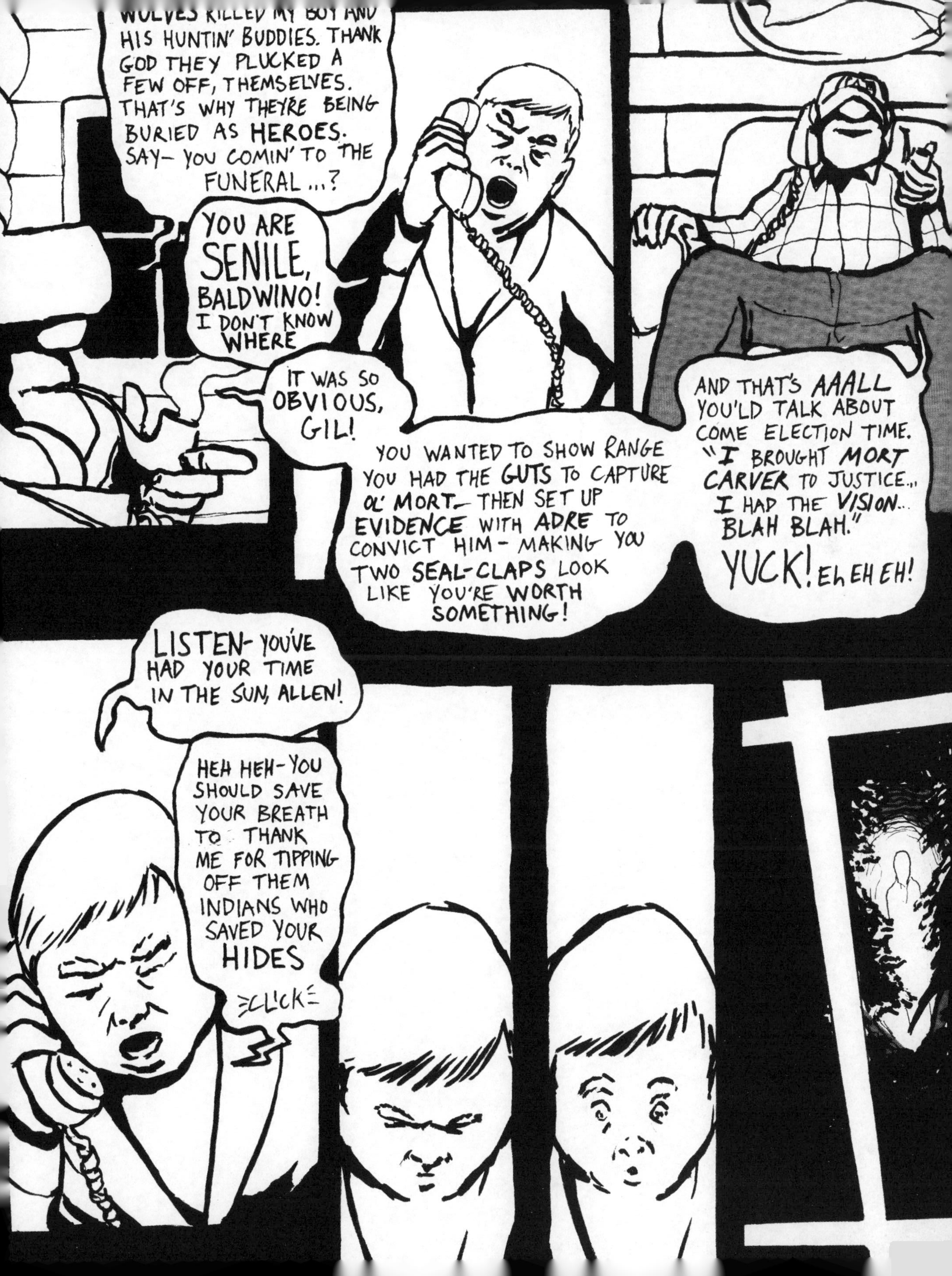
WOLVES KILLED MY BOY AND HIS HUNTIN' BUDDIES. THANK GOD THEY PLUCKED A FEW OFF, THEMSELVES. THAT'S WHY THEY'RE BEING BURIED AS HEROES. SAY— YOU COMIN' TO THE FUNERAL ...?
YOU ARE SENILE, BALDWINO! I DON'T KNOW WHERE
IT WAS SO OBVIOUS, GIL!
YOU WANTED TO SHOW RANGE YOU HAD THE GUTS TO CAPTURE OL' MORT— THEN SET UP EVIDENCE WITH ADRE TO CONVICT HIM - MAKING YOU TWO SEAL-CLAPS LOOK LIKE YOU'RE WORTH SOMETHING!
AND THAT'S AAALL YOU'LD TALK ABOUT COME ELECTION TIME. "I BROUGHT MORT CARVER TO JUSTICE... I HAD THE VISION... BLAH BLAH."
YUCK! EH EH EH!
LISTEN- YOU'VE HAD YOUR TIME IN THE SUN, ALLEN!
HEH HEH- YOU SHOULD SAVE YOUR BREATH TO THANK ME FOR TIPPING OFF THEM INDIANS WHO SAVED YOUR HIDES
CLICK

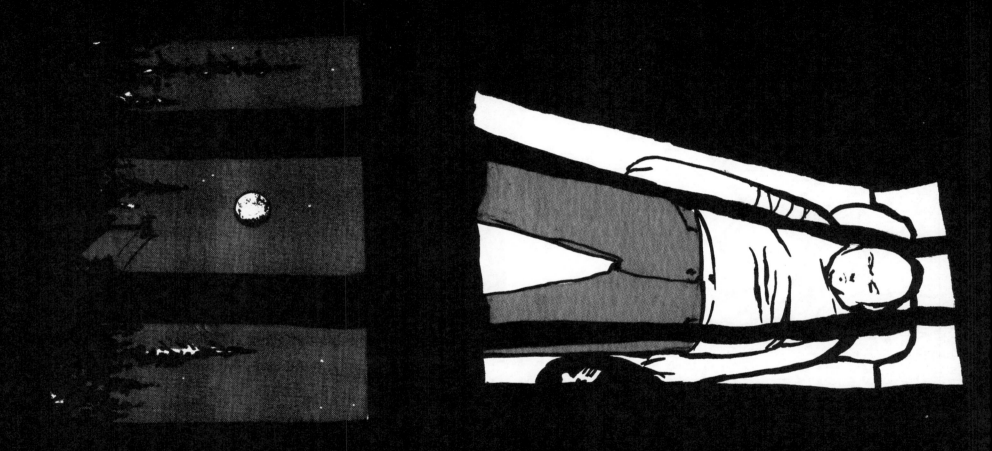

4.
ALL SOULS

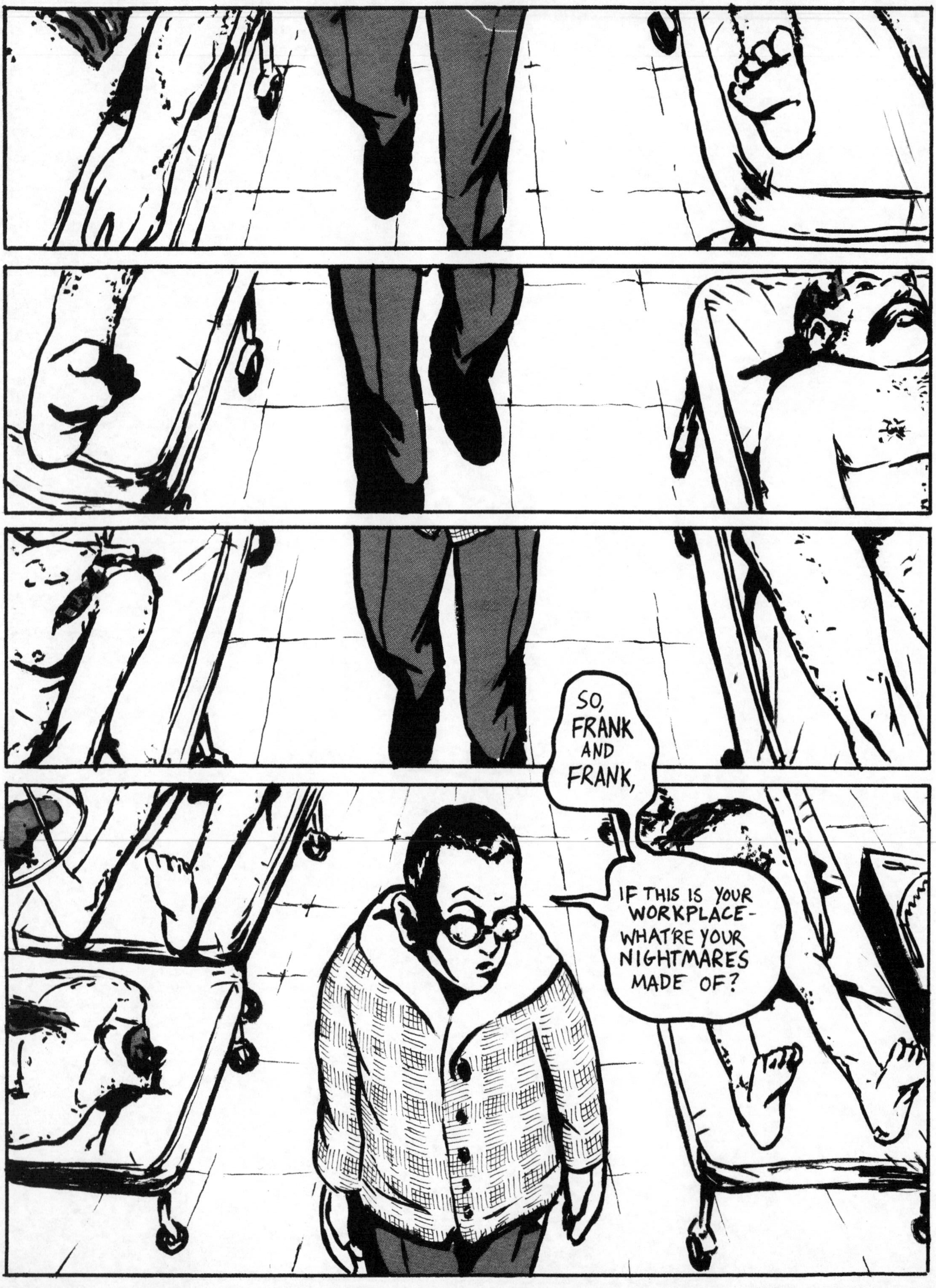
SO, FRANK AND FRANK,
IF THIS IS YOUR WORKPLACE- WHAT'RE YOUR NIGHTMARES MADE OF?

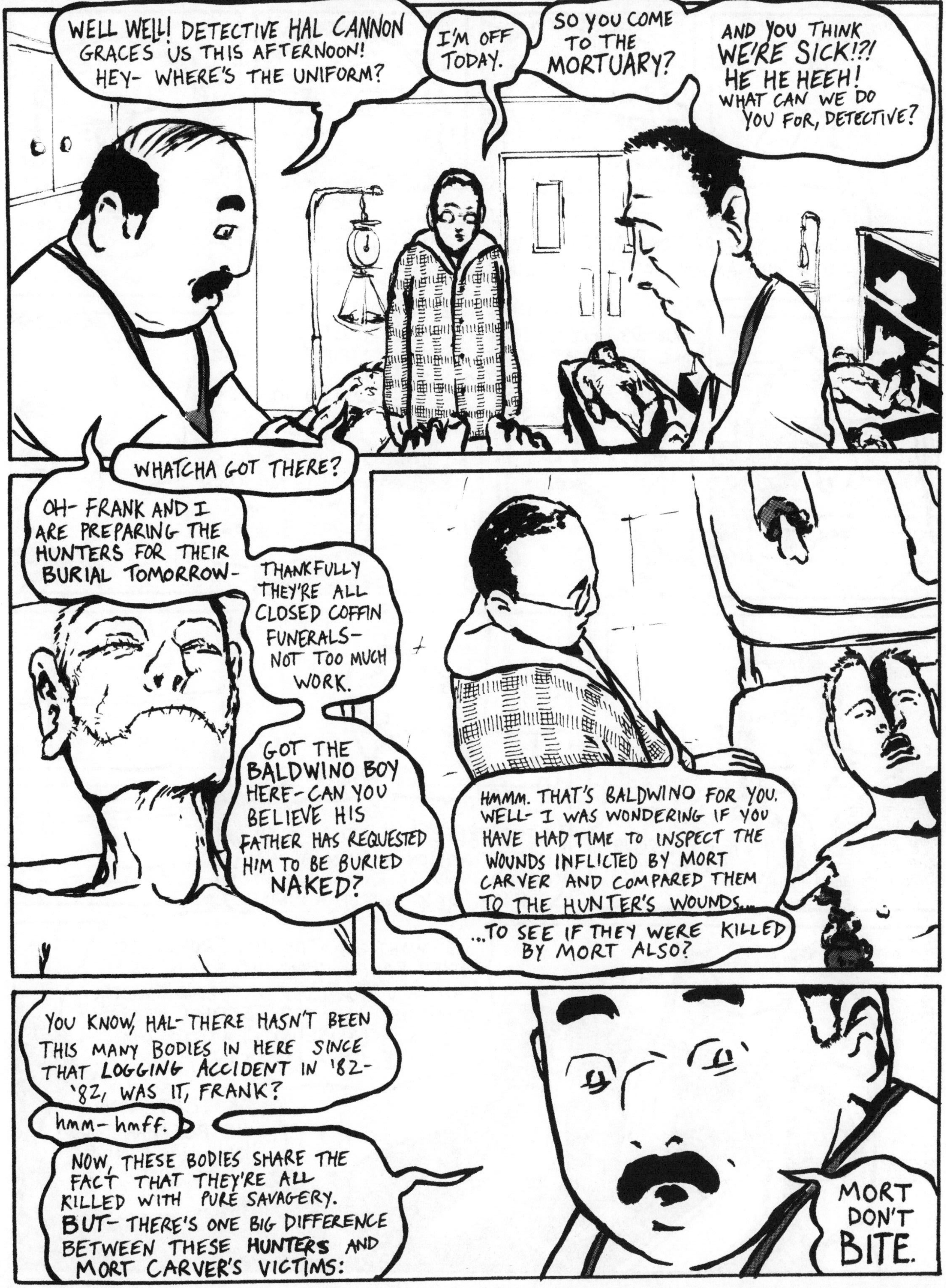
WELL WELL! DETECTIVE HAL CANNON GRACES US THIS AFTERNOON! HEY- WHERE'S THE UNIFORM?
I'M OFF TODAY.
SO YOU COME TO THE MORTUARY?
AND YOU THINK WE'RE SICK!?! HE HE HEEH! WHAT CAN WE DO YOU FOR, DETECTIVE?
WHATCHA GOT THERE?
OH- FRANK AND I ARE PREPARING THE HUNTERS FOR THEIR BURIAL TOMORROW-
THANKFULLY THEY'RE ALL CLOSED COFFIN FUNERALS- NOT TOO MUCH WORK.
GOT THE BALDWINO BOY HERE- CAN YOU BELIEVE HIS FATHER HAS REQUESTED HIM TO BE BURIED NAKED?
HMMM. THAT'S BALDWINO FOR YOU. WELL- I WAS WONDERING IF YOU HAVE HAD TIME TO INSPECT THE WOUNDS INFLICTED BY MORT CARVER AND COMPARED THEM TO THE HUNTER'S WOUNDS...
...TO SEE IF THEY WERE KILLED BY MORT ALSO?
YOU KNOW, HAL- THERE HASN'T BEEN THIS MANY BODIES IN HERE SINCE THAT LOGGING ACCIDENT IN '82- '82, WAS IT, FRANK?
hmm-hmff.
NOW, THESE BODIES SHARE THE FACT THAT THEY'RE ALL KILLED WITH PURE SAVAGERY. BUT- THERE'S ONE BIG DIFFERENCE BETWEEN THESE HUNTERS AND MORT CARVER'S VICTIMS:
MORT DON'T BITE.

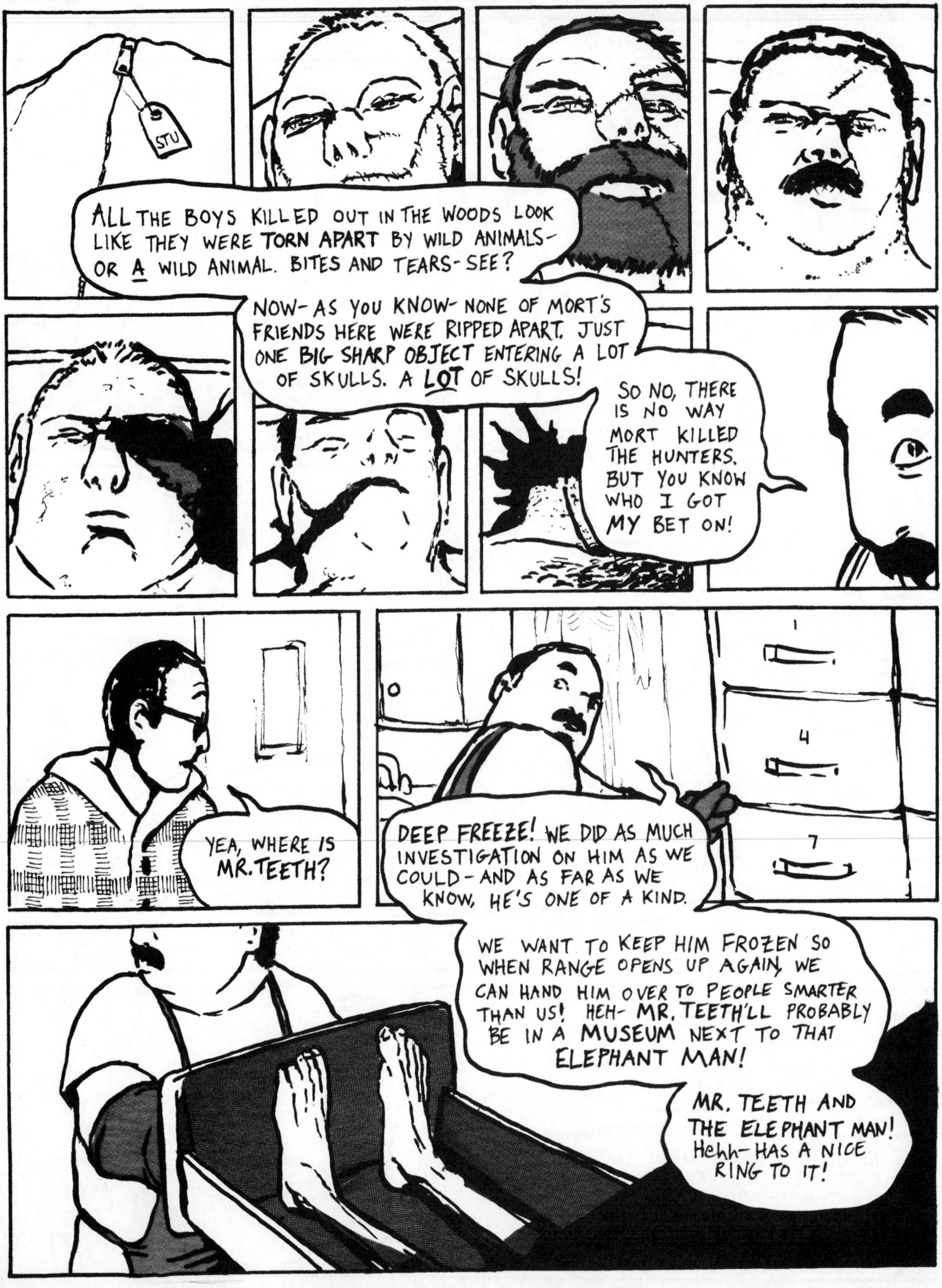
STU
ALL THE BOYS KILLED OUT IN THE WOODS LOOK LIKE THEY WERE TORN APART BY WILD ANIMALS- OR A WILD ANIMAL. BITES AND TEARS- SEE?
NOW- AS YOU KNOW- NONE OF MORT'S FRIENDS HERE WERE RIPPED APART. JUST ONE BIG SHARP OBJECT ENTERING A LOT OF SKULLS. A LOT OF SKULLS!
SO NO, THERE IS NO WAY MORT KILLED THE HUNTERS. BUT YOU KNOW WHO I GOT MY BET ON!
YEA, WHERE IS MR. TEETH?
1
4
7
DEEP FREEZE! WE DID AS MUCH INVESTIGATION ON HIM AS WE COULD- AND AS FAR AS WE KNOW, HE'S ONE OF A KIND.
WE WANT TO KEEP HIM FROZEN SO WHEN RANGE OPENS UP AGAIN, WE CAN HAND HIM OVER TO PEOPLE SMARTER THAN US! HEH- MR. TEETH'LL PROBABLY BE IN A MUSEUM NEXT TO THAT ELEPHANT MAN!
MR. TEETH AND THE ELEPHANT MAN! Hehh- HAS A NICE RING TO IT!

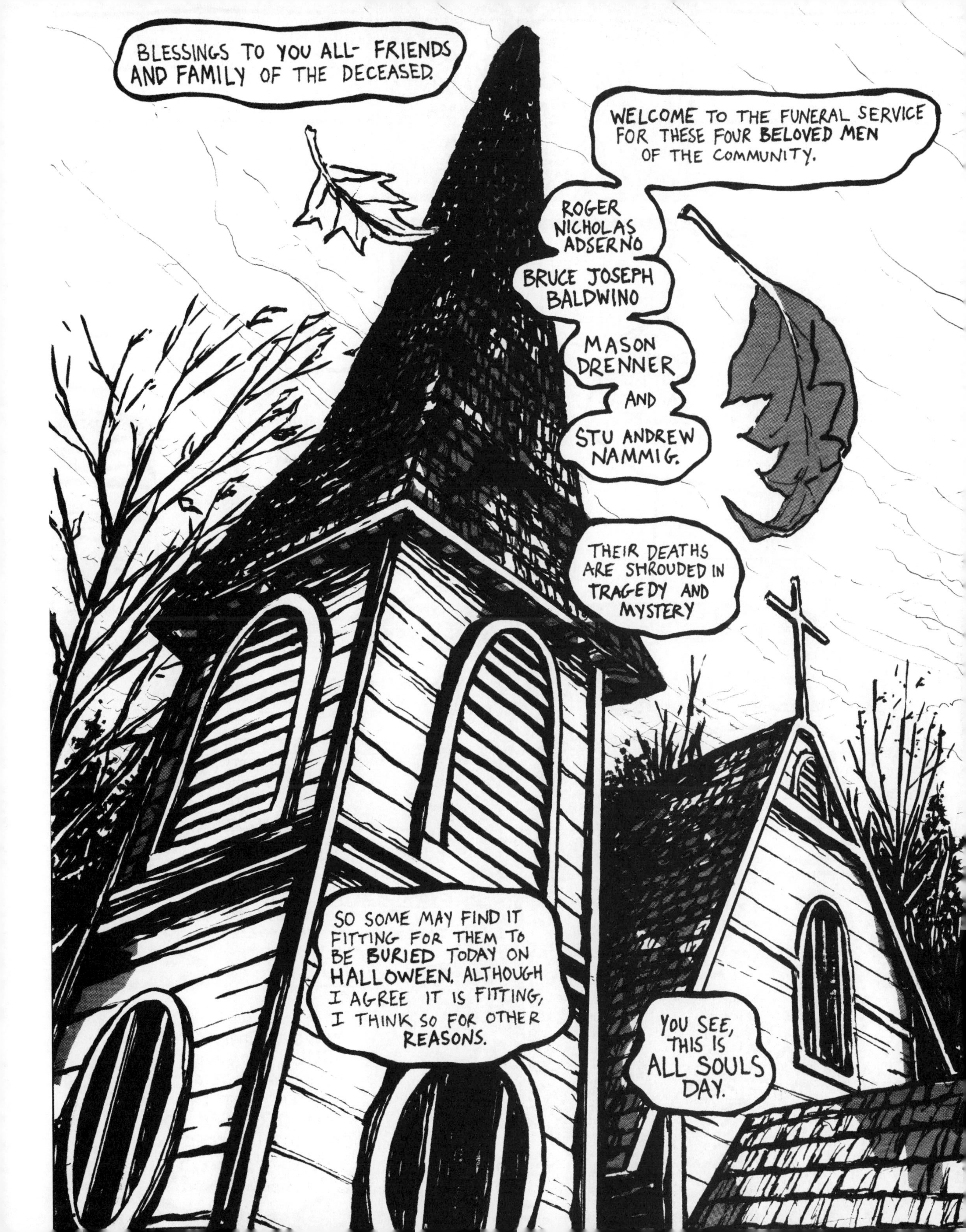
BLESSINGS TO YOU ALL- FRIENDS AND FAMILY OF THE DECEASED.
WELCOME TO THE FUNERAL SERVICE FOR THESE FOUR BELOVED MEN OF THE COMMUNITY.
ROGER NICHOLAS ADSERNO
BRUCE JOSEPH BALDWINO
MASON DRENNER
AND
STU ANDREW NAMMIG.
THEIR DEATHS ARE SHROUDED IN TRAGEDY AND MYSTERY
SO SOME MAY FIND IT FITTING FOR THEM TO BE BURIED TODAY ON HALLOWEEN. ALTHOUGH I AGREE IT IS FITTING, I THINK SO FOR OTHER REASONS.
YOU SEE, THIS IS ALL SOULS DAY.

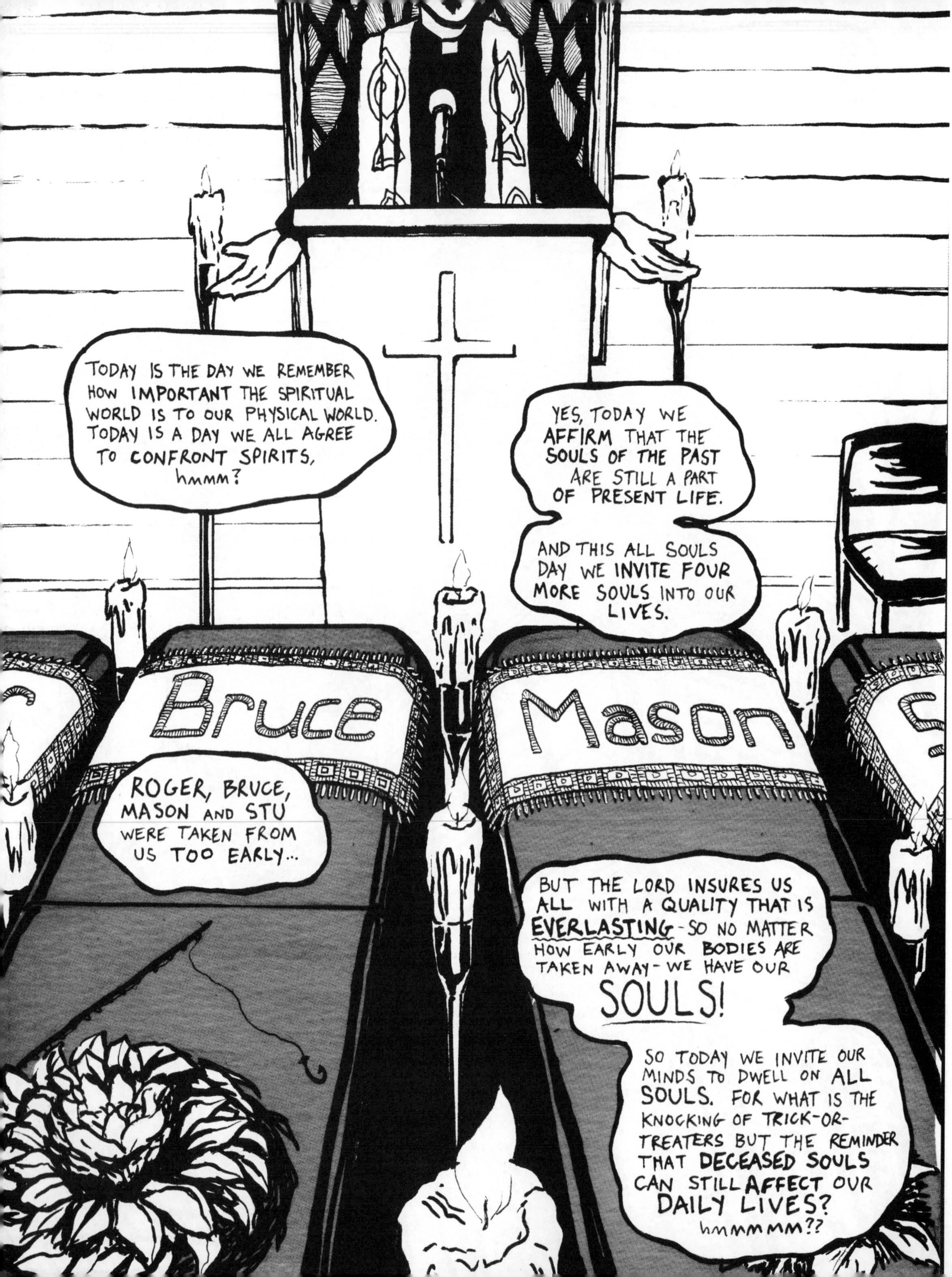
TODAY IS THE DAY WE REMEMBER HOW IMPORTANT THE SPIRITUAL WORLD IS TO OUR PHYSICAL WORLD. TODAY IS A DAY WE ALL AGREE TO CONFRONT SPIRITS, hmmm?
YES, TODAY WE AFFIRM THAT THE SOULS OF THE PAST ARE STILL A PART OF PRESENT LIFE.
AND THIS ALL SOULS DAY WE INVITE FOUR MORE SOULS INTO OUR LIVES.
Bruce
Mason
ROGER, BRUCE, MASON AND STU WERE TAKEN FROM US TOO EARLY...
BUT THE LORD INSURES US ALL WITH A QUALITY THAT IS EVERLASTING - SO NO MATTER HOW EARLY OUR BODIES ARE TAKEN AWAY - WE HAVE OUR SOULS!
SO TODAY WE INVITE OUR MINDS TO DWELL ON ALL SOULS. FOR WHAT IS THE KNOCKING OF TRICK-OR-TREATERS BUT THE REMINDER THAT DECEASED SOULS CAN STILL AFFECT OUR DAILY LIVES? hmmmmm??

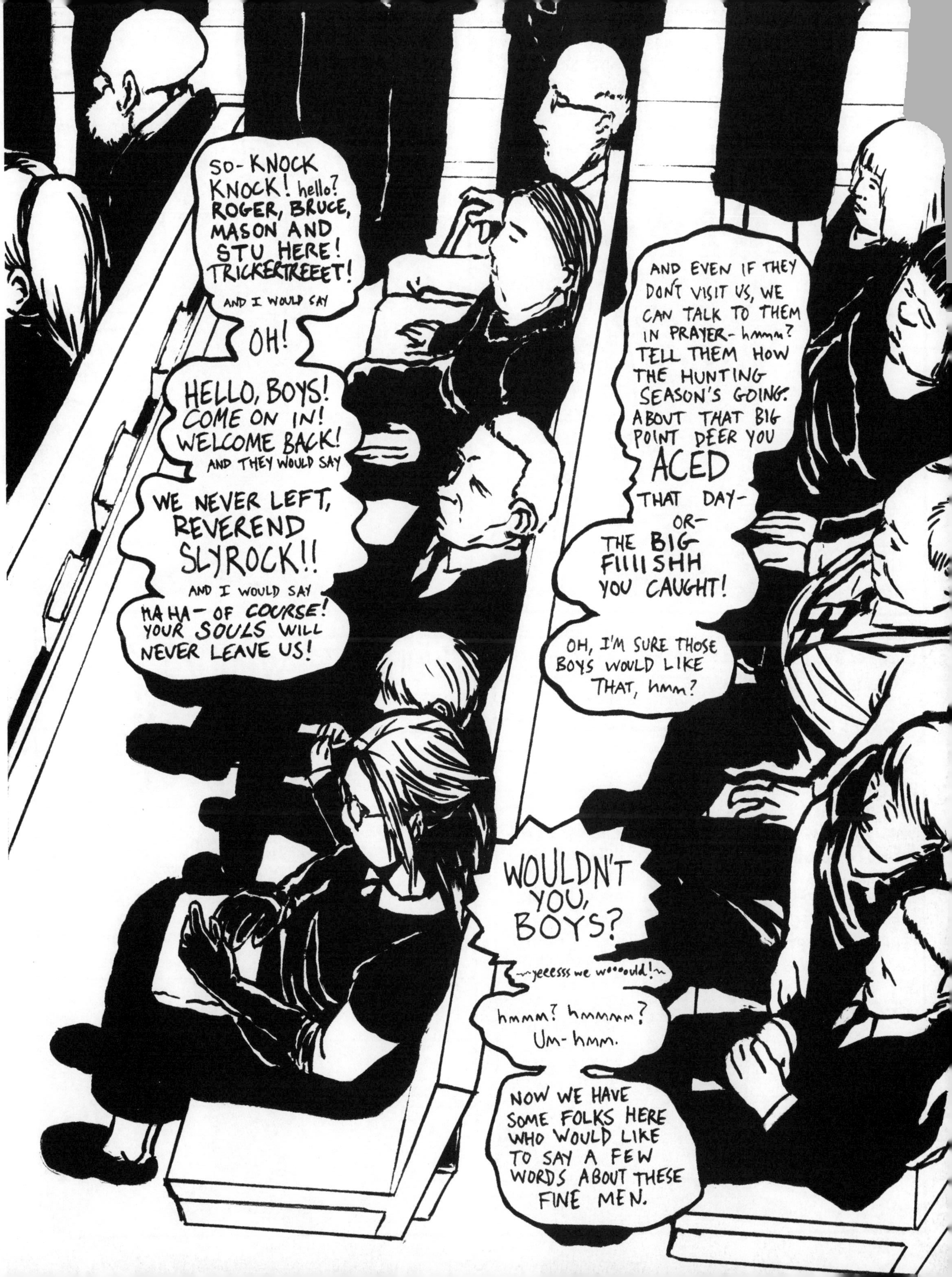
SO- KNOCK KNOCK! hello? ROGER, BRUCE, MASON AND STU HERE! TRICKERTREEET!
AND I WOULD SAY
OH!
HELLO, BOYS! COME ON IN! WELCOME BACK!
AND THEY WOULD SAY
WE NEVER LEFT, REVEREND SLYROCK!!
AND I WOULD SAY
HA HA- OF COURSE! YOUR SOULS WILL NEVER LEAVE US!
AND EVEN IF THEY DON'T VISIT US, WE CAN TALK TO THEM IN PRAYER- hmmm? TELL THEM HOW THE HUNTING SEASON'S GOING. ABOUT THAT BIG POINT DEER YOU ACED THAT DAY-
OR-
THE BIG FIIIISHH YOU CAUGHT!
OH, I'M SURE THOSE BOYS WOULD LIKE THAT, hmm?
WOULDN'T YOU, BOYS?
~yeeesss we woooould!~
hmmm? hmmmm? Um-hmm.
NOW WE HAVE SOME FOLKS HERE WHO WOULD LIKE TO SAY A FEW WORDS ABOUT THESE FINE MEN.

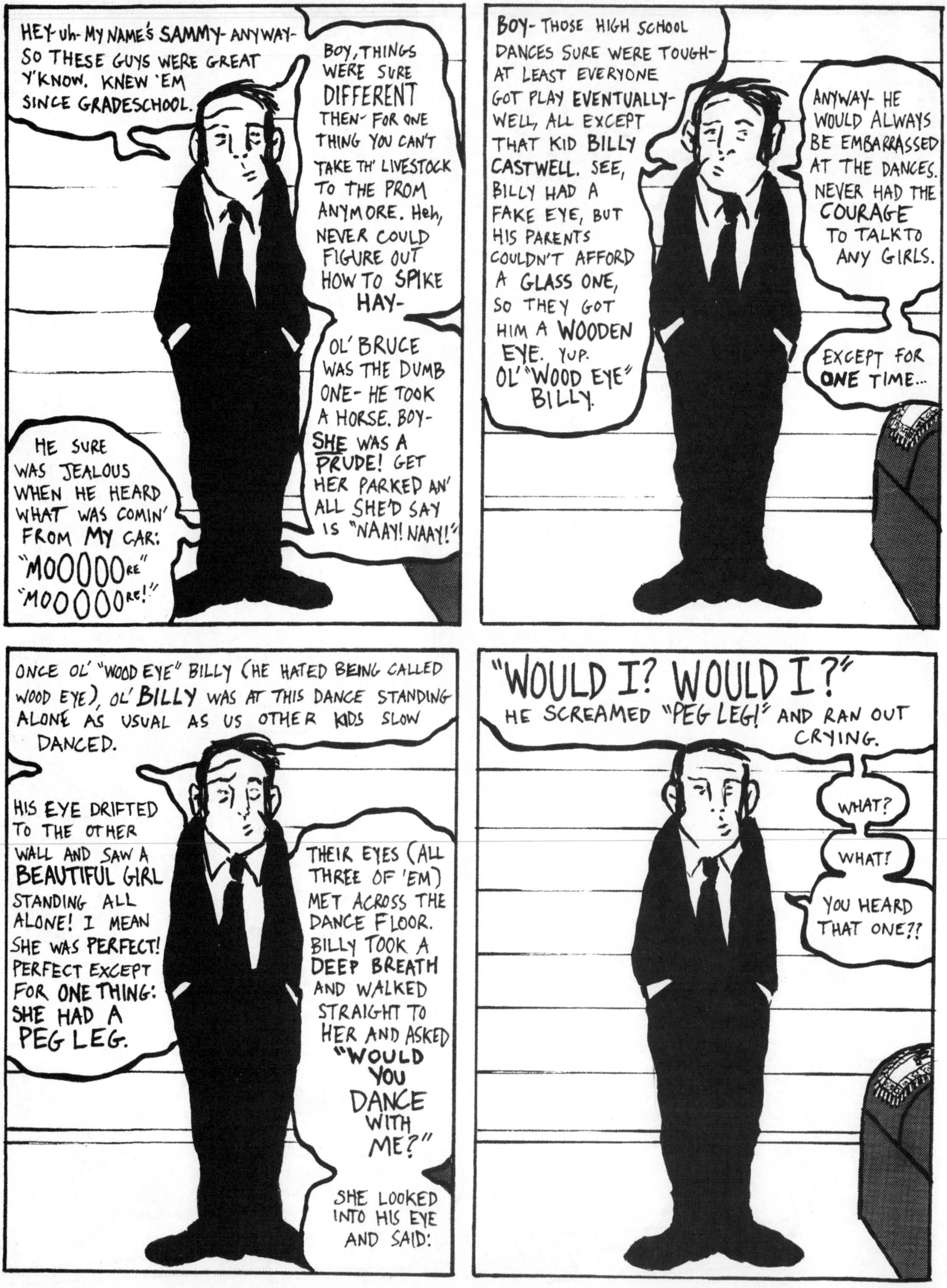
HEY-uh-MY NAME'S SAMMY-ANYWAY-SO THESE GUYS WERE GREAT Y'KNOW. KNEW 'EM SINCE GRADESCHOOL.
BOY, THINGS WERE SURE DIFFERENT THEN- FOR ONE THING YOU CAN'T TAKE TH' LIVESTOCK TO THE PROM ANYMORE. Heh, NEVER COULD FIGURE OUT HOW TO SPIKE HAY-
OL' BRUCE WAS THE DUMB ONE- HE TOOK A HORSE. BOY- SHE WAS A PRUDE! GET HER PARKED AN' ALL SHE'D SAY IS "NAAY! NAAY!"
HE SURE WAS JEALOUS WHEN HE HEARD WHAT WAS COMIN' FROM MY CAR: "MOOOOOre" "MOOOOOre!"
BOY- THOSE HIGH SCHOOL DANCES SURE WERE TOUGH- AT LEAST EVERYONE GOT PLAY EVENTUALLY- WELL, ALL EXCEPT THAT KID BILLY CASTWELL. SEE, BILLY HAD A FAKE EYE, BUT HIS PARENTS COULDN'T AFFORD A GLASS ONE, SO THEY GOT HIM A WOODEN EYE. YUP. OL' "WOOD EYE" BILLY.
ANYWAY- HE WOULD ALWAYS BE EMBARRASSED AT THE DANCES. NEVER HAD THE COURAGE TO TALK TO ANY GIRLS.
EXCEPT FOR ONE TIME...
ONCE OL' "WOOD EYE" BILLY (HE HATED BEING CALLED WOOD EYE), OL' BILLY WAS AT THIS DANCE STANDING ALONE AS USUAL AS US OTHER KIDS SLOW DANCED.
HIS EYE DRIFTED TO THE OTHER WALL AND SAW A BEAUTIFUL GIRL STANDING ALL ALONE! I MEAN SHE WAS PERFECT! PERFECT EXCEPT FOR ONE THING: SHE HAD A PEG LEG.
THEIR EYES (ALL THREE OF 'EM) MET ACROSS THE DANCE FLOOR. BILLY TOOK A DEEP BREATH AND WALKED STRAIGHT TO HER AND ASKED "WOULD YOU DANCE WITH ME?"
SHE LOOKED INTO HIS EYE AND SAID:
"WOULD I? WOULD I?" HE SCREAMED "PEG LEG!" AND RAN OUT CRYING.
WHAT?
WHAT?
YOU HEARD THAT ONE??

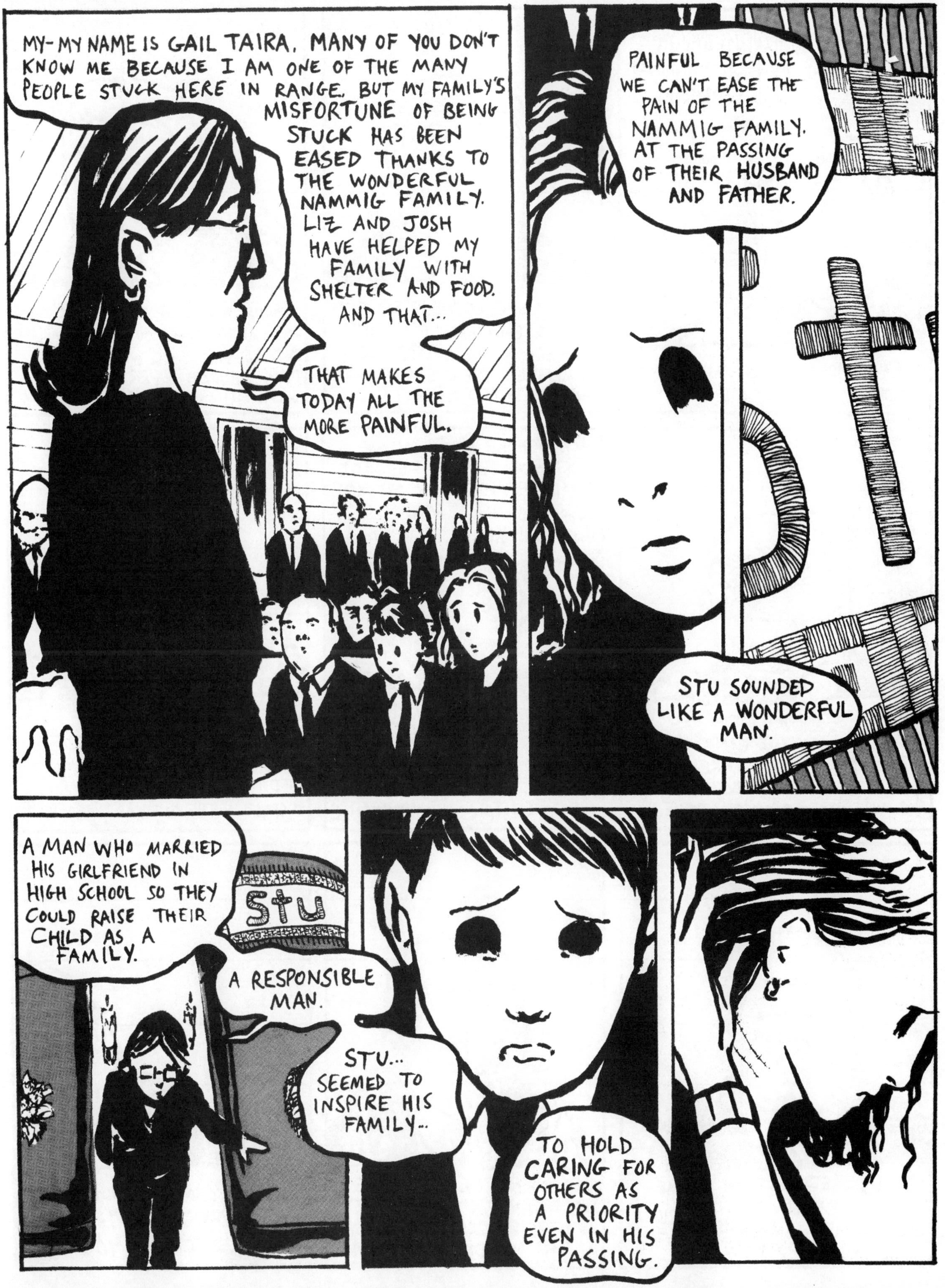
MY-MY NAME IS GAIL TAIRA. MANY OF YOU DON'T KNOW ME BECAUSE I AM ONE OF THE MANY PEOPLE STUCK HERE IN RANGE. BUT MY FAMILY'S MISFORTUNE OF BEING STUCK HAS BEEN EASED THANKS TO THE WONDERFUL NAMMIG FAMILY. LIZ AND JOSH HAVE HELPED MY FAMILY WITH SHELTER AND FOOD. AND THAT...
THAT MAKES TODAY ALL THE MORE PAINFUL.
PAINFUL BECAUSE WE CAN'T EASE THE PAIN OF THE NAMMIG FAMILY. AT THE PASSING OF THEIR HUSBAND AND FATHER.
STU SOUNDED LIKE A WONDERFUL MAN.
A MAN WHO MARRIED HIS GIRLFRIEND IN HIGH SCHOOL SO THEY COULD RAISE THEIR CHILD AS A FAMILY.
STU
A RESPONSIBLE MAN.
STU... SEEMED TO INSPIRE HIS FAMILY...
TO HOLD CARING FOR OTHERS AS A PRIORITY EVEN IN HIS PASSING.

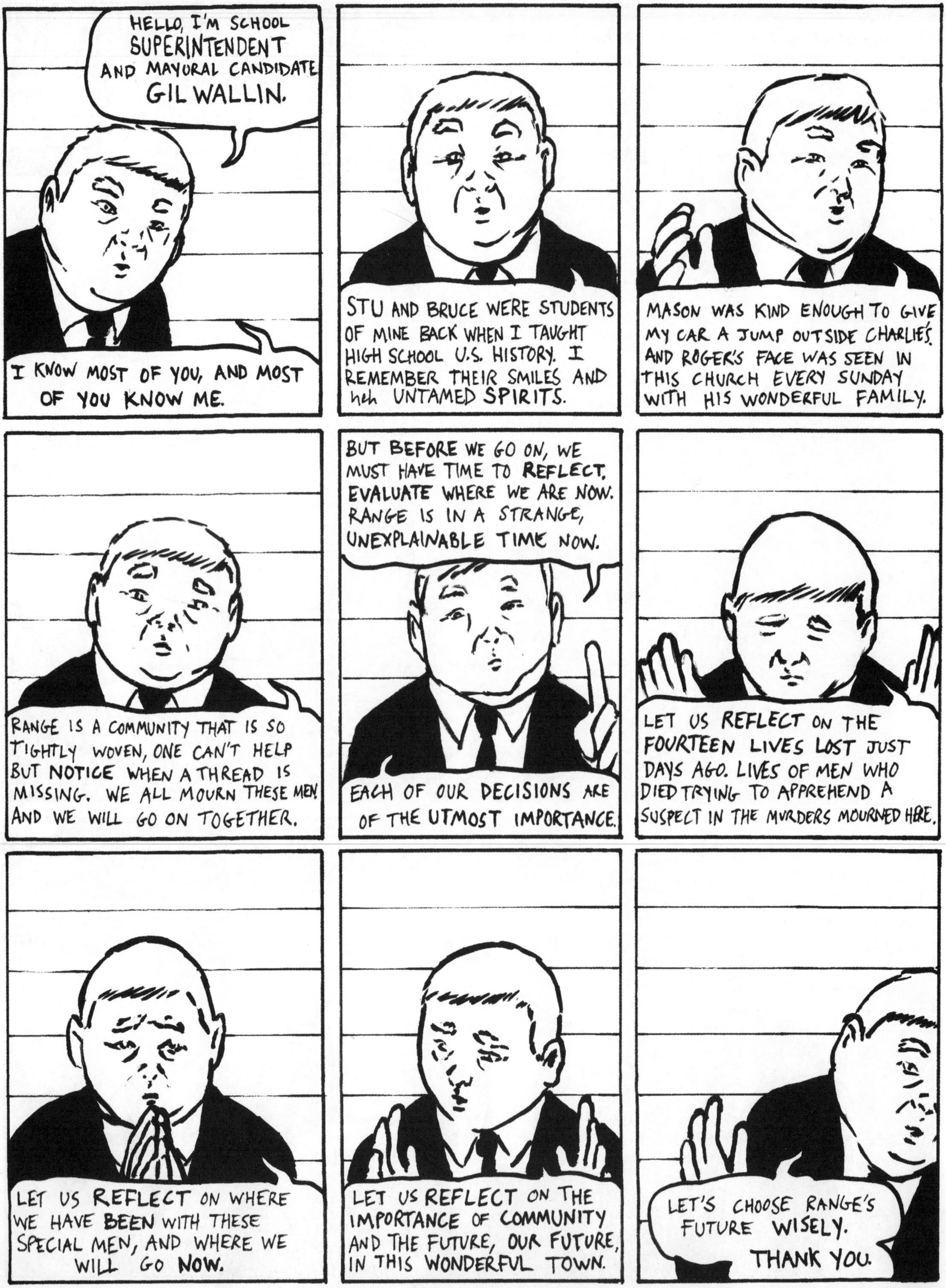
HELLO, I'M SCHOOL SUPERINTENDENT AND MAYORAL CANDIDATE GIL WALLIN.
I KNOW MOST OF YOU, AND MOST OF YOU KNOW ME.
STU AND BRUCE WERE STUDENTS OF MINE BACK WHEN I TAUGHT HIGH SCHOOL U.S. HISTORY. I REMEMBER THEIR SMILES AND UNTAMED SPIRITS.
MASON WAS KIND ENOUGH TO GIVE MY CAR A JUMP OUTSIDE CHARLIE'S. AND ROGER'S FACE WAS SEEN IN THIS CHURCH EVERY SUNDAY WITH HIS WONDERFUL FAMILY.
RANGE IS A COMMUNITY THAT IS SO TIGHTLY WOVEN, ONE CAN'T HELP BUT NOTICE WHEN A THREAD IS MISSING. WE ALL MOURN THESE MEN. AND WE WILL GO ON TOGETHER.
BUT BEFORE WE GO ON, WE MUST HAVE TIME TO REFLECT, EVALUATE WHERE WE ARE NOW. RANGE IS IN A STRANGE, UNEXPLAINABLE TIME NOW.
EACH OF OUR DECISIONS ARE OF THE UTMOST IMPORTANCE.
LET US REFLECT ON THE FOURTEEN LIVES LOST JUST DAYS AGO. LIVES OF MEN WHO DIED TRYING TO APPREHEND A SUSPECT IN THE MURDERS MOURNED HERE.
LET US REFLECT ON WHERE WE HAVE BEEN WITH THESE SPECIAL MEN, AND WHERE WE WILL GO NOW.
LET US REFLECT ON THE IMPORTANCE OF COMMUNITY AND THE FUTURE, OUR FUTURE, IN THIS WONDERFUL TOWN.
LET'S CHOOSE RANGE'S FUTURE WISELY.
THANK YOU.

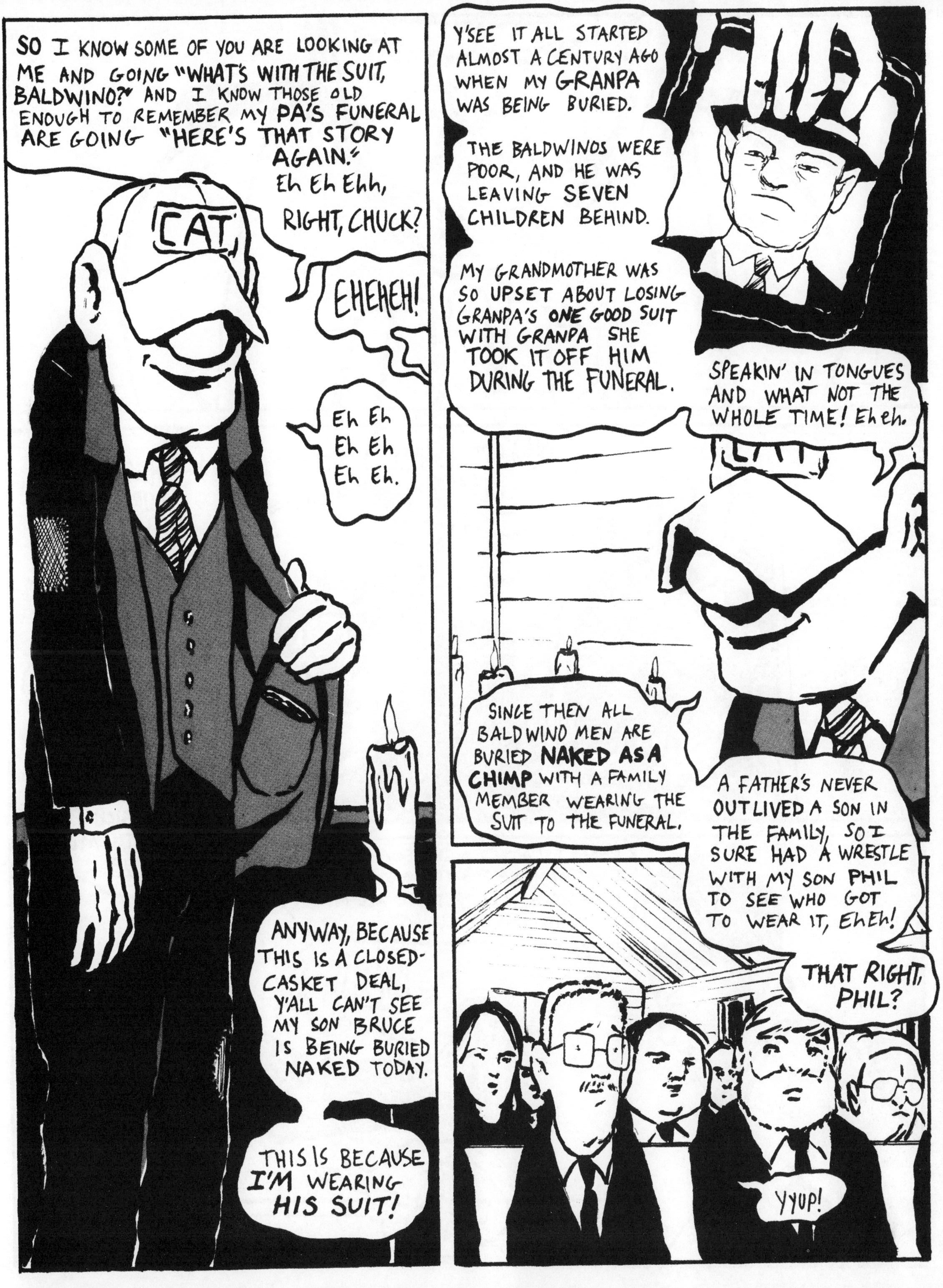
SO I KNOW SOME OF YOU ARE LOOKING AT ME AND GOING "WHAT'S WITH THE SUIT, BALDWINO?" AND I KNOW THOSE OLD ENOUGH TO REMEMBER MY PA'S FUNERAL ARE GOING "HERE'S THAT STORY AGAIN." Eh Eh Ehh, RIGHT, CHUCK?
CAT
EHEHEH!
Eh Eh Eh Eh Eh Eh.
ANYWAY, BECAUSE THIS IS A CLOSED-CASKET DEAL, Y'ALL CAN'T SEE MY SON BRUCE IS BEING BURIED NAKED TODAY.
THIS IS BECAUSE I'M WEARING HIS SUIT!
Y'SEE IT ALL STARTED ALMOST A CENTURY AGO WHEN MY GRANPA WAS BEING BURIED.
THE BALDWINOS WERE POOR, AND HE WAS LEAVING SEVEN CHILDREN BEHIND.
MY GRANDMOTHER WAS SO UPSET ABOUT LOSING GRANPA'S ONE GOOD SUIT WITH GRANPA SHE TOOK IT OFF HIM DURING THE FUNERAL.
SPEAKIN' IN TONGUES AND WHAT NOT THE WHOLE TIME! Eheh.
SINCE THEN ALL BALDWINO MEN ARE BURIED NAKED AS A CHIMP WITH A FAMILY MEMBER WEARING THE SUIT TO THE FUNERAL.
A FATHER'S NEVER OUTLIVED A SON IN THE FAMILY, SO I SURE HAD A WRESTLE WITH MY SON PHIL TO SEE WHO GOT TO WEAR IT, EhEh!
THAT RIGHT, PHIL?
YYUP!

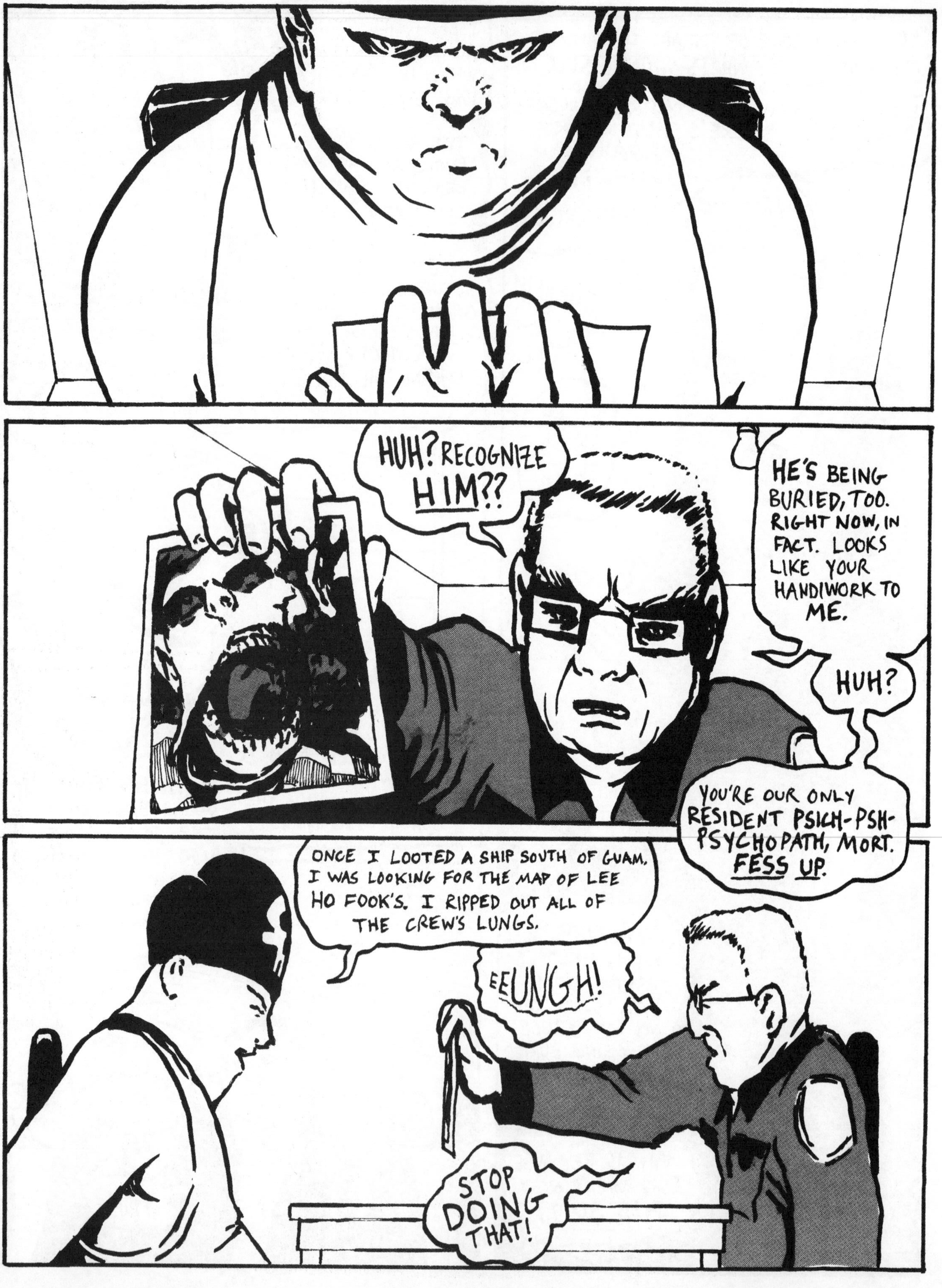
HUH? RECOGNIZE HIM??
HE'S BEING BURIED, TOO. RIGHT NOW, IN FACT. LOOKS LIKE YOUR HANDIWORK TO ME.
HUH?
YOU'RE OUR ONLY RESIDENT PSICH-PSH-PSYCHOPATH, MORT. FESS UP.
ONCE I LOOTED A SHIP SOUTH OF GUAM. I WAS LOOKING FOR THE MAP OF LEE HO FOOK'S. I RIPPED OUT ALL OF THE CREW'S LUNGS.
EEUNGH!
STOP DOING THAT!

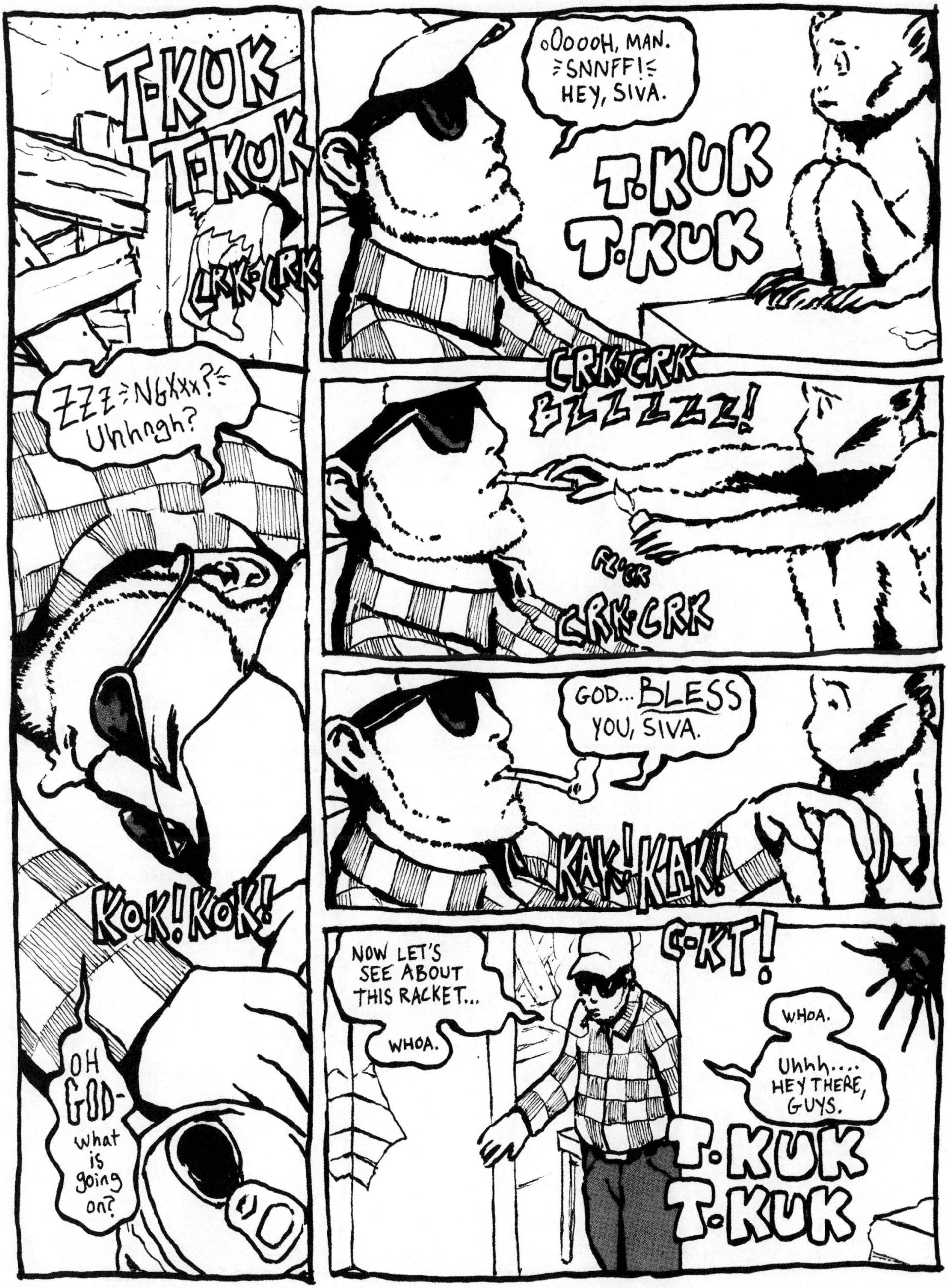
T-KUK
T-KUK
CRK-CRK
ZZZ NGXXX?
Uhhngh?
KOK! KOK!
OH GOD-
what is going on?
oOOOOH, MAN.
SNNFF!
HEY, SIVA.
T.KUK
T.KUK
CRK-CRK
BZZZZZZ!
FLICK
CRK-CRK
GOD... BLESS YOU, SIVA.
KAK! KAK!
C-KT!
NOW LET'S SEE ABOUT THIS RACKET...
WHOA.
WHOA.
Uhhh.... HEY THERE, GUYS.
T.KUK
T.KUK

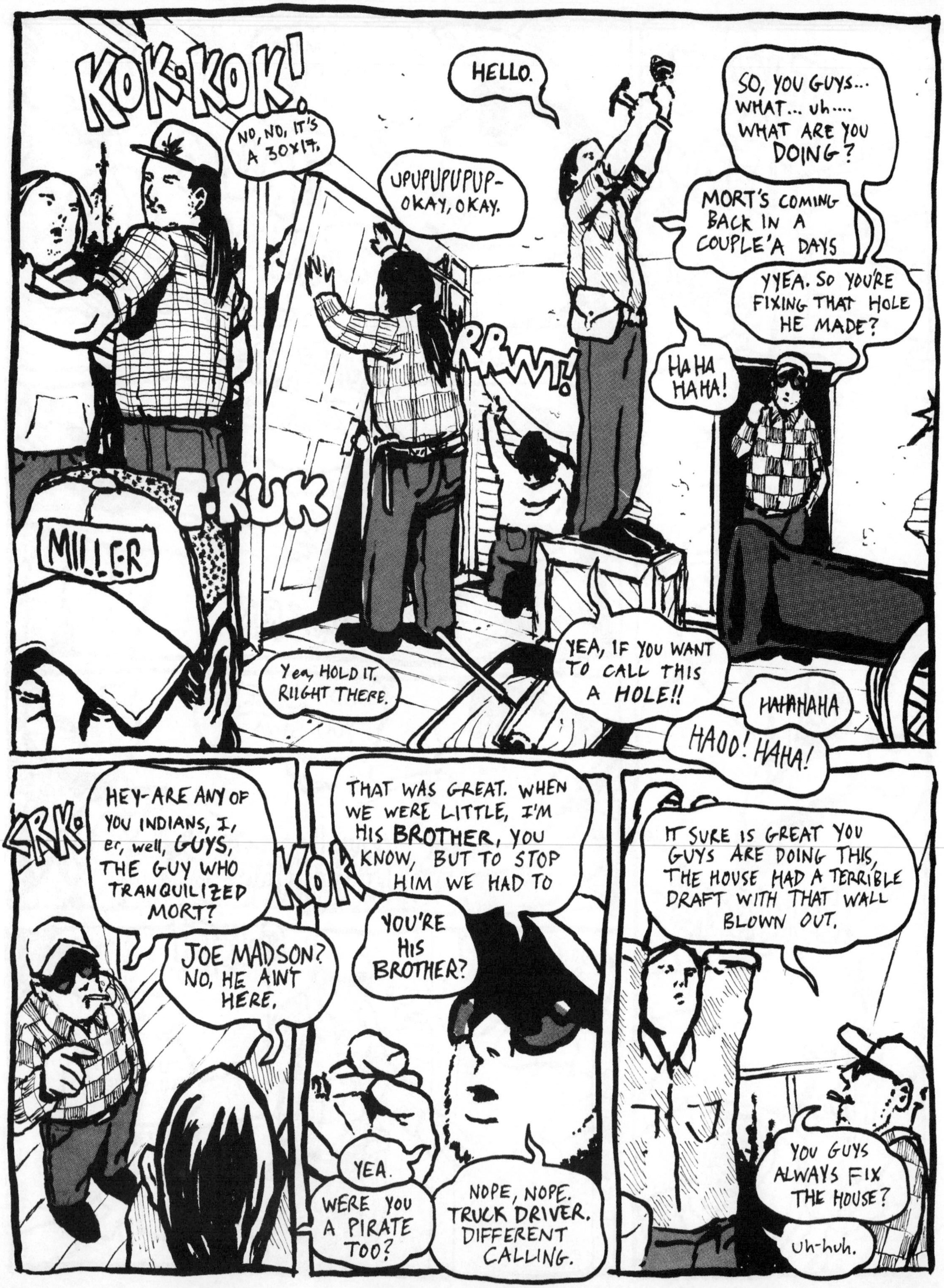
KOK-KOK!
NO, NO, IT'S A 30X17.
HELLO.
UPUPUPUPUP- OKAY, OKAY.
SO, YOU GUYS... WHAT... uh.... WHAT ARE YOU DOING?
MORT'S COMING BACK IN A COUPLE'A DAYS
YYEA. SO YOU'RE FIXING THAT HOLE HE MADE?
RRANT!
HAHA HAHA!
T-KUK
MILLER
Yea, HOLD IT. RIIGHT THERE.
YEA, IF YOU WANT TO CALL THIS A HOLE!!
HAHAHAHA
HAOO! HAHA!
CRK.
HEY-ARE ANY OF YOU INDIANS, I, er, well, GUYS, THE GUY WHO TRANQUILIZED MORT?
JOE MADSON? NO, HE AIN'T HERE.
KOK
THAT WAS GREAT. WHEN WE WERE LITTLE, I'M HIS BROTHER, YOU KNOW, BUT TO STOP HIM WE HAD TO
YOU'RE HIS BROTHER?
YEA.
WERE YOU A PIRATE TOO?
NOPE, NOPE. TRUCK DRIVER. DIFFERENT CALLING.
IT SURE IS GREAT YOU GUYS ARE DOING THIS, THE HOUSE HAD A TERRIBLE DRAFT WITH THAT WALL BLOWN OUT.
YOU GUYS ALWAYS FIX THE HOUSE?
Uh-huh.

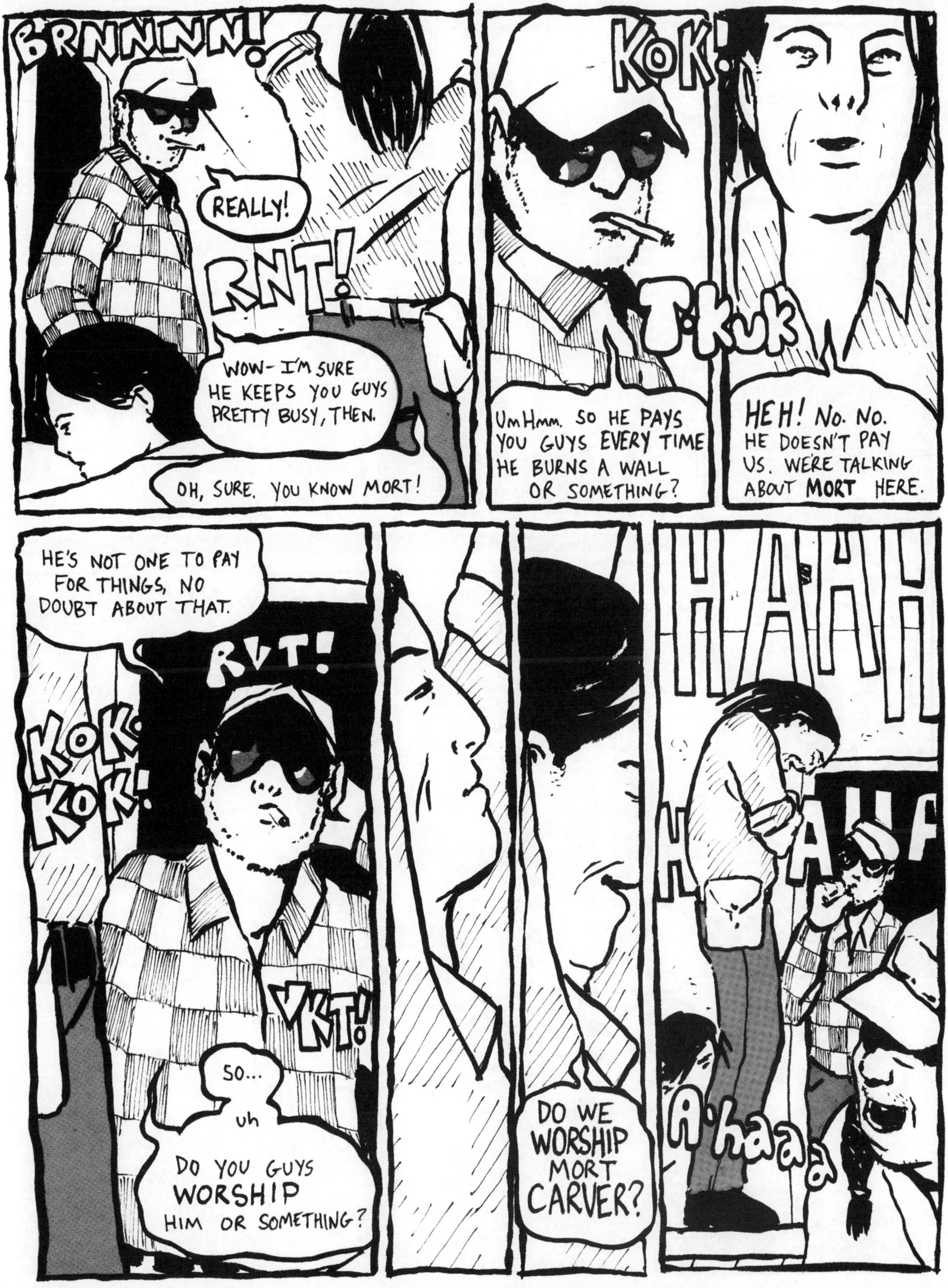
BRNNNN!
REALLY!
RNT!
WOW- I'M SURE HE KEEPS YOU GUYS PRETTY BUSY, THEN.
OH, SURE. YOU KNOW MORT!
KOK!
T-KUK
UMHMM. SO HE PAYS YOU GUYS EVERY TIME HE BURNS A WALL OR SOMETHING?
HEH! NO. NO. HE DOESN'T PAY US. WE'RE TALKING ABOUT MORT HERE.
HE'S NOT ONE TO PAY FOR THINGS, NO DOUBT ABOUT THAT.
RVT!
KOK KOK!
VKT!
SO...
UH
DO YOU GUYS WORSHIP HIM OR SOMETHING?
DO WE WORSHIP MORT CARVER?
HAHAH
HAHA
A-HAAAA

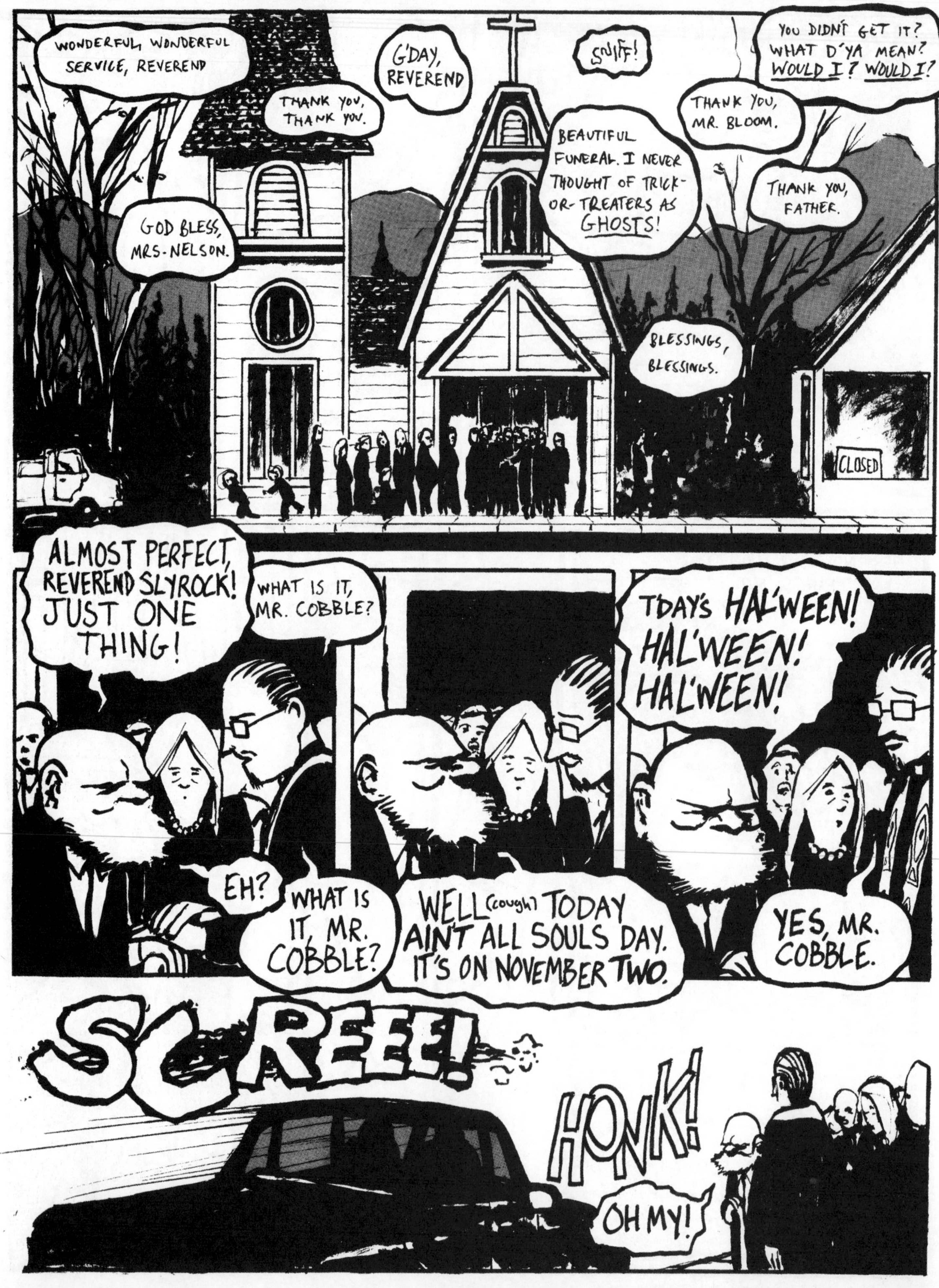
WONDERFUL, WONDERFUL SERVICE, REVEREND
THANK YOU, THANK YOU.
G'DAY, REVEREND
SNIFF!
YOU DIDN'T GET IT? WHAT D'YA MEAN? WOULD I? WOULD I?
THANK YOU, MR. BLOOM.
GOD BLESS, MRS. NELSON.
BEAUTIFUL FUNERAL. I NEVER THOUGHT OF TRICK-OR-TREATERS AS GHOSTS!
THANK YOU, FATHER.
BLESSINGS, BLESSINGS.
CLOSED
ALMOST PERFECT, REVEREND SLYROCK! JUST ONE THING!
WHAT IS IT, MR. COBBLE?
EH?
WHAT IS IT, MR. COBBLE?
WELL (cough) TODAY AIN'T ALL SOULS DAY. IT'S ON NOVEMBER TWO.
TODAY'S HAL'WEEN! HAL'WEEN! HAL'WEEN!
YES, MR. COBBLE.
SCREEE!
HONK!
OH MY!

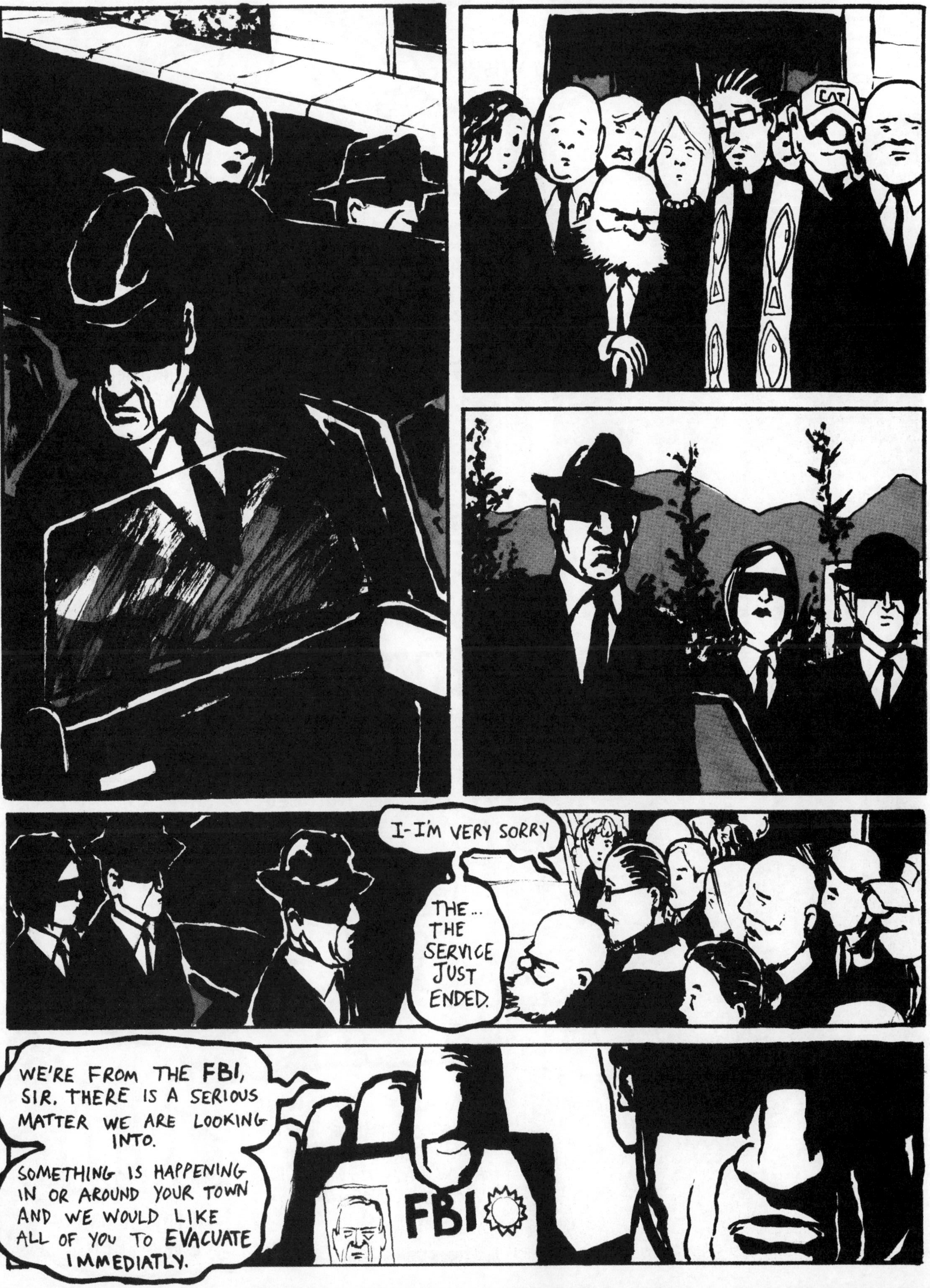
I-I'M VERY SORRY
THE... THE SERVICE JUST ENDED.
WE'RE FROM THE FBI, SIR. THERE IS A SERIOUS MATTER WE ARE LOOKING INTO.
SOMETHING IS HAPPENING IN OR AROUND YOUR TOWN AND WE WOULD LIKE ALL OF YOU TO EVACUATE IMMEDIATLY.
FBI

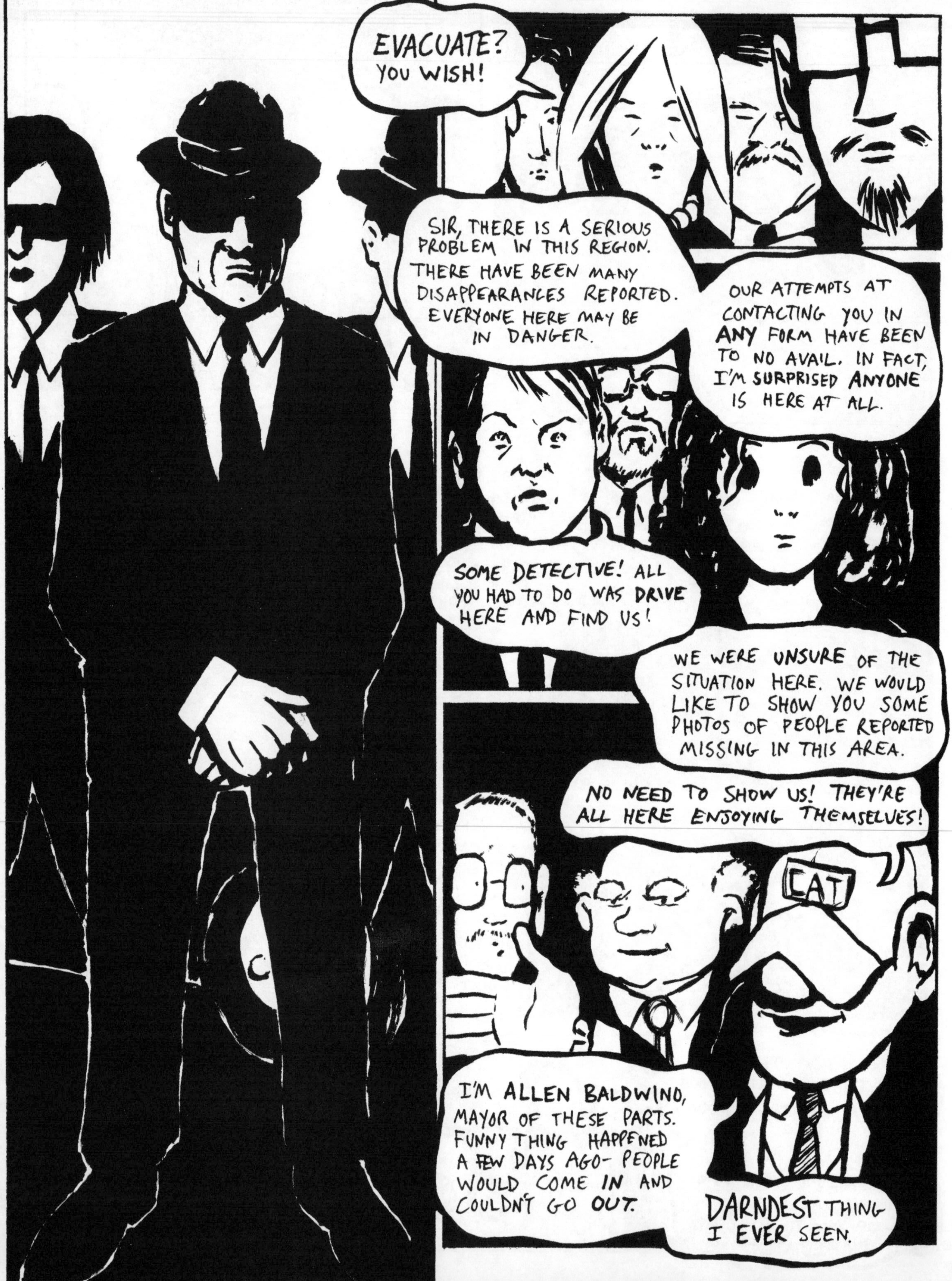
EVACUATE? YOU WISH!
SIR, THERE IS A SERIOUS PROBLEM IN THIS REGION. THERE HAVE BEEN MANY DISAPPEARANCES REPORTED. EVERYONE HERE MAY BE IN DANGER.
OUR ATTEMPTS AT CONTACTING YOU IN ANY FORM HAVE BEEN TO NO AVAIL. IN FACT, I'M SURPRISED ANYONE IS HERE AT ALL.
SOME DETECTIVE! ALL YOU HAD TO DO WAS DRIVE HERE AND FIND US!
WE WERE UNSURE OF THE SITUATION HERE. WE WOULD LIKE TO SHOW YOU SOME PHOTOS OF PEOPLE REPORTED MISSING IN THIS AREA.
NO NEED TO SHOW US! THEY'RE ALL HERE ENJOYING THEMSELVES!
CAT
I'M ALLEN BALDWIND, MAYOR OF THESE PARTS. FUNNY THING HAPPENED A FEW DAYS AGO- PEOPLE WOULD COME IN AND COULDN'T GO OUT.
DARNDEST THING I EVER SEEN.

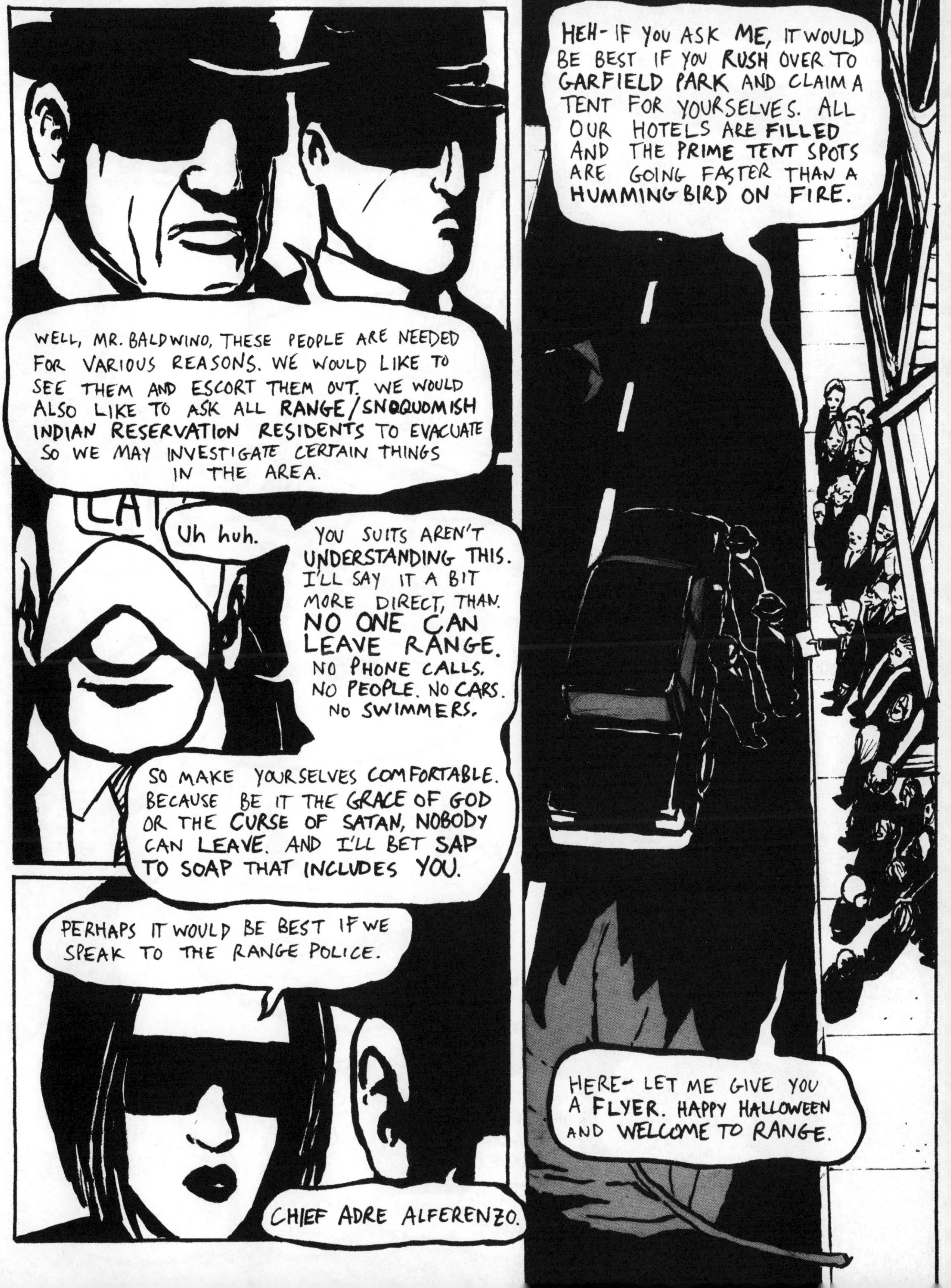
WELL, MR. BALDWINO, THESE PEOPLE ARE NEEDED FOR VARIOUS REASONS. WE WOULD LIKE TO SEE THEM AND ESCORT THEM OUT. WE WOULD ALSO LIKE TO ASK ALL RANGE/SNOQUOMISH INDIAN RESERVATION RESIDENTS TO EVACUATE SO WE MAY INVESTIGATE CERTAIN THINGS IN THE AREA.
Uh huh.
YOU SUITS AREN'T UNDERSTANDING THIS. I'LL SAY IT A BIT MORE DIRECT, THAN. NO ONE CAN LEAVE RANGE. NO PHONE CALLS. NO PEOPLE. NO CARS. NO SWIMMERS.
SO MAKE YOURSELVES COMFORTABLE. BECAUSE BE IT THE GRACE OF GOD OR THE CURSE OF SATAN, NOBODY CAN LEAVE. AND I'LL BET SAP TO SOAP THAT INCLUDES YOU.
PERHAPS IT WOULD BE BEST IF WE SPEAK TO THE RANGE POLICE.
CHIEF ADRE ALFERENZO.
HEH- IF YOU ASK ME, IT WOULD BE BEST IF YOU RUSH OVER TO GARFIELD PARK AND CLAIM A TENT FOR YOURSELVES. ALL OUR HOTELS ARE FILLED AND THE PRIME TENT SPOTS ARE GOING FASTER THAN A HUMMING BIRD ON FIRE.
HERE- LET ME GIVE YOU A FLYER. HAPPY HALLOWEEN AND WELCOME TO RANGE.

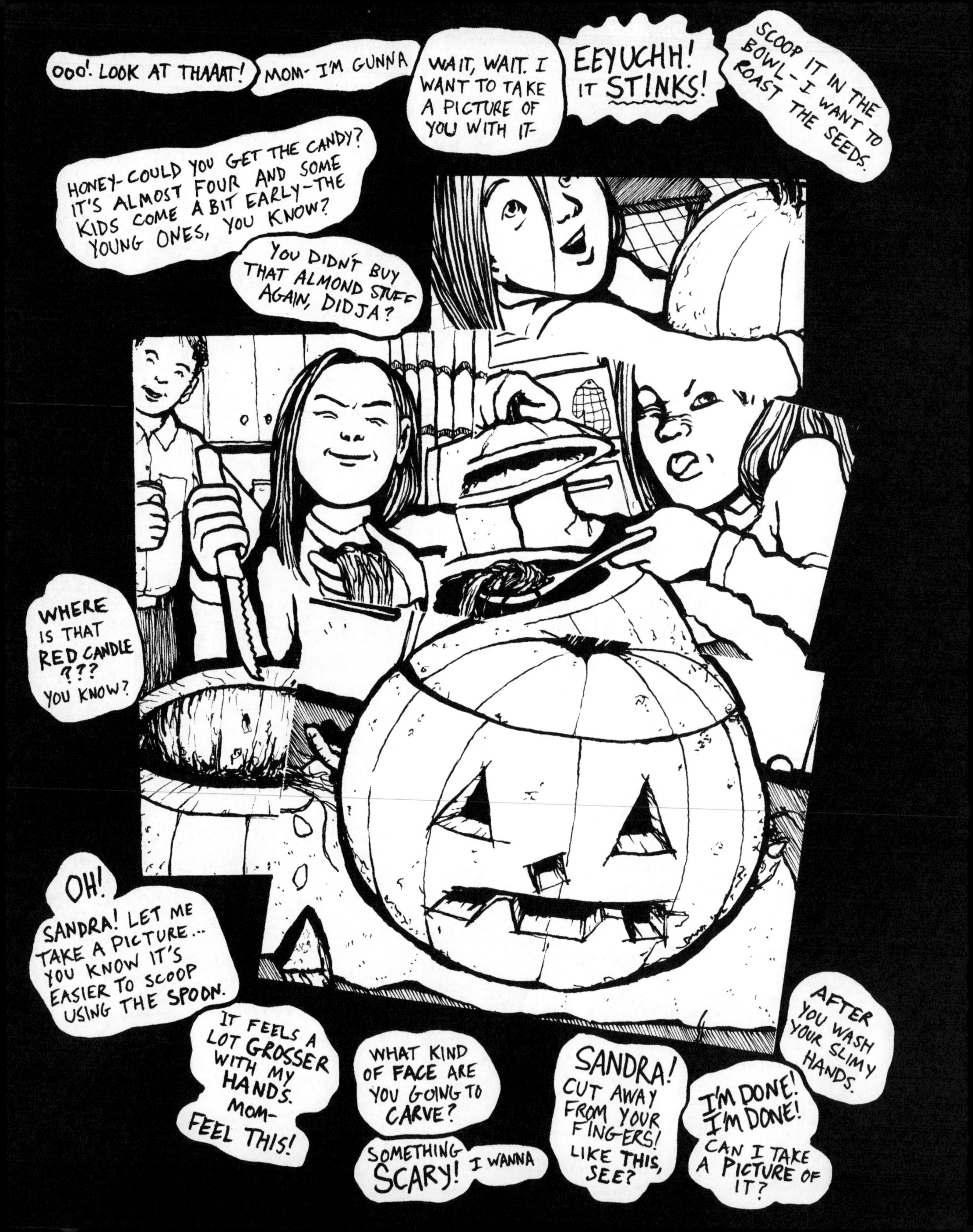
OOO! LOOK AT THAAAT!
MOM- I'M GUNNA
WAIT, WAIT. I WANT TO TAKE A PICTURE OF YOU WITH IT-
EEYUCHH! IT STINKS!
SCOOP IT IN THE BOWL- I WANT TO ROAST THE SEEDS.
HONEY- COULD YOU GET THE CANDY? IT'S ALMOST FOUR AND SOME KIDS COME A BIT EARLY- THE YOUNG ONES, YOU KNOW?
YOU DIDN'T BUY THAT ALMOND STUFF AGAIN, DIDJA?
WHERE IS THAT RED CANDLE ??? YOU KNOW?
OH!
SANDRA! LET ME TAKE A PICTURE... YOU KNOW IT'S EASIER TO SCOOP USING THE SPOON.
IT FEELS A LOT GROSSER WITH MY HANDS. MOM- FEEL THIS!
WHAT KIND OF FACE ARE YOU GOING TO CARVE?
SOMETHING SCARY! I WANNA
SANDRA! CUT AWAY FROM YOUR FINGERS! LIKE THIS, SEE?
I'M DONE! I'M DONE! CAN I TAKE A PICTURE OF IT?
AFTER YOU WASH YOUR SLIMY HANDS.

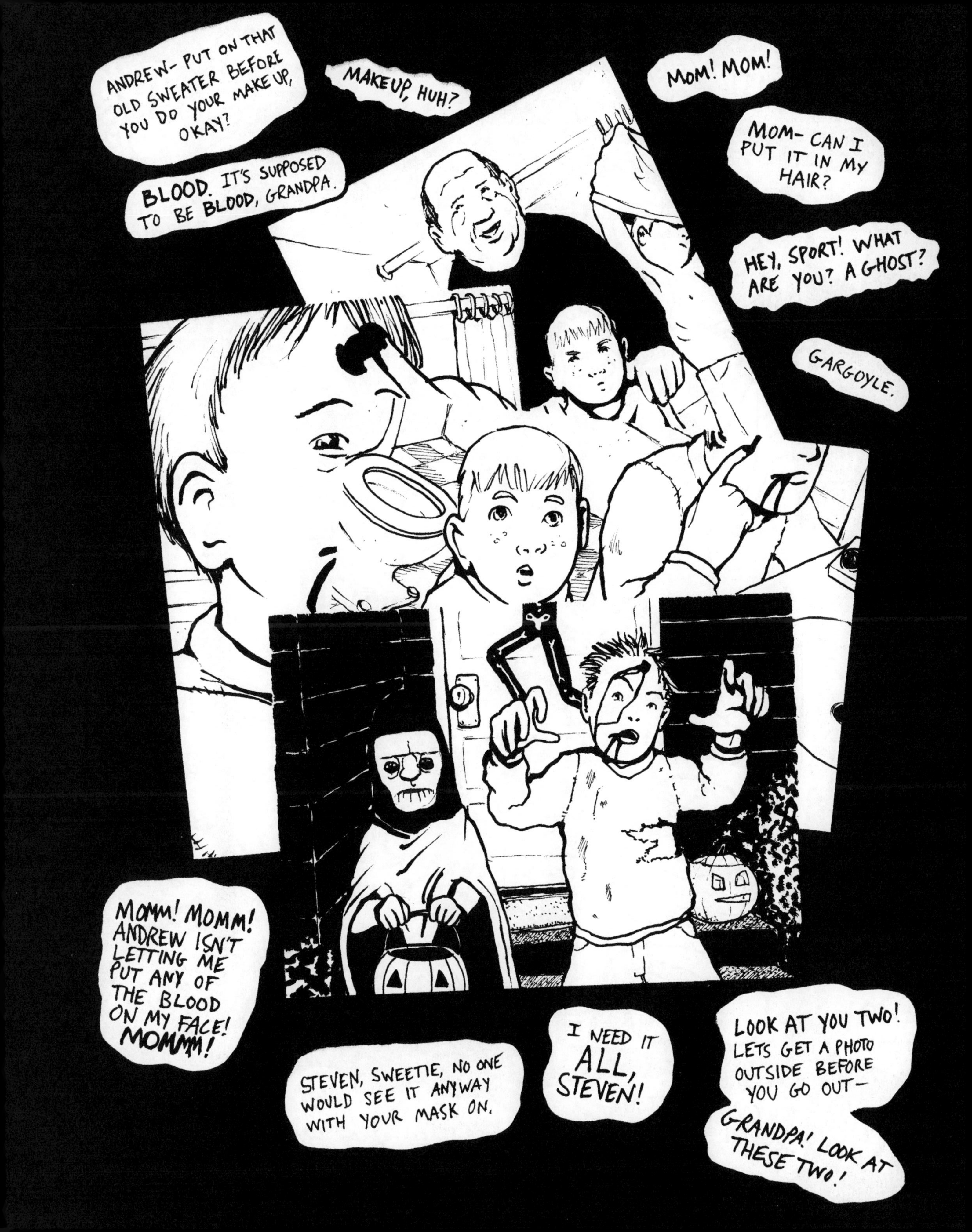
ANDREW- PUT ON THAT OLD SWEATER BEFORE YOU DO YOUR MAKE UP, OKAY?
MAKEUP, HUH?
BLOOD. IT'S SUPPOSED TO BE BLOOD, GRANDPA.
MOM! MOM!
MOM- CAN I PUT IT IN MY HAIR?
HEY, SPORT! WHAT ARE YOU? A GHOST?
GARGOYLE.
MOMM! MOMM! ANDREW ISN'T LETTING ME PUT ANY OF THE BLOOD ON MY FACE! MOMMM!
STEVEN, SWEETIE, NO ONE WOULD SEE IT ANYWAY WITH YOUR MASK ON.
I NEED IT ALL, STEVEN!
LOOK AT YOU TWO! LETS GET A PHOTO OUTSIDE BEFORE YOU GO OUT-
GRANDPA! LOOK AT THESE TWO!

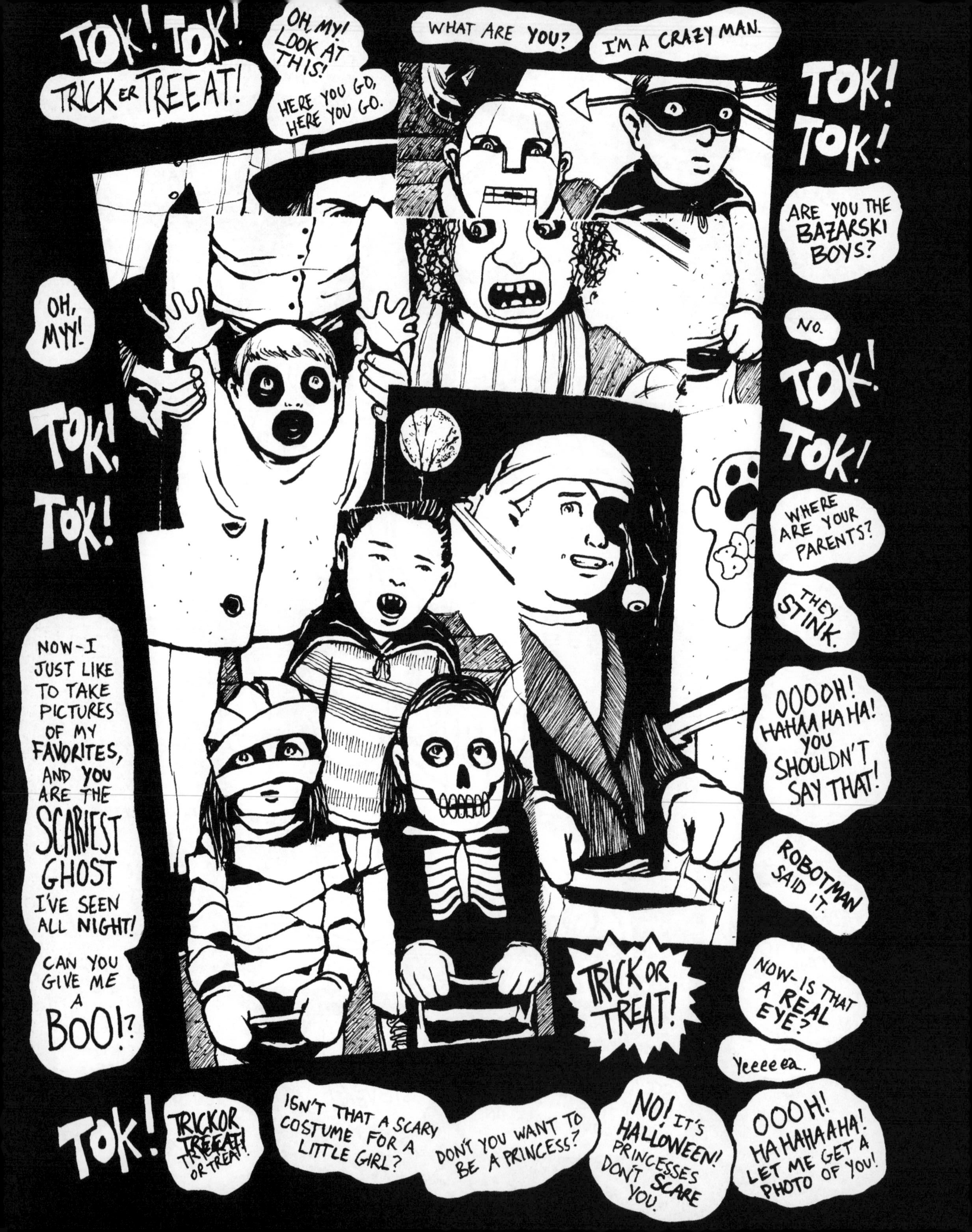
TOK! TOK!
TRICK ER TREEAT!
OH, MY! LOOK AT THIS!
HERE YOU GO, HERE YOU GO.
WHAT ARE YOU?
I'M A CRAZY MAN.
TOK! TOK!
ARE YOU THE BAZARSKI BOYS?
NO.
OH, MYY!
TOK! TOK!
TOK! TOK!
WHERE ARE YOUR PARENTS?
THEY STINK.
NOW-I JUST LIKE TO TAKE PICTURES OF MY FAVORITES, AND YOU ARE THE SCARIEST GHOST I'VE SEEN ALL NIGHT!
CAN YOU GIVE ME A BOO!?
OOOOH! HAHAAHAHA! YOU SHOULDN'T SAY THAT!
ROBOTMAN SAID IT.
TRICK OR TREAT!
NOW-IS THAT A REAL EYE?
Yeeeeea.
TOK!
TRICKOR TREEAT! TREAT! OR TREAT!
ISN'T THAT A SCARY COSTUME FOR A LITTLE GIRL?
DON'T YOU WANT TO BE A PRINCESS?
NO! IT'S HALLOWEEN! PRINCESSES DON'T SCARE YOU.
OOOH! HAHAHAAHA! LET ME GET A PHOTO OF YOU!

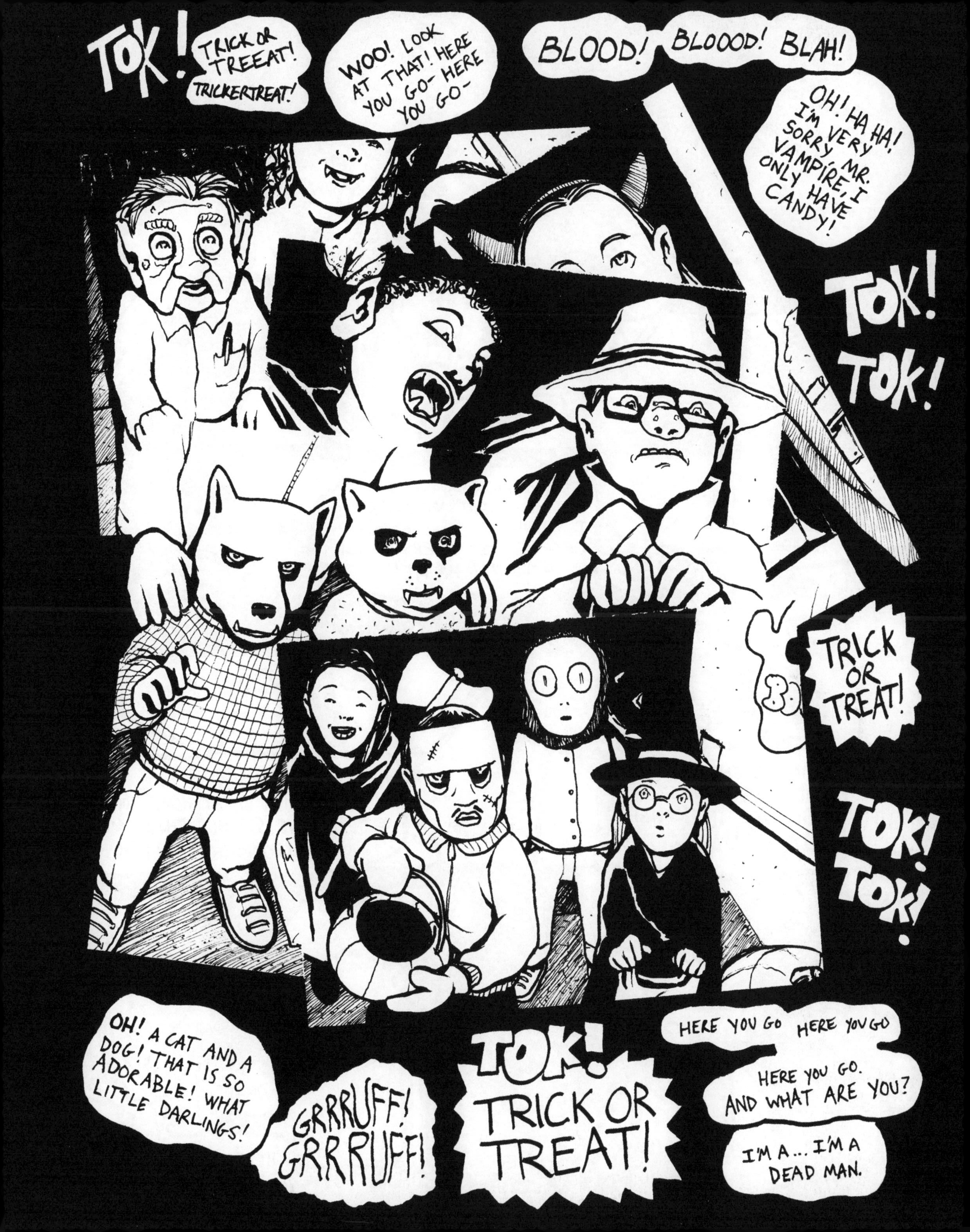
TOK!
TRICK OR TREEAT! TRICKERTREAT!
WOO! LOOK AT THAT! HERE YOU GO- HERE YOU GO-
BLOOD! BLOOOD! BLAH!
OH! HA HA! I'M VERY SORRY, MR. VAMPIRE, I ONLY HAVE CANDY!
TOK! TOK!
TRICK OR TREAT!
TOK! TOK!
OH! A CAT AND A DOG! THAT IS SO ADORABLE! WHAT LITTLE DARLINGS!
GRRRUFF! GRRRUFF!
TOK! TRICK OR TREAT!
HERE YOU GO HERE YOU GO
HERE YOU GO. AND WHAT ARE YOU?
I'M A... I'M A DEAD MAN.

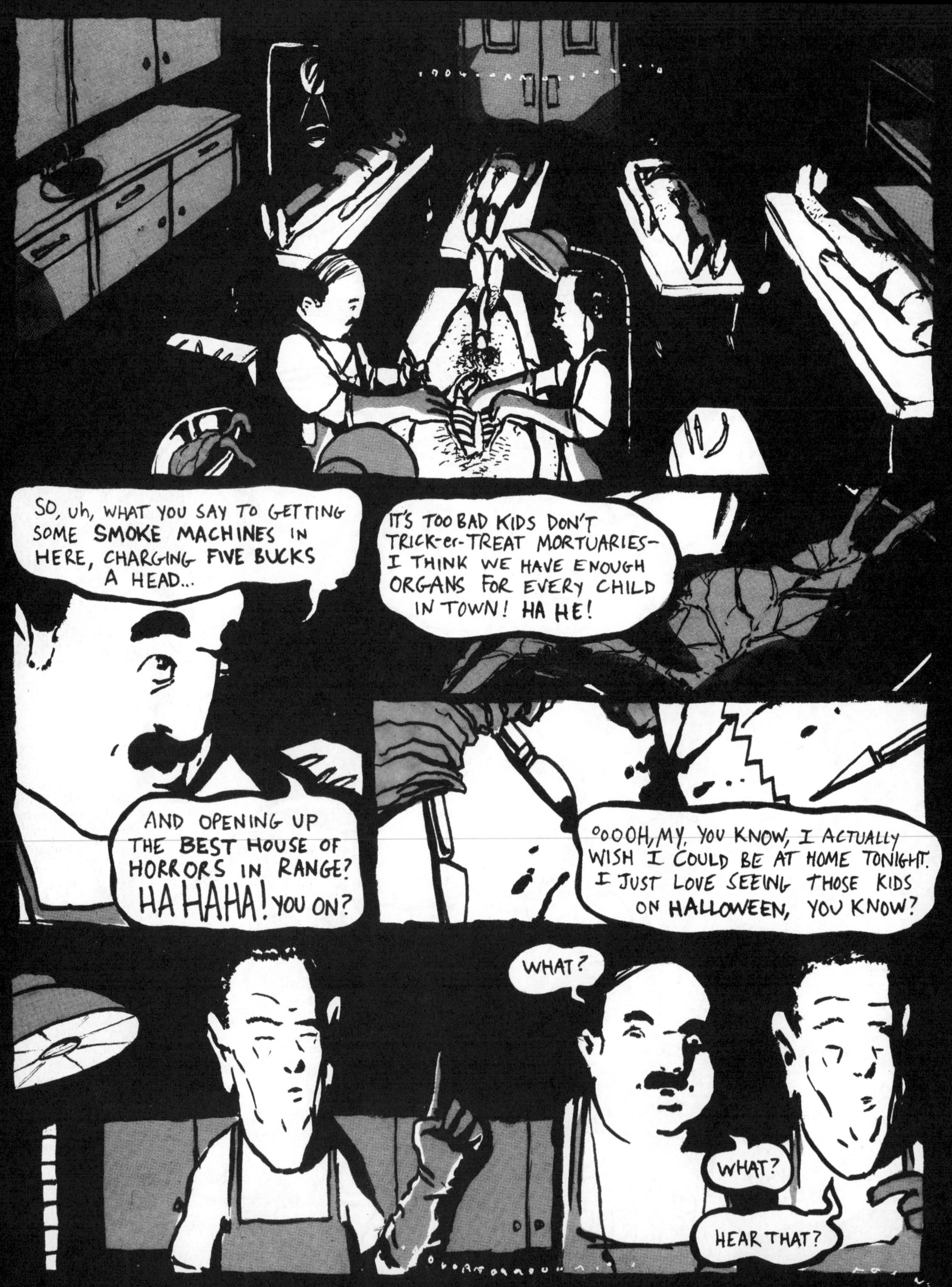
SO, uh, WHAT YOU SAY TO GETTING SOME SMOKE MACHINES IN HERE, CHARGING FIVE BUCKS A HEAD...
IT'S TOO BAD KIDS DON'T TRICK-er-TREAT MORTUARIES– I THINK WE HAVE ENOUGH ORGANS FOR EVERY CHILD IN TOWN! HA HE!
AND OPENING UP THE BEST HOUSE OF HORRORS IN RANGE? HA HAHA! YOU ON?
OOOOH, MY, YOU KNOW, I ACTUALLY WISH I COULD BE AT HOME TONIGHT. I JUST LOVE SEEING THOSE KIDS ON HALLOWEEN, YOU KNOW?
WHAT?
WHAT?
HEAR THAT?

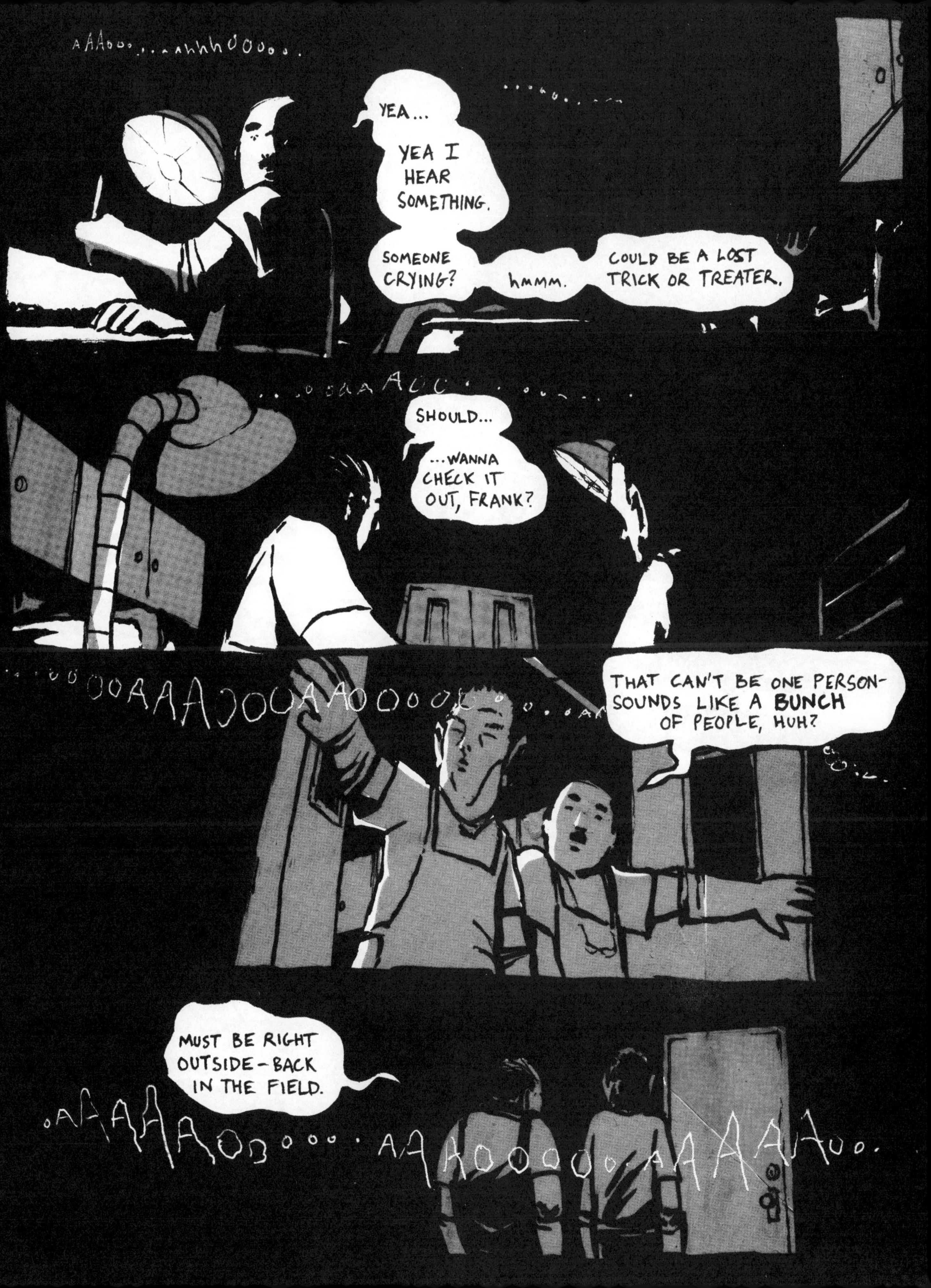
AAAooo.....ahhhOOooo..
YEA...
YEA I HEAR SOMETHING.
SOMEONE CRYING?
hmmm.
COULD BE A LOST TRICK OR TREATER.
SHOULD...
...WANNA CHECK IT OUT, FRANK?
THAT CAN'T BE ONE PERSON-SOUNDS LIKE A **BUNCH** OF PEOPLE, HUH?
MUST BE RIGHT OUTSIDE-BACK IN THE FIELD.

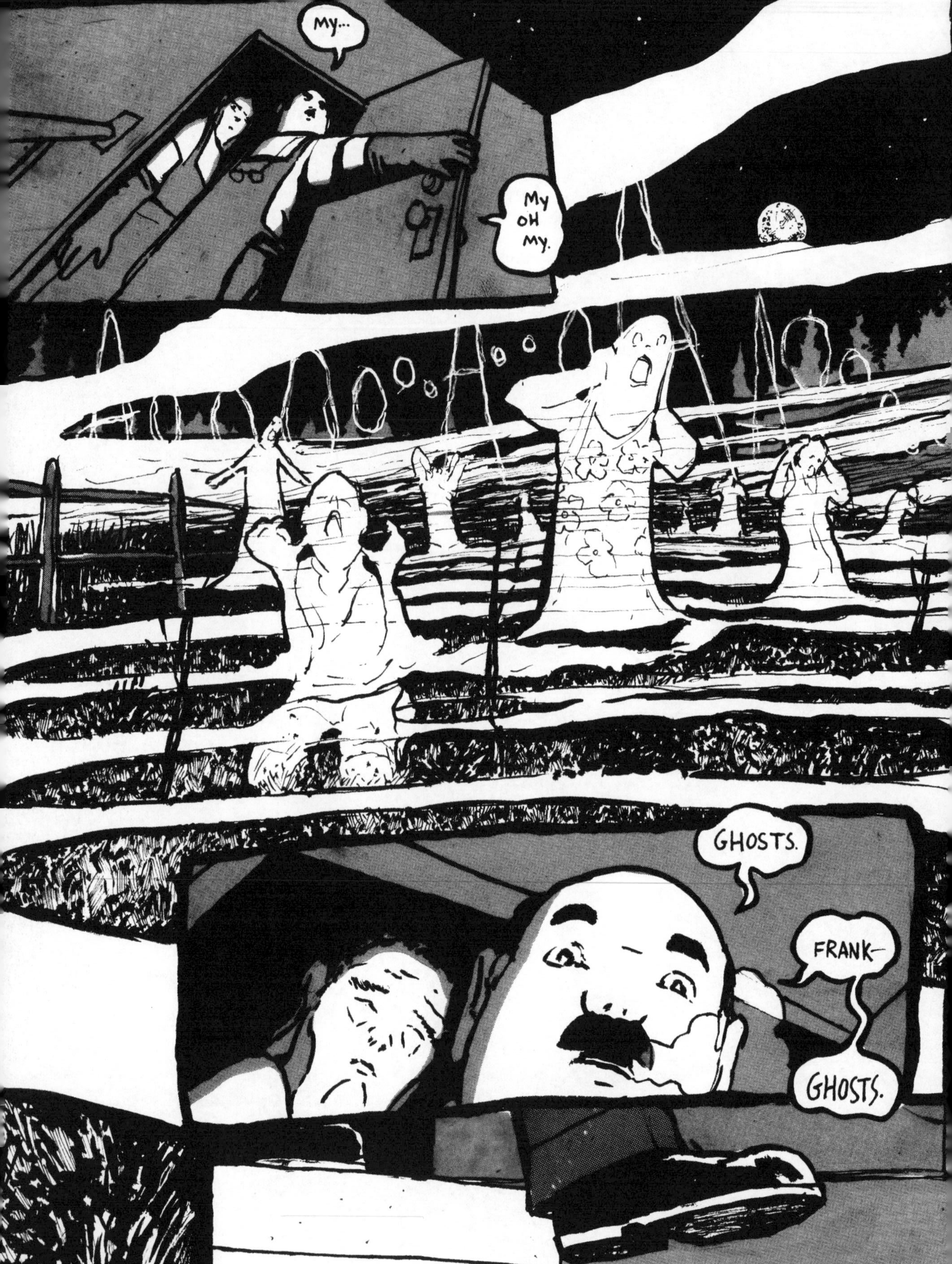
My...
My oh my.
GHOSTS.
FRANK—
GHOSTS.

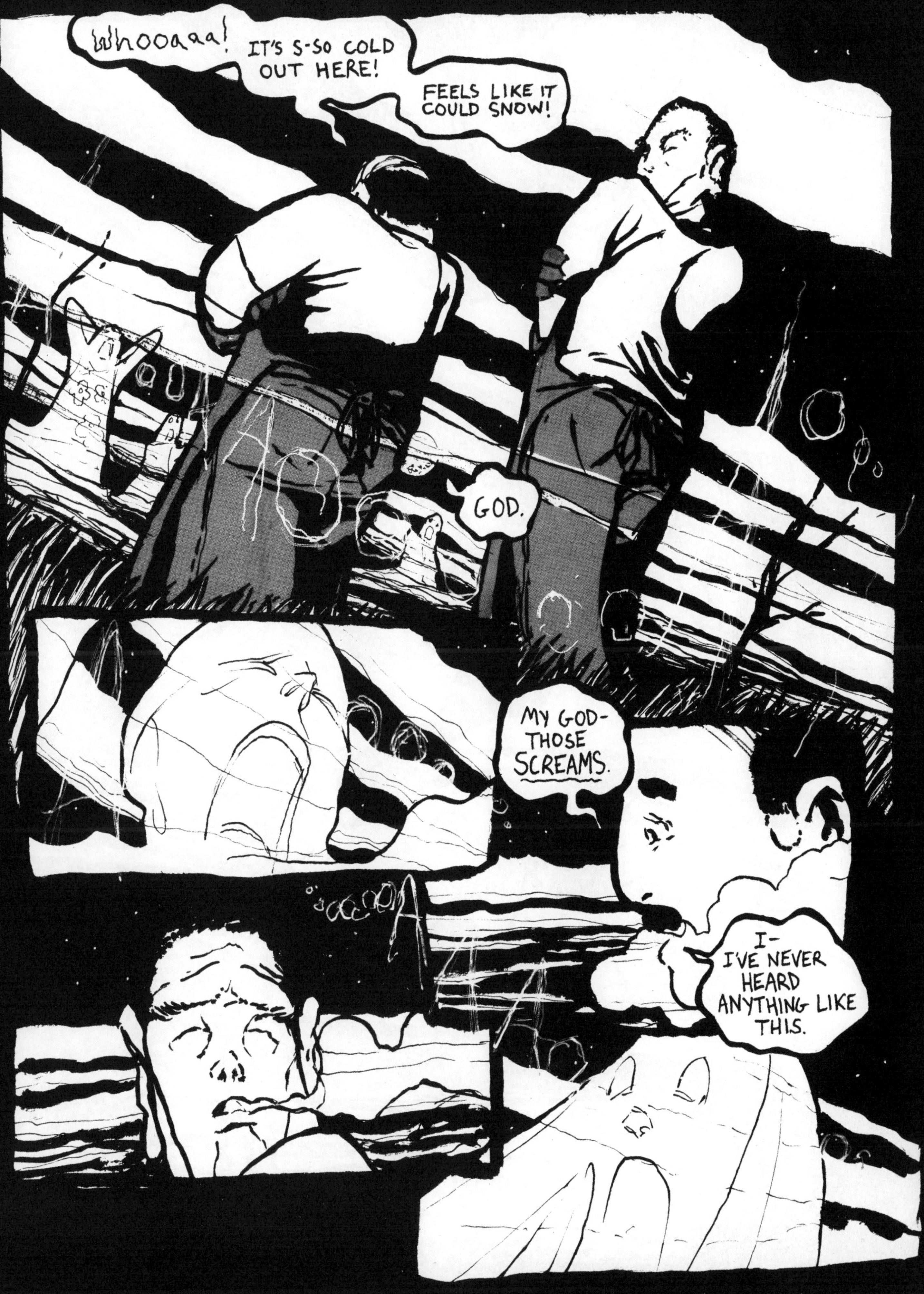
Whooaaa!
IT'S S-SO COLD OUT HERE!
FEELS LIKE IT COULD SNOW!
GOD.
MY GOD- THOSE SCREAMS.
I- I'VE NEVER HEARD ANYTHING LIKE THIS.

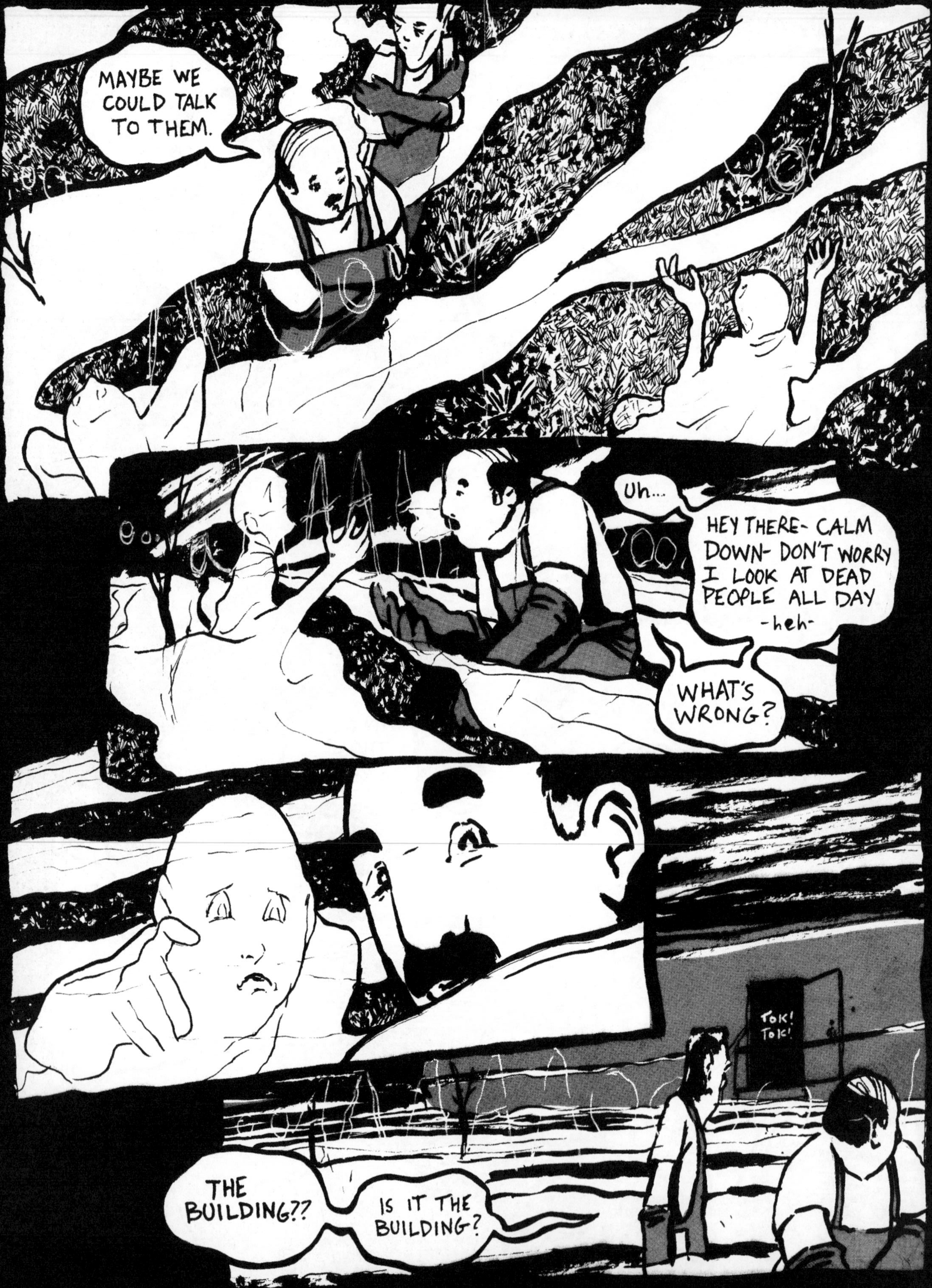
MAYBE WE COULD TALK TO THEM.
Uh...
HEY THERE- CALM DOWN- DON'T WORRY I LOOK AT DEAD PEOPLE ALL DAY -heh-
WHAT'S WRONG?
TOK! TOK!
THE BUILDING??
IS IT THE BUILDING?

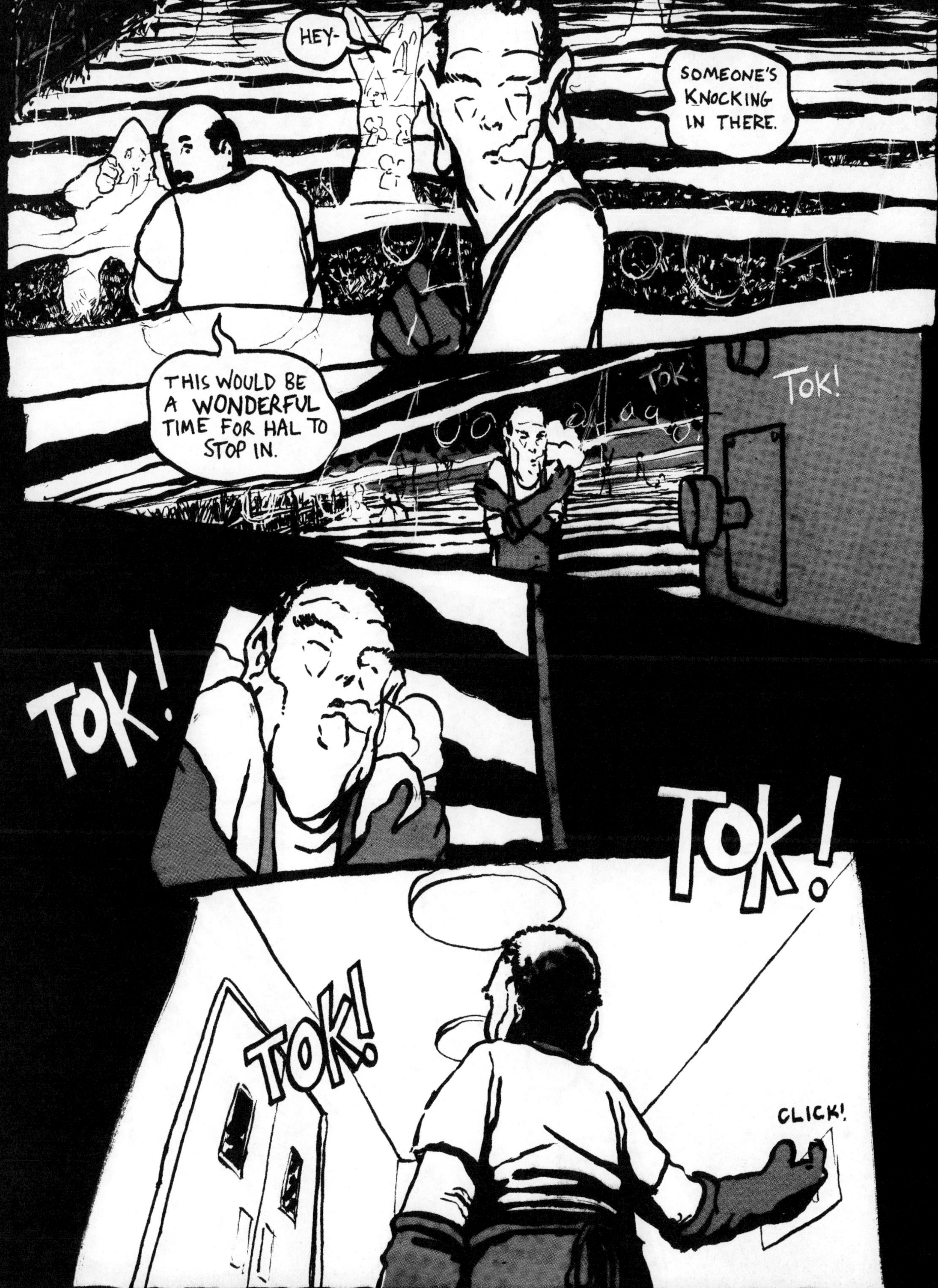
HEY-
SOMEONE'S KNOCKING IN THERE.
THIS WOULD BE A WONDERFUL TIME FOR HAL TO STOP IN.
TOK!
TOK!
TOK!
TOK!
TOK!
TOK!
CLICK!

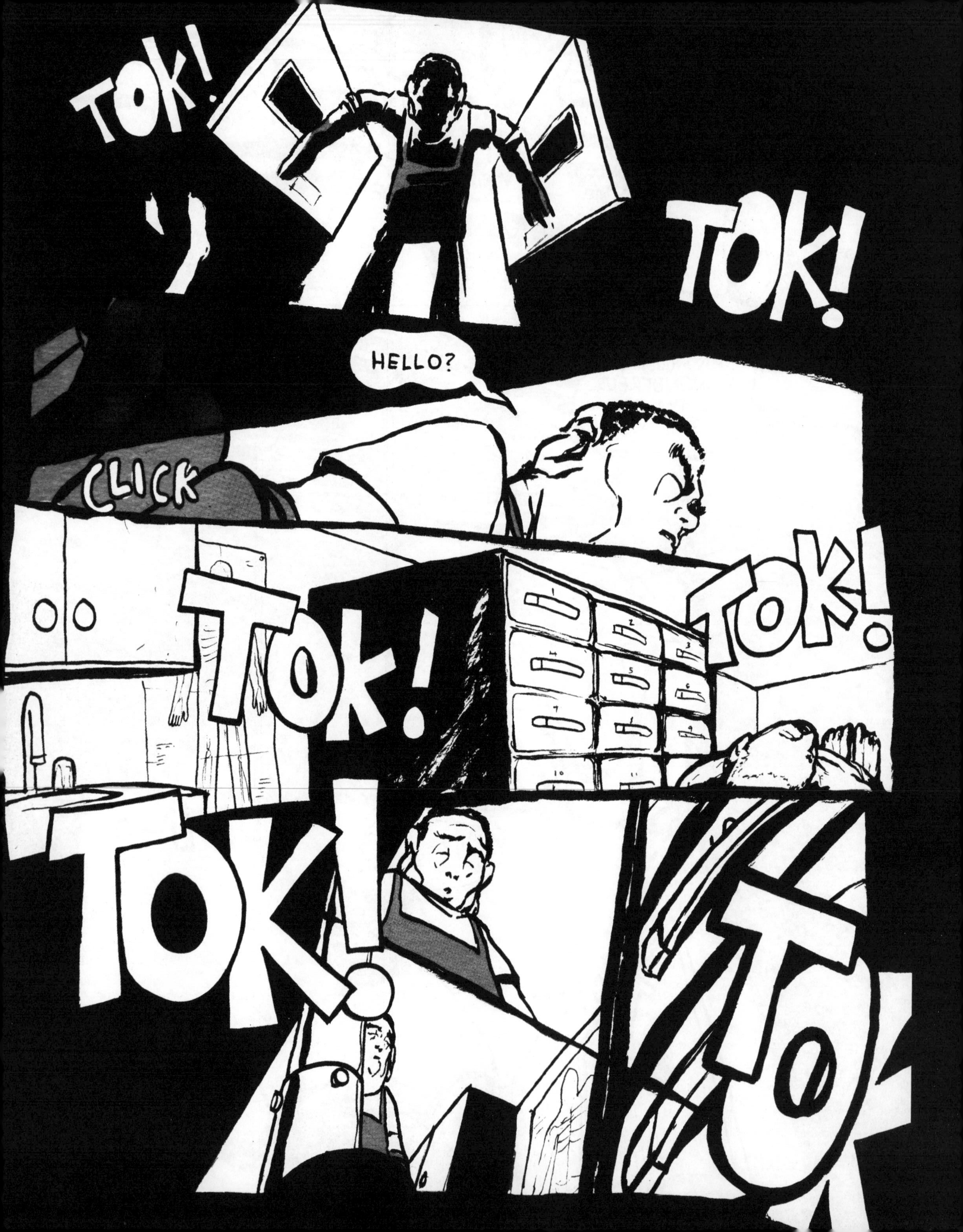
TOK!
TOK!
HELLO?
CLICK
TOK!
TOK!
TOK!

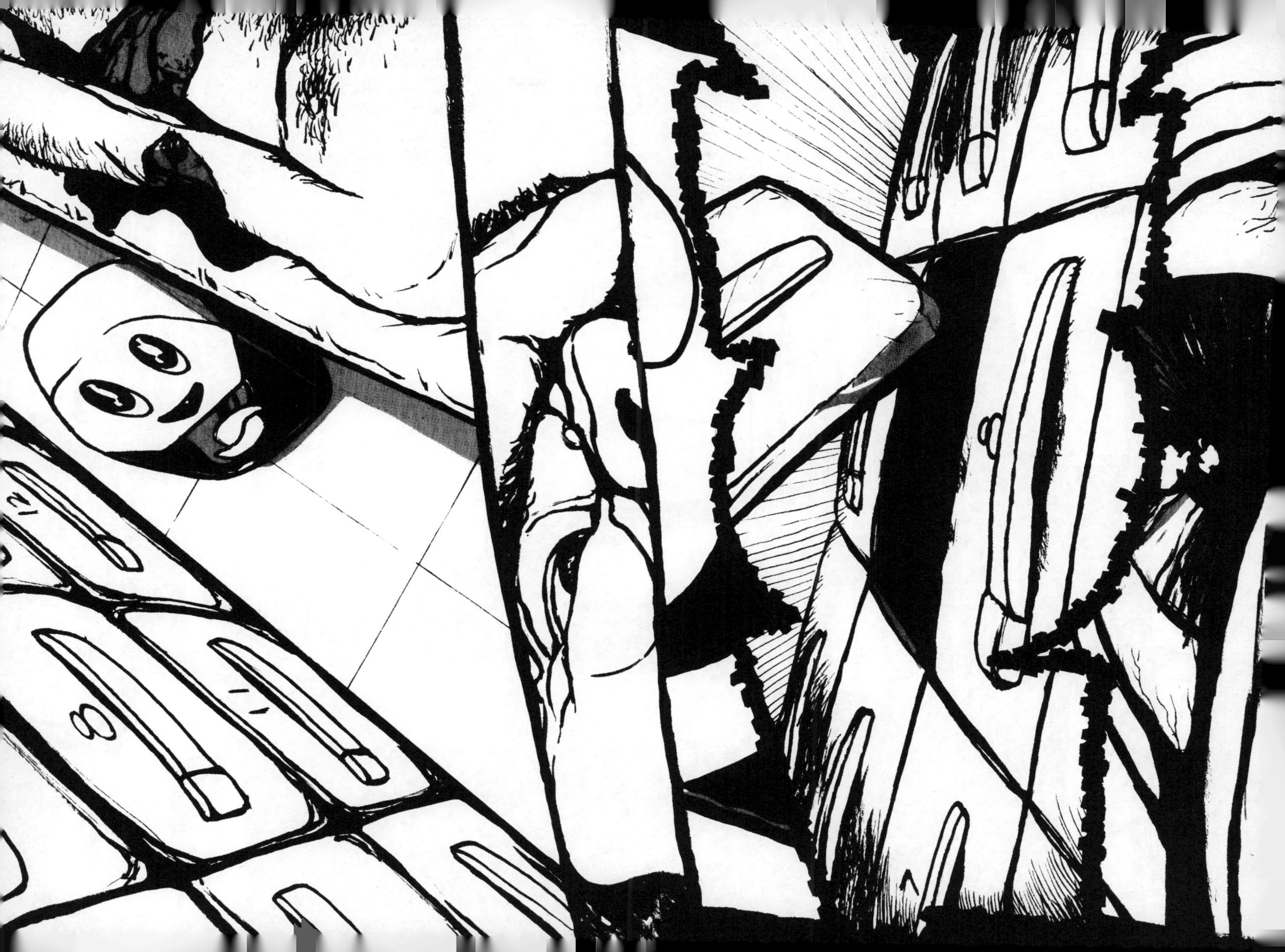

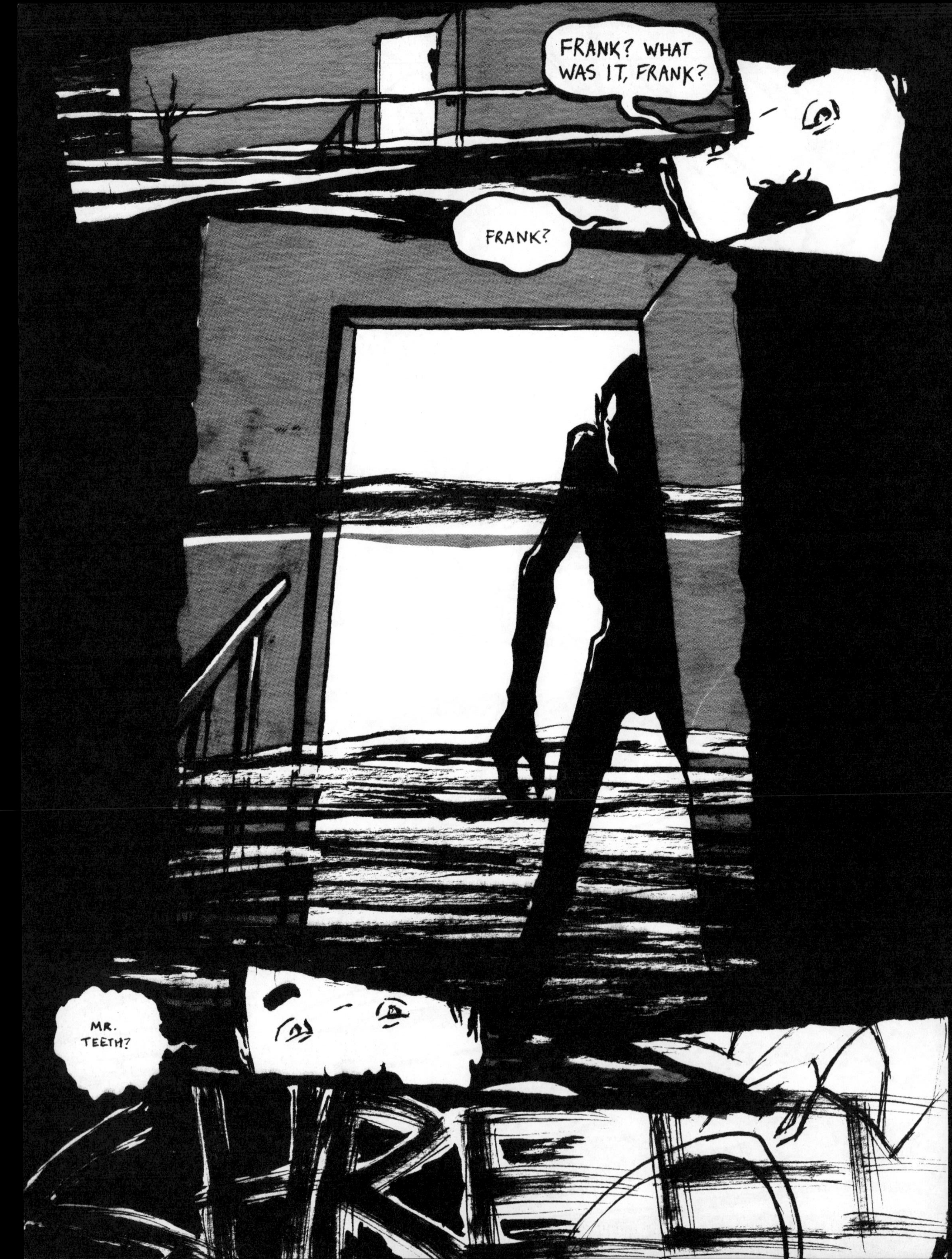
FRANK? WHAT WAS IT, FRANK?
FRANK?
MR. TEETH?

5.
LUNATIC

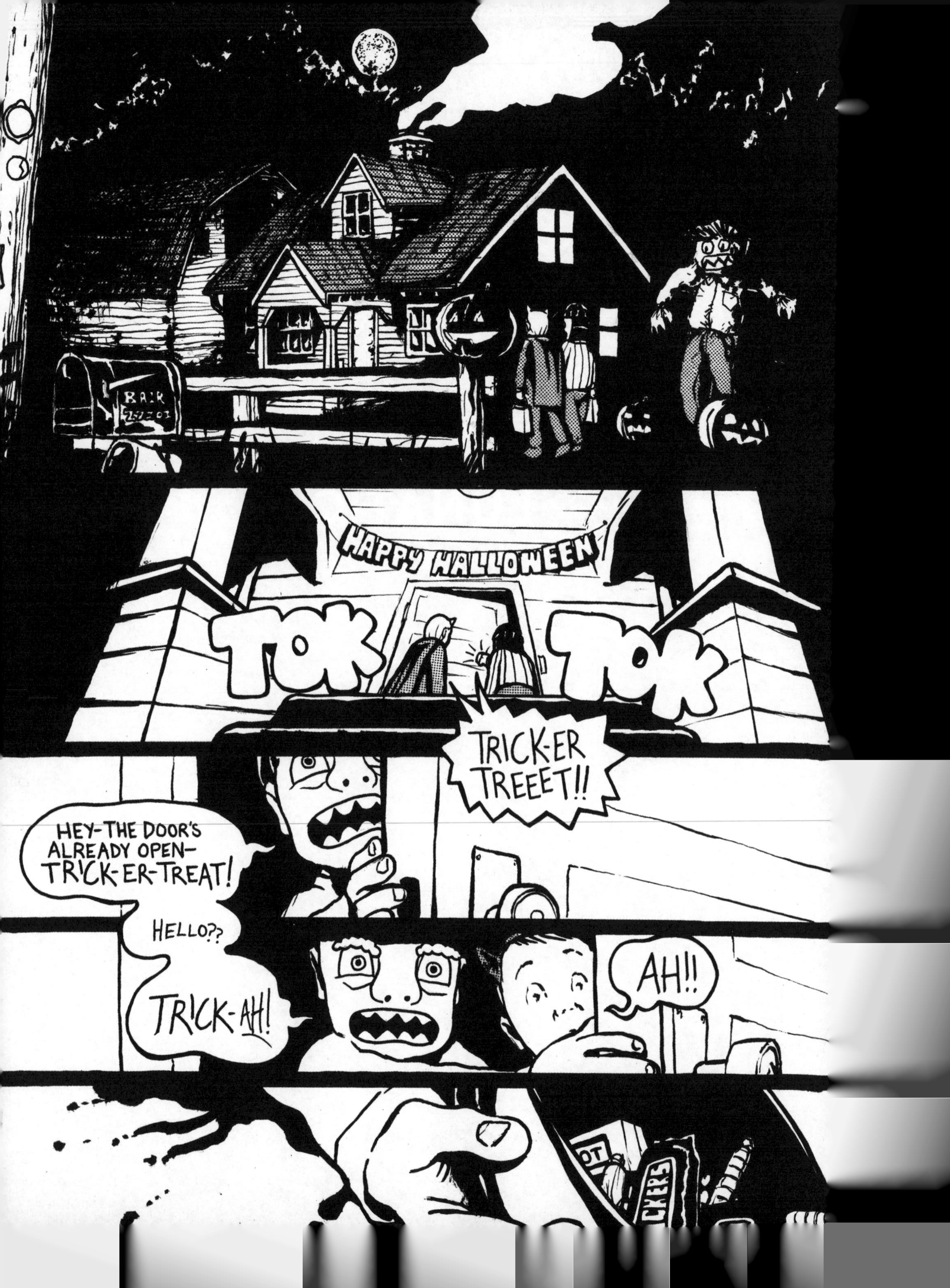
BAIR
HAPPY HALLOWEEN
TOK TOK
TRICK-ER TREEET!!
HEY-THE DOOR'S ALREADY OPEN- TRICK-ER-TREAT!
HELLO??
TRICK-AH!
AH!!

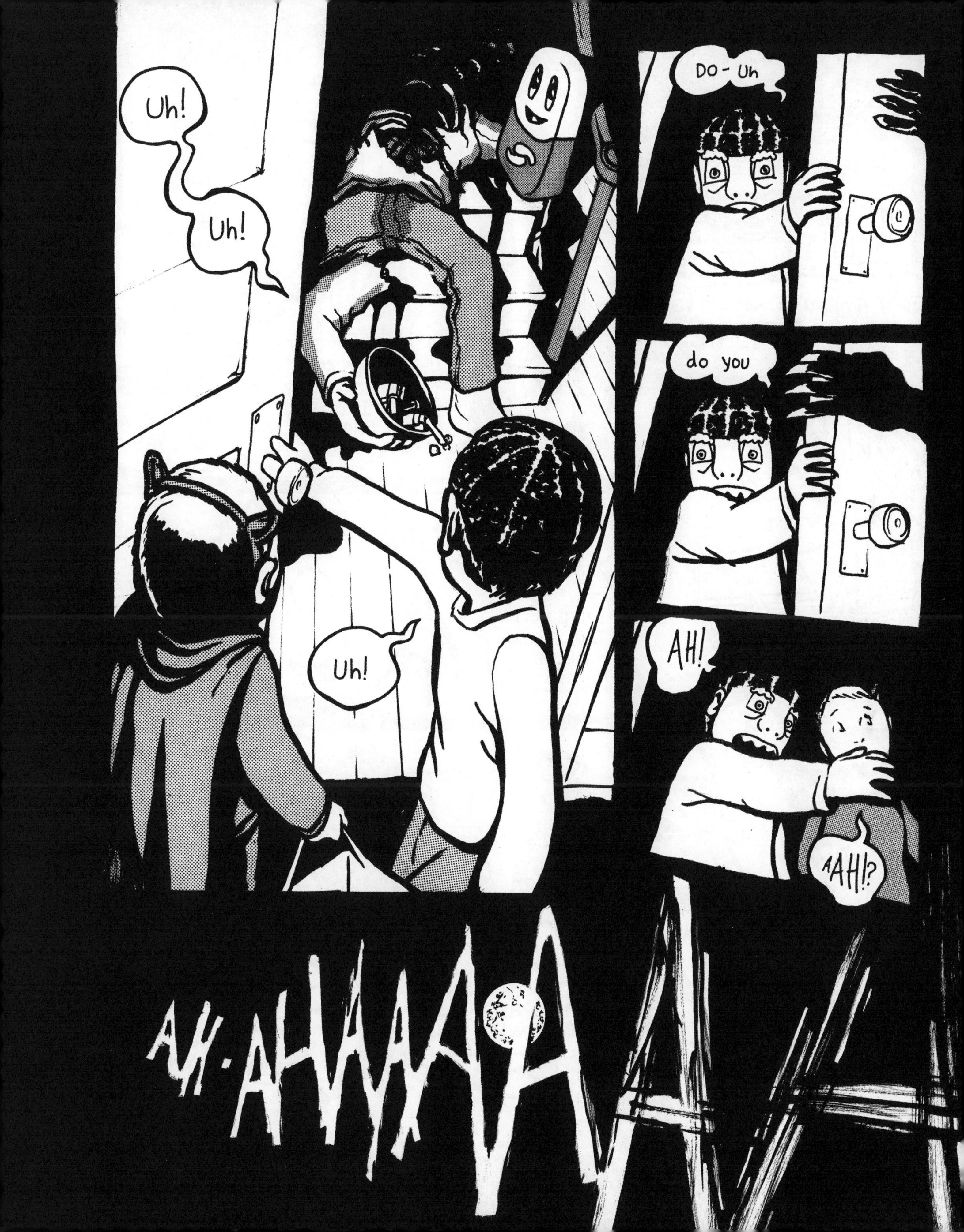
Uh!
Uh!
Uh!
DO-Uh
do you
AH!
AAH!?
AH-AHAAAAAA

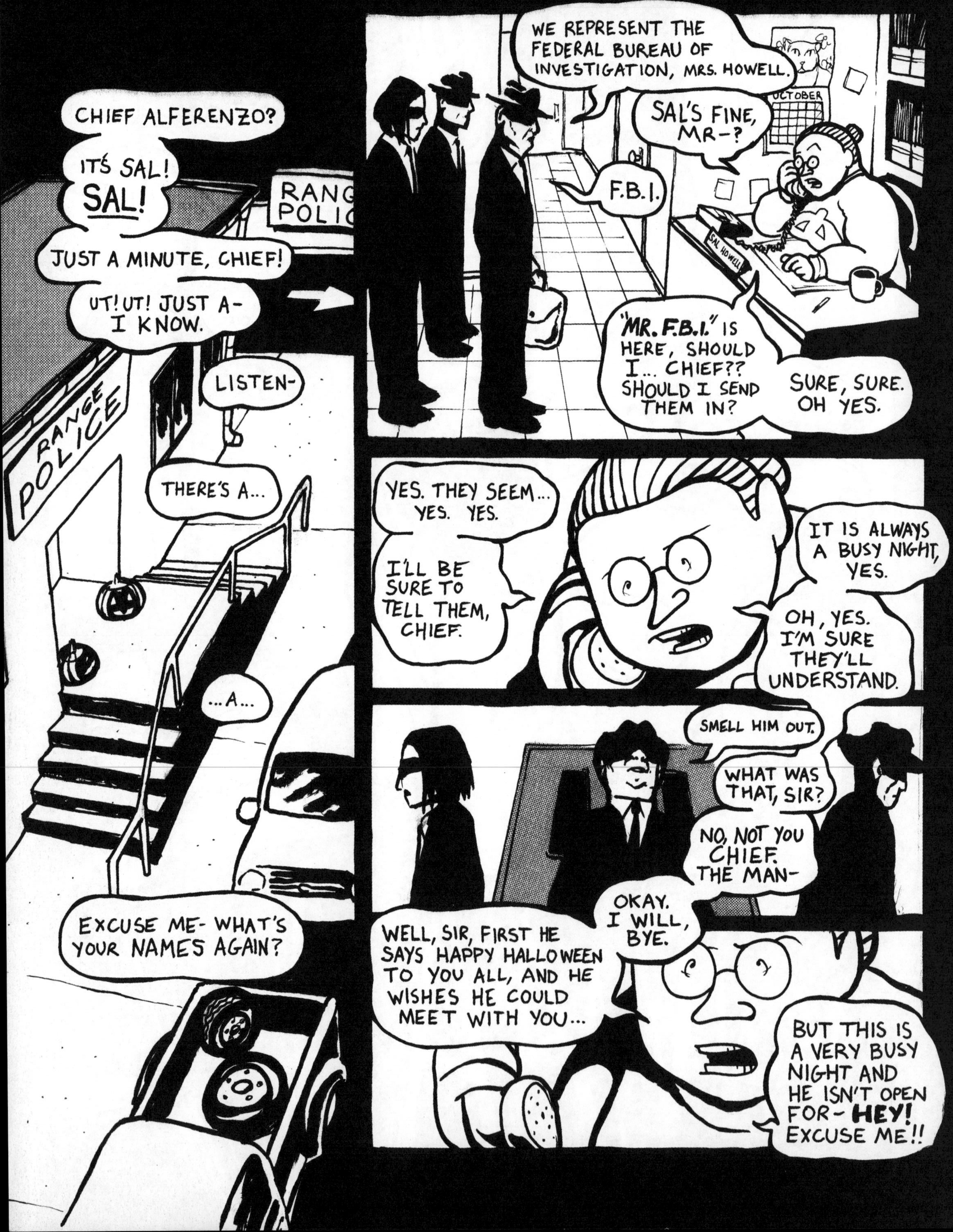
CHIEF ALFERENZO?
IT'S SAL! SAL!
JUST A MINUTE, CHIEF!
UT! UT! JUST A- I KNOW.
LISTEN-
THERE'S A...
...A...
EXCUSE ME- WHAT'S YOUR NAMES AGAIN?
RANGE POLICE
RANG POLIC
WE REPRESENT THE FEDERAL BUREAU OF INVESTIGATION, MRS. HOWELL.
SAL'S FINE, MR-?
F.B.I.
OCTOBER
SAL HOWELL
"MR. F.B.I." IS HERE, SHOULD I... CHIEF?? SHOULD I SEND THEM IN?
SURE, SURE. OH YES.
YES. THEY SEEM... YES. YES.
I'LL BE SURE TO TELL THEM, CHIEF.
IT IS ALWAYS A BUSY NIGHT, YES.
OH, YES. I'M SURE THEY'LL UNDERSTAND.
SMELL HIM OUT.
WHAT WAS THAT, SIR?
NO, NOT YOU CHIEF. THE MAN-
OKAY. I WILL, BYE.
WELL, SIR, FIRST HE SAYS HAPPY HALLOWEEN TO YOU ALL, AND HE WISHES HE COULD MEET WITH YOU...
BUT THIS IS A VERY BUSY NIGHT AND HE ISN'T OPEN FOR- HEY! EXCUSE ME!!

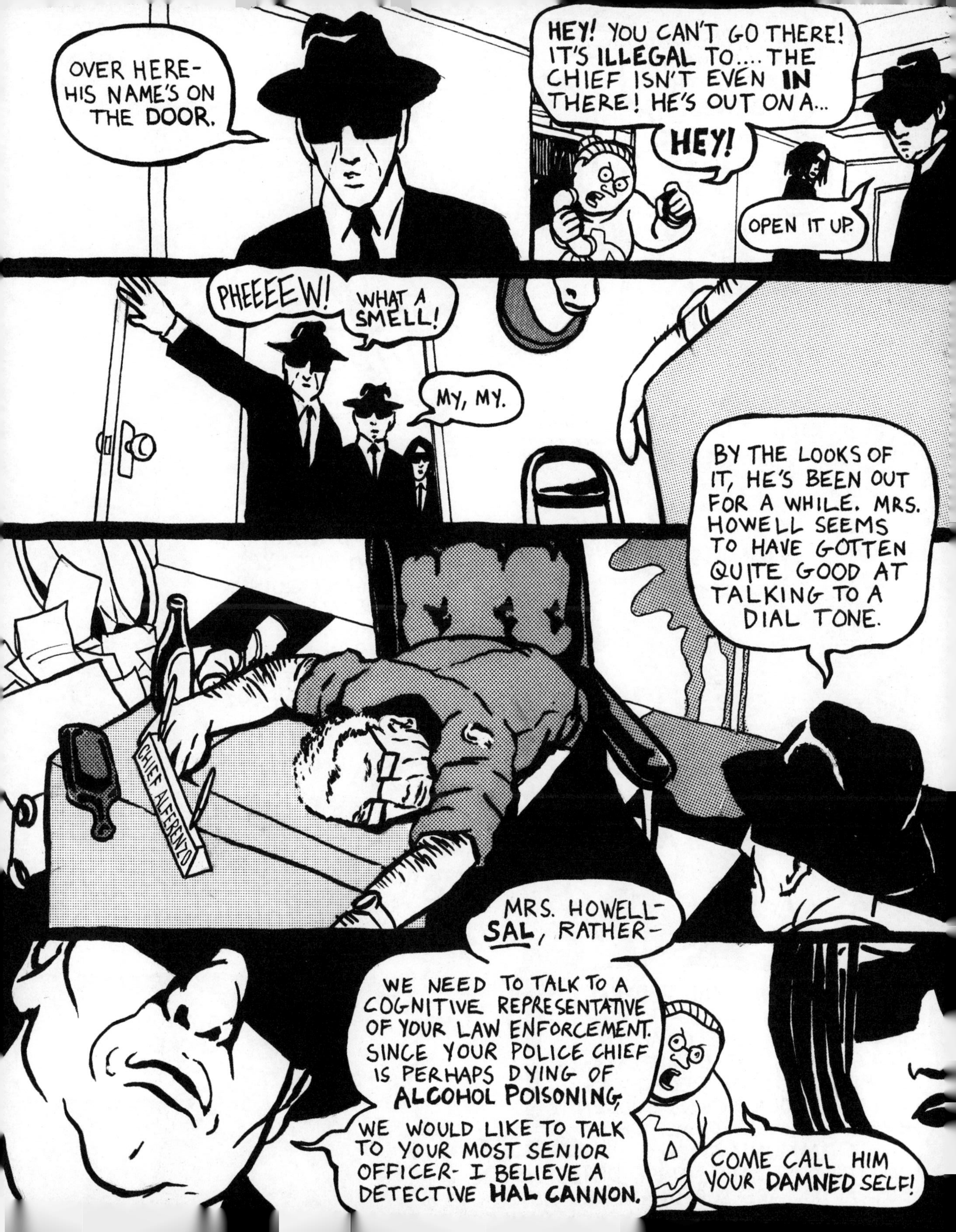
OVER HERE- HIS NAME'S ON THE DOOR.
HEY! YOU CAN'T GO THERE! IT'S ILLEGAL TO.... THE CHIEF ISN'T EVEN IN THERE! HE'S OUT ON A...
HEY!
OPEN IT UP.
PHEEEEW!
WHAT A SMELL!
MY, MY.
BY THE LOOKS OF IT, HE'S BEEN OUT FOR A WHILE. MRS. HOWELL SEEMS TO HAVE GOTTEN QUITE GOOD AT TALKING TO A DIAL TONE.
CHIEF ALFERENZO
MRS. HOWELL- SAL, RATHER-
WE NEED TO TALK TO A COGNITIVE REPRESENTATIVE OF YOUR LAW ENFORCEMENT. SINCE YOUR POLICE CHIEF IS PERHAPS DYING OF ALCOHOL POISONING,
WE WOULD LIKE TO TALK TO YOUR MOST SENIOR OFFICER- I BELIEVE A DETECTIVE HAL CANNON.
COME CALL HIM YOUR DAMNED SELF!

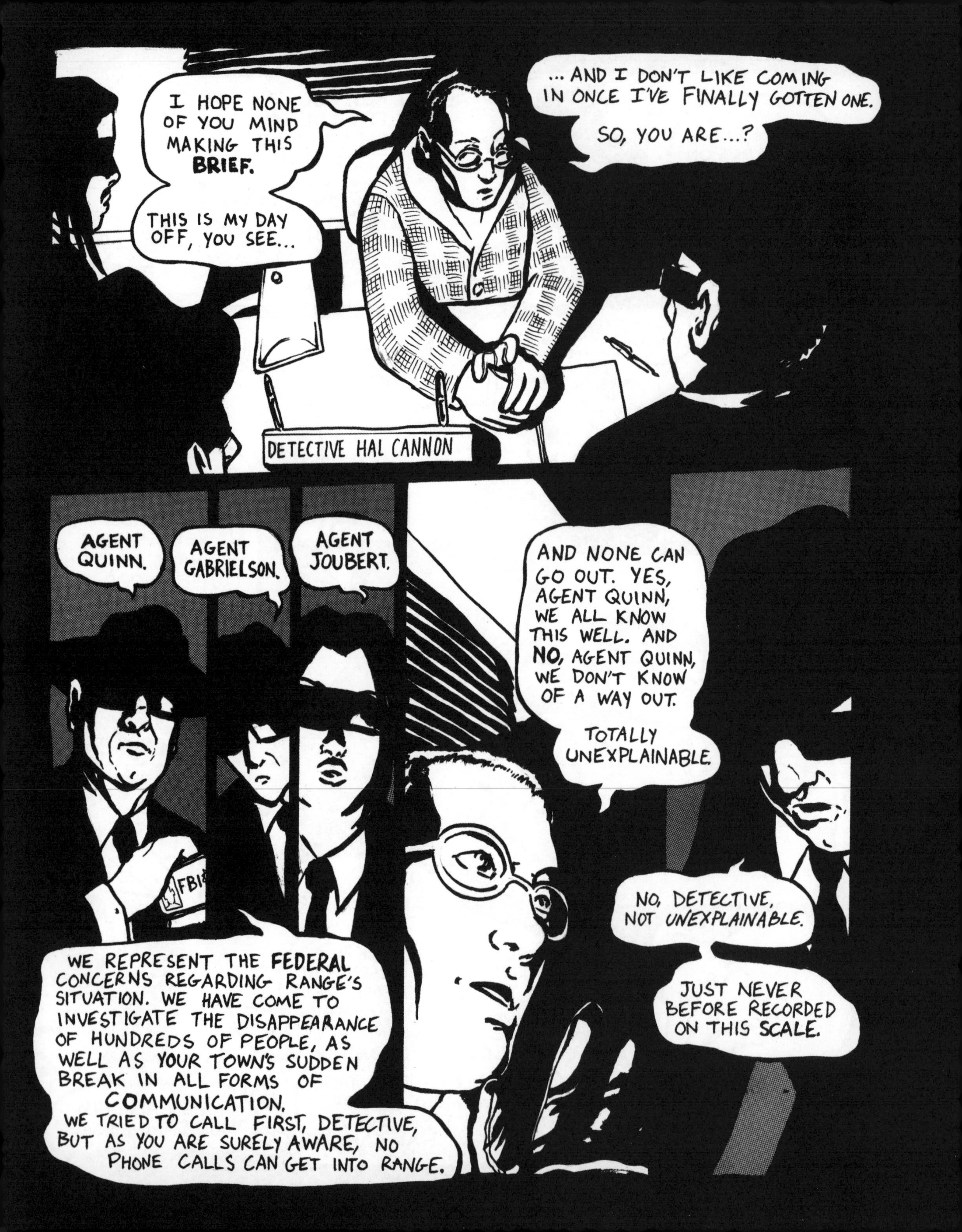
I HOPE NONE OF YOU MIND MAKING THIS **BRIEF.**
THIS IS MY DAY OFF, YOU SEE...
... AND I DON'T LIKE COMING IN ONCE I'VE FINALLY GOTTEN ONE.
SO, YOU ARE...?
DETECTIVE HAL CANNON
AGENT QUINN.
AGENT GABRIELSON.
AGENT JOUBERT.
WE REPRESENT THE **FEDERAL** CONCERNS REGARDING RANGE'S SITUATION. WE HAVE COME TO INVESTIGATE THE DISAPPEARANCE OF HUNDREDS OF PEOPLE, AS WELL AS YOUR TOWN'S SUDDEN BREAK IN ALL FORMS OF **COMMUNICATION.**
WE TRIED TO CALL FIRST, DETECTIVE, BUT AS YOU ARE SURELY AWARE, NO PHONE CALLS CAN GET INTO RANGE.
AND NONE CAN GO OUT. YES, AGENT QUINN, WE ALL KNOW THIS WELL. AND **NO,** AGENT QUINN, WE DON'T KNOW OF A WAY OUT.
TOTALLY UNEXPLAINABLE.
NO, DETECTIVE, NOT *UNEXPLAINABLE.*
JUST NEVER BEFORE RECORDED ON THIS **SCALE.**

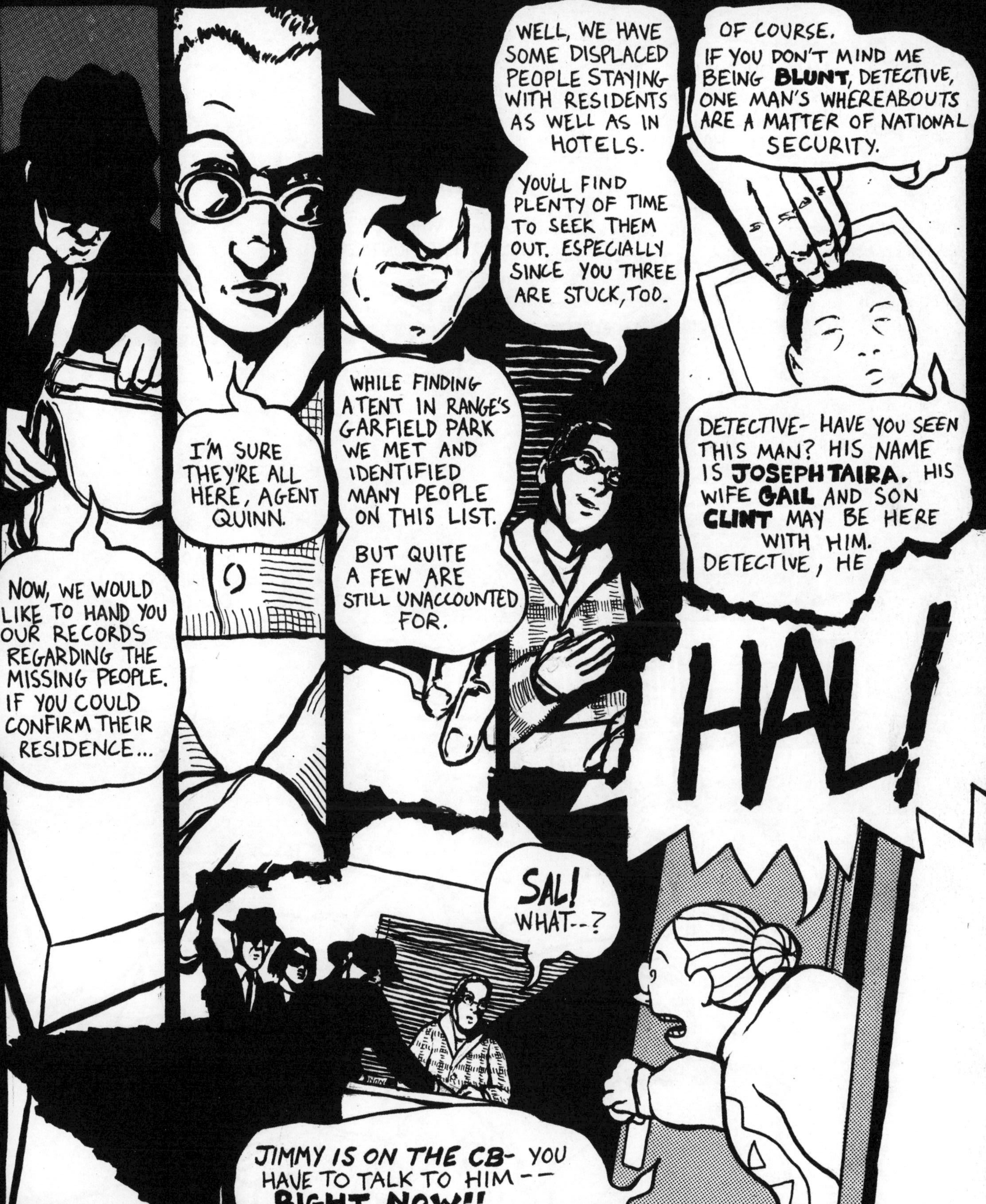
NOW, WE WOULD LIKE TO HAND YOU OUR RECORDS REGARDING THE MISSING PEOPLE. IF YOU COULD CONFIRM THEIR RESIDENCE...
I'M SURE THEY'RE ALL HERE, AGENT QUINN.
WHILE FINDING ATENT IN RANGE'S GARFIELD PARK WE MET AND IDENTIFIED MANY PEOPLE ON THIS LIST.
BUT QUITE A FEW ARE STILL UNACCOUNTED FOR.
WELL, WE HAVE SOME DISPLACED PEOPLE STAYING WITH RESIDENTS AS WELL AS IN HOTELS.
YOU'LL FIND PLENTY OF TIME TO SEEK THEM OUT. ESPECIALLY SINCE YOU THREE ARE STUCK, TOO.
OF COURSE.
IF YOU DON'T MIND ME BEING **BLUNT**, DETECTIVE, ONE MAN'S WHEREABOUTS ARE A MATTER OF NATIONAL SECURITY.
DETECTIVE- HAVE YOU SEEN THIS MAN? HIS NAME IS **JOSEPH TAIRA.** HIS WIFE **GAIL** AND SON **CLINT** MAY BE HERE WITH HIM.
DETECTIVE, HE
HAL!
SAL! WHAT--?
JIMMY IS ON THE CB- YOU HAVE TO TALK TO HIM -- **RIGHT NOW!!**

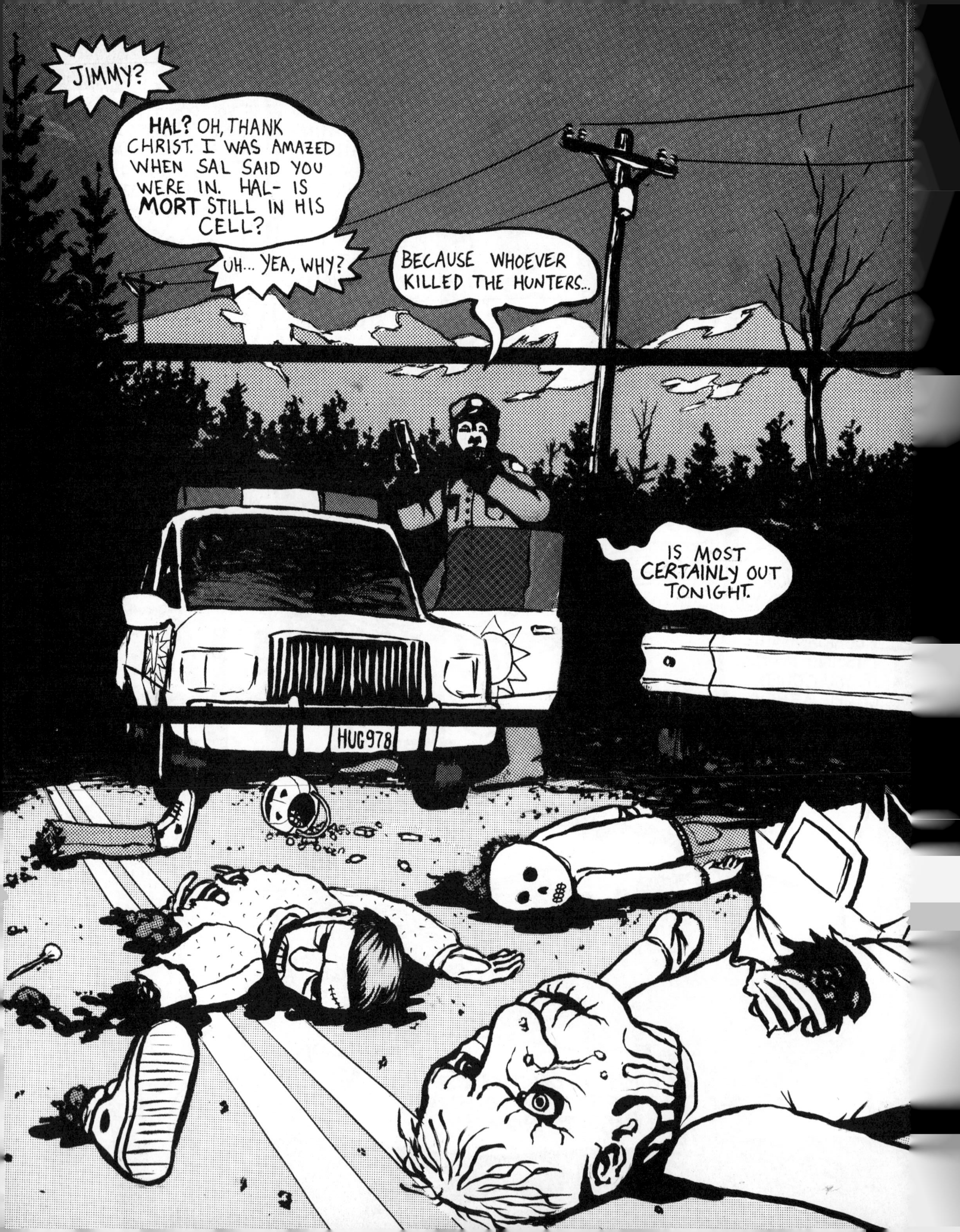
JIMMY?
HAL? OH, THANK CHRIST. I WAS AMAZED WHEN SAL SAID YOU WERE IN. HAL- IS MORT STILL IN HIS CELL?
UH... YEA, WHY?
BECAUSE WHOEVER KILLED THE HUNTERS...
IS MOST CERTAINLY OUT TONIGHT.
HUG978

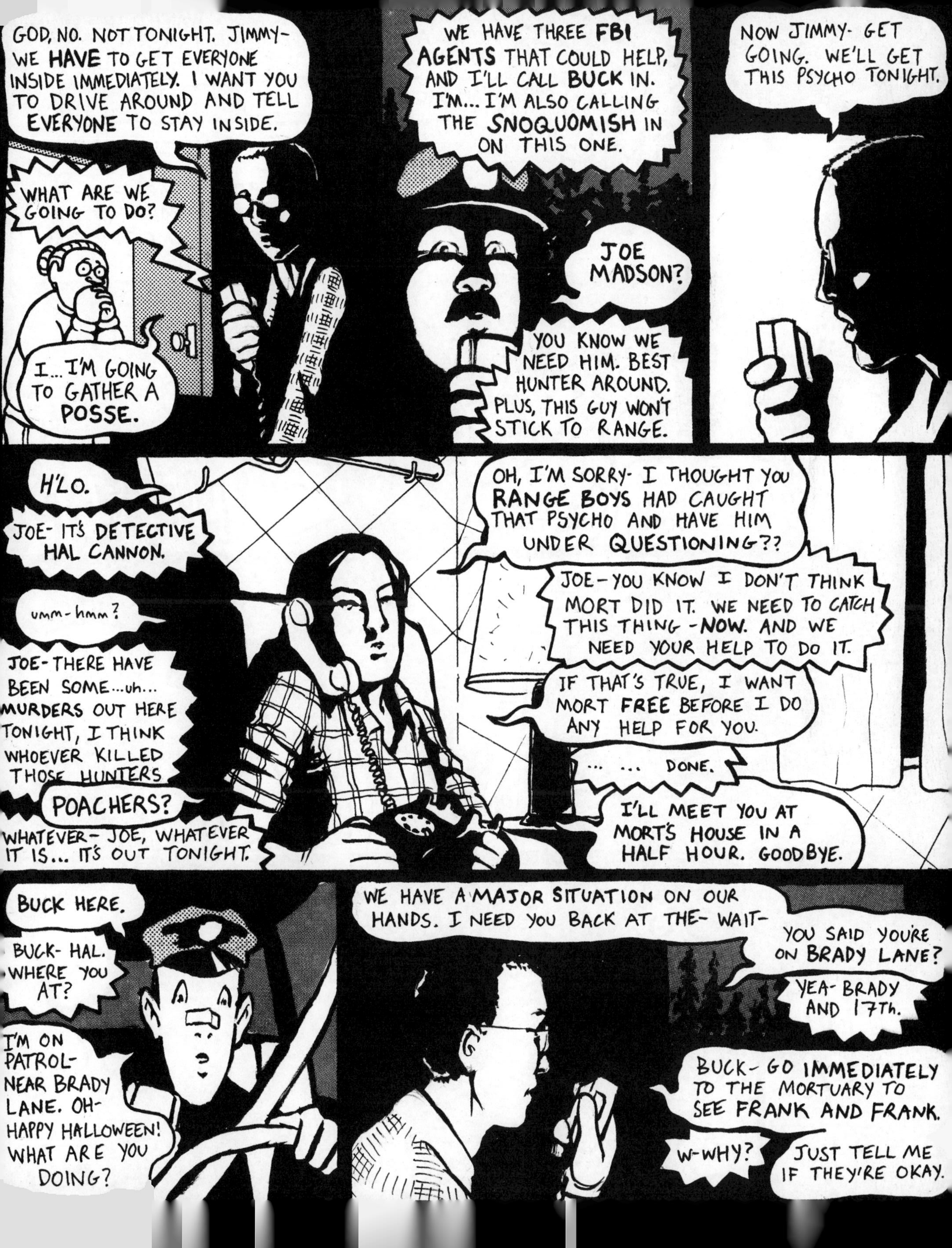
GOD, NO. NOT TONIGHT. JIMMY- WE HAVE TO GET EVERYONE INSIDE IMMEDIATELY. I WANT YOU TO DRIVE AROUND AND TELL EVERYONE TO STAY INSIDE.
WHAT ARE WE GOING TO DO?
I... I'M GOING TO GATHER A POSSE.
WE HAVE THREE FBI AGENTS THAT COULD HELP, AND I'LL CALL BUCK IN. I'M... I'M ALSO CALLING THE SNOQUOMISH IN ON THIS ONE.
JOE MADSON?
YOU KNOW WE NEED HIM. BEST HUNTER AROUND. PLUS, THIS GUY WON'T STICK TO RANGE.
NOW JIMMY- GET GOING. WE'LL GET THIS PSYCHO TONIGHT.
H'LO.
JOE- IT'S DETECTIVE HAL CANNON.
umm-hmm?
JOE- THERE HAVE BEEN SOME...uh... MURDERS OUT HERE TONIGHT, I THINK WHOEVER KILLED THOSE HUNTERS
POACHERS?
WHATEVER- JOE, WHATEVER IT IS... IT'S OUT TONIGHT.
OH, I'M SORRY- I THOUGHT YOU RANGE BOYS HAD CAUGHT THAT PSYCHO AND HAVE HIM UNDER QUESTIONING??
JOE- YOU KNOW I DON'T THINK MORT DID IT. WE NEED TO CATCH THIS THING- NOW. AND WE NEED YOUR HELP TO DO IT.
IF THAT'S TRUE, I WANT MORT FREE BEFORE I DO ANY HELP FOR YOU.
... ... DONE.
I'LL MEET YOU AT MORT'S HOUSE IN A HALF HOUR. GOODBYE.
BUCK HERE.
BUCK- HAL. WHERE YOU AT?
I'M ON PATROL- NEAR BRADY LANE. OH- HAPPY HALLOWEEN! WHAT ARE YOU DOING?
WE HAVE A MAJOR SITUATION ON OUR HANDS. I NEED YOU BACK AT THE- WAIT-
YOU SAID YOU'RE ON BRADY LANE?
YEA- BRADY AND 17th.
BUCK- GO IMMEDIATELY TO THE MORTUARY TO SEE FRANK AND FRANK.
W-WHY?
JUST TELL ME IF THEY'RE OKAY.

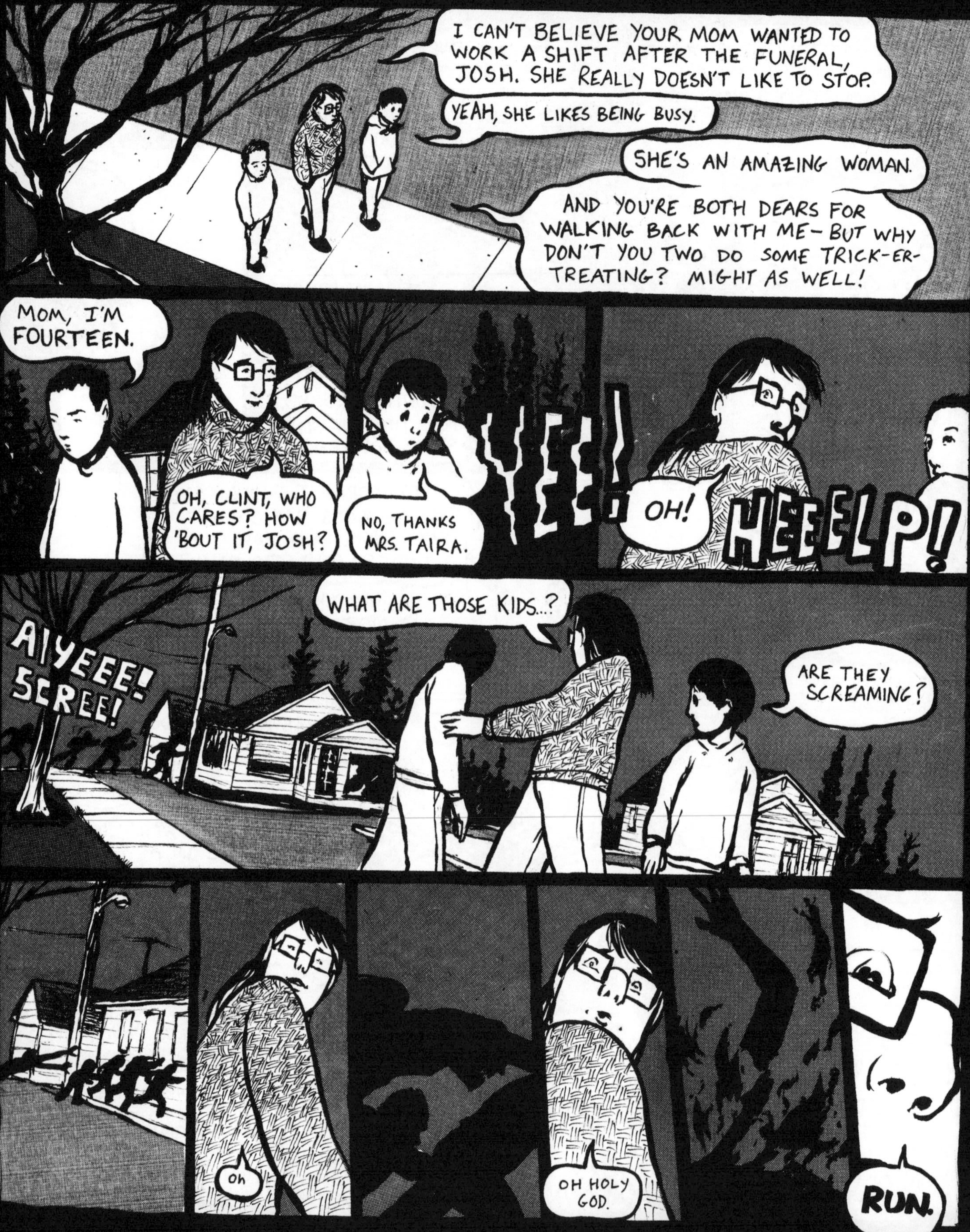
I CAN'T BELIEVE YOUR MOM WANTED TO WORK A SHIFT AFTER THE FUNERAL, JOSH. SHE REALLY DOESN'T LIKE TO STOP.
YEAH, SHE LIKES BEING BUSY.
SHE'S AN AMAZING WOMAN.
AND YOU'RE BOTH DEARS FOR WALKING BACK WITH ME— BUT WHY DON'T YOU TWO DO SOME TRICK-ER-TREATING? MIGHT AS WELL!
MOM, I'M FOURTEEN.
OH, CLINT, WHO CARES? HOW 'BOUT IT, JOSH?
NO, THANKS MRS. TAIRA.
YEE!
OH!
HEEELP!
AIYEEE! SCREE!
WHAT ARE THOSE KIDS...?
ARE THEY SCREAMING?
Oh
OH HOLY GOD.
RUN.

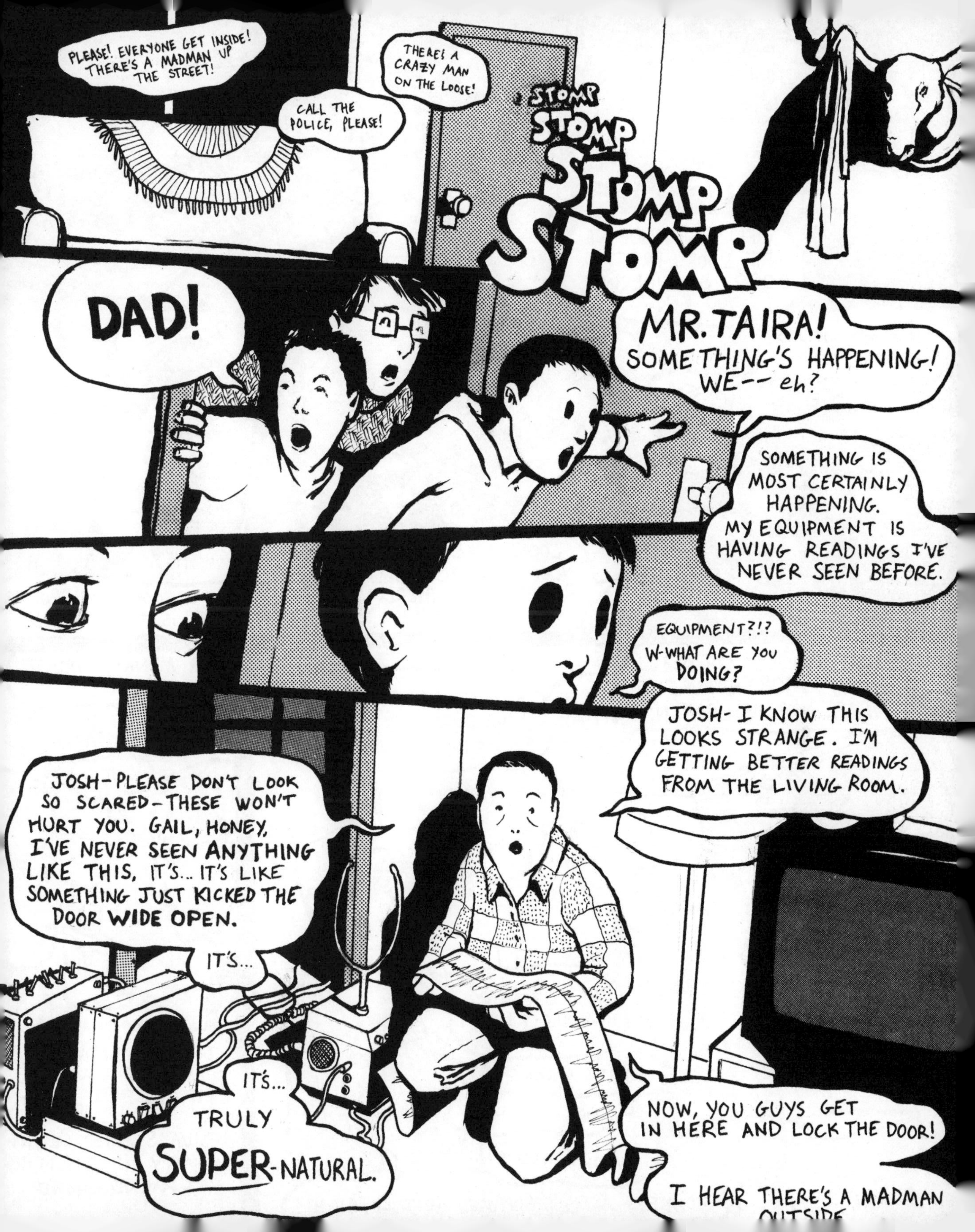
PLEASE! EVERYONE GET INSIDE! THERE'S A MADMAN UP THE STREET!
CALL THE POLICE, PLEASE!
THERE'S A CRAZY MAN ON THE LOOSE!
STOMP
STOMP
STOMP
STOMP
DAD!
MR. TAIRA! SOMETHING'S HAPPENING! WE-- eh?
SOMETHING IS MOST CERTAINLY HAPPENING. MY EQUIPMENT IS HAVING READINGS I'VE NEVER SEEN BEFORE.
EQUIPMENT?!? W-WHAT ARE YOU DOING?
JOSH- I KNOW THIS LOOKS STRANGE. I'M GETTING BETTER READINGS FROM THE LIVING ROOM.
JOSH- PLEASE DON'T LOOK SO SCARED- THESE WON'T HURT YOU. GAIL, HONEY, I'VE NEVER SEEN ANYTHING LIKE THIS, IT'S... IT'S LIKE SOMETHING JUST KICKED THE DOOR WIDE OPEN.
IT'S...
IT'S... TRULY SUPER-NATURAL.
NOW, YOU GUYS GET IN HERE AND LOCK THE DOOR!
I HEAR THERE'S A MADMAN

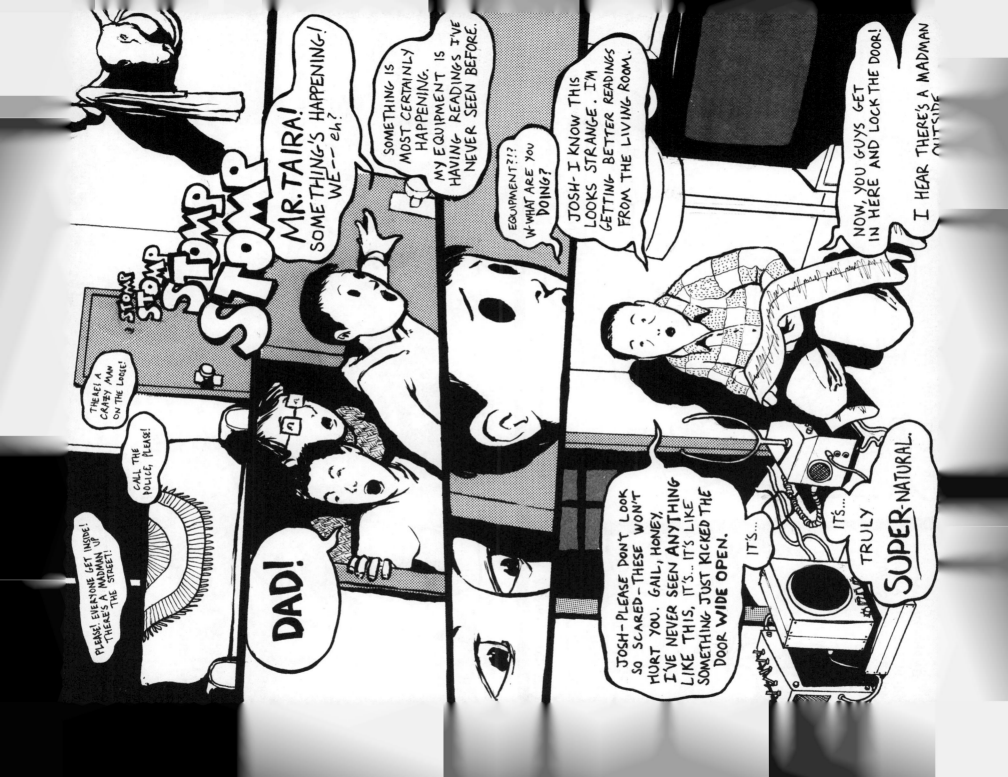

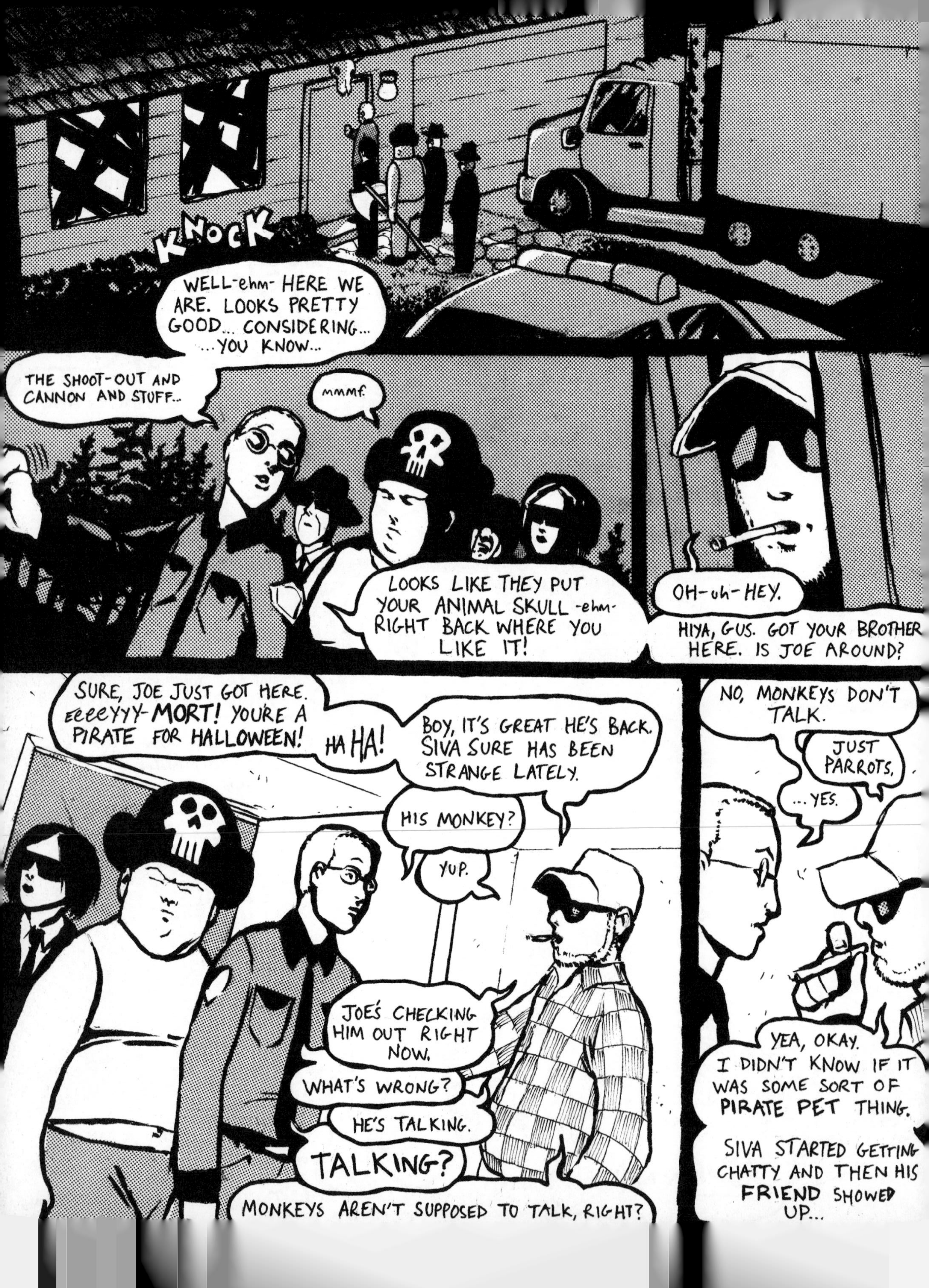
KNOCK
WELL-ehm- HERE WE ARE. LOOKS PRETTY GOOD... CONSIDERING... ...YOU KNOW...
THE SHOOT-OUT AND CANNON AND STUFF...
mmmf.
LOOKS LIKE THEY PUT YOUR ANIMAL SKULL -ehm- RIGHT BACK WHERE YOU LIKE IT!
OH-uh-HEY.
HIYA, GUS. GOT YOUR BROTHER HERE. IS JOE AROUND?
SURE, JOE JUST GOT HERE. EEEEYYY-MORT! YOU'RE A PIRATE FOR HALLOWEEN!
HA HA!
BOY, IT'S GREAT HE'S BACK. SIVA SURE HAS BEEN STRANGE LATELY.
HIS MONKEY?
YUP.
JOE'S CHECKING HIM OUT RIGHT NOW.
WHAT'S WRONG?
HE'S TALKING.
TALKING?
MONKEYS AREN'T SUPPOSED TO TALK, RIGHT?
NO, MONKEYS DON'T TALK.
JUST PARROTS,
...YES.
YEA, OKAY. I DIDN'T KNOW IF IT WAS SOME SORT OF PIRATE PET THING.
SIVA STARTED GETTING CHATTY AND THEN HIS FRIEND SHOWED UP...

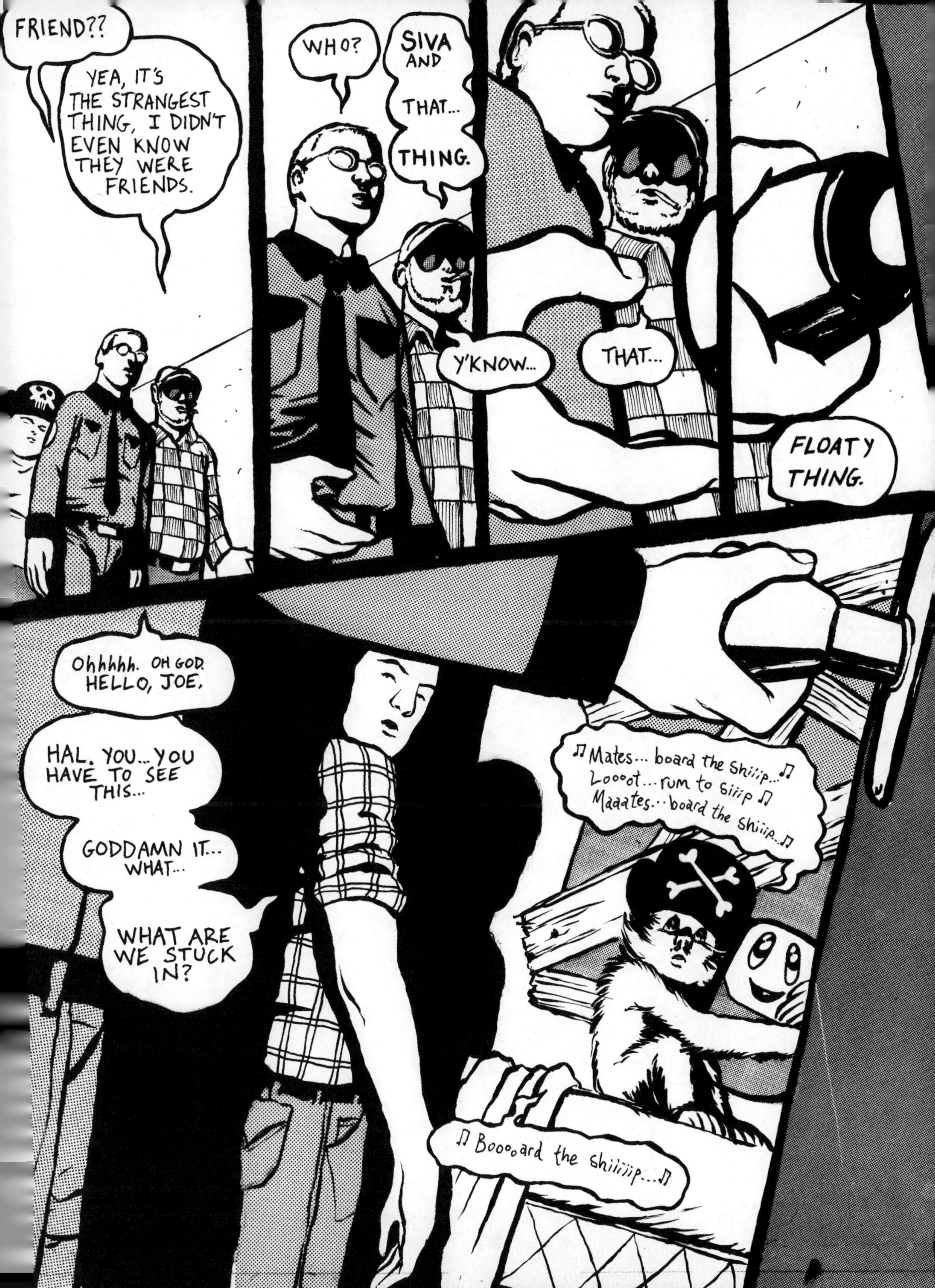

FRIEND??
YEA, IT'S THE STRANGEST THING, I DIDN'T EVEN KNOW THEY WERE FRIENDS.
WHO?
SIVA AND THAT... THING.
Y'KNOW...
THAT...
FLOATY THING.
Ohhhhh. OH GOD. HELLO, JOE.
HAL. YOU... YOU HAVE TO SEE THIS...
GODDAMN IT... WHAT...
WHAT ARE WE STUCK IN?
♫ Mates... board the shiiip... ♫ Loooot... rum to siiip ♫ Maaates... board the shiiip... ♫
♫ Booooard the shiiiiip... ♫

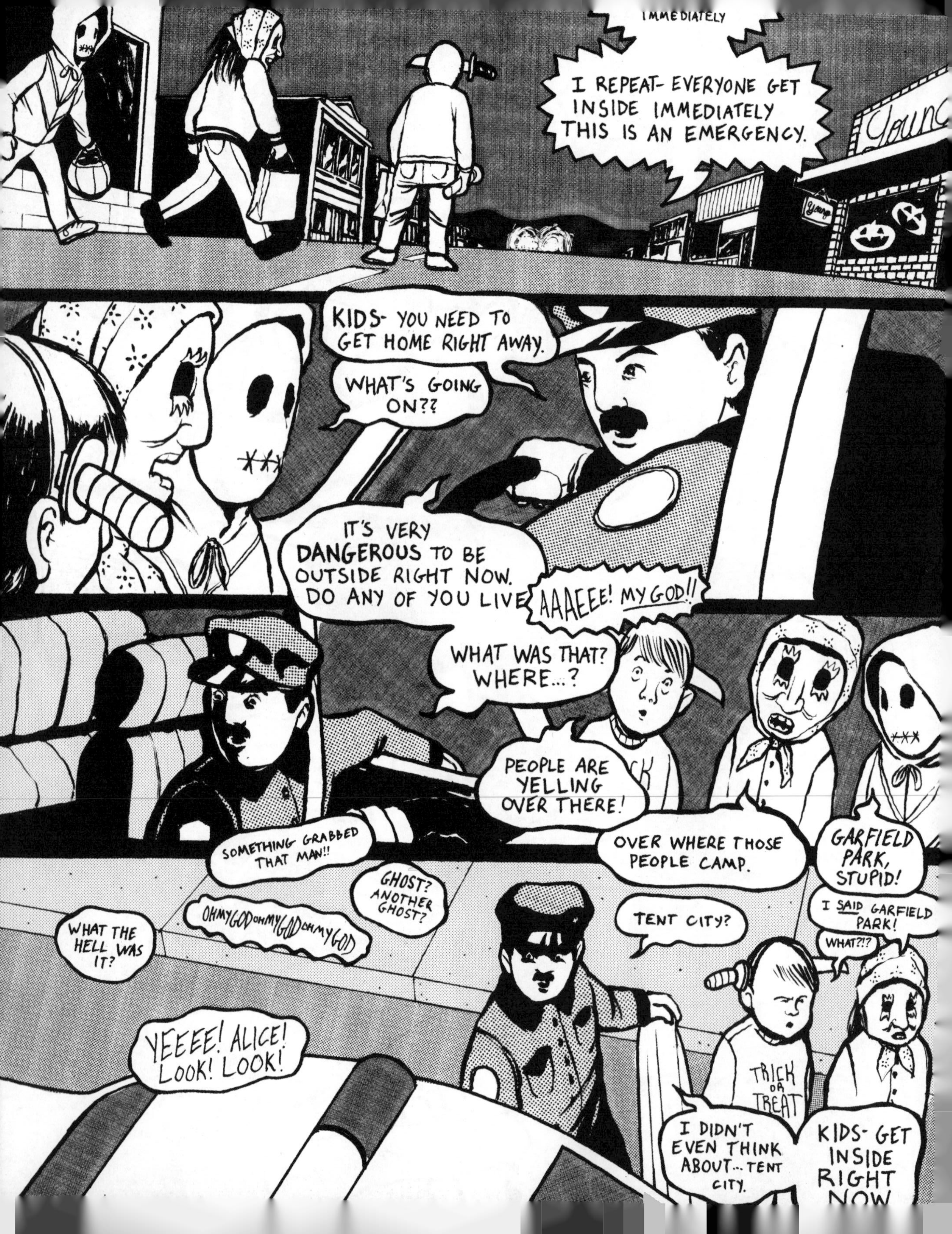

IMMEDIATELY
I REPEAT- EVERYONE GET INSIDE IMMEDIATELY THIS IS AN EMERGENCY.
KIDS- YOU NEED TO GET HOME RIGHT AWAY.
WHAT'S GOING ON??
IT'S VERY DANGEROUS TO BE OUTSIDE RIGHT NOW. DO ANY OF YOU LIVE
AAAEEE! MY GOD!!
WHAT WAS THAT? WHERE...?
PEOPLE ARE YELLING OVER THERE!
SOMETHING GRABBED THAT MAN!!
OVER WHERE THOSE PEOPLE CAMP.
GARFIELD PARK, STUPID!
GHOST? ANOTHER GHOST?
OHMYGODOHMYGODOHMYGOD
WHAT THE HELL WAS IT?
TENT CITY?
I SAID GARFIELD PARK!
WHAT?!?
YEEEE! ALICE! LOOK! LOOK!
TRICK OR TREAT
I DIDN'T EVEN THINK ABOUT... TENT CITY.
KIDS- GET INSIDE RIGHT NOW

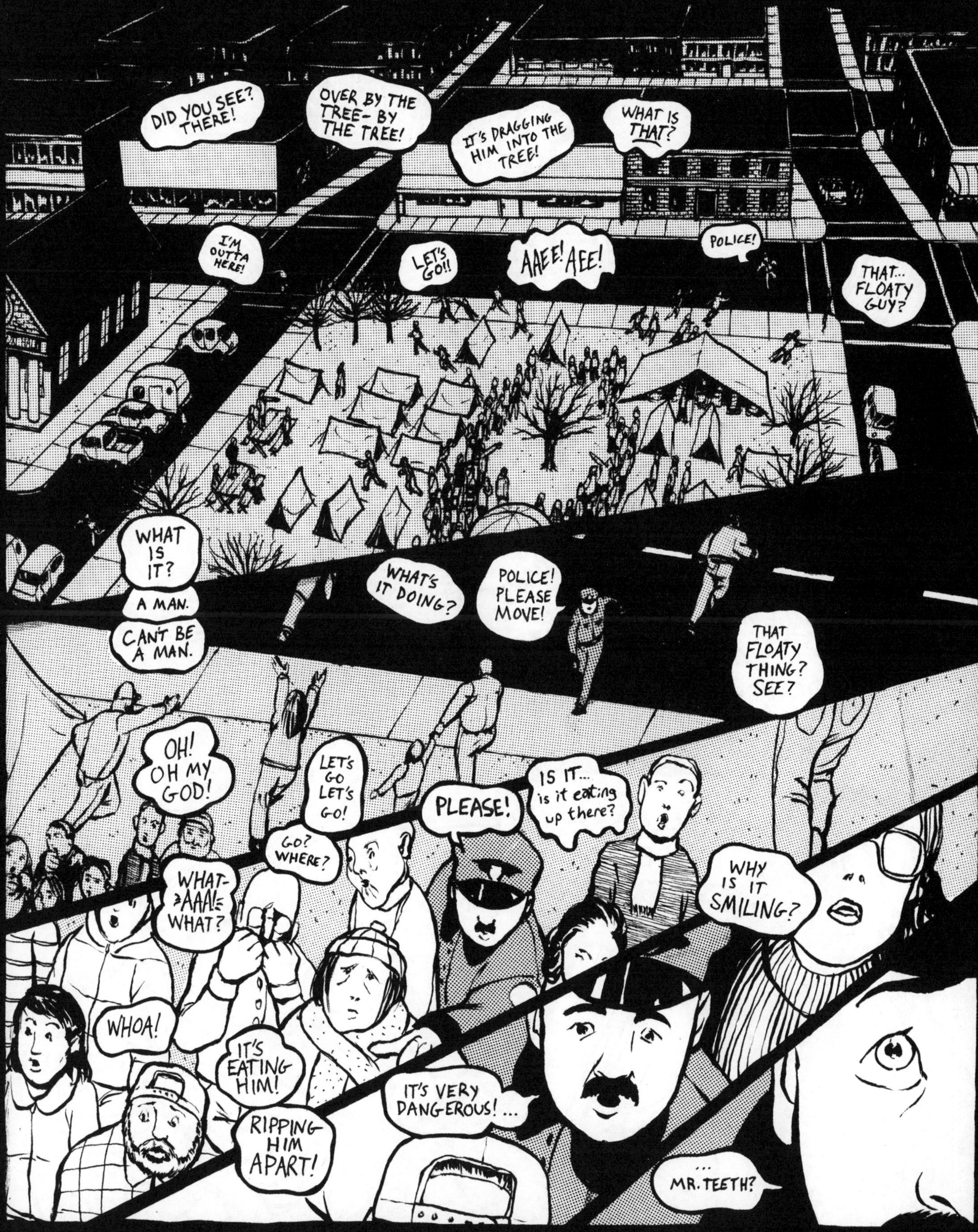
DID YOU SEE? THERE!
OVER BY THE TREE- BY THE TREE!
IT'S DRAGGING HIM INTO THE TREE!
WHAT IS THAT?
I'M OUTTA HERE!
LET'S GO!!
AAEE! AEE!
POLICE!
THAT... FLOATY GUY?
WHAT IS IT?
A MAN.
CAN'T BE A MAN.
WHAT'S IT DOING?
POLICE! PLEASE MOVE!
THAT FLOATY THING? SEE?
OH! OH MY GOD!
LET'S GO LET'S GO!
PLEASE!
IS IT... is it eating up there?
GO? WHERE?
WHAT- AAA! WHAT?
WHY IS IT SMILING?
WHOA!
IT'S EATING HIM!
RIPPING HIM APART!
IT'S VERY DANGEROUS! ...
... MR. TEETH?

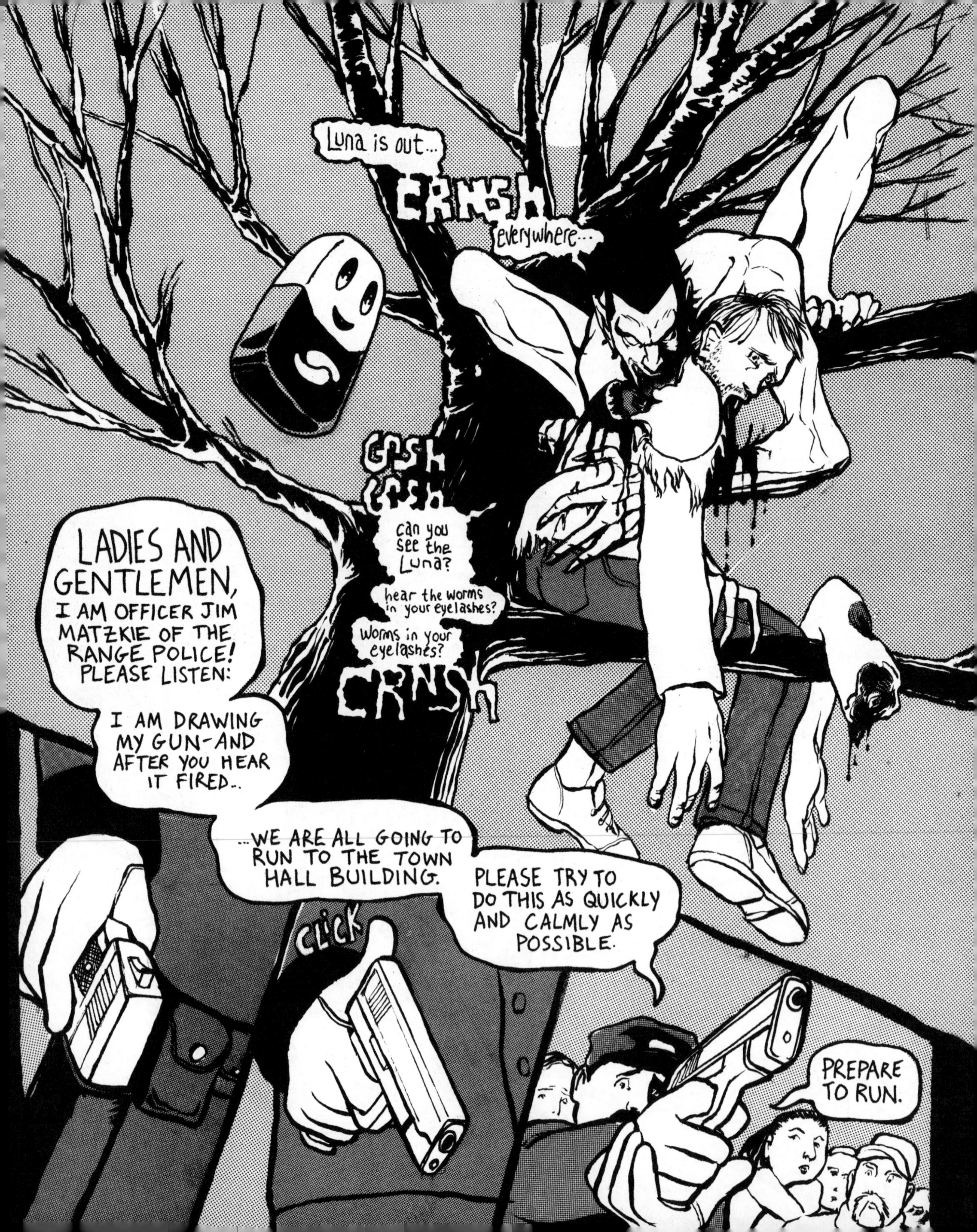
Luna is out...
CRNSH
everywhere...
GSH
GSH
can you see the Luna?
hear the worms in your eyelashes?
Worms in your eyelashes?
CRNSH
LADIES AND GENTLEMEN, I AM OFFICER JIM MATZKIE OF THE RANGE POLICE! PLEASE LISTEN:
I AM DRAWING MY GUN-AND AFTER YOU HEAR IT FIRED..
...WE ARE ALL GOING TO RUN TO THE TOWN HALL BUILDING.
PLEASE TRY TO DO THIS AS QUICKLY AND CALMLY AS POSSIBLE.
CLICK
PREPARE TO RUN.

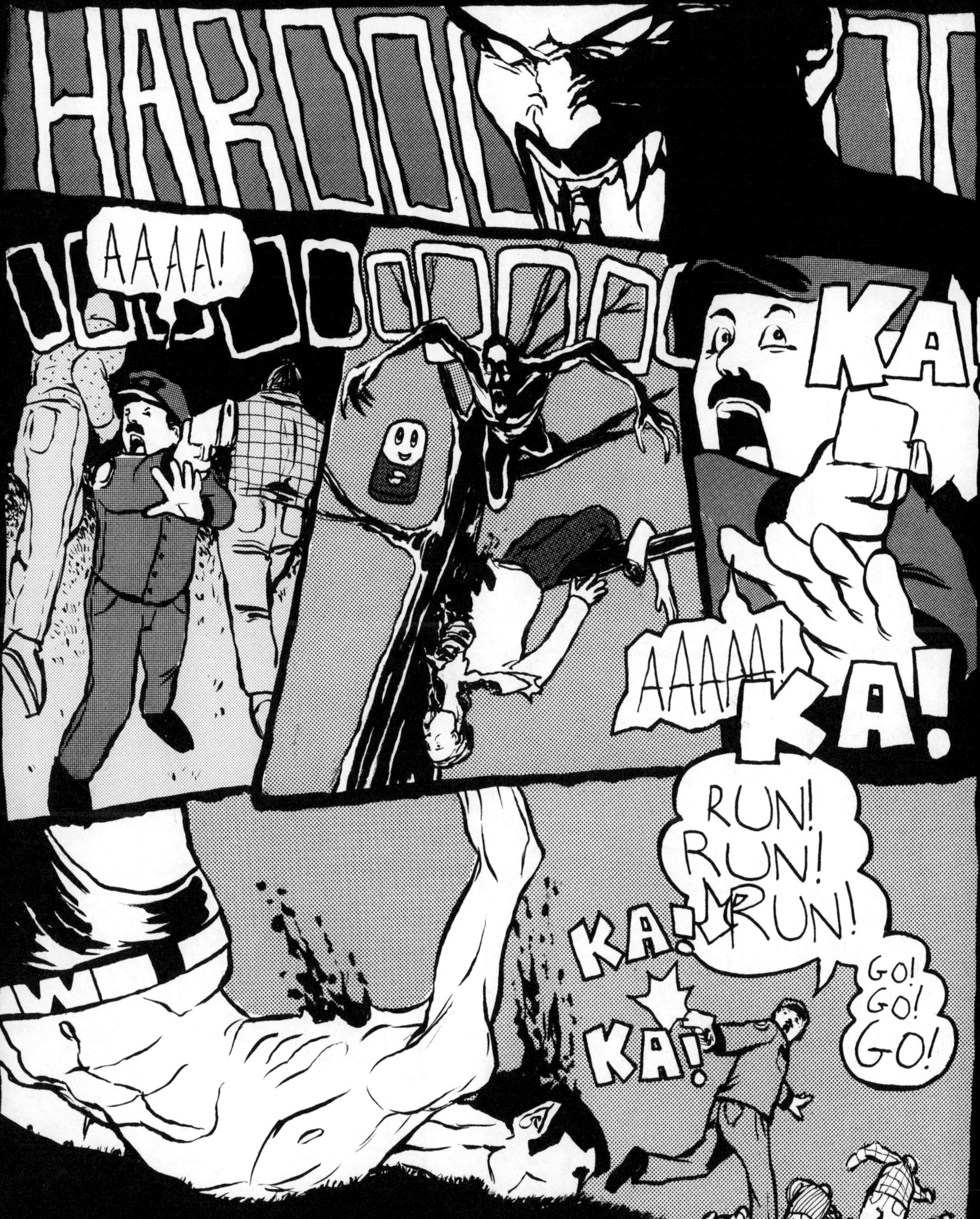
HAROOOOOOOOOOOO
AAAA!
KA!
AAAAA!
KA!
RUN! RUN! RUN!
KA!
KA!
GO! GO! GO!

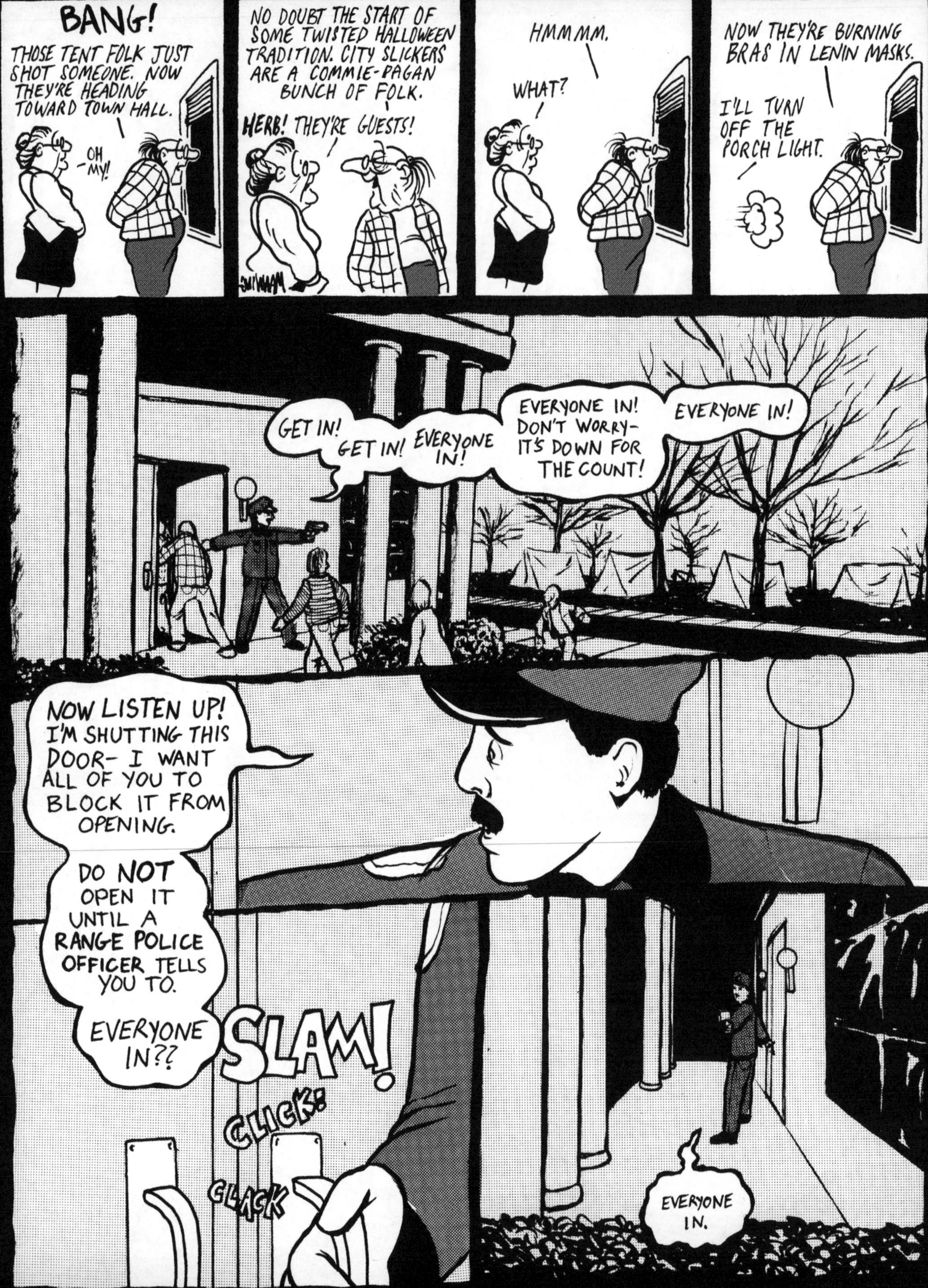

BANG!
THOSE TENT FOLK JUST SHOT SOMEONE. NOW THEY'RE HEADING TOWARD TOWN HALL.
OH -MY!
NO DOUBT THE START OF SOME TWISTED HALLOWEEN TRADITION. CITY SLICKERS ARE A COMMIE-PAGAN BUNCH OF FOLK.
HERB! THEY'RE GUESTS!
HMMMM.
WHAT?
NOW THEY'RE BURNING BRAS IN LENIN MASKS.
I'LL TURN OFF THE PORCH LIGHT.
GET IN!
GET IN! EVERYONE IN!
EVERYONE IN! DON'T WORRY- IT'S DOWN FOR THE COUNT!
EVERYONE IN!
NOW LISTEN UP! I'M SHUTTING THIS DOOR- I WANT ALL OF YOU TO BLOCK IT FROM OPENING.
DO NOT OPEN IT UNTIL A RANGE POLICE OFFICER TELLS YOU TO.
EVERYONE IN??
SLAM!
CLICK!
GLACK
EVERYONE IN.

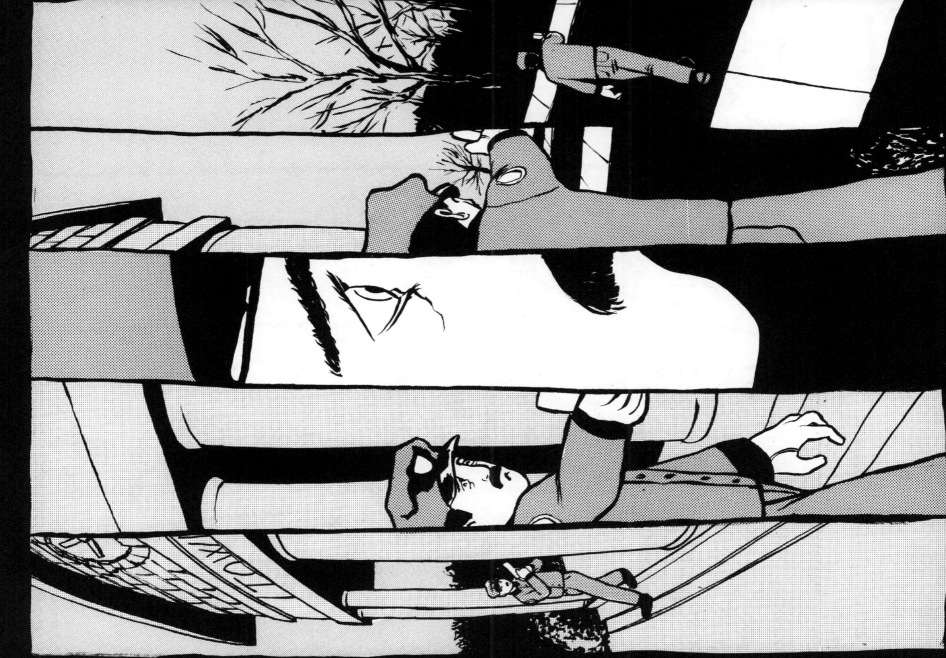

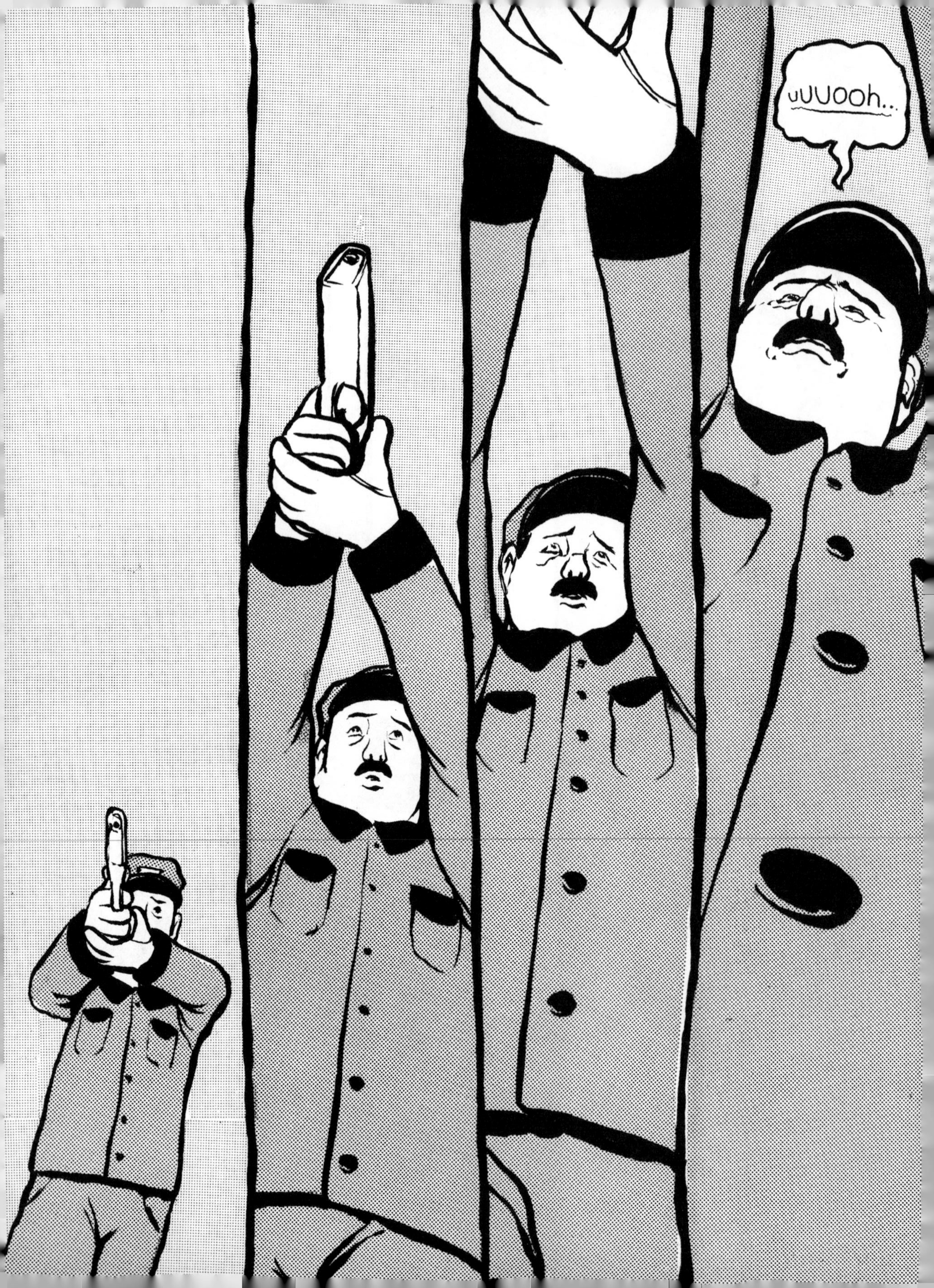
uUUOOh...

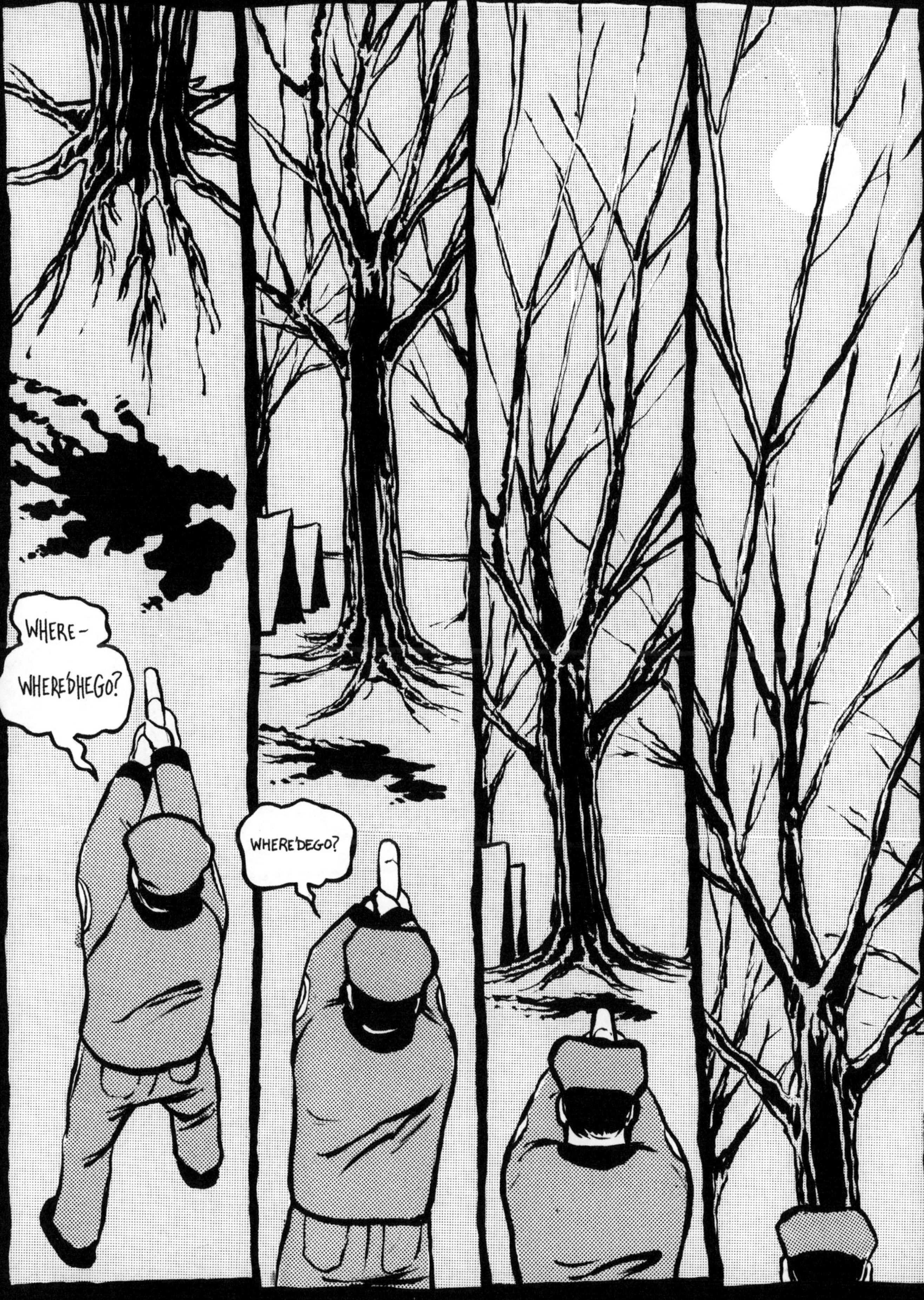
WHERE-
WHERE'D HE GO?
WHERE'D E GO?

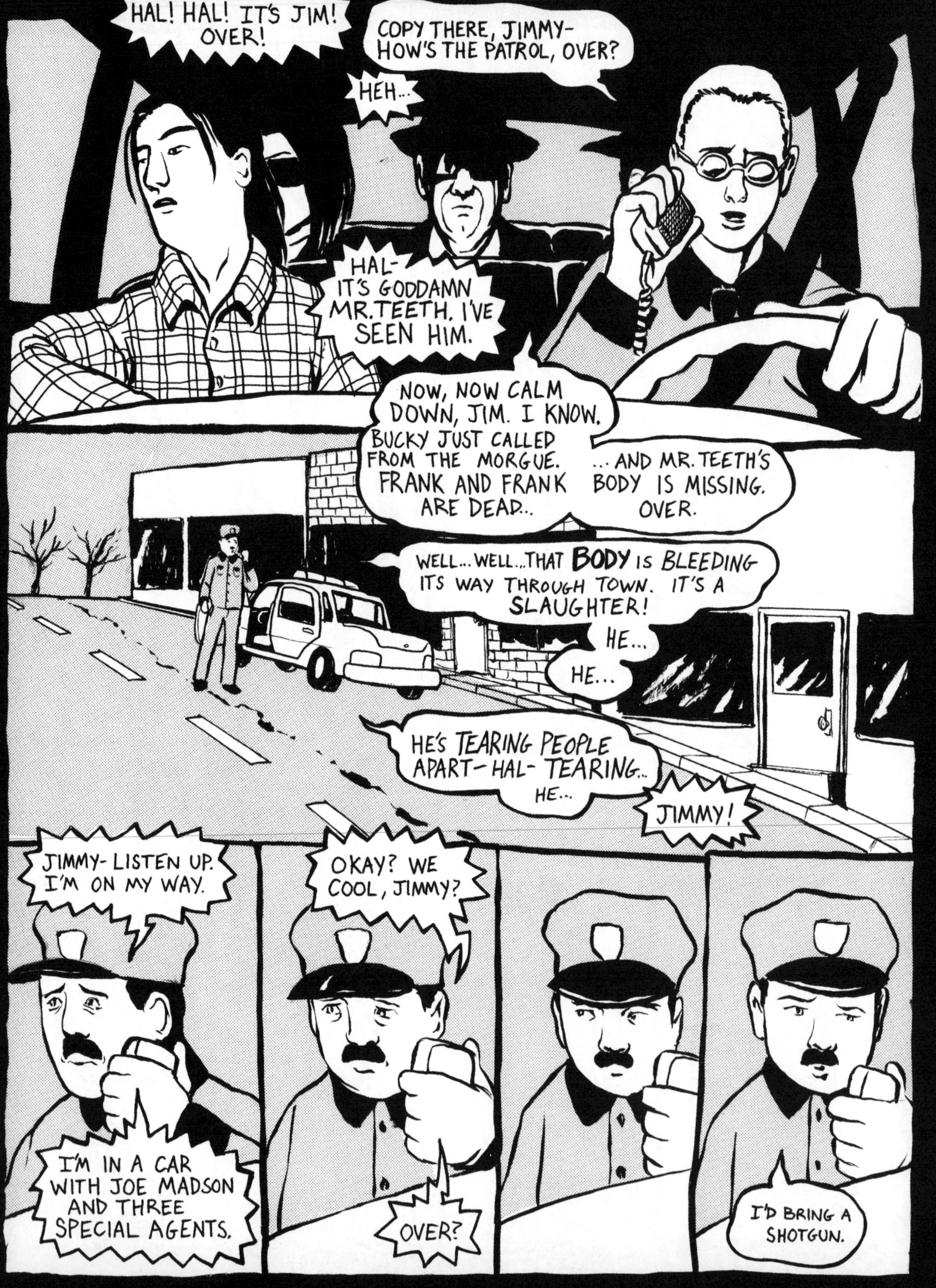
HAL! HAL! IT'S JIM! OVER!
COPY THERE, JIMMY- HOW'S THE PATROL, OVER?
HEH...
HAL- IT'S GODDAMN MR. TEETH. I'VE SEEN HIM.
NOW, NOW CALM DOWN, JIM. I KNOW. BUCKY JUST CALLED FROM THE MORGUE. FRANK AND FRANK ARE DEAD...
...AND MR. TEETH'S BODY IS MISSING. OVER.
WELL... WELL... THAT BODY IS BLEEDING ITS WAY THROUGH TOWN. IT'S A SLAUGHTER!
HE...
HE...
HE'S TEARING PEOPLE APART- HAL- TEARING... HE...
JIMMY!
JIMMY- LISTEN UP. I'M ON MY WAY.
I'M IN A CAR WITH JOE MADSON AND THREE SPECIAL AGENTS.
OKAY? WE COOL, JIMMY?
OVER?
I'D BRING A SHOTGUN.

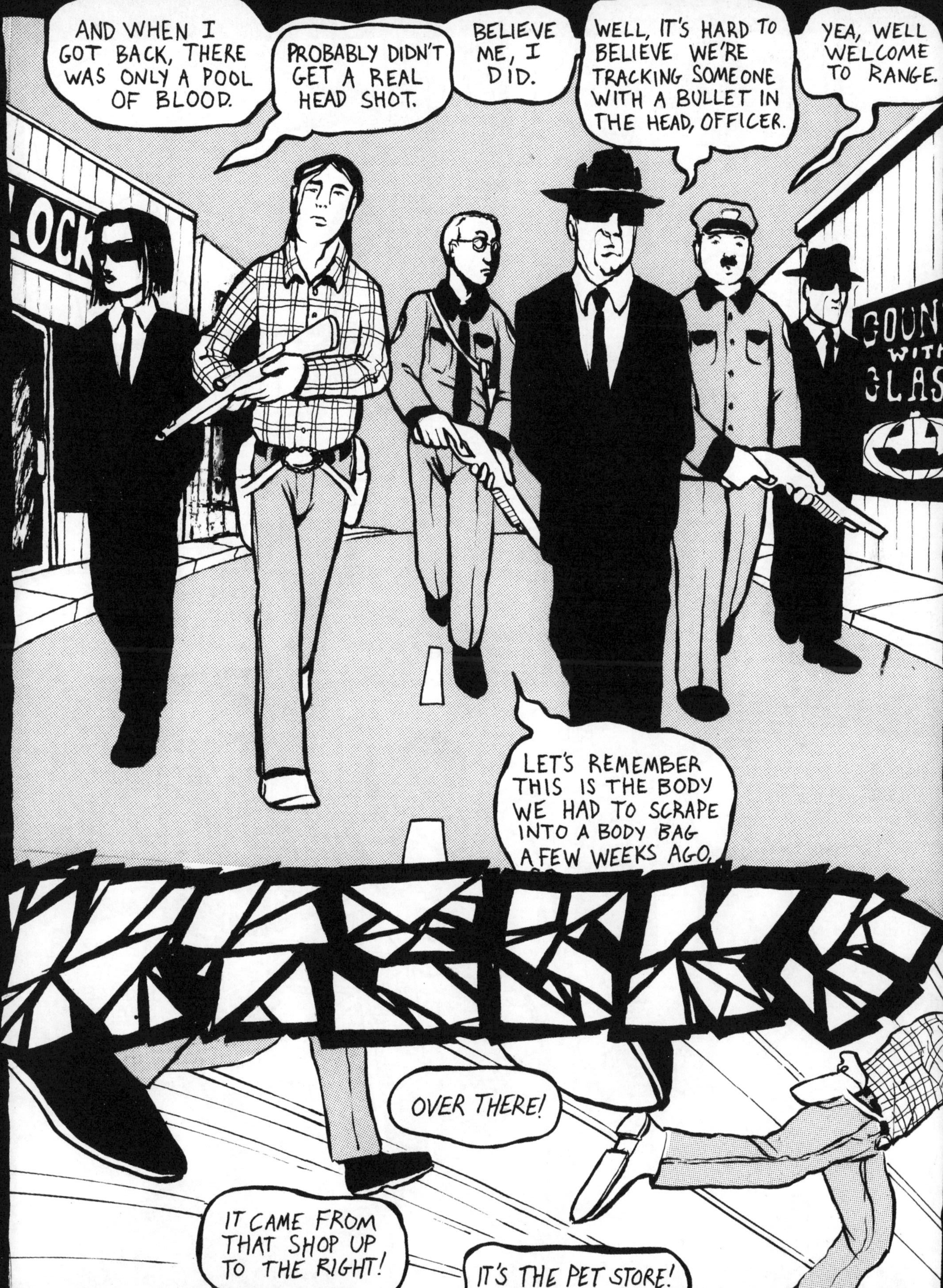
AND WHEN I GOT BACK, THERE WAS ONLY A POOL OF BLOOD.
PROBABLY DIDN'T GET A REAL HEAD SHOT.
BELIEVE ME, I DID.
WELL, IT'S HARD TO BELIEVE WE'RE TRACKING SOMEONE WITH A BULLET IN THE HEAD, OFFICER.
YEA, WELL WELCOME TO RANGE.
LET'S REMEMBER THIS IS THE BODY WE HAD TO SCRAPE INTO A BODY BAG A FEW WEEKS AGO,
OVER THERE!
IT CAME FROM THAT SHOP UP TO THE RIGHT!
IT'S THE PET STORE! THE PET STORE!

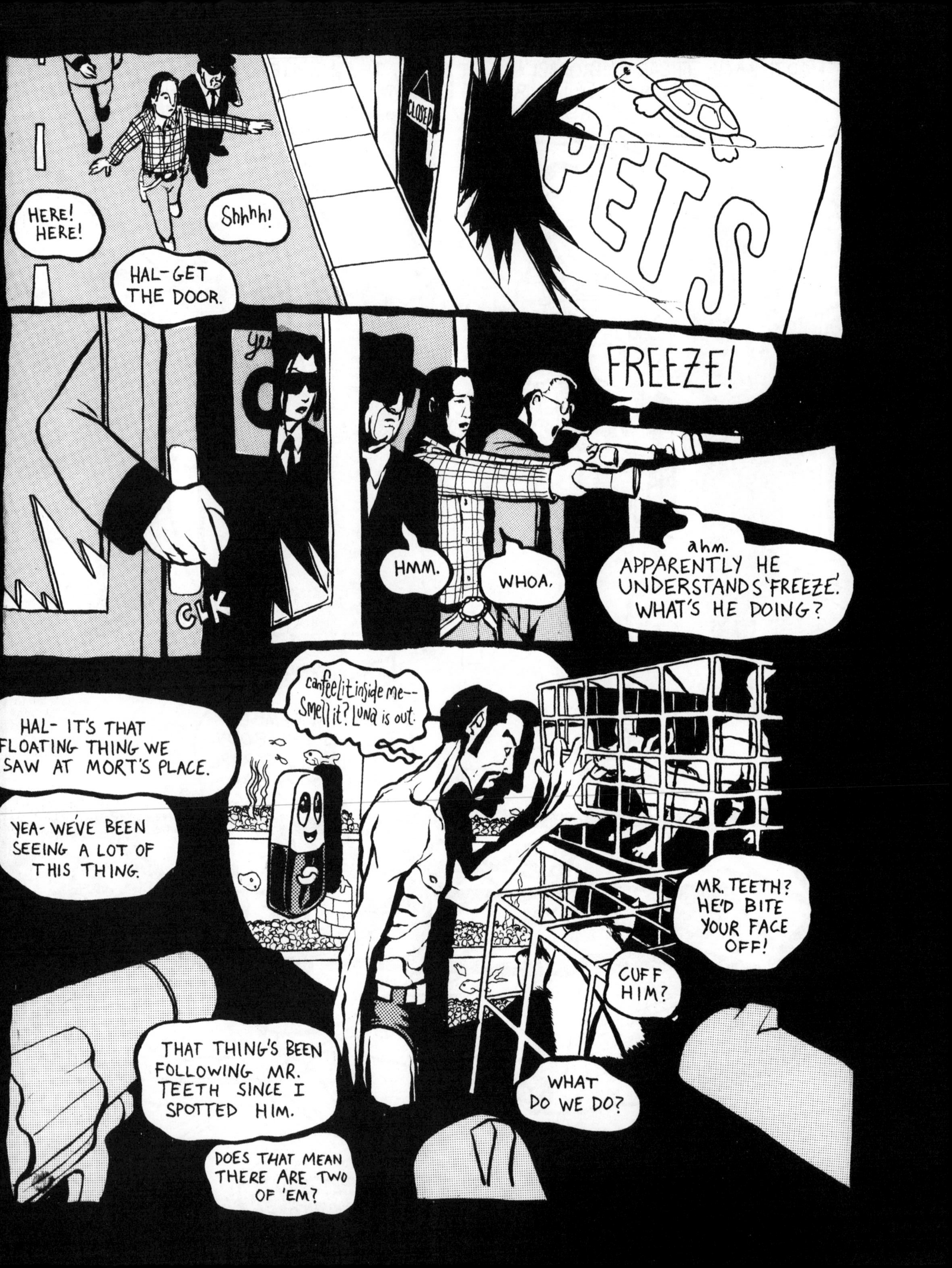
HERE! HERE!
Shhhh!
HAL-GET THE DOOR.
CLOSED
PETS
CLK
FREEZE!
HMM.
WHOA.
ahm. APPARENTLY HE UNDERSTANDS 'FREEZE'. WHAT'S HE DOING?
HAL- IT'S THAT FLOATING THING WE SAW AT MORT'S PLACE.
YEA- WE'VE BEEN SEEING A LOT OF THIS THING.
canfeel it inside me-- Smell it? Luna is out.
MR. TEETH? HE'D BITE YOUR FACE OFF!
CUFF HIM?
THAT THING'S BEEN FOLLOWING MR. TEETH SINCE I SPOTTED HIM.
WHAT DO WE DO?
DOES THAT MEAN THERE ARE TWO OF 'EM?

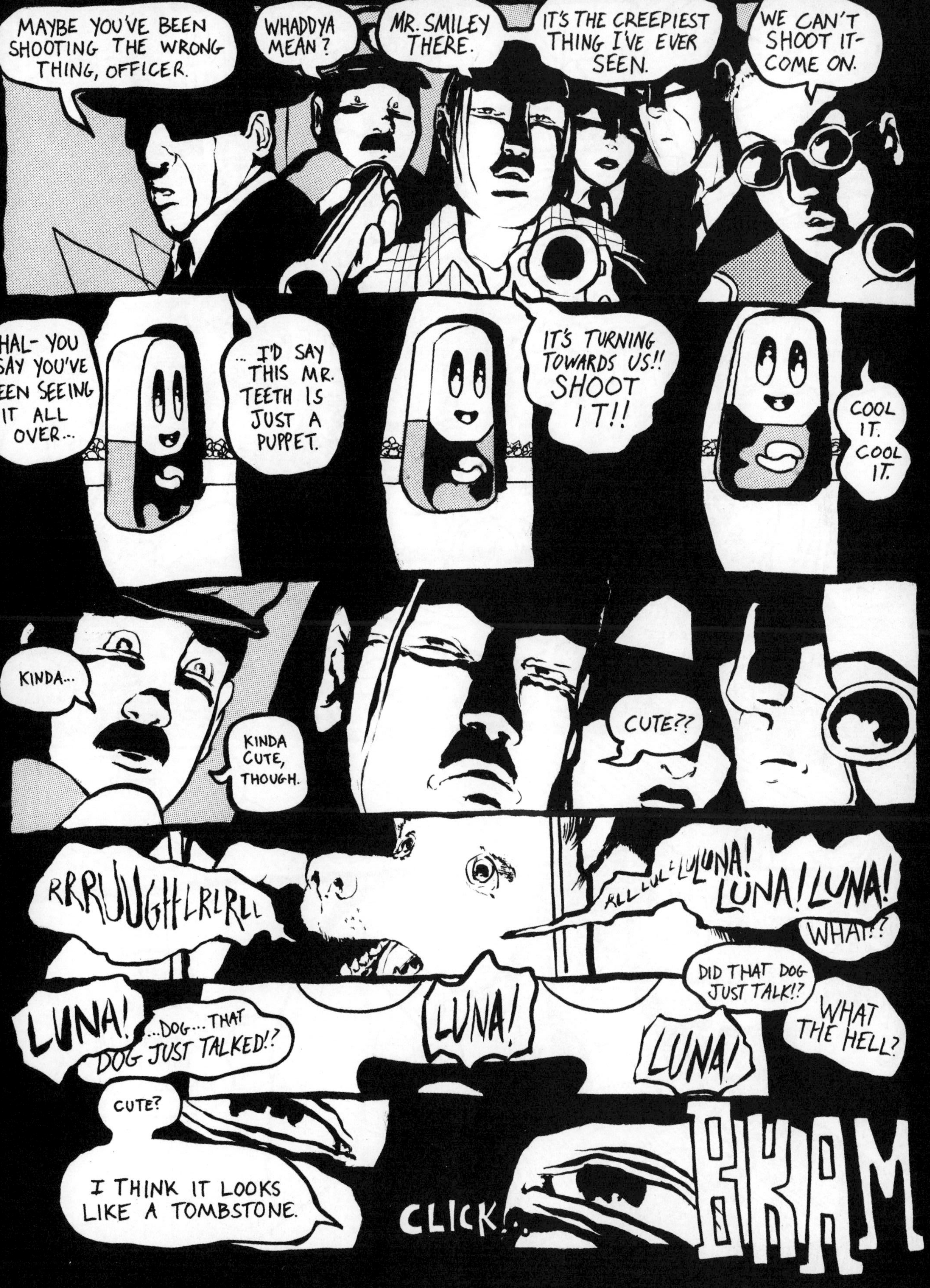
MAYBE YOU'VE BEEN SHOOTING THE WRONG THING, OFFICER.
WHADDYA MEAN?
MR. SMILEY THERE.
IT'S THE CREEPIEST THING I'VE EVER SEEN.
WE CAN'T SHOOT IT- COME ON.
HAL- YOU SAY YOU'VE BEEN SEEING IT ALL OVER...
...I'D SAY THIS MR. TEETH IS JUST A PUPPET.
IT'S TURNING TOWARDS US!! SHOOT IT!!
COOL IT. COOL IT.
KINDA...
KINDA CUTE, THOUGH.
CUTE??
RRRRUUGHLRLRLL
ALL LUL LULUNA! LUNA! LUNA!
WHAT!?
LUNA!
...DOG... THAT DOG JUST TALKED!?
LUNA!
DID THAT DOG JUST TALK!?
LUNA!
WHAT THE HELL?
CUTE?
I THINK IT LOOKS LIKE A TOMBSTONE.
CLICK...
BKAM

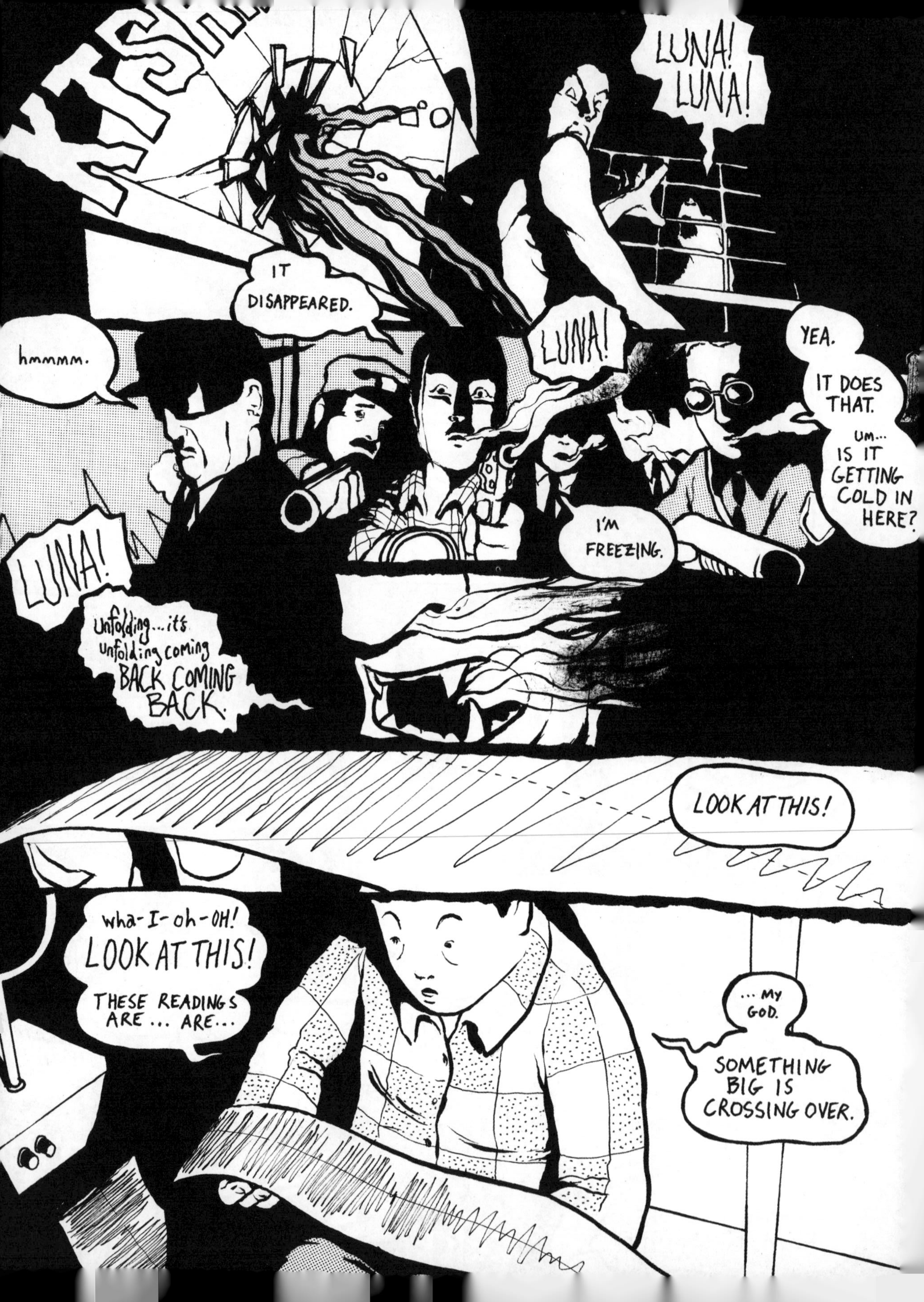
LUNA! LUNA!
IT DISAPPEARED.
hmmmm.
LUNA!
YEA.
IT DOES THAT.
UM... IS IT GETTING COLD IN HERE?
I'M FREEZING.
LUNA!
unfolding...its unfolding coming BACK COMING BACK.
LOOK AT THIS!
wha-I-oh-OH! LOOK AT THIS!
THESE READINGS ARE... ARE...
...MY GOD.
SOMETHING BIG IS CROSSING OVER.

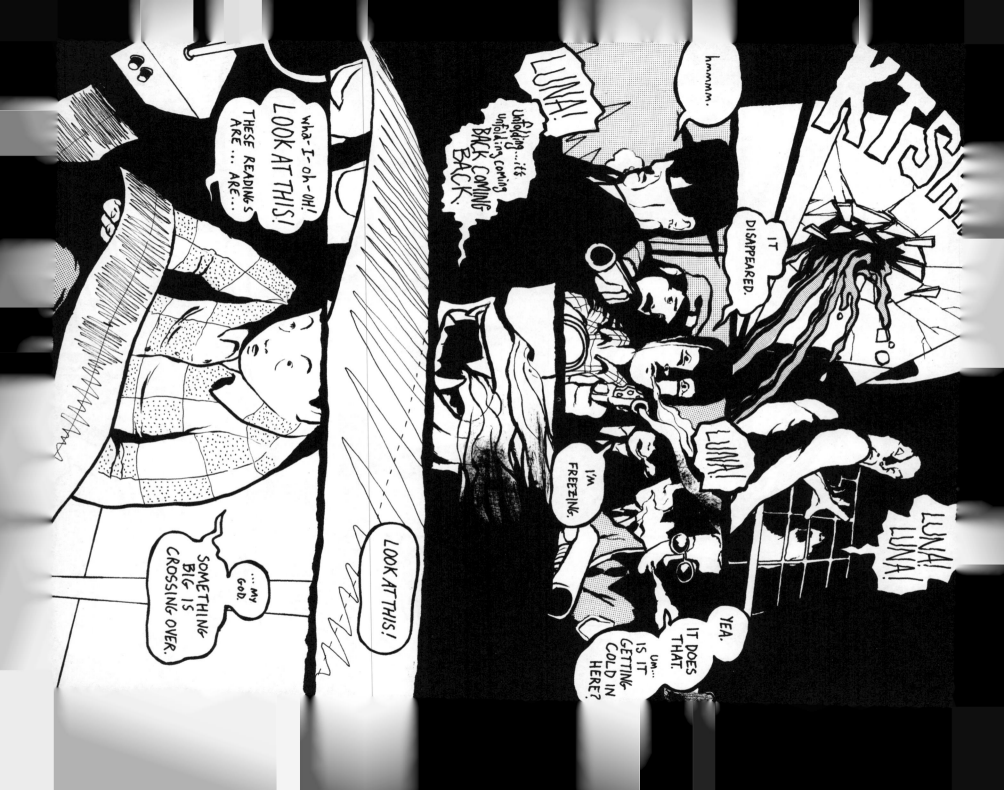

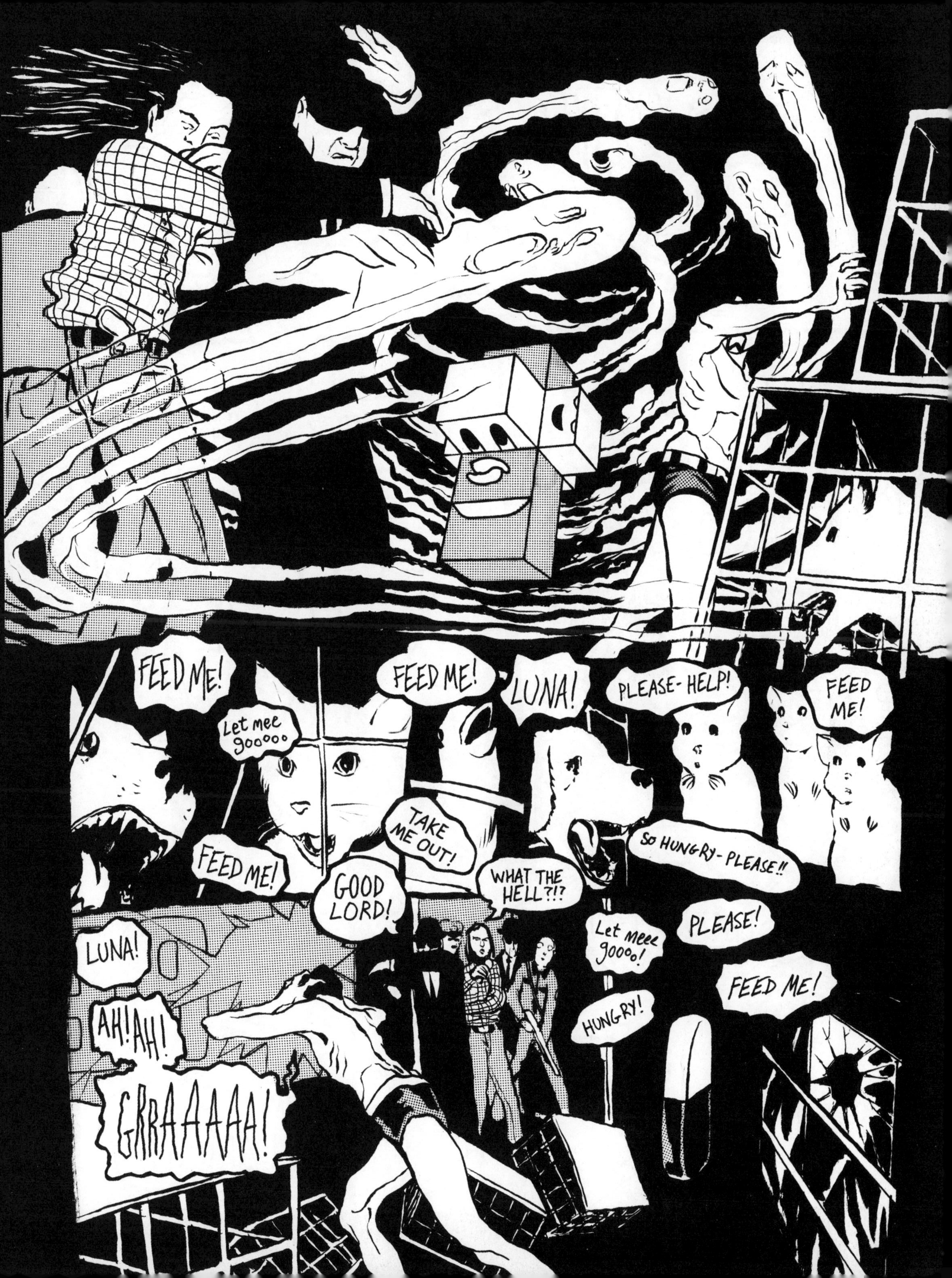
FEED ME!
FEED ME!
LUNA!
PLEASE- HELP!
FEED ME!
Let mee gooooo
TAKE ME OUT!
FEED ME!
SO HUNGRY- PLEASE!!
GOOD LORD!
WHAT THE HELL?!?
LUNA!
Let mee goooo!
PLEASE!
FEED ME!
HUNGRY!
AH! AH!
GRRAAAAA!

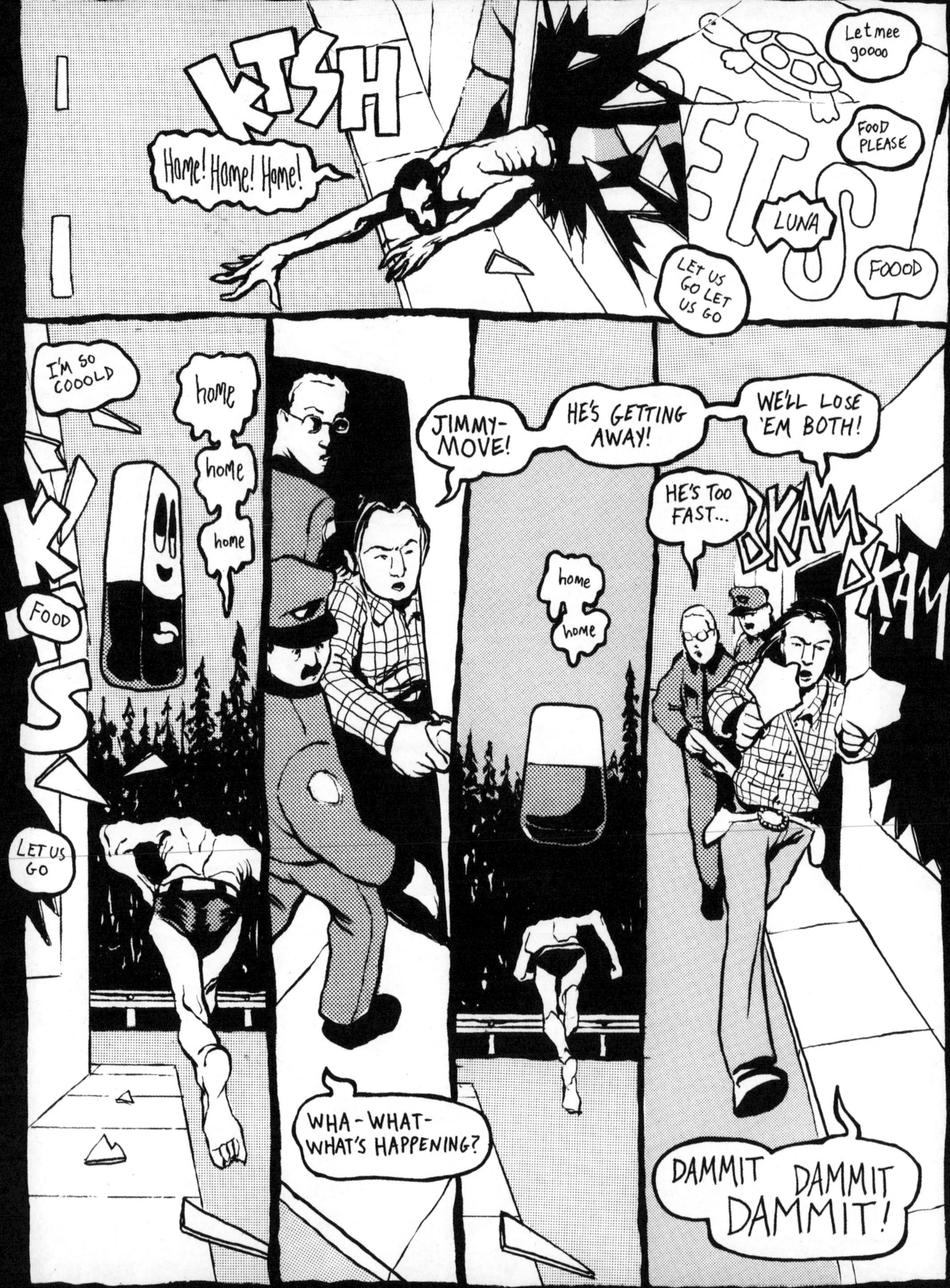
KTSH
Home! Home! Home!
Let mee goooo
FOOD PLEASE
LUNA
FOOOD
LET US GO LET US GO
I'M SO COOOLD
home
home
home
FOOD
LET US GO
JIMMY- MOVE!
HE'S GETTING AWAY!
WE'LL LOSE 'EM BOTH!
WHA-WHAT-WHAT'S HAPPENING?
home
home
HE'S TOO FAST...
BKAM
BKAM
DAMMIT DAMMIT DAMMIT!

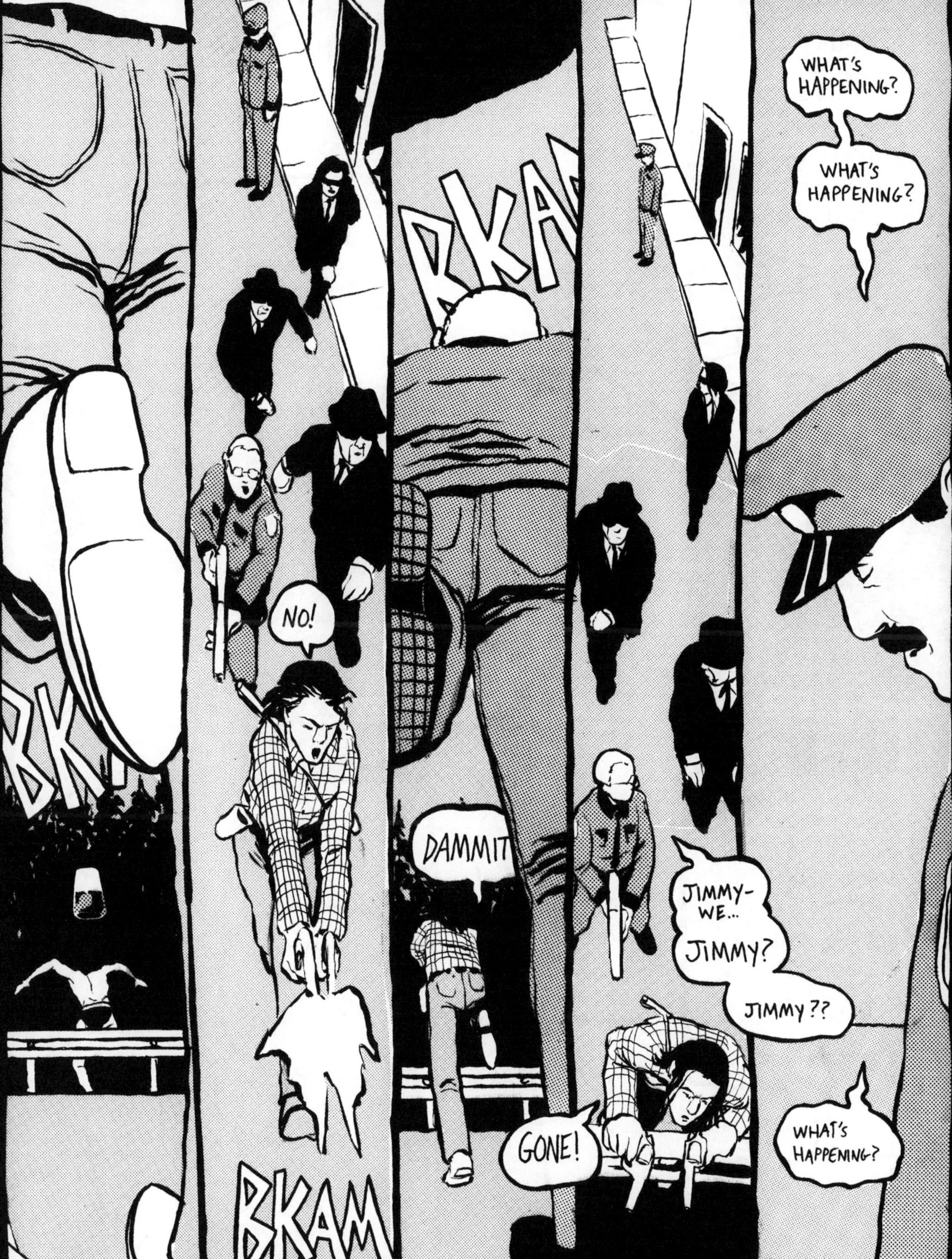

BK
NO!
BKAM
BKA
DAMMIT
GONE!
JIMMY-
WE...
JIMMY?
JIMMY??
WHAT'S HAPPENING?
WHAT'S HAPPENING?
WHAT'S HAPPENING?

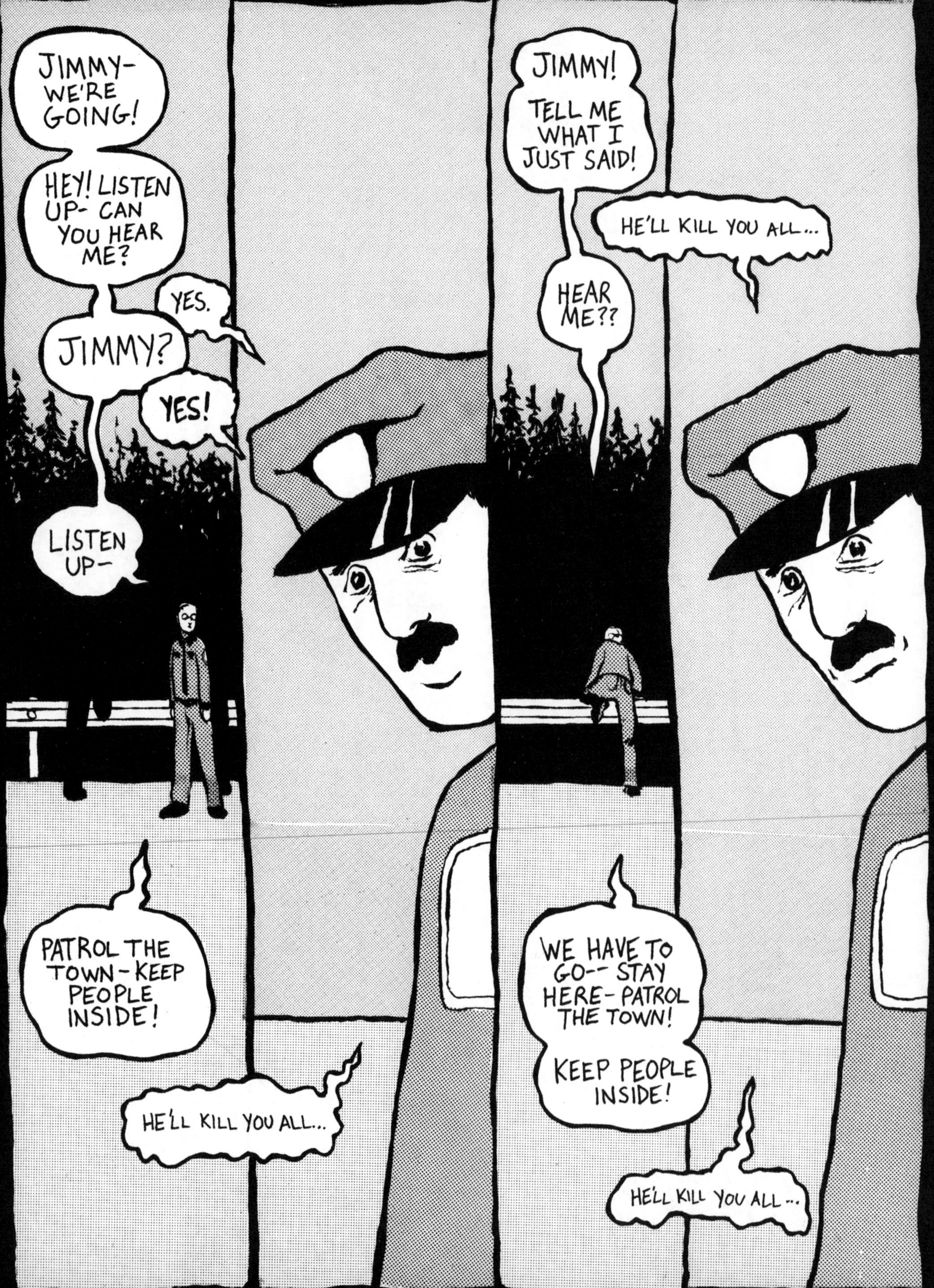
JIMMY- WE'RE GOING!
HEY! LISTEN UP- CAN YOU HEAR ME?
YES.
JIMMY?
YES!
LISTEN UP-
PATROL THE TOWN- KEEP PEOPLE INSIDE!
HE'LL KILL YOU ALL...
JIMMY!
TELL ME WHAT I JUST SAID!
HE'LL KILL YOU ALL...
HEAR ME??
WE HAVE TO GO-- STAY HERE- PATROL THE TOWN!
KEEP PEOPLE INSIDE!
HE'LL KILL YOU ALL...

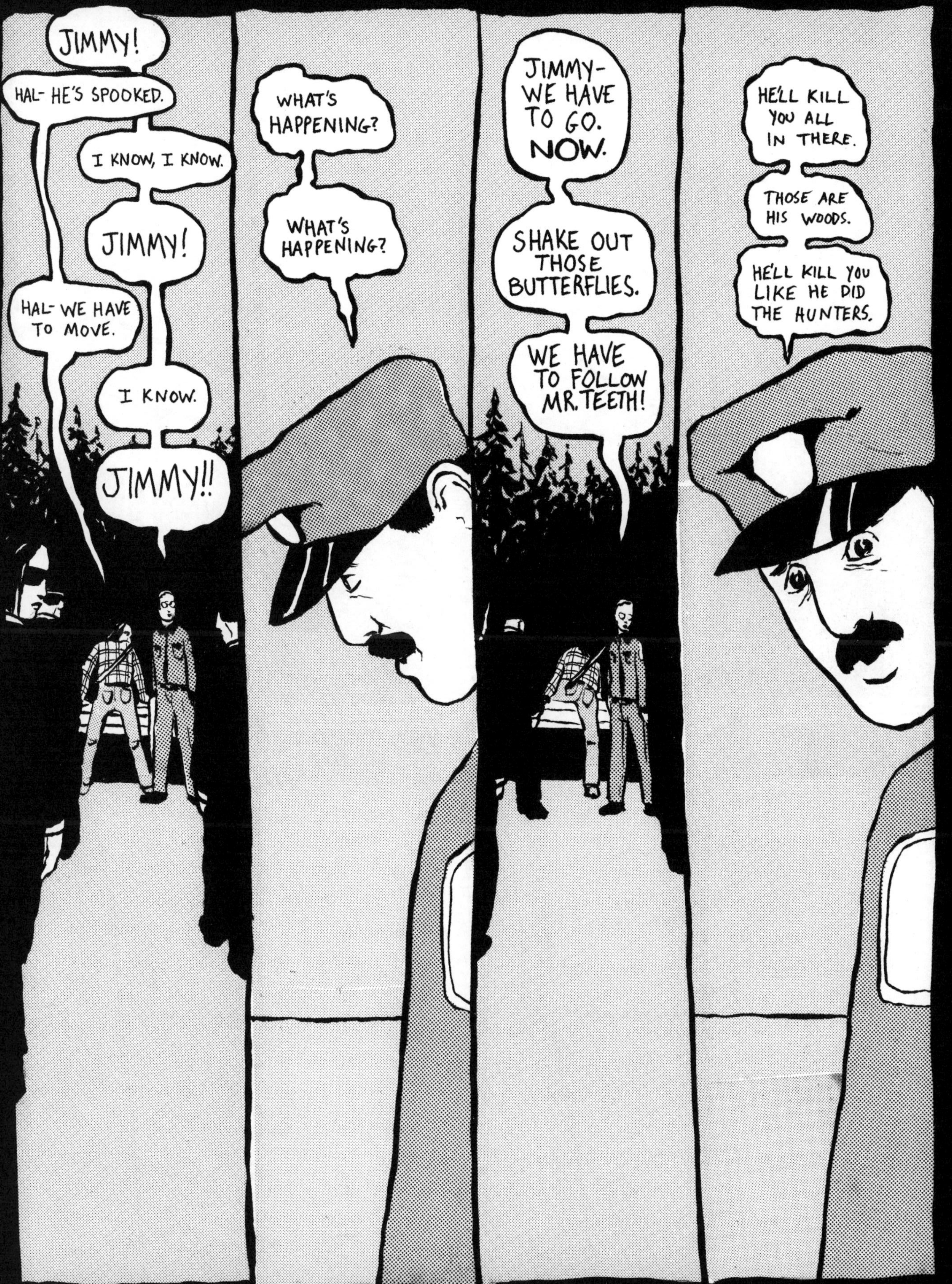
JIMMY!
HAL- HE'S SPOOKED.
I KNOW, I KNOW.
JIMMY!
HAL- WE HAVE TO MOVE.
I KNOW.
JIMMY!!
WHAT'S HAPPENING?
WHAT'S HAPPENING?
JIMMY- WE HAVE TO GO. NOW.
SHAKE OUT THOSE BUTTERFLIES.
WE HAVE TO FOLLOW MR. TEETH!
HE'LL KILL YOU ALL IN THERE.
THOSE ARE HIS WOODS.
HE'LL KILL YOU LIKE HE DID THE HUNTERS.

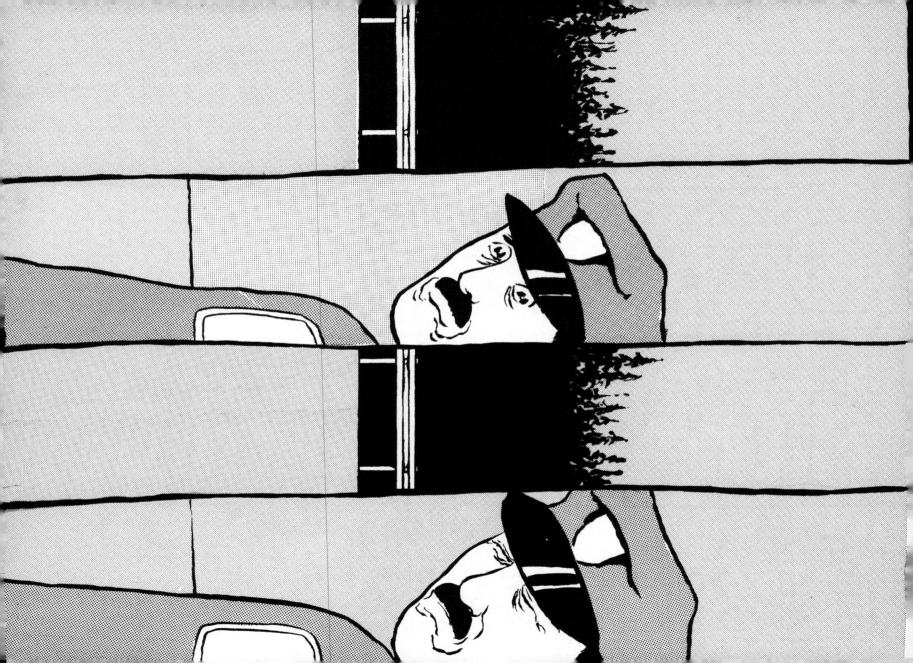

6.
TRESPASS

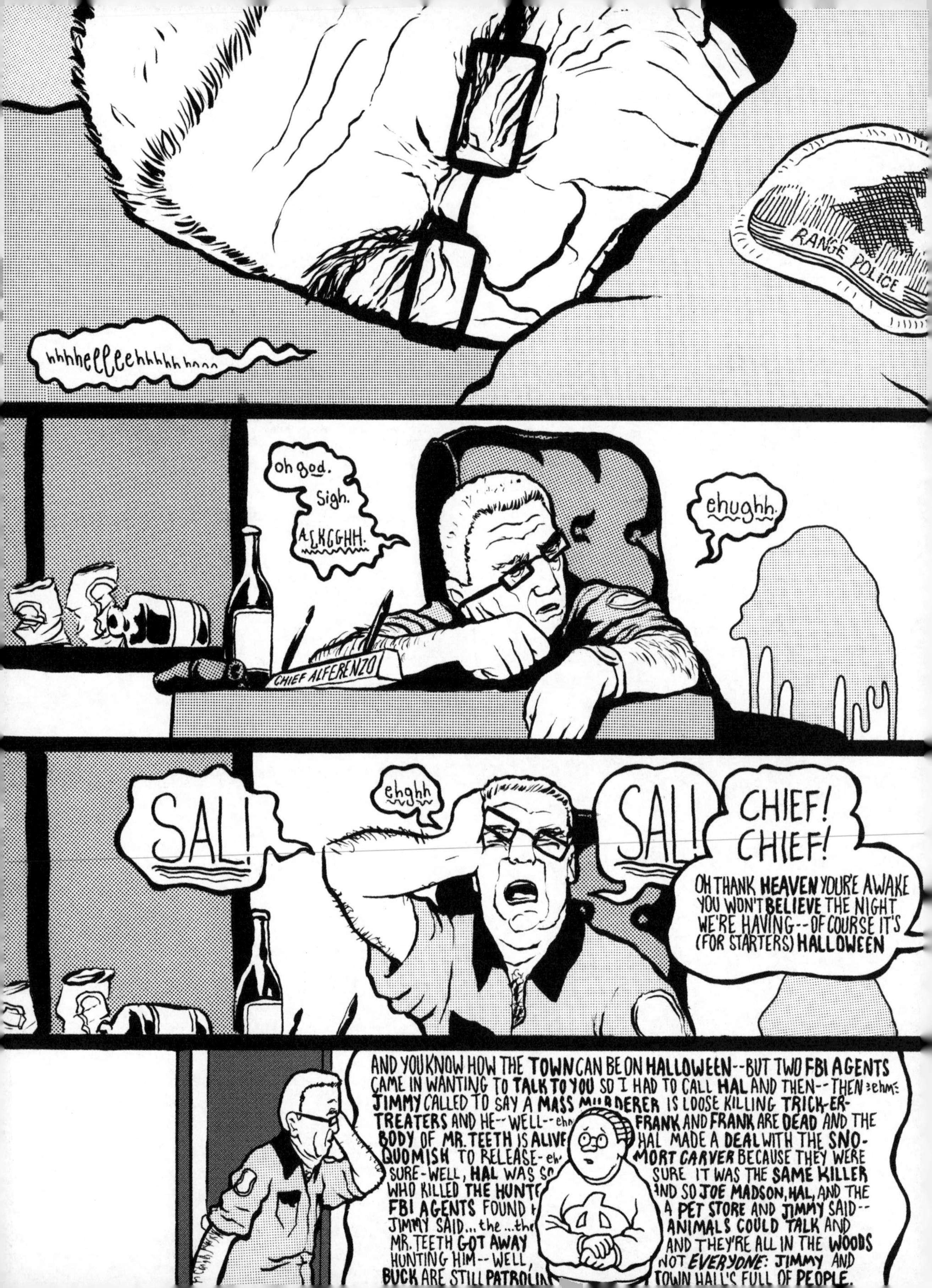
RANGE POLICE
hhhhelleehhhhhhooo
oh god.
Sigh.
ACKGHH.
CHIEF ALFERENZO
ehughh.
SAL!
ehghh
SAL!
CHIEF! CHIEF!
OH THANK HEAVEN YOU'RE AWAKE YOU WON'T BELIEVE THE NIGHT WE'RE HAVING--OF COURSE IT'S (FOR STARTERS) HALLOWEEN
AND YOU KNOW HOW THE TOWN CAN BE ON HALLOWEEN--BUT TWO FBI AGENTS CAME IN WANTING TO TALK TO YOU SO I HAD TO CALL HAL AND THEN--THEN ehm JIMMY CALLED TO SAY A MASS MURDERER IS LOOSE KILLING TRICK-ER-TREATERS AND HE--WELL--ehm FRANK AND FRANK ARE DEAD AND THE BODY OF MR. TEETH IS ALIVE HAL MADE A DEAL WITH THE SNOQUOMISH TO RELEASE-eh MORT CARVER BECAUSE THEY WERE SURE-WELL, HAL WAS SURE IT WAS THE SAME KILLER WHO KILLED THE HUNTE AND SO JOE MADSON, HAL, AND THE FBI AGENTS FOUND A PET STORE AND JIMMY SAID--JIMMY SAID... the... the ANIMALS COULD TALK AND MR. TEETH GOT AWAY AND THEY'RE ALL IN THE WOODS HUNTING HIM--WELL, NOT EVERYONE: JIMMY AND BUCK ARE STILL PATROLIN TOWN HALL'S FULL OF PEOPLE.

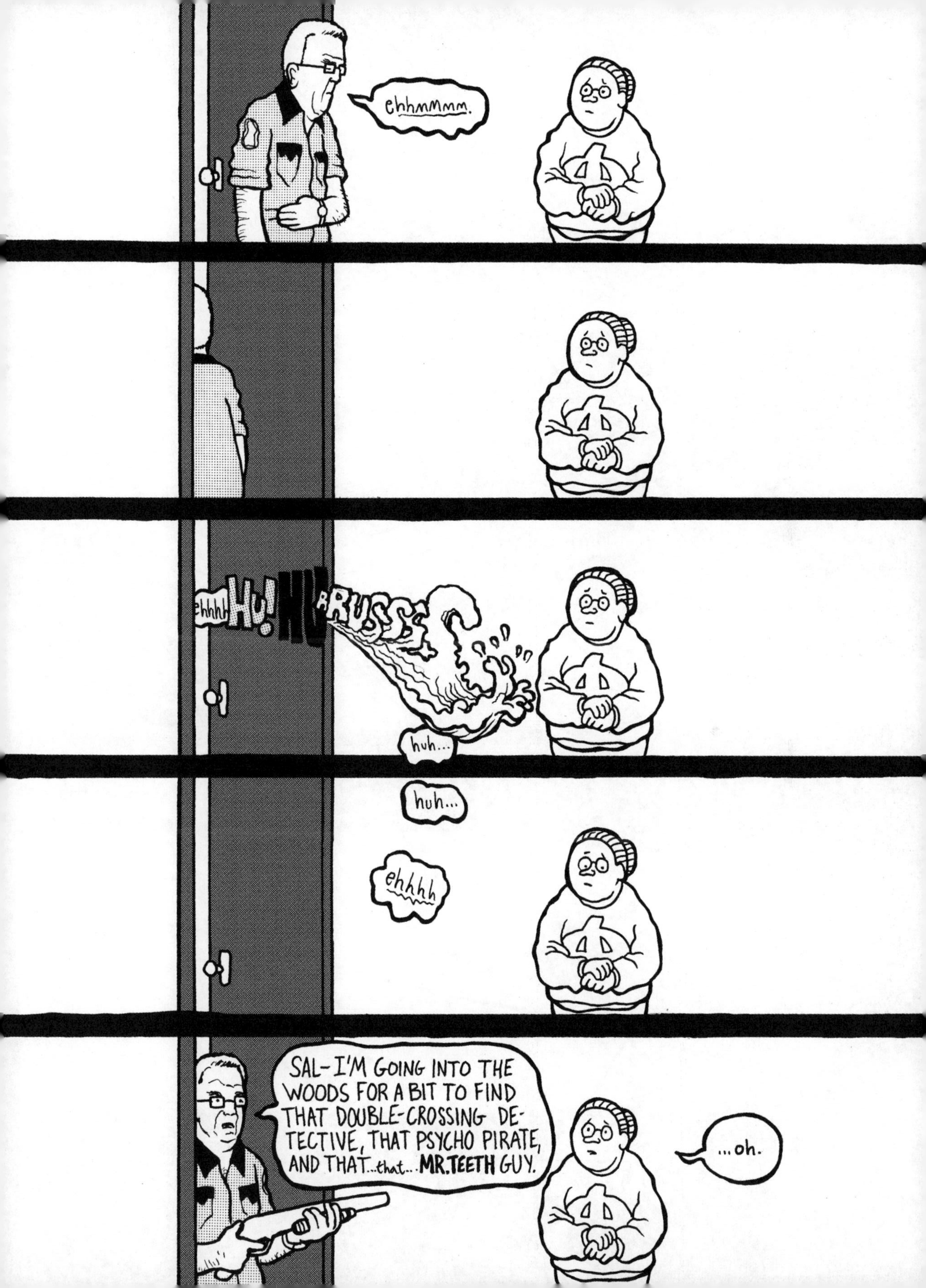
ehhmmmm.
ehhhhHU!HU
BRUSSS
huh...
huh...
ehhhh
SAL—I'M GOING INTO THE WOODS FOR A BIT TO FIND THAT DOUBLE-CROSSING DETECTIVE, THAT PSYCHO PIRATE, AND THAT...that... MR. TEETH GUY.
...oh.

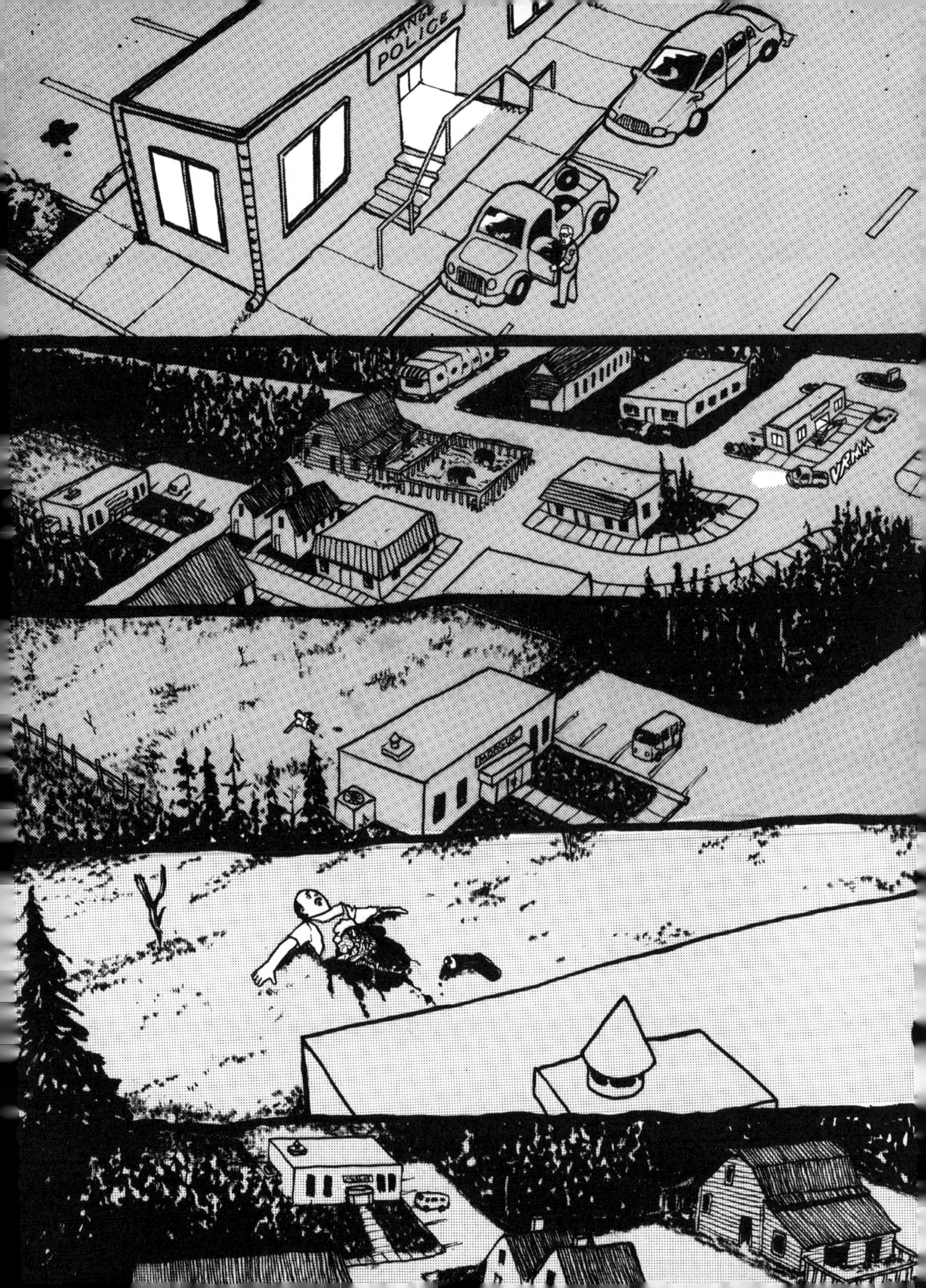
POLICE
VRMM

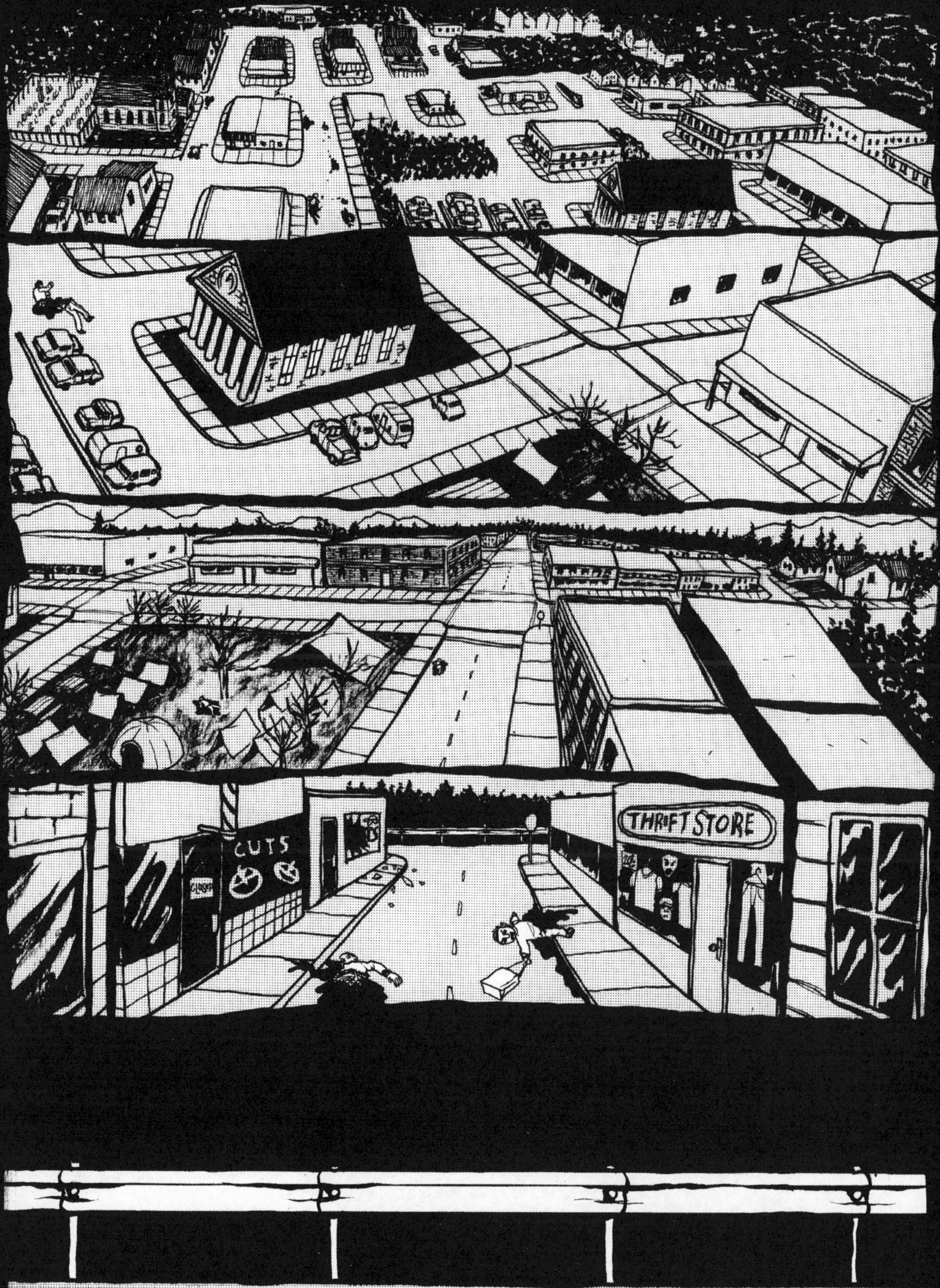
CUTS
THRIFT STORE

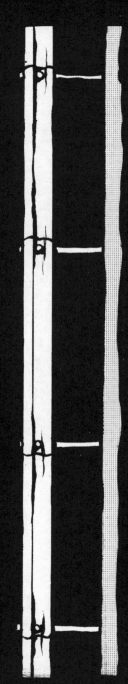

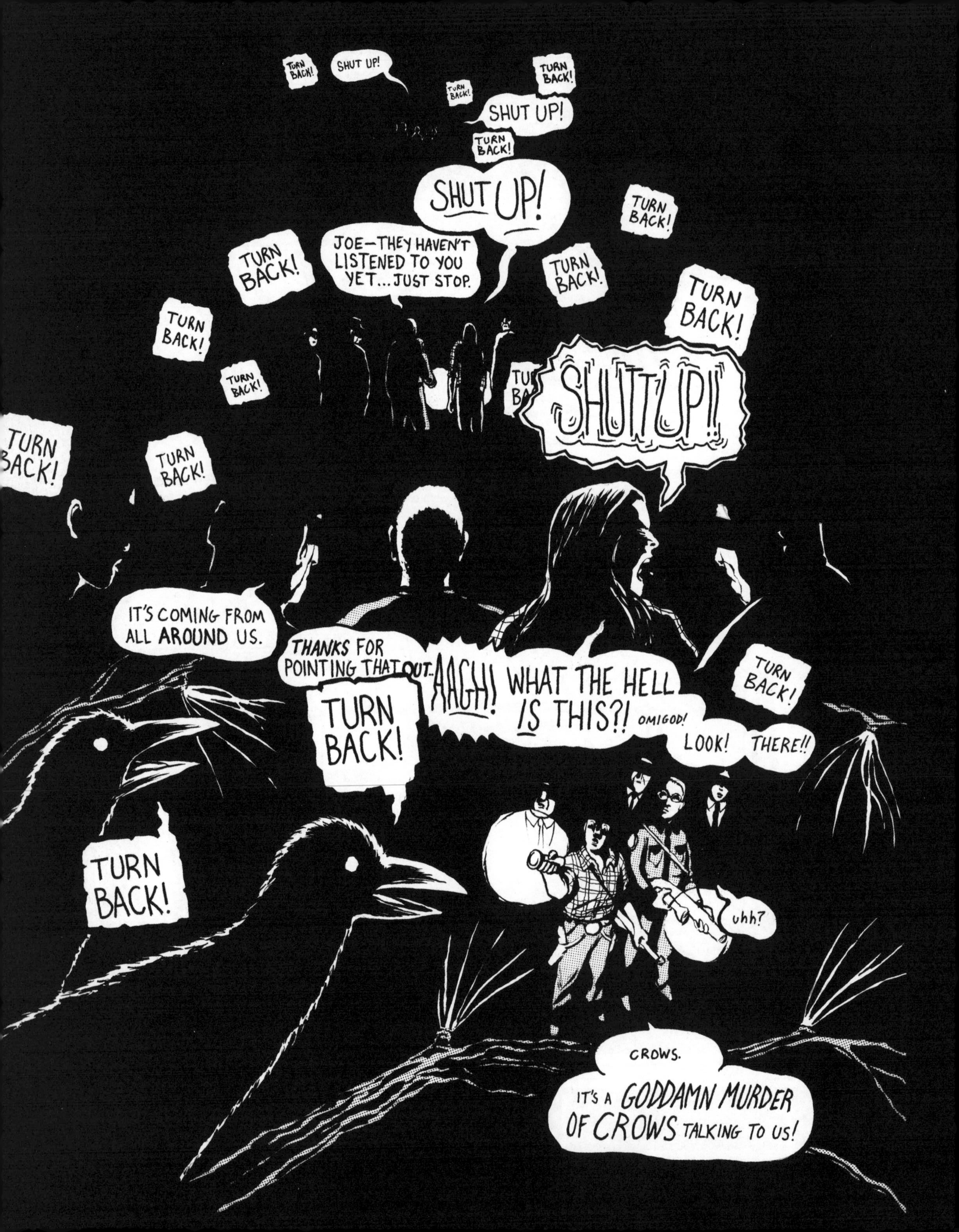
TURN BACK!
SHUT UP!
TURN BACK!
TURN BACK!
SHUT UP!
TURN BACK!
SHUT UP!
TURN BACK!
TURN BACK!
JOE—THEY HAVEN'T LISTENED TO YOU YET... JUST STOP.
TURN BACK!
TURN BACK!
TURN BACK!
TURN BACK!
SHUT UP!!
TURN BACK!
TURN BACK!
IT'S COMING FROM ALL AROUND US.
THANKS FOR POINTING THAT OUT.
AAGH! WHAT THE HELL IS THIS?!
TURN BACK!
TURN BACK!
OMIGOD!
LOOK!
THERE!!
TURN BACK!
uhh?
CROWS.
IT'S A GODDAMN MURDER OF CROWS TALKING TO US!

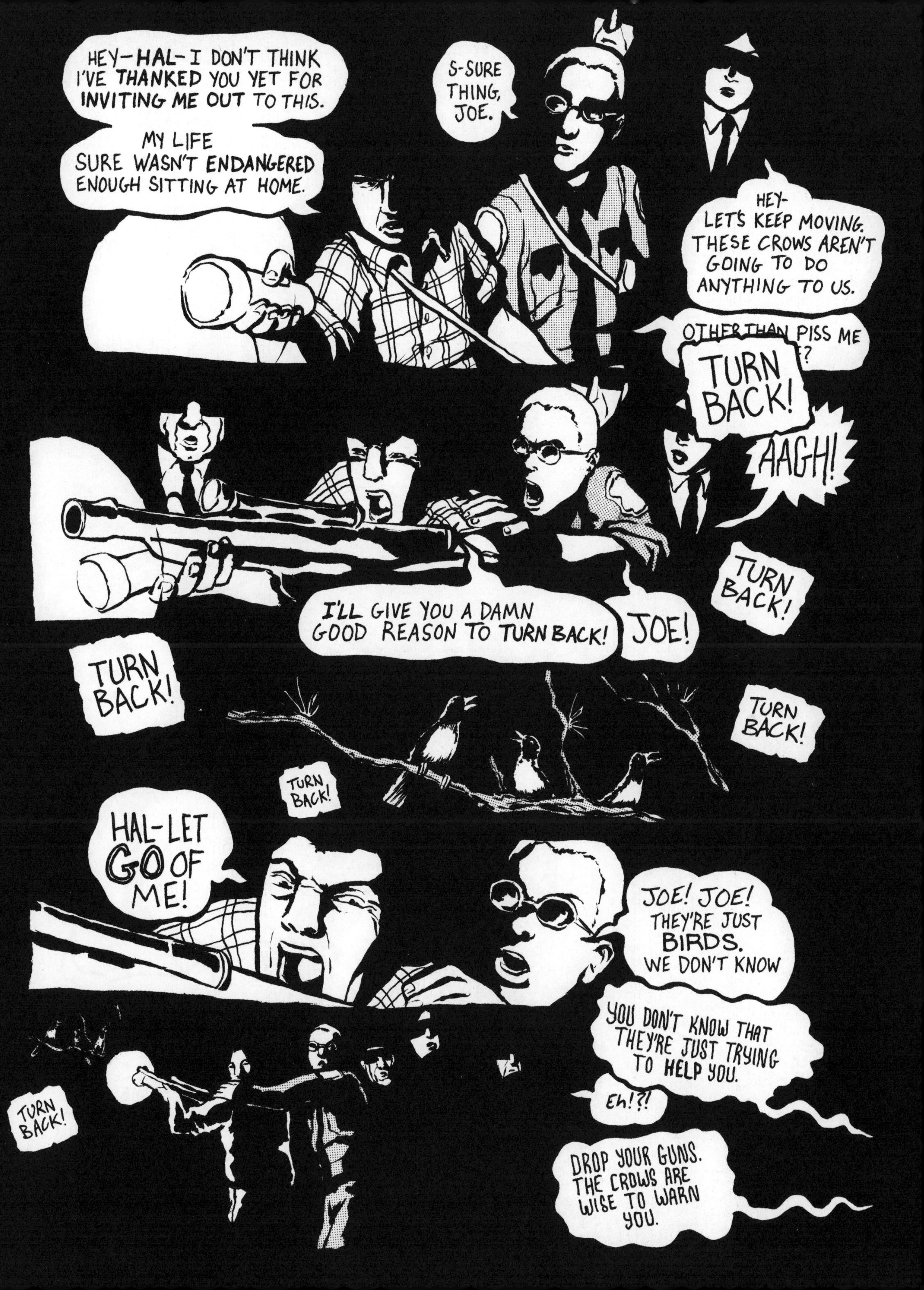
HEY—HAL—I DON'T THINK I'VE THANKED YOU YET FOR INVITING ME OUT TO THIS.
MY LIFE SURE WASN'T ENDANGERED ENOUGH SITTING AT HOME.
S-SURE THING, JOE.
HEY- LET'S KEEP MOVING. THESE CROWS AREN'T GOING TO DO ANYTHING TO US.
OTHER THAN PISS ME
TURN BACK!
AAGH!
TURN BACK!
I'LL GIVE YOU A DAMN GOOD REASON TO TURN BACK!
JOE!
TURN BACK!
TURN BACK!
TURN BACK!
HAL-LET GO OF ME!
JOE! JOE! THEY'RE JUST BIRDS. WE DON'T KNOW
YOU DON'T KNOW THAT THEY'RE JUST TRYING TO HELP YOU.
Eh!?!
TURN BACK!
DROP YOUR GUNS. THE CROWS ARE WISE TO WARN YOU.

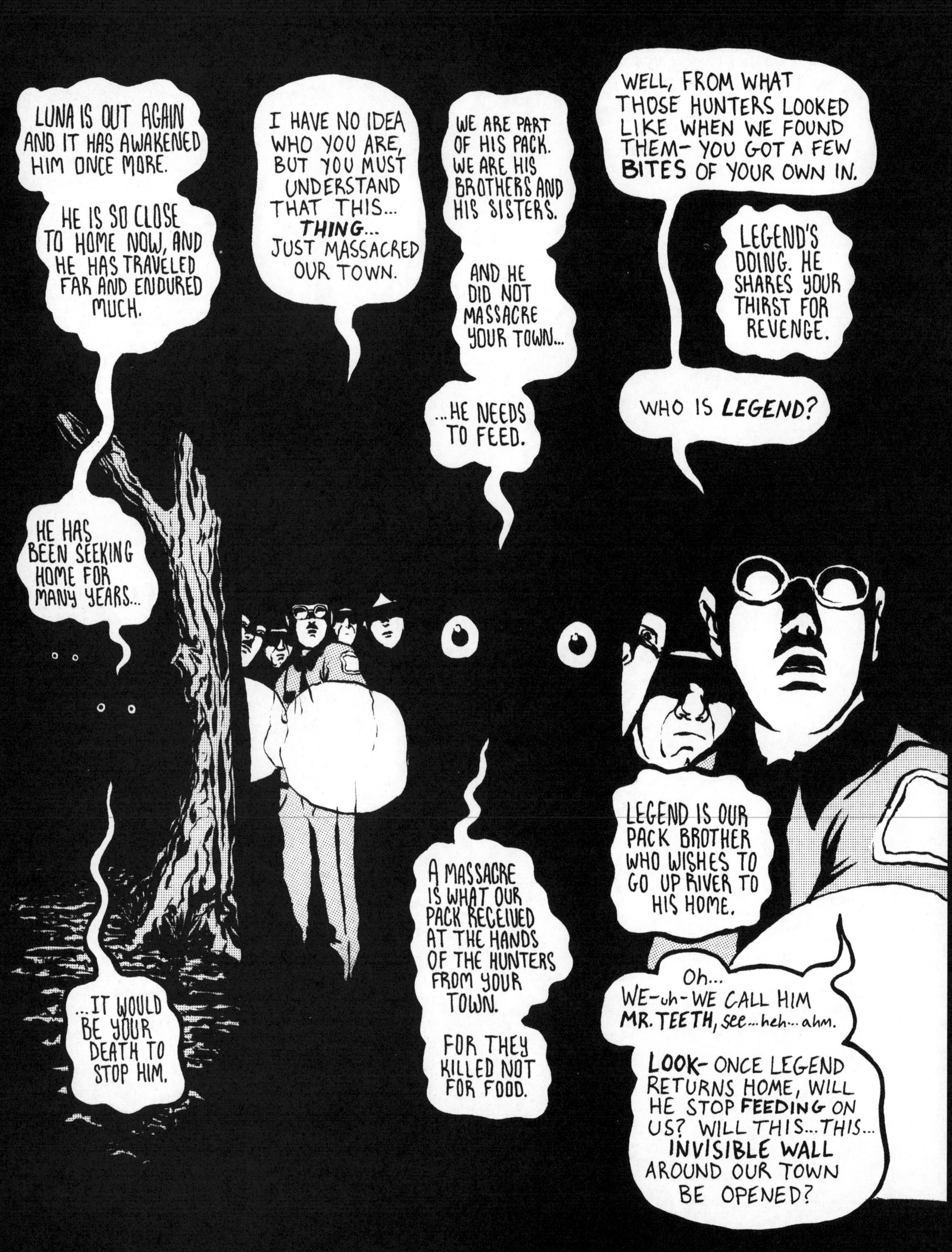
LUNA IS OUT AGAIN AND IT HAS AWAKENED HIM ONCE MORE.
HE IS SO CLOSE TO HOME NOW, AND HE HAS TRAVELED FAR AND ENDURED MUCH.
I HAVE NO IDEA WHO YOU ARE, BUT YOU MUST UNDERSTAND THAT THIS... THING... JUST MASSACRED OUR TOWN.
WE ARE PART OF HIS PACK. WE ARE HIS BROTHERS AND HIS SISTERS.
AND HE DID NOT MASSACRE YOUR TOWN...
...HE NEEDS TO FEED.
WELL, FROM WHAT THOSE HUNTERS LOOKED LIKE WHEN WE FOUND THEM- YOU GOT A FEW BITES OF YOUR OWN IN.
LEGEND'S DOING. HE SHARES YOUR THIRST FOR REVENGE.
WHO IS LEGEND?
HE HAS BEEN SEEKING HOME FOR MANY YEARS...
...IT WOULD BE YOUR DEATH TO STOP HIM.
A MASSACRE IS WHAT OUR PACK RECEIVED AT THE HANDS OF THE HUNTERS FROM YOUR TOWN.
FOR THEY KILLED NOT FOR FOOD.
LEGEND IS OUR PACK BROTHER WHO WISHES TO GO UP RIVER TO HIS HOME.
Oh... WE-uh-WE CALL HIM MR. TEETH, see...heh...ahm.
LOOK- ONCE LEGEND RETURNS HOME, WILL HE STOP FEEDING ON US? WILL THIS...THIS... INVISIBLE WALL AROUND OUR TOWN BE OPENED?

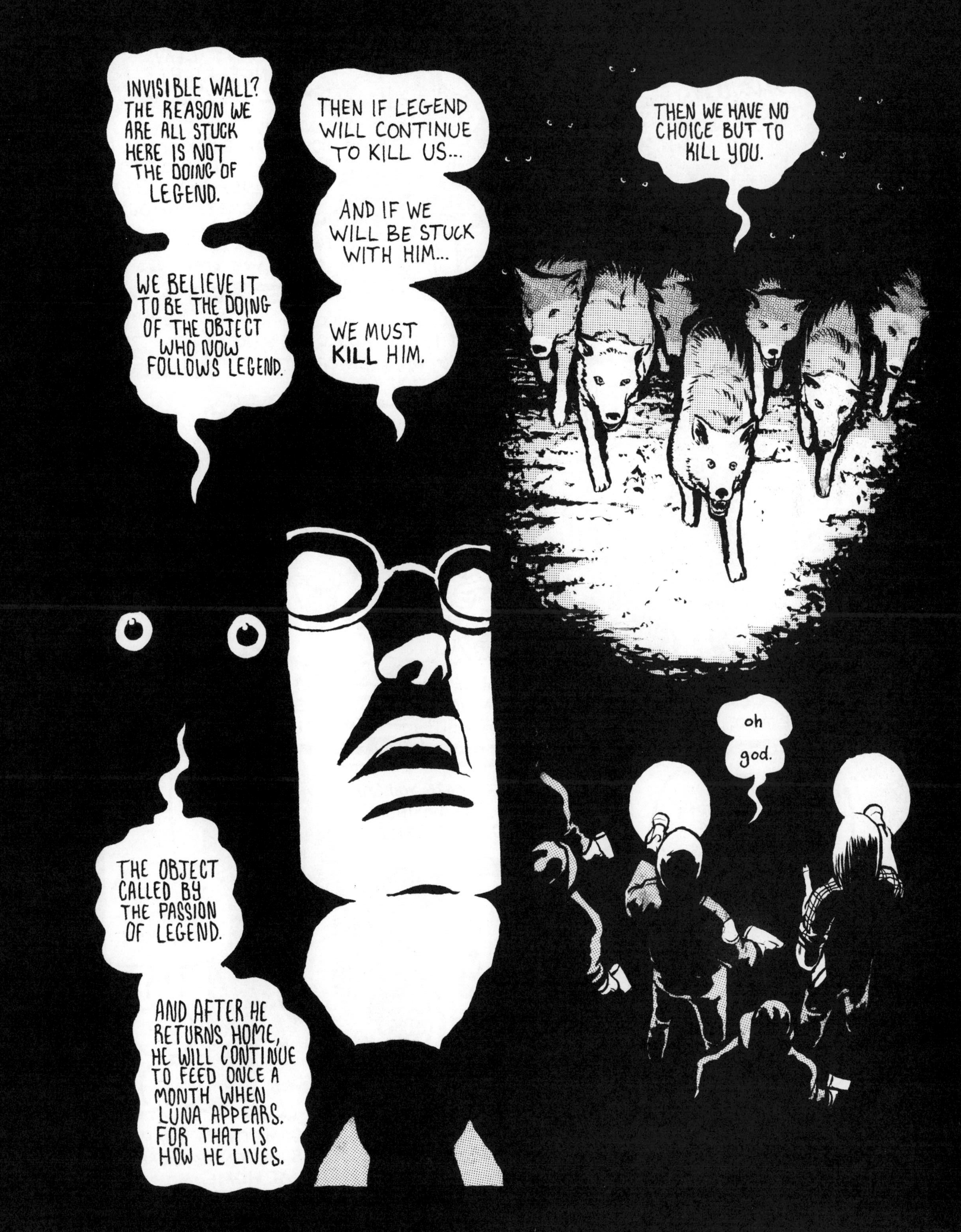
INVISIBLE WALL? THE REASON WE ARE ALL STUCK HERE IS NOT THE DOING OF LEGEND.
WE BELIEVE IT TO BE THE DOING OF THE OBJECT WHO NOW FOLLOWS LEGEND.
THEN IF LEGEND WILL CONTINUE TO KILL US...
AND IF WE WILL BE STUCK WITH HIM...
WE MUST **KILL** HIM.
THE OBJECT CALLED BY THE PASSION OF LEGEND.
AND AFTER HE RETURNS HOME, HE WILL CONTINUE TO FEED ONCE A MONTH WHEN LUNA APPEARS. FOR THAT IS HOW HE LIVES.
THEN WE HAVE NO CHOICE BUT TO KILL YOU.
oh god.

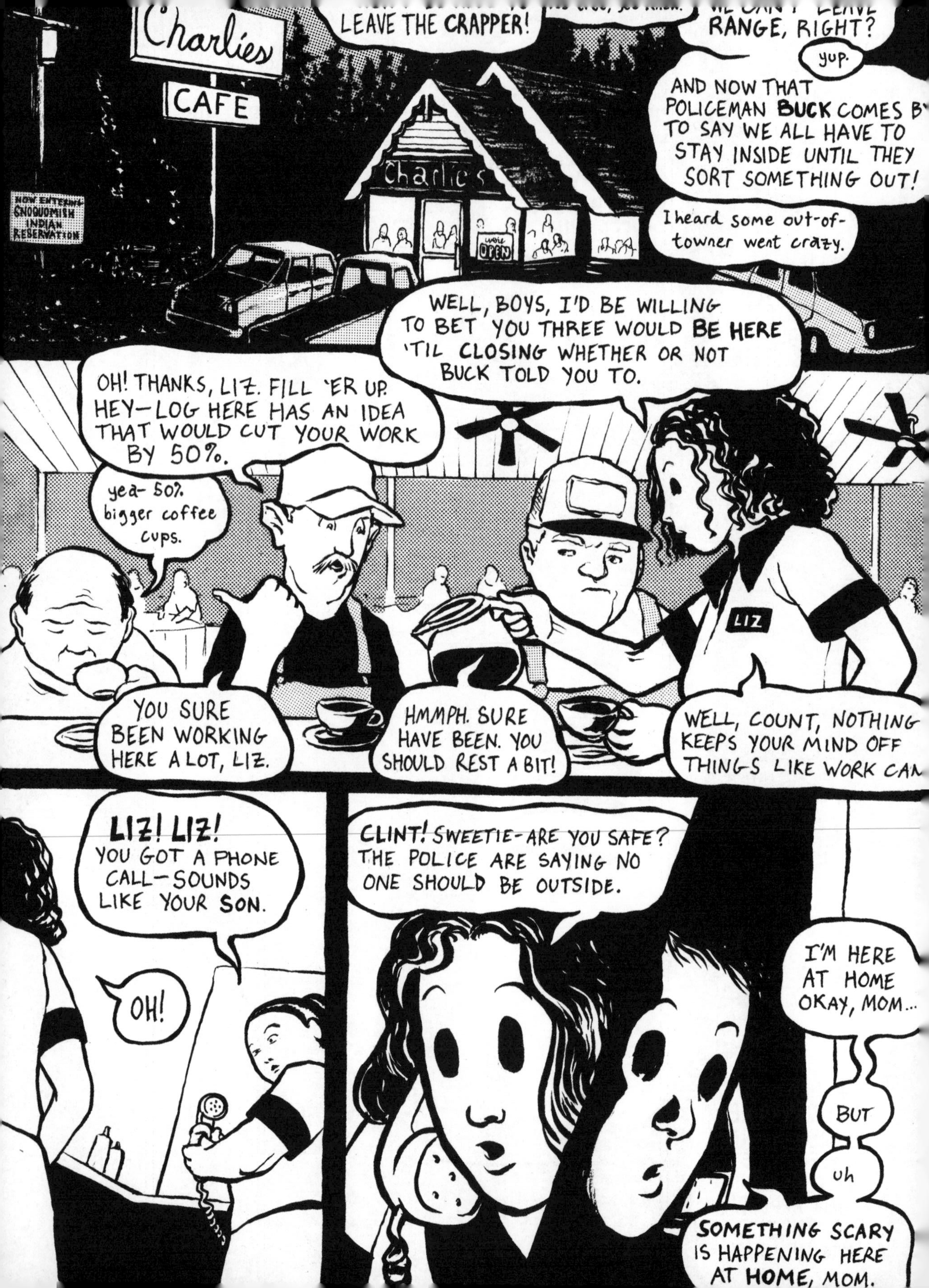
Charlie's
CAFE
LEAVE THE CRAPPER!
RANGE, RIGHT?
yup.
AND NOW THAT POLICEMAN BUCK COMES BY TO SAY WE ALL HAVE TO STAY INSIDE UNTIL THEY SORT SOMETHING OUT!
I heard some out-of-towner went crazy.
NOW ENTERING SNOQUOMISH INDIAN RESERVATION
Charlie's
OPEN
WELL, BOYS, I'D BE WILLING TO BET YOU THREE WOULD BE HERE 'TIL CLOSING WHETHER OR NOT BUCK TOLD YOU TO.
OH! THANKS, LIZ. FILL 'ER UP. HEY—LOG HERE HAS AN IDEA THAT WOULD CUT YOUR WORK BY 50%.
yea- 50% bigger coffee cups.
LIZ
YOU SURE BEEN WORKING HERE A LOT, LIZ.
HMMPH. SURE HAVE BEEN. YOU SHOULD REST A BIT!
WELL, COUNT, NOTHING KEEPS YOUR MIND OFF THINGS LIKE WORK CAN
LIZ! LIZ! YOU GOT A PHONE CALL—SOUNDS LIKE YOUR SON.
OH!
CLINT! SWEETIE-ARE YOU SAFE? THE POLICE ARE SAYING NO ONE SHOULD BE OUTSIDE.
I'M HERE AT HOME OKAY, MOM...
BUT
uh
SOMETHING SCARY IS HAPPENING HERE AT HOME, MOM.

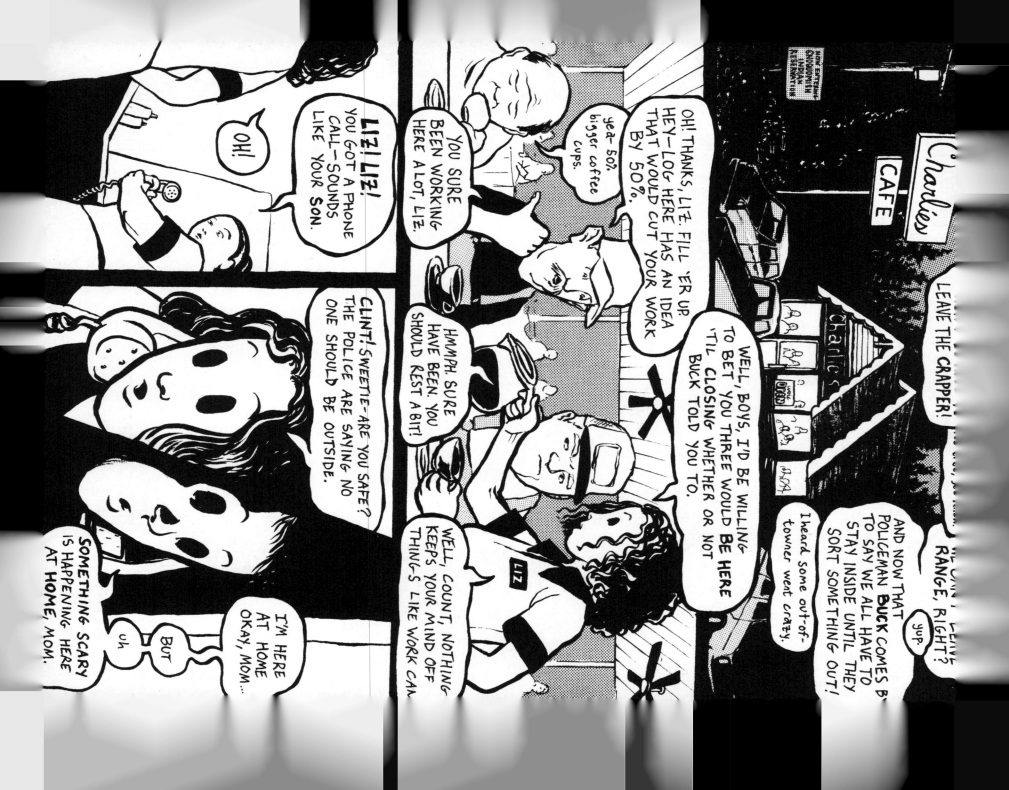

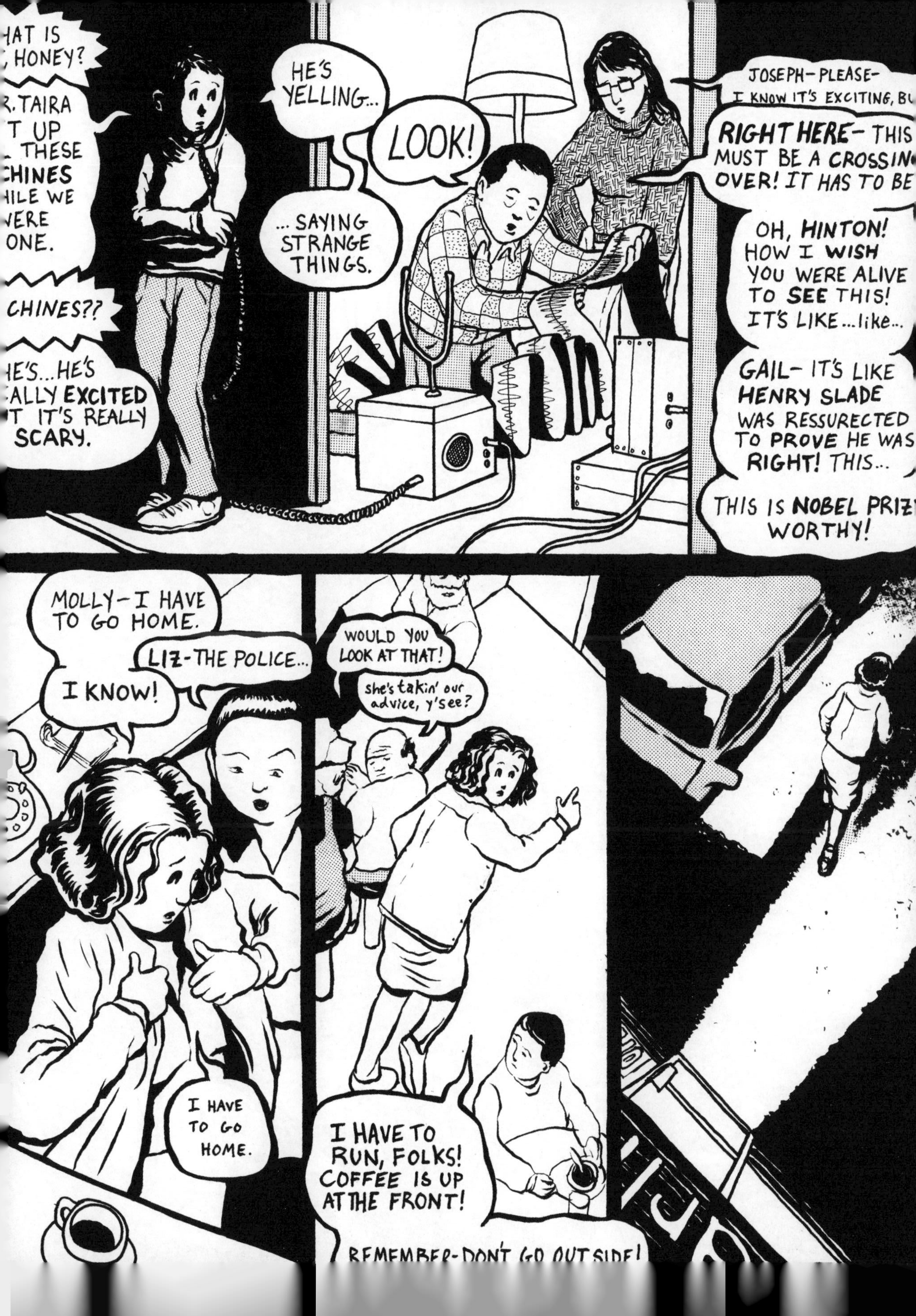
HAT IS
HONEY?
R. TAIRA
T UP
THESE
CHINES
HILE WE
VERE
ONE.
CHINES??
HE'S...HE'S
ALLY EXCITED
T IT'S REALLY
SCARY.
HE'S YELLING...
...SAYING STRANGE THINGS.
LOOK!
JOSEPH—PLEASE—
I KNOW IT'S EXCITING, BU
RIGHT HERE—THIS MUST BE A CROSSIN
OVER! IT HAS TO BE
OH, HINTON! HOW I WISH YOU WERE ALIVE TO SEE THIS! IT'S LIKE...like...
GAIL—IT'S LIKE HENRY SLADE WAS RESSURECTED TO PROVE HE WAS RIGHT! THIS...
THIS IS NOBEL PRIZ
WORTHY!
MOLLY—I HAVE TO GO HOME.
LIZ—THE POLICE...
I KNOW!
I HAVE TO GO HOME.
WOULD YOU LOOK AT THAT!
she's takin' our advice, y'see?
I HAVE TO RUN, FOLKS! COFFEE IS UP AT THE FRONT!
REMEMBER—DON'T GO OUTSIDE!

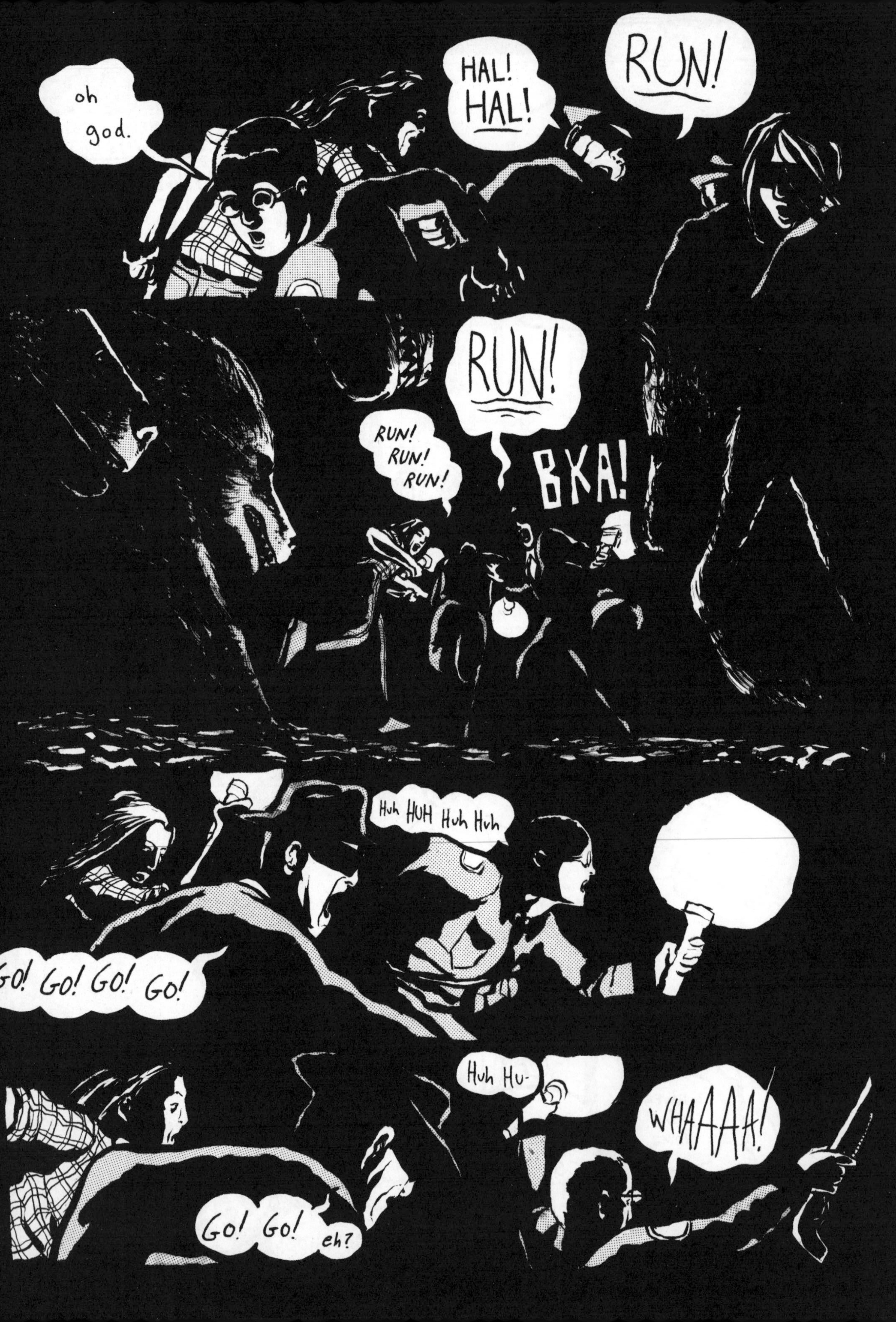
oh god.
HAL! HAL!
RUN!
RUN!
RUN! RUN! RUN!
BKA!
Huh HUH Huh Huh
GO! GO! GO! GO!
Huh Hu-
WHAAAA!
Go! Go! eh?

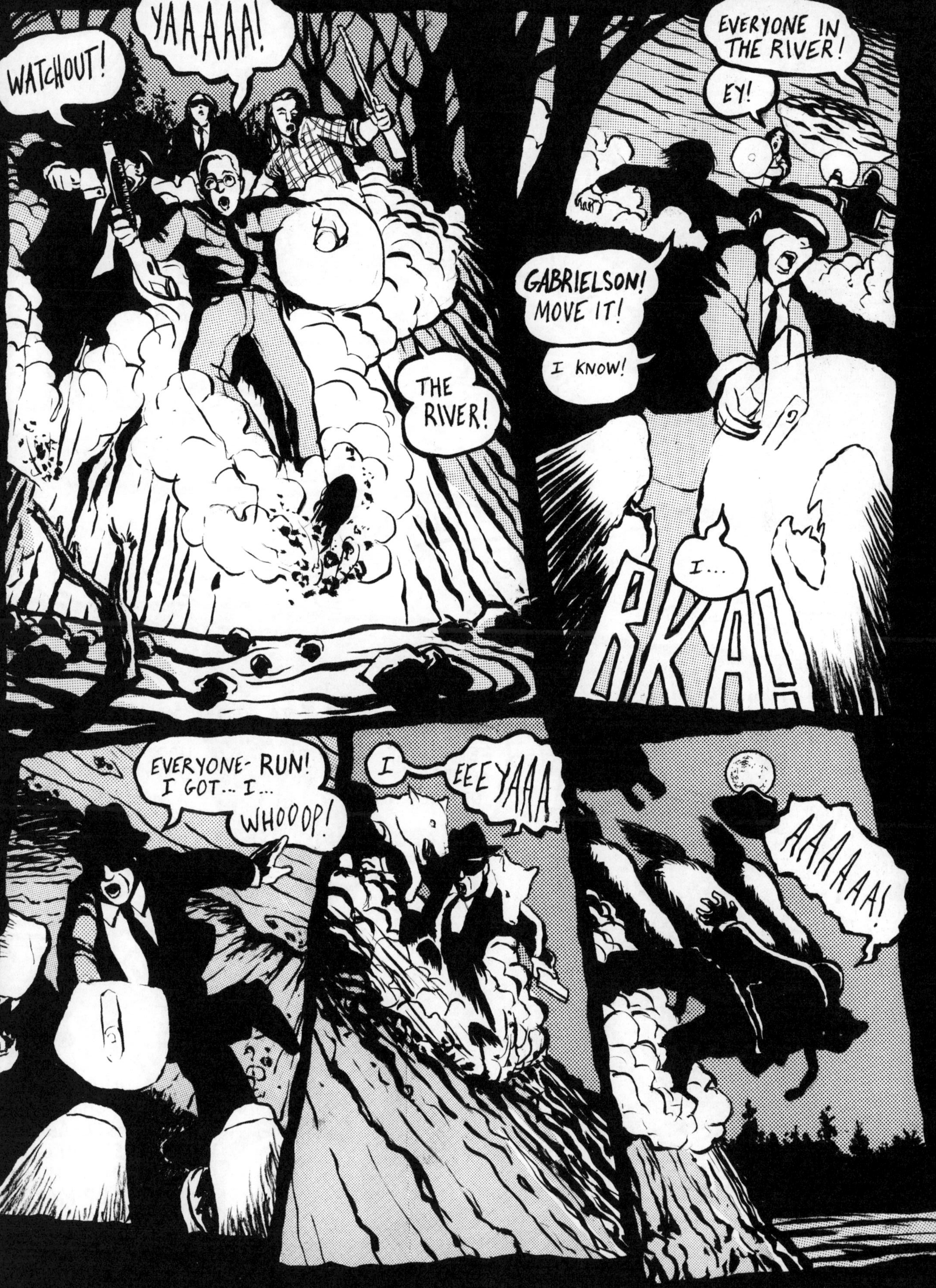
WATCHOUT!
YAAAAA!
THE RIVER!
EVERYONE IN THE RIVER!
EY!
GABRIELSON! MOVE IT!
I KNOW!
I...
RKA!
EVERYONE- RUN! I GOT... I... WHOOOP!
I
EEEYAAA
AAAAAA!

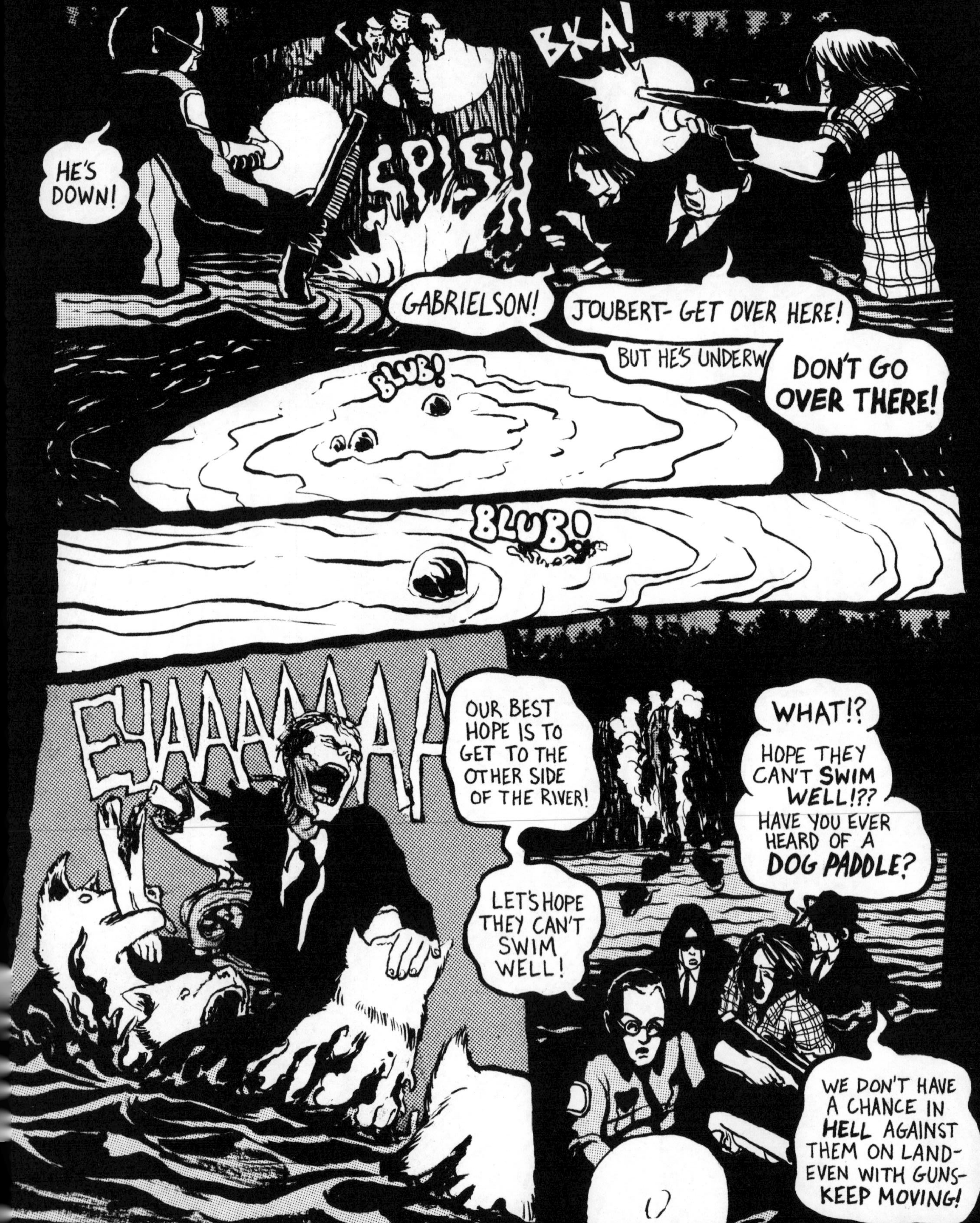
HE'S DOWN!
BKA!
SPLISH
GABRIELSON!
JOUBERT- GET OVER HERE!
BUT HE'S UNDERW
DON'T GO **OVER THERE!**
BLUB!
BLUB!
EYAAAAAAA
OUR BEST HOPE IS TO GET TO THE OTHER SIDE OF THE RIVER!
LET'S HOPE THEY CAN'T SWIM WELL!
WHAT!?
HOPE THEY CAN'T **SWIM WELL**!??
HAVE YOU EVER HEARD OF A **DOG PADDLE?**
WE DON'T HAVE A CHANCE IN **HELL** AGAINST THEM ON LAND- EVEN WITH GUNS- **KEEP MOVING!**

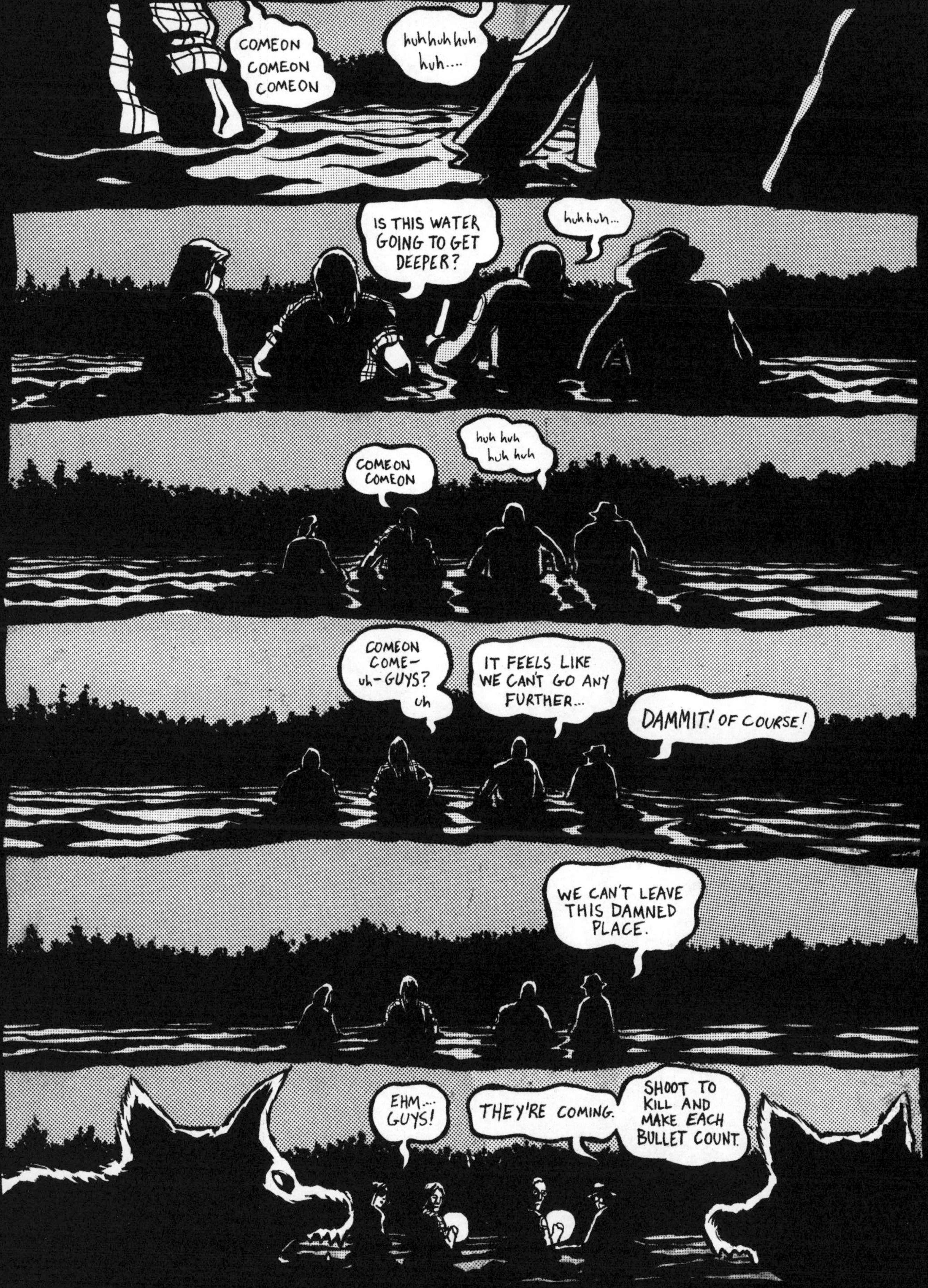
COMEON COMEON COMEON
huhhuhhuh huh....
IS THIS WATER GOING TO GET DEEPER?
huhhuh...
COMEON COMEON
huh huh huh huh
COMEON COME- uh-GUYS? uh
IT FEELS LIKE WE CAN'T GO ANY FURTHER...
DAMMIT! OF COURSE!
WE CAN'T LEAVE THIS DAMNED PLACE.
EHM... GUYS!
THEY'RE COMING.
SHOOT TO KILL AND MAKE EACH BULLET COUNT.

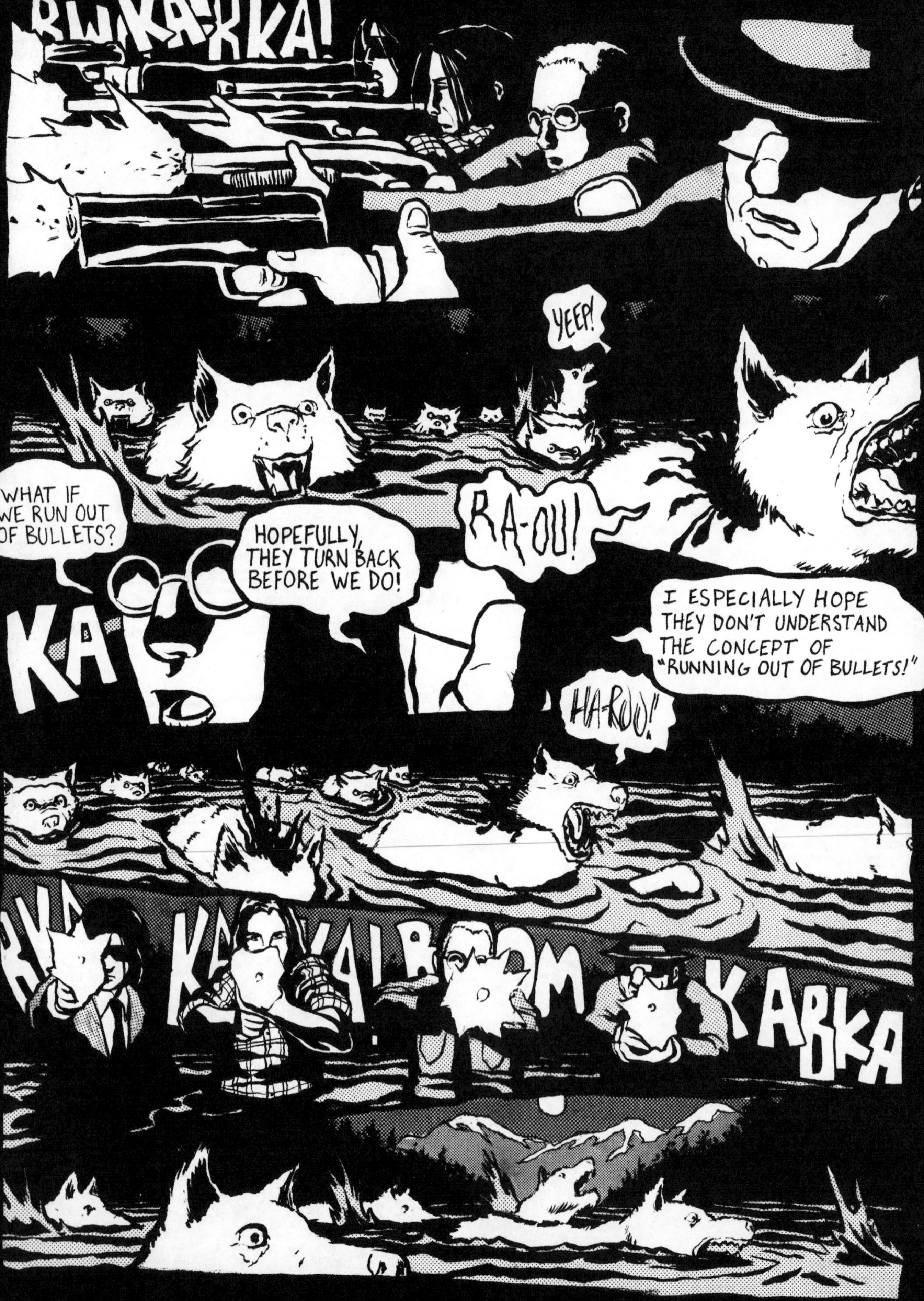

BWKA!RKA!
YEEP!
WHAT IF WE RUN OUT OF BULLETS?
HOPEFULLY, THEY TURN BACK BEFORE WE DO!
RA-OU!
KA-
I ESPECIALLY HOPE THEY DON'T UNDERSTAND THE CONCEPT OF "RUNNING OUT OF BULLETS!"
HA-ROO!
KABKA

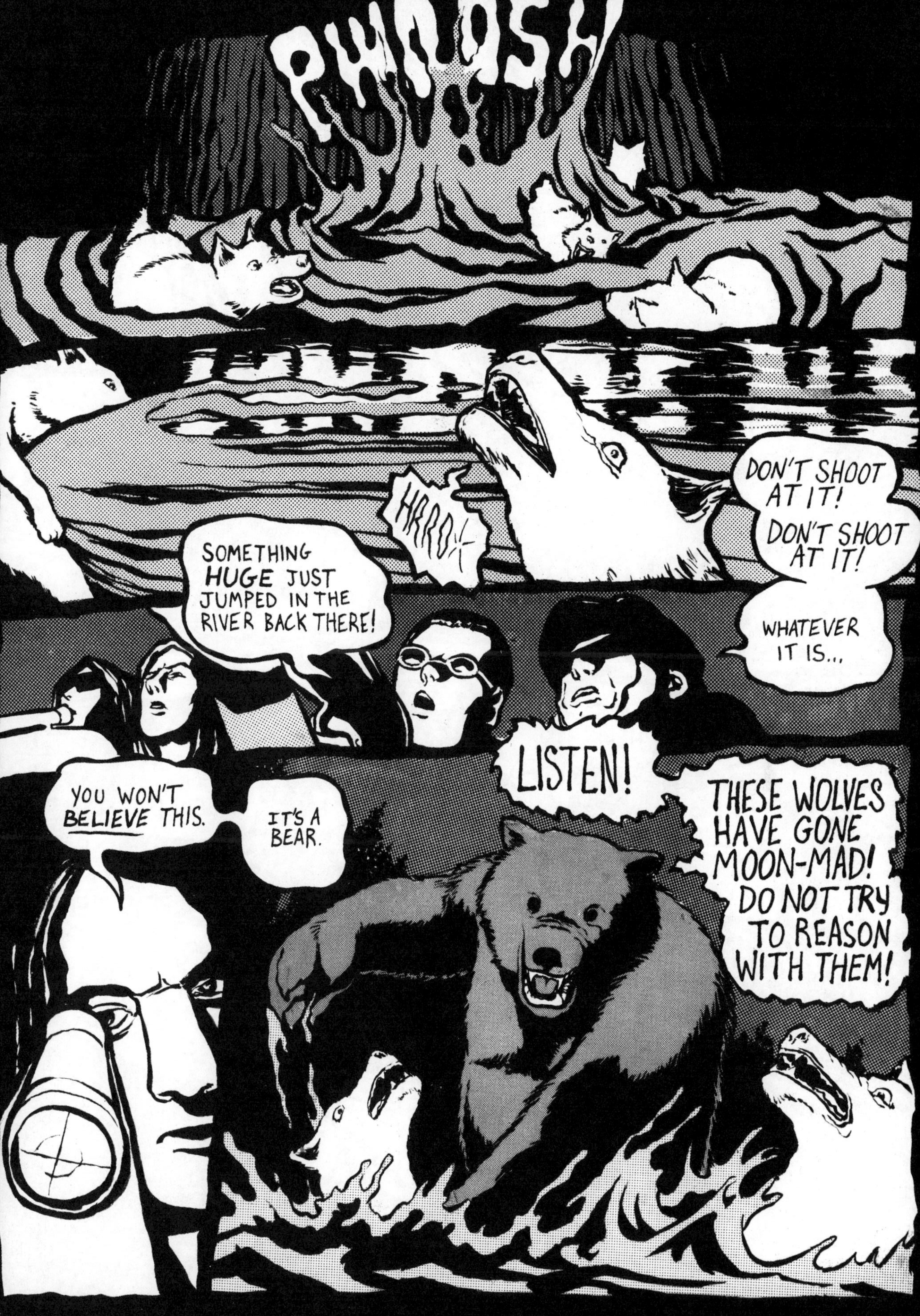
PHOOSH!
HRROO!
DON'T SHOOT AT IT!
DON'T SHOOT AT IT!
SOMETHING HUGE JUST JUMPED IN THE RIVER BACK THERE!
WHATEVER IT IS...
LISTEN!
THESE WOLVES HAVE GONE MOON-MAD! DO NOT TRY TO REASON WITH THEM!
YOU WON'T BELIEVE THIS.
IT'S A BEAR.

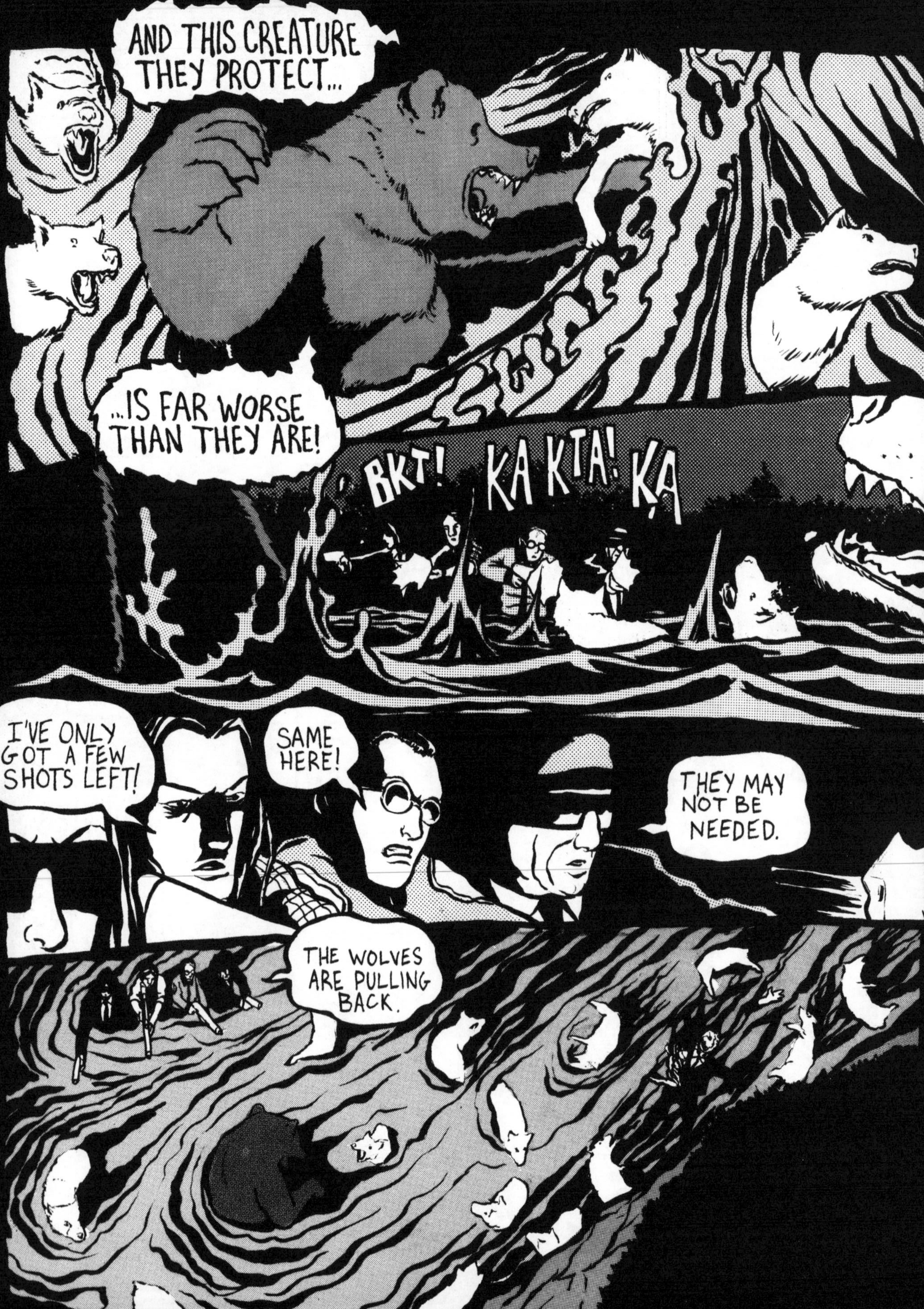
AND THIS CREATURE THEY PROTECT...
...IS FAR WORSE THAN THEY ARE!
BKT! KA KTA! KA
I'VE ONLY GOT A FEW SHOTS LEFT!
SAME HERE!
THEY MAY NOT BE NEEDED.
THE WOLVES ARE PULLING BACK.

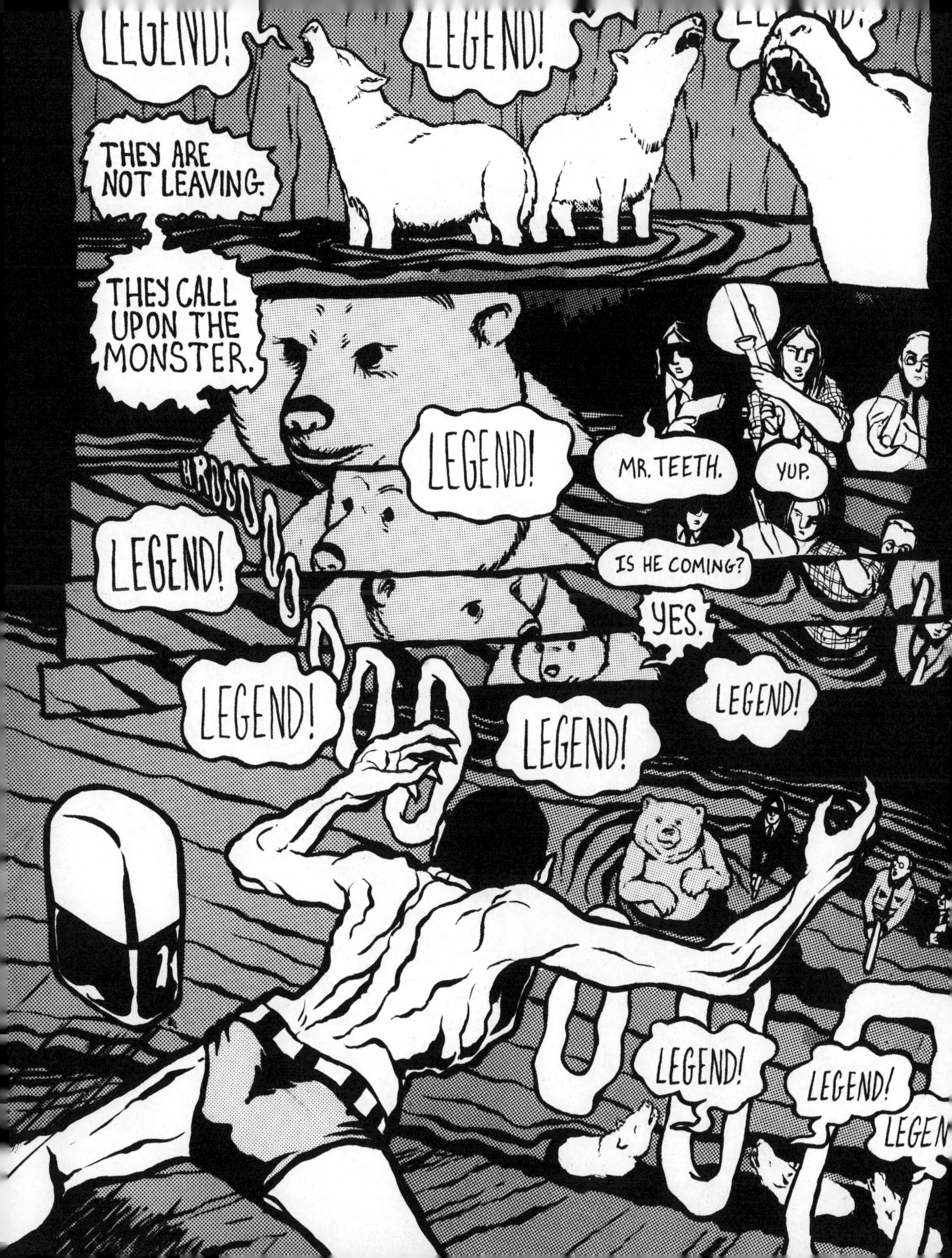
LEGEND!
LEGEND!
THEY ARE NOT LEAVING.
THEY CALL UPON THE MONSTER.
LEGEND!
HROOOO
LEGEND!
MR. TEETH.
YUP.
IS HE COMING?
YES.
LEGEND!
LEGEND!
LEGEND!
LEGEND!
LEGEND!
LEGEN

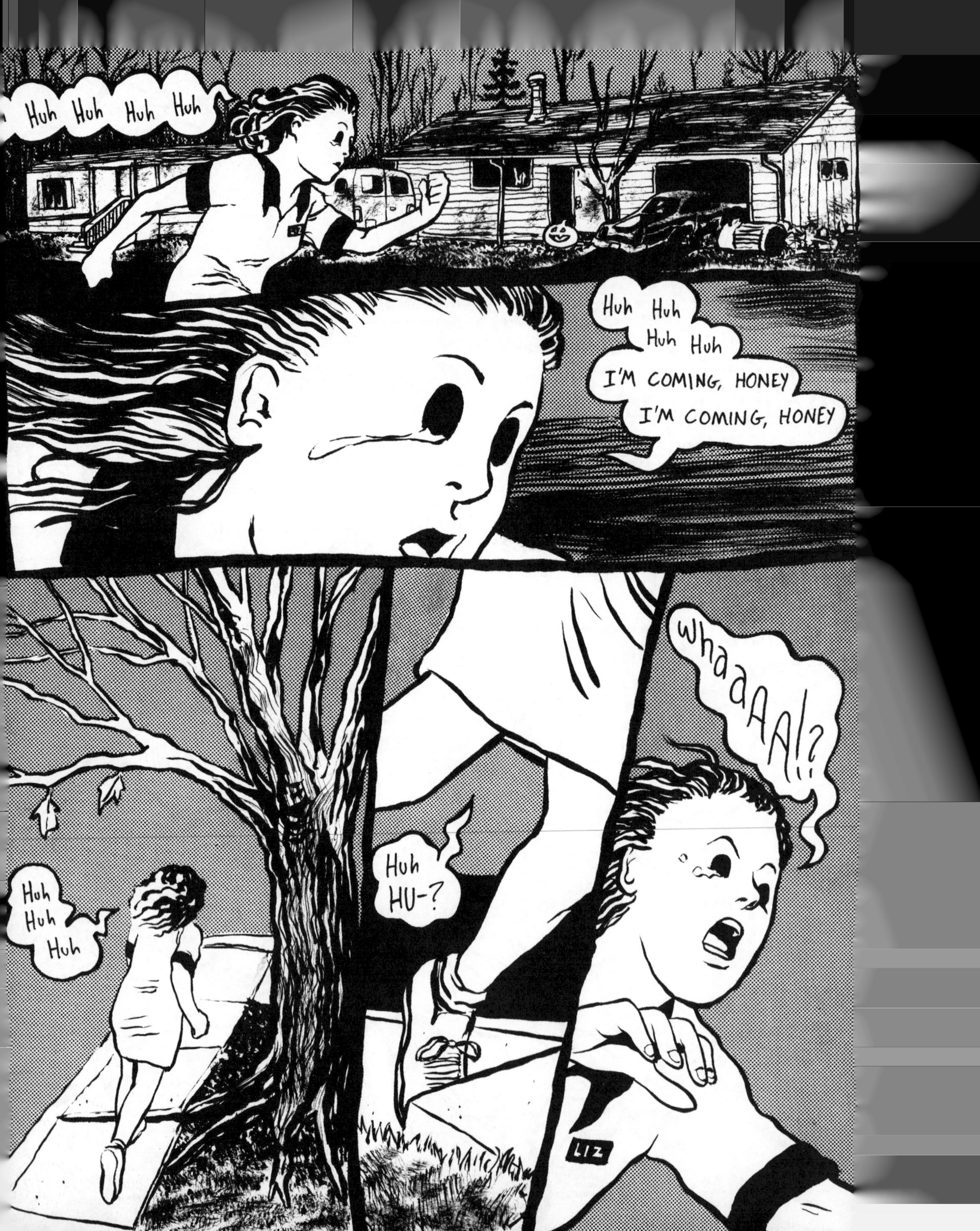
Huh Huh Huh Huh
Huh Huh Huh Huh I'M COMING, HONEY I'M COMING, HONEY
Huh Huh Huh
Huh HU-?
whaaAA!?
LIZ

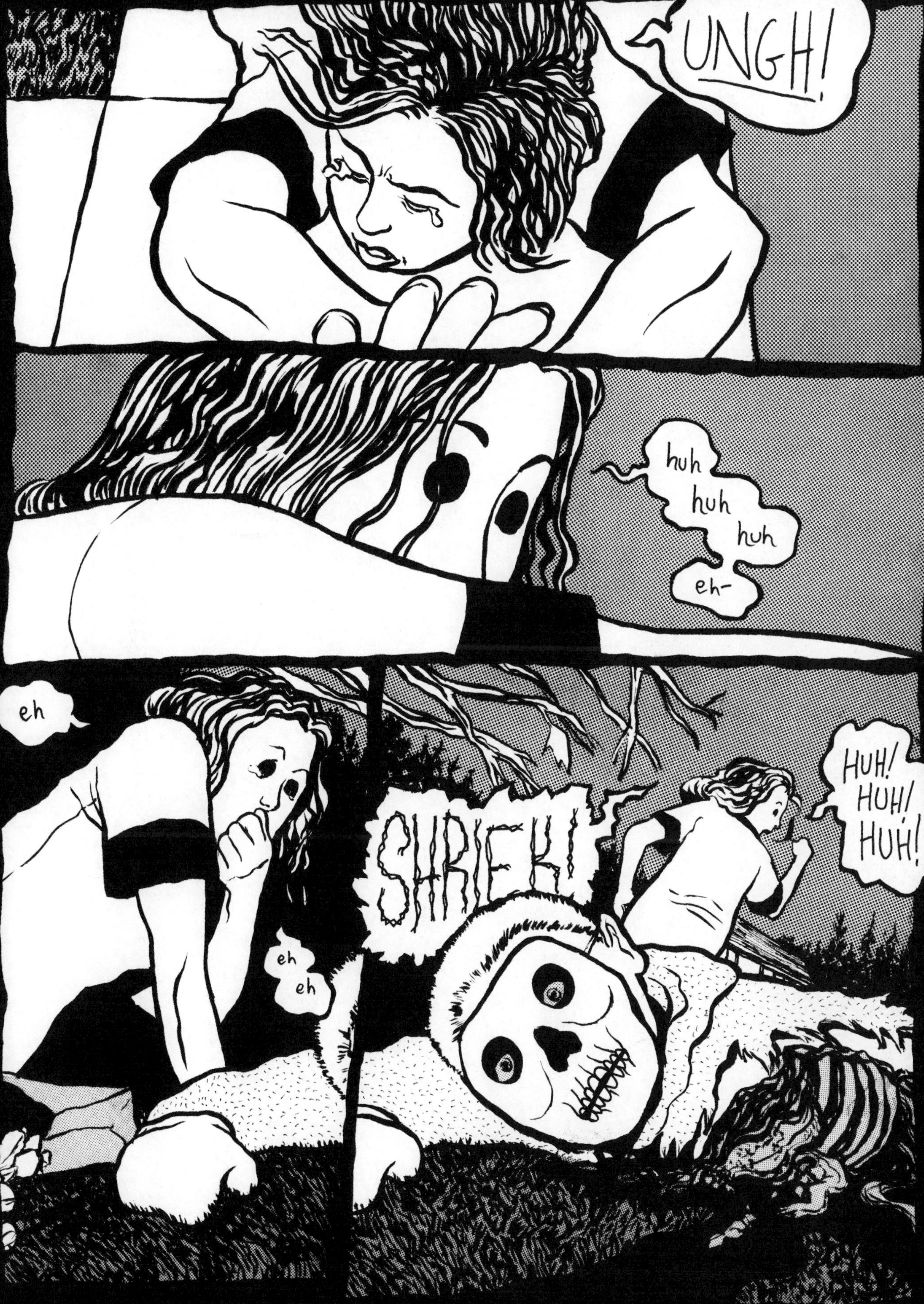
UNGH!
huh huh huh eh-
eh
eh eh
SHRIEK!
HUH! HUH! HUH!

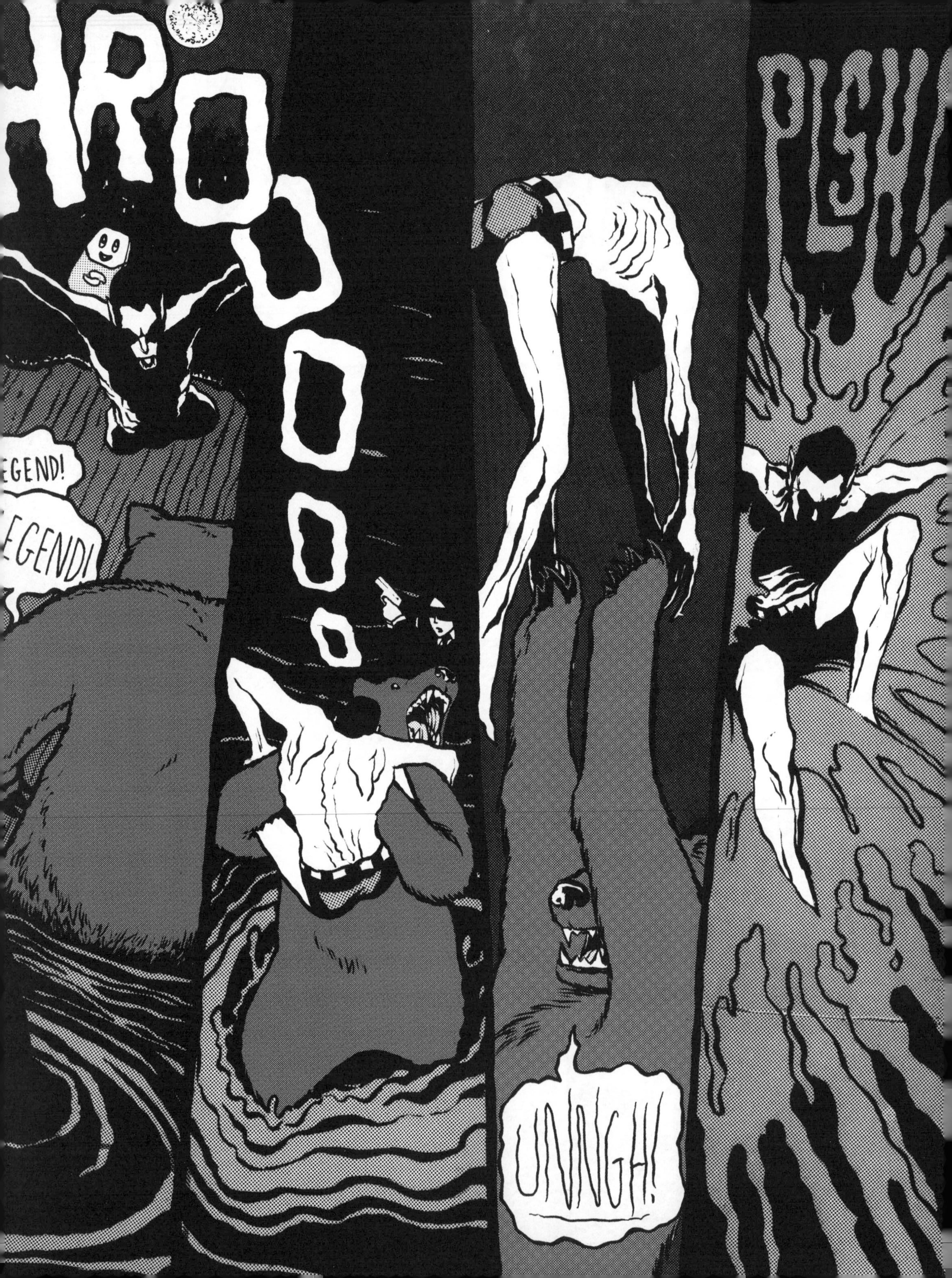

HROOOOOOO
EGEND!
EGEND!
UNNGH!
PLSH!

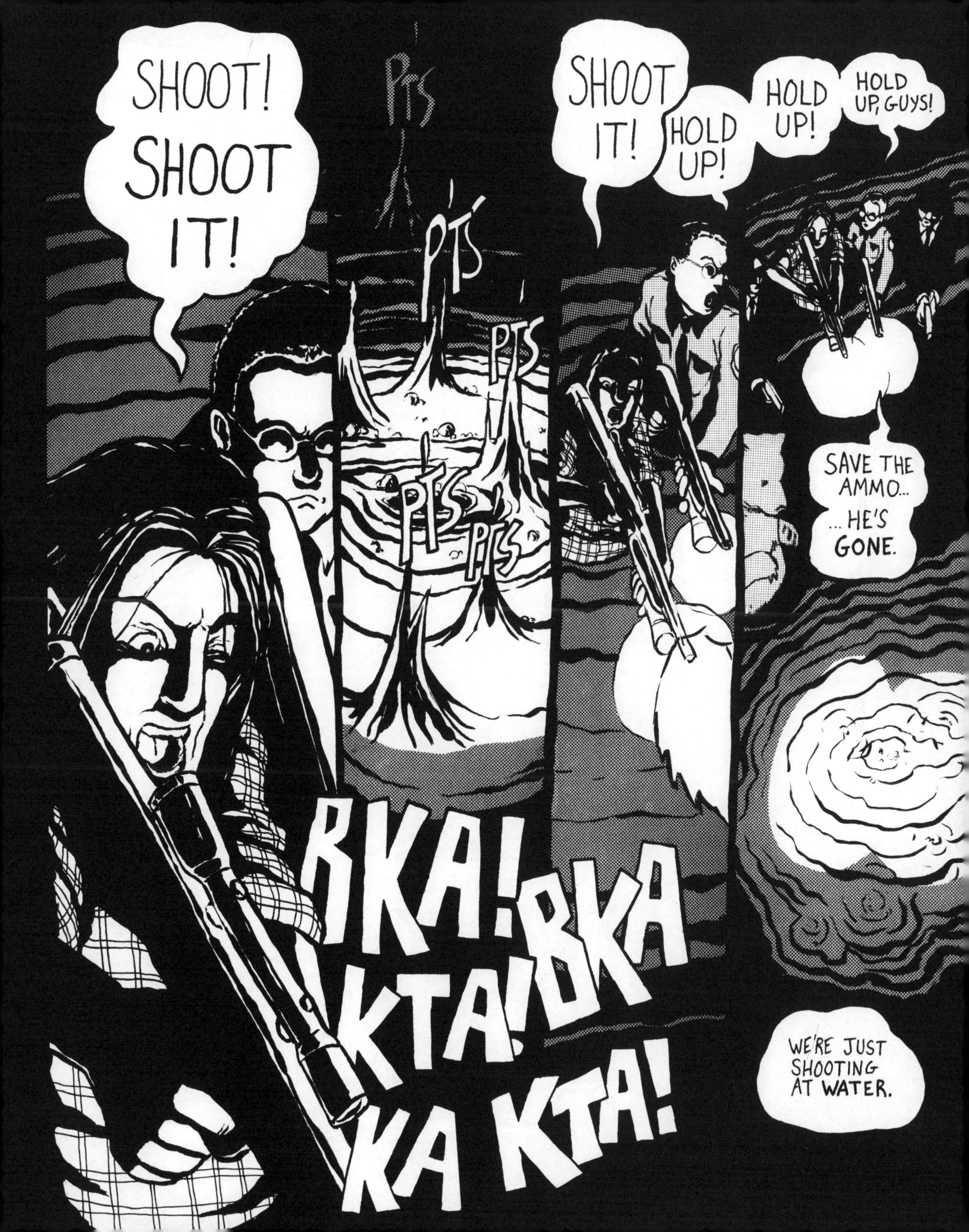
SHOOT! SHOOT IT!
PTS
PTS
PTS
PTS
PTS
SHOOT IT!
HOLD UP!
HOLD UP!
HOLD UP, GUYS!
SAVE THE AMMO... ...HE'S GONE.
BKA! KTA! BKA KTA! KA KTA!
WE'RE JUST SHOOTING AT WATER.

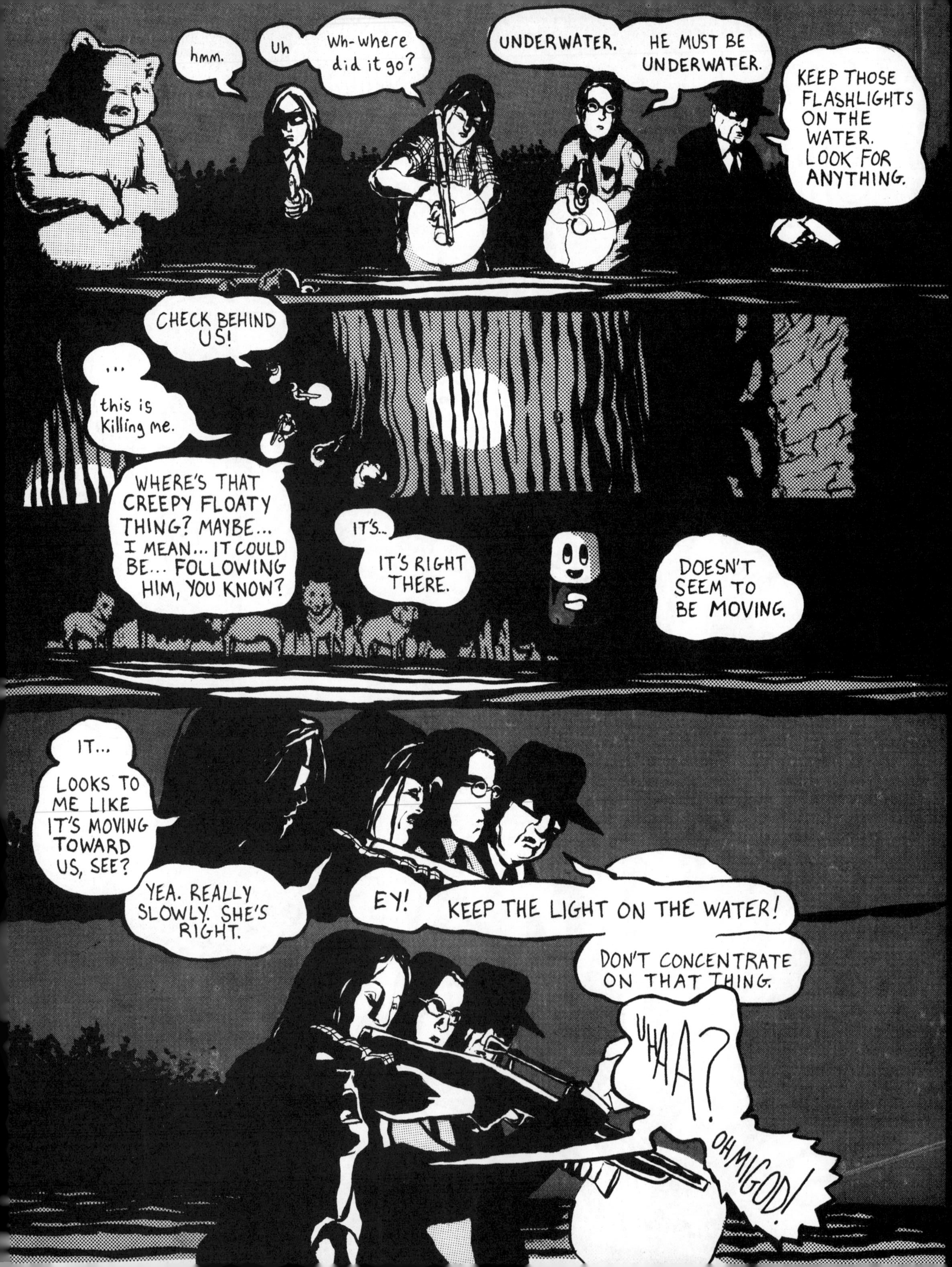
hmm.
Uh
Wh-where did it go?
UNDERWATER.
HE MUST BE UNDERWATER.
KEEP THOSE FLASHLIGHTS ON THE WATER. LOOK FOR ANYTHING.
CHECK BEHIND US!
...
this is killing me.
WHERE'S THAT CREEPY FLOATY THING? MAYBE... I MEAN... IT COULD BE... FOLLOWING HIM, YOU KNOW?
IT'S..
IT'S RIGHT THERE.
DOESN'T SEEM TO BE MOVING.
IT...
LOOKS TO ME LIKE IT'S MOVING TOWARD US, SEE?
YEA. REALLY SLOWLY. SHE'S RIGHT.
EY!
KEEP THE LIGHT ON THE WATER!
DON'T CONCENTRATE ON THAT THING.
UHAA?
OHMIGOD!

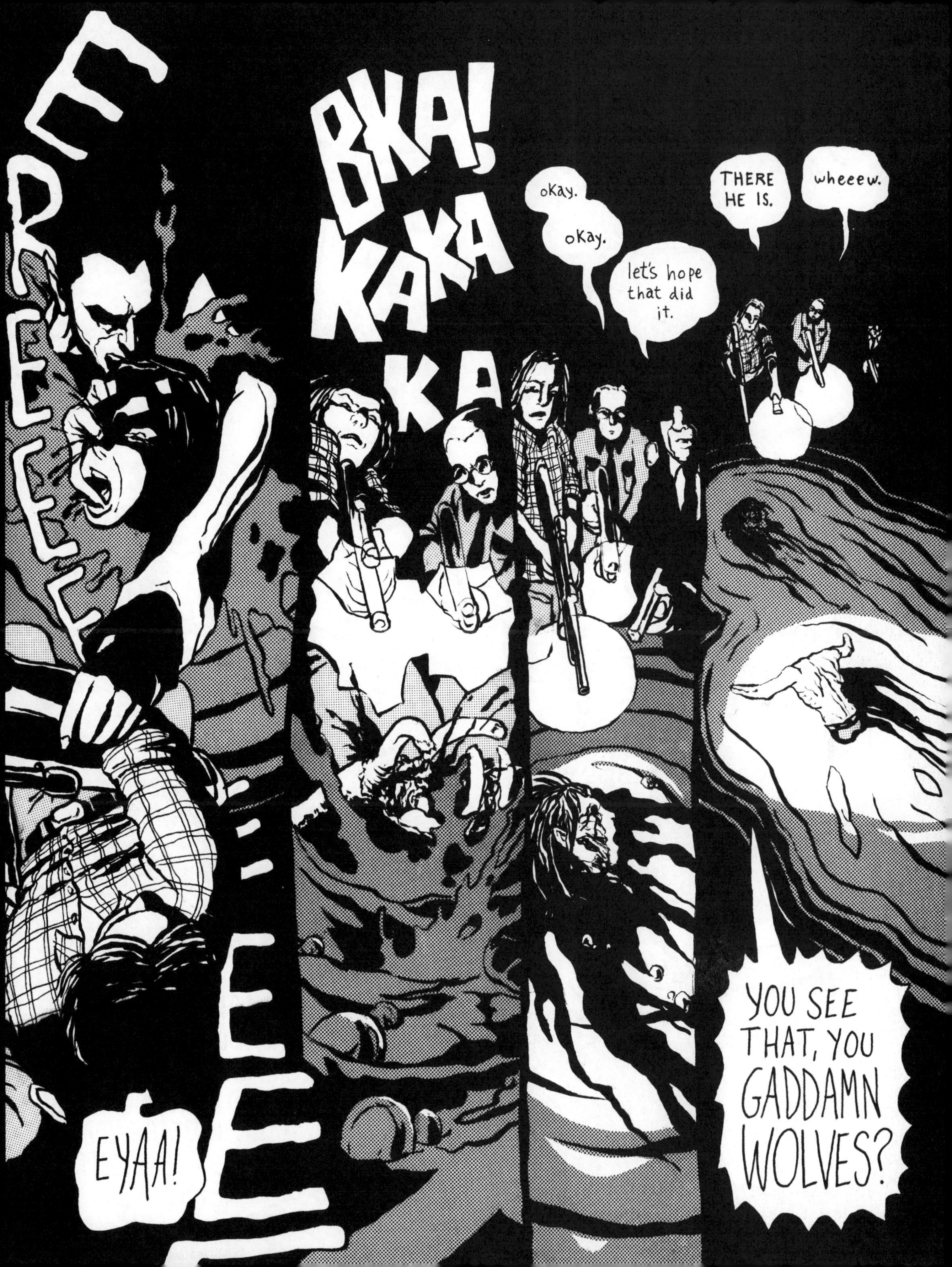
EREEEEEE...EEE
EYAA!
BKA! KAKA KA
okay.
okay.
let's hope that did it.
THERE HE IS.
wheeew.
YOU SEE THAT, YOU GADDAMN WOLVES?

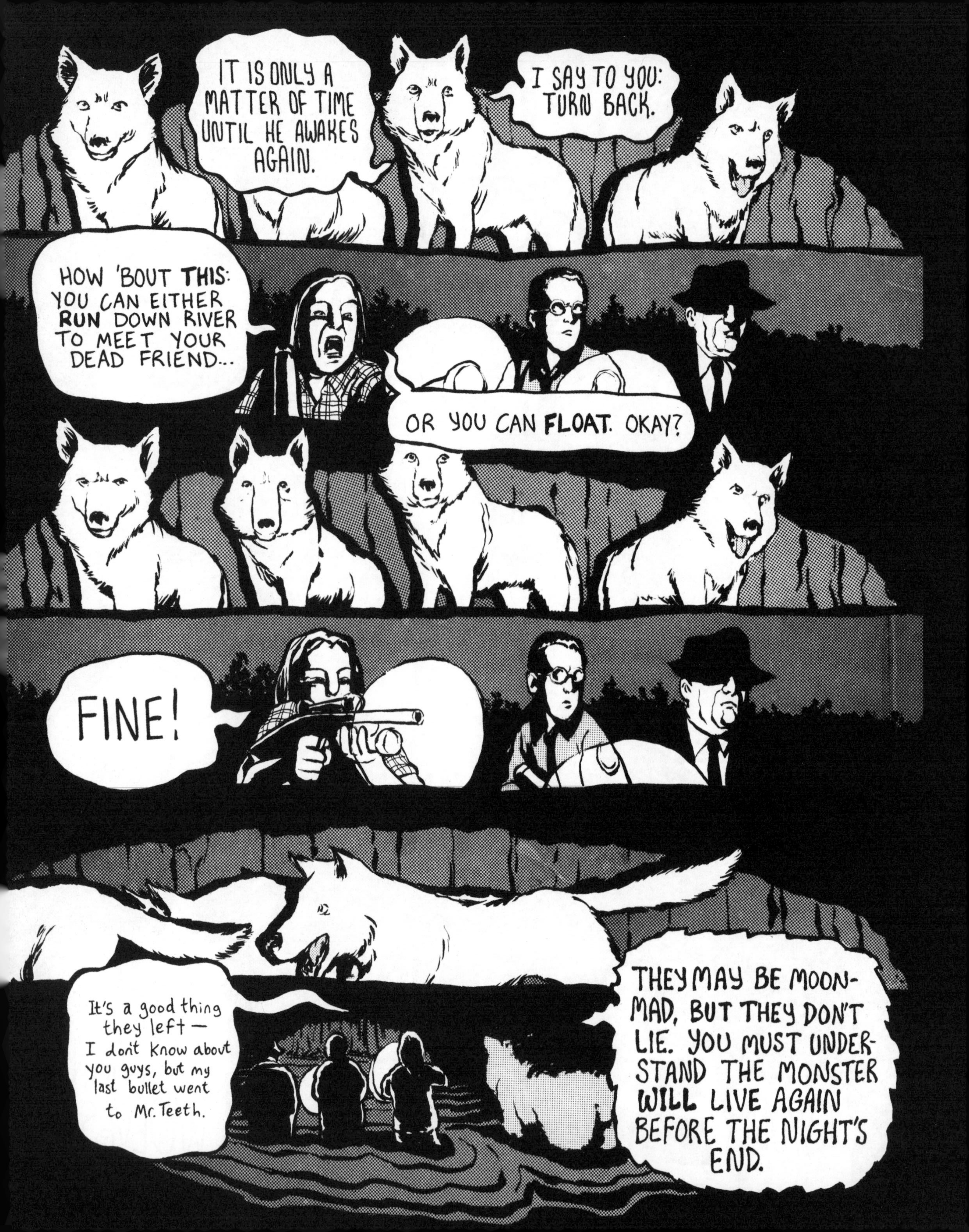
IT IS ONLY A MATTER OF TIME UNTIL HE AWAKES AGAIN.
I SAY TO YOU: TURN BACK.
HOW 'BOUT **THIS**: YOU CAN EITHER **RUN** DOWN RIVER TO MEET YOUR DEAD FRIEND...
OR YOU CAN **FLOAT**. OKAY?
FINE!
THEY MAY BE MOON-MAD, BUT THEY DON'T LIE. YOU MUST UNDER-STAND THE MONSTER **WILL** LIVE AGAIN BEFORE THE NIGHT'S END.
It's a good thing they left — I don't know about you guys, but my last bullet went to Mr. Teeth.

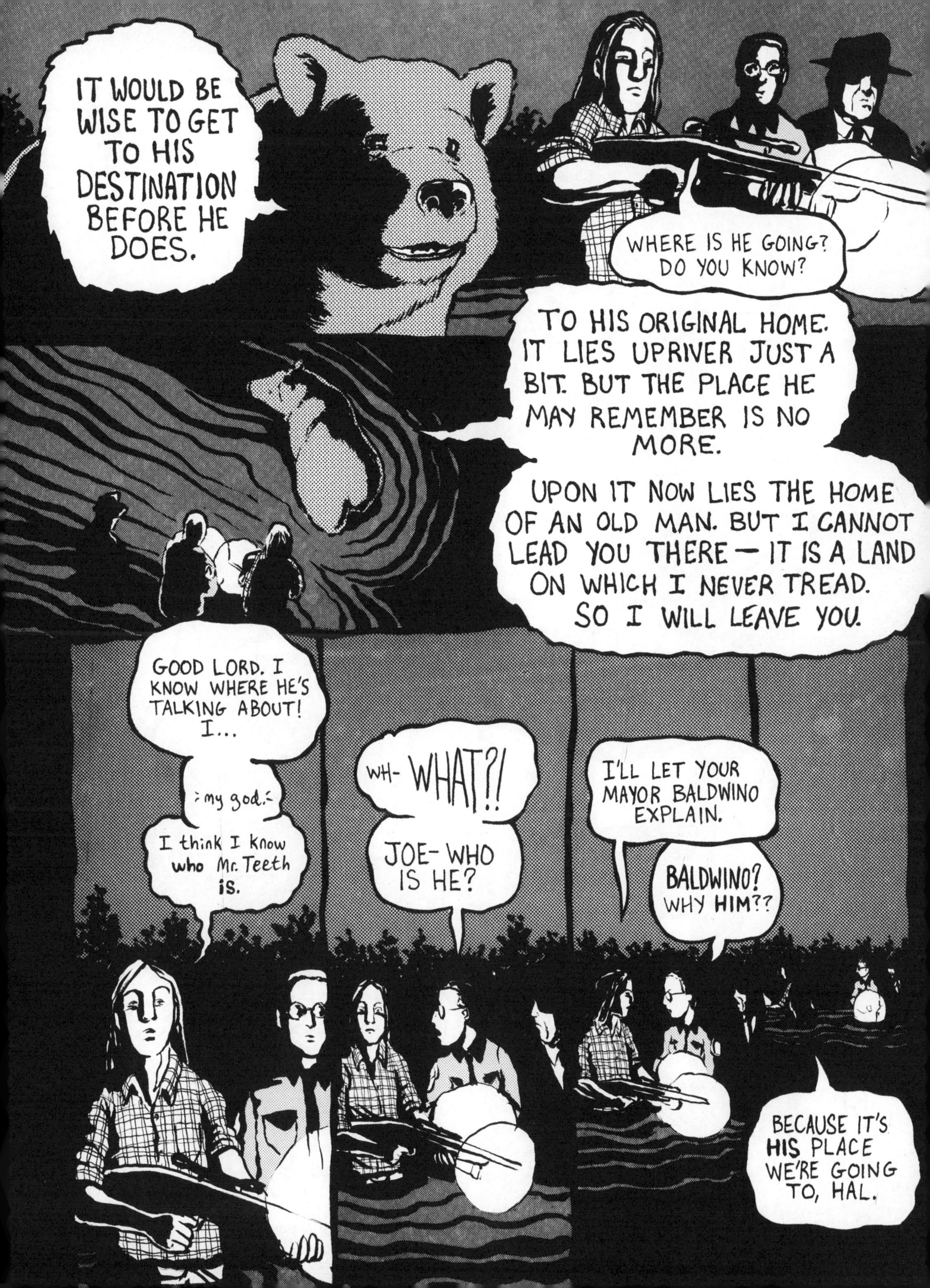
IT WOULD BE WISE TO GET TO HIS DESTINATION BEFORE HE DOES.
WHERE IS HE GOING? DO YOU KNOW?
TO HIS ORIGINAL HOME. IT LIES UPRIVER JUST A BIT. BUT THE PLACE HE MAY REMEMBER IS NO MORE.
UPON IT NOW LIES THE HOME OF AN OLD MAN. BUT I CANNOT LEAD YOU THERE — IT IS A LAND ON WHICH I NEVER TREAD. SO I WILL LEAVE YOU.
GOOD LORD. I KNOW WHERE HE'S TALKING ABOUT! I...
:my god.:
I think I know who Mr. Teeth **is.**
WH- WHAT?!
JOE- WHO IS HE?
I'LL LET YOUR MAYOR BALDWINO EXPLAIN.
BALDWINO? WHY **HIM**??
BECAUSE IT'S **HIS** PLACE WE'RE GOING TO, HAL.

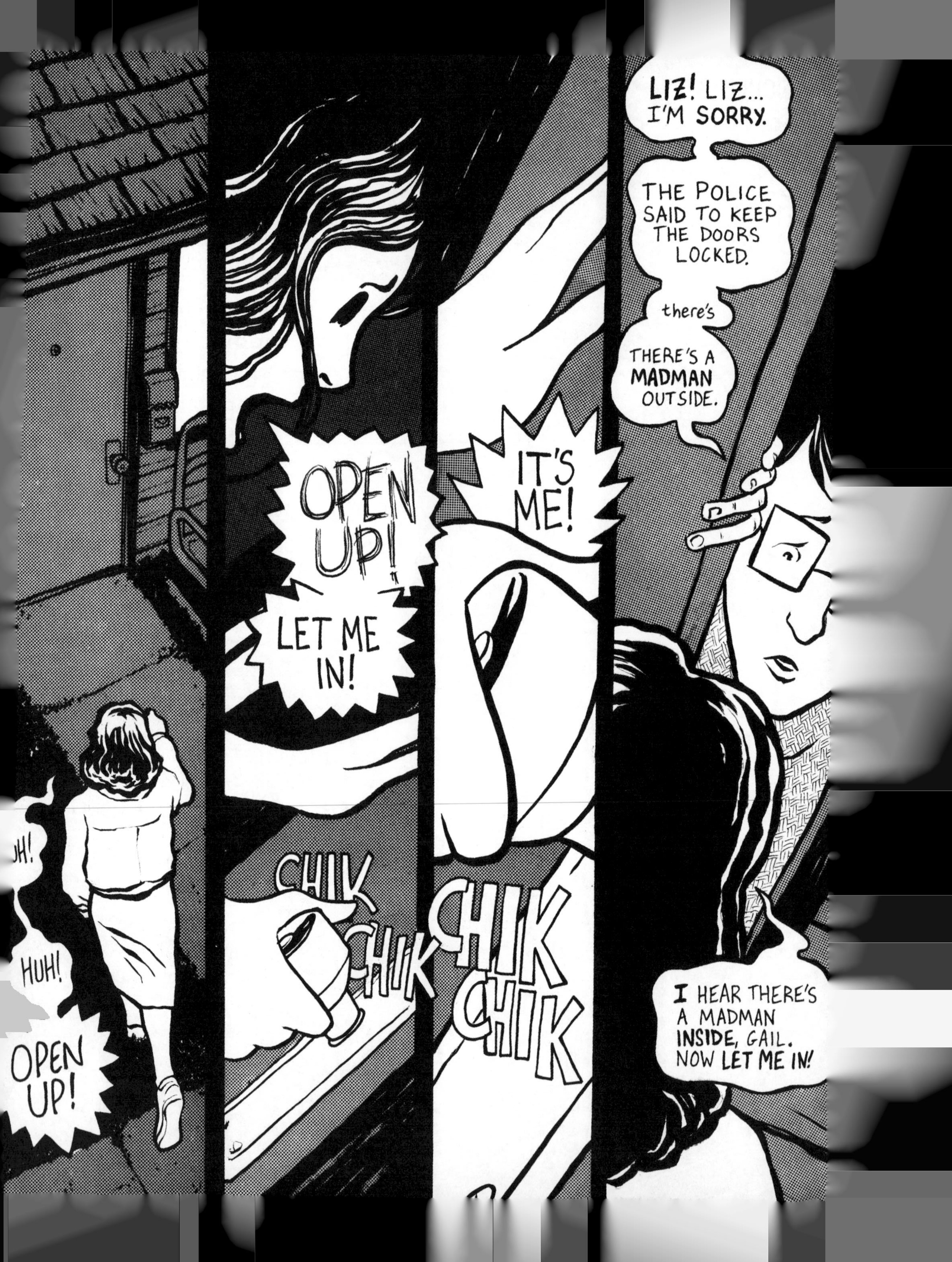
UH!
HUH!
OPEN UP!
OPEN UP!
LET ME IN!
CHIK CHIK
IT'S ME!
CHIK CHIK
LIZ! LIZ... I'M SORRY.
THE POLICE SAID TO KEEP THE DOORS LOCKED.
there's
THERE'S A MADMAN OUTSIDE.
I HEAR THERE'S A MADMAN INSIDE, GAIL. NOW LET ME IN!

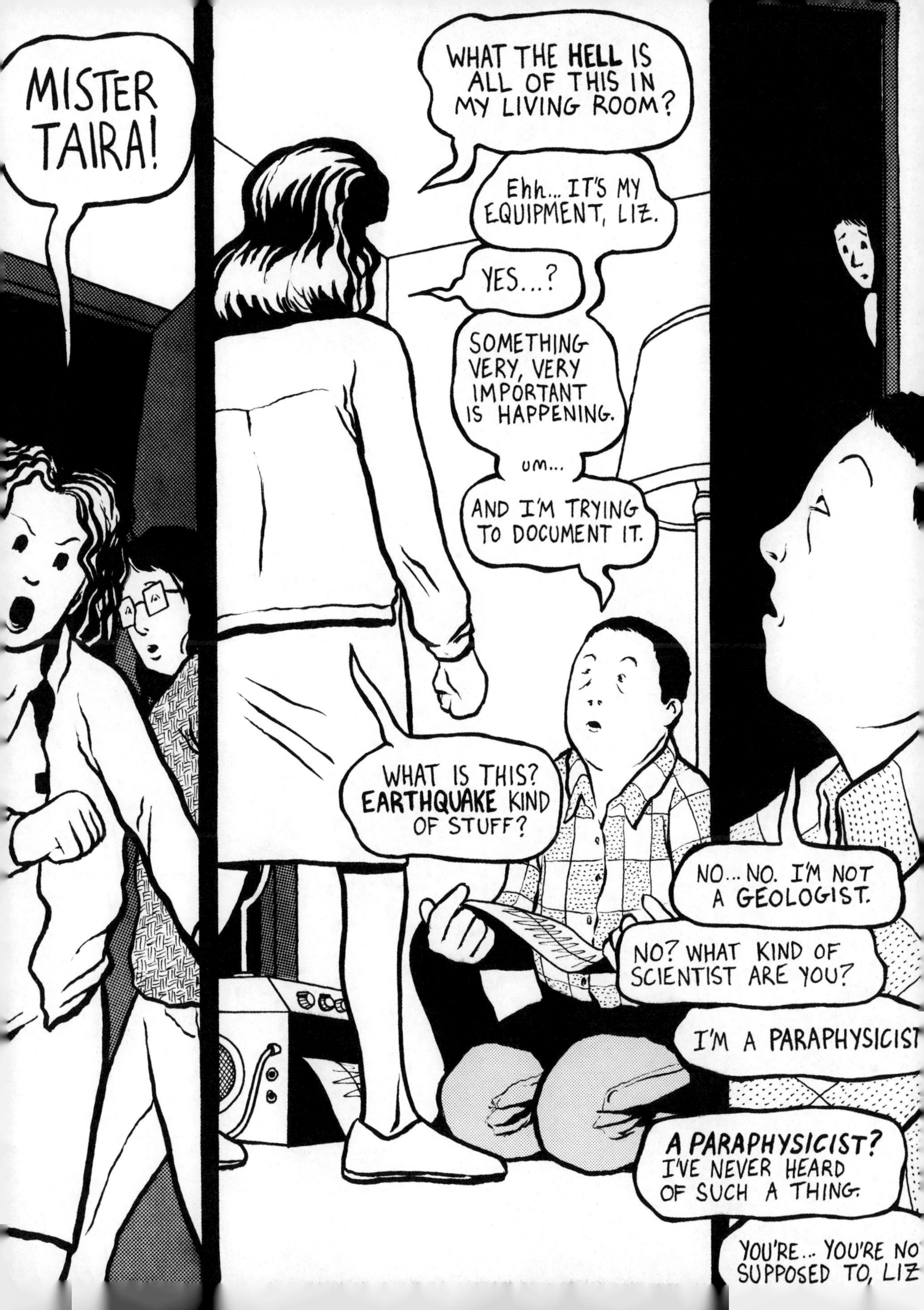
MISTER TAIRA!
WHAT THE **HELL** IS ALL OF THIS IN MY LIVING ROOM?
Ehh... IT'S MY EQUIPMENT, LIZ.
YES...?
SOMETHING VERY, VERY IMPORTANT IS HAPPENING.
um...
AND I'M TRYING TO DOCUMENT IT.
WHAT IS THIS? **EARTHQUAKE** KIND OF STUFF?
NO... NO. I'M NOT A **GEOLOGIST.**
NO? WHAT KIND OF SCIENTIST ARE YOU?
I'M A **PARAPHYSICIST**
A PARAPHYSICIST? I'VE NEVER HEARD OF SUCH A THING.
YOU'RE... YOU'RE NO SUPPOSED TO, LIZ

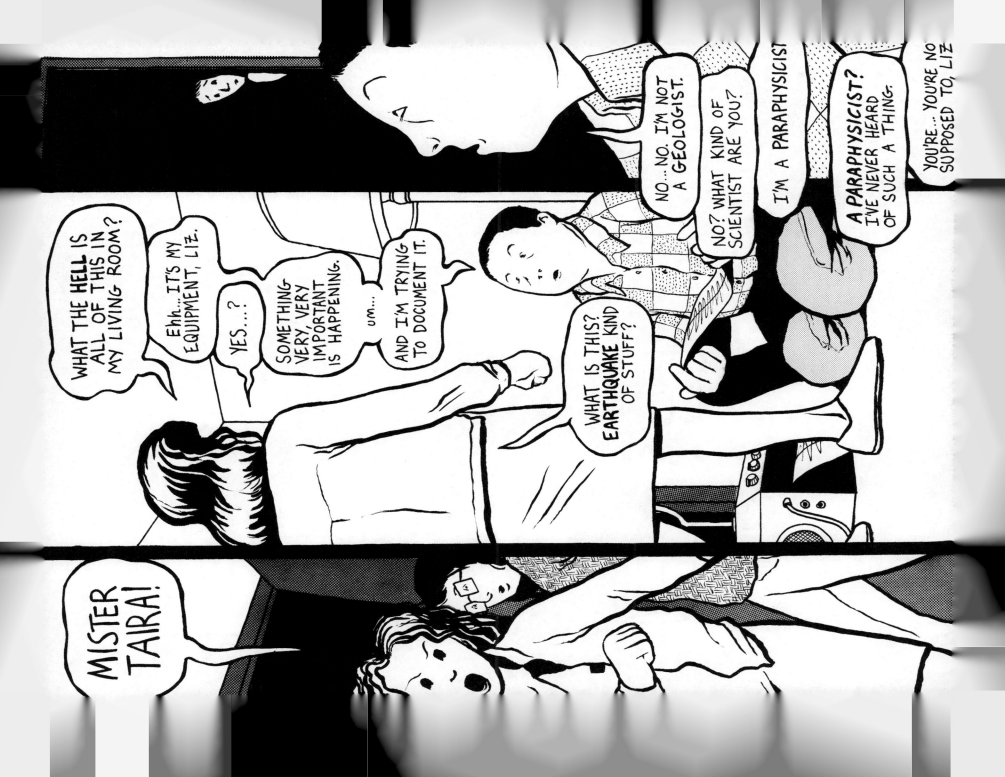

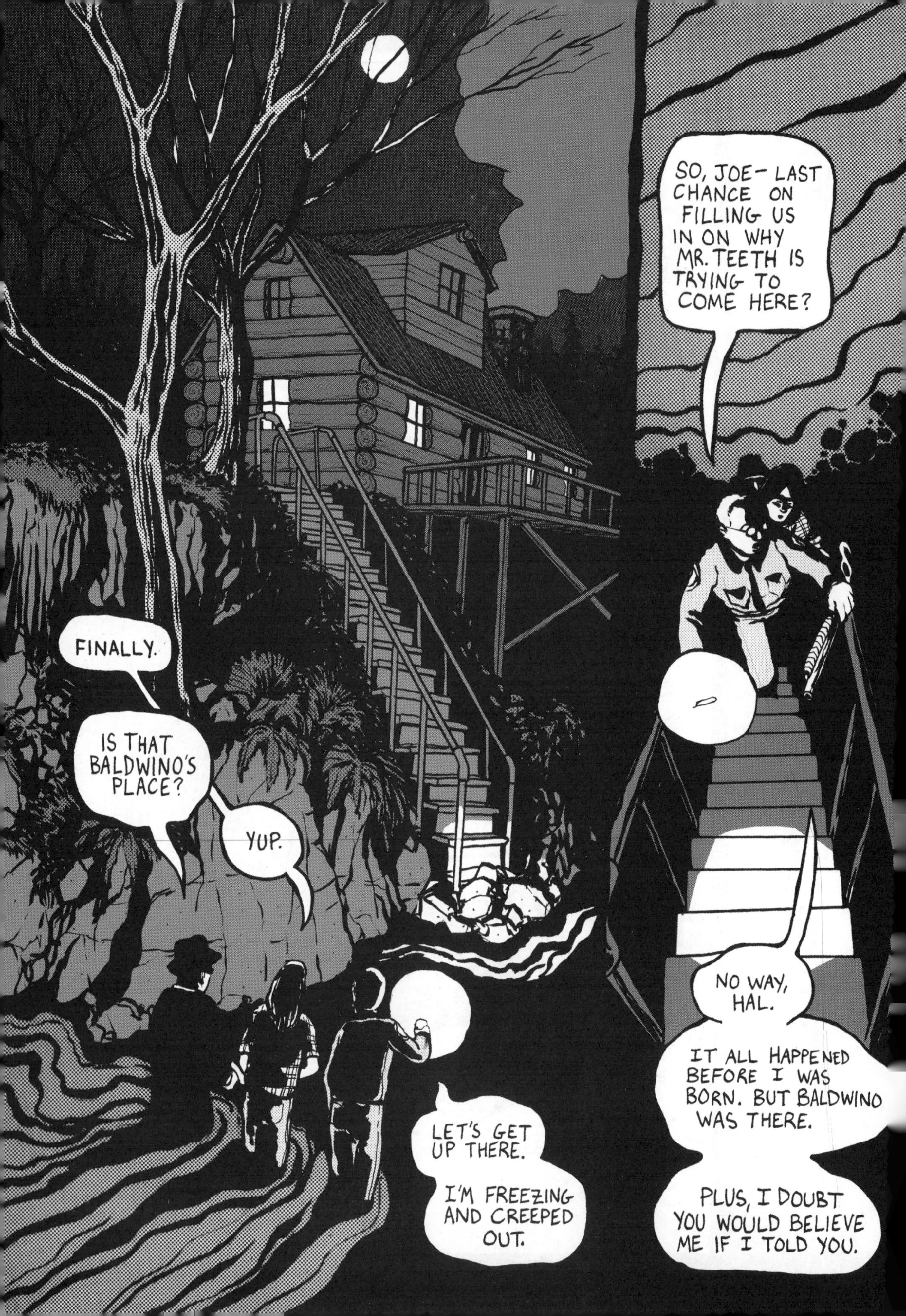
FINALLY.
IS THAT BALDWINO'S PLACE?
YUP.
LET'S GET UP THERE.
I'M FREEZING AND CREEPED OUT.
SO, JOE- LAST CHANCE ON FILLING US IN ON WHY MR. TEETH IS TRYING TO COME HERE?
NO WAY, HAL.
IT ALL HAPPENED BEFORE I WAS BORN. BUT BALDWINO WAS THERE.
PLUS, I DOUBT YOU WOULD BELIEVE ME IF I TOLD YOU.

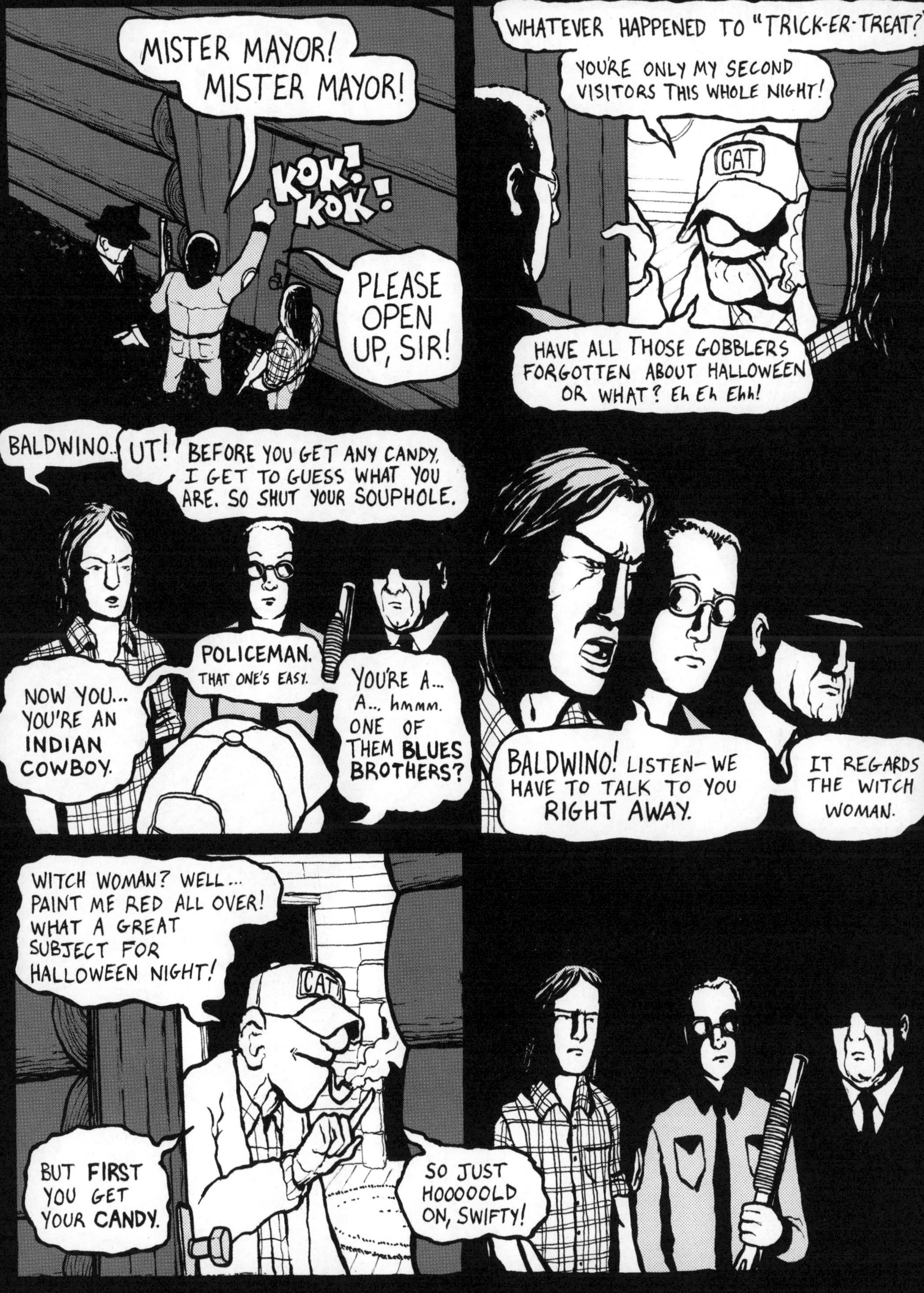
MISTER MAYOR! MISTER MAYOR!
KOK! KOK!
PLEASE OPEN UP, SIR!
WHATEVER HAPPENED TO "TRICK-ER-TREAT?"
YOU'RE ONLY MY SECOND VISITORS THIS WHOLE NIGHT!
CAT
HAVE ALL THOSE GOBBLERS FORGOTTEN ABOUT HALLOWEEN OR WHAT? Eh Eh Ehh!
BALDWINO..
UT!
BEFORE YOU GET ANY CANDY, I GET TO GUESS WHAT YOU ARE. SO SHUT YOUR SOUPHOLE.
NOW YOU... YOU'RE AN INDIAN COWBOY.
POLICEMAN. THAT ONE'S EASY.
YOU'RE A... A..., hmmm. ONE OF THEM BLUES BROTHERS?
BALDWINO! LISTEN— WE HAVE TO TALK TO YOU RIGHT AWAY.
IT REGARDS THE WITCH WOMAN.
WITCH WOMAN? WELL... PAINT ME RED ALL OVER! WHAT A GREAT SUBJECT FOR HALLOWEEN NIGHT!
CAT
BUT FIRST YOU GET YOUR CANDY.
SO JUST HOOOOOLD ON, SWIFTY!

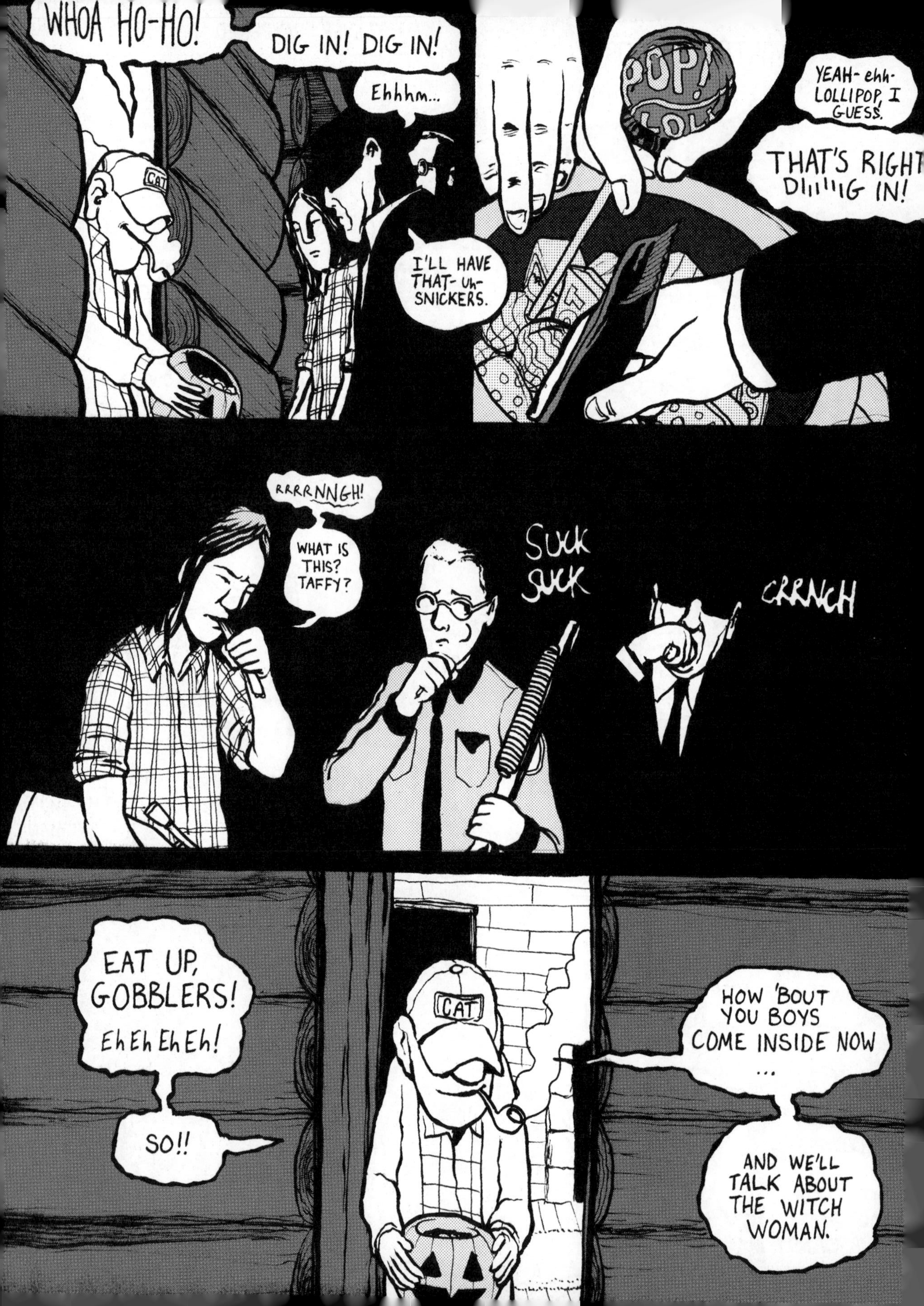
WHOA HO-HO!
DIG IN! DIG IN!
Ehhhm...
I'LL HAVE THAT- uh- SNICKERS.
POP! LOLL
YEAH- ehh- LOLLIPOP, I GUESS.
THAT'S RIGHT DIIIIIG IN!
RRRRNNGH!
WHAT IS THIS? TAFFY?
SUCK SUCK
CRRNCH
EAT UP, GOBBLERS!
EhEhEhEh!
SO!!
CAT
HOW 'BOUT YOU BOYS COME INSIDE NOW ...
AND WE'LL TALK ABOUT THE WITCH WOMAN.

7.
HOME

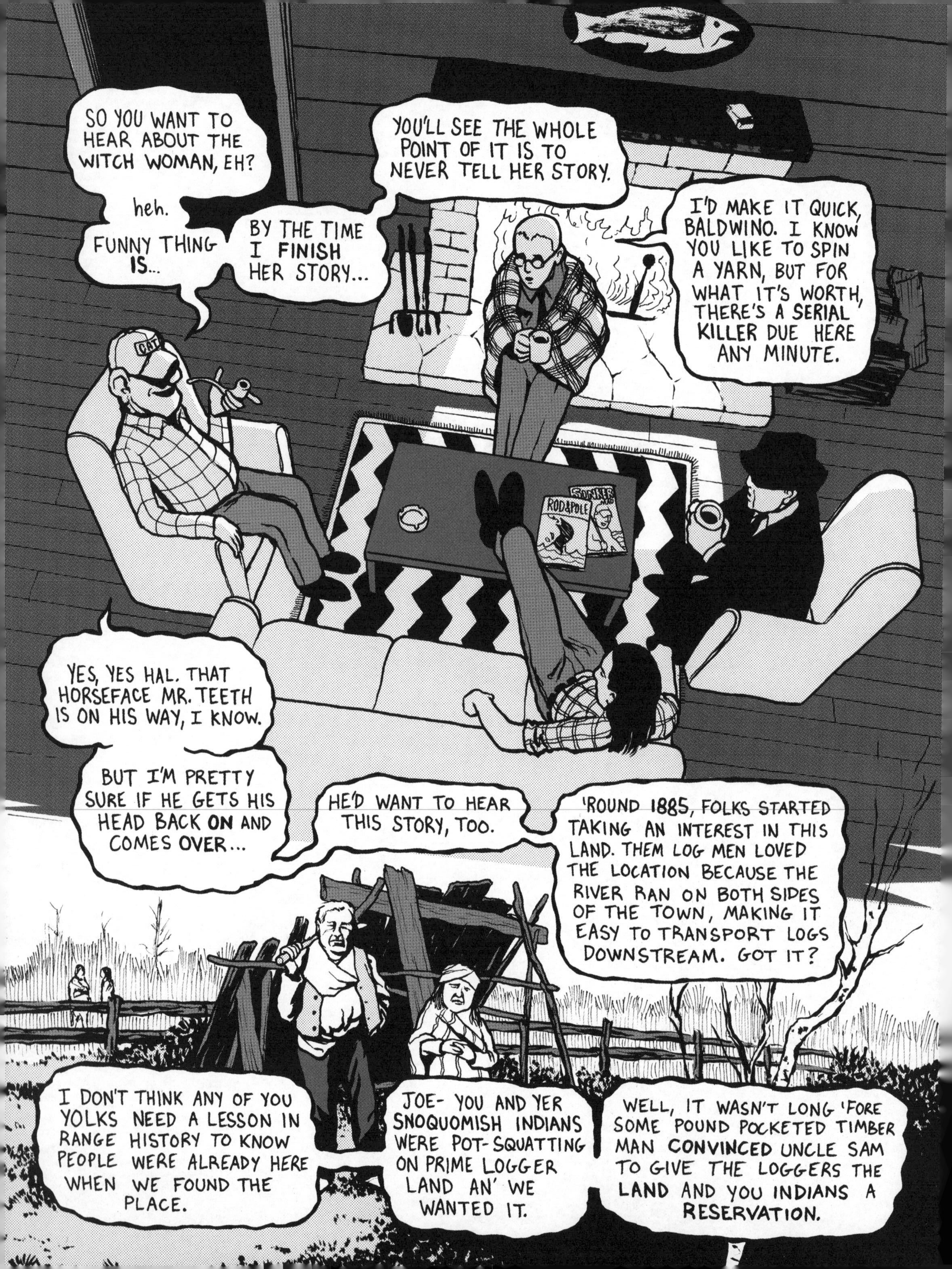
SO YOU WANT TO HEAR ABOUT THE WITCH WOMAN, EH?
heh.
FUNNY THING IS...
BY THE TIME I FINISH HER STORY...
YOU'LL SEE THE WHOLE POINT OF IT IS TO NEVER TELL HER STORY.
I'D MAKE IT QUICK, BALDWINO. I KNOW YOU LIKE TO SPIN A YARN, BUT FOR WHAT IT'S WORTH, THERE'S A SERIAL KILLER DUE HERE ANY MINUTE.
YES, YES HAL. THAT HORSEFACE MR. TEETH IS ON HIS WAY, I KNOW.
BUT I'M PRETTY SURE IF HE GETS HIS HEAD BACK ON AND COMES OVER...
HE'D WANT TO HEAR THIS STORY, TOO.
ROD&POLE
'ROUND 1885, FOLKS STARTED TAKING AN INTEREST IN THIS LAND. THEM LOG MEN LOVED THE LOCATION BECAUSE THE RIVER RAN ON BOTH SIDES OF THE TOWN, MAKING IT EASY TO TRANSPORT LOGS DOWNSTREAM. GOT IT?
I DON'T THINK ANY OF YOU YOLKS NEED A LESSON IN RANGE HISTORY TO KNOW PEOPLE WERE ALREADY HERE WHEN WE FOUND THE PLACE.
JOE- YOU AND YER SNOQUOMISH INDIANS WERE POT-SQUATTING ON PRIME LOGGER LAND AN' WE WANTED IT.
WELL, IT WASN'T LONG 'FORE SOME POUND POCKETED TIMBER MAN CONVINCED UNCLE SAM TO GIVE THE LOGGERS THE LAND AND YOU INDIANS A RESERVATION.

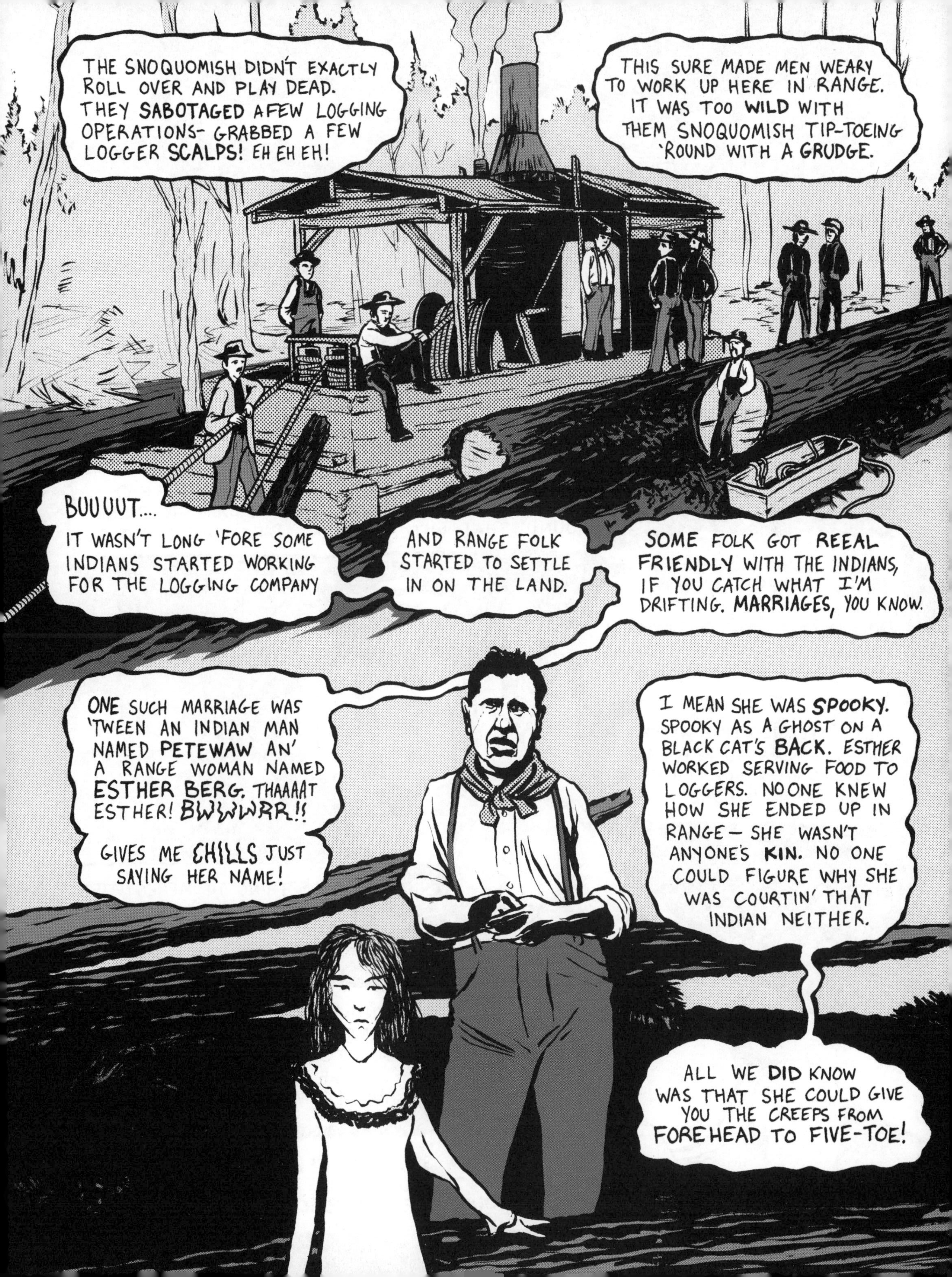
THE SNOQUOMISH DIDN'T EXACTLY ROLL OVER AND PLAY DEAD. THEY SABOTAGED AFEW LOGGING OPERATIONS- GRABBED A FEW LOGGER SCALPS! EH EH EH!
THIS SURE MADE MEN WEARY TO WORK UP HERE IN RANGE. IT WAS TOO WILD WITH THEM SNOQUOMISH TIP-TOEING 'ROUND WITH A GRUDGE.
BUUUUT....
IT WASN'T LONG 'FORE SOME INDIANS STARTED WORKING FOR THE LOGGING COMPANY
AND RANGE FOLK STARTED TO SETTLE IN ON THE LAND.
SOME FOLK GOT REEAL FRIENDLY WITH THE INDIANS, IF YOU CATCH WHAT I'M DRIFTING. MARRIAGES, YOU KNOW.
ONE SUCH MARRIAGE WAS 'TWEEN AN INDIAN MAN NAMED PETEWAW AN' A RANGE WOMAN NAMED ESTHER BERG. THAAAAT ESTHER! BWWWRR!!
GIVES ME CHILLS JUST SAYING HER NAME!
I MEAN SHE WAS SPOOKY. SPOOKY AS A GHOST ON A BLACK CAT'S BACK. ESTHER WORKED SERVING FOOD TO LOGGERS. NOONE KNEW HOW SHE ENDED UP IN RANGE- SHE WASN'T ANYONE'S KIN. NO ONE COULD FIGURE WHY SHE WAS COURTIN' THAT INDIAN NEITHER.
ALL WE DID KNOW WAS THAT SHE COULD GIVE YOU THE CREEPS FROM FOREHEAD TO FIVE-TOE!

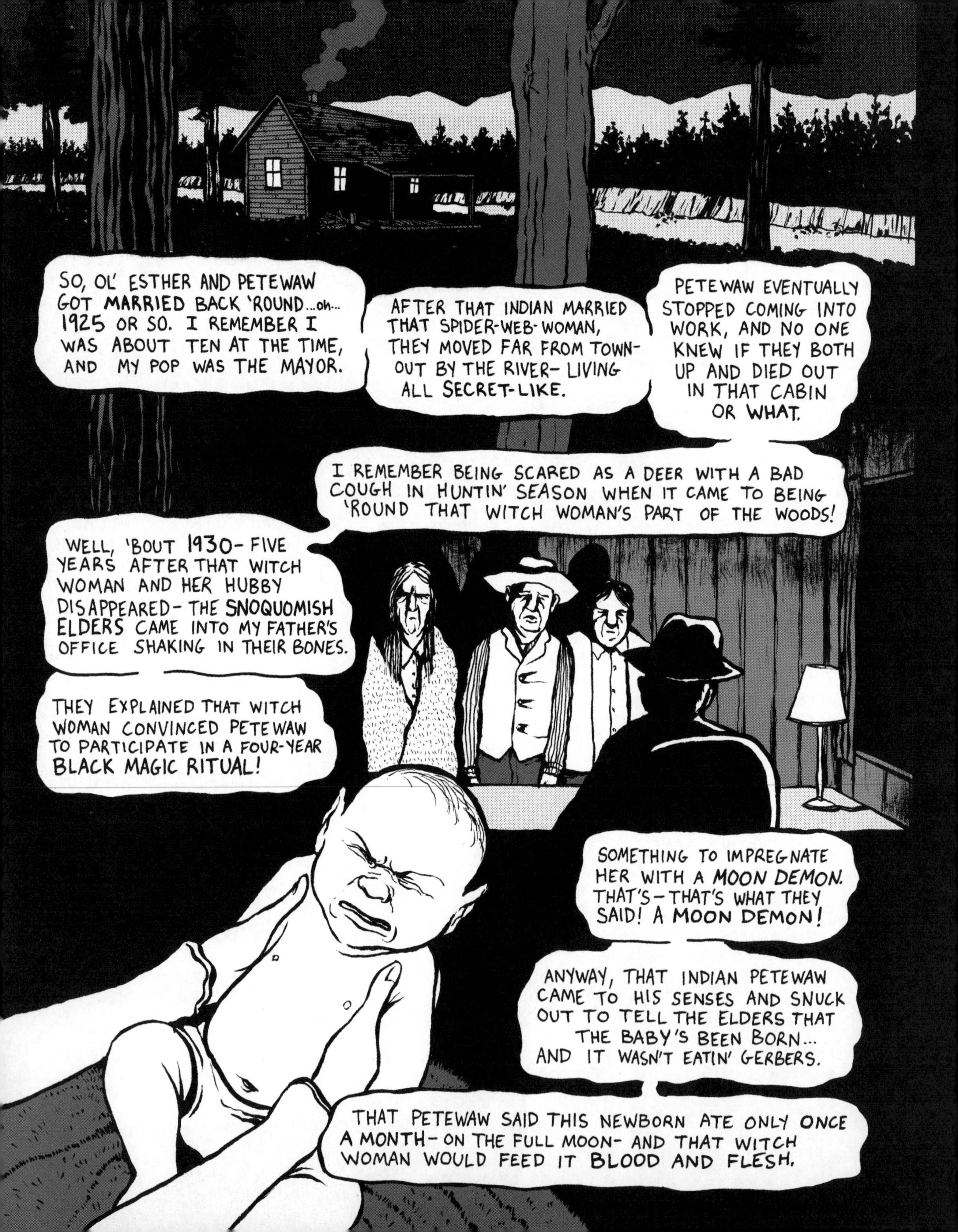
SO, OL' ESTHER AND PETEWAW GOT MARRIED BACK 'ROUND...oh... 1925 OR SO. I REMEMBER I WAS ABOUT TEN AT THE TIME, AND MY POP WAS THE MAYOR.
AFTER THAT INDIAN MARRIED THAT SPIDER-WEB-WOMAN, THEY MOVED FAR FROM TOWN- OUT BY THE RIVER- LIVING ALL SECRET-LIKE.
PETEWAW EVENTUALLY STOPPED COMING INTO WORK, AND NO ONE KNEW IF THEY BOTH UP AND DIED OUT IN THAT CABIN OR WHAT.
I REMEMBER BEING SCARED AS A DEER WITH A BAD COUGH IN HUNTIN' SEASON WHEN IT CAME TO BEING 'ROUND THAT WITCH WOMAN'S PART OF THE WOODS!
WELL, 'BOUT 1930- FIVE YEARS AFTER THAT WITCH WOMAN AND HER HUBBY DISAPPEARED- THE SNOQUOMISH ELDERS CAME INTO MY FATHER'S OFFICE SHAKING IN THEIR BONES.
THEY EXPLAINED THAT WITCH WOMAN CONVINCED PETEWAW TO PARTICIPATE IN A FOUR-YEAR BLACK MAGIC RITUAL!
SOMETHING TO IMPREGNATE HER WITH A MOON DEMON. THAT'S- THAT'S WHAT THEY SAID! A MOON DEMON!
ANYWAY, THAT INDIAN PETEWAW CAME TO HIS SENSES AND SNUCK OUT TO TELL THE ELDERS THAT THE BABY'S BEEN BORN... AND IT WASN'T EATIN' GERBERS.
THAT PETEWAW SAID THIS NEWBORN ATE ONLY ONCE A MONTH- ON THE FULL MOON- AND THAT WITCH WOMAN WOULD FEED IT BLOOD AND FLESH.

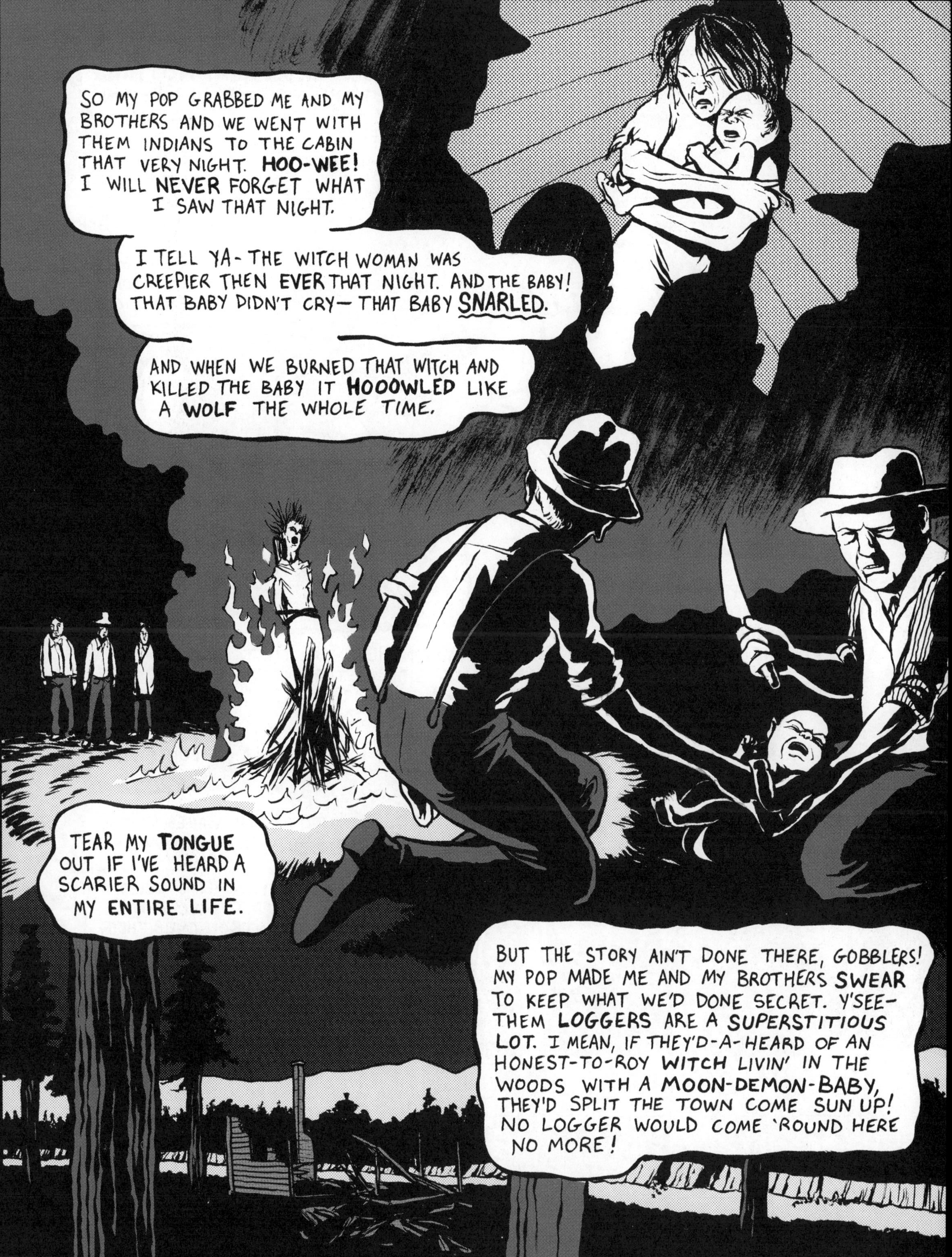
SO MY POP GRABBED ME AND MY BROTHERS AND WE WENT WITH THEM INDIANS TO THE CABIN THAT VERY NIGHT. HOO-WEE! I WILL NEVER FORGET WHAT I SAW THAT NIGHT.
I TELL YA- THE WITCH WOMAN WAS CREEPIER THEN EVER THAT NIGHT. AND THE BABY! THAT BABY DIDN'T CRY— THAT BABY SNARLED.
AND WHEN WE BURNED THAT WITCH AND KILLED THE BABY IT HOOOWLED LIKE A WOLF THE WHOLE TIME.
TEAR MY TONGUE OUT IF I'VE HEARD A SCARIER SOUND IN MY ENTIRE LIFE.
BUT THE STORY AIN'T DONE THERE, GOBBLERS! MY POP MADE ME AND MY BROTHERS SWEAR TO KEEP WHAT WE'D DONE SECRET. Y'SEE- THEM LOGGERS ARE A SUPERSTITIOUS LOT. I MEAN, IF THEY'D-A-HEARD OF AN HONEST-TO-ROY WITCH LIVIN' IN THE WOODS WITH A MOON-DEMON-BABY, THEY'D SPLIT THE TOWN COME SUN UP! NO LOGGER WOULD COME 'ROUND HERE NO MORE!

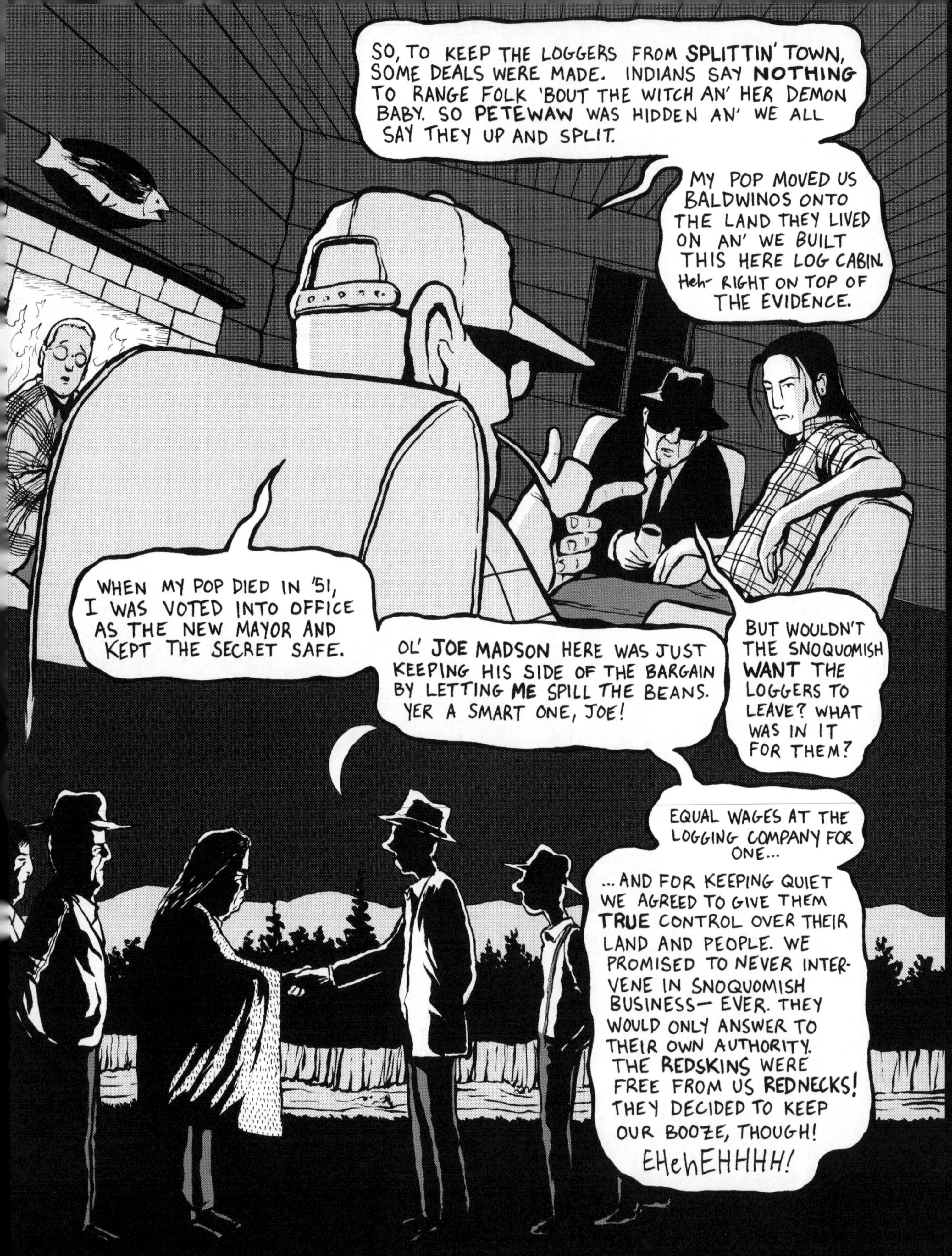
SO, TO KEEP THE LOGGERS FROM SPLITTIN' TOWN, SOME DEALS WERE MADE. INDIANS SAY NOTHING TO RANGE FOLK 'BOUT THE WITCH AN' HER DEMON BABY. SO PETEWAW WAS HIDDEN AN' WE ALL SAY THEY UP AND SPLIT.
MY POP MOVED US BALDWINOS ONTO THE LAND THEY LIVED ON AN' WE BUILT THIS HERE LOG CABIN. Heh- RIGHT ON TOP OF THE EVIDENCE.
WHEN MY POP DIED IN '51, I WAS VOTED INTO OFFICE AS THE NEW MAYOR AND KEPT THE SECRET SAFE.
OL' JOE MADSON HERE WAS JUST KEEPING HIS SIDE OF THE BARGAIN BY LETTING ME SPILL THE BEANS. YER A SMART ONE, JOE!
BUT WOULDN'T THE SNOQUOMISH WANT THE LOGGERS TO LEAVE? WHAT WAS IN IT FOR THEM?
EQUAL WAGES AT THE LOGGING COMPANY FOR ONE...
...AND FOR KEEPING QUIET WE AGREED TO GIVE THEM TRUE CONTROL OVER THEIR LAND AND PEOPLE. WE PROMISED TO NEVER INTERVENE IN SNOQUOMISH BUSINESS— EVER. THEY WOULD ONLY ANSWER TO THEIR OWN AUTHORITY. THE REDSKINS WERE FREE FROM US REDNECKS! THEY DECIDED TO KEEP OUR BOOZE, THOUGH!
EHehEHHHH!

WHOA—MORT!?? THIS IS PART OF THE REASON YOU GAVE AMNESTY TO THAT GUY??

I'VE GOT AN IDEA. AN' I'D TELL YA IF YOU'D JUST MOVE YER MUD-MUSHERS.

EY, JOE— WE'RE NOT THE ONES WHO DECIDED TO TEST THE WATERS BY ADOPTING A PSYCHO PIRATE.

THERE'S THAT RANGE "RESPECT" WE'VE LEARNED TO EXPECT, BALDWINO.

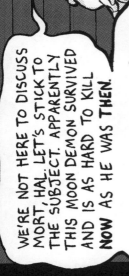

WE'RE NOT HERE TO DISCUSS MORT, HAL. LET'S STICK TO THE SUBJECT. APPARENTLY THIS MOON DEMON SURVIVED AND IS AS HARD TO KILL **NOW** AS HE WAS **THEN.**

IT SEEMS HE WANTS TO RETURN TO WHERE HE WAS BORN—HERE. SO HOW DO WE STOP HIM?

mud

mushers?

...

YER FEET.

OH!

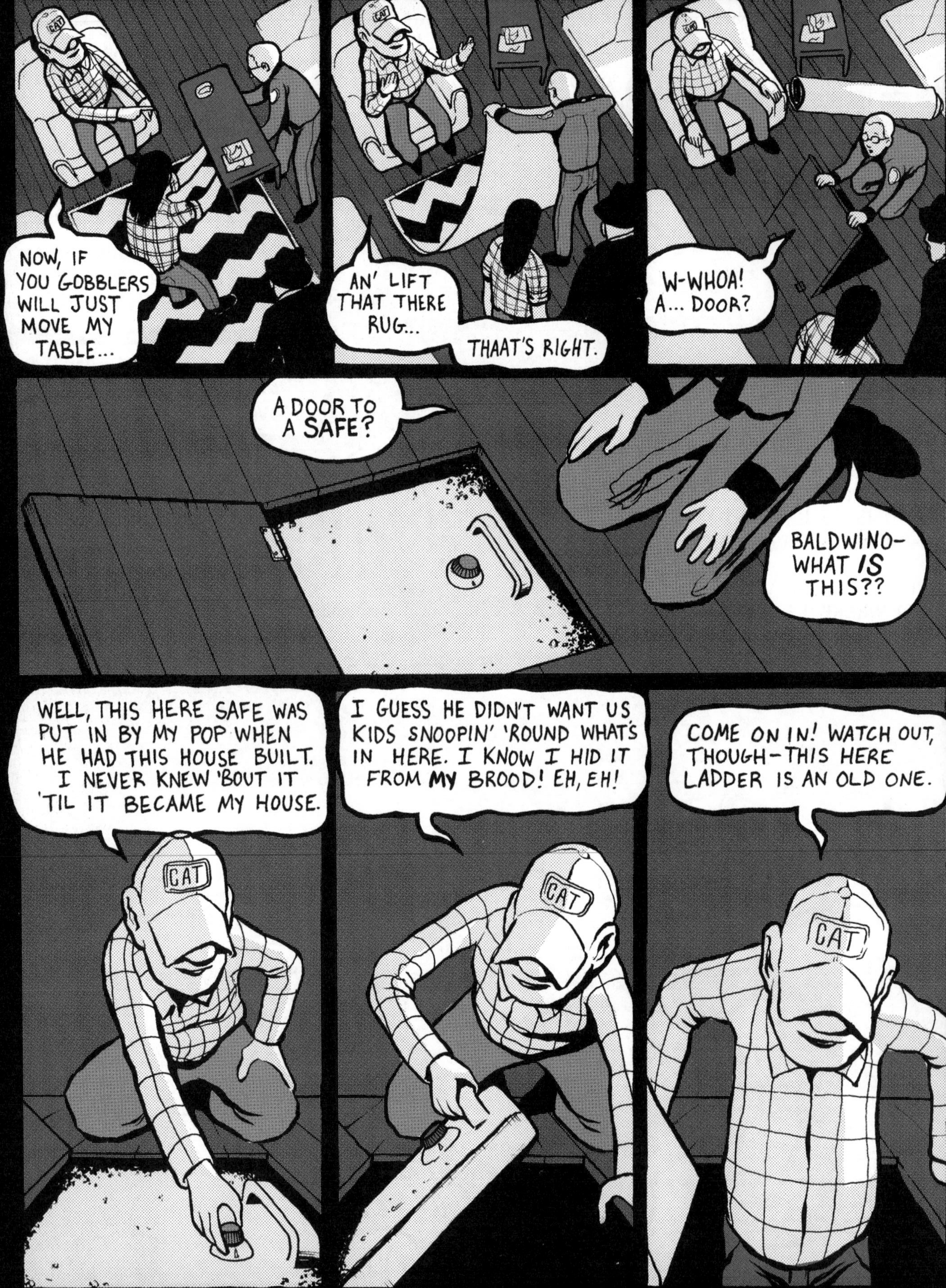
NOW, IF YOU GOBBLERS WILL JUST MOVE MY TABLE...
AN' LIFT THAT THERE RUG...
THAAT'S RIGHT.
W-WHOA! A... DOOR?
A DOOR TO A SAFE?
BALDWINO— WHAT IS THIS??
WELL, THIS HERE SAFE WAS PUT IN BY MY POP WHEN HE HAD THIS HOUSE BUILT. I NEVER KNEW 'BOUT IT 'TIL IT BECAME MY HOUSE.
I GUESS HE DIDN'T WANT US KIDS SNOOPIN' 'ROUND WHAT'S IN HERE. I KNOW I HID IT FROM MY BROOD! EH, EH!
COME ON IN! WATCH OUT, THOUGH—THIS HERE LADDER IS AN OLD ONE.

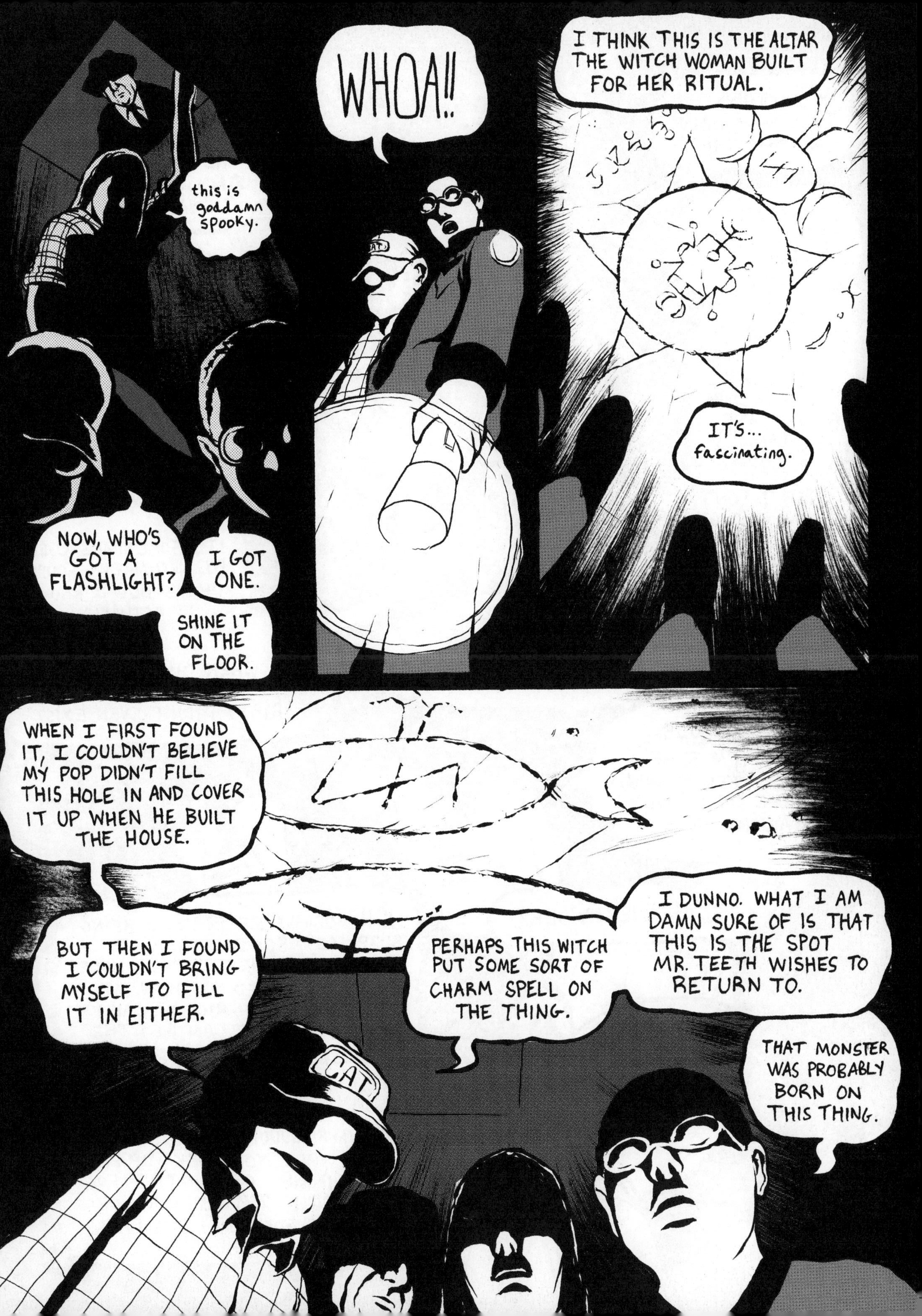
this is goddamn spooky.
NOW, WHO'S GOT A FLASHLIGHT?
I GOT ONE.
SHINE IT ON THE FLOOR.
WHOA!!
I THINK THIS IS THE ALTAR THE WITCH WOMAN BUILT FOR HER RITUAL.
IT'S... fascinating.
WHEN I FIRST FOUND IT, I COULDN'T BELIEVE MY POP DIDN'T FILL THIS HOLE IN AND COVER IT UP WHEN HE BUILT THE HOUSE.
BUT THEN I FOUND I COULDN'T BRING MYSELF TO FILL IT IN EITHER.
PERHAPS THIS WITCH PUT SOME SORT OF CHARM SPELL ON THE THING.
I DUNNO. WHAT I AM DAMN SURE OF IS THAT THIS IS THE SPOT MR. TEETH WISHES TO RETURN TO.
THAT MONSTER WAS PROBABLY BORN ON THIS THING.

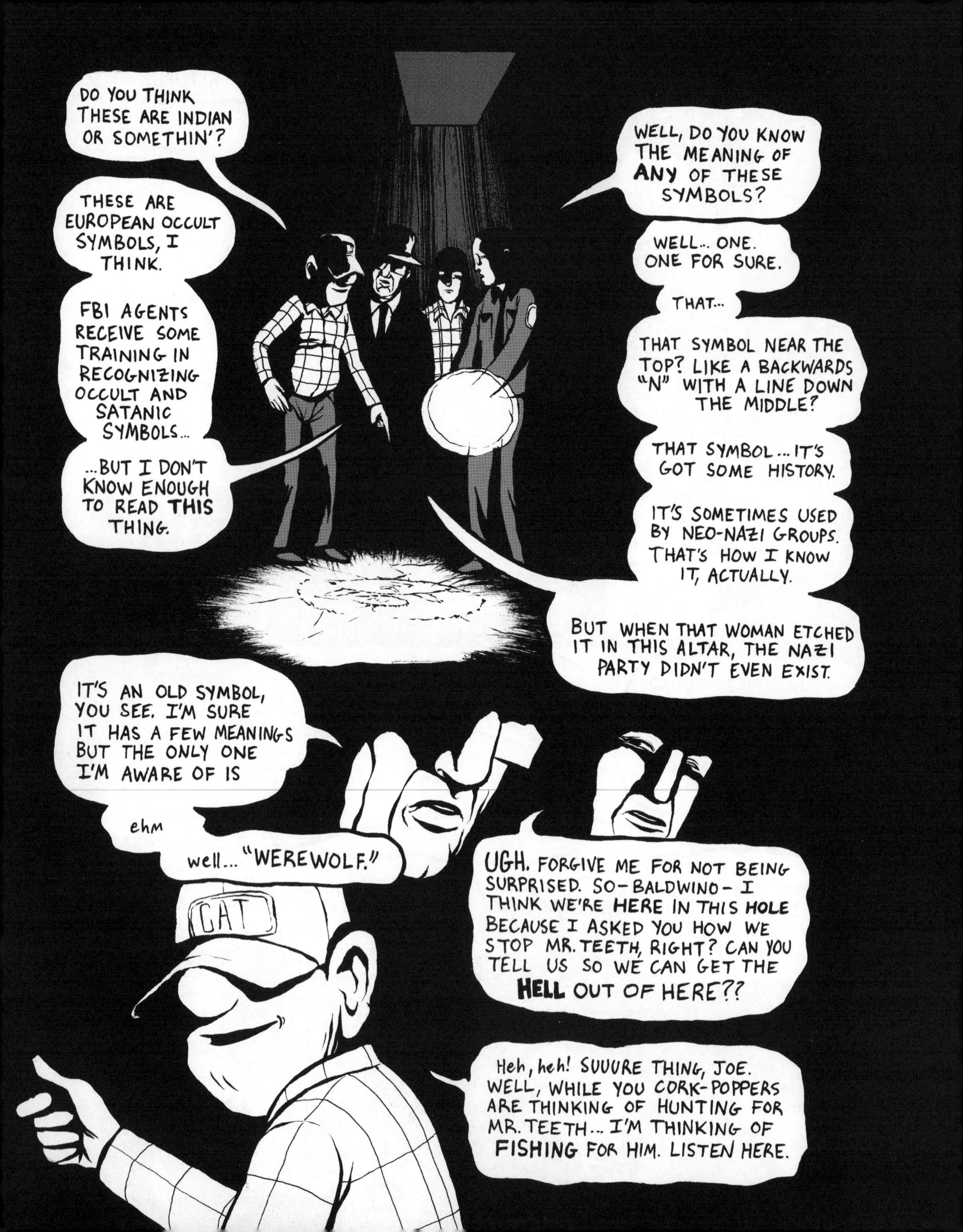
DO YOU THINK THESE ARE INDIAN OR SOMETHIN'?
THESE ARE EUROPEAN OCCULT SYMBOLS, I THINK.
FBI AGENTS RECEIVE SOME TRAINING IN RECOGNIZING OCCULT AND SATANIC SYMBOLS...
...BUT I DON'T KNOW ENOUGH TO READ **THIS** THING.
WELL, DO YOU KNOW THE MEANING OF **ANY** OF THESE SYMBOLS?
WELL... ONE. ONE FOR SURE.
THAT...
THAT SYMBOL NEAR THE TOP? LIKE A BACKWARDS "N" WITH A LINE DOWN THE MIDDLE?
THAT SYMBOL... IT'S GOT SOME HISTORY.
IT'S SOMETIMES USED BY NEO-NAZI GROUPS. THAT'S HOW I KNOW IT, ACTUALLY.
BUT WHEN THAT WOMAN ETCHED IT IN THIS ALTAR, THE NAZI PARTY DIDN'T EVEN EXIST.
IT'S AN OLD SYMBOL, YOU SEE. I'M SURE IT HAS A FEW MEANINGS BUT THE ONLY ONE I'M AWARE OF IS
ehm
well... "WEREWOLF."
UGH. FORGIVE ME FOR NOT BEING SURPRISED. SO-BALDWINO- I THINK WE'RE **HERE** IN THIS **HOLE** BECAUSE I ASKED YOU HOW WE STOP MR. TEETH, RIGHT? CAN YOU TELL US SO WE CAN GET THE **HELL** OUT OF HERE??
GAT
Heh, heh! SUUURE THING, JOE. WELL, WHILE YOU CORK-POPPERS ARE THINKING OF HUNTING FOR MR. TEETH... I'M THINKING OF **FISHING** FOR HIM. LISTEN HERE.

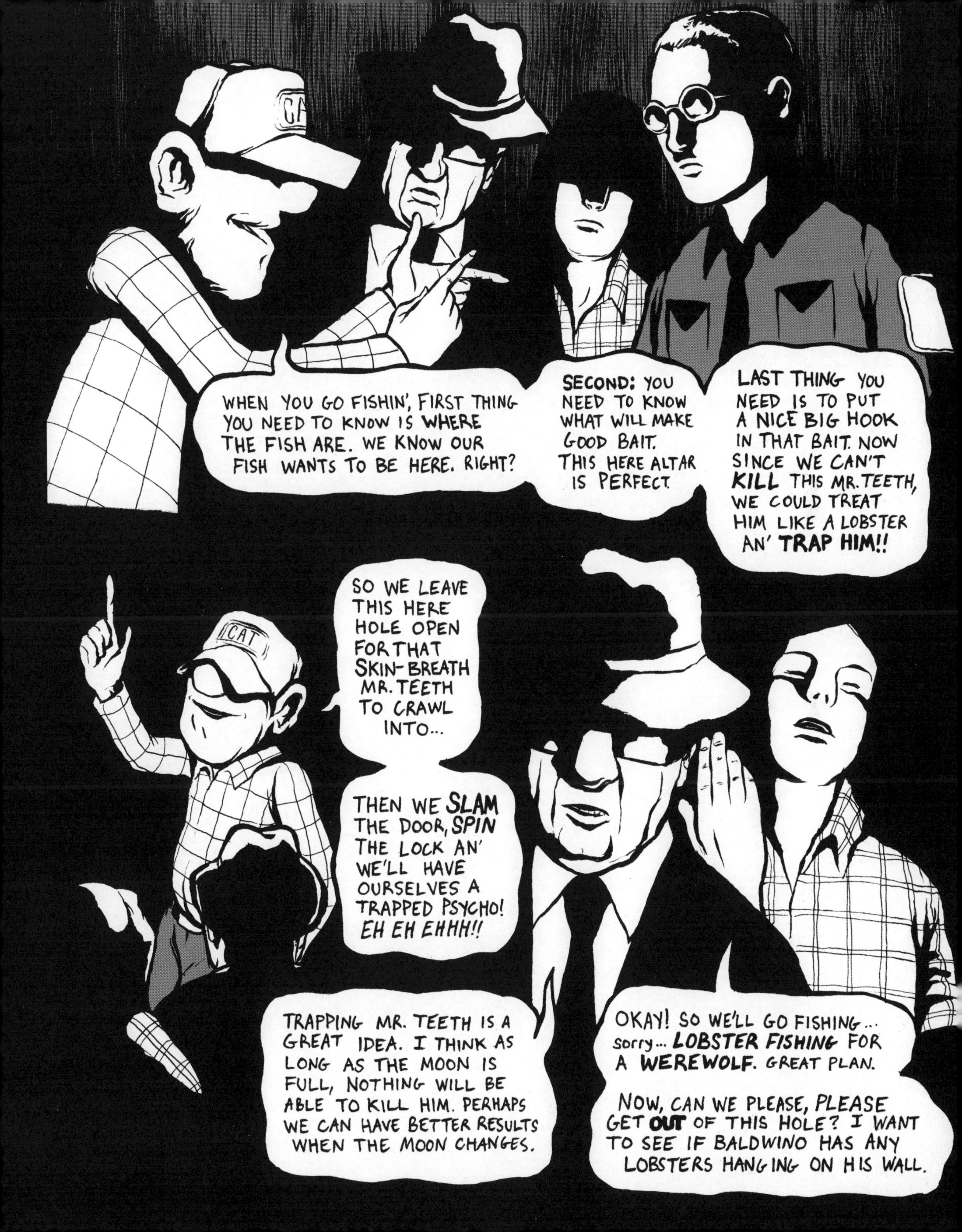
WHEN YOU GO FISHIN', FIRST THING YOU NEED TO KNOW IS WHERE THE FISH ARE. WE KNOW OUR FISH WANTS TO BE HERE. RIGHT?
SECOND: YOU NEED TO KNOW WHAT WILL MAKE GOOD BAIT. THIS HERE ALTAR IS PERFECT.
LAST THING YOU NEED IS TO PUT A NICE BIG HOOK IN THAT BAIT. NOW SINCE WE CAN'T KILL THIS MR. TEETH, WE COULD TREAT HIM LIKE A LOBSTER AN' TRAP HIM!!
SO WE LEAVE THIS HERE HOLE OPEN FOR THAT SKIN-BREATH MR. TEETH TO CRAWL INTO...
THEN WE SLAM THE DOOR, SPIN THE LOCK AN' WE'LL HAVE OURSELVES A TRAPPED PSYCHO! EH EH EHHH!!
TRAPPING MR. TEETH IS A GREAT IDEA. I THINK AS LONG AS THE MOON IS FULL, NOTHING WILL BE ABLE TO KILL HIM. PERHAPS WE CAN HAVE BETTER RESULTS WHEN THE MOON CHANGES.
OKAY! SO WE'LL GO FISHING... sorry... LOBSTER FISHING FOR A WEREWOLF. GREAT PLAN.
NOW, CAN WE PLEASE, PLEASE GET OUT OF THIS HOLE? I WANT TO SEE IF BALDWINO HAS ANY LOBSTERS HANGING ON HIS WALL.

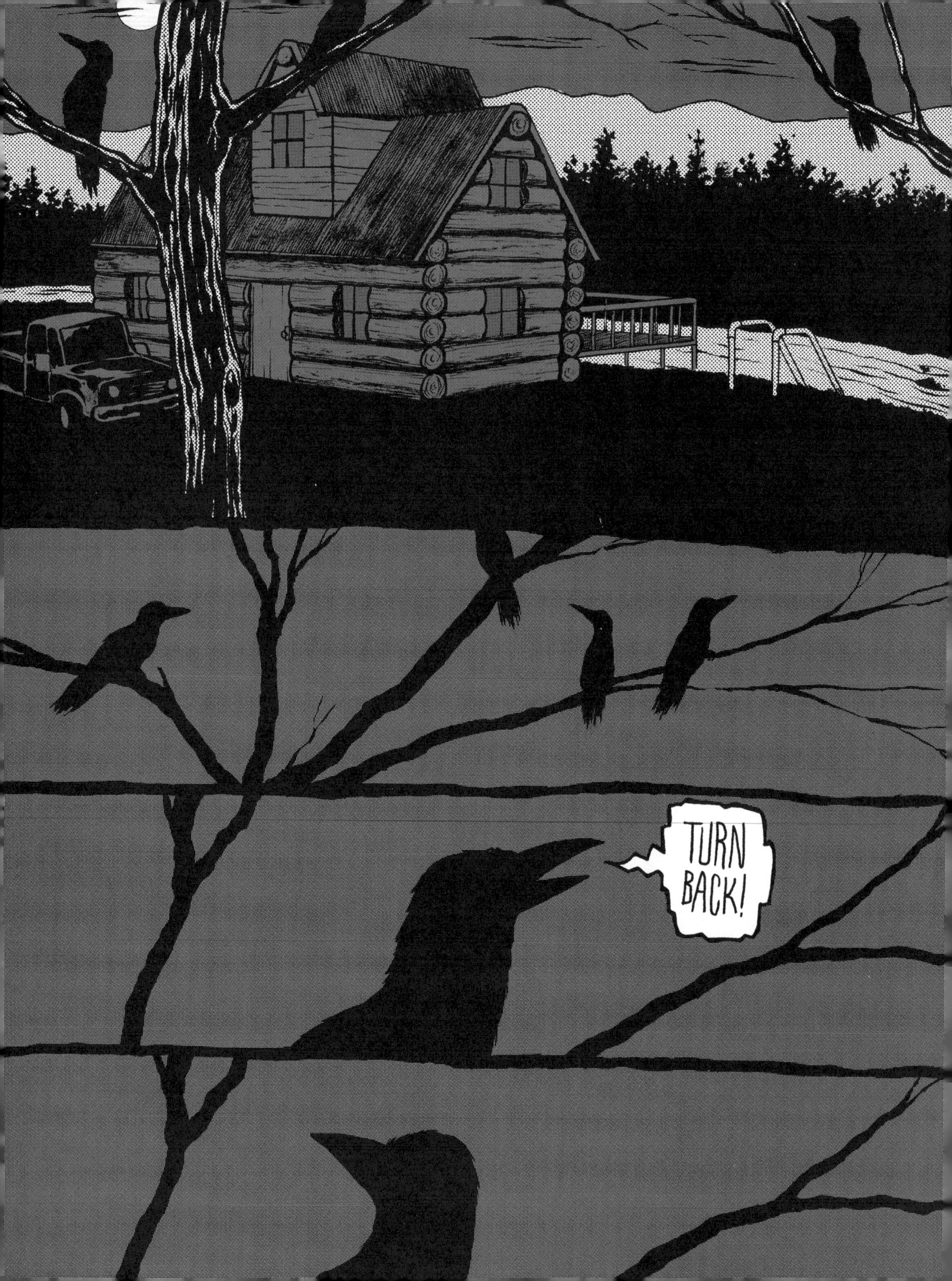
TURN BACK!

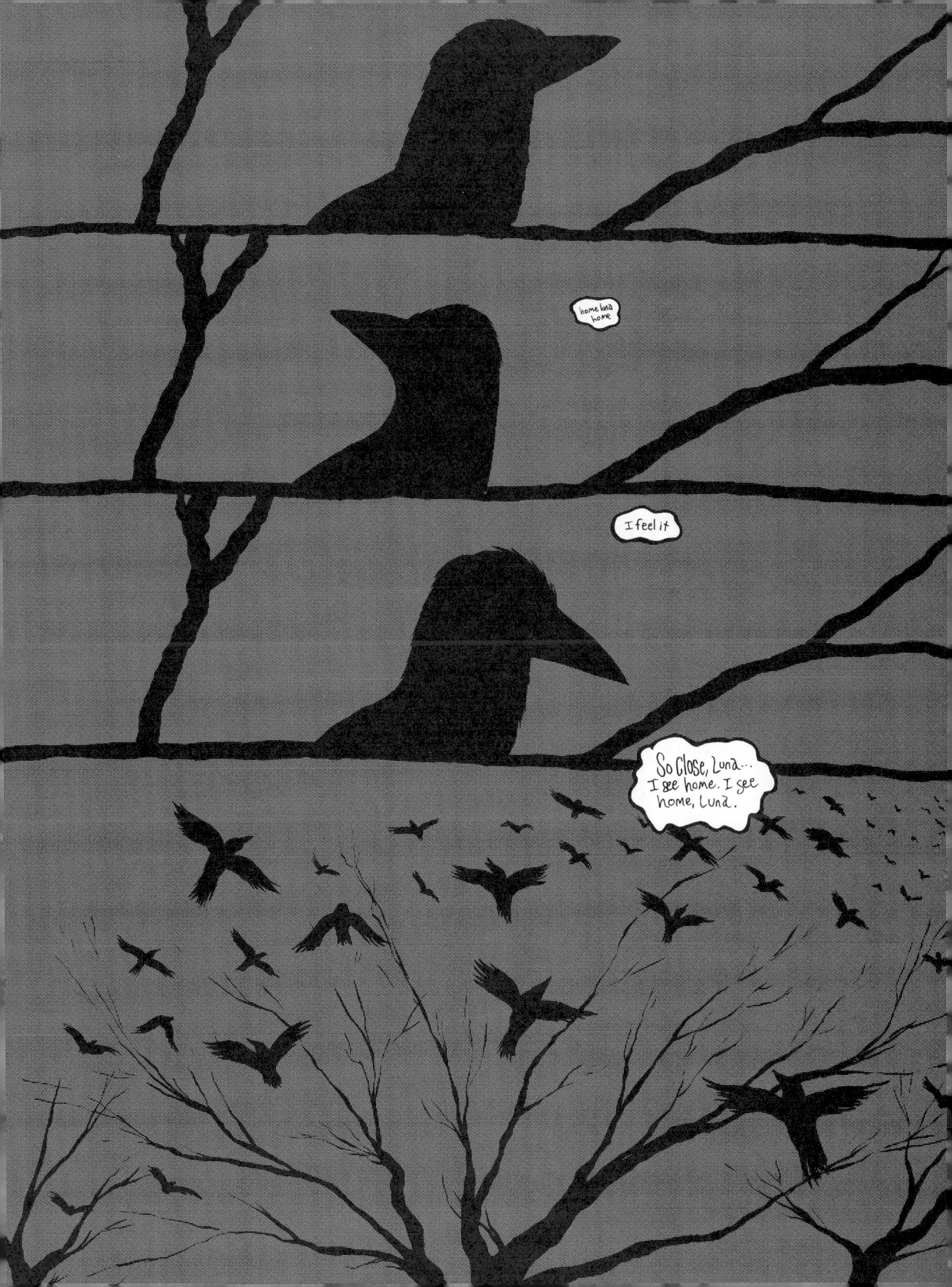
home luna home
I feel it
So Close, Luna... I see home. I see home, Luna.

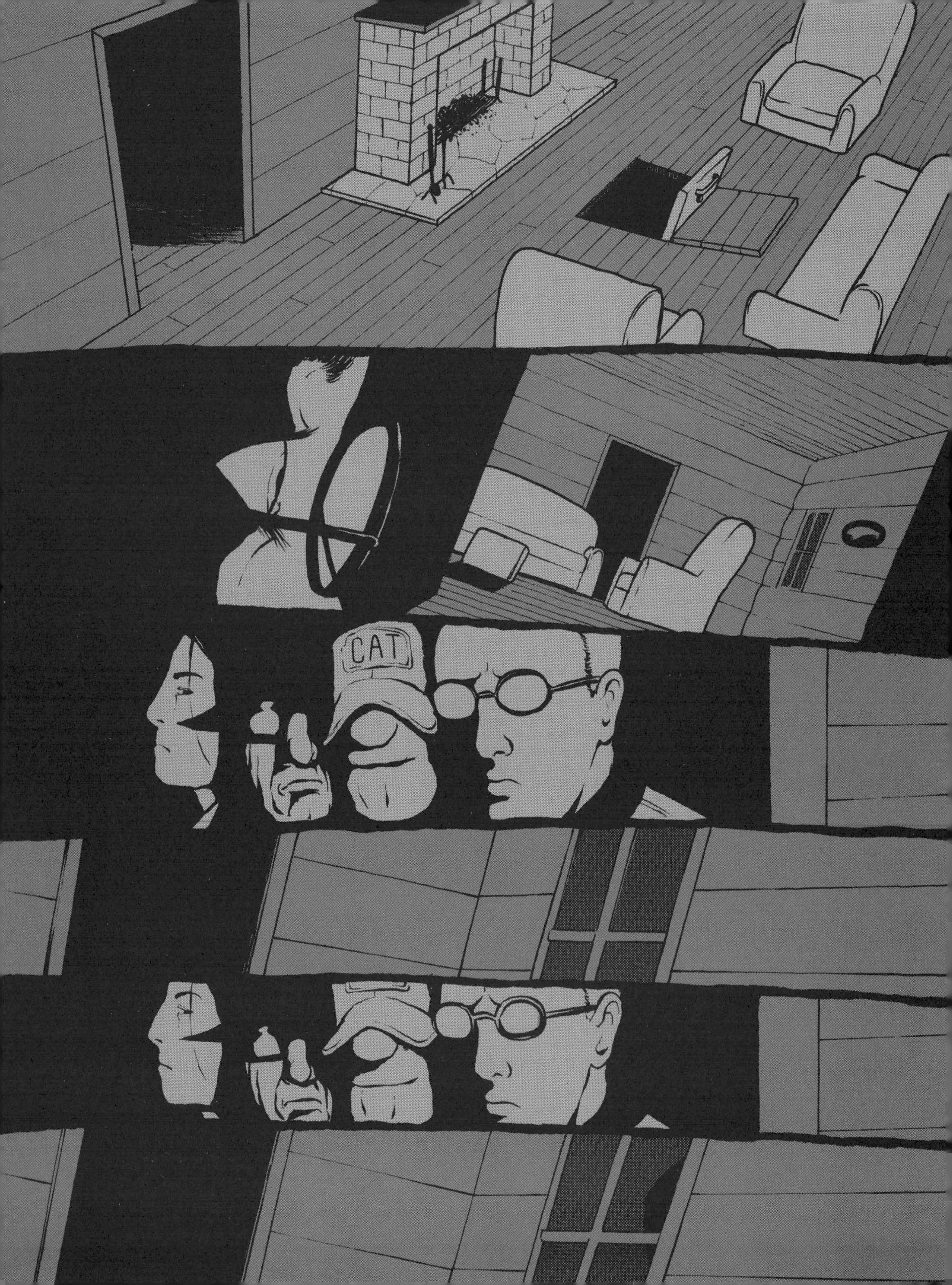
CAT

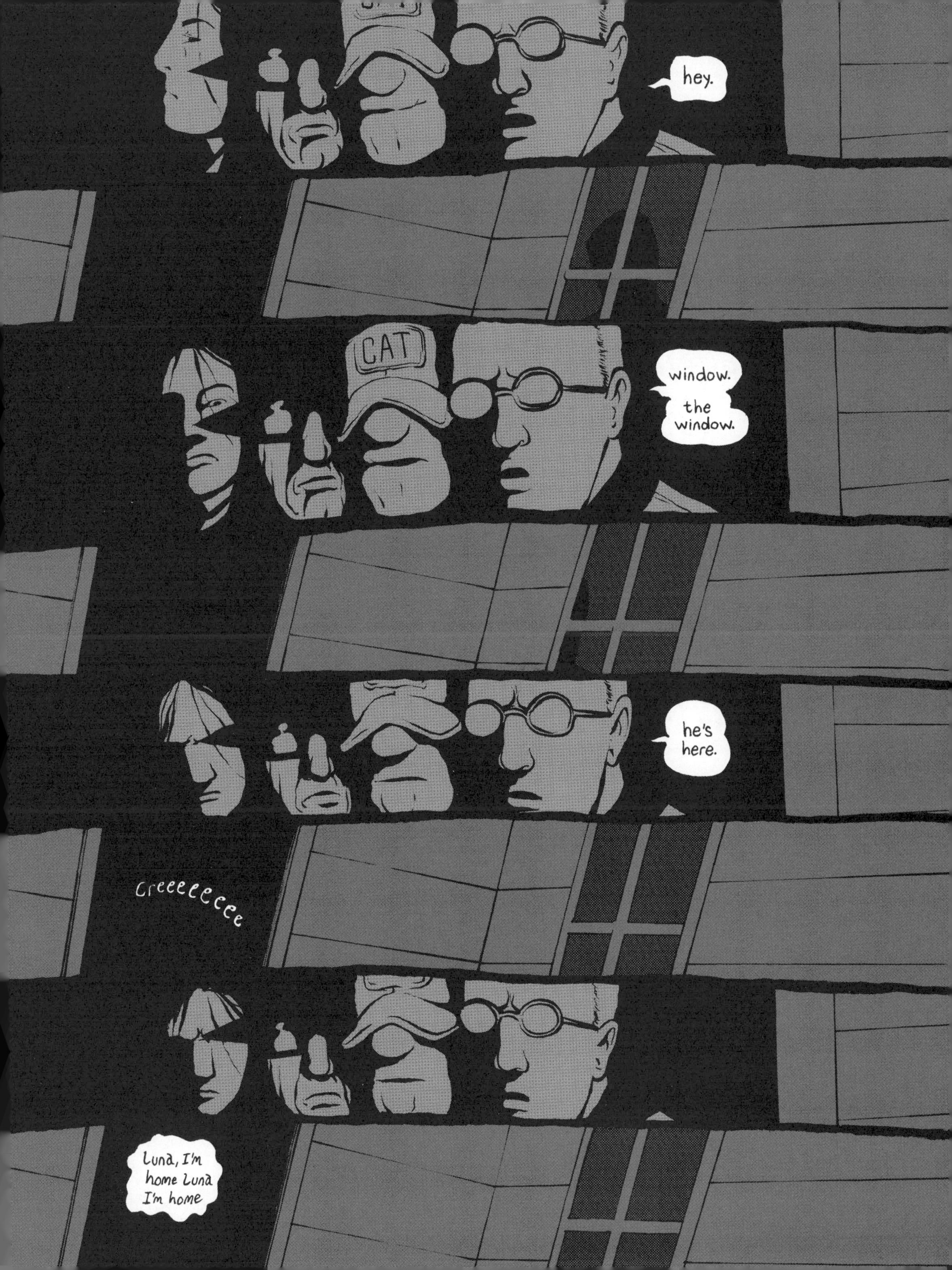
hey.
window.
the window.
he's here.
Creeeeeeeee
Luna, I'm home Luna I'm home

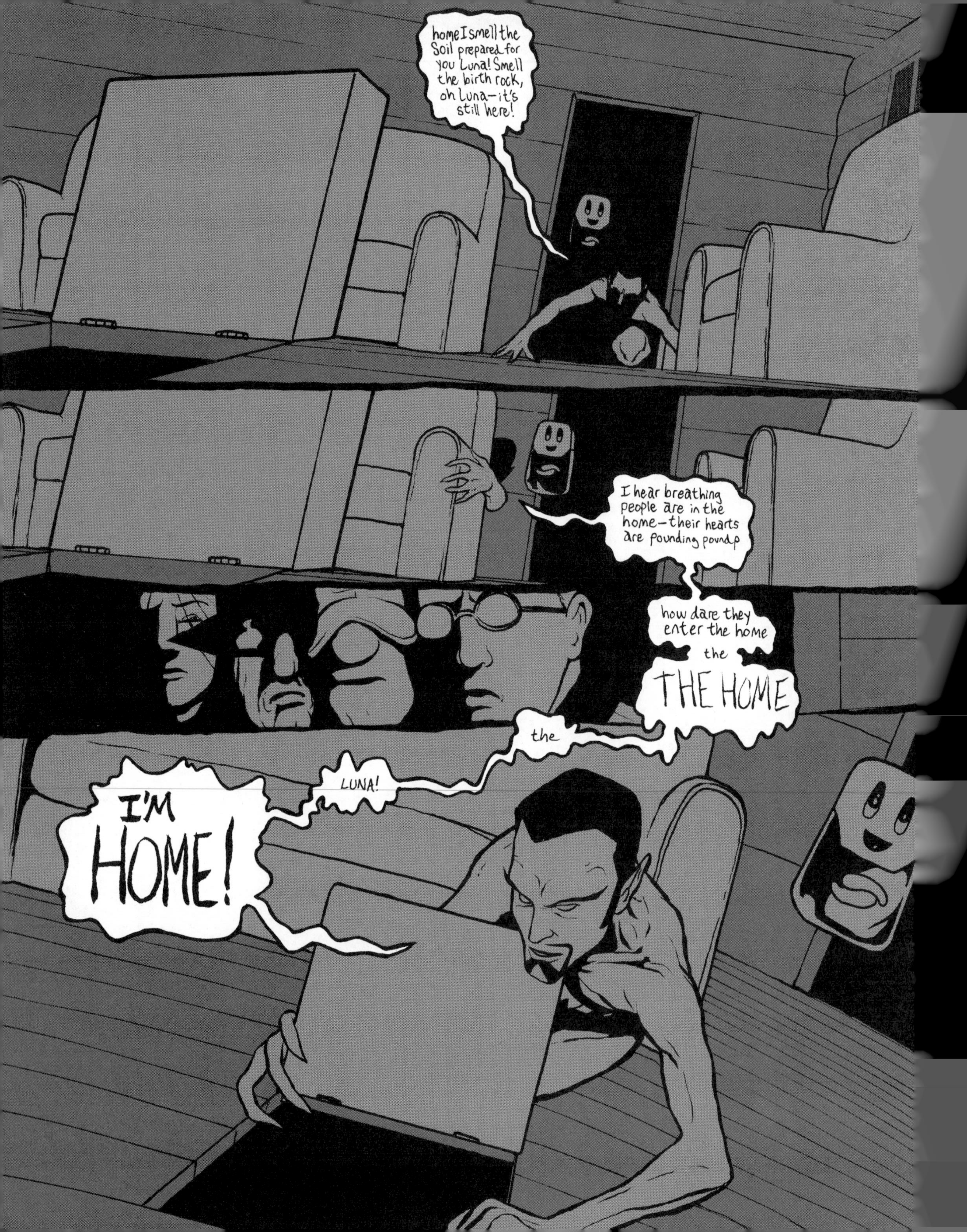
home I smell the Soil prepared for you Luna! Smell the birth rock, oh Luna—it's still here!
I hear breathing people are in the home—their hearts are pounding pound.p
how dare they enter the home
the
THE HOME
the
LUNA!
I'M HOME!

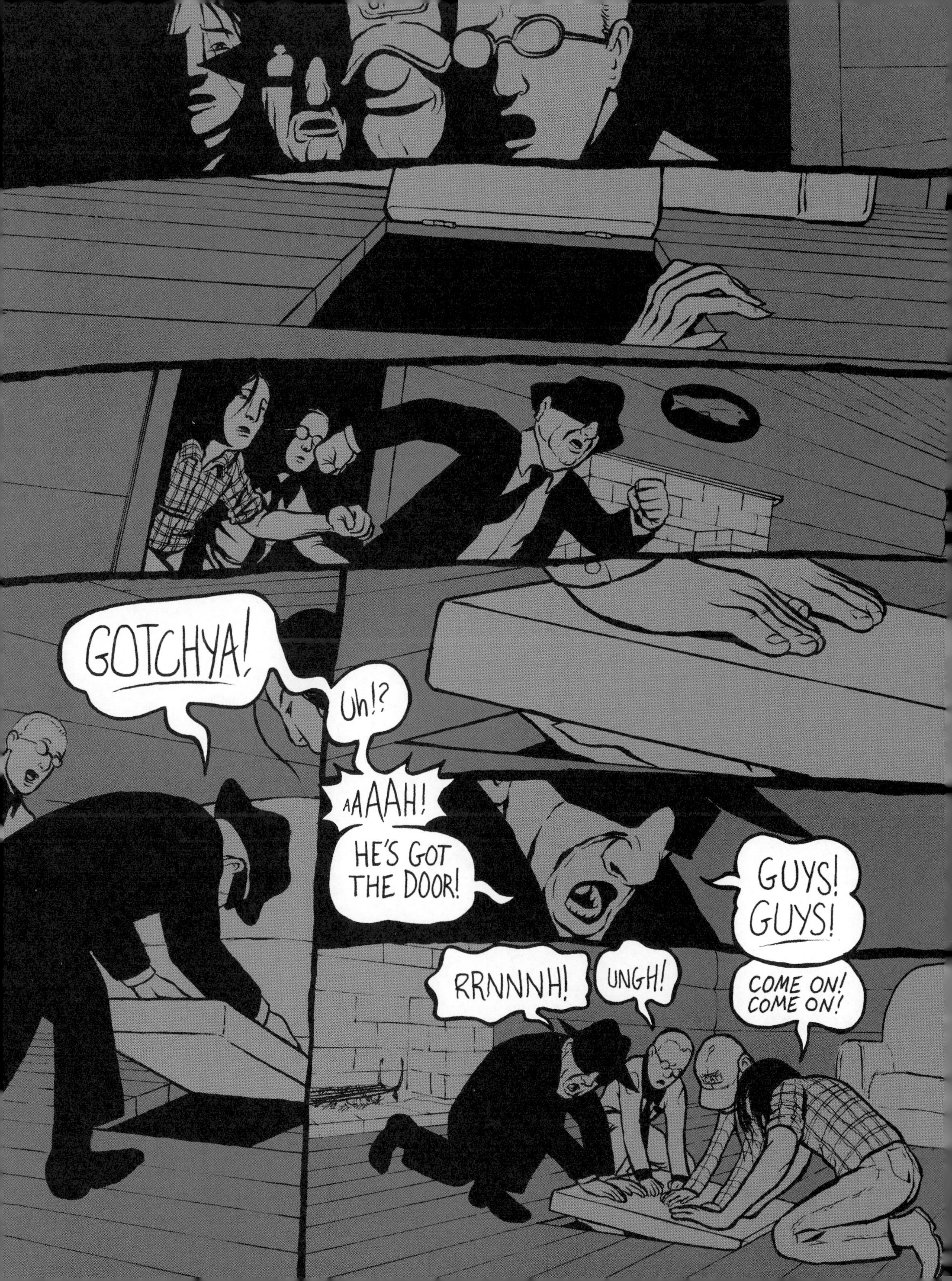
GOTCHYA!
Uh!?
AAAAH!
HE'S GOT THE DOOR!
GUYS! GUYS!
RRNNNH!
UNGH!
COME ON! COME ON!

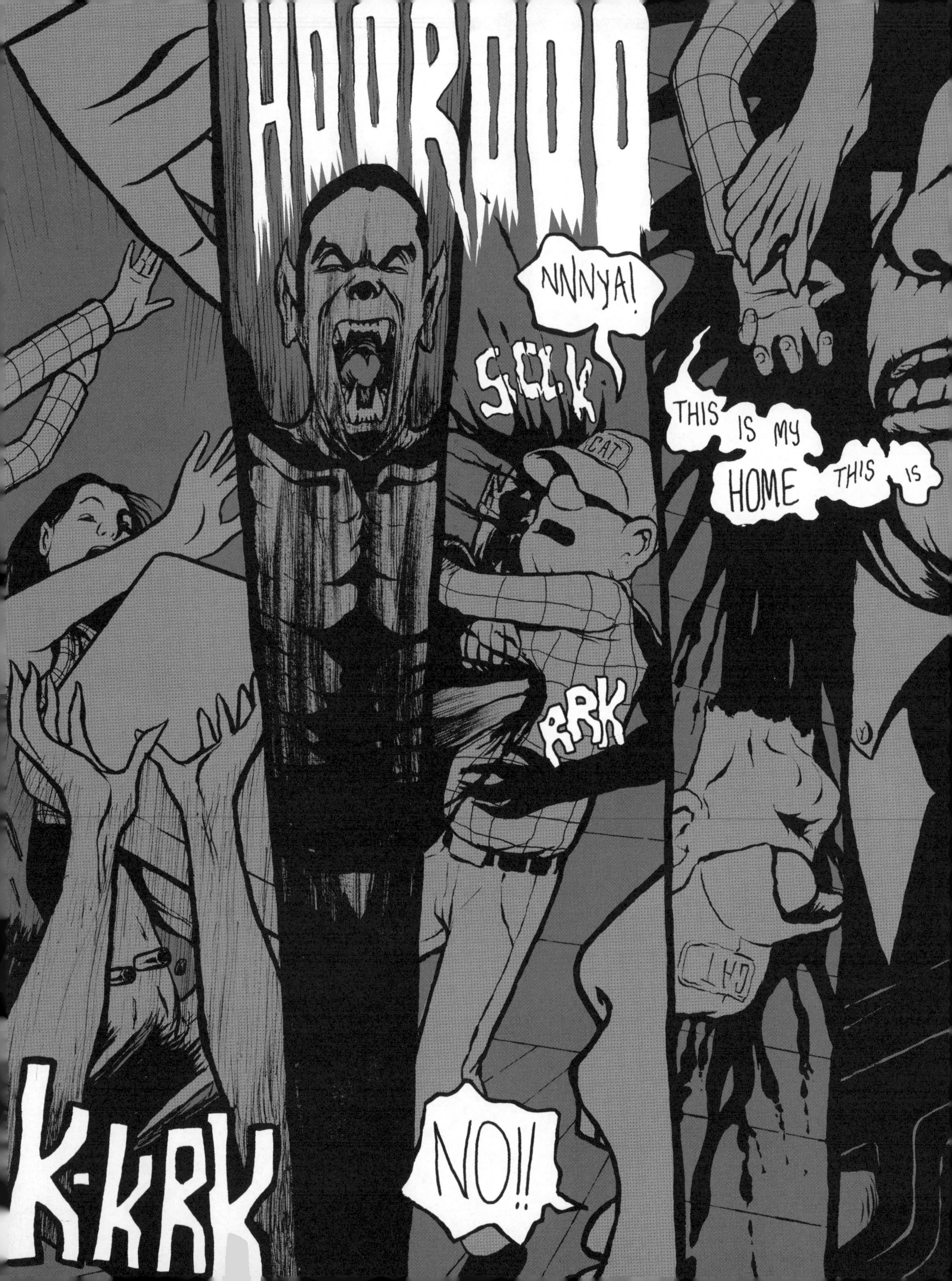
HOOROOO
NNNYA!
SCLK
THIS IS MY HOME THIS IS
RRK
K-KRK
NO!!

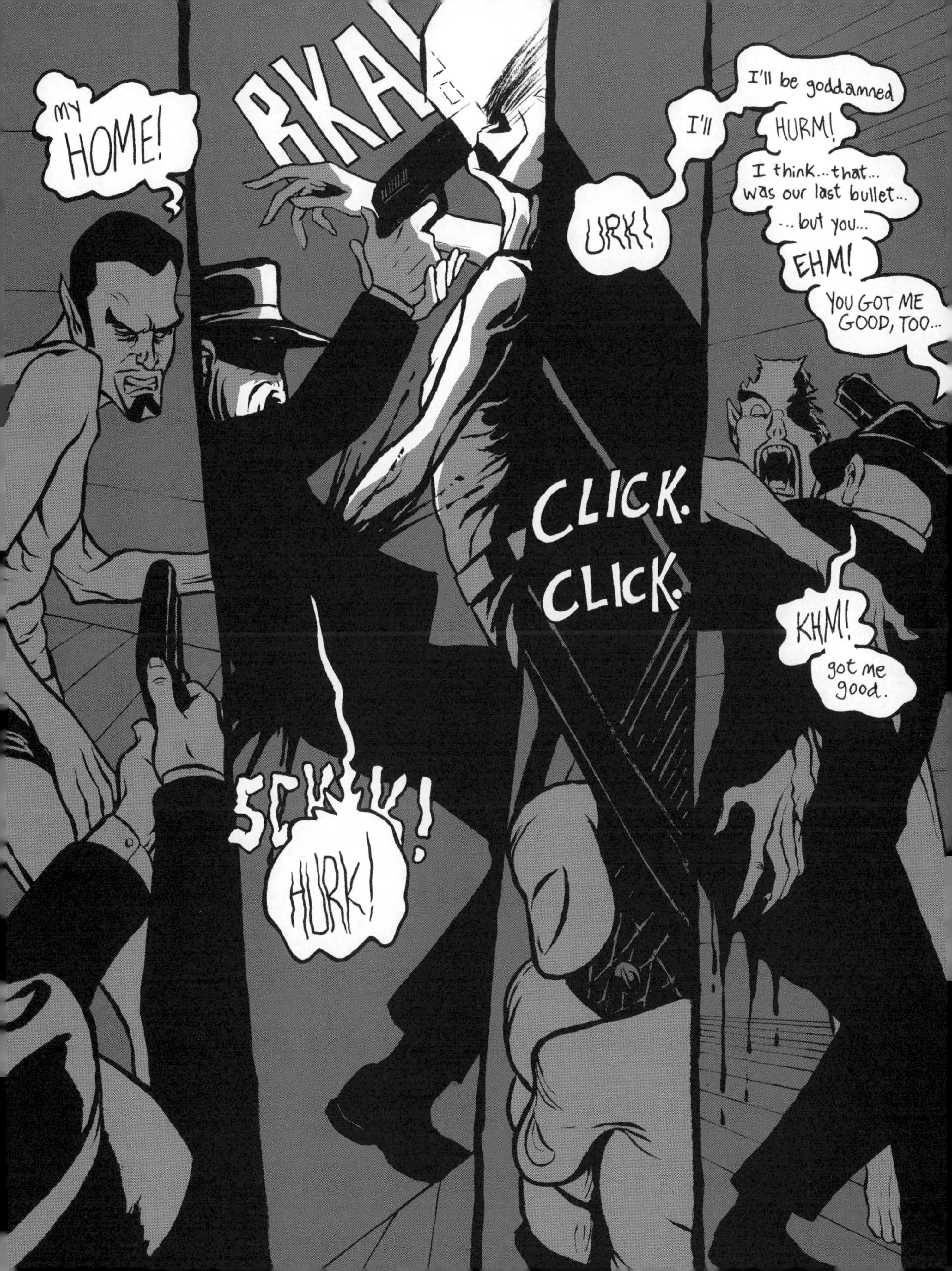
my HOME!
URK!
I'll
I'll be goddamned
HURM!
I think... that... was our last bullet...
... but you...
EHM!
YOU GOT ME GOOD, TOO...
CLICK.
CLICK.
KHM!
got me good.
HURK!

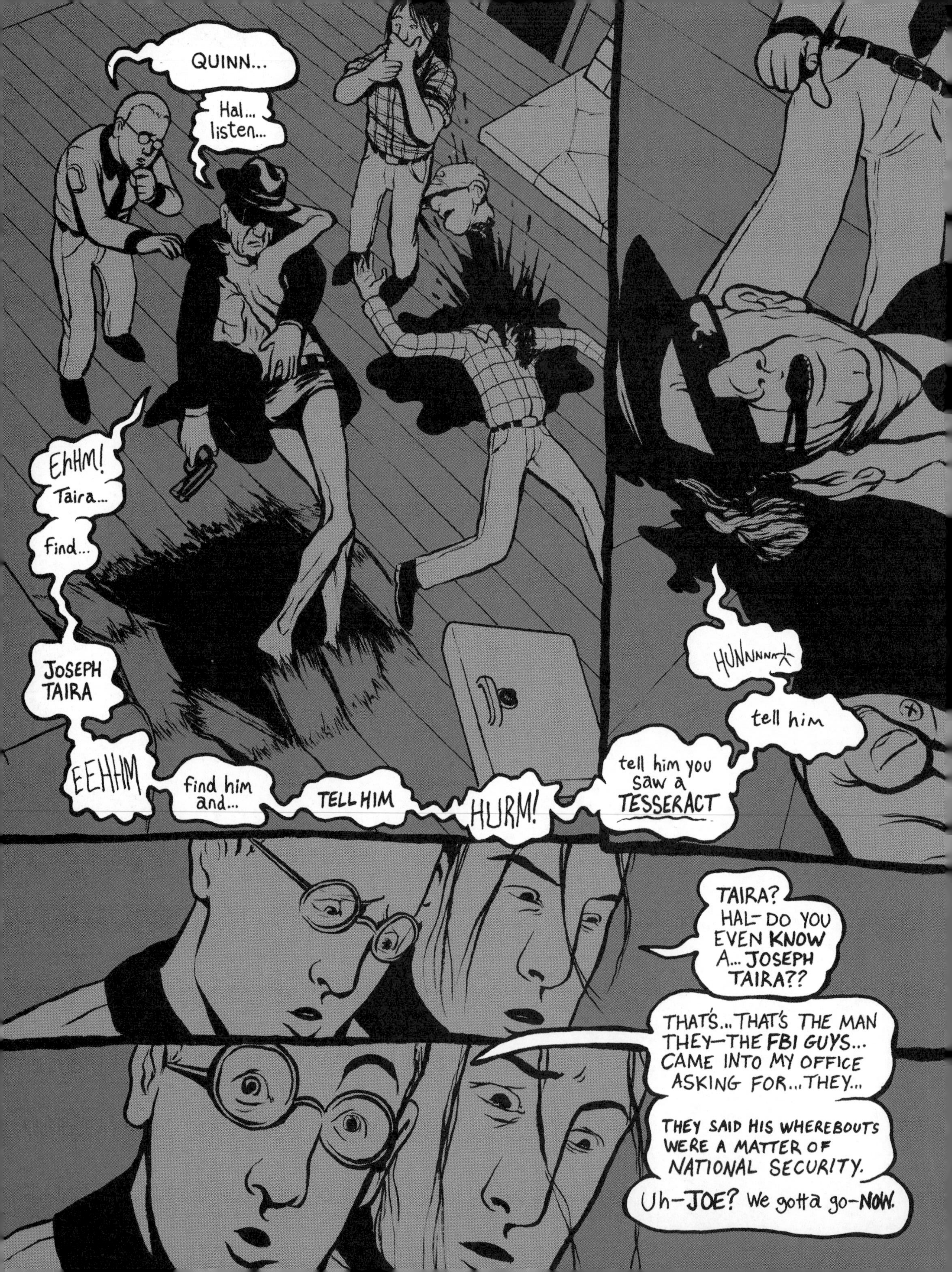
QUINN...
Hal... listen...
EhHM! Taira...
find...
JOSEPH TAIRA
EEHHM
find him and...
TELL HIM
HURM!
tell him you saw a TESSERACT
HUNNNNNN
tell him
TAIRA? HAL-DO YOU EVEN KNOW A... JOSEPH TAIRA??
THAT'S... THAT'S THE MAN THEY—THE FBI GUYS... CAME INTO MY OFFICE ASKING FOR... THEY...
THEY SAID HIS WHEREBOUTS WERE A MATTER OF NATIONAL SECURITY.
Uh—JOE? We gotta go—NOW.

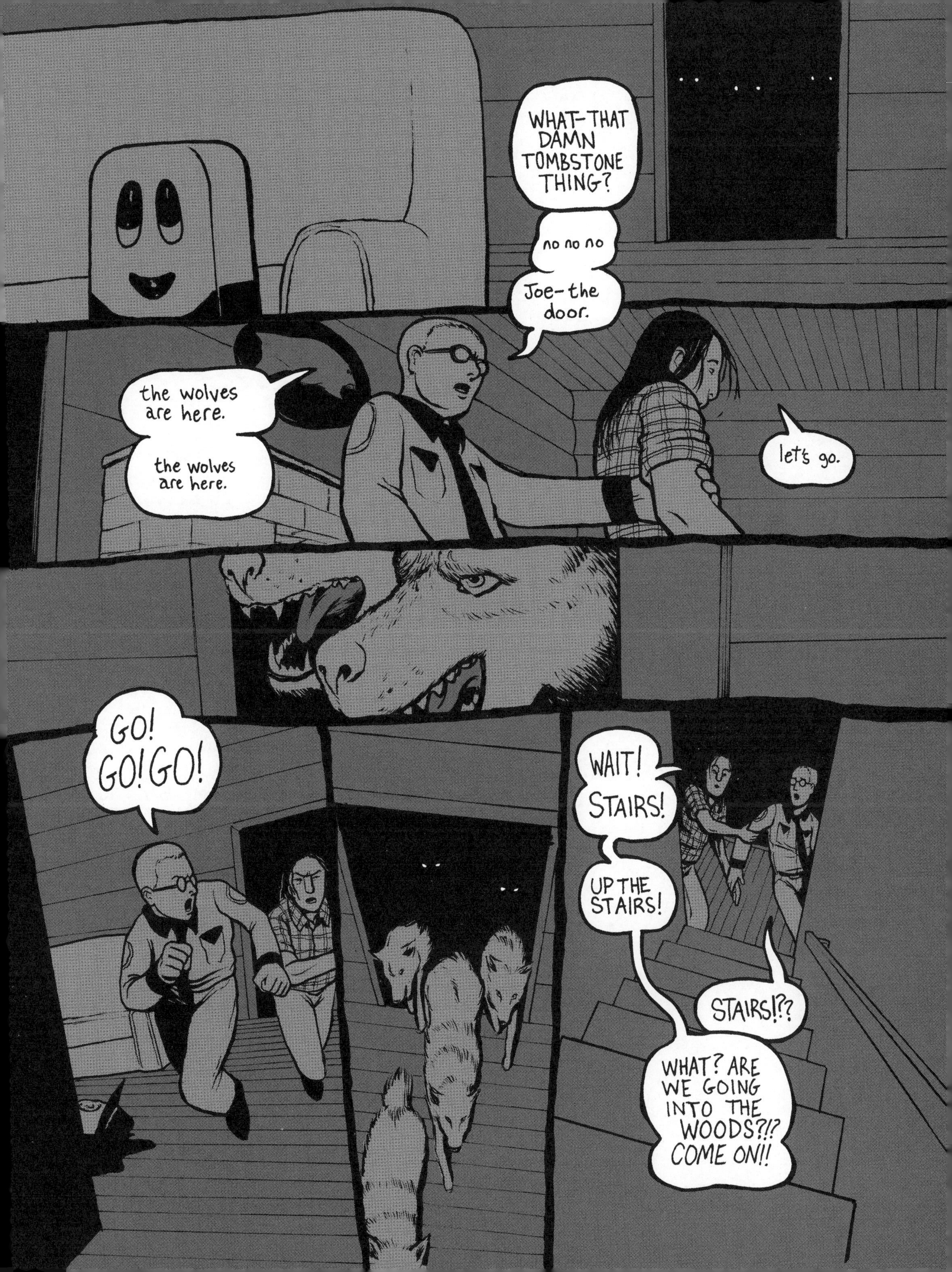
WHAT-THAT DAMN TOMBSTONE THING?
no no no
Joe-the door.
the wolves are here.
the wolves are here.
let's go.
GO! GO! GO!
WAIT! STAIRS!
UP THE STAIRS!
STAIRS!??
WHAT? ARE WE GOING INTO THE WOODS?!? COME ON!!

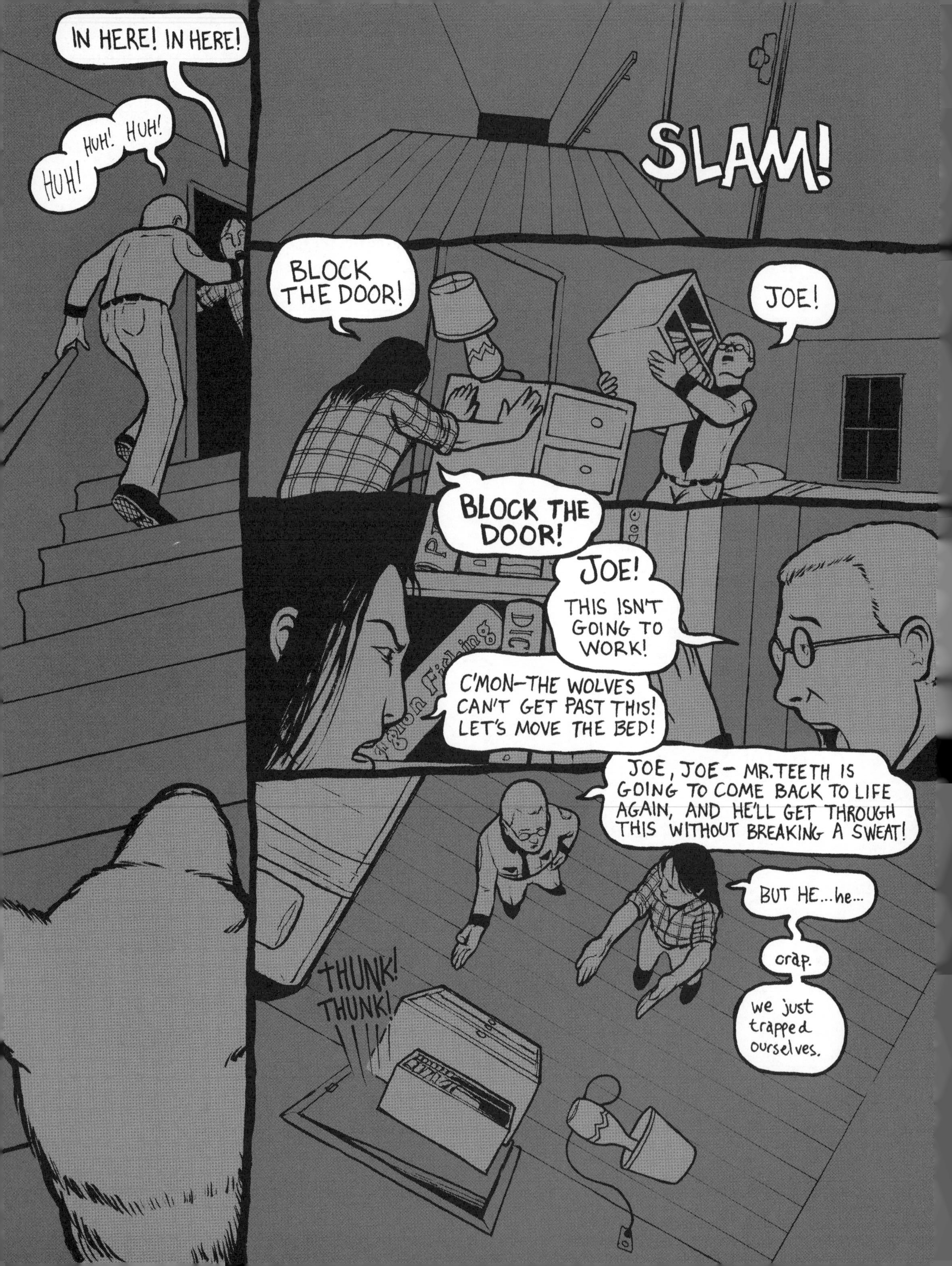
IN HERE! IN HERE!
HUH! HUH! HUH!
SLAM!
BLOCK THE DOOR!
JOE!
BLOCK THE DOOR!
JOE!
THIS ISN'T GOING TO WORK!
C'MON—THE WOLVES CAN'T GET PAST THIS! LET'S MOVE THE BED!
JOE, JOE – MR. TEETH IS GOING TO COME BACK TO LIFE AGAIN, AND HE'LL GET THROUGH THIS WITHOUT BREAKING A SWEAT!
BUT HE...he...
crap.
we just trapped ourselves.
THUNK! THUNK!

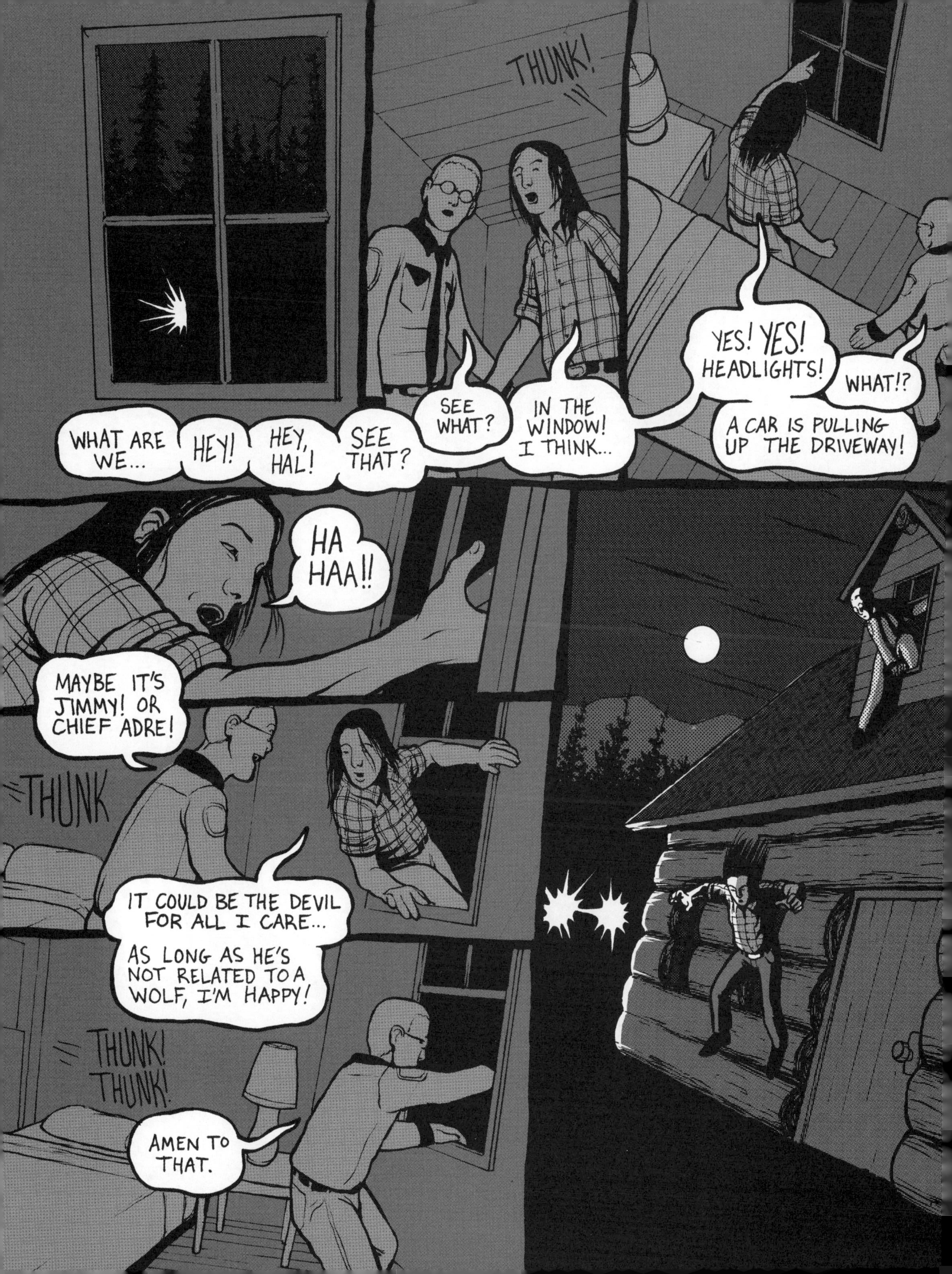
THUNK!
WHAT ARE WE...
HEY!
HEY, HAL!
SEE THAT?
SEE WHAT?
IN THE WINDOW! I THINK...
YES! YES! HEADLIGHTS!
A CAR IS PULLING UP THE DRIVEWAY!
WHAT!?
HA HAA!!
MAYBE IT'S JIMMY! OR CHIEF ADRE!
THUNK
IT COULD BE THE DEVIL FOR ALL I CARE...
AS LONG AS HE'S NOT RELATED TO A WOLF, I'M HAPPY!
THUNK! THUNK!
AMEN TO THAT.

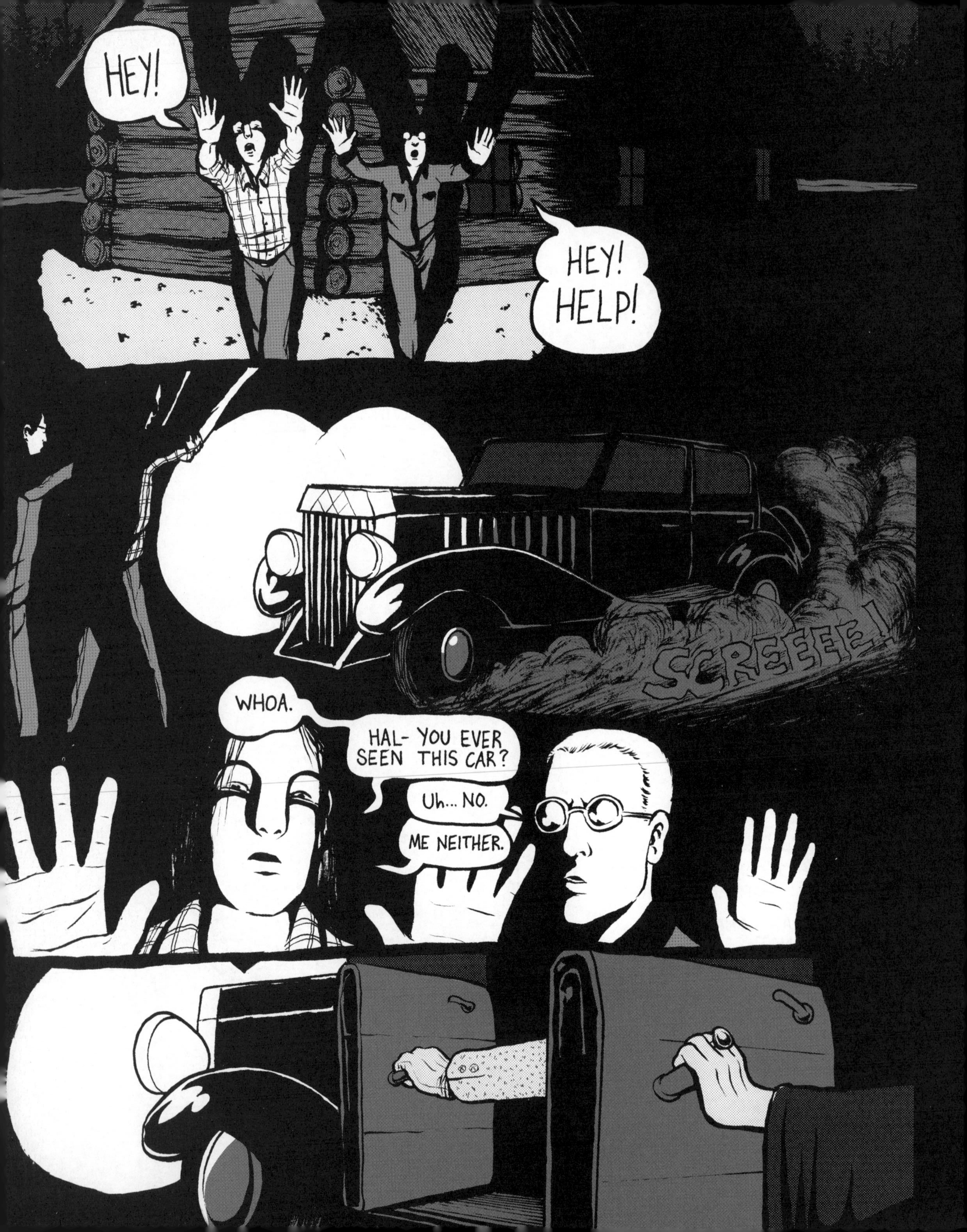
HEY!
HEY! HELP!
SCREEEE!
WHOA.
HAL- YOU EVER SEEN THIS CAR?
Uh... NO.
ME NEITHER.

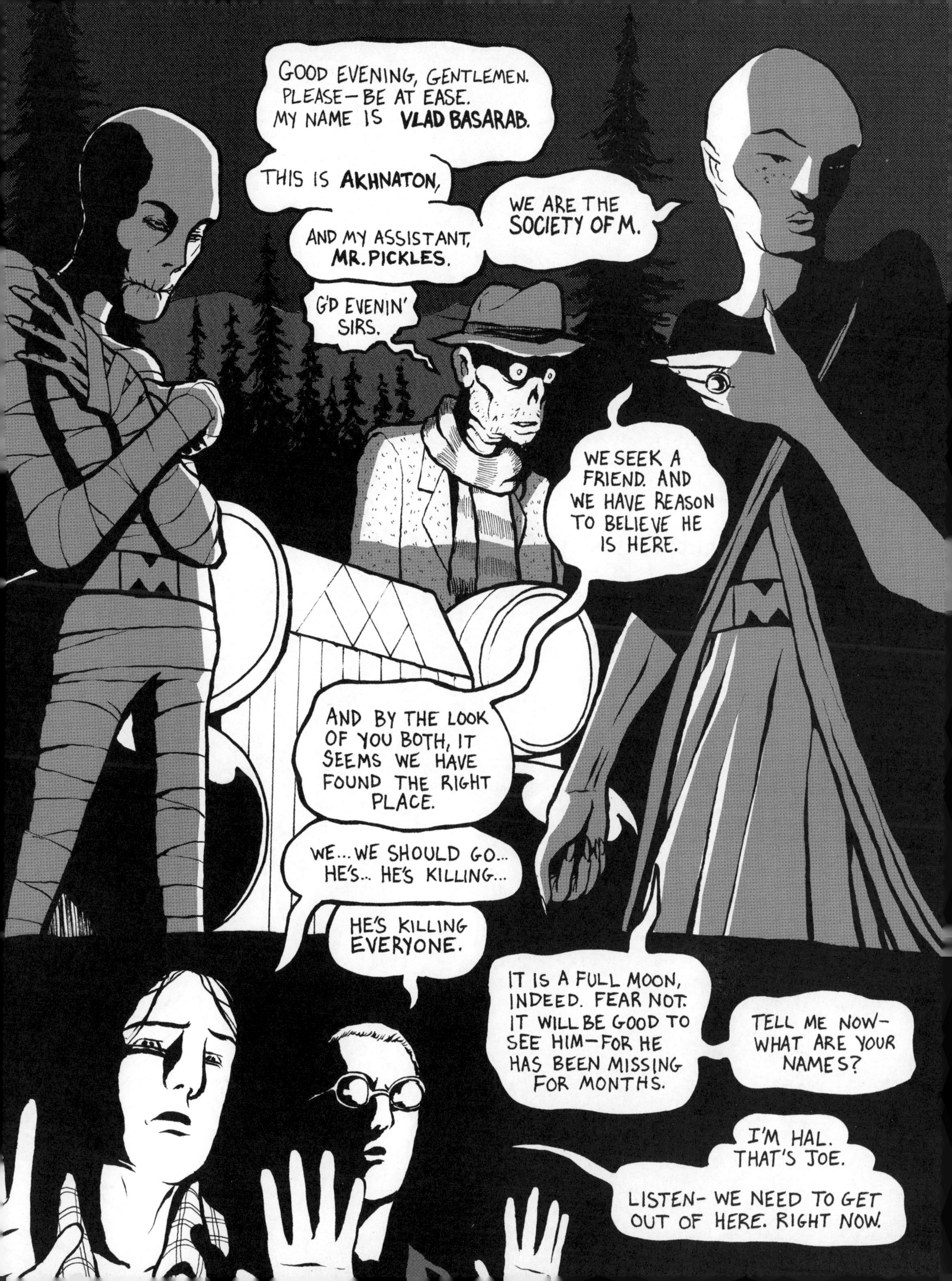
GOOD EVENING, GENTLEMEN. PLEASE—BE AT EASE. MY NAME IS **VLAD BASARAB.**
THIS IS **AKHNATON,**
AND MY ASSISTANT, **MR. PICKLES.**
WE ARE THE SOCIETY OF M.
G'D EVENIN' SIRS.
WE SEEK A FRIEND. AND WE HAVE REASON TO BELIEVE HE IS HERE.
AND BY THE LOOK OF YOU BOTH, IT SEEMS WE HAVE FOUND THE RIGHT PLACE.
WE... WE SHOULD GO... HE'S... HE'S KILLING...
HE'S KILLING EVERYONE.
IT IS A FULL MOON, INDEED. FEAR NOT. IT WILL BE GOOD TO SEE HIM—FOR HE HAS BEEN MISSING FOR MONTHS.
TELL ME NOW—WHAT ARE YOUR NAMES?
I'M HAL. THAT'S JOE.
LISTEN- WE NEED TO GET OUT OF HERE. RIGHT NOW.

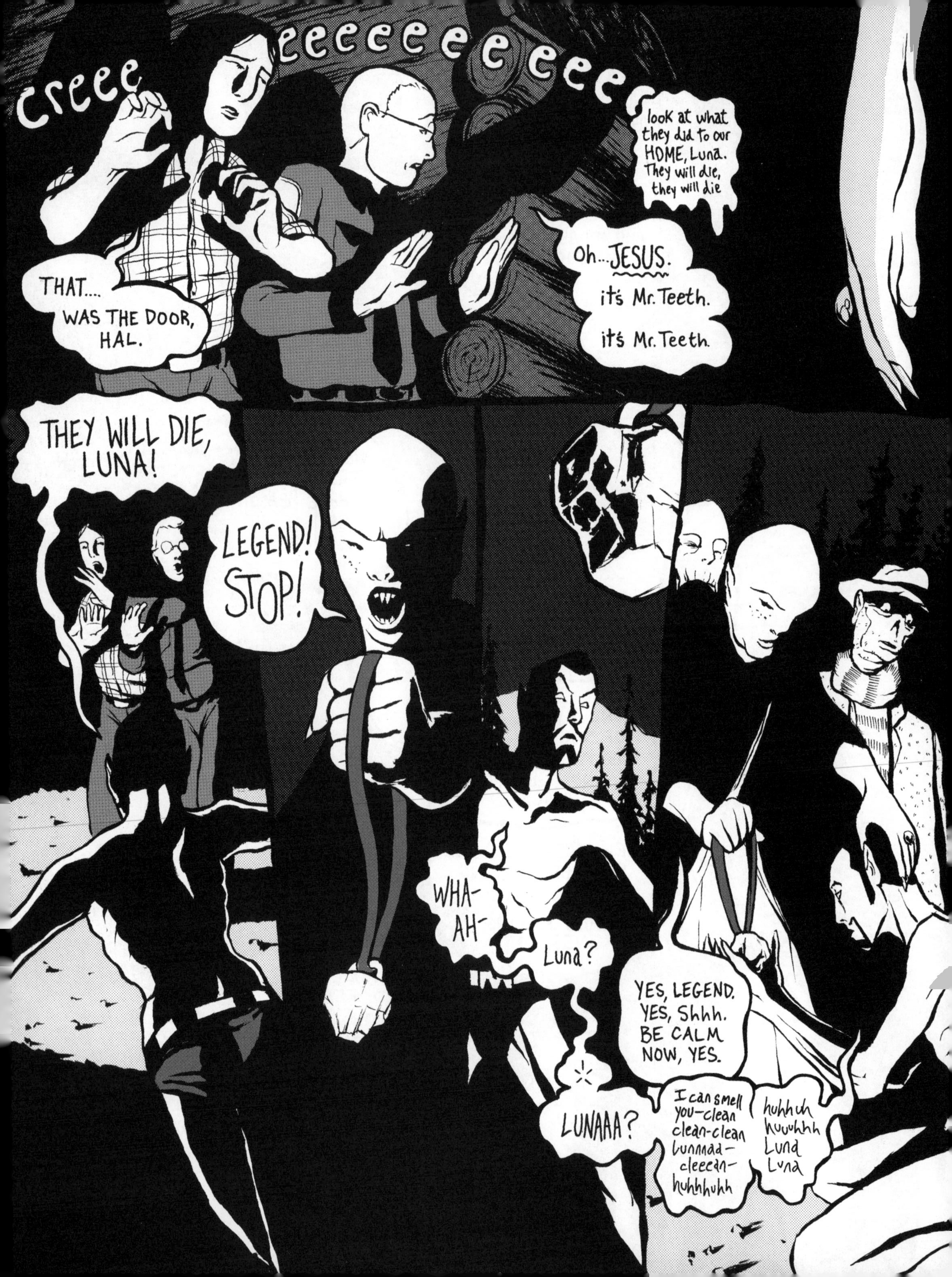
Creeeeeeeeeeeeeee
THAT.... WAS THE DOOR, HAL.
look at what they did to our HOME, Luna. They will die, they will die
Oh... JESUS.
it's Mr. Teeth.
it's Mr. Teeth.
THEY WILL DIE, LUNA!
LEGEND! STOP!
WHA- AH-
Luna?
!
LUNAAA?
YES, LEGEND. YES, Shhh. BE CALM NOW, YES.
I can smell you—clean clean-clean Lunnaa-cleeean-huhhhuhh
huhhuh huuuhhh Luna Luna

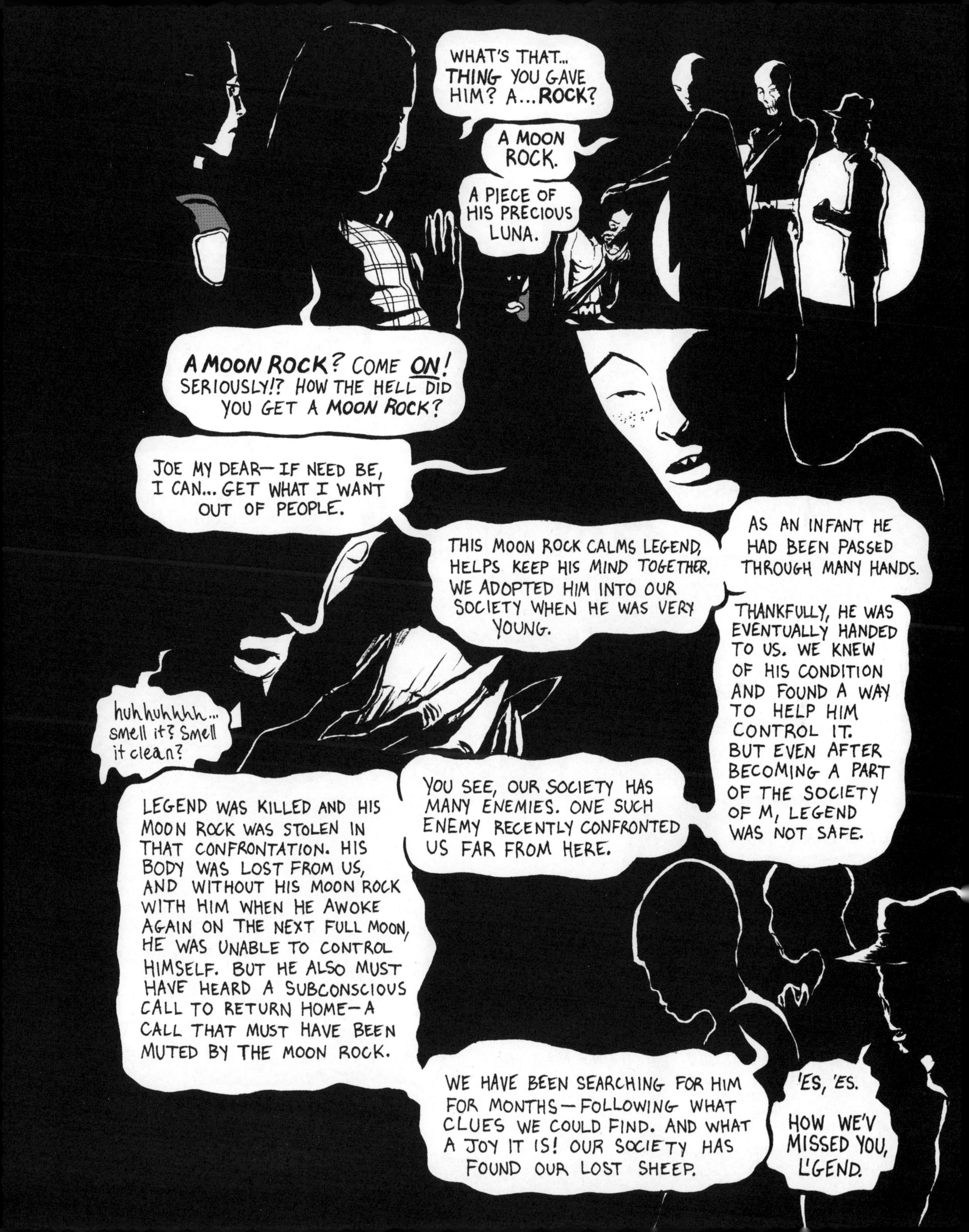
WHAT'S THAT... THING YOU GAVE HIM? A... ROCK?
A MOON ROCK.
A PIECE OF HIS PRECIOUS LUNA.
A MOON ROCK? COME ON! SERIOUSLY!? HOW THE HELL DID YOU GET A MOON ROCK?
JOE MY DEAR—IF NEED BE, I CAN... GET WHAT I WANT OUT OF PEOPLE.
THIS MOON ROCK CALMS LEGEND, HELPS KEEP HIS MIND TOGETHER. WE ADOPTED HIM INTO OUR SOCIETY WHEN HE WAS VERY YOUNG.
AS AN INFANT HE HAD BEEN PASSED THROUGH MANY HANDS.
THANKFULLY, HE WAS EVENTUALLY HANDED TO US. WE KNEW OF HIS CONDITION AND FOUND A WAY TO HELP HIM CONTROL IT. BUT EVEN AFTER BECOMING A PART OF THE SOCIETY OF M, LEGEND WAS NOT SAFE.
huhhuhhhh... smell it? Smell it clean?
YOU SEE, OUR SOCIETY HAS MANY ENEMIES. ONE SUCH ENEMY RECENTLY CONFRONTED US FAR FROM HERE.
LEGEND WAS KILLED AND HIS MOON ROCK WAS STOLEN IN THAT CONFRONTATION. HIS BODY WAS LOST FROM US, AND WITHOUT HIS MOON ROCK WITH HIM WHEN HE AWOKE AGAIN ON THE NEXT FULL MOON, HE WAS UNABLE TO CONTROL HIMSELF. BUT HE ALSO MUST HAVE HEARD A SUBCONSCIOUS CALL TO RETURN HOME—A CALL THAT MUST HAVE BEEN MUTED BY THE MOON ROCK.
WE HAVE BEEN SEARCHING FOR HIM FOR MONTHS—FOLLOWING WHAT CLUES WE COULD FIND. AND WHAT A JOY IT IS! OUR SOCIETY HAS FOUND OUR LOST SHEEP.
'ES, 'ES.
HOW WE'V MISSED YOU, L'GEND.

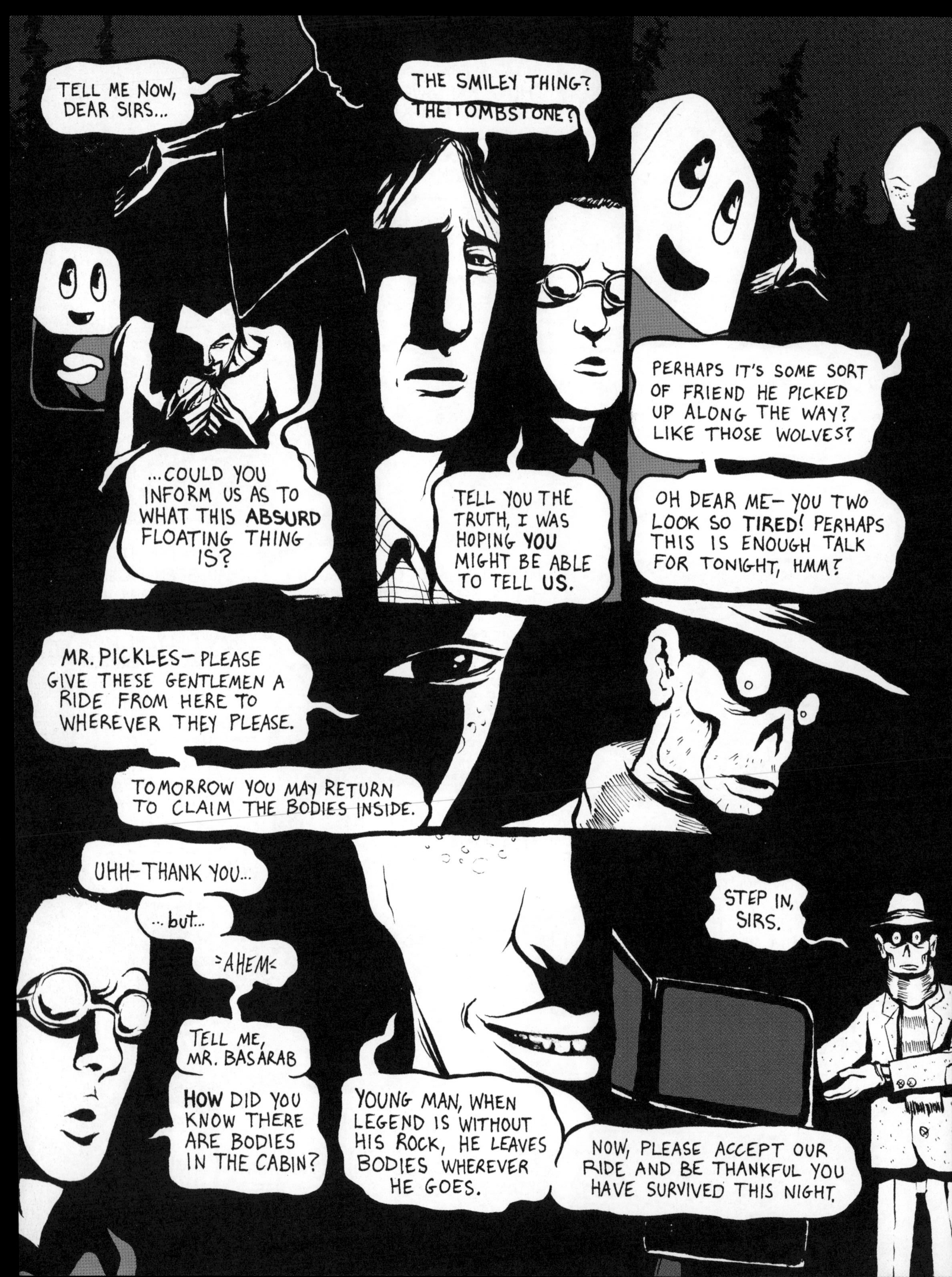
TELL ME NOW, DEAR SIRS...
...COULD YOU INFORM US AS TO WHAT THIS **ABSURD** FLOATING THING IS?
THE SMILEY THING? THE TOMBSTONE?
TELL YOU THE TRUTH, I WAS HOPING **YOU** MIGHT BE ABLE TO TELL **US.**
PERHAPS IT'S SOME SORT OF FRIEND HE PICKED UP ALONG THE WAY? LIKE THOSE WOLVES?
OH DEAR ME— YOU TWO LOOK SO **TIRED!** PERHAPS THIS IS ENOUGH TALK FOR TONIGHT, HMM?
MR. PICKLES— PLEASE GIVE THESE GENTLEMEN A RIDE FROM HERE TO WHEREVER THEY PLEASE.
TOMORROW YOU MAY RETURN TO CLAIM THE BODIES INSIDE.
UHH—THANK YOU...
...but...
>AHEM<
TELL ME, MR. BASARAB
HOW DID YOU KNOW THERE ARE BODIES IN THE CABIN?
YOUNG MAN, WHEN LEGEND IS WITHOUT HIS ROCK, HE LEAVES BODIES WHEREVER HE GOES.
NOW, PLEASE ACCEPT OUR RIDE AND BE THANKFUL YOU HAVE SURVIVED THIS NIGHT.
STEP IN, SIRS.

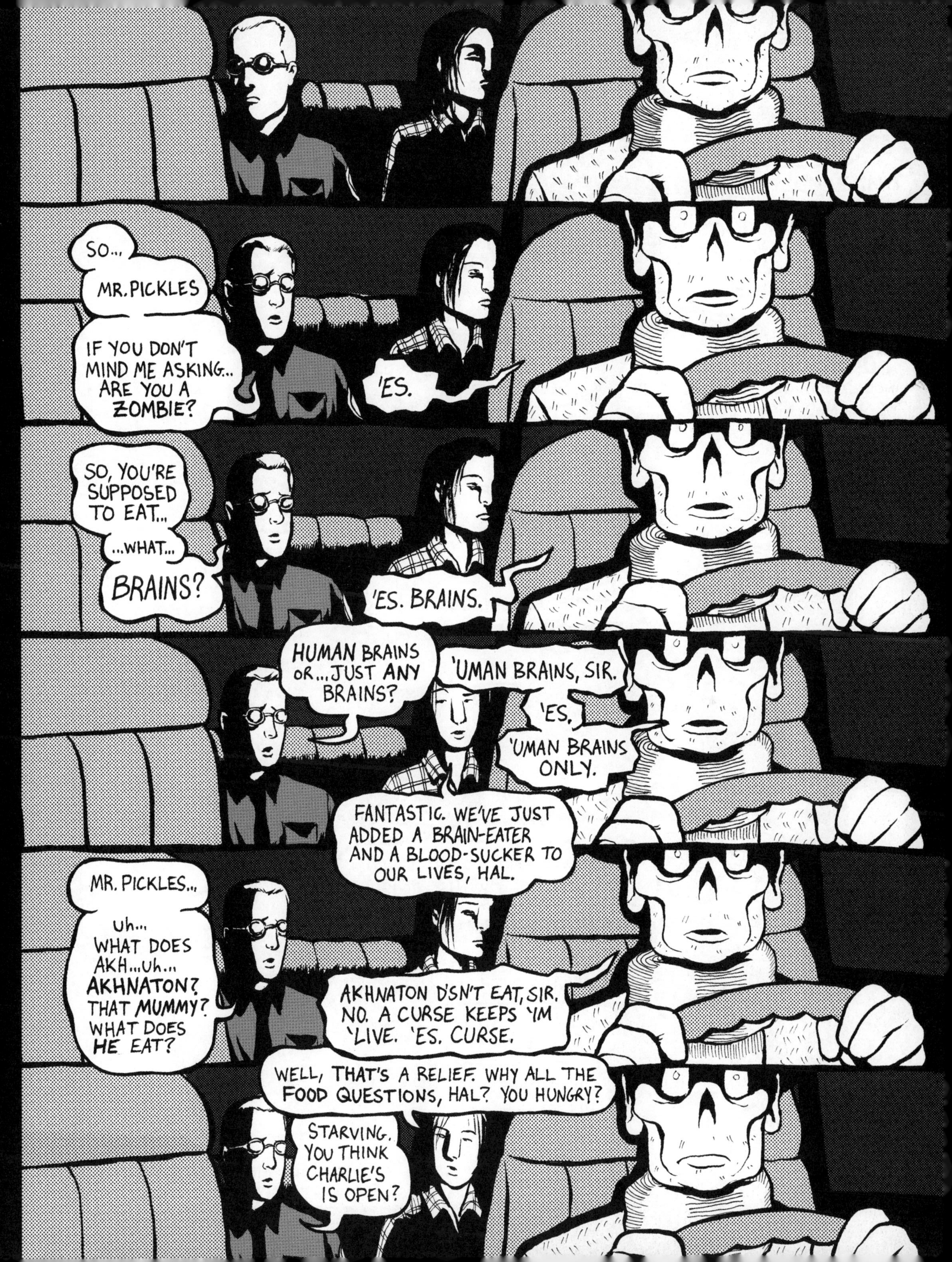
SO...
MR. PICKLES
IF YOU DON'T MIND ME ASKING... ARE YOU A ZOMBIE?
'ES.
SO, YOU'RE SUPPOSED TO EAT...
...WHAT...
BRAINS?
'ES. BRAINS.
HUMAN BRAINS OR...JUST ANY BRAINS?
'UMAN BRAINS, SIR.
'ES.
'UMAN BRAINS ONLY.
FANTASTIC. WE'VE JUST ADDED A BRAIN-EATER AND A BLOOD-SUCKER TO OUR LIVES, HAL.
MR. PICKLES...
Uh... WHAT DOES AKH...Uh... AKHNATON? THAT MUMMY? WHAT DOES HE EAT?
AKHNATON D'SN'T EAT, SIR. NO. A CURSE KEEPS 'IM 'LIVE. 'ES. CURSE.
WELL, THAT'S A RELIEF. WHY ALL THE FOOD QUESTIONS, HAL? YOU HUNGRY?
STARVING. YOU THINK CHARLIE'S IS OPEN?

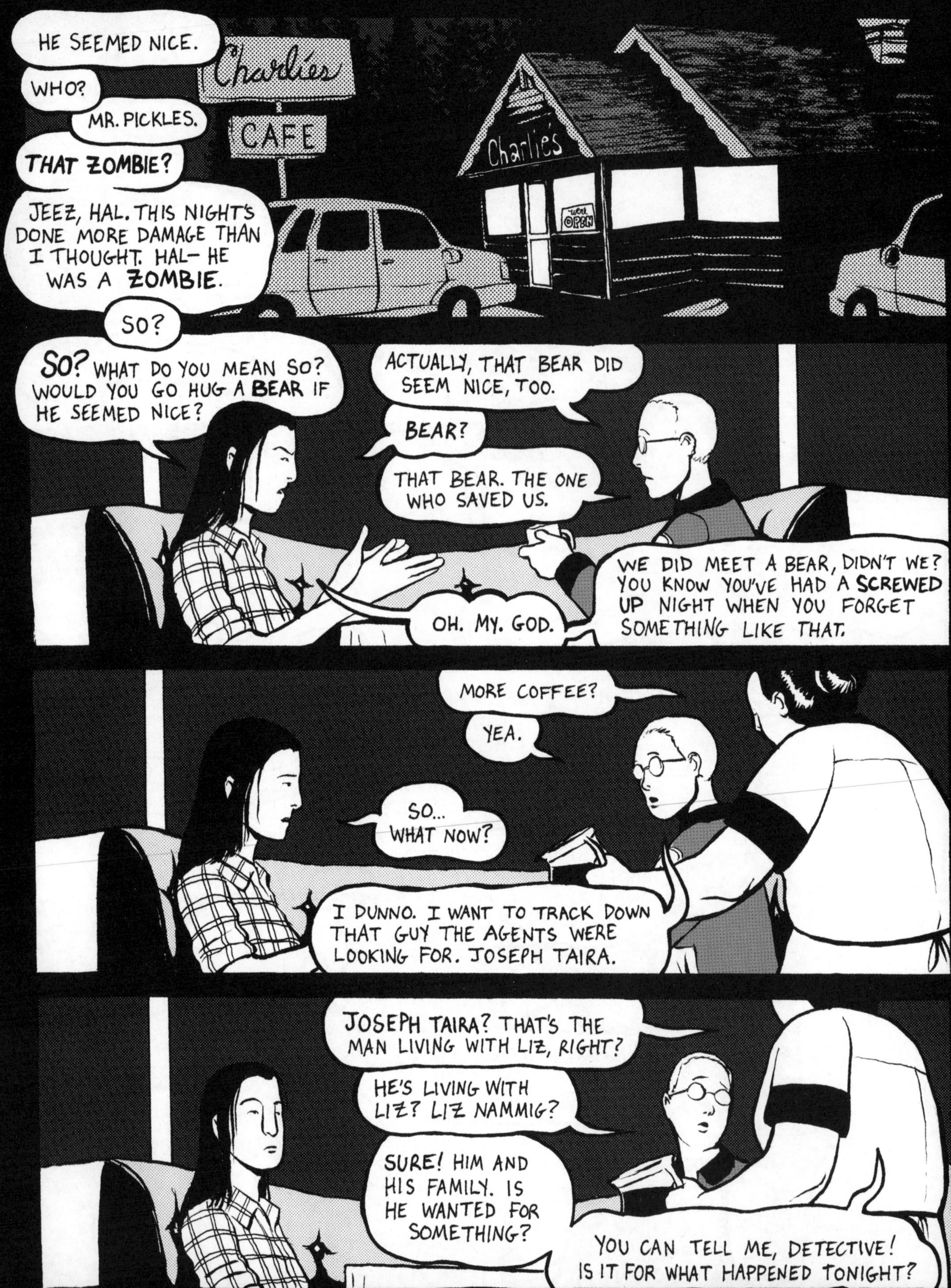
HE SEEMED NICE.
WHO?
MR. PICKLES.
Charlie's
CAFE
THAT ZOMBIE?
Charlie's
OPEN
JEEZ, HAL. THIS NIGHT'S DONE MORE DAMAGE THAN I THOUGHT. HAL— HE WAS A ZOMBIE.
SO?
SO? WHAT DO YOU MEAN SO? WOULD YOU GO HUG A BEAR IF HE SEEMED NICE?
ACTUALLY, THAT BEAR DID SEEM NICE, TOO.
BEAR?
THAT BEAR. THE ONE WHO SAVED US.
WE DID MEET A BEAR, DIDN'T WE? YOU KNOW YOU'VE HAD A SCREWED UP NIGHT WHEN YOU FORGET SOMETHING LIKE THAT.
OH. MY. GOD.
MORE COFFEE?
YEA.
SO... WHAT NOW?
I DUNNO. I WANT TO TRACK DOWN THAT GUY THE AGENTS WERE LOOKING FOR. JOSEPH TAIRA.
JOSEPH TAIRA? THAT'S THE MAN LIVING WITH LIZ, RIGHT?
HE'S LIVING WITH LIZ? LIZ NAMMIG?
SURE! HIM AND HIS FAMILY. IS HE WANTED FOR SOMETHING?
YOU CAN TELL ME, DETECTIVE! IS IT FOR WHAT HAPPENED TONIGHT?

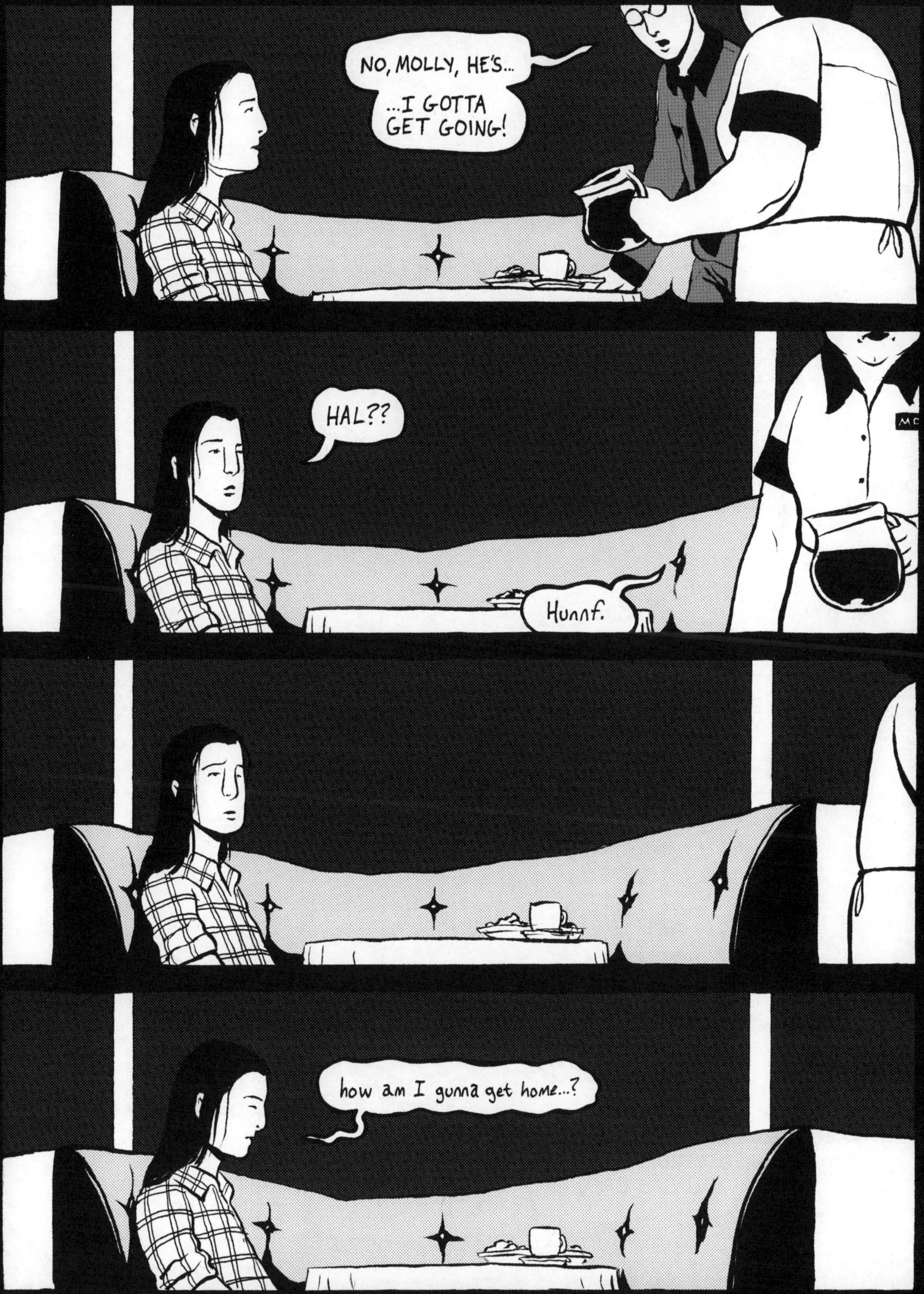
NO, MOLLY, HE'S...
...I GOTTA GET GOING!
HAL??
Hunnf.
how am I gunna get home...?

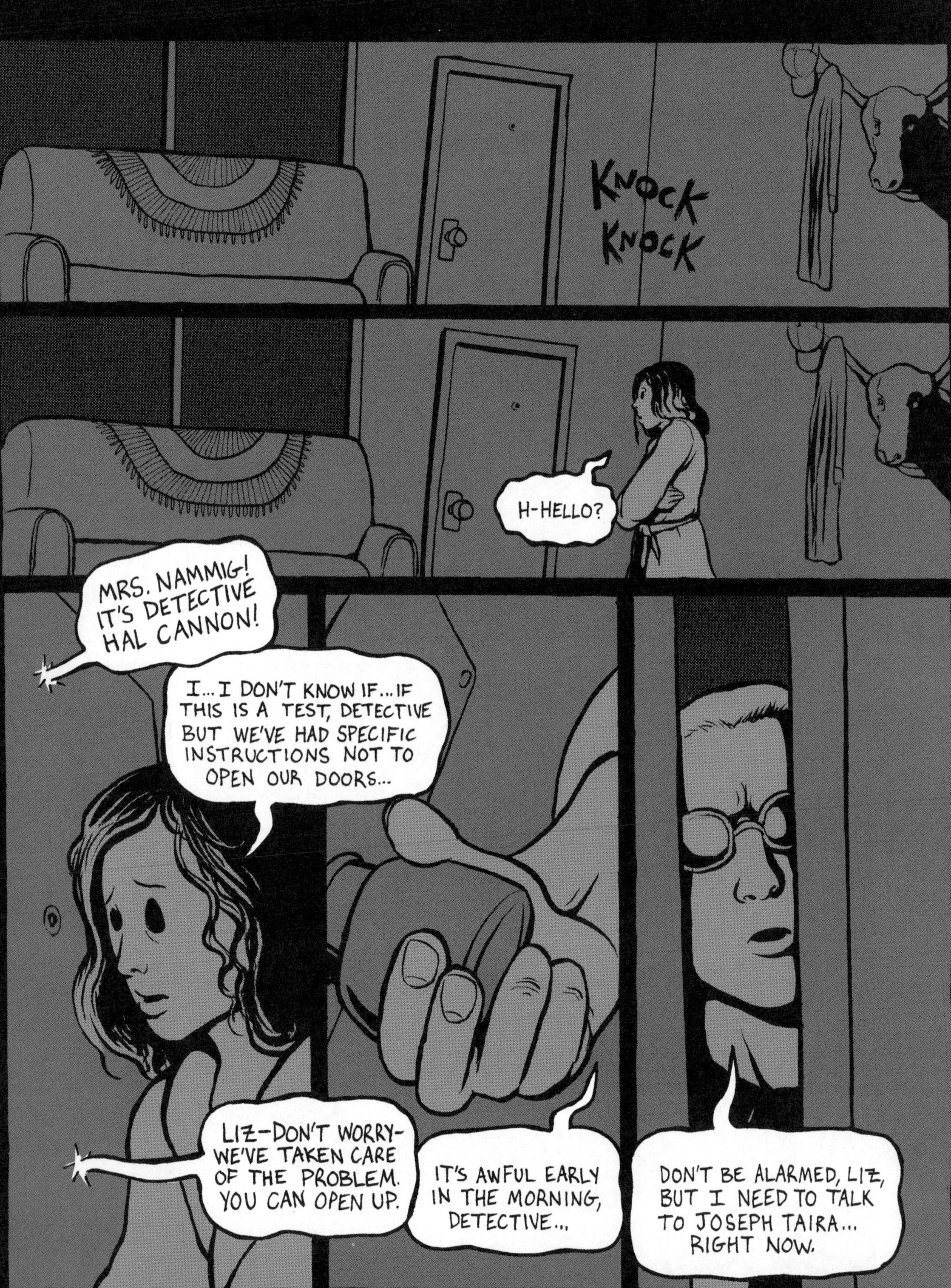
KNOCK KNOCK
H-HELLO?
MRS. NAMMIG! IT'S DETECTIVE HAL CANNON!
I... I DON'T KNOW IF... IF THIS IS A TEST, DETECTIVE BUT WE'VE HAD SPECIFIC INSTRUCTIONS NOT TO OPEN OUR DOORS...
LIZ–DON'T WORRY–WE'VE TAKEN CARE OF THE PROBLEM. YOU CAN OPEN UP.
IT'S AWFUL EARLY IN THE MORNING, DETECTIVE...
DON'T BE ALARMED, LIZ, BUT I NEED TO TALK TO JOSEPH TAIRA... RIGHT NOW.

8.
COMMUNE

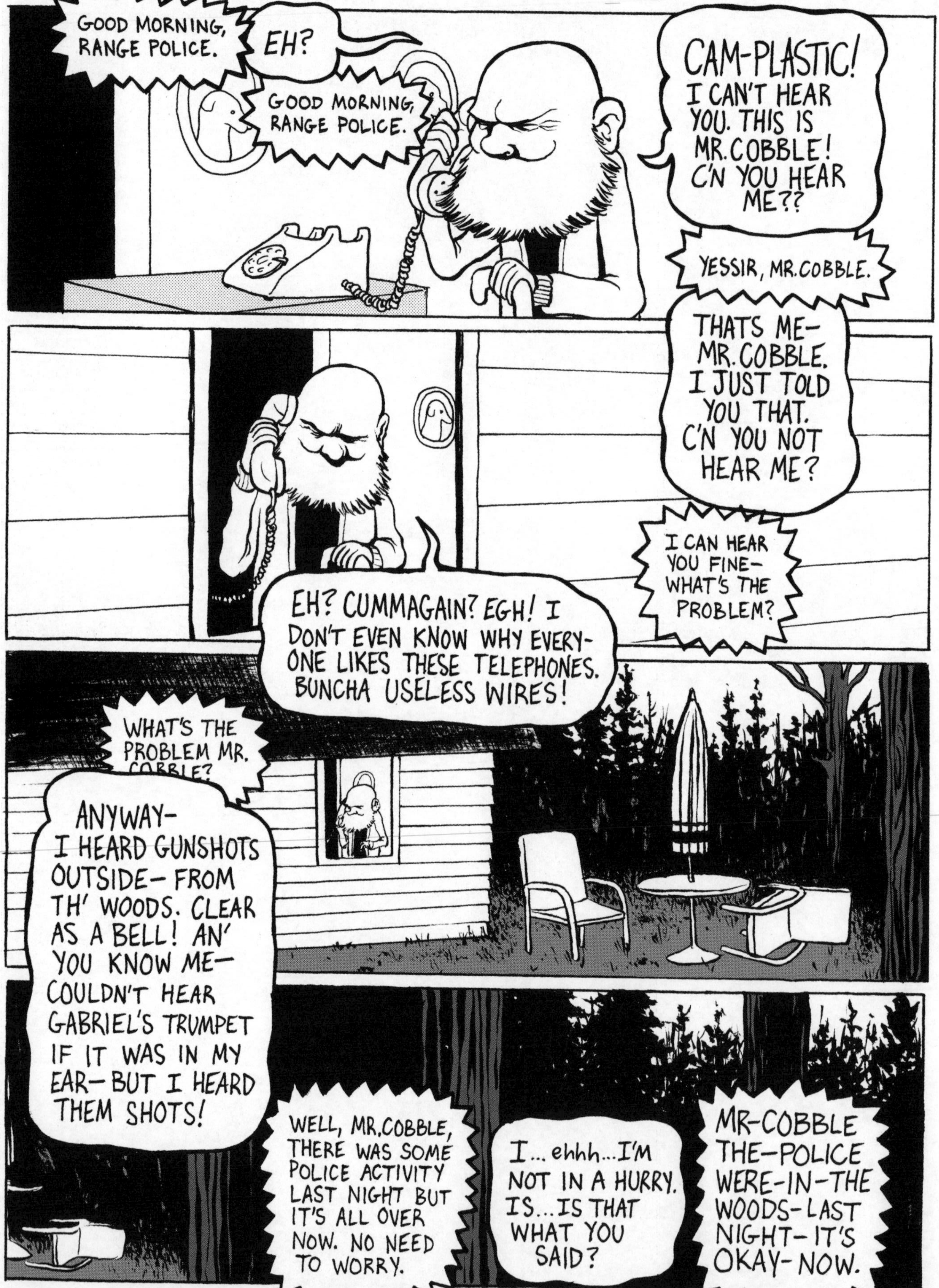
GOOD MORNING, RANGE POLICE.
EH?
GOOD MORNING, RANGE POLICE.
CAM-PLASTIC! I CAN'T HEAR YOU. THIS IS MR. COBBLE! C'N YOU HEAR ME??
YESSIR, MR. COBBLE.
THATS ME- MR. COBBLE. I JUST TOLD YOU THAT. C'N YOU NOT HEAR ME?
I CAN HEAR YOU FINE- WHAT'S THE PROBLEM?
EH? CUMMAGAIN? EGH! I DON'T EVEN KNOW WHY EVERY-ONE LIKES THESE TELEPHONES. BUNCHA USELESS WIRES!
WHAT'S THE PROBLEM MR. COBBLE?
ANYWAY- I HEARD GUNSHOTS OUTSIDE- FROM TH' WOODS. CLEAR AS A BELL! AN' YOU KNOW ME- COULDN'T HEAR GABRIEL'S TRUMPET IF IT WAS IN MY EAR- BUT I HEARD THEM SHOTS!
WELL, MR. COBBLE, THERE WAS SOME POLICE ACTIVITY LAST NIGHT BUT IT'S ALL OVER NOW. NO NEED TO WORRY.
I... ehhh... I'M NOT IN A HURRY. IS... IS THAT WHAT YOU SAID?
MR-COBBLE THE-POLICE WERE-IN-THE WOODS-LAST NIGHT-IT'S OKAY-NOW.

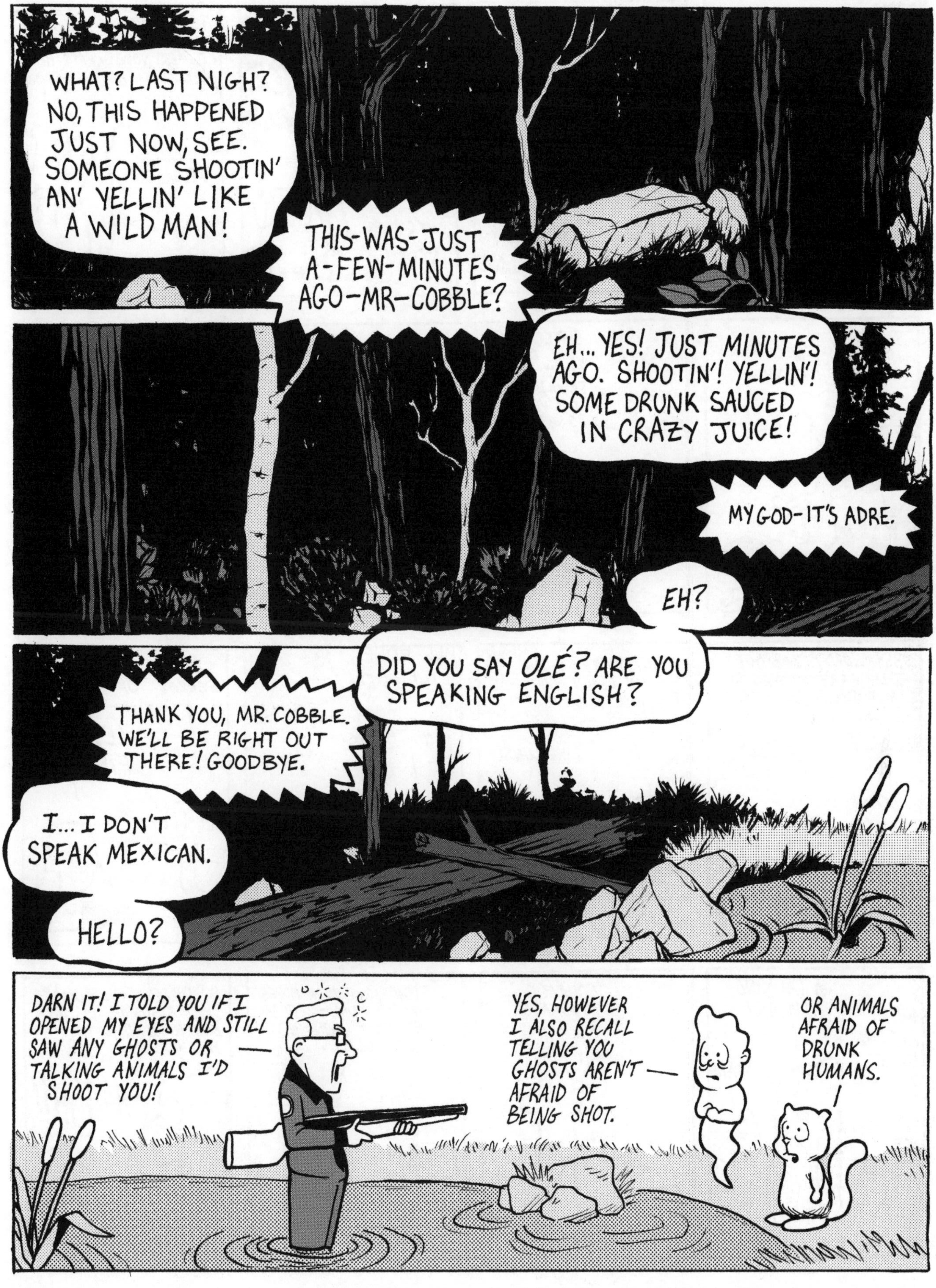
WHAT? LAST NIGH? NO, THIS HAPPENED JUST NOW, SEE. SOMEONE SHOOTIN' AN' YELLIN' LIKE A WILD MAN!
THIS-WAS-JUST A-FEW-MINUTES AGO-MR-COBBLE?
EH... YES! JUST MINUTES AGO. SHOOTIN'! YELLIN'! SOME DRUNK SAUCED IN CRAZY JUICE!
MY GOD-IT'S ADRE.
EH?
DID YOU SAY OLÉ? ARE YOU SPEAKING ENGLISH?
THANK YOU, MR. COBBLE. WE'LL BE RIGHT OUT THERE! GOODBYE.
I... I DON'T SPEAK MEXICAN.
HELLO?
DARN IT! I TOLD YOU IF I OPENED MY EYES AND STILL SAW ANY GHOSTS OR TALKING ANIMALS I'D SHOOT YOU!
YES, HOWEVER I ALSO RECALL TELLING YOU GHOSTS AREN'T AFRAID OF BEING SHOT.
OR ANIMALS AFRAID OF DRUNK HUMANS.

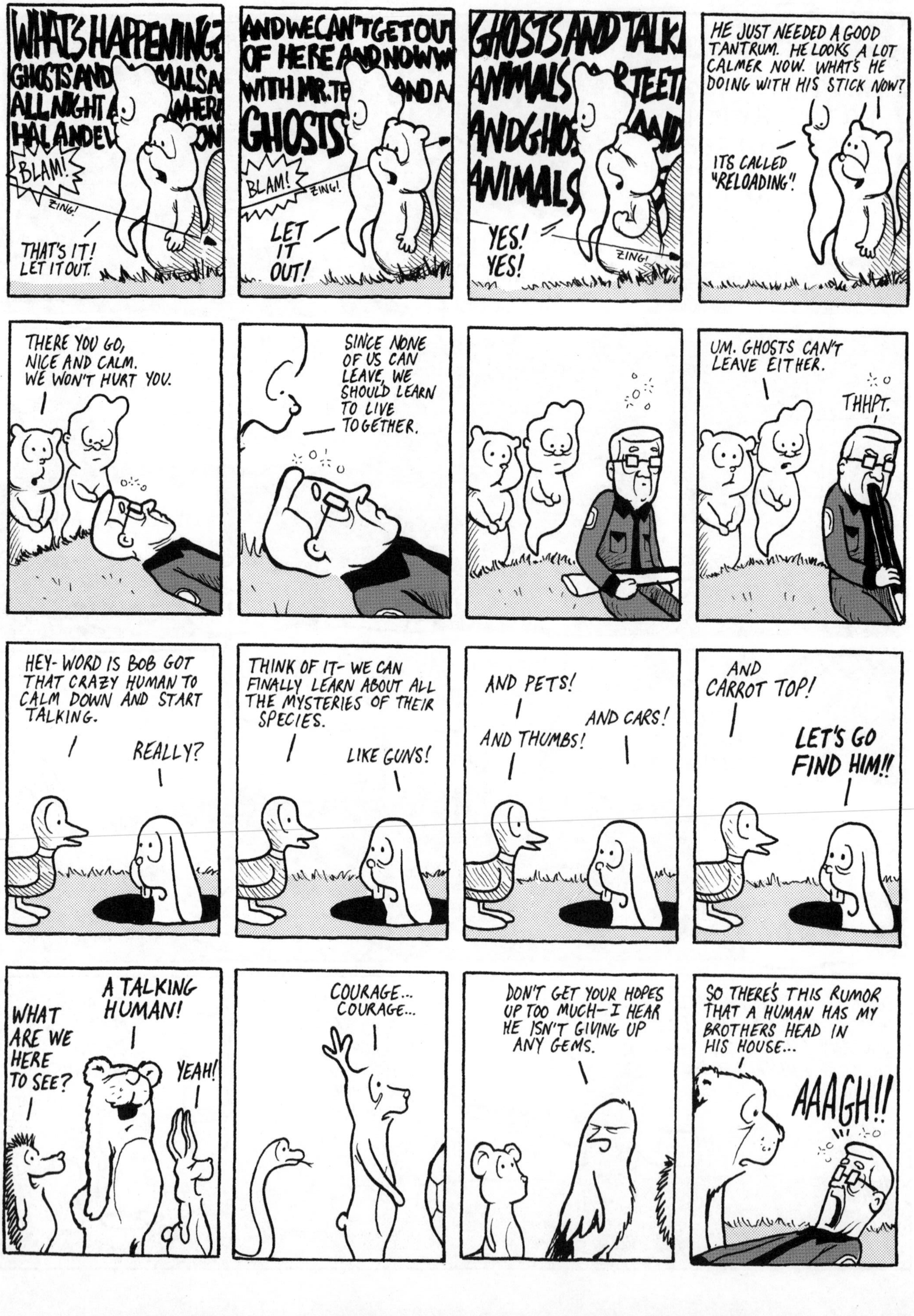
WHAT'S HAPPENING?
GHOSTS AND
ALL NIGHT
BLAM!
ZING!
THAT'S IT! LET IT OUT.
AND WE CAN'T GET OUT
OF HERE AND NOW
WITH MR.
GHOSTS
BLAM!
ZING!
LET IT OUT!
GHOSTS AND
ANIMALS
ANIMALS
YES! YES!
ZING!
HE JUST NEEDED A GOOD TANTRUM. HE LOOKS A LOT CALMER NOW. WHAT'S HE DOING WITH HIS STICK NOW?
ITS CALLED "RELOADING".
THERE YOU GO, NICE AND CALM. WE WON'T HURT YOU.
SINCE NONE OF US CAN LEAVE, WE SHOULD LEARN TO LIVE TOGETHER.
UM. GHOSTS CAN'T LEAVE EITHER.
THHPT.
HEY- WORD IS BOB GOT THAT CRAZY HUMAN TO CALM DOWN AND START TALKING.
REALLY?
THINK OF IT- WE CAN FINALLY LEARN ABOUT ALL THE MYSTERIES OF THEIR SPECIES.
LIKE GUNS!
AND PETS!
AND THUMBS!
AND CARS!
AND CARROT TOP!
LET'S GO FIND HIM!!
WHAT ARE WE HERE TO SEE?
A TALKING HUMAN!
YEAH!
COURAGE... COURAGE...
DON'T GET YOUR HOPES UP TOO MUCH- I HEAR HE ISN'T GIVING UP ANY GEMS.
SO THERE'S THIS RUMOR THAT A HUMAN HAS MY BROTHERS HEAD IN HIS HOUSE...
AAAGH!!

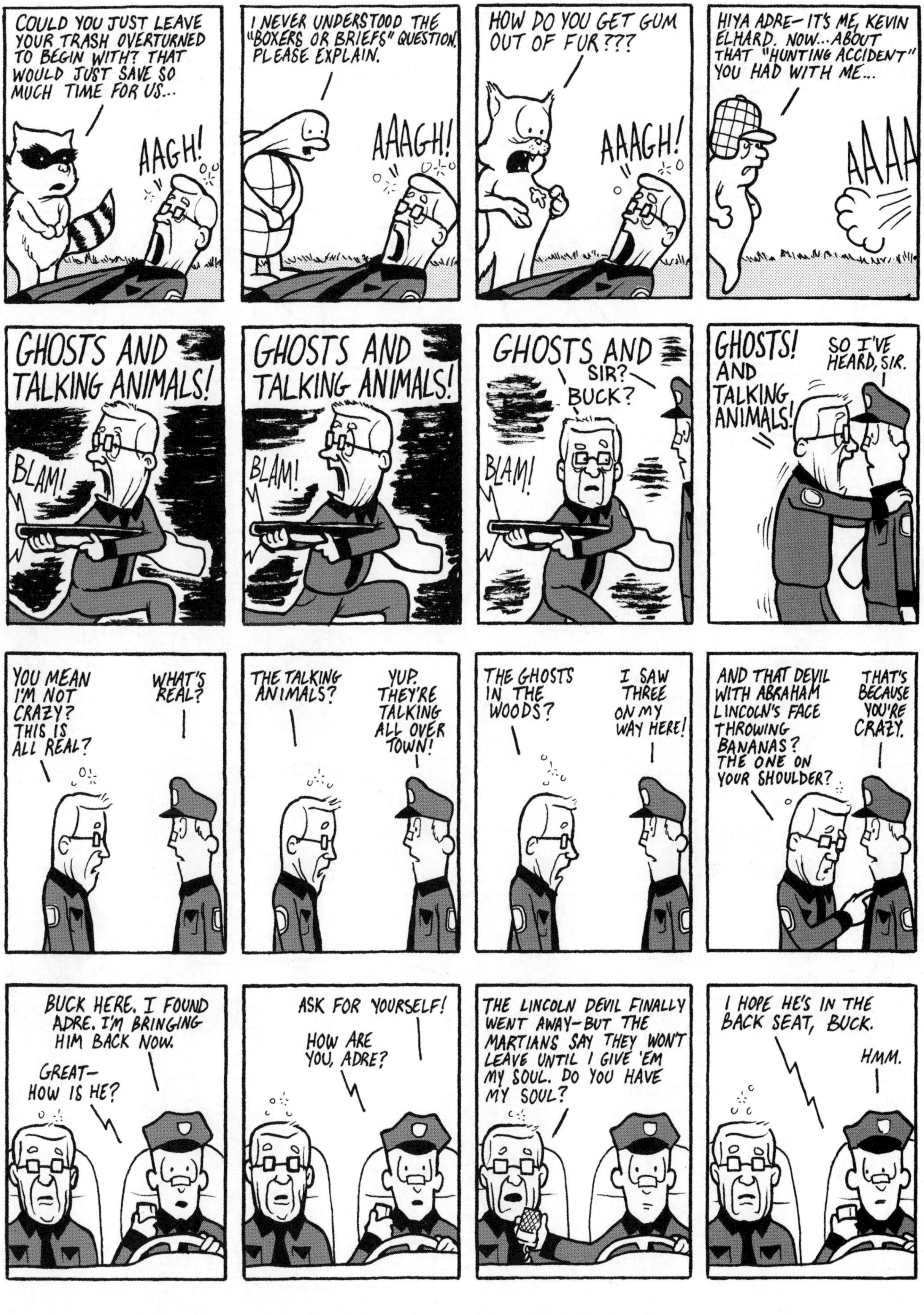
COULD YOU JUST LEAVE YOUR TRASH OVERTURNED TO BEGIN WITH? THAT WOULD JUST SAVE SO MUCH TIME FOR US...
AAGH!
I NEVER UNDERSTOOD THE "BOXERS OR BRIEFS" QUESTION. PLEASE EXPLAIN.
AAAGH!
HOW DO YOU GET GUM OUT OF FUR???
AAAGH!
HIYA ADRE— IT'S ME, KEVIN ELHARD. NOW... ABOUT THAT "HUNTING ACCIDENT" YOU HAD WITH ME...
AAAA
GHOSTS AND TALKING ANIMALS!
BLAM!
GHOSTS AND TALKING ANIMALS!
BLAM!
GHOSTS AND
SIR?
BUCK?
BLAM!
GHOSTS! AND TALKING ANIMALS!
SO I'VE HEARD, SIR.
YOU MEAN I'M NOT CRAZY? THIS IS ALL REAL?
WHAT'S REAL?
THE TALKING ANIMALS?
YUP. THEY'RE TALKING ALL OVER TOWN!
THE GHOSTS IN THE WOODS?
I SAW THREE ON MY WAY HERE!
AND THAT DEVIL WITH ABRAHAM LINCOLN'S FACE THROWING BANANAS? THE ONE ON YOUR SHOULDER?
THAT'S BECAUSE YOU'RE CRAZY.
BUCK HERE. I FOUND ADRE. I'M BRINGING HIM BACK NOW.
GREAT— HOW IS HE?
ASK FOR YOURSELF!
HOW ARE YOU, ADRE?
THE LINCOLN DEVIL FINALLY WENT AWAY— BUT THE MARTIANS SAY THEY WON'T LEAVE UNTIL I GIVE 'EM MY SOUL. DO YOU HAVE MY SOUL?
I HOPE HE'S IN THE BACK SEAT, BUCK.
HMM.

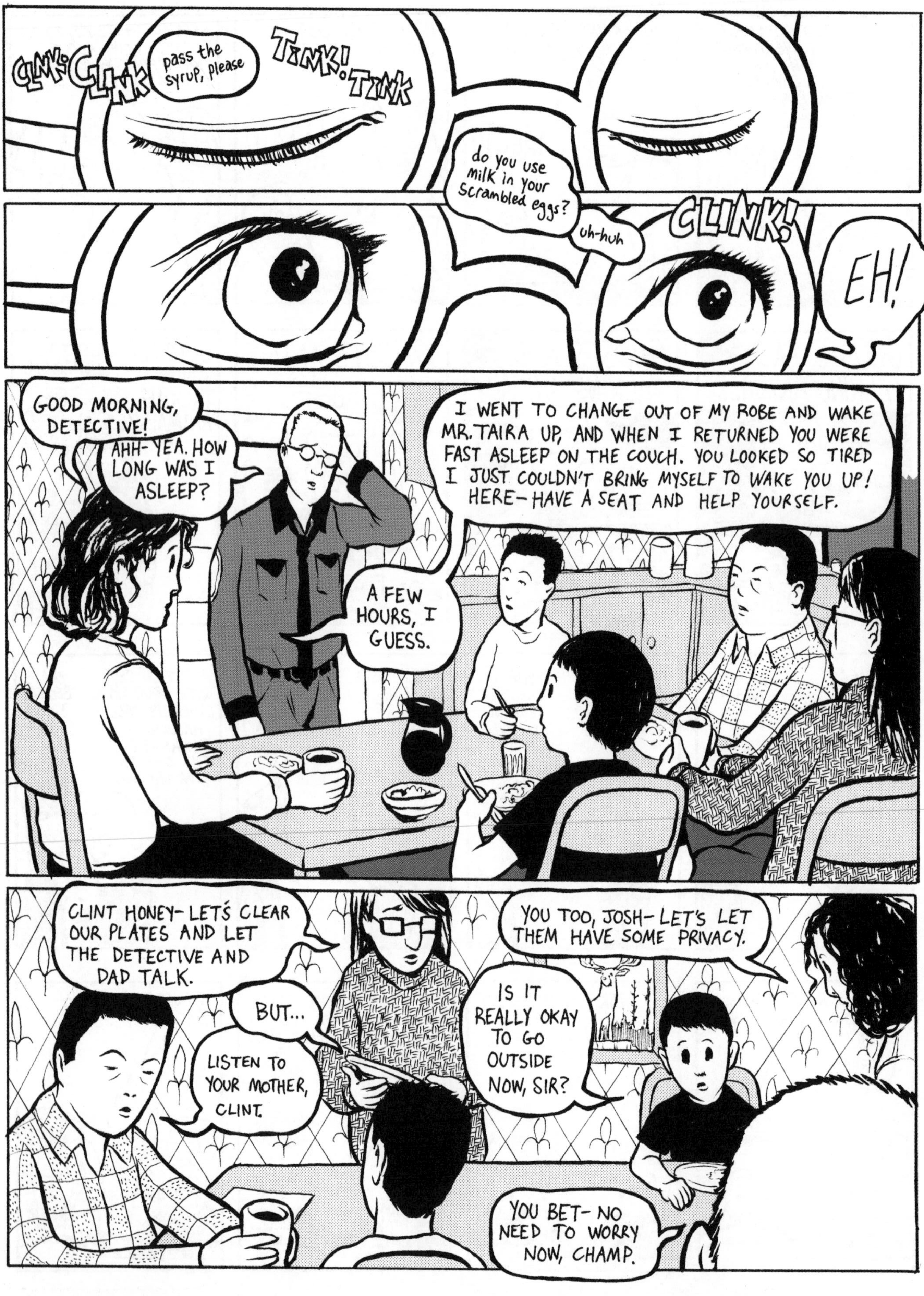
CLINK CLINK
pass the syrup, please
TINK! TINK
do you use milk in your scrambled eggs?
uh-huh
CLINK!
EH!
GOOD MORNING, DETECTIVE!
AHH- YEA. HOW LONG WAS I ASLEEP?
I WENT TO CHANGE OUT OF MY ROBE AND WAKE MR. TAIRA UP, AND WHEN I RETURNED YOU WERE FAST ASLEEP ON THE COUCH. YOU LOOKED SO TIRED I JUST COULDN'T BRING MYSELF TO WAKE YOU UP! HERE- HAVE A SEAT AND HELP YOURSELF.
A FEW HOURS, I GUESS.
CLINT HONEY- LET'S CLEAR OUR PLATES AND LET THE DETECTIVE AND DAD TALK.
BUT...
LISTEN TO YOUR MOTHER, CLINT.
YOU TOO, JOSH- LET'S LET THEM HAVE SOME PRIVACY.
IS IT REALLY OKAY TO GO OUTSIDE NOW, SIR?
YOU BET- NO NEED TO WORRY NOW, CHAMP.

SO— WHAT'S FOR BREAKFAST HERE?

NORWEGIAN PANCAKES. THAT'S WHAT LIZ CALLS 'EM.

MR. TAIRA—

JOSEPH, PLEASE.

JOSEPH.

I'M DETECTIVE HAL CANNON.

SURE, SURE. IT'S IN MY AREA OF STUDY. WELL, A TESSERACT IS A HARD THING TO DEFINE.

BUT ESSENTIALLY IT'S A SHAPE— LET ME EXPLAIN...

IT SOUNDS TO ME LIKE IT'S A QUESTION YOU KNOW THE ANSWER TO, HOWEVER.

A TESSERACT? LIKE A HYPERCUBE? THAT'S AN INTERESTING FIRST QUESTION.

THEY'RE PRETTY GOOD. SO... JOSEPH... WHAT IS A TESSERACT?

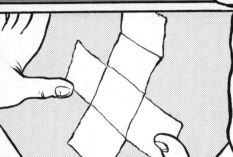

AND WE CAN TELL THE 2-D PEOPLE THAT THIS CROSS SHAPE MAY NOT BE A CUBE, BUT IT IS A CUBE UNFOLDED INTO THEIR DIMENSIONAL TERMS. IF THEY COULD FIND THE MENTAL GYMNASTICS TO IMAGINE HOW THIS SHAPE WOULD FOLD TO FORM A CUBE, THEY COULD VISUALIZE 3-D SPACE!

LET'S SAY THIS TABLE TOP IS A LAND OF 2-D PEOPLE. WHEN THIS CUBE SITS ON THEIR LAND, THEY SEE IT AS A SQUARE. BUT WHEN I UNFOLD THIS CUBE THEY SUDDENLY SEE THIS CROSS-LIKE SHAPE APPEAR.

A CUBE IS EASY FOR US TO VISUALIZE BECAUSE IT'S A 3-DIMENSIONAL OBJECT AND WE'RE 3-DIMENSIONAL PEOPLE. BUT IT WOULD BE IMPOSSIBLE FOR A 2-DIMENSIONAL PERSON TO VISUALIZE THIS CUBE, BUT WE CAN GIVE THEM A HINT.

THE TESSERACT CAME FROM THE WORK OF AN ENGLISH MATHEMATICIAN BY THE NAME OF *CHARLES HINTON*. HINTON WAS INTERESTED IN THE IDEA OF VISUALIZING THE FOURTH DIMENSION.

VISUALIZE? HOW?

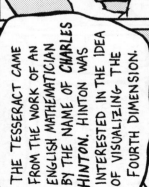

OKAY— LET ME TEAR THIS PAPER NAPKIN AND SHOW YOU SOMETHING. I'M GOING TO MAKE A CUBE OUT OF IT.

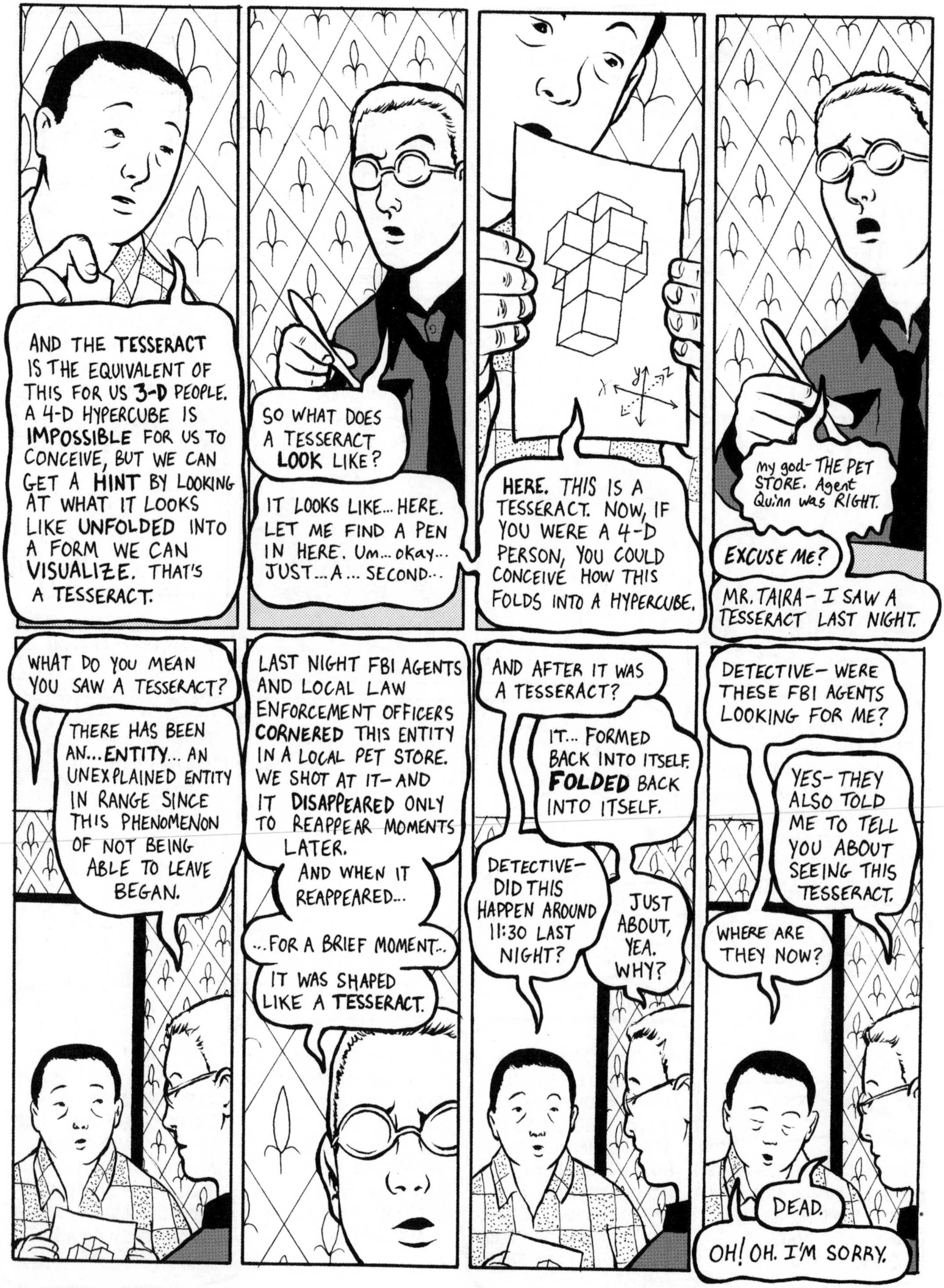
AND THE TESSERACT IS THE EQUIVALENT OF THIS FOR US 3-D PEOPLE. A 4-D HYPERCUBE IS IMPOSSIBLE FOR US TO CONCEIVE, BUT WE CAN GET A HINT BY LOOKING AT WHAT IT LOOKS LIKE UNFOLDED INTO A FORM WE CAN VISUALIZE. THAT'S A TESSERACT.
SO WHAT DOES A TESSERACT LOOK LIKE?
IT LOOKS LIKE... HERE. LET ME FIND A PEN IN HERE. Um... okay... JUST... A ... SECOND...
HERE. THIS IS A TESSERACT. NOW, IF YOU WERE A 4-D PERSON, YOU COULD CONCEIVE HOW THIS FOLDS INTO A HYPERCUBE.
My god- THE PET STORE. Agent Quinn was RIGHT.
EXCUSE ME?
MR. TAIRA- I SAW A TESSERACT LAST NIGHT.
WHAT DO YOU MEAN YOU SAW A TESSERACT?
THERE HAS BEEN AN... ENTITY... AN UNEXPLAINED ENTITY IN RANGE SINCE THIS PHENOMENON OF NOT BEING ABLE TO LEAVE BEGAN.
LAST NIGHT FBI AGENTS AND LOCAL LAW ENFORCEMENT OFFICERS CORNERED THIS ENTITY IN A LOCAL PET STORE. WE SHOT AT IT- AND IT DISAPPEARED ONLY TO REAPPEAR MOMENTS LATER.
AND WHEN IT REAPPEARED...
...FOR A BRIEF MOMENT...
IT WAS SHAPED LIKE A TESSERACT.
AND AFTER IT WAS A TESSERACT?
IT... FORMED BACK INTO ITSELF. FOLDED BACK INTO ITSELF.
DETECTIVE- DID THIS HAPPEN AROUND 11:30 LAST NIGHT?
JUST ABOUT, YEA. WHY?
DETECTIVE- WERE THESE FBI AGENTS LOOKING FOR ME?
YES- THEY ALSO TOLD ME TO TELL YOU ABOUT SEEING THIS TESSERACT.
WHERE ARE THEY NOW?
DEAD.
OH! OH. I'M SORRY.

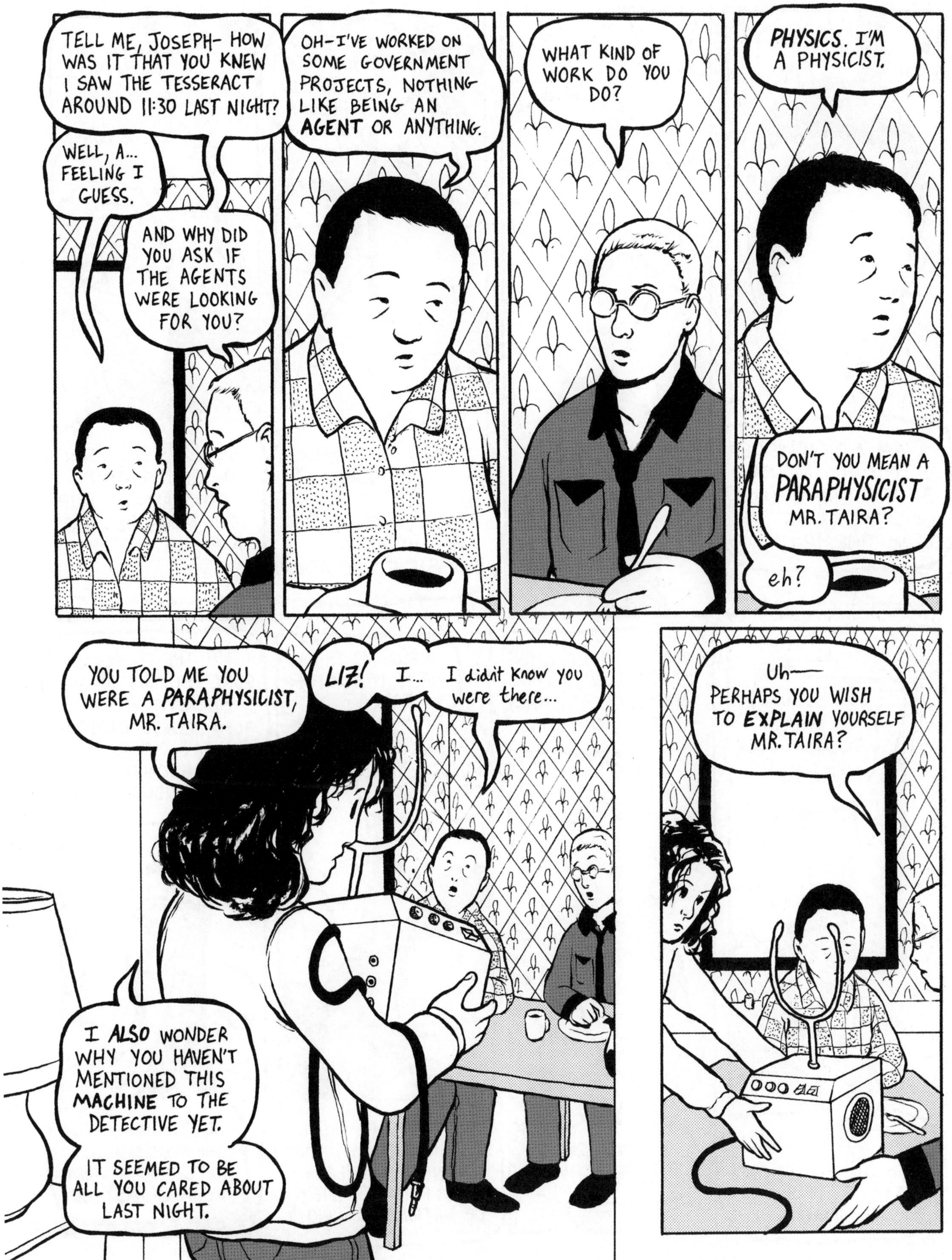
TELL ME, JOSEPH- HOW WAS IT THAT YOU KNEW I SAW THE TESSERACT AROUND 11:30 LAST NIGHT?
WELL, A... FEELING I GUESS.
AND WHY DID YOU ASK IF THE AGENTS WERE LOOKING FOR YOU?
OH-I'VE WORKED ON SOME GOVERNMENT PROJECTS, NOTHING LIKE BEING AN AGENT OR ANYTHING.
WHAT KIND OF WORK DO YOU DO?
PHYSICS. I'M A PHYSICIST.
DON'T YOU MEAN A PARAPHYSICIST MR. TAIRA?
eh?
YOU TOLD ME YOU WERE A PARAPHYSICIST, MR. TAIRA.
LIZ!
I... I didn't know you were there...
I ALSO WONDER WHY YOU HAVEN'T MENTIONED THIS MACHINE TO THE DETECTIVE YET.
IT SEEMED TO BE ALL YOU CARED ABOUT LAST NIGHT.
Uh— PERHAPS YOU WISH TO EXPLAIN YOURSELF MR. TAIRA?

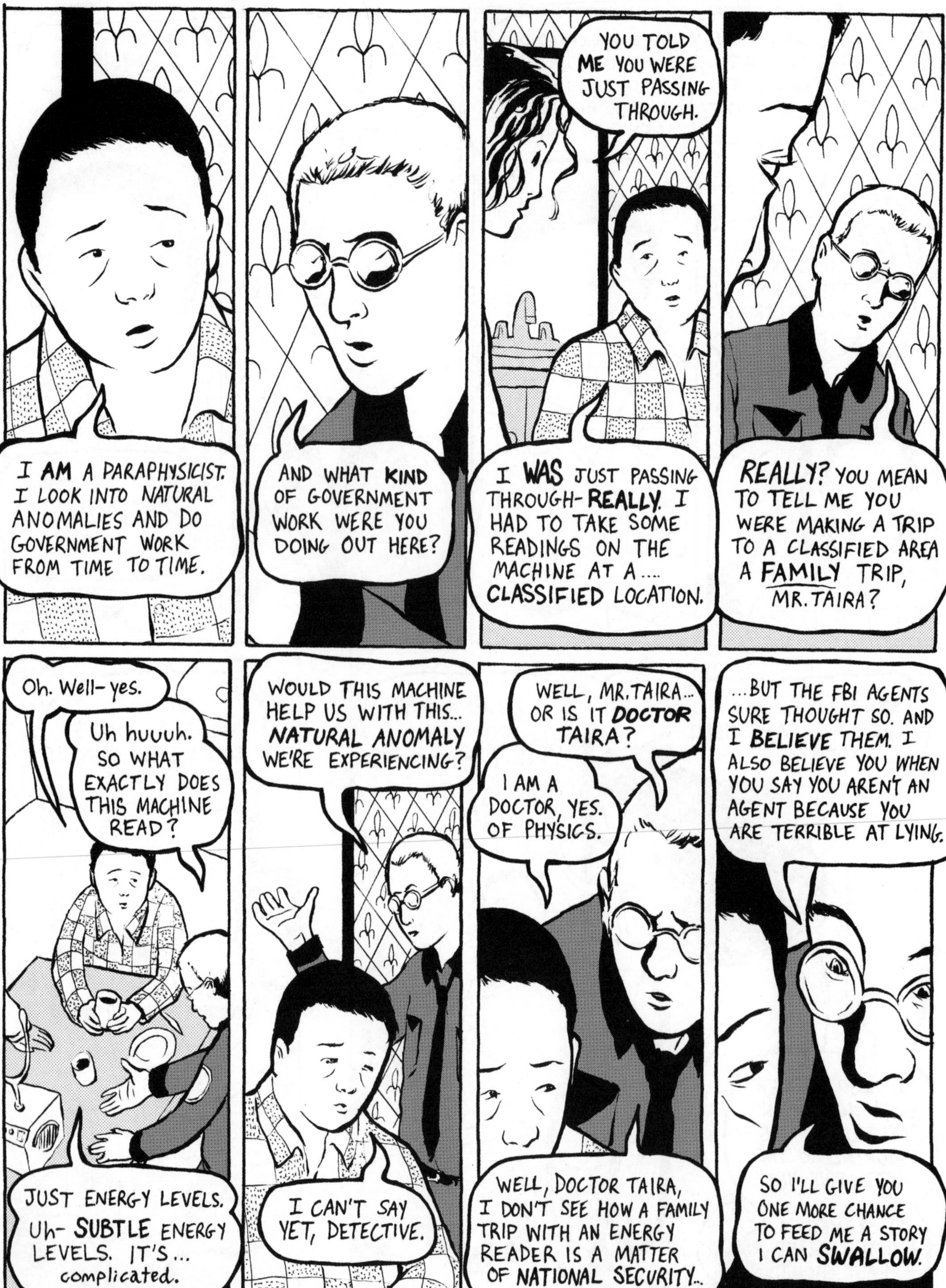
I AM A PARAPHYSICIST. I LOOK INTO NATURAL ANOMALIES AND DO GOVERNMENT WORK FROM TIME TO TIME.
AND WHAT KIND OF GOVERNMENT WORK WERE YOU DOING OUT HERE?
YOU TOLD ME YOU WERE JUST PASSING THROUGH.
I WAS JUST PASSING THROUGH- REALLY. I HAD TO TAKE SOME READINGS ON THE MACHINE AT A.... CLASSIFIED LOCATION.
REALLY? YOU MEAN TO TELL ME YOU WERE MAKING A TRIP TO A CLASSIFIED AREA A FAMILY TRIP, MR. TAIRA?
Oh. Well- yes.
Uh huuuh. SO WHAT EXACTLY DOES THIS MACHINE READ?
JUST ENERGY LEVELS. Uh- SUBTLE ENERGY LEVELS. IT'S... complicated.
WOULD THIS MACHINE HELP US WITH THIS... NATURAL ANOMALY WE'RE EXPERIENCING?
I CAN'T SAY YET, DETECTIVE.
WELL, MR. TAIRA... OR IS IT DOCTOR TAIRA?
I AM A DOCTOR, YES. OF PHYSICS.
WELL, DOCTOR TAIRA, I DON'T SEE HOW A FAMILY TRIP WITH AN ENERGY READER IS A MATTER OF NATIONAL SECURITY...
...BUT THE FBI AGENTS SURE THOUGHT SO. AND I BELIEVE THEM. I ALSO BELIEVE YOU WHEN YOU SAY YOU AREN'T AN AGENT BECAUSE YOU ARE TERRIBLE AT LYING.
SO I'LL GIVE YOU ONE MORE CHANCE TO FEED ME A STORY I CAN SWALLOW.

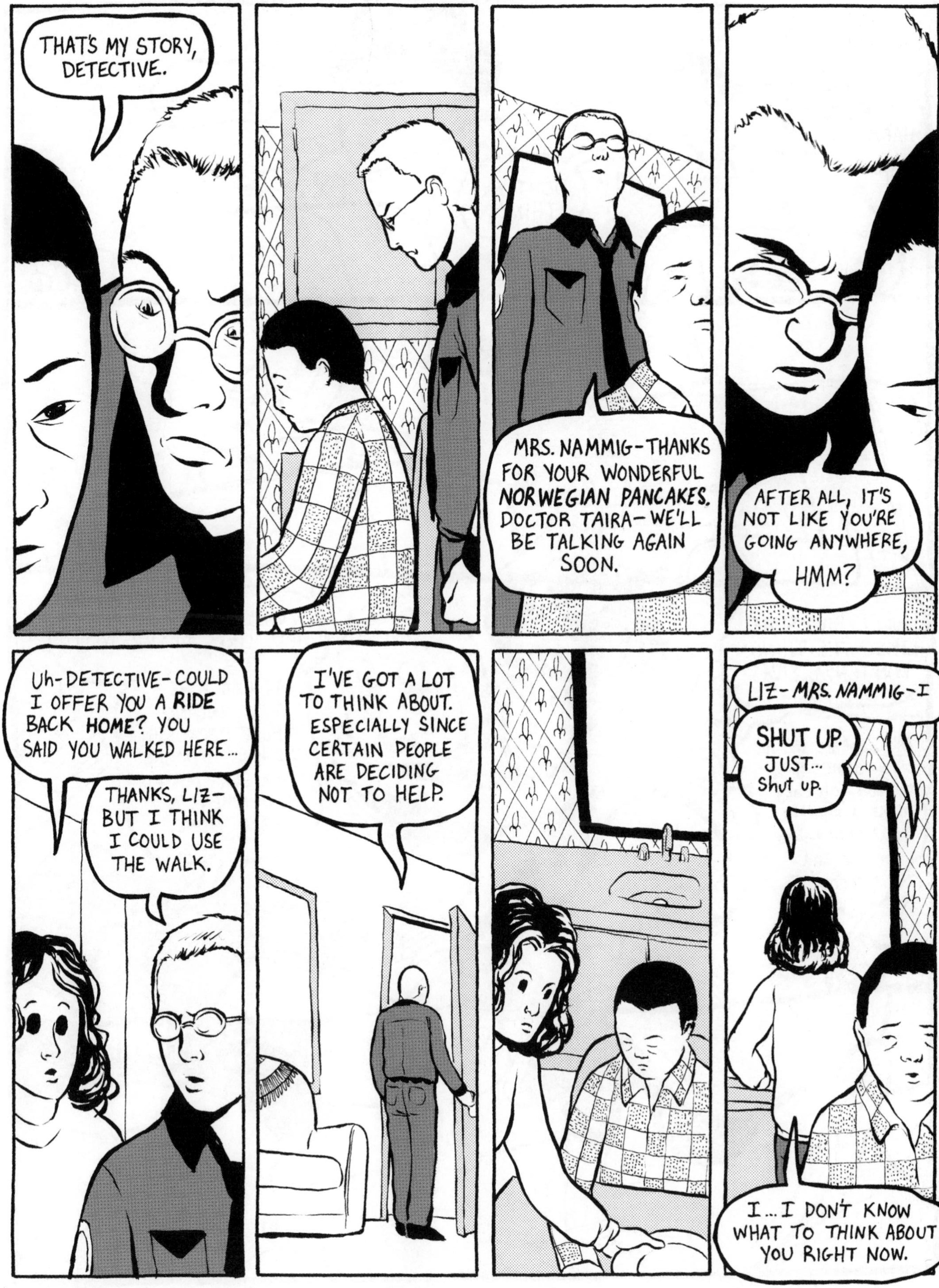
THAT'S MY STORY, DETECTIVE.
MRS. NAMMIG–THANKS FOR YOUR WONDERFUL **NORWEGIAN PANCAKES.** DOCTOR TAIRA–WE'LL BE TALKING AGAIN SOON.
AFTER ALL, IT'S NOT LIKE YOU'RE GOING ANYWHERE,
HMM?
Uh-DETECTIVE-COULD I OFFER YOU A **RIDE** BACK **HOME**? YOU SAID YOU WALKED HERE...
THANKS, LIZ–BUT I THINK I COULD USE THE WALK.
I'VE GOT A LOT TO THINK ABOUT. ESPECIALLY SINCE CERTAIN PEOPLE ARE DECIDING NOT TO HELP.
LIZ–*MRS. NAMMIG*–I
SHUT UP. JUST... Shut up.
I... I DON'T KNOW WHAT TO THINK ABOUT YOU RIGHT NOW.

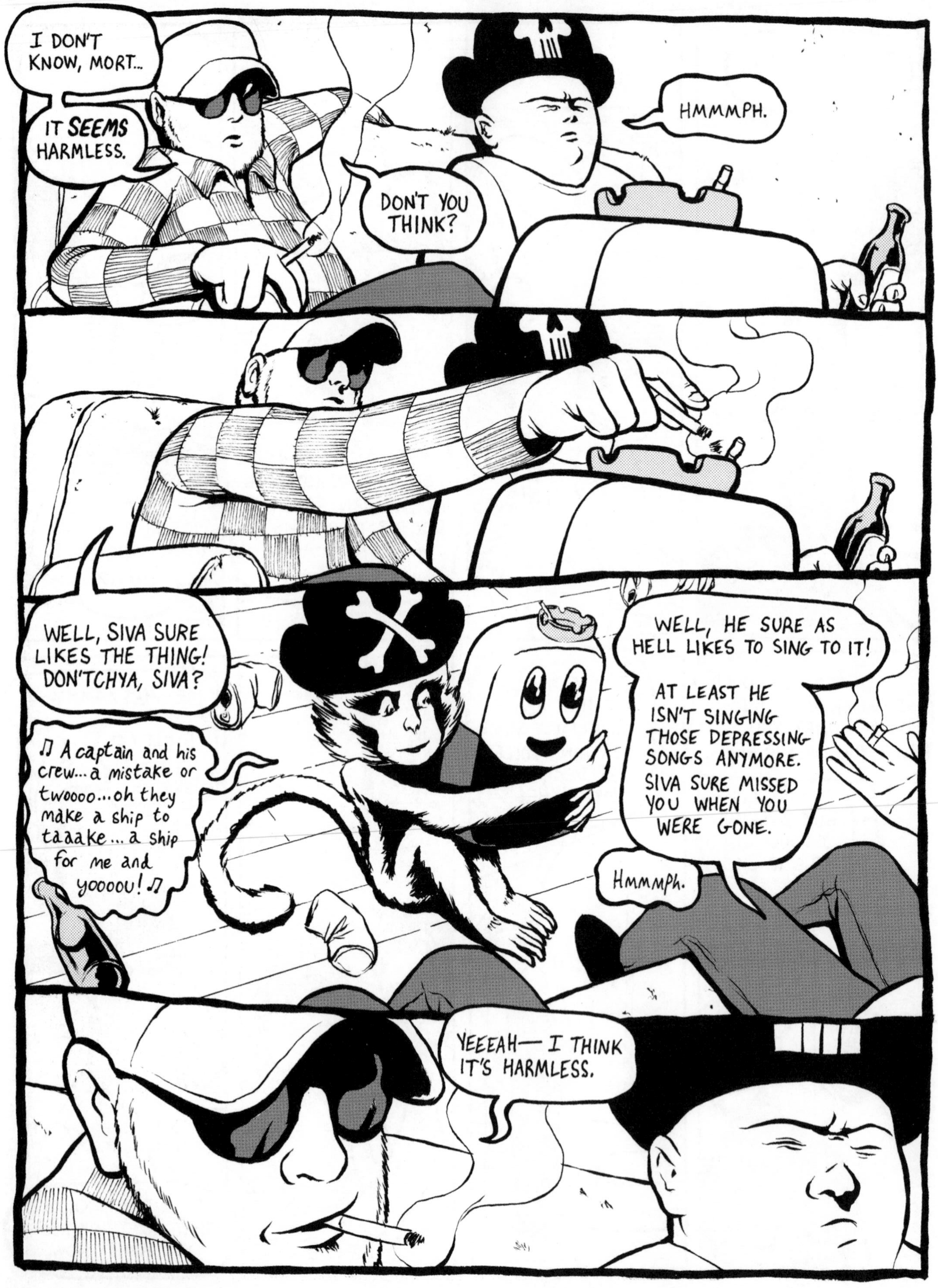
I DON'T KNOW, MORT...
IT SEEMS HARMLESS.
DON'T YOU THINK?
HMMMPH.
WELL, SIVA SURE LIKES THE THING! DON'TCHYA, SIVA?
♫ A captain and his crew... a mistake or twoooo... oh they make a ship to taaake... a ship for me and yoooou! ♫
WELL, HE SURE AS HELL LIKES TO SING TO IT!
AT LEAST HE ISN'T SINGING THOSE DEPRESSING SONGS ANYMORE. SIVA SURE MISSED YOU WHEN YOU WERE GONE.
Hmmmph.
YEEEAH— I THINK IT'S HARMLESS.

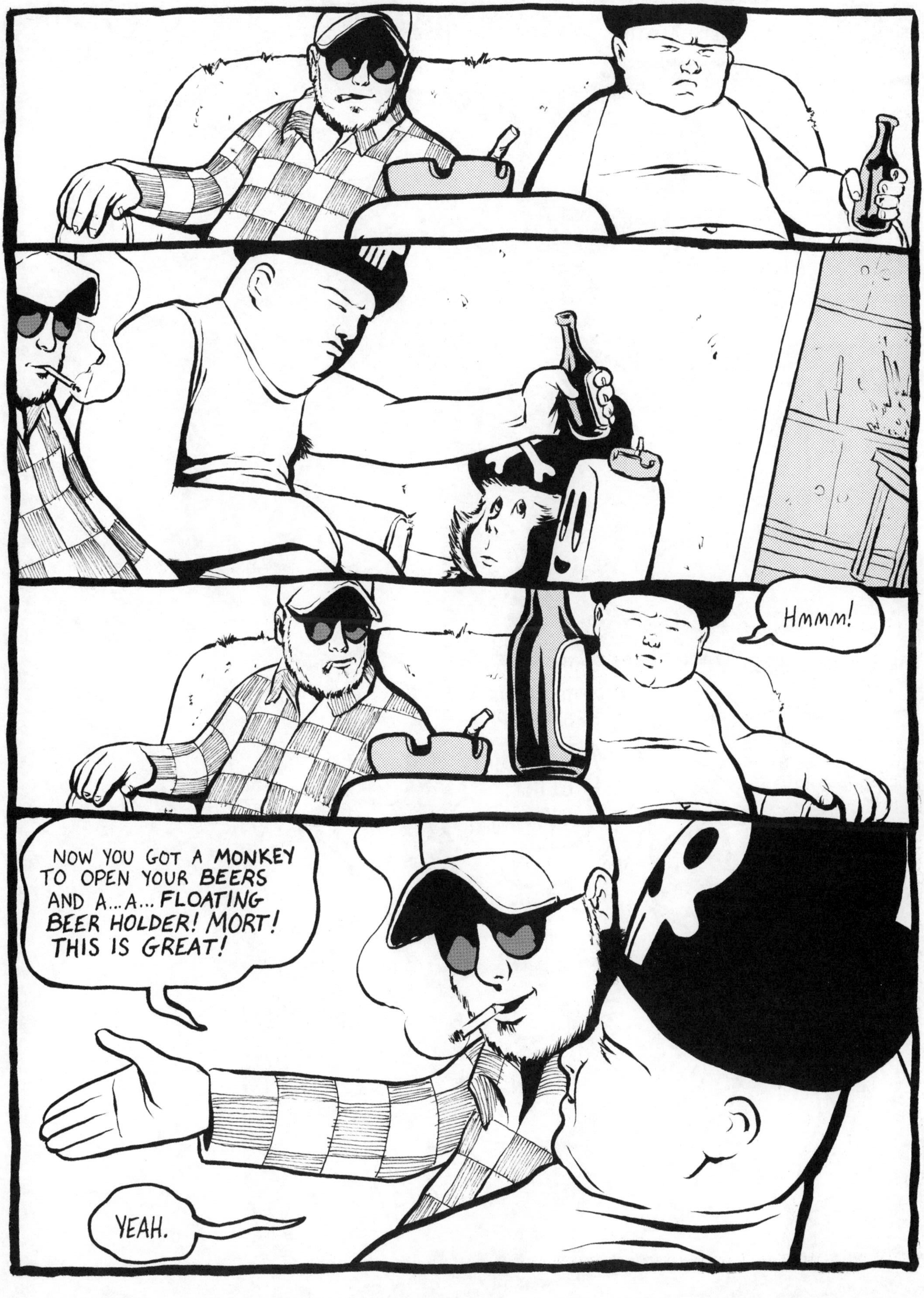
Hmmm!
NOW YOU GOT A MONKEY TO OPEN YOUR BEERS AND A...A... FLOATING BEER HOLDER! MORT! THIS IS GREAT!
YEAH.

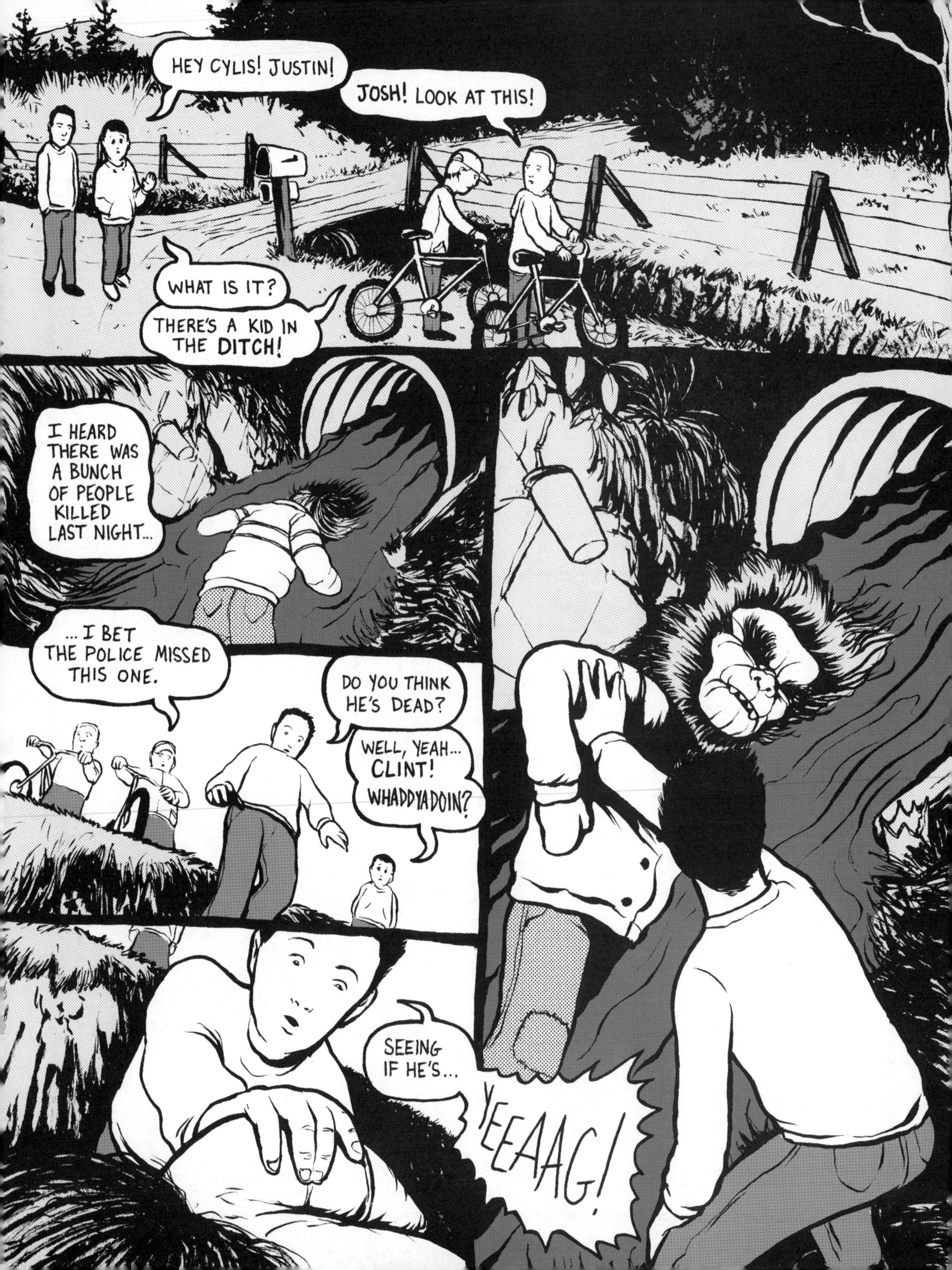
HEY CYLIS! JUSTIN!
JOSH! LOOK AT THIS!
WHAT IS IT?
THERE'S A KID IN THE DITCH!
I HEARD THERE WAS A BUNCH OF PEOPLE KILLED LAST NIGHT...
... I BET THE POLICE MISSED THIS ONE.
DO YOU THINK HE'S DEAD?
WELL, YEAH... CLINT! WHADDYADOIN?
SEEING IF HE'S...
YEEAAG!

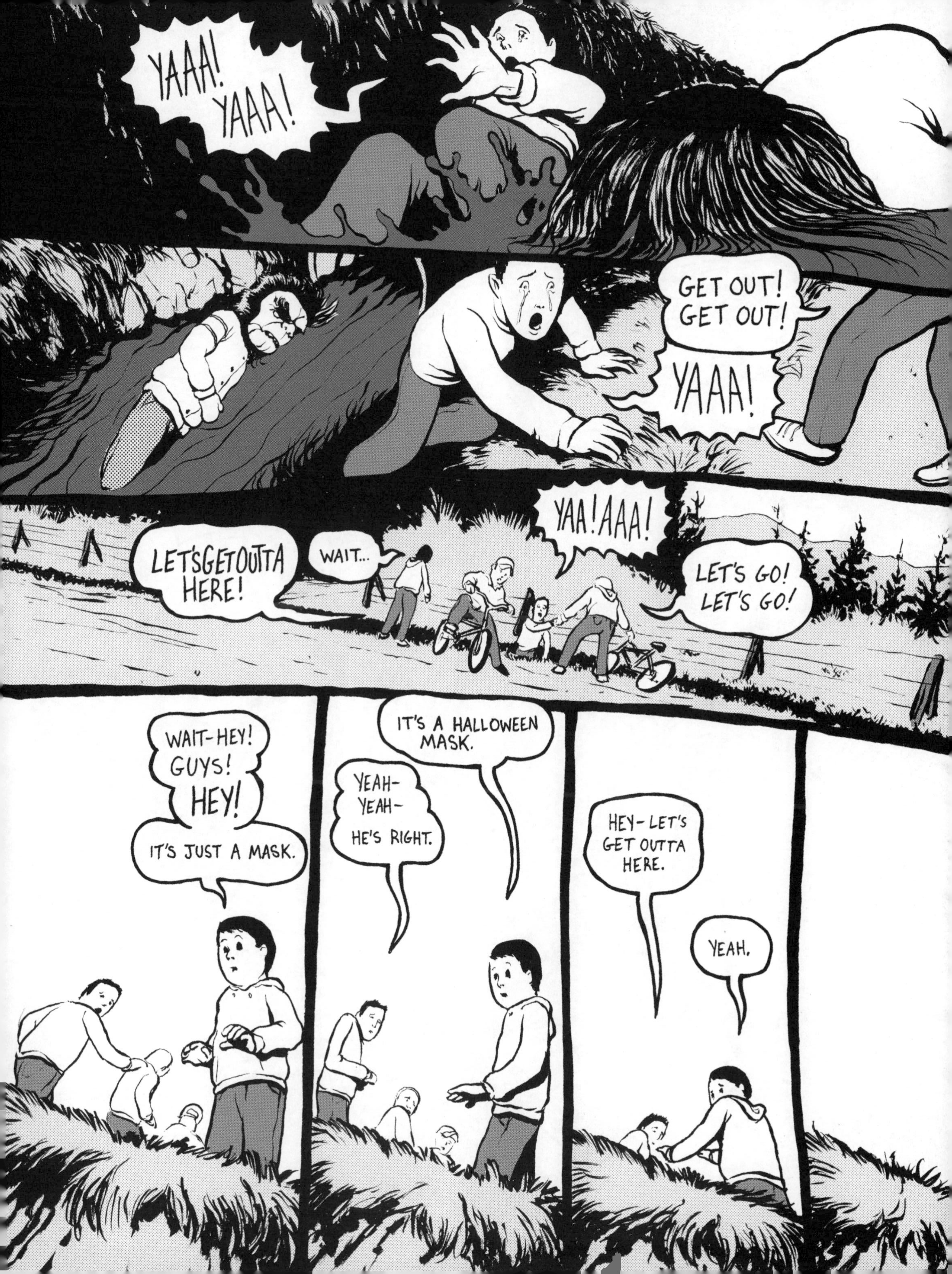
YAAA! YAAA!
GET OUT! GET OUT!
YAAA!
LET'SGETOUTTA HERE!
WAIT...
YAA!AAA!
LET'S GO! LET'S GO!
WAIT-HEY! GUYS! HEY!
IT'S JUST A MASK.
IT'S A HALLOWEEN MASK.
YEAH- YEAH- HE'S RIGHT.
HEY-LET'S GET OUTTA HERE.
YEAH.

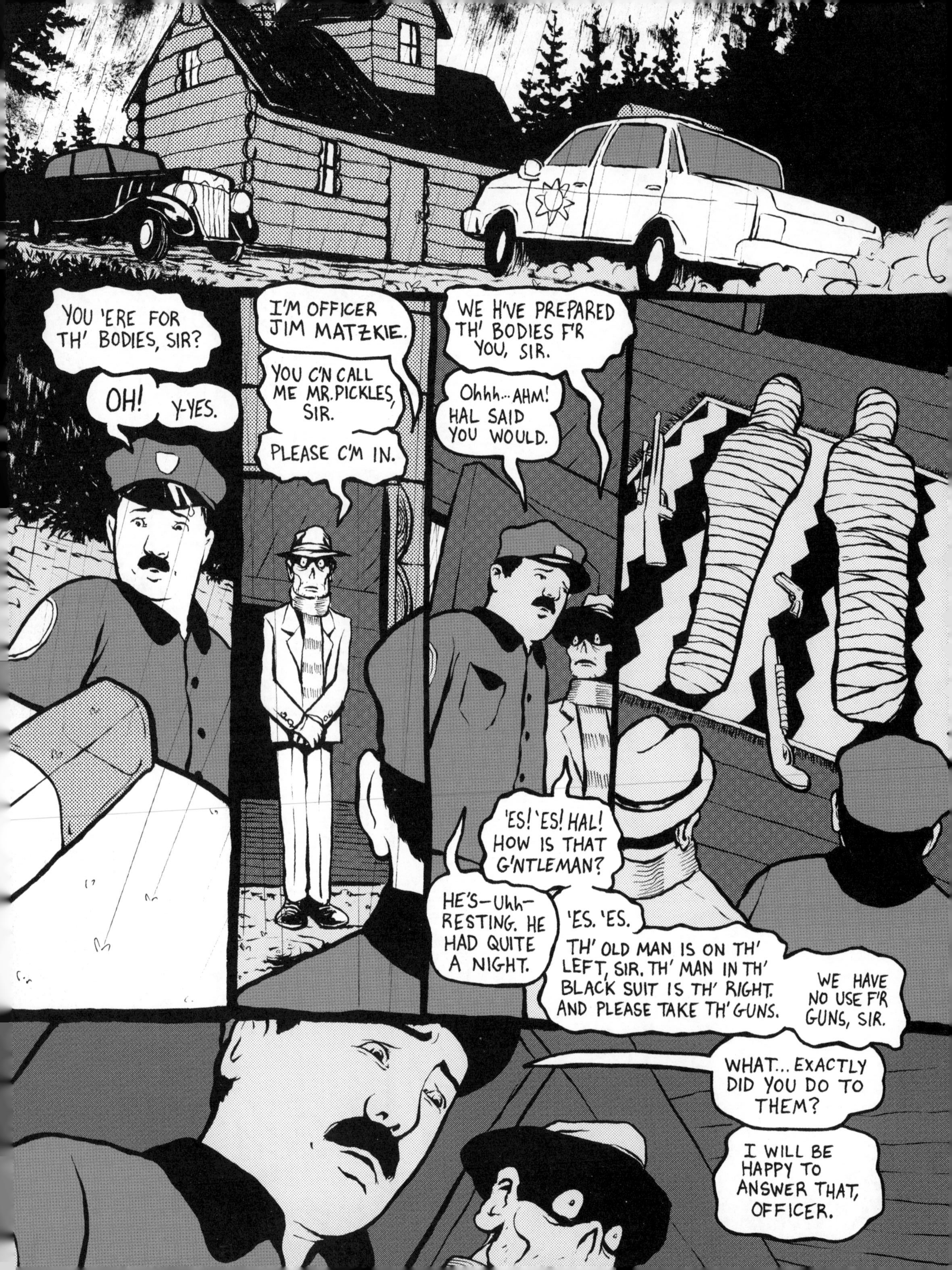

YOU 'ERE FOR TH' BODIES, SIR?
OH!
Y-YES.
I'M OFFICER JIM MATZKIE.
YOU C'N CALL ME MR.PICKLES, SIR.
PLEASE C'M IN.
WE H'VE PREPARED TH' BODIES F'R YOU, SIR.
Ohhh... AHM! HAL SAID YOU WOULD.
'ES! 'ES! HAL! HOW IS THAT G'NTLEMAN?
HE'S—Uhh— RESTING. HE HAD QUITE A NIGHT.
'ES. 'ES.
TH' OLD MAN IS ON TH' LEFT, SIR. TH' MAN IN TH' BLACK SUIT IS TH' RIGHT. AND PLEASE TAKE TH' GUNS.
WE HAVE NO USE F'R GUNS, SIR.
WHAT... EXACTLY DID YOU DO TO THEM?
I WILL BE HAPPY TO ANSWER THAT, OFFICER.

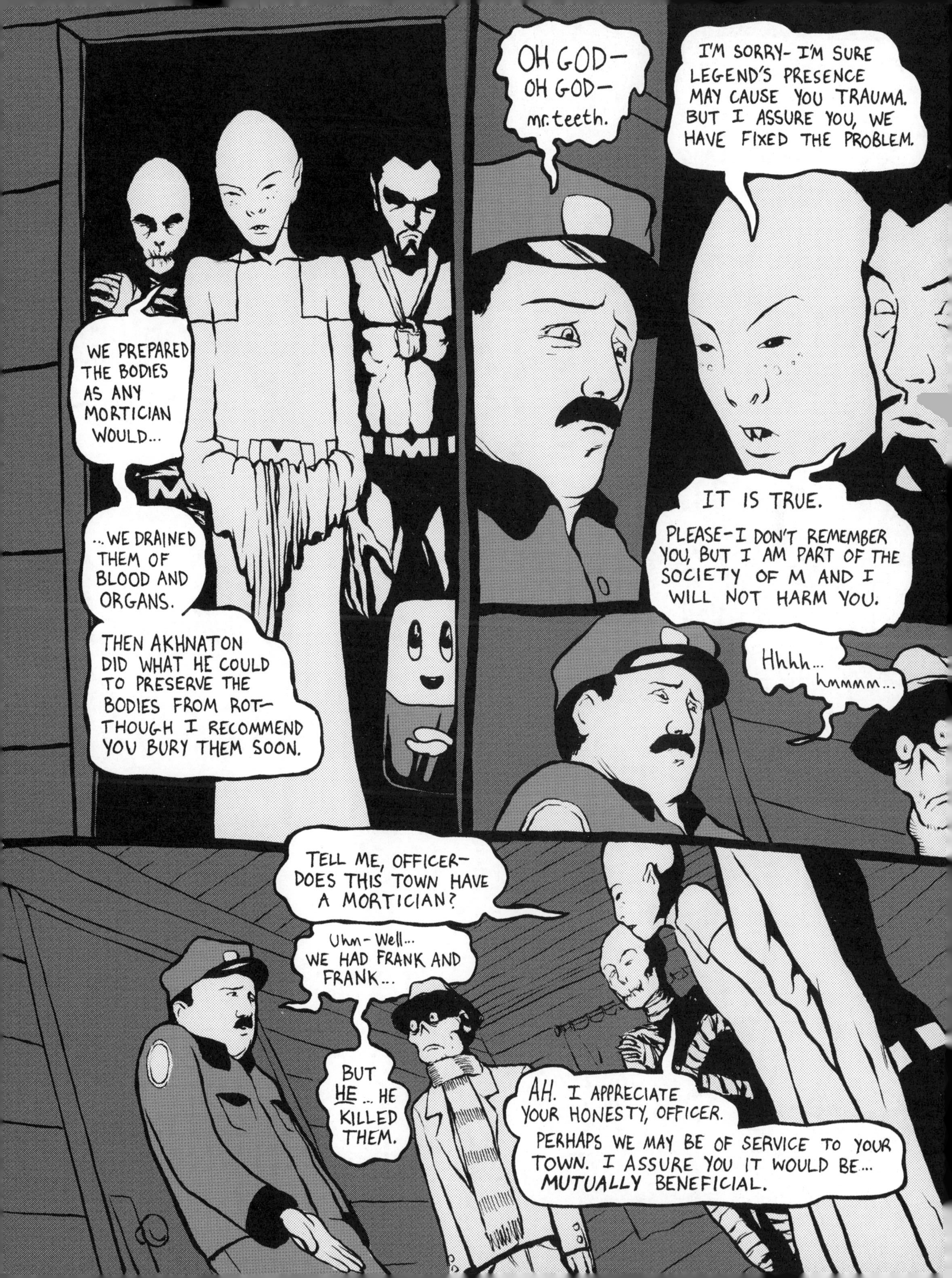
WE PREPARED THE BODIES AS ANY MORTICIAN WOULD...
...WE DRAINED THEM OF BLOOD AND ORGANS.
THEN AKHNATON DID WHAT HE COULD TO PRESERVE THE BODIES FROM ROT-THOUGH I RECOMMEND YOU BURY THEM SOON.
OH GOD—
OH GOD—
mr. teeth.
I'M SORRY- I'M SURE LEGEND'S PRESENCE MAY CAUSE YOU TRAUMA. BUT I ASSURE YOU, WE HAVE FIXED THE PROBLEM.
IT IS TRUE.
PLEASE-I DON'T REMEMBER YOU, BUT I AM PART OF THE SOCIETY OF M AND I WILL NOT HARM YOU.
Hhhh... hmmmm...
TELL ME, OFFICER- DOES THIS TOWN HAVE A MORTICIAN?
Uhm- Well... WE HAD FRANK AND FRANK...
BUT HE ... HE KILLED THEM.
AH. I APPRECIATE YOUR HONESTY, OFFICER.
PERHAPS WE MAY BE OF SERVICE TO YOUR TOWN. I ASSURE YOU IT WOULD BE... MUTUALLY BENEFICIAL.

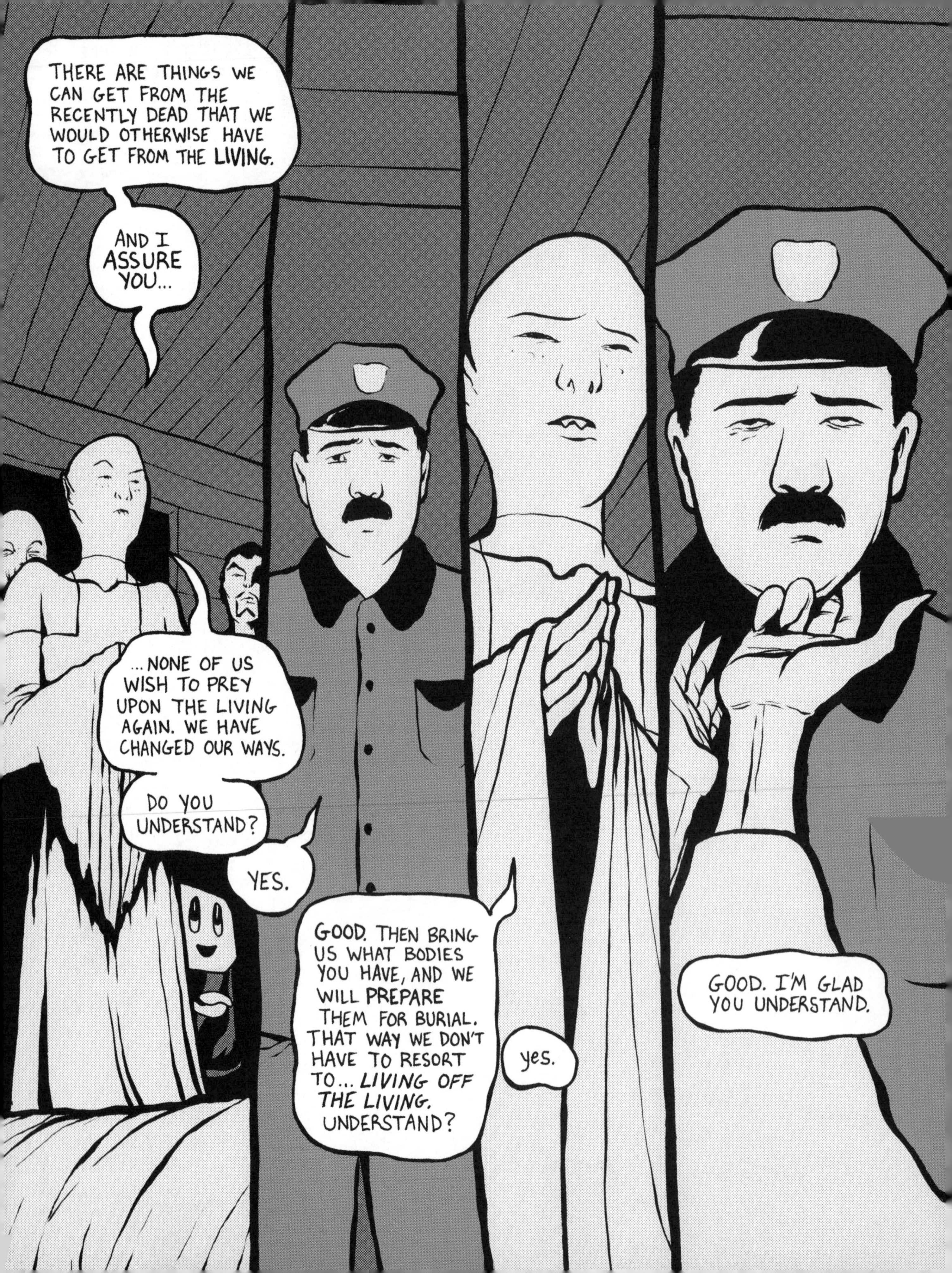
THERE ARE THINGS WE CAN GET FROM THE RECENTLY DEAD THAT WE WOULD OTHERWISE HAVE TO GET FROM THE **LIVING**.
AND I **ASSURE** YOU...
...NONE OF US WISH TO PREY UPON THE LIVING AGAIN. WE HAVE CHANGED OUR WAYS.
DO YOU UNDERSTAND?
YES.
GOOD. THEN BRING US WHAT BODIES YOU HAVE, AND WE WILL **PREPARE** THEM FOR BURIAL. THAT WAY WE DON'T HAVE TO RESORT TO... ***LIVING OFF THE LIVING.*** UNDERSTAND?
yes.
GOOD. I'M GLAD YOU UNDERSTAND.

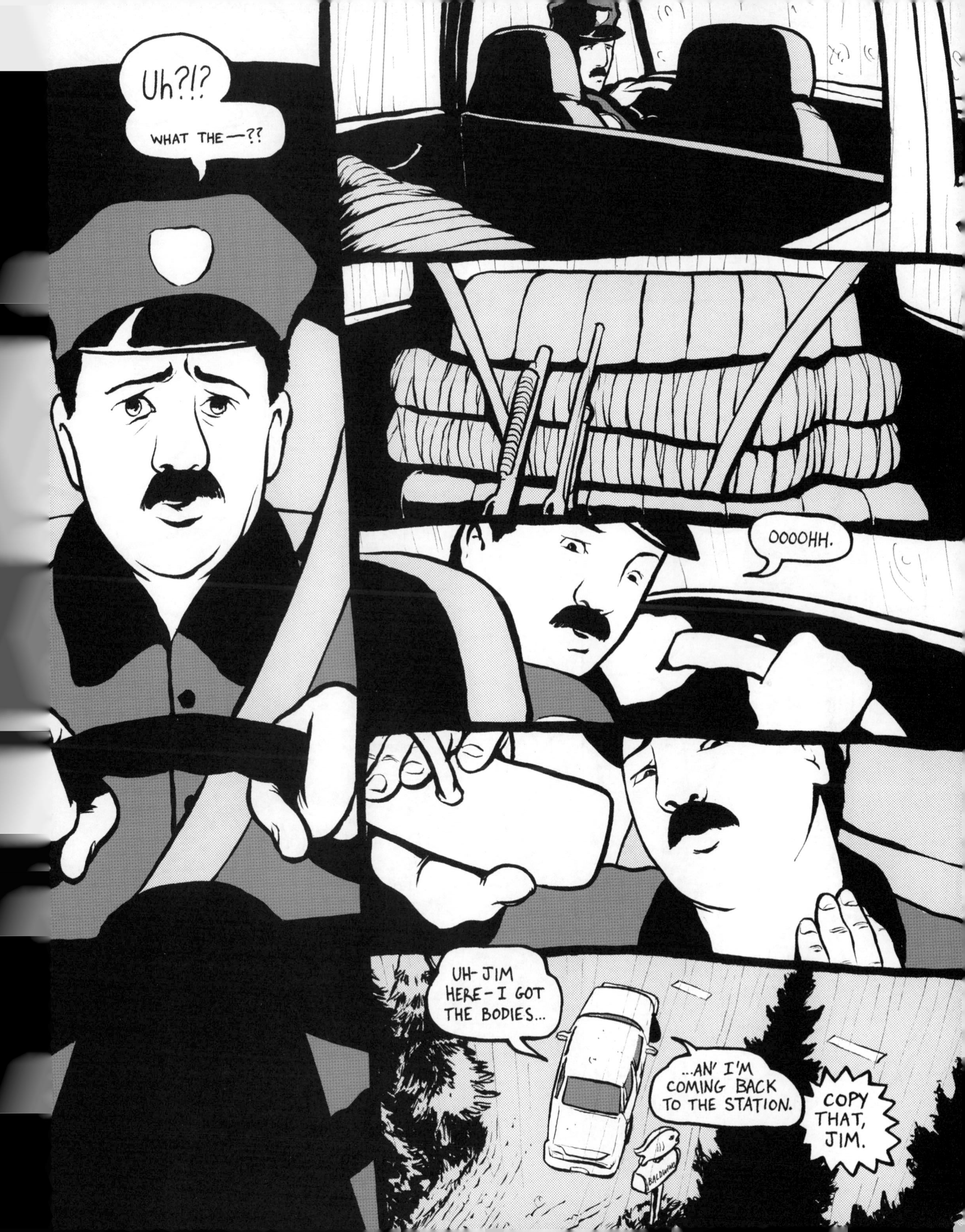
Uh?!?
WHAT THE—??
OOOOHH.
UH-JIM HERE-I GOT THE BODIES...
...AN' I'M COMING BACK TO THE STATION.
COPY THAT, JIM.

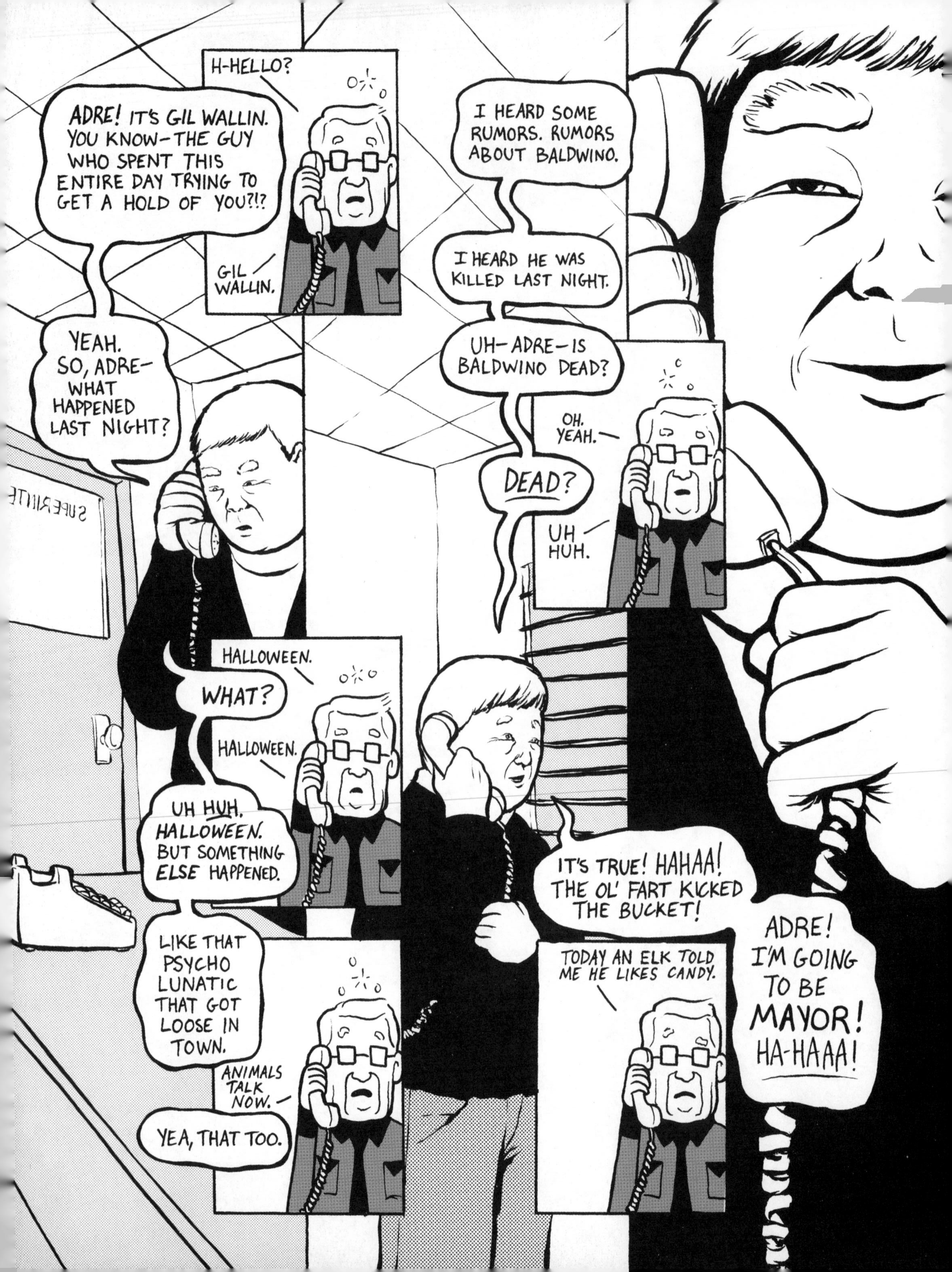
H-HELLO?
GIL WALLIN.
ADRE! IT'S GIL WALLIN. YOU KNOW—THE GUY WHO SPENT THIS ENTIRE DAY TRYING TO GET A HOLD OF YOU?!?
YEAH. SO, ADRE—WHAT HAPPENED LAST NIGHT?
HALLOWEEN.
WHAT?
HALLOWEEN.
UH HUH. HALLOWEEN. BUT SOMETHING ELSE HAPPENED.
LIKE THAT PSYCHO LUNATIC THAT GOT LOOSE IN TOWN.
ANIMALS TALK NOW.
YEA, THAT TOO.
I HEARD SOME RUMORS. RUMORS ABOUT BALDWINO.
I HEARD HE WAS KILLED LAST NIGHT.
UH—ADRE—IS BALDWINO DEAD?
OH. YEAH.
DEAD?
UH HUH.
IT'S TRUE! HAHAA! THE OL' FART KICKED THE BUCKET!
TODAY AN ELK TOLD ME HE LIKES CANDY.
ADRE! I'M GOING TO BE MAYOR! HA-HAAA!

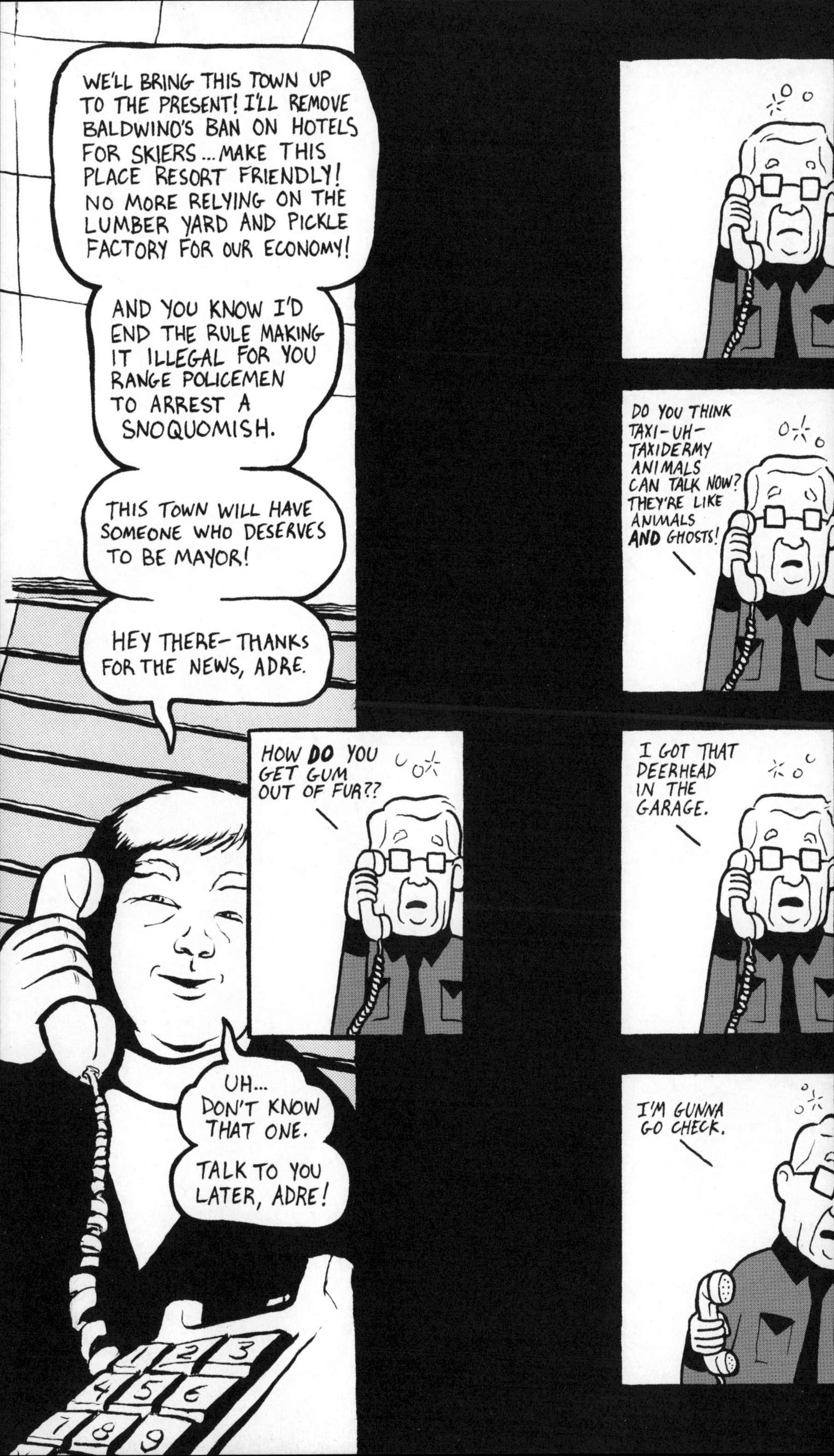
WE'LL BRING THIS TOWN UP TO THE PRESENT! I'LL REMOVE BALDWINO'S BAN ON HOTELS FOR SKIERS... MAKE THIS PLACE RESORT FRIENDLY! NO MORE RELYING ON THE LUMBER YARD AND PICKLE FACTORY FOR OUR ECONOMY!
AND YOU KNOW I'D END THE RULE MAKING IT ILLEGAL FOR YOU RANGE POLICEMEN TO ARREST A SNOQUOMISH.
THIS TOWN WILL HAVE SOMEONE WHO DESERVES TO BE MAYOR!
HEY THERE– THANKS FOR THE NEWS, ADRE.
HOW **DO** YOU GET GUM OUT OF FUR??
UH... DON'T KNOW THAT ONE.
TALK TO YOU LATER, ADRE!
DO YOU THINK TAXI–UH– TAXIDERMY ANIMALS CAN TALK NOW? THEY'RE LIKE ANIMALS **AND** GHOSTS!
I GOT THAT DEERHEAD IN THE GARAGE.
I'M GUNNA GO CHECK.

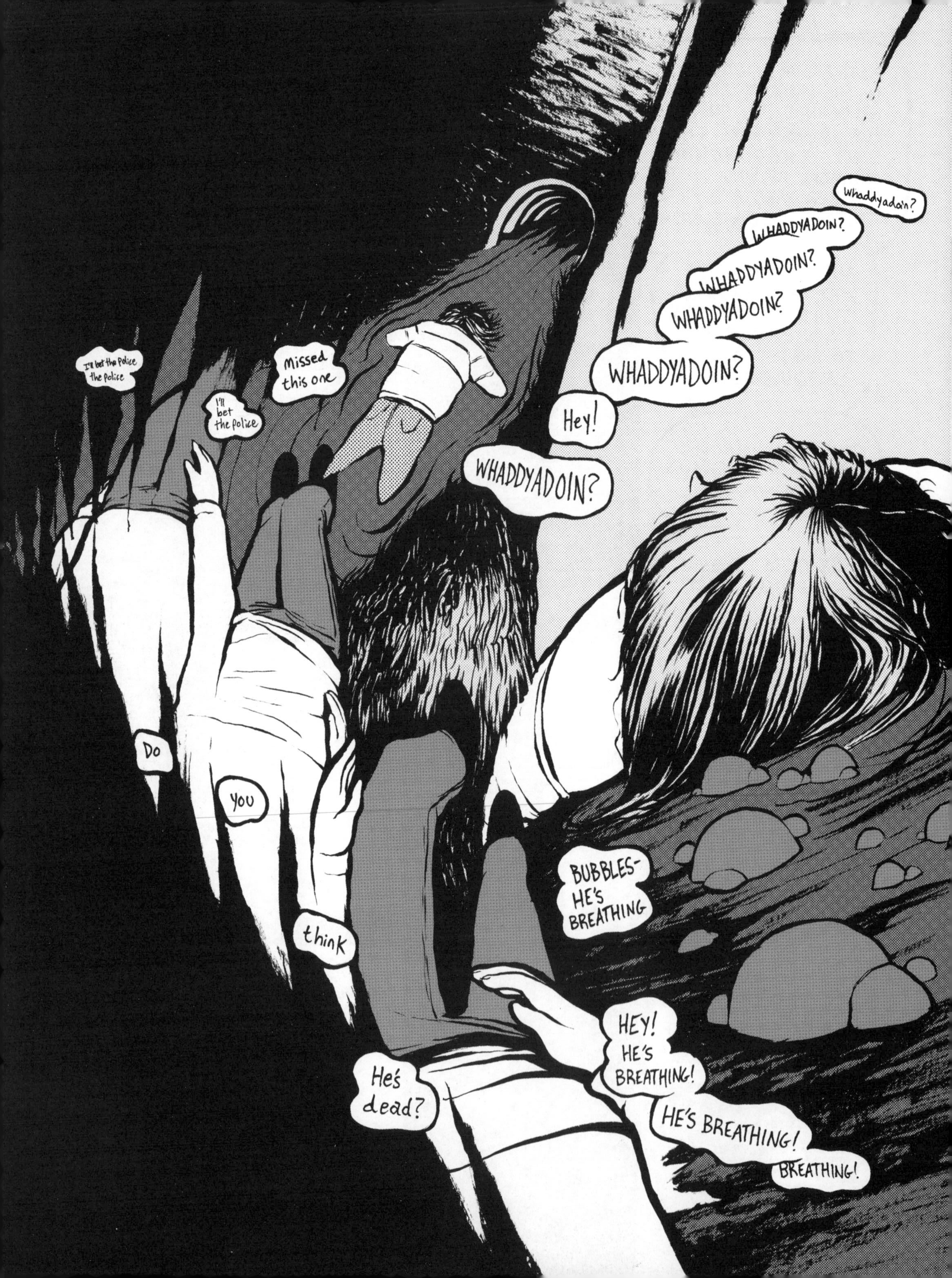

I'll bet the Police the police
I'll bet the police
missed this one
Do
you
think
He's dead?
WHADDYADOIN?
Hey!
WHADDYADOIN?
WHADDYADOIN?
WHADDYADOIN?
WHADDYADOIN?
Whaddyadoin?
BUBBLES- HE'S BREATHING
HEY! HE'S BREATHING!
HE'S BREATHING!
BREATHING!

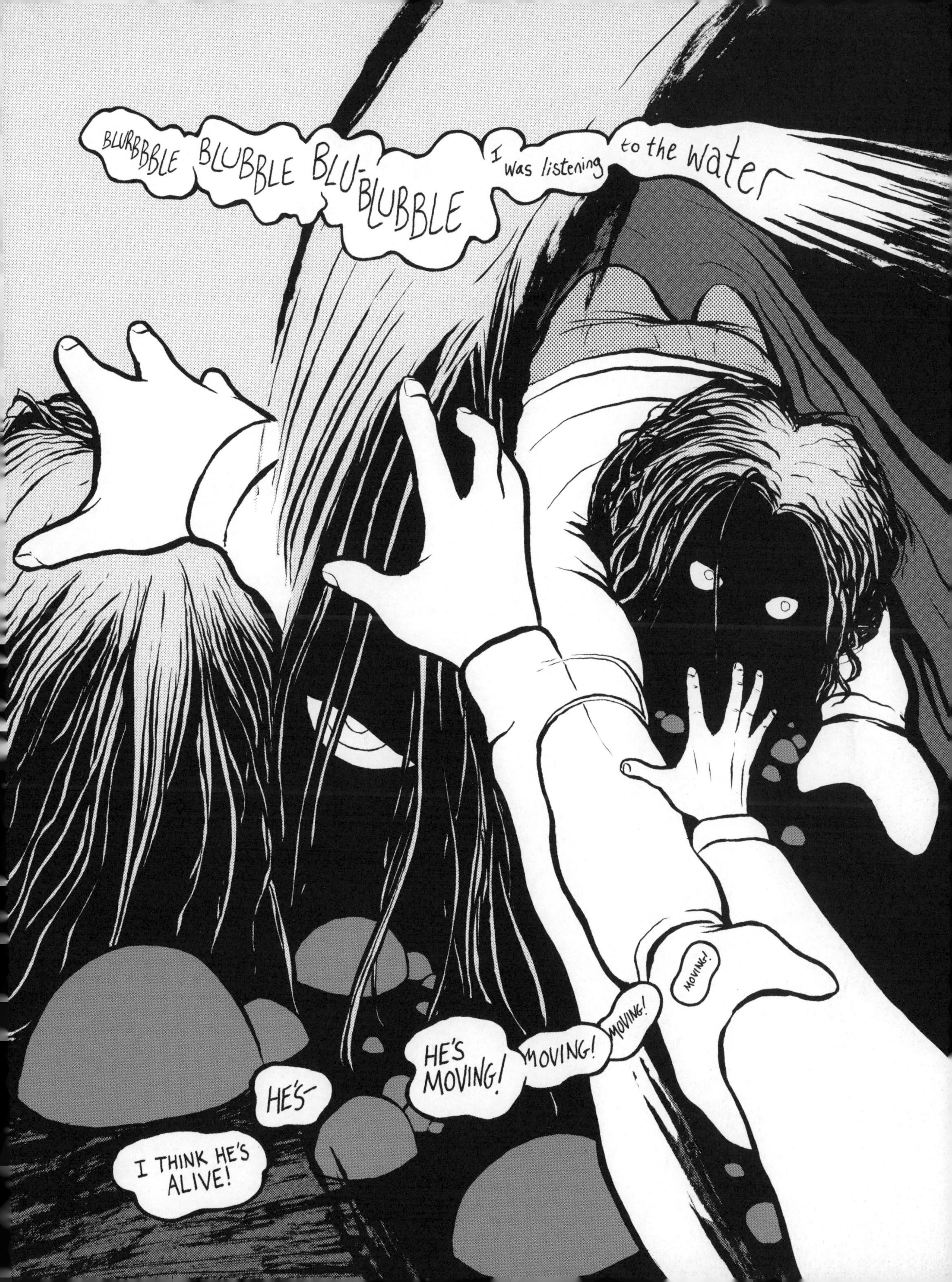
BLURBBBLE BLUBBLE BLU-BLUBBLE
I was listening to the water
I THINK HE'S ALIVE!
HE'S-
HE'S MOVING!
MOVING!
MOVING!
MOVING!

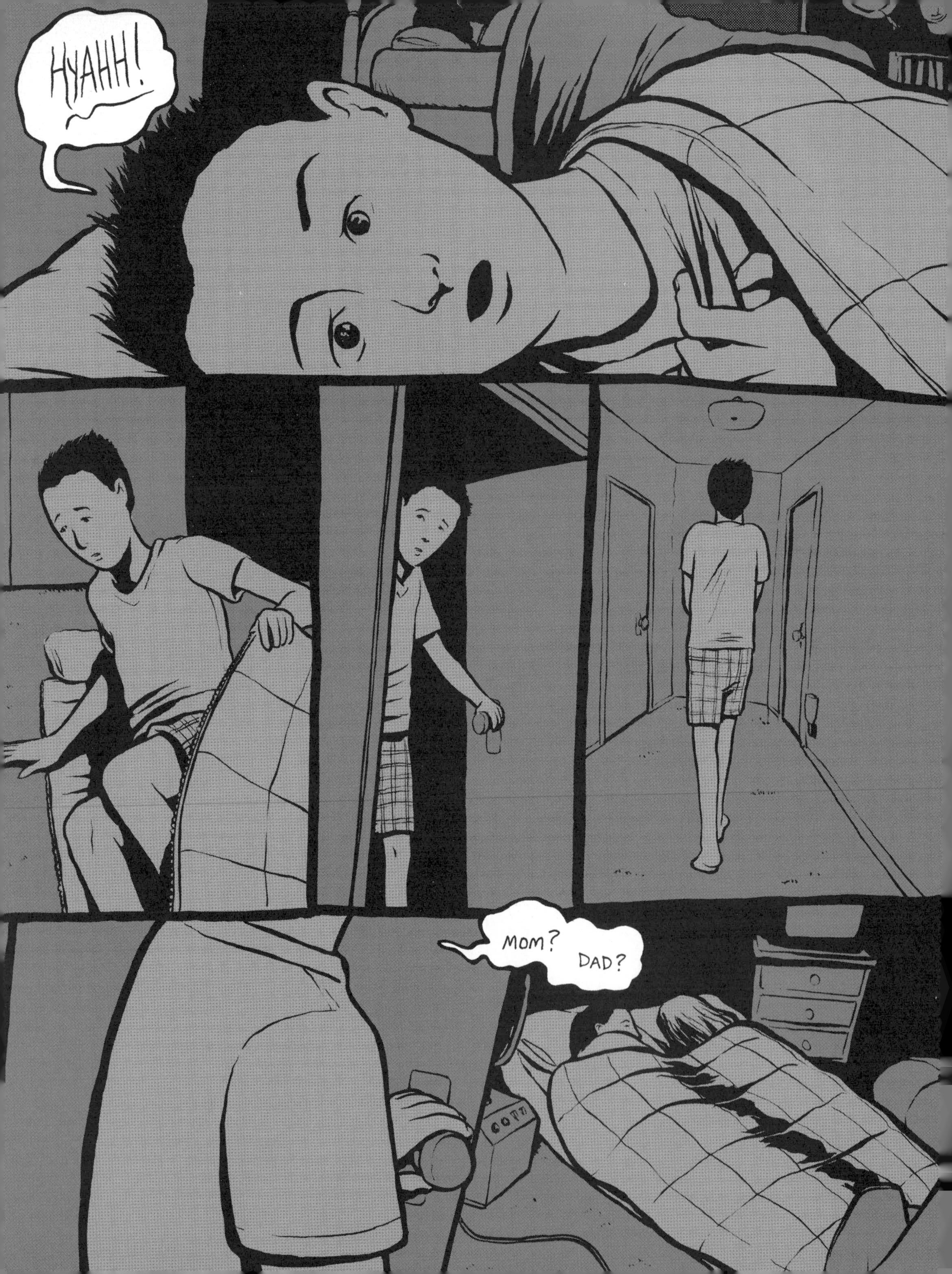
HYAHH!
MOM? DAD?

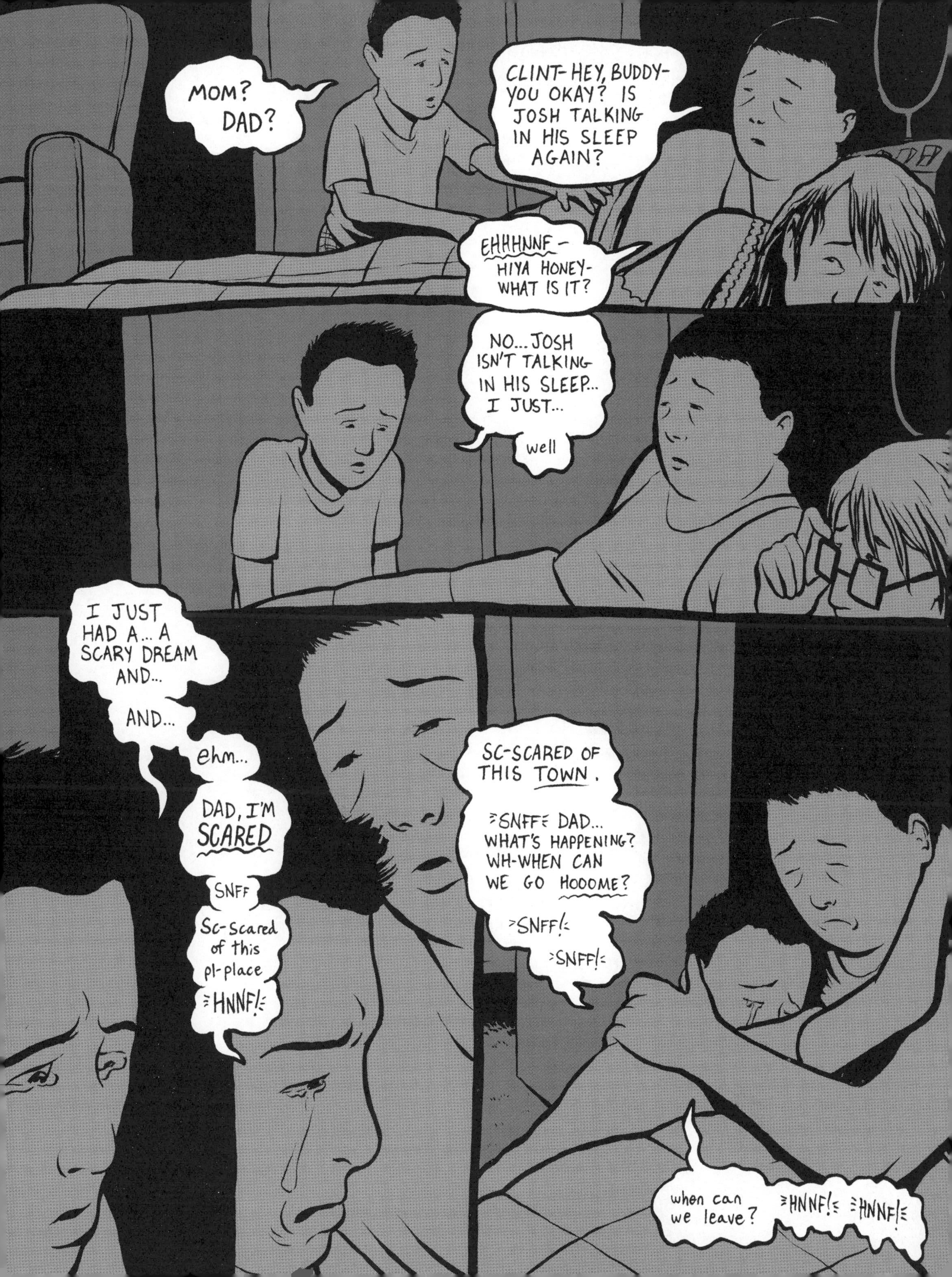
MOM? DAD?
CLINT- HEY, BUDDY- YOU OKAY? IS JOSH TALKING IN HIS SLEEP AGAIN?
EHHHNNF- HIYA HONEY- WHAT IS IT?
NO... JOSH ISN'T TALKING IN HIS SLEEP... I JUST...
well
I JUST HAD A... A SCARY DREAM AND...
AND...
ehm...
DAD, I'M SCARED
SNFF
Sc-Scared of this pl-place
HNNF!
SC-SCARED OF THIS TOWN.
SNFF DAD... WHAT'S HAPPENING? WH-WHEN CAN WE GO HOOOME?
SNFF!
SNFF!
when can we leave?
HNNF!
HNNF!

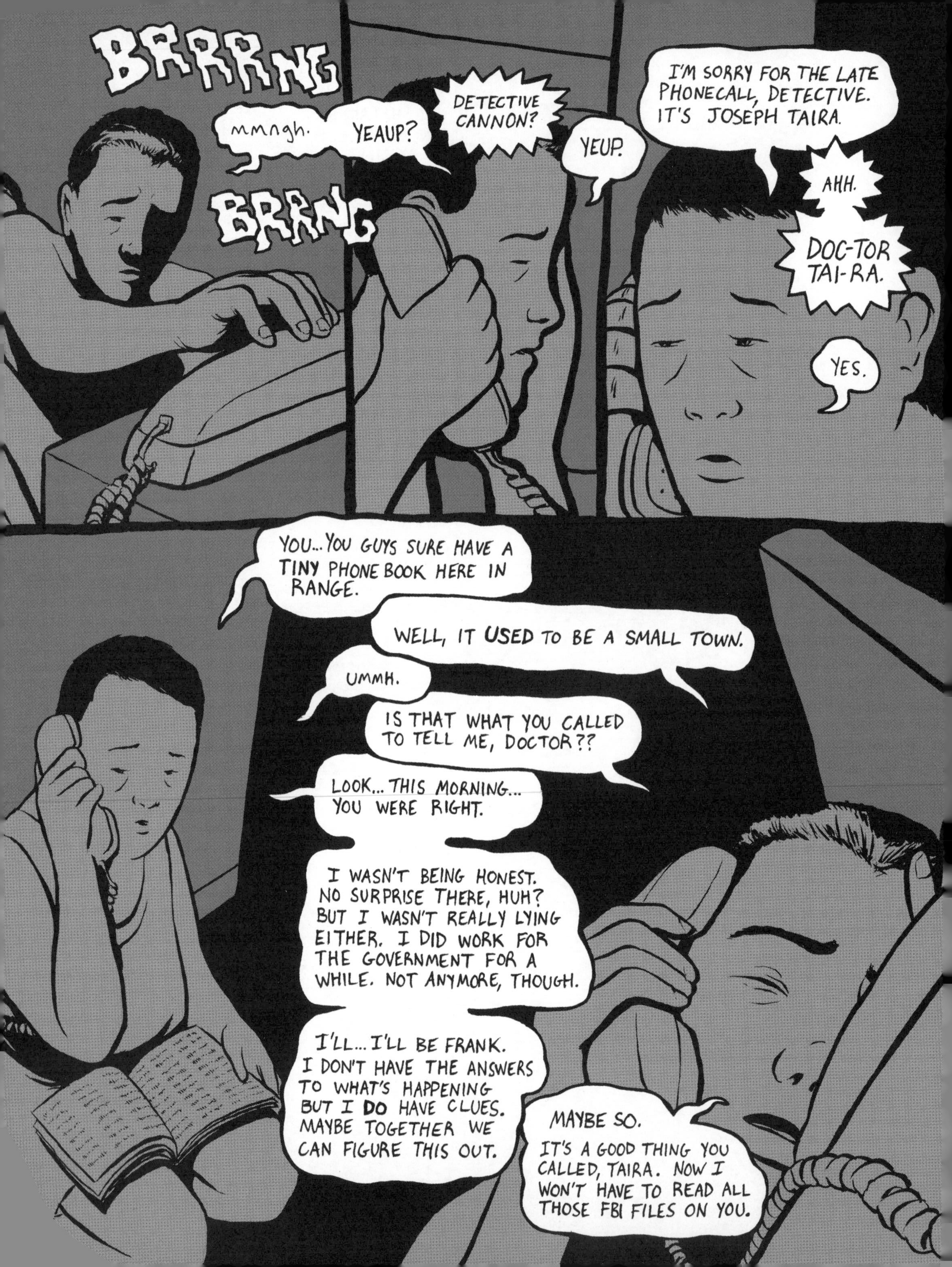
BRRRNG
mmngh.
YEAUP?
BRRNG
DETECTIVE CANNON?
YEUP.
I'M SORRY FOR THE LATE PHONECALL, DETECTIVE. IT'S JOSEPH TAIRA.
AHH.
DOC-TOR TAI-RA.
YES.
YOU... YOU GUYS SURE HAVE A TINY PHONE BOOK HERE IN RANGE.
WELL, IT USED TO BE A SMALL TOWN.
UMMH.
IS THAT WHAT YOU CALLED TO TELL ME, DOCTOR??
LOOK... THIS MORNING... YOU WERE RIGHT.
I WASN'T BEING HONEST. NO SURPRISE THERE, HUH? BUT I WASN'T REALLY LYING EITHER. I DID WORK FOR THE GOVERNMENT FOR A WHILE. NOT ANYMORE, THOUGH.
I'LL... I'LL BE FRANK. I DON'T HAVE THE ANSWERS TO WHAT'S HAPPENING BUT I DO HAVE CLUES. MAYBE TOGETHER WE CAN FIGURE THIS OUT.
MAYBE SO.
IT'S A GOOD THING YOU CALLED, TAIRA. NOW I WON'T HAVE TO READ ALL THOSE FBI FILES ON YOU.

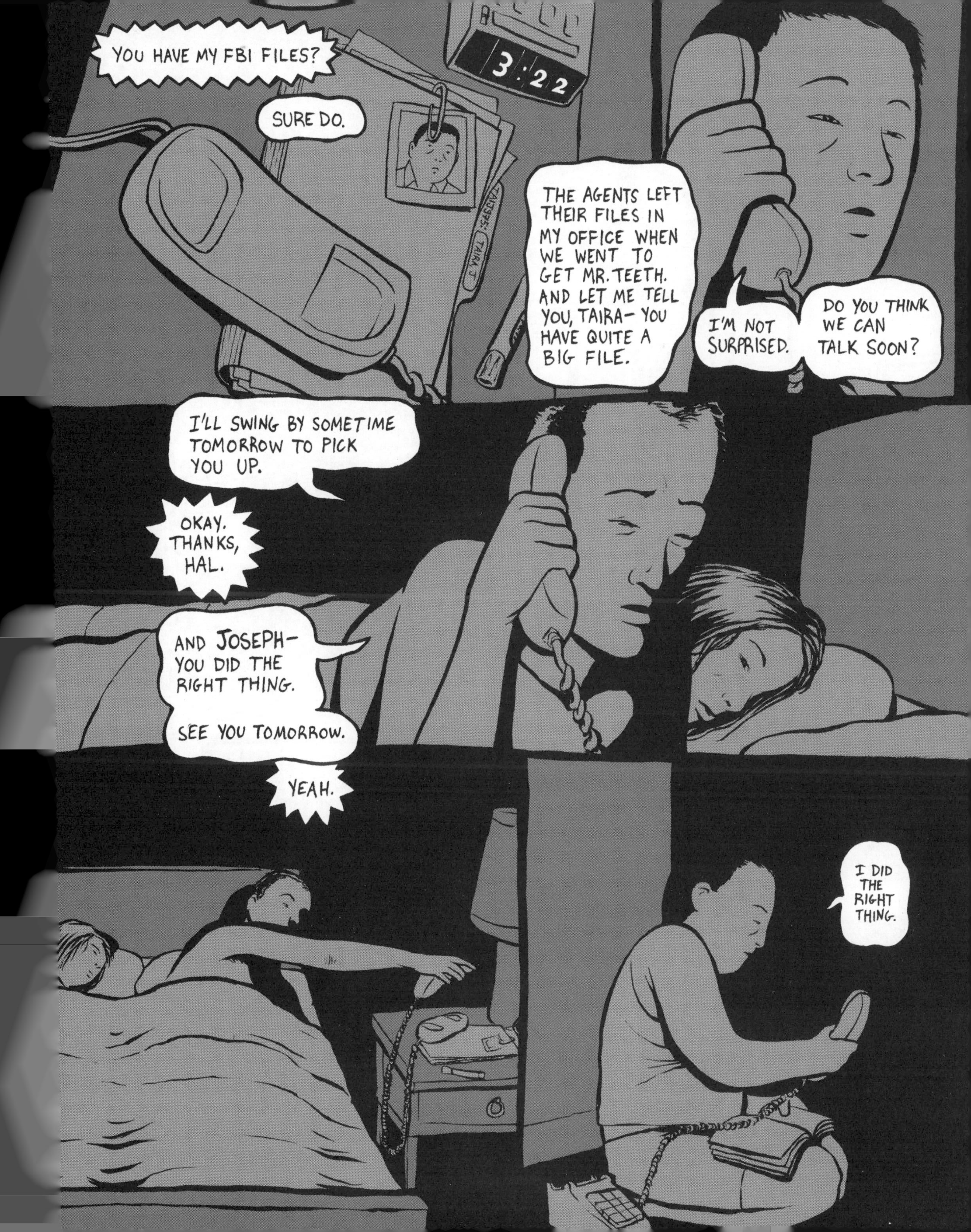
YOU HAVE MY FBI FILES?
SURE DO.
3:22
TAIRA J
THE AGENTS LEFT THEIR FILES IN MY OFFICE WHEN WE WENT TO GET MR. TEETH. AND LET ME TELL YOU, TAIRA– YOU HAVE QUITE A BIG FILE.
I'M NOT SURPRISED.
DO YOU THINK WE CAN TALK SOON?
I'LL SWING BY SOMETIME TOMORROW TO PICK YOU UP.
OKAY. THANKS, HAL.
AND JOSEPH– YOU DID THE RIGHT THING.
SEE YOU TOMORROW.
YEAH.
I DID THE RIGHT THING.

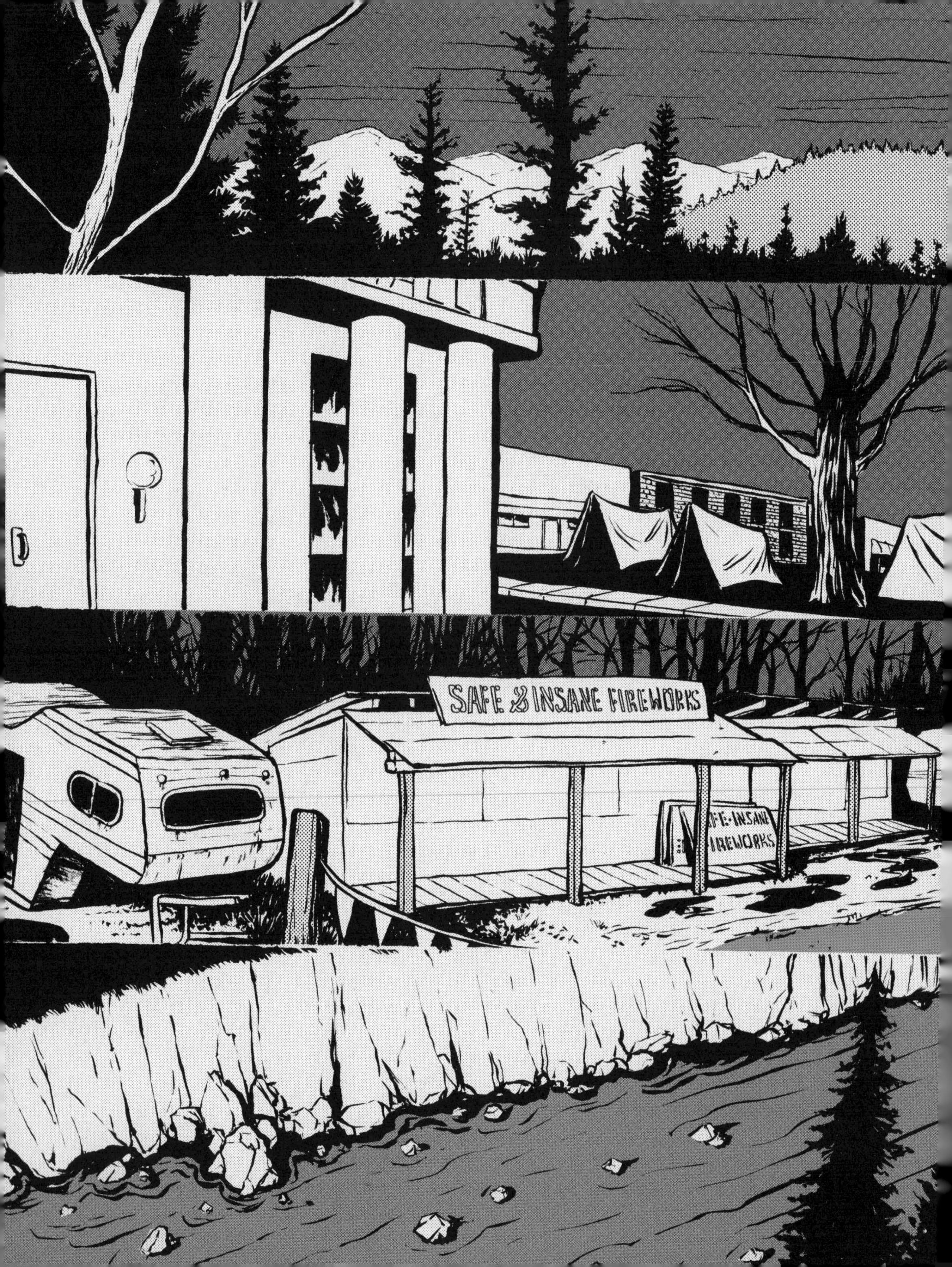
SAFE & INSANE FIREWORKS
AFE·INSANE
IREWORKS

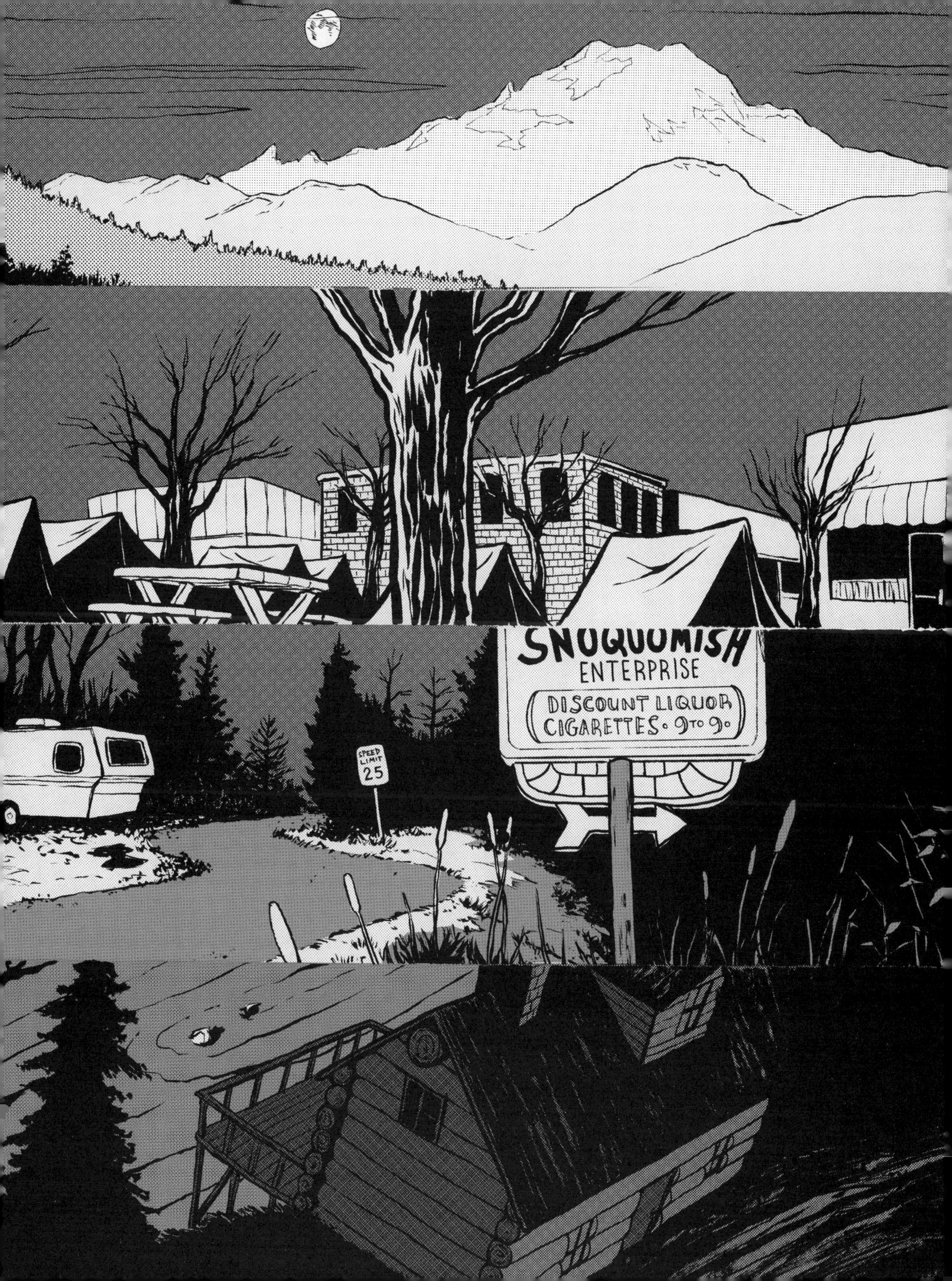
SNOQUOMISH
ENTERPRISE
DISCOUNT LIQUOR
CIGARETTES. 9 TO 9.
SPEED LIMIT 25

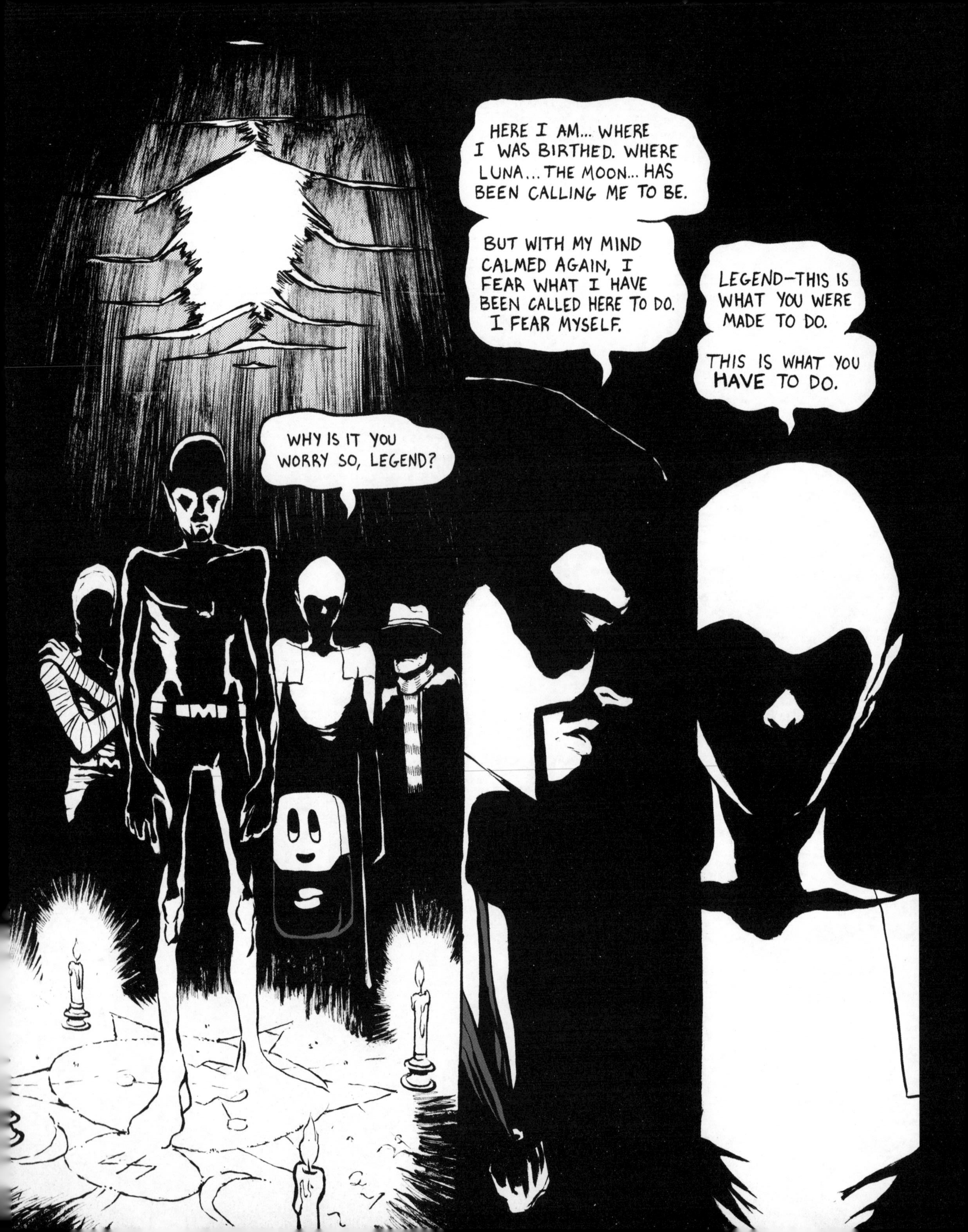
HERE I AM... WHERE I WAS BIRTHED. WHERE LUNA... THE MOON... HAS BEEN CALLING ME TO BE.
BUT WITH MY MIND CALMED AGAIN, I FEAR WHAT I HAVE BEEN CALLED HERE TO DO. I FEAR MYSELF.
LEGEND—THIS IS WHAT YOU WERE MADE TO DO.
THIS IS WHAT YOU **HAVE** TO DO.
WHY IS IT YOU WORRY SO, LEGEND?

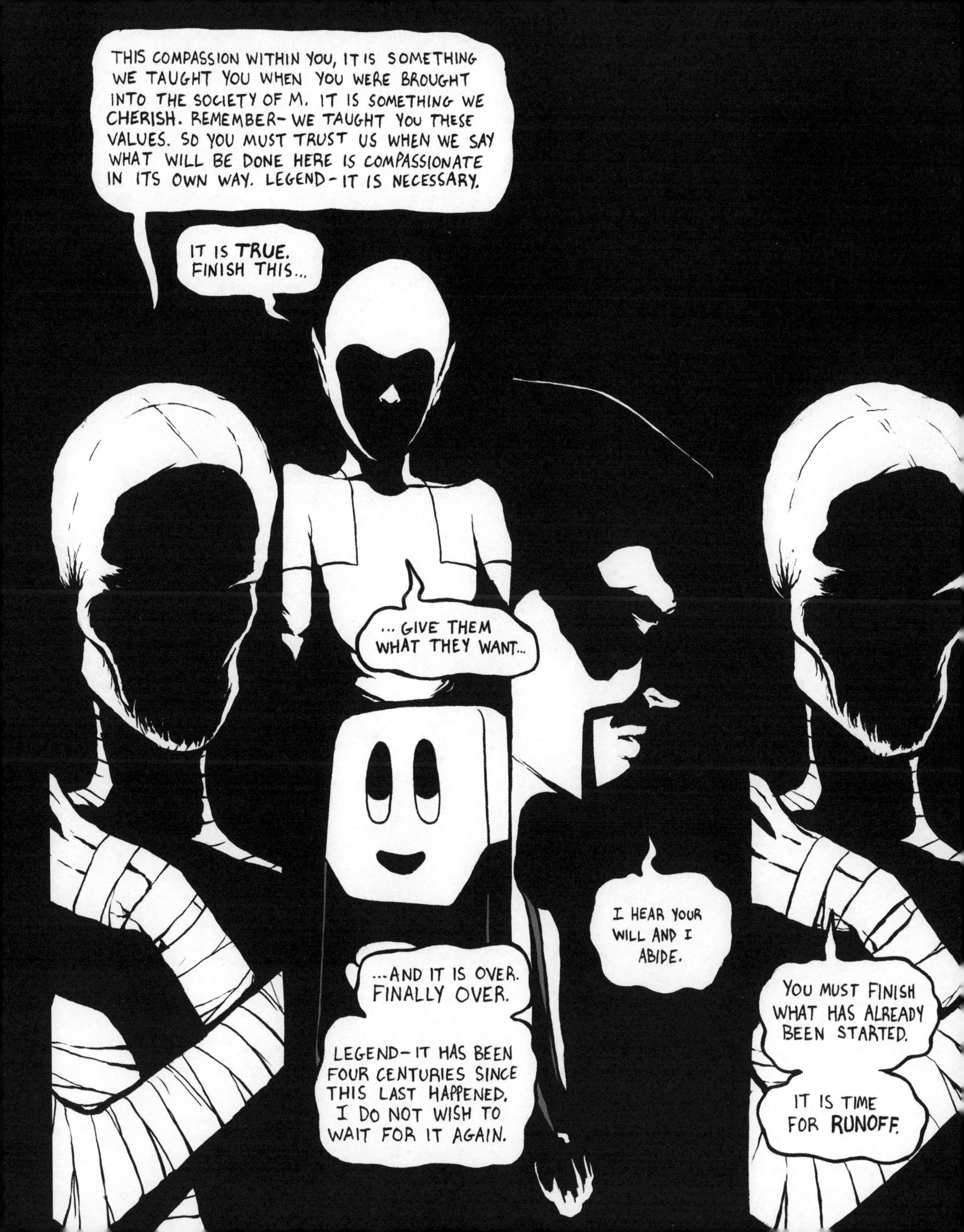
THIS COMPASSION WITHIN YOU, IT IS SOMETHING WE TAUGHT YOU WHEN YOU WERE BROUGHT INTO THE SOCIETY OF M. IT IS SOMETHING WE CHERISH. REMEMBER- WE TAUGHT YOU THESE VALUES. SO YOU MUST TRUST US WHEN WE SAY WHAT WILL BE DONE HERE IS COMPASSIONATE IN ITS OWN WAY. LEGEND - IT IS NECESSARY.
IT IS TRUE. FINISH THIS...
... GIVE THEM WHAT THEY WANT...
...AND IT IS OVER. FINALLY OVER.
LEGEND- IT HAS BEEN FOUR CENTURIES SINCE THIS LAST HAPPENED. I DO NOT WISH TO WAIT FOR IT AGAIN.
I HEAR YOUR WILL AND I ABIDE.
YOU MUST FINISH WHAT HAS ALREADY BEEN STARTED.
IT IS TIME FOR RUNOFF.

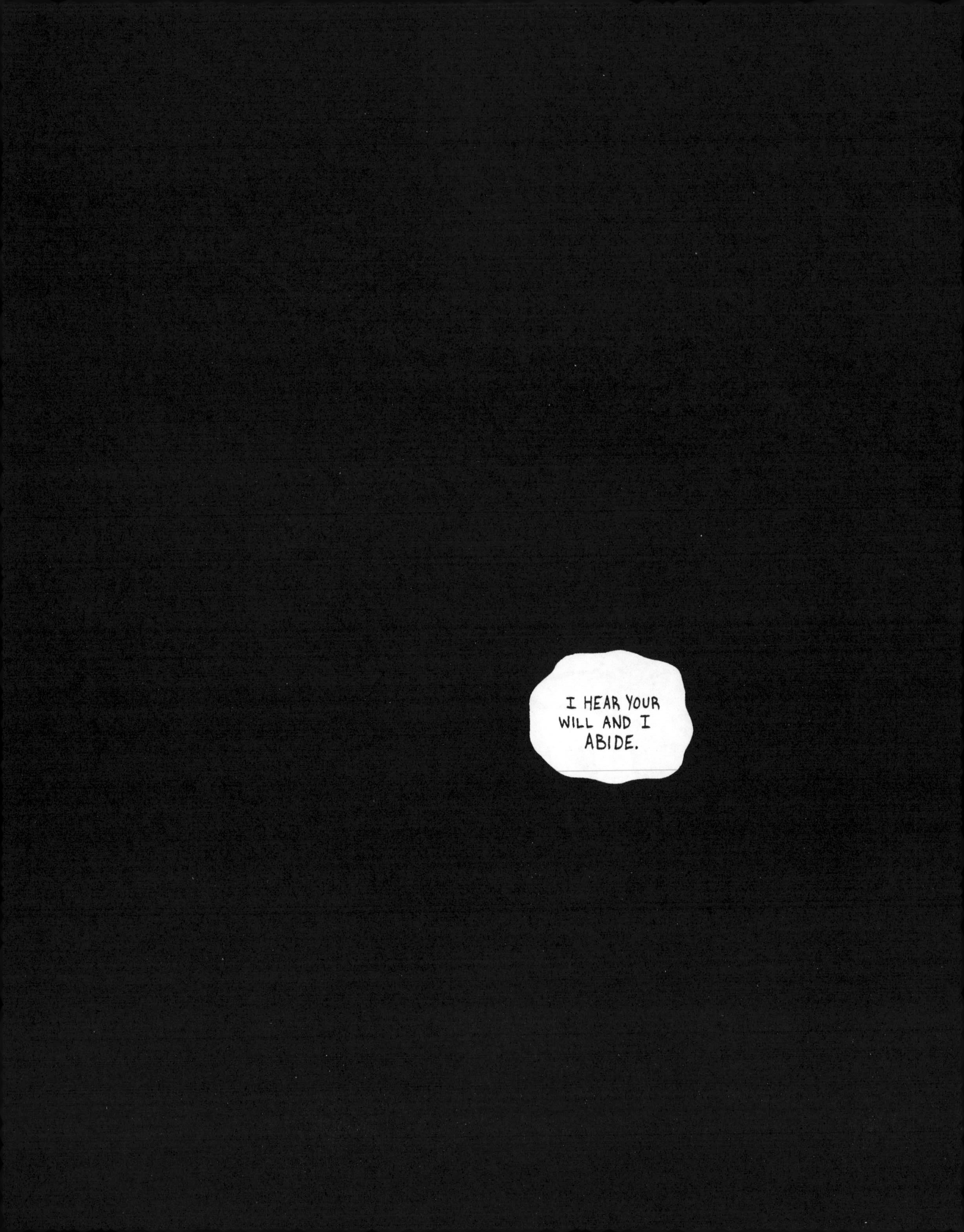
I HEAR YOUR WILL AND I ABIDE.

9.
APPARITION

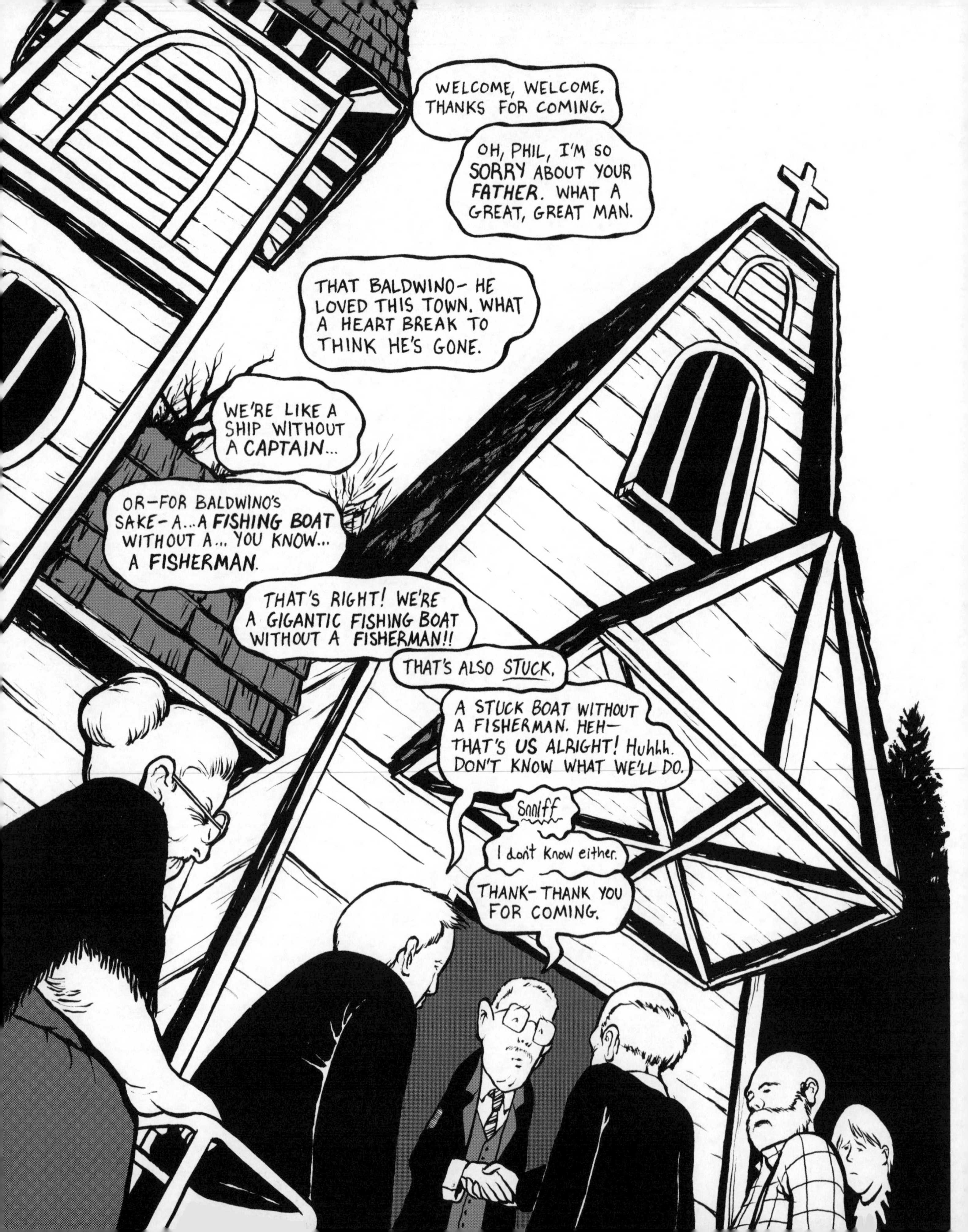
WELCOME, WELCOME. THANKS FOR COMING.
OH, PHIL, I'M SO SORRY ABOUT YOUR FATHER. WHAT A GREAT, GREAT MAN.
THAT BALDWINO- HE LOVED THIS TOWN. WHAT A HEART BREAK TO THINK HE'S GONE.
WE'RE LIKE A SHIP WITHOUT A CAPTAIN...
OR—FOR BALDWINO'S SAKE- A...A FISHING BOAT WITHOUT A... YOU KNOW... A FISHERMAN.
THAT'S RIGHT! WE'RE A GIGANTIC FISHING BOAT WITHOUT A FISHERMAN!!
THAT'S ALSO STUCK.
A STUCK BOAT WITHOUT A FISHERMAN. HEH— THAT'S US ALRIGHT! Huhhh. DON'T KNOW WHAT WE'LL DO.
Sniff
I don't know either.
THANK- THANK YOU FOR COMING.

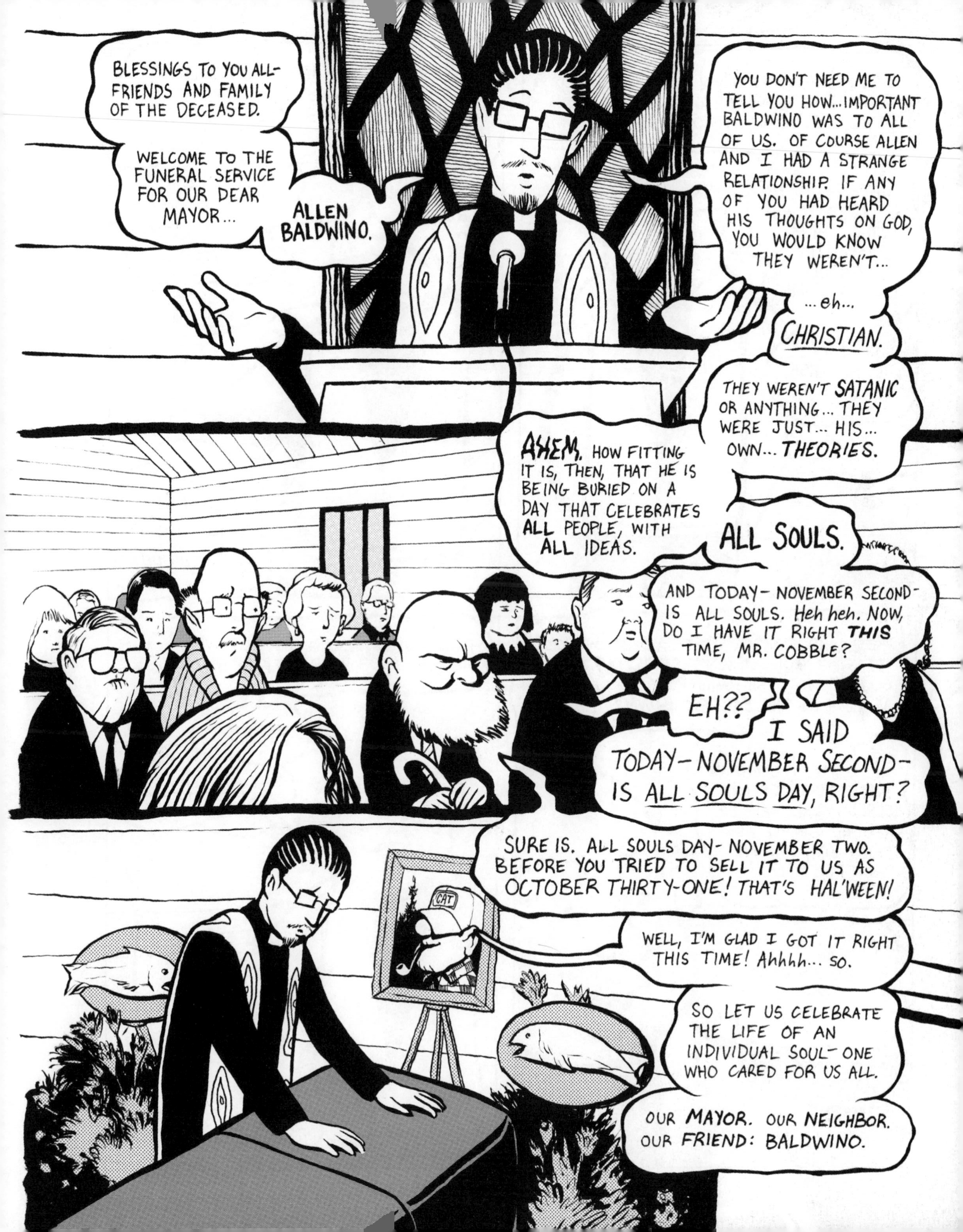
BLESSINGS TO YOU ALL- FRIENDS AND FAMILY OF THE DECEASED.
WELCOME TO THE FUNERAL SERVICE FOR OUR DEAR MAYOR...
ALLEN BALDWINO.
YOU DON'T NEED ME TO TELL YOU HOW...IMPORTANT BALDWINO WAS TO ALL OF US. OF COURSE ALLEN AND I HAD A STRANGE RELATIONSHIP. IF ANY OF YOU HAD HEARD HIS THOUGHTS ON GOD, YOU WOULD KNOW THEY WEREN'T...
...eh...
CHRISTIAN.
THEY WEREN'T SATANIC OR ANYTHING... THEY WERE JUST... HIS... OWN... THEORIES.
AHEM. HOW FITTING IT IS, THEN, THAT HE IS BEING BURIED ON A DAY THAT CELEBRATES ALL PEOPLE, WITH ALL IDEAS.
ALL SOULS.
AND TODAY- NOVEMBER SECOND- IS ALL SOULS. Heh heh. NOW, DO I HAVE IT RIGHT THIS TIME, MR. COBBLE?
EH??
I SAID TODAY- NOVEMBER SECOND- IS ALL SOULS DAY, RIGHT?
SURE IS. ALL SOULS DAY- NOVEMBER TWO. BEFORE YOU TRIED TO SELL IT TO US AS OCTOBER THIRTY-ONE! THAT'S HAL'WEEN!
WELL, I'M GLAD I GOT IT RIGHT THIS TIME! Ahhhh... so.
SO LET US CELEBRATE THE LIFE OF AN INDIVIDUAL SOUL- ONE WHO CARED FOR US ALL.
OUR MAYOR. OUR NEIGHBOR. OUR FRIEND: BALDWINO.
CAT

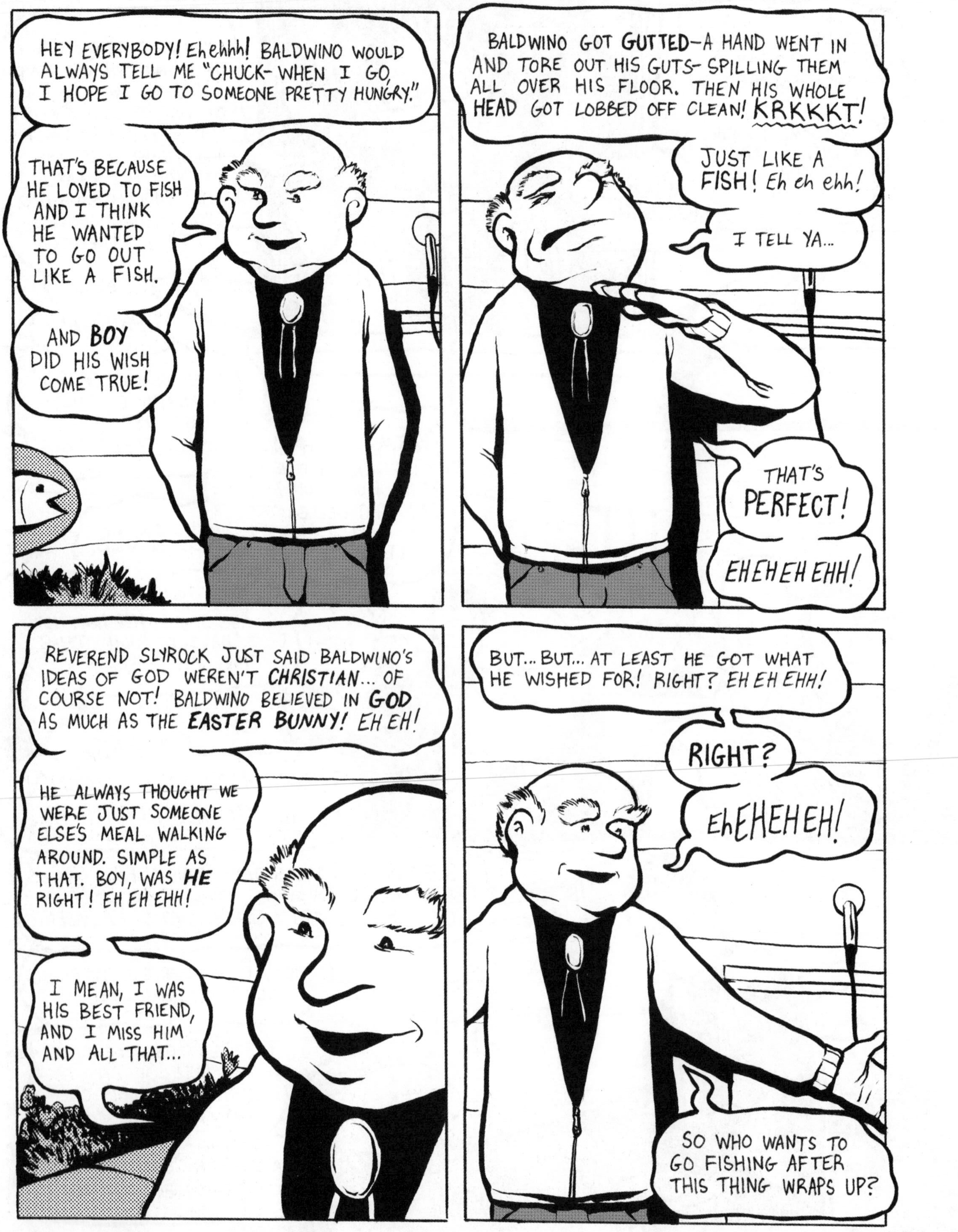
HEY EVERYBODY! Ehehhh! BALDWINO WOULD ALWAYS TELL ME "CHUCK- WHEN I GO, I HOPE I GO TO SOMEONE PRETTY HUNGRY."
THAT'S BECAUSE HE LOVED TO FISH AND I THINK HE WANTED TO GO OUT LIKE A FISH.
AND BOY DID HIS WISH COME TRUE!
BALDWINO GOT GUTTED—A HAND WENT IN AND TORE OUT HIS GUTS- SPILLING THEM ALL OVER HIS FLOOR. THEN HIS WHOLE HEAD GOT LOBBED OFF CLEAN! KRKKKT!
JUST LIKE A FISH! Eh eh ehh!
I TELL YA...
THAT'S PERFECT!
EHEHEH EHH!
REVEREND SLYROCK JUST SAID BALDWINO'S IDEAS OF GOD WEREN'T CHRISTIAN... OF COURSE NOT! BALDWINO BELIEVED IN GOD AS MUCH AS THE EASTER BUNNY! EH EH!
HE ALWAYS THOUGHT WE WERE JUST SOMEONE ELSE'S MEAL WALKING AROUND. SIMPLE AS THAT. BOY, WAS HE RIGHT! EH EH EHH!
I MEAN, I WAS HIS BEST FRIEND, AND I MISS HIM AND ALL THAT...
BUT... BUT... AT LEAST HE GOT WHAT HE WISHED FOR! RIGHT? EH EH EHH!
RIGHT?
EhEHEHEH!
SO WHO WANTS TO GO FISHING AFTER THIS THING WRAPS UP?

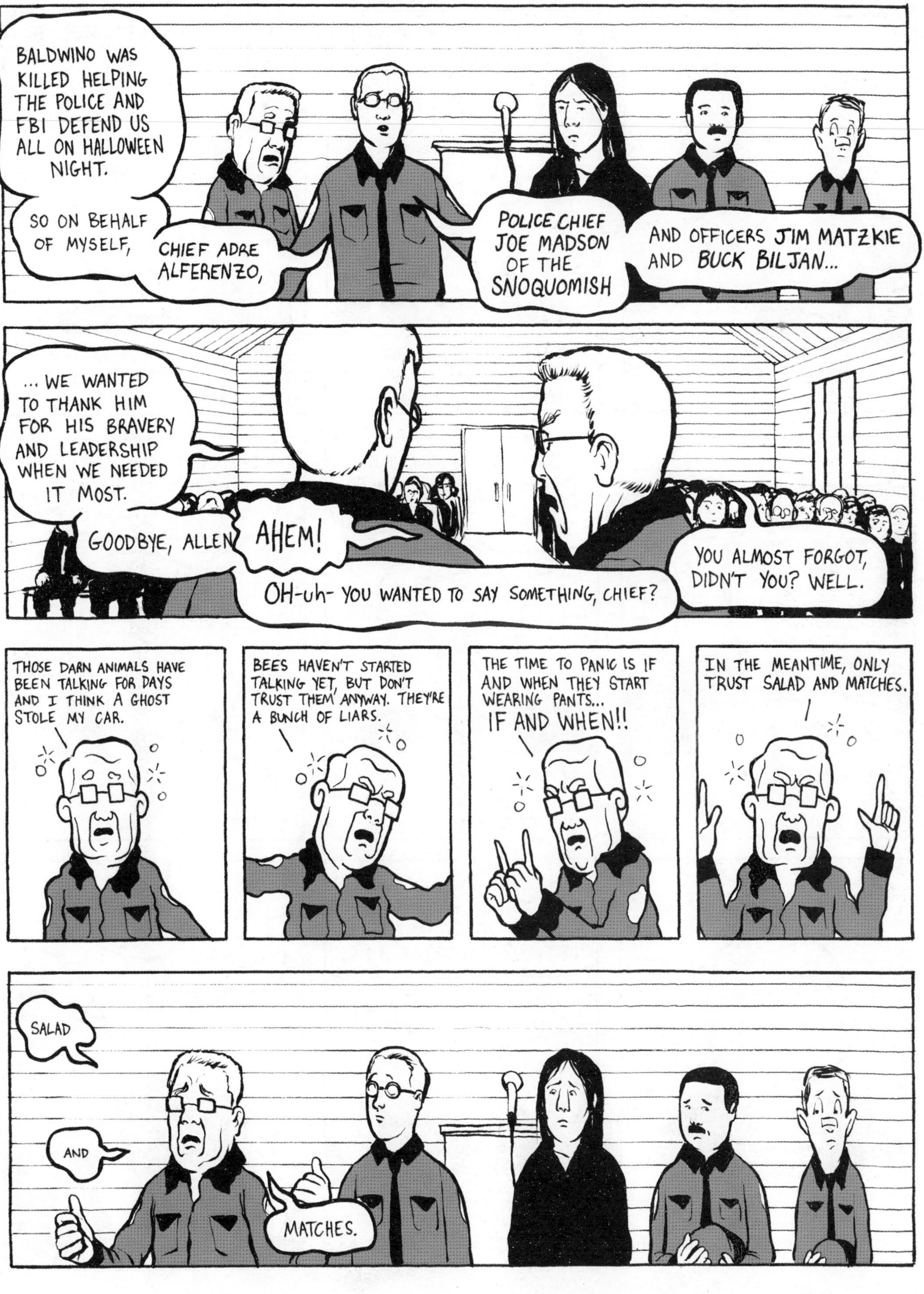
BALDWINO WAS KILLED HELPING THE POLICE AND FBI DEFEND US ALL ON HALLOWEEN NIGHT.
SO ON BEHALF OF MYSELF,
CHIEF ADRE ALFERENZO,
POLICE CHIEF JOE MADSON OF THE SNOQUOMISH
AND OFFICERS JIM MATZKIE AND BUCK BILJAN...
... WE WANTED TO THANK HIM FOR HIS BRAVERY AND LEADERSHIP WHEN WE NEEDED IT MOST.
GOODBYE, ALLEN
AHEM!
OH-uh- YOU WANTED TO SAY SOMETHING, CHIEF?
YOU ALMOST FORGOT, DIDN'T YOU? WELL.
THOSE DARN ANIMALS HAVE BEEN TALKING FOR DAYS AND I THINK A GHOST STOLE MY CAR.
BEES HAVEN'T STARTED TALKING YET, BUT DON'T TRUST THEM ANYWAY. THEY'RE A BUNCH OF LIARS.
THE TIME TO PANIC IS IF AND WHEN THEY START WEARING PANTS... IF AND WHEN!!
IN THE MEANTIME, ONLY TRUST SALAD AND MATCHES.
SALAD
AND
MATCHES.

HELLO, I'M SCHOOL SUPERINTENDENT AND MAYORAL CANDIDATE GIL WALLIN.

I KNOW MOST OF YOU, AND MOST OF YOU KNOW ME.

BUT ALMOST AS A...

REMINDER OF HOPE

BALDWINO PASSED AWAY JUST A WEEK BEFORE OUR MAYORAL ELECTIONS.

I WANT TO MAKE SURE YOU ALL PARTICIPATE IN THE UPCOMING MAYORAL ELECTION.

WE ARE HERE TODAY HONORING ALLEN FOR HIS LIFE AND HIS MANY *ACCOMPLISHMENTS*.

ONE OF WHICH WAS DEFEATING ME EVERY TIME I RAN AGAINST HIM—ha ha hh.

AND FOR THE FIRST TIME IN AGES ALLEN BALDWINO WILL NOT BE ON THE BALLOT.

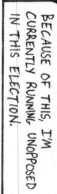

BECAUSE OF THIS, I'M CURRENTLY RUNNING UNOPPOSED IN THIS ELECTION.

I WANT TO ANNOUNCE HERE THAT I'LL BE HOLDING A MEETING AT TOWN HALL NOVEMBER FOURTH AT 8 PM.

THERE I WILL LAY OUT MY PLANS TO LEAD RANGE THROUGH THESE TOUGH TIMES

DURING THE MANY DECADES HE ACTED AS OUR MAYOR, HE LED US WITH HIS QUIRKY, HUMOR AND WONDERFUL INSIGHT.

AND WITH HIS PASSING COMES AN END TO HIS SERVICE TO US—AND BLESS HIM FOR IT.

ALTHOUGH I KNOW WE ARE ALL FRIGHTENED BECAUSE OF RANGE'S SITUATION...

NONE OF US BEING ABLE TO LEAVE, THE TALKING ANIMALS, GHOSTS...erm... KILLERS...

AND INTO A *BRIGHTER* FUTURE.

THANK YOU.

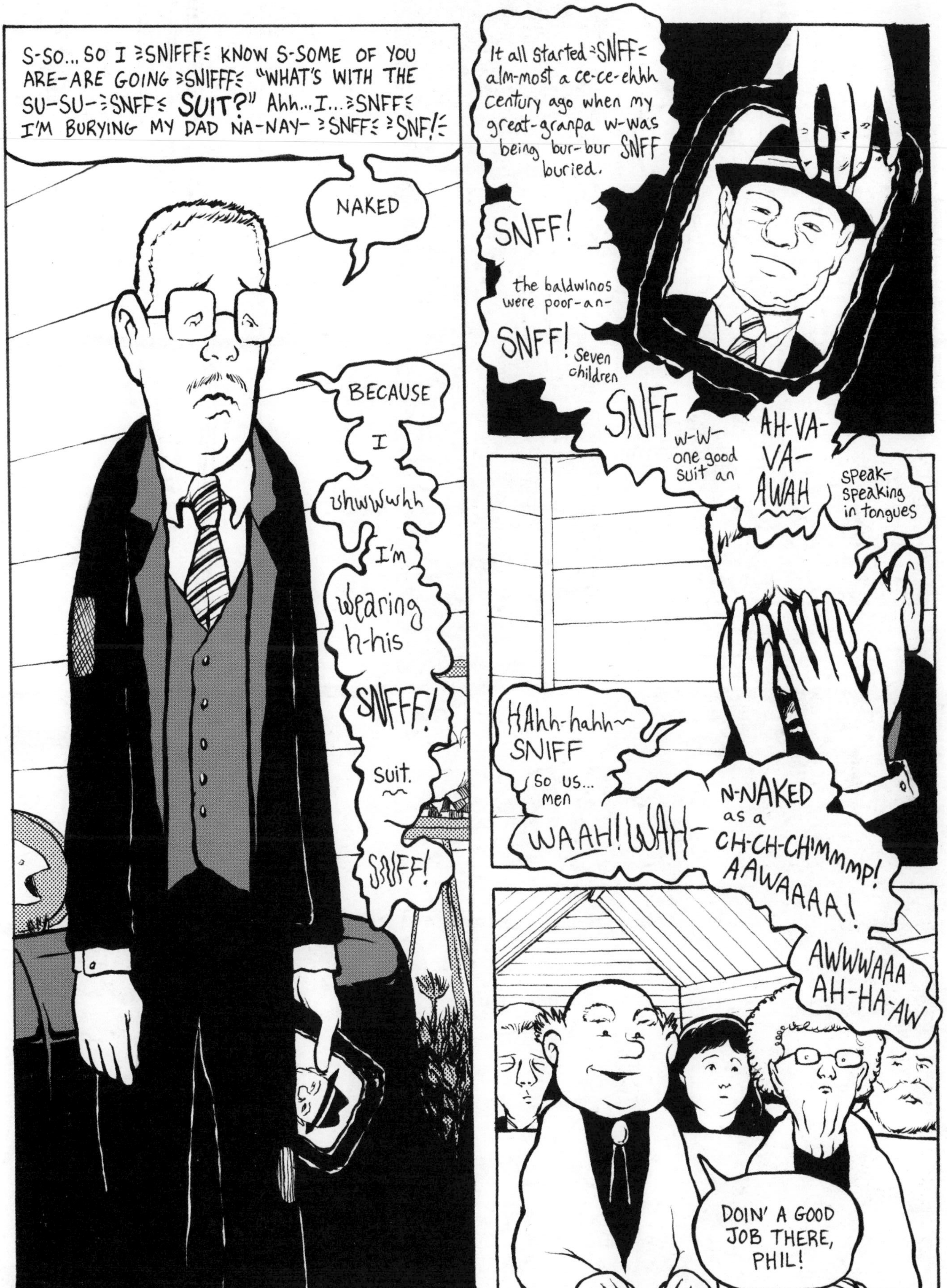
S-SO... SO I ⋛SNIFFF⋚ KNOW S-SOME OF YOU ARE-ARE GOING ⋛SNIFFF⋚ "WHAT'S WITH THE SU-SU-⋛SNFF⋚ SUIT?" Ahh... I... ⋛SNFF⋚ I'M BURYING MY DAD NA-NAY- ⋛SNFF⋚ ⋛SNF!⋚
NAKED
BECAUSE
I
uhwwwhh
I'm
wearing
h-his
SNFFF!
suit.
SNFF!
It all started ⋛SNFF⋚ alm-most a ce-ce-ehhh century ago when my great-granpa w-was being bur-bur SNFF buried.
SNFF!
the baldwinos were poor-an-
SNFF!
Seven children
SNFF
w-w- one good suit an
AH-VA-VA-AWAH
speak-speaking in tongues
HAhh-hahh~ SNIFF
so us... men
WAAH! WAH-
N-NAKED as a CH-CH-CHIMMMP! AAWAAAAA!
AWWWAAA AH-HA-AW
DOIN' A GOOD JOB THERE, PHIL!

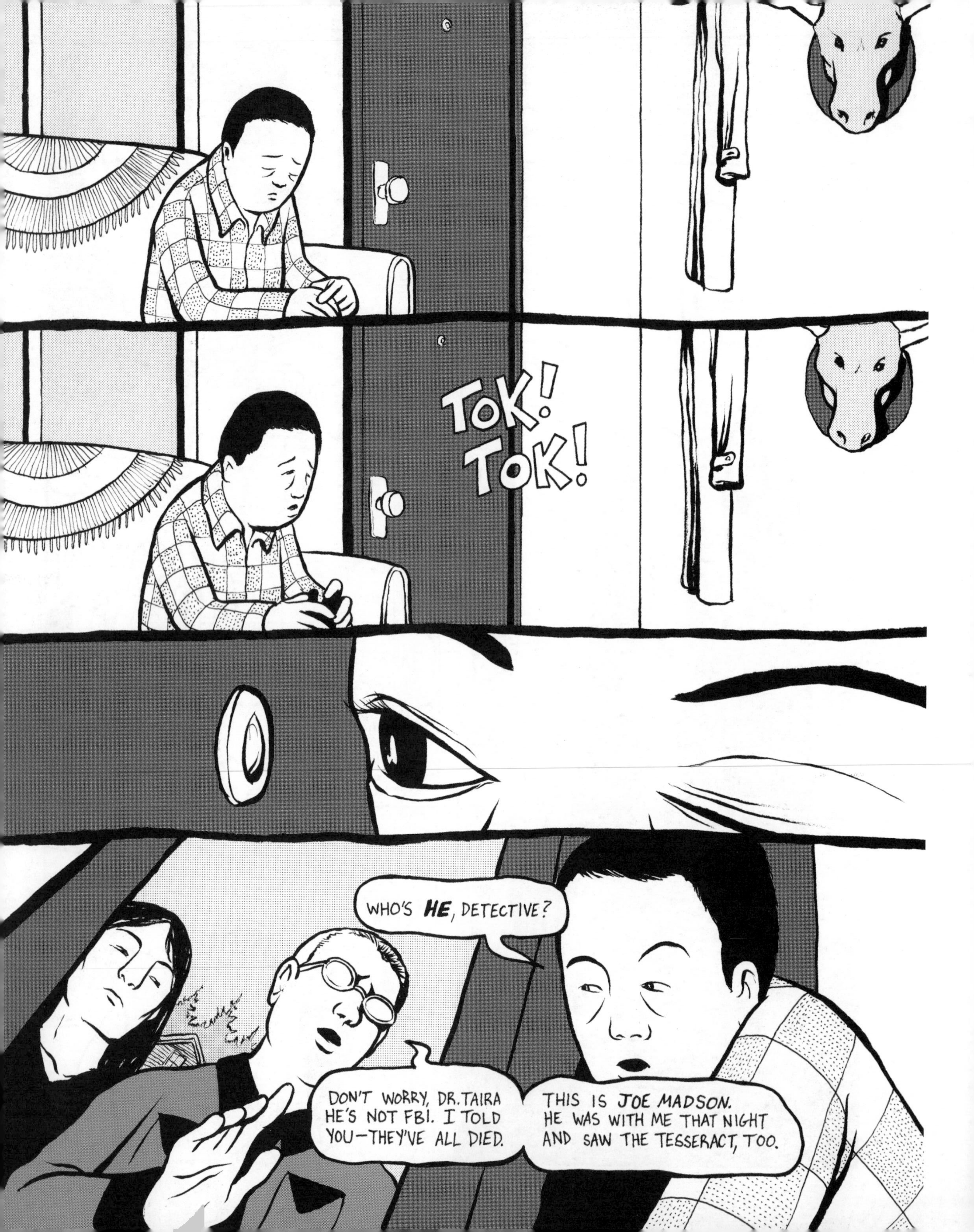
TOK! TOK!
WHO'S HE, DETECTIVE?
DON'T WORRY, DR. TAIRA HE'S NOT FBI. I TOLD YOU—THEY'VE ALL DIED.
THIS IS JOE MADSON. HE WAS WITH ME THAT NIGHT AND SAW THE TESSERACT, TOO.

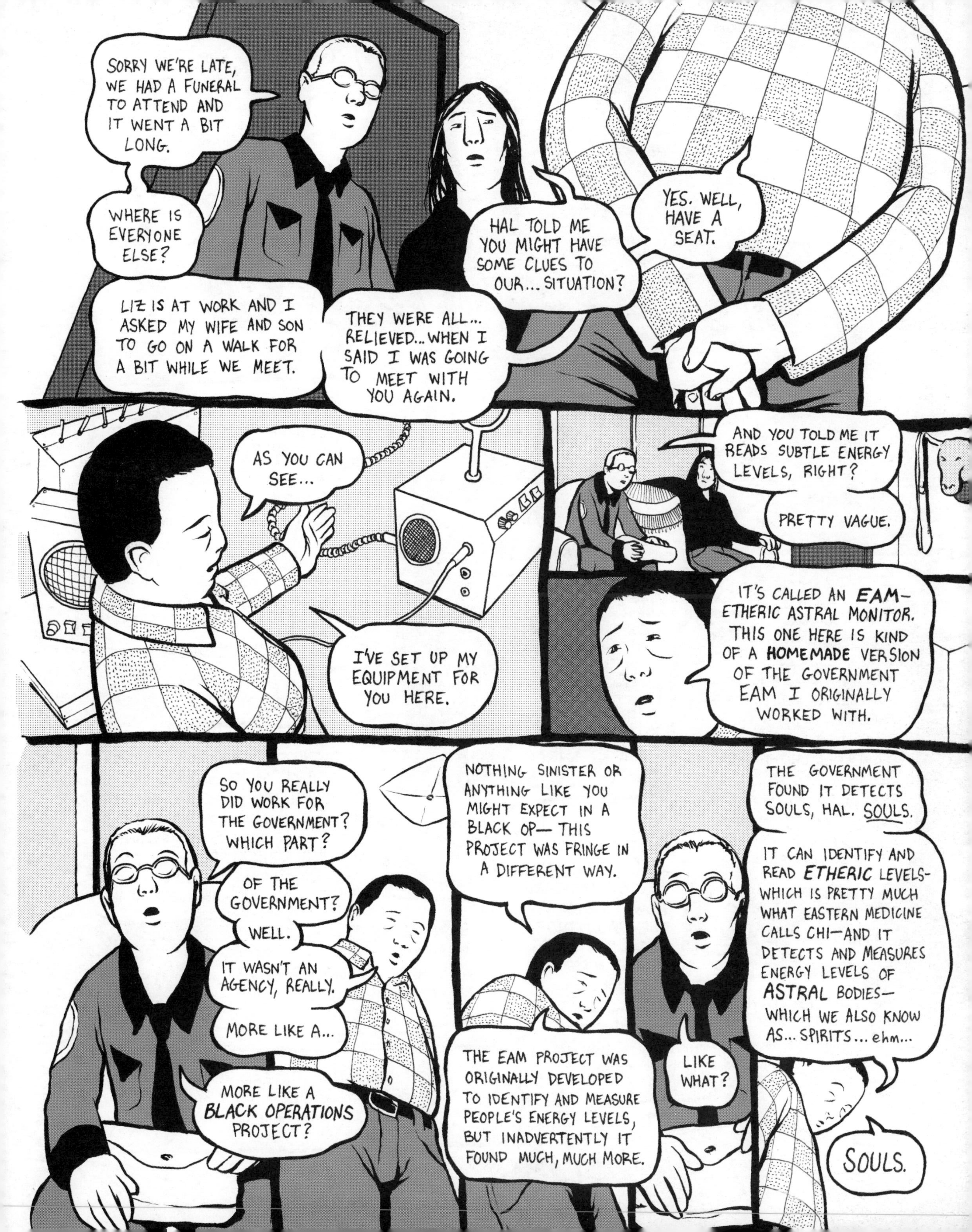
SORRY WE'RE LATE, WE HAD A FUNERAL TO ATTEND AND IT WENT A BIT LONG.
WHERE IS EVERYONE ELSE?
LIZ IS AT WORK AND I ASKED MY WIFE AND SON TO GO ON A WALK FOR A BIT WHILE WE MEET.
THEY WERE ALL... RELIEVED... WHEN I SAID I WAS GOING TO MEET WITH YOU AGAIN.
HAL TOLD ME YOU MIGHT HAVE SOME CLUES TO OUR... SITUATION?
YES. WELL, HAVE A SEAT.
AS YOU CAN SEE...
I'VE SET UP MY EQUIPMENT FOR YOU HERE.
AND YOU TOLD ME IT READS SUBTLE ENERGY LEVELS, RIGHT?
PRETTY VAGUE.
IT'S CALLED AN **EAM**—ETHERIC ASTRAL MONITOR. THIS ONE HERE IS KIND OF A **HOMEMADE** VERSION OF THE GOVERNMENT EAM I ORIGINALLY WORKED WITH.
SO YOU REALLY DID WORK FOR THE GOVERNMENT? WHICH PART?
OF THE GOVERNMENT?
WELL.
IT WASN'T AN AGENCY, REALLY.
MORE LIKE A...
MORE LIKE A BLACK OPERATIONS PROJECT?
NOTHING SINISTER OR ANYTHING LIKE YOU MIGHT EXPECT IN A BLACK OP— THIS PROJECT WAS FRINGE IN A DIFFERENT WAY.
THE EAM PROJECT WAS ORIGINALLY DEVELOPED TO IDENTIFY AND MEASURE PEOPLE'S ENERGY LEVELS, BUT INADVERTENTLY IT FOUND MUCH, MUCH MORE.
LIKE WHAT?
THE GOVERNMENT FOUND IT DETECTS SOULS, HAL. SOULS.
IT CAN IDENTIFY AND READ **ETHERIC** LEVELS—WHICH IS PRETTY MUCH WHAT EASTERN MEDICINE CALLS CHI—AND IT DETECTS AND MEASURES ENERGY LEVELS OF ASTRAL BODIES—WHICH WE ALSO KNOW AS... SPIRITS... ehm...
SOULS.

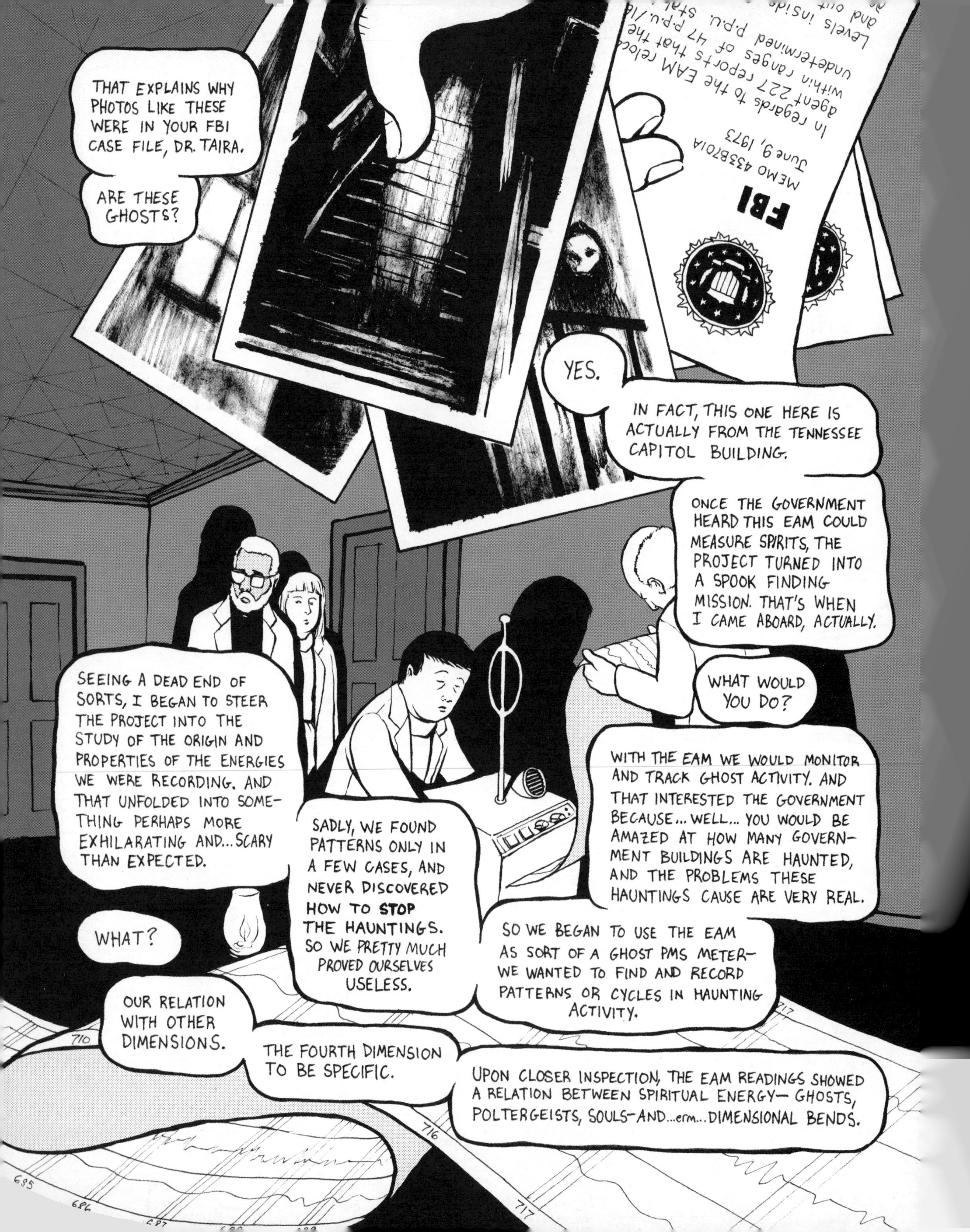
THAT EXPLAINS WHY PHOTOS LIKE THESE WERE IN YOUR FBI CASE FILE, DR. TAIRA.
ARE THESE GHOSTS?
FBI
MEMO 433B701A
June 9, 1973
In regards to the EAM reloc
agent 227 reports that the
within ranges of 47 p.p.u./l
undetermined p.p.u. sta
Levels insid
and out
YES.
IN FACT, THIS ONE HERE IS ACTUALLY FROM THE TENNESSEE CAPITOL BUILDING.
ONCE THE GOVERNMENT HEARD THIS EAM COULD MEASURE SPIRITS, THE PROJECT TURNED INTO A SPOOK FINDING MISSION. THAT'S WHEN I CAME ABOARD, ACTUALLY.
WHAT WOULD YOU DO?
WITH THE EAM WE WOULD MONITOR AND TRACK GHOST ACTIVITY. AND THAT INTERESTED THE GOVERNMENT BECAUSE... WELL... YOU WOULD BE AMAZED AT HOW MANY GOVERNMENT BUILDINGS ARE HAUNTED, AND THE PROBLEMS THESE HAUNTINGS CAUSE ARE VERY REAL.
SO WE BEGAN TO USE THE EAM AS SORT OF A GHOST PMS METER— WE WANTED TO FIND AND RECORD PATTERNS OR CYCLES IN HAUNTING ACTIVITY.
SADLY, WE FOUND PATTERNS ONLY IN A FEW CASES, AND NEVER DISCOVERED HOW TO **STOP** THE HAUNTINGS. SO WE PRETTY MUCH PROVED OURSELVES USELESS.
SEEING A DEAD END OF SORTS, I BEGAN TO STEER THE PROJECT INTO THE STUDY OF THE ORIGIN AND PROPERTIES OF THE ENERGIES WE WERE RECORDING. AND THAT UNFOLDED INTO SOMETHING PERHAPS MORE EXHILARATING AND... SCARY THAN EXPECTED.
WHAT?
OUR RELATION WITH OTHER DIMENSIONS.
THE FOURTH DIMENSION TO BE SPECIFIC.
UPON CLOSER INSPECTION, THE EAM READINGS SHOWED A RELATION BETWEEN SPIRITUAL ENERGY— GHOSTS, POLTERGEISTS, SOULS—AND...erm... DIMENSIONAL BENDS.
710
716
717
685
686

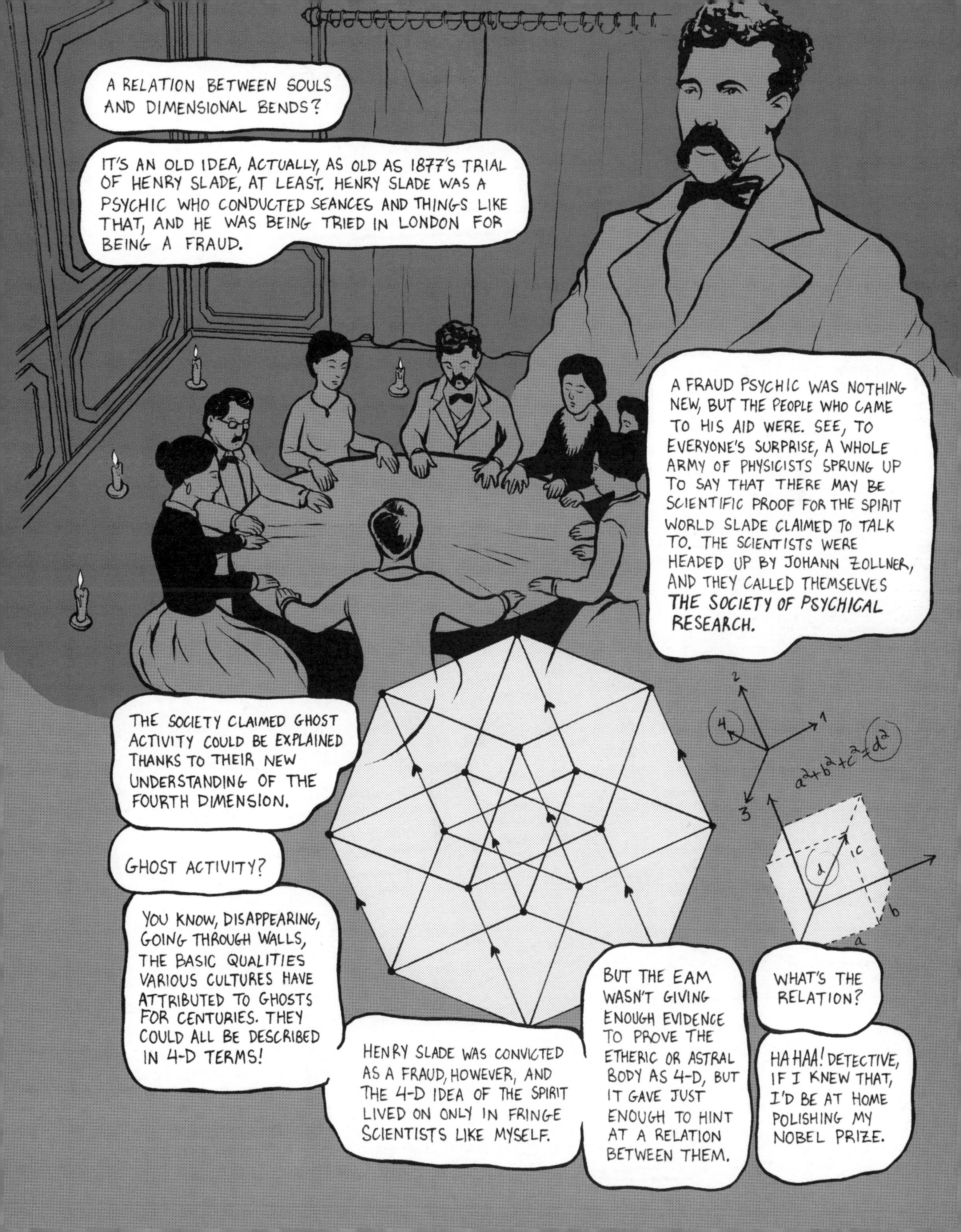
A RELATION BETWEEN SOULS AND DIMENSIONAL BENDS?
IT'S AN OLD IDEA, ACTUALLY, AS OLD AS 1877'S TRIAL OF HENRY SLADE, AT LEAST. HENRY SLADE WAS A PSYCHIC WHO CONDUCTED SEANCES AND THINGS LIKE THAT, AND HE WAS BEING TRIED IN LONDON FOR BEING A FRAUD.
A FRAUD PSYCHIC WAS NOTHING NEW, BUT THE PEOPLE WHO CAME TO HIS AID WERE. SEE, TO EVERYONE'S SURPRISE, A WHOLE ARMY OF PHYSICISTS SPRUNG UP TO SAY THAT THERE MAY BE SCIENTIFIC PROOF FOR THE SPIRIT WORLD SLADE CLAIMED TO TALK TO. THE SCIENTISTS WERE HEADED UP BY JOHANN ZOLLNER, AND THEY CALLED THEMSELVES **THE SOCIETY OF PSYCHICAL RESEARCH.**
THE SOCIETY CLAIMED GHOST ACTIVITY COULD BE EXPLAINED THANKS TO THEIR NEW UNDERSTANDING OF THE FOURTH DIMENSION.
GHOST ACTIVITY?
YOU KNOW, DISAPPEARING, GOING THROUGH WALLS, THE BASIC QUALITIES VARIOUS CULTURES HAVE ATTRIBUTED TO GHOSTS FOR CENTURIES. THEY COULD ALL BE DESCRIBED IN 4-D TERMS!
HENRY SLADE WAS CONVICTED AS A FRAUD, HOWEVER, AND THE 4-D IDEA OF THE SPIRIT LIVED ON ONLY IN FRINGE SCIENTISTS LIKE MYSELF.
BUT THE EAM WASN'T GIVING ENOUGH EVIDENCE TO PROVE THE ETHERIC OR ASTRAL BODY AS 4-D, BUT IT GAVE JUST ENOUGH TO HINT AT A RELATION BETWEEN THEM.
WHAT'S THE RELATION?
HAHAA! DETECTIVE, IF I KNEW THAT, I'D BE AT HOME POLISHING MY NOBEL PRIZE.
1
2
3
4
$a^2+b^2+c^2=d^2$
a
b
c
d

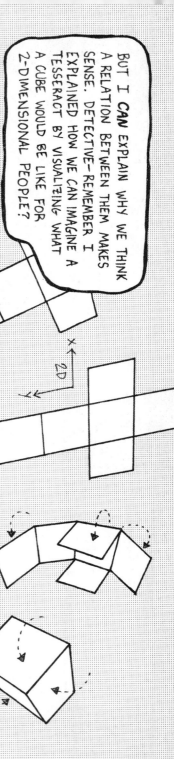

BUT I **CAN** EXPLAIN WHY WE THINK A RELATION BETWEEN THEM MAKES SENSE. DETECTIVE—REMEMBER I EXPLAINED HOW WE CAN IMAGINE A TESSERACT BY VISUALIZING WHAT A CUBE WOULD BE LIKE FOR 2-DIMENSIONAL PEOPLE?

WELL, YOU SAID 2-D PEOPLE COULD SEE A CUBE IF IT WAS UNFOLDED, BUT WOULD FIND IT HARD TO IMAGINE HOW IT WOULD FOLD TO FORM A CUBE BECAUSE THEY CAN'T COMPREHEND A THIRD DIMENSION.

THAT'S RIGHT, DETECTIVE. NOW HERE'S ANOTHER BRAIN TEASE: LET'S PRETEND WE ARE 2-D PEOPLE WHO EXIST IN OUR FLAT LAND—AND A 3-D CONE PASSES THROUGH OUR LAND, STARTING AT THE TIP. NOW... AS IT PASSES THROUGH, WHAT DO WE SEE?

UM... WE WOULD SEE A SMALL CIRCLE AT FIRST, AND IT... THEN IT WOULD **LARGER** AS THE CONE GOES THROUGH OUR LAND?

YES—THAT'S RIGHT! A CIRCLE WOULD APPEAR—OUT OF _NOWHERE_—AND INEXPLICABLY GROW LARGER AND LARGER. QUITE A STRANGE PHENOMENON FOR US 2-D PEOPLE.

AND WHAT WOULD HAPPEN WHEN THE CONE PASSES ALL THE WAY THROUGH OUR 2-D LAND? THE CIRCLE WOULD BE AT ITS LARGEST... THEN?

Uh... I DUNNO.

IT WOULD **DISAPPEAR**! **POOF**! ONCE THIS CONE PASSED THROUGH OUR 2-D PLANE, IT WOULD SEEM TO HAVE JUST DISAPPEARED.

AND THAT'S BECAUSE OBJECTS OF A HIGHER DIMENSION EXHIBIT PROPERTIES THAT SEEM IMPOSSIBLE IN A LOWER DIMENSION.

THEY COULD APPEAR OUT OF NOWHERE, DISAPPEAR, GROW, SHRINK, MULTIPLY, PASS THROUGH BOUNDARIES... UNDERSTAND? WELL, NEEDLESS TO SAY, WE SAW SUCH ANOMALIES IN THE ETHERIC AND ASTRAL ENERGIES WE STUDIED WITH THE EAM.

LOOK, DOCTOR, I DON'T KNOW IF I'M TOTALLY UNDERSTANDING THIS. BUT... BUT LET'S MOVE ON. SO WHAT HAPPENED TO THE EAM PROJECT? WHY IS THE FBI LOOKING FOR YOU?

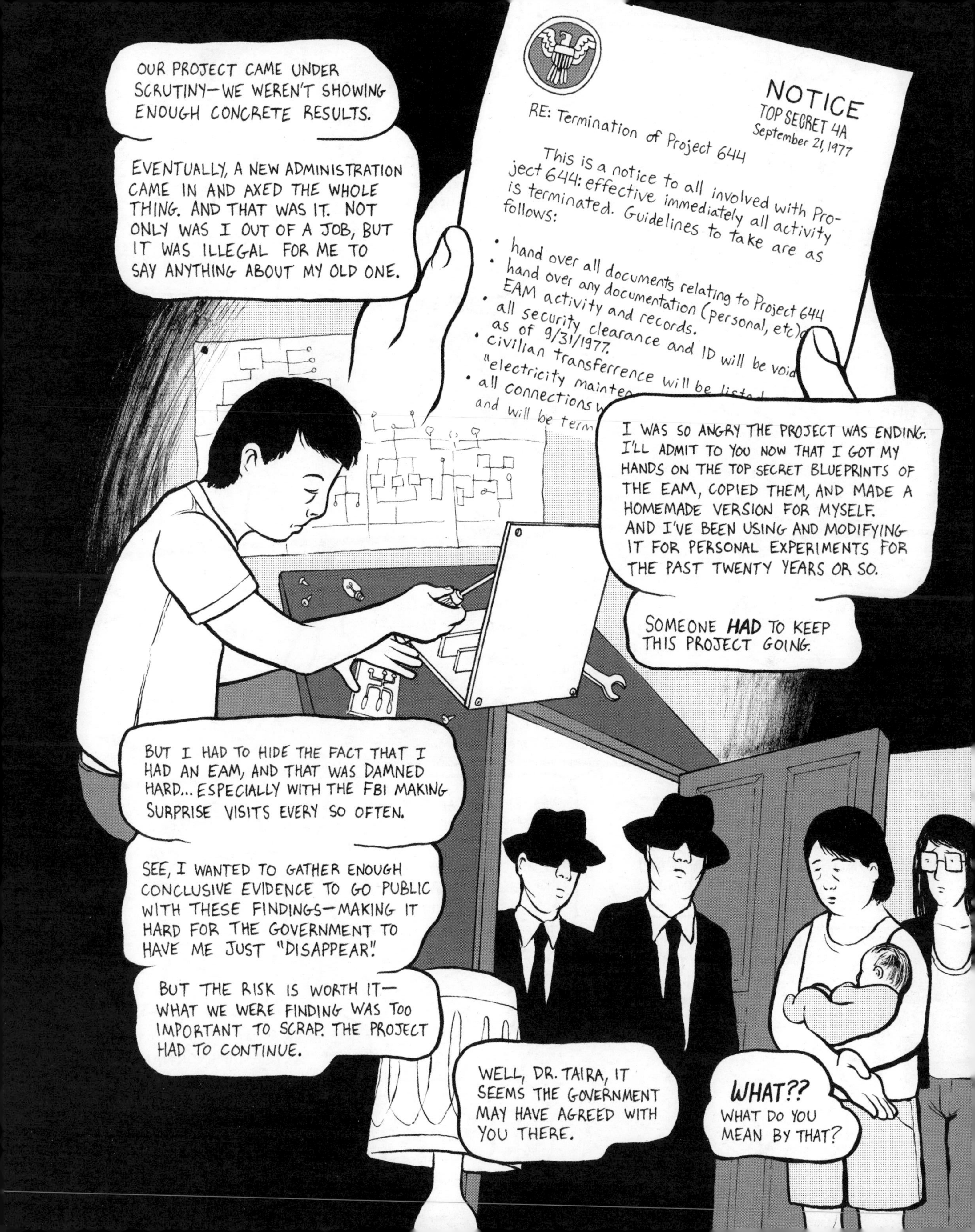

OUR PROJECT CAME UNDER SCRUTINY—WE WEREN'T SHOWING ENOUGH CONCRETE RESULTS.
EVENTUALLY, A NEW ADMINISTRATION CAME IN AND AXED THE WHOLE THING. AND THAT WAS IT. NOT ONLY WAS I OUT OF A JOB, BUT IT WAS ILLEGAL FOR ME TO SAY ANYTHING ABOUT MY OLD ONE.
NOTICE
TOP SECRET 4A
September 21, 1977
RE: Termination of Project 644
This is a notice to all involved with Project 644: effective immediately all activity is terminated. Guidelines to take are as follows:
• hand over all documents relating to Project 644
• hand over any documentation (personal, etc) of EAM activity and records.
• all security clearance and ID will be void as of 9/31/1977.
• civilian transferrence will be listed
"electricity mainte
• all connections w
and will be term
I WAS SO ANGRY THE PROJECT WAS ENDING. I'LL ADMIT TO YOU NOW THAT I GOT MY HANDS ON THE TOP SECRET BLUEPRINTS OF THE EAM, COPIED THEM, AND MADE A HOMEMADE VERSION FOR MYSELF. AND I'VE BEEN USING AND MODIFYING IT FOR PERSONAL EXPERIMENTS FOR THE PAST TWENTY YEARS OR SO.
SOMEONE HAD TO KEEP THIS PROJECT GOING.
BUT I HAD TO HIDE THE FACT THAT I HAD AN EAM, AND THAT WAS DAMNED HARD... ESPECIALLY WITH THE FBI MAKING SURPRISE VISITS EVERY SO OFTEN.
SEE, I WANTED TO GATHER ENOUGH CONCLUSIVE EVIDENCE TO GO PUBLIC WITH THESE FINDINGS—MAKING IT HARD FOR THE GOVERNMENT TO HAVE ME JUST "DISAPPEAR."
BUT THE RISK IS WORTH IT—WHAT WE WERE FINDING WAS TOO IMPORTANT TO SCRAP. THE PROJECT HAD TO CONTINUE.
WELL, DR. TAIRA, IT SEEMS THE GOVERNMENT MAY HAVE AGREED WITH YOU THERE.
WHAT?? WHAT DO YOU MEAN BY THAT?

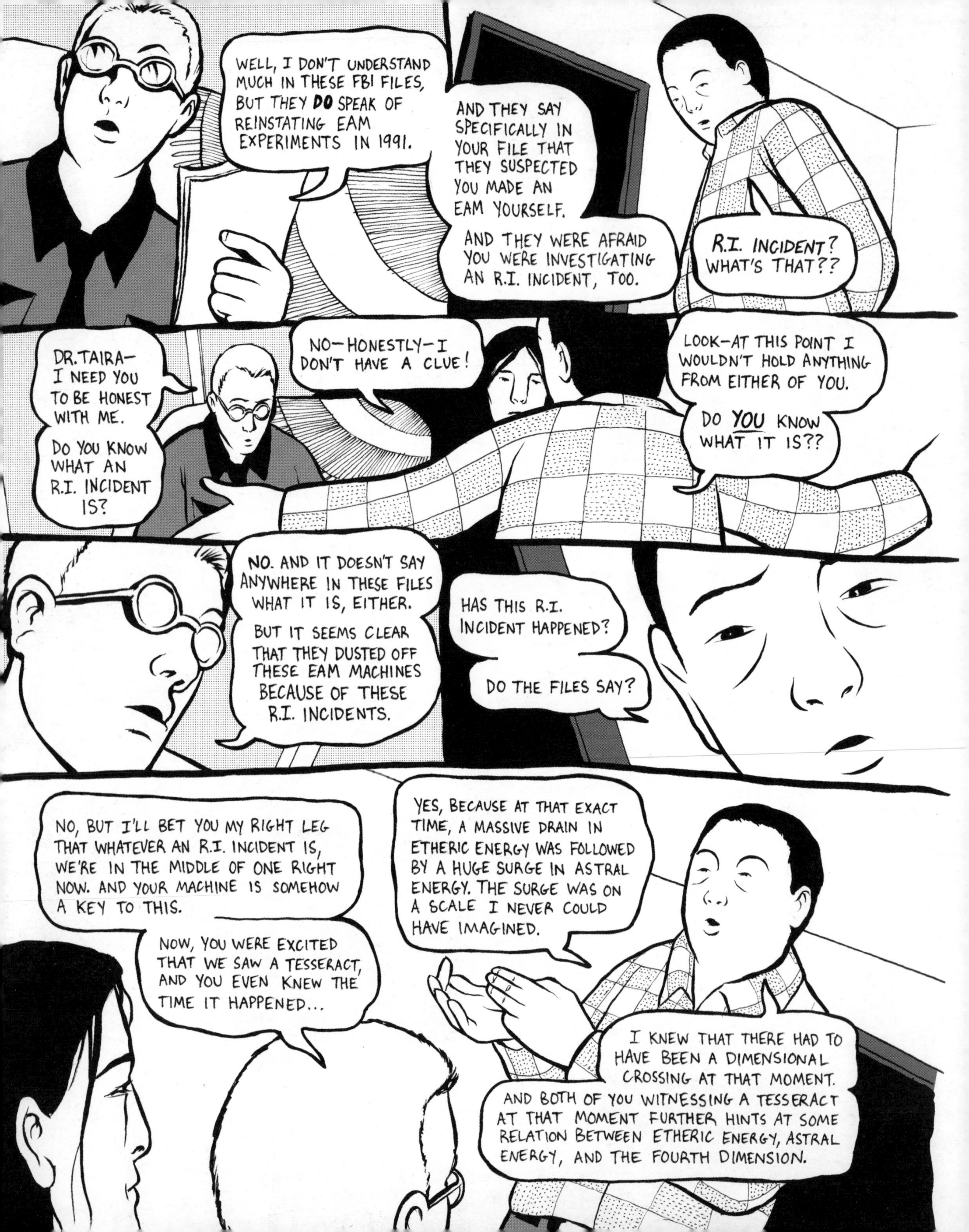
WELL, I DON'T UNDERSTAND MUCH IN THESE FBI FILES, BUT THEY **DO** SPEAK OF REINSTATING EAM EXPERIMENTS IN 1991.
AND THEY SAY SPECIFICALLY IN YOUR FILE THAT THEY SUSPECTED YOU MADE AN EAM YOURSELF.
AND THEY WERE AFRAID YOU WERE INVESTIGATING AN R.I. INCIDENT, TOO.
R.I. INCIDENT? WHAT'S THAT??
DR. TAIRA—I NEED YOU TO BE HONEST WITH ME.
DO YOU KNOW WHAT AN R.I. INCIDENT IS?
NO—HONESTLY—I DON'T HAVE A CLUE!
LOOK—AT THIS POINT I WOULDN'T HOLD ANYTHING FROM EITHER OF YOU.
DO **YOU** KNOW WHAT IT IS??
NO. AND IT DOESN'T SAY ANYWHERE IN THESE FILES WHAT IT IS, EITHER.
BUT IT SEEMS CLEAR THAT THEY DUSTED OFF THESE EAM MACHINES BECAUSE OF THESE R.I. INCIDENTS.
HAS THIS R.I. INCIDENT HAPPENED?
DO THE FILES SAY?
NO, BUT I'LL BET YOU MY RIGHT LEG THAT WHATEVER AN R.I. INCIDENT IS, WE'RE IN THE MIDDLE OF ONE RIGHT NOW. AND YOUR MACHINE IS SOMEHOW A KEY TO THIS.
NOW, YOU WERE EXCITED THAT WE SAW A TESSERACT, AND YOU EVEN KNEW THE TIME IT HAPPENED...
YES, BECAUSE AT THAT EXACT TIME, A MASSIVE DRAIN IN ETHERIC ENERGY WAS FOLLOWED BY A HUGE SURGE IN ASTRAL ENERGY. THE SURGE WAS ON A SCALE I NEVER COULD HAVE IMAGINED.
I KNEW THAT THERE HAD TO HAVE BEEN A DIMENSIONAL CROSSING AT THAT MOMENT.
AND BOTH OF YOU WITNESSING A TESSERACT AT THAT MOMENT FURTHER HINTS AT SOME RELATION BETWEEN ETHERIC ENERGY, ASTRAL ENERGY, AND THE FOURTH DIMENSION.

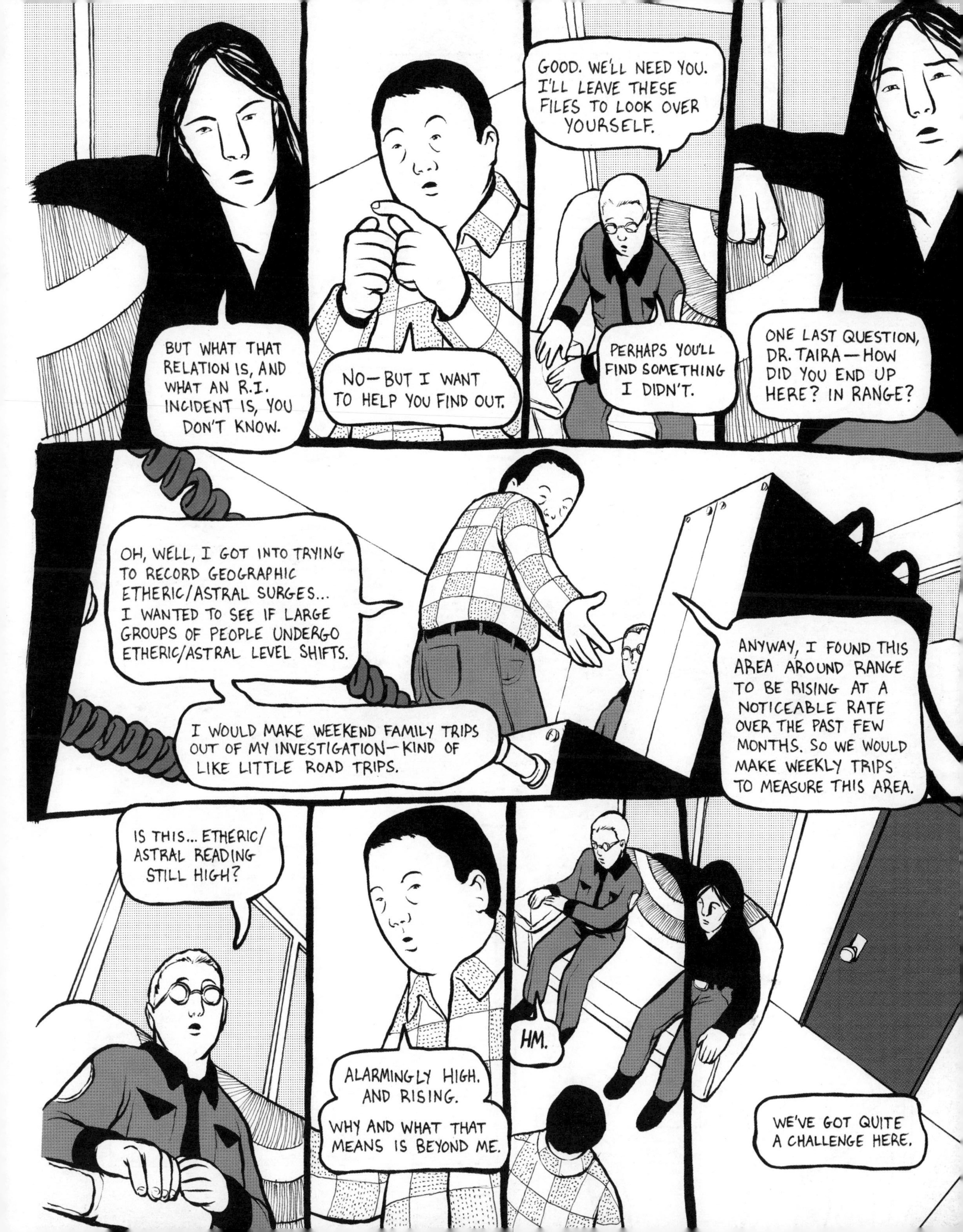
BUT WHAT THAT RELATION IS, AND WHAT AN R.I. INCIDENT IS, YOU DON'T KNOW.
NO—BUT I WANT TO HELP YOU FIND OUT.
GOOD. WE'LL NEED YOU. I'LL LEAVE THESE FILES TO LOOK OVER YOURSELF.
PERHAPS YOU'LL FIND SOMETHING I DIDN'T.
ONE LAST QUESTION, DR. TAIRA—HOW DID YOU END UP HERE? IN RANGE?
OH, WELL, I GOT INTO TRYING TO RECORD GEOGRAPHIC ETHERIC/ASTRAL SURGES... I WANTED TO SEE IF LARGE GROUPS OF PEOPLE UNDERGO ETHERIC/ASTRAL LEVEL SHIFTS.
I WOULD MAKE WEEKEND FAMILY TRIPS OUT OF MY INVESTIGATION—KIND OF LIKE LITTLE ROAD TRIPS.
ANYWAY, I FOUND THIS AREA AROUND RANGE TO BE RISING AT A NOTICEABLE RATE OVER THE PAST FEW MONTHS. SO WE WOULD MAKE WEEKLY TRIPS TO MEASURE THIS AREA.
IS THIS... ETHERIC/ ASTRAL READING STILL HIGH?
ALARMINGLY HIGH. AND RISING.
WHY AND WHAT THAT MEANS IS BEYOND ME.
HM.
WE'VE GOT QUITE A CHALLENGE HERE.

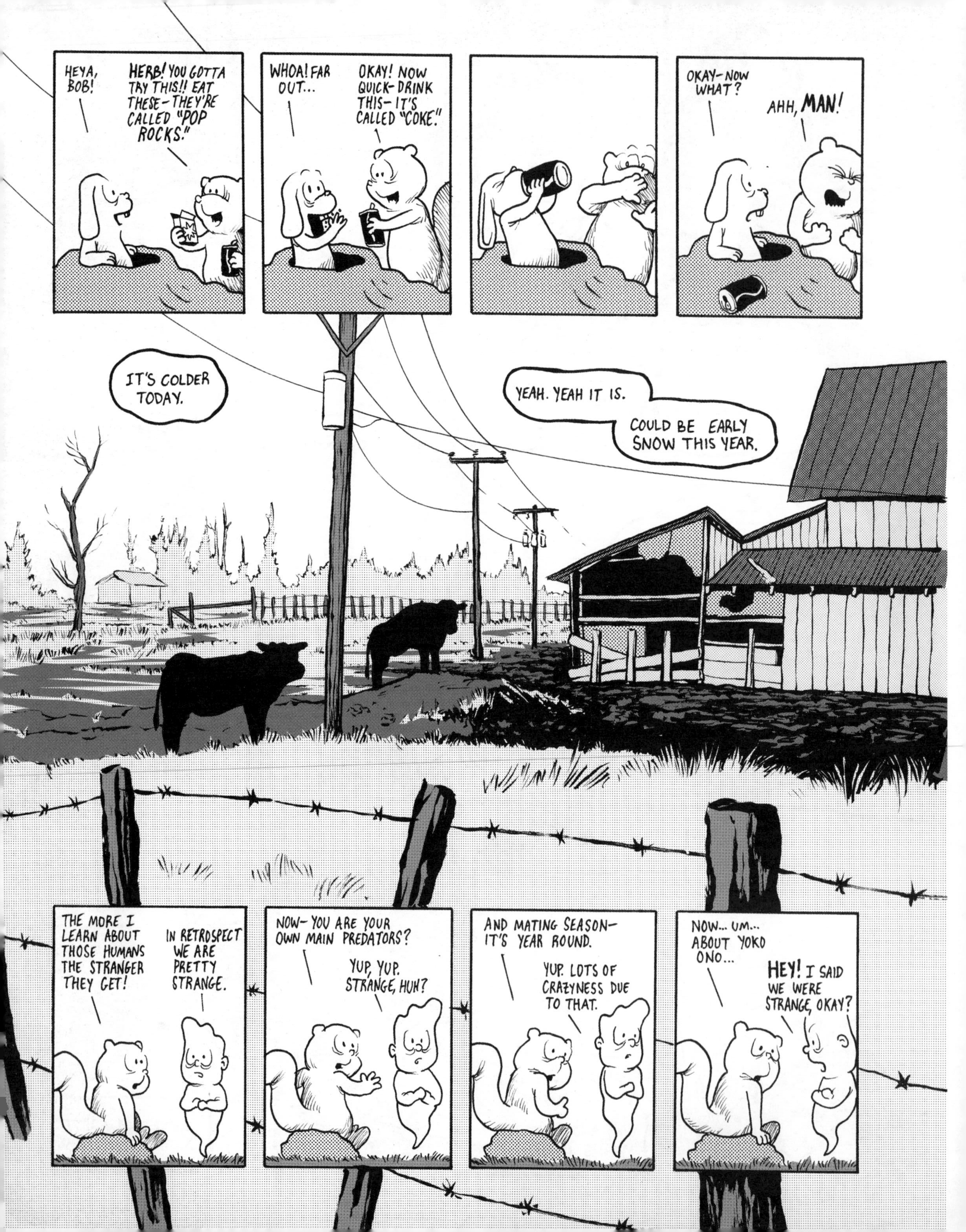
HEYA, BOB!
HERB! YOU GOTTA TRY THIS!! EAT THESE—THEY'RE CALLED "POP ROCKS."
WHOA! FAR OUT...
OKAY! NOW QUICK-DRINK THIS—IT'S CALLED "COKE."
OKAY—NOW WHAT?
AHH, MAN!
IT'S COLDER TODAY.
YEAH. YEAH IT IS.
COULD BE EARLY SNOW THIS YEAR.
THE MORE I LEARN ABOUT THOSE HUMANS THE STRANGER THEY GET!
IN RETROSPECT WE ARE PRETTY STRANGE.
NOW—YOU ARE YOUR OWN MAIN PREDATORS?
YUP, YUP. STRANGE, HUH?
AND MATING SEASON—IT'S YEAR ROUND.
YUP. LOTS OF CRAZYNESS DUE TO THAT.
NOW... UM... ABOUT YOKO ONO...
HEY! I SAID WE WERE STRANGE, OKAY?

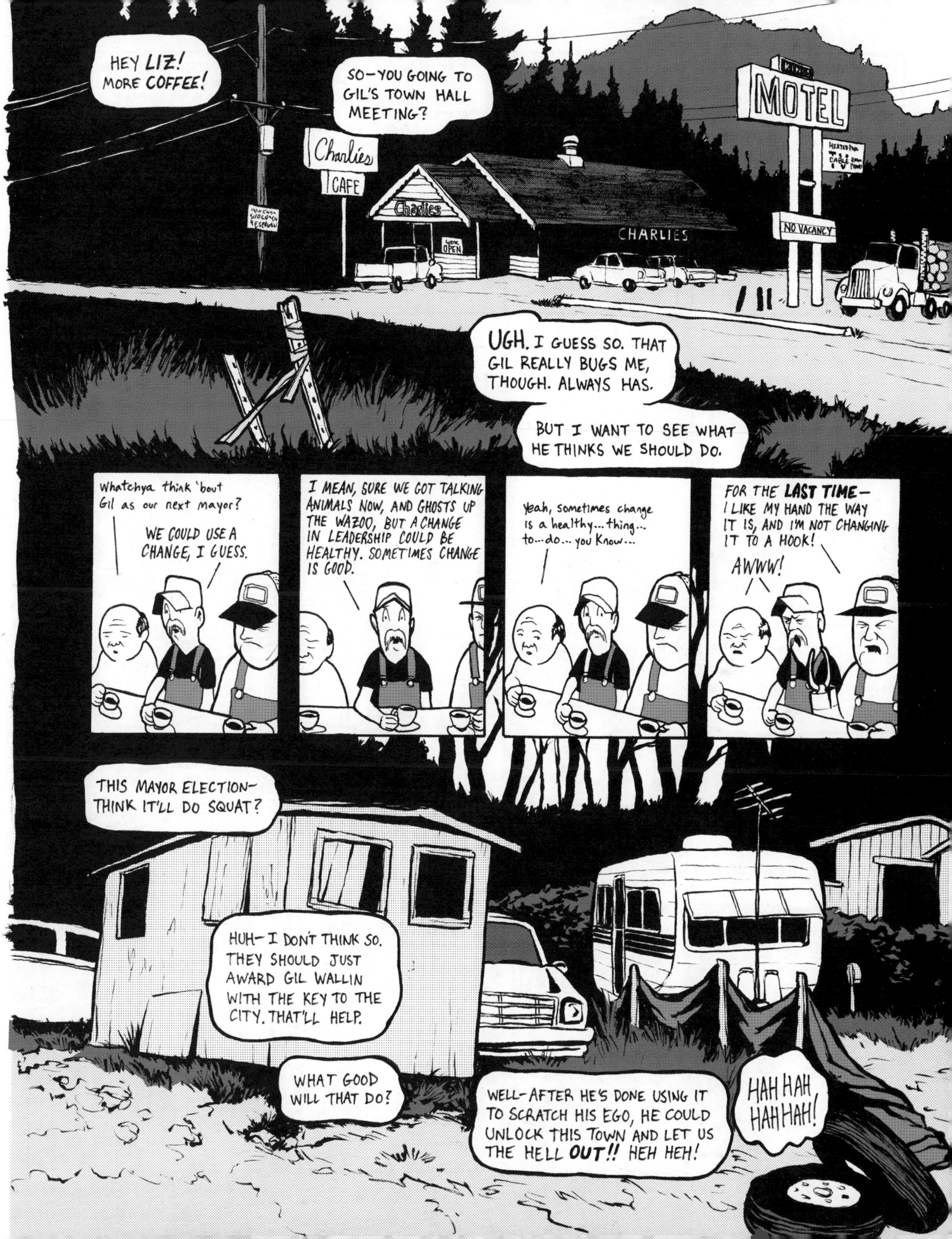
HEY LIZ! MORE COFFEE!
SO—YOU GOING TO GIL'S TOWN HALL MEETING?
Charlie's
CAFE
Charlies
OPEN
CHARLIES
KING
MOTEL
NO VACANCY
UGH. I GUESS SO. THAT GIL REALLY BUGS ME, THOUGH. ALWAYS HAS.
BUT I WANT TO SEE WHAT HE THINKS WE SHOULD DO.
Whatchya think 'bout Gil as our next mayor?
WE COULD USE A CHANGE, I GUESS.
I MEAN, SURE WE GOT TALKING ANIMALS NOW, AND GHOSTS UP THE WAZOO, BUT A CHANGE IN LEADERSHIP COULD BE HEALTHY. SOMETIMES CHANGE IS GOOD.
Yeah, sometimes change is a healthy... thing... to...do... you know...
FOR THE LAST TIME— I LIKE MY HAND THE WAY IT IS, AND I'M NOT CHANGING IT TO A HOOK!
AWWW!
THIS MAYOR ELECTION— THINK IT'LL DO SQUAT?
HUH— I DON'T THINK SO. THEY SHOULD JUST AWARD GIL WALLIN WITH THE KEY TO THE CITY. THAT'LL HELP.
WHAT GOOD WILL THAT DO?
WELL—AFTER HE'S DONE USING IT TO SCRATCH HIS EGO, HE COULD UNLOCK THIS TOWN AND LET US THE HELL OUT!! HEH HEH!
HAH HAH HAH HAH!

A TRUE MATCH MADE IN THE DEPTHS OF HELL—THE PRODUCT OF THE FIVE CLOVES OF THE ABRAHAM LINCOLN GOAT—GHOSTS AND TALKING ANIMALS EVERYWHERE! I'M WATCHING. YES. WATCHING. YES.
CHIEF AIE
XXX
WATCHING FOR WHICH WITCH SWITCHED. WHICH WITCH SWITCHED!? NOW WE'RE IN THE FATE OF HOBO HIM AND HIS GOOD GRACES. ANIMALS EAT GRASS. GHOSTS EAT SOULS. WATCHING BOTH. WATCHING.
GOTTA KEEP ONE EYE ON THE GRASS. ONE ON THE SOUL. HOBO HIM SAID HE'D RETURN WITH THE SPACESHIP BY NOW. MY GOD—HE LIED AGAIN!! OF COURSE HE DID!! IT WAS FORETOLD BY THE SNAKE AND SCROLL!!
HEY CHIEF—GIL WALLIN WANTS TO SEE YOU. IS...IS THIS AN OKAY TIME?
SURE! AS OKAY AS ANY!
HEY, ADRE! GREAT TO SEE YOU—AND HEY—THANKS FOR TAKING THE TIME.
YEAH.
NOW, I WANTED TO MAKE SURE YOU REMEMBERED OUR DISCUSSION OF "LOSING" ANY APPLICATIONS SUBMITTED BY PEOPLE LOOKING TO RUN AGAINST ME.
JUST A LITTLE SAFEGUARD THAT MY ONLY OPPONENT REMAINS A DEAD ONE! SAY—YOU'RE LOOKING PRETTY PALE, ADRE—HAVE YOU EATEN TODAY??
I HAD SOME...PLASTERBOARD... ABOUT TWO HOURS AGO. IT'S NOT SITTING SO WELL.
I SEE.
RANGE POLICE—HOW MAY I HELP YOU? YOUR CAT SAID WHAT ABOUT YOU? WELL, I DON'T KNOW WHAT WE CAN DO ABOUT THAT...
RANGE POLICE
RANGE POLICE—HOW MAY I HELP YOU? YES—WE'RE HAVING POWER PROBLEMS IN THAT AREA. I CAN'T SAY WHEN IT WILL BE FIXED. SEE, WE USED TO HAVE A GUY COME UP FROM AUBURN FOR THIS STUFF.
RANGE POLICE. YES, I'M AWARE THERE ISN'T ANY MILK IN TOWN.
ADRE SURE IS TRAUMATIZED BY WHAT HAPPENED HALLOWEEN NIGHT, HUH?
OH, MY YES!
SAL HOWELL
HE'S TERRIFIED OF THE GHOSTS AND TALKING ANIMALS
BLAM!!
SAL HOWELL
SAL!! I'M ALL OUT OF SHELLS AND I THINK A RACCOON'S IN HERE!! QUICK! QUICK!
SIGH.
SAL HOWELL
DON'T WORRY, WE SWITCHED HIM TO BLANKS YESTERDAY.
AH!
SHELLS
SAL HOWELL

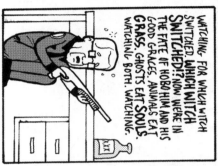

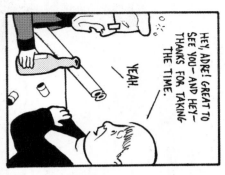

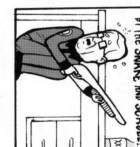

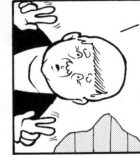

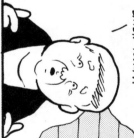

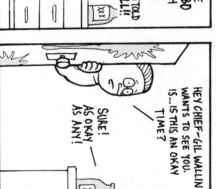

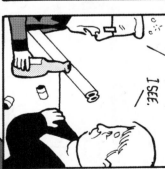

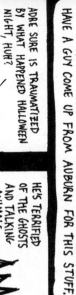

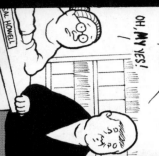

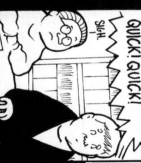

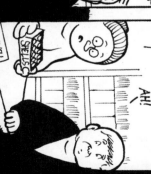

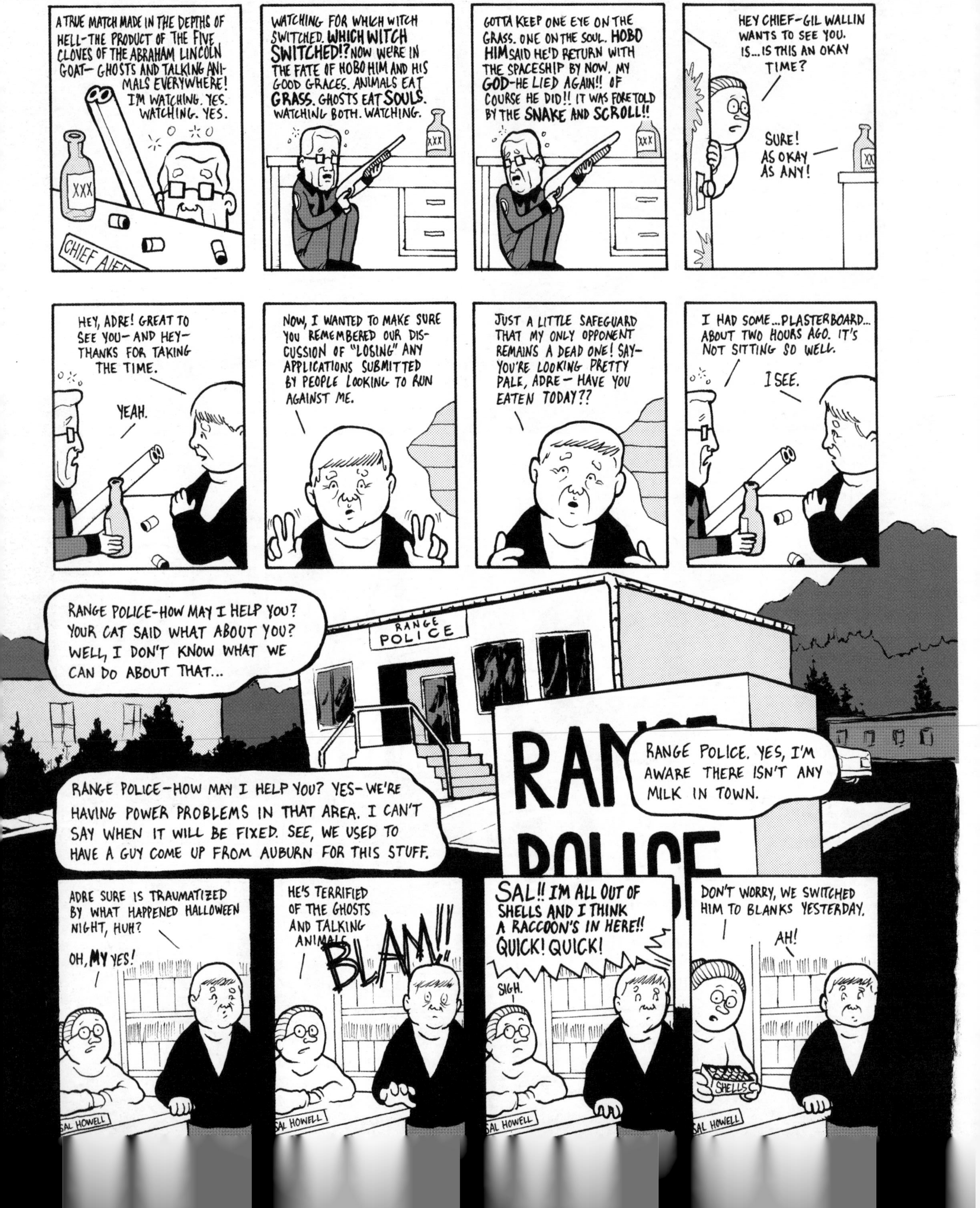

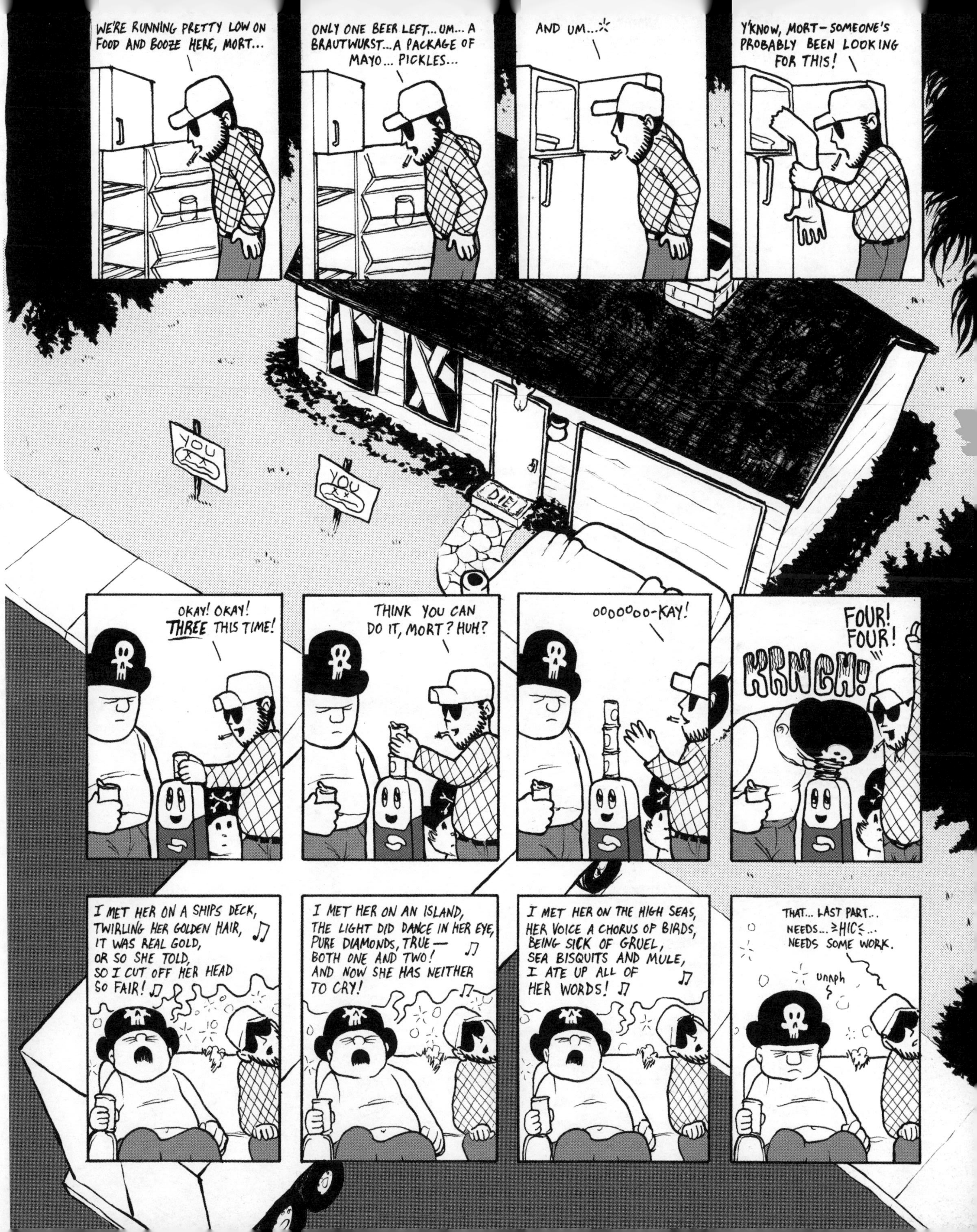
WE'RE RUNNING PRETTY LOW ON FOOD AND BOOZE HERE, MORT...
ONLY ONE BEER LEFT... UM... A BRAUTWURST... A PACKAGE OF MAYO... PICKLES...
AND UM...
Y'KNOW, MORT– SOMEONE'S PROBABLY BEEN LOOKING FOR THIS!
YOU
YOU
DIE!
OKAY! OKAY! THREE THIS TIME!
THINK YOU CAN DO IT, MORT? HUH?
OOOOOOO-KAY!
KRNCH!
FOUR! FOUR!
I MET HER ON A SHIPS DECK, TWIRLING HER GOLDEN HAIR, IT WAS REAL GOLD, OR SO SHE TOLD, SO I CUT OFF HER HEAD SO FAIR!
I MET HER ON AN ISLAND, THE LIGHT DID DANCE IN HER EYE, PURE DIAMONDS, TRUE— BOTH ONE AND TWO! AND NOW SHE HAS NEITHER TO CRY!
I MET HER ON THE HIGH SEAS, HER VOICE A CHORUS OF BIRDS, BEING SICK OF GRUEL, SEA BISQUITS AND MULE, I ATE UP ALL OF HER WORDS!
THAT... LAST PART... NEEDS... ≥HIC≤... NEEDS SOME WORK.
UNNPH

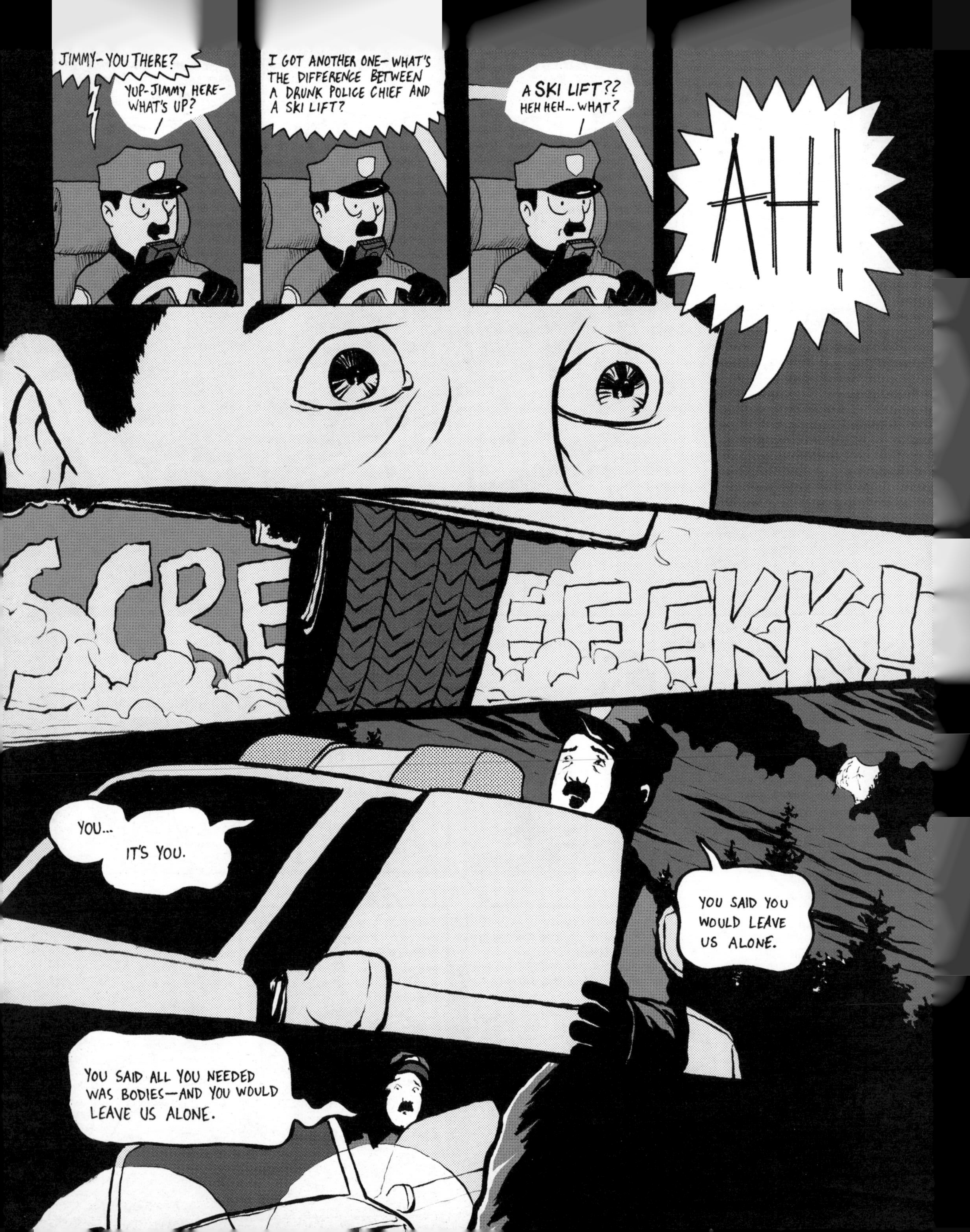
JIMMY- YOU THERE?
YUP- JIMMY HERE- WHAT'S UP?
I GOT ANOTHER ONE- WHAT'S THE DIFFERENCE BETWEEN A DRUNK POLICE CHIEF AND A SKI LIFT?
A SKI LIFT?? HEH HEH... WHAT?
AH!
SCREEEEKK!
YOU... IT'S YOU.
YOU SAID YOU WOULD LEAVE US ALONE.
YOU SAID ALL YOU NEEDED WAS BODIES—AND YOU WOULD LEAVE US ALONE.

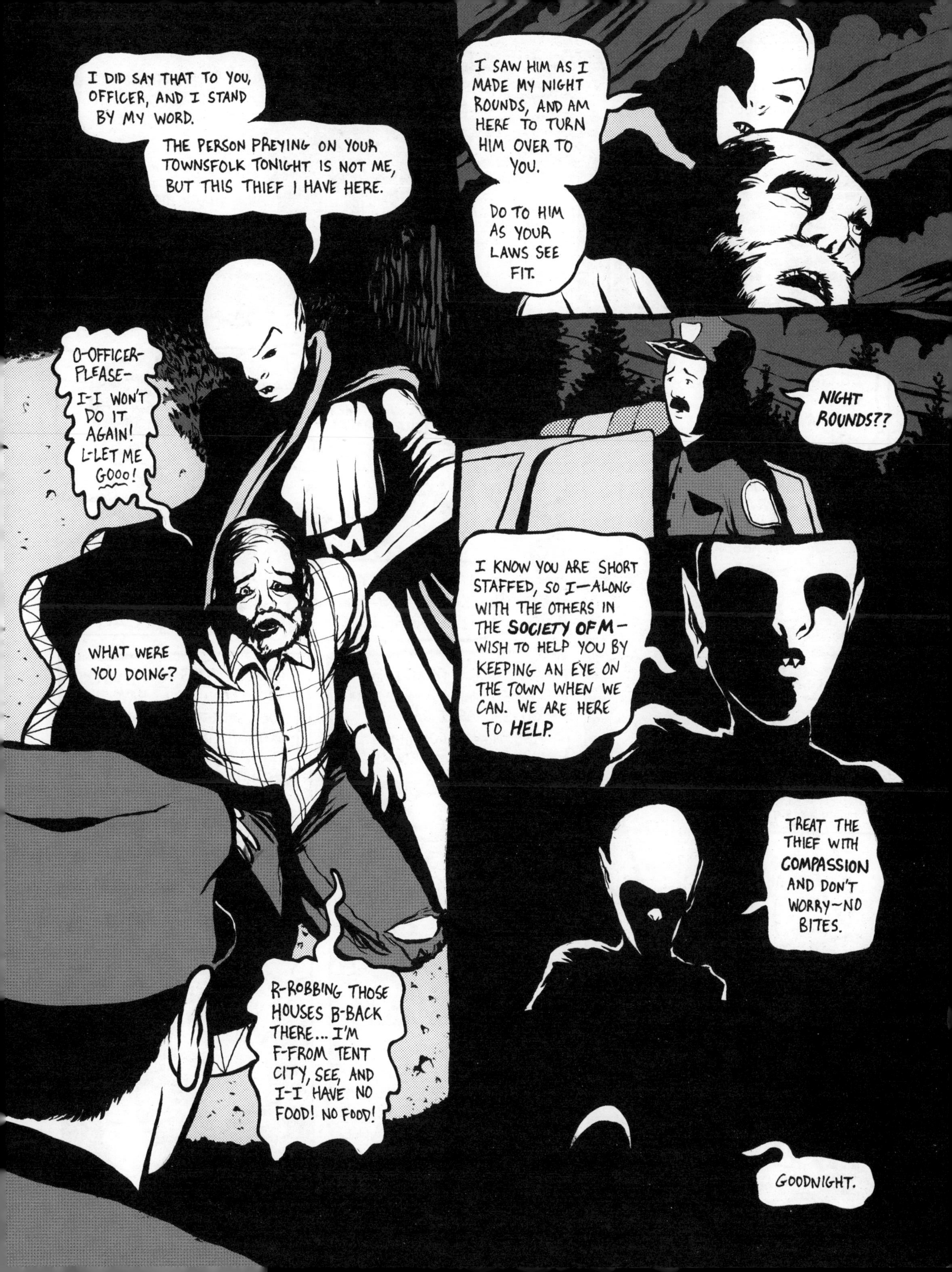
I DID SAY THAT TO YOU, OFFICER, AND I STAND BY MY WORD.
THE PERSON PREYING ON YOUR TOWNSFOLK TONIGHT IS NOT ME, BUT THIS THIEF I HAVE HERE.
O-OFFICER-PLEASE-
I-I WON'T DO IT AGAIN! L-LET ME GOOO!
WHAT WERE YOU DOING?
R-ROBBING THOSE HOUSES B-BACK THERE... I'M F-FROM TENT CITY, SEE, AND I-I HAVE NO FOOD! NO FOOD!
I SAW HIM AS I MADE MY NIGHT ROUNDS, AND AM HERE TO TURN HIM OVER TO YOU.
DO TO HIM AS YOUR LAWS SEE FIT.
NIGHT ROUNDS??
I KNOW YOU ARE SHORT STAFFED, SO I—ALONG WITH THE OTHERS IN THE SOCIETY OF M—WISH TO HELP YOU BY KEEPING AN EYE ON THE TOWN WHEN WE CAN. WE ARE HERE TO HELP.
TREAT THE THIEF WITH COMPASSION AND DON'T WORRY—NO BITES.
GOODNIGHT.

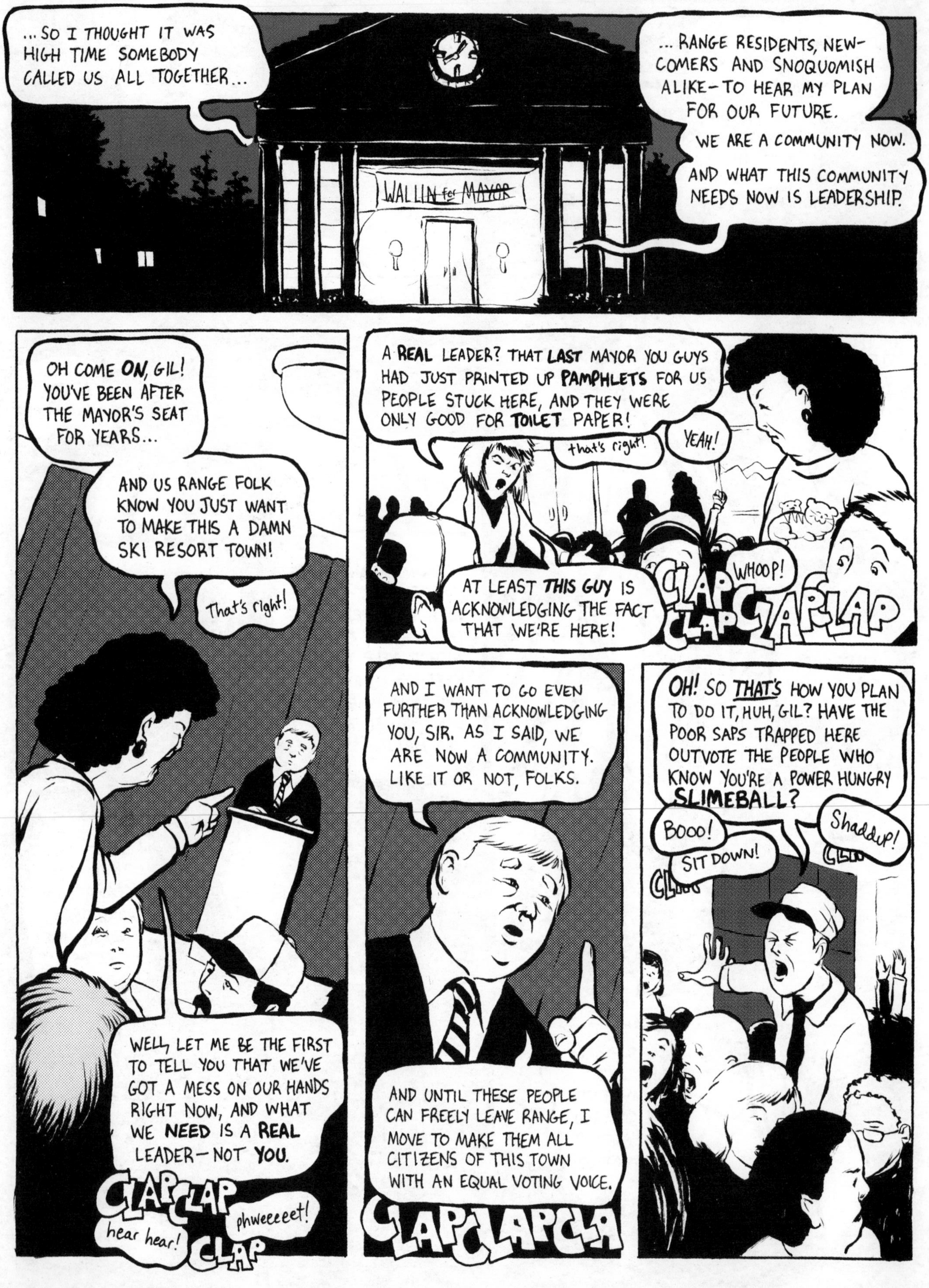
...SO I THOUGHT IT WAS HIGH TIME SOMEBODY CALLED US ALL TOGETHER...
WALLIN for MAYOR
...RANGE RESIDENTS, NEW-COMERS AND SNOQUOMISH ALIKE—TO HEAR MY PLAN FOR OUR FUTURE.
WE ARE A COMMUNITY NOW.
AND WHAT THIS COMMUNITY NEEDS NOW IS LEADERSHIP.
OH COME ON, GIL! YOU'VE BEEN AFTER THE MAYOR'S SEAT FOR YEARS...
AND US RANGE FOLK KNOW YOU JUST WANT TO MAKE THIS A DAMN SKI RESORT TOWN!
That's right!
WELL, LET ME BE THE FIRST TO TELL YOU THAT WE'VE GOT A MESS ON OUR HANDS RIGHT NOW, AND WHAT WE NEED IS A REAL LEADER—NOT YOU.
CLAPCLAP
phweeeeet!
hear hear!
CLAP
A REAL LEADER? THAT LAST MAYOR YOU GUYS HAD JUST PRINTED UP PAMPHLETS FOR US PEOPLE STUCK HERE, AND THEY WERE ONLY GOOD FOR TOILET PAPER!
that's right!
YEAH!
AT LEAST THIS GUY IS ACKNOWLEDGING THE FACT THAT WE'RE HERE!
CLAP CLAP
WHOOP!
CLAPCLAP
AND I WANT TO GO EVEN FURTHER THAN ACKNOWLEDGING YOU, SIR. AS I SAID, WE ARE NOW A COMMUNITY. LIKE IT OR NOT, FOLKS.
AND UNTIL THESE PEOPLE CAN FREELY LEAVE RANGE, I MOVE TO MAKE THEM ALL CITIZENS OF THIS TOWN WITH AN EQUAL VOTING VOICE.
CLAPCLAPCLA
OH! SO THAT'S HOW YOU PLAN TO DO IT, HUH, GIL? HAVE THE POOR SAPS TRAPPED HERE OUTVOTE THE PEOPLE WHO KNOW YOU'RE A POWER HUNGRY SLIMEBALL?
Booo!
Shaddup!
SIT DOWN!

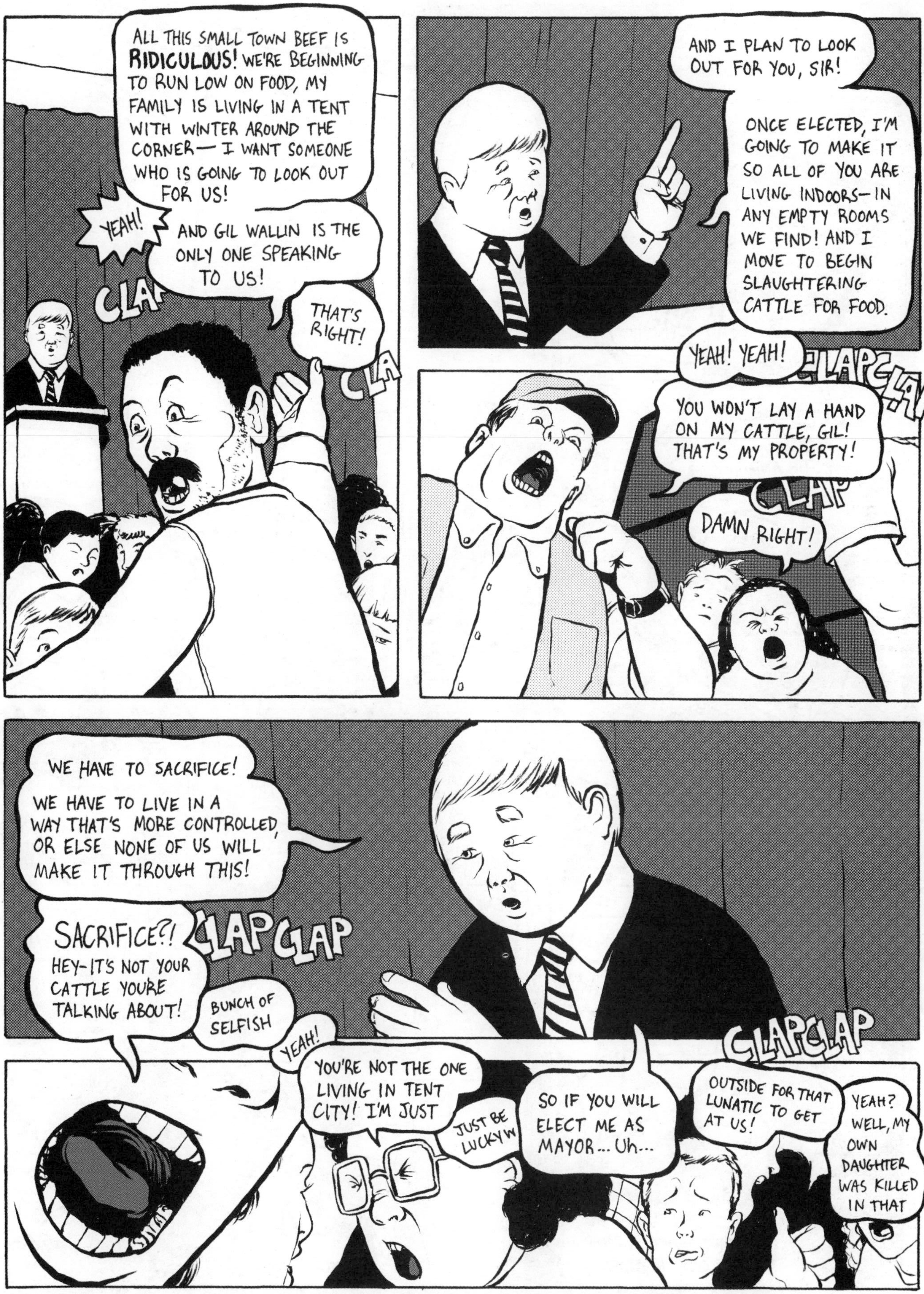
ALL THIS SMALL TOWN BEEF IS **RIDICULOUS!** WE'RE BEGINNING TO RUN LOW ON FOOD, MY FAMILY IS LIVING IN A TENT WITH WINTER AROUND THE CORNER— I WANT SOMEONE WHO IS GOING TO LOOK OUT FOR US!
YEAH!
AND GIL WALLIN IS THE ONLY ONE SPEAKING TO US!
CLA
THAT'S RIGHT!
CLA
AND I PLAN TO LOOK OUT FOR YOU, SIR!
ONCE ELECTED, I'M GOING TO MAKE IT SO ALL OF YOU ARE LIVING INDOORS—IN ANY EMPTY ROOMS WE FIND! AND I MOVE TO BEGIN SLAUGHTERING CATTLE FOR FOOD.
YEAH! YEAH!
CLAPCLAP
YOU WON'T LAY A HAND ON MY CATTLE, GIL! THAT'S MY PROPERTY!
CLAP
DAMN RIGHT!
WE HAVE TO SACRIFICE!
WE HAVE TO LIVE IN A WAY THAT'S MORE CONTROLLED, OR ELSE NONE OF US WILL MAKE IT THROUGH THIS!
SACRIFICE?! HEY-IT'S NOT YOUR CATTLE YOU'RE TALKING ABOUT!
CLAPCLAP
BUNCH OF SELFISH
YEAH!
YOU'RE NOT THE ONE LIVING IN TENT CITY! I'M JUST
JUST BE LUCKY W
SO IF YOU WILL ELECT ME AS MAYOR... Uh...
CLAPCLAP
OUTSIDE FOR THAT LUNATIC TO GET AT US!
YEAH? WELL, MY OWN DAUGHTER WAS KILLED IN THAT

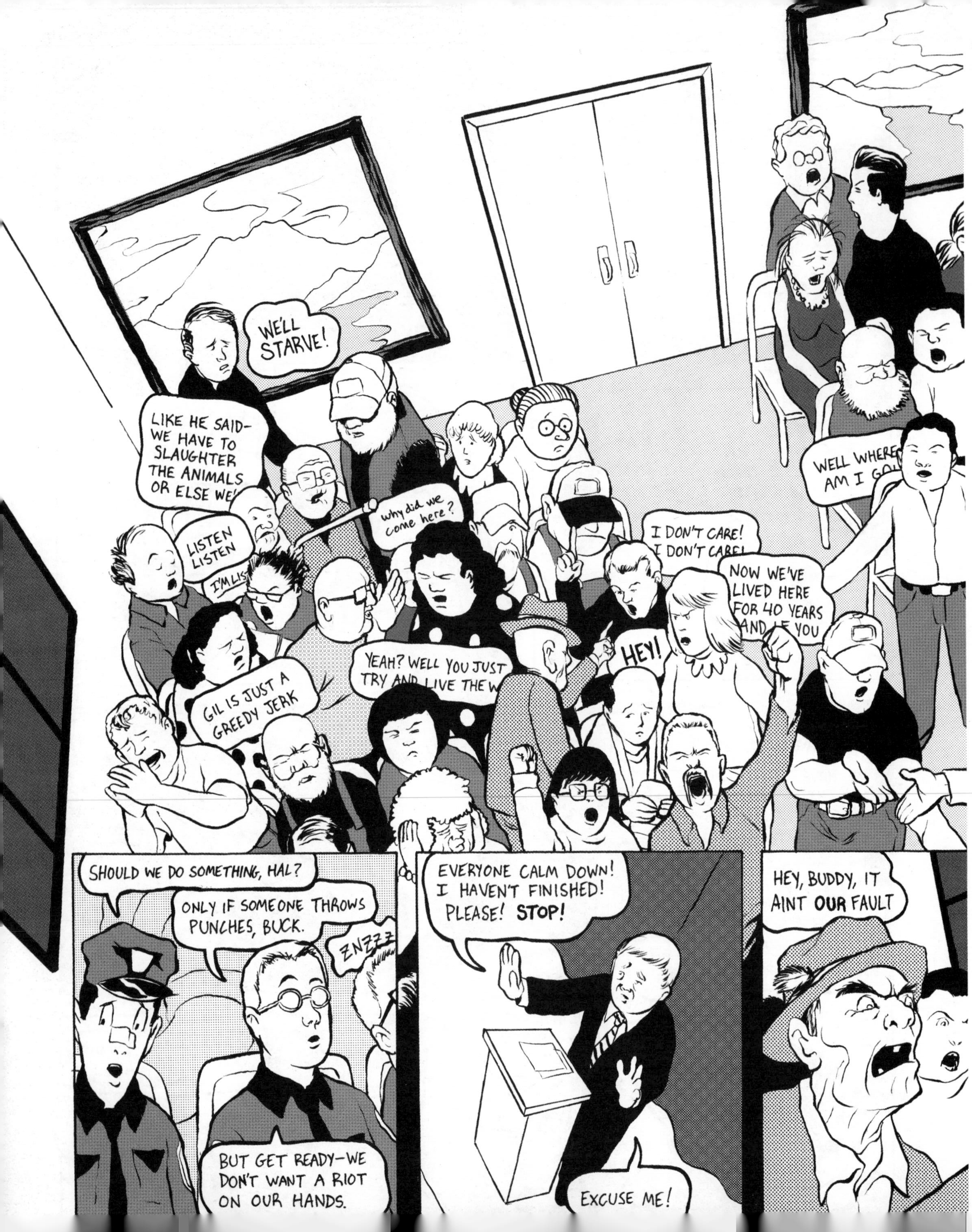
WE'LL STARVE!
LIKE HE SAID- WE HAVE TO SLAUGHTER THE ANIMALS OR ELSE WE
LISTEN LISTEN
I'M LIS
why did we come here?
I DON'T CARE! I DON'T CARE!
NOW WE'VE LIVED HERE FOR 40 YEARS AND
WELL WHERE AM I
YEAH? WELL YOU JUST TRY AND LIVE THE
HEY!
GIL IS JUST A GREEDY JERK
SHOULD WE DO SOMETHING, HAL?
ONLY IF SOMEONE THROWS PUNCHES, BUCK.
ZNZZZ
BUT GET READY—WE DON'T WANT A RIOT ON OUR HANDS.
EVERYONE CALM DOWN! I HAVEN'T FINISHED! PLEASE! **STOP!**
EXCUSE ME!
HEY, BUDDY, IT AINT **OUR** FAULT

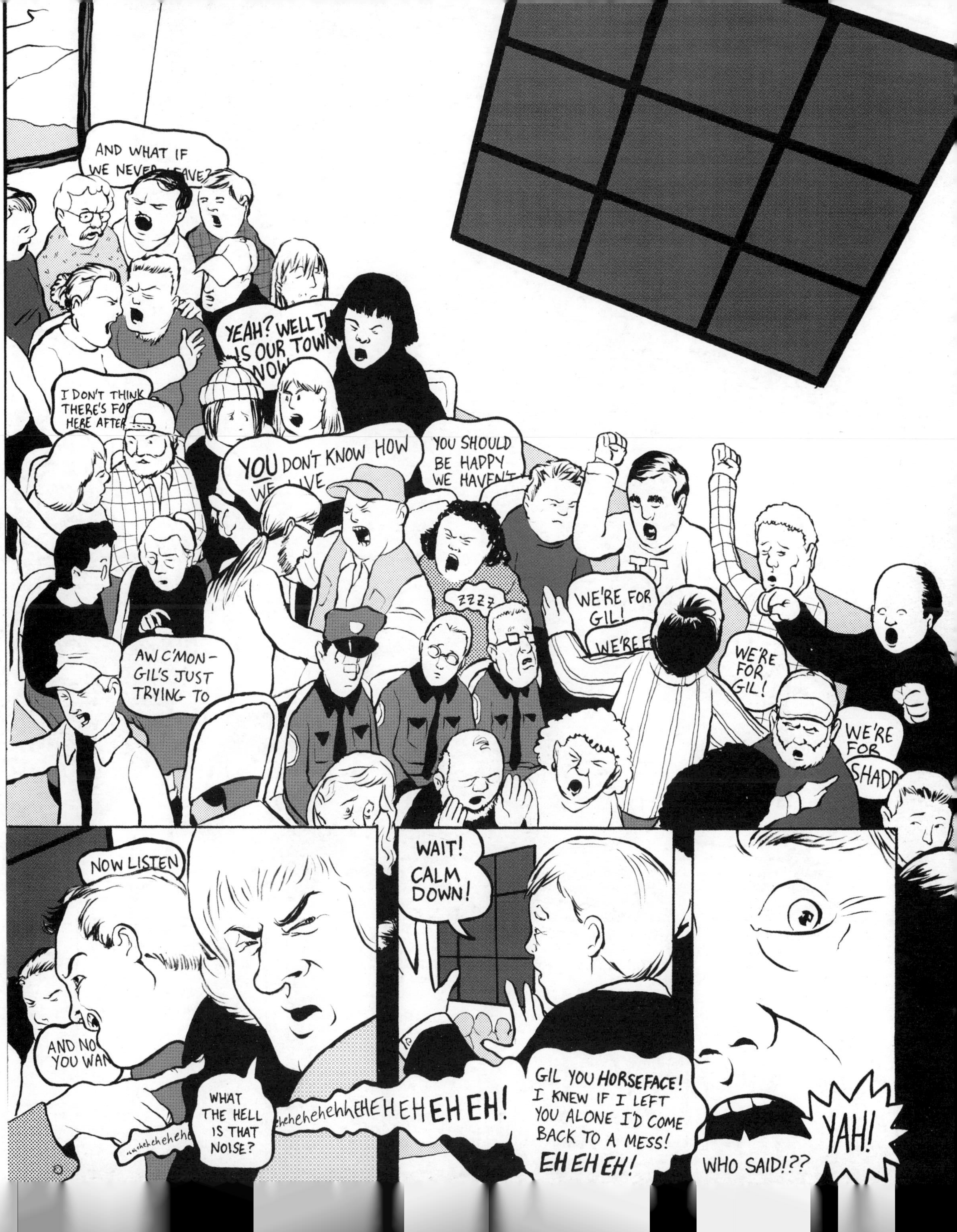
AND WHAT IF WE NEVER LEAVE?
YEAH? WELL TH IS OUR TOWN NOW
I DON'T THINK THERE'S FO HERE AFTER
YOU DON'T KNOW HOW WE LIVE
YOU SHOULD BE HAPPY WE HAVEN'T
ZZZZ
WE'RE FOR GIL!
WE'RE F
WE'RE FOR GIL!
WE'RE FOR SHADD
AW C'MON-GIL'S JUST TRYING TO
NOW LISTEN
AND NO YOU WAN
WHAT THE HELL IS THAT NOISE?
ehehehehehehehehehehhEHEHEHEHEH!
WAIT! CALM DOWN!
GIL YOU HORSEFACE! I KNEW IF I LEFT YOU ALONE I'D COME BACK TO A MESS! EHEHEH!
WHO SAID!??
YAH!

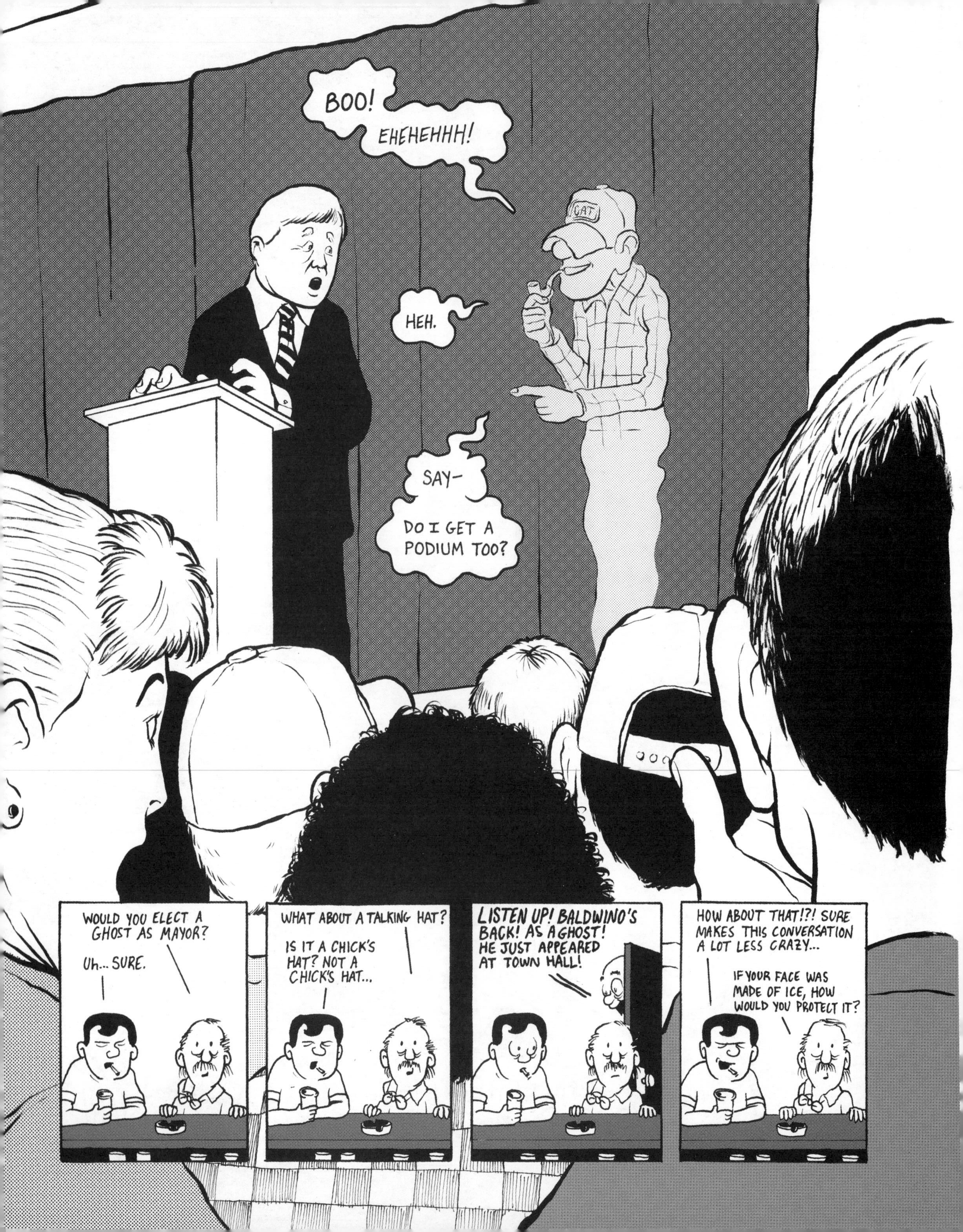
BOO!
EHEHEHHH!
HEH.
SAY-
DO I GET A PODIUM TOO?
CAT
WOULD YOU ELECT A GHOST AS MAYOR?
Uh... SURE.
WHAT ABOUT A TALKING HAT?
IS IT A CHICK'S HAT? NOT A CHICK'S HAT...
LISTEN UP! BALDWINO'S BACK! AS A GHOST! HE JUST APPEARED AT TOWN HALL!
HOW ABOUT THAT!?! SURE MAKES THIS CONVERSATION A LOT LESS CRAZY...
IF YOUR FACE WAS MADE OF ICE, HOW WOULD YOU PROTECT IT?

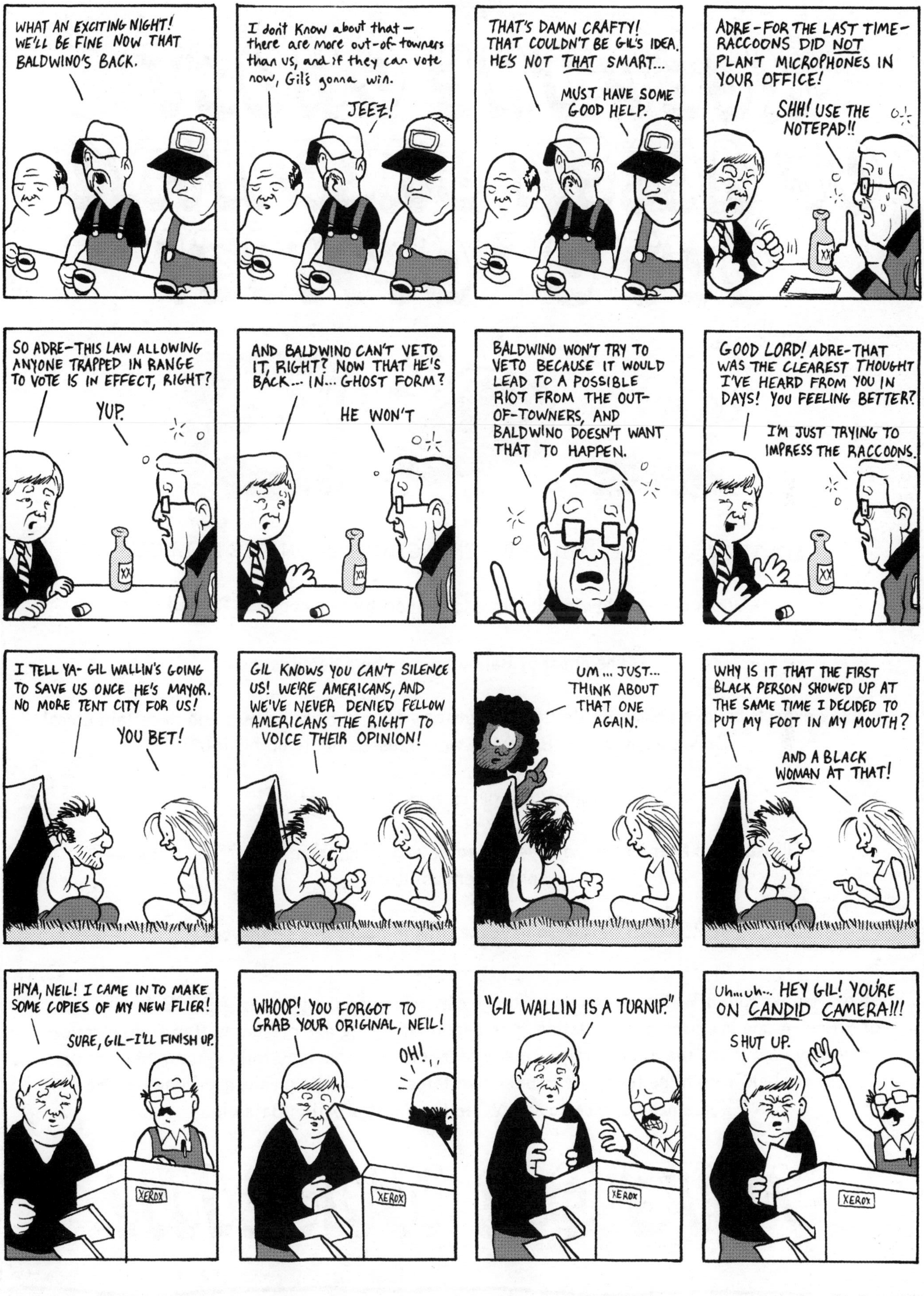

WHAT AN EXCITING NIGHT! WE'LL BE FINE NOW THAT BALDWINO'S BACK.
I don't know about that — there are more out-of-towners than us, and if they can vote now, Gil's gonna win.
JEEZ!
THAT'S DAMN CRAFTY! THAT COULDN'T BE GIL'S IDEA. HE'S NOT THAT SMART...
MUST HAVE SOME GOOD HELP.
ADRE — FOR THE LAST TIME — RACCOONS DID NOT PLANT MICROPHONES IN YOUR OFFICE!
SHH! USE THE NOTEPAD!!
SO ADRE — THIS LAW ALLOWING ANYONE TRAPPED IN RANGE TO VOTE IS IN EFFECT, RIGHT?
YUP.
AND BALDWINO CAN'T VETO IT, RIGHT? NOW THAT HE'S BACK... IN... GHOST FORM?
HE WON'T
BALDWINO WON'T TRY TO VETO BECAUSE IT WOULD LEAD TO A POSSIBLE RIOT FROM THE OUT-OF-TOWNERS, AND BALDWINO DOESN'T WANT THAT TO HAPPEN.
GOOD LORD! ADRE — THAT WAS THE CLEAREST THOUGHT I'VE HEARD FROM YOU IN DAYS! YOU FEELING BETTER?
I'M JUST TRYING TO IMPRESS THE RACCOONS.
I TELL YA — GIL WALLIN'S GOING TO SAVE US ONCE HE'S MAYOR. NO MORE TENT CITY FOR US!
YOU BET!
GIL KNOWS YOU CAN'T SILENCE US! WE'RE AMERICANS, AND WE'VE NEVER DENIED FELLOW AMERICANS THE RIGHT TO VOICE THEIR OPINION!
UM... JUST... THINK ABOUT THAT ONE AGAIN.
WHY IS IT THAT THE FIRST BLACK PERSON SHOWED UP AT THE SAME TIME I DECIDED TO PUT MY FOOT IN MY MOUTH?
AND A BLACK WOMAN AT THAT!
HIYA, NEIL! I CAME IN TO MAKE SOME COPIES OF MY NEW FLIER!
SURE, GIL — I'LL FINISH UP.
XEROX
WHOOP! YOU FORGOT TO GRAB YOUR ORIGINAL, NEIL!
OH!
XEROX
"GIL WALLIN IS A TURNIP."
XEROX
Uh... uh... HEY GIL! YOU'RE ON CANDID CAMERA!!!
SHUT UP.
XEROX

KEEP THE GHOST OF ALLEN BALDWINO OUT OF OFFICE!

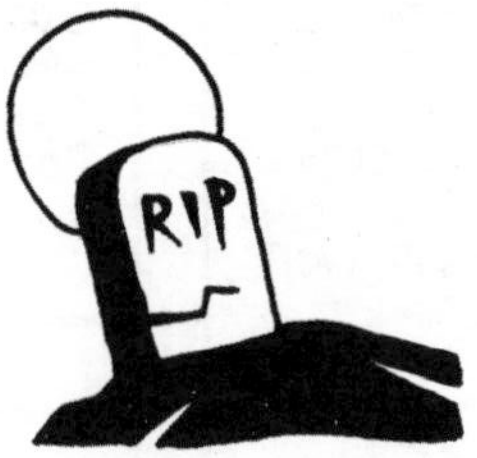
RIP
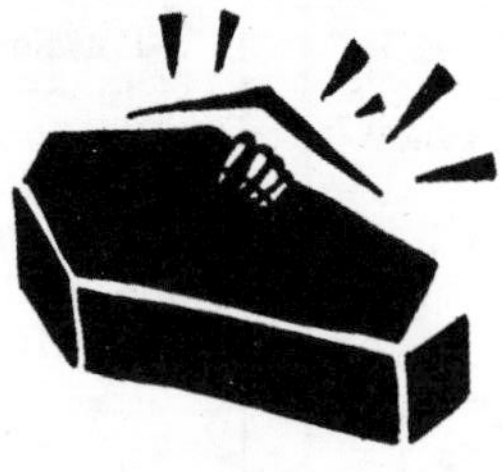
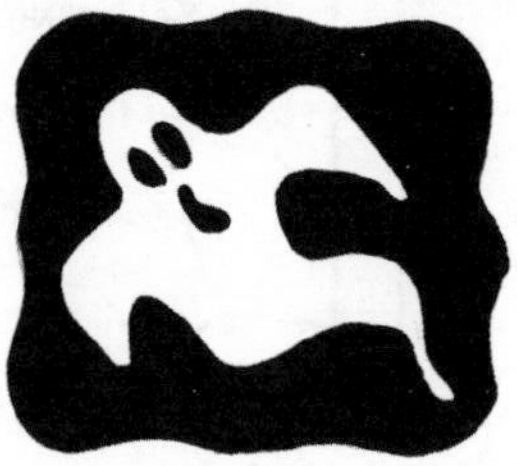

SIX THINGS TO CONSIDER WHEN A GHOST IS ON THE BALLOT:

- When alive, Baldwino did little to support those trapped in Range!
- The ghost of Baldwino may be a demon!
- Many experts believe ghosts are limited to appearing only in certain times and in certain areas! Do we want to give Baldwino *more* reasons not to do his job?
- A ghost has never won an election!
- Ghosts have been known to possess people and make them do horrible things—even innocent children!
- How will Baldwino have the time to haunt *and* be mayor?

Now, thanks to Gil Wallin, *everyone* in Range can help keep the ghost of Allen Baldwino out of office! A law has been passed stating "any person of voting age present in Range on election day may vote in the mayoral election, or any other election that may follow, until they are no longer held within the town due to unknown forces." And this means everyone will be guaranteed a voice to say NO to the ghost of Allen Baldwino!

VOTE GIL WALLIN!

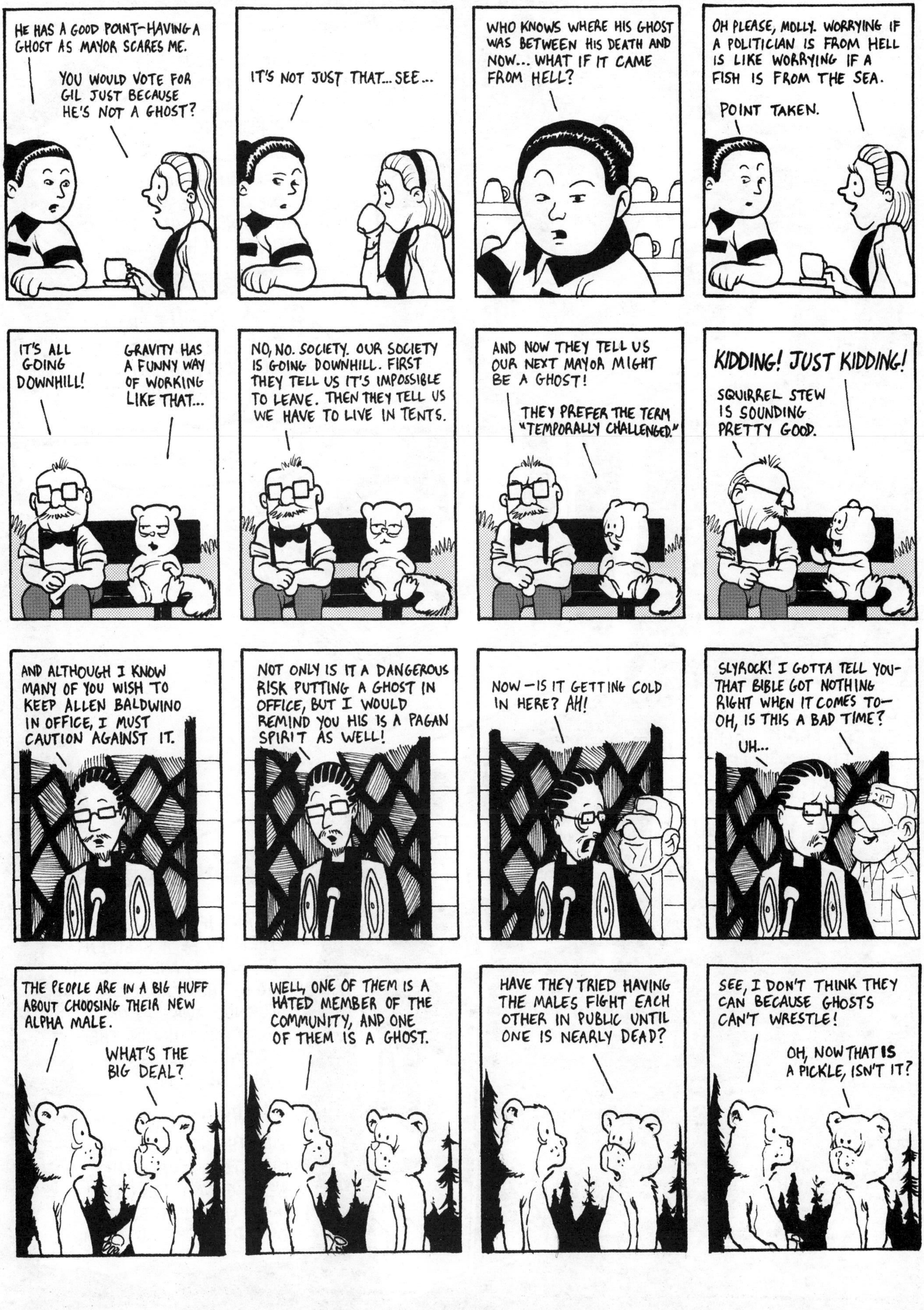
HE HAS A GOOD POINT—HAVING A GHOST AS MAYOR SCARES ME.
YOU WOULD VOTE FOR GIL JUST BECAUSE HE'S NOT A GHOST?
IT'S NOT JUST THAT... SEE...
WHO KNOWS WHERE HIS GHOST WAS BETWEEN HIS DEATH AND NOW... WHAT IF IT CAME FROM HELL?
OH PLEASE, MOLLY. WORRYING IF A POLITICIAN IS FROM HELL IS LIKE WORRYING IF A FISH IS FROM THE SEA.
POINT TAKEN.
IT'S ALL GOING DOWNHILL!
GRAVITY HAS A FUNNY WAY OF WORKING LIKE THAT...
NO, NO. SOCIETY. OUR SOCIETY IS GOING DOWNHILL. FIRST THEY TELL US IT'S IMPOSSIBLE TO LEAVE. THEN THEY TELL US WE HAVE TO LIVE IN TENTS.
AND NOW THEY TELL US OUR NEXT MAYOR MIGHT BE A GHOST!
THEY PREFER THE TERM "TEMPORALLY CHALLENGED."
KIDDING! JUST KIDDING!
SQUIRREL STEW IS SOUNDING PRETTY GOOD.
AND ALTHOUGH I KNOW MANY OF YOU WISH TO KEEP ALLEN BALDWINO IN OFFICE, I MUST CAUTION AGAINST IT.
NOT ONLY IS IT A DANGEROUS RISK PUTTING A GHOST IN OFFICE, BUT I WOULD REMIND YOU HIS IS A PAGAN SPIRIT AS WELL!
NOW—IS IT GETTING COLD IN HERE? AH!
SLYROCK! I GOTTA TELL YOU—THAT BIBLE GOT NOTHING RIGHT WHEN IT COMES TO—OH, IS THIS A BAD TIME?
UH...
THE PEOPLE ARE IN A BIG HUFF ABOUT CHOOSING THEIR NEW ALPHA MALE.
WHAT'S THE BIG DEAL?
WELL, ONE OF THEM IS A HATED MEMBER OF THE COMMUNITY, AND ONE OF THEM IS A GHOST.
HAVE THEY TRIED HAVING THE MALES FIGHT EACH OTHER IN PUBLIC UNTIL ONE IS NEARLY DEAD?
SEE, I DON'T THINK THEY CAN BECAUSE GHOSTS CAN'T WRESTLE!
OH, NOW THAT IS A PICKLE, ISN'T IT?

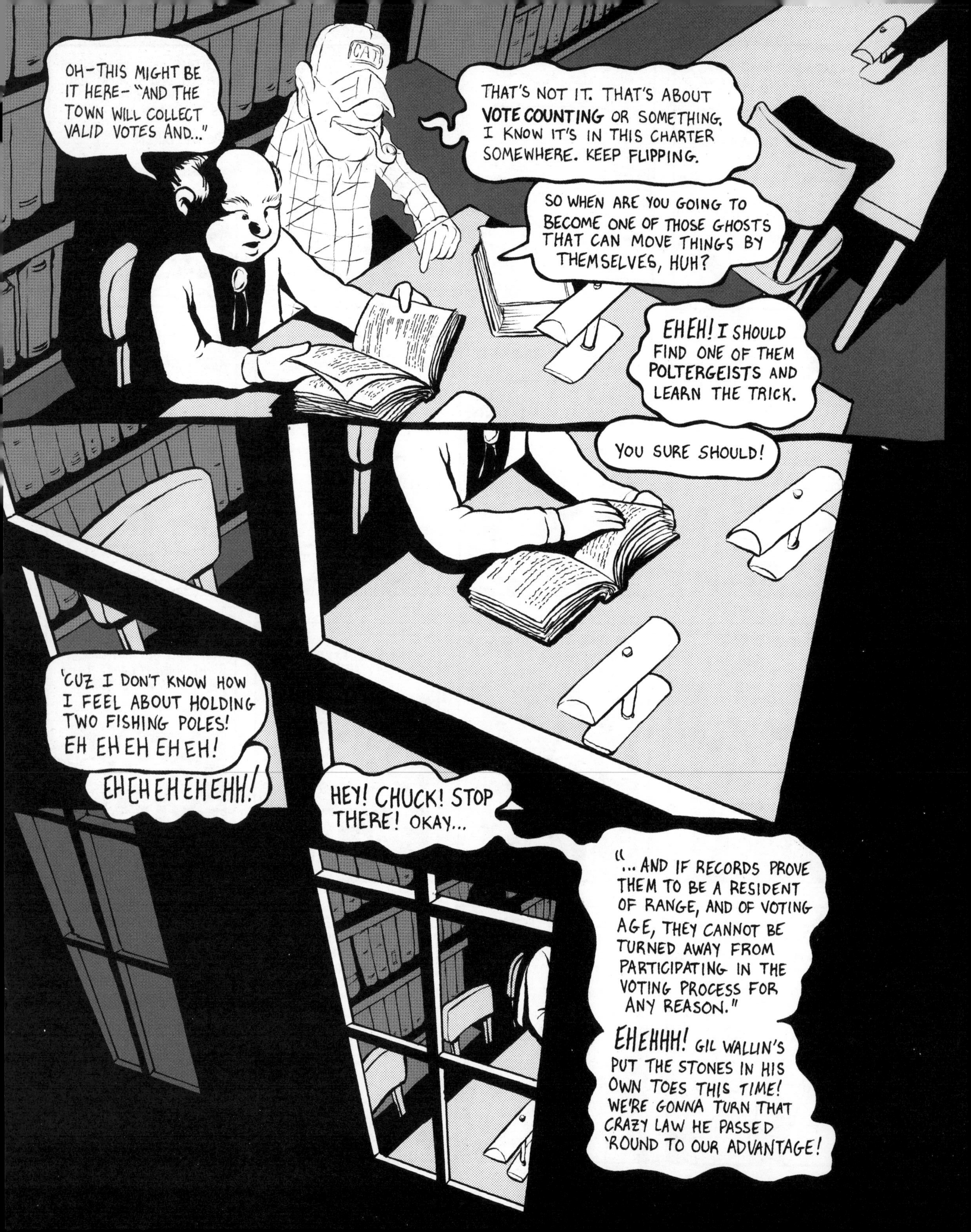
OH-THIS MIGHT BE IT HERE- "AND THE TOWN WILL COLLECT VALID VOTES AND..."
THAT'S NOT IT. THAT'S ABOUT **VOTE COUNTING** OR SOMETHING. I KNOW IT'S IN THIS CHARTER SOMEWHERE. KEEP FLIPPING.
SO WHEN ARE YOU GOING TO BECOME ONE OF THOSE GHOSTS THAT CAN MOVE THINGS BY THEMSELVES, HUH?
EHEH! I SHOULD FIND ONE OF THEM POLTERGEISTS AND LEARN THE TRICK.
YOU SURE SHOULD!
'CUZ I DON'T KNOW HOW I FEEL ABOUT HOLDING TWO FISHING POLES! EH EH EH EH EH!
EHEHEHEHEHH!
HEY! CHUCK! STOP THERE! OKAY...
"...AND IF RECORDS PROVE THEM TO BE A RESIDENT OF RANGE, AND OF VOTING AGE, THEY CANNOT BE TURNED AWAY FROM PARTICIPATING IN THE VOTING PROCESS FOR ANY REASON."
EHEHHH! GIL WALLIN'S PUT THE STONES IN HIS OWN TOES THIS TIME! WE'RE GONNA TURN THAT CRAZY LAW HE PASSED 'ROUND TO OUR ADVANTAGE!

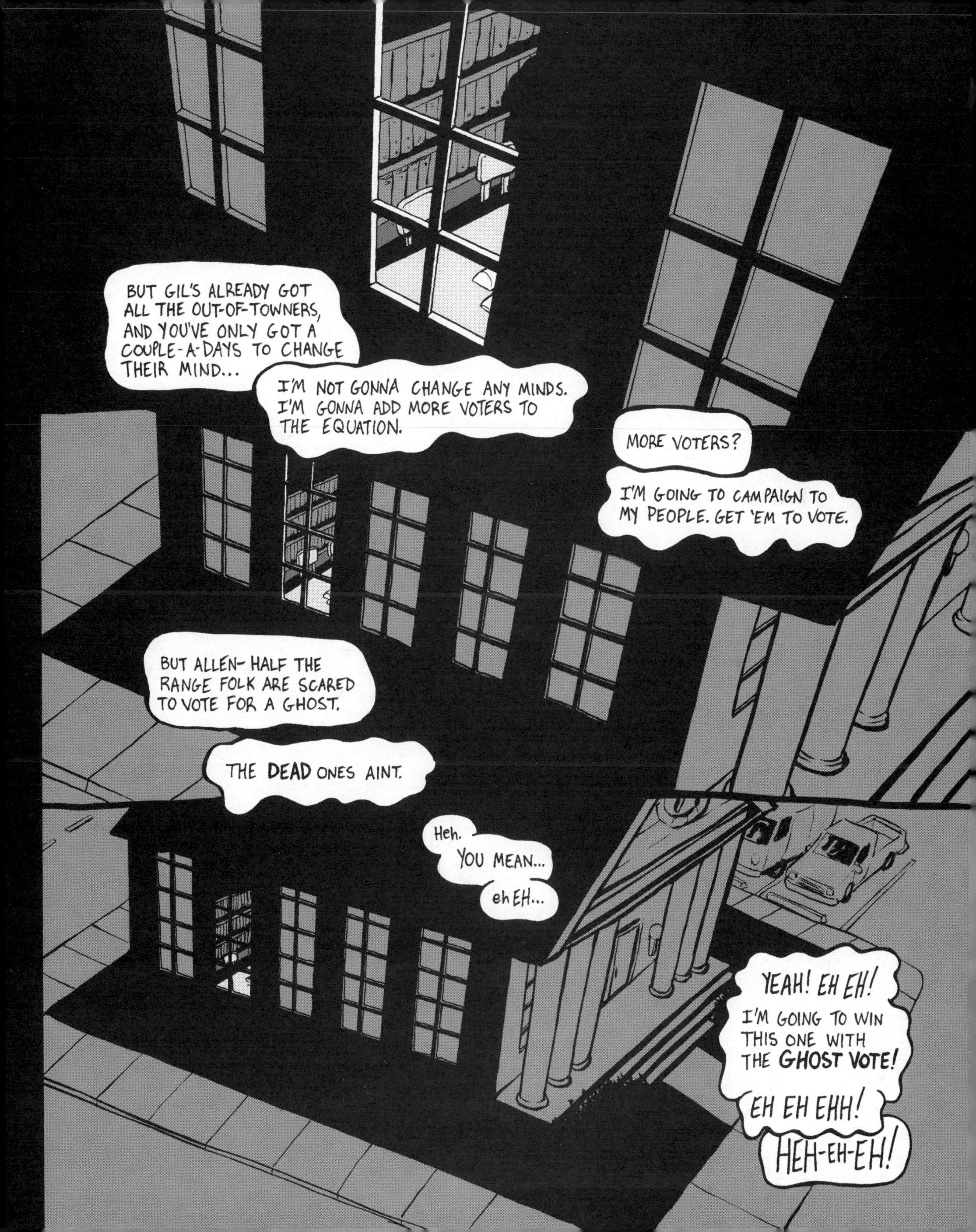
BUT GIL'S ALREADY GOT ALL THE OUT-OF-TOWNERS, AND YOU'VE ONLY GOT A COUPLE-A-DAYS TO CHANGE THEIR MIND...
I'M NOT GONNA CHANGE ANY MINDS. I'M GONNA ADD MORE VOTERS TO THE EQUATION.
MORE VOTERS?
I'M GOING TO CAMPAIGN TO MY PEOPLE. GET 'EM TO VOTE.
BUT ALLEN- HALF THE RANGE FOLK ARE SCARED TO VOTE FOR A GHOST.
THE **DEAD** ONES AINT.
Heh.
YOU MEAN...
eh EH...
YEAH! EH EH!
I'M GOING TO WIN THIS ONE WITH THE **GHOST VOTE**!
EH EH EHH!
HEH-EH-EH!

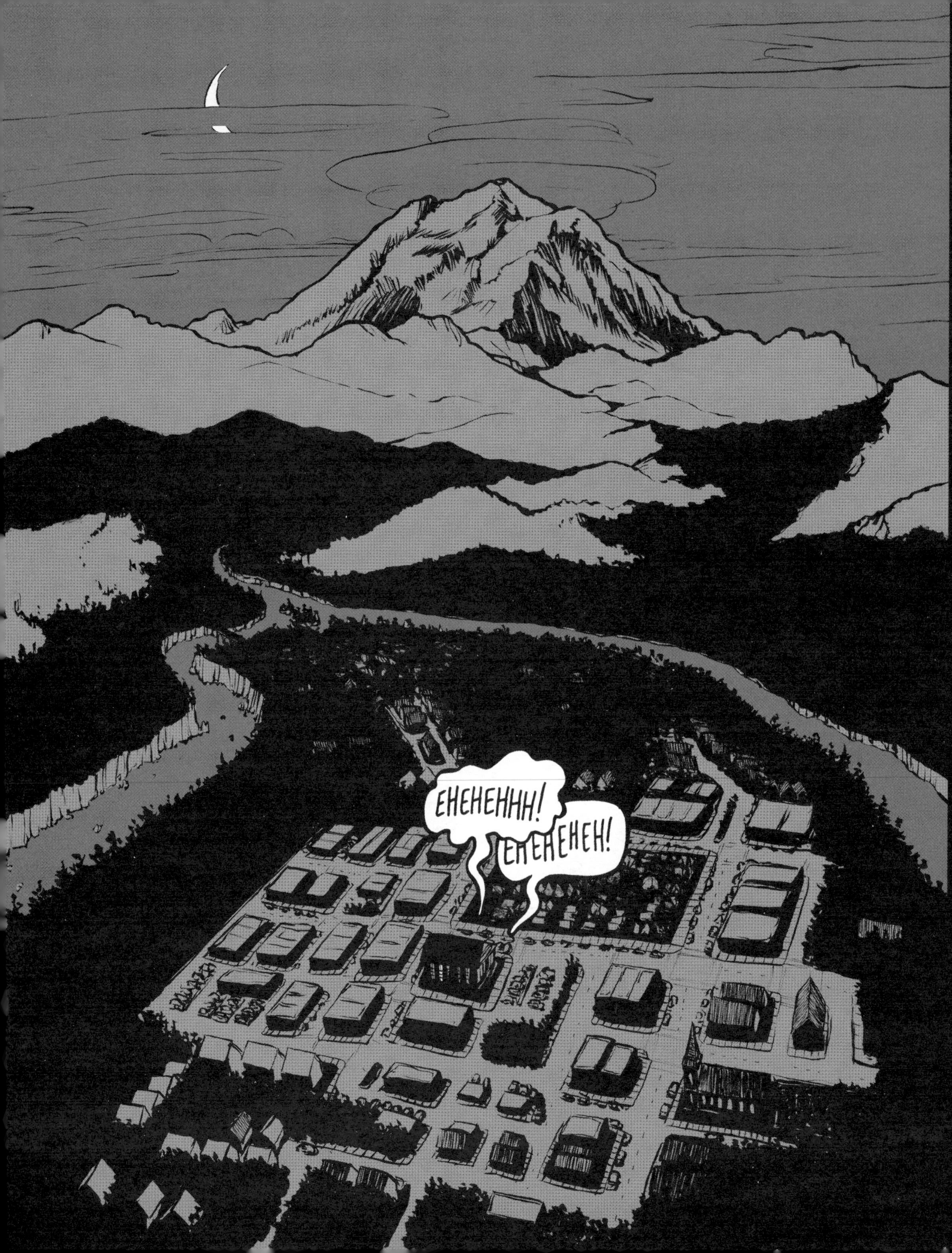
EHEHEHHH!
EHEHEHEH!

10.
ELECTION

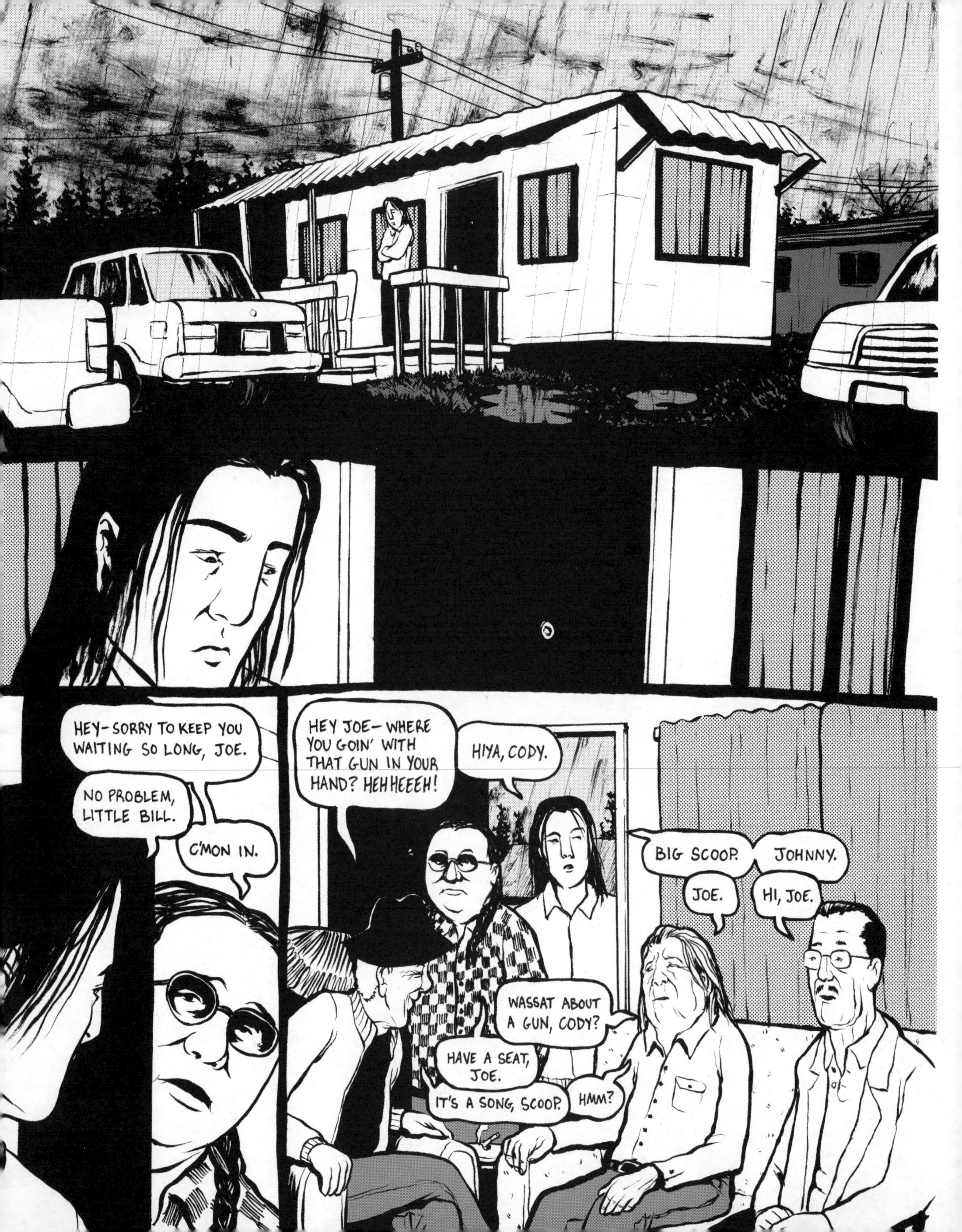
HEY- SORRY TO KEEP YOU WAITING SO LONG, JOE.
NO PROBLEM, LITTLE BILL.
C'MON IN.
HEY JOE- WHERE YOU GOIN' WITH THAT GUN IN YOUR HAND? HEHHEEEH!
HIYA, CODY.
BIG SCOOP.
JOE.
JOHNNY.
HI, JOE.
WASSAT ABOUT A GUN, CODY?
HAVE A SEAT, JOE.
IT'S A SONG, SCOOP.
HMM?

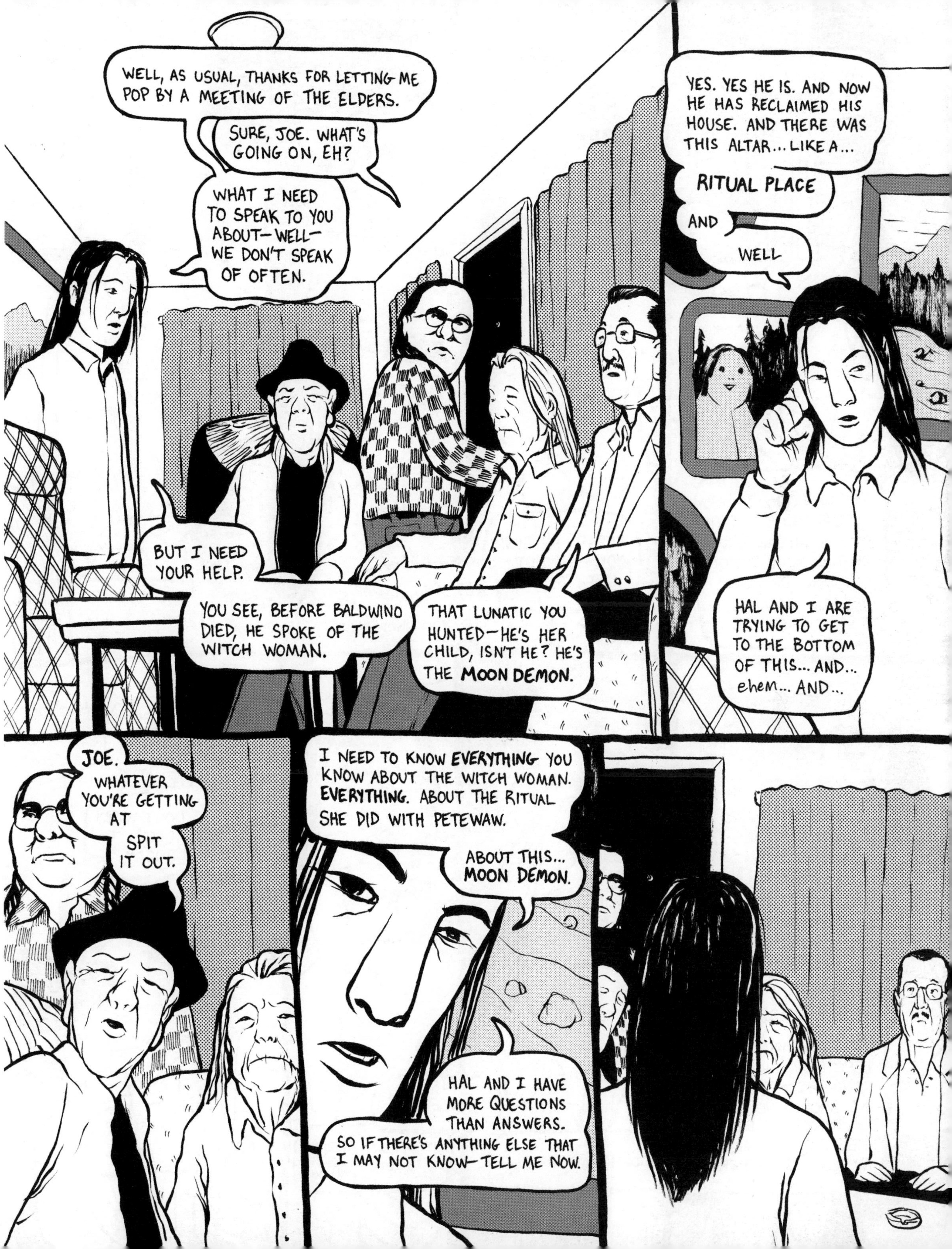
WELL, AS USUAL, THANKS FOR LETTING ME POP BY A MEETING OF THE ELDERS.
SURE, JOE. WHAT'S GOING ON, EH?
WHAT I NEED TO SPEAK TO YOU ABOUT—WELL— WE DON'T SPEAK OF OFTEN.
BUT I NEED YOUR HELP.
YOU SEE, BEFORE BALDWIND DIED, HE SPOKE OF THE WITCH WOMAN.
THAT LUNATIC YOU HUNTED—HE'S HER CHILD, ISN'T HE? HE'S THE **MOON DEMON.**
YES. YES HE IS. AND NOW HE HAS RECLAIMED HIS HOUSE. AND THERE WAS THIS ALTAR... LIKE A...
RITUAL PLACE
AND
WELL
HAL AND I ARE TRYING TO GET TO THE BOTTOM OF THIS... AND... ehem... AND...
JOE.
WHATEVER YOU'RE GETTING AT
SPIT IT OUT.
I NEED TO KNOW **EVERYTHING** YOU KNOW ABOUT THE WITCH WOMAN. **EVERYTHING.** ABOUT THE RITUAL SHE DID WITH PETEWAW.
ABOUT THIS... **MOON DEMON.**
HAL AND I HAVE MORE QUESTIONS THAN ANSWERS.
SO IF THERE'S ANYTHING ELSE THAT I MAY NOT KNOW—TELL ME NOW.

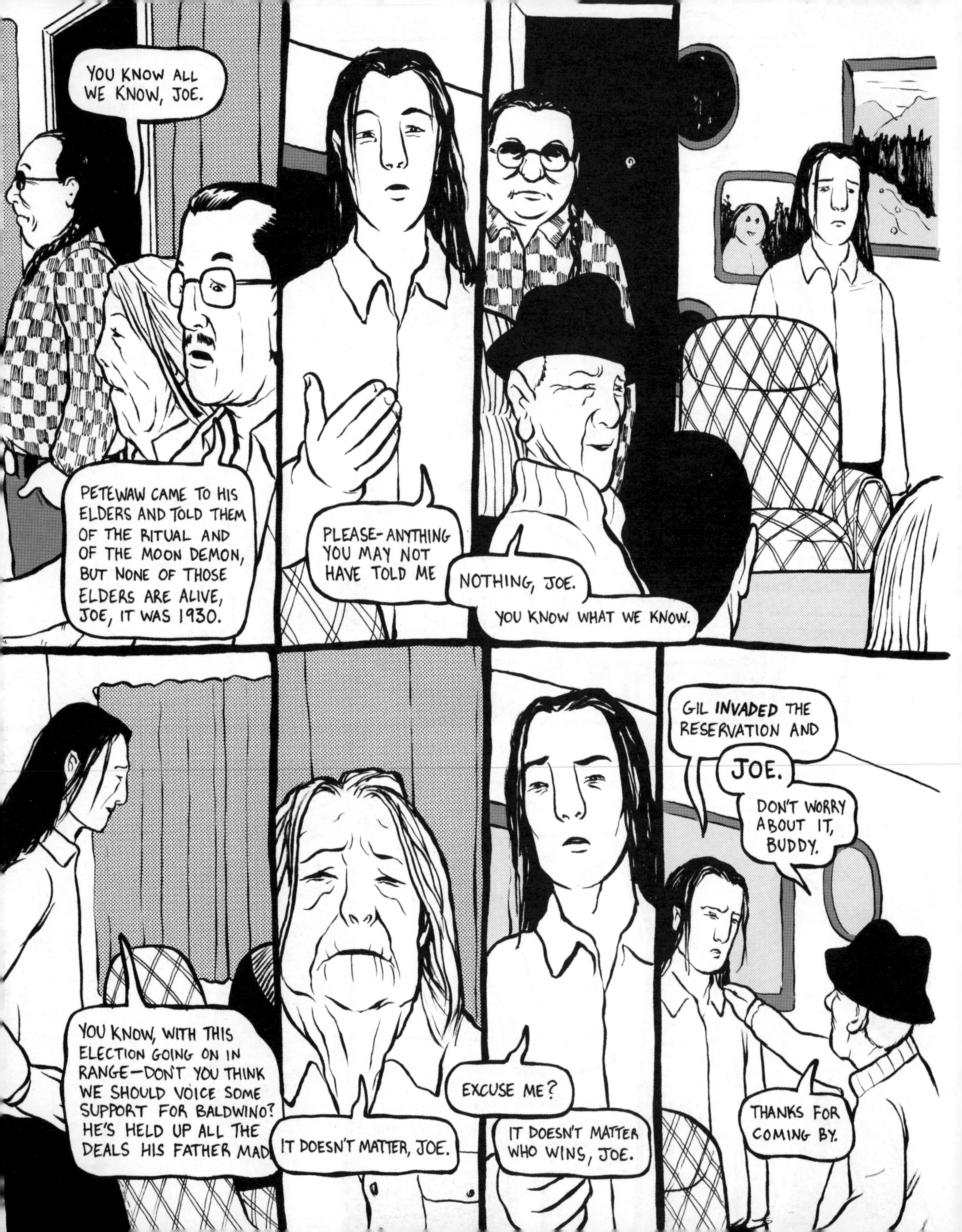
YOU KNOW ALL WE KNOW, JOE.
PETEWAW CAME TO HIS ELDERS AND TOLD THEM OF THE RITUAL AND OF THE MOON DEMON, BUT NONE OF THOSE ELDERS ARE ALIVE, JOE, IT WAS 1930.
PLEASE-ANYTHING YOU MAY NOT HAVE TOLD ME
NOTHING, JOE.
YOU KNOW WHAT WE KNOW.
YOU KNOW, WITH THIS ELECTION GOING ON IN RANGE—DON'T YOU THINK WE SHOULD VOICE SOME SUPPORT FOR BALDWINO? HE'S HELD UP ALL THE DEALS HIS FATHER MAD
IT DOESN'T MATTER, JOE.
EXCUSE ME?
IT DOESN'T MATTER WHO WINS, JOE.
GIL INVADED THE RESERVATION AND
JOE.
DON'T WORRY ABOUT IT, BUDDY.
THANKS FOR COMING BY.

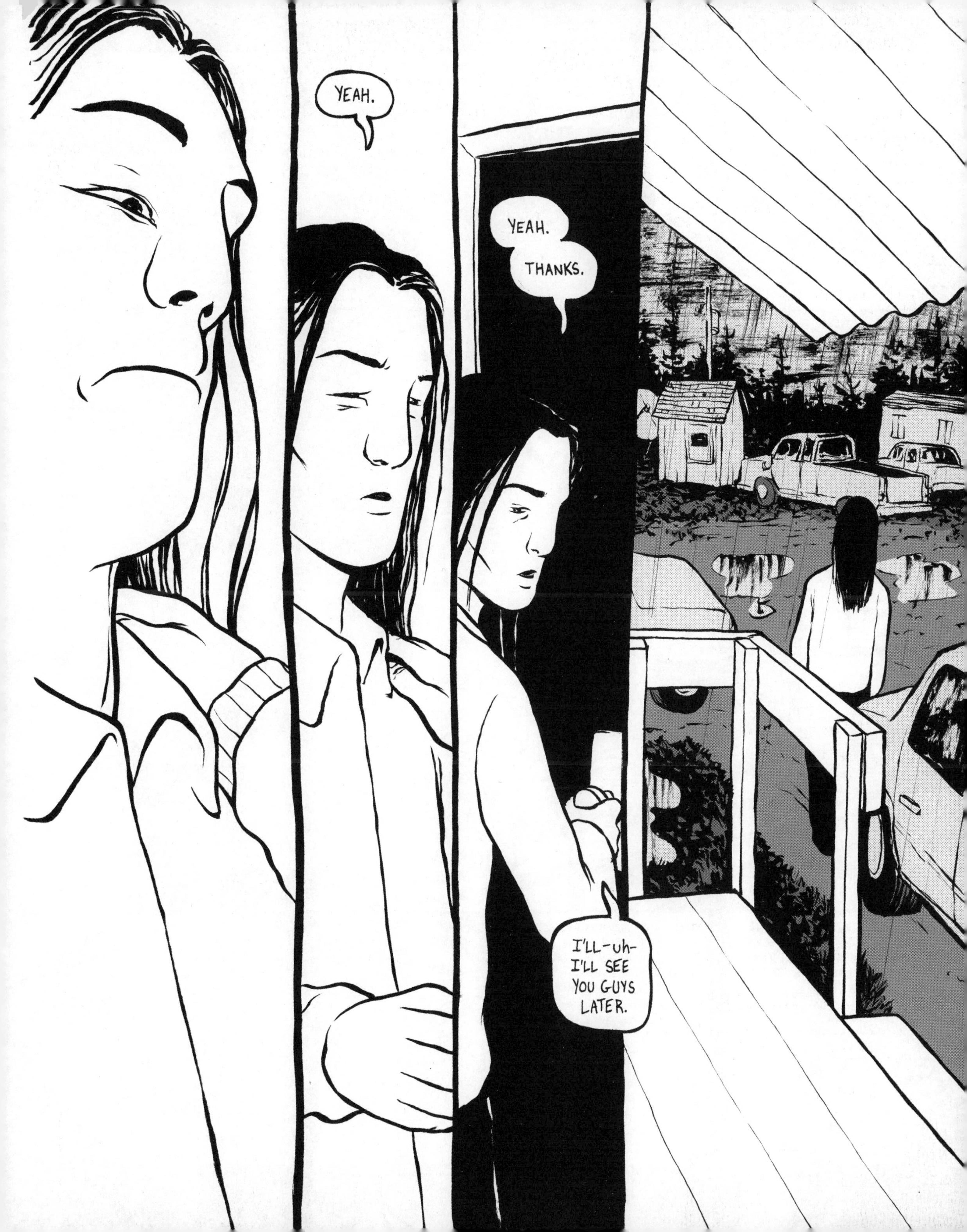
YEAH.
YEAH.
THANKS.
I'LL-uh-
I'LL SEE
YOU GUYS
LATER.

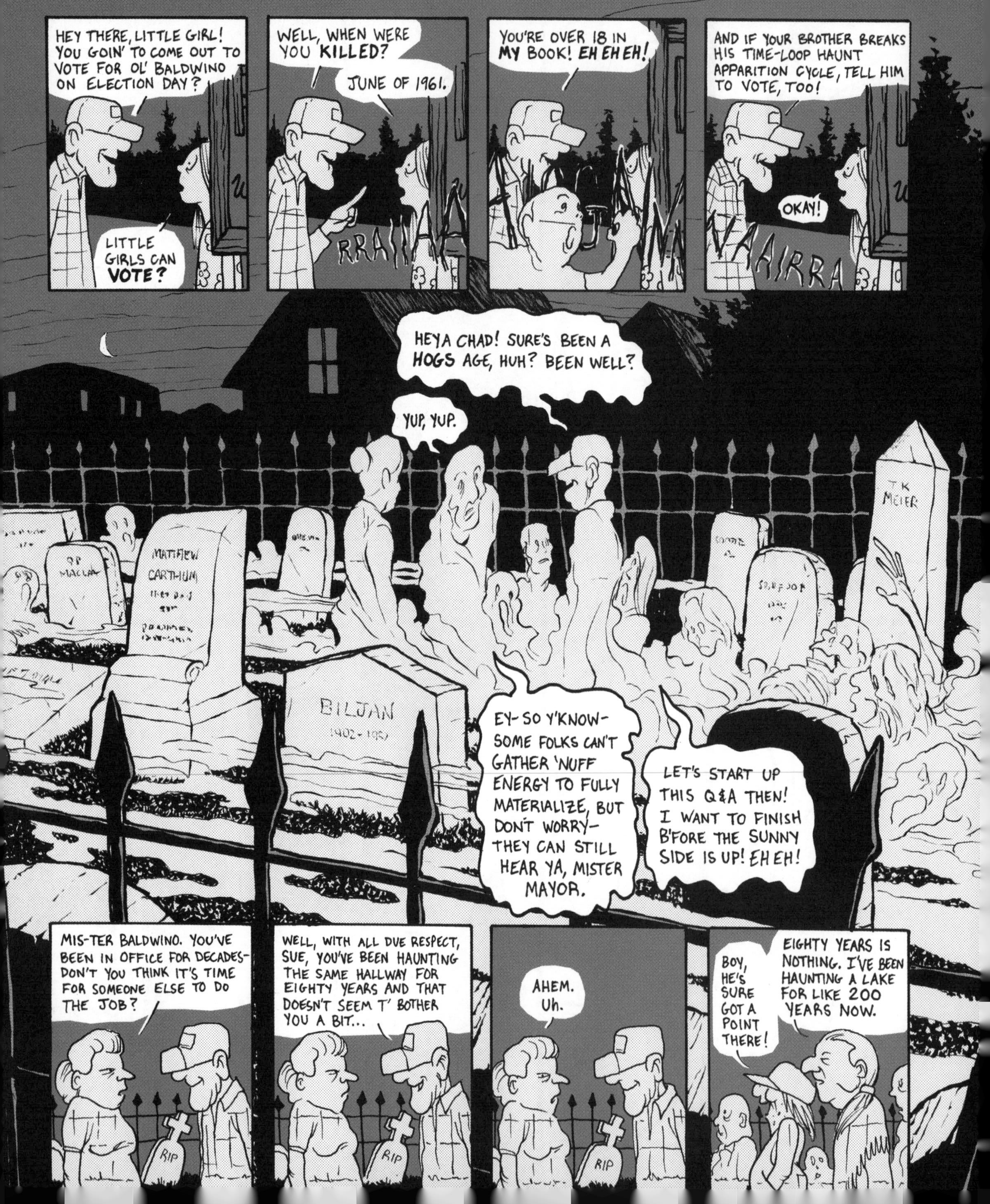
HEY THERE, LITTLE GIRL! YOU GOIN' TO COME OUT TO VOTE FOR OL' BALDWINO ON ELECTION DAY?
LITTLE GIRLS CAN VOTE?
WELL, WHEN WERE YOU KILLED?
JUNE OF 1961.
RRAIIAA
YOU'RE OVER 18 IN MY BOOK! EH EH EH!
AND IF YOUR BROTHER BREAKS HIS TIME-LOOP HAUNT APPARITION CYCLE, TELL HIM TO VOTE, TOO!
OKAY!
VAAIRRA
HEYA CHAD! SURE'S BEEN A HOGS AGE, HUH? BEEN WELL?
YUP, YUP.
T.K. MEIER
MATTHEW CARTHUM
BILJAN
1902–1951
EY- SO Y'KNOW- SOME FOLKS CAN'T GATHER 'NUFF ENERGY TO FULLY MATERIALIZE, BUT DON'T WORRY- THEY CAN STILL HEAR YA, MISTER MAYOR.
LET'S START UP THIS Q&A THEN! I WANT TO FINISH B'FORE THE SUNNY SIDE IS UP! EH EH!
MIS-TER BALDWINO. YOU'VE BEEN IN OFFICE FOR DECADES- DON'T YOU THINK IT'S TIME FOR SOMEONE ELSE TO DO THE JOB?
RIP
WELL, WITH ALL DUE RESPECT, SUE, YOU'VE BEEN HAUNTING THE SAME HALLWAY FOR EIGHTY YEARS AND THAT DOESN'T SEEM T' BOTHER YOU A BIT...
RIP
AHEM. Uh.
RIP
EIGHTY YEARS IS NOTHING. I'VE BEEN HAUNTING A LAKE FOR LIKE 200 YEARS NOW.
BOY, HE'S SURE GOT A POINT THERE!

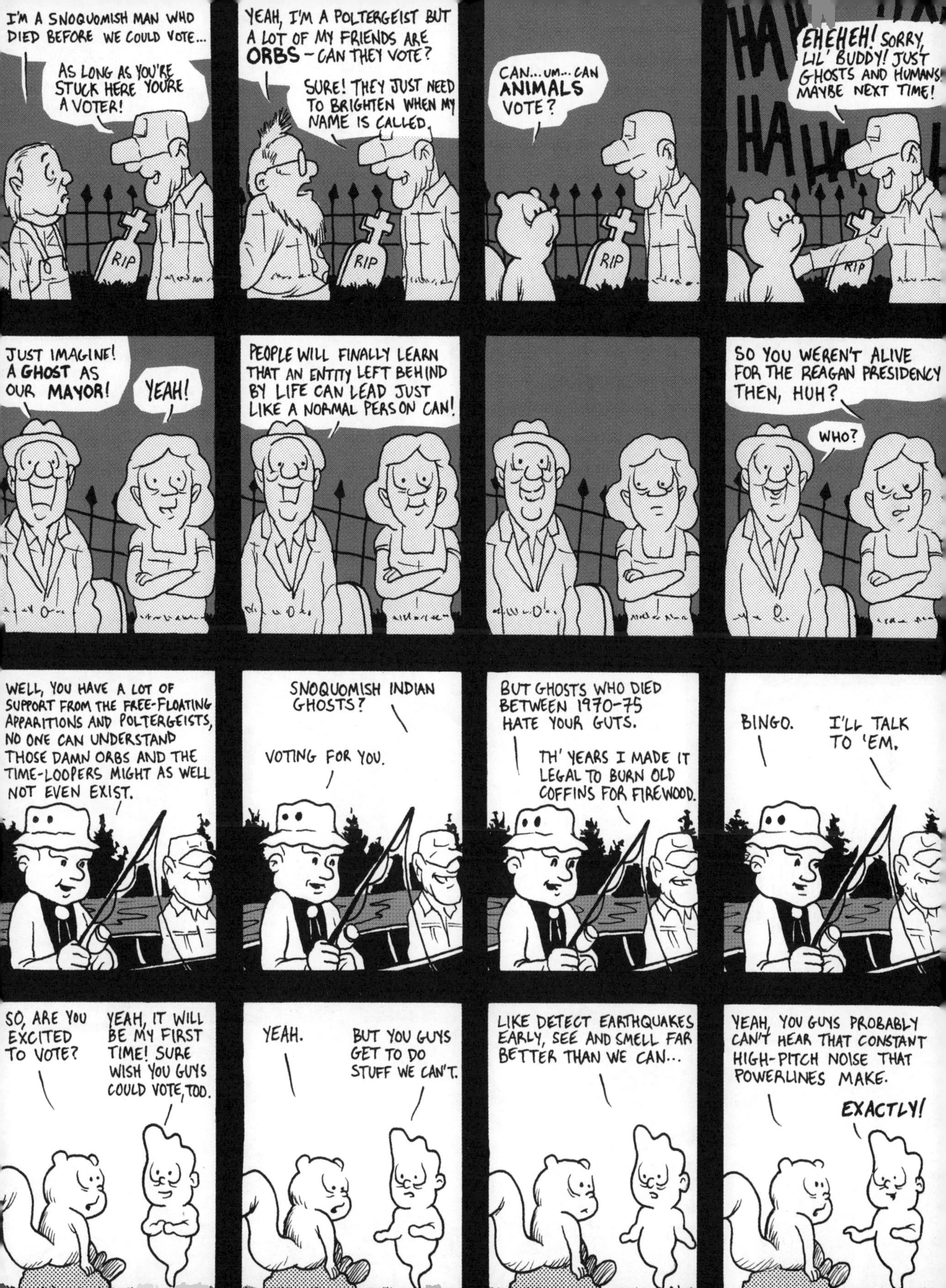
I'M A SNOQUOMISH MAN WHO DIED BEFORE WE COULD VOTE...
AS LONG AS YOU'RE STUCK HERE YOU'RE A VOTER!
YEAH, I'M A POLTERGEIST BUT A LOT OF MY FRIENDS ARE ORBS – CAN THEY VOTE?
SURE! THEY JUST NEED TO BRIGHTEN WHEN MY NAME IS CALLED.
CAN... UM... CAN ANIMALS VOTE?
HA HA HA
EHEHEH! SORRY, LIL' BUDDY! JUST GHOSTS AND HUMANS! MAYBE NEXT TIME!
JUST IMAGINE! A GHOST AS OUR MAYOR!
YEAH!
PEOPLE WILL FINALLY LEARN THAT AN ENTITY LEFT BEHIND BY LIFE CAN LEAD JUST LIKE A NORMAL PERSON CAN!
SO YOU WEREN'T ALIVE FOR THE REAGAN PRESIDENCY THEN, HUH?
WHO?
WELL, YOU HAVE A LOT OF SUPPORT FROM THE FREE-FLOATING APPARITIONS AND POLTERGEISTS, NO ONE CAN UNDERSTAND THOSE DAMN ORBS AND THE TIME-LOOPERS MIGHT AS WELL NOT EVEN EXIST.
SNOQUOMISH INDIAN GHOSTS?
VOTING FOR YOU.
BUT GHOSTS WHO DIED BETWEEN 1970-75 HATE YOUR GUTS.
TH' YEARS I MADE IT LEGAL TO BURN OLD COFFINS FOR FIREWOOD.
BINGO.
I'LL TALK TO 'EM.
SO, ARE YOU EXCITED TO VOTE?
YEAH, IT WILL BE MY FIRST TIME! SURE WISH YOU GUYS COULD VOTE, TOO.
YEAH.
BUT YOU GUYS GET TO DO STUFF WE CAN'T.
LIKE DETECT EARTHQUAKES EARLY, SEE AND SMELL FAR BETTER THAN WE CAN...
YEAH, YOU GUYS PROBABLY CAN'T HEAR THAT CONSTANT HIGH-PITCH NOISE THAT POWERLINES MAKE.
EXACTLY!

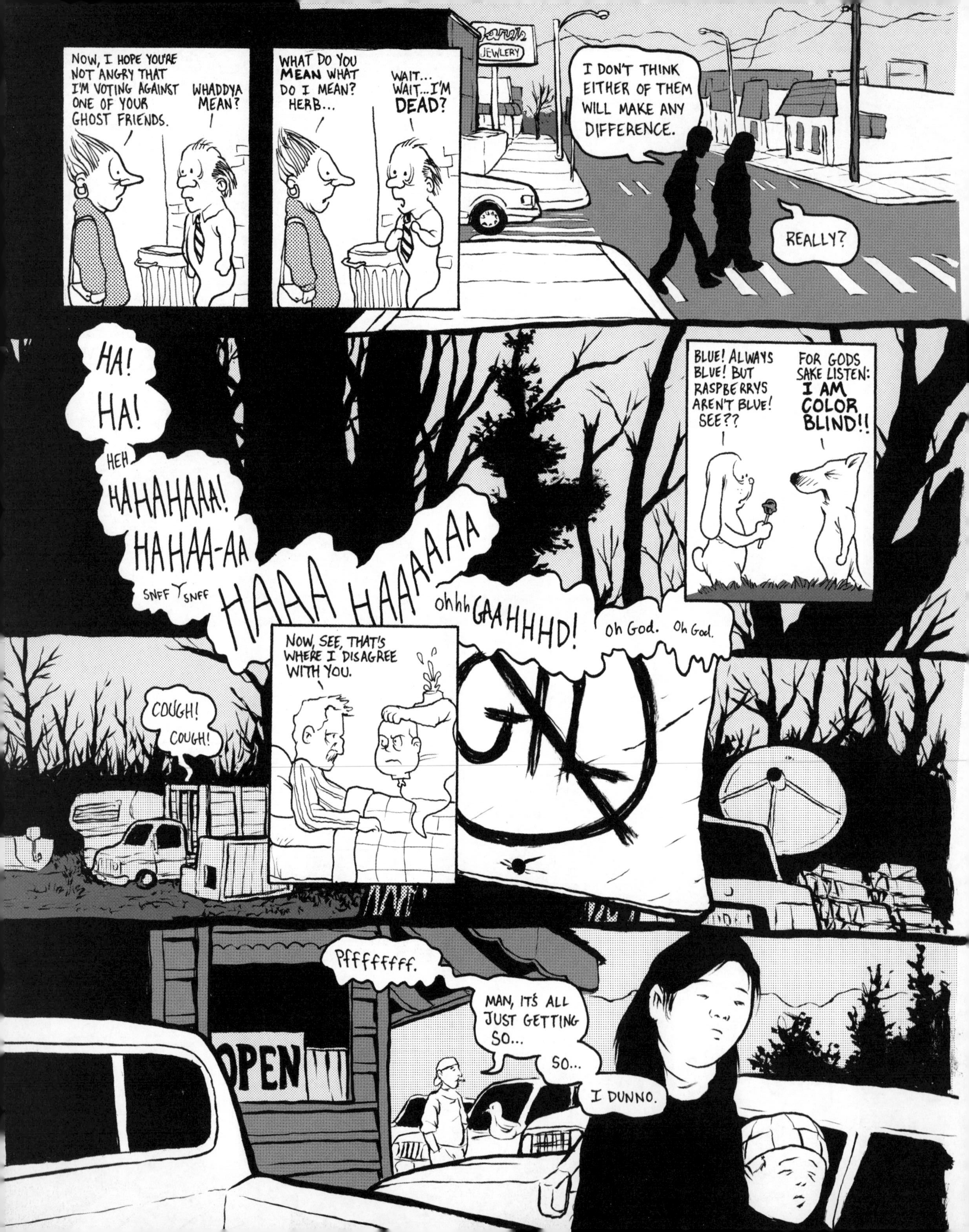
NOW, I HOPE YOU'RE NOT ANGRY THAT I'M VOTING AGAINST ONE OF YOUR GHOST FRIENDS.
WHADDYA MEAN?
WHAT DO YOU MEAN WHAT DO I MEAN? HERB...
WAIT... WAIT...I'M DEAD?
JEWLERY
I DON'T THINK EITHER OF THEM WILL MAKE ANY DIFFERENCE.
REALLY?
HA!
HA!
HEH
HAHAHAAA!
HAHAA-AA
SNFF SNFF
HAAA HAAAAAA
ohhh GAAHHHD!
Oh God. Oh God.
BLUE! ALWAYS BLUE! BUT RASPBERRYS AREN'T BLUE! SEE??
FOR GODS SAKE LISTEN: I AM COLOR BLIND!!
COUGH! COUGH!
NOW, SEE, THAT'S WHERE I DISAGREE WITH YOU.
OPEN
Pfffffff.
MAN, IT'S ALL JUST GETTING SO...
SO...
I DUNNO.

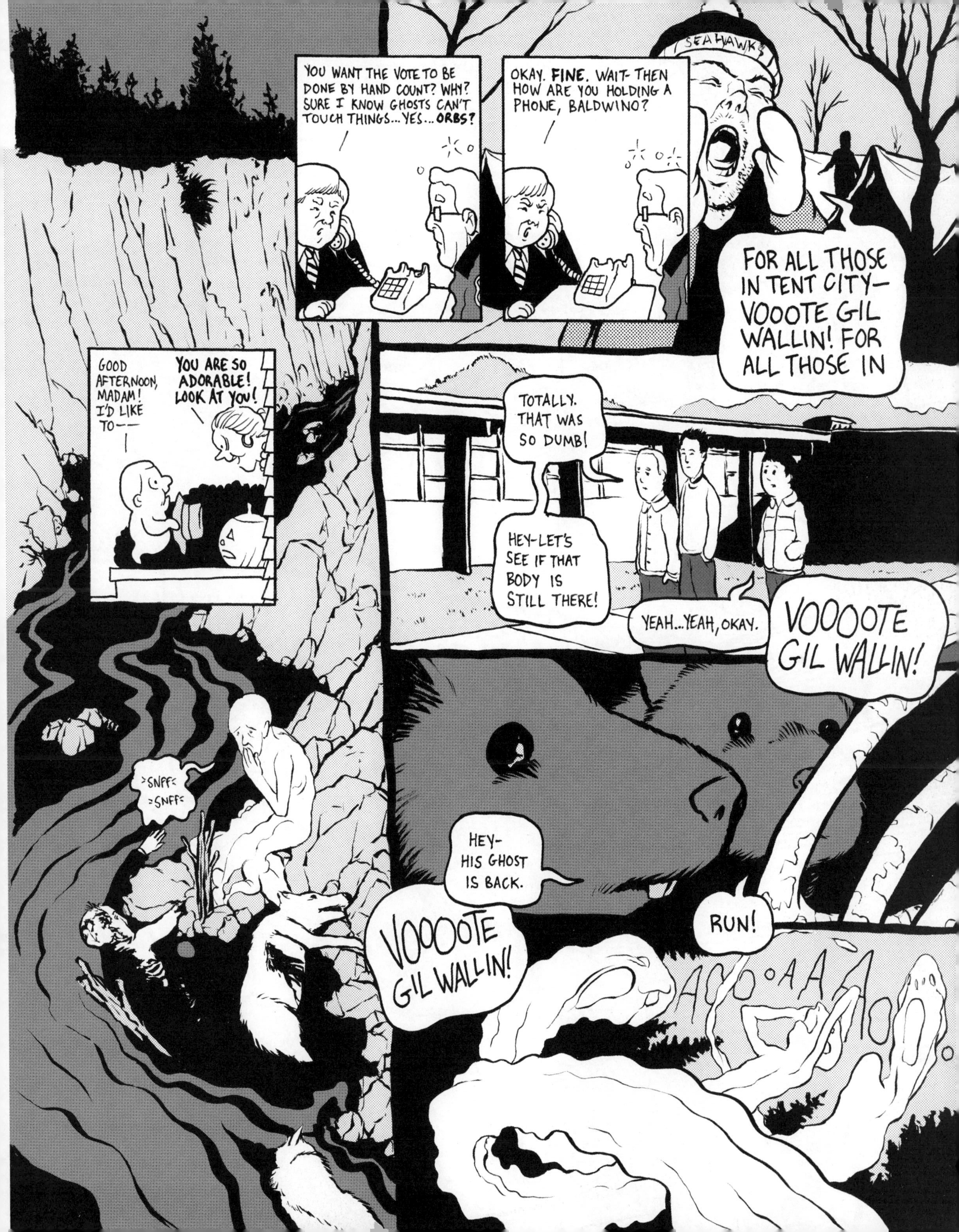
YOU WANT THE VOTE TO BE DONE BY HAND COUNT? WHY? SURE I KNOW GHOSTS CAN'T TOUCH THINGS... YES... **ORBS?**
OKAY. **FINE.** WAIT- THEN HOW ARE YOU HOLDING A PHONE, BALDWINO?
SEAHAWKS
FOR ALL THOSE IN TENT CITY- VOOOTE GIL WALLIN! FOR ALL THOSE IN
GOOD AFTERNOON, MADAM! I'D LIKE TO--
YOU ARE SO ADORABLE! LOOK AT YOU!
TOTALLY. THAT WAS SO DUMB!
HEY-LET'S SEE IF THAT BODY IS STILL THERE!
YEAH... YEAH, OKAY.
VOOOOTE GIL WALLIN!
>SNFF<
>SNFF<
HEY- HIS GHOST IS BACK.
VOOOOTE GIL WALLIN!
RUN!

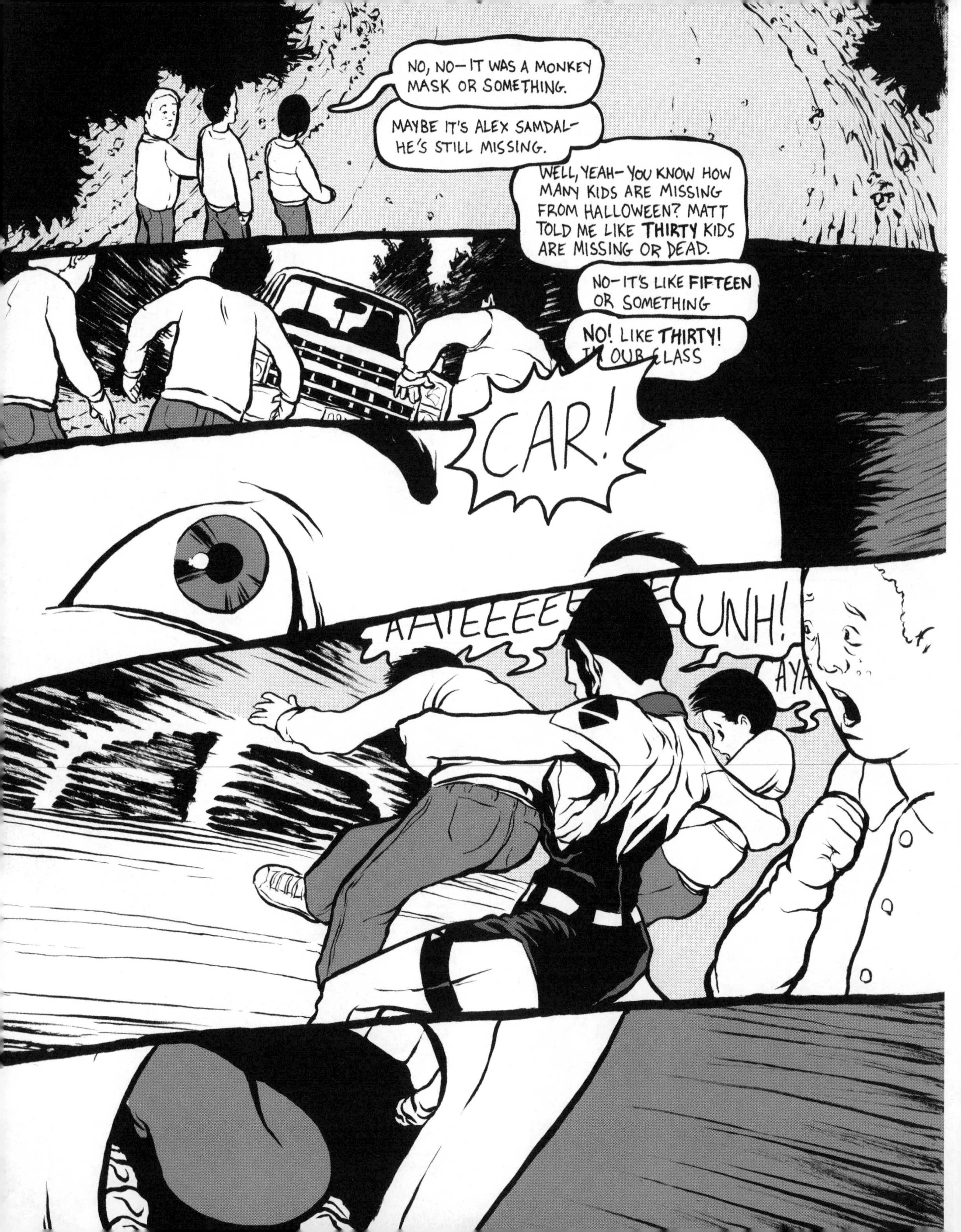
NO, NO— IT WAS A MONKEY MASK OR SOMETHING.
MAYBE IT'S ALEX SAMDAL— HE'S STILL MISSING.
WELL, YEAH— YOU KNOW HOW MANY KIDS ARE MISSING FROM HALLOWEEN? MATT TOLD ME LIKE THIRTY KIDS ARE MISSING OR DEAD.
NO— IT'S LIKE FIFTEEN OR SOMETHING
NO! LIKE THIRTY!
OUR CLASS
CAR!
AAIEEEEE
UNH!

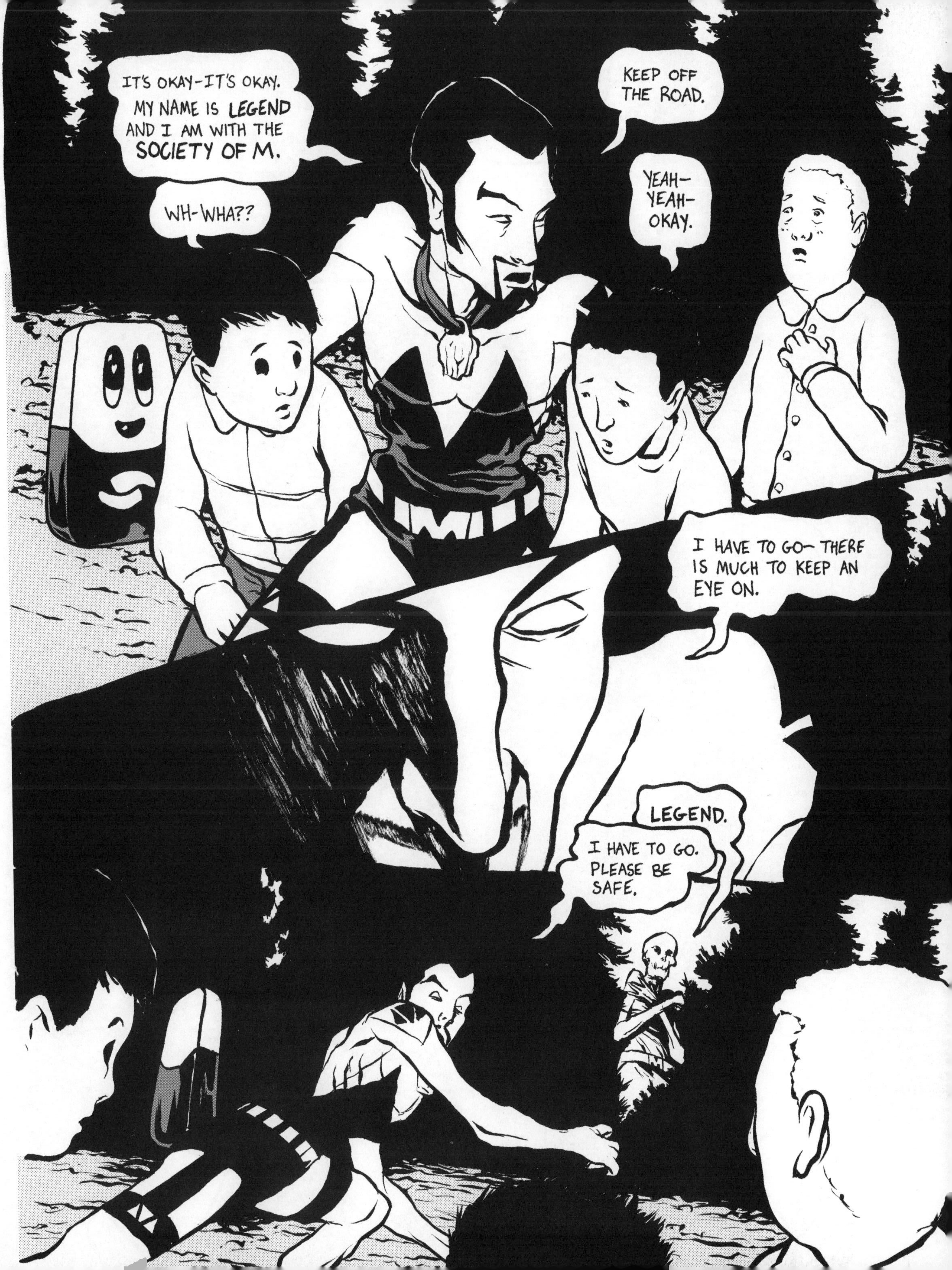
IT'S OKAY-IT'S OKAY.
MY NAME IS LEGEND AND I AM WITH THE SOCIETY OF M.
WH-WHA??
KEEP OFF THE ROAD.
YEAH-YEAH-OKAY.
I HAVE TO GO- THERE IS MUCH TO KEEP AN EYE ON.
LEGEND.
I HAVE TO GO. PLEASE BE SAFE.

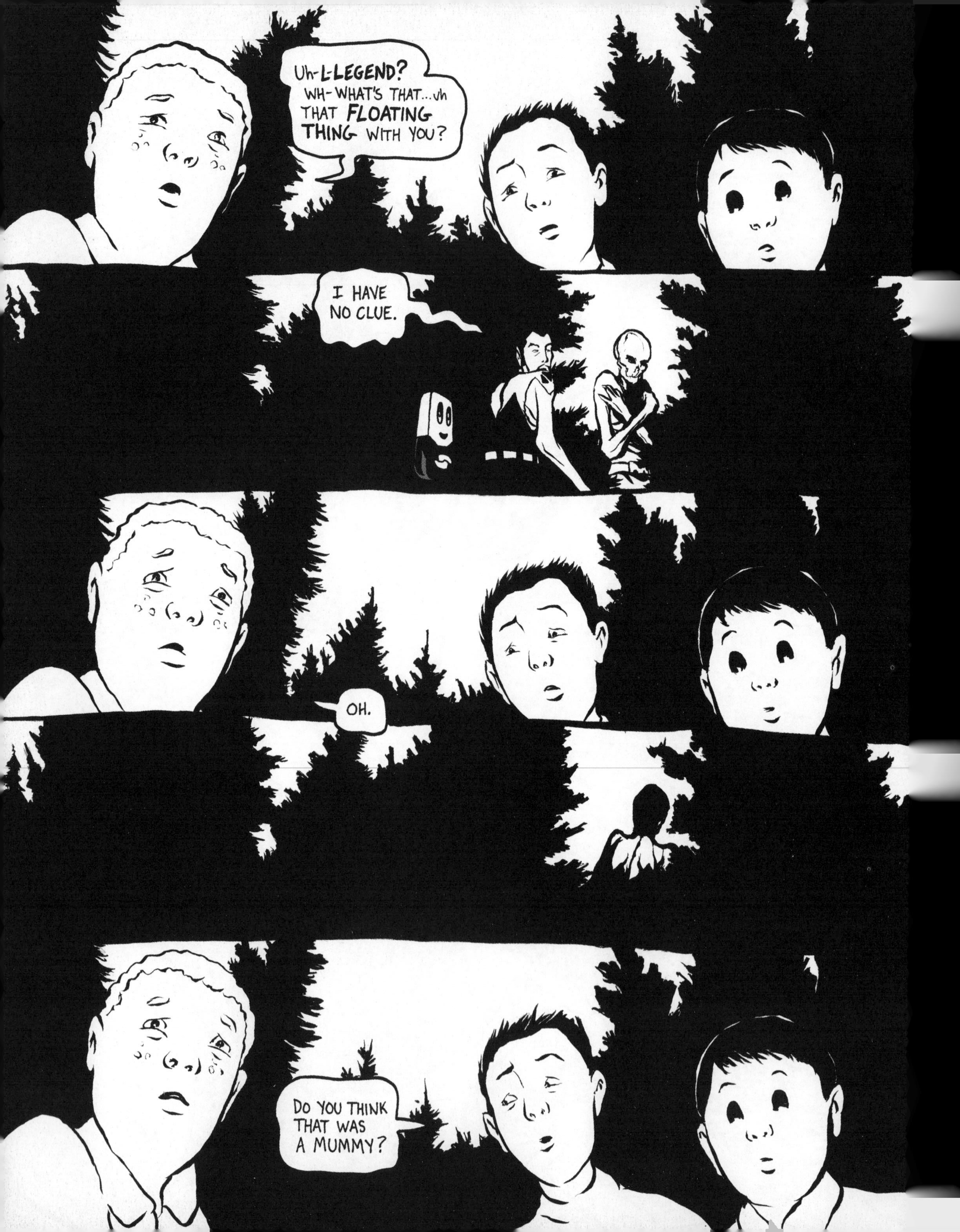
Uh-L-LEGEND? WH-WHAT'S THAT...uh THAT FLOATING THING WITH YOU?
I HAVE NO CLUE.
OH.
DO YOU THINK THAT WAS A MUMMY?

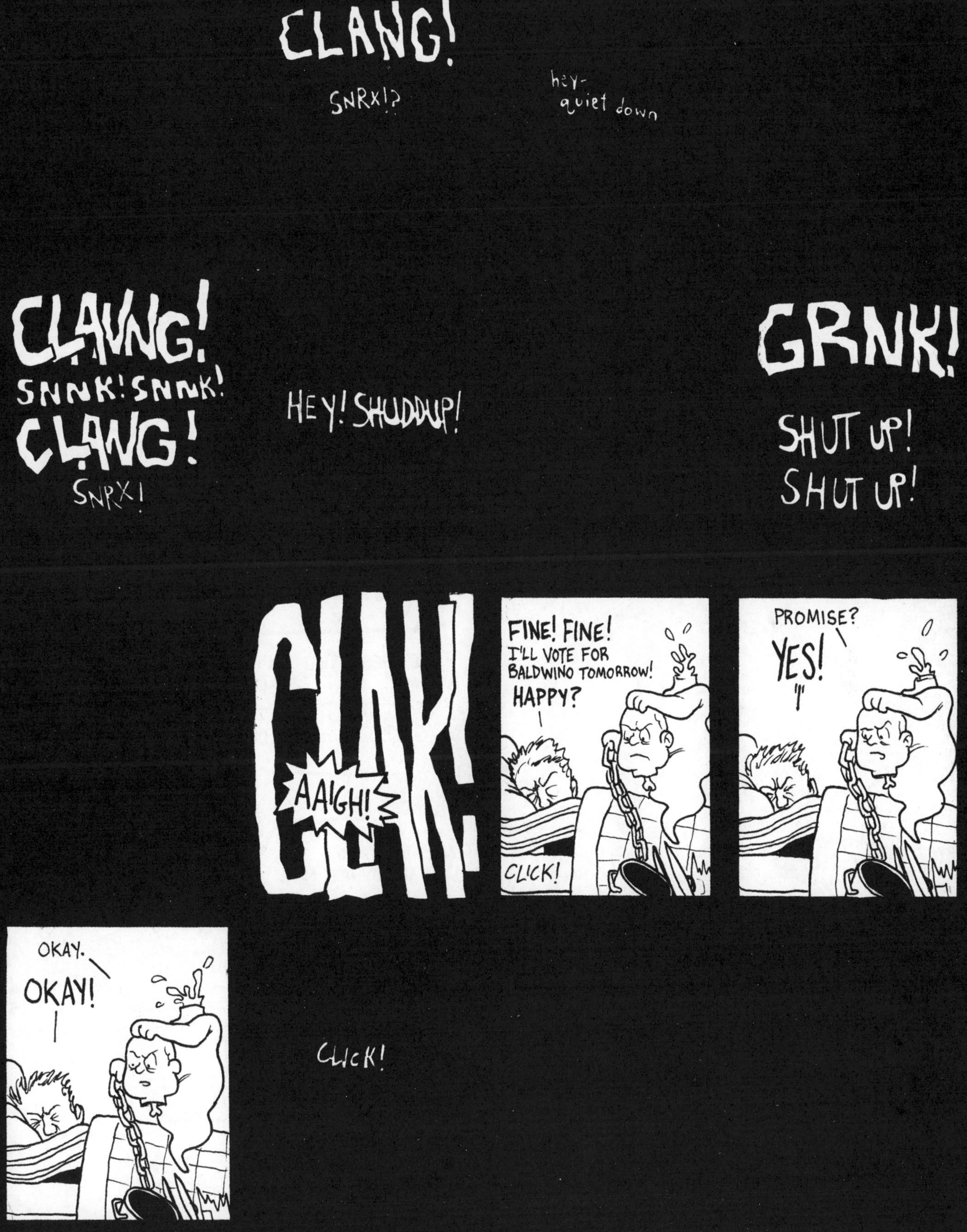
CLANG!
SNRX!?
hey-
quiet down
CLAUNG!
SNNK! SNNK!
CLANG!
SNRX!
HEY! SHUDDUP!
GRNK!
SHUT UP!
SHUT UP!
CLNK!
AAIGH!
FINE! FINE!
I'LL VOTE FOR BALDWINO TOMORROW!
HAPPY?
CLICK!
PROMISE?
YES!
OKAY.
OKAY!
CLICK!

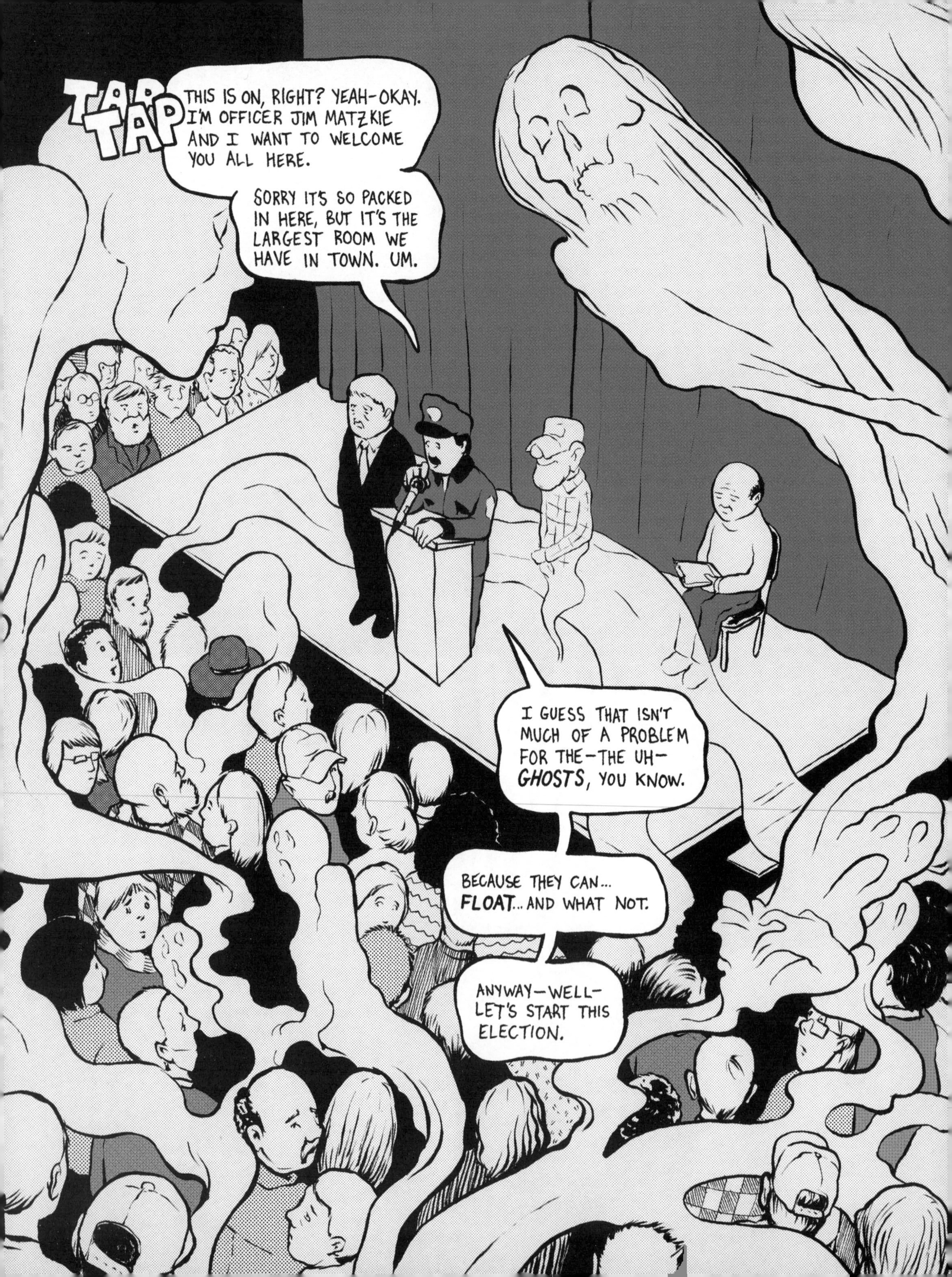
TAP TAP
THIS IS ON, RIGHT? YEAH-OKAY. I'M OFFICER JIM MATZKIE AND I WANT TO WELCOME YOU ALL HERE.
SORRY IT'S SO PACKED IN HERE, BUT IT'S THE LARGEST ROOM WE HAVE IN TOWN. UM.
I GUESS THAT ISN'T MUCH OF A PROBLEM FOR THE—THE UH—*GHOSTS*, YOU KNOW.
BECAUSE THEY CAN... **FLOAT**... AND WHAT NOT.
ANYWAY—WELL—LET'S START THIS ELECTION.

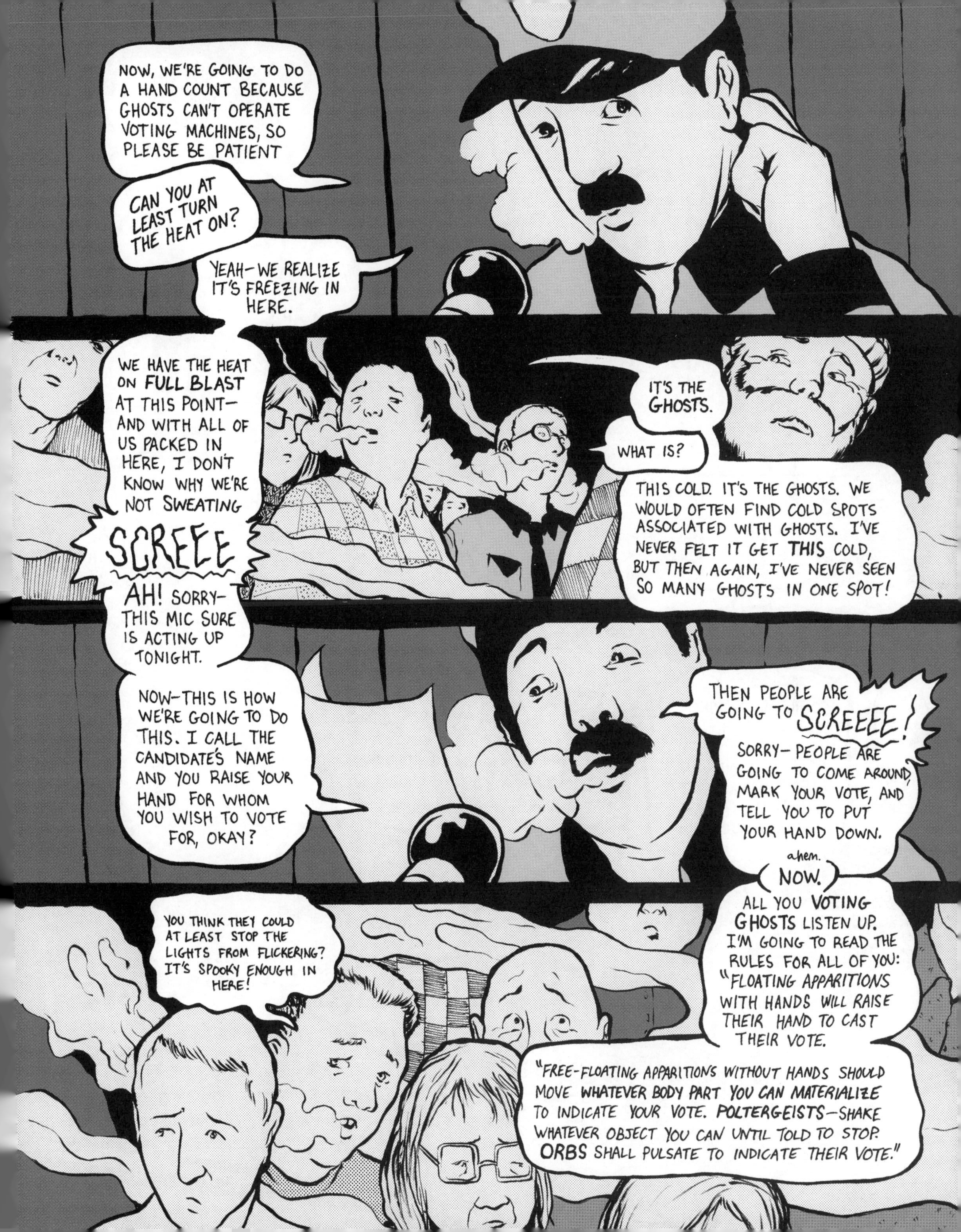
NOW, WE'RE GOING TO DO A HAND COUNT BECAUSE GHOSTS CAN'T OPERATE VOTING MACHINES, SO PLEASE BE PATIENT
CAN YOU AT LEAST TURN THE HEAT ON?
YEAH—WE REALIZE IT'S FREEZING IN HERE.
WE HAVE THE HEAT ON FULL BLAST AT THIS POINT—AND WITH ALL OF US PACKED IN HERE, I DON'T KNOW WHY WE'RE NOT SWEATING
SCREEE
AH! SORRY—THIS MIC SURE IS ACTING UP TONIGHT.
IT'S THE GHOSTS.
WHAT IS?
THIS COLD. IT'S THE GHOSTS. WE WOULD OFTEN FIND COLD SPOTS ASSOCIATED WITH GHOSTS. I'VE NEVER FELT IT GET THIS COLD, BUT THEN AGAIN, I'VE NEVER SEEN SO MANY GHOSTS IN ONE SPOT!
NOW—THIS IS HOW WE'RE GOING TO DO THIS. I CALL THE CANDIDATE'S NAME AND YOU RAISE YOUR HAND FOR WHOM YOU WISH TO VOTE FOR, OKAY?
THEN PEOPLE ARE GOING TO SCREEEE!
SORRY—PEOPLE ARE GOING TO COME AROUND, MARK YOUR VOTE, AND TELL YOU TO PUT YOUR HAND DOWN.
ahem.
NOW.
ALL YOU VOTING GHOSTS LISTEN UP. I'M GOING TO READ THE RULES FOR ALL OF YOU: "FLOATING APPARITIONS WITH HANDS WILL RAISE THEIR HAND TO CAST THEIR VOTE.
YOU THINK THEY COULD AT LEAST STOP THE LIGHTS FROM FLICKERING? IT'S SPOOKY ENOUGH IN HERE!
"FREE-FLOATING APPARITIONS WITHOUT HANDS SHOULD MOVE WHATEVER BODY PART YOU CAN MATERIALIZE TO INDICATE YOUR VOTE. POLTERGEISTS—SHAKE WHATEVER OBJECT YOU CAN UNTIL TOLD TO STOP. ORBS SHALL PULSATE TO INDICATE THEIR VOTE."

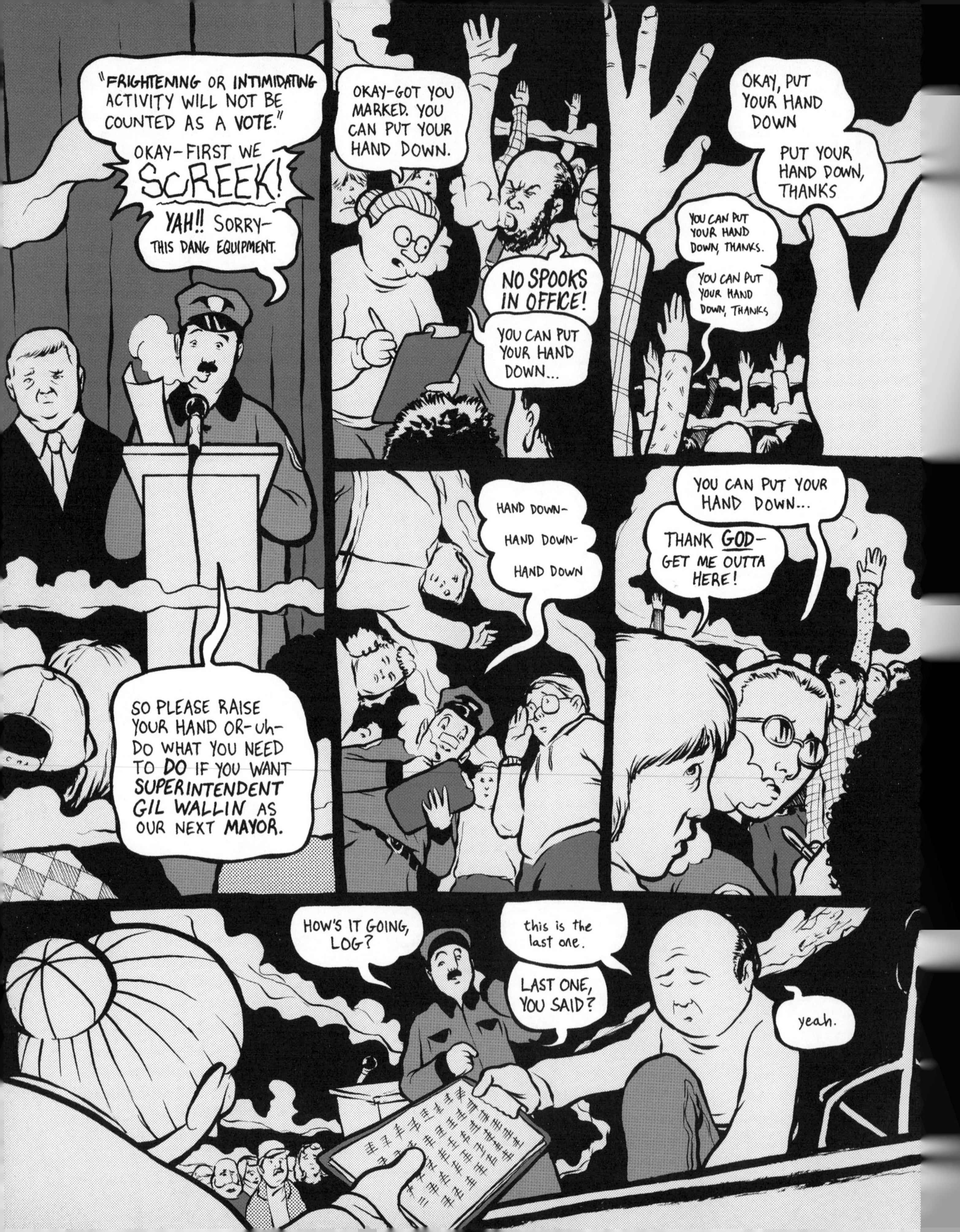
"FRIGHTENING OR INTIMIDATING ACTIVITY WILL NOT BE COUNTED AS A VOTE."
OKAY—FIRST WE
SCREEK!
YAH!! SORRY— THIS DANG EQUIPMENT.
SO PLEASE RAISE YOUR HAND OR—uh— DO WHAT YOU NEED TO DO IF YOU WANT SUPERINTENDENT GIL WALLIN AS OUR NEXT MAYOR.
OKAY—GOT YOU MARKED. YOU CAN PUT YOUR HAND DOWN.
NO SPOOKS IN OFFICE!
YOU CAN PUT YOUR HAND DOWN...
OKAY, PUT YOUR HAND DOWN
PUT YOUR HAND DOWN, THANKS
YOU CAN PUT YOUR HAND DOWN, THANKS.
YOU CAN PUT YOUR HAND DOWN, THANKS
HAND DOWN—
HAND DOWN—
HAND DOWN
YOU CAN PUT YOUR HAND DOWN...
THANK GOD— GET ME OUTTA HERE!
HOW'S IT GOING, LOG?
this is the last one.
LAST ONE, YOU SAID?
yeah.

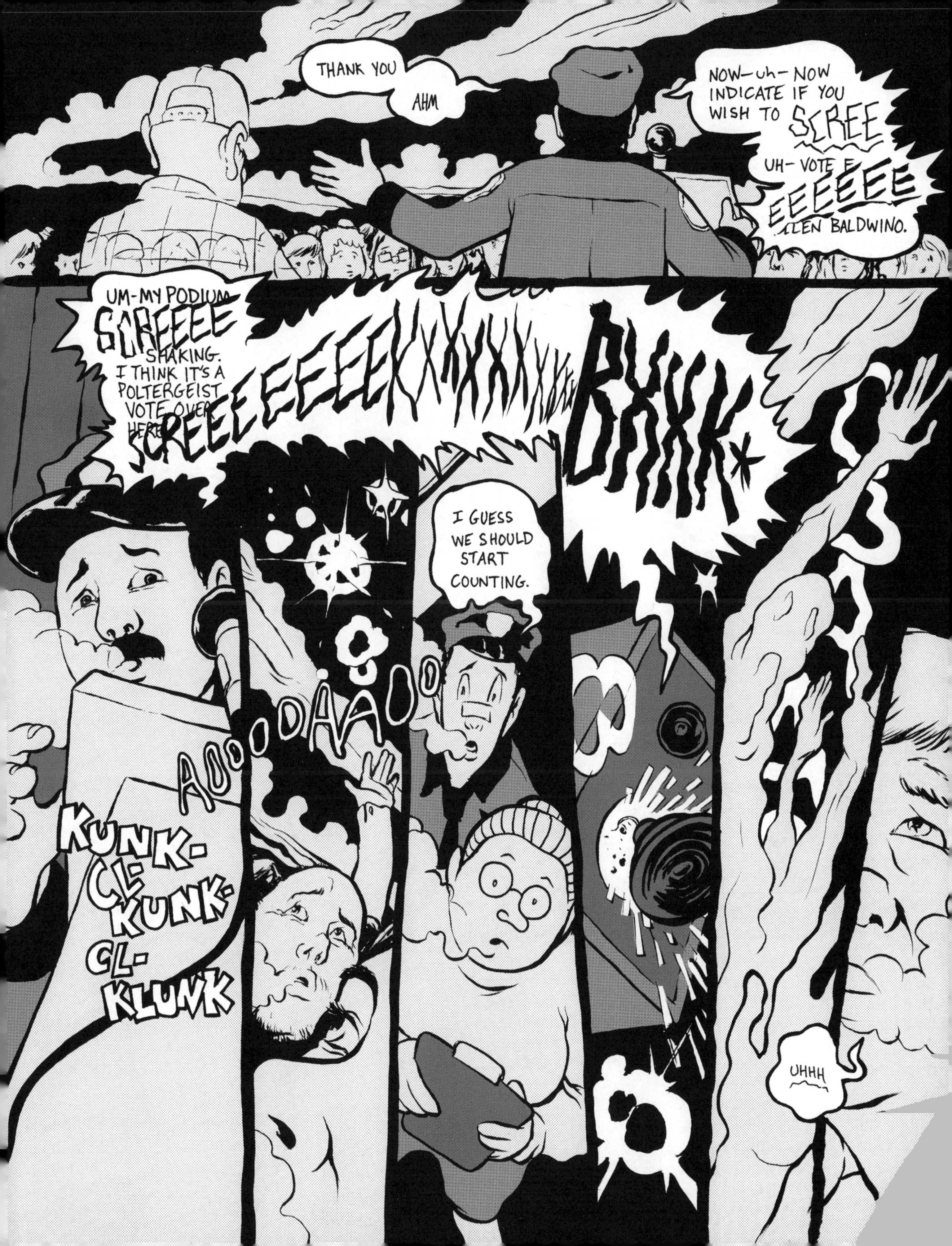
THANK YOU
AHM
NOW—uh—NOW INDICATE IF YOU WISH TO SCREE
UH—VOTE EEEEEE
UM-MY PODIUM SCREEEE SHAKING. I THINK IT'S A POLTERGEIST VOTE OVER HERE
SCREEEEEEEEKXXXXXXX
BXXXK*
I GUESS WE SHOULD START COUNTING.
AOOOODAAAOO
KUNK-CL-KUNK-CL-KLUNK
UHHH

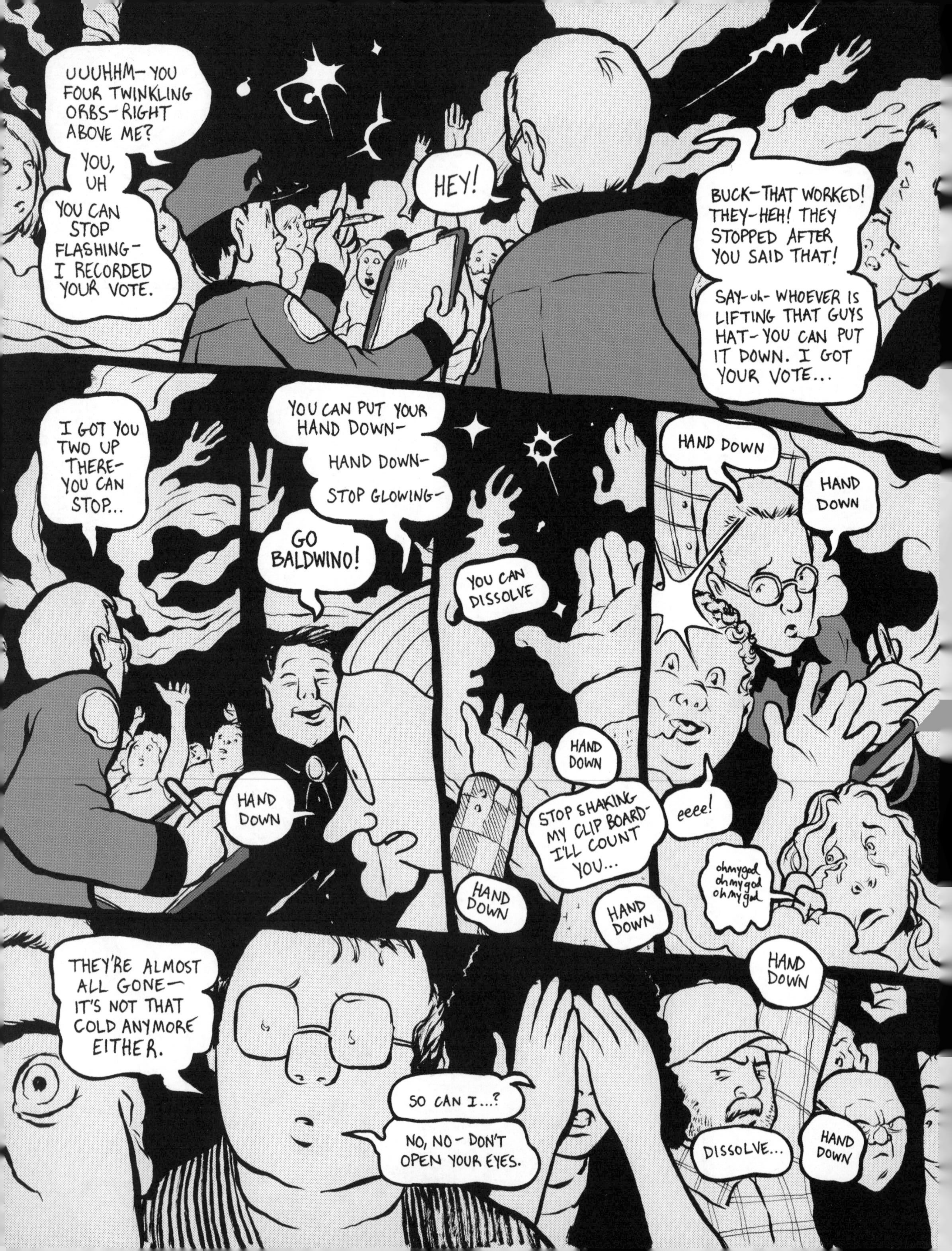
UUUHHM—YOU FOUR TWINKLING ORBS—RIGHT ABOVE ME?
YOU, UH
YOU CAN STOP FLASHING—I RECORDED YOUR VOTE.
HEY!
BUCK—THAT WORKED! THEY—HEH! THEY STOPPED AFTER YOU SAID THAT!
SAY-uh- WHOEVER IS LIFTING THAT GUYS HAT—YOU CAN PUT IT DOWN. I GOT YOUR VOTE...
I GOT YOU TWO UP THERE—YOU CAN STOP...
HAND DOWN
YOU CAN PUT YOUR HAND DOWN—
HAND DOWN—
STOP GLOWING—
GO BALDWINO!
YOU CAN DISSOLVE
HAND DOWN
HAND DOWN
STOP SHAKING MY CLIP BOARD—I'LL COUNT YOU...
HAND DOWN
HAND DOWN
HAND DOWN
eeee!
ohmygod ohmygod ohmygod
THEY'RE ALMOST ALL GONE—IT'S NOT THAT COLD ANYMORE EITHER.
SO CAN I...?
NO, NO—DON'T OPEN YOUR EYES.
HAND DOWN
DISSOLVE...
HAND DOWN

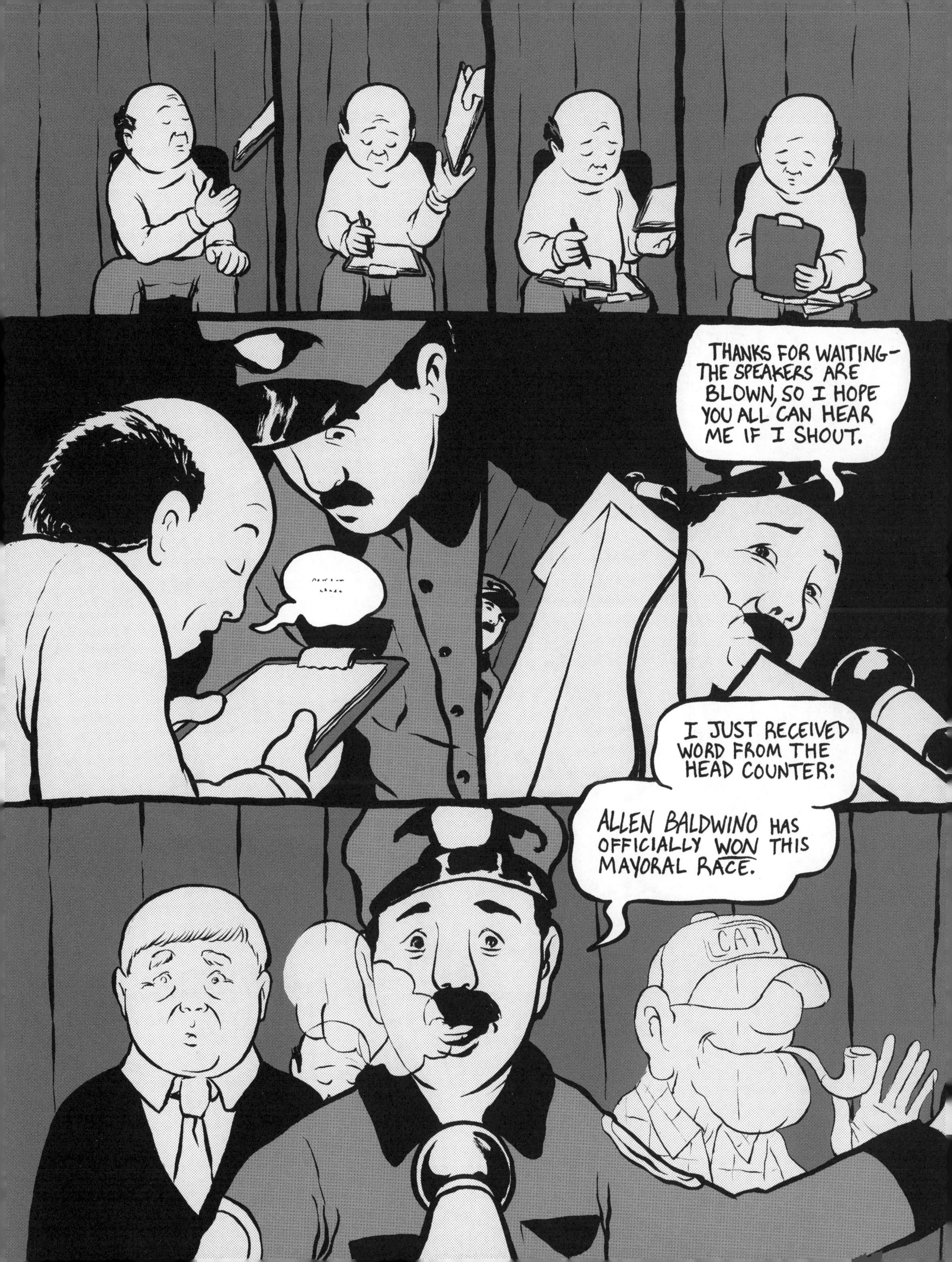
THANKS FOR WAITING- THE SPEAKERS ARE BLOWN, SO I HOPE YOU ALL CAN HEAR ME IF I SHOUT.
I JUST RECEIVED WORD FROM THE HEAD COUNTER:
ALLEN BALDWINO HAS OFFICIALLY WON THIS MAYORAL RACE.
CAT

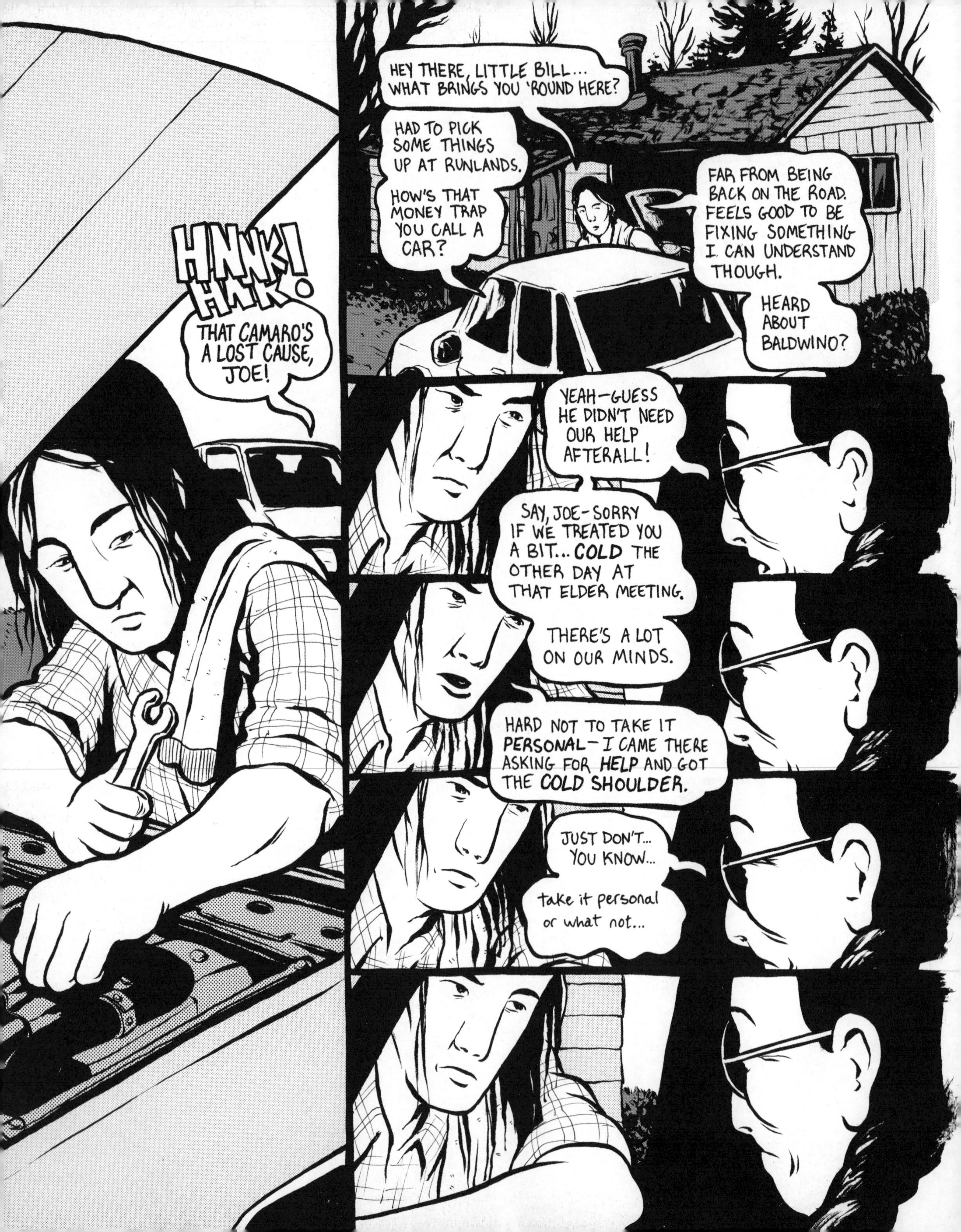
HNNK! HNK!
THAT CAMARO'S A LOST CAUSE, JOE!
HEY THERE, LITTLE BILL... WHAT BRINGS YOU 'ROUND HERE?
HAD TO PICK SOME THINGS UP AT RUNLANDS.
HOW'S THAT MONEY TRAP YOU CALL A CAR?
FAR FROM BEING BACK ON THE ROAD. FEELS GOOD TO BE FIXING SOMETHING I CAN UNDERSTAND THOUGH.
HEARD ABOUT BALDWINO?
YEAH—GUESS HE DIDN'T NEED OUR HELP AFTERALL!
SAY, JOE-SORRY IF WE TREATED YOU A BIT... **COLD** THE OTHER DAY AT THAT ELDER MEETING.
THERE'S A LOT ON OUR MINDS.
HARD NOT TO TAKE IT **PERSONAL**—I CAME THERE ASKING FOR **HELP** AND GOT THE **COLD SHOULDER**.
JUST DON'T... YOU KNOW...
take it personal or what not...

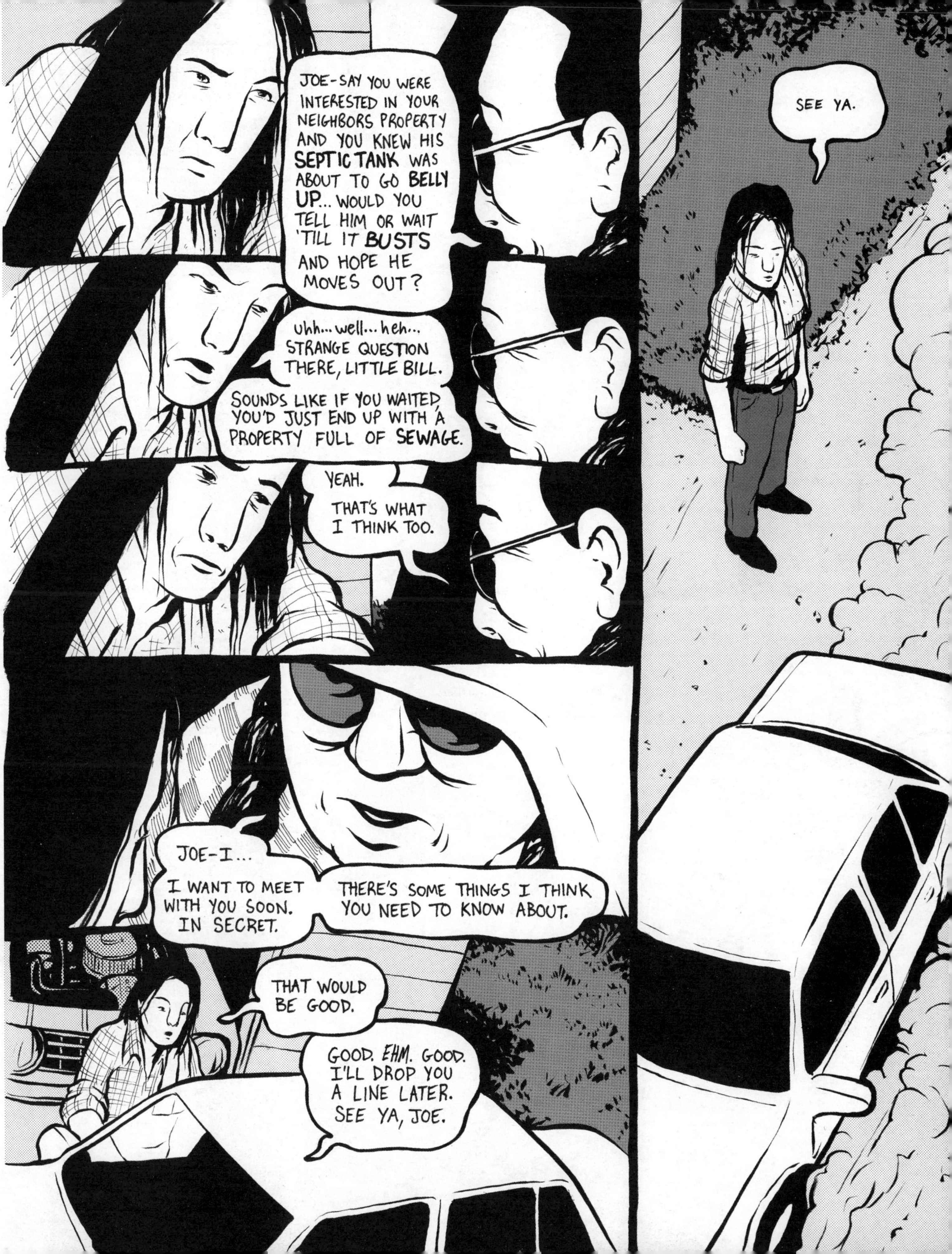
JOE-SAY YOU WERE INTERESTED IN YOUR NEIGHBORS PROPERTY AND YOU KNEW HIS SEPTIC TANK WAS ABOUT TO GO BELLY UP... WOULD YOU TELL HIM OR WAIT 'TILL IT BUSTS AND HOPE HE MOVES OUT?
uhh... well... heh... STRANGE QUESTION THERE, LITTLE BILL.
SOUNDS LIKE IF YOU WAITED YOU'D JUST END UP WITH A PROPERTY FULL OF SEWAGE.
YEAH.
THAT'S WHAT I THINK TOO.
JOE-I...
I WANT TO MEET WITH YOU SOON. IN SECRET.
THERE'S SOME THINGS I THINK YOU NEED TO KNOW ABOUT.
THAT WOULD BE GOOD.
GOOD. EHM. GOOD. I'LL DROP YOU A LINE LATER. SEE YA, JOE.
SEE YA.

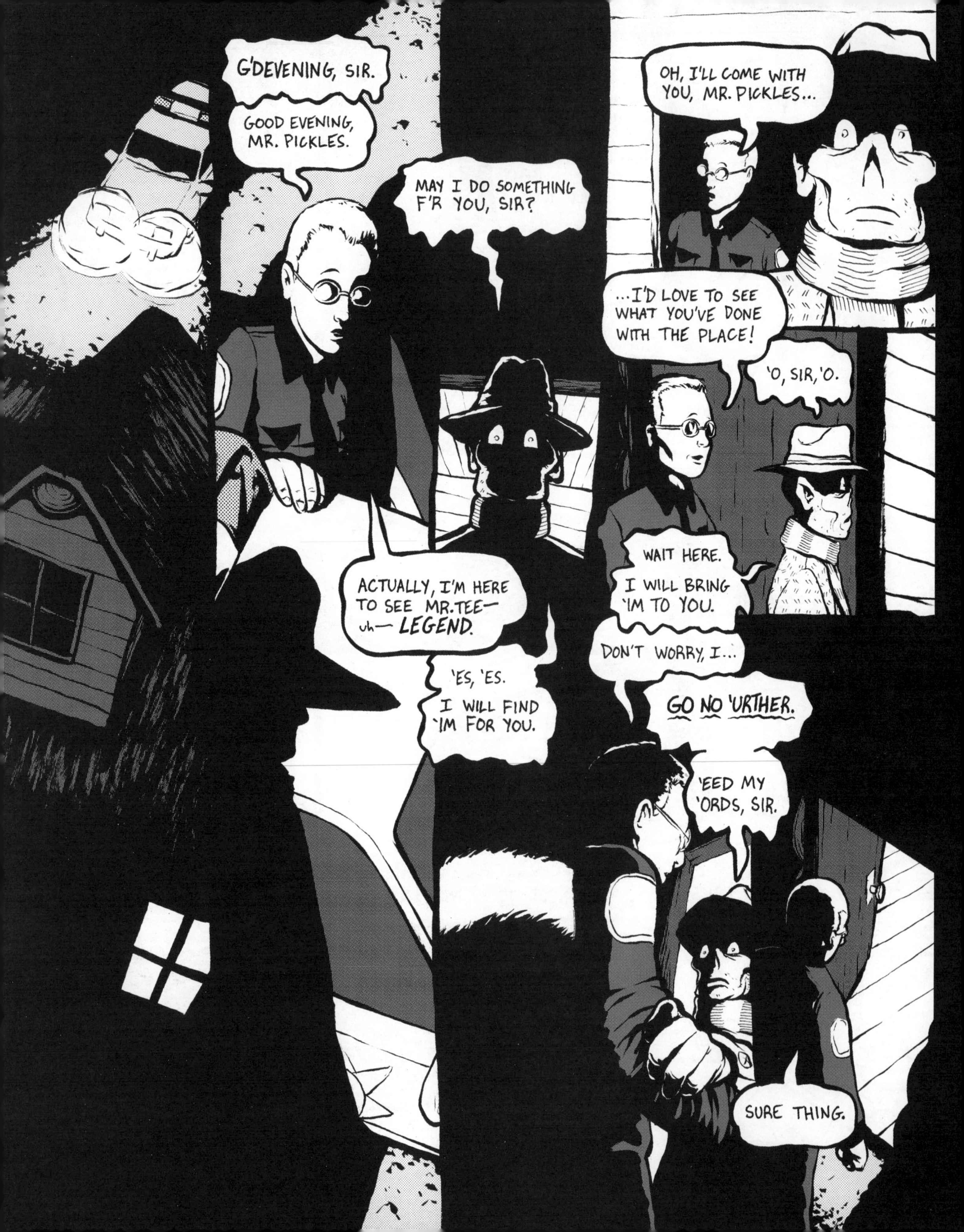
G'DEVENING, SIR.
GOOD EVENING, MR. PICKLES.
MAY I DO SOMETHING F'R YOU, SIR?
ACTUALLY, I'M HERE TO SEE MR. TEE— uh— LEGEND.
'ES, 'ES. I WILL FIND 'IM FOR YOU.
OH, I'LL COME WITH YOU, MR. PICKLES...
...I'D LOVE TO SEE WHAT YOU'VE DONE WITH THE PLACE!
'O, SIR, 'O.
WAIT HERE. I WILL BRING 'IM TO YOU.
DON'T WORRY, I...
GO NO 'URTHER.
'EED MY 'ORDS, SIR.
SURE THING.

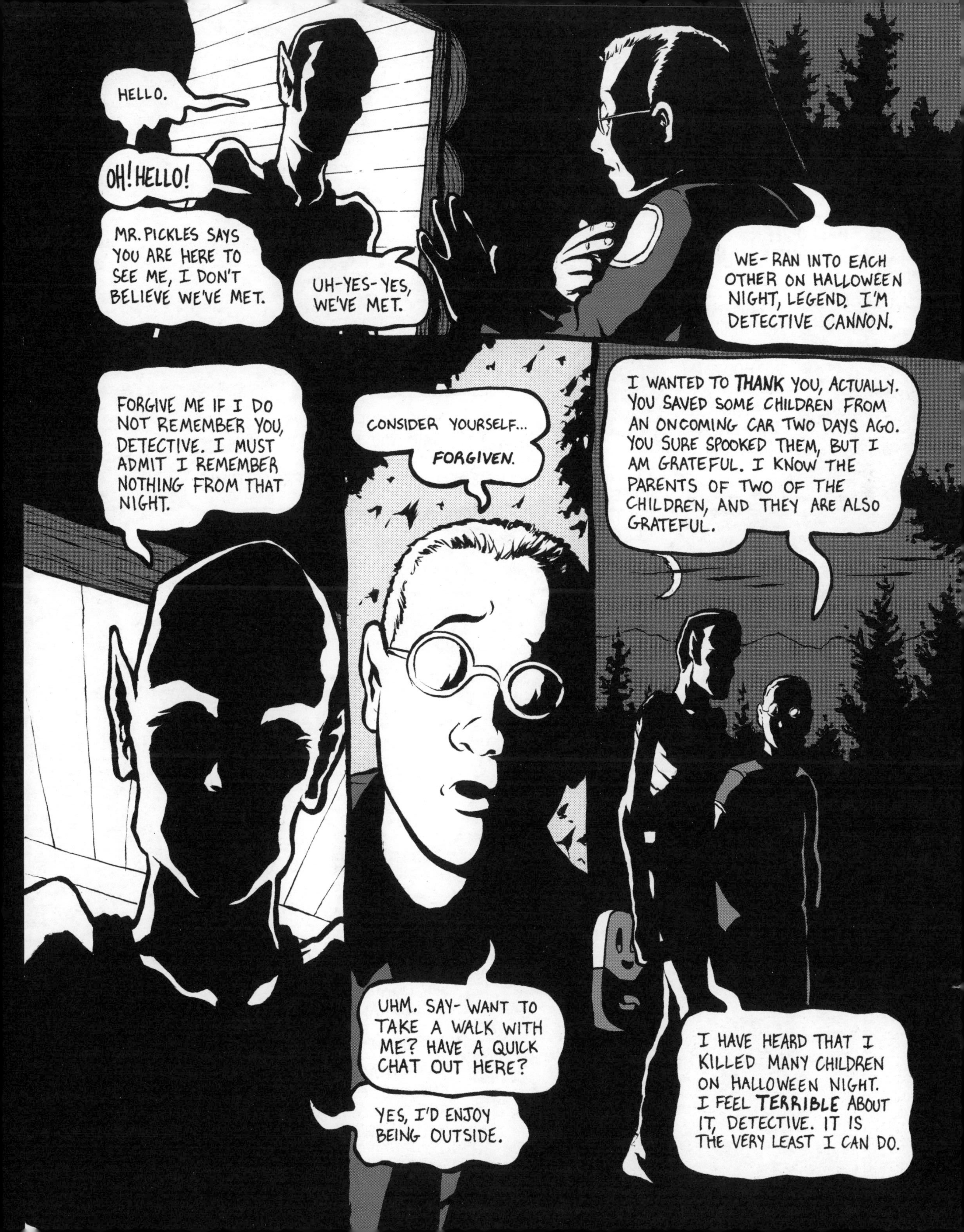
HELLO.
OH! HELLO!
MR. PICKLES SAYS YOU ARE HERE TO SEE ME, I DON'T BELIEVE WE'VE MET.
UH-YES-YES, WE'VE MET.
WE-RAN INTO EACH OTHER ON HALLOWEEN NIGHT, LEGEND. I'M DETECTIVE CANNON.
FORGIVE ME IF I DO NOT REMEMBER YOU, DETECTIVE. I MUST ADMIT I REMEMBER NOTHING FROM THAT NIGHT.
CONSIDER YOURSELF... FORGIVEN.
I WANTED TO THANK YOU, ACTUALLY. YOU SAVED SOME CHILDREN FROM AN ONCOMING CAR TWO DAYS AGO. YOU SURE SPOOKED THEM, BUT I AM GRATEFUL. I KNOW THE PARENTS OF TWO OF THE CHILDREN, AND THEY ARE ALSO GRATEFUL.
UHM. SAY- WANT TO TAKE A WALK WITH ME? HAVE A QUICK CHAT OUT HERE?
YES, I'D ENJOY BEING OUTSIDE.
I HAVE HEARD THAT I KILLED MANY CHILDREN ON HALLOWEEN NIGHT. I FEEL TERRIBLE ABOUT IT, DETECTIVE. IT IS THE VERY LEAST I CAN DO.

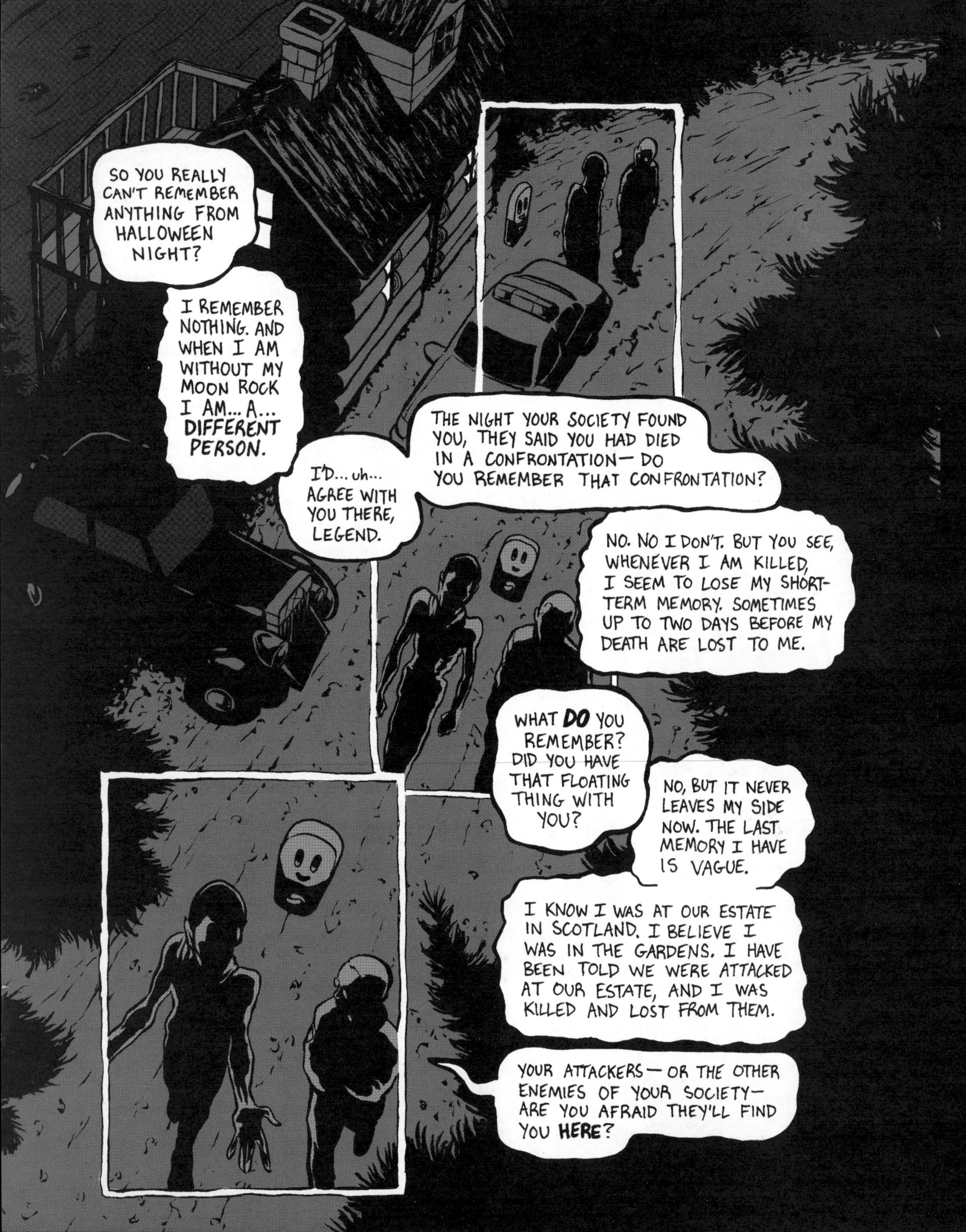
SO YOU REALLY CAN'T REMEMBER ANYTHING FROM HALLOWEEN NIGHT?
I REMEMBER NOTHING. AND WHEN I AM WITHOUT MY MOON ROCK I AM... A... **DIFFERENT PERSON.**
I'D... uh... AGREE WITH YOU THERE, LEGEND.
THE NIGHT YOUR SOCIETY FOUND YOU, THEY SAID YOU HAD DIED IN A CONFRONTATION— DO YOU REMEMBER THAT CONFRONTATION?
NO. NO I DON'T. BUT YOU SEE, WHENEVER I AM KILLED, I SEEM TO LOSE MY SHORT-TERM MEMORY. SOMETIMES UP TO TWO DAYS BEFORE MY DEATH ARE LOST TO ME.
WHAT **DO** YOU REMEMBER? DID YOU HAVE THAT FLOATING THING WITH YOU?
NO, BUT IT NEVER LEAVES MY SIDE NOW. THE LAST MEMORY I HAVE IS VAGUE.
I KNOW I WAS AT OUR ESTATE IN SCOTLAND. I BELIEVE I WAS IN THE GARDENS. I HAVE BEEN TOLD WE WERE ATTACKED AT OUR ESTATE, AND I WAS KILLED AND LOST FROM THEM.
YOUR ATTACKERS— OR THE OTHER ENEMIES OF YOUR SOCIETY— ARE YOU AFRAID THEY'LL FIND YOU **HERE**?

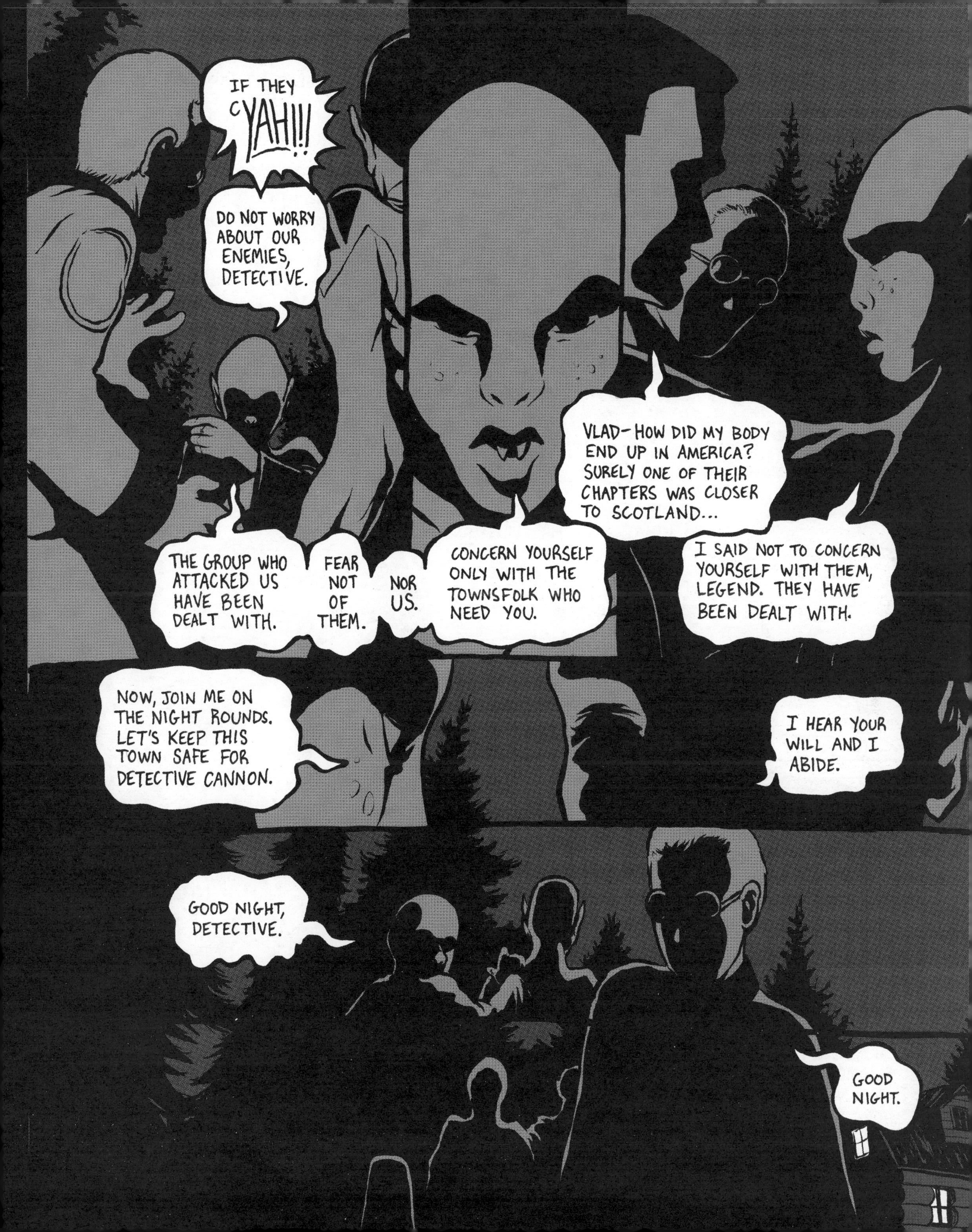
IF THEY C
YAH!!!
DO NOT WORRY ABOUT OUR ENEMIES, DETECTIVE.
THE GROUP WHO ATTACKED US HAVE BEEN DEALT WITH.
FEAR NOT OF THEM.
NOR US.
CONCERN YOURSELF ONLY WITH THE TOWNSFOLK WHO NEED YOU.
VLAD- HOW DID MY BODY END UP IN AMERICA? SURELY ONE OF THEIR CHAPTERS WAS CLOSER TO SCOTLAND...
I SAID NOT TO CONCERN YOURSELF WITH THEM, LEGEND. THEY HAVE BEEN DEALT WITH.
NOW, JOIN ME ON THE NIGHT ROUNDS. LET'S KEEP THIS TOWN SAFE FOR DETECTIVE CANNON.
I HEAR YOUR WILL AND I ABIDE.
GOOD NIGHT, DETECTIVE.
GOOD NIGHT.

HAL HERE— I JUST LEFT THE CABIN, OVER.

OH, HAL! GOOD TO HEAR YOU. IT'S BUCK. GET ANYTHING FROM MR. TEETH? OVER!

I GOT INTERRUPTED BEFORE HE COULD SAY MUCH. GOT ME THINKING, THOUGH. OVER.

THE ASTRAL ENERGY READINGS FOR RANGE ARE **GIGANTIC** AND **EXPONENTIALLY GROWING.** AND THE MORE OUR ASTRAL ENERGY LEVEL GROWS, THE MORE IT DRAWS FROM THE ENVIRONMENTAL ENERGY.

YOU FOLLOWING? OVER??

JUST TELL ME WHAT IT MEANS, TAIRA.

THEY CAN CONVERT ATMOSPHERIC AND ELECTRICAL ENERGY INTO ASTRAL ENERGY. WE ALSO BELIEVED THEY COULD USE EMOTIONAL ENERGY TOO, THOUGH THAT WAS MUCH HARDER TO PROVE. NOW—EHM—

MY POINT IS...WELL...OUR REASONING FOR THESE TEMPERATURE SHIFTS WAS THAT GHOSTS DREW UPON ENVIRONMENTAL ENERGY TO MANIFEST THEMSELVES.

WHAT'S YOUR POINT, TAIRA?

I—I WAS THINKING ABOUT THAT AND...HAL— DID YOU KNOW THAT FOR THE PAST WEEK RANGE HAS BEEN ABOUT **TEN DEGREES COOLER** THAN AVERAGE? OVER?

SURE.

DOCTOR TAIRA HERE. THE ELECTION— REMEMBER I SAID THE GHOSTS WERE MAKING THE ROOM COLD? UH— OVER?

HAL!

PUT HIM ON.

HAL— THAT GUY TAIRA CAME INTO THE STATION WANTING TO TALK TO YOU— SAYS IT'S IMPORTANT. OVER.

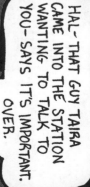

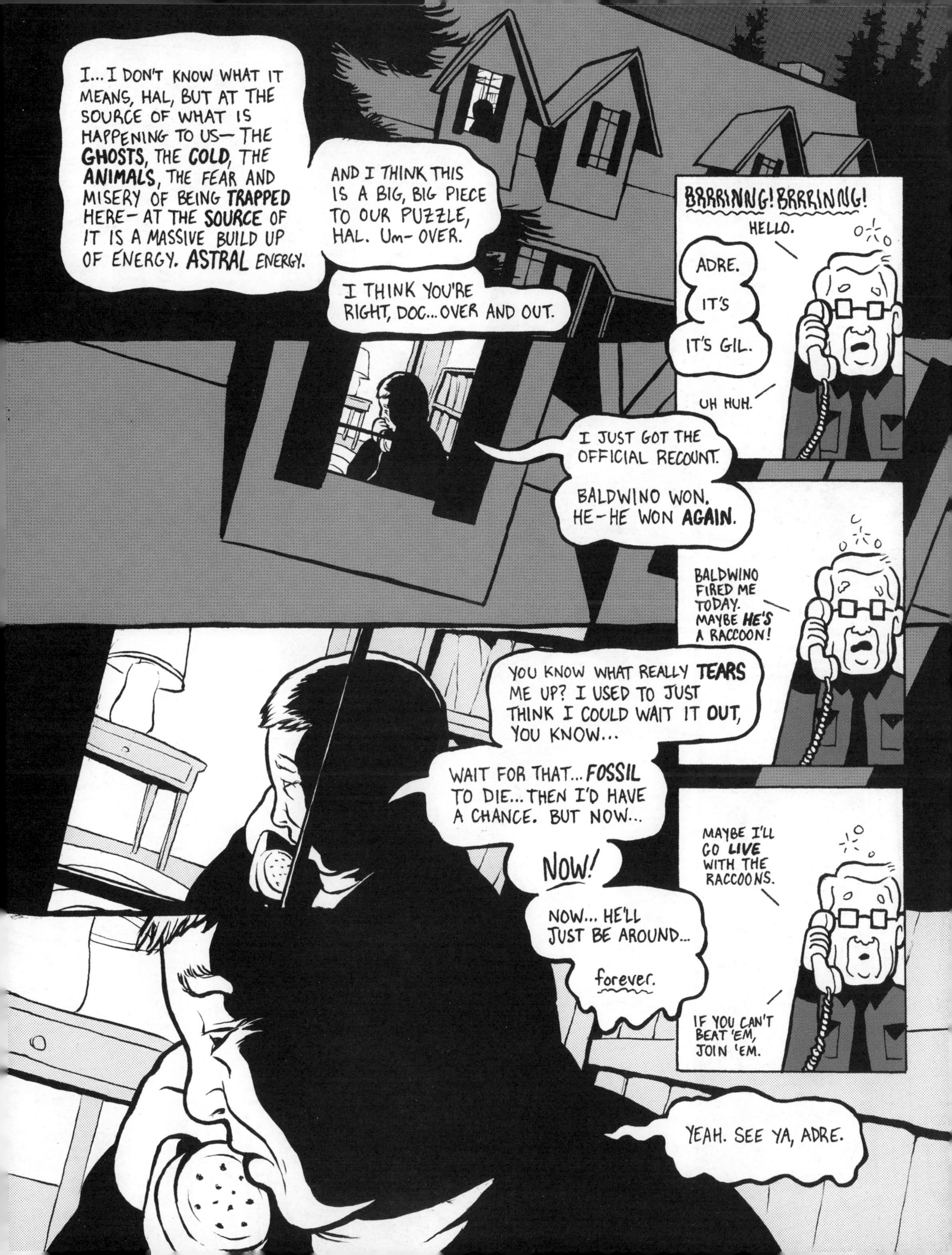
I... I DON'T KNOW WHAT IT MEANS, HAL, BUT AT THE SOURCE OF WHAT IS HAPPENING TO US— THE **GHOSTS**, THE **COLD**, THE **ANIMALS**, THE FEAR AND MISERY OF BEING **TRAPPED** HERE— AT THE **SOURCE** OF IT IS A MASSIVE BUILD UP OF ENERGY. **ASTRAL** ENERGY.
AND I THINK THIS IS A BIG, BIG PIECE TO OUR PUZZLE, HAL. Um- OVER.
I THINK YOU'RE RIGHT, DOC... OVER AND OUT.
BRRRINNG! BRRRINNG!
HELLO.
ADRE.
IT'S
IT'S GIL.
UH HUH.
I JUST GOT THE OFFICIAL RECOUNT.
BALDWINO WON. HE-HE WON **AGAIN**.
BALDWINO FIRED ME TODAY. MAYBE **HE'S** A RACCOON!
YOU KNOW WHAT REALLY **TEARS** ME UP? I USED TO JUST THINK I COULD WAIT IT **OUT**, YOU KNOW...
WAIT FOR THAT... **FOSSIL** TO DIE... THEN I'D HAVE A CHANCE. BUT NOW...
MAYBE I'LL GO **LIVE** WITH THE RACCOONS.
NOW!
NOW... HE'LL JUST BE AROUND...
forever.
IF YOU CAN'T BEAT 'EM, JOIN 'EM.
YEAH. SEE YA, ADRE.

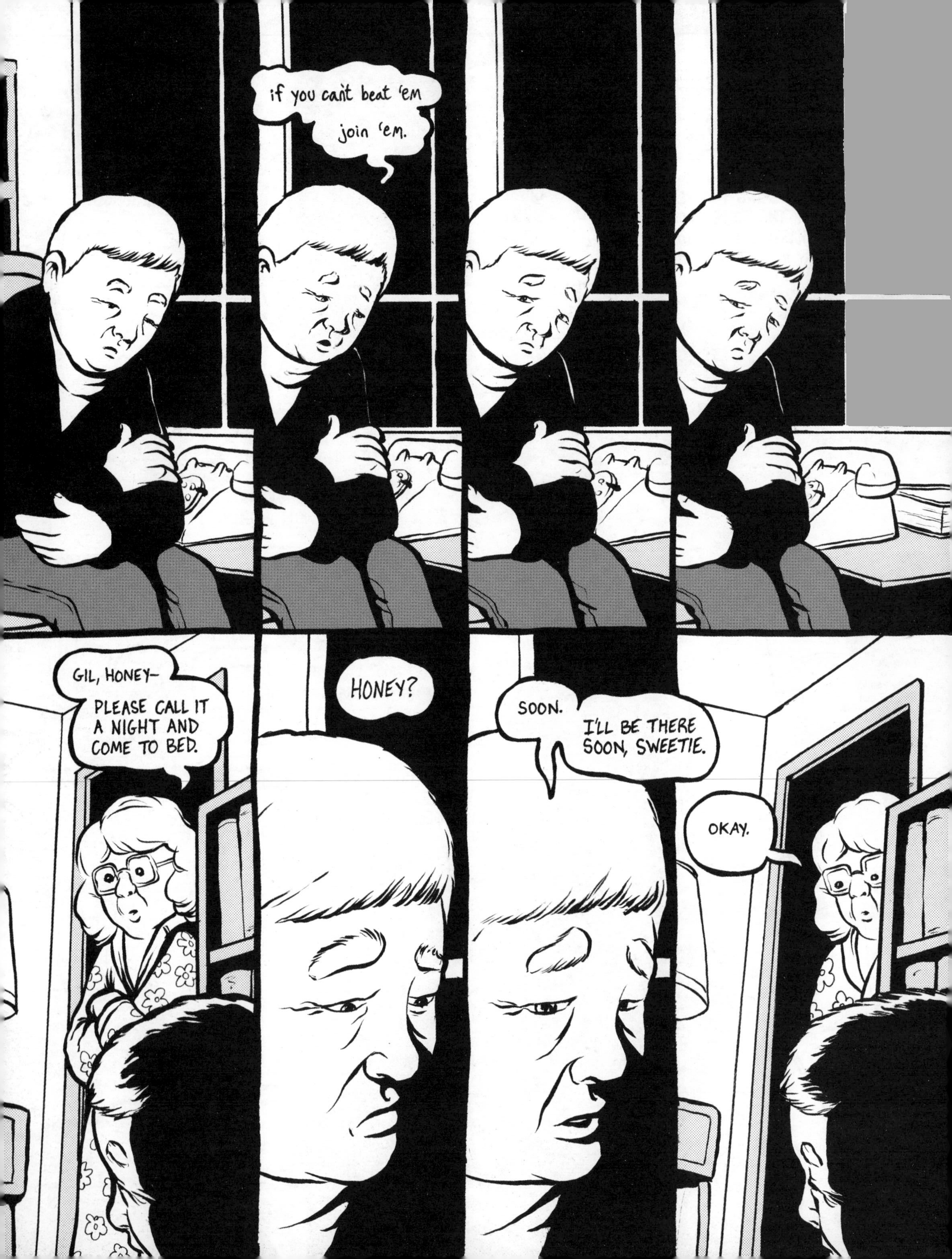
if you can't beat 'em
join 'em.
GIL, HONEY–
PLEASE CALL IT A NIGHT AND COME TO BED.
HONEY?
SOON.
I'LL BE THERE SOON, SWEETIE.
OKAY.

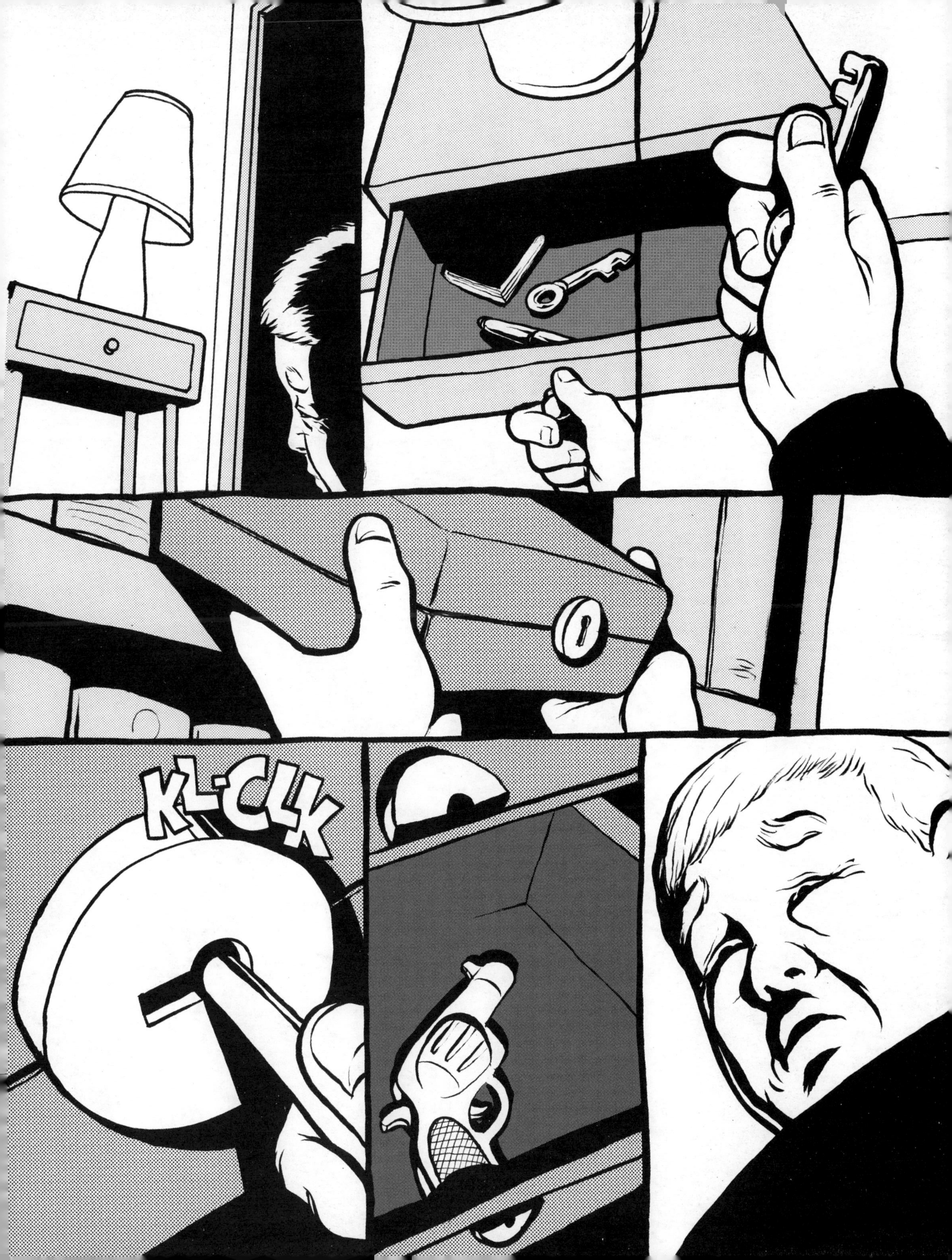
KL-CLK

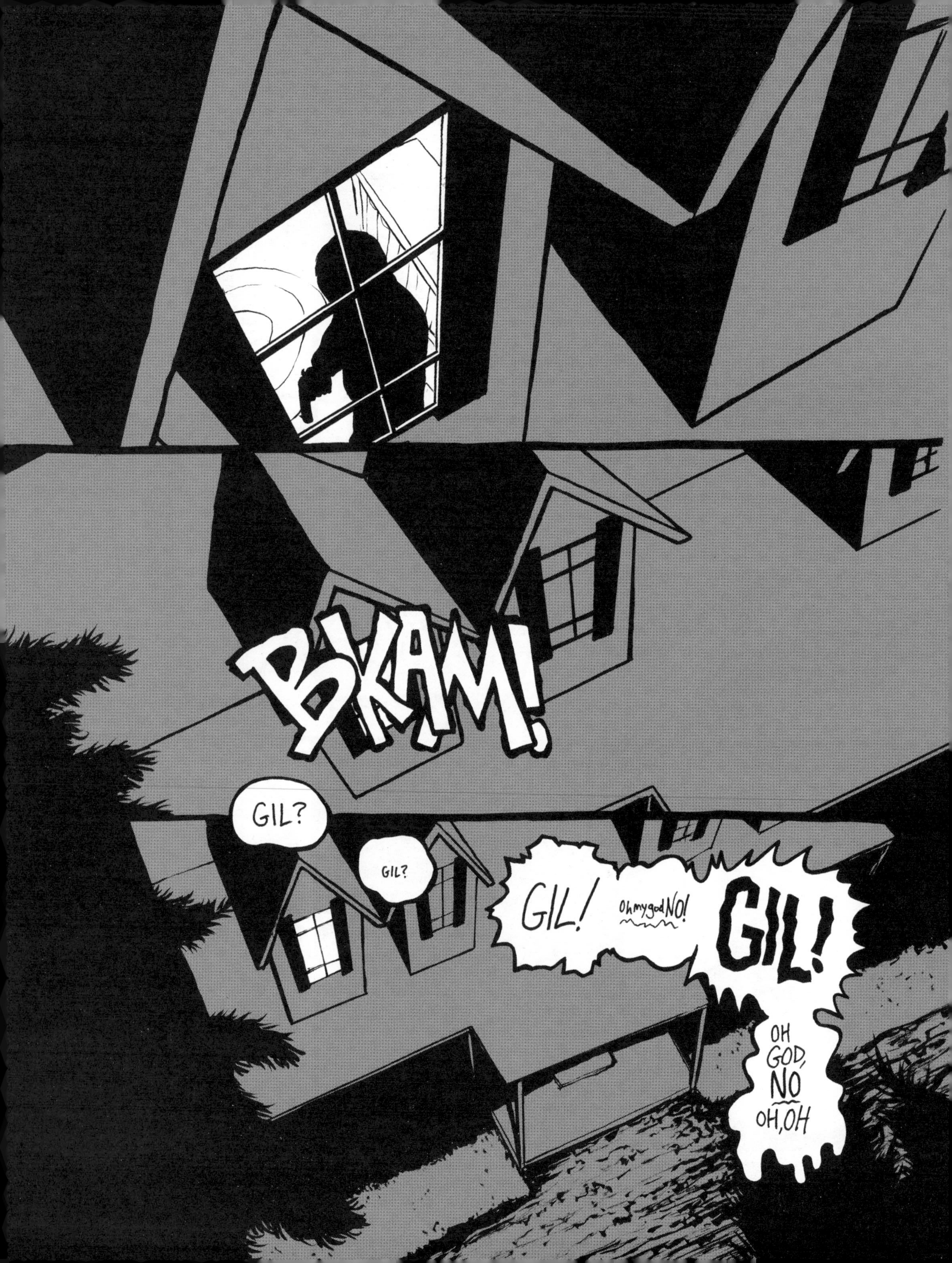
BKAM!
GIL?
GIL?
GIL!
OhmygodNO!
GIL!
OH GOD, NO OH,OH

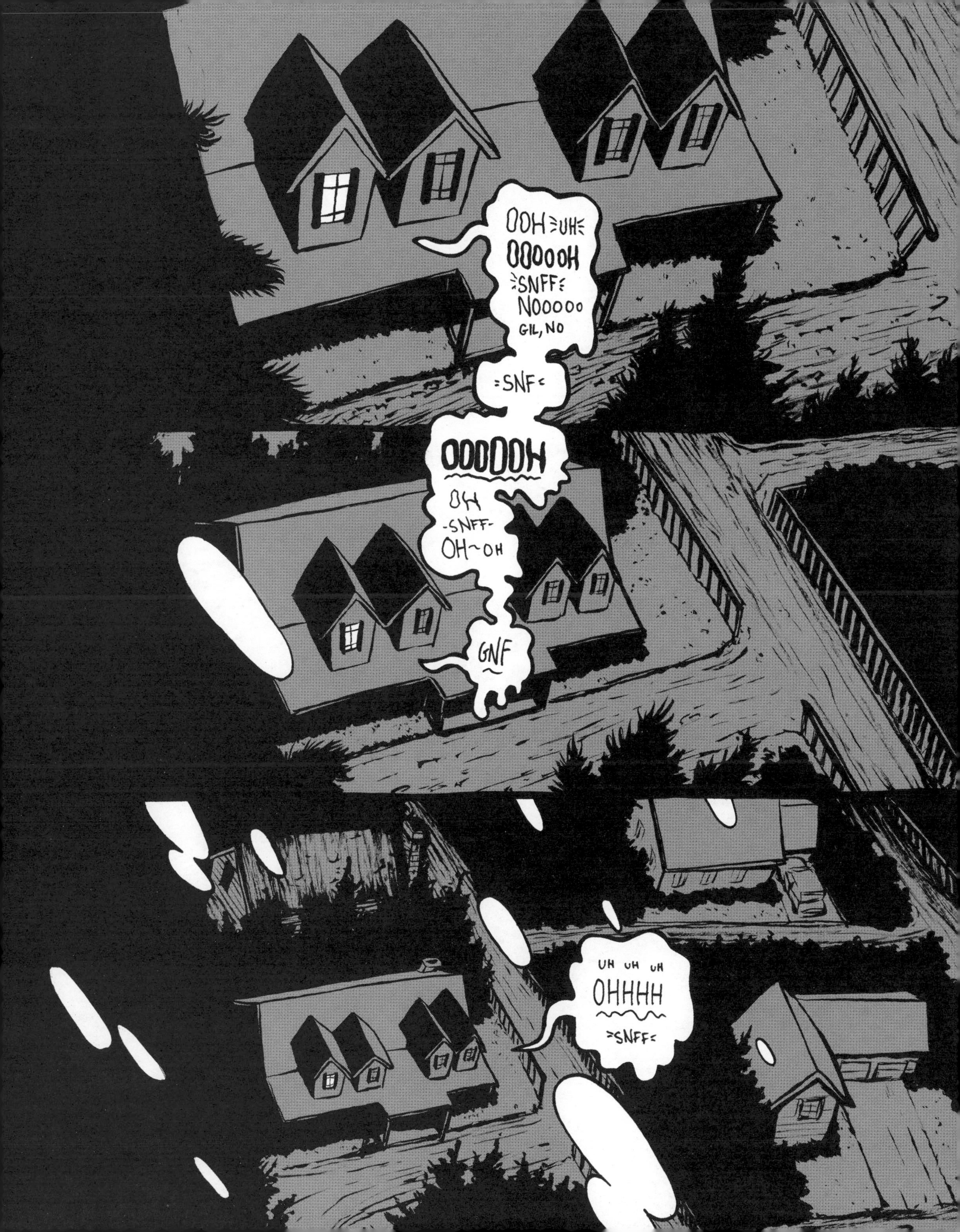
OOH =UH= OOOOOH =SNFF= NOOOOO GIL, NO
=SNF=
OOODOH
OH -SNFF- OH~OH
GNF
UH UH UH OHHHH =SNFF=

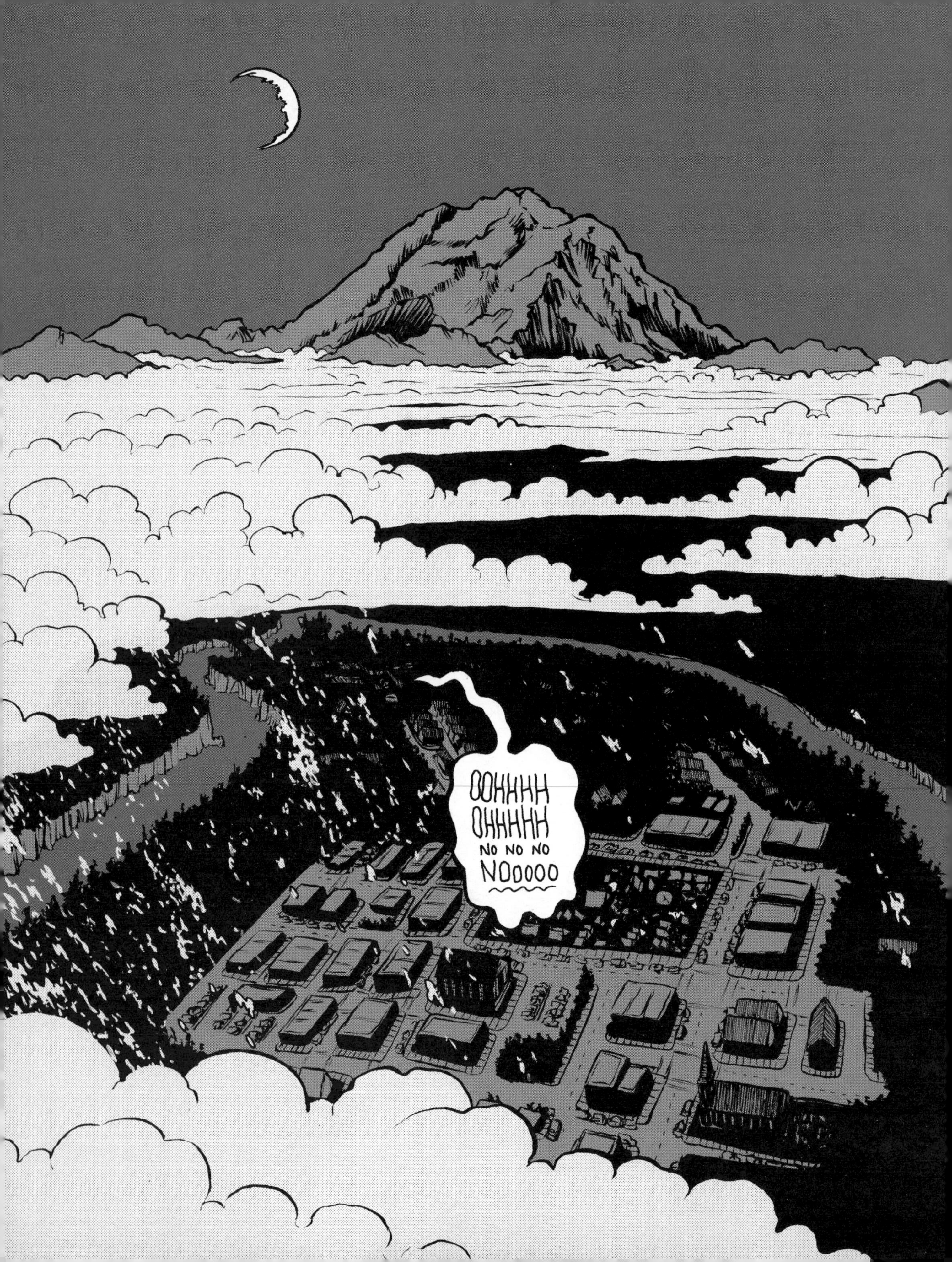
OOHHHH OHHHHH NO NO NO NOoooo

11.
REVELATIONS

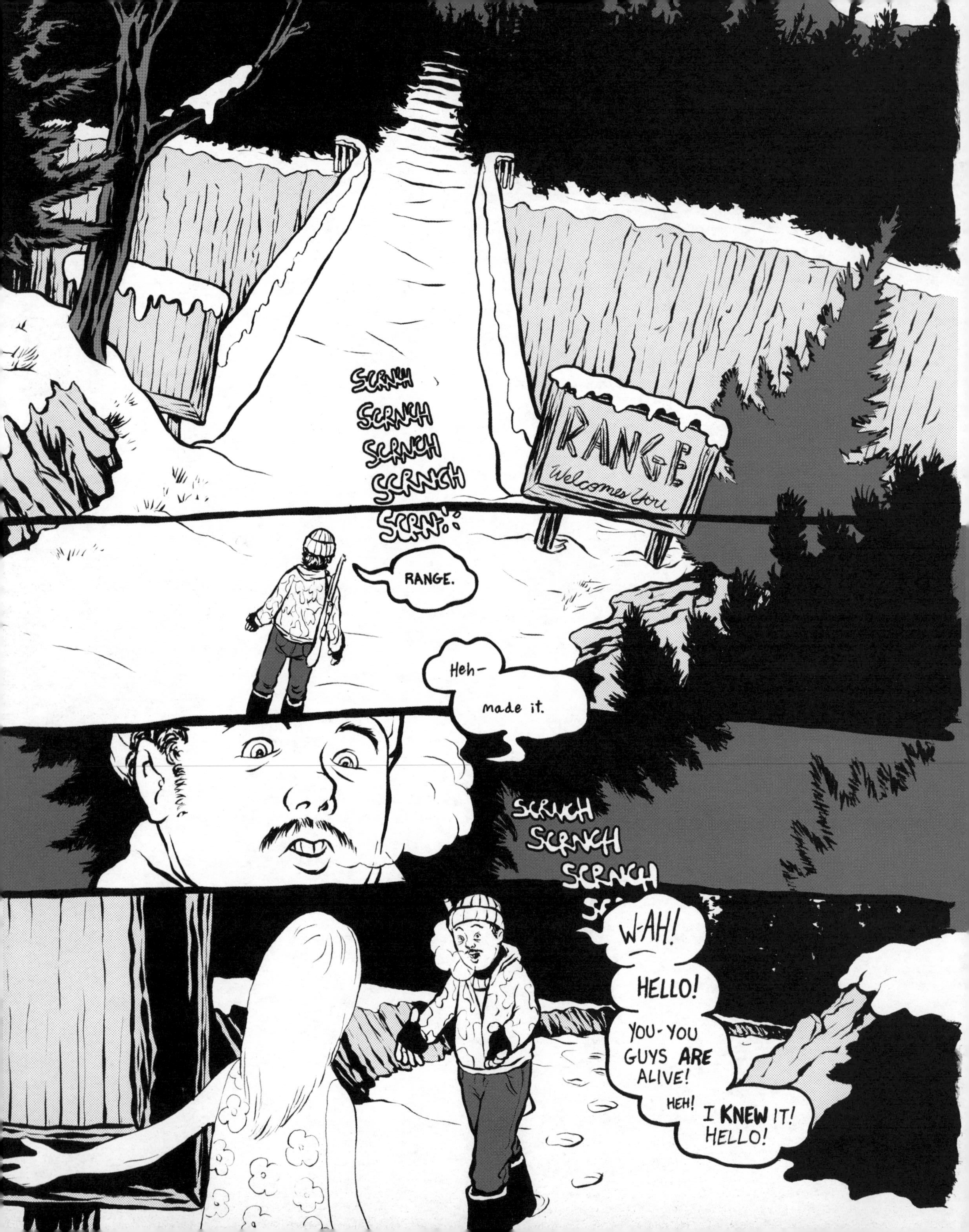
SCRNCH
SCRNCH
SCRNCH
SCRNCH
SCRN...
RANGE
Welcomes You
RANGE.
Heh-
made it.
SCRNCH
SCRNCH
SCRNCH
W-AH!
HELLO!
YOU-YOU GUYS ARE ALIVE!
HEH!
I KNEW IT! HELLO!

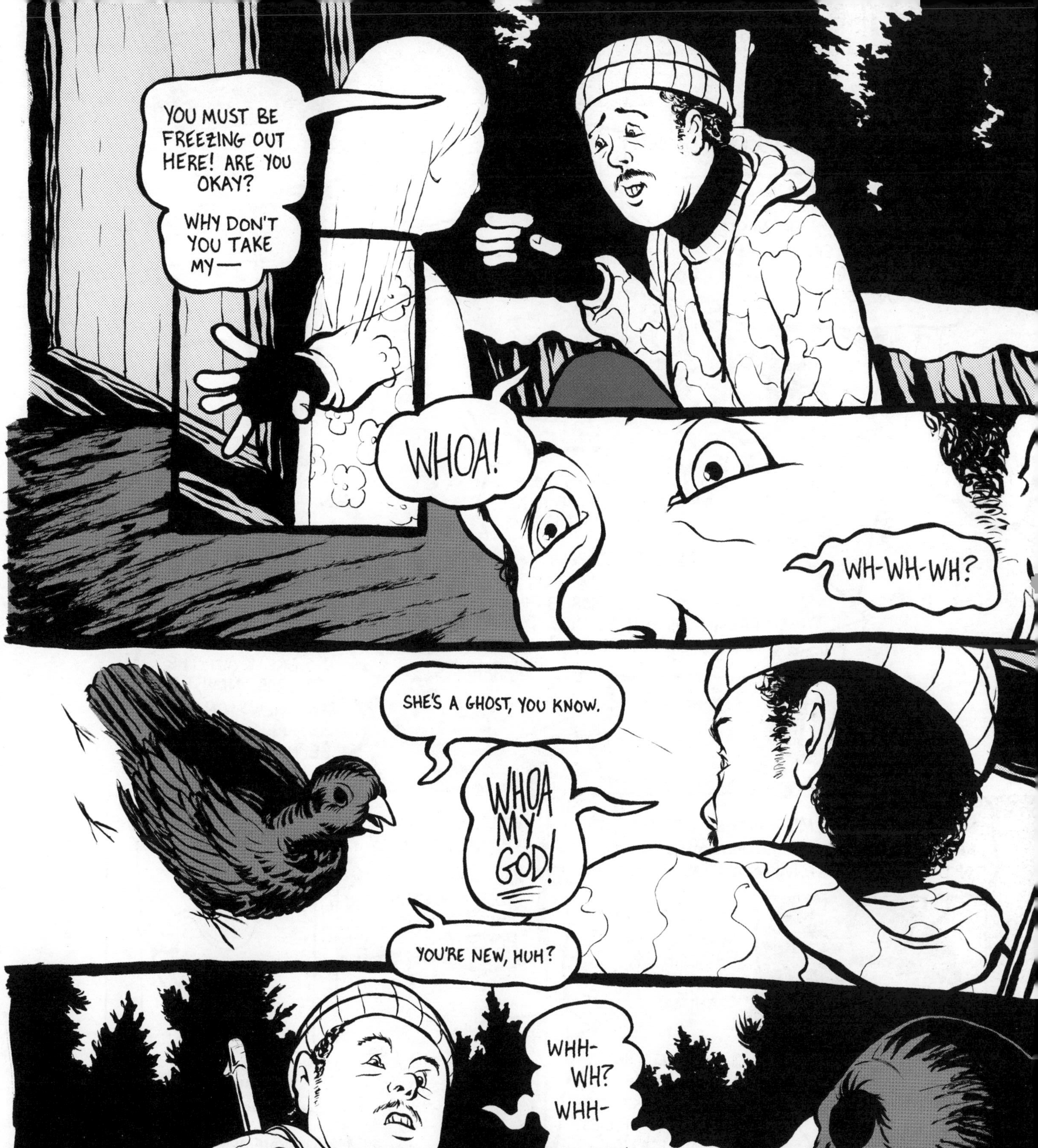
YOU MUST BE FREEZING OUT HERE! ARE YOU OKAY?
WHY DON'T YOU TAKE MY—
WHOA!
WH-WH-WH?
SHE'S A GHOST, YOU KNOW.
WHOA MY GOD!
YOU'RE NEW, HUH?
WHH- WH? WHH-
WHAT'S?
what'sgoingon?

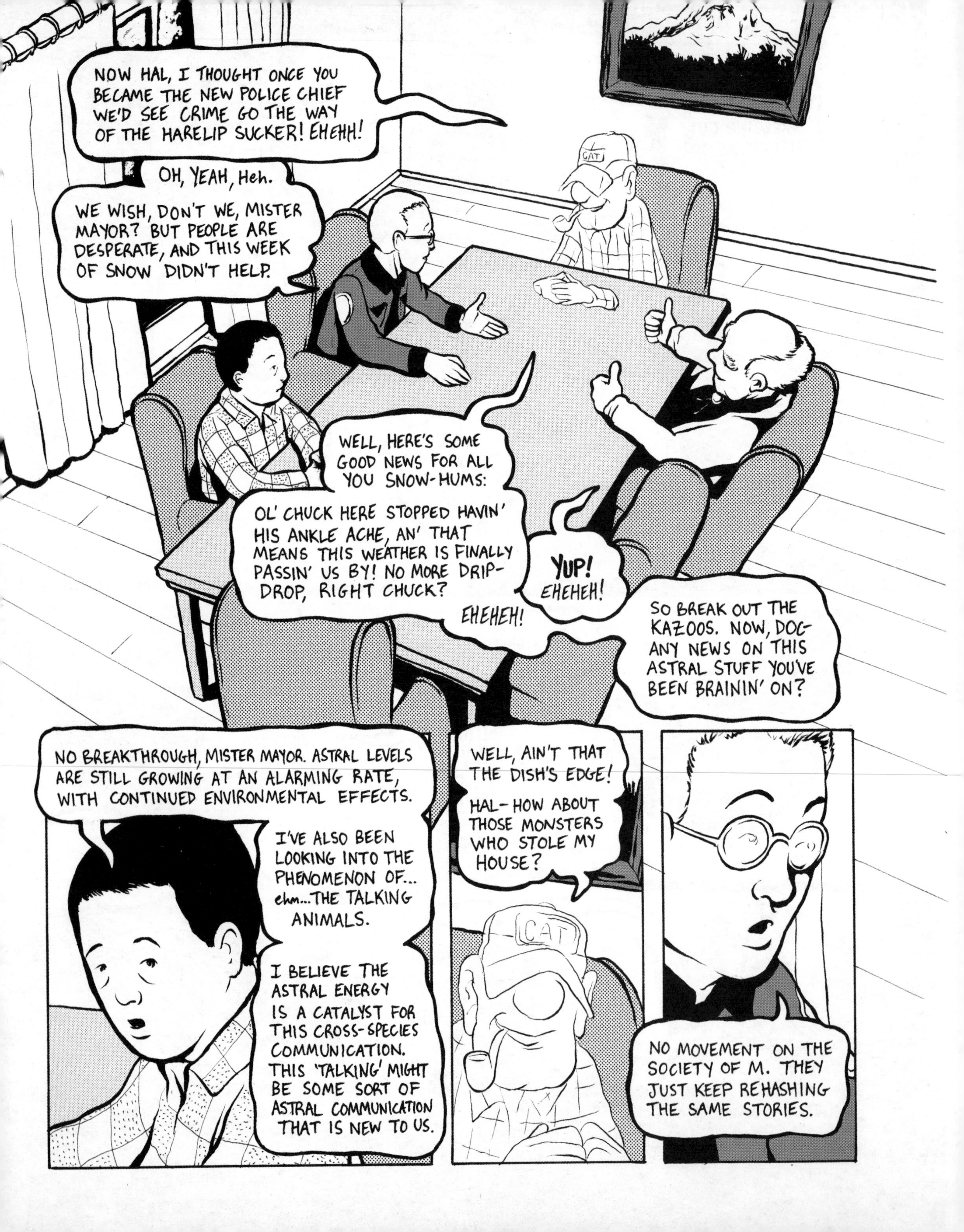
NOW HAL, I THOUGHT ONCE YOU BECAME THE NEW POLICE CHIEF WE'D SEE CRIME GO THE WAY OF THE HARELIP SUCKER! EHEHH!
OH, YEAH, Heh.
WE WISH, DON'T WE, MISTER MAYOR? BUT PEOPLE ARE DESPERATE, AND THIS WEEK OF SNOW DIDN'T HELP.
WELL, HERE'S SOME GOOD NEWS FOR ALL YOU SNOW-HUMS:
OL' CHUCK HERE STOPPED HAVIN' HIS ANKLE ACHE, AN' THAT MEANS THIS WEATHER IS FINALLY PASSIN' US BY! NO MORE DRIP-DROP, RIGHT CHUCK?
EHEHEH!
YUP! EHEHEH!
SO BREAK OUT THE KAZOOS. NOW, DOC- ANY NEWS ON THIS ASTRAL STUFF YOU'VE BEEN BRAININ' ON?
NO BREAKTHROUGH, MISTER MAYOR. ASTRAL LEVELS ARE STILL GROWING AT AN ALARMING RATE, WITH CONTINUED ENVIRONMENTAL EFFECTS.
I'VE ALSO BEEN LOOKING INTO THE PHENOMENON OF... ehm... THE TALKING ANIMALS.
I BELIEVE THE ASTRAL ENERGY IS A CATALYST FOR THIS CROSS-SPECIES COMMUNICATION. THIS 'TALKING' MIGHT BE SOME SORT OF ASTRAL COMMUNICATION THAT IS NEW TO US.
WELL, AIN'T THAT THE DISH'S EDGE!
HAL- HOW ABOUT THOSE MONSTERS WHO STOLE MY HOUSE?
NO MOVEMENT ON THE SOCIETY OF M. THEY JUST KEEP REHASHING THE SAME STORIES.

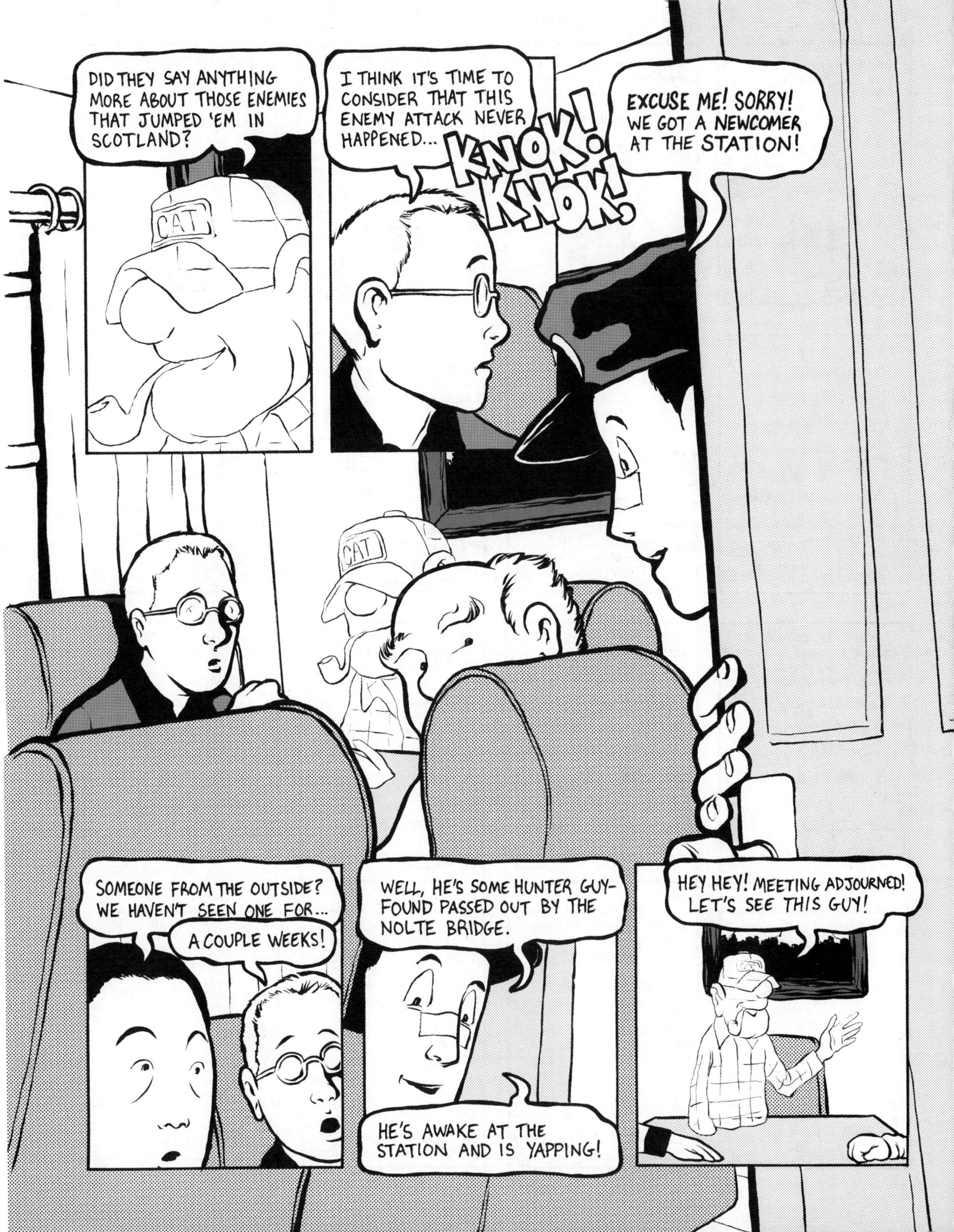
DID THEY SAY ANYTHING MORE ABOUT THOSE ENEMIES THAT JUMPED 'EM IN SCOTLAND?
I THINK IT'S TIME TO CONSIDER THAT THIS ENEMY ATTACK NEVER HAPPENED...
KNOK! KNOK!
EXCUSE ME! SORRY! WE GOT A NEWCOMER AT THE STATION!
CAT
CAT
SOMEONE FROM THE OUTSIDE? WE HAVEN'T SEEN ONE FOR...
A COUPLE WEEKS!
WELL, HE'S SOME HUNTER GUY-FOUND PASSED OUT BY THE NOLTE BRIDGE.
HE'S AWAKE AT THE STATION AND IS YAPPING!
HEY HEY! MEETING ADJOURNED! LET'S SEE THIS GUY!

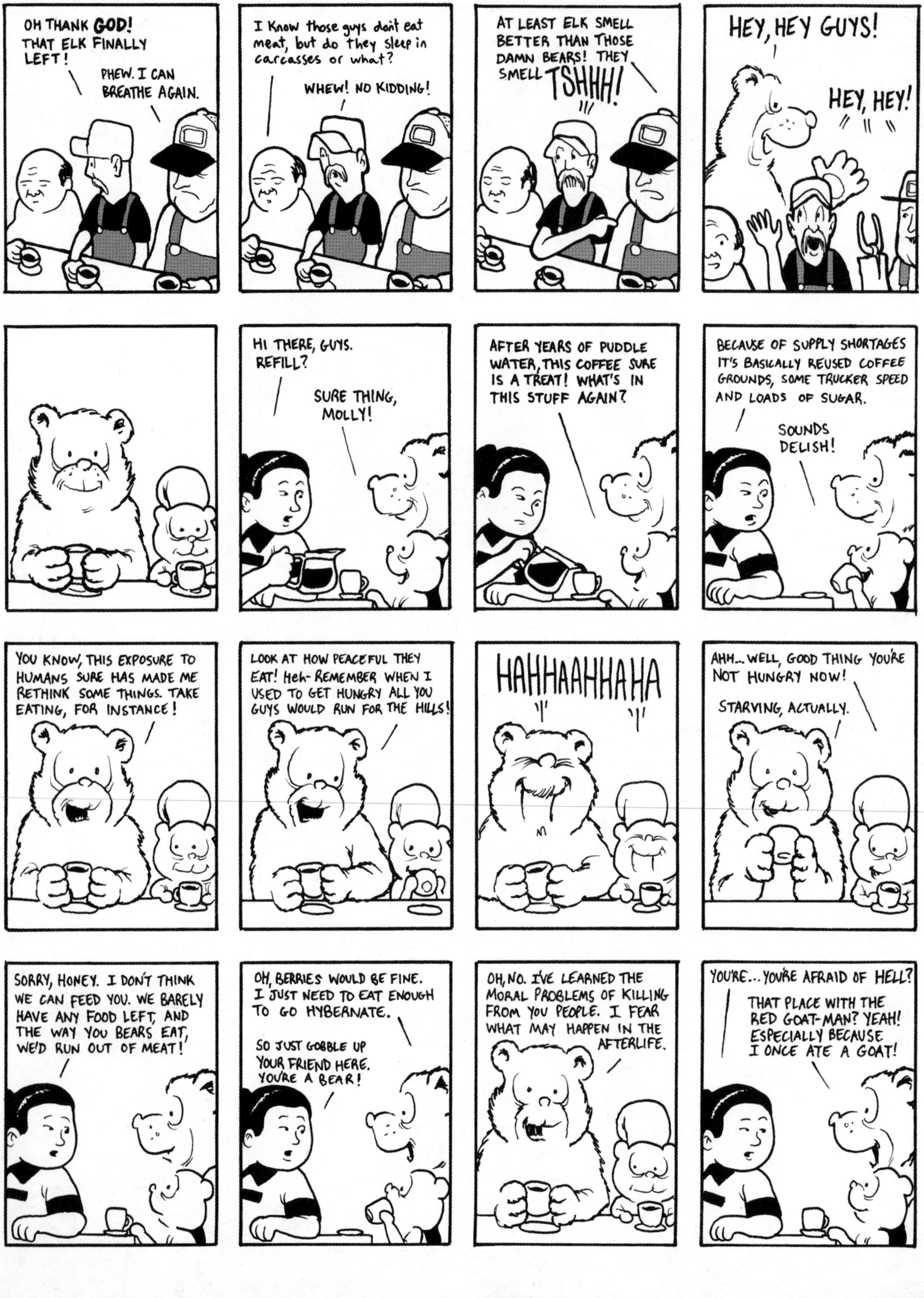
OH THANK GOD! THAT ELK FINALLY LEFT!
PHEW. I CAN BREATHE AGAIN.
I Know those guys don't eat meat, but do they sleep in carcasses or what?
WHEW! NO KIDDING!
AT LEAST ELK SMELL BETTER THAN THOSE DAMN BEARS! THEY SMELL TSHHH!
HEY, HEY GUYS!
HEY, HEY!
HI THERE, GUYS. REFILL?
SURE THING, MOLLY!
AFTER YEARS OF PUDDLE WATER, THIS COFFEE SURE IS A TREAT! WHAT'S IN THIS STUFF AGAIN?
BECAUSE OF SUPPLY SHORTAGES IT'S BASICALLY REUSED COFFEE GROUNDS, SOME TRUCKER SPEED AND LOADS OF SUGAR.
SOUNDS DELISH!
YOU KNOW, THIS EXPOSURE TO HUMANS SURE HAS MADE ME RETHINK SOME THINGS. TAKE EATING, FOR INSTANCE!
LOOK AT HOW PEACEFUL THEY EAT! Heh- REMEMBER WHEN I USED TO GET HUNGRY ALL YOU GUYS WOULD RUN FOR THE HILLS!
HAHHAAHHAHA
AHH... WELL, GOOD THING YOU'RE NOT HUNGRY NOW!
STARVING, ACTUALLY.
SORRY, HONEY. I DON'T THINK WE CAN FEED YOU. WE BARELY HAVE ANY FOOD LEFT, AND THE WAY YOU BEARS EAT, WE'D RUN OUT OF MEAT!
OH, BERRIES WOULD BE FINE. I JUST NEED TO EAT ENOUGH TO GO HYBERNATE.
SO JUST GOBBLE UP YOUR FRIEND HERE. YOU'RE A BEAR!
OH, NO. I'VE LEARNED THE MORAL PROBLEMS OF KILLING FROM YOU PEOPLE. I FEAR WHAT MAY HAPPEN IN THE AFTERLIFE.
YOU'RE... YOU'RE AFRAID OF HELL?
THAT PLACE WITH THE RED GOAT-MAN? YEAH! ESPECIALLY BECAUSE I ONCE ATE A GOAT!

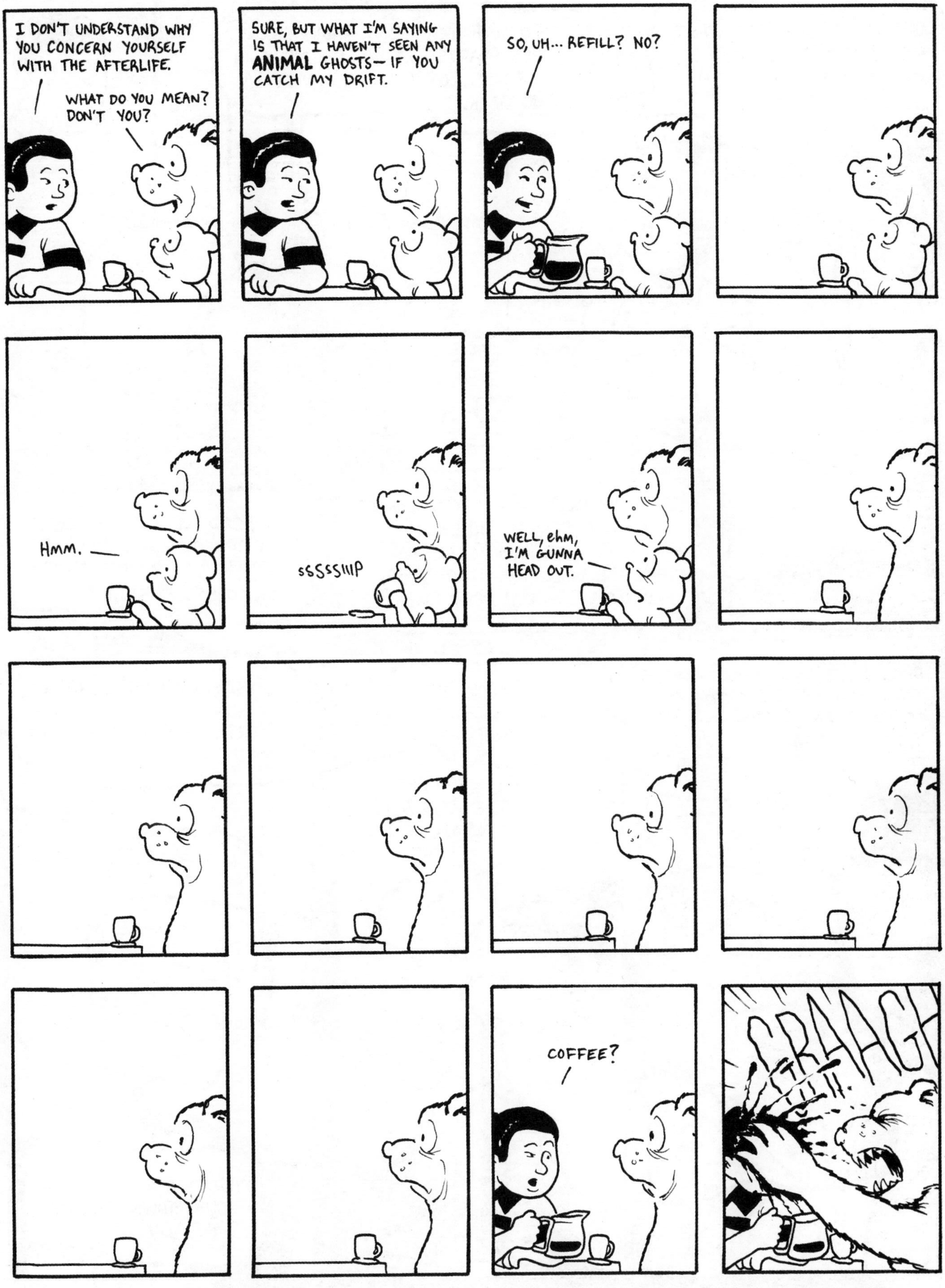
I DON'T UNDERSTAND WHY YOU CONCERN YOURSELF WITH THE AFTERLIFE.
WHAT DO YOU MEAN? DON'T YOU?
SURE, BUT WHAT I'M SAYING IS THAT I HAVEN'T SEEN ANY **ANIMAL** GHOSTS— IF YOU CATCH MY DRIFT.
SO, UH... REFILL? NO?
Hmm.
SSSSSIIIP
WELL, ehm, I'M GUNNA HEAD OUT.
COFFEE?

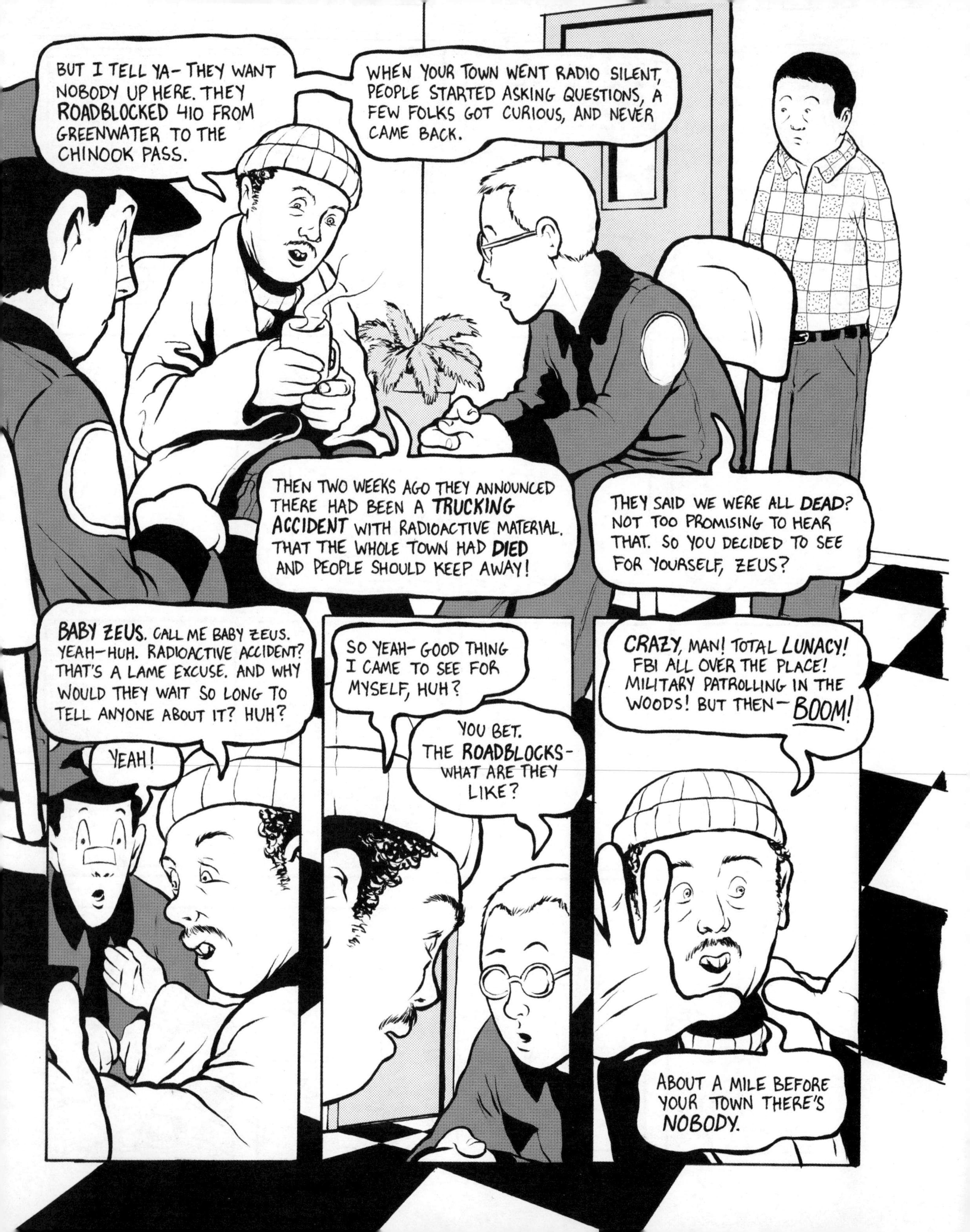
BUT I TELL YA- THEY WANT NOBODY UP HERE. THEY ROADBLOCKED 410 FROM GREENWATER TO THE CHINOOK PASS.
WHEN YOUR TOWN WENT RADIO SILENT, PEOPLE STARTED ASKING QUESTIONS, A FEW FOLKS GOT CURIOUS, AND NEVER CAME BACK.
THEN TWO WEEKS AGO THEY ANNOUNCED THERE HAD BEEN A TRUCKING ACCIDENT WITH RADIOACTIVE MATERIAL. THAT THE WHOLE TOWN HAD DIED AND PEOPLE SHOULD KEEP AWAY!
THEY SAID WE WERE ALL DEAD? NOT TOO PROMISING TO HEAR THAT. SO YOU DECIDED TO SEE FOR YOURSELF, ZEUS?
BABY ZEUS. CALL ME BABY ZEUS. YEAH-HUH. RADIOACTIVE ACCIDENT? THAT'S A LAME EXCUSE. AND WHY WOULD THEY WAIT SO LONG TO TELL ANYONE ABOUT IT? HUH?
YEAH!
SO YEAH- GOOD THING I CAME TO SEE FOR MYSELF, HUH?
YOU BET. THE ROADBLOCKS- WHAT ARE THEY LIKE?
CRAZY, MAN! TOTAL LUNACY! FBI ALL OVER THE PLACE! MILITARY PATROLLING IN THE WOODS! BUT THEN- BOOM!
ABOUT A MILE BEFORE YOUR TOWN THERE'S NOBODY.

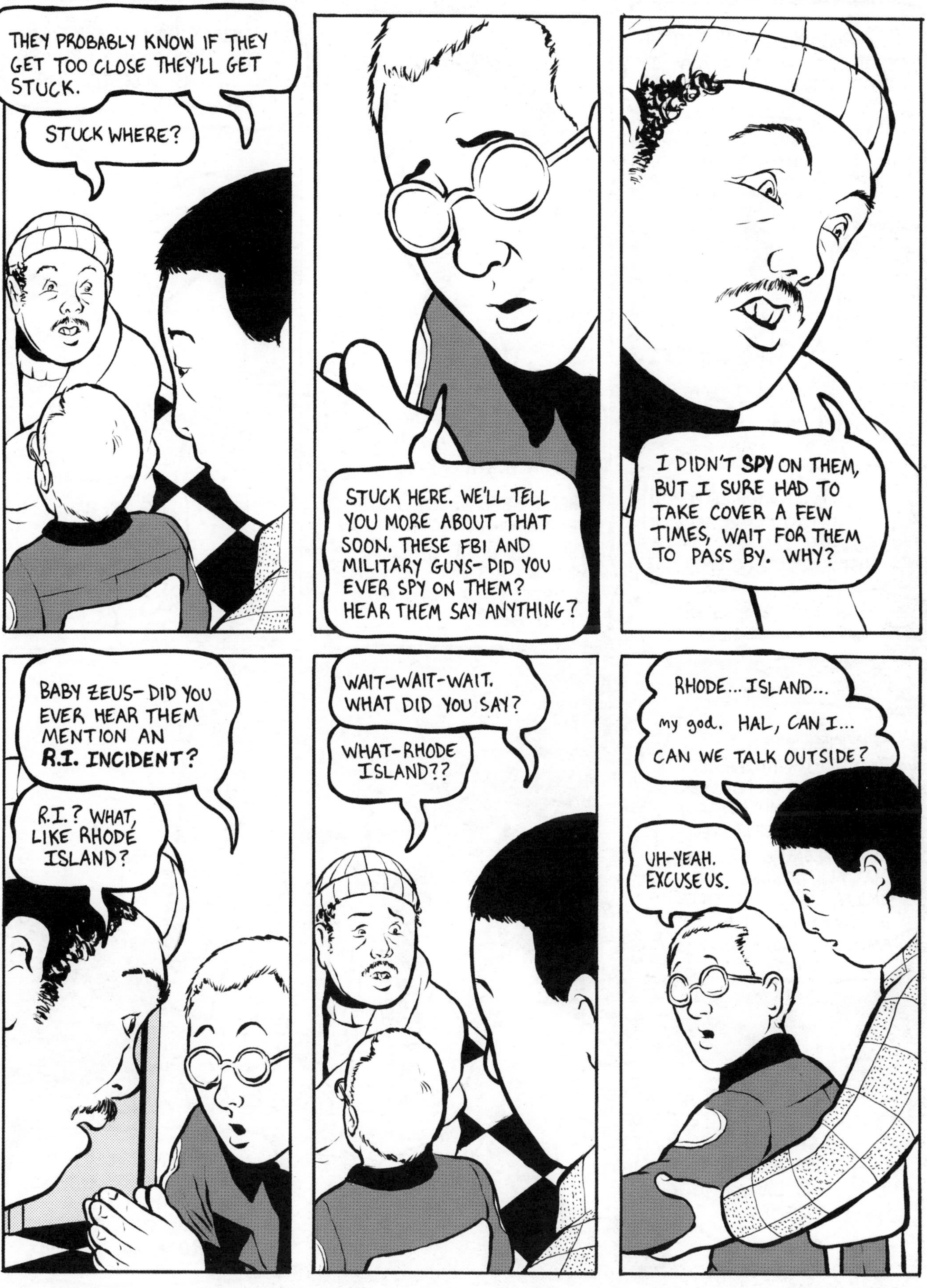
THEY PROBABLY KNOW IF THEY GET TOO CLOSE THEY'LL GET STUCK.
STUCK WHERE?
STUCK HERE. WE'LL TELL YOU MORE ABOUT THAT SOON. THESE FBI AND MILITARY GUYS- DID YOU EVER SPY ON THEM? HEAR THEM SAY ANYTHING?
I DIDN'T **SPY** ON THEM, BUT I SURE HAD TO TAKE COVER A FEW TIMES, WAIT FOR THEM TO PASS BY. WHY?
BABY ZEUS- DID YOU EVER HEAR THEM MENTION AN **R.I. INCIDENT**?
R.I.? WHAT, LIKE RHODE ISLAND?
WAIT-WAIT-WAIT. WHAT DID YOU SAY?
WHAT-RHODE ISLAND??
RHODE... ISLAND... my god. HAL, CAN I... CAN WE TALK OUTSIDE?
UH-YEAH. EXCUSE US.

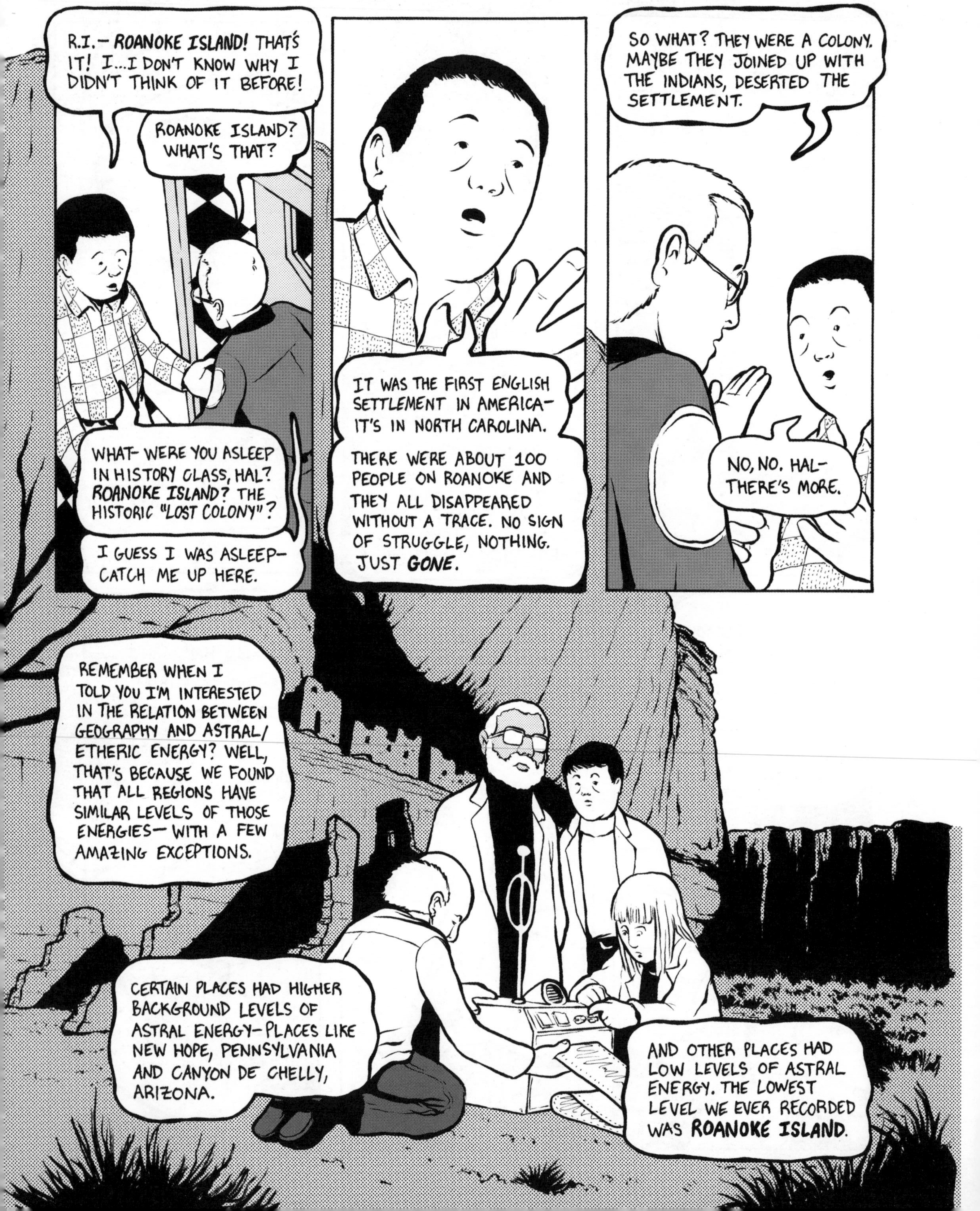
R.I.—**ROANOKE ISLAND!** THAT'S IT! I...I DON'T KNOW WHY I DIDN'T THINK OF IT BEFORE!
ROANOKE ISLAND? WHAT'S THAT?
WHAT- WERE YOU ASLEEP IN HISTORY CLASS, HAL? **ROANOKE ISLAND**? THE HISTORIC "LOST COLONY"?
I GUESS I WAS ASLEEP- CATCH ME UP HERE.
IT WAS THE FIRST ENGLISH SETTLEMENT IN AMERICA- IT'S IN NORTH CAROLINA.
THERE WERE ABOUT 100 PEOPLE ON ROANOKE AND THEY ALL DISAPPEARED WITHOUT A TRACE. NO SIGN OF STRUGGLE, NOTHING. JUST **GONE**.
SO WHAT? THEY WERE A COLONY. MAYBE THEY JOINED UP WITH THE INDIANS, DESERTED THE SETTLEMENT.
NO, NO. HAL- THERE'S MORE.
REMEMBER WHEN I TOLD YOU I'M INTERESTED IN THE RELATION BETWEEN GEOGRAPHY AND ASTRAL/ ETHERIC ENERGY? WELL, THAT'S BECAUSE WE FOUND THAT ALL REGIONS HAVE SIMILAR LEVELS OF THOSE ENERGIES—WITH A FEW AMAZING EXCEPTIONS.
CERTAIN PLACES HAD HIGHER BACKGROUND LEVELS OF ASTRAL ENERGY—PLACES LIKE NEW HOPE, PENNSYLVANIA AND CANYON DE CHELLY, ARIZONA.
AND OTHER PLACES HAD LOW LEVELS OF ASTRAL ENERGY. THE LOWEST LEVEL WE EVER RECORDED WAS **ROANOKE ISLAND**.

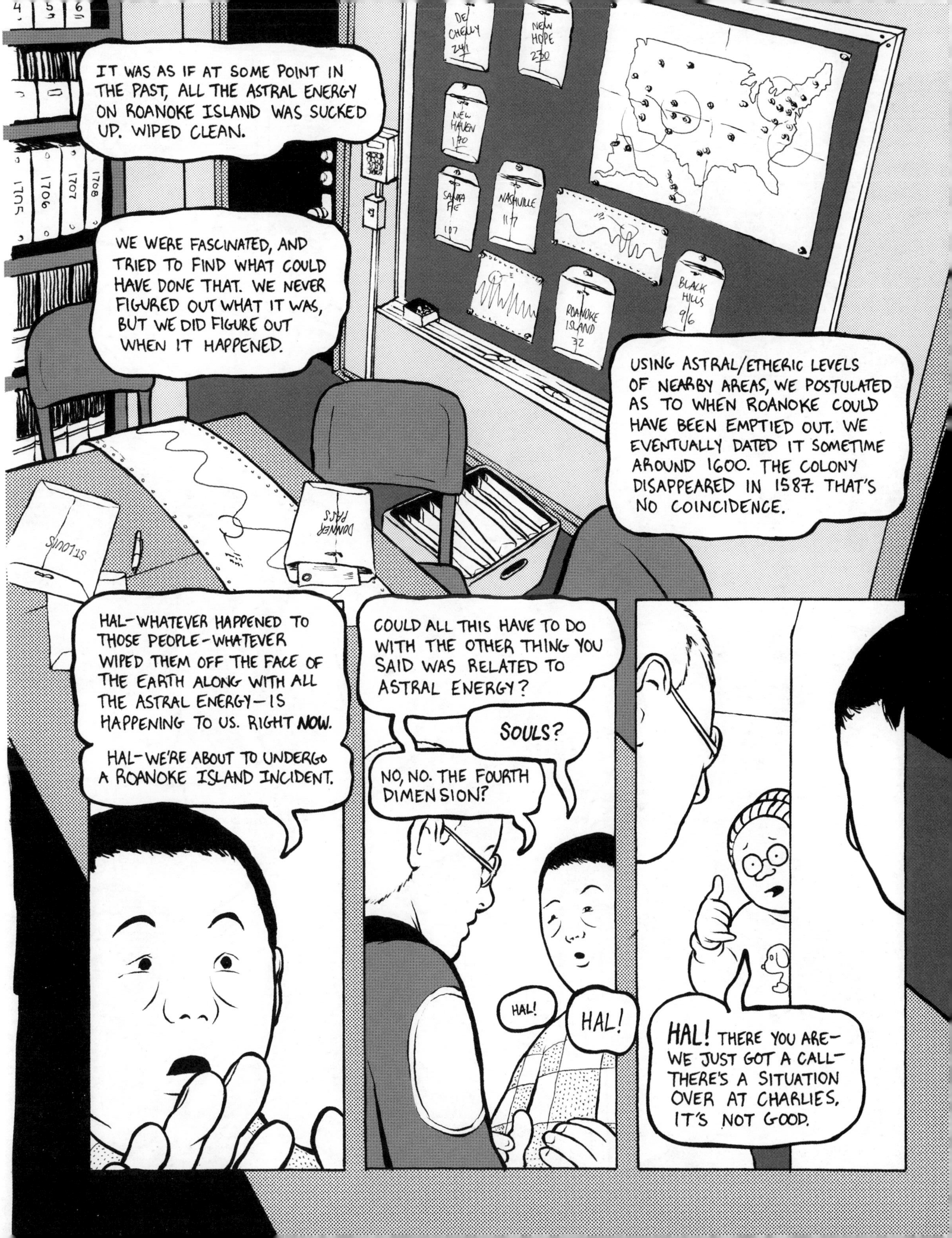
IT WAS AS IF AT SOME POINT IN THE PAST, ALL THE ASTRAL ENERGY ON ROANOKE ISLAND WAS SUCKED UP. WIPED CLEAN.
WE WERE FASCINATED, AND TRIED TO FIND WHAT COULD HAVE DONE THAT. WE NEVER FIGURED OUT WHAT IT WAS, BUT WE DID FIGURE OUT WHEN IT HAPPENED.
DE CHELLY 241
NEW HOPE 230
NEW HAVEN 170
SANTA FE 107
NASHVILLE 117
BLACK HILLS 96
ROANOKE ISLAND 32
DONNER PASS
ST. LOUIS
1705
1706
1707
1708
USING ASTRAL/ETHERIC LEVELS OF NEARBY AREAS, WE POSTULATED AS TO WHEN ROANOKE COULD HAVE BEEN EMPTIED OUT. WE EVENTUALLY DATED IT SOMETIME AROUND 1600. THE COLONY DISAPPEARED IN 1587. THAT'S NO COINCIDENCE.
HAL—WHATEVER HAPPENED TO THOSE PEOPLE—WHATEVER WIPED THEM OFF THE FACE OF THE EARTH ALONG WITH ALL THE ASTRAL ENERGY—IS HAPPENING TO US. RIGHT **NOW**.
HAL—WE'RE ABOUT TO UNDERGO A ROANOKE ISLAND INCIDENT.
COULD ALL THIS HAVE TO DO WITH THE OTHER THING YOU SAID WAS RELATED TO ASTRAL ENERGY?
SOULS?
NO, NO. THE FOURTH DIMENSION?
HAL!
HAL!
HAL! THERE YOU ARE—WE JUST GOT A CALL—THERE'S A SITUATION OVER AT CHARLIES. IT'S NOT GOOD.

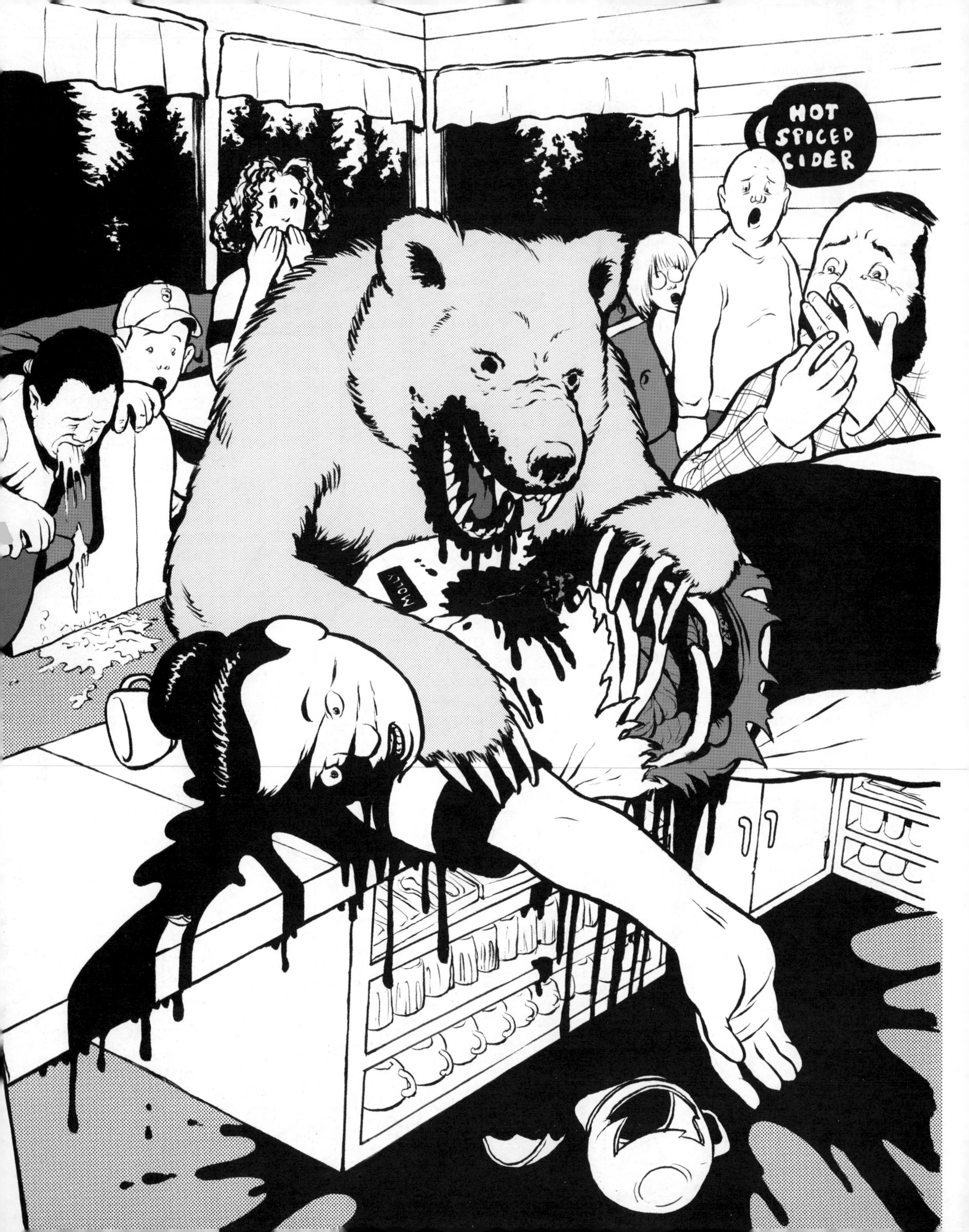
HOT SPICED CIDER
MOLLY

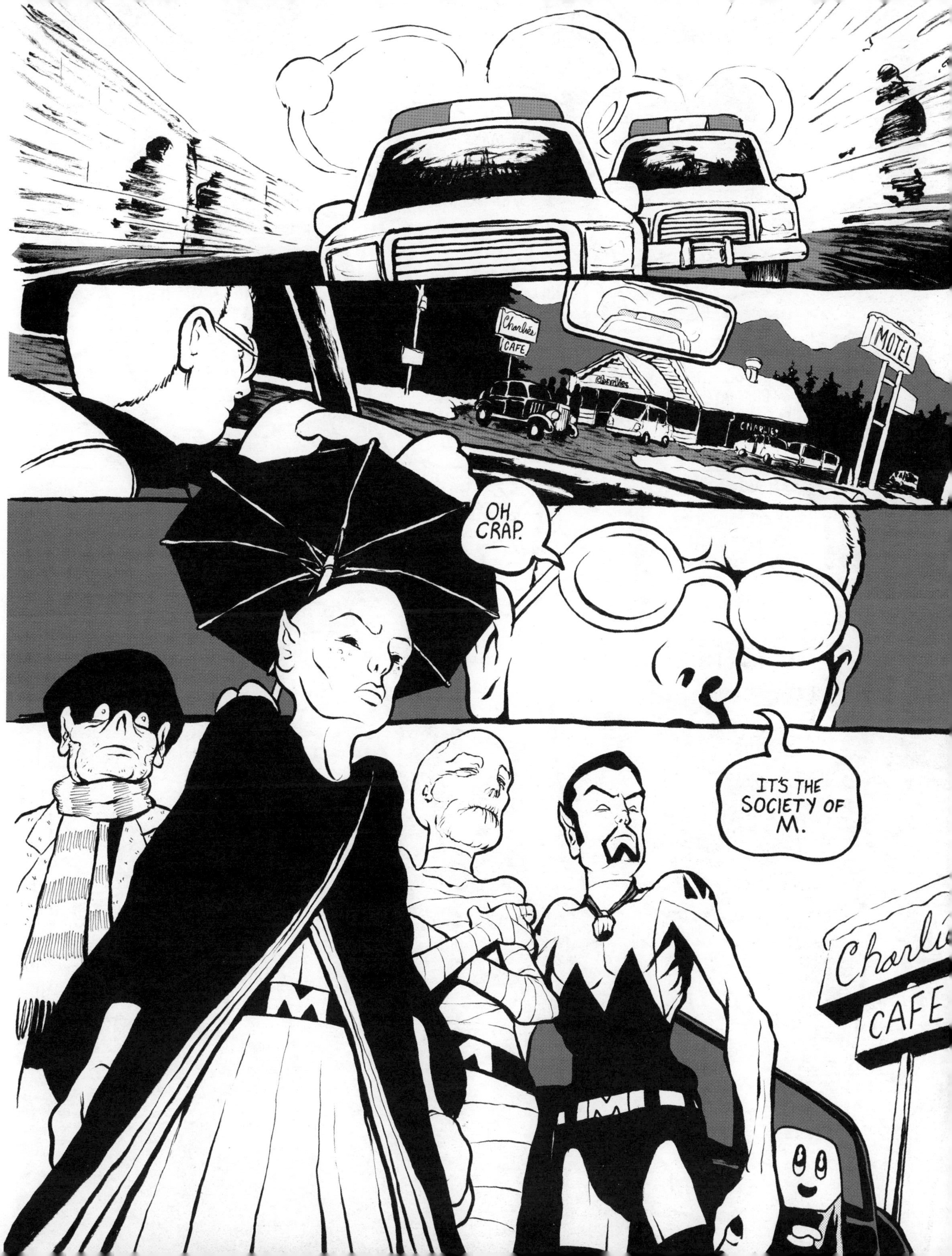

Charlie's
CAFE
MOTEL
OH CRAP.
IT'S THE SOCIETY OF M.
CAFE

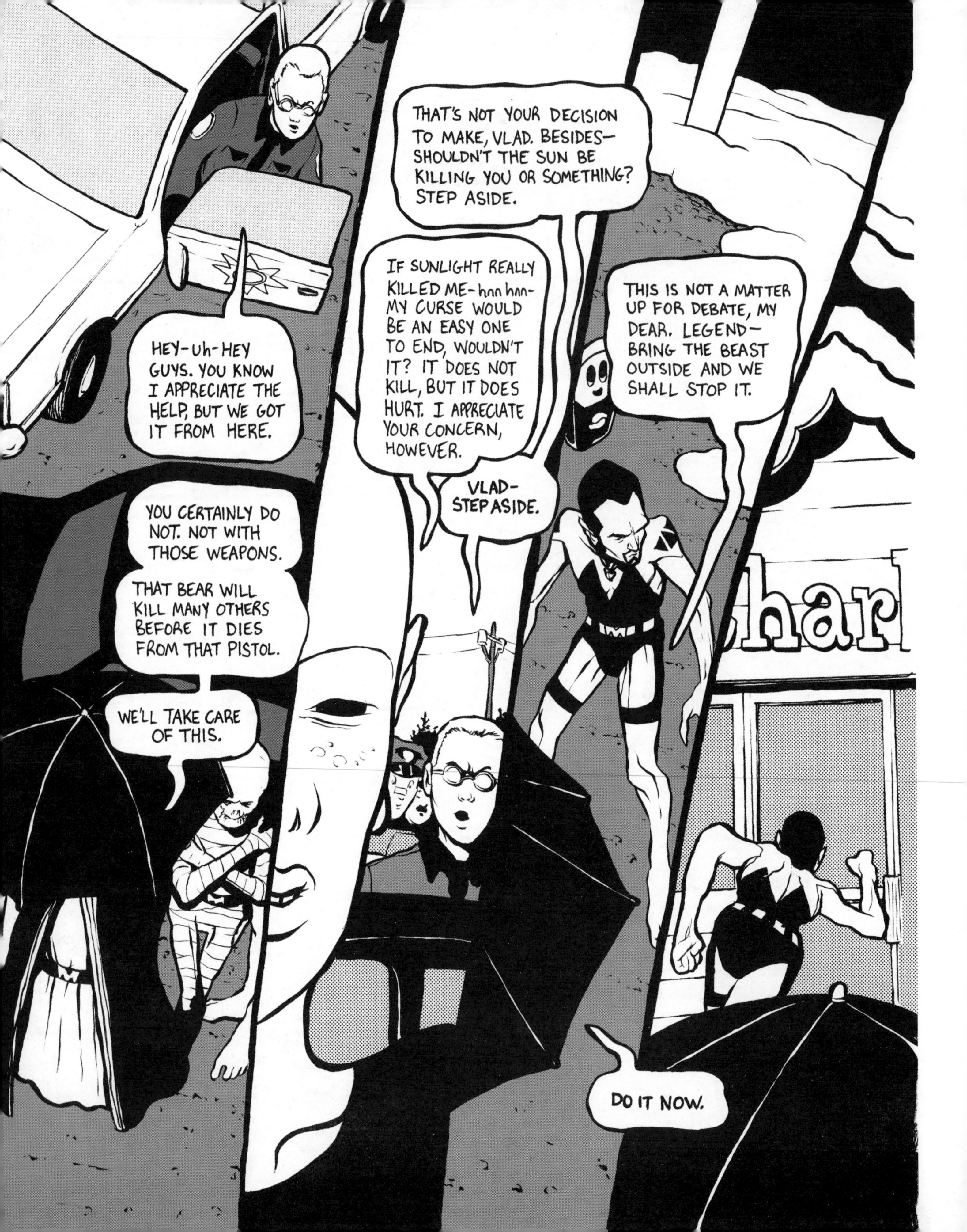
HEY-uh-HEY GUYS. YOU KNOW I APPRECIATE THE HELP, BUT WE GOT IT FROM HERE.
YOU CERTAINLY DO NOT. NOT WITH THOSE WEAPONS.
THAT BEAR WILL KILL MANY OTHERS BEFORE IT DIES FROM THAT PISTOL.
WE'LL TAKE CARE OF THIS.
THAT'S NOT YOUR DECISION TO MAKE, VLAD. BESIDES—SHOULDN'T THE SUN BE KILLING YOU OR SOMETHING? STEP ASIDE.
IF SUNLIGHT REALLY KILLED ME-hnn hnn- MY CURSE WOULD BE AN EASY ONE TO END, WOULDN'T IT? IT DOES NOT KILL, BUT IT DOES HURT. I APPRECIATE YOUR CONCERN, HOWEVER.
VLAD- STEP ASIDE.
THIS IS NOT A MATTER UP FOR DEBATE, MY DEAR. LEGEND—BRING THE BEAST OUTSIDE AND WE SHALL STOP IT.
DO IT NOW.

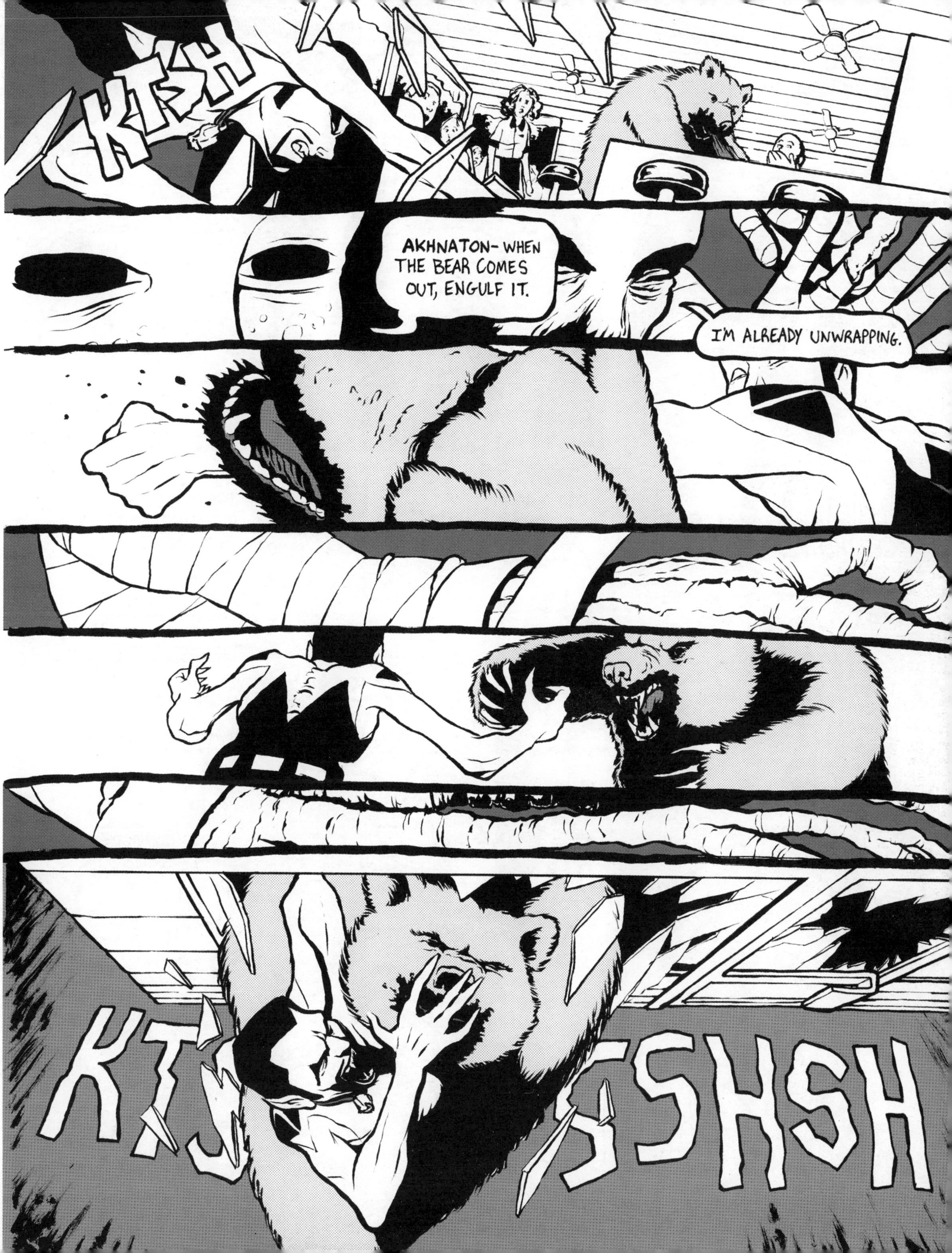
KTSH
AKHNATON- WHEN THE BEAR COMES OUT, ENGULF IT.
I'M ALREADY UNWRAPPING.
KT
SSHSH

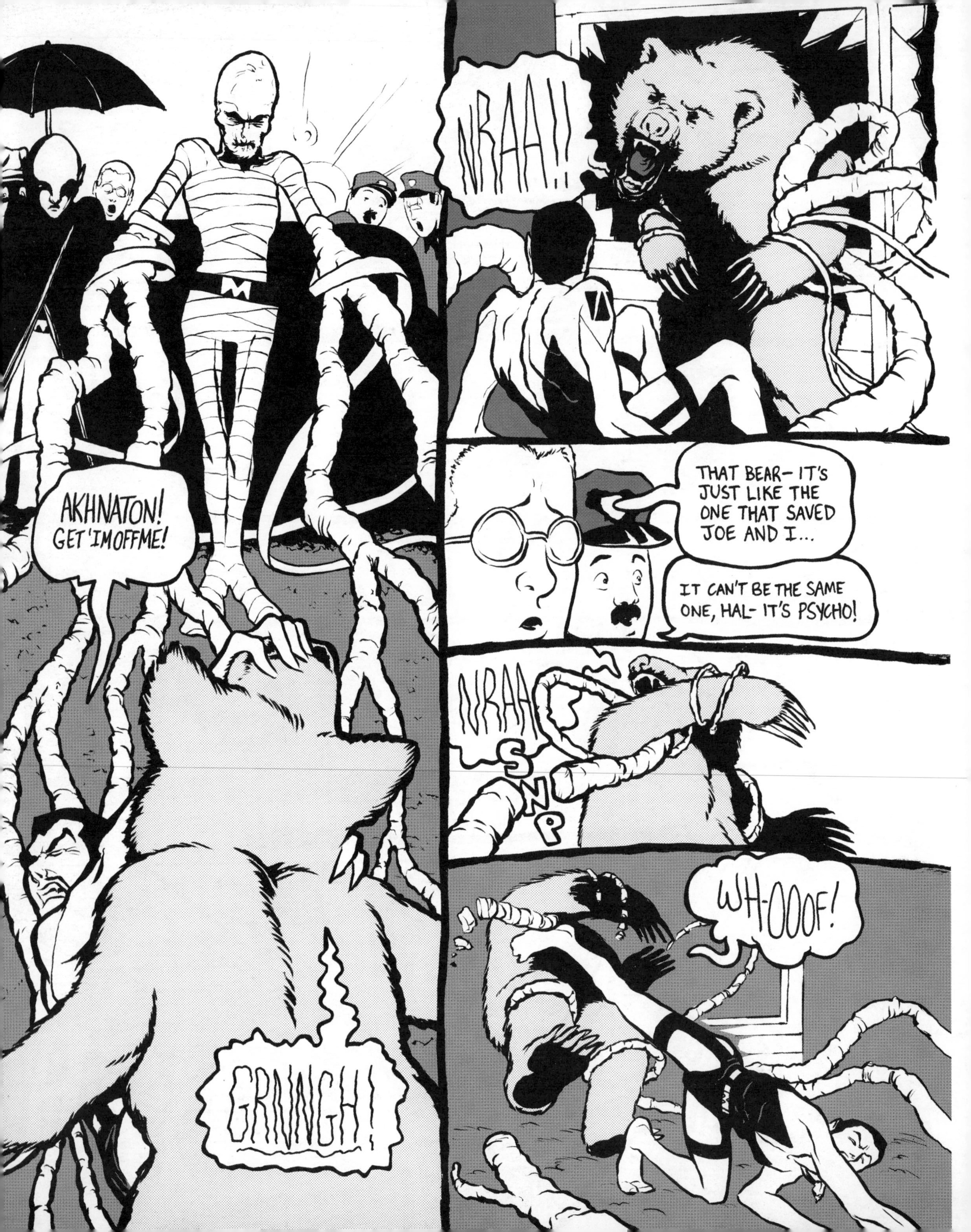
AKHNATON! GET 'IMOFFME!
GRNNGH!
NRAA!!
THAT BEAR— IT'S JUST LIKE THE ONE THAT SAVED JOE AND I...
IT CAN'T BE THE SAME ONE, HAL— IT'S PSYCHO!
NRAA
SNP
WH-OOOF!

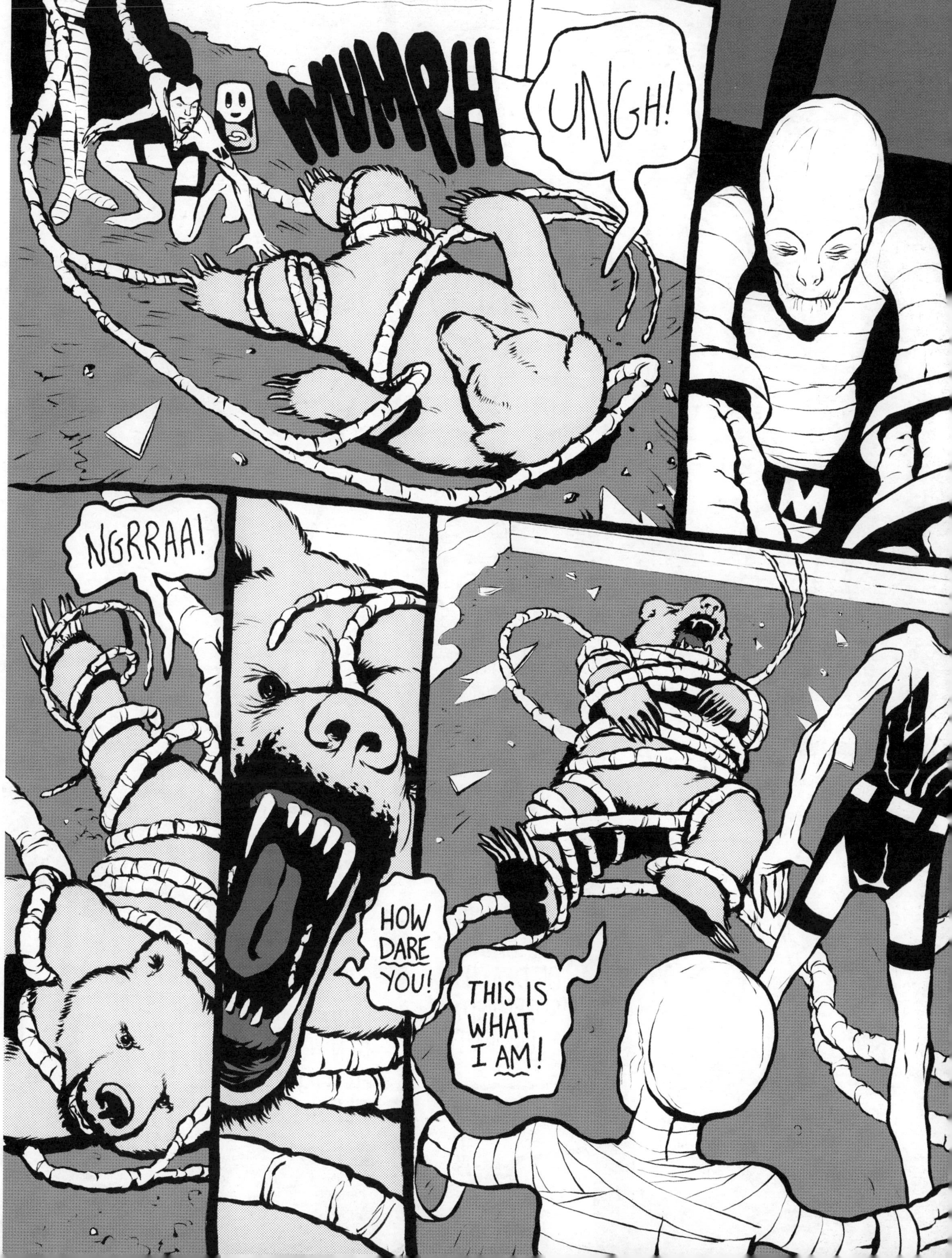
WUMPH
UNGH!
NGRRAA!
HOW DARE YOU!
THIS IS WHAT I AM!

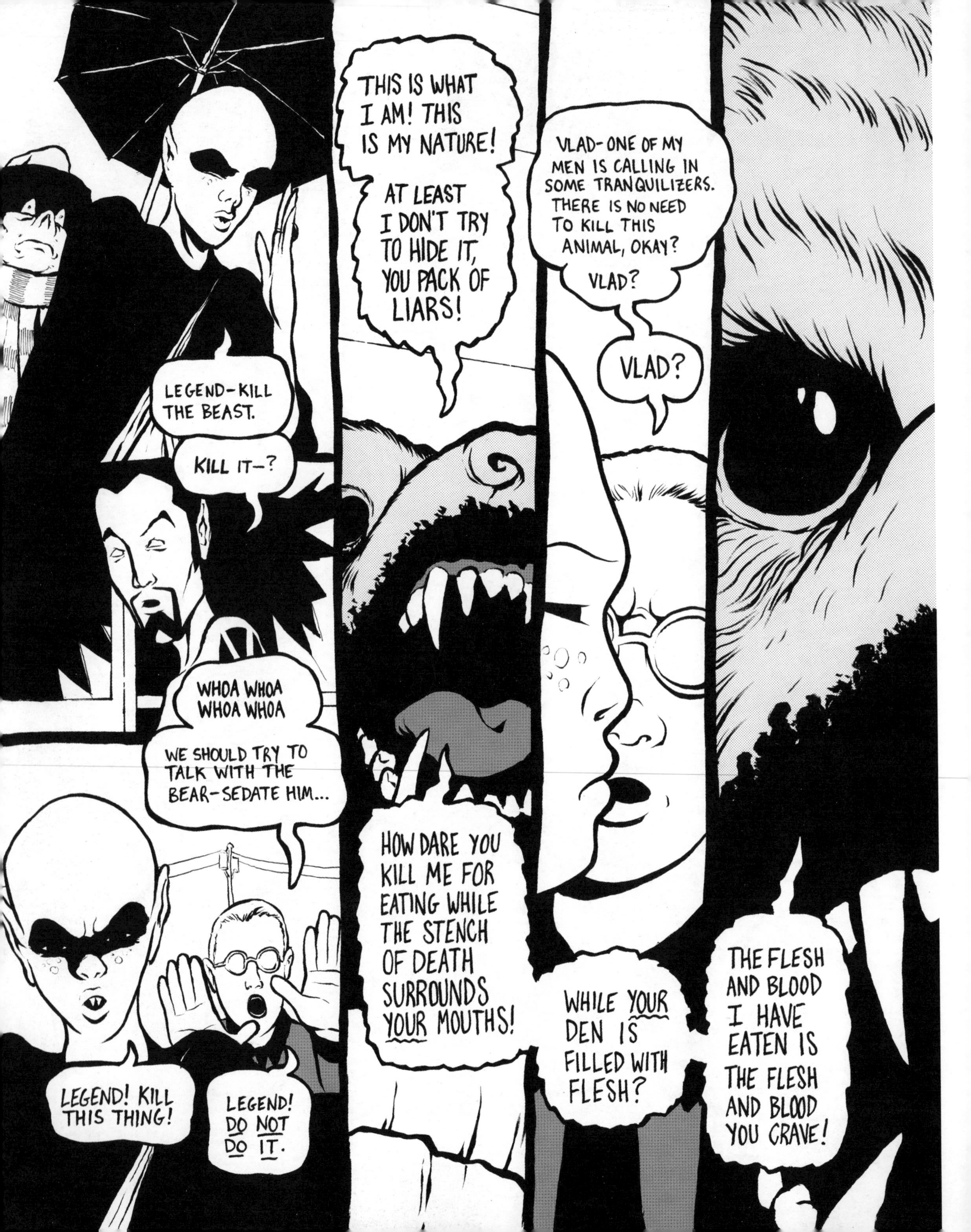
LEGEND–KILL THE BEAST.
KILL IT–?
WHOA WHOA WHOA WHOA
WE SHOULD TRY TO TALK WITH THE BEAR–SEDATE HIM...
LEGEND! KILL THIS THING!
LEGEND! DO NOT DO IT.
THIS IS WHAT I AM! THIS IS MY NATURE!
AT LEAST I DON'T TRY TO HIDE IT, YOU PACK OF LIARS!
HOW DARE YOU KILL ME FOR EATING WHILE THE STENCH OF DEATH SURROUNDS YOUR MOUTHS!
VLAD–ONE OF MY MEN IS CALLING IN SOME TRANQUILIZERS. THERE IS NO NEED TO KILL THIS ANIMAL, OKAY?
VLAD?
VLAD?
WHILE YOUR DEN IS FILLED WITH FLESH?
THE FLESH AND BLOOD I HAVE EATEN IS THE FLESH AND BLOOD YOU CRAVE!

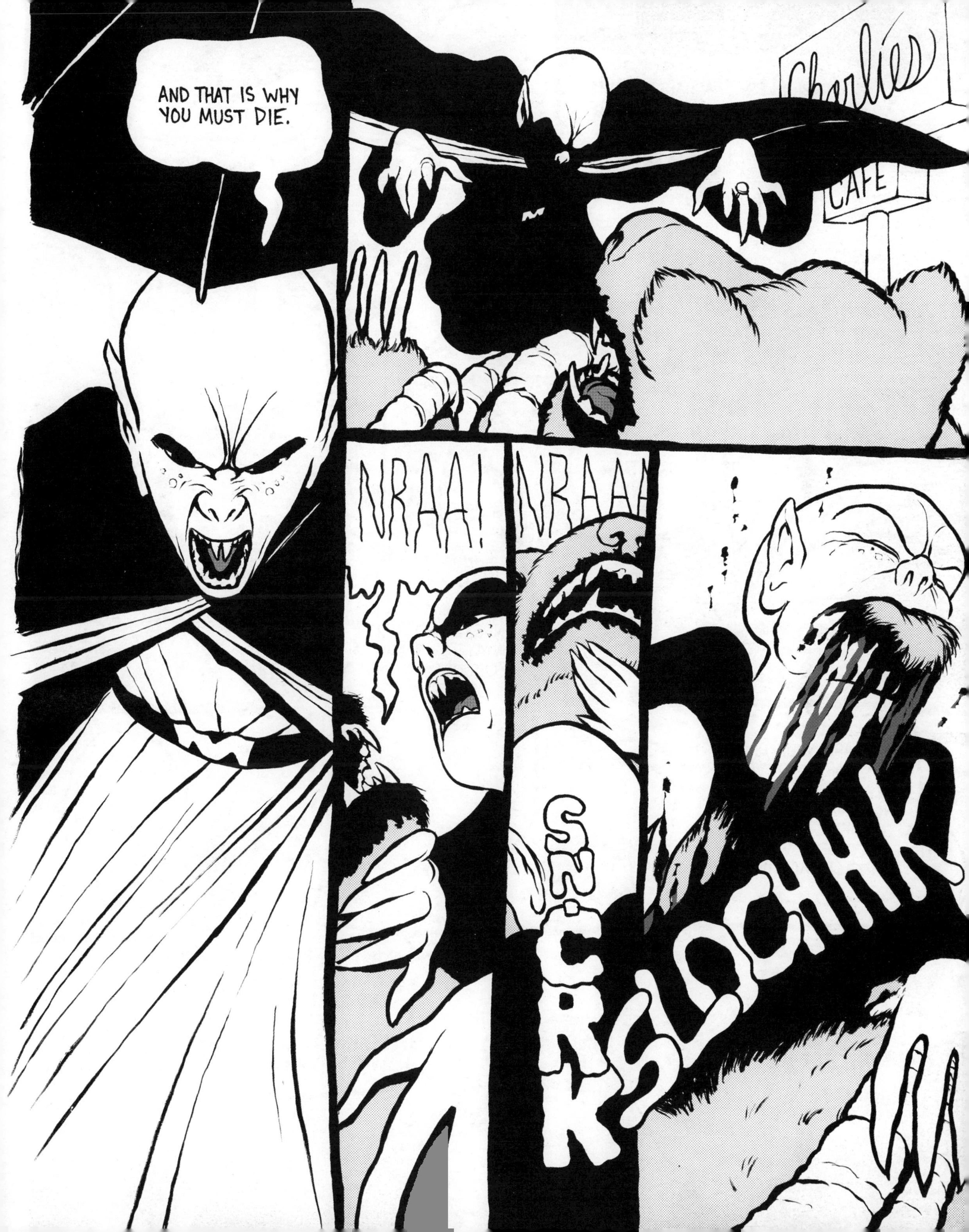
AND THAT IS WHY YOU MUST DIE.
Charlie's
CAFE
NRAA!
NRAAA
SN·CRK
SLOCHHK

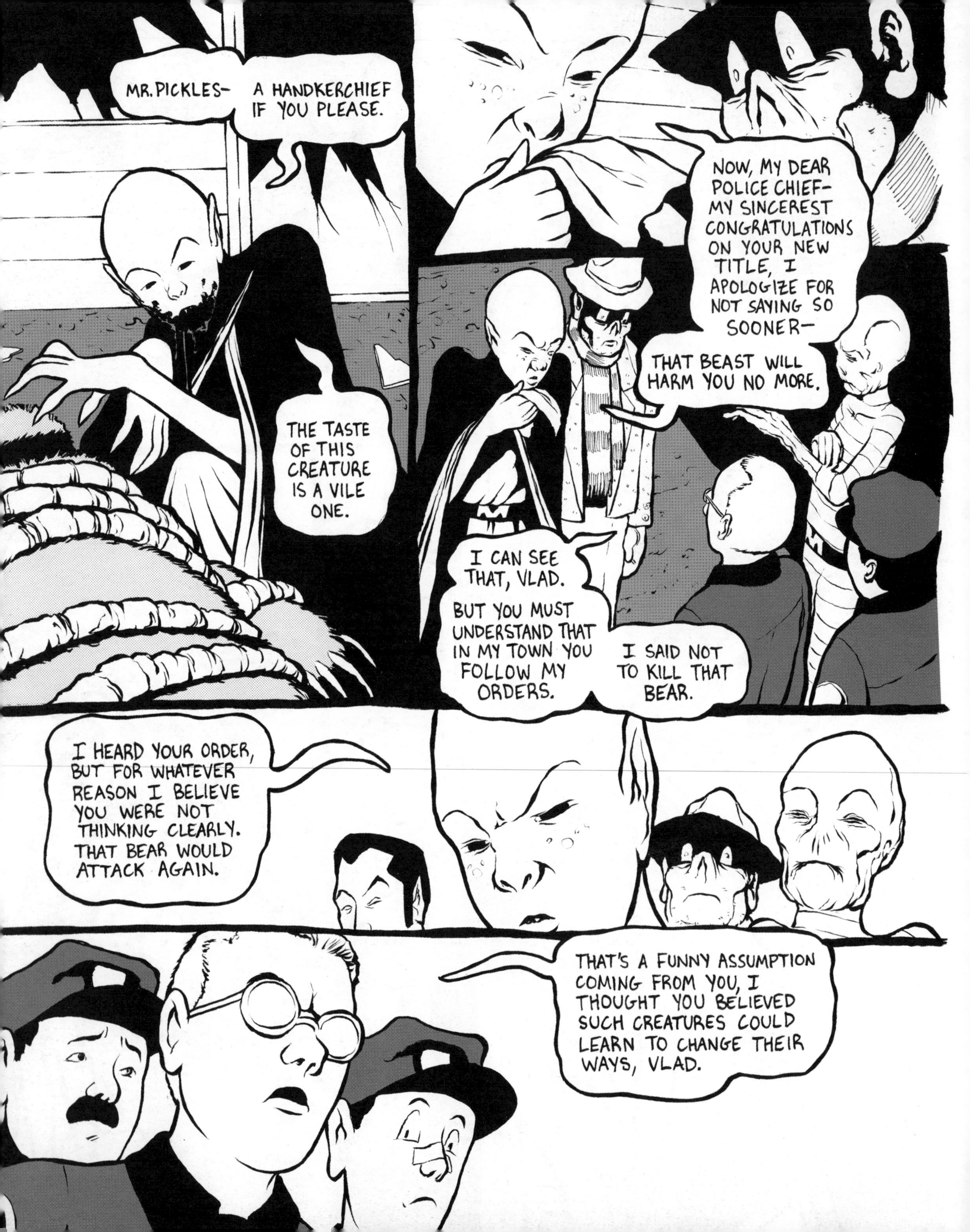
MR. PICKLES—
A HANDKERCHIEF IF YOU PLEASE.
THE TASTE OF THIS CREATURE IS A VILE ONE.
NOW, MY DEAR POLICE CHIEF— MY SINCEREST CONGRATULATIONS ON YOUR NEW TITLE, I APOLOGIZE FOR NOT SAYING SO SOONER—
THAT BEAST WILL HARM YOU NO MORE.
I CAN SEE THAT, VLAD.
BUT YOU MUST UNDERSTAND THAT IN MY TOWN YOU FOLLOW MY ORDERS.
I SAID NOT TO KILL THAT BEAR.
I HEARD YOUR ORDER, BUT FOR WHATEVER REASON I BELIEVE YOU WERE NOT THINKING CLEARLY. THAT BEAR WOULD ATTACK AGAIN.
THAT'S A FUNNY ASSUMPTION COMING FROM YOU, I THOUGHT YOU BELIEVED SUCH CREATURES COULD LEARN TO CHANGE THEIR WAYS, VLAD.

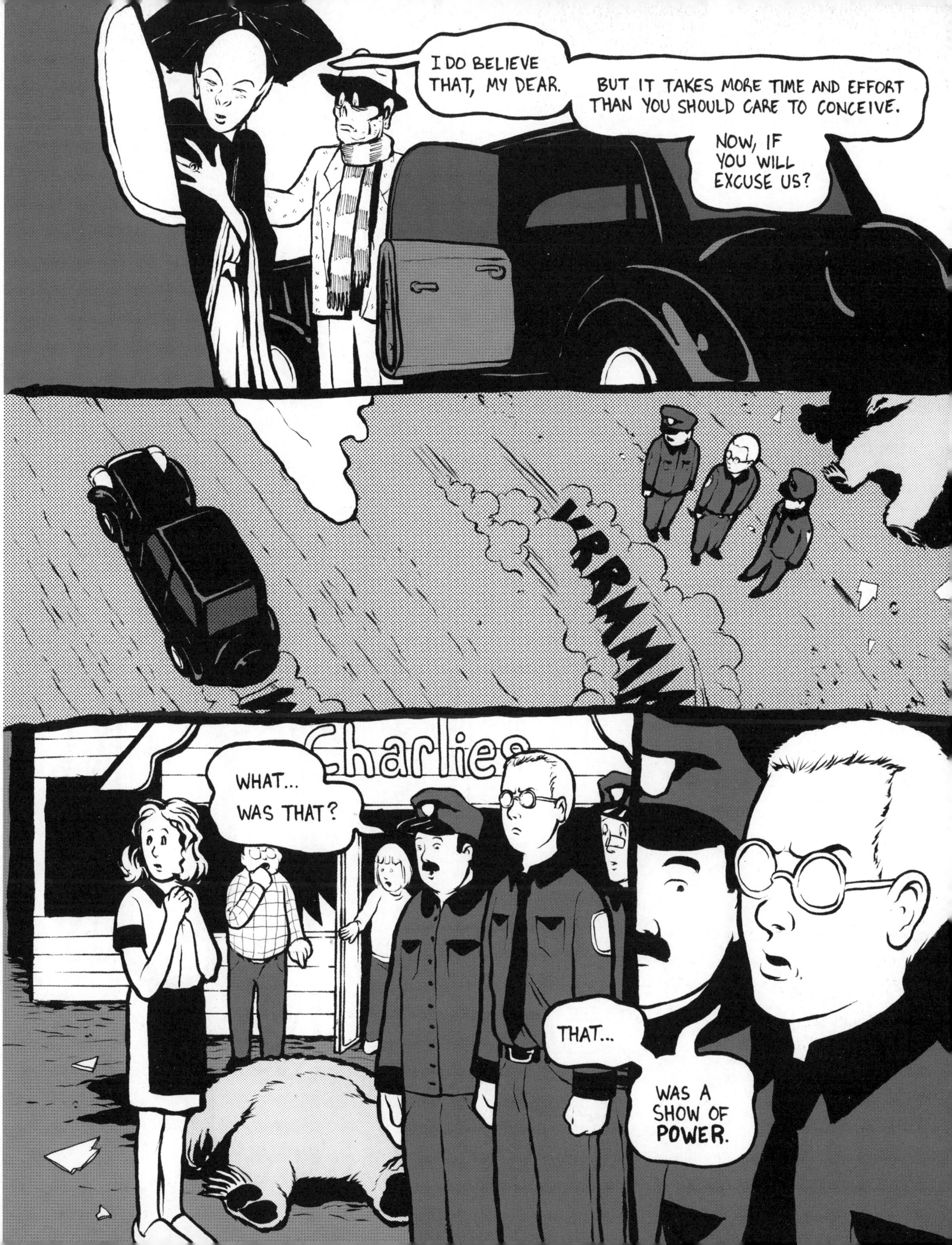
I DO BELIEVE THAT, MY DEAR.
BUT IT TAKES MORE TIME AND EFFORT THAN YOU SHOULD CARE TO CONCEIVE.
NOW, IF YOU WILL EXCUSE US?
KRRMMM
Charlies
WHAT... WAS THAT?
THAT...
WAS A SHOW OF POWER.

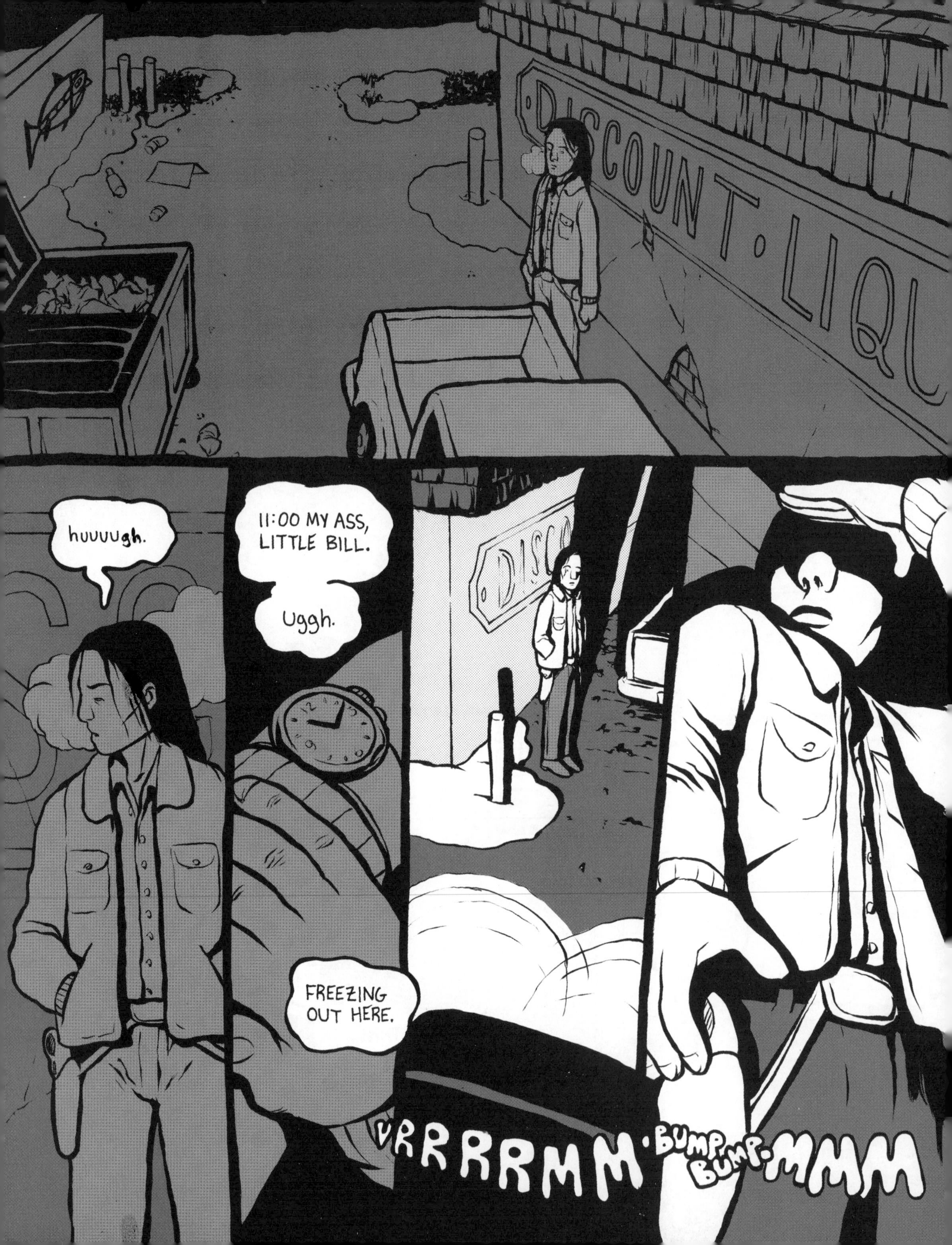
DISCOUNT LIQU
huuuugh.
11:00 MY ASS, LITTLE BILL.
Uggh.
FREEZING OUT HERE.
DISCO
VRRRRRMM·BUMP BUMP·MMMM

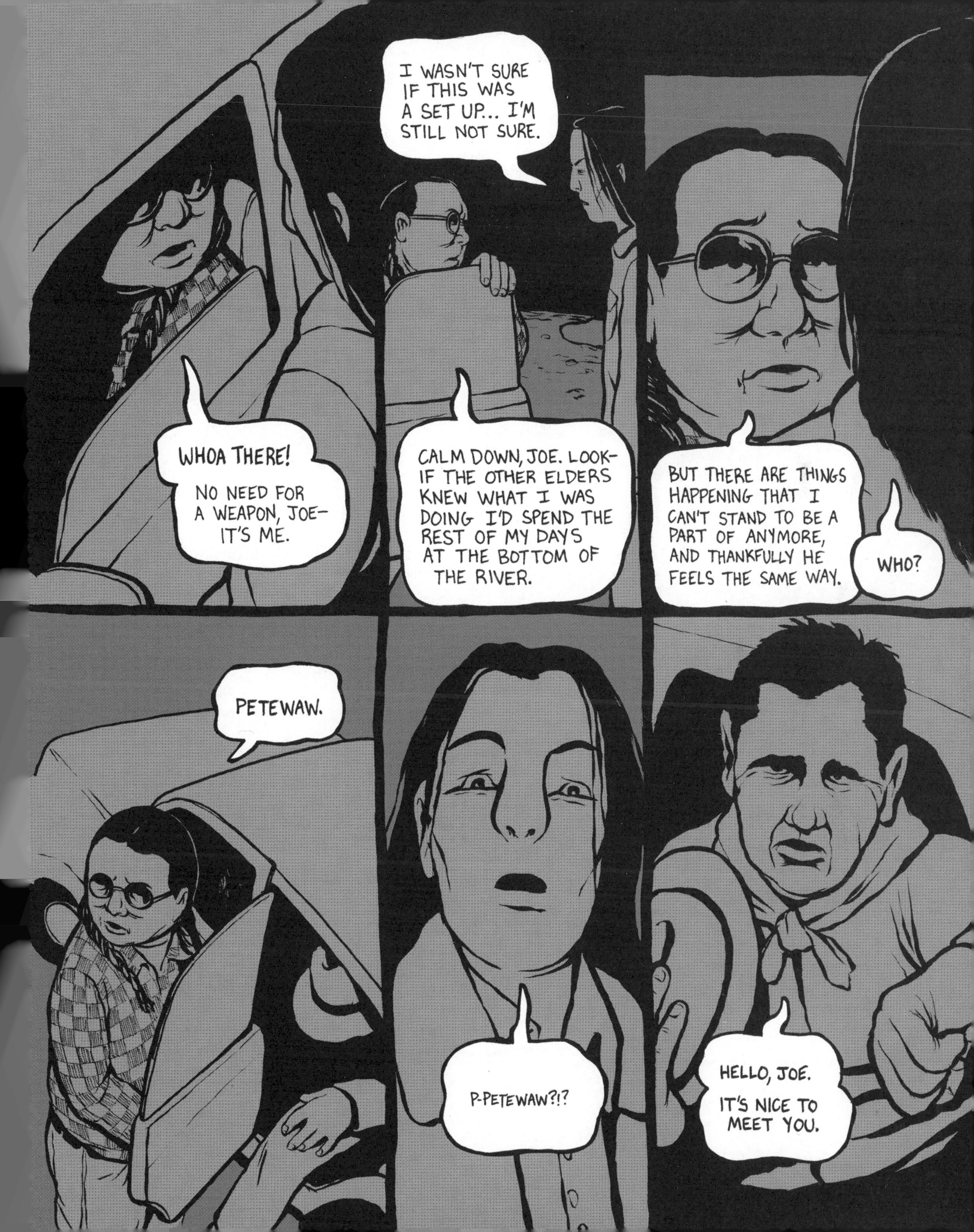
WHOA THERE!
NO NEED FOR A WEAPON, JOE- IT'S ME.
I WASN'T SURE IF THIS WAS A SET UP... I'M STILL NOT SURE.
CALM DOWN, JOE. LOOK- IF THE OTHER ELDERS KNEW WHAT I WAS DOING I'D SPEND THE REST OF MY DAYS AT THE BOTTOM OF THE RIVER.
BUT THERE ARE THINGS HAPPENING THAT I CAN'T STAND TO BE A PART OF ANYMORE, AND THANKFULLY HE FEELS THE SAME WAY.
WHO?
PETEWAW.
P-PETEWAW?!?
HELLO, JOE.
IT'S NICE TO MEET YOU.

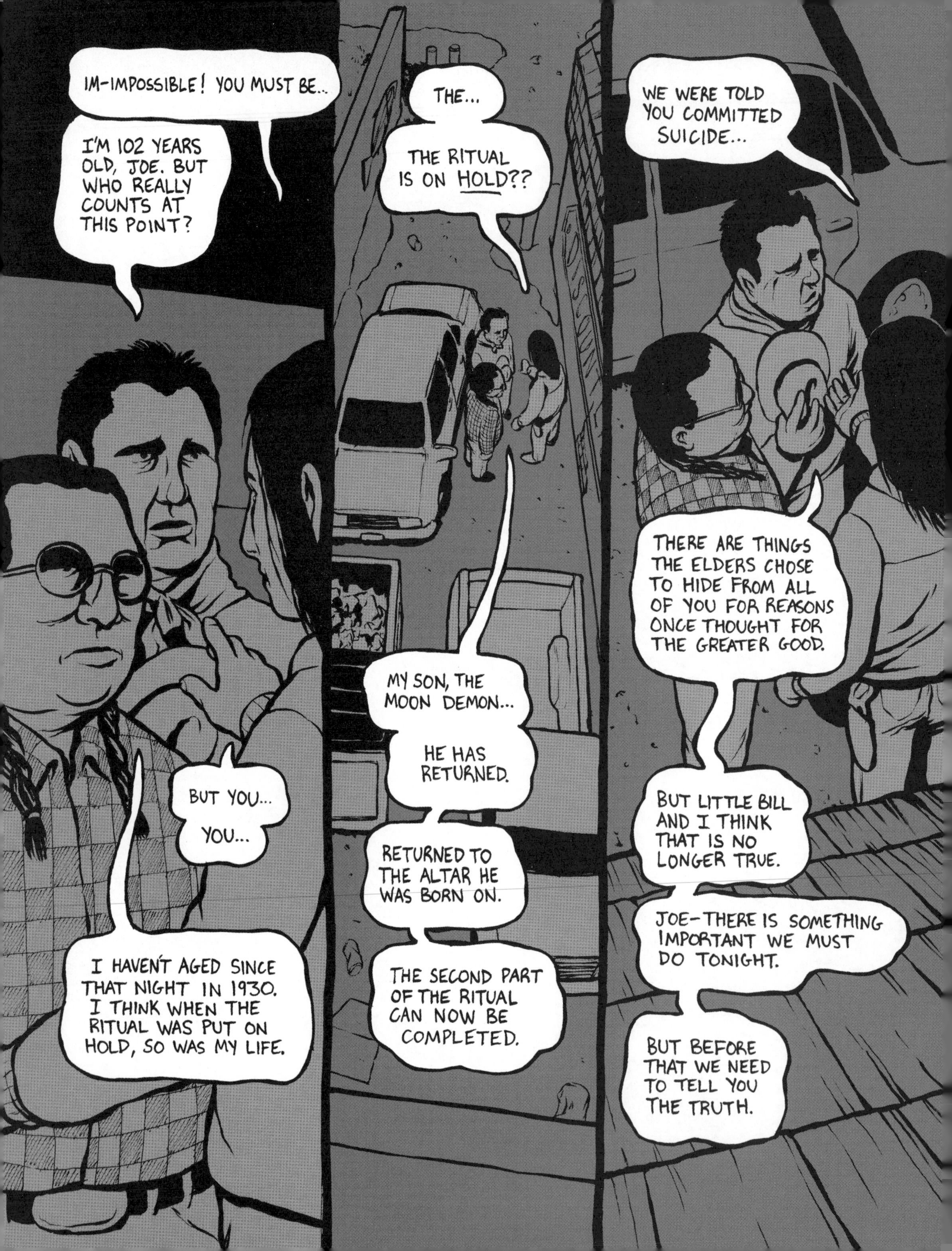
IM-IMPOSSIBLE! YOU MUST BE...
I'M 102 YEARS OLD, JOE. BUT WHO REALLY COUNTS AT THIS POINT?
BUT YOU...
YOU...
I HAVEN'T AGED SINCE THAT NIGHT IN 1930. I THINK WHEN THE RITUAL WAS PUT ON HOLD, SO WAS MY LIFE.
THE...
THE RITUAL IS ON HOLD??
MY SON, THE MOON DEMON...
HE HAS RETURNED.
RETURNED TO THE ALTAR HE WAS BORN ON.
THE SECOND PART OF THE RITUAL CAN NOW BE COMPLETED.
WE WERE TOLD YOU COMMITTED SUICIDE...
THERE ARE THINGS THE ELDERS CHOSE TO HIDE FROM ALL OF YOU FOR REASONS ONCE THOUGHT FOR THE GREATER GOOD.
BUT LITTLE BILL AND I THINK THAT IS NO LONGER TRUE.
JOE–THERE IS SOMETHING IMPORTANT WE MUST DO TONIGHT.
BUT BEFORE THAT WE NEED TO TELL YOU THE TRUTH.

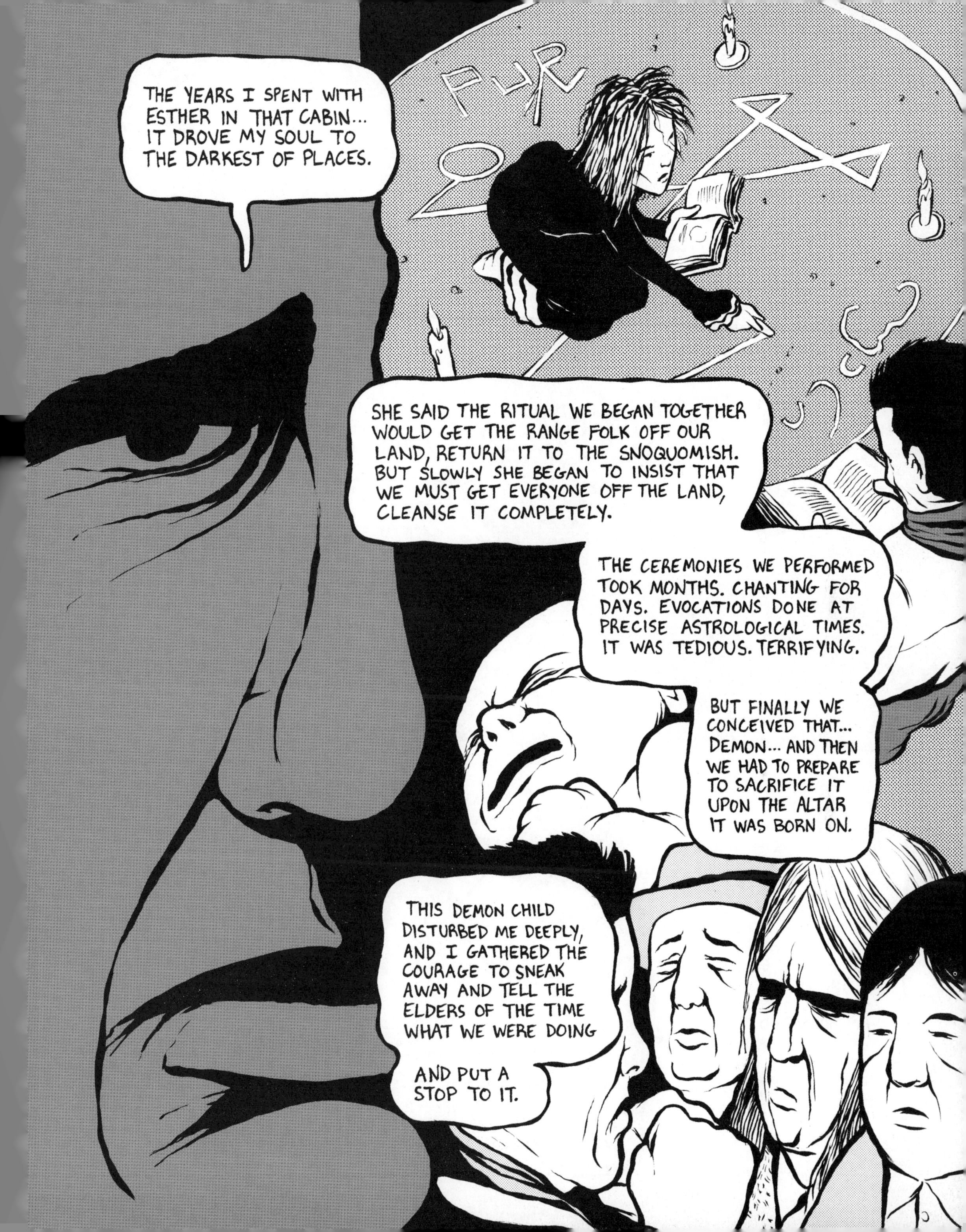
THE YEARS I SPENT WITH ESTHER IN THAT CABIN... IT DROVE MY SOUL TO THE DARKEST OF PLACES.
SHE SAID THE RITUAL WE BEGAN TOGETHER WOULD GET THE RANGE FOLK OFF OUR LAND, RETURN IT TO THE SNOQUOMISH. BUT SLOWLY SHE BEGAN TO INSIST THAT WE MUST GET EVERYONE OFF THE LAND, CLEANSE IT COMPLETELY.
THE CEREMONIES WE PERFORMED TOOK MONTHS. CHANTING FOR DAYS. EVOCATIONS DONE AT PRECISE ASTROLOGICAL TIMES. IT WAS TEDIOUS. TERRIFYING.
BUT FINALLY WE CONCEIVED THAT... DEMON... AND THEN WE HAD TO PREPARE TO SACRIFICE IT UPON THE ALTAR IT WAS BORN ON.
THIS DEMON CHILD DISTURBED ME DEEPLY, AND I GATHERED THE COURAGE TO SNEAK AWAY AND TELL THE ELDERS OF THE TIME WHAT WE WERE DOING
AND PUT A STOP TO IT.

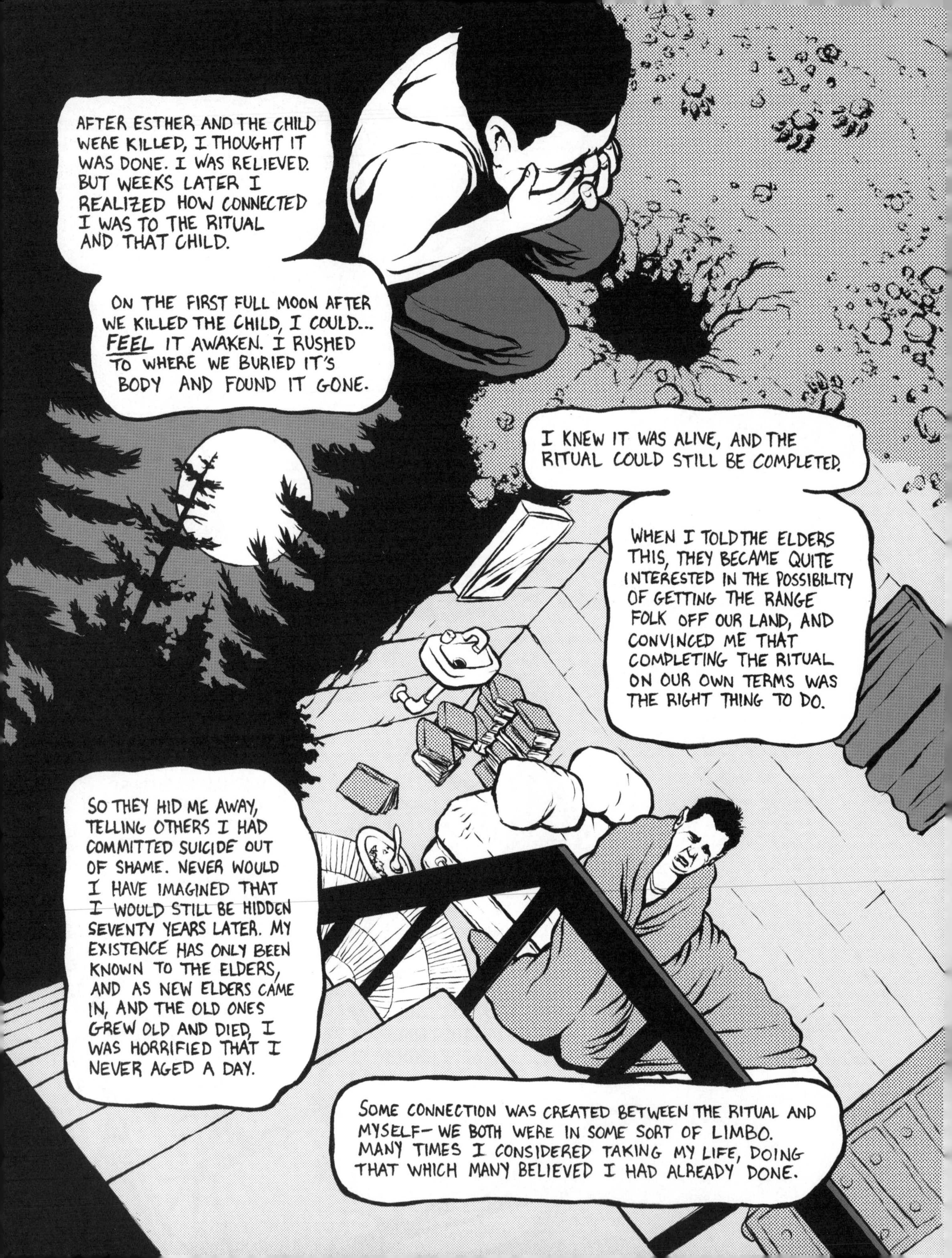
AFTER ESTHER AND THE CHILD WERE KILLED, I THOUGHT IT WAS DONE. I WAS RELIEVED. BUT WEEKS LATER I REALIZED HOW CONNECTED I WAS TO THE RITUAL AND THAT CHILD.
ON THE FIRST FULL MOON AFTER WE KILLED THE CHILD, I COULD... FEEL IT AWAKEN. I RUSHED TO WHERE WE BURIED IT'S BODY AND FOUND IT GONE.
I KNEW IT WAS ALIVE, AND THE RITUAL COULD STILL BE COMPLETED.
WHEN I TOLD THE ELDERS THIS, THEY BECAME QUITE INTERESTED IN THE POSSIBILITY OF GETTING THE RANGE FOLK OFF OUR LAND, AND CONVINCED ME THAT COMPLETING THE RITUAL ON OUR OWN TERMS WAS THE RIGHT THING TO DO.
SO THEY HID ME AWAY, TELLING OTHERS I HAD COMMITTED SUICIDE OUT OF SHAME. NEVER WOULD I HAVE IMAGINED THAT I WOULD STILL BE HIDDEN SEVENTY YEARS LATER. MY EXISTENCE HAS ONLY BEEN KNOWN TO THE ELDERS, AND AS NEW ELDERS CAME IN, AND THE OLD ONES GREW OLD AND DIED, I WAS HORRIFIED THAT I NEVER AGED A DAY.
SOME CONNECTION WAS CREATED BETWEEN THE RITUAL AND MYSELF— WE BOTH WERE IN SOME SORT OF LIMBO. MANY TIMES I CONSIDERED TAKING MY LIFE, DOING THAT WHICH MANY BELIEVED I HAD ALREADY DONE.

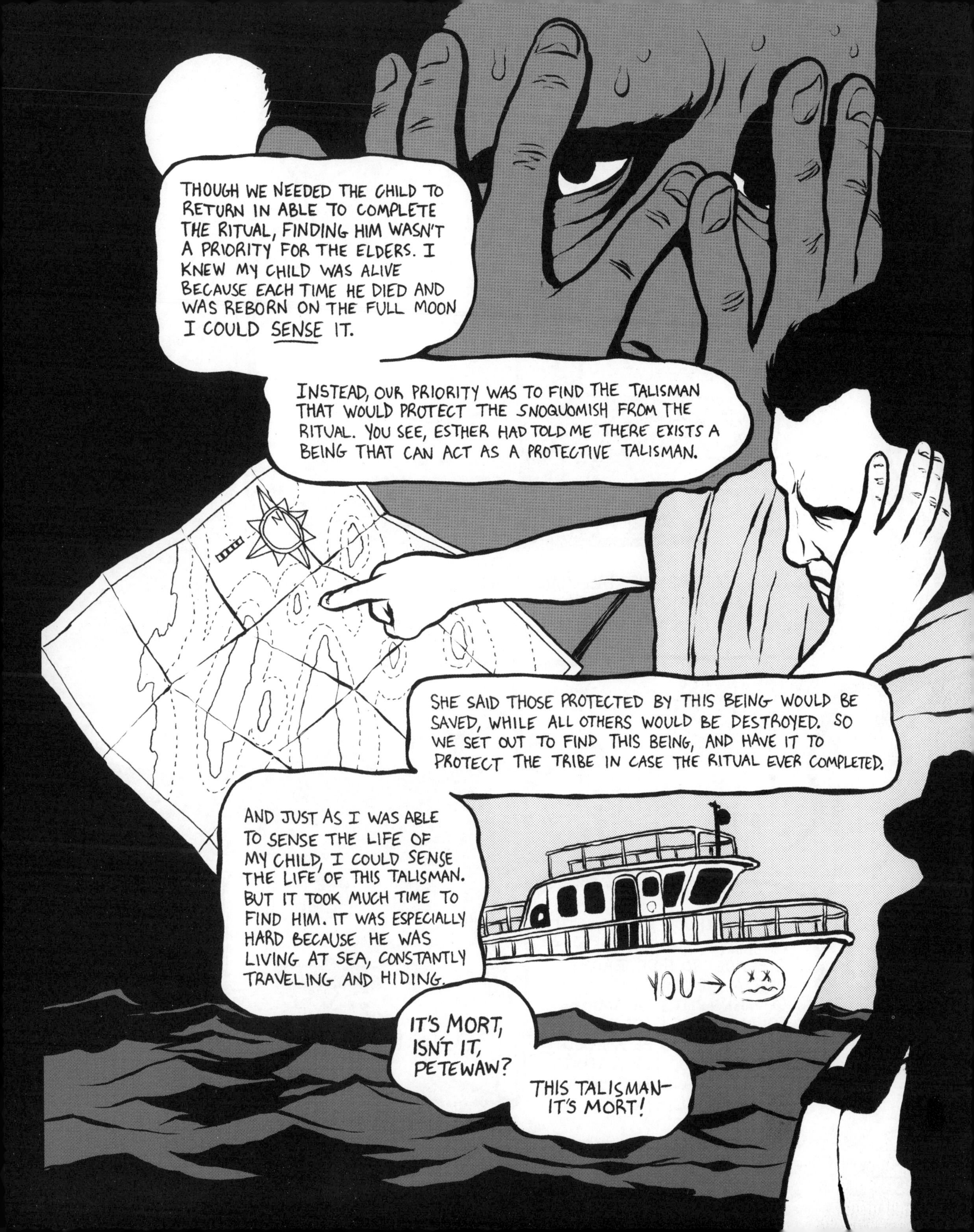
THOUGH WE NEEDED THE CHILD TO RETURN IN ABLE TO COMPLETE THE RITUAL, FINDING HIM WASN'T A PRIORITY FOR THE ELDERS. I KNEW MY CHILD WAS ALIVE BECAUSE EACH TIME HE DIED AND WAS REBORN ON THE FULL MOON I COULD SENSE IT.
INSTEAD, OUR PRIORITY WAS TO FIND THE TALISMAN THAT WOULD PROTECT THE SNOQUOMISH FROM THE RITUAL. YOU SEE, ESTHER HAD TOLD ME THERE EXISTS A BEING THAT CAN ACT AS A PROTECTIVE TALISMAN.
SHE SAID THOSE PROTECTED BY THIS BEING WOULD BE SAVED, WHILE ALL OTHERS WOULD BE DESTROYED. SO WE SET OUT TO FIND THIS BEING, AND HAVE IT TO PROTECT THE TRIBE IN CASE THE RITUAL EVER COMPLETED.
AND JUST AS I WAS ABLE TO SENSE THE LIFE OF MY CHILD, I COULD SENSE THE LIFE OF THIS TALISMAN. BUT IT TOOK MUCH TIME TO FIND HIM. IT WAS ESPECIALLY HARD BECAUSE HE WAS LIVING AT SEA, CONSTANTLY TRAVELING AND HIDING.
YOU →
IT'S MORT, ISN'T IT, PETEWAW?
THIS TALISMAN- IT'S MORT!

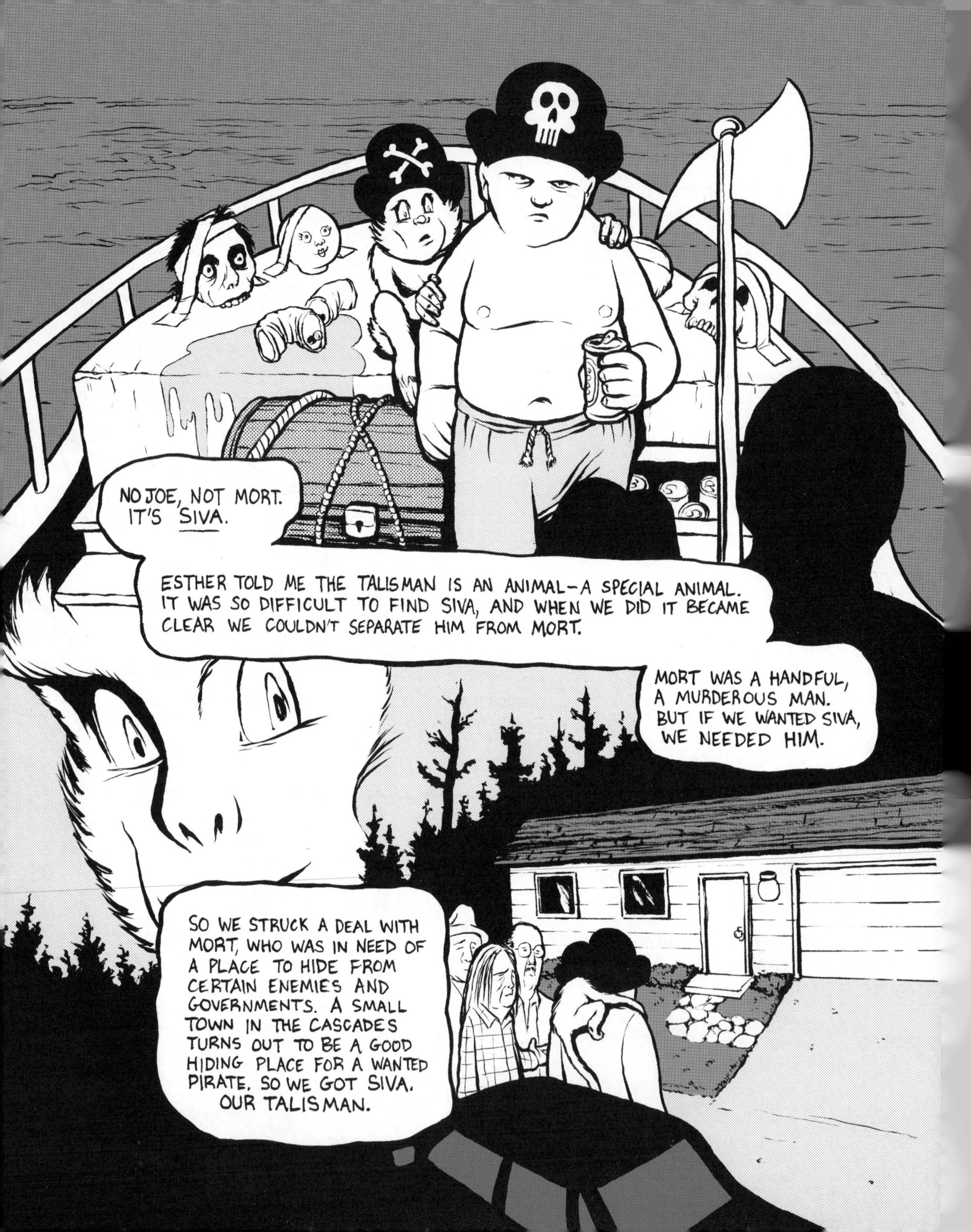
NO JOE, NOT MORT. IT'S SIVA.
ESTHER TOLD ME THE TALISMAN IS AN ANIMAL—A SPECIAL ANIMAL. IT WAS SO DIFFICULT TO FIND SIVA, AND WHEN WE DID IT BECAME CLEAR WE COULDN'T SEPARATE HIM FROM MORT.
MORT WAS A HANDFUL, A MURDEROUS MAN. BUT IF WE WANTED SIVA, WE NEEDED HIM.
SO WE STRUCK A DEAL WITH MORT, WHO WAS IN NEED OF A PLACE TO HIDE FROM CERTAIN ENEMIES AND GOVERNMENTS. A SMALL TOWN IN THE CASCADES TURNS OUT TO BE A GOOD HIDING PLACE FOR A WANTED PIRATE. SO WE GOT SIVA. OUR TALISMAN.

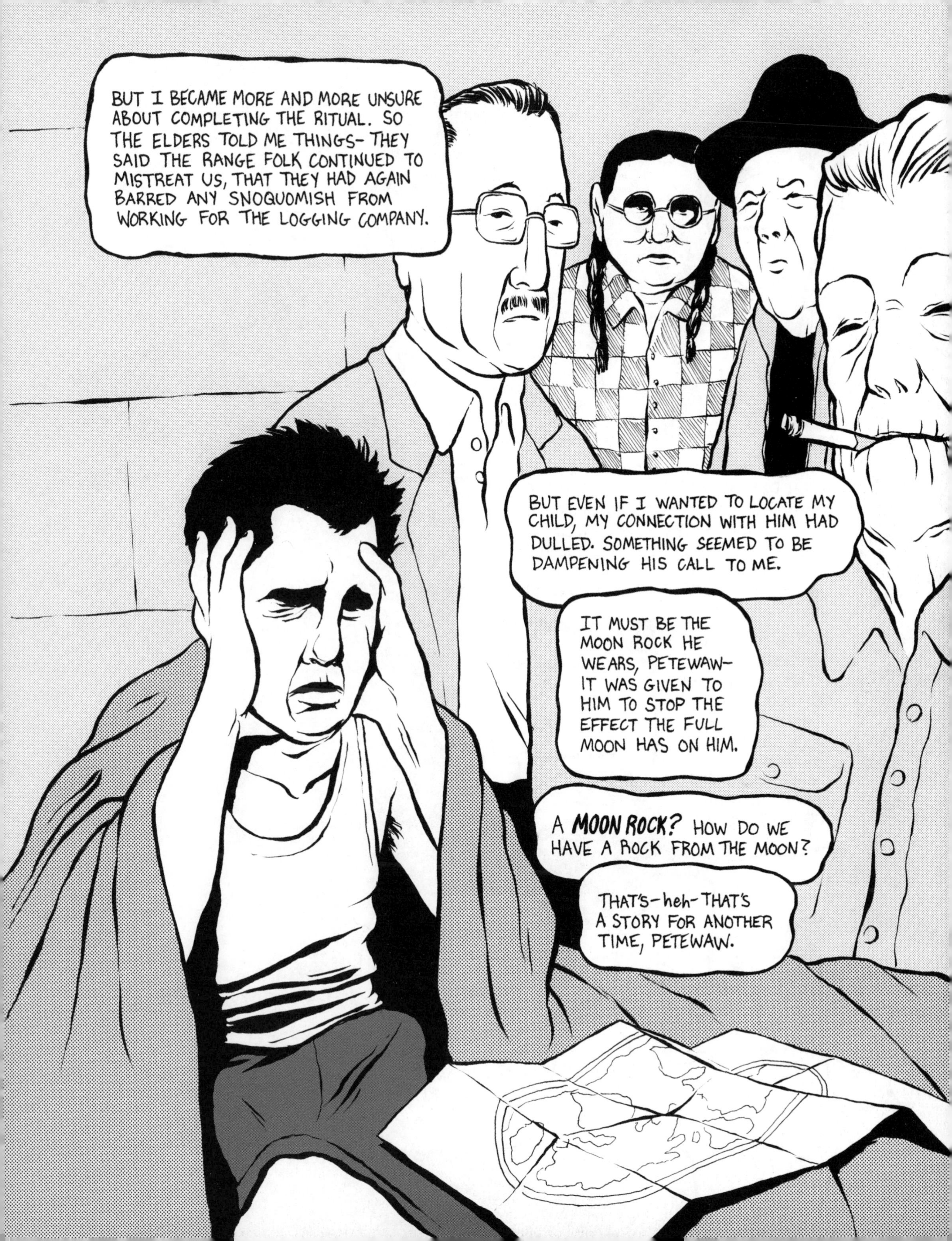
BUT I BECAME MORE AND MORE UNSURE ABOUT COMPLETING THE RITUAL. SO THE ELDERS TOLD ME THINGS- THEY SAID THE RANGE FOLK CONTINUED TO MISTREAT US, THAT THEY HAD AGAIN BARRED ANY SNOQUOMISH FROM WORKING FOR THE LOGGING COMPANY.
BUT EVEN IF I WANTED TO LOCATE MY CHILD, MY CONNECTION WITH HIM HAD DULLED. SOMETHING SEEMED TO BE DAMPENING HIS CALL TO ME.
IT MUST BE THE MOON ROCK HE WEARS, PETEWAW- IT WAS GIVEN TO HIM TO STOP THE EFFECT THE FULL MOON HAS ON HIM.
A MOON ROCK? HOW DO WE HAVE A ROCK FROM THE MOON?
THAT'S-heh-THAT'S A STORY FOR ANOTHER TIME, PETEWAW.

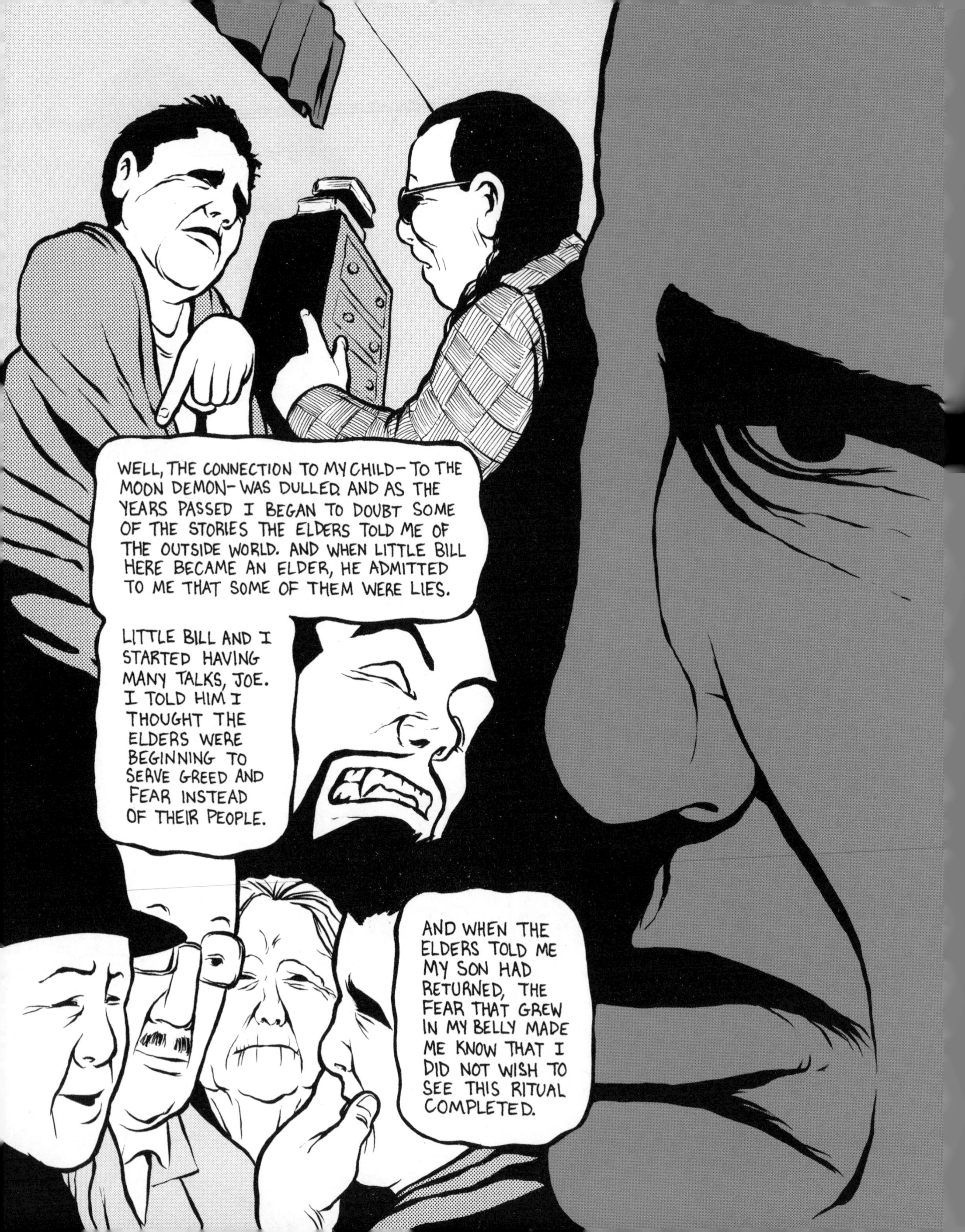
WELL, THE CONNECTION TO MY CHILD— TO THE MOON DEMON— WAS DULLED. AND AS THE YEARS PASSED I BEGAN TO DOUBT SOME OF THE STORIES THE ELDERS TOLD ME OF THE OUTSIDE WORLD. AND WHEN LITTLE BILL HERE BECAME AN ELDER, HE ADMITTED TO ME THAT SOME OF THEM WERE LIES.
LITTLE BILL AND I STARTED HAVING MANY TALKS, JOE. I TOLD HIM I THOUGHT THE ELDERS WERE BEGINNING TO SERVE GREED AND FEAR INSTEAD OF THEIR PEOPLE.
AND WHEN THE ELDERS TOLD ME MY SON HAD RETURNED, THE FEAR THAT GREW IN MY BELLY MADE ME KNOW THAT I DID NOT WISH TO SEE THIS RITUAL COMPLETED.

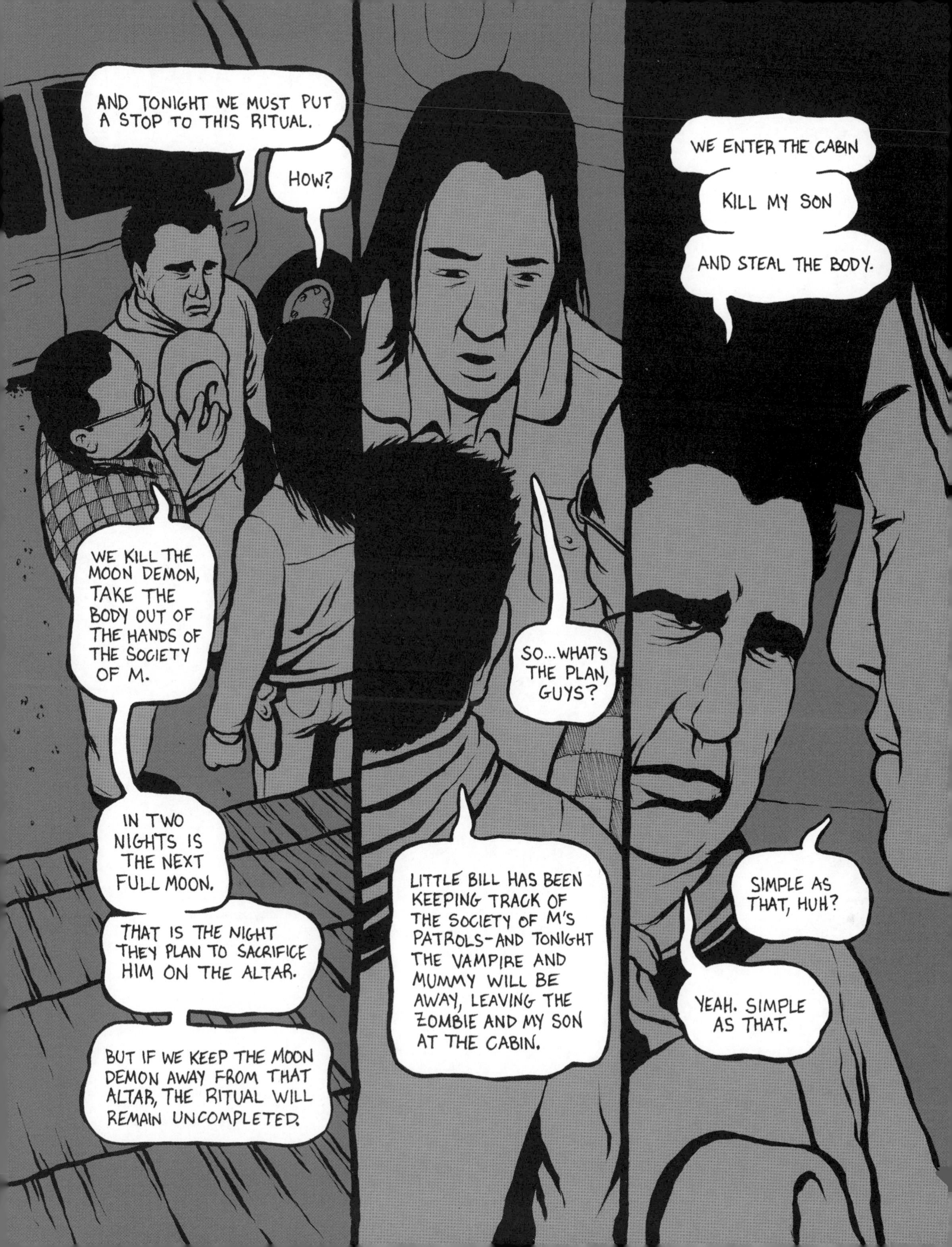
AND TONIGHT WE MUST PUT A STOP TO THIS RITUAL.
HOW?
WE KILL THE MOON DEMON, TAKE THE BODY OUT OF THE HANDS OF THE SOCIETY OF M.
IN TWO NIGHTS IS THE NEXT FULL MOON.
THAT IS THE NIGHT THEY PLAN TO SACRIFICE HIM ON THE ALTAR.
BUT IF WE KEEP THE MOON DEMON AWAY FROM THAT ALTAR, THE RITUAL WILL REMAIN UNCOMPLETED.
SO...WHAT'S THE PLAN, GUYS?
LITTLE BILL HAS BEEN KEEPING TRACK OF THE SOCIETY OF M'S PATROLS-AND TONIGHT THE VAMPIRE AND MUMMY WILL BE AWAY, LEAVING THE ZOMBIE AND MY SON AT THE CABIN.
WE ENTER THE CABIN
KILL MY SON
AND STEAL THE BODY.
SIMPLE AS THAT, HUH?
YEAH. SIMPLE AS THAT.

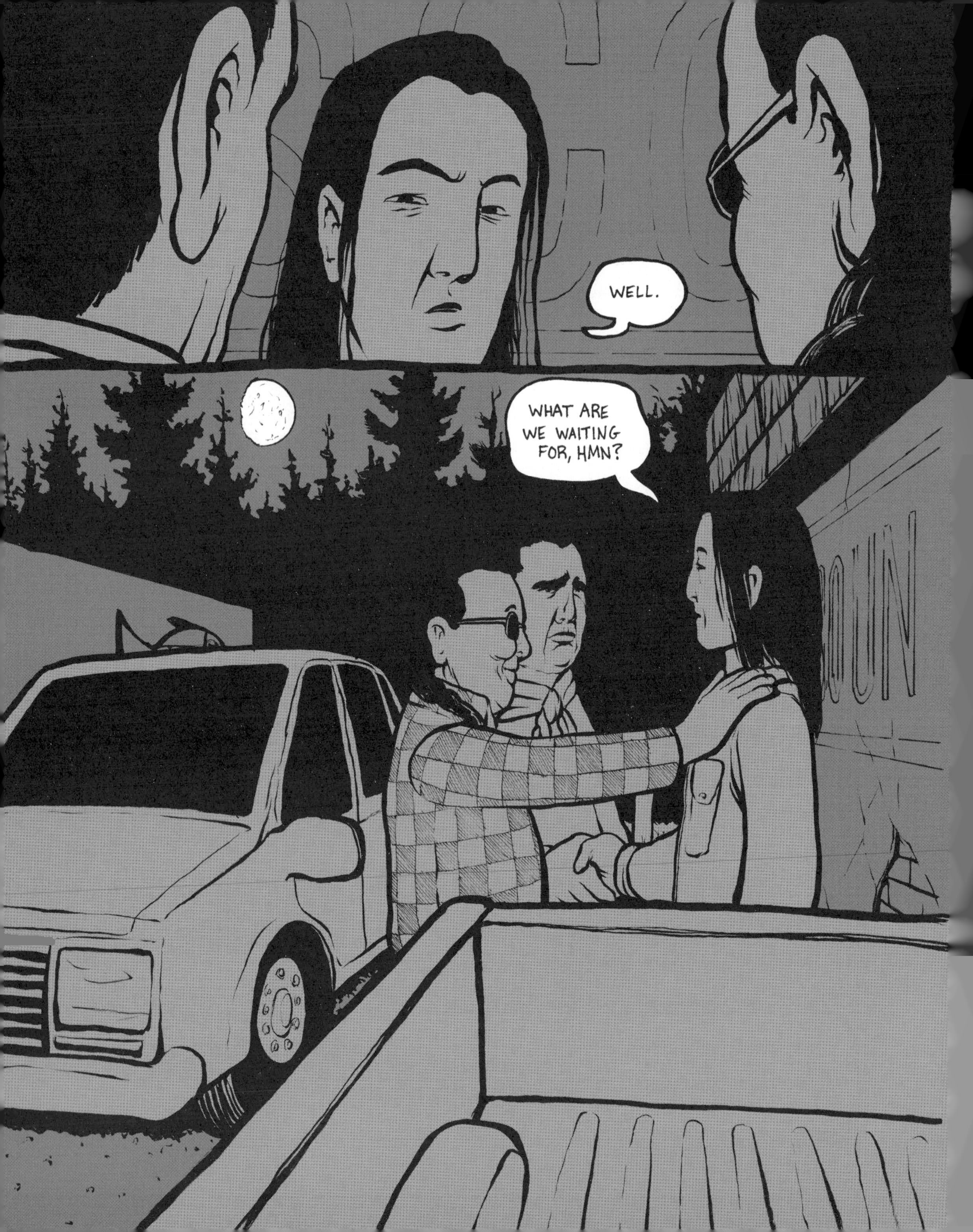
WELL.
WHAT ARE WE WAITING FOR, HMN?

12.
REVOLUTIONS

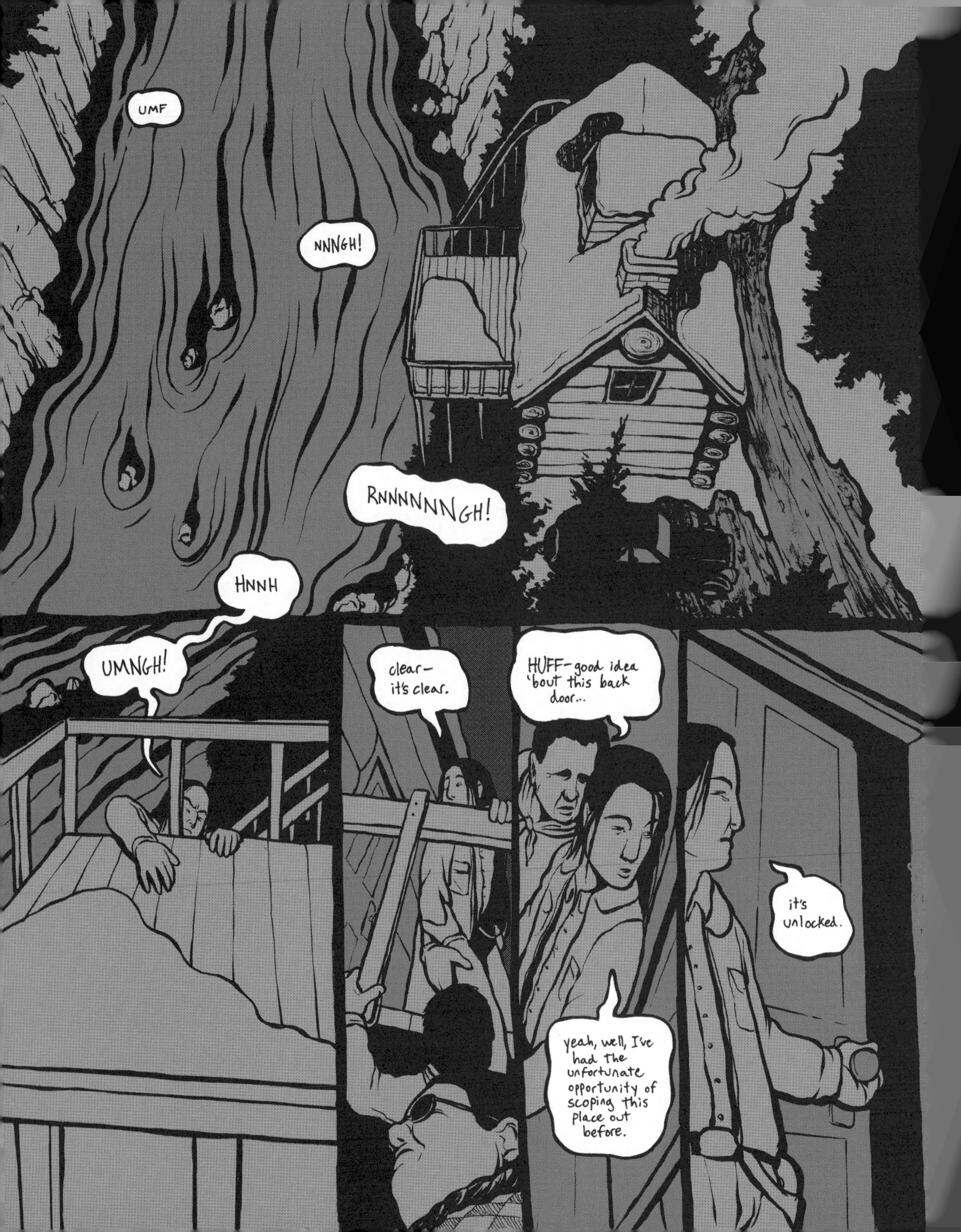
UMF
NNNGH!
RNNNNNNNGH!
HNNH
UMNGH!
clear— it's clear.
HUFF—good idea 'bout this back door...
yeah, well, I've had the unfortunate opportunity of scoping this place out before.
it's unlocked.

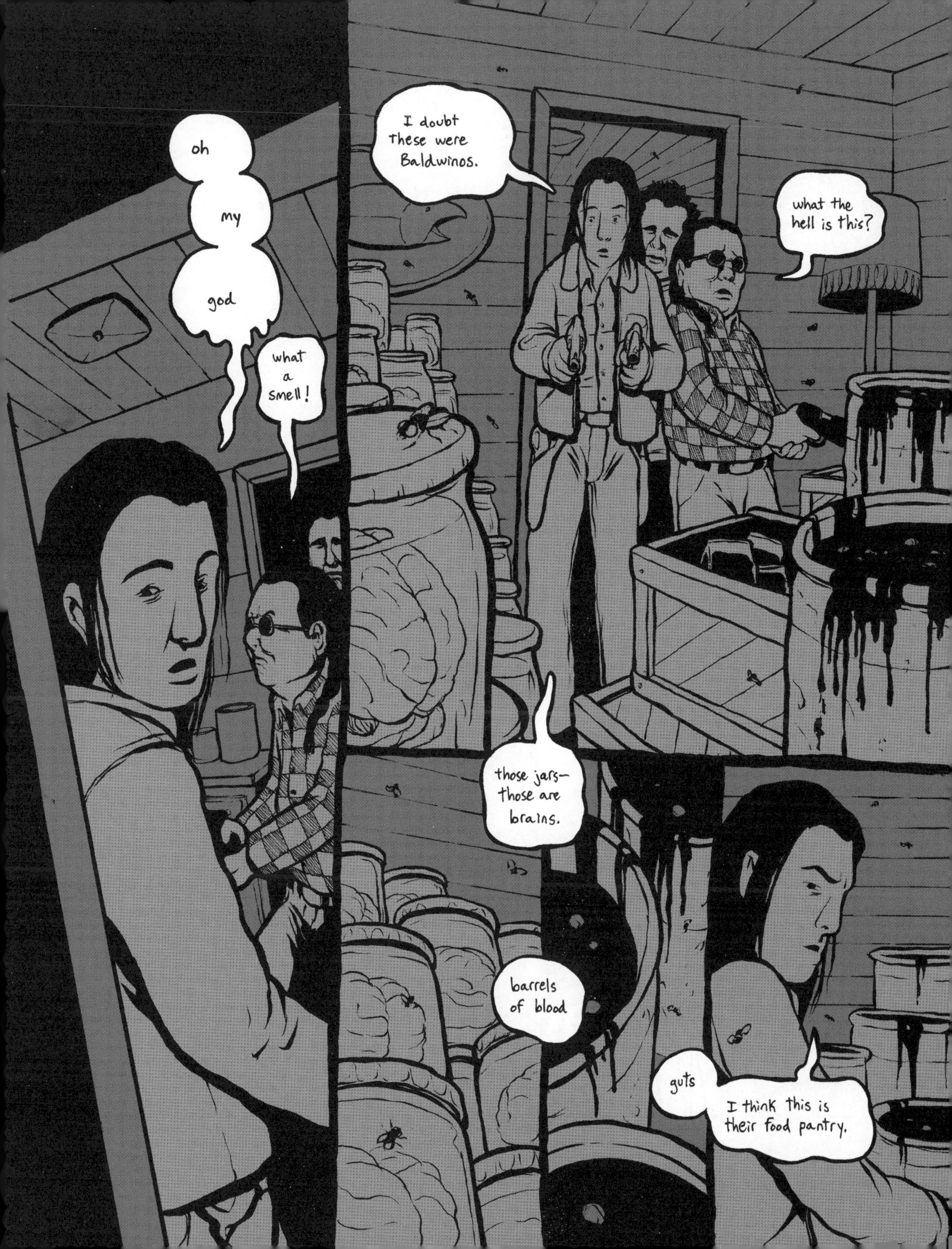
oh
my
god
what a smell!
I doubt these were Baldwinos.
what the hell is this?
those jars— those are brains.
barrels of blood
guts
I think this is their food pantry.

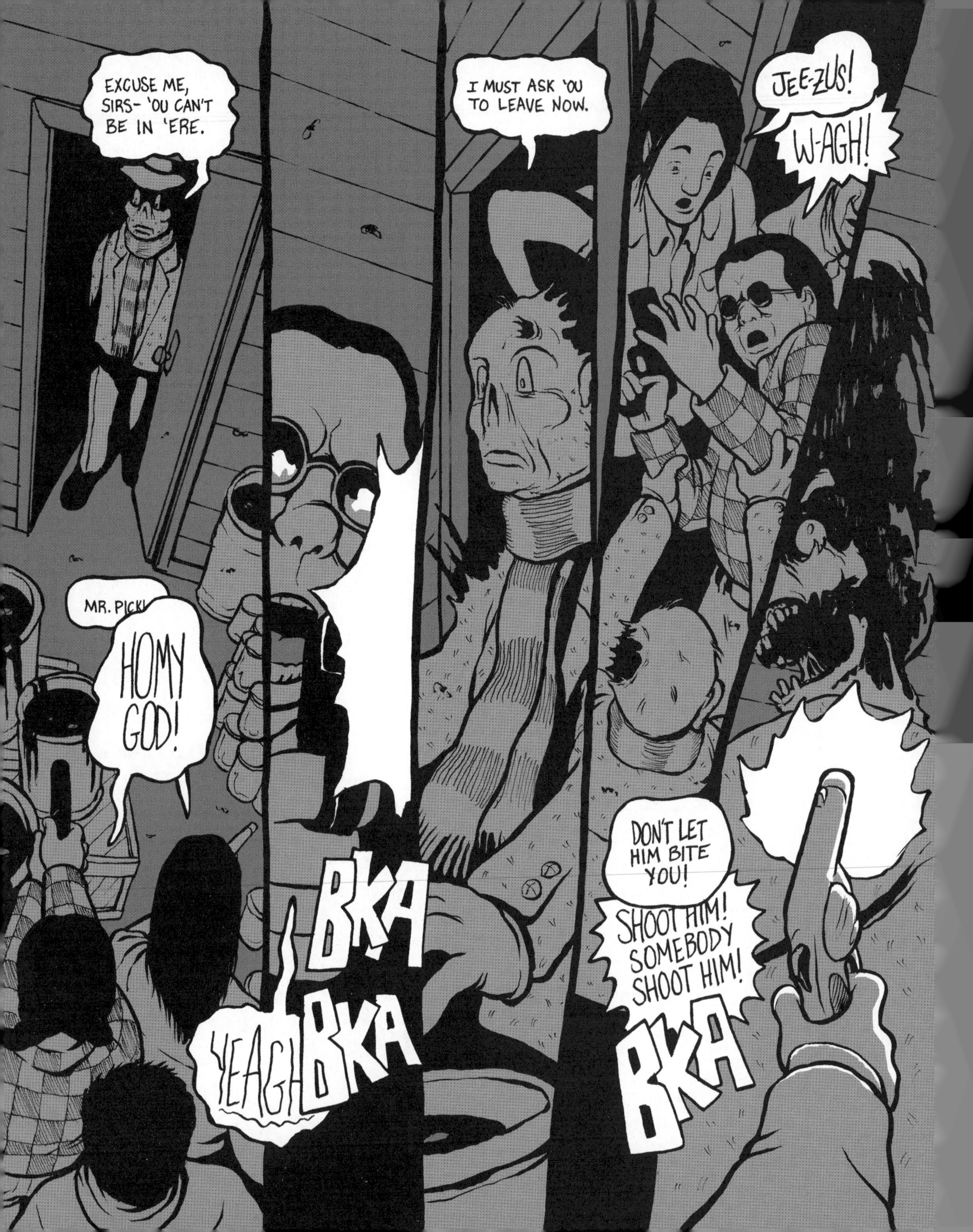
EXCUSE ME, SIRS- 'OU CAN'T BE IN 'ERE.
I MUST ASK 'OU TO LEAVE NOW.
JEE-ZUS!
W-AGH!
MR. PICKL
HOMY GOD!
BKA
YEAGH
BKA
DON'T LET HIM BITE YOU!
SHOOT HIM! SOMEBODY SHOOT HIM!
BKA

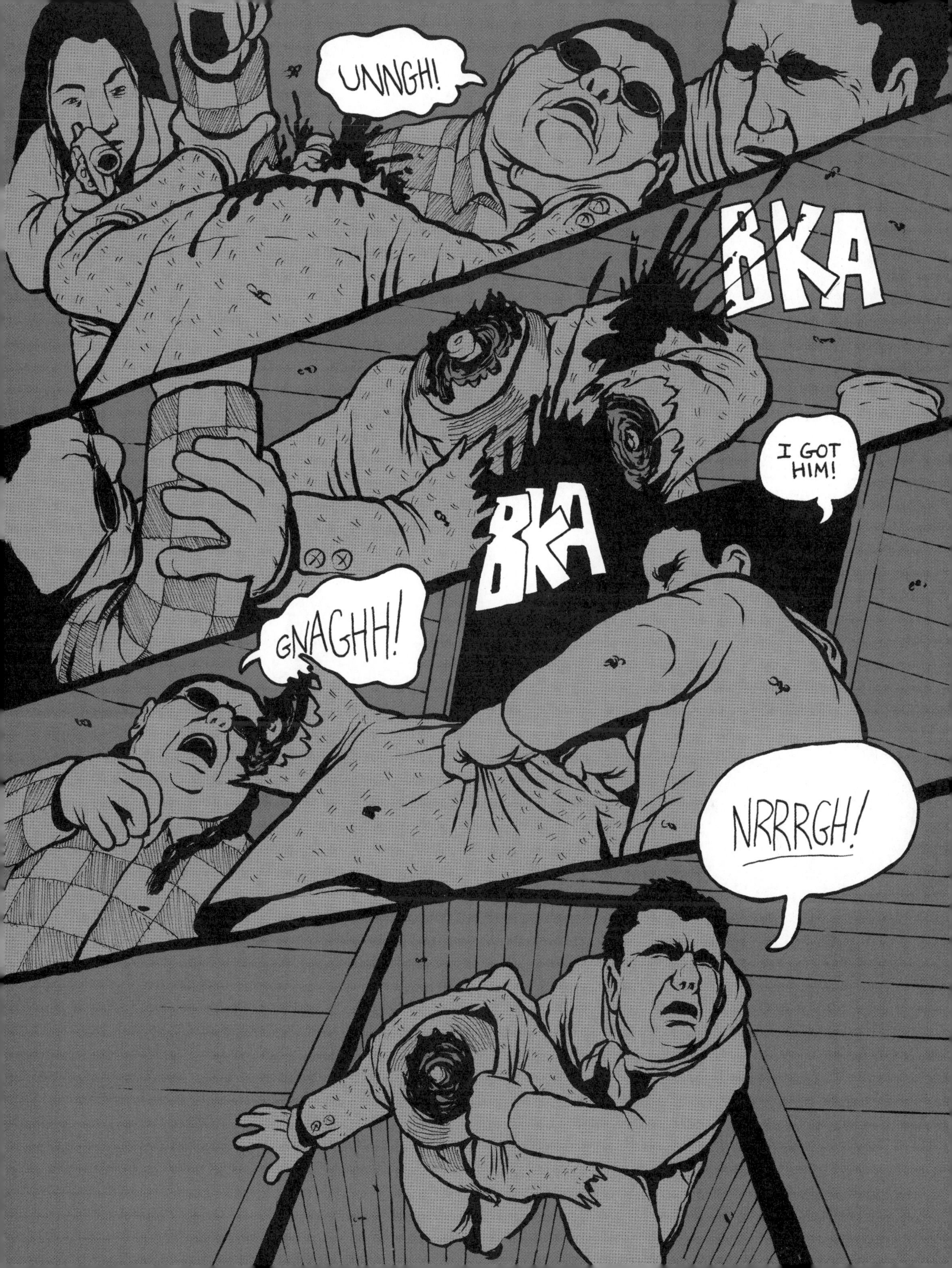
UNNGH!
BKA
I GOT HIM!
BKA
GNAGHH!
NRRRGH!

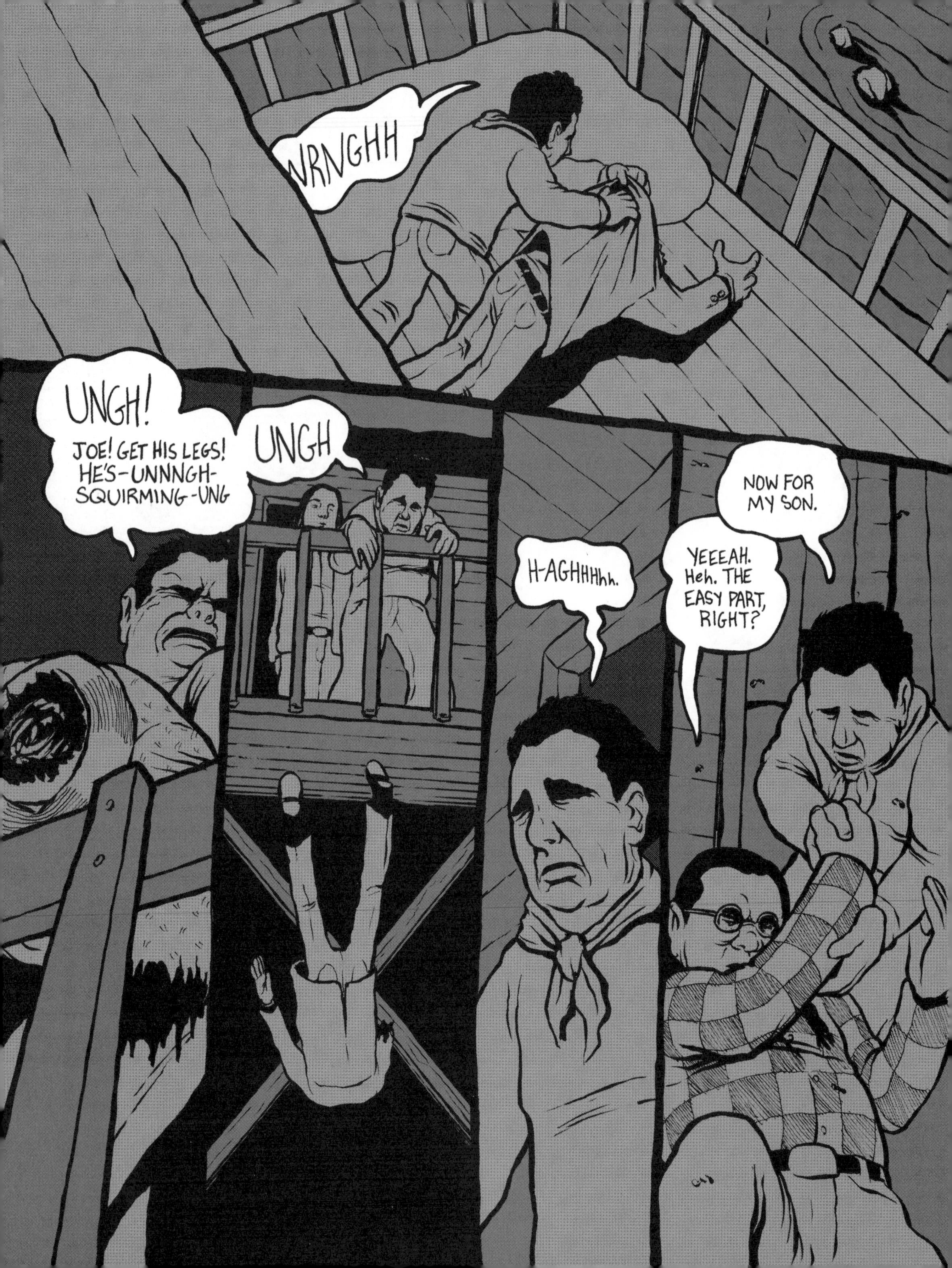
WRNGHH
UNGH!
JOE! GET HIS LEGS! HE'S-UNNNGH-SQUIRMING-UNG
UNGH
H-AGHHHhh.
NOW FOR MY SON.
YEEEAH. Heh. THE EASY PART, RIGHT?

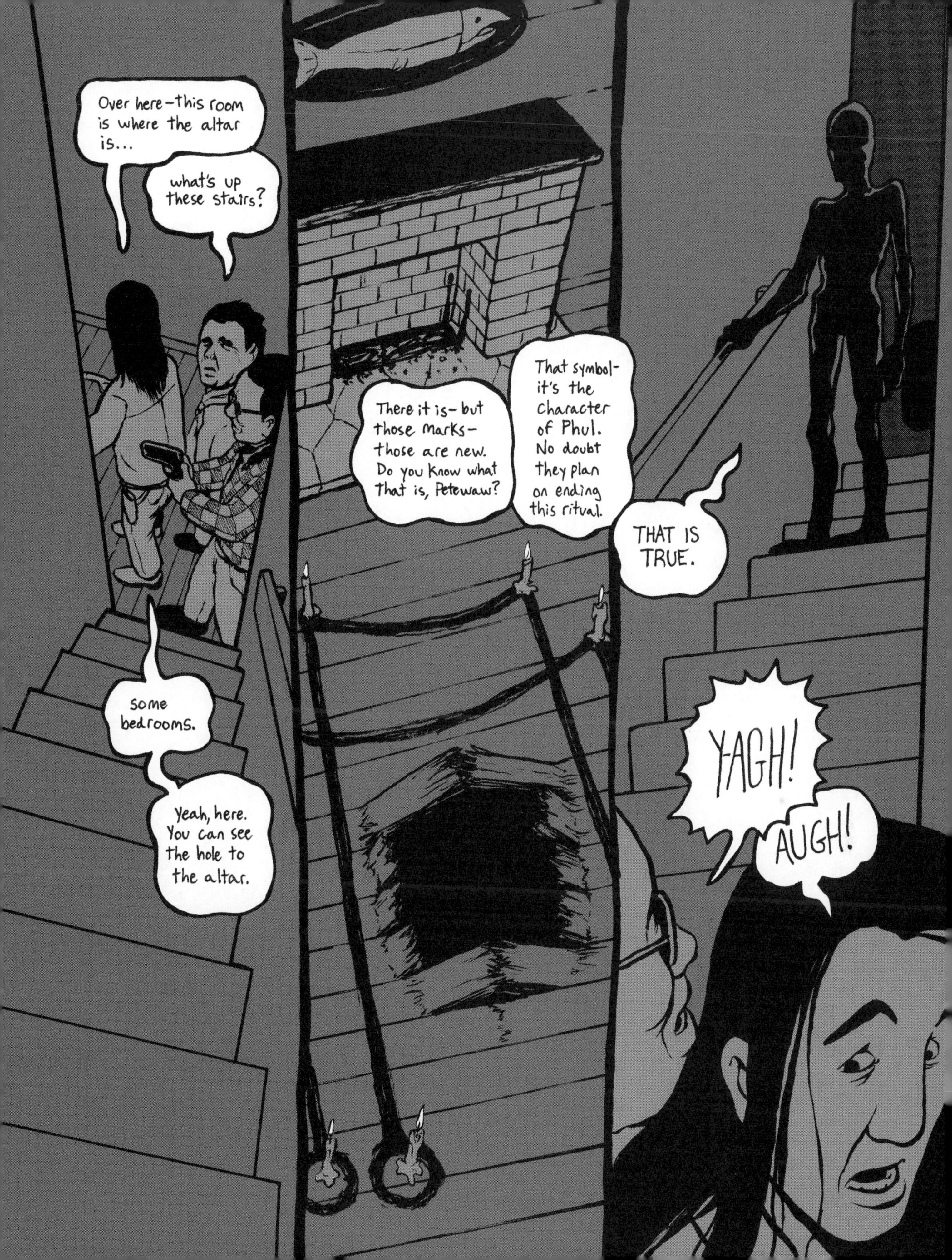

Over here—this room is where the altar is...
what's up these stairs?
some bedrooms.
Yeah, here. You can see the hole to the altar.
There it is—but those marks—those are new. Do you know what that is, Petewaw?
That symbol—it's the character of Phul. No doubt they plan on ending this ritual.
THAT IS TRUE.
Y-AGH!
AUGH!

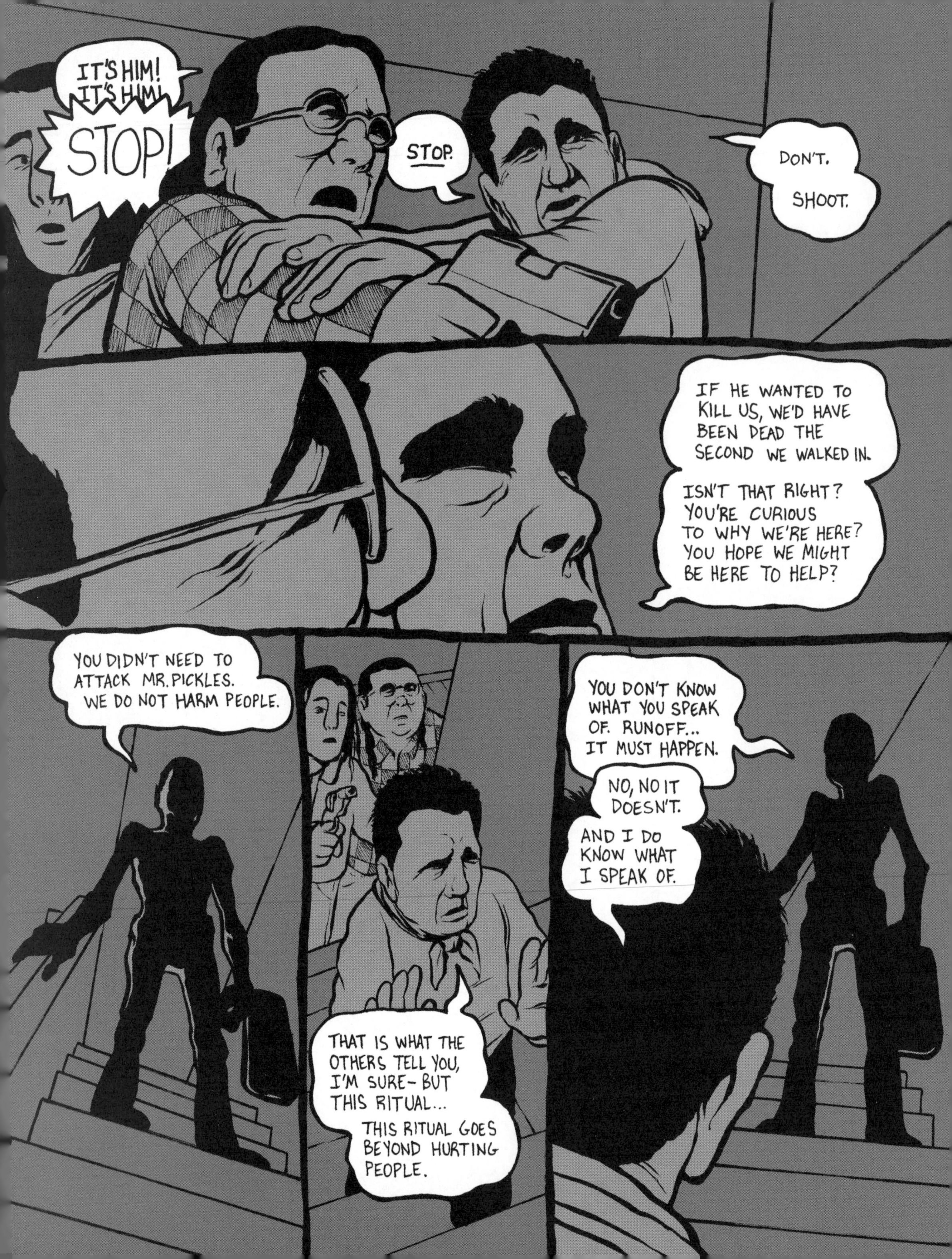
IT'S HIM! IT'S HIM!
STOP!
STOP.
DON'T. SHOOT.
IF HE WANTED TO KILL US, WE'D HAVE BEEN DEAD THE SECOND WE WALKED IN.
ISN'T THAT RIGHT? YOU'RE CURIOUS TO WHY WE'RE HERE? YOU HOPE WE MIGHT BE HERE TO HELP?
YOU DIDN'T NEED TO ATTACK MR. PICKLES. WE DO NOT HARM PEOPLE.
THAT IS WHAT THE OTHERS TELL YOU, I'M SURE- BUT THIS RITUAL...
THIS RITUAL GOES BEYOND HURTING PEOPLE.
YOU DON'T KNOW WHAT YOU SPEAK OF. RUNOFF... IT MUST HAPPEN.
NO, NO IT DOESN'T.
AND I DO KNOW WHAT I SPEAK OF.

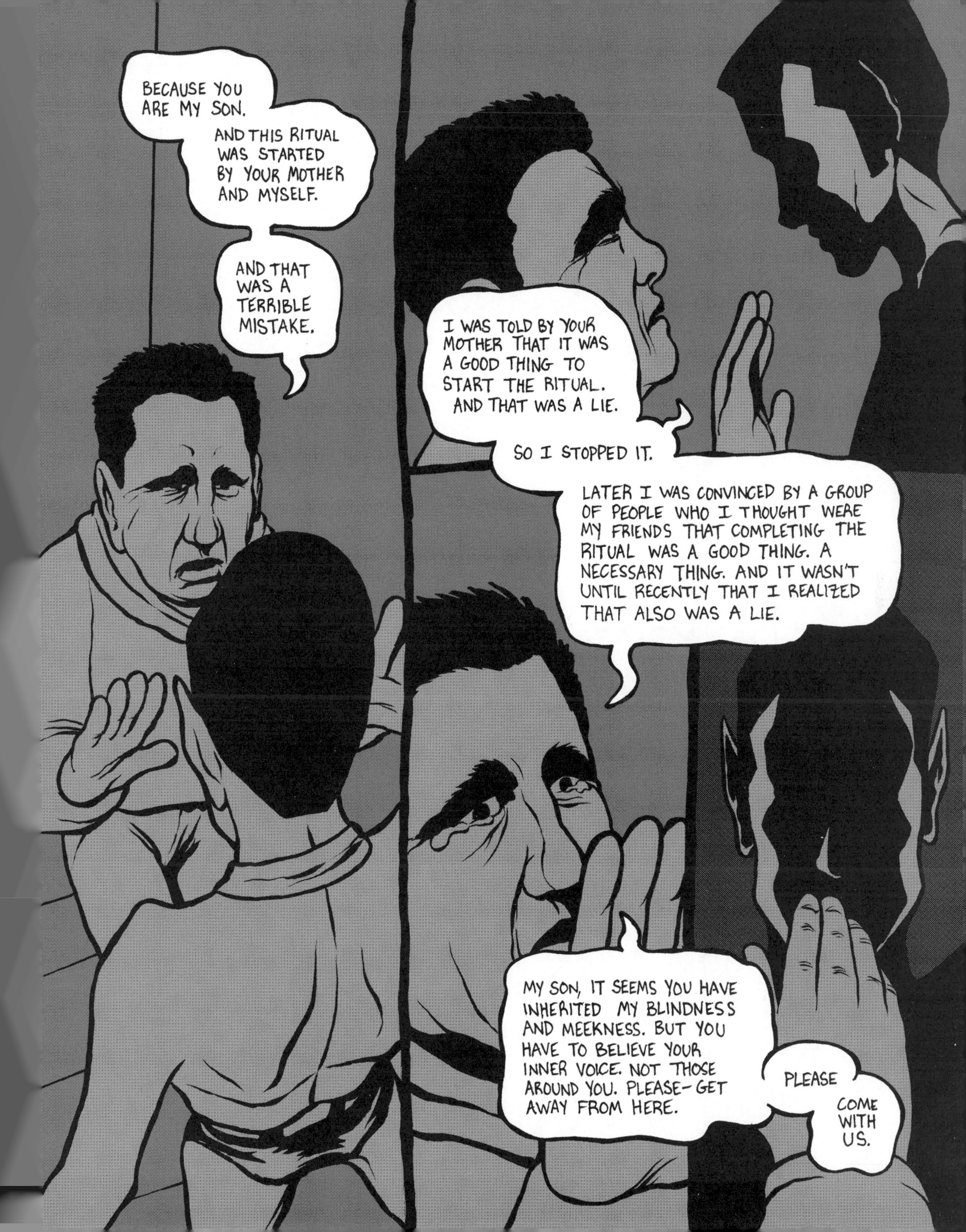
BECAUSE YOU ARE MY SON.
AND THIS RITUAL WAS STARTED BY YOUR MOTHER AND MYSELF.
AND THAT WAS A TERRIBLE MISTAKE.
I WAS TOLD BY YOUR MOTHER THAT IT WAS A GOOD THING TO START THE RITUAL. AND THAT WAS A LIE.
SO I STOPPED IT.
LATER I WAS CONVINCED BY A GROUP OF PEOPLE WHO I THOUGHT WERE MY FRIENDS THAT COMPLETING THE RITUAL WAS A GOOD THING. A NECESSARY THING. AND IT WASN'T UNTIL RECENTLY THAT I REALIZED THAT ALSO WAS A LIE.
MY SON, IT SEEMS YOU HAVE INHERITED MY BLINDNESS AND MEEKNESS. BUT YOU HAVE TO BELIEVE YOUR INNER VOICE. NOT THOSE AROUND YOU. PLEASE- GET AWAY FROM HERE.
PLEASE
COME WITH US.

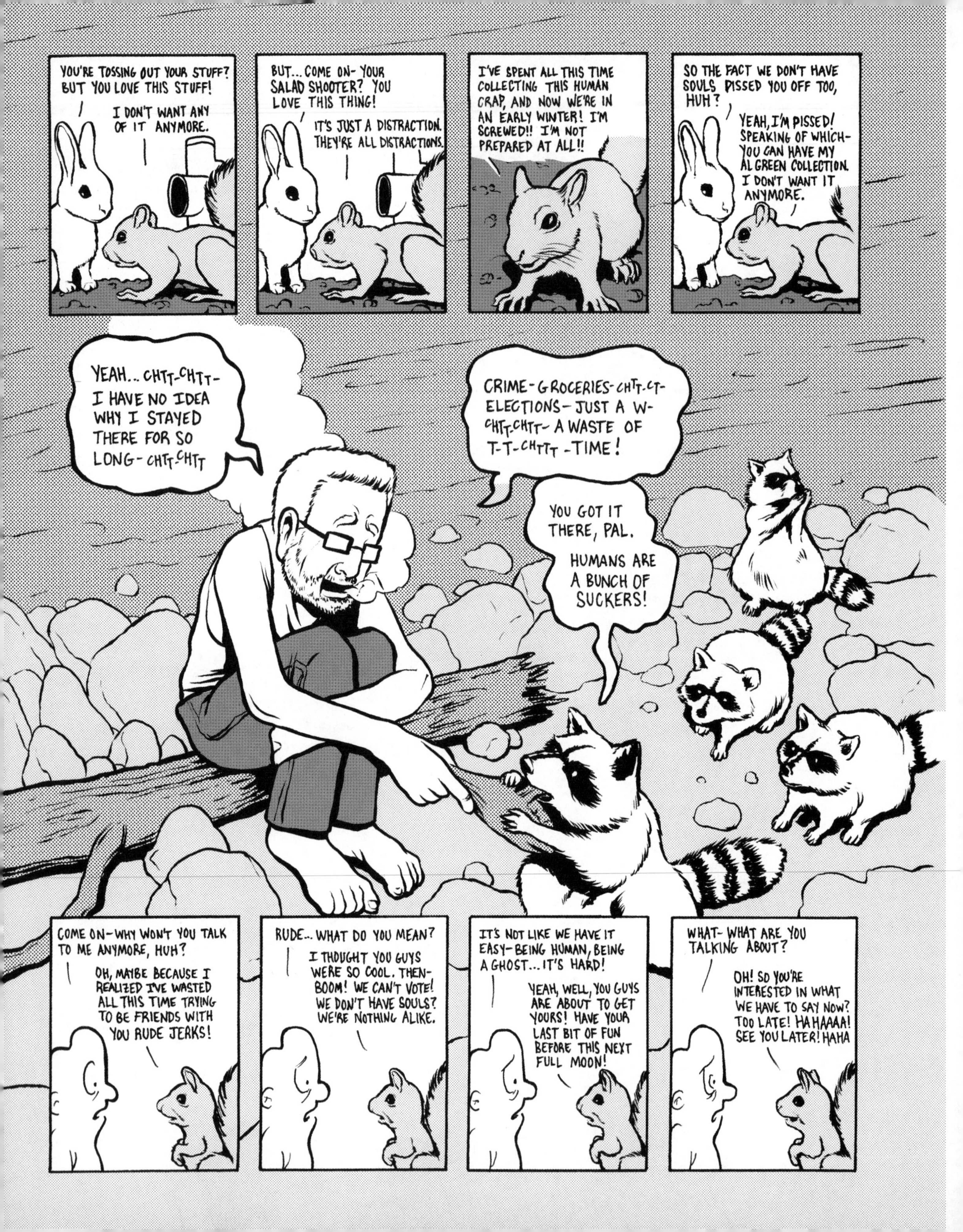
YOU'RE TOSSING OUT YOUR STUFF? BUT YOU LOVE THIS STUFF!
I DON'T WANT ANY OF IT ANYMORE.
BUT... COME ON- YOUR SALAD SHOOTER? YOU LOVE THIS THING!
IT'S JUST A DISTRACTION. THEY'RE ALL DISTRACTIONS.
I'VE SPENT ALL THIS TIME COLLECTING THIS HUMAN CRAP, AND NOW WE'RE IN AN EARLY WINTER! I'M SCREWED!! I'M NOT PREPARED AT ALL!!
SO THE FACT WE DON'T HAVE SOULS PISSED YOU OFF TOO, HUH?
YEAH, I'M PISSED! SPEAKING OF WHICH- YOU CAN HAVE MY AL GREEN COLLECTION. I DON'T WANT IT ANYMORE.
YEAH... CHTT-CHTT- I HAVE NO IDEA WHY I STAYED THERE FOR SO LONG- CHTT-CHTT
CRIME- GROCERIES- CHTT-CT- ELECTIONS- JUST A W- CHTT-CHTT- A WASTE OF T-T-CHTTT -TIME!
YOU GOT IT THERE, PAL.
HUMANS ARE A BUNCH OF SUCKERS!
COME ON- WHY WON'T YOU TALK TO ME ANYMORE, HUH?
OH, MAYBE BECAUSE I REALIZED I'VE WASTED ALL THIS TIME TRYING TO BE FRIENDS WITH YOU RUDE JERKS!
RUDE... WHAT DO YOU MEAN?
I THOUGHT YOU GUYS WERE SO COOL. THEN- BOOM! WE CAN'T VOTE! WE DON'T HAVE SOULS? WE'RE NOTHING ALIKE.
IT'S NOT LIKE WE HAVE IT EASY- BEING HUMAN, BEING A GHOST... IT'S HARD!
YEAH, WELL, YOU GUYS ARE ABOUT TO GET YOURS! HAVE YOUR LAST BIT OF FUN BEFORE THIS NEXT FULL MOON!
WHAT- WHAT ARE YOU TALKING ABOUT?
OH! SO YOU'RE INTERESTED IN WHAT WE HAVE TO SAY NOW? TOO LATE! HAHAAAA! SEE YOU LATER! HAHA

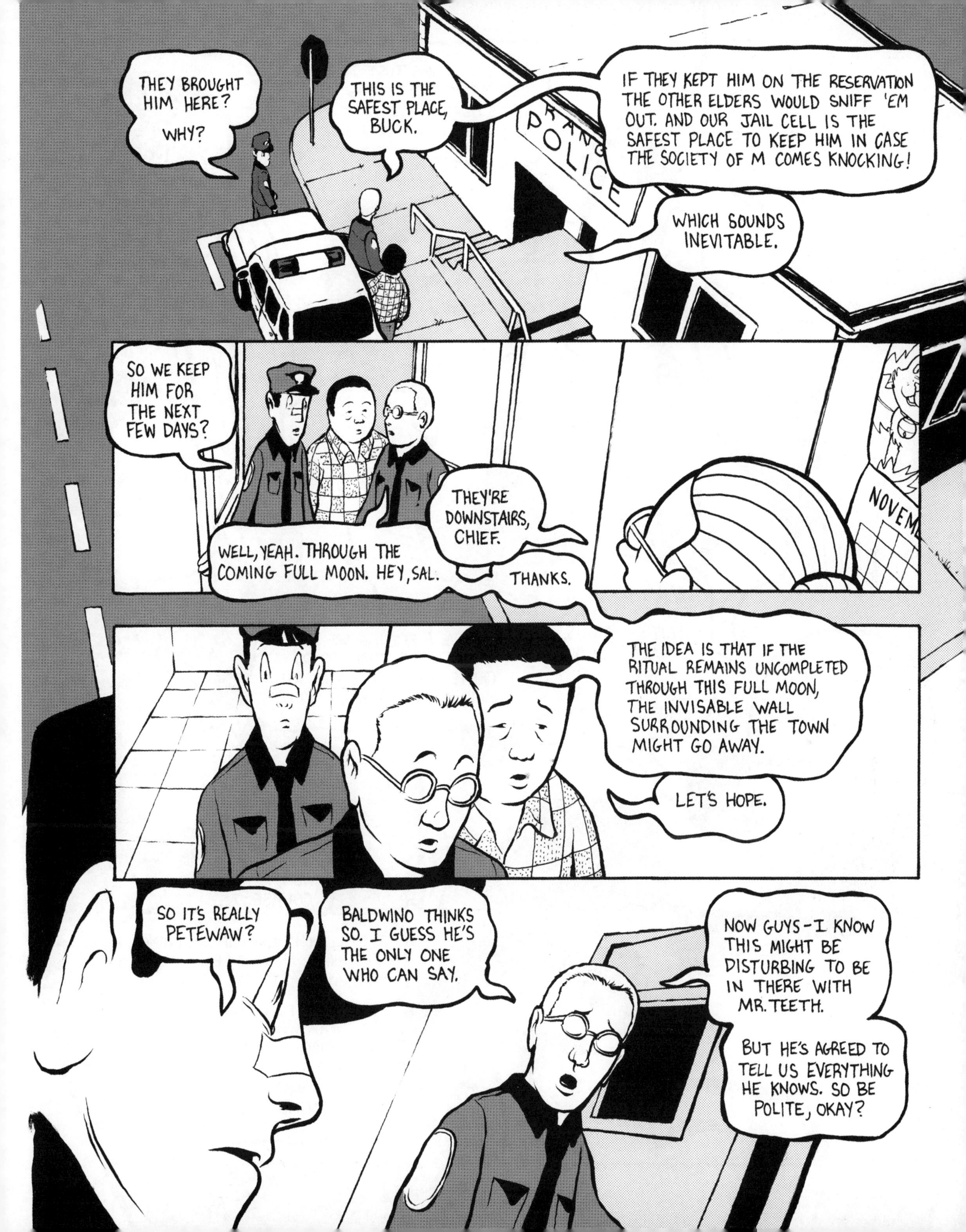
THEY BROUGHT HIM HERE? WHY?
THIS IS THE SAFEST PLACE, BUCK.
IF THEY KEPT HIM ON THE RESERVATION THE OTHER ELDERS WOULD SNIFF 'EM OUT. AND OUR JAIL CELL IS THE SAFEST PLACE TO KEEP HIM IN CASE THE SOCIETY OF M COMES KNOCKING!
POLICE
WHICH SOUNDS INEVITABLE.
SO WE KEEP HIM FOR THE NEXT FEW DAYS?
WELL, YEAH. THROUGH THE COMING FULL MOON. HEY, SAL.
THEY'RE DOWNSTAIRS, CHIEF.
THANKS.
NOVEM
THE IDEA IS THAT IF THE RITUAL REMAINS UNCOMPLETED THROUGH THIS FULL MOON, THE INVISABLE WALL SURROUNDING THE TOWN MIGHT GO AWAY.
LET'S HOPE.
SO IT'S REALLY PETEWAW?
BALDWINO THINKS SO. I GUESS HE'S THE ONLY ONE WHO CAN SAY.
NOW GUYS - I KNOW THIS MIGHT BE DISTURBING TO BE IN THERE WITH MR. TEETH.
BUT HE'S AGREED TO TELL US EVERYTHING HE KNOWS. SO BE POLITE, OKAY?

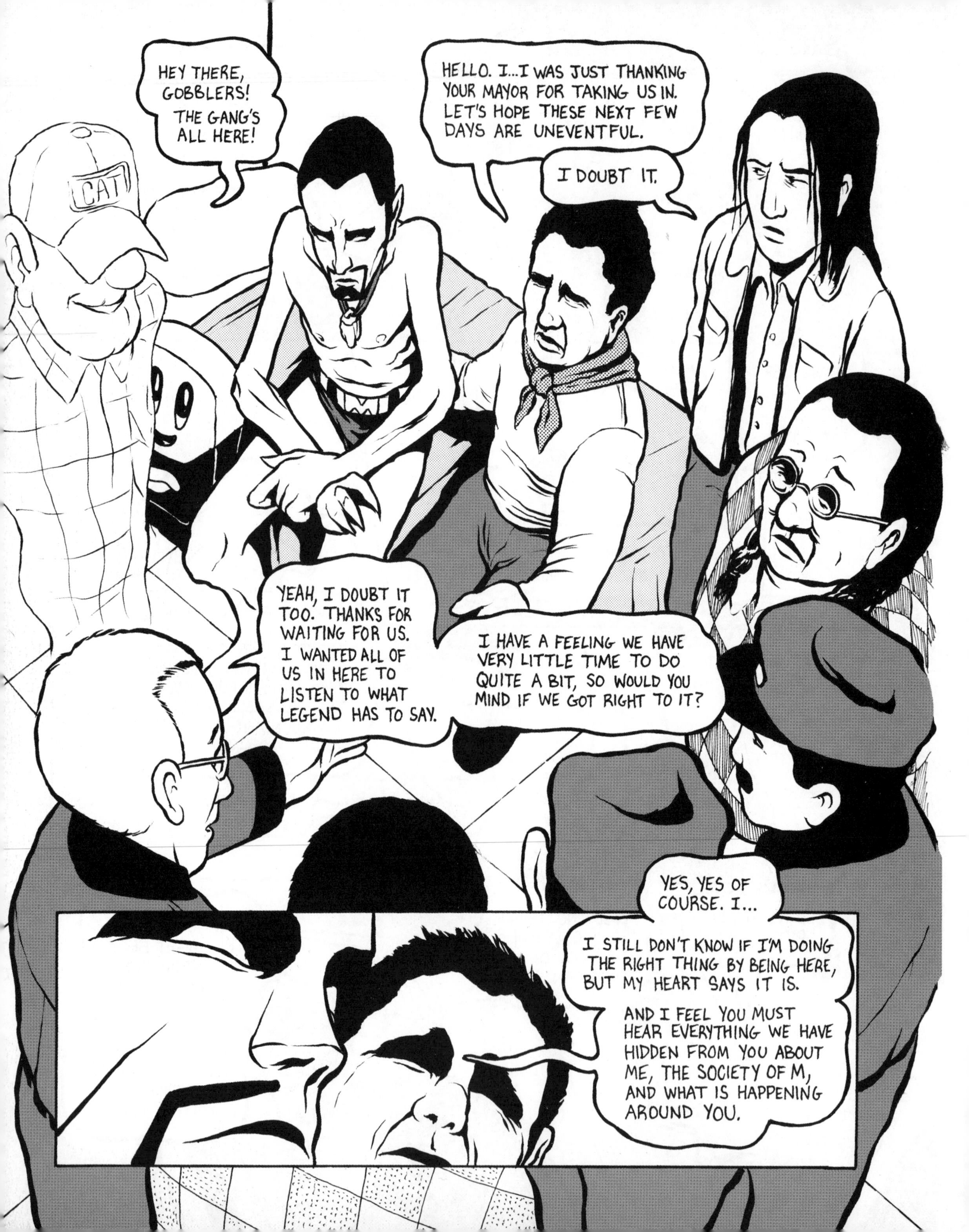
HEY THERE, GOBBLERS!
THE GANG'S ALL HERE!
HELLO. I...I WAS JUST THANKING YOUR MAYOR FOR TAKING US IN. LET'S HOPE THESE NEXT FEW DAYS ARE UNEVENTFUL.
I DOUBT IT.
YEAH, I DOUBT IT TOO. THANKS FOR WAITING FOR US. I WANTED ALL OF US IN HERE TO LISTEN TO WHAT LEGEND HAS TO SAY.
I HAVE A FEELING WE HAVE VERY LITTLE TIME TO DO QUITE A BIT, SO WOULD YOU MIND IF WE GOT RIGHT TO IT?
YES, YES OF COURSE. I...
I STILL DON'T KNOW IF I'M DOING THE RIGHT THING BY BEING HERE, BUT MY HEART SAYS IT IS.
AND I FEEL YOU MUST HEAR EVERYTHING WE HAVE HIDDEN FROM YOU ABOUT ME, THE SOCIETY OF M, AND WHAT IS HAPPENING AROUND YOU.

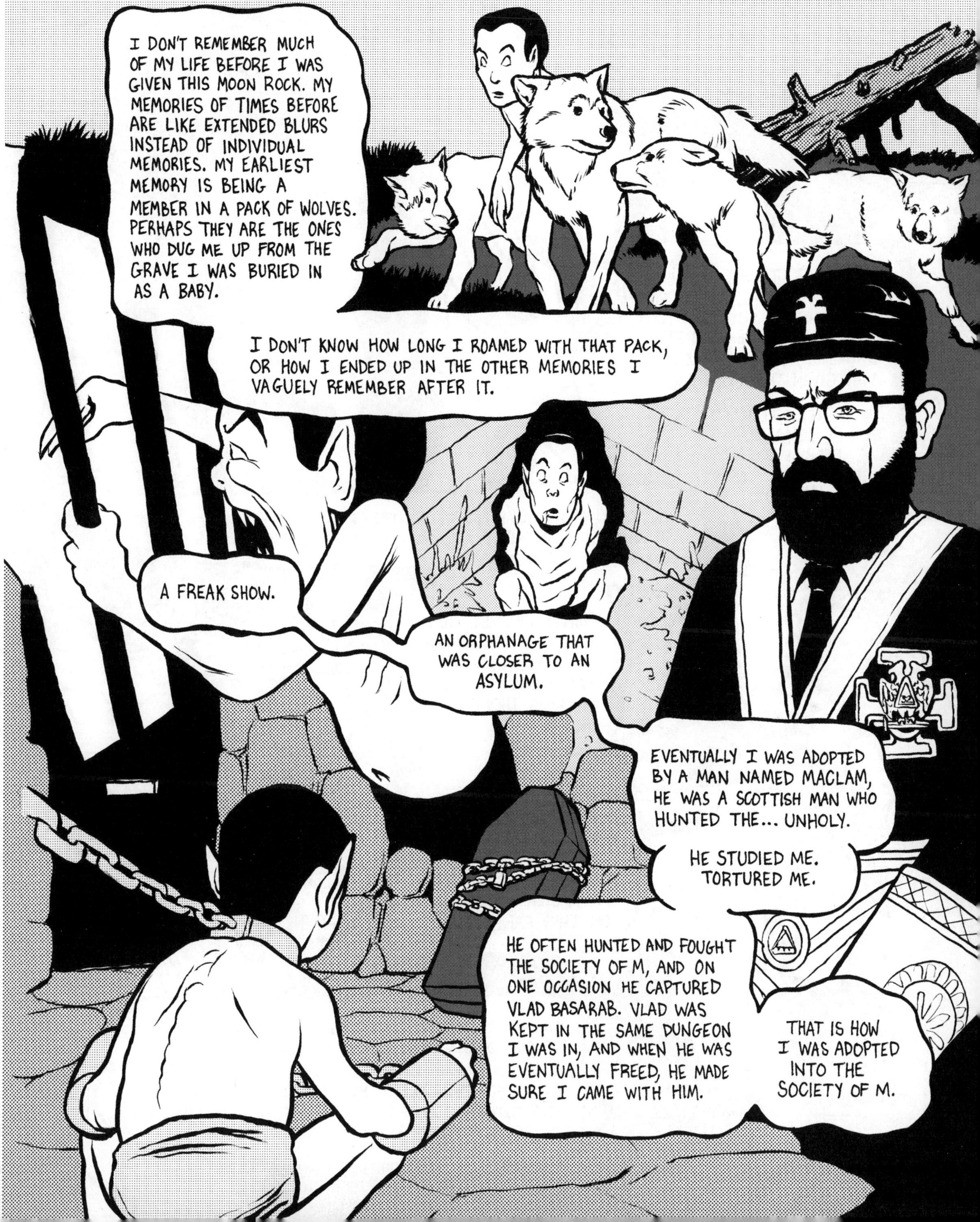
I DON'T REMEMBER MUCH OF MY LIFE BEFORE I WAS GIVEN THIS MOON ROCK. MY MEMORIES OF TIMES BEFORE ARE LIKE EXTENDED BLURS INSTEAD OF INDIVIDUAL MEMORIES. MY EARLIEST MEMORY IS BEING A MEMBER IN A PACK OF WOLVES. PERHAPS THEY ARE THE ONES WHO DUG ME UP FROM THE GRAVE I WAS BURIED IN AS A BABY.
I DON'T KNOW HOW LONG I ROAMED WITH THAT PACK, OR HOW I ENDED UP IN THE OTHER MEMORIES I VAGUELY REMEMBER AFTER IT.
A FREAK SHOW.
AN ORPHANAGE THAT WAS CLOSER TO AN ASYLUM.
EVENTUALLY I WAS ADOPTED BY A MAN NAMED MACLAM, HE WAS A SCOTTISH MAN WHO HUNTED THE... UNHOLY.
HE STUDIED ME. TORTURED ME.
HE OFTEN HUNTED AND FOUGHT THE SOCIETY OF M, AND ON ONE OCCASION HE CAPTURED VLAD BASARAB. VLAD WAS KEPT IN THE SAME DUNGEON I WAS IN, AND WHEN HE WAS EVENTUALLY FREED, HE MADE SURE I CAME WITH HIM.
THAT IS HOW I WAS ADOPTED INTO THE SOCIETY OF M.

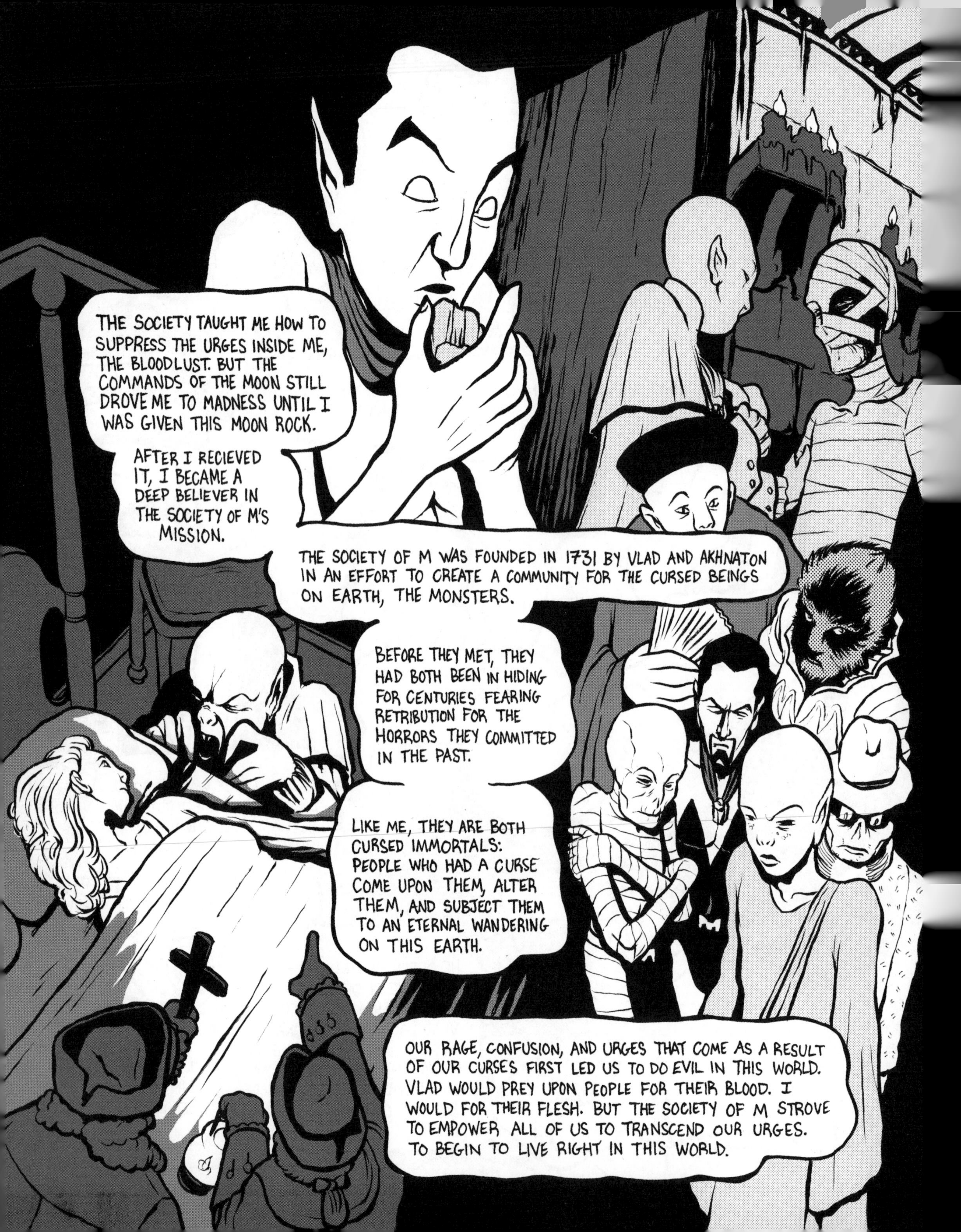
THE SOCIETY TAUGHT ME HOW TO SUPPRESS THE URGES INSIDE ME, THE BLOODLUST. BUT THE COMMANDS OF THE MOON STILL DROVE ME TO MADNESS UNTIL I WAS GIVEN THIS MOON ROCK.
AFTER I RECIEVED IT, I BECAME A DEEP BELIEVER IN THE SOCIETY OF M'S MISSION.
THE SOCIETY OF M WAS FOUNDED IN 1731 BY VLAD AND AKHNATON IN AN EFFORT TO CREATE A COMMUNITY FOR THE CURSED BEINGS ON EARTH, THE MONSTERS.
BEFORE THEY MET, THEY HAD BOTH BEEN IN HIDING FOR CENTURIES FEARING RETRIBUTION FOR THE HORRORS THEY COMMITTED IN THE PAST.
LIKE ME, THEY ARE BOTH CURSED IMMORTALS: PEOPLE WHO HAD A CURSE COME UPON THEM, ALTER THEM, AND SUBJECT THEM TO AN ETERNAL WANDERING ON THIS EARTH.
OUR RAGE, CONFUSION, AND URGES THAT COME AS A RESULT OF OUR CURSES FIRST LED US TO DO EVIL IN THIS WORLD. VLAD WOULD PREY UPON PEOPLE FOR THEIR BLOOD. I WOULD FOR THEIR FLESH. BUT THE SOCIETY OF M STROVE TO EMPOWER ALL OF US TO TRANSCEND OUR URGES. TO BEGIN TO LIVE RIGHT IN THIS WORLD.

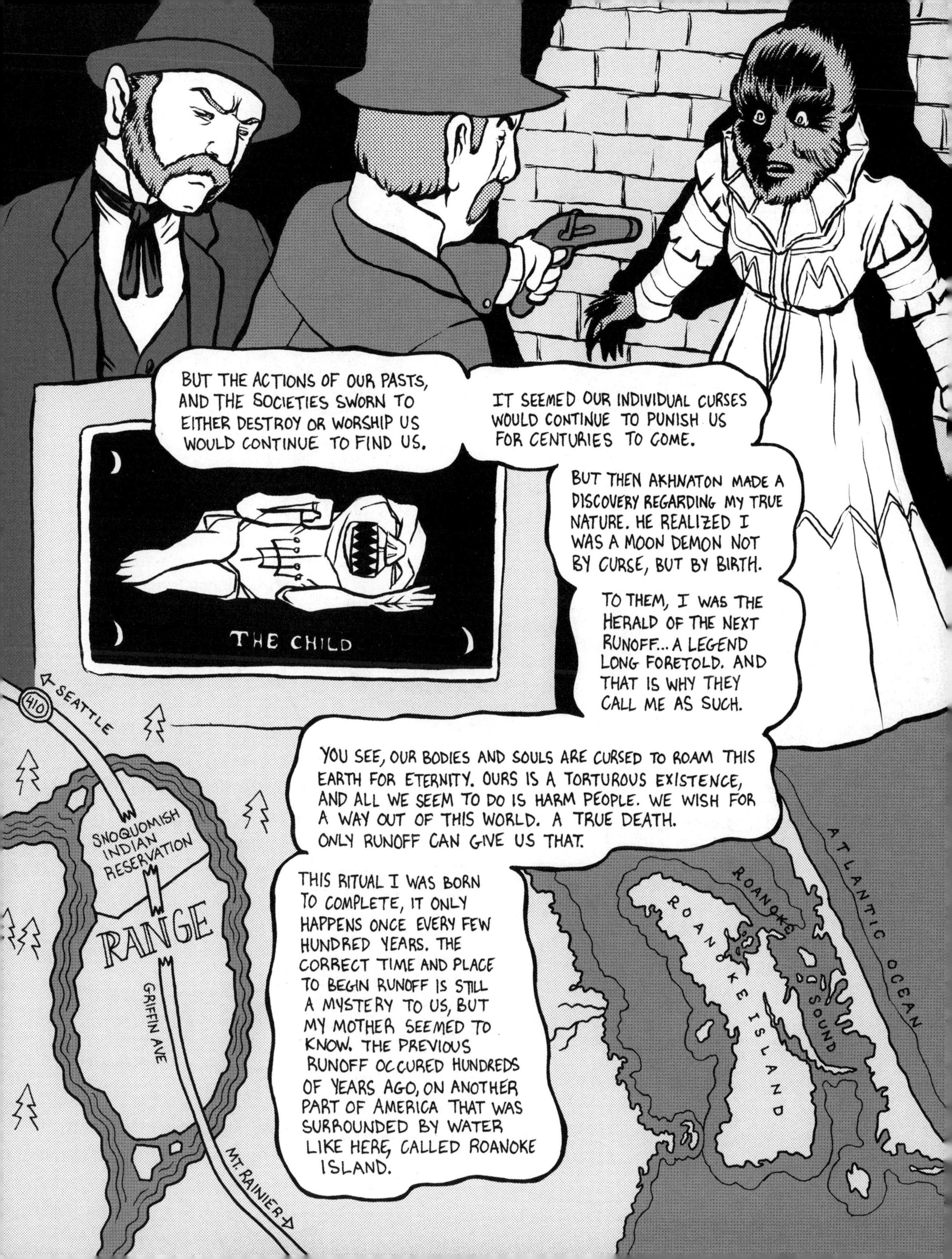
BUT THE ACTIONS OF OUR PASTS, AND THE SOCIETIES SWORN TO EITHER DESTROY OR WORSHIP US WOULD CONTINUE TO FIND US.
IT SEEMED OUR INDIVIDUAL CURSES WOULD CONTINUE TO PUNISH US FOR CENTURIES TO COME.
BUT THEN AKHNATON MADE A DISCOVERY REGARDING MY TRUE NATURE. HE REALIZED I WAS A MOON DEMON NOT BY CURSE, BUT BY BIRTH.
TO THEM, I WAS THE HERALD OF THE NEXT RUNOFF... A LEGEND LONG FORETOLD. AND THAT IS WHY THEY CALL ME AS SUCH.
THE CHILD
410
SEATTLE
SNOQUOMISH INDIAN RESERVATION
RANGE
GRIFFIN AVE
MT. RAINIER
YOU SEE, OUR BODIES AND SOULS ARE CURSED TO ROAM THIS EARTH FOR ETERNITY. OURS IS A TORTUROUS EXISTENCE, AND ALL WE SEEM TO DO IS HARM PEOPLE. WE WISH FOR A WAY OUT OF THIS WORLD. A TRUE DEATH. ONLY RUNOFF CAN GIVE US THAT.
THIS RITUAL I WAS BORN TO COMPLETE, IT ONLY HAPPENS ONCE EVERY FEW HUNDRED YEARS. THE CORRECT TIME AND PLACE TO BEGIN RUNOFF IS STILL A MYSTERY TO US, BUT MY MOTHER SEEMED TO KNOW. THE PREVIOUS RUNOFF OCCURED HUNDREDS OF YEARS AGO, ON ANOTHER PART OF AMERICA THAT WAS SURROUNDED BY WATER LIKE HERE, CALLED ROANOKE ISLAND.
ROANOKE
ROANOKE ISLAND
ROANOKE SOUND
ATLANTIC OCEAN

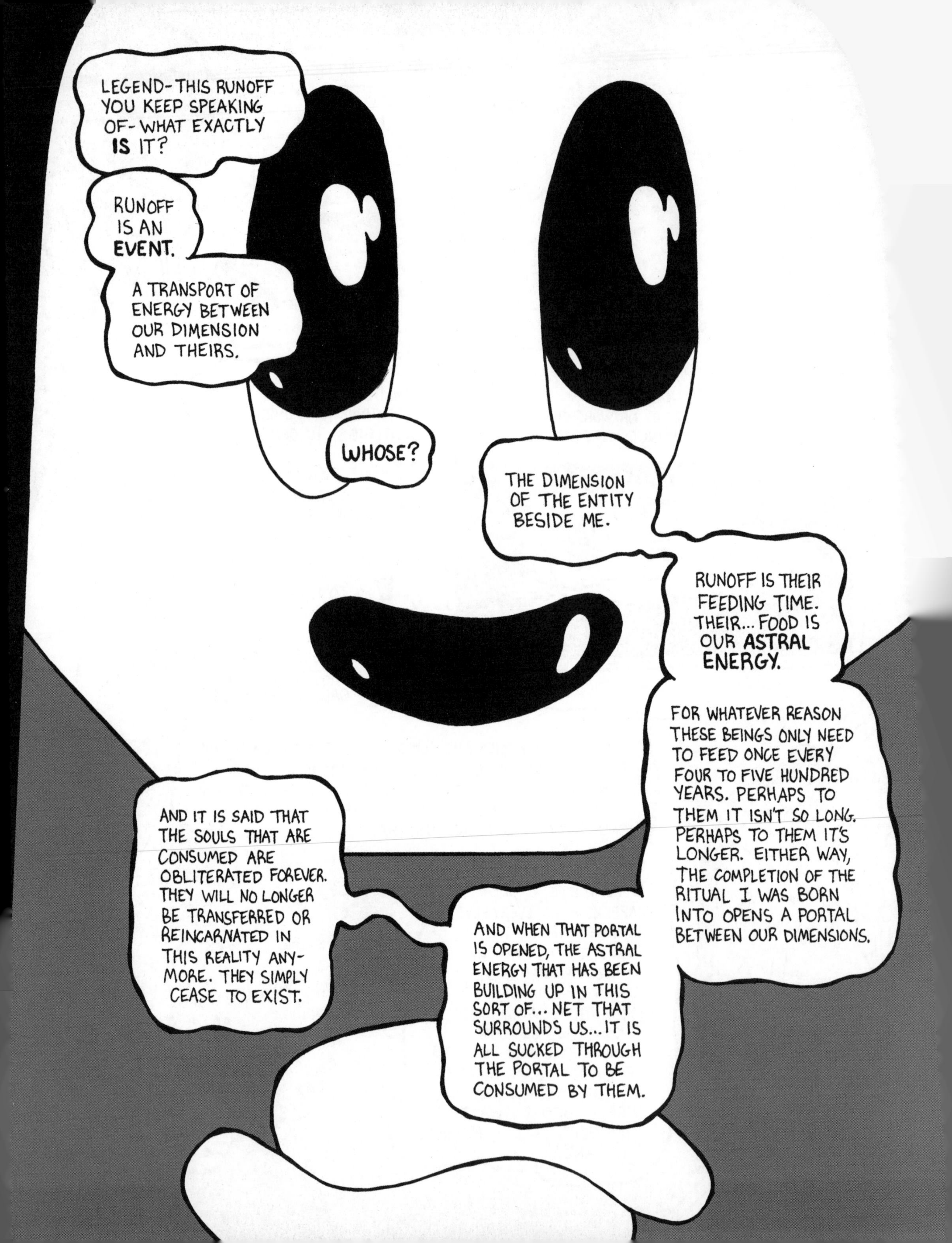
LEGEND- THIS RUNOFF YOU KEEP SPEAKING OF- WHAT EXACTLY **IS** IT?
RUNOFF IS AN **EVENT.**
A TRANSPORT OF ENERGY BETWEEN OUR DIMENSION AND THEIRS.
WHOSE?
THE DIMENSION OF THE ENTITY BESIDE ME.
RUNOFF IS THEIR FEEDING TIME. THEIR... FOOD IS OUR **ASTRAL ENERGY.**
FOR WHATEVER REASON THESE BEINGS ONLY NEED TO FEED ONCE EVERY FOUR TO FIVE HUNDRED YEARS. PERHAPS TO THEM IT ISN'T SO LONG. PERHAPS TO THEM IT'S LONGER. EITHER WAY, THE COMPLETION OF THE RITUAL I WAS BORN INTO OPENS A PORTAL BETWEEN OUR DIMENSIONS.
AND WHEN THAT PORTAL IS OPENED, THE ASTRAL ENERGY THAT HAS BEEN BUILDING UP IN THIS SORT OF... NET THAT SURROUNDS US... IT IS ALL SUCKED THROUGH THE PORTAL TO BE CONSUMED BY THEM.
AND IT IS SAID THAT THE SOULS THAT ARE CONSUMED ARE OBLITERATED FOREVER. THEY WILL NO LONGER BE TRANSFERRED OR REINCARNATED IN THIS REALITY ANY-MORE. THEY SIMPLY CEASE TO EXIST.

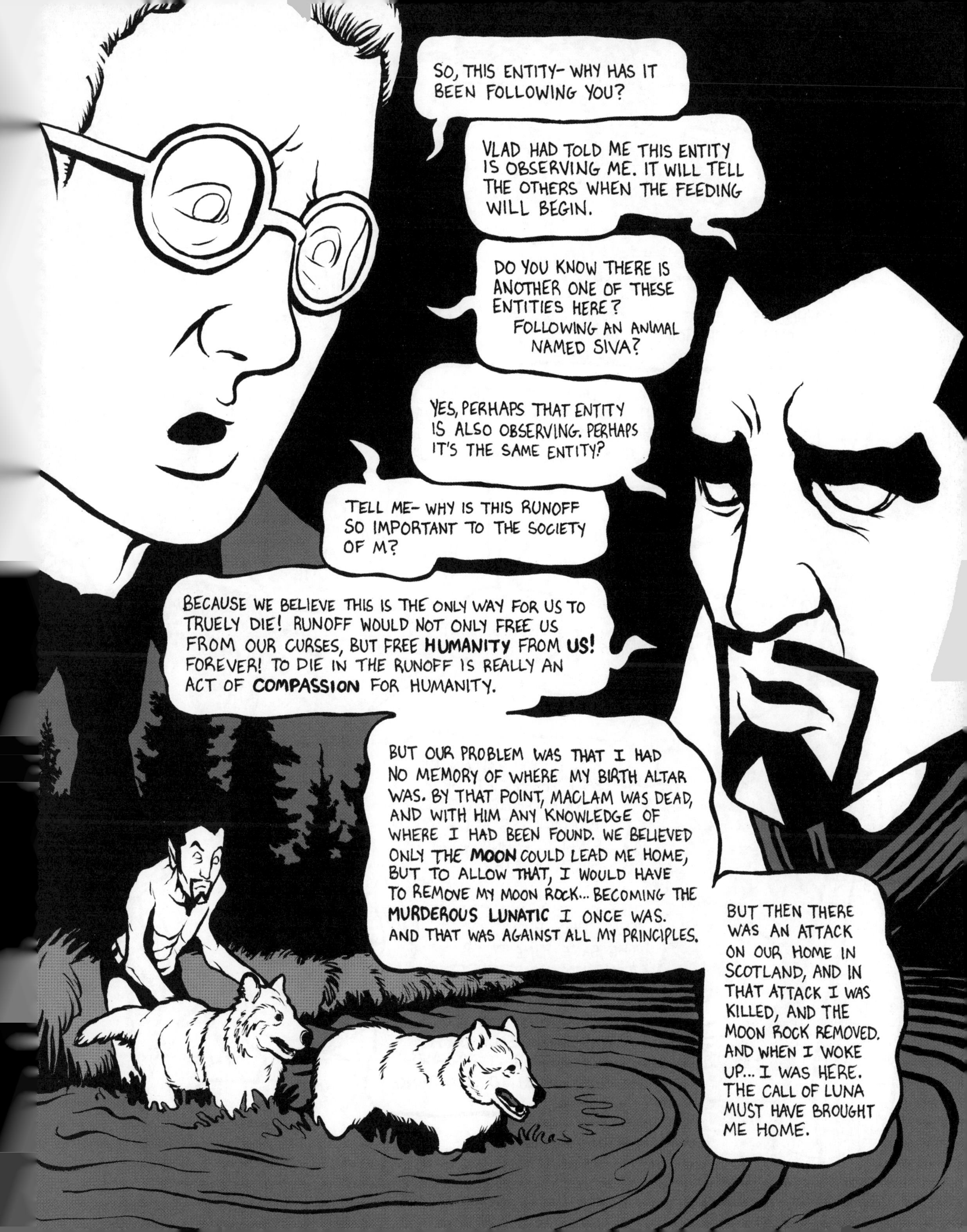
SO, THIS ENTITY- WHY HAS IT BEEN FOLLOWING YOU?
VLAD HAD TOLD ME THIS ENTITY IS OBSERVING ME. IT WILL TELL THE OTHERS WHEN THE FEEDING WILL BEGIN.
DO YOU KNOW THERE IS ANOTHER ONE OF THESE ENTITIES HERE? FOLLOWING AN ANIMAL NAMED SIVA?
YES, PERHAPS THAT ENTITY IS ALSO OBSERVING. PERHAPS IT'S THE SAME ENTITY?
TELL ME- WHY IS THIS RUNOFF SO IMPORTANT TO THE SOCIETY OF M?
BECAUSE WE BELIEVE THIS IS THE ONLY WAY FOR US TO TRUELY DIE! RUNOFF WOULD NOT ONLY FREE US FROM OUR CURSES, BUT FREE **HUMANITY** FROM **US!** FOREVER! TO DIE IN THE RUNOFF IS REALLY AN ACT OF **COMPASSION** FOR HUMANITY.
BUT OUR PROBLEM WAS THAT I HAD NO MEMORY OF WHERE MY BIRTH ALTAR WAS. BY THAT POINT, MACLAM WAS DEAD, AND WITH HIM ANY KNOWLEDGE OF WHERE I HAD BEEN FOUND. WE BELIEVED ONLY THE **MOON** COULD LEAD ME HOME, BUT TO ALLOW THAT, I WOULD HAVE TO REMOVE MY MOON ROCK... BECOMING THE **MURDEROUS LUNATIC** I ONCE WAS. AND THAT WAS AGAINST ALL MY PRINCIPLES.
BUT THEN THERE WAS AN ATTACK ON OUR HOME IN SCOTLAND, AND IN THAT ATTACK I WAS KILLED, AND THE MOON ROCK REMOVED. AND WHEN I WOKE UP... I WAS HERE. THE CALL OF LUNA MUST HAVE BROUGHT ME HOME.

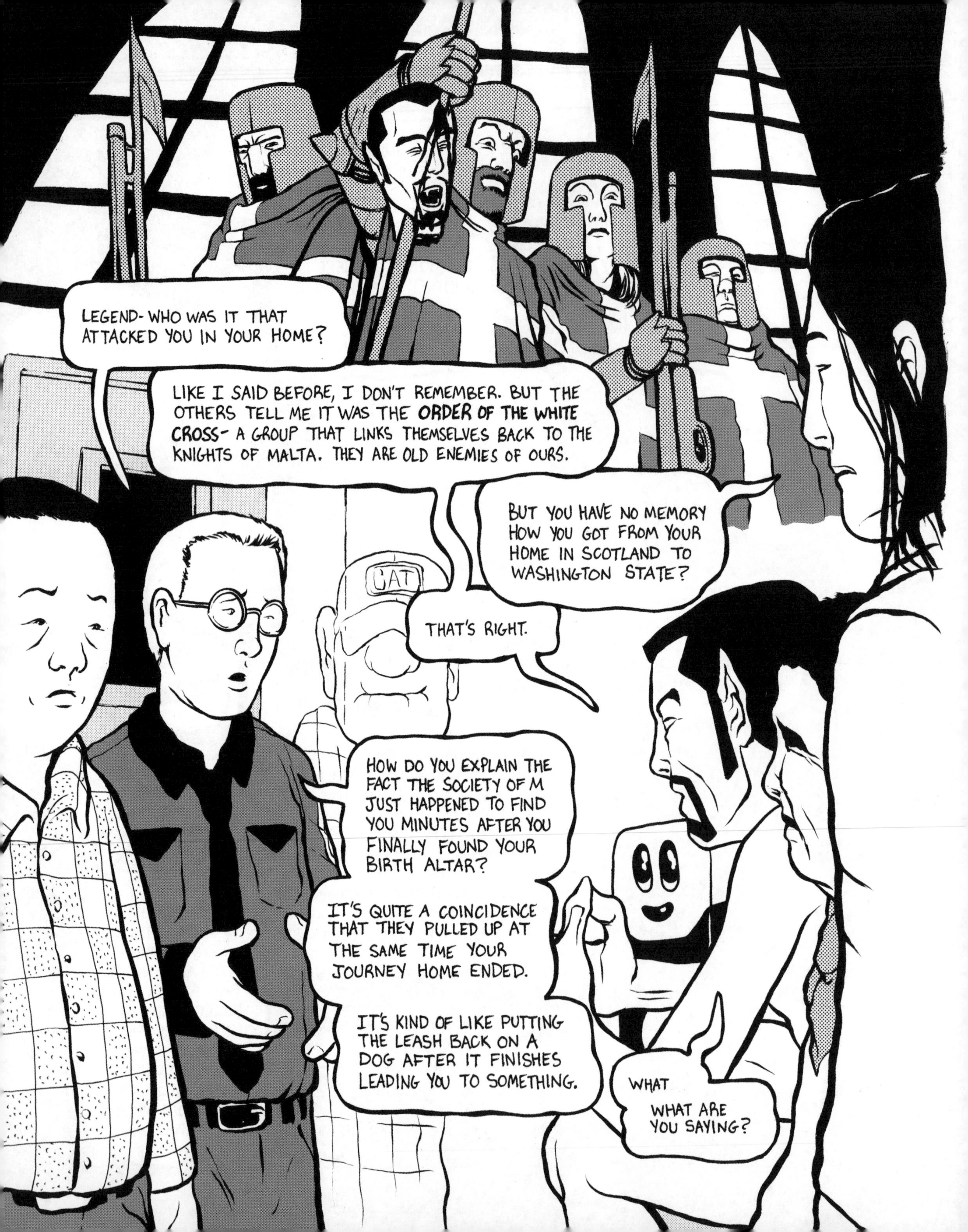
LEGEND- WHO WAS IT THAT ATTACKED YOU IN YOUR HOME?
LIKE I SAID BEFORE, I DON'T REMEMBER. BUT THE OTHERS TELL ME IT WAS THE **ORDER OF THE WHITE CROSS**- A GROUP THAT LINKS THEMSELVES BACK TO THE KNIGHTS OF MALTA. THEY ARE OLD ENEMIES OF OURS.
BUT YOU HAVE NO MEMORY HOW YOU GOT FROM YOUR HOME IN SCOTLAND TO WASHINGTON STATE?
THAT'S RIGHT.
CAT
HOW DO YOU EXPLAIN THE FACT THE SOCIETY OF M JUST HAPPENED TO FIND YOU MINUTES AFTER YOU FINALLY FOUND YOUR BIRTH ALTAR?
IT'S QUITE A COINCIDENCE THAT THEY PULLED UP AT THE SAME TIME YOUR JOURNEY HOME ENDED.
IT'S KIND OF LIKE PUTTING THE LEASH BACK ON A DOG AFTER IT FINISHES LEADING YOU TO SOMETHING.
WHAT
WHAT ARE YOU SAYING?

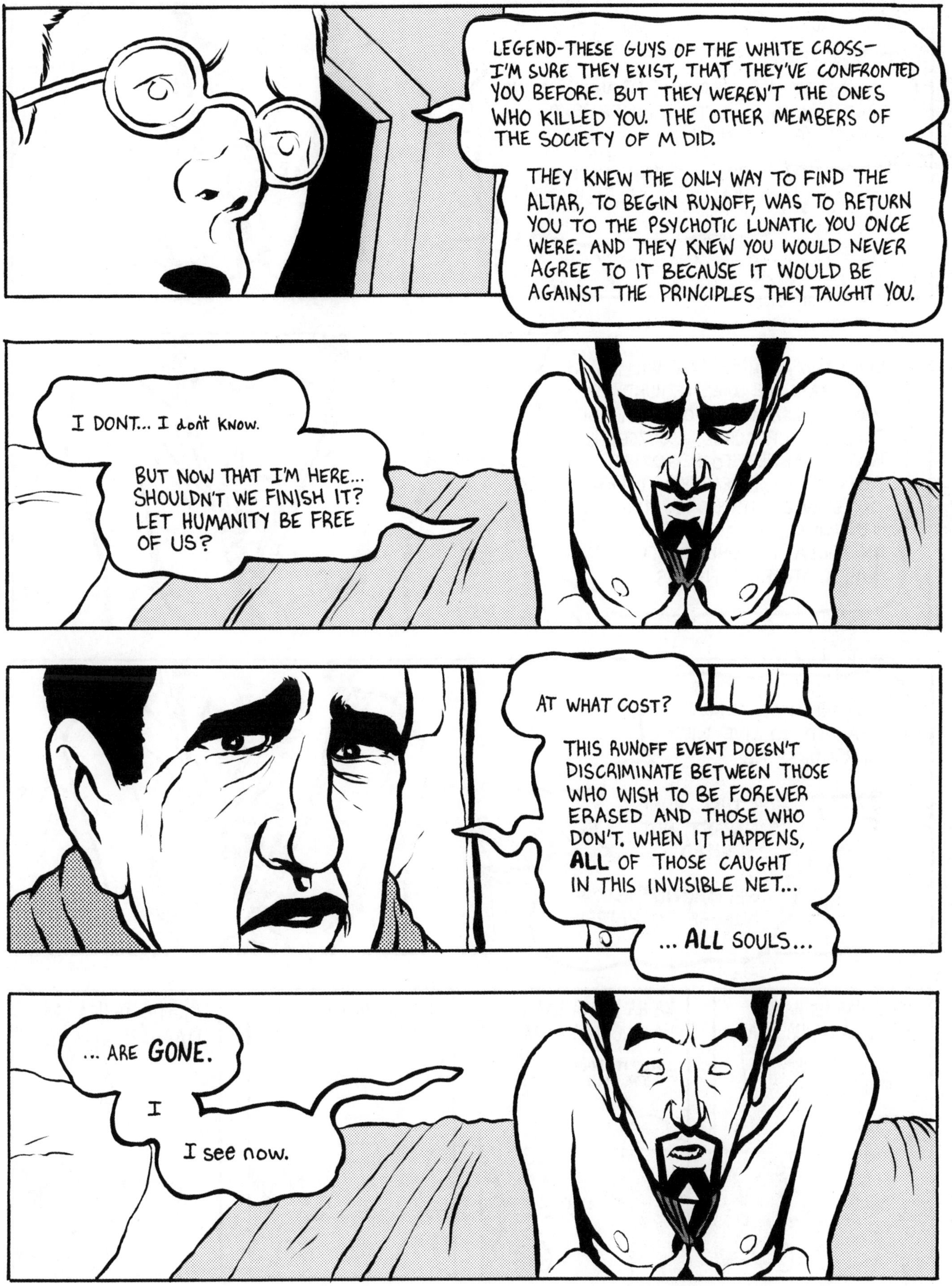
LEGEND-THESE GUYS OF THE WHITE CROSS- I'M SURE THEY EXIST, THAT THEY'VE CONFRONTED YOU BEFORE. BUT THEY WEREN'T THE ONES WHO KILLED YOU. THE OTHER MEMBERS OF THE SOCIETY OF M DID.
THEY KNEW THE ONLY WAY TO FIND THE ALTAR, TO BEGIN RUNOFF, WAS TO RETURN YOU TO THE PSYCHOTIC LUNATIC YOU ONCE WERE. AND THEY KNEW YOU WOULD NEVER AGREE TO IT BECAUSE IT WOULD BE AGAINST THE PRINCIPLES THEY TAUGHT YOU.
I DONT... I don't know.
BUT NOW THAT I'M HERE... SHOULDN'T WE FINISH IT? LET HUMANITY BE FREE OF US?
AT WHAT COST?
THIS RUNOFF EVENT DOESN'T DISCRIMINATE BETWEEN THOSE WHO WISH TO BE FOREVER ERASED AND THOSE WHO DON'T. WHEN IT HAPPENS, **ALL** OF THOSE CAUGHT IN THIS INVISIBLE NET...
... **ALL** SOULS...
... ARE **GONE.**
I
I see now.

MY SOCIETY HAS TOLD ME THAT ANNIHILATING OURSELVES THROUGH THE RUNOFF IS A SERVICE TO HUMANITY...

BUT IN TRUTH IT'S THE HEIGHT OF SELFISHNESS!

VLAD AND AKHNATON ARE WILLING TO OBLITERATE THE SOULS OF HUNDREDS, MAYBE THOUSANDS, SO WE CAN BE FREE OF OUR CURSE. A CURSE WE HAVE LEARNED TO NEGOTIATE ANYWAY. WE'VE LEARNED TO FEED OURSELVES WITHOUT PREYING ON THE LIVING... LEARNED TO LIVE IN ISOLATION, ONLY DISTURBED WHEN OTHERS FIND US.

IF... WE HAVE ALREADY LEARNED TO LIVE WITH OUR CURSES...

FOR THEM, RUNOFF IS A **WANT**, NOT A **NEED**.

WE **CANNOT** ALLOW RUNOFF TO HAPPEN.

HA HA HAA HA HA HA HA HAAA HA HA HAA!

SHUT UP. SHUT UP! STOP LAUGHING...

HA HA HAAAA HAA HA HA HA HA HAAAAA !

STOP IT! LOOK... I'M GOING.

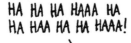

HA HA HA HAAA HA HA HAA HA HA HAAA!

AHA HA HA HAAAAA HAAHA HAAHAAA

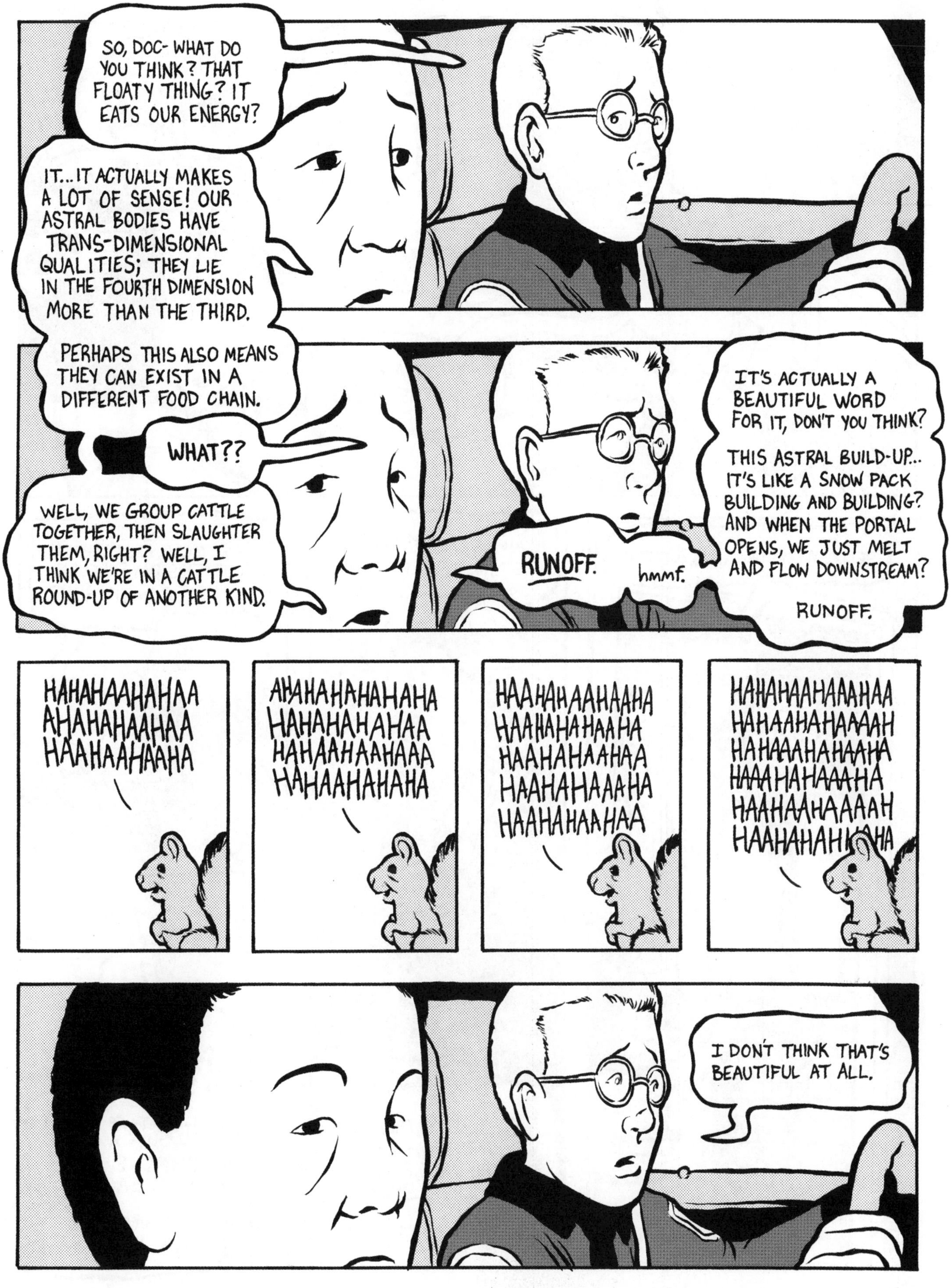
SO, DOC- WHAT DO YOU THINK? THAT FLOATY THING? IT EATS OUR ENERGY?
IT... IT ACTUALLY MAKES A LOT OF SENSE! OUR ASTRAL BODIES HAVE TRANS-DIMENSIONAL QUALITIES; THEY LIE IN THE FOURTH DIMENSION MORE THAN THE THIRD.
PERHAPS THIS ALSO MEANS THEY CAN EXIST IN A DIFFERENT FOOD CHAIN.
WHAT??
WELL, WE GROUP CATTLE TOGETHER, THEN SLAUGHTER THEM, RIGHT? WELL, I THINK WE'RE IN A CATTLE ROUND-UP OF ANOTHER KIND.
RUNOFF.
hmmf.
IT'S ACTUALLY A BEAUTIFUL WORD FOR IT, DON'T YOU THINK?
THIS ASTRAL BUILD-UP... IT'S LIKE A SNOW PACK BUILDING AND BUILDING? AND WHEN THE PORTAL OPENS, WE JUST MELT AND FLOW DOWNSTREAM?
RUNOFF.
HAHAHAAHAHAA AHAHAHAAHAA HAAHAAHAAHA
AHAHAHAHAHAHA HAHAHAHAHAA HAHAAHAAHAAA HAHAAHAHAHA
HAAHAHAAHAAHA HAAHAHAHAAHA HAAHAHAAHAA HAAHAHAAAHA HAAHAHAAHAA
HAHAHAAHAAAHAA HAHAAHAHAAAAH HAHAAAHAHAAHA HAAAHAHAAAHA HAAHAAHAAAAH
I DON'T THINK THAT'S BEAUTIFUL AT ALL.

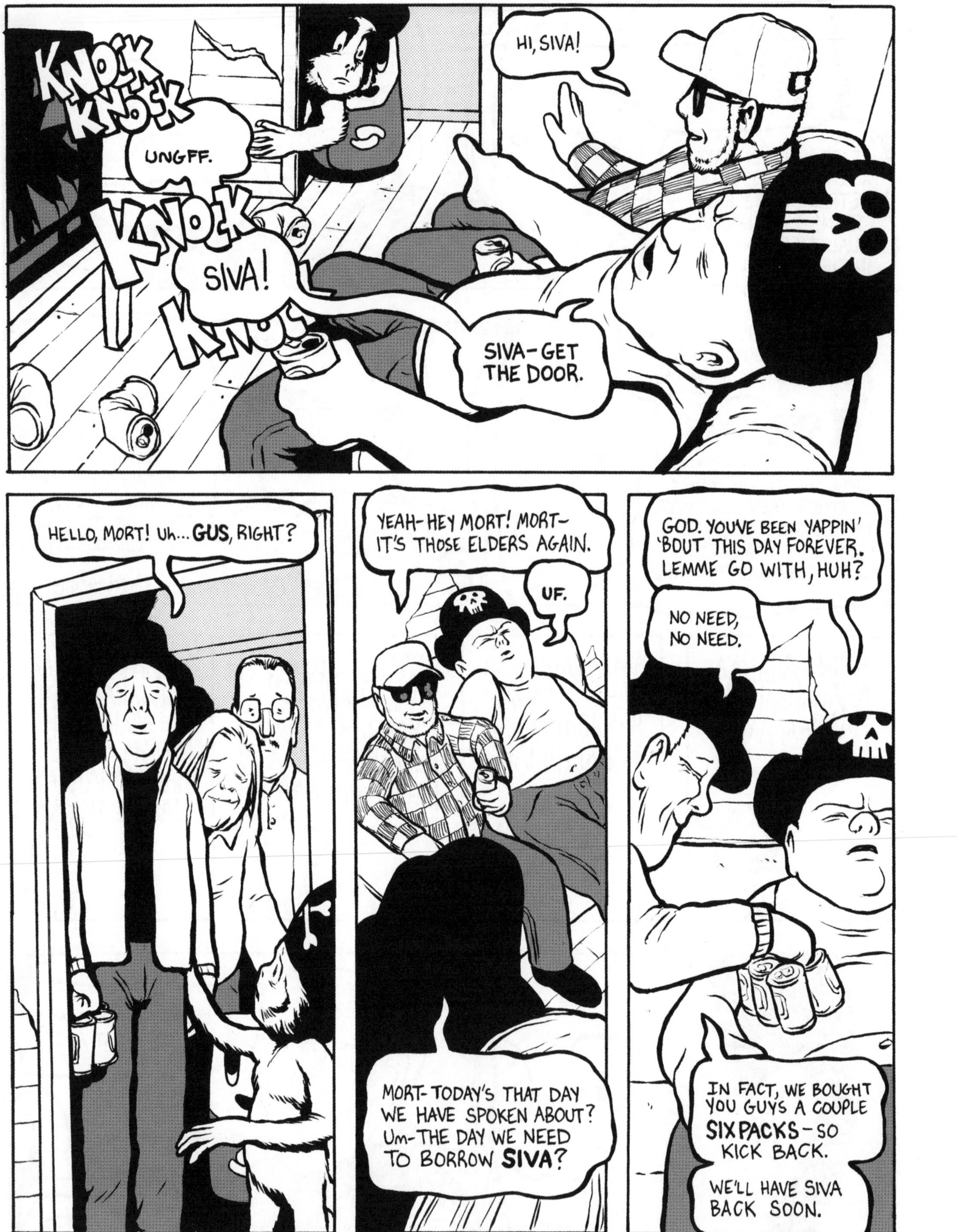
KNOCK KNOCK
UNGFF.
KNOCK
SIVA!
KNOCK
HI, SIVA!
SIVA-GET THE DOOR.
HELLO, MORT! Uh... GUS, RIGHT?
YEAH-HEY MORT! MORT-IT'S THOSE ELDERS AGAIN.
UF.
MORT-TODAY'S THAT DAY WE HAVE SPOKEN ABOUT? Um-THE DAY WE NEED TO BORROW SIVA?
GOD. YOU'VE BEEN YAPPIN' 'BOUT THIS DAY FOREVER. LEMME GO WITH, HUH?
NO NEED, NO NEED.
IN FACT, WE BOUGHT YOU GUYS A COUPLE SIXPACKS-SO KICK BACK.
WE'LL HAVE SIVA BACK SOON.

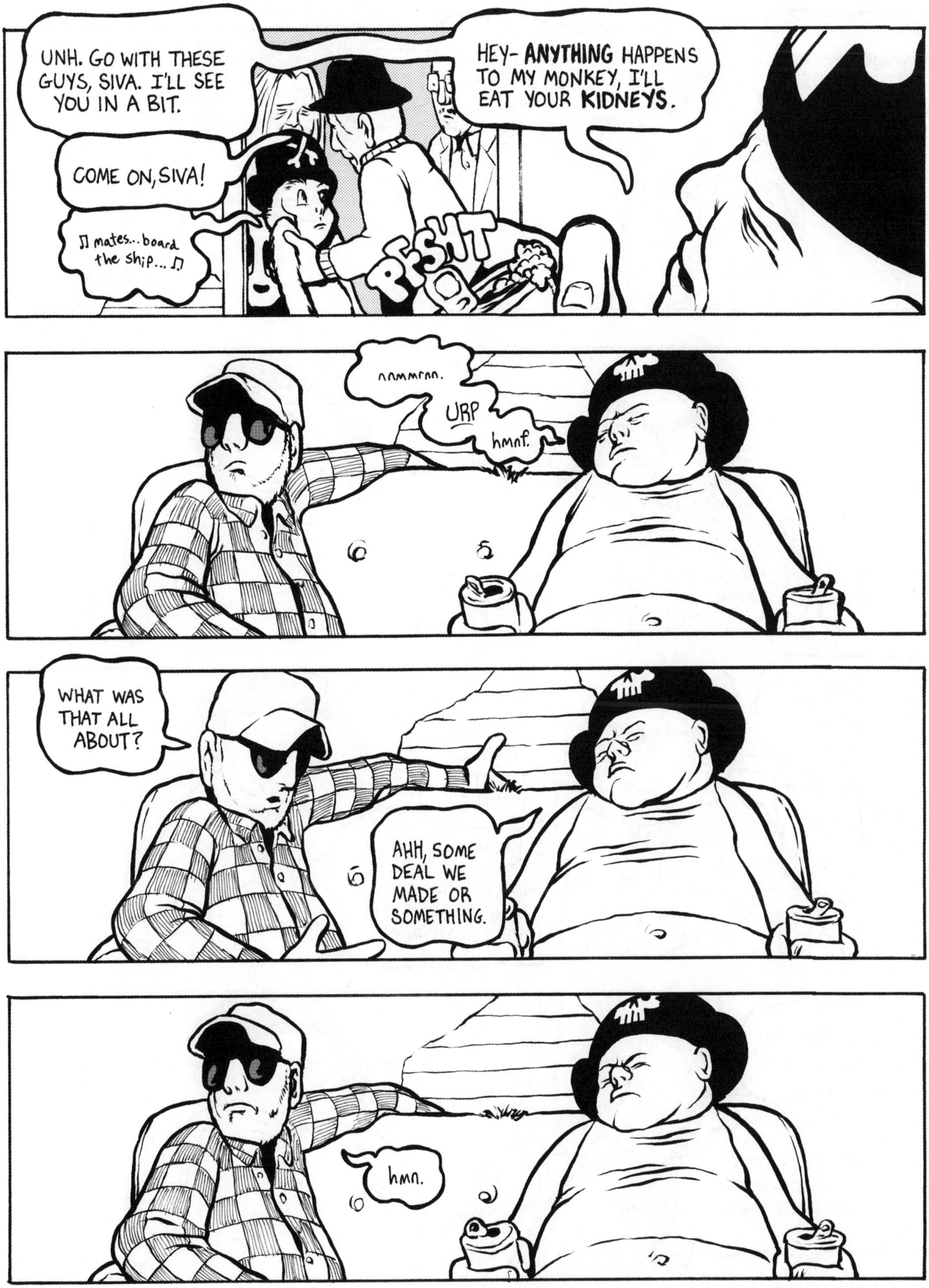
UNH. GO WITH THESE GUYS, SIVA. I'LL SEE YOU IN A BIT.
HEY- ANYTHING HAPPENS TO MY MONKEY, I'LL EAT YOUR KIDNEYS.
COME ON, SIVA!
♫ mates... board the ship... ♫
PFSHT
nnmmrnn.
URP
hmnf.
WHAT WAS THAT ALL ABOUT?
AHH, SOME DEAL WE MADE OR SOMETHING.
hmn.

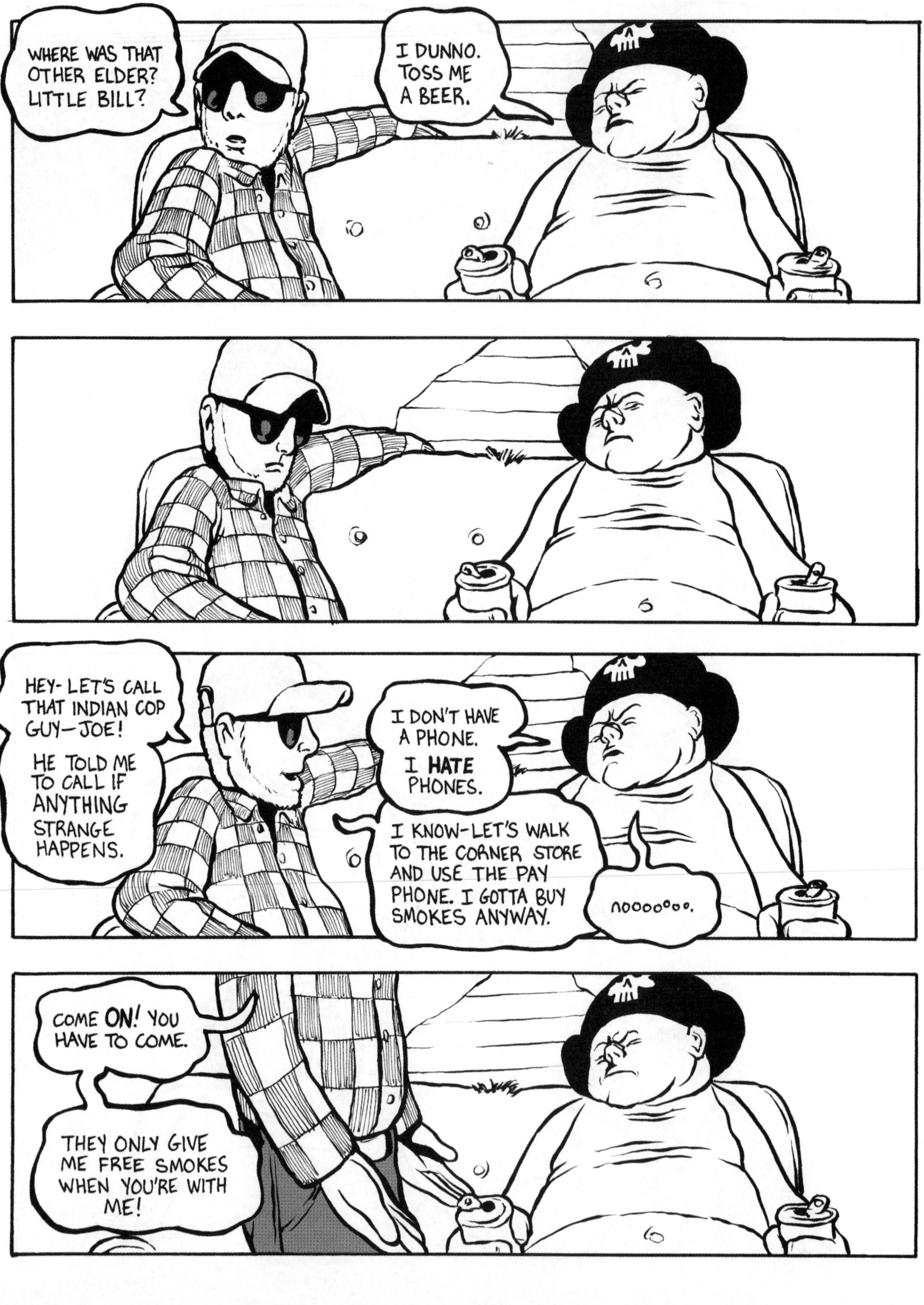
WHERE WAS THAT OTHER ELDER? LITTLE BILL?
I DUNNO. TOSS ME A BEER.
HEY- LET'S CALL THAT INDIAN COP GUY—JOE!
HE TOLD ME TO CALL IF ANYTHING STRANGE HAPPENS.
I DON'T HAVE A PHONE.
I **HATE** PHONES.
I KNOW-LET'S WALK TO THE CORNER STORE AND USE THE PAY PHONE. I GOTTA BUY SMOKES ANYWAY.
nooooººº.
COME **ON**! YOU HAVE TO COME.
THEY ONLY GIVE ME FREE SMOKES WHEN YOU'RE WITH ME!

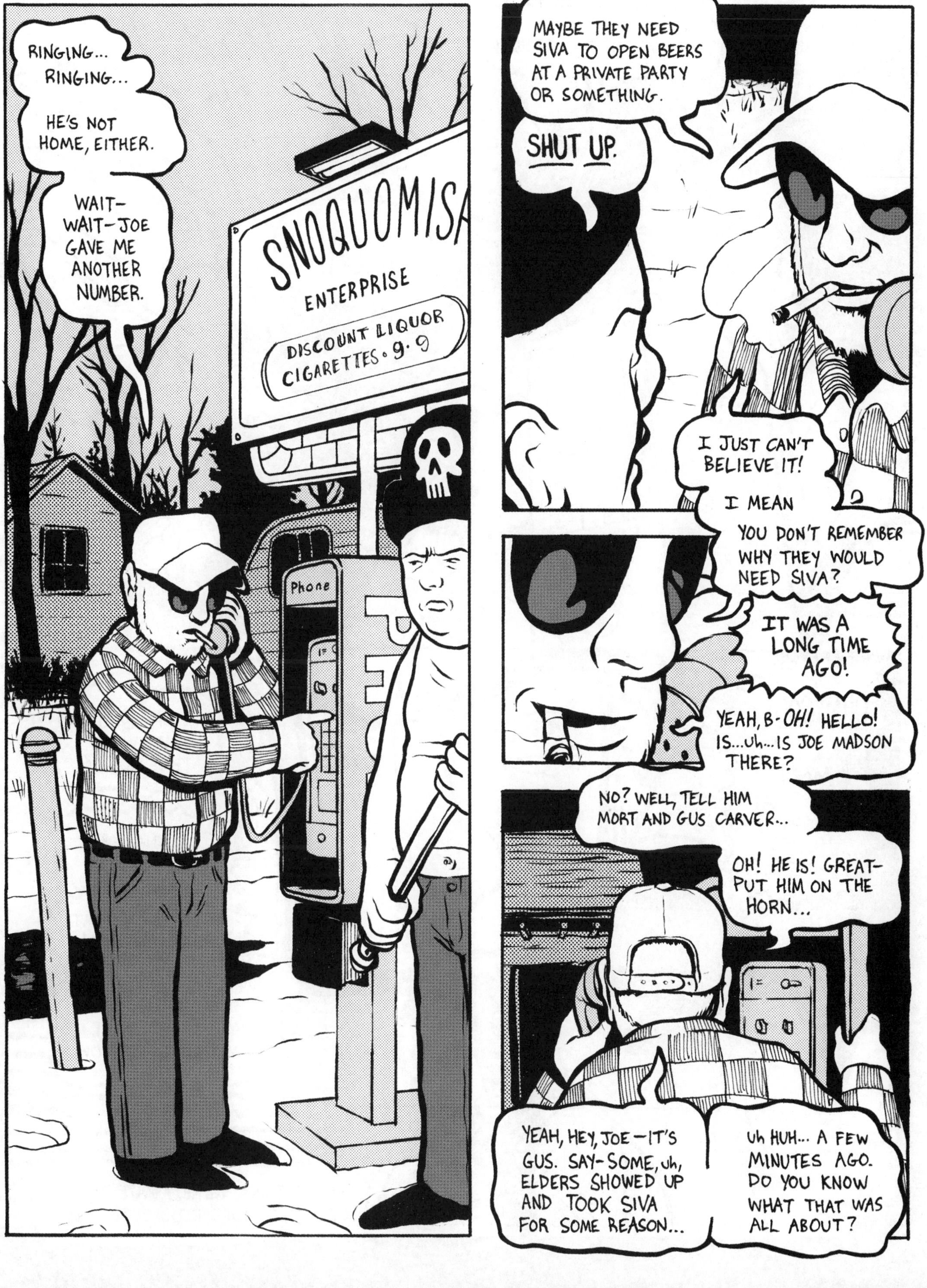
RINGING... RINGING...
HE'S NOT HOME, EITHER.
WAIT- WAIT- JOE GAVE ME ANOTHER NUMBER.
SNOQUOMISA
ENTERPRISE
DISCOUNT LIQUOR CIGARETTES • 9 - 9
Phone
MAYBE THEY NEED SIVA TO OPEN BEERS AT A PRIVATE PARTY OR SOMETHING.
SHUT UP.
I JUST CAN'T BELIEVE IT!
I MEAN
YOU DON'T REMEMBER WHY THEY WOULD NEED SIVA?
IT WAS A LONG TIME AGO!
YEAH, B- OH! HELLO! IS...uh...IS JOE MADSON THERE?
NO? WELL, TELL HIM MORT AND GUS CARVER...
OH! HE IS! GREAT- PUT HIM ON THE HORN...
YEAH, HEY, JOE — IT'S GUS. SAY- SOME, uh, ELDERS SHOWED UP AND TOOK SIVA FOR SOME REASON...
uh HUH... A FEW MINUTES AGO. DO YOU KNOW WHAT THAT WAS ALL ABOUT?

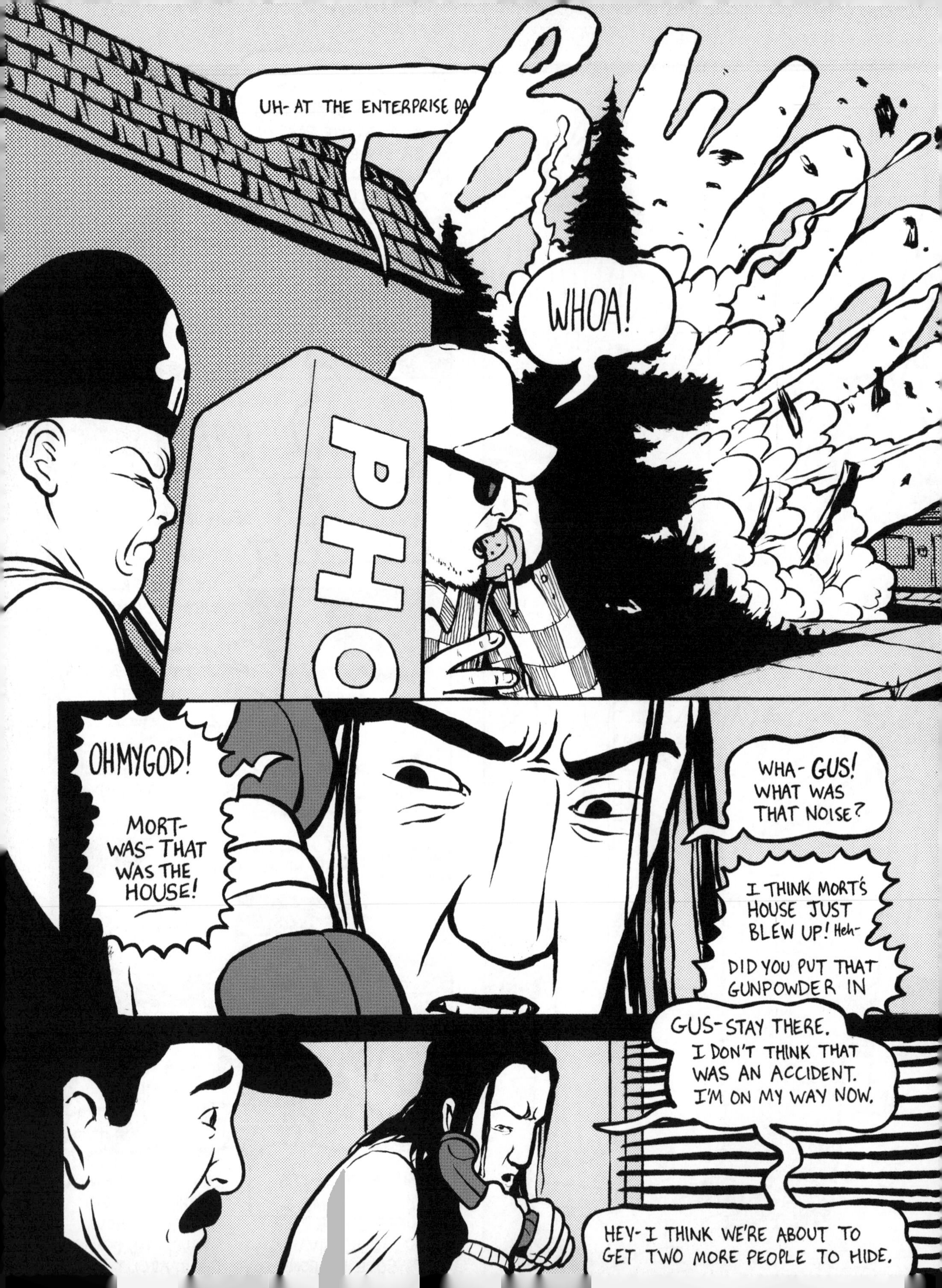
UH- AT THE ENTERPRISE PA
WHOA!
PHO
OHMYGOD!
MORT- WAS- THAT WAS THE HOUSE!
WHA- GUS! WHAT WAS THAT NOISE?
I THINK MORT'S HOUSE JUST BLEW UP! Heh-
DID YOU PUT THAT GUNPOWDER IN
GUS- STAY THERE. I DON'T THINK THAT WAS AN ACCIDENT. I'M ON MY WAY NOW.
HEY- I THINK WE'RE ABOUT TO GET TWO MORE PEOPLE TO HIDE.

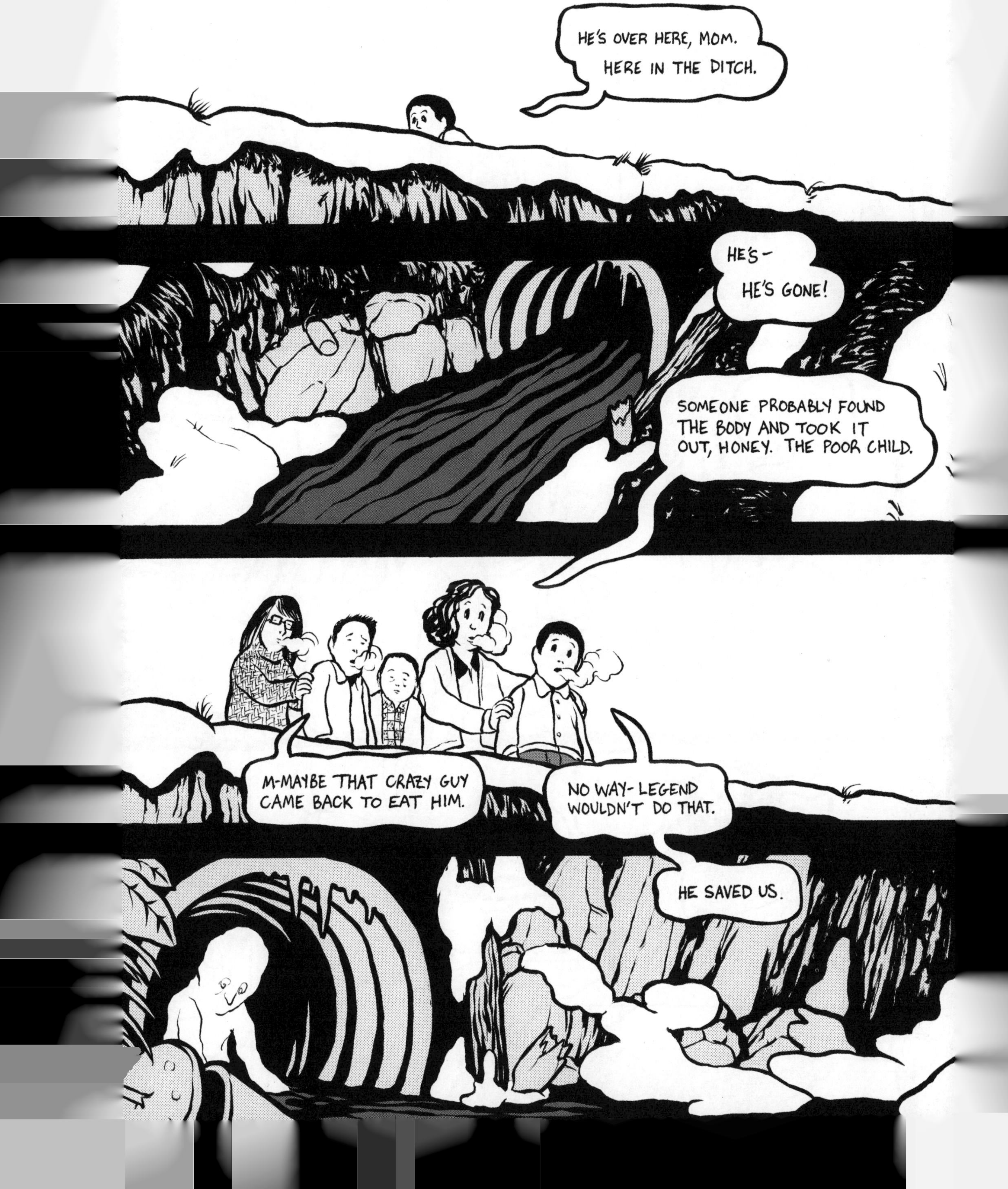
HE'S OVER HERE, MOM. HERE IN THE DITCH.
HE'S - HE'S GONE!
SOMEONE PROBABLY FOUND THE BODY AND TOOK IT OUT, HONEY. THE POOR CHILD.
M-MAYBE THAT CRAZY GUY CAME BACK TO EAT HIM.
NO WAY- LEGEND WOULDN'T DO THAT.
HE SAVED US.

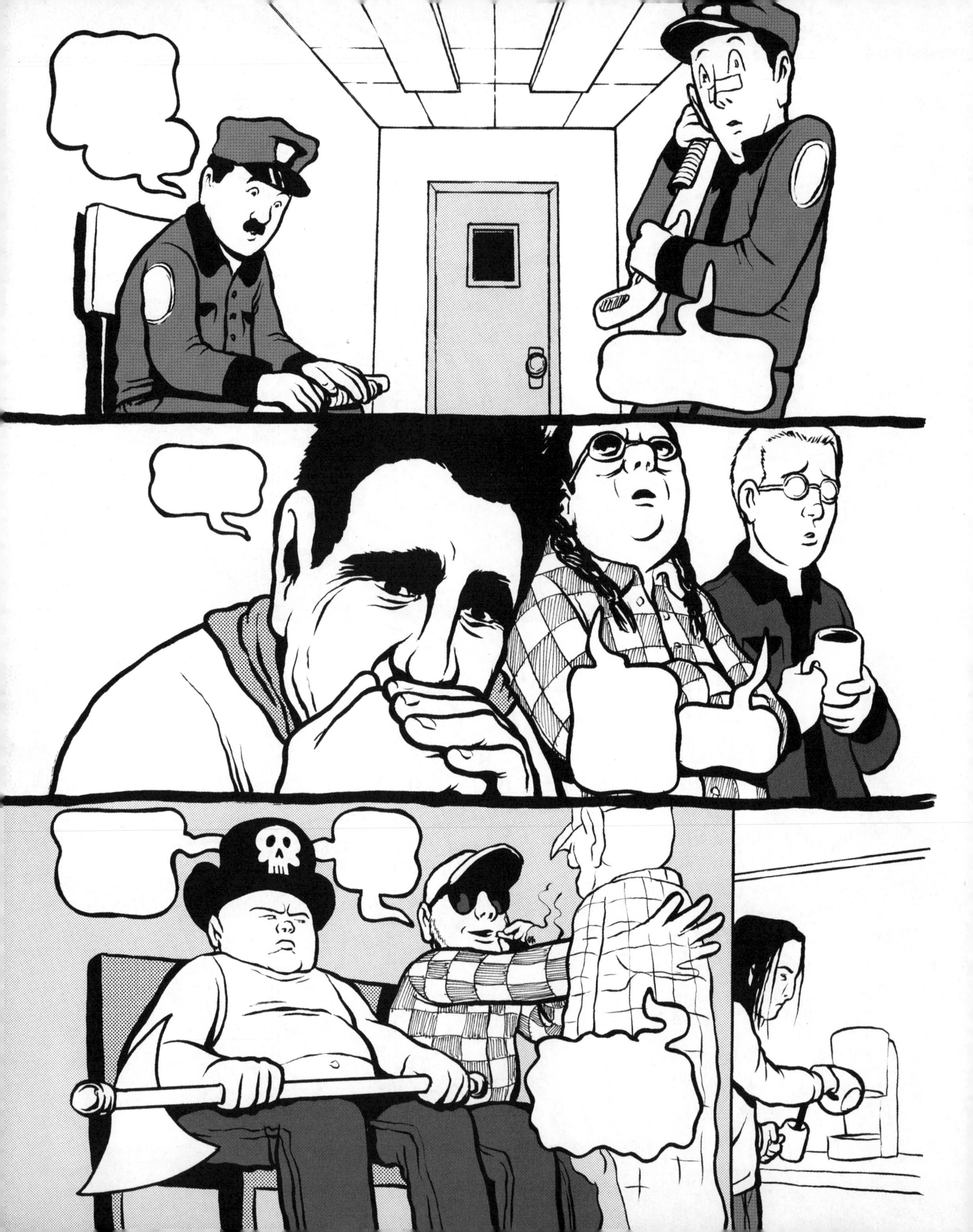

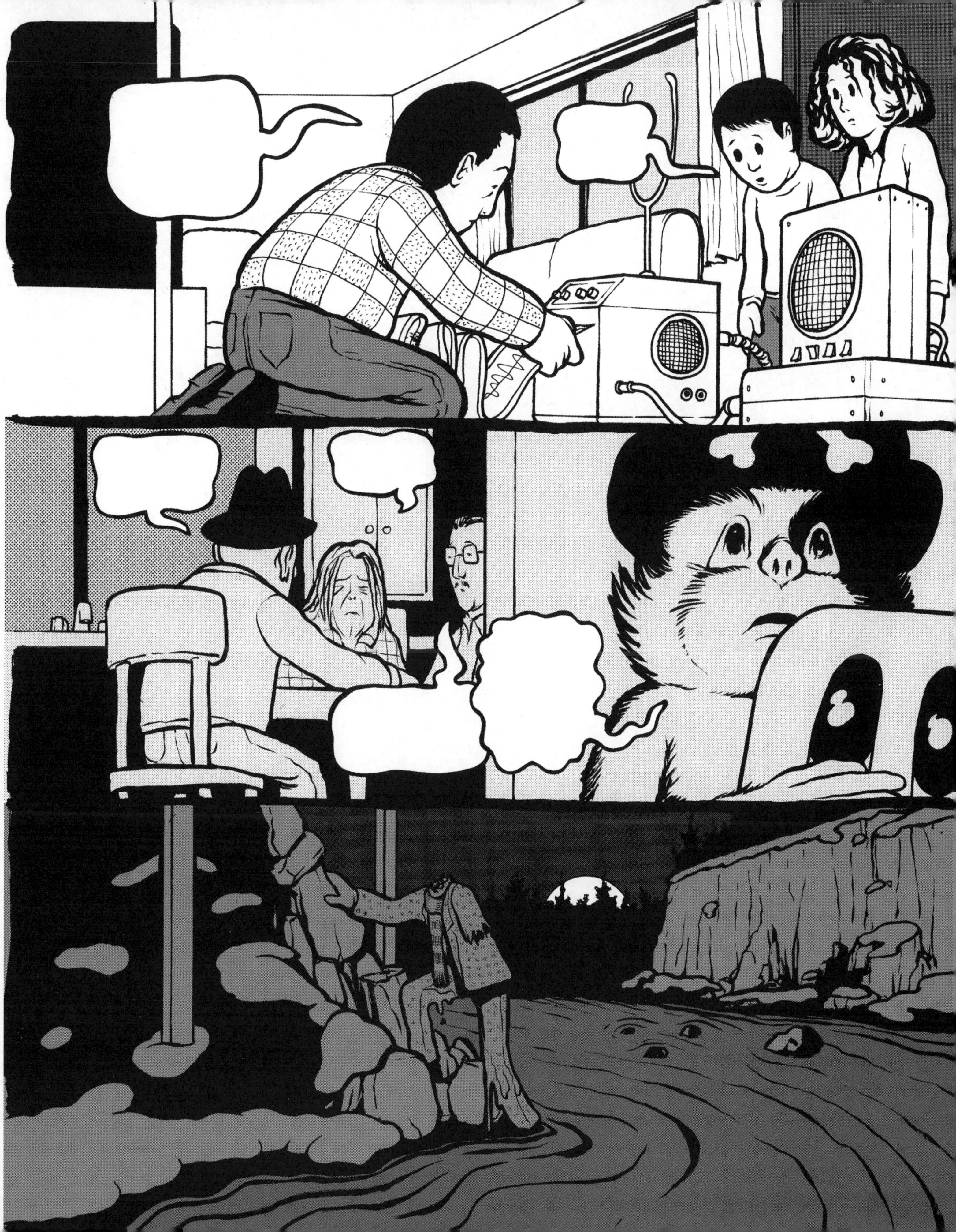

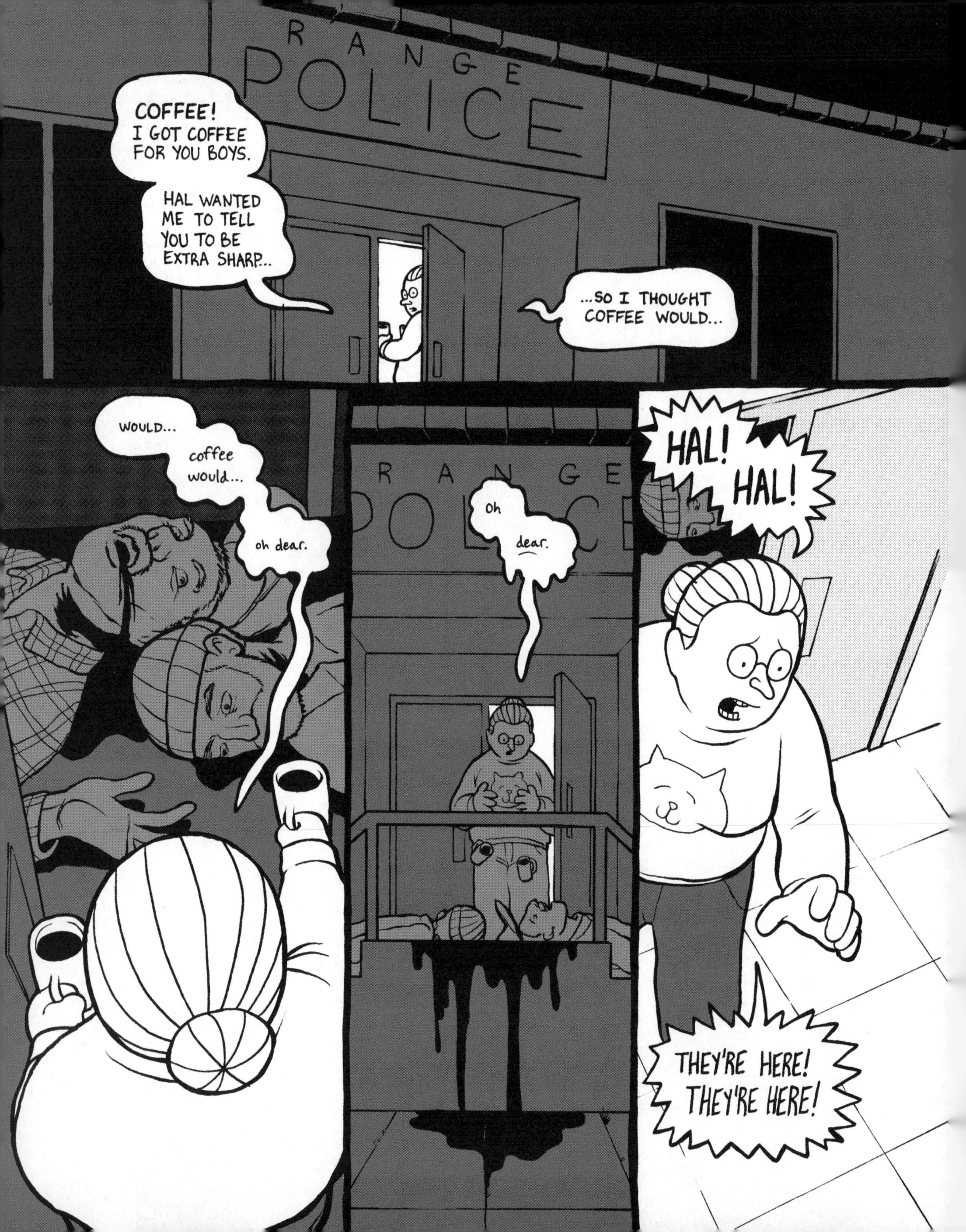
RANGE POLICE
COFFEE! I GOT COFFEE FOR YOU BOYS.
HAL WANTED ME TO TELL YOU TO BE EXTRA SHARP...
...SO I THOUGHT COFFEE WOULD...
WOULD... coffee would... oh dear.
RANGE POLICE
oh dear.
HAL! HAL!
THEY'RE HERE! THEY'RE HERE!

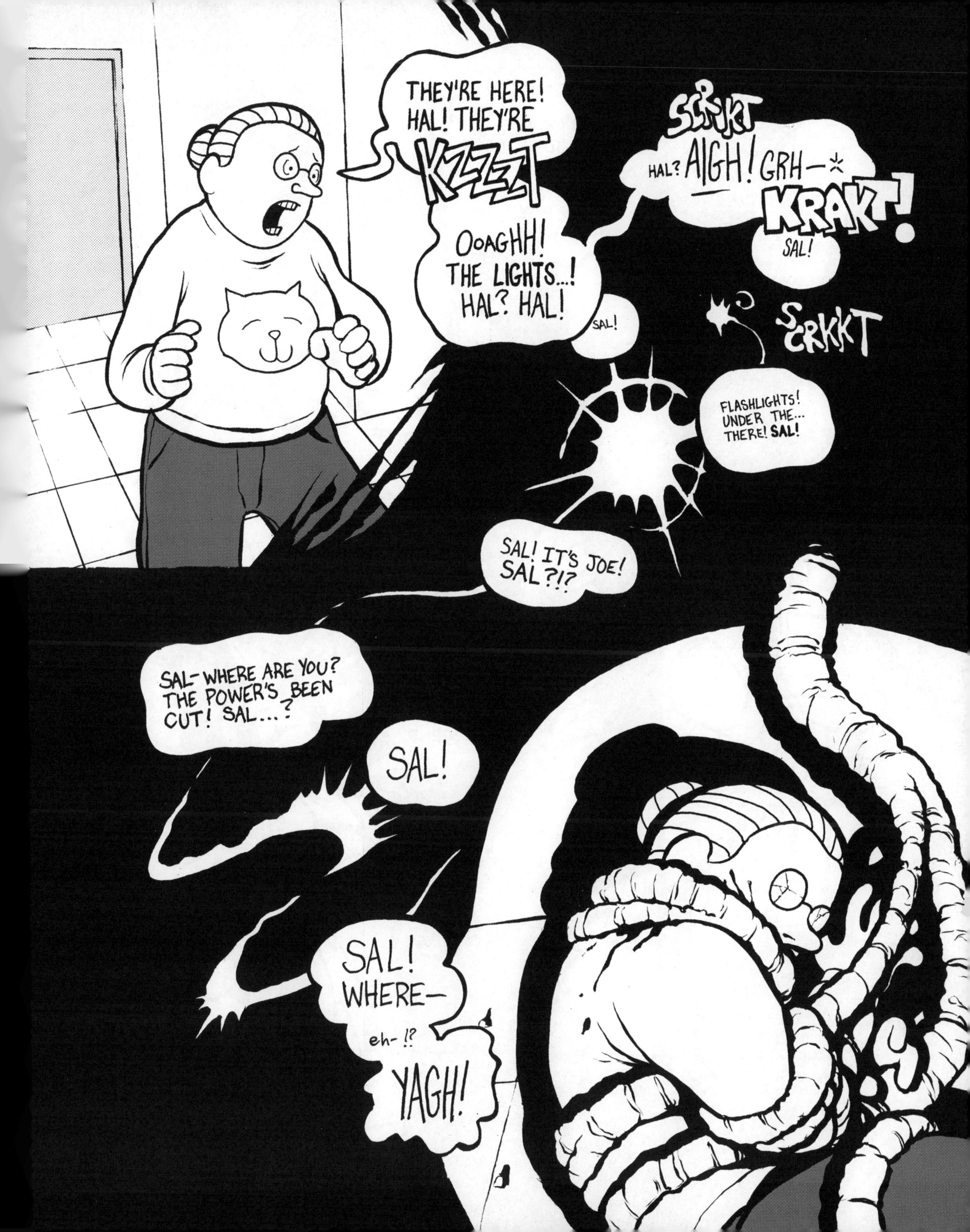
THEY'RE HERE! HAL! THEY'RE
KZZZZT
OOAGHH! THE LIGHTS...! HAL? HAL!
SCRKKT
HAL? AIGH! GRH—
KRAKT!
SAL!
SAL!
SCRKKT
FLASHLIGHTS! UNDER THE... THERE! SAL!
SAL! IT'S JOE! SAL?!?
SAL- WHERE ARE YOU? THE POWER'S BEEN CUT! SAL...?
SAL!
SAL! WHERE—
eh- !?
YAGH!

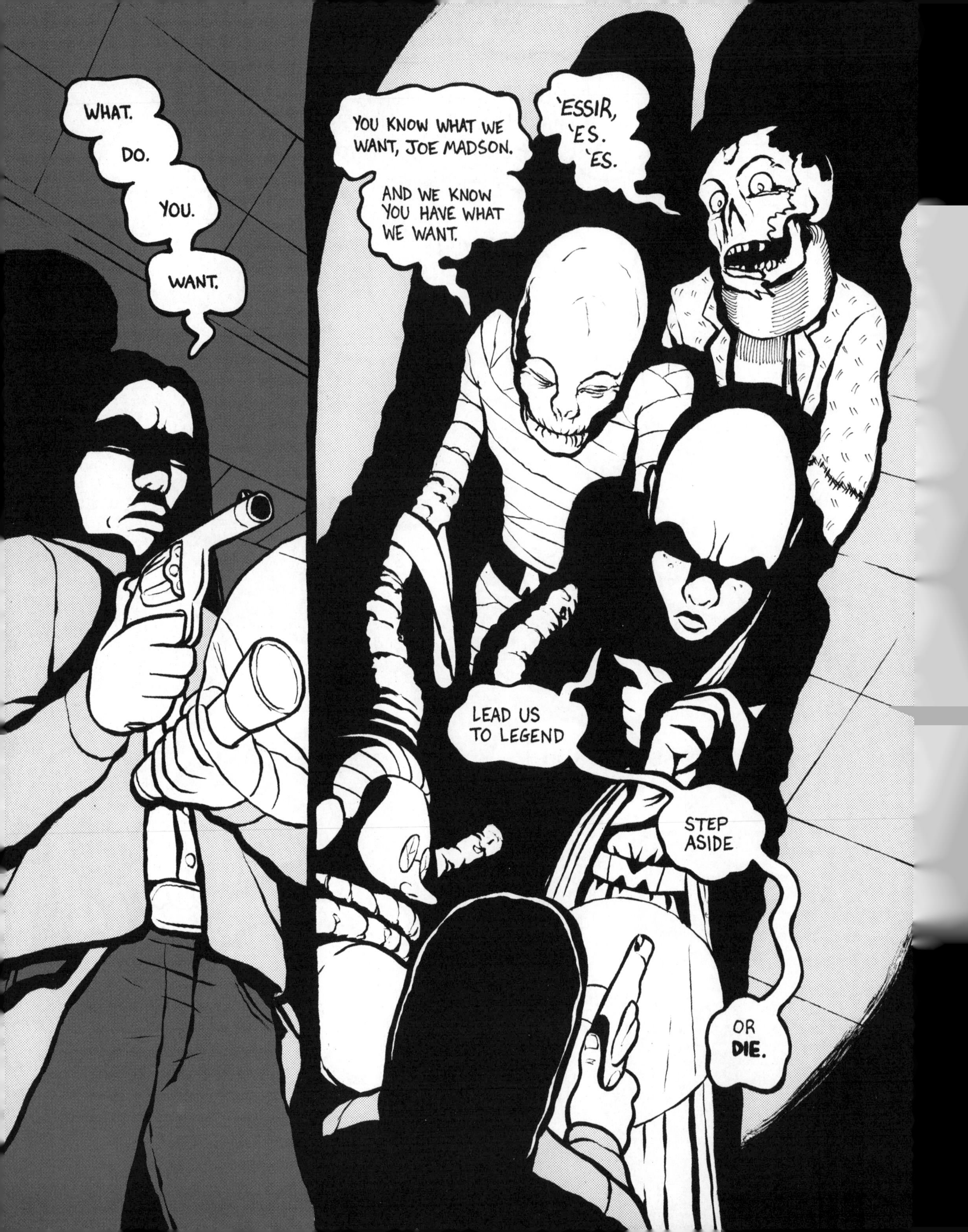
WHAT.
DO.
YOU.
WANT.
YOU KNOW WHAT WE WANT, JOE MADSON.
AND WE KNOW YOU HAVE WHAT WE WANT.
`ESSIR, `ES. `ES.
LEAD US TO LEGEND
STEP ASIDE
OR **DIE.**

13.
RUNOFF

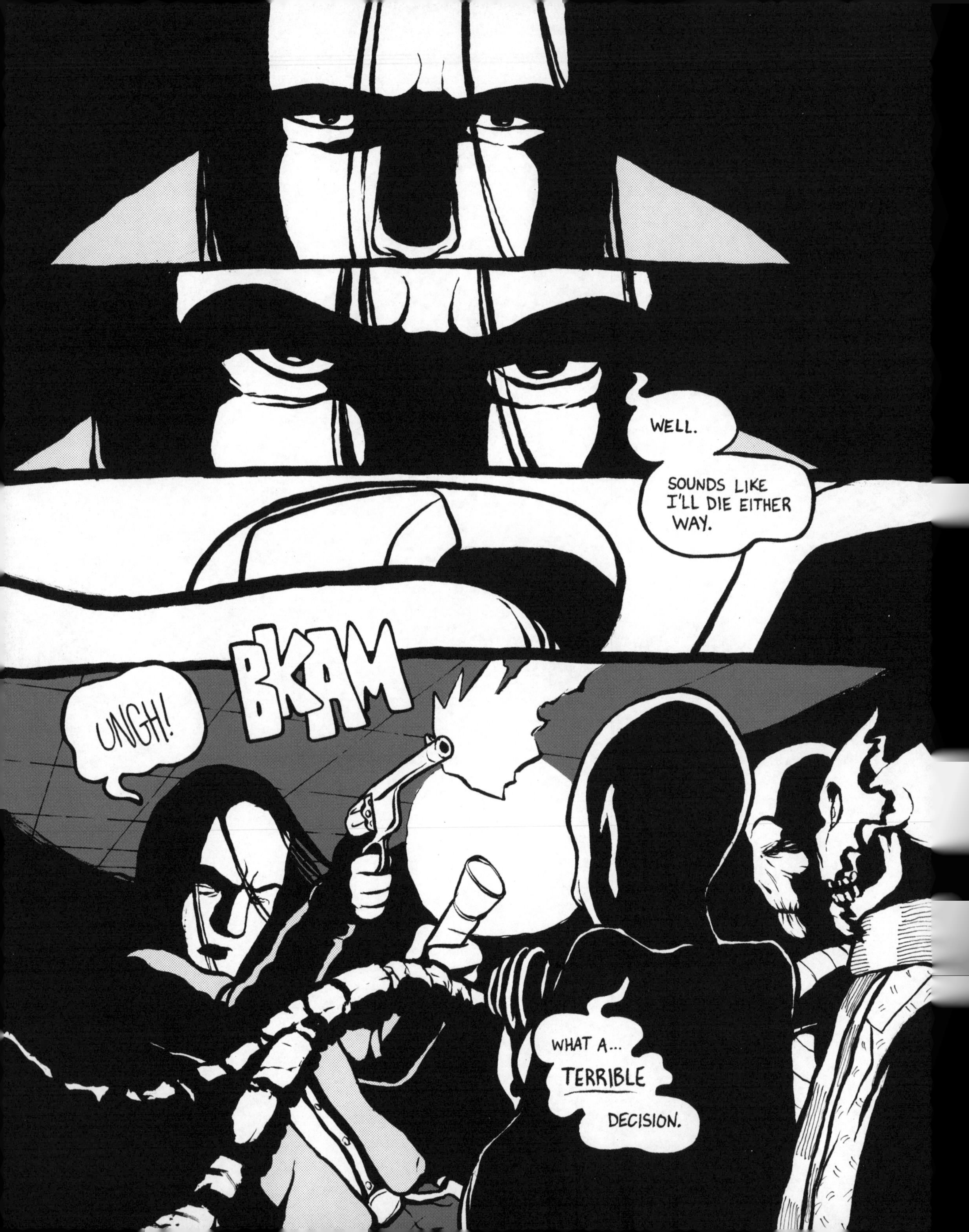
WELL.
SOUNDS LIKE I'LL DIE EITHER WAY.
UNGH!
BKAM
WHAT A... TERRIBLE DECISION.

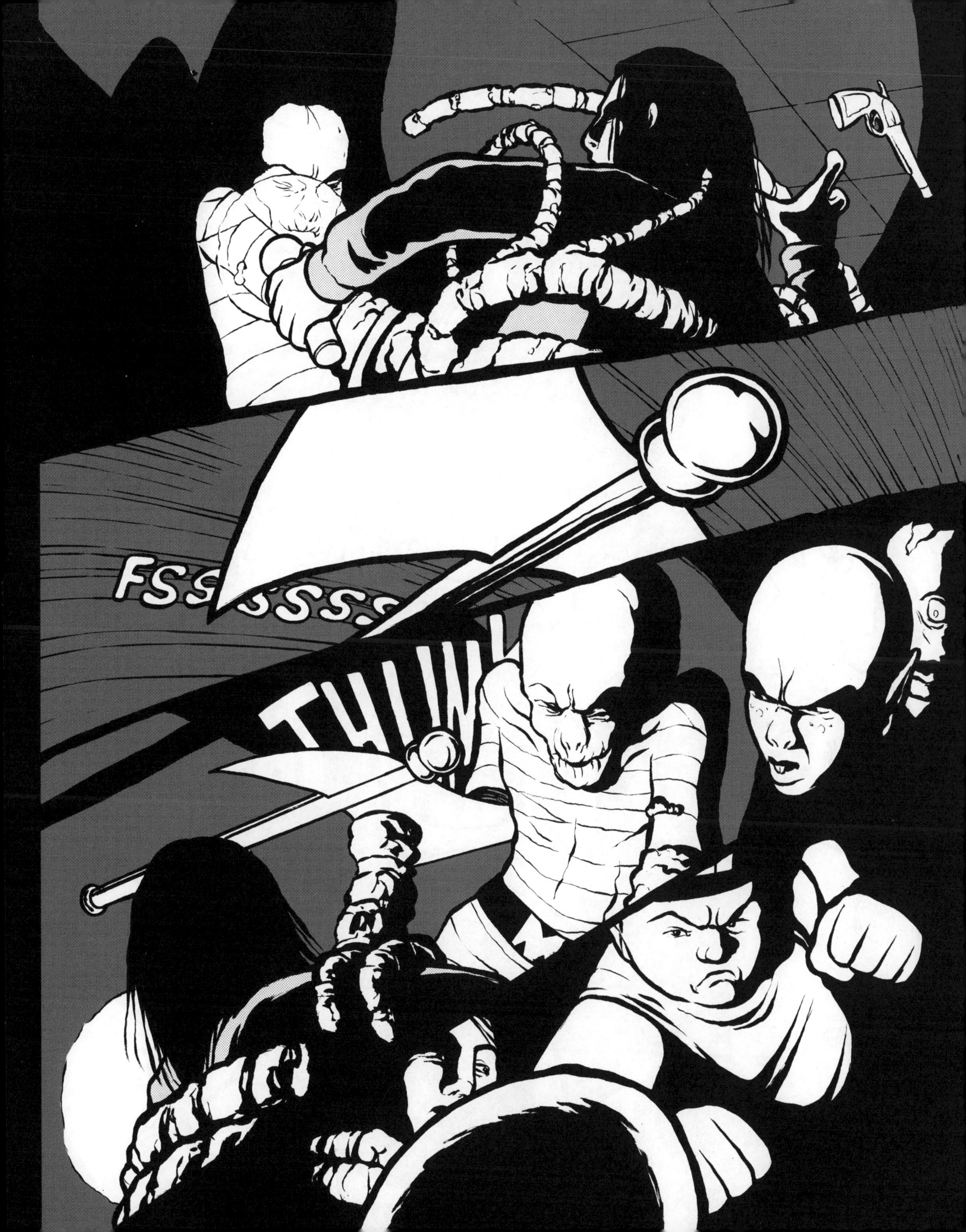
FSSSSSS
THUN

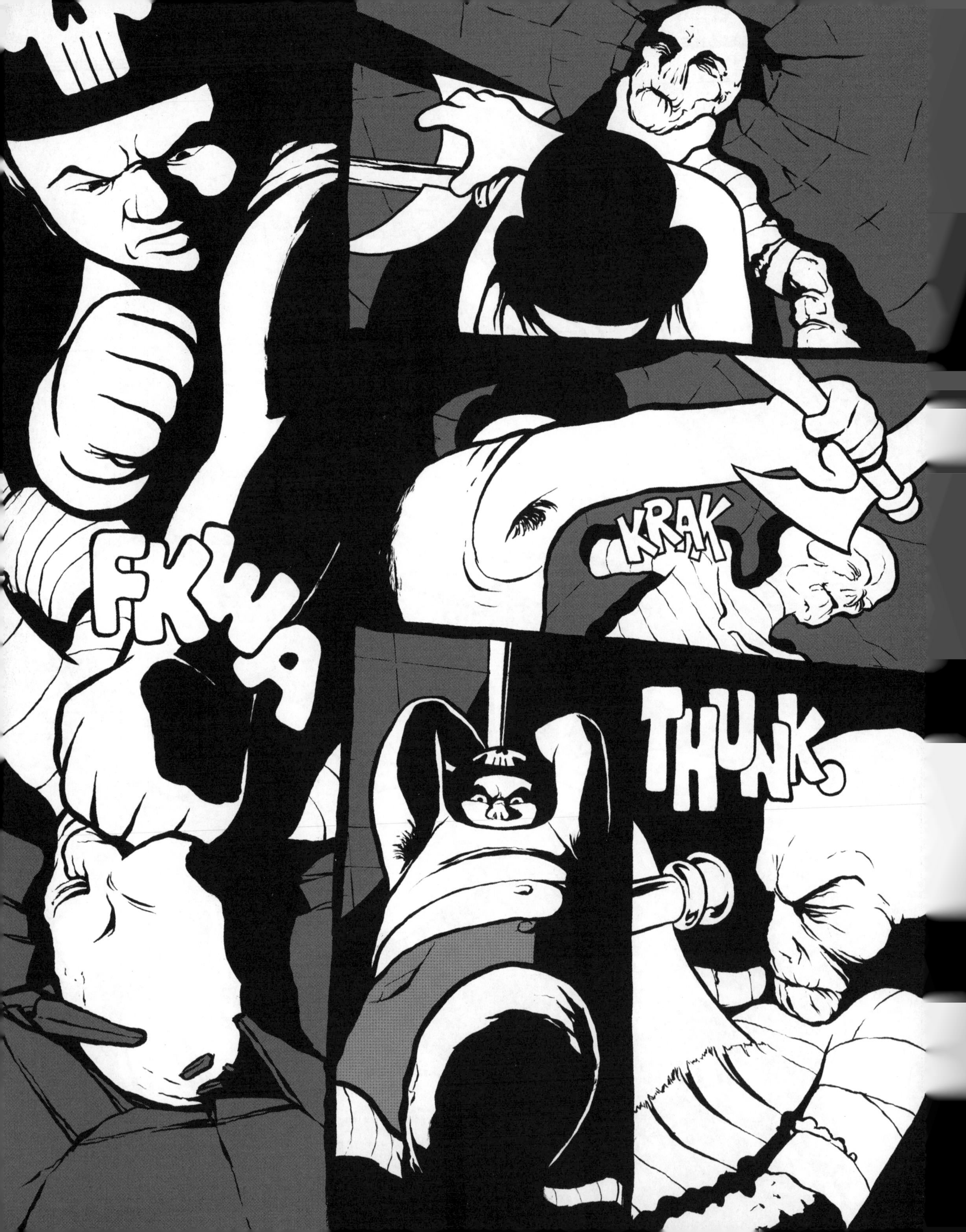
FKWA
KRAK
THUNK

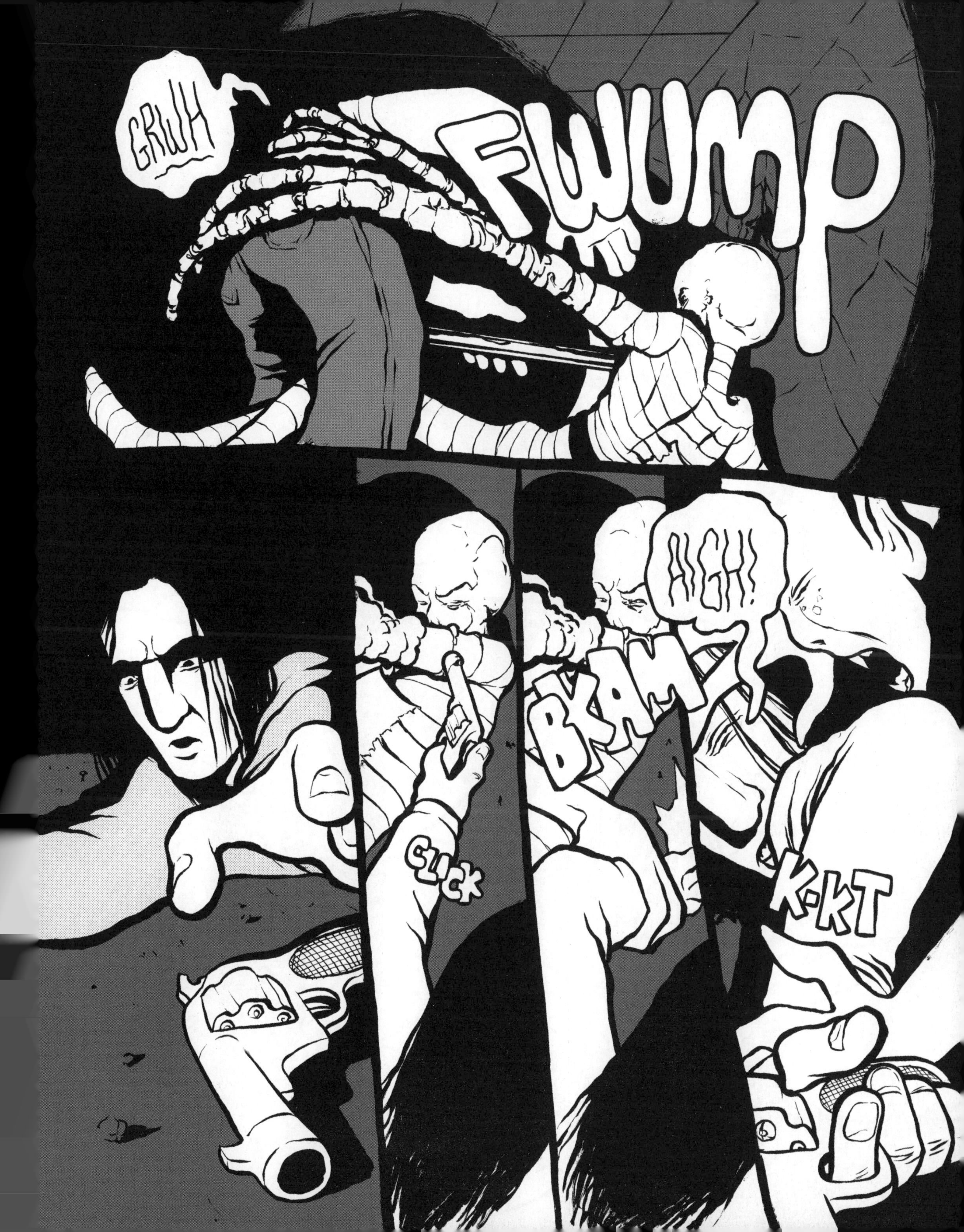
GRWH
FWUMP
CLICK
BKAM
AIGH!
K-KT

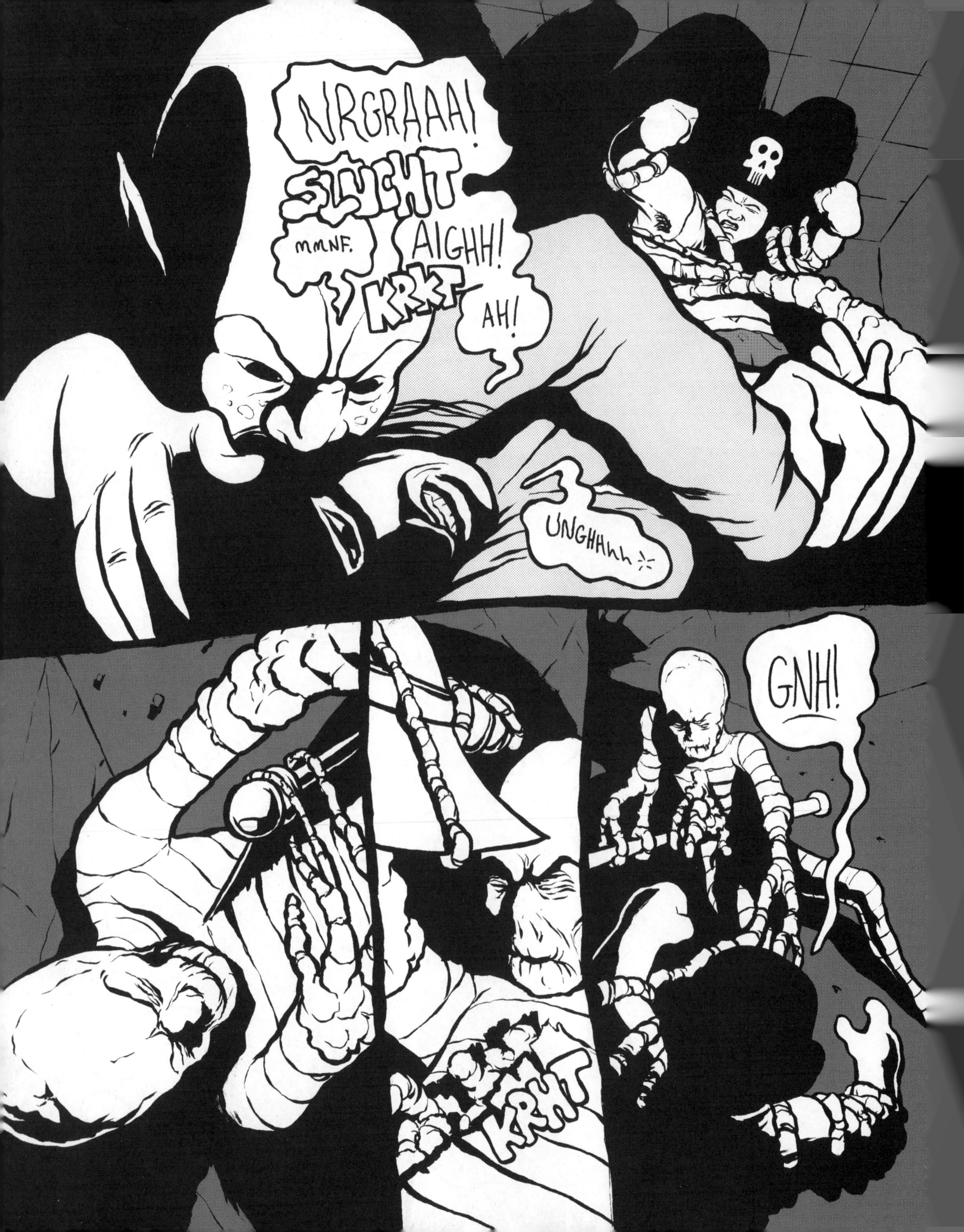
NRGRAAA!
SLUCHT
MMNF.
AIGHH!
KRKT
AH!
UNGHHhhh
GNH!
KRKT

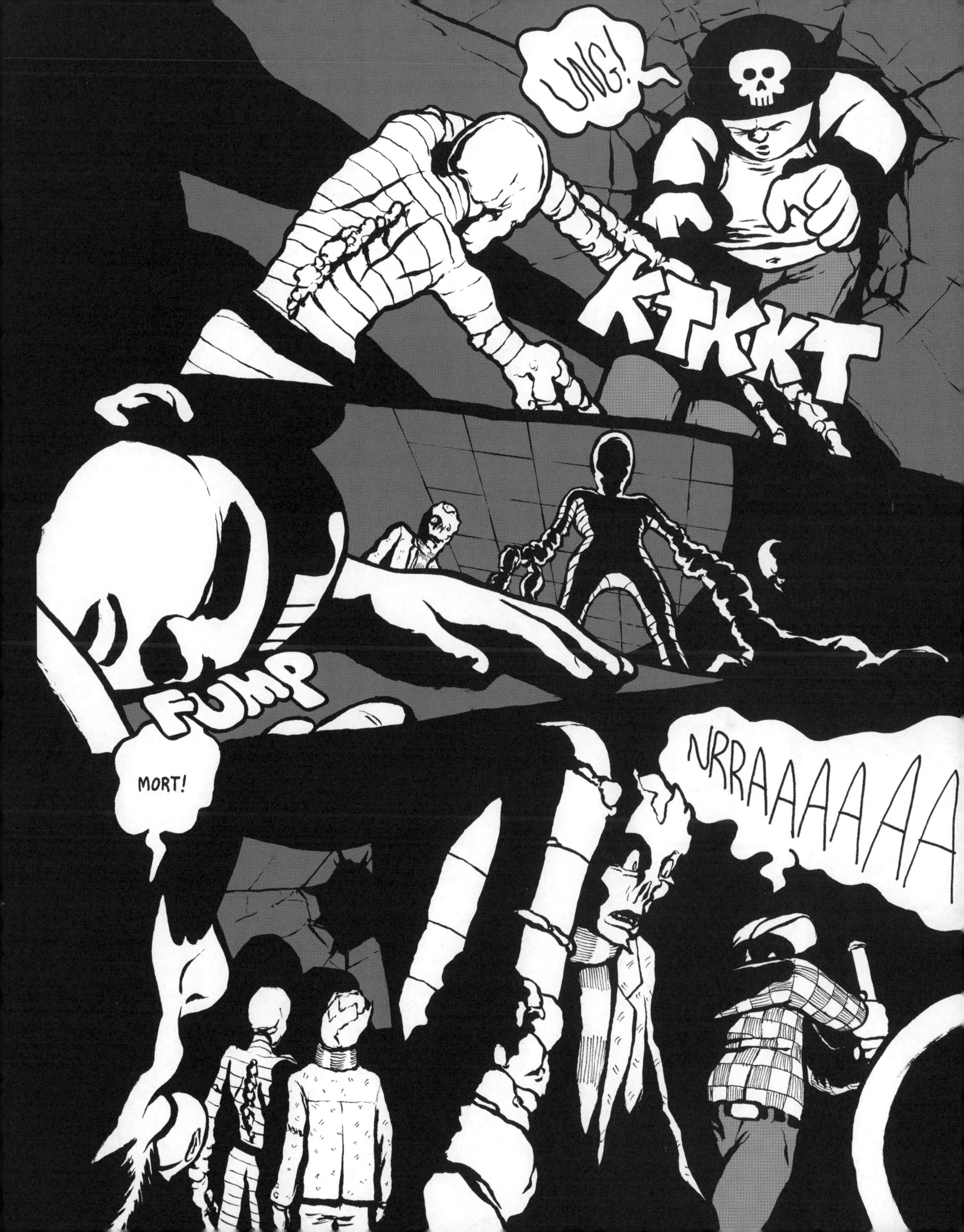
UNG!
KTKKT
FUMP
MORT!
NRRAAAAAAA

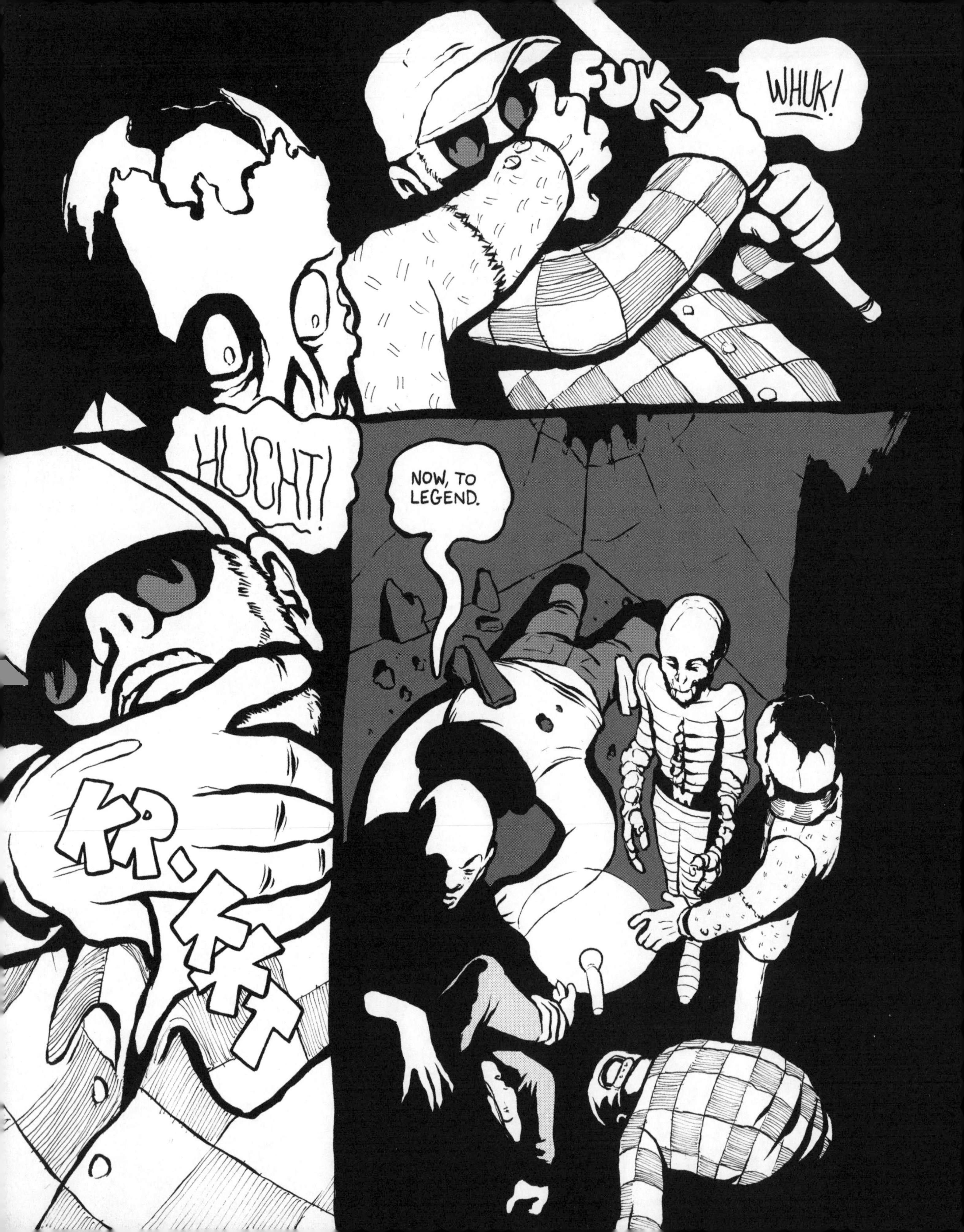
FUK!
WHUK!
HUCHT!
NOW, TO LEGEND.
KR.
KKT

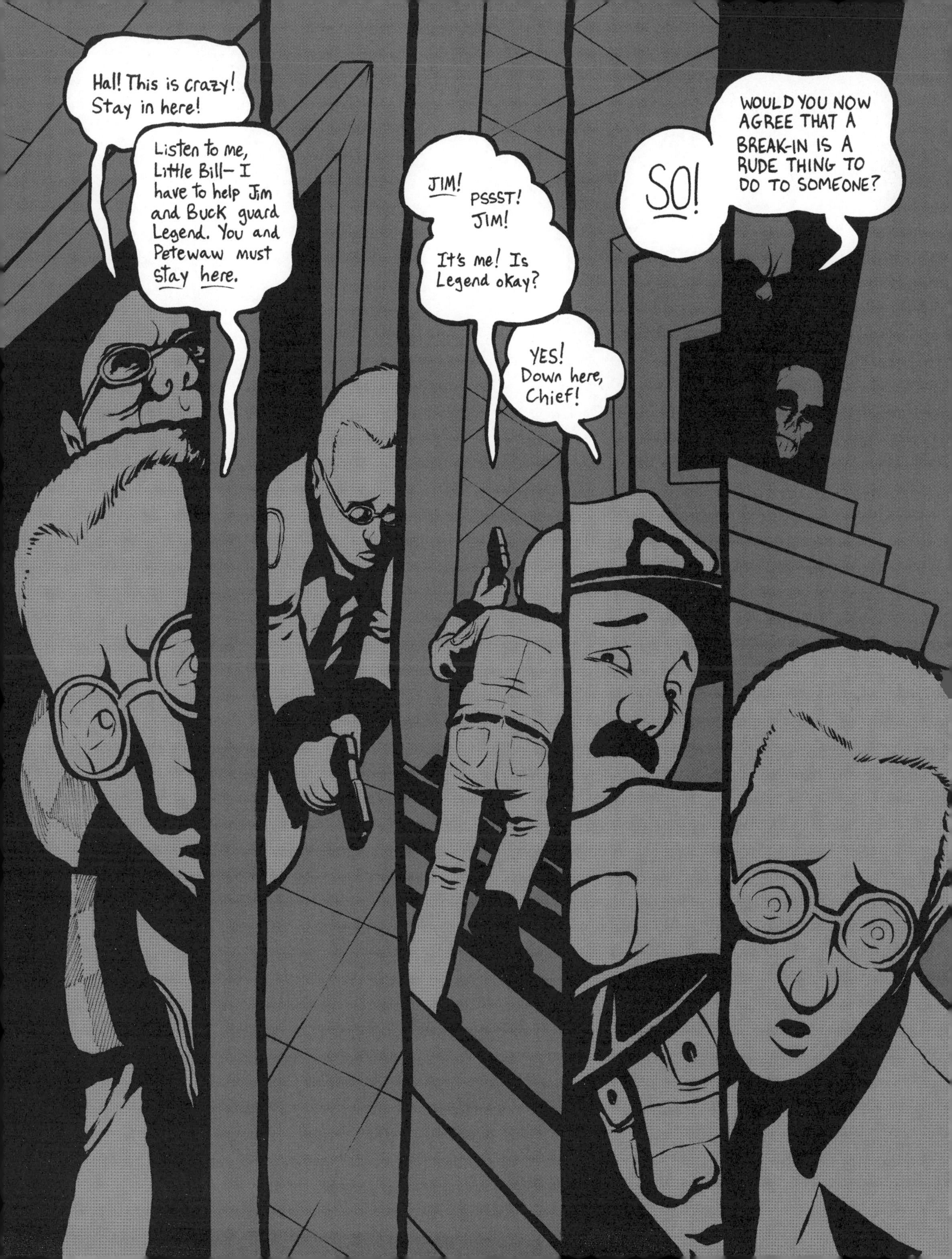
Hal! This is crazy! Stay in here!
Listen to me, Little Bill— I have to help Jim and Buck guard Legend. You and Petewaw must stay here.
JIM! PSSST! JIM!
It's me! Is Legend okay?
YES! Down here, Chief!
SO!
WOULD YOU NOW AGREE THAT A BREAK-IN IS A RUDE THING TO DO TO SOMEONE?

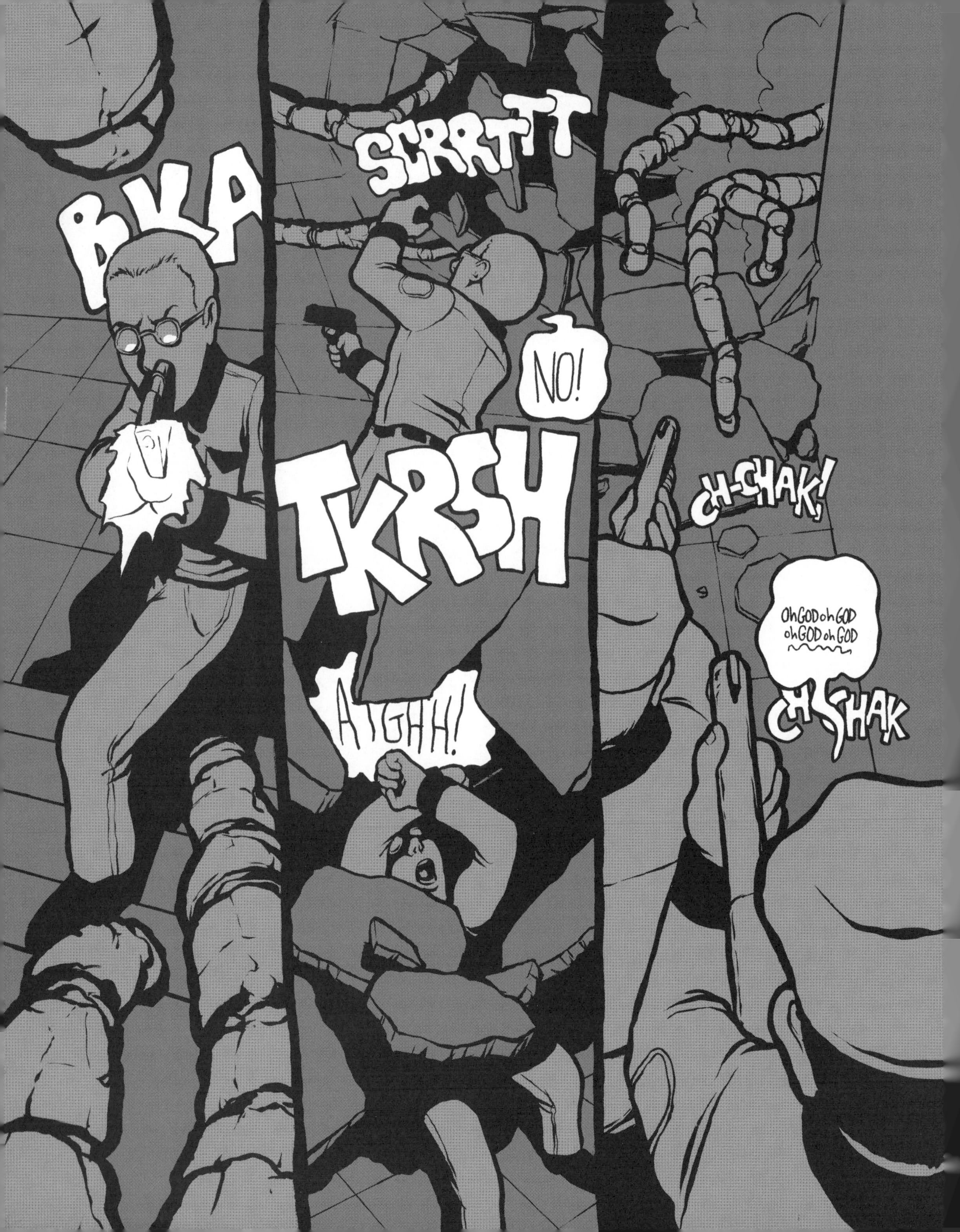
BKA
SCRRTTT
NO!
TKRSH
AIGHH!
CH-CHAK!
OhGOD oh GOD
ohGOD oh GOD
CH-SHAK

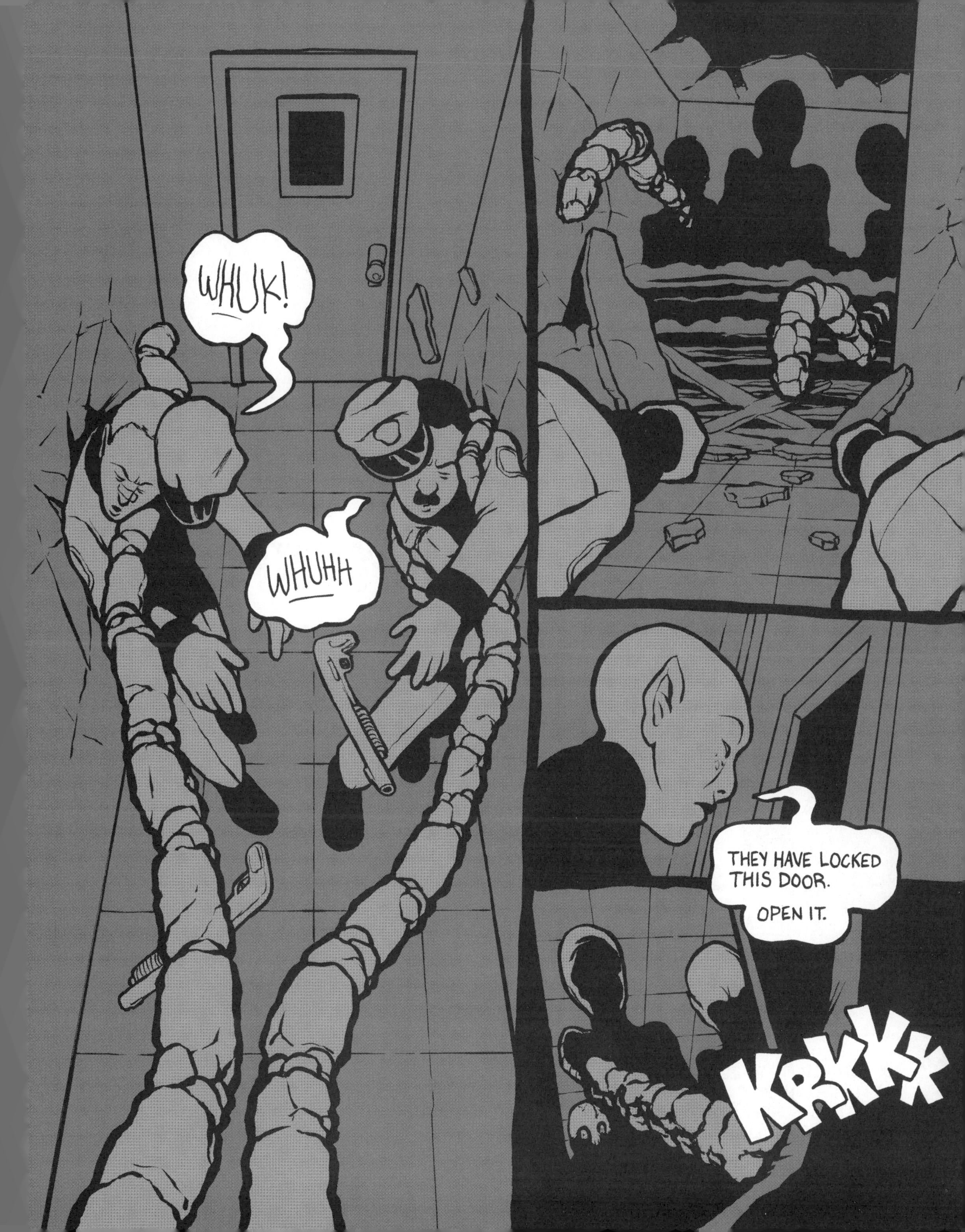
WHUK!
WHUHH
THEY HAVE LOCKED THIS DOOR.
OPEN IT.
KRKKK

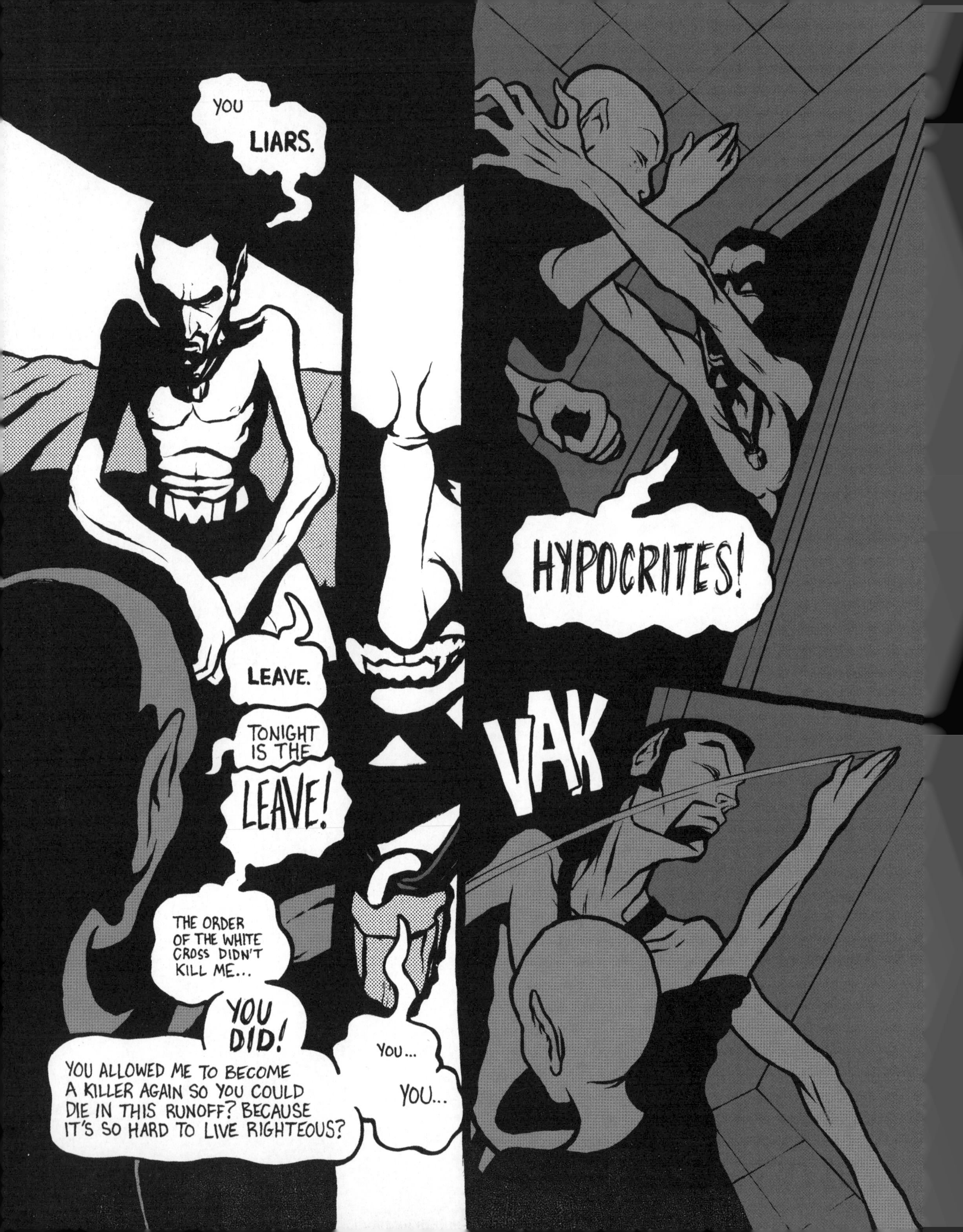
YOU LIARS.
HYPOCRITES!
LEAVE.
TONIGHT IS THE
LEAVE!
VAK
THE ORDER OF THE WHITE CROSS DIDN'T KILL ME...
YOU DID!
YOU ALLOWED ME TO BECOME A KILLER AGAIN SO YOU COULD DIE IN THIS RUNOFF? BECAUSE IT'S SO HARD TO LIVE RIGHTEOUS?
YOU...
YOU...

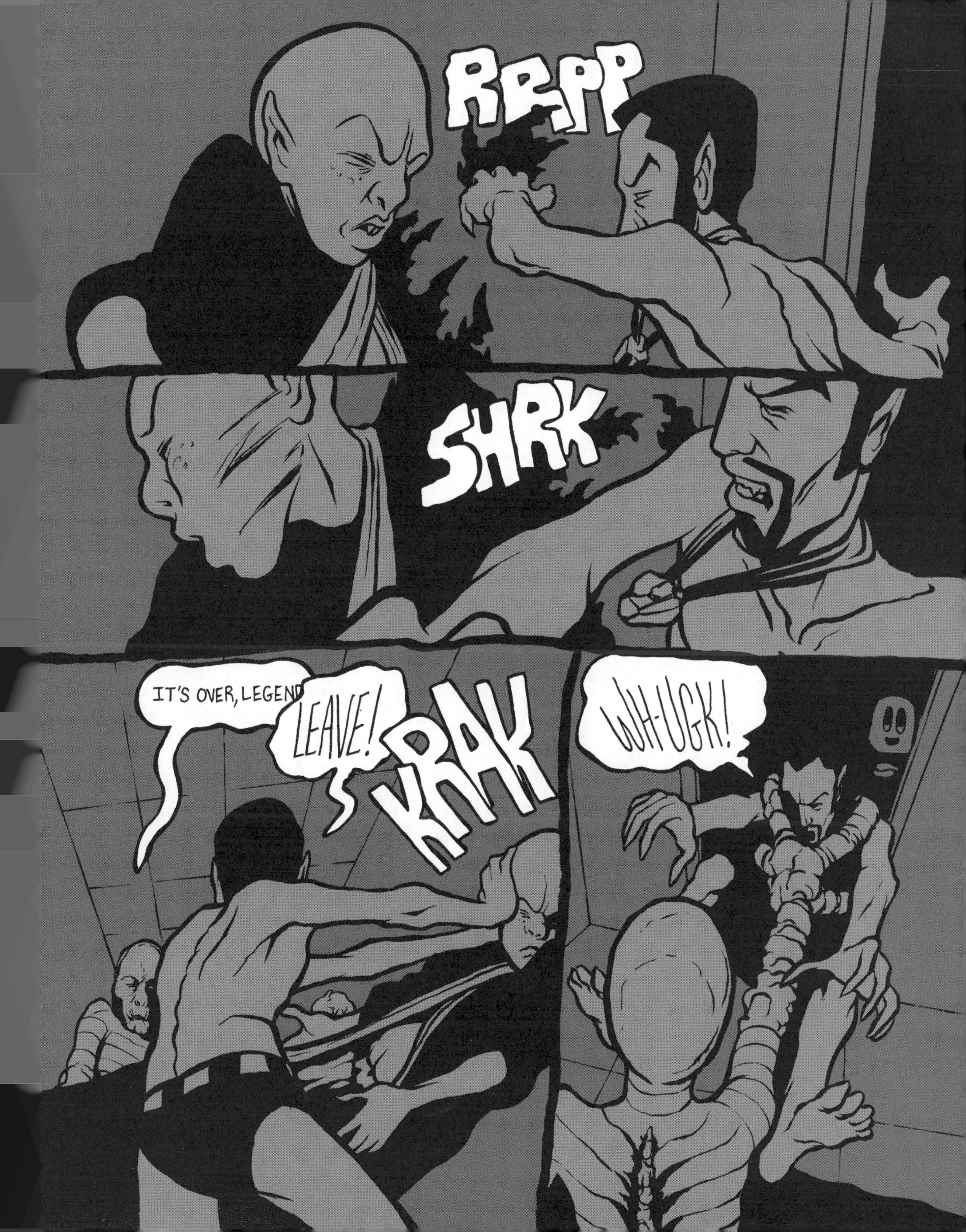
RRPP
SHRK
IT'S OVER, LEGEND
LEAVE!
KRAK
WH-UGK!

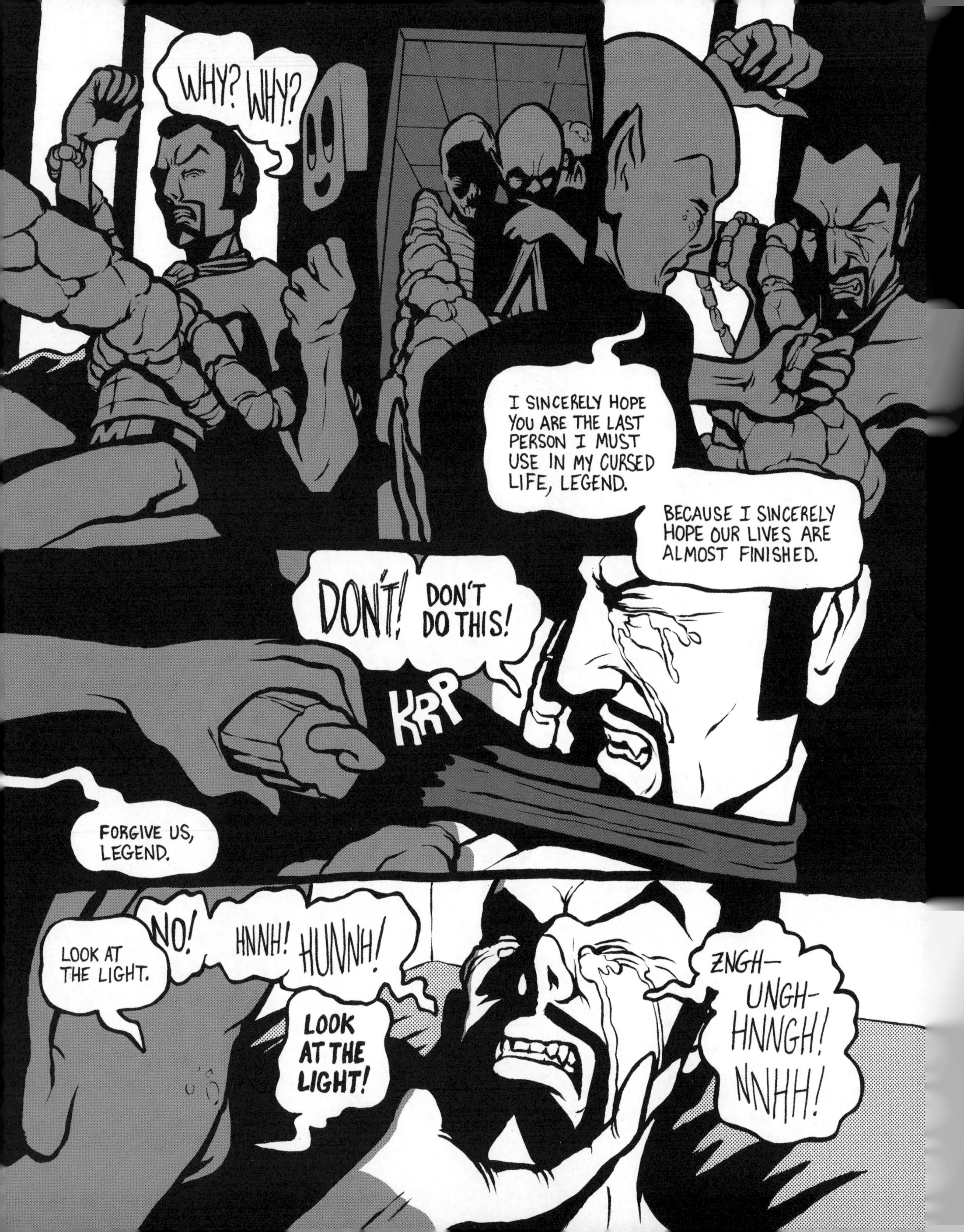
WHY? WHY?
I SINCERELY HOPE YOU ARE THE LAST PERSON I MUST USE IN MY CURSED LIFE, LEGEND.
BECAUSE I SINCERELY HOPE OUR LIVES ARE ALMOST FINISHED.
DON'T! DON'T DO THIS!
KRP
FORGIVE US, LEGEND.
LOOK AT THE LIGHT.
NO! HNNH! HUNNH!
LOOK AT THE LIGHT!
ZNGH- UNGH- HNNGH! NNHH!

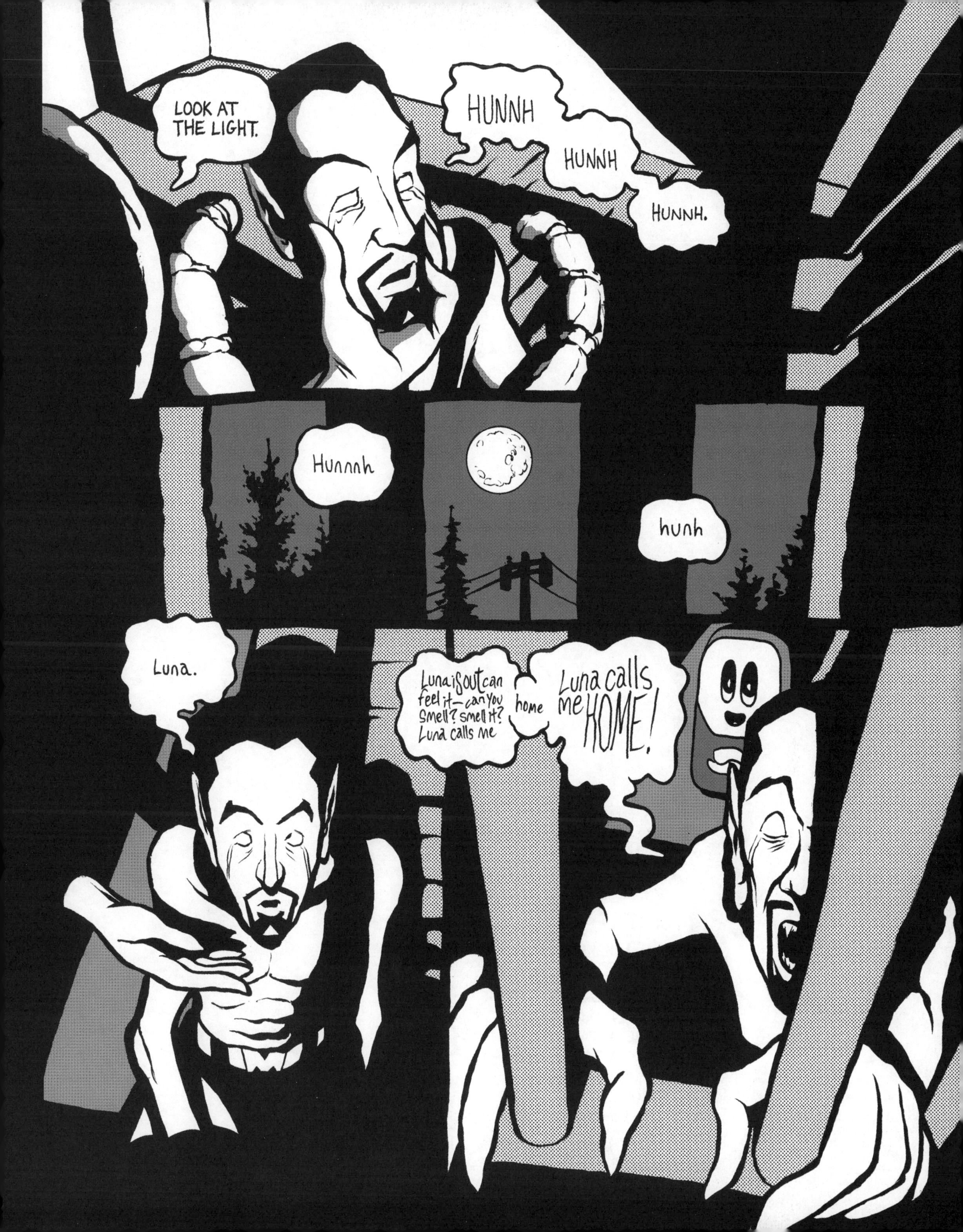
LOOK AT THE LIGHT.
HUNNH
HUNNH
HUNNH.
Hunnnh
hunh
Luna.
Luna is out can feel it—can you smell? smell it? Luna calls me
home
Luna calls me HOME!

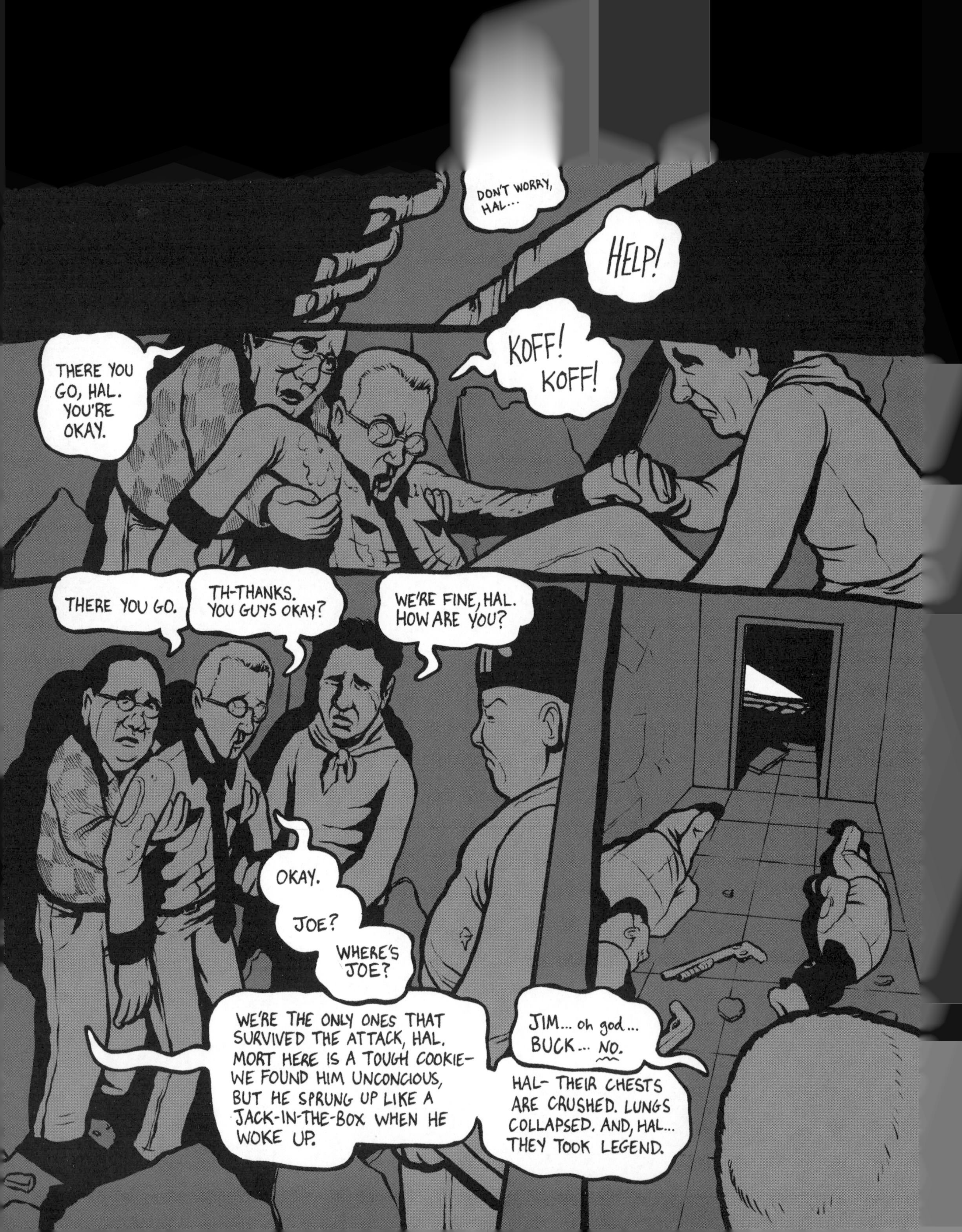
DON'T WORRY, HAL...
HELP!
THERE YOU GO, HAL. YOU'RE OKAY.
KOFF! KOFF!
THERE YOU GO.
TH-THANKS. YOU GUYS OKAY?
WE'RE FINE, HAL. HOW ARE YOU?
OKAY.
JOE?
WHERE'S JOE?
WE'RE THE ONLY ONES THAT SURVIVED THE ATTACK, HAL. MORT HERE IS A TOUGH COOKIE- WE FOUND HIM UNCONCIOUS, BUT HE SPRUNG UP LIKE A JACK-IN-THE-BOX WHEN HE WOKE UP.
JIM... oh god... BUCK... NO.
HAL- THEIR CHESTS ARE CRUSHED. LUNGS COLLAPSED. AND, HAL... THEY TOOK LEGEND.

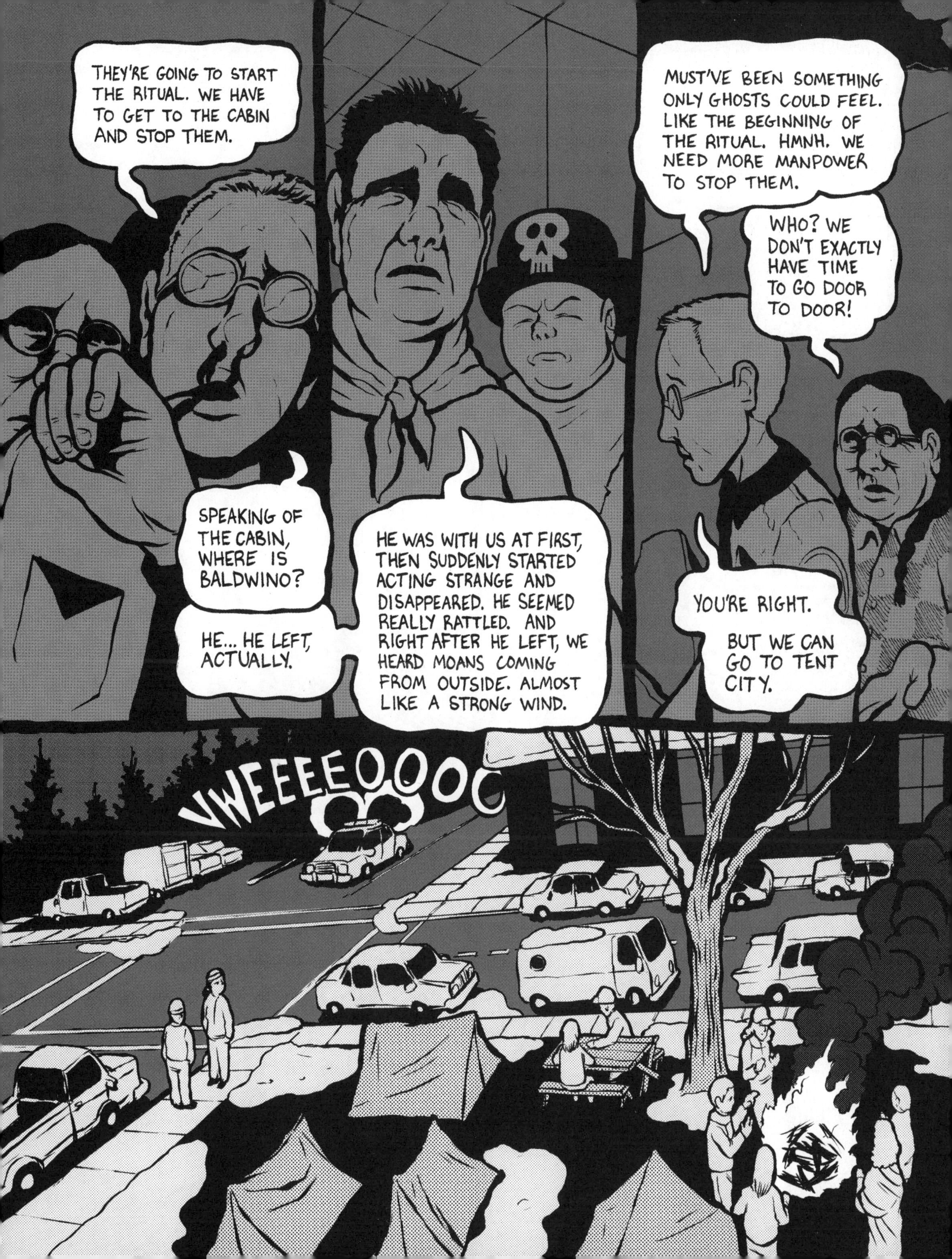
THEY'RE GOING TO START THE RITUAL. WE HAVE TO GET TO THE CABIN AND STOP THEM.
MUST'VE BEEN SOMETHING ONLY GHOSTS COULD FEEL. LIKE THE BEGINNING OF THE RITUAL. HMNH. WE NEED MORE MANPOWER TO STOP THEM.
WHO? WE DON'T EXACTLY HAVE TIME TO GO DOOR TO DOOR!
SPEAKING OF THE CABIN, WHERE IS BALDWINO?
HE... HE LEFT, ACTUALLY.
HE WAS WITH US AT FIRST, THEN SUDDENLY STARTED ACTING STRANGE AND DISAPPEARED. HE SEEMED REALLY RATTLED. AND RIGHT AFTER HE LEFT, WE HEARD MOANS COMING FROM OUTSIDE. ALMOST LIKE A STRONG WIND.
YOU'RE RIGHT.
BUT WE CAN GO TO TENT CITY.
VWEEEEOOOO

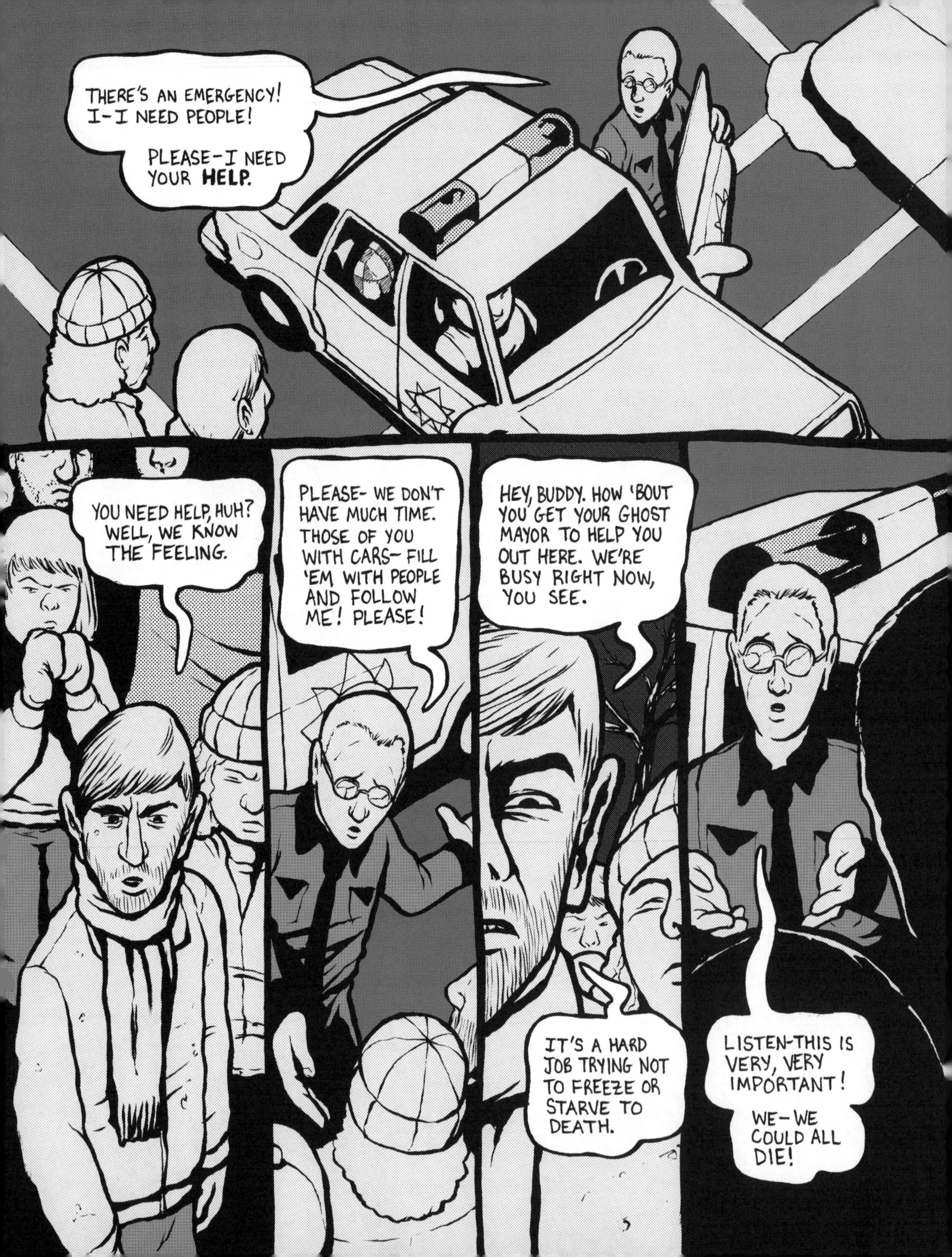
THERE'S AN EMERGENCY! I-I NEED PEOPLE!
PLEASE-I NEED YOUR **HELP**.
YOU NEED HELP, HUH? WELL, WE KNOW THE FEELING.
PLEASE- WE DON'T HAVE MUCH TIME. THOSE OF YOU WITH CARS- FILL 'EM WITH PEOPLE AND FOLLOW ME! PLEASE!
HEY, BUDDY. HOW 'BOUT YOU GET YOUR GHOST MAYOR TO HELP YOU OUT HERE. WE'RE BUSY RIGHT NOW, YOU SEE.
IT'S A HARD JOB TRYING NOT TO FREEZE OR STARVE TO DEATH.
LISTEN-THIS IS VERY, VERY IMPORTANT!
WE-WE COULD ALL DIE!

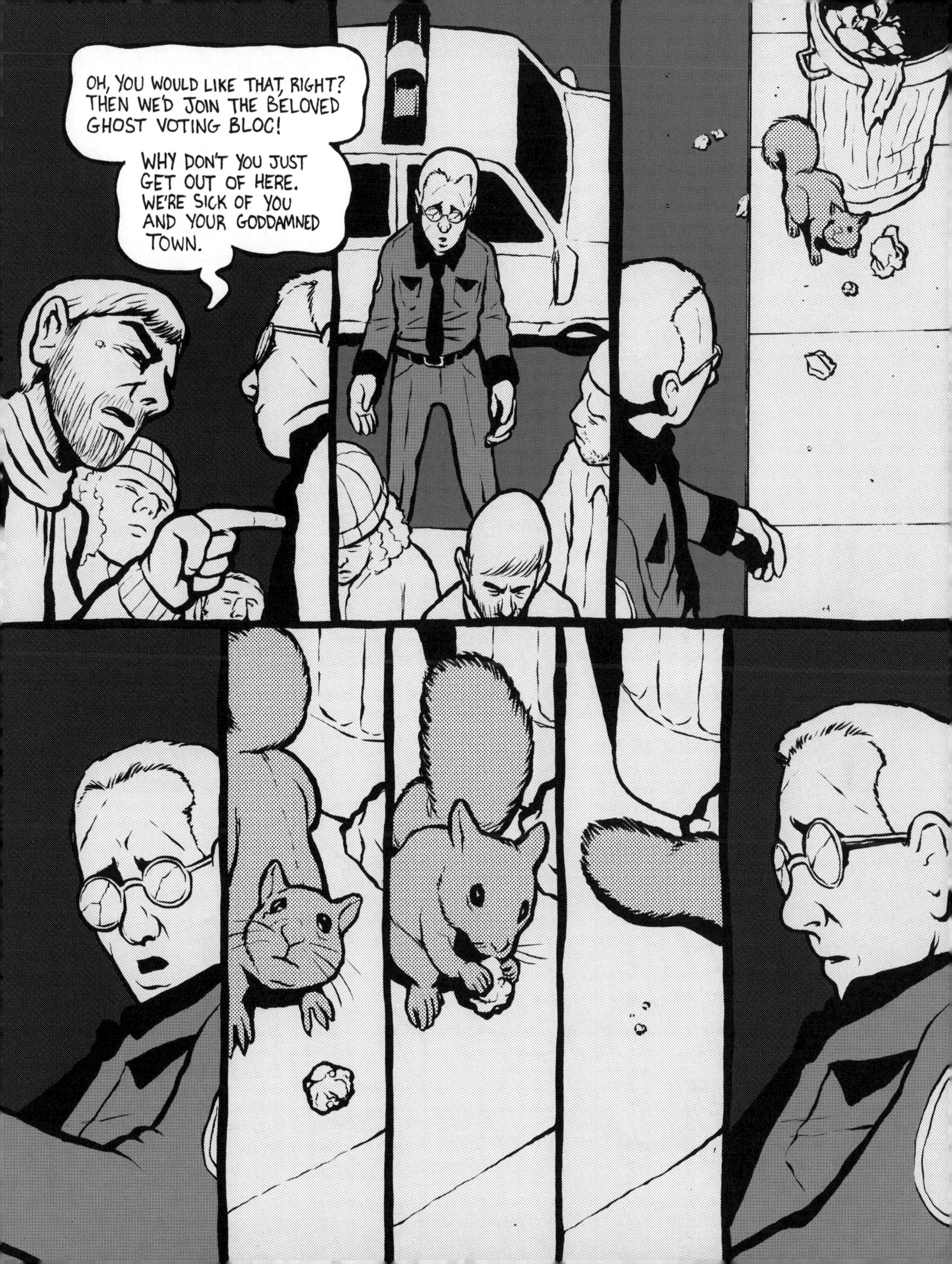
OH, YOU WOULD LIKE THAT, RIGHT? THEN WE'D JOIN THE BELOVED GHOST VOTING BLOC!
WHY DON'T YOU JUST GET OUT OF HERE. WE'RE SICK OF YOU AND YOUR GODDAMNED TOWN.

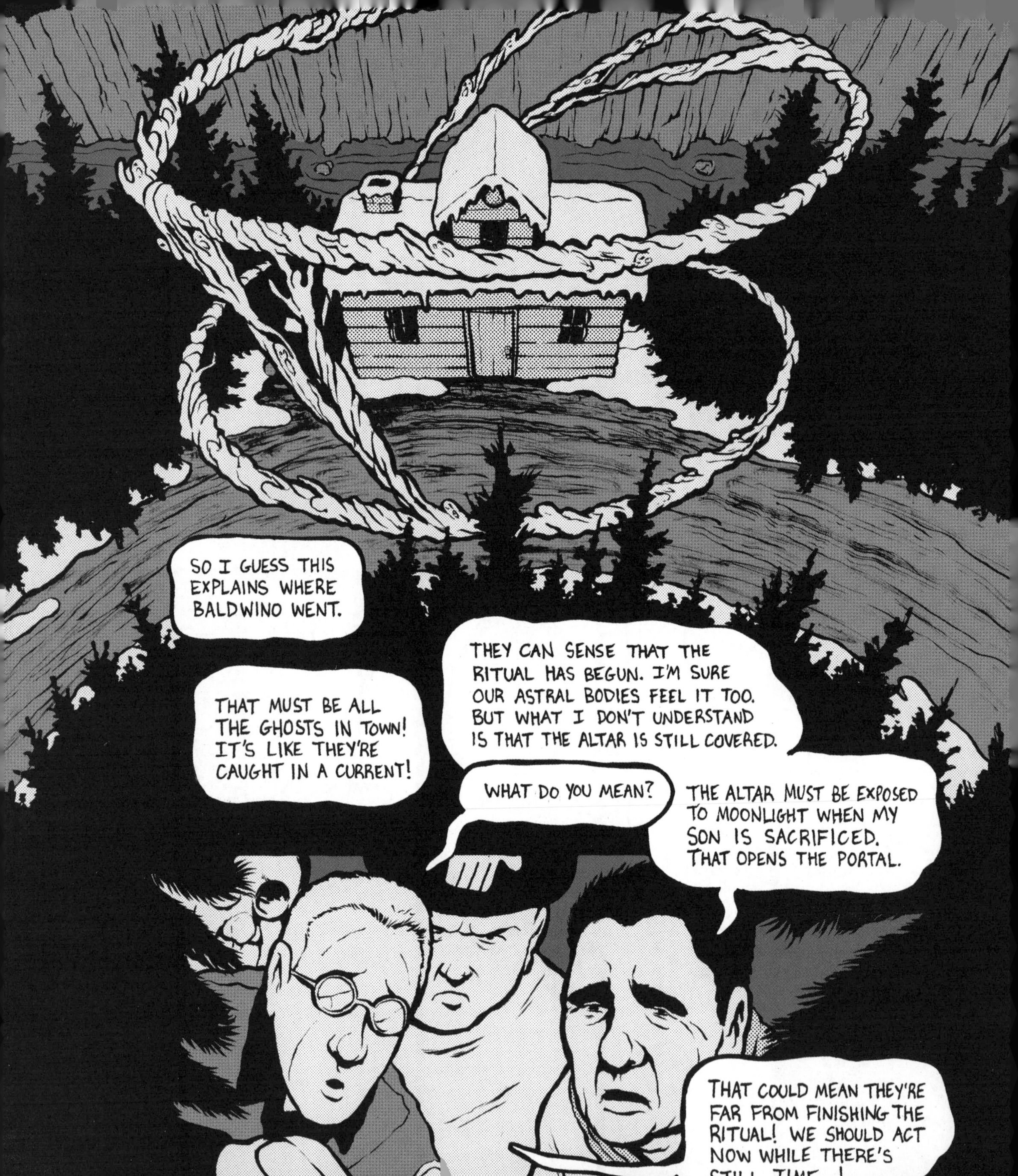
SO I GUESS THIS EXPLAINS WHERE BALDWINO WENT.
THAT MUST BE ALL THE GHOSTS IN TOWN! IT'S LIKE THEY'RE CAUGHT IN A CURRENT!
THEY CAN SENSE THAT THE RITUAL HAS BEGUN. I'M SURE OUR ASTRAL BODIES FEEL IT TOO. BUT WHAT I DON'T UNDERSTAND IS THAT THE ALTAR IS STILL COVERED.
WHAT DO YOU MEAN?
THE ALTAR MUST BE EXPOSED TO MOONLIGHT WHEN MY SON IS SACRIFICED. THAT OPENS THE PORTAL.
THAT COULD MEAN THEY'RE FAR FROM FINISHING THE RITUAL! WE SHOULD ACT NOW WHILE THERE'S STILL TIME...!

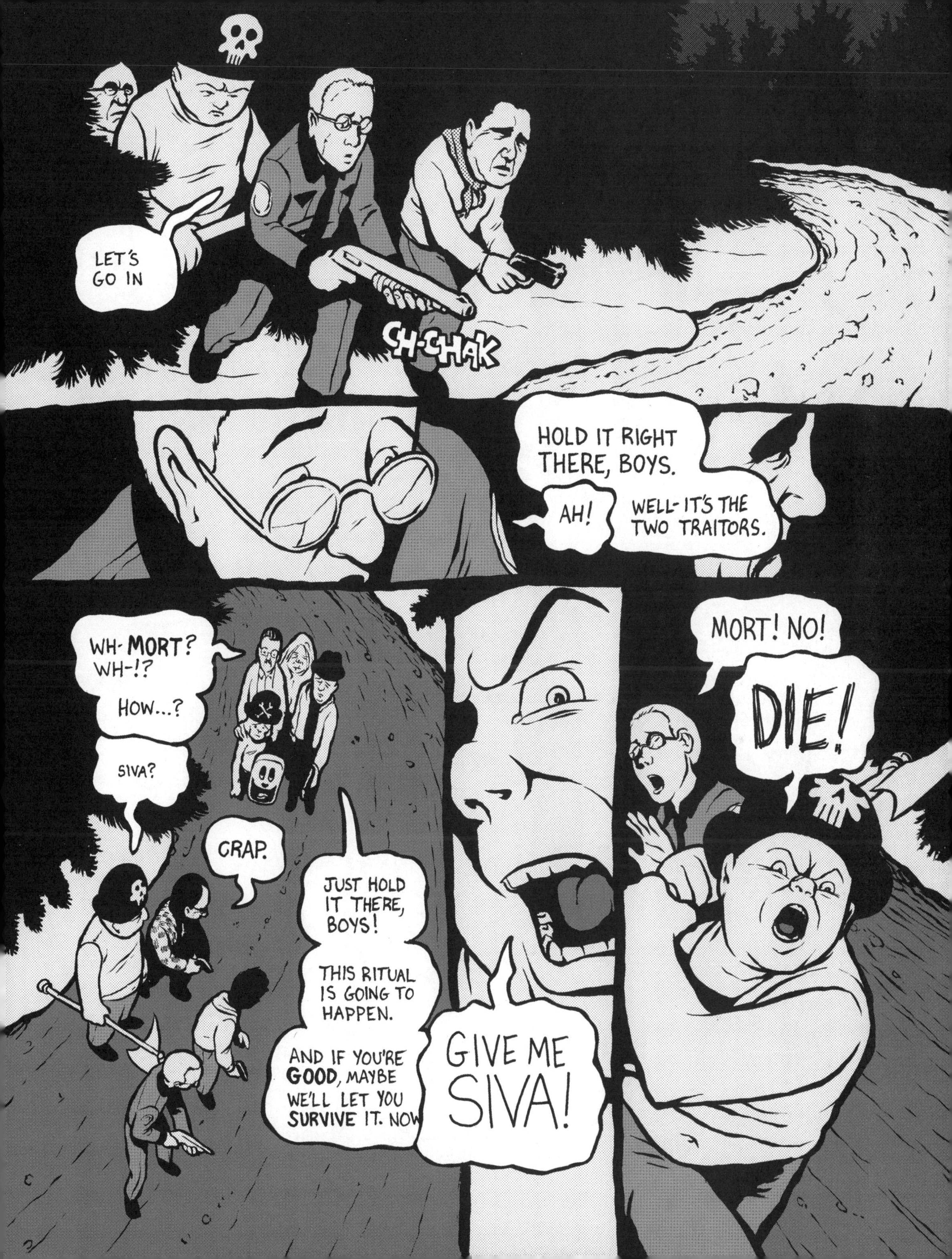
LET'S GO IN
CH-CHAK
HOLD IT RIGHT THERE, BOYS.
AH!
WELL- IT'S THE TWO TRAITORS.
WH- MORT? WH-!?
HOW...?
SIVA?
CRAP.
JUST HOLD IT THERE, BOYS!
THIS RITUAL IS GOING TO HAPPEN.
AND IF YOU'RE GOOD, MAYBE WE'LL LET YOU SURVIVE IT. NOW
GIVE ME SIVA!
MORT! NO!
DIE!

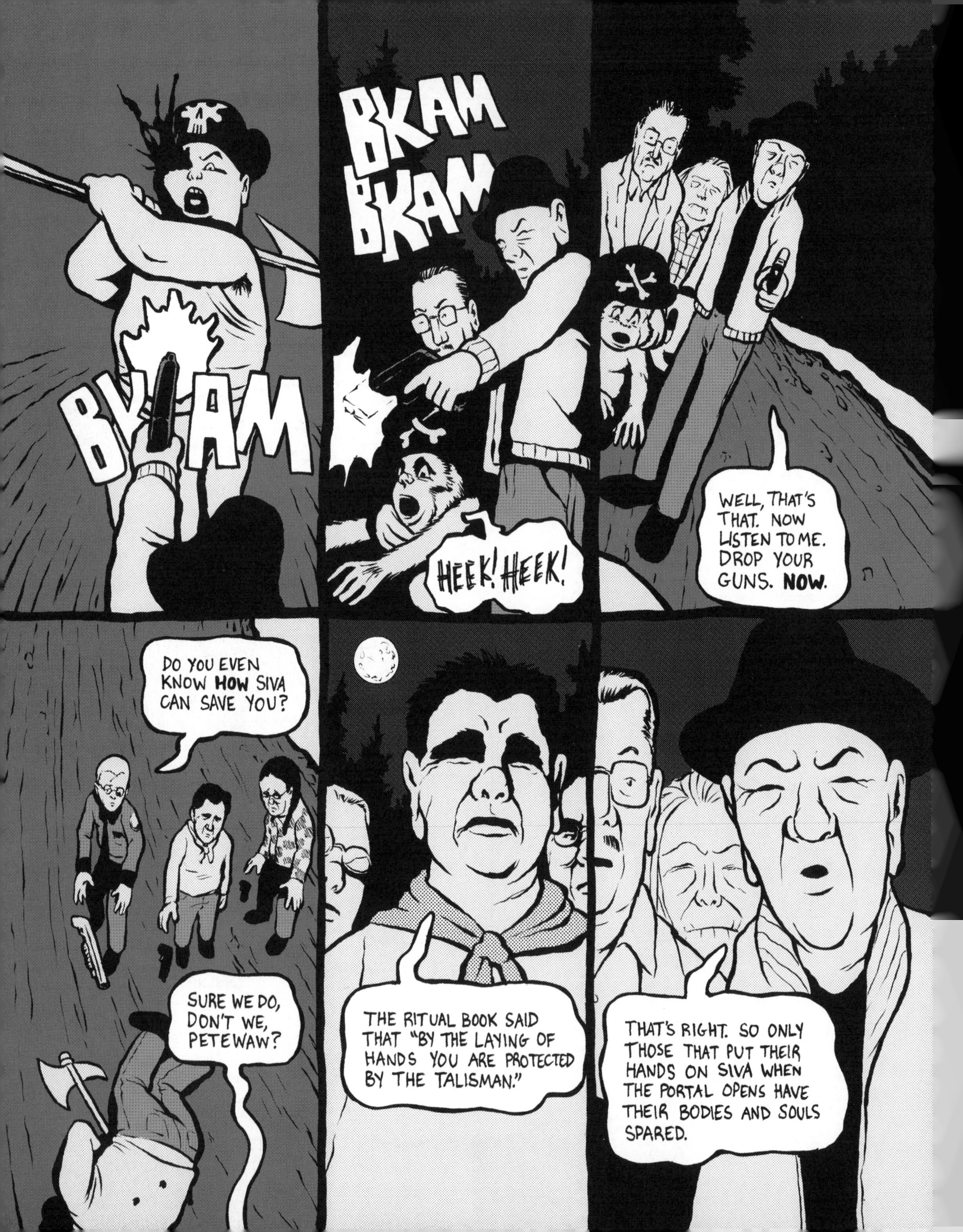
BLAM
BKAM BKAM
HEEK! HEEK!
WELL, THAT'S THAT. NOW LISTEN TO ME. DROP YOUR GUNS. **NOW**.
DO YOU EVEN KNOW **HOW** SIVA CAN SAVE YOU?
SURE WE DO, DON'T WE, PETEWAW?
THE RITUAL BOOK SAID THAT "BY THE LAYING OF HANDS YOU ARE PROTECTED BY THE TALISMAN."
THAT'S RIGHT. SO ONLY THOSE THAT PUT THEIR HANDS ON SIVA WHEN THE PORTAL OPENS HAVE THEIR BODIES AND SOULS SPARED.

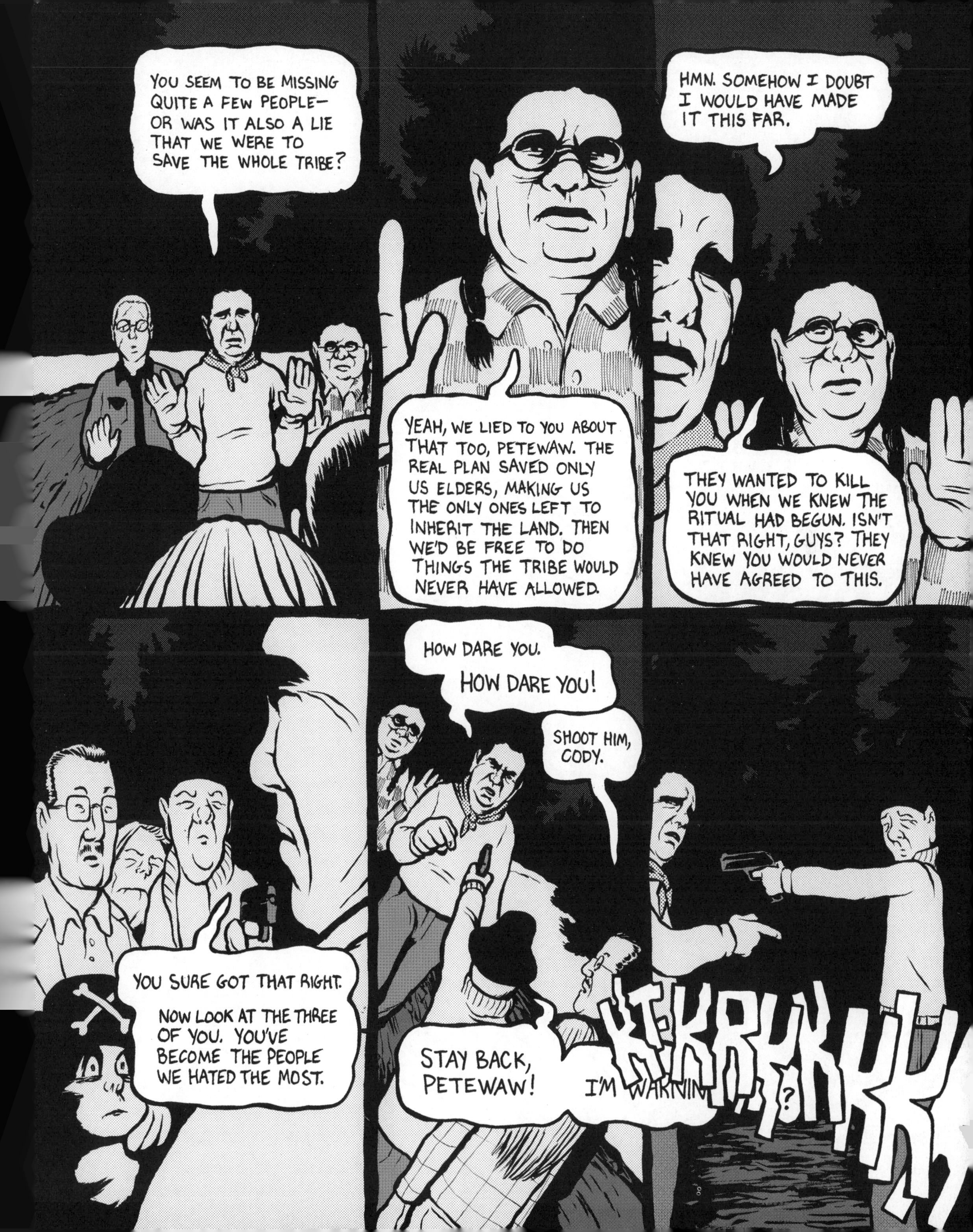
YOU SEEM TO BE MISSING QUITE A FEW PEOPLE— OR WAS IT ALSO A LIE THAT WE WERE TO SAVE THE WHOLE TRIBE?
YEAH, WE LIED TO YOU ABOUT THAT TOO, PETEWAW. THE REAL PLAN SAVED ONLY US ELDERS, MAKING US THE ONLY ONES LEFT TO INHERIT THE LAND. THEN WE'D BE FREE TO DO THINGS THE TRIBE WOULD NEVER HAVE ALLOWED.
HMN. SOMEHOW I DOUBT I WOULD HAVE MADE IT THIS FAR.
THEY WANTED TO KILL YOU WHEN WE KNEW THE RITUAL HAD BEGUN. ISN'T THAT RIGHT, GUYS? THEY KNEW YOU WOULD NEVER HAVE AGREED TO THIS.
YOU SURE GOT THAT RIGHT.
NOW LOOK AT THE THREE OF YOU. YOU'VE BECOME THE PEOPLE WE HATED THE MOST.
HOW DARE YOU.
HOW DARE YOU!
SHOOT HIM, CODY.
STAY BACK, PETEWAW!
I'M WARNIN
?
KT-KRKK

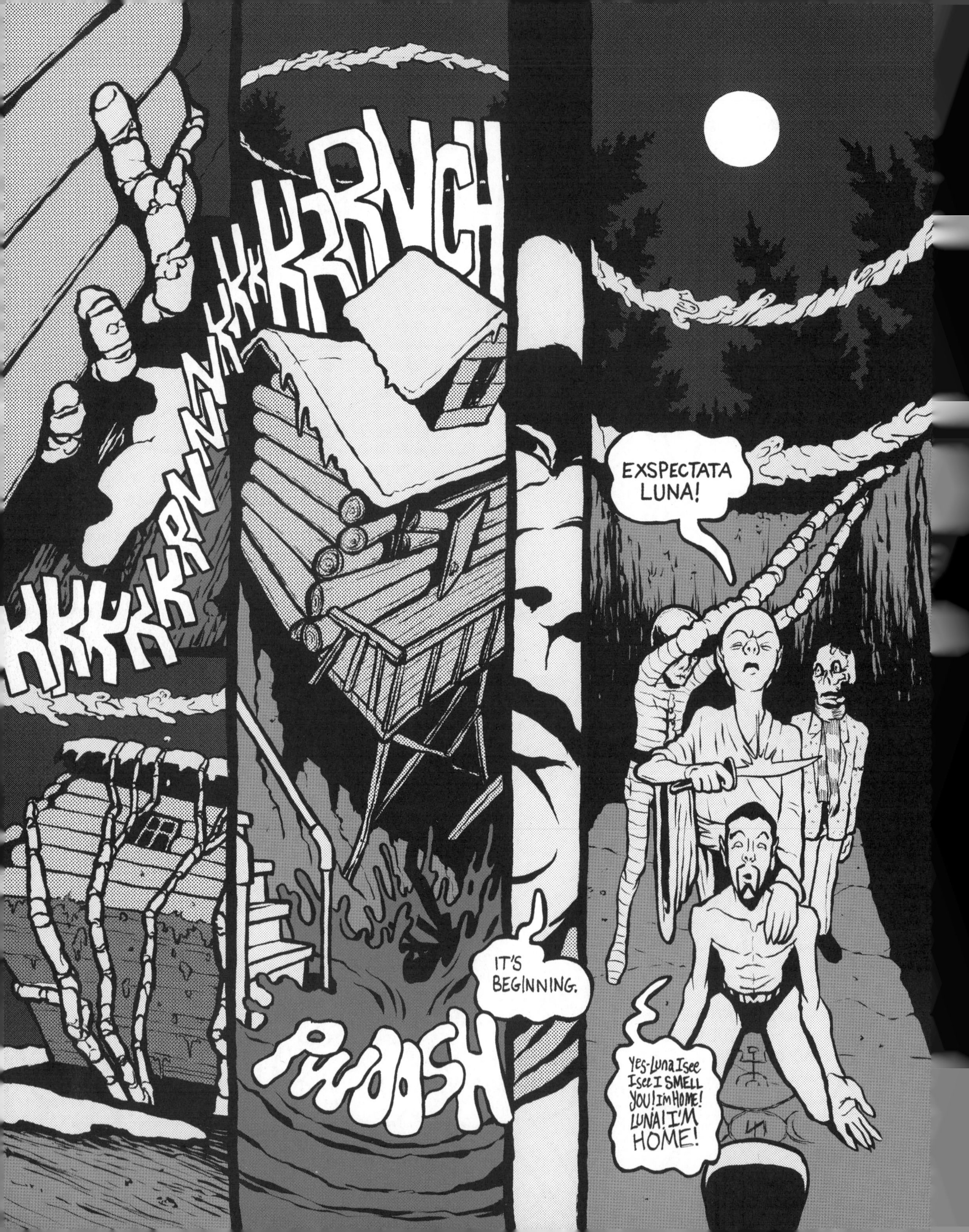
KKKKKRRNNNKKKKRRRNCH
PWOOSH
IT'S BEGINNING.
EXSPECTATA LUNA!
Yes-Luna Isee Isee I SMELL YOU! I'M HOME! LUNA! I'M HOME!

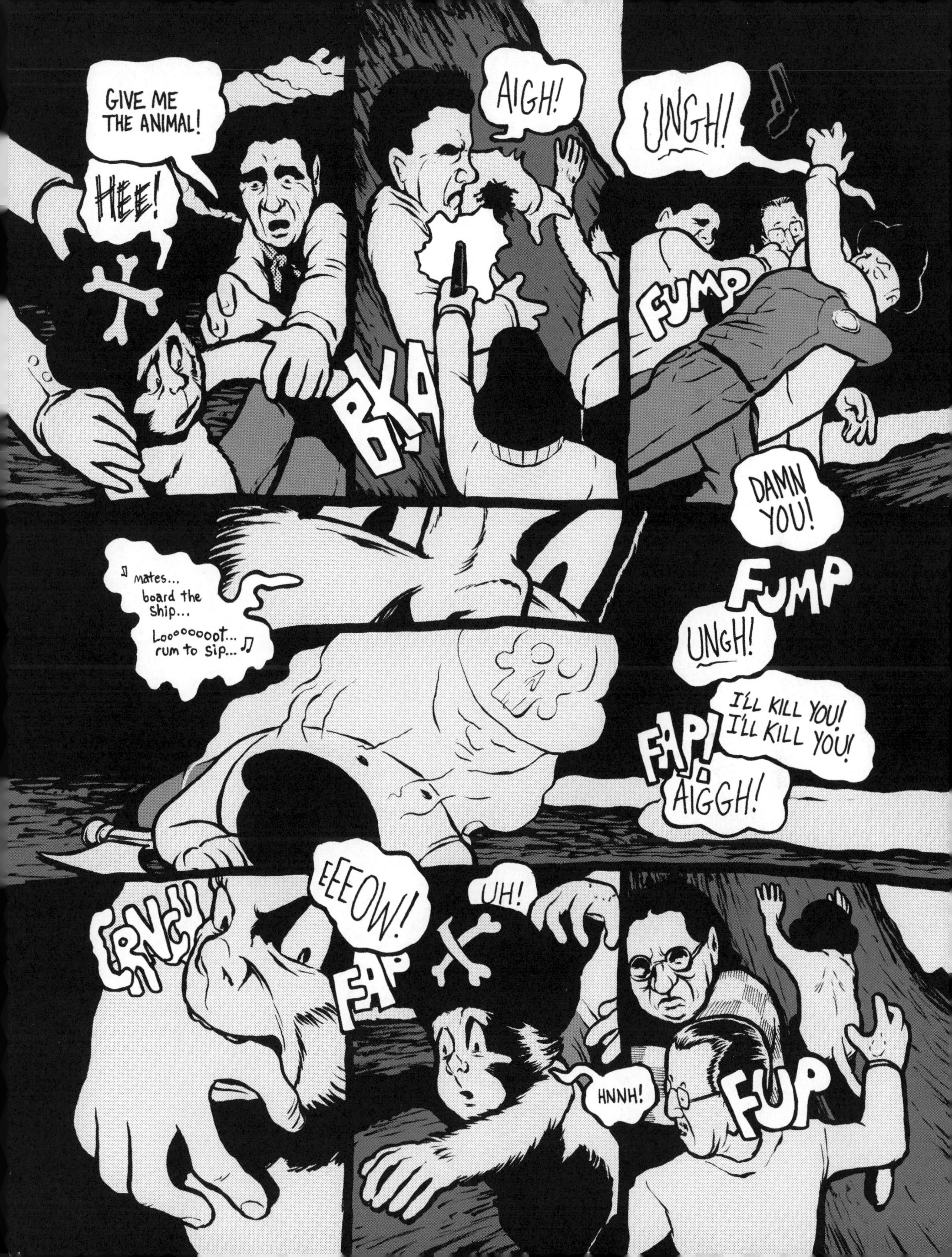
GIVE ME THE ANIMAL!
HEE!
BKA
AIGH!
UNGH!
FUMP
DAMN YOU!
♫ mates... board the ship... Looooooot... rum to sip... ♫
FUMP
UNGH!
I'LL KILL YOU! I'LL KILL YOU!
FAP!
AIGGH!
CRNCH
EEEOW!
UH!
FAP
HNNH!
FUP

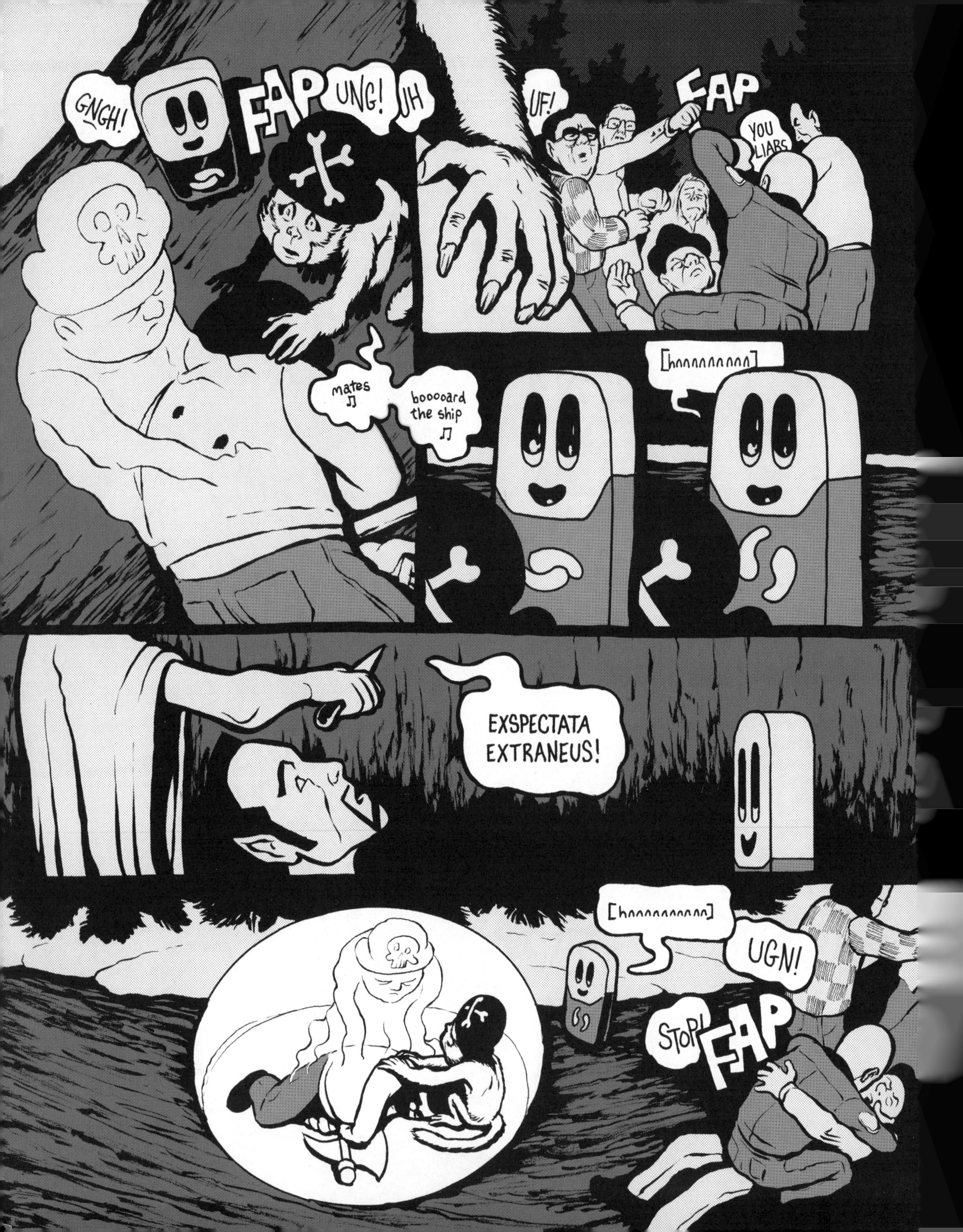
GNGH!
FAP
UNG!
UH
UF!
FAP
YOU LIARS
mates ♫
boooaard the ship ♫
[hnnnnnnnnn]
EXSPECTATA EXTRANEUS!
[hnnnnnnnnnn]
UGN!
STOP!
FAP

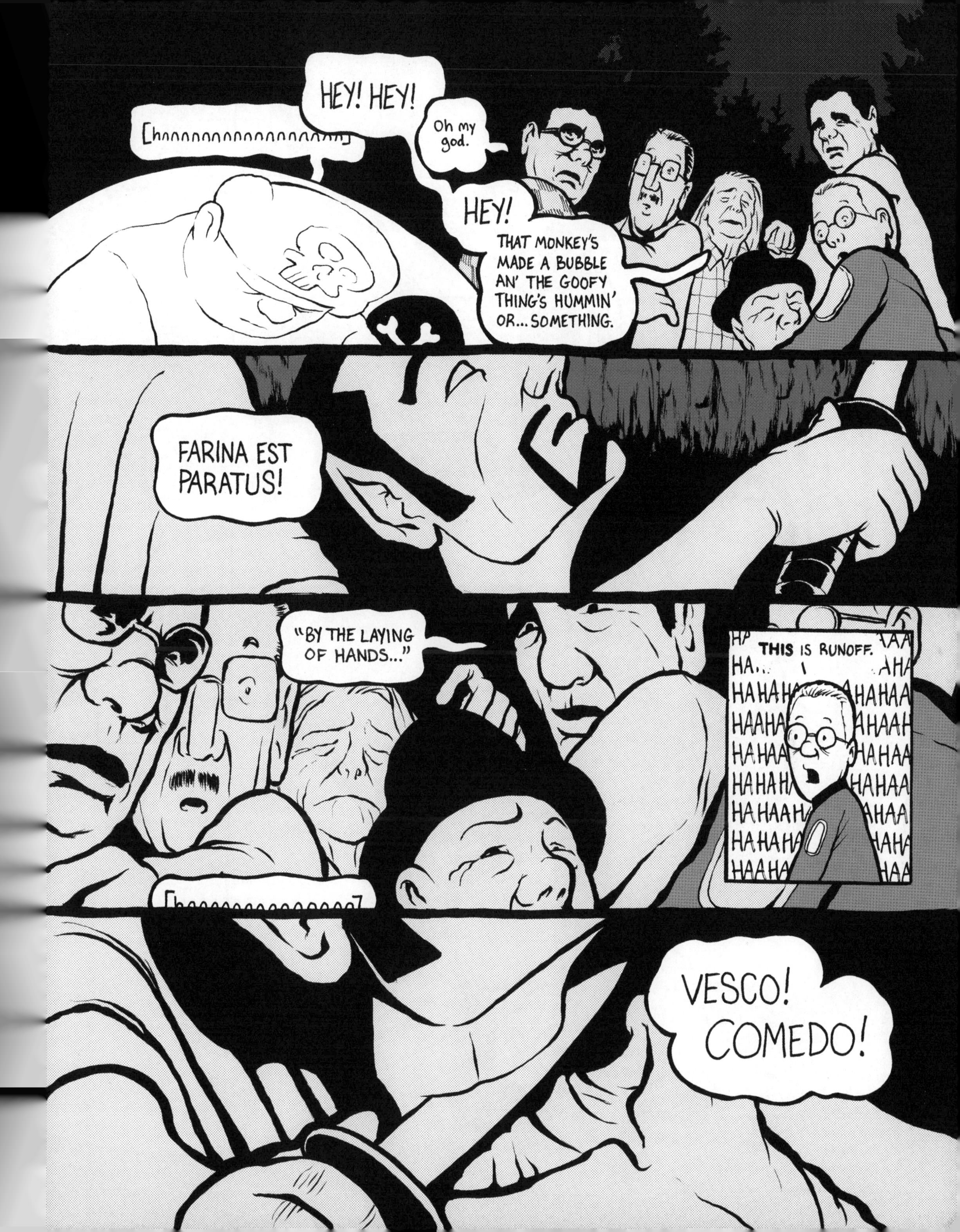
[hnnnnnnnnnnnnnnnnnnn]
HEY! HEY!
Oh my god.
HEY!
THAT MONKEY'S MADE A BUBBLE AN' THE GOOFY THING'S HUMMIN' OR... SOMETHING.
FARINA EST PARATUS!
"BY THE LAYING OF HANDS..."
THIS IS RUNOFF.
[hnnnnnnnnnnnnnnnn]
VESCO! COMEDO!

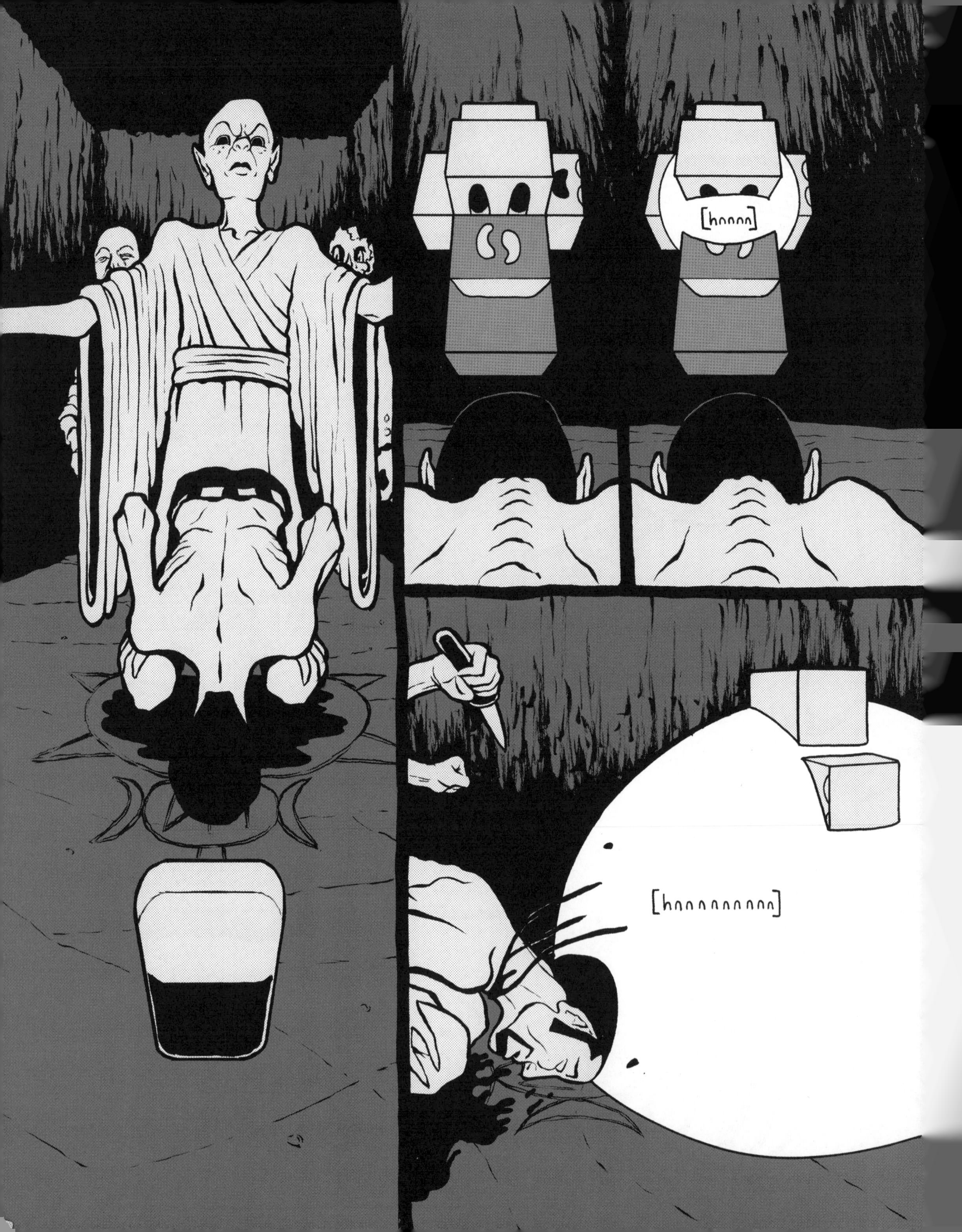
[hnnnn]
[hnnnnnnnnn]

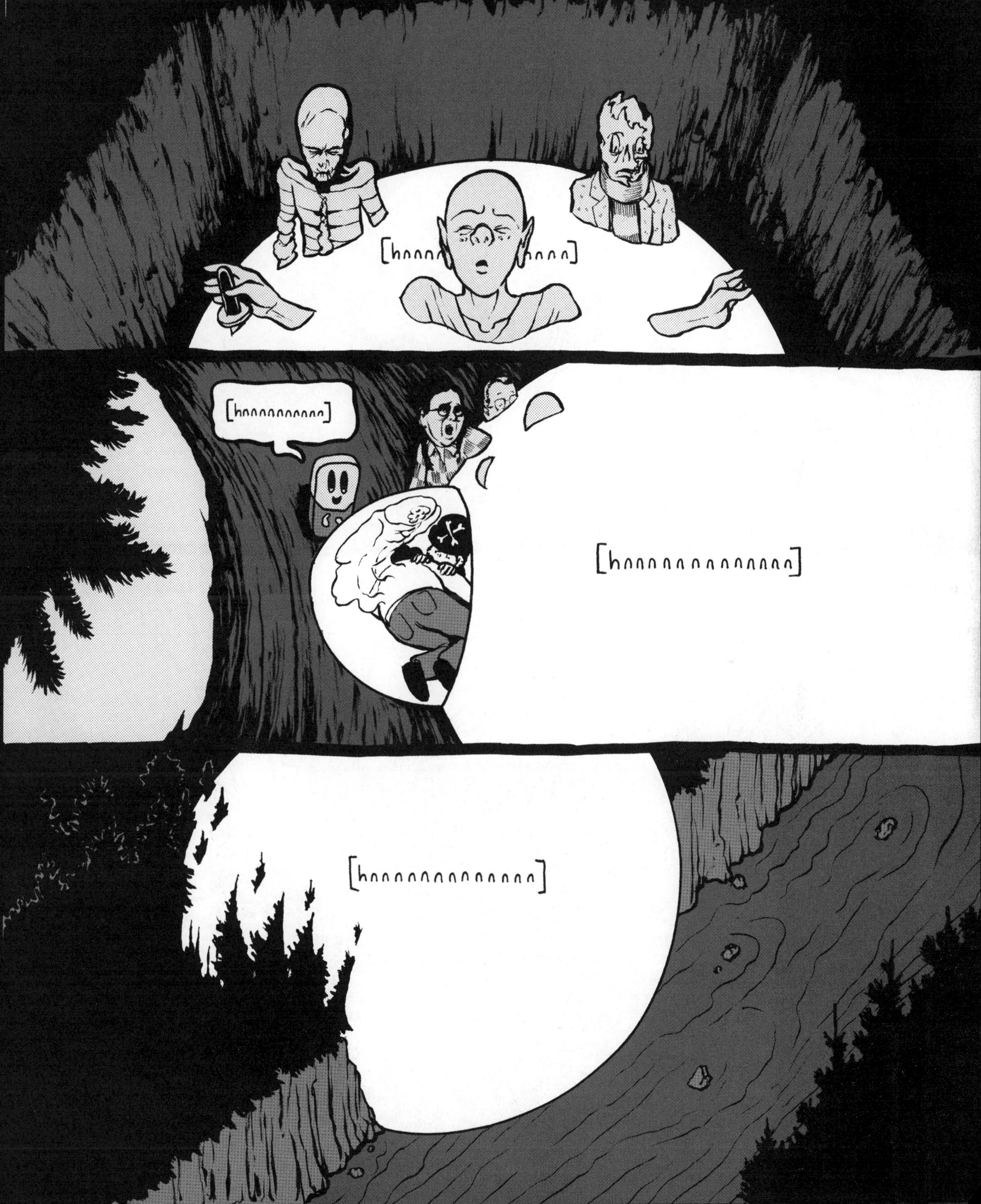
[hnnn
nnnn]
[hnnnnnnnnnn]
[hnnnnnnnnnnnnnn]
[hnnnnnnnnnnnnnn]

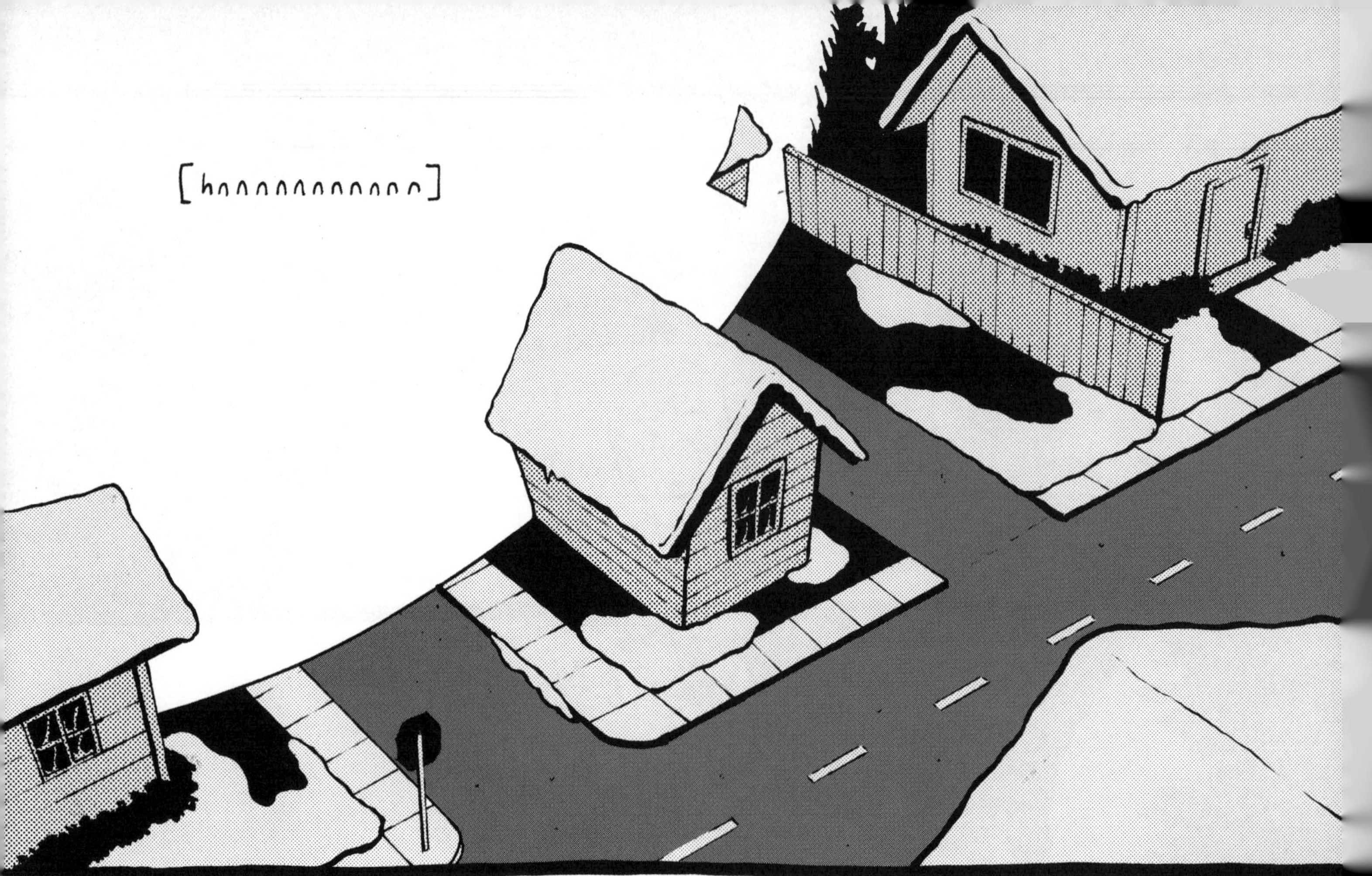
[hnnnnnnnnnnn]

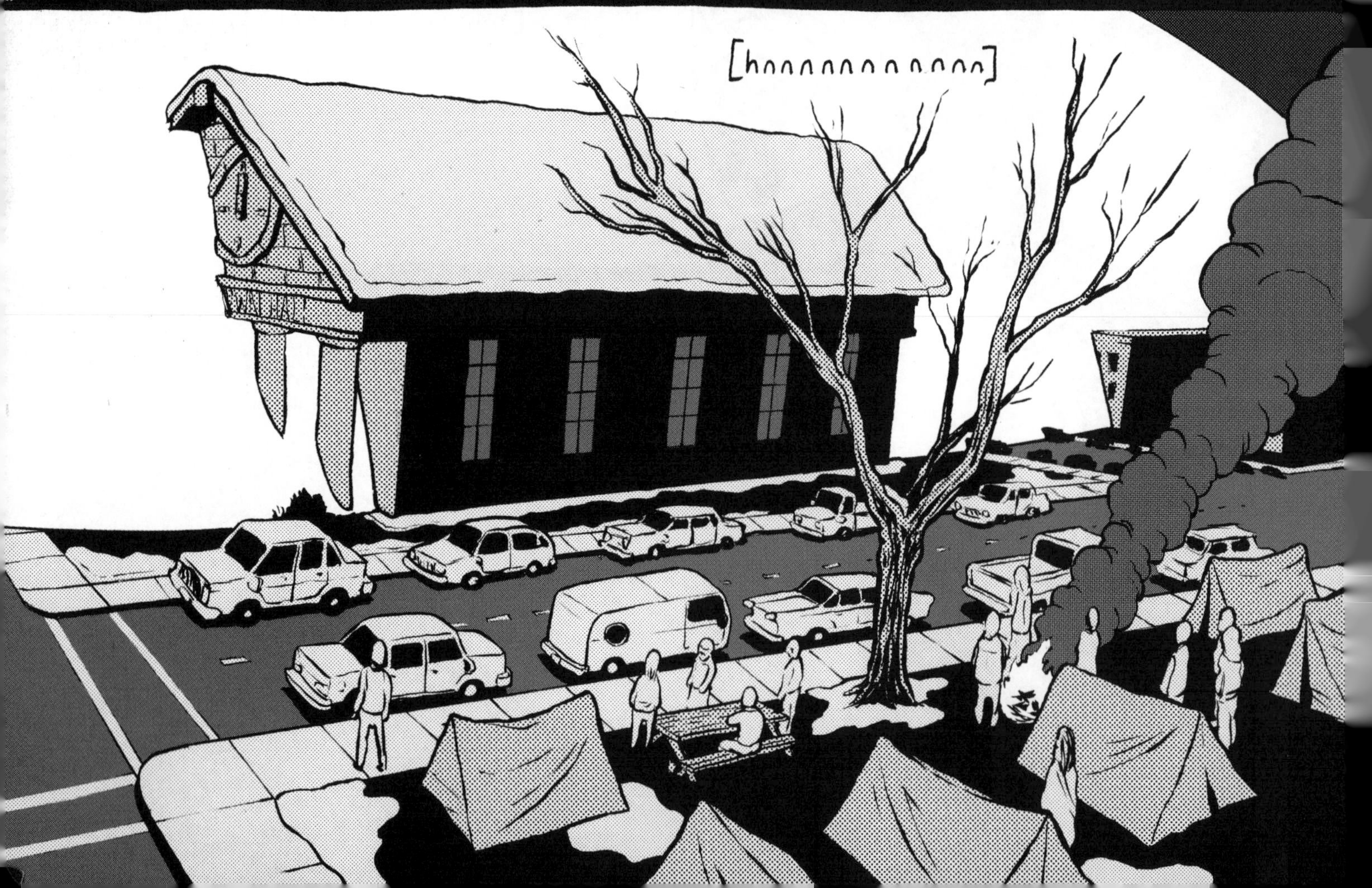
[hnnnnnnnnnnn]

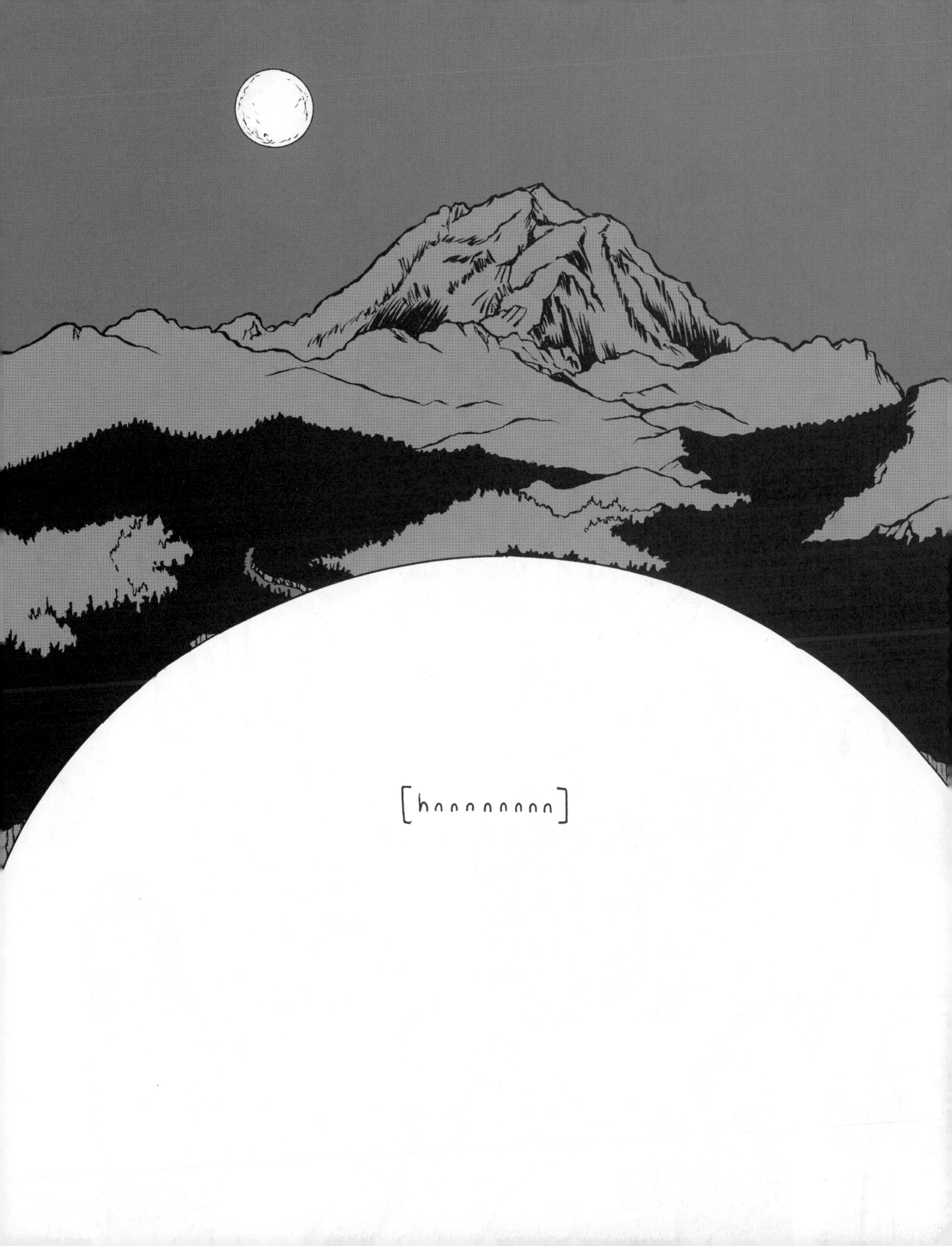
[hnnnnnnnn]

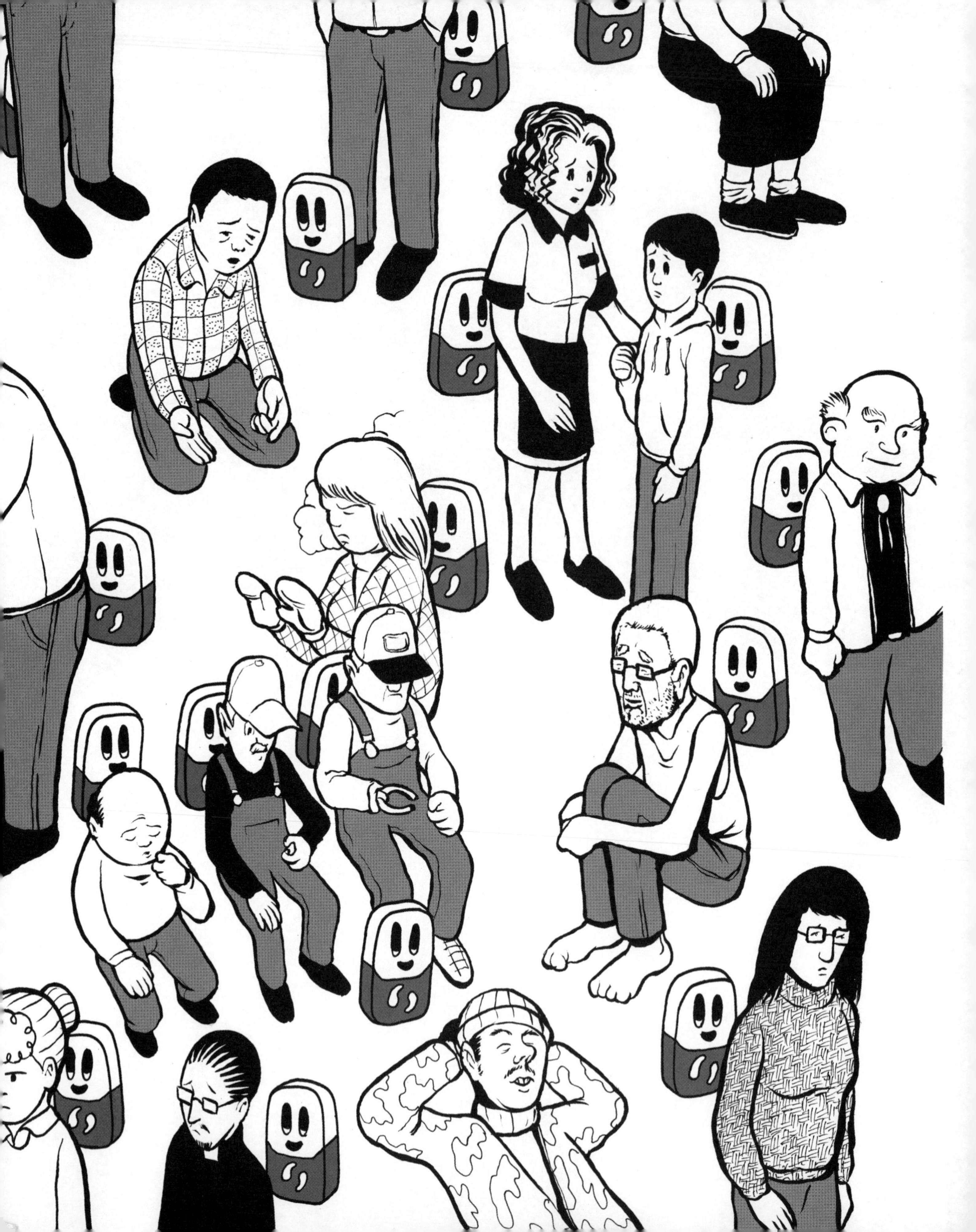

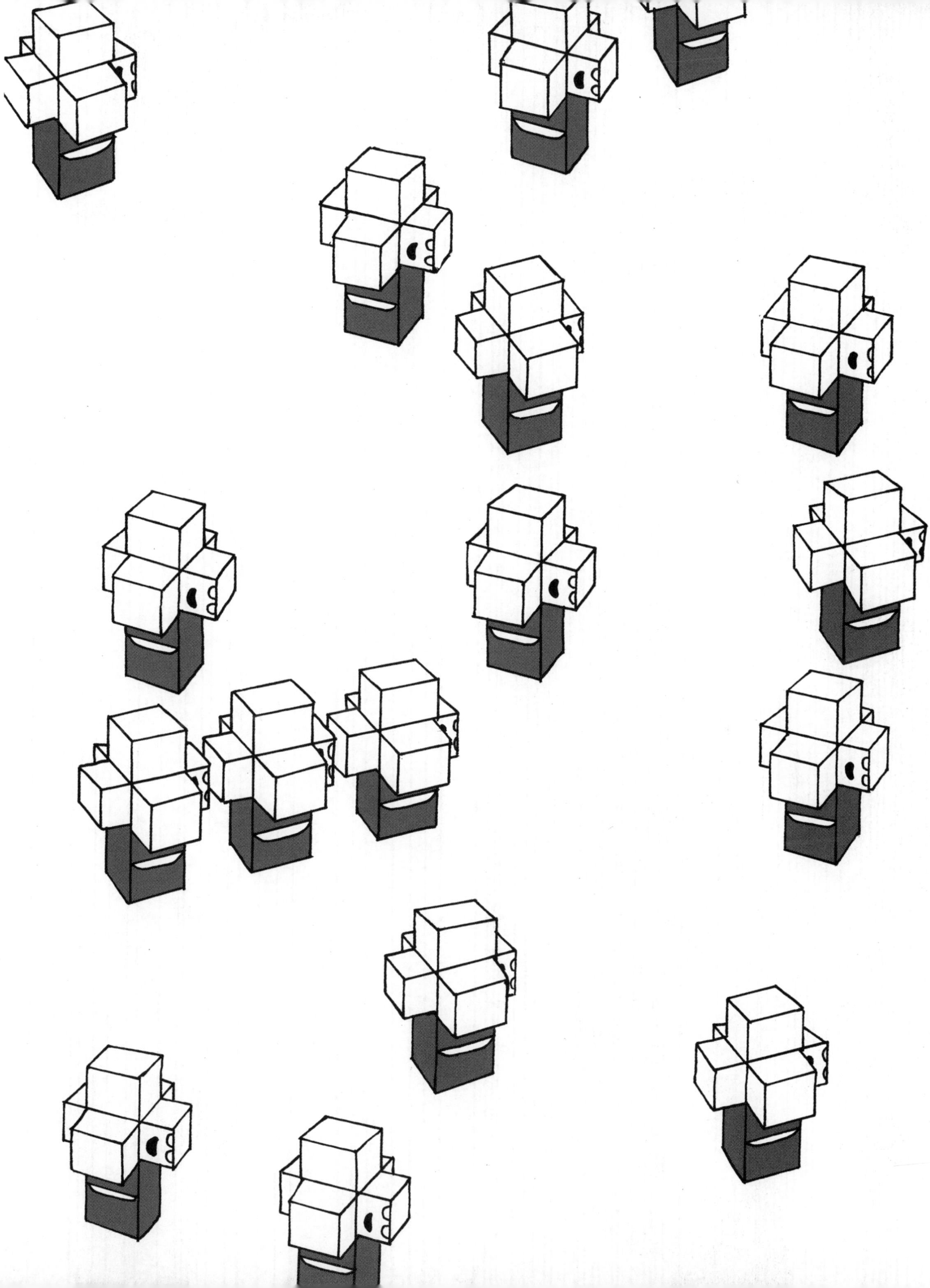

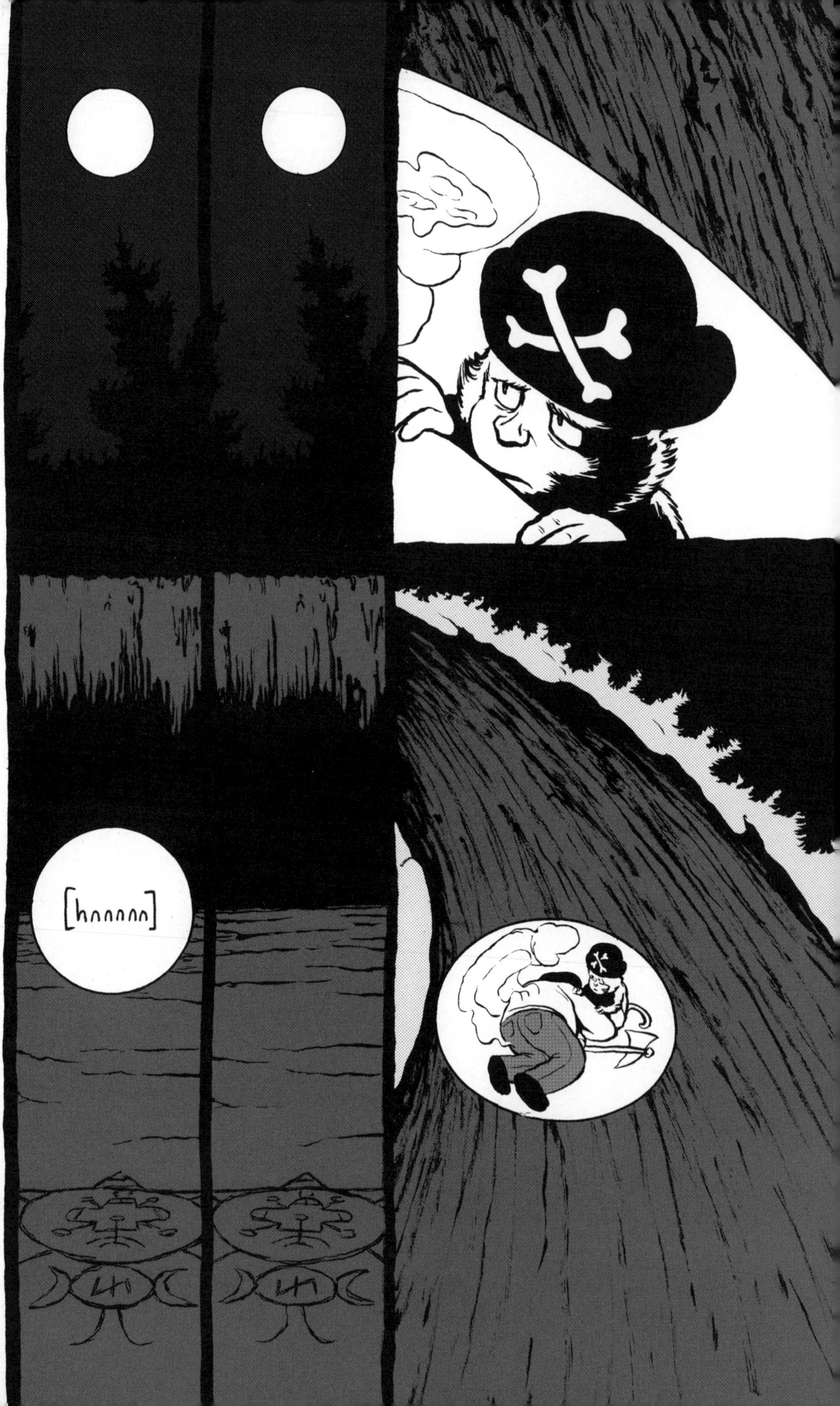
[hnnnnn]
[hnnnnn]

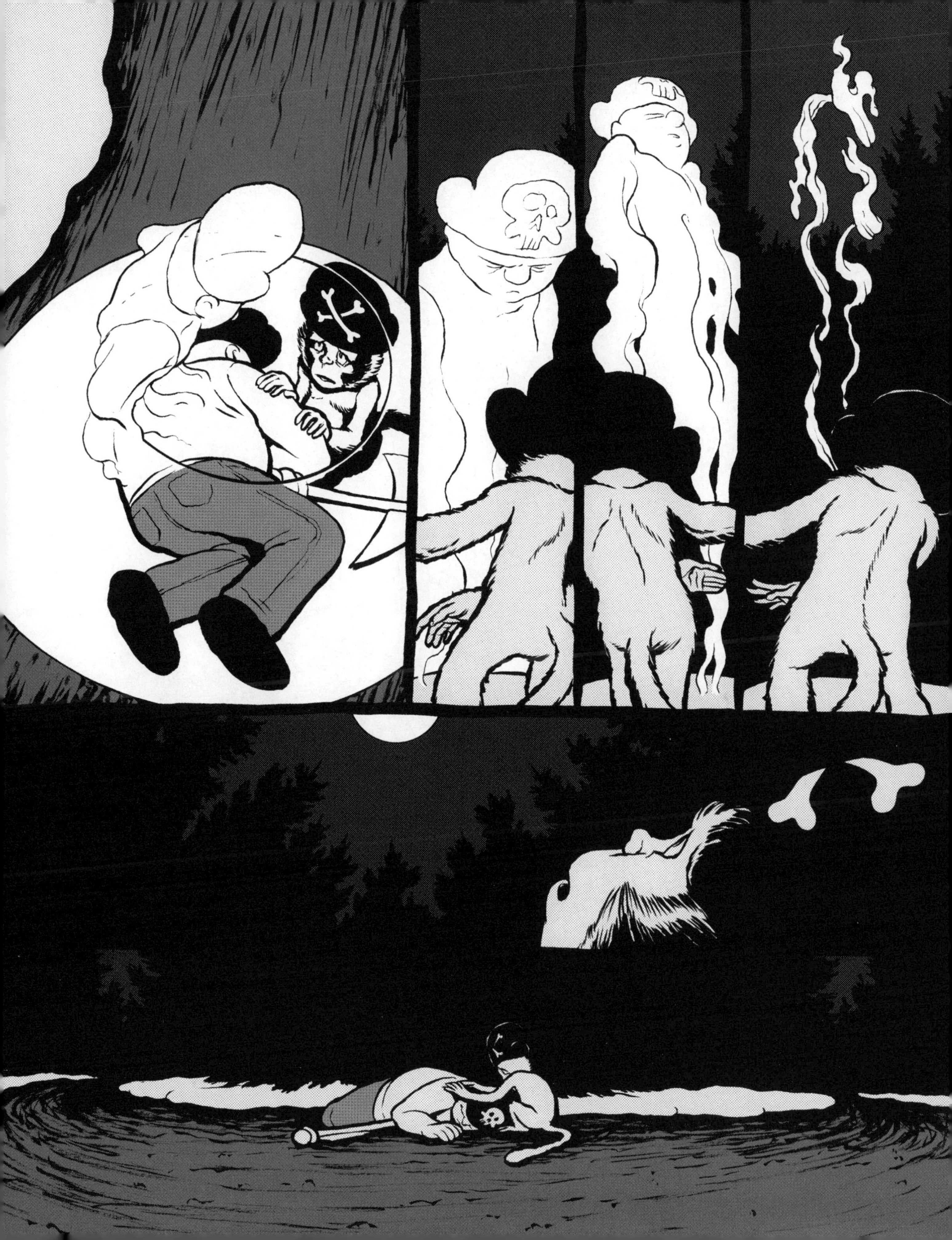

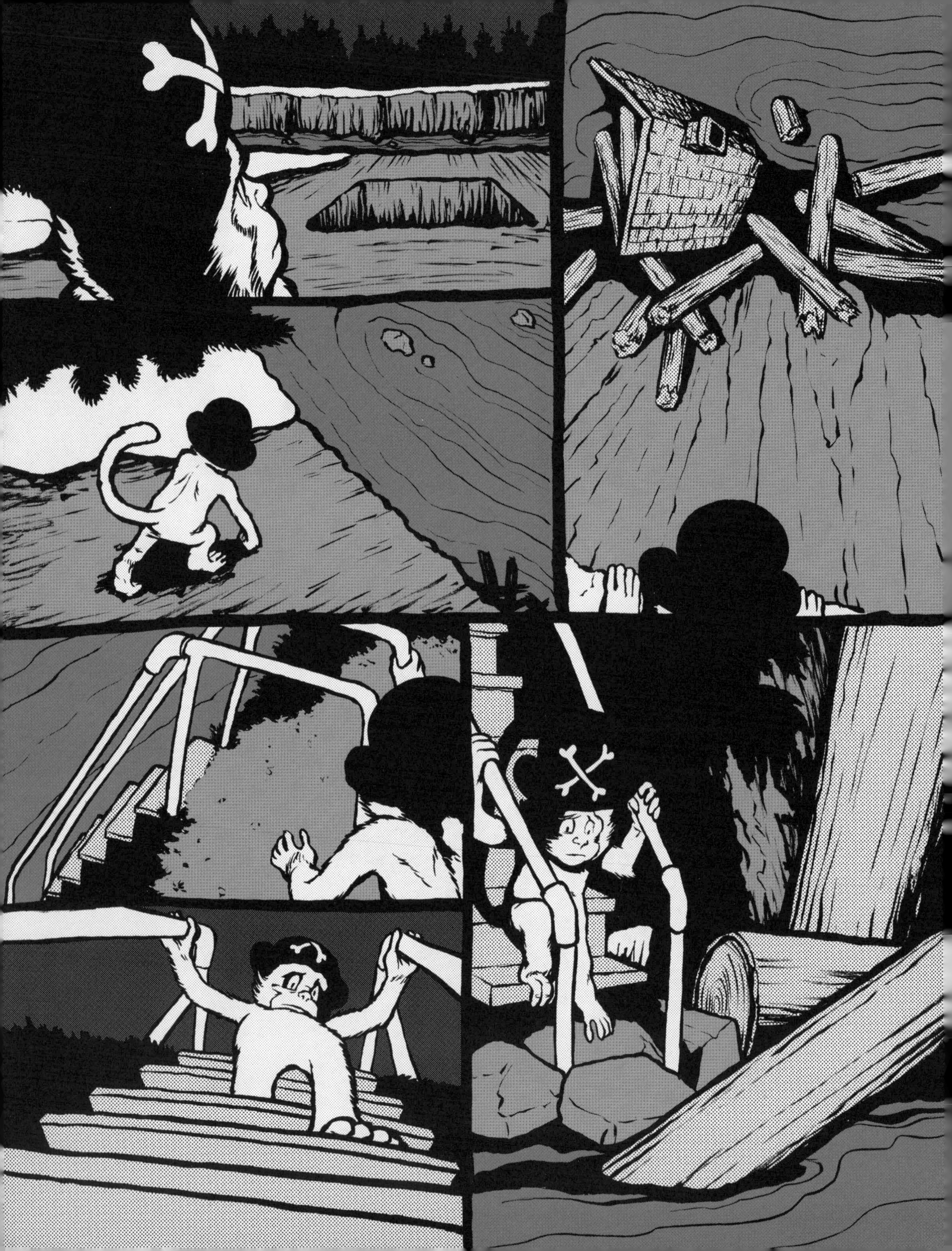

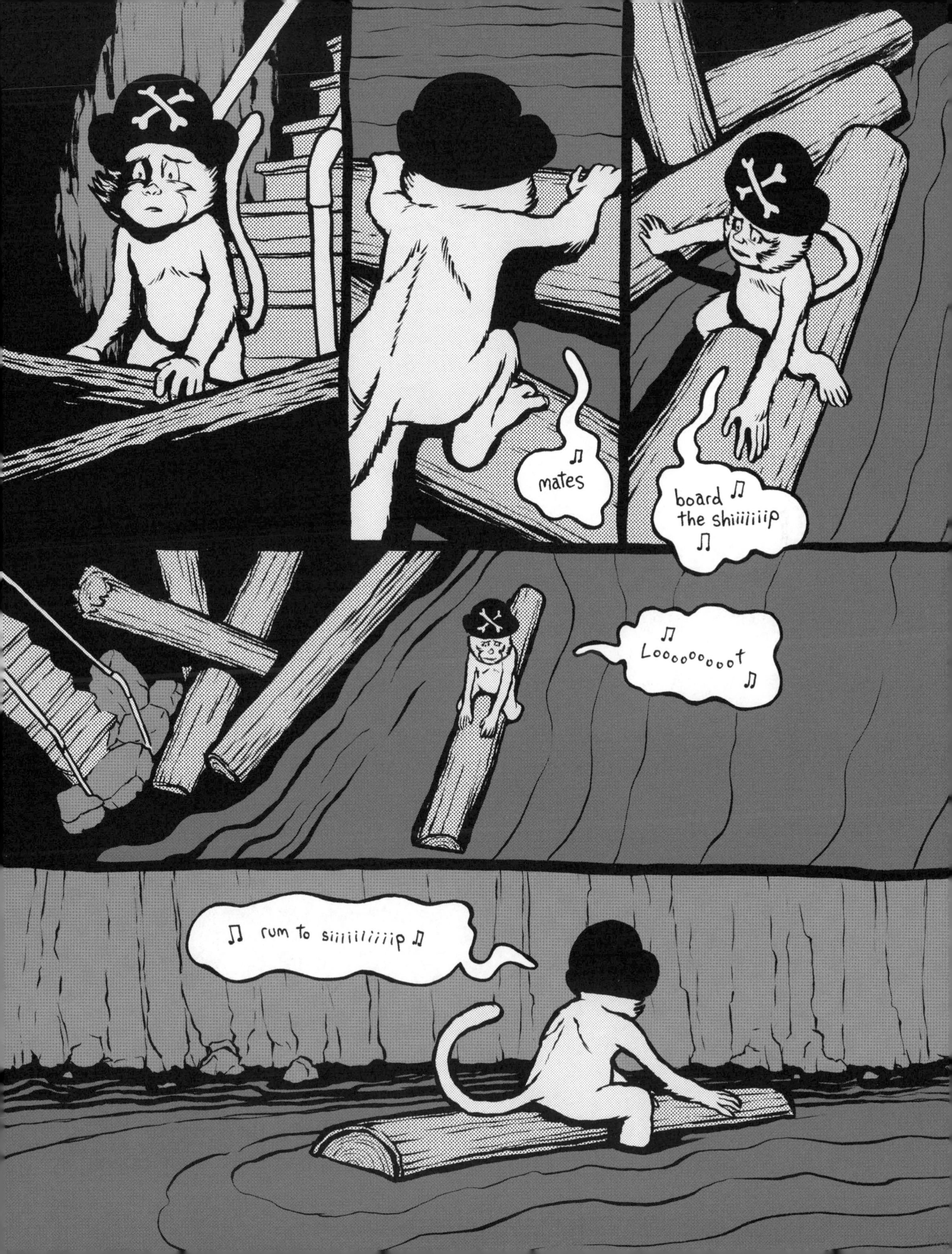
♫ mates
board ♫ the shiiiiiiip ♫
♫ Looooooooot ♫
♫ rum to siiiiiiiiiip ♫

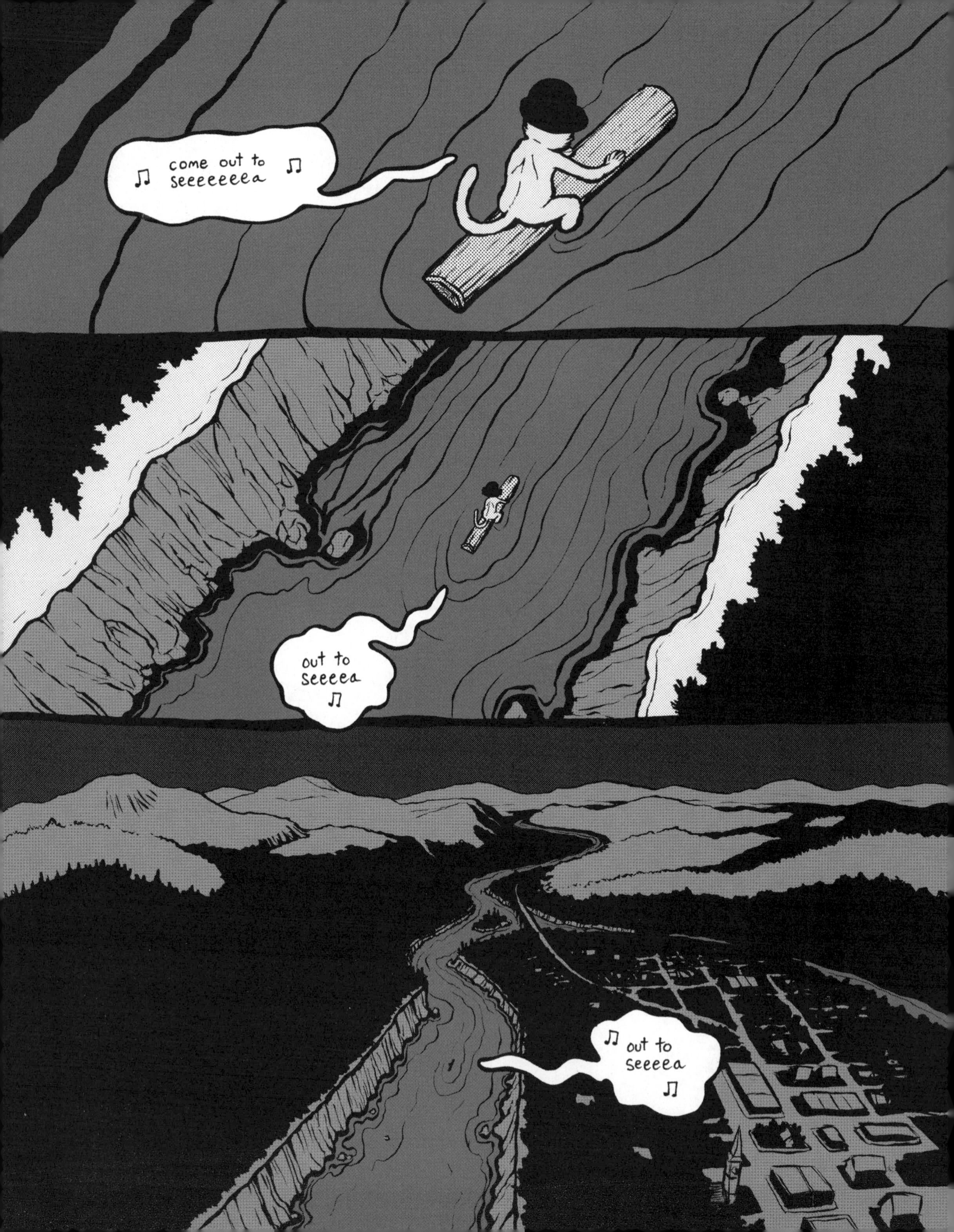
♫ come out to seeeeeeea ♫
out to seeeea ♫
♫ out to seeeea ♫

THE END

ABOUT THE AUTHOR

Tom Manning was raised in Enumclaw,
Washington. His first graphic novel, *RACECAR*,
was published in 1999. Manning currently
lives in Oakland, California with his wife Stacy
and children. He enjoys cats, Earl Grey tea,
his parents, and ghost stories. His hobbies
include work.